20th Century Theatre

Volume II

For my mother,
Marion Busher Loney

20th Century Theatre

Volume II

by Glenn Loney

Facts On File Publications
460 Park Avenue South
New York, N.Y. 10016

20th Century Theatre

Volume II

Glenn Loney

Library of Congress Cataloging in Publication Data

Loney, Glenn Meredith, 1928–
   20th century theater.

   Includes index.
      1. Theater—History—20th century.   I. Title.
II. Title: Twentieth century theater.
PN2189.L65   792'.09'04   81-19587
ISBN 0-87196-463-5   AACR2
ISBN 0-87196-807-X   Vol 1.
ISBN 0-87196-808-8   Vol 2.

10 9 8 7 6 5 4 3 2 1

Printed in the United States of America

20th Century Theatre

Volume II

Jan 14 *Strange Bedfellows* (NY—Morosco—Comedy). Joan Tetzel plays a militant suffragette in the Gay Nineties, in Florence Ryerson and Colin Clements' comedy. Carl Benton Reid plays opposite for the 229 performances.

Jan 15 *Make Mine Manhattan* (NY—Broadhurst—Revue). Sid Caesar heads the cast in this musical revue which runs almost 53 weeks. Sketches are by Arnold Horwitt, music by Richard Levine. Hassard Short stages.

Jan 29 *Look, Ma, I'm Dancin'* (NY—Adelphi—Musical). Jerome Robbins has the idea, Jerome Lawrence and Robert E. Lee devise the book, and Hugh Martin provides music and lyrics ("Gotta Dance") for this tale of a brewery heiress (Nancy Walker) who takes over a ballet company. George Abbott and Robbins stage. There are 188 showings.

Feb. 18 *Mister Roberts* (NY—Alvin—Comedy). Henry Fonda scores a hit (1,157 performances) as a lieutenant who champions his men against the paranoid policies of his captain (William Harrigan), in Thomas Heggen and Joshua Logan's play based on a Heggen novel. The hit comes to London at the Coliseum on July 19, 1950, with Tyrone Power heading the cast. But it has only 211 performances.

Feb 26 *Me and Molly* (NY—Belasco—Comedy). Gertrude Berg, known for her radio show *The Goldbergs*, repeats her radio role of Molly in this saga of the Goldberg family during 1919. There are 156 performances.

March 16 *The Respectful Prostitute* (NY—Cort—Drama). Jean-Paul Sartre's play about a Northern prostitute learning the ways of white supremacy in the South, has 348 performances. Meg Mundy plays the prostitute. Mary Hunter stages.

April 30 *Inside the U.S.A.* (NY—Century—Revue). The title is taken from a recent book of political reportage by John Gunther. It is scripted by Moss Hart, Arnold Auerbach, and Arnold Horwitt, with songs by Howard Dietz and Arthur Schwartz. Helen Tamiris choreographs; Jay Blackton conducts; Lemuel Ayers designs the sets, and the costumes are by Castillo and Eleanor Goldsmith. In the cast are Beatrice Lillie—leading a choral ode to Pittsburgh, Herb Shriner, Valerie Bettis, Jack Haley, John Tyers, Thelma Carpenter, Rod Alexander, and Carl Reiner. The cast cuts the show album during tryouts, to beat the deadline for the ASCAP strike, when composers and lyricists forbid the recording of their works. There are 399 performances.

May 9 *Ballet Ballads* (NY—Maxine Elliott—Musical). With music by Jerome Moross, lyrics by John LaTouche, and choreography by Hanya Holm, among others, three ballads are presented in a limited six-performance showing by the Experimental Theatre (ANTA). The following week the show moves to the Music Box Theatre for a total run of 69 performances.

Sep 15 *Small Wonder* (NY—Coronet—Revue). Jack Cassidy and Mary McCarty are in the cast of this intimate revue which runs nearly 17 weeks. Gower Champion choreographs; George Axelrod and others write the sketches; Burt Shevelove stages.

Sep 20 *Magdalena* (NY—Ziegfield—Musical). A lavish vision of village life on the banks of Columbia's Magdalena River, with score by Heitor Villa-Lobos and choreography by Jack Cole, this musical gets mixed reviews and runs only 11 weeks. Homer Auran and Frederick Brennan write the book, Jules Dassin directs.

Sep 30 *Edward, My Son.* See L premiere, 1947.

Oct 6 *Summer and Smoke* (NY—Music Box—Drama). Atkinson (*NY Times*) calls playwright Tennessee Williams's insight "almost unbearably lucid" in this new play about a repressed woman in love. Margaret Phillips and Tod Andrews head the cast. The show runs 102 performances. It opens in London at the Duchess on Jan 23, 1952 following a run at the Lyric, Hammersmith. Margaret Johnston and William Sylvester play the leads. It has only 43 performances at the Duchess.

Oct 7 *Love Life* (NY—46th Street—Musical). Kurt Weill creates the score for Alan Jay Lerner's book about the complexities of marriage, set against six eras of American history. Ray Middleton and Nanette Fabray head the cast; Elia Kazan stages; Cheryl Crawford produces. There are 252 performances.

Oct 11 *Where's Charley* (NY—St. James—Musical). Ray Bolger and Allyn Ann McLerie are the lovers in George Abbott's musical adaptation and staging of Brandon Thomas's *Charley's Aunt*. Frank Loesser writes the songs ("Once in Love with Amy"). George Balanchine choreographs. It has 792 performances. On Feb 20, 1958, the show opens at London's Palace with Norman Wisdom in the title role. There are 404 showings.

Oct. 20 *Life With Mother* (NY—Empire—Comedy). Howard Lindsay and Russel Crouse's sequel to *Life With Father* has 265 performances, compared with the latter's 3,224. Lindsay and his wife Dorothy Stickney play the parents. Guthrie McClintic stages.

Nov 3 *Set My People Free* (NY—Hudson—Drama). The *New York Post* calls Dorothy Heyward's historical drama about a planned slave uprising in Charleston, "absorbing," but it has only 36 performances. Canada Lee is in the cast, directed by Martin Ritt.

Nov 17 *Goodbye, My Fancy* (NY—Morosco—Comedy). Kay Fanin wins 446 performances and inclusion in *Best Plays* for her comedy about a Congresswoman's return to her Alma Mater. Madeleine Carroll, Sam Wanamaker, and Shirley Booth head the cast. Wanamaker directs.

Nov 18 *Light Up the Sky* (NY—Royale—Comedy). Moss Hart's comedy, about a play in rehearsal, runs for 27 weeks. Among the cast are Audrey Christie, Glenn Anders, and Virginia Field. Hart stages.

Nov 24 *The Silver Whistle* (NY—Biltmore—Comedy). Jose Ferrer plays a drifter

MR. ROBERTS

SMALL WONDER

who brings hope and humor into the lives of some old people in Robert McEnroe's fantasy offered by the Theatre Guild. There are 219 showings. On the other side of the Atlantic, the show has only 15 performances following its premiere at the Duchess on May 1, 1956.

Dec 8 *Anne of the Thousand Days* (NY—Shuberg—Drama). Rex Harrison and Joyce Redman play the leads in Maxwell Anderson's poetic drama about the marriage of Anne Boleyn and Henry VIII. There are 286 performances. The Playwrights' Company and Leland Hayward produce; H.C. Potter stages.

Dec 16 *Lend an Ear* (NY—National—Revue). Charol Channing, Gene Nelson, and Yvonne Adair are in the cast of this revue which has 460 showings. Gower Champion and Hal Gerson do the staging. Raoul Pene DuBois designs.

Dec 27 *The Madwoman of Chaillot* (NY—Belasco—Comedy). Martita Hunt and Estelle Winwood draw appreciative reviews in Jean Giraudoux's portrait of shrewd Parisian madwomen capable of sending the greedy to their doom. There are 368 showings. On Feb 15, 1951, the comedy opens at London's St. James's with Hunt again in the lead. It has only 68 performances.

Dec 30 *Kiss Me, Kate* (NY—New Century—Musical). Together, Cole Porter's songs and Sam and Bella Spewack's adaptation create a contemporary musical version of Shakespeare's *Taming of the Shrew* that runs for 1,077 performances. Alfred Drake and Patricia Morrison are the squabbling duo. The show opens at the Coliseum in London on March 8, 1951, with Bill Johnson and Morrison in the leads. It runs 501 performances.

1948 BRITISH PREMIERES

Jan 24 *Diamond Lil.* See NY premiere, 1928.

March 2 *I Remember Mama.* See NY premiere, 1944.

March 10 *Carissma* (L—Palace—Musical). Shirl Conway and Maxine Audley are in the cast of this musical romance, staged by Reginald Tate. It runs for 466 performances. Hans May provides the score for Erich Maschwitz's book and lyrics.

March 11 *Four, Five, Six!* (L—Duke of York's—Revue). Binnie Hale, Bobby Howes, and Vida Hope are among the cast of this revue which runs almost ten months.

March 20 *Rocket To the Moon.* See NY premiere, 1938.

March 29 *The Happiest Days of Your Life* (L—Apollo—Comedy). Margaret Rutherford appears in John Deighton's popular farce about schooldays. It wins a run of 605 performances. Richard Bird directs.

April 8 *Little Lambs Eat Ivy* (L—Ambassadors'—Comedy). Margot Lister is among the cast of Noel Langley's comedy, which runs for 48 weeks. Charles Hickman stages.

April 10 *Hellzapoppin'.* See NY premiere, 1938.

April 21 *Frenzy* (L—St. Martin's—Drama). Peter Ustinov bases his new drama on a Swedish original by Ingmar Bergman, and takes the lead as a tormenting schoolmaster. Joan Greenwood, Denholm Elliott, and Alan Badel are also in the cast. Murray MacDonald stages.

May 5 *Bob's Your Uncle* (L—Saville—Musical). Author Austin Melford calls this a "musical farce," and it has 363 performances. Noel Gay composes the score, with lyrics by Frank Eyton. Leslie Henson heads the cast, which he co-directs with Melford.

May 11 *All My Sons.* See NY premiere, 1947.

June 2 *Traveller's Joy* (L—Criterion—Comedy). Yvonne Arnaud and Arthur Macrae have a run of 954 performances in Macrae's comedy about rich travelers in Sweden who run out of their legal traveling allowance. Richard Bird directs.

June 3 *The Giaconda Smile* (L—New—Drama). Author Aldous Huxley earns a run of 297 performances, with Pamela Brown and Clive Brooke in leading roles.

June 3 *A Caribbean Rhapsody* (L—Prince of Wales's—Revue). Dancer Katherine Dunham and her company present dances and customs of the West Indies in this revue which has 148 performances.

June 17 *A La Carte* (L—Savoy—Revue). Hermoine Baddeley heads the cast of Alan Melville's revue, which runs for almost 31 weeks. Norman Marshall stages, with music by Charles Zwar.

June 18 *Cage Me a Peacock* (L—Strand—Musical). Yolande Donlan, Linda Gray, and Bill O'Connor are in the cast of Noel Langley's musical based on mythical characters such as Mercury and Cassandra. Charles Hickman stages, and it runs for 42 weeks.

July 28 *The Glass Menagerie.* See NY premiere, 1945.

Sep 2 *Don't Listen, Ladies* (L—St. James's—Comedy). Constance Cummings and Denholm Elliott head the cast of Stephen Powys and Guy Bolton's comedy, based on a French original by Sacha Guitry. William Armstrong stages. It runs nearly seven months.

Sep 8 *Playbill* (L—Phoenix—Drama). Eric Portman and Mary Ellis star in two Terence Rattigan plays, directed by Peter Glenville. In the first, *The Browning Version*, Portman plays a severe, repressed teacher being forced into early retirement. Ellis plays his wife. In the second, *A Harlequinade*, the pair play an aging acting duo. The production runs nearly 31 weeks. The double-bill opens in New York at the Coronet on Oct 12, 1949, with Maurice Evans and Edna Best. The run is nearly nine weeks.

Sep 11 *The Perfect Woman* (L—Playhouse—Comedy). Sonnie Hale and Gordon Craig are among the cast of Wallace Geoffrey and Basil Mitchell's comedy, which runs for seven months. J.H. Roberts stages.

Sep 30 *The Kid From Stratford* (L—Princes—Musical). Comedian Arthur Askey is in the cast of Barbara Gordon and Basil Thomas' musical, which has a score by Manning Sherwin. William Mollison stages. There are 234 performances.

Oct 11 *Lute Song.* See NY premiere, 1946.

Nov 16 *The Solitary Lover* (L—Winter Garden—Drama). Donald Wolfitt plays the writer and cleric Dean Jonathan Swift in this drama, which he also directs. Patricia Jessel and Rosalind Iden play the women in Swift's life.

Dec 8 *One Wild Oat* (L—Garrick—Comedy). Robertson Hare, Constance Lorne, and June Sylvaine animate Vernon Sylvaine's farce, which has 508 performances. Richard Bird directs.

Dec 15 *September Tide* (L—Aldwych—Drama). Gertrude Lawrence stars in Daphne Du Maurier's play, which runs almost 34 weeks. Bryan Forbes, Michael Gough, and Dandy Nichols are also in the cast. Irene Hentschel directs.

Dec 22 *High Button Shoes.* See NY premiere, 1947.

1948 REVIVALS/REPERTORIES

Jan 4 Lee Strasberg directs John Garfield in Jan DeHartog's play *Skipper Next to God* for the Experimental Theatre, an ANTA project at the Maxine Elliott Theatre. The show is so well received that it moves on Jan 29 to the Playhouse for a total of 93 showings. The play closes because Garfield must return to Hollywood.

Jan 8 At New York's City Center, Jose Ferrer and John Carradine star in a revival of Ben Jonson's *Volpone.* Richard Barr directs the 14 performances. In a 14-performance revival of Hamilton's *Angel Street* on Jan 22, Ferrer plays the fiendish husband, Uta Hagen his wife. Again Barr stages. On Feb 5, there are performances of four Chekov comedies.

Feb 3 At the New Theatre in London, the Old Vic ensemble revives Gogol's *The Government Inspector,* staged by John Burrell, with Alec Guinness and Renee Asherson. On March 31, the company revives *Coriolanus,* with E. Martin Browne as director. Guinness plays the title-role.

Feb 8 Randolph Goodman and Walter Carroll adapt Gorki's *The Lower Depths* as *A Long Way from Home,* which opens at the Maxine Elliott Theatre, under the auspices of Experimental Theatre (ANTA). The locale is now Durham, North Carolina, and the cast is black. Catherine Ayers, Josh White and Ruby Dee are among the company. Alan Schneider directs. As agreed with the theatre unions, there are only six performances.

Feb 10 Dublin's Gate Theatre Company arrives in New York at the Mansfield Theatre with a repertory including Shaw's *John Bull's Other Island,* Denis Johnstone's *The Old Lady Says "NO!",* and Micheal macLiammoir's *Where Stars Walk.* Hilton Edwards, a leading actor in the troupe, stages. There are only 30 performances.

Feb 24 Eva LeGallienne revives Ibsen's *Ghosts* for ten performances on Broadway at the Cort Theatre. This is followed by a revival of *Hedda Gabler,* for 15 per-

formances. Margaret Webster stages for the American Repertory Theatre.

March 16 Shaw's *You Never Can Tell* is revived on Broadway at the Martin Beck Theatre for five weeks, produced by the Theatre Guild. Leo G. Carroll is in the ensemble, directed by Peter Ashmore.

April 15 *King John* opens the season at the Shakespeare Memorial Theatre in Stratford-upon-Avon. Michael Benthall directs, as he does *Hamlet, The Merchant of Venice,* and *The Taming of the Shrew.* Anthony Quayle stages *The Winter's Tale* and *Troilus and Cressida. Othello* is directed by Godfrey Tearle. *Hamlet* has Paul Scofield and Robert Helpmann alternating in the title role. At the end of the season Barry Jackson resigns as festival director and Anthony Quayle takes over.

April 23 Katherine Garrison Chapin's play, *Sojourner Truth,* about a courageous black woman and her struggle for her people, opens at New York's American Negro Theatre Playhouse. Osceola Archer directs for this Harlem-based black theatre group.

May 6 *The Barretts of Wimpole Street* take up residence in London at the Garrick Theatre. This revival of Rudolf Besier's popular drama of the love-affair between Robert (Alec Clunes) and Elizabeth Barrett Browning (Margaret Johnston) is staged by H. K. Ayliff.

May 6 Jose Ferrer, as director of the New York City Theatre Company—at the City Center, opens the spring season with Ben Jonson's *The Alchemist.* Morton DaCosta stages a troupe which includes Ferrer and George Coulouris. The show has 14 performances, as does its successor, Eugene O'Neill's four sea-plays, titled *S.S. Glencairn.*

May 14 Ibsen's *The Master Builder,* staged by Peter Cotes, is revived at the Westminster Theatre in London, with Donald Wolfit in the title role.

May 22 *Tit-Coq,* by Gratien Gelinas, opens at Montreal's Monument National. The premiere marks the beginning of indigenous French-Canadian drama. In English translation, the play is produced at the Theatre du Gesu (Montreal, 1950) and in New York at the Broadhurst Theatre (Feb 8, 1951). *Tit-Coq* will become the longest-running play in Canadian theatre history. The second longest-running will be *Bousille et les Justes,* also by Gelinas.

June 1 The Liverpool Repertory Company comes to London's St. James's Theatre with their production of Chekhov's *The Cherry Orchard,* staged by John Fernald. On June 15, they are replaced by the Sheffield Repretory Company with Alfred Sangster's *The Brontes,* staged by Geoffrey Ost. On June 29, the Birmingham Repertory Company offers Sheridan's *The Rivals,* staged by William Stoker. The Bristol Old Vic arrives on July 13 to play *Hamlet,* staged by Hugh Hunt.

ALL MY SONS

June 3 At the New York City Center, the City Theatre Company offers a two-week revival of Karel and Josef Capek's *The Insect Comedy*. Jose Ferrer stages, with dances by Hanya Holm. Among the company are Ferrer, Tom Poston, George Coulouris, and Rita Gam.

June 7 At London's Sadler's Wells Theatre, the D'Oyly Carte Opera Company opens its Gilbert and Sullivan repertory with *The Gondoliers*, followed by *The Mikado* (June 9), *Iolanthe* (June 11), *Trial by Jury* and *The Pirates of Penzance* (June 12), *The Yeoman of the Guard* (June 15), *Patience* (June 17), *Cox and Box* and *H.M.S. Pinafore* (June 18).

June 8 In London's Regent's Park, the Open Air Theatre offers Robert Atkins' production of *As You Like It*. On July 6, *King John* opens. *A Midsummer Night's Dream* follows on July 27.

her Nurse. On the 24th, Tyrone Guthrie stages a 16th century Scottish play, *The Thrie Estaites*, on an open stage in the Assembly Hall. This experiment will bear fruit in Guthrie's concept of a theatre for Stratford in Canada—which will, in its turn, influence the design of other new theatre-spaces. From Paris's Theatre Marigny, comes the Compagnie Madeleine Renaud et Jean-Louis Barrault, with three productions. *Hamlet* has been translated by Andre Gide. Barrault plays the lead. *Les Fausses Confidences*, is staged by Barrault, who plays opposite Renaud. Prevert's *Baptiste* is staged and choreographed by Barrault, with Renaud. Also in the troupe is Marcel Marceau. Laurence Olivier's film version of *Hamlet* is shown at the Edinburgh Film Festival. Operas presented are Mozart's *Don Giovanni* and *Cosi fan Tutte*, from the Glyn-

Third Man—previously known as *Jealousy*—on Nov 10. She and Marius Goring are the entire cast in this Louis Verneuil play. Esme Percy directs the next Arts production, James Bridie's *Gog and MacGog*, with Alec Clunes.

Sep 19 Alec Guinness directs *Twelfth Night* in its current Old Vic revival at London's New Theatre, with Cedric Hardwicke. *Dr. Faustus* revives on Oct 7, staged by John Burrell, with Hardwicke and Faith Brook. On the 21st, Congreve's *The Way of the World* is staged by Burrell, with Edith Evans. On Nov 25, the play is Chekhov's *The Cherry Orchard* directed by Hugh Hunt.

Sep 27 The Dublin Gate Theatre opens its season with Mrs. H. T. Lowe-Porter's *Abdication*, staged by Hilton Edwards. Other shows include Micheal mac-Liammoir's *The Mountains Look Different* and a revival of *The Drunkard*, a 19th century melodrama.

Oct 4 John C. Wilson revives Noel Coward's *Private Lives* with an extensive tour for the star, Tallulah Bankhead, before the show opens tonight on Broadway at the Plymouth Theatre. It runs 31 weeks.

Oct 11 The Comedie Française arrives from Paris to present some of its traditional repertoire at London's Cambridge Theatre. Today, there are two plays opening: *La Navette* and *Le Misanthrope*. On Oct 18, another two plays open: *Un Caprice* and *Andromaque*. And on Oct 25, a further two plays: *La Bouquet* and *Le Malade Imaginaire*.

Oct 13 Shaw's *Captain Brassbound's Conversion* is revived at London's Lyric, Hammersmith, staged by John Counsell, with Flora Robson. Other autumnal revivals include James Bridie's *The Anatomist*, staged by Alastair Sim at the Westminster Theatre on Nov 2; Ibsen's *The Wild Duck*, staged by Michael Benthall, with Fay Compton on the next day at St. Martin's Theatre; Pirandello's *Naked* on the 20th, at the Torch Theatre; St. John Hankin's *The Return of the Prodigal* at the Globe Theatre on Nov 24; Eugene O'Neill's *Beyond the Horizon* on the 29th, at the New Lindsey Theatre, and on Nov 30, Strindberg's *The Father* at the Embassy Theatre, with Michael Redgrave.

Dec 7 Gian-Carlo Menotti's *The Medium* and *The Telephone* are revived at popular prices at the New York City Center for five weeks. Marie Powers and Margery Mayer alternate as the fraudulent medium.

Dec 20 Christmas is almost here, so the Old Vic's Young Vic Company opens its pantomime of *The Snow Queen*. Michel Saint-Denis and Suria Magito direct. Emile Littler's *Humpty-Dumpty* opens the next day at the Casino Theatre, with Julie Andrews in the title-role. *Where The Rainbow Ends* bows on Dec 22 at the Cambridge Theatre. On the 23rd, at the Prince's Theatre it's *Babes in the Wood*;

LEE STRASBERG

June 17 Jean-Paul Sartre's *Crime Passionel*, translated by Kitty Black, opens at London's Lyric, Hammersmith, staged by Peter Glenville. The cast includes Joyce Redman and Roger Livesy. On August 4, the production transfers to the West End's Garrick Theatre.

July 8 It's revival time at the Arts Theatre in London. Ibsen's *Rosmersholm*, staged by Peter Powell, leads off. On July 20, Shaw's *Too True To Be Good* is revived in an Esme Percy staging. On Aug 3, the play is *Tartuffe*.

Aug 11 In its new Elizabethan Theatre, the Oregon Shakespeare Festival offers to Ashland visitors Angus Bowmer's staging of *Othello* and *Love's Labour's Lost*. Allen Fletcher next directs *King John*, succeeded by *The Merchant of Venice*, with Bowmer staging.

Aug 22 Britain's Edinburgh International Festival opens. On the following day, Robinson Jeffers' version of Euripides' *Medea* is shown at the Royal Lyceum Theatre, staged by John Gielgud. Eileen Herlie plays Medea, with Cathleen Nesbitt as

debourne Festival. The Sadler's Wells Ballet returns.

Aug 26 J. B. Priestley's *Eden End*, staged by Michael MacOwen, gets a revival in London at the Duchess Theatre. Angela Baddeley plays the lead. On Aug 27, at the Boltons Theatre, Leslie and Sewell Stokes' *Oscar Wilde* is revived, directed by Leslie Stokes.

Sep 6 John Gay's *The Beggar's Opera* is revived at London's Sadler's Wells Theatre, staged by Tyrone Guthrie. Peter Pears and Nancy Evans head the cast.

Sep 7 Bessie Breuer's *Sundown Beach* is the first commercial venture of a new group, the Actor's Studio, at New York's Belasco Theatre. Lee Strasberg is the group's mentor; the director is Elia Kazan. The cast includes Martin Balsam, Phyllis Thaxter, Julie Harris, and Cloris Leachman.

Sep 9 Chekhov's *The Cherry Orchard*, staged by Peter Powell, is revived in London at the Arts Theatre. On Oct 14, Lucie Mannheim directs Chekhov's *The Bear* and Gogol's *Marriage*. She also stages *The*

260

at His Majesty's, *Charley's Aunt*, and at the Fortune Theatre, *Treasure Island*. Joan Hopkins is Peter Pan in the Barrie revival on the 24th at the Scala Theatre. *Cinderella* is on view at the King's, Hammersmith; at the Palladium, and at the Embassy Theatre. Other shows include *Jack and the Beanstalk* (Wimbledon), *The Wizard of Oz* (Strand), *Mother Goose* (Golders Green Hippodrome), *Puss in Boots* (Richmond), *A Kiss for Cinderella* (Queen's) and *The Land of the Christmas Stocking* (Duke of York's).

1948 BIRTHS/DEATHS/DEBUTS

Feb 9 American drama critic and author Burns Mantle (b. 1873) dies in Forest Hills, New York. In 1919 he inaugurated the *Best Plays* series which he edited and published annually. From 1922 until his retirement in 1943, Mantle was critic of the New York *Daily News*. He was the author of *American Playwrights of Today*.

April 11 English actor-manager and dramatist (Alexander) Matheson Lang (b. 1879) is dead in Barbados. Lang's first success was in *The Christian* in 1907 at the Lyceum Theatre. In 1913 he appeared in *Mr. Wu*, which gave title to his autobiography, *Mr. Wu Looks Back*, published in 1940.

May 9 Choreographer-dancer-director Hanya Holm makes her Broadway debut as choreographer of *The Eccentricities of Davey Crockett*, one of the John Latouche-Jerome Moross set of *Ballet Ballads* at Maxine Elliott's Theatre.

May 9 Actress Viola Allen (b. 1867) dies in New York. Allen was a member of Charles Frohman's stock company at the Empire Theatre. She appeared in many Shakespeare productions, and her role as Viola in *Twelfth Night* was acclaimed by critics.

May 22 Actor-playwright Gratien Gelinas was born in St. Tite, Quebec, Canada, Dec 8, 1909. He became known in 1937 for his comic monologue character, Fridolin, an irreverent kid from East End Montreal. Fridolin has his own weekly radio show and stars in an annual satirical revue, *Les Fridolinons*. Gelinas writes and acts in his own plays: *Tit-Coq, Bousille et les Justes, Hier, les Enfants Dansaient*. Founder of La Comédie Canadienne, Gelinas will also become President of the Canadian Theatre Centre and will help found the National Theatre School.

May 29 Dame May Whitty (b. 1865) dies in Hollywood. Whitty made her first stage appearance in London in 1881. She first came to America with Henry Irving in 1895. In 1918 Whitty was made a Dame Commander of the British Empire for charitable work. Her husband was actor Ben Webster.

June 17 American producer, playwright, and songwriter Earl Carroll (b. 1892) dies in airplane crash near Mount Carmel, Pennsylvania.

July 27 American playwright-novelist Susan Glaspell (b. 1882) dies in Provincetown, Massachusetts. Glaspell was active in the formation of the Provincetown Players where several of her plays were produced. She is best remembered for her Pulitzer Prize-winning *Alison's House*.

Nov 1 Canadian-born actor Arthur Hill makes his stage debut as Finch in Arthur Laurents' *Home of the Brave* at London's Westminster Theatre.

Dec 10 American-born British poet-playwright T.S. Eliot is awarded the Nobel Prize for Literature.

1948 THEATERS/PRODUCTIONS

In Britain, a patent is granted to O. Heller for a rain-effect, in which water runs downward on a mirrored surface which reflects the image on a scenic background.

April Members of ASCAP, the union protecting the rights of composers and lyricists, strike for better terms for royalties on recordings and radio broadcasting of their works. Since radio is currently the best way to boost the popularity of a show-song, this hurts Broadway musicals and revues.

May 29 Tonight *Oklahoma!*, the longest-running show to date on either side of the Atlantic, closes after 2,248 performances at the St. James on Broadway.

June 1 Compiling 1947–48 Broadway season statistics, *Best Plays* editor John Chapman reports the *NY Times* count is 43 new plays, nine musicals, three revues, 30 revivals, and four shows which are called "miscellaneous." Chapman pays special note to the growing importance of Off-Broadway productions. Chapman's selection of ten *Best Plays* includes: Williams' *A Streetcar Named Desire*, Heggen and Logan's *Mr. Roberts*, Haines' *Command Decision*, Rattigan's *The Winslow Boy*, the Goetzes' *The Heiress*, Rogers and Hammerstein's *Allegro*, Gardner's *Eastward in Eden*, De Hartog's *Skipper Next To God*, Priestley's *An Inspector Calls*, and Berg's *Me and Molly*. Tennessee Williams' *A Streetcar Named Desire* wins both the Pulitzer Prize and the Drama Critics' Circle Award.

Nov 13 Flamboyant producer Mike Todd takes $340,000 to mount *As the Girls Go* at New York's Winter Garden, a burlesque musical romp, with Bobby Clark as the husband of the first woman President of the United States (Irene Rich). But after nearly a year's run, the show fails to pay back its investment.

EVE LEGALLIENNE

Jan 13 *Along Fifth Avenue* (NY—Broadhurst—Revue). Nancy Walker and Jackie Gleason are among the cast of this revue which has 180 performances. Music is by Gordon Jenkins, with lyrics from Tom Adair. Charles Friedman stages.

Feb 10 *Death of a Salesman* (NY—Morosco—Drama). Arthur Miller wins the Pulitzer Prize, the Drama Critics' Circle Award, and a run of 742 performances with this drama of a salesman who dreams the American dream but can't make it work for him. Lee J. Cobb, Mildred Dunnock, Cameron Mitchell, and Arthur Kennedy get raves. The show premieres on July 28, 1949 in London at the Phoenix with Paul Muni in the lead. There are 204 performances.

Feb 24 *The Big Knife* (NY—National—Drama). Lee Strasberg directs John Garfield in Clifford Odets's drama about a Hollywood star being blackmailed by his studio. It runs nearly 14 weeks. On Jan 1, 1954, the play opens in the West End at the Duke of York's with Sam Wanamaker in the lead. The production has 138 showings.

March 2 *Two Blind Mice* (NY—Cort—Comedy). Melvyn Douglas and Jan Sterling head the cast of Sam Spewack's comedy about Washington bureaucracy. Spewack stages; it runs 157 performances.

March 8 *At War with the Army* (NY—Booth—Comedy). Gary Merrill plays a 1st sergeant in this comedy about life in an army training-camp written by a playwriting student, James B. Allardice. It wins 151 performances. Ezra Stone stages.

March 23 *Detective Story* (NY—Hudson—Drama). There are 581 performances of Sidney Kingsley's melodrama about a detective, driven by internal stresses who acts as judge and jury. Ralph Bellamy, Maureen Stapleton, and Lee Grant head the cast. The play opens in London at the Prince's on March 25, 1950, with Douglas Montgomery in the lead. It has only 41 showings.

March 27 *The Whole World Over* (NY—Biltmore—Comedy). Uta Hagen, Sanford Meisner, and Jo Van Fleet are in the cast of Konstantine Simonov's domestic comedy about a housing shortage in Moscow. Harold Clurman directs the 100 performances.

April 4 *The Traitor* (NY—48th Street—Drama). Herman Wouk's play about an American atomic scientist who believes he can prevent war by passing secrets to the Russians so both sides have the bomb, runs only 67 performances. Walter Hampden and Jean Hagen are in the cast, directed by Jed Harris.

April 7 *South Pacific* (NY—Majestic—Musical). A smash hit, Joshua Logan and Oscar Hammerstein II's book, based on

DEATH OF A SALESMAN

James Michener's *Tales of the South Pacific*, wins 1,925 performances and the Pulitzer Prize. Richard Rodgers composes a lavish score, with Hammerstein lyrics. Mary Martin and Ezio Pinza star. The show is a hit in England as well. It opens at the Drury Lane on Nov 1, 1951, for 1,830 performances. Martin and Wilbur Evans head the cast.

July 15 *Miss Liberty* (NY—Imperial—Musical). Bartholdi's statue is about to be dedicated in New York harbor in this Robert E. Sherwood musical, with songs by Irving Berlin and choreography by Jerome Robbins. Allyn McLerie, Mary McCarty, and Eddie Albert are among the cast. Moss Hart and Robbins stage for 308 showings.

Oct 12 *The Browning Version/Harlequinade*. See L premiere *(Playbill)*, 1948.

Oct 13 *Touch and Go* (NY—Broadhurst—Revue). Jean and Walter Kerr's revue has a large cast, including Kyle MacDonnell and Daniel Nagrin, and a score by Jay Gorney. It runs 22 weeks. The show premieres in London on May 19, 1950, at the Prince of Wales's where it runs for 11 months. Kaye Ballard, Helen Gallagher, and Carole Lynne are among the cast.

Oct 29 *Montserrat* (NY—Fulton—Drama). Emlyn Williams, Julie Harris, and William Redfield head the cast in this Lillian Hellman adaptation of Emmanuel Robles French play about Simon Bolivar. Hellman stages, but it runs just two months. Richard Burton plays Monstserrat in Lon-

don at the Lyric, when it opens there on April 8, 1952.

Oct 30 *Lost in the Stars* (NY—Music Box—Musical). Kurt Weill provides the score for Maxwell Anderson's adaptation of Alan Paton's novel of black suffering in South Africa, *Cry, the Beloved Country*. Todd Duncan and Julian Mayfield head the cast. Rouben Mamoulian stages the 273 performances.

Oct 31 *Regina* (NY—46th-Street—Musical). Composer-librettist Marc Blitzstein creates a modern opera by adapting Lillian Hellman's *The Little Foxes*. Jane Pickens plays Regina. Robert Lewis stages, Cheryl Crawford produces the seven week run.

Nov 22 *That Lady* (NY—Martin Beck—Drama). Katharine Cornell plays a princess in the court of King Philip of Spain, confined in her castle by the jealous monarch. Kate O'Brien's stage adaptation of her novel, says critic John Chapman, is a "lead-footed bore." It has only 78 showings. Guthrie McClintic stages.

Nov 25 *Texas, Li'l Darlin'* (NY—Mark Hellinger—Musical). Kenny Delmar plays a Texas politician running for election in Sam Moore and John Whedon's book, with music by Robert Emmett Dolan and lyrics by Johnny Mercer. Paul Crabtree stages. It runs beyond the season's end.

Dec 3 *Clutterbuck*. See L premiere, 1946.

Dec 8 *Gentlemen Prefer Blondes* (NY—Ziegfeld—Musical). Carol Channing plays the wide-eyed Lorelei in Anita Loos and

Herbert Fields' adaptation of Loos' satiric novel set in the 20's. Jule Styne writes the score, with Leo Robin's lyrics ("Diamonds Are a Girl's Best Friend"). John C. Wilson stages the show which runs beyond the season's end.

Dec 26 *The Velvet Glove* (NY—Booth—Comedy). Grace George plays a wise nun in a convent school who saves the job of a liberal young lay teacher. Rosemary Casey's play runs 19 weeks. Guthrie McClintic directs.

1949 BRITISH PREMIERES

Jan 5 *Harvey*. See NY premiere, 1944.

Jan 26 *Oranges and Lemons* (L—Globe—Revue). Diana Churchill, Max Adrian, and Elisabeth Welch are among the cast of this Laurier Lister revue, which transfers from the Lyric, Hammersmith, and earns a run of 116 performances.

Feb 1 *The Heiress*. See NY premiere, 1947.

Feb 2 *The Damask Cheek*. See NY premiere, 1942.

Feb 23 *The Foolish Gentlewoman* (L—Duchess—Drama). Sybil Thorndike and her actor-husband Lewis Casson head the cast of Margery Sharp's play, which runs for 180 performances. Michael MacOwan stages.

March 17 *Adventure Story* (L—St. James's—Drama). Terence Rattigan wanders somewhat afield from his usual British turf. Noel William is Darius the Great; Paul Scofield, Alexander; Raymond Westwell, Ptolemy; Roberty Flemyng, Philotas; William Devlin, Bessus, and Gwen Ffrangcon-Davies, the Queen Mother of Persia. Directed by Peter Glenville, this historical fiction has a run of 107 performances.

March 19 *Latin Quarter* (L—Casino—Revue). Robert Nesbitt devises and stages this musical revue which has 445 performances. Georges Guetary and Frances Day are in the company.

March 23 *Daphne Laureola* (L—Wyndham's—Comedy). Edith Evans and Felix Aylmer have leads in James Bridie's comedy about an amiable eccentric who marries her butler when her aged husband dies. It runs 46 weeks. The show opens at the Music Box on Broadway on Sep 18, 1950, with Evans repeating her role. It runs only seven weeks.

April 14 *Brigadoon*. See NY premiere, 1947.

May 3 *Black Chiffon* (L—Westminster—Drama). Flora Robson stars in Lesley Storm's play about a woman who steals a black chiffon nightgown. It runs 51 weeks. On Sep 27, 1950, the play opens at New York's 48th Street Theatre with Robson again in the lead. The show has 109 performances.

May 11 *The Lady's Not for Burning* (L—Globe—Comedy). Christopher Fry's verse-drama of witch-burning runs 37 weeks. Pamela Brown and John Gielgud head the cast in this comedy first seen at the Arts Theatre in 1948. The play opens in New York at the Royale on Nov 8, 1950, with the same cast. It runs for 151 performances.

May 18 *Sauce Tartare* (L—Cambridge—Revue). There are 433 performances of this Cecil Landau revue. Renee Houston, Zoe Gail and Ronald Frankau are among the cast. Geoffrey Parsons and Berkeley Fase provide the music.

May 20 *Ann Veronica* (L—Piccadilly—Drama). Wendy Hiller and Cyril Ritchard play the leads in Ronald Gow's adaptation of H. G. Wells' novel. Peter Ashmore directs. The play runs nearly four months.

June 1 *On Monday Next . . .* (L—Comedy—Comedy). Henry Kendall plays the director of a bad play by a timid author. It's in rehearsal in Philip's King's comedy which has 444 performances. Kendall and Shaun Sutton co-direct.

June 13 *The Third Visitor* (L—Duke of York's—Drama). Sonia Dresdel plays a wife involved in a mysterious murder in Gerald Anstruther's thriller, which runs for 33 weeks. Ellen Pollock stages.

June 22 *Her Excellency* (L—Hippodrome—Musical). Cicely Courtneidge plays Britain's first woman ambassador. With book by Archie Menzies and Max Kester and songs by Manning Sherwin and Harry Parr-Davies, the show runs nearly eight months. Jack Hulbert stages.

June 27 *The Male Animal*. See NY premiere, 1940.

July 7 *Young Wives' Tale* (L—Savoy—Comedy). Ronald Jeans' comedy of errors about the housing shortage, runs for almost 47 weeks. Joan Greenwood and Naunton Wayne head the cast. Michael MacOwan stages.

July 28 *Death of a Salesman*. See NY premiere, 1949.

Aug 31 *Tobacco Road*. See NY premiere, 1933.

Sep 1 *Master of Arts* (L—Strand—Comedy). William Douglas Home's comedy about a schoolboy who tries to blackmail his housemaster runs for 107 performances. Roland Culver is in the cast. Michael Benthall stages.

Sep 14 *Treasure Hunt* (L—Apollo—Comedy). Sybil Thorndike, Alan Webb, and Marie Löhr head the cast of M.J. Farrell and John Perry's comedy about an aristocratic pair who decide to take in paying-guests to maintain their almost bankrupt estate. John Gielgud stages. It runs for 11 months.

Sep 15 *King's Rhapsody* (L—Palace—Musical). There are 839 performances of Ivor Novello's popular new musical romance. Novello, Phyllis Dare, and Vanessa Lee head the cast. Christopher Hassall provides lyrics for Novello's music, Murray MacDonald stages.

Sep 27 *Folies Bergere Revue* (L—Hippodrome—Revue). Dick Hurran adapts the Paris book of Paul Derval and Michael Gyarmathy in this lavish revue which has 881 performances. Comedian Michael Bentine is among the cast.

Oct 10 *Bouyant Billions* (L—Prince's—Comedy). George Bernard Shaw's play, staged by Esme Percy, runs only five weeks, despite a cast that includes Frances Day and Denholm Elliott.

Oct 11 *A Streetcar Named Desire*. See NY premiere, 1947.

Nov 3 *Queen Elizabeth Slept Here* (L—Strand—Comedy). Husband-and-wife team Dulcie Gray and Michael Denison play a young couple who spend all their savings on a run-down house, only to risk losing it, in Talbot Rothwell's British adaptation of George S. Kaufman and Moss Hart's farce, *George Washington Slept Here*. Richard Bird stages the 11-month run.

Dec 1 *The Philadelphia Story*. See NY premiere, 1939.

Dec 6 *Bonaventure* (L—Vaudeville—Drama). Fay Compton plays a nun who turns amateur detective and solves a murder, in Charlotte Hastings' play which has 149 performances. Charles Hickman stages.

Dec 7 *Castle in the Air* (L—Adelphi—Comedy). Jack Buchanan and Coral

MISS LIBERTY

Browne head the cast of Alan Melville's comedy about an earl whose plans to sell his decaying castle are almost foiled by Coal Board bureaucrats who want the castle as a holiday home for miners. Roy Rich directs the nine-month run.

Dec 14 *Murder at the Vicarage* (L—Playhouse—Drama). Barbara Mullen plays Miss Marple, Agatha Christie's sleuth, in this Moie Charles and Barbara Toy adaptation of a Christie novel. It has 127 performances. Reginald Tate stages.

1949 REVIVALS/REPERTORIES

Jan 3 The Old Vic's Young Vic Company offers London *As You Like It*, staged by Glen Byam Shaw.

Jan 4 Sydney Grundy's *A Pair of Spectacles* is revived in London at the Arts Theatre, staged by Alec Clunes. Esme Percy directs the revival of Shaw's *Widowers' Houses* on Feb 2. John Fernald stages Jean-Jacques Bernard's *The Unquiet Spirit* on the 24th, followed on March 22, by W. Somerset Maugham's *Caroline*, directed by Joan Swinstead. Roy Rich stages Goldsmith's *She Stoops To Conquer* on April 19, with Megs Jenkins and Brenda Bruce. Rich also stages *The Male Animal*, by Thurber and Nugent, on May 18, with Arthur Hill and Bessie Love. On June 21, director Swinstead revives Hubert Henry Davies' *The Mollusc*.

Jan 18 Strindberg's *The Father*—destined for the Duchess Theatre on the 24th, comes to London's Embassy Theatre with Michael Redgrave in the lead. On Feb 15, Jerome K. Jerome's *The Passing of the Third Floor Back* is revived by director Wyndham Goldie. Albert Camus' *Caligula* opens on March 8, staged by Alexis Solomis, with Theodore Bikel. On March 22, the play revived is Max Catto's *They Walk Alone*, staged by Laurence Payne. Philip King's *On Monday Next . . .* opens on April 5, followed on the 26th by *A Woman in Love*, by Georges de Porto-Riche, which Michael Redgrave stages and translates with Diana Gould.

Jan 20 Laurence Olivier stages this Old Vic revival of Sheridan's *The School for Scandal* at the New Theatre in London. He and Vivian Leigh star. On Jan 26, Olivier is *Richard III*, with Leigh as Lady Anne, in the staging of John Burrell. Olivier directs Jean Anouilh's *Antigone* and plays the Chorus on Feb 10, with Leigh as Antigone. Chekhov's *The Proposal* is a curtain-raiser.

Jan 25 At the New York City Center, the Theatre Guild revives Rodgers and Hammerstein's *Carousel* for an engagement at popular prices, followed by a move to the Majestic Theatre on Broadway for a total of six weeks. On May 2, Judith Anderson returns from her national tour with Robinson Jeffers' *Medea* for a two-week engagement. On May 16, Maurice Evans returns from his national tour with Shaw's *Man and Superman*, for 16 performances.

Feb Continuing its season, the Dublin Gate Theatre offers Strindberg's *The Father*, followed by Forzano's *To Live in Peace*, and macLiammoir's *Ill Met by Moonlight*.

Feb 9 Lilli Palmer and Jean Pierre Aumont star in Aumont's romantic comedy *My Name is Aquilon*, adapted by Philip Barry, in a Theatre Guild production at New York's Lyceum. The cast also includes Phyllis Kirk, Arlene Francis, and Doe Avedon. This Robert Sinclair staging lasts only four weeks.

Feb 24 Franz Schubert's melodies are heard again in London. At his Majesty's Theatre, *Blossom Time* has John Lewis as the composer.

April 16 Actor-director Anthony Quayle becomes director of the Shakespeare Memorial Theatre in Stratford-upon-Avon. The season opens today with his staging of *Macbeth*. *A Midsummer Night's Dream* and *Cymbeline* are staged by Michael Benthall. John Gielgud directs *Much Ado About Nothing*. Tyrone Guthrie directs *Henry VIII*. Godfrey Tearle's *Othello* is revived from last season.

May 5 John Clements revives Farquhar's Restoration comedy, *The Beaux' Stratagem* in London at the Phoenix Theatre. Clements and his wife Kay Hammond head the cast.

May 16 The D'Oyly Carte Opera Company returns to London for a season of its traditional Gilbert & Sullivan repertory at Sadler's Wells Theatre: *Ruddigore*, *Trial by Jury* and *The Pirates of Penzance*, *The Mikado*, *The Yeomen of the Guard*, *The Gondoliers*, *Cox and Box* and *H. M. S. Pinafore*, *Iolanthe* and *Patience*.

Summer In San Diego, the Old Globe Theatre comes to life again as the home of the San Diego National Shakespeare Festival. The theatre was intended by Thomas Wood Stevens to suggest Shakespeare's original London playhouse.

June 2 In London's Regent's Park the summer drama season gets underway in the Open Air Theatre with a production of *Much Ado about Nothing*, staged by Robert Atkins. On June 27, the play is *The Comedy of Errors*. *Two Gentlemen of Verona*, is the next production offered in an Atkins staging. On July 18, Atkins presents *The Tempest*. Goethe's *Faust*, translated by Graham and Tristan Rawson, opens on Aug 9.

June 14 From Glasgow the Citizens' Theatre company comes to London to show its production of *Let Wives Tak Tent*, a "free translation into Scottish" of Moliere's *L'Ecole des Femmes*. John Casson directs. On June 28, the Nottingham Theatre Company offers *Othello*, staged by Andre Van Gyseghem. Leo McKern and Maxine Audley are in the ensemble. On July 12, the troupe is the Bristol Old Vic with Peter Watling's *Wilderness of Monkeys*, staged by Allan Davis. The Embassy Theatre is the venue.

June 15 Terence Rattigan's very successful early comedy, *French Without Tears*, is revived in London at the Vaudeville Theatre. Robert Flemyng stages. Flemyng and Moira Lister head the cast.

July 11 *Song of Norway*, Wright and Forrest's reworking of the music and life of Edvard Grieg, gets a revival in London at the Palace Theatre.

Aug 1 William Douglas Home's *The Chiltern Hundreds* has a revival at the Strand Theatre in London. At the Aldwych Theatre on Aug 10, David Belasco's *The Return of Peter Grimm* is revived, staged by Robert Henderson.

Aug 2 *Romeo and Juliet*, staged by Richard Graham, opens the annual Oregon Shakespeare Festival in Ashland. James Sandoe directs *Richard II* and *A Midsummer Night's Dream*. These are followed by Allen Fletcher's stagings of *Othello* and *The Taming of the Shrew*. All are presented uncut, without intermission.

Aug 21 Britain's Edinburgh International Festival opens. *The Thrie Estaites*, given an innovative staging last season by Tyrone Guthrie, is revived. The Scottish Theatre also presents Allan Ramsay's *The Gentle Shepherd*, staged by Guthrie. T. S. Elliot's *The Cocktail Party* is premiered, staged by E. Martin Browne. In the cast are Alec Guinness, Cathleen Nesbitt, Ursula Jeans, and Irene Worth. Peter Ustinov stages his play, *The Man in the Raincoat*. Mary Ellis and George Coulouris are among the cast. The distinguished German actor-director, Gustaf Gruendgens comes to the Festival with the Dusseldorf Schauspielhuas ensemble in his production of Goethe's *Faust*. Verdi's *Un Ballo in Maschera* and Mozart's *Cosi fan Tutte* are presented by the Glyndebourne Festival Opera.

Oct 4 Chekhov's *The Seagull*, staged by Irene Hentschel, is revived at London's Lyric Theatre, Hammersmith. (On Nov 16, it moves to St. James's Theatre). Paul Scofield and Mai Zetterling head the cast. Other autumn revivals include *Lady Audley's Secret* at the Bedford Theatre on Oct 17; *The Diary of a Scoundrel*, by Ostrovsky, at the Arts Theatre on the 19th; *Hindle Wakes*, by Houghton, at the Arts on Nov 23; and the musical, *Me and My Girl*, at the Winter Garden on Dec 12, staged by Lupino Lane.

Oct 11 It's another season with the Old Vic Company in its temporary West End home, London's New Theatre. *Love's Labour's Lost*, staged by Hugh Hunt, opens, with Michael Redgrave, Paul Rogers, and

Yvonne Mitchell. On Oct 18, the company offers Goldsmith's *She Stoops To Conquer*, directed by Michael Benthall. On Nov 30, Redgrave plays Rakitin in Turgenev's *A Month in the Country*, staged by Michel Saint-Denis.

Nov 2 S. N. Behrman adapts Marcel Achard's *I Know My Love* at New York's Shubert Theatre for Alfred Lunt and Lynn Fontanne, celebrating 25 years of acting as a romantic duo. The Theatre Guild production has 246 performances. Lunt stages.

Nov 29 The two Hermiones, Gingold and Baddeley, join forces in a London revival of Noel Coward's *Fallen Angels*, directed by Willard Stocker. *Fumed Oak* is the curtain-raiser. There are 299 performances at the Ambassadors'.

Dec 20 At London's Players' Club, the Christmas pantomime is a revival of the 19th century *Beauty and the Beast*, by J. R. Planche. At the Mercury Theatre, the following day, the title is the same, but the script is by Nicholas Stuart Gray. At the Casino Theatre, Emile Littler offers his *Little Miss Muffet*. On Dec 22, *The Silver Curlew* is revived at the Arts Theatre. Other holiday treats include *Cinderella Comes of Age* (Torch), *Puss in Boots* (Palladium), *Dick Whittington* (Prince's, Wimbledon, King's Hammersmith), *Charley's Aunt* (Piccadilly), *Peter Pan* (Scala, with Margaret Lockwood as Peter), *Christmas Party* (Cambridge), *Treasure Island* (Fortune), *Where the Rainbow Ends* (Comedy), *Aladdin* (Richmond), *Cinderella* (People's Palace), *A*

ADVENTURE STORY

Midsummer Night's Dream (St. Martin's), and *Snow White and the Seven Dwarfs* (Victoria Palace).

Dec 21 Cedric Hardwicke stages this revival of Shaw's *Caesar and Cleopatra* on Broadway at the National Theatre, with Lilli Palmer as Cleopatra. It has 149 performances.

Dec 28 At the New York City Center, the City Theatre Company revives Goldsmith's *She Stoops To Conquer* for two weeks, staged by Morton DaCosta. Maurice Evans, acting as volunteer Artistic Director, gets Ezra Stone, Burl Ives, Carmen Mathews, and Brian Aherne to rehearse and act for $50 a week.

agency qualified to send an official theatre delegation to a meeting of the International Theatre Institute." Atkinson is referring to the UNESCO organization which makes possible the exchange throughout the world of information, experience, and ideas about theatre.

May 29 The current Broadway season, ending the decade of the 1940s, is summed up today by the *NY Times*. Of the 70-production total, 43 have been plays; 8, musicals; 5, revues; 5, revivals; and 9, miscellaneous. This season has had 19 fewer productions than last.

June 1 At the end of the 1948–49 Broadway season, as reported by *Variety*, there are fifteen distinct box-office hits, costing a total of $1,940,000 to produce. By this date, they have returned $2,176,000, but not all have yet recouped their original investment. *Edward, My Son* has earned a profit of $130,000 on an initial $70,000 investment. Tallulah Bankhead's *Private Lives* revival has returned its $25,000 costs five-fold. *As the Girls Go*, produced for an impressive $340,000 has already earned all of that, save $10,000, with the end of its run nowhere in sight. There are 47 failures though, with a total loss of $4,535,000. *Magdalena* and *Heaven on Earth* between them have lost $650,000.

June 1 John Chapman's annual selection of the ten *Best Plays* is: Miller's *Death of a Salesman*, Anderson's *Anne of the Thousand Days*, Giraudoux's *The Madwoman of Chaillot*, Kingsley's *Detective Story*, Morley and Langley's *Edward, My Son*, Lindsay and Crouse's *Life With Mother*, Hart's *Light Up the Sky*, McEnroe's *The Silver Whistle*, Spewack's *Two Blind Mice*, and Kanin's *Goodbye, My Fancy*. Miller's *Death of a Salesman* wins both the Drama Critics' Circle Award and the Pulitzer Prize.

1949   BIRTHS/DEATHS/DEBUTS

April 6 Actor-manager Sir John Martin Harvey (b., 1863) is dead. Sir John made his first appearance on stage in 1881. In 1889 Sir John inaugurated his own management at the Lyceum Theatre. Among his later productions were *Everyman*, *Hamlet*, and *Henry V*. In 1912 he was acclaimed for his performance in the Max Reinhardt production of *Oedipus Rex*. His autobiography was published in 1933.

April 6 English actor-manager and dramatist Sir Edward Seymour Hicks (b. 1871) dies in Hampshire. England. With Charles Brookfield, he produced *Under the Clock*, the first review seen in London. He published several volumes of reminiscences as well as a number of plays.

April 21 American drama critic and his-

torian Lloyd Lewis (b. 1891) dies in Libertyville, Illinois. Lewis was critic and film and drama editor of the *Chicago Daily News*. He is also the author of the play, *Jayhawker*, in collaboration with Sinclair Lewis.

Nov 25 American stage and screen actor and dancer Bill Robinson (b.1878) dies in New York. Robinson first gained a reputation as a dancer in vaudeville

Dec 3 American playwright Philip Barry (b. 1896) dies in New York. Barry, whose metier was high comedy, wrote such works as *Holiday*, *Here Come the Clowns*, and *The Philadelphia Story*. *Second Threshold*, an unfinished comedy, was completed by Robert Sherwood.

1949   THEATERS/PRODUCTIONS

New York's Drama Desk is founded. Membership includes critics, reporters, editors, and commentators in all media on the New York theatre.

Jan 30 The *NY Times*' drama critic Brooks Atkinson writes about "National Theatre," commenting: "...We are the only first-class nation without a government

Jan 5 *The Member of the Wedding* (NY—Empire—Drama). Julie Harris stars in Carson McCuller's atmospheric exploration of children growing up in the South. It wins 501 showings. The *New York Times* says it "has incomparable insight, grace and beauty." It's produced in London at the Royal Court Theatre on Feb 4, 1957, with Geraldine McEwan as Frankie. Tony Richardson directs.

Jan 18 *The Enchanted* (NY—Lyceum—Comedy). Leueen McGrath appears in Maurice Valency's adaptation of Jean Giraudoux's script, staged by George S. Kaufman. John Chapman names it one of the year's ten "Best Plays," but this blend of French fantasy achieves only 45 performances.

Jan 21 *The Cocktail Party* (NY—Henry Miller—Drama). T.S. Eliot's poetic mysticism, brought from the Edinburgh Festival by Gilbert Miller and Henry Sherek, features Alec Guinness, Irene Worth, and Cathleen Nesbitt. An immediate success, it runs 409 performances, but Brooks Atkinson notes it leaves "a theatregoer impressed without being enlightened." The show opens at London's New Theatre on May 3, with Rex Harrison, Ian Hunter, and Alison Leggatt in the cast. It has a run of 10 months.

Jan 24 *The Happy Time* (NY—Plymouth—Comedy). Samuel Taylor adapts the popular book by Robert Fontaine, dealing with an Ottawa boy's youth in a loving French-Canadian family. Johnny Stewart, Claude Dauphin, and Eva Gabor lead

MEMBER OF THE WEDDING

the cast. Produced by Richard Rodgers and Oscar Hammerstein II, it runs for 614 performances. The comedy opens in London at the St. James's on Jan 30, 1952, with Andrew Ray, Peter Finch, and Rachel Kempson. The play is not popular, surviving only four weeks.

Feb 1 *The Innocents* (NY—Playhouse—Drama). William Archibald makes a stageworthy adaption of Henry James's *The Turn of the Screw* with Beatrice Straight playing the governess. Brooks Atkinson calls Peter Glenville's direction "a work of art," but it runs only 141 performances because Straight is expecting a child. On July 3, the drama opens at London's His Majesty's with Flora Robson in the lead. The production runs nearly six months.

Feb 15 *Come Back, Little Sheba.* (NY—Booth—Drama). In William Inge's tale of a disillusioned couple, Shirley Booth plays the slatternly but romantic Lola, with Sidney Blackmer as Doc, her hard-drinking husband. Their lost hopes are symbolised in the title, a reference to Lola's forlorn call for her lost pet Sheba, which she finally realizes will never come back. There are 191 performances.

March 15 *The Consul* (NY—Ethel Barrymore—Musical). Gian-Carlo Menotti wins the Pulitzer Prize for music with this opera, and the Drama Critics' Circle votes it the season's "Best Musical." Patricia Neway and Marie Powers take leading roles. There are 269 performances. Menotti's stark drama of a desperate woman trying to get a visa to join her husband in exile comes to London's Cambridge on Feb 7, 1951, where it has only 85 performances.

March 29 *The Wisteria Trees* (NY—Martin Beck—Drama). "Southern Fried Chekhov" is one pundit's verdict on Joshua Logan's attempt to restage *The Cherry Orchard* in the American postbellum South. Helen Hayes plays Lucy Ransdell, the American Ranyevskaya. It runs nearly 21 weeks.

April 26 Much is hoped in New York for *A Phoenix Too Frequent*, by the British poet, Christopher Fry, but this tale of a mourning widow, brought back to the love of life by a soldier who finds her in her husband's tomb plays only five times. Nina Foch is the widow.

April 27 *Tickets, Please!* (NY—Coronet—Revue). Led by Grace and Paul Hartman, this revue gets off to a lively start by panning the critics. Produced by Arthur Klein, it runs nearly 31 weeks.

June 28 *Peepshow* (NY—Winter (NY—Winter Garden—Revue). Producer Mike Todd presents yards of scantily-clad girls and suggestive burlesque comics, and is asked to tone down some of the material by the Commissioner of Licenses. Has-

WISTERIA TREES — HELEN HAYES

sard Short and Bobby Clark stage. It runs nearly 35 weeks.

Sep 18 *Daphne Laureola.* See L premiere, 1949.

Sept 25 *Affairs of State* (NY—Royale—Comedy). This romantic comedy is set in official Washington. Written by Louis Verneuil, it stars Celeste Holm. It plays 610 performances. The comedy opens at the Cambridge in London on Aug 21, 1952, with Coral Browne, Hugh Williams, Wilfrid Hyde White and Joyce Redman in the cast. There are 612 showings.

Sep 27 *Black Chiffon.* See L premiere, 1949.

Oct 7 *The Gioconda Smile.* See L premiere, 1948.

Oct 12 *Call Me Madam* (NY—Imperial—Musical). Ethel Merman plays an exuberant, party-giving American ambassador. Songs are by Irving Berlin, libretto by Howard Lindsay and Russel Crouse. Jerome Robbins choreographs. The show runs 644 performances. It opens in London at the Coliseum on March 15, 1952, with Billie Worth. There are 485 showings.

Oct 18 *Burning Bright* (NY—Broadhurst—Drama). Kent Smith plays Joe, who loves Mordeen (Barbara Bel Geddes). She knows he's sterile and gives him a child by another. Written by John Steinbeck, produced by Rodgers and Hammerstein, it runs just two weeks.

Oct 24 *The Curious Savage* (NY—Martin Beck—Comedy). The critics pan John Patrick's new show about a wealthy widow (Lillian Gish) who's spending her $10 million inheritance by allowing people to induge their favorite foolish fantasies. It has only 31 performances.

Nov 8 *The Lady's Not for Burning*. See L premiere, 1949.

Nov 10 *The Country Girl* (NY—Lyceum—Drama). Clifford Odets stages his own drama about a talented actor who's become a lying drunk. Uta Hagen plays the desperate wife and Paul Kelly the thespian. It has 235 performances. Odets's drama, this time called *Winter Journey*, opens in the West End at the St. James's on April 3, 1952, with Michael Redgrave and Googie Withers. The production runs over 30 weeks.

Nov 14 *Bell, Book, and Candle* (NY—Ethel Barrymore—Comedy). John Van Druten stages his new play about a coven of very sophisticated New York witches, one of whom (Lilli Palmer) is falling in love with a non-witch (Rex Harrison). It runs 29 weeks. The show comes to London's Phoenix on Oct 5, 1954, with Palmer and Harrison repeating their roles. There are 486 showings.

Nov 23 *Ring Round the Moon* (NY—Martin Beck—Comedy). Jean Anouilh's French fantasy, translated by Christopher Fry, is staged by Gilbert Miller and features Denholm Elliott. But the story is fragile, and the play endures only 68 performances.

Nov 24 *Guys and Dolls* (NY—46th Street—Musical). Jo Swerling and Abe Burrows base their book on Damon Runyan's stories of New York street characters. Frank Loesser creates the music. Robert Alda and Isabel Bigley star. It has a smashing 1,200 performances. The show comes to the Coliseum in London on May 28, 1953, with Jerry Wayne and Lizbeth Webb. There are 555 performances.

Dec 21 *Out of This World* (NY—New Century—Musical). Cole Porter creates the songs ("Climb Up the Mountain") for this musical version of Giraudoux's *Amphytrion 38*, with George Jongeyans and Charlotte Greenwood. Agnes de Mille stages. The show only garners 157 performances.

They play a group of women at a holiday camp and the audience loves it for 1,361 performances.

March 18 *Latin Quarter, 1950* (L—Casino—Revue). Robert Nesbitt creates and stages the material. Vic Oliver heads the cast, supported by Sylvie St. Clair and others. A group of young French singers, Les Compagnons de la Chanson, nearly steal the show which earns 456 performances.

March 25 *Detective Story*. See NY premiere, 1949.

May 3 *The Cocktail Party*. See NY premiere, 1950.

May 10 *The Holly and the Ivy* (L—Duchess—Drama). It's Christmas in a country vicarage and Margaret (Daphne Arthur) and Mich (Bryan Forbes) come home to visit their remote father (Herbert Lomas) and elder sister (Jane Baxter). Written by Wynyard Browne, it runs a year.

May 19 *Touch and Go*. See NY premiere, 1949.

May 23 *His Excellency* (L—Prince's—Drama). In Dorothy and Campbell Christie's drama, Eric Portman plays a Socialist trades union leader promoted to governor of a colony. There are 452 performances.

June 7 *Carousel*. See NY premiere, 1945.

June 14 *Seagulls Over Sorrento* (L—Apollo—Comedy). Hugh Hastings' play has over 1,550 performances. John Grigson, Nigel Stock, Bernard Lee, and Ronald Shiner play Royal Navy volunteers, and William Hartnell scores a success as a sadistic Petty Officer who goads them into rebellion.

June 28 *The Dish Ran Away* (L—Whitehall—Comedy). Graham Fraser's farce is based on a French play. There are some moral objections to theme—a wife shelters her husband's mistress, who is the mother of his child. Betty Paul and Frank Leighton are featured. It runs nearly 37 weeks.

1950 BRITISH PREMIERES

Jan 18 *Venus Observed* (L—St. James's Comedy). Laurence Olivier, managing the theatre, stages Christopher Fry's new poetic drama and plays the leading role of the Duke of Altair, seeking a likely stepmother for his grown son (Denholm Elliott), when the beautiful Perpetua (Heather Stannard) comes on the scene, quite distracting him. Also in the cast are Rachel Kempson, Brenda De Banzie, and Valerie Taylor. Roger Furse designs. There are 230 showings. On Feb 13, 1952, the play opens in New York at the Century Theatre. Rex Harrison plays the Duke, and the show has a run of 86 performances.

Jan 25 *A Lady Mislaid* (L—St. Martin's—Comedy). Kenneth Horne's play about two sisters (Avice Landone and Gwen Watford), who buy a cottage only to find it may conceal a corpse, is staged by Anthony Hawtrey and runs 148 performances.

Jan 26 *Ring Round the Moon* (L—Globe—Comedy). Paul Scofield, Claire Bloom, and Margaret Rutherford animate Christopher Fry's adaptation of Jean Anouilh's comedy about scheming twins. Peter Brook stages. The score is by Richard Addinsell; sets and costumes by Oliver Messel. There are 682 performances.

Feb 7 *Larger Than Life* (L—Duke of York's—Comedy). Guy Bolton adapts W. Somerset Maugham's novel *Theatre* and Jessie Royce Landis scores a success as a middle-aged trouper trying to win back her former husband, an actor (Reginald Denny). There are 118 performances.

March 2 *The Way Things Go* (L—Phoenix—Comedy). Frederick Lonsdale's comedy about an impoverished aristocratic family is staged by Anthony Pelissier and has a run of nearly five months. Among the cast are Glynis Johns, Kenneth More, and Ronald Squire.

March 7 *Home At Seven* (L—Wyndham's—Drama). Ralph Richardson plays a victim of amnesia, suspected of murder, in R.C. Sherriff's new play. Staged by Murray MacDonald, with decor by Tanya Moiseiwitsch, the drama runs 43 weeks.

March 9 *Mr. Gillie* (L—Garrick—Drama). Alastair Sim plays an over-eager Scottish schoolmaster in James Bridie's play, which has a novel Prologue and Epilogue set in Heaven. It runs 147 performances.

March 16 *Knights of Madness* (L—Victoria Palace—Revue). This slap-happy revue features the Crazy Gang, also known as Jimmy Nervo, Teddy Knox, Bud Flanagan, Charlie Naughton and Jimmy Gold.

CALL ME MADAME — ETHEL MERMAN

July 3 *The Innocents.* See NY premiere, 1950.

July 7 *Ace of Clubs* (L—Cambridge—Musical). Noel Coward stages his new show set in a Soho nightclub. Songs include "My Kind of Man" and "Chase Me, Charlie." "The Juvenile Delinquents" number is a show-stopper. Pat Kirkwood stars. There are 211 performances.

July 19 *Mister Roberts.* See NY premiere, 1948.

Aug 9 *Captain Carvallo* (L—St. James's—Comedy). Denis Cannan's "traditional comedy," directed by Laurence Olivier, has Shavian overtones, including a hero who goes to war carrying a potted geranium. James Donald and Diana Wynyard appear. There is a six-month run.

Aug 23 *The Little Hut* (L—Lyric—Comedy). Nancy Mitford adapts Andre Roussin's slight comedy in which a husband, a wife, and her lover are shipwrecked on a desert island. Robert Morley, Joan Tetzel, and David Tomlinson are directed by Peter Brook. The show has over 1,260 performances. It opens at New York's Coronet on Oct 7, 1953, with Anne Vernon, Colin Gordon, and Roland Culver. It has only 29 performances.

Sep 6 *Will Any Gentleman?* (L—Strand—Comedy). Robertson Hare plays a mild bank clerk whose hidden Dr. Jekyll complex comes to the fore when's he's hypnotized at a music hall. Vernon Sylvaine's farce, with Constance Lorne, earns a 45-week run.

Sep 7 *Accolade* (L—Aldwych—Drama). Emlyn Williams takes the lead in his play about an author, soon to be knighted, who's confronted by a blackmailer and a scandal in his past. Diana Churchill plays his wife. Williams withdraws, due to illness, after 180 performances.

Sep 12 *Reluctant Heroes* (L—Whitehall—Comedy). One of the long-running Whitehall farces (over 1,622 performances), Colin Morris' script has Wally Patch playing an army sergeant and Brian Rix, Larry Noble, and Dermot Walsh as hopeless rookies.

Oct 12 *The Fourposter* (L—Ambassadors'—Comedy). Michael Denison and Dulcie Gray play a married couple during various periods of their marriage in Jan de Hartog's play. It has 68 performances. The show opens at the Barrymore in New York on Oct 24, 1951, with Jessica Tandy and Hume Cronyn. It receives 632 showings, but Walter Kerr says it is "a shade too familiar for a thoroughly winning evening in the theatre."

Oct 13 *Dear Miss Phoebe* (L—Phoenix—Musical). Christopher Hassal bases his libretto on J.J. Barrie's play *Quality Street*, with music by Harry Parr-Davies. Carol Ray plays Miss Phoebe; Peter Graves, her lover. Charles Hickman stages. The show runs nearly nine months.

Oct 24 *Who Is Sylvia?* (L—Criterion—Comedy). Terence Rattigan, not Shakespeare, asks the question as his philandering hero (Robert Flemyng) pursues his quest for the Ideal Beauty. Anthony Quale stages. It has 381 performances.

Oct 31 *Take It From Us* (L—Adelphi—Revue). The popular radio team of Jimmy Edwards, Jay Nichols, and Dick Bentley, with Wallas Easton, amuse audiences for 570 performances—twice daily. There are sketches by Frank Muir and Denis Norden among others.

Nov 23 *To Dorothy, A Son* (L—Savoy—Comedy). Roger MacDougall's play is called "parturition behind a partition" by one critic. Sheila Sim plays the pregnant Dorothy, unseen but certainly heard; Richard Attenborough, her husband, and Yolande Donlan, his first wife. It plays over 500 performances. The show premieres at New York's Golden on Nov 19, 1951, where it has a run of only one week.

Dec 14 *Lace on Her Petticoat* (L—Ambassadors'—Drama). Class distinctions create a gap between milliner's daughter (Eleanor Macready) and marquis's daughter (Perlita Neilson) which almost results in tragedy. Aimee Stuart's play, set in turn-of-the-century Scotland, earns 190 performances.

Dec 26 *Point of Departure* (L—Duke of York's—Drama) Kitty Black translates Jean Anouilh's *Eurydice* with a new title. In this version of the Greek myth, Mai Zetterling plays an experienced Eurydice to Dirk Bogarde's virginal Orpheus. It runs five months.

1950 REVIVALS/REPERTORIES

Jan 11 Maurice Evans continues his program of two-week play-revivals at popular prices at the New York City Center. This evening it's Emlyn Williams' *The Corn Is Green*, with Eva LeGallienne. It is followed on January 25 by Evans as Dick Dudgeon in Shaw's *The Devil's Disciple*, which is so successful, it's given a commercial production on Broadway at the Royale on February 21. *The Heiress* is the last of the current series, with Margaret Philips and Basil Rathbone. It opens February 8.

Jan 17 The Old Vic Company, at London's New Theatre, offers Miles Malleson's adaptation of Moliere's *The Miser*, staged by Tyrone Guthrie, with Malleson in the title-role. On February 2, the revival is Shakespeare's *Hamlet*, in a Hugh Hunt staging, with Michael Redgrave as the Dane. The production is a triumph for Redgrave.

Jan 19 The night after Christopher Fry's *Venus Observed* opens in the West End, his *The Boy with a Cart* opens in Hammersmith at the Lyric Theatre, staged by John Gielgud, with Richard Burton in the title-role. J. M. Barrie's *Shall We Join the Ladies?* is the curtain-raiser.

Jan 24 A series of 19th century revivals opens at London's Bedford Theatre with Dion Boucicault's Irish play, *The Shaughran*, directed by Judith Furse, with Bill Shine, Dirk Bogarde, and Lucienne Hill. *East Lynne*, from Mrs. Henry Wood's melodramatic novel, opens on March 27, staged by Gordon Crier. Paul Potter's adaptation of Du Maurier's *Trilby* follows on April 17, staged by Furse. On May 8, Henry Arthur Jones and Henry Hermann's *The Silver King* comes to life, staged by Crier, with John Justin and Rosemary Scott. On May 29, Kenneth Tynan stages a revival of *The Bells*, a Henry Irving melodramatic vehicle by Leopold Lewis. Paired with this play is Henry Byron's *The Rosebud of Stingingnettle Farm*. Douglas Jerrold's *Black-Eyed Susan* is revived on June 19.

Jan 25 At the Arts Theatre in London, Bernard Shaw's *Mrs. Warren's Profession* has a revival, staged by Roy Rich. Ibsen's *John Gabriel Borkman*, staged by John Fernald, is presented on March 1. Vanbrugh's *The Provoked Wife*, staged by Max Adrian, opens on the 22nd. On April 20, the play is Chekhov's *Ivanov*, staged by Fernald, with Michael Hordern in the title-role.

Jan 26 Katharine Hepburn returns to Broadway as Rosalind in *As You Like It*. Michael Benthall conceives and stages for the Theatre Guild.

March 9 Peter Brook's production of *Measure for Measure* opens the season at England's Stratford-upon-Avon Shakespeare Memorial Theatre. The director of the festival and the theatre, Anthony Quayle, co-directs two plays: *King Lear*, with John Gielgud, and *Julius Caesar*, with Michael Langham. Gielgud's *Much Ado About Nothing* and the Tyrone Guthrie *Henry VIII* are revived from last season. When the season closes on October 28, renovations costing $65,854 begin on the theatre; seating is increasing to 1,301, with 76 standees.

April 24 Roger L. Stevens, with Peter Lawrence, revives James Barrie's *Peter Pan* on Broadway at the Imperial Theatre for 321 showings. Jean Arthur is Peter; Boris Karloff plays Captain Hook.

May 2 At the New York City Center, Cheryl Crawford revives the Lerner and Loewe musical *Brigadoon* for three weeks. It is to become one of the most popular musicals at City Center, as frequently as twice in the same year. On May 23, Williams' *A Streetcar Named Desire* is revived, starring Uta Hagen and Anthony Quinn, with Elia Kazan staging.

May 22 At the Sadler's Wells Theatre in

CAPTAIN CARVALLO

London, the Gilbert & Sullivan season opens with the D'Oyly Carte Opera Company's production of *The Mikado*, followed by *Trial by Jury* and *The Pirates of Penzance*, *The Yeomen of the Guard*, *Iolanthe*, *Patience*, *The Gondoliers*, *Ruddigore*, and *Cox and Box* and *H. M. S. Pinafore*.

May 25 The Open Air Theatre in London's Regent's Park opens its annual fair-weather season with *The Winter's Tale*, staged by the veteran Shakespeare director and actor, Robert Atkins. *The Merchant of Venice* appears on June 19; *The Taming of the Shrew*, on July 17.

June 8 Alec Clunes revives *Macbeth* at London's Arts Theatre playing the title-role. John Fernald stages Bernard Shaw's *Heartbreak House* on July 5. Roy Rich directs Maugham's *Home and Beauty* in an August 31 revival. On Sep 27, it opens at St. Martin's Theatre.

June 13 After a 20-week national tour, Alfred de Liagre, Jr., brings his production of Giraudoux's *The Madwoman of Chaillot* to the New York City Center for a two-week run at popular prices.

June 27 The Bristol Old Vic comes to the Lyric, Hammersmith, with its production of Molière's *Tartuffe*. On July 17, Benjamin Britten's English Opera Group performs Britten's version of John Gay's *The Beggar's Opera*.

July 1 Kermit Hunter's drama *Unto These Hills* is performed by Cherokee Indians in their outdoor theatre in Cherokee, North Carolina. The production becomes an annual event, attracting visitors from all over the United States.

July 24 At the Fulton Theatre on Broadway, Sam Wanamaker and Terese Hayden inaugurate the "Festival Theatre" with Henri Becque's *La Parisienne*, adapted by Ashley Dukes. On August 7, they revive Ibsen's *The Lady From the Sea*, followed on August 21, by Lynn Riggs' *Borned in Texas*. The three casts include such talents as Luise Rainer, Herbert Berghof, Francis Lederer, Faye Emerson, and An-

thony Quinn. Wanamaker directs.

July 25 Ibsen's *Rosmersholm* is revived on August 22 at the St. Martin's Theatre. On the 29th, at the Haymarket, Eileen Herlie is Paula in Pinero's *The Second Mrs. Tanqueray*.

Aug In Ashland, the Oregon Shakespeare Festival offers four plays: *Anthony and Cleopatra*, *As You Like It*, *The Comedy of Errors* and *Henry IV, Part 1*.

August 5 Paul Green's *Faith of Our Fathers*, opens in Washington, D.C. The story is centered on a critical period in the first American President's life. The production is intended to run for ten years but closes in two—with losses.

Aug 20 Britain's Edinburgh International Festival opens. The Old Vic Company presents Jonson's *Bartholomew Fair*, staged by George Devine. Among the cast are Dorothy Tutin, Paul Rogers, Richard Pasco, and Alec Clunes. The Glasgow Citizens' Theatre offers James Bridie's *The Queen's Comedy*, staged by Tyrone Guthrie and John Casson. Eric Linklater's *The Atom Doctor* and John Home's classic Scots play, *Douglas*, with Sybil Thorndike, complete their repertory.

Sep 6 George Bernard Shaw offers *Farfetched Fables*—six in all—to London audiences at the Watergate Theatre. Esmé Percy directs and appears in them.

Sep 19 John Fernald stages C. B. Fernald's *The Mask and the Face*, revived at London's Arts Theatre. In the ensemble are Eileen Thorndike, Alec McCowen, Eric Berry, and Patricia Jessel. On Oct 10, Hugh Williamson's *Queen Elizabeth* comes alive. On Nov 15, the play is Pinero's *Preserving Mr. Panmure*. *Lady Precious Stream* is revived on Dec 13.

Oct 4 London's autumnal revivals include tonight's production of *The Old Ladies*, based on Hugh Walpole's novel by Rodney Ackland, at the Lyric, Hammersmith. On the next night, R. C. Sherriff's *Journey's End* is brought back, at the Westminster Theatre. Ashley Dukes' *Man With a Load of Mischief* is revived at the

Embassy Theatre. At the same theatre, on November 21, Pirandello's *Six Characters in Search of an Author* is shown, staged by mystery-writer Ngaio Marsh. Frank Marcus directs Shaw's *The Man of Destiny* at the Chepstow Theatre on November 28, playing Bonaparte himself. Scribe's *A Glass of Water* is revived at the Mercury Theatre on Dec 11.

Nov 14 London's Old Vic Company reopens at its newly restored and improved home, previously closed because of war damage. On December 18, George Devine directs Jonson's *Bartholomew Fair*—first seen at the Edinburgh Festival.

Nov 22 Cyril Ritchard revives Sir John Vanbrugh's Restoration comedy, *The Relapse, or Virtue in Danger*, on Broadway at the Morosco Theatre. This Theatre Guild production, partly inspired by Anthony Quayle's 1948 London mounting, is New York's first professional production. There are only 30 showings.

Nov 26 *The Tower Beyond Tragedy* is the inaugural production of the new American National Theatre at New York's renamed Guild Theatre, now the ANTA. Judith Anderson plays Clytemnestra in this Robinson Jeffers verse drama, based on the *Oresteia* of Aeschylus.

Dec 19 London's first pantomime of the season is *Ali Baba* at the Players' Theatre. Don Gemmel stages, also playing Cassim Baba to Eric Chitty's Ali. There's also a traditional Harlequinade. At the Westminster Theatre, *Beauty and the Beast* opens. *Goody Two Shoes* bows at the Casino Theatre on the next day, followed on the 21st by *Peter Pan* (Scala, with Margaret Lockwood as Peter), *The Ghost Train* (Embassy), *Charley's Aunt* (Saville), and *Aladdin* (Finsbury Park Empire). Later shows include *The Silver Curlew* (Fortune), *Red Riding Hood* (Golder's Green Hippodrome), *Babes in the Wood* (Palladium), *Mother Goose* (Prince's), *Where the Rainbow Ends* (Stoll), and *Treasure Island* (Theatre Royal, Stratford East, St. James's).

Dec 24 José Ferrer and Gloria Swanson revive *Twentieth Century*, by Ben Hecht and Charles MacArthur, for the season at the ANTA Threatre on Broadway. After the limited run, Ferrer, as director and star, moves the production to the Fulton Theatre for an extended engagement.

Dec 25 Louis Calhern begins a six-week revival of Shakespeare's *King Lear* on Broadway at the National Theatre.

Dec 27 Artistic Director Maurice Evans opens the 1950-1951 season of the Theatre Company at New York City Center with a revival of Shaw's *Captain Brassbound's Conversion*, with John Archer and Edna Best. Morton DaCosta directs.

Dec 28 At Broadway's Broadhurst Theatre, Arthur Miller offers his revision of Ibsen's *An Enemy of the People*, with Fredric March and Florence Eldridge. (There are only 36 performances.)

Jan 20 Playwright Robert Anderson's sketch, "The Lunts are the Lunts," is one of the features in the revue, *Dance Me a Song*, opening tonight at the Royale Theatre. This is his first contribution to a Broadway production.

Jan 22 American stage and screen actor Alan Hale is dead in Hollywood at age 57.

Feb 16 English dramatist Charles Rann Kennedy (b. 1871) dies in Los Angeles. A long-time U.S. resident, Kennedy's plays include: *The Servant in the House*, *The Winterfeast*, and *The Terrible Meek*.

Feb 26 Scottish comedian and music hall star Sir Harry Lauder (b. 1870) dies in Scotland. Lauder made his first appearance in London in 1900, and later toured extensively in the United States, South Africa, and Australia. He received a knighthood in 1919.

March 22 American producer and playwright Arthur Hopkins (b. 1878) dies in New York. Hopkin's first production was *The Poor Little Rich Girl*, followed by O'Neill's *Anna Christie* and *The Hairy Ape*, *Hamlet*, *What Price Glory*, and others. He is also the author of *How's Your Second Act?*, *To a Lonely Boy*, and *Reference Point*.

April 3 German-born composer Kurt Weill (b. 1900) dies in New York. Among Weill's noted compositions are *The Threepenny Opera*, *Mahagony*, *The Seven Deadly Sins*, *Knickerbocker Holiday*, *Lady in the Dark*, and *One Touch of Venus*.

April 7 American actor Walter Huston (b. 1884) dies in Beverly Hills, California. Huston made his first appearance on stage in Toronto in 1902. He later played in *Desire Under the Elms*, *Kongo*, *Dodsworth*, and *Knickerbocker Holiday*. He

began his film career in 1928.

June 22 American actress Jane Cowl (b. 1884) dies in Santa Monica, Calif. Cowl appeared in a number of Belasco productions including *The Music Master*. She was acclaimed for her interpretations of Juliet and Cleopatra.

Sep 13 Irish actress Sara Allgood (b. 1883) dies in Woodland Hills, California. Allgood appeared for some years at the Abbey Theatre. Two of her finest performances were in O'Casey's *Juno and the Paycock* and *The Plough and the Stars*. She made her last stage appearance in New York in 1940, then turned to film acting.

Sep 17 Actor Pedro de Cordoba is dead in Hollywood.

Sep 19 American actress Chrystal Herne (b. 1883) dies in Boston. Herne made her professional debut at age 16 in her father's play, *Griffith Davenport*. Three of her outstanding roles were in *Craig's Wife*, *The Trojan Women*, and *Our Betters*.

Oct 10 American actress Pauline Lord (b. 1890) dies in Alamogordo, New Mexico. She made her first appearance in *Are You a Mason?* in San Francisco in 1903. Her

most notable roles were in *Samson and Delilah*, *Anna Christie*, and *Ethan Frome*.

Oct 23 American actor and singer Al Jolson (b. 1886) dies in San Francisco. Jolson first appeared on stage as one of the mob in *Children of the Ghetto*. For several years he performed with various circus and minstrel companies. Jolson's film career began in 1927 with his appearance in the first "talking" picture, *The Jazz Singer*.

Nov 2 At 94, Britain's famed playwright, critic and social reformer, George Bernard Shaw (b. 1856), is dead. Among his many plays are *Saint Joan*, *Candida*, *Major Barbara*, *Arms and the Man*, *Pygmalion*, and *Back to Mathuselah*. In 1925, he was awarded the Nobel Prize for Literature.

Nov 12 American actress Julia Marlowe (b. 1866) dies in New York City. In 1911 she married actor E. H. Sothern, after which the Sothern-Marlowe team toured in Shakespeare repertory in both England and America. Morlowe retired from the stage in 1924.

Nov 24 Robert Alda makes his Broadway debut as Sky Masterson in Frank Loesser's *Guys and Dolls* at the 46th Street Theatre. He made his debut as a singer in vaudeville in 1933 at the RKO in New York City.

1950 THEATERS/PRODUCTIONS

A patent is granted to A. Perrottet and E. Stroecklin for a theatre-structure in which the audience sits in the center on a revolving platform which can be stopped at any portion of the annular stage surrounding it. Several such systems are to be patented in Britain and America. The concept will be used in some corporate shows at world's fairs and other expositions.

June 3 The 62 productions mounted in New York during the 1949-1950 season are an all-time low. John Chapman, critic for the *New York Daily News*, blames rising production costs. Even with good reviews and runs of 100—200 performances, he notes, some plays still have lost money. The seasonal Broadway gross is $28,614,500, of which $2,553,800 is earned by *South Pacific*, taking in $50,600 per week. Investors have lost about $2.5 million, with the $200,000 *Dance Me a Song* cost to produce the largest of the losses.

June 3 At the close of the 1949-1950 season, John Chapman sums up activity Off Broadway. He reports a statistic: 264 play-producing groups in New York which are on record for the season, with a possible further 50 not registered. Actors work for as little as $5 per week, with Equity's permission. In April, 53 groups merge to find a theatre for year-round production.

June 3 John Chapman, editing the *Burns Mantle Best Plays* series, chooses the ten best dramas of the Broadway season 1949-1950. They are Eliot's *The Cocktail Party*, McCullers' *The Member of the Wedding*, Archibald's *The Innocents*, Anderson and Weill's *Lost in the Stars*, Inge's *Come Back, Little Sheba*, Taylor's *The Happy Time*, Logan's *The Wisteria Trees*, Behrman's *I Know My Love*, Giraudoux's *The Enchanted*, and Levy's *Clutterbuck*.

Aug 16 In Washington, D. C., the Arena Stage comes into existence with the production of *She Stoops To Conquer*, by Oliver Goldsmith. A group of dedicated young people are the founders; they include Edward Mangum, Vera and Pernell Roberts, and Zelda and Thomas Fichhandler. Zelda Fichhandler is Producing Director of the venture and is later, with her husband as managing director, to build it into one of America's most distinctive and adventurous regional theatre complexes. In 1961, the Arena Theatre will have a new 811-seat home near the Potomac.

Nov 14 London's Old Vic re-opens. It has been closed since May 1941, when it suffered bomb damage. The reconstruction was made to the designs of architect Douglas W. Rowntree and the theatre now seats 948.

WALTER HUSTON & NAN SUNDERLAND

Jan 2 *Second Threshold* (NY—Morosco—Comedy). Robert E. Sherwood revises the late Philip Barry's last play about a retired senator (Clive Brook) who threatens suicide over his daughter's (Margaret Phillips) plans to marry a man twice her age. The show runs 126 performances. On Sep 24, 1952, it opens in London at the Vaudeville with Clive Brook and Margaret Johnston. It runs only 69 performances.

Jan 13 *Darkness at Noon* (NY—Alvin—Drama). Sidney Kingsley adapts and stages Arthur Koestler's haunting novel about the Stalinist purges. The cast is headed by Claude Rains. It runs 23 weeks and wins the Drama Critics' Circle Award.

Feb 3 *The Rose Tattoo* (NY—Martin Beck—Comedy). The *NY Times* calls Tennessee Williams's new play " . . . the loveliest idyll written for the stage in some time." Maureen Stapleton plays a grieving widow who finds a comical but loving suitor, played by Eli Wallach. Sal Mineo and Martin Balsam are also in the cast. It runs 38 weeks. On Jan 15, 1959, the comedy opens at London's New Theatre with Lea Padovani in the lead. There are only 92 performances.

Feb 10 *Billy Budd* (NY—Biltmore—Drama). Charles Nolte plays the young seaman Billy, sentenced to death for an accidental killing, in this adaptation of Herman Melville's novella by Louis O. Coxe and Robert Chapman. The play runs 105 performances. Under the title *The Good Sailor*, the play has a brief run of 21 performances at the Lyric, Hammersmith beginning April 4, 1956.

March 7 *The Autumn Garden* (NY—Coronet—Drama). Lillian Hellman's new play explores wasted lives and missed opportunities, but, says the *New York Daily Mirror*, " . . . it never focuses to an effective point." It stars Fredric March and Florence Eldridge, and runs only 13 weeks.

March 8 *The Moon is Blue* (NY—Henry Miller—Comedy). F. Hugh Herbert's romantic comedy, with Barbara Bel Geddes and Barry Nelson, causes quite a stir among the moralists. Bel Geddes plays a virgin in circumstances which might lead to a change of designation. The comedy comes to the Duke of York's in the West End on July 7, 1953, with Diana Lynn and Biff McGuire. It earns a run of 175 performances.

March 29 *The King and I* (NY—St. James—Musical). Richard Rodgers (music) and Oscar Hammerstein II (book and lyrics) base this hit show (1,246 performances) on Margaret Landon's book *Anna and the King of Siam*. When an English governess (Gertrude Lawrence) is engaged to tutor Siam's Crown Prince, she also effects a

THE KING & I

change in the austere King (Yul Brynner). Jerome Robbins choreographs. There are 946 performances for this hit when it is presented in London at the Drury Lane beginning Oct 8, 1953. Valerie Hobson and Herbert Lom are Anna and the King.

April 18 *Make a Wish* (NY—Winter Garden—Musical). Nanette Fabray takes the lead in Preston Sturges' adaptation of Ferenc Molnar's *The Good Fairy*, with some additional doctoring by Abe Burrows. Music and lyrics are by Hugh Martin and choreography by Gower Champion. It runs only 13 weeks.

April 19 *A Tree Grows in Brooklyn* (NY—Alvin—Musical). George Abbott produces, stages, and helps Betty Smith adapt her best-selling novel about Irish family life in turn-of-the-century Brooklyn. Shirley Booth stops the show with "He Had Refinement," one of the songs by Dorothy Fields and Arthur Schwartz. It earns a 34-week run.

May 8 *Stalag 17* (NY—48th Street—Comedy). Pompous Nazis and wise-cracking American GI's animate this Donald Bevan and Edmund Trzcinski comedy set in a prison-camp. Staged by Jose Ferrer, with John Ericson, Robert Strauss, and Harvey Lembeck among the cast, it runs 472 performances. The show opens at the Prince's in the West End on April 4, 1953, where it has only 11 performances.

May 14 *Flahooley* (NY—Broadhurst—Musical). Yma Sumac, a singer with a vocal range of four octaves, is the most interesting part of this E.Y. Harburg and Fred Saidy musical, which runs just 5 weeks. The music is by Sammy Fain.

June 21 *Seventeen* (NY—Broadhurst—Musical). Booth Tarkington's novel becomes a musical set in Indianapolis in

1907, in this Sally Benson adaptation, with music and lyrics by Walter Kent and Kim Gannon. Kenneth Nelson and Ann Crowley are the leads. The show runs almost 23 weeks.

July 19 *Two on the Aisle* (NY—Mark Hellinger—Revue). Bert Lahr plays a famous baseball player talking about booze and broads while being interviewed on a children's program in this revue by Betty Comden, Adolph Green, and other others. Abe Burrows stages. The music is by Jule Styne; dances by Ted Cappy. It has a 35-week run.

Sep 12 *Bagels and Yox* (NY—Holiday—Revue). This American-Yiddish review, with its pun on lox and theatre-slang for laughs, runs 26 weeks.

Oct 3 *Remains to Be Seen* (NY—Morosco—Comedy). Leland Hayward produces Howard Lindsay and Russel Crouse's play about a murderer, a girl singer, and a jazz-loving apartment superintendant. Starring Jackie Cooper and Janis Paige, it runs 199 performances. It receives only seven performances following its London premiere at Her Majesty's on Dec 16, 1952.

Oct 16 *A Sleep of Prisoners.* See L premiere, 1951.

Oct 24 *The Fourposter.* See L premiere, 1950.

Oct 31 *Barefoot in Athens* (NY—Martin Beck—Drama). Admired by most critics, this Maxwell Anderson drama about Socrates, the late 5th century B.C. philosopher, runs only 30 performances. Barry Jones and Lotte Lenya appear. Alan Anderson directs.

Nov 1 *Top Banana* (NY—Winter Garden—Musical). Burlesque comics make a

TWO ON THE AISLE

comeback on television in Hy Kraft's book, with songs by Johnny Mercer. Phil Silvers heads a large cast which includes Jack Albertson, Herbie Faye, and Judy Lynn. The show runs nearly 11 months.

Nov 12 *Paint Your Wagon* (NY—Shubert—Musical). Alan Jay Lerner (book) and Frederick Loewe (score) use an old Bret Harte tale, *The Millionaire of Rough and Ready*, as the basis for this rousing show about an 1853 gold-strike in a California cemetery. James Barton leads the cast with Olga San Juan. Agnes de Mille choreographs. It runs nine months. On Feb 11,

1953, the musical opens at Her Majesty's with Bobby Howes and his daughter Sally Ann Howes in the leads. It has 478 performances.

Nov 24 *Gigi* (NY—Fulton—Comedy). Audrey Hepburn plays Gigi, Cathleen Nesbitt her Aunt, and Michael Evans the debonaire Gaston in this Anita Loos play based on a novel by Colette. The show has 219 performances on Broadway and then tours. Leslie Caron has the title role in the London production which opens on May 23, 1956, at the New Theatre. The show runs for 10 months.

Nov 28 *I Am A Camera* (NY—Empire—Drama). The *NY Times* calls Julie Harris "stunning" as the flamboyant Sally Bowles in John Van Druten's adaptation of Christopher Isherwood's stories of Berlin between the world wars. William Prince plays Isherwood. A 27-week run is followed by a tour. It opens at London's New Theatre on March 12, 1954, with Dorothy Tutin and Michael Gwynn. The show runs 43 weeks. Later the play becomes a musical, *Cabaret*.

Dec 13 *Point of No Return* (NY—Alvin—Comedy). Henry Fonda plays an executive who has striven to conform but now insists on being his own man, in this Paul Osborn adaptation of the J.P. Marquand novel. Leora Dana plays his wife. H.C. Potter stages. It runs nearly 46 weeks.

Dec 26 *Legend of Lovers* (NY—Plymouth—Drama). Dorothy McGuire, Richard Burton, and Hugh Griffith head the cast of this Jean Anouilh version of the Orpheus myth. Peter Ashmore directs. But the play baffles some critics; and it runs only 22 performances.

1951 BRITISH PREMIERES

Feb 7 *The Consul*. See NY premiere, 1950.

Feb 15 *The Madwoman of Chaillot*. See NY premiere, 1948.

March 1 *A Penny for a Song* (L—Haymarket—Comedy). Peter Brook directs this John Whiting farce which includes such players as Ronald Squire, Alan Webb, and Virginia McKenna.

March 6 *Folies Bergère, 1951* (L—Hippodrome—Revue). Playing twice daily, this show runs 579 performances with numbers based on the original Paris revue, devised by Paul Derval and Marcel Gyarmathy. It's staged by Dick Hurran.

March 8 *Kiss Me, Kate*. See NY premiere, 1948.

March 10 *Latin Quarter, 1951* (L—Casino—Revue). Songs, exotic dances, humorous sketches and lavish decor, add up to a revue that, playing twice-daily, achieves a run of 468 performances. Robert Nesbitt stages, with dances devised by Hazel Gee.

March 14 *The Seventh Veil* (L—Prince's—Drama). Ann Todd, Herbert Lom and Leo Genn star in the Muriel and Sydney Box melodrama about a concert pianist who fears she will never play again. Despite being adapted by the Boxs' from their successful screenplay, with Todd recreating her film role, it runs only 68 performances.

April 4 *Who Goes There!* (L—Vaudeville—Comedy). Nigel Patrick and Geraldine McEwan take the leads in John Dighton's comedy focusing on lovers' mixups. John Counsell stages. There are 222 performances.

April 19 *Waters of the Moon* (L—Haymarket—Drama). With a cast that includes Edith Evans, Sybil Thorndike, and Wendy Hiller, and a script by N.C. Hunter that is called Chekhovian, this play about the inmates of a country resident hotel achieves 835 performances. It's staged by Frith Banbury.

May 15 *Fancy Free* (L—Prince of Wales's—Revue). Comedian Tommy Trinder and musical actress Pat Kirkwood liven this revue staged by Charles Henry. Sketches and lyrics are by Barbara Gordon and Basil Thomas. It has 369 performances.

May 15 *A Sleep of Prisoners* (L—St. Thomas's Church—Drama). Christopher Fry's play shows war prisoners being held in a church who dream they are characters from the Bible. The drama is staged in the sanctuary by Michael MacOwan. Leonard White, Denholm Elliott, Stanley Baker, and Hugh Pryse are featured. The play is given at St. James's Church in New York beginning Oct 16, with most of the British cast. It is shown for four weeks and later tours the nation.

May 28 *The Love of Four Colonels* (L—Wyndham's—Comedy). Peter Ustinov stars in his own highly successful play (812 performances) which examines how men of different nationalities respond to women when they are in love. The four colonels are played by Alan Gifford, Colin Gordon, Eugene Deckers, and Theodore Bikel. The play opens in New York at the Shubert on Jan 15, 1953, with Larry Gates, Robert Coote, George Voskovec, and Stefan Schnabel. This Theatre Guild production runs nearly 18 weeks and is voted "Best Foreign Play" by the Drama Critics' Circle.

June 7 *The Hollow* (L—Fortune—Drama). This Agatha Christie whodunit set in a handsome country house is staged by Hubert Gregg. George Thorpe, Jeanne de Casalis, Ernest Clark and Joan Newell are among the cast. Later transferred to the Ambassadors' Theatre, the show runs just over 47 weeks.

June 28 *Penny Plain* (L—St. Martin's—Revue). Joyce Grenfell and Max Adrian head the cast of this colorful revue which runs 443 performances. It has been devised by Laurier Lister, with material by Grenfell, Richard Addinsell, Paul Dehn, and Michael Flanders and Donald Swann.

July 19 *My Wife's Lodger* (L—Comedy—Comedy). Queenie Barratt plays the lead in Dominic Roche's farce, staged by Vyvian Hall, who also takes a leading role. There are 258 performances.

Aug 14 *The Biggest Thief in Town* (L—Duchess—Comedy). Dalton Trumbo's tale of a Colorado undertaker who steals the body of a rich man, hoping to make a killing on the funeral expenses, moves to the West End after a tryout at the New Boltons in July. It later transfers to the Fortune, with a total run of nearly 22 weeks. Hartley Power scores a hit as the undertaker and is succeeded in the role by Liam Redmond, and by J. Edward Bromberg, the American actor, who dies during the run.

Aug 30 *Ardele* (L—Vaudeville—Drama). Jean Anouilh's satiric play about varieties of love is directed by Anthony Pelissier, with a cast headed by Isabel Jeans.

There are 67 performances.

Sep 21 *Rainbow Square* (L—Stoll—Musical). Robert Stolz provides the score for Guy Bolton and Harold Purcell's book and lyrics about life in present-day occupied Vienna. Robert Nesbitt stages. The large cast includes Sonnie Hale and Alfred Marks. It runs nearly 19 weeks.

Oct 11 *The White Sheep of the Family* (L—Piccadilly—Comedy). L. du Garde Peach and Ian Hay's play about a family of professional criminals wins a run of 34 weeks. Derek Blomfield, Rona Anderson, Jack Hulbert and Joyce Carey are in the cast.

Oct 16 *Figure of Fun* (L—Aldwych—Comedy). Arthur Macrae adapts Andre Roussin's Parisian romantic comedy. John Mills plays an actor whose wife (Natasha Parry) leaves him in order to discover if he really loves her. Staged by Peter Ashmore, it runs 211 performances.

Oct 17 *And So To Bed* (L—New—Musical). Vivian Ellis' musical version of J.B. Fagan's play about Samuel Pepys' visit to a mistress of King Charles—in which he's caught out by the king and suitably chastened—runs over 10 months. Leslie Henson, Keith Michell, and Jessie Royce Landis take leading roles. Wendy Toye stages.

Oct 20 *Zip Goes a Million* (L—Palace—Musical). Popular music hall comedian George Formby plays a man who must give away a million dollars in order to inherit even more millions in this musical version of the American play *Brewster's Millions* (1907). Charles Hickman stages the book by Eric Maschwitz and score by George Posford. The show runs 543 performances.

Nov 1 *South Pacific.* See NY premiere, 1949.

Nov 7 *Women of Twilight* (L—Vaudeville—Drama). Sylvia Rayman's play about a home for unwed mothers, run by a "baby-farmer" posing as a nurse, offers strong roles for Barbara Couper, Rene Ray, and Miriam Karlin among others. Anthony Hawtrey directs, and the play runs a year.

Nov 28 *Relative Values* (L—Savoy—Comedy). Noel Coward stages his new play which wins 477 performances. Gladys Cooper plays the Countess of Marshwood, hostess to a Hollywood film star (Judy Campbell) who seeks to marry her son and heir (Ralph Michael). Richard Leech and Angela Baddeley also appear.

Dec 13 *Colombe* (L—New—Drama). Peter Brook stages Jean Anouilh's cynical play about the instability of love, with Joyce Redman, Michael Gough, and Yvonne Arnaud. It runs nearly four months. The show opens at New York's Longacre on Jan 6, 1954, as *Mademoiselle Colombe* with Julie Harris, Edna Best, Eli Wallach, and Sam Jaffee, but there are only 61 performances.

1951   REVIVALS/REPERTORIES

Jan 7 Continuing the premiere season of the newly named ANTA Theatre, Federico Garcia Lorca's *The House of Bernarda Alba* opens with the "First Lady of the Greek National Theatre," Katina Paxinou as Bernarda. Paul Green's version of Ibsen's *Peer Gynt* opens on Jan 28, staged by Lee Strasberg, with John Garfield, Karl Malden, Sono Osato, Mildred Dunnock, and others. John Sti directs J. M. Barries' *Mary Rose*, opening March 4, with Bethel Leslie in the title role. On March 18, Louis Jouvet and his Paris troupe offer Moliere's *L'Ecole des Femmes*. Critic Edmund Wilson's drama, *The Little Blue Light*, is presented on April 29, staged by Albert Marre. The cast includes Melvyn Douglas, Burgess Meredith, Martin Gabel, and Arlene Frances. Bernard Shaw's *Getting Married* opens at the ANTA on May 7, with Peggy Wood, Bramwell Fletcher, and Arthur Treacher in the company.

Jan 9 At London's Embassy Theatre, the Spanish classic, *Celestina*, in an Ashley Dukes adaptation, is revived. On January 23, Michael Langham stages a revival of Shaw's *Pygmalion*, with Yvonne Mitchell. Val Gielgud's *Iron Curtain*, opens on February 6. *The Late Christopher Bean* is revived by Peter Powell on the 20th. On March 6, the revival is Ardrey's *Thunder Rock*. Michael Hutton's *The Happy Family* is played on March 20.

Jan 10 At the New York City Center, *The Royal Family*, by Kaufman and Ferber, is revived for a two-week run with Ethel Griffies and John Emery. On January 24, Maurice Evans plays *Richard II* for two weeks. On April 25, *The Taming of the Shrew* opens, with Claire Luce as Katherina. On May 9, Elmer Rice's *Dream Girl* is revived, with July Holliday in the title role. On May 23, Robert E. Sherwood's *Idiot's Delight* is presented.

Jan 17 Ibsen's *Hedda Gabler* is revived in London at the Arts Theatre, with Jean Forbes-Robertson. Roy Rich directs. On March 21, Jean Cocteau's *Les Parents Terribles* comes to the stage in an English version by Charles Frank, called *Intimate Relations*.

Jan 23 During the Festival of Britain, *Merrie England*, a comic opera by Basil Hood (book) and Edward German (score), is presented at London's Coliseum by the National Light Opera Company. Joan Wood plays Queen Elizabeth I; Ralph Reader stages. The show plays two weeks.

Jan 24 At London's Garrick Theatre Michael Langham directs *The Gay Invalid*, an adaptation of Moliere's *Le Malade Imaginaire*. A. E. Matthews, Elizabeth Bergner, Peter Cushing, and Daphne Slater appear. Graham Stark, as Scaramouche, heads a troupe of *Commedia* players used in the production. There are 69 performances.

Jan 26 *Medusa's Raft* a German play by Georg Kaiser, is presented at London's Watergate Theatre.

Jan 29 On Broadway at the St. James Theatre, London's D'Oyly Carte Opera Company opens a run of Gilbert & Sullivan productions beginning with *The Mikado*, with Martyn Green as Ko-Ko. Isadore Godfrey conducts. *Iolanthe, H. M. S. Pinafore, Trial by Jury*, are among the other works offered.

Jan 30 At London's Old Vic, *Henry V*, with Alec Clunes, is staged by Glen Byam Shaw. A Festival of Britain presentation, the show is designed by Motley. Among the company are Roger Livesey, Richard Pasco, Tony van Bridge, and Dorothy Tutin. On March 13, the company offers a twin-bill of Sophocles' *Electra* and Chekhov's *The Wedding*. Barbara Hepworth designs the tragedy for director Michel Saint-Denis. Motley designs the comedy for George Devine. Peggy Ashcroft is Electra to Catherine Lacey's Clytemnestra. On April 17, Shaw's *Captain Brassbound's Conversion* is revived, staged by Hugh Hunt and designed by Voytek. Ursula Jeans is Lady Cicely, with Livesey as Brassbound. On May 31, *The Merry Wives of Windsor*, with Livesey as Falstaff, is staged by Hunt and designed by Ann Barlow.

Jan 31 John Galsworthy's *The Silver Box* is revived by director Frith Banbury at London's Lyric.

Feb Dublin's Gate Theatre continues its 22nd season with Hugh Walpole's *The Old Ladies*, staged by Hilton Edwards. Other plays include Shakespeare's *Richard II*, Laverty's *Liffey Lane*, and Miller's *Death of a Salesman*. Strong's *The Director*, opening on May 28, is the last show of the season.

Feb 12 Among London's Shaw revivals this winter and spring is Peter Cotes's staging of *Candida*, with Joan Miller, at the New Boltons Theatre. On April 3 at St. Martin's Theatre, Ellen Pollock presents *Shavings*, three Shaw one-act plays: *The Man of Destiny, Village Wooing*, and *The Dark Lady of the Sonnets*. On April 26, the Arts Theatre opens a two-program Shaw Festival: The first series of plays contains *Great Catherine, How He Lied To Her Husband, Passion, Poison*, and *Petrification*, and *The Admirable Bashville*. The directors offer a second series on May 16, consisting of *The Inca of Perusalem, The Fascinating Foundling, The Shewing-Up of Blanco Posnet*, and *Press Cuttings*.

Feb 14 Bernard Shaw's *Man and Superman*, staged by John Clements, is handsomely revived at London's New Theatre, with decor by Laurence Irving. Clements plays John Tanner, Kay Hammond plays Ann Whitefield. The production has a run of 255 performances.

March 10 Douglass Watson and Olivia De Havilland play Romeo and Juliet on Broadway at the Broadhurst Theatre. They are supported, for 49 showings, by such players as Jack Hawkins, Evelyn Varden, Isobel Elsom, and Michael Higgins. Peter Glenville stages, with sets and costumes by Oliver Messel.

March 15 Marc Connelly stages a revival of his 1930 play, *The Green Pastures*, at the Broadway Theatre in New York, there are only 44 performances.

March 20 *The Passing Day*, an Irish play by George Shiels, is brought to London's Lyric by the Northern Ireland Festival Company. Tyrone Guthrie directs this and John Stewart's *Danger, Men Working*, opening on April 2. On April 23, Charles Shadwell's *The Sham Prince* is presented in a Guthrie staging.

March 24 Antony Quayle's production of *Richard II*, with Michael Redgrave, opens this year's Shakespeare Festival at the newly renovated Memorial Theatre in Stratford-upon-Avon. It is part of a four-unit history cycle, including *Henry IV, Part 1* (staged by Quayle and John Kidd), *Henry IV, Part 2* (directed by Michael Redgrave), and *Henry V* (staged by Quayle). Richard Burton makes a Stratford debut as Prince Hal and Henry V. Michael Benthall stages *The Tempest*. The season closes October 27.

April 30 *Three Sisters*, Chekhov's comedy, opens at London's Aldwych Theatre, a special Festival of Britain revival. The sisters are played by Celia Johnston, Margaret Leighton, and Renee Asherson. There are 140 performances.

May 7 At London's Savoy Theatre, the D'Oyly Carte Opera Comapny opens its season of Gilbert & Sullivan revivals with *The Mikado*. *The Yeoman of the Guard* is also presented, followed by *Cox and Box* and *The Pirates of Penzance*.

May 9 In London, Basil Dean revives his 1923 success, James Elroy Flecker's spectacular poetic epic, *Hassan*, but it's not a hit.

May 10 London's St. James's Theatre presents Laurence Olivier and Vivien Leigh in Bernard Shaw's *Caesar and Cleopatra* directed by Michael Benthall. Supporting them are Robert Helpmann, Elspeth March, Niall MacGinnis, Wilfrid Hyde White, Norman Wooland, Maxine Audley, Jill Bennett, and Edmund Purdom. On May 11 the Oliviers play Shakespeare's *Antony and Cleopatra*, also directed by Benthall. Helpmann plays Octavius, with Elizabeth Kentish as Octavia. Roger Furse designs the settings. There

are 155 performances and later a visit to Broadway.

May 17 Alec Guinness takes the role of the Dane in Shakespeare's *Hamlet* at London's New Theatre. It's performed uncut and is apparently underrehearsed. Critics complain about the nontraditional sets and costumes, the lighting, Lydia Sherwood's Gertrude, Kenneth Tynan's First Player, and Guinness's decision to play Hamlet bearded. Later, he removes the beard, but it doesn't save the life of the production, which has only 49 performances.

Summer The first Pitlochry Festival opens in Scotland, founded by John Stewart and played under a marquee or tent. Stewart's dream is to have a "theatre in the hills." On the 30th anniversary, May 19, 1981, a new theatre will be formally opened.

June 20 The third program of London's Arts Theatre's Shaw Festival opens with *Augustus Does His Bit*, *Village Wooing*, *Annajanska, the Bolshevik Empress*, *The Glimpse of Reality*, and *Overruled*. Roy Rich and John Fernald share directorial duties. Among the players are Brenda Bruce, Rachel Gurney, David Bird, Alan MacNaughton, and Vivienne Bennett. On June 27, the fourth program is presented: *O'Flaherty, V. C.*, *The Six of Calais*, *The Man of Destiny*, *The Music-Cure*, and *The Dark Lady of the Sonnets*.

June 27 Offered as a Festival of Britain attraction, Peter Brook's staging of Shakespeare's *The Winter Tale* becomes a solid box-office success, with a run of nearly 27 weeks and a trip to the Edinburgh Festival. John Gielgud is Leontes; Diana Wynyard, his Hermione.

July 6 Arthur Wing Pinero's *His House in Order* (1906) is revived in London at the New Theatre as a Festival of Britain attraction. John Counsell stages, with Martin Battersby's decors. Godfrey Tearle, Mary Kerridge, and Sebastian Shaw are in the cast.

Aug 1 In Ashland, the Oregon Shakespeare Festival opens with *Twelfth Night*, directed by Richard Graham. James Sandoe's staging of *Measure for Measure* comes next, followed by *King Lear*, directed by Angus Bowmer, the festival's founder. Philip Hanson stages King *Henry IV, Part 2*.

Aug 19 Britain's Edinburgh International Festival opens, with some competition from other cities for this is the year of the Festival of Britain. Ian Hunter, the Artistic Director, imports the New York Philharmonic, conducted by Bruno Walter. *The Thrie Estaites*, a 16th century Scots play, returns for the third time, produced by the Glasgow Citizens' Theatre. Producer Henry Sherek offers a revival of Bernard Shaw's *Pygmalion*, with Margaret Lockwood and Alan Webb. Peter Brook's production of *The Winter's Tale* has music by Christopher Fry, and a cast including John Gielgud, Flora Robson,

Diana Wynyard, and George Rose. Sophie Fedorovitch designs. From Paris comes the company of the Theatre de L'Atélier, with Henry Monnier's *L'Enterrement* and Jean Anouilh's *Le Bal des Voleurs (Thieves' Carnival)* and *Le Rendez-Vous de Senlis*. André Barsacq directs.

Sep 5 At London's Arts Theatre, John Whiting's play, *Saint's Day*, is staged by Stephen Murray. Among the players are Michael Hordern, and Donald Pleasance.

Sep 9 Bernard Miles revives Henry Purcell's opera, *Dido and Aeneas* in his London Mermaid Theatre, a new venture. Sarah Miles plays Spring in the Prologue. The opera cast includes Kirsten Flagstad, Thomas Hemsley, Maggie Teyte, and Murray Dickie. Miles stages. On September 17, Miles is Caliban in the Mermaid revival of *The Tempest*, directed by Julius Gellner.

Sep 24 At London's Old Vic Theatre, the fall season features this revival of Marlowe's *Tamburlaine the Great*, staged by Tyrone Guthrie, with Donald Wolfit in the lead. Margaret Rawlings is Zabina. Michael Langham directs Douglas Campbell in *Othello*, opening on Oct 31 and offering a contrast to Orson Welles' Moor at the St. James's Theatre. Paul Rogers is Iago; Coral Browne, Desdemona. On Dec 5, Wolfit plays the lead in the Colman-Garrick 18th century comedy, *The Clandestine Marriage*, with Hilton Edwards directing. On Dec 26, Guthrie provides a holiday revival of *A Midsummer Night's Dream*, with Rogers as Bottom. Others include Irene Worth, Robert Shaw, Alan Badel, and Terry Wale.

Sep 25 Paris's La Compagnie Madeleine Renaud, with Jean-Louis Barrault, opens at London's St. James's Theatre with a double-bill: Marivaux's *Les fausses Confidences* and Jacques Prevert's pantomime-ballet, *Baptiste*, in which Barrault plays the title role. On September 27, they offer another double-bill, Armand Salacrou's *Les Nuits de la Colère*, staged by Barrault, and André Gide's *Oedipe*, directed by Jean Vilar. On October 1, Claudel's *Partage de Midi* is presented. On October 5, the bill is Molière's *Amphitryon* and *Les Fourberies de Scapin*, the latter staged by Louis Jouvet.

Sep 26 In *The Lyric Revue*, comedians Dora Bryan, Joan Heal, and Ian Carmichael transfer from the Lyric Theatre, Hammersmith, to London's Globe for a 39-week West End run. William Chappell directs songs, spoofs, and sketches.

Sep 27 Christopher Fry's *A Phoenix Too Frequent* and *Thor, With Angels* are staged by Michael MacOwan at London's Lyric, Hammersmith. The cast includes Diana Churchill, Jessie Evans, Jack Hawkins, Eric Porter, and Dorothy Tutin.

Sep 28 At London's Arts Theatre, W. Somerset Maugham's *Mrs. Dot* is revived in a production mounted by Joan Swinstead. Arnold Bennett's *The Great Ad-*

venture is revived on December 4, with John Fernald staging.

Oct 4 New York's Theatre Guild begins its season with an attractive revival of Shaw's *Saint Joan*, with Uta Hagen as the Maid. It runs nearly 18 weeks, staged by Margaret Webster.

Oct 8 The Dublin Gate Theatre opens *Tolka Row*, by Maura Laverty, directed by Hilton Edwards. This is the company's 23rd season, Donagh MacDonagh's *God's Gentry* is the Christmas production this year.

Oct 18 Under Laurence Olivier's management, Orson Welles directs and plays the leading role in Shakespeare's *Othello* at London's St. James's Theatre. Gudrun Ure is Desdemona. Peter Finch plays Iago. The production runs two months, with a number of critics calling Welles one of the best Othellos of the time.

Oct 22 Charles Laughton stages *Don Juan in Hell*, the third act of Shaw's *Man and Superman* at New York's Carnegie Hall for one night before going on tour. Charles Boyer is Don Juan; Agnes Moorhead, Donna Anna; Charles Laughton, the Devil, and Cedric Hardwicke, the Statue. On November 29, it briefly returns to New York, to the Century Theatre, and again tours, returning April 6 to the Plymouth Theatre for a total of 105 performances.

Nov 6 A program of Grand Guignol is presented at London's Irving Theatre. Ken Tynan stages Eugene O'Neill's *Before Breakfast* and *Andronicus*, an abridgement of *Titus Andronicus*. Ellen Pollock

directs the other three plays: *The Mask, Coals of Fire,* and *Dalgarni*. On December 11, the program transfers to the Embassy Theatre.

Nov 14 The Earl of Longford's translation of Molière's *The School for Wives* opens at the New Boltons Theatre.

Dec 18 London's holiday season opens at the Players' Theatre with J. R. Planché's *Riquet with the Tuft*, adapted by Hattie Jacques and Joan Sterndale-Bennett, who play Fairy Queen and Fay Daze. On the 19th, *Aladdin*, with Julie Andrews, opens at the Casino Theatre. At the St. James's Theatre, it's *Snow White* on December 20. Joan Greenwood plays Peter Pan at the Scala Theatre, opening on the 21st. Other productions include *Cinderella* (Prince's), *Humpty Dumpty* (Palladium, with Terry-Thomas, Gillian Lynne, and Peggy Mount), *Where the Rainbow Ends* (Winter Garden), *The Sleeping Beauty* (Golder's Green Hippodrome), and two seasonal revues: *Ring in the New*, at the New Lindsay Theatre, and *Archie Andrews' Christmas Party* at the Prince of Wales's Theatre.

Dec 26 At London's People's Palace, the D'Oyly Carte Opera Company opens with *The Mikado*, from their Gilbert & Sullivan repertory. On December 31, they offer *The Yeoman of the Guard*. This is followed, on January 2, by *The Gondoliers*.

Dec 26 George Schaefer presents the New York City Theatre Company in a revival of Ibsen's *The Wild Duck*, staged by Morton DaCosta at the City Center.

Feb 15 The Circle In The Square's first production, *Dark of the Moon*, opens in the new theatre space at 5 Sheridan Square, a former nightclub, in New York City. Theodore Mann is the Artistic Director.

June John Chapman, surveying the theatre-scene at the end of the 1950–1951 Broadway season, notes a gradual artistic and economic decline, the latter caused by inflation which puts tickets beyond the budgets of many. This season there are 87 professional productions, 39 of them new plays, with 14 new musicals. There are eight musical revivals and 26 play revivals. Chapman is uneasy about the new plays and musicals because so many of them are adaptations of novels, stories, and other plays.

June 1 At the close of the current season on Broadway, 1950-1951, John Chapman again selects the ten "Best Plays." His candidates this year are Burrows and Loesser's *Guys and Dolls*, Kingsley's *Darkness at Noon*, Coxe and Chapman's *Billy Budd*, Hellman's *The Autumn Garden*, Van Druten's *Bell, Book, and Candle*, Odet's *The Country Girl*, Williams' *The Rose Tattoo*, Gibbs' *Season in the Sun*, Verneuil's *Affairs of State*, and Barry's *Second Threshold*. There is no play thought worthy of the Pulitzer Prize. The Drama Critics Circle gives its annual Best Play Award to *Darkness at Noon*; *Guys and Dolls* is voted Best Musical.

July 10 Connecticut's Governor John Davis Lodge signs into law the bill creating the American Shakespeare Festival Theatre and Academy and allocating $500,000 for its use. The proposed theatre-building, envisioned as a modernized Globe Theatre, is to cost $250,000.

July 13 Queen Elizabeth lays the foundation stone for the proposed National Theatre on the South Bank of the Thames. It will be years before the National Theatre becomes a reality, and it will not be constructed on this site.

July 15 The stage, backstage area, and dressing-rooms of the Abbey Theatre in Dublin are destroyed by fire. A new rebuilt Abbey will not be ready for use until 1966.

Dec 2 With $6,000 inherited from an aunt, Julian Beck and his wife, Judith Malina, open their first New York performances at the Cherry Lane Theatre in Greenwich Village. Their Living Theatre is to become celebrated—even notorious—as one of the most experimental of avant garde stages.

1951   BIRTHS/DEATHS/DEBUTS

Jan 20 American producer Dwight Deere Wiman (b. 1895) dies in Hudson, New York. With William A. Brady, Jr., Wiman produced such plays as *The Road to Rome* and *Command to Love*. Independently he managed a number of plays including *The Vinegar Tree*.

Feb 20 English actor-manager Cyril Maude (b. 1862) dies in Torquay, England. Maude excelled in "old-men" roles, such as Bob Acres in *The Rivals* and Lord Ogleby in *The Clandestine Marriage*. For many years he was president of the Royal Academy of Dramatic Art.

April 5 English stage and screen actor Edward Rigby (b. 1879) dies. In the 1930s he played in *The Tempest, Anna Christie*, and *Ghosts*, among others.

May 14 Actress-singer Barbara Cook makes her Broadway debut as Sandy in E. Y. Harburg's *Flahooley* at the Broadhurst Theatre.

May 29 American actress Fanny Brice (b. 1891) dies in Hollywood. Brice was first engaged by Florenz Ziegfeld for his *Follies* series in 1910. She began her film career in 1928.

June 27 Actor David Warfield (b. 1866) dies in New York. At the height of his fame, Warfield was associated with David Belasco, who starred him in *The Auctioneer* and the 1922 production of *The Merchant of Venice*.

Oct 12 Veteran comedian Leon Errol (b. 1881) dies in Hollywood.

1951   THEATERS/PRODUCTIONS

1951 Norman Ginsbury and Eric Maschwitz have written a musical about Queen Victoria and Prince Albert. The Lord Chamberlain bans its public performance owing to alleged historical inaccuracies, among them the portrayal of the Queen singing.

Jan This is the Bicentennial Year of the American Theatre—1751–1951.

Jan 15 *The Shrike* (NY—Cort—Drama). Joseph Kramm wins the Pulitzer Prize and is called "most promising new playwright" for this drama about a vengeful wife, played by Judith Evelyn. Jose Ferrer co-stars, stages, and produces. It runs 20 weeks. The psychological melodrama comes to London's Prince's on Feb 13, 1953, with Constance Cummings as his wife. There are only 43 performances.

Feb 1 *Jane.* See L premiere, 1947.

Feb 4 Emlyn Williams, in the character of Charles Dickens, offers some of Dickens' own readings, at the Golden Theatre on Broadway. They include *The Signal Man, Mr. Chops,* and *The Fancy Ball.* Sol Hurok presents Williams, who tours this show.

Feb 13 *Venus Observed.* See L premiere, 1950.

Feb 20 *Mrs. McThing* (NY—ANTA—Comedy). Helen Hayes plays the title-role. Mary Chase's play is intended for children but the two-week run is extended to 350 performances as adults flock to the theatre as well. The cast includes Brandon de Wilde, Ernest Borgnine, and Enid Markey. The show goes on to Central City, Colorado for its summer festival.

March 14 *Paris '90* (NY—Booth—Revue). Cornelia Otis Skinner presents a gallery of celebrated Parisiennes of La Belle Epoque in this handsomely mounted and staged series of impersonations. There are 87 performances.

March 18 *Flight Into Egypt* (NY—Music Box—Drama). Elia Kazan directs Zero Mostel, Jo Van Fleet, Joseph Anthony, and Paul Mann in George Tabori's dream of Viennese refugees striving to get to America. There are just 46 performances.

March 27 *The Grass Harp* (NY—Martin Beck—Comedy). Some think this Truman Capote fantasy about Dorothy Talbo (Mildred Natwick) who lives in a tree with her friends to escape life's complications, is charming. Others do not, as the mere 36 performances testify. Robert Lewis stages with designs by Cecil Beaton.

May 16 *New Faces of 1952* (NY—Royale—Revue). Leonard Sillman's show wins 365 performances and a national tour. Memorable is Eartha Kitt's rendition of "Monotonous." Other cast members include Ronny Graham, Alice Ghostley, and Carol Lawrence. John Murray stages.

June 25 *Wish You Were Here* (NY—Imperial—Musical). Director Joshua Logan and designer Jo Mielziner put a real swimming pool on stage for this reworking of Arthur Kober's *Having Wonderful Time,* set in a summer camp in the Catskills. Patricia Marland and Jack Cassidy head the cast. There are 598 performances. The musical comes to London's

Casino on Oct 10, 1953, with Elizabeth Larner and Joe Robinson in the cast. It runs 35 weeks.

Oct 2 *An Evening with Beatrice Lillie* (NY—Booth—Revue). Lillie is supported by Reginald Gardiner in this collage of music and sketches which runs nearly 35 weeks. Lillie opens in London at the Globe on Nov 24, 1954, for a run of 196 performances.

Oct 15 *The Time of the Cuckoo* (NY—Empire—Comedy). Shirley Booth wins praise as a lonely American spinster, on vacation in Venice, who falls in love with a married store-keeper (Dino DiLuca). Later it will be a film and a musical. Harold Clurman stages Arthur Laurents' play. It runs 35 weeks.

Oct 16 *Bernardine* (NY—Playhouse—Comedy). Pulitzer Prize-winner Mary Chase *(Harvey)* whips up a fantasy about a group of teenage boys who yearn for older, more experienced women. Johnny Stewart and John Kerr are in the cast. Staged by Guthrie McClintic, it runs nearly 20 weeks.

Oct 29 *Dial "M" for Murder.* See L premiere, 1952.

Nov 5 *The Deep Blue Sea.* See L premiere, 1952.

Nov 13 *The Climate of Eden* (NY—Martin Beck—Drama). Although chosen as one of the season's "Best Plays," it earns only 20 showings. Moss Hart bases it on Edgar Mittelholzer's novel *Shadows Move Among Them,* about an unorthodox missionary in British Guiana. The cast includes Earle Hyman, Lee Montague, and Rosemary Harris.

Nov 20 *The Seven Year Itch* (NY—Fulton—Comedy). Seven years of marriage have brought playwright George Axelrod's hero (Tom Ewell) to a dangerous point. His wife's away; there's a pretty

THE SHRIKE

girl (Vanessa Brown) upstairs, and he has a lively imagination. Staged by John Gerstad, the show earns a run of 1,141 performances. On May 14, 1953, it opens in London at the Aldwych, staged by Gerstad, but with Brian Reece and Rosemary Harris in the roles. It has 331 showings. Later, the story provides a memorable cinema vehicle for Marilyn Monroe.

Nov 26 *Time Out for Ginger* (NY—Lyceum—Comedy). Ronald Alexander's heroine is a tomboy (Nancy Malone) who wants to be on the high school football team. Father (Melvyn Douglas) backs her up. Directed by Shepard Traube, it runs 31 weeks.

Dec 15 *Two's Company* (NY—Alvin—Revue). Bette Davis comes to Broadway, and there are 90 performances. The show's skits are by Peter DeVries and Charles Sherman; music is by Vernon Duke, with lyrics by Ogden Nash and Sammy Cahn. Jerome Robbins choreographs.

1952 BRITISH PREMIERES

Jan 23 *Summer and Smoke.* See NY premiere, 1948.

Jan 29 *The Firstborn* (L—Winter Garden—Drama). Christopher Fry's play, first seen at the Edinburgh Festival, has Alec Clunes as Moses contesting with Egypt's Pharaoh (Mark Dignam) to free the Israelites from bondage. John Fernald directs; there are 46 showings. On April 30, 1958, the play opens in New York at the Coronet, saluting Israel's 10th anniversary. Anthony Quayle and Katharine Cornell take the leading roles.

Jan 30 *The Happy Time.* See NY premiere, 1950.

Feb 18 *Bet Your Life* (L—Hippodrome—

Musical). Comedian Arthur Askey plays a jockey with psychic gifts. Sally Ann Howes and Brian Reece are also in the cast. Alan Melville devises the plot and lyrics, with music by Kenneth Leslie-Smith and Charles Zwar. Richard Bird directs; the show runs 45 weeks.

Feb 27 *Nightmare Abbey* (L—Westminster—Comedy). Thomas Love Peacock's satiric novel on the romantic movement is cleverly adapted by Anthony Sharp and staged by John Fernald. It runs nearly 11 weeks with Charles Lloyd Pack and Alan MacNaughton among the cast.

March 6 *The Deep Blue Sea* (L—Duchess—Drama). Peggy Ashcroft plays a woman distraught because she has left her husband for a man who does not love her. Terence Rattigan's play runs 513 performances. On Nov 5, it opens on Broadway at the Morosco with Margaret Sullavan. The play lasts 132 performances.

March 8 *Excitement* (L—Casino—Revue). Robert Nesbitt stages comedians Jimmy Jewel and Ben Warriss in this new Latin Quarter revue which runs a year.

March 15 *Call Me Madam.* See NY premiere, 1950.

April 2 *The Young Elizabeth* (L—New—Drama). As Elizabeth II ascends Britain's throne, this timely play by two Americans, Jennette Dowling and Francis Letton, explores the early life of the first Queen Elizabeth. Mary Morris stars, with staging by Charles Hickman. It runs for 498 performances.

April 2 *London Laughs* (L—Adelphi—Revue). Britain's wartime "sweetheart" Vera Lynn and comedians Jimmy Edwards and Tony Hancock head the cast of this long-running show (1,113 performances). Alec Shanks and Joan Davis stage the musical numbers.

April 3 *Winter Journey.* See NY premiere, 1950.

April 8 *Montserrat.* See NY premiere, 1949.

April 12 *Paris To Piccadilly* (L—Prince of Wales's—Revue). With popular comic Norman Wisdom heading the cast, this Folies Bergere revue runs 846 performances. It is staged by Dick Hurran and Charles Henry.

April 23 *Under the Sycamore Tree* (L—Aldwych—Comedy). Alec Guinness plays an ant scientist in an ant-hill under a tree somewhere in America. He borrows from Man to make the ants' lives more easy and progressive, but he has no luck trying to share ant-wisdom with Man. Diana Churchill is his Ant Queen. Peter Glenville directs Sam Spewack's American fable, with decors by Oliver Messel. This runs nearly six months.

May 21 *Sweet Madness* (L—Vaudeville—Comedy). Richard Attenborough plays a health faddist who consults a psychiatrist to find an ideal wife. Geraldine McEwan co-stars. Peter Jones' farce is staged by Jack Minster and runs four months.

May 27 *Meet Mr. Callaghan* (L—Garrick—Comedy). Gerald Verner adapts Peter Cheney's novel *The Urgent Hangman* to create a comedy-thriller that runs for 339 performances. Derrick de Marney directs the cast, which includes Terence de Marney and Trevor Reid.

June 11 *The Gay Dog* (L—Piccadilly—Comedy). Joseph Colton's farce, staged by Wallace Douglas, has a cast headed by Megs Jenkins and radio personality Wilfred Pickles. It runs 35 weeks.

July 10 *The Globe Revue* (L—Globe—Revue). Comedians Dora Bryan and Ian Carmichael animate the show, with sketches and songs by Noel Coward and Richard Addinsell among others. Staged by William Chappell, who also choreographs and designs the costumes, it runs 29 weeks.

June 19 *Dial "M" for Murder* (L—Westminster—Drama). Frederick Knott's popular thriller generates suspense with the possibility that a character whom the audience knows to be innocent will be convicted of murder. The cast includes Emrys Jones and Jane Baxter. There are 425 performances. John Fernald directs. On Oct 29, the show comes to Broadway's Plymouth with Maurice Evans in the lead. It enjoys a run of 552 performances.

July 3 *The Innocents.* See NY premiere, 1950.

Aug 7 *The Happy Marriage* (L—Duke of York's—Comedy). John Clements adapts, directs, and stars in this play from Jean Bernard Luc's farce *Le Complexe de Philemon*, about a psychiatrist's meddling in a happy marriage. Kay Hammond co-stars. It has 367 performances.

Aug 11 *The Bride of Denmark Hill* (L—Comedy—Drama). Transferring from the Royal Court Theatre, this play by Lawrence Williams and Nell O'Day about the private life of writer and art critic John Ruskin has a run of 666 performances. The cast is headed by Andrew Osborn and Dorothy Green.

Aug 21 *Affairs of State.* See NY premiere, 1950.

Sep 12 *Quadrille* (L—Phoenix—Comedy). Written and directed by Noel Coward, this comedy about an American railway magnate of the 1870s, whose wife is enticed away by another man, stars Alfred Lunt and Lynn Fontanne. It runs for 329 performances. The show opens on Broadway at the Coronet on Nov 3, 1954, with the Lunts repeating their roles. The production lasts 19 weeks.

Sep 23 *Hanging Judge* (L—New—Drama). Raymond Massey bases his play about a severe judge, who finds himself falsely accused of murder, on Bruce Hamilton's book *Let Him Have Judgement*. Michael Powell directs Godfrey Tearle as the judge. It runs for 3 months.

Sep 24 *Second Threshold.* See NY premiere, 1951.

Sep 25 *Love From Judy* (L—Saville—Musical). This is Jean Webster's beloved novel and play, *Daddy Long-Legs*, adapted for British tastes by Eric Maschwitz, with songs by Hugh Martin and Jack Gray. Charles Hickman stages, with the colorful settings of Berkeley Sutcliffe. Jean Carson wins praise as Judy, the orphan who falls in love with her guardian. There are 594 performances.

NEW FACES OF 1952

HAPPY TIME

Oct 21 *Wonderful Time* (L—Palladium—Revue) Twice-daily shows give 344 performances to this mixture of music and comedy, featuring comedian Max Bygraves.

Oct 28 *The River Line* (L—Strand—Drama). Charles Morgan's play, about the experiences of three escapees from wartime France, comes to the West End by way of the Edinburgh Festival and the Lyric, Hammersmith. Directed by Michael MacOwan, the cast is headed by Pamela Brown, Paul Scofield, and Virginia McKenna. It runs 150 performances.

Nov 6 *Wild Horses* (L—Aldwych—Comedy). Veteran farceurs Ralph Lynn and Robertson Hare play ex-convicts trying to stay out of jail in Ben Travers' new comedy. Staged by Charles Hickman, it has 179 performances.

Nov 25 *The Mousetrap* (L—Ambassadors'—Drama). Richard Attenborough and his off-stage wife Sheila Sim open in Agatha Christie's mystery-thriller, set in a snowbound manor house. It is destined to become the longest-running play ever, still playing as this book is published. Peter Cotes stages.

Dec 16 *Remains To Be Seen.* See NY premiere, 1951.

Dec 17 *For Better, For Worse . . .* (L—Comedy—Comedy). Geraldine McEwan and Leslie Phillips play a young couple trying to find a decent place to live during a housing shortage in Arthur Watkyn's lighthearted play which runs 607 performances. John Counsell directs.

Dec 18 *Dear Charles* (L—New—Comedy). Yvonne Arnaud earns 466 performances as a lady trying to decide which of her children's three different fathers she should marry. Alan Melville adapts the play from Marc-Gilbert Sauvajon's *Les Enfants d'Edouard*, which in turn is based on an English play by Frederick Jackson. On Sep 15, 1954, the comedy opens at New York's Morosco with Tallulah Bankhead in the lead. The show runs 20 weeks and then tours.

1952   REVIVALS/REPERTORIES

Jan 3 At London's Arts Theatre, Jean Anouilh's *Thieves' Carnival* is revived, with Roy Rich staging. Marcel Marceau's program, *Essays in Mime* and *The Pantomimes of Bip*, follows on January 30.

Jan 9 At the New York City Center, Eugene O'Neill's *Anna Christie* has a two-week run, with Celeste Holm. The show is then moved to Broadway's Lyceum Theatre for a brief run.

Jan 11 John Gielgud's Stratford production of *Much Ado About Nothing* opens in London at the Phoenix Theatre for a seven-month run. Gielgud heads the cast, which includes Dorothy Tutin, and Paul Scofield.

Jan 16 At New York's ANTA Theatre, the series of revivals continues with Eugene O'Neill's *Desire Under the Elm*, staged by Harold Clurman. Karl Malden and Douglass Watson are the Cabots, father and son. On March 12, John Garfield plays the title-role in Clifford Odets' *Golden Boy*, directed by Odets himself. On April 16, the composer Virgil Thomson shows his revival of *Four Saints in Three Acts*, the opera he composed to a Gertrude Stein text. He is both musical and artistic director. Leontyne Price is St. Cecilia.

Feb 4 *Christ's Emperor*, a religious epic by mystery-writer Dorothy L. Sayers, opens in London's St. Thomas's Church. Sayers and Graham Suter co-direct.

Feb 5 Strindberg's *The Creditors* is revived in London at the New Lindsay Theatre. On February 21 at the Watergate, Sandy Wilson offers a new revue, *See You Again*, staged by Vida Hope. J. B. Priestley's *Treasure on Pelican* opens at the Golder's Green Hippodrome on February 25. On February 28, at the New Boltons Theatre, two plays by the American novelist, Henry James, are staged by Basil Ashmore: *Still Waters* and *The High Bid*.

Feb 19 The Bristol Old Vic comes to London's Old Vic with *Two Two Gentlemen of Verona*, staged by Denis Carey.

March 3 The Old Vic's *King Lear* revival opens with Stephen Murray in the title-role, instead of Donald Wolfit, who has bowed out of both production and ensemble. Hugh Hunt stages, with designs by Reece Pemberton. Tyrone Guthrie stages the revival of *Timon of Athens* on May 28, with Andre Morell as Timon.

March 4 Noel Coward's early play, *The Vortex*, is revived at London's Lyric, Hammersmith, with a cast including Adrianne Allen, Isabel Jeans, and Dirk Bogarde as Nicky Lancaster. It transfers to the Criterion on April 9. On March 11, *The Song of the Centipede*, by Peter Jones, is heard from the stage of the Q Theatre, with Geraldine McEwan in the cast; this becomes *Sweet Madness* in May at the Vaudeville. On March 11, at the Embassy Theatre, Sylvia Regan's *The Golden Door* is revived. On the 18th, Lally Bowers is Hera in *Believe It Or Not* at the Watergate. Chekhov's *Uncle Vanya* is revived on March 27 at the Arts. At the New Boltons on the 28th, the play is *Lady Susan*, based on Jane Austen's novel paired with St. John Hankin's *The Constant Lover*. On the 31st, the Players offer *The Castle Spectre*.

March 11 Dorothy and Campbell Christie's *His Excellency* opens at the Dublin Gate Theatre. Langley's *Ninotchka*, and a revival of Laverty's *Tolka Row* follow. After a Danish tour, the company's production of *Hamlet* opens at the Olympia Theatre.

March 13 Glen Byam Shaw's production of *Coriolanus* opens the season at the Shakespeare Memorial Theatre in Stratford-upon-Avon. He also stages *As You Like It*. Other productions include John Gielgud's mounting of *Macbeth* and George Devine's staging of Jonson's *Volpone*. *The Tempest* is revived from last season. The ensemble includes such players as Ralph Richardson, Margaret Leighton, May Ellis, Michael Hordern, Laurence Harvey, and Siobhan McKenna.

April 14 Franz Lehar's *The Merry Widow*, staged by Richard Bird, is revived at London's Stoll Theatre. Margaret Mitchell and Peter Graves play the leads.

April 22 After a fairly successful tour, Olivia de Havilland opens on Broadway in a revival of Shaw's *Candida*, staged by Herman Shumlin. The run is only 31 performances.

April 24 In Greenwich Village, Jose Quintero's staging of the Circle in the Square's revival of Tennessee Williams' *Summer and Smoke*, with Geraldine Page as Alma, becomes a hit. Some critics say it's the first big success below 42nd Street in 30 years. Atkinson of the *NY Times* raves.

April 30 At the New York City Center, *The Male Animal,* by James Thurber and Elliott Nugent, is staged by Michael Gordon, with Nugent, Robert Preston, and Martha Scott. Intended as a two-week revival, the production is so successful, John Golden moves it to the Music Box Theatre for a total run of 317 performances. On May 14, Robert E. Sherwood's *Tovarich* enjoys a two-week revival, with Uta Hagen, staged and set by Harry Horner. On May 28, George S. Kaufman and Katherine Dayton's *First Lady* is revived for two weeks.

May 5 At New York's Zeigfeld Theatre, *Of Thee I Sing* achieves a nine-week run in a revival staged by George S. Kaufman, with Jack Carson and Paul Hartman.

May 6 At London's Arts Theatre, Harley Granville Barker's *The Voysey Inheritance* returns, staged by John Fernald. Alec McCowen, and Rachel Gurney are cast. On May 14, Barbara Jefford plays the title-role in a revival of Pinero's *Trelawny of the' Wells'* at the Lyric, Hammersmith. Wilde's *Salomé* is revived on May 20 at the New Torch Theatre.

May 12 Joan Littlewood stages Ewan MacColl's *Uranium 235* at the Embassy Theatre for the Theatre Workshop. Among the cast are Avis Bunnage and Harry Corbett. The play transfers to the Comedy Theatre on June 18.

May 29 London's Regent's Park Open Air Theatre opens its season with Shakespeare's *As You Like It.* Robert Atkins stages. On July 29, the fare changes; Christopher Fry's *The Boy With a Cart* is paired with John Milton's masque of *Comus.*

June 4 At London's Arts Theatre, Harold Brighouse's *Hobson's Choice* is revived, staged by Roy Rich, with Donald Pleasance. On June 16, Vivien Merchant is in Elmer Harris's *Johnny Belinda* at the Wimbledon Theatre.

June 27 Katharine Hepburn plays the title-role in Bernard Shaw's *The Millionairess,* revived in London at the New Theatre. Staged by Michael Benthall, it has James Bailey settings and a cast including Cyril Ritchard and Robert Helpmann. There are 98 performances. On Oct 17, the show opens on Broadway as a Theatre Guild presentation at the Shubert. This time there are only 38 showings for Hepburn, Ritchard, and Helpmann.

June 27 Kermit Hunter's *Horn in the West* opens in a landscaped outdoor theatre in Boone, North Carolina. A drama involving Daniel Boone and other early settlers, the production becomes an annual summer event.

June 30 At London's Old Vic Theatre, the Bristol Old Vic shows its production of *The Two Gentlemen of Verona.* On July 21, the Birmingham Repertory Company presents its mounting of *Henry VI, Part 3,* directed by Douglas Seale.

July 4 *Thunderland* opens at Ashville, North Carolina. Robert Hayes' play has Daniel Boone as its hero.

July 26 Bernard Shaw's *Village Wooing* serves as a curtain-raiser at London's Royal Court Theatre for H. F. Rubinstein's comedy, *Bernard Shaw in Heaven.* Diarmuid Kelly plays Shaw, with Catherine Lacey as Candida. Ellen Pollock directs.

Aug *The Tempest* opens this season's Oregon Shakespeare Festival in the outdoor Elizabethan Theatre in Ashland. Richard Graham directs. *Henry V* follows directed by Philip Hanson. Festival founder Angus Bowmer stages *Much Ado About Nothing.* Allen Fletcher directs *Julius Caesar.*

Aug 17 Britain's Edinburgh International Festival opens. *The River Line,* by Charles Morgan, is staged by Michael MacOwan. The cast includes Pamela Brown, Paul Scofield, and Virginia McKenna. Emlyn Williams appears as Charles Dickens, reading his adaptation of *Bleak House.* Christopher Hassall's *The Player King* has Cathleen Nesbitt among its cast. Norman Marshall directs. In the Assembly Hall, Tyrone Guthrie stages Joseph Mitchell's *The Highland Fair* for the Glasgow Citizens' Theatre. The Old Vic offers *Romeo and Juliet,* with Alan Badel and Claire Bloom as the lovers. Peter Finch is Mercutio. Hugh Hunt stages.

Sep 3 Emlyn Williams presents his reading of *Bleak House,* in the character of Charles Dickens. The production has a run of 69 performances at London's Ambassadors' Theatre.

Sep 8 At London's Arts Theatre, Alec Clunes directs Bernard Shaw's *Don Juan in Hell,* playing the Don. On the 10th, at Bernard Miles' Mermaid Theatre, Miles plays Macbeth, with his wife Josephine Wilson as Lady Macbeth, directed by Joan Swinstead. At the Royal Court Theatre on the 16th, the play is *Ebb Tide,* by actor Donald Pleasance. On September 24 at the Arts Theatre, the controversial Dorothy and Howard Baker drama about lesbian attraction, *Two Loves I have . . .* opens, with Elizabeth Henson and Sonia Dresdel. F. Hugh Herbert's *For Love or Money,* with Geraldine McEwan, opens on September 30 at the Q Theatre.

Sep 11 Florette Henri's play *The Sword of Gideon* is presented in Kings Mountain National Military Park.

Sep 15 At London's Old Vic *Romeo and Juliet,* opens with Claire Bloom and Alan Badel. Athene Seyler is the nurse. Peter Finch is Mercutio. Hugh Hunt directs, with sets and costumes by Roger Furse. Eugene Labiche's *An Italian Straw Hat* is the company's next production on November 18, staged by Denis Carey.

Sep 29 The 24th season of the Dublin's Gate Theatre offers Arthur Koestler's *Darkness at Noon,* followed by Laverty's *A Tree in the Crescent,* macLiammoir's *Where Stars Walk,* and Anouilh's *Ring Round the Moon.* Hilton Edwards directs the plays.

Oct 6 At London's Mermaid Theatre, Bernard Miles heads the cast in Thomas Middleton's *A Trick To Catch the Old One.* At the Embassy Theatre, on October 22, William Douglas Home's play, *Caro William,* is staged. On the 29th, Jean Genet's *Les Bonnes (The Maids)* is performed in French at the Mercury Theatre, in a Peter Zadek staging. J. B. Priestley's *The Long Mirror* has its debut at the Royal Court on October 29, staged by Andre van Gyseghem.

Oct 7 *Lord Arthur Saville's Crime* opens at the Royal Court Theatre. Jack Hulbert stages. On October 23, a different version of Wilde's story, but with the same title, opens at the Arts Theatre. This is the work of adaptors Basil Dawson and St. John Clowes. Stephen Murray directs. The cast includes David Markham and Adrianne Allen.

MOUSETRAP

Oct 9 Robert Breen's American touring production of *Porgy and Bess,* with Leontyne Price and William Warfield, delights London audiences at the Stoll Theatre. The show has a run of 18 weeks.

Oct 20 At Broadway's Mark Hellinger

Theatre, S. M. Charto presents his Gilbert & Sullivan Company for a month's repertory of favorites such as *The Mikado, Iolanthe,* and *H. M. S. Pinafore.* Martyn Green, the D'Oyly Carte star, is in the ensemble.

Oct 27 *My Darlin' Aida,* Charles Friedman's adaptation of Verdi's *Aida* opens at New York's Winter Garden. He moves the locale from Egypt to the American South. The show lasts 11 weeks.

Nov 12 From Paris come Jean-Louis Barrault and Madeleine Renaud with their troupe for a limited Broadway engagement at the Ziegfeld Theatre.

Nov 12 *Ring Out the Bells* opens at London's Victoria Palace. The Crazy Gang are at it again in this show, with songs by Ross Parker and staging by Alec Shanks and Charles Henry. There are 997 performances.

Nov 19 On Broadway for a brief engagement at the Mark Hellinger Theatre. Katina Paxinou plays Sophocles' *Electra,* leading the ensemble of the National Theatre of Greece. Her husband Alexis Minotis appears on November 24 as *Oedipus* in the Sophoclean tragedy, supported by Paxinou as Jocasta. The music is composed by Dimitri Mitropoulis. The plays are performed in modern Greek.

Dec 16 The Players' Theatre opens the holiday season of pantomimes with *Babes in the Wood and the Good Little Fairy-Birds!* Don Gemmell directs. On the 18th,

the Embassy Theatre offers *The Dancing Princess.* At the Casino, *Jack and Jill* opens, with Hy Hazell as Jack. Other holiday treats are *Where the Rainbow Ends* (Princes), *Beauty and the Beast* (Mercury), *The Bewitching Witch* (Boltons), *Peter Pan* (Scala, with Brenda Bruce as Peter), *Dick Whittington* (Palladium, with Vanessa Lee as Dick and Frankie Howard as Idle Jack), *Humpty Dumpty* (Streatham Hill), *Cinderella* (Golders Green Hippodrome), and two intimate revues: *Lighting a Torch,* at the New Torch

Theatre, and *Intimacy at Eight,* at the New Lindsay Theatre.

Dec 18 Producer Kermit Bloomgarden revives Lillian Hellman's *The Children's Hour.* Hellman stages, with Kim Hunter and Patricia Neal heading the cast. The production runs beyond the season's close.

Dec 24 John Guilgud revives *Richard II* at London's Lyric, Hammersmith, directing Paul Scofield as the tragic king. Herbert Lomas and Eric Porter are among the cast.

1952 BIRTHS/DEATHS/DEBUTS

Jan 30 English actress Glynis Johns makes her New York debut playing the title role in Enid Bagnold's *Gertie* at the Plymouth Theatre.

May 8 American actress and author Elizabeth Robins (b. 1865) is dead. Robins played nearly three hundred roles with the Boston Museum Stock Company. Her play, *Votes For Women,* was produced in 1907.

May 8 American actor Canada Lee (b. 1907) dies in New York City. Lee came to prominence at the Civic Repertory Theater in 1934. He later played in *Macbeth, Anna Lucasta,* and *The Tempest.* Lee's first film appearance was in *Lifeboat* in 1944.

May 13 English actor-manager E. Vivian Reynolds (b. 1886) is dead. From 1901 to 1917 Reynolds was stage manager of the St. James's Theatre where he also played in many of its productions. During the 1930s he appeared in *The Streets of London,* and *London After Dark,* among others.

May 16 Actor, director, and writer Paul Lynde makes his Broadway debut in Leonard Sillman's *New Faces of 1952.*

May 21 Stage and screen actor John Garfield (b. 1913 as Jules Garfinkel) dies in

New York. He first won attention working with the Group Theatre.

June 25 Actress-singer Florence Henderson makes her Broadway debut as the New Girl in Arthur Kober and Joshua Logan's musical, *Wish You Were Here,* at the Imperial Theatre.

July 22 Libby Holman, the American songstylist, opens in London at the Lyric, Hammersmith.

Sep 6 English actress Gertrude Lawrence (b. 1898) dies in New York City. She starred in several plays by Noel Coward, notably *Private Lives, To-Night at 8:30,* and *Blithe Spirit.* Her last Broadway role was Anna in *The King and I.* She was married to producer Richard Aldrich. Her memoir, *A Star Danced,* was published in 1945.

Sep 22 British playwright and novelist Ian Hay (b. 1876) dies in Hampshire, England. Hay dramatized his own light novels, such as *Happy-Go-Lucky* and *Housemaster.* Much of his later work was in collaboration with other writers, among them P. G. Wodehouse.

Oct 20 English actor Basil Radford (b. 1897) dies. He toured extensively in the 1920s throughout Australia, New Zealand, Vancouver, and the United States.

1952 THEATERS/PRODUCTIONS

I AM A CAMERA

In a loft over a judo academy this year, Jules Irving and Herbert Blau, drama faculty members at San Francisco State College, launch a new theatre ensemble, The Actors' Workshop. The troupe has the distinction of presenting tbe American premiere of Brecht's *Mother Courage,* and Pinter's *The Caretaker* and *The Birthday Party* before they are seen on Broadway. The Actors' Workshop is invited to represent American regional theatre at the world's fairs in Brussels and in Seattle. Such credits ultimately bring Blau and Irving to Lincoln Center to open the new Vivian Beaumont Theatre.

June 1 With the Broadway season of 1951–1952 now closed, John Chapman

selects the ten "Best Plays." They are Chase's *Mrs. McThing,* Kramm's *The Shrike,* Van Druten's *I Am a Camera,* DeHartog's *The Fourposter,* Osborn's *Point of No Return,* Anderson's *Barefoot in Athens,* Fry's *Venus Observed,* Behrman's *Jane,* Loos' *Gigi,* and Lindsay and Crouse's *Remains to Be Seen.* Kramm's *The Shrike* wins the Pulitzer Prize, with the Drama Critics' Circle Award going to Van Druten's *I Am a Camera.* Only nine new plays have had more than 100 performances this season.

July 2 The Royal Court Theatre on Sloane Square, closed since the 1940 blitz, reopens with *The Bride of Denmark Hill.*

Jan 15 *The Love of Four Colonels.* See L premiere, 1951.

Jan 21 *Mid-Summer* (NY—Vanderbilt—Drama). Geraldine Page's performance is admired in Vina Delmar's play about a poor young New York couple in 1907. Paul Crabtree directs and co-produces. There are 109 performances.

Jan 22 *The Crucible* (NY—Martin Beck—Drama). Arthur Miller's fierce drama about Salem's witchcraft trials of 1692 premiers, as political witch-hunts go on in Washington. Arthur Kennedy and Madeleine Sherwood head the cast: " . . . the acting is at a high pitch of bitterness, anger and fear," says the *New York Times.* Jed Harris stages the nearly 25-week run.

Jan 23 *The Fifth Season* (NY—Cort—Comedy). Sylvia Regan's farce about New York's garment industry stars Menasha Skulnik and runs 654 performances. It comes to the West End on Feb 24, 1954, at the Cambridge. Joseph Buloff has the lead for the 101 performances.

Feb 9 *The Emperor's New Clothes* (NY—Barrymore—Drama). George Tabori has only a two-week run with his play about a poverty-stricken professor and his son, but it's chosen as one of the season's ten best. Harold Clurman directs Lee J. Cobb, Brandon de Wilde, and Maureen Stapleton.

Feb 11 *Hazel Flagg* (NY—Mark Hellinger—Musical). Ben Hecht bases his book on the film *Nothing Sacred* and a story by James Street. Helen Gallagher is Hazel, thought to be dying and brought to New York for a last round of pleasure. Jule Styne composes the score. It runs nearly 24 weeks.

Feb 19 *Picnic* (NY—Music Box—Drama). The Drama Critics' Circle chooses William Inge's play about a handsome drifter who stirs female passions in a small Kansas town, Best American Play. Ralph Meeker, Kim Stanley, and Paul Newman are among the cast. Joshua Logan stages. There are 477 performances.

Feb 25 *Wonderful Town* (NY—Winter Garden—Musical). Rosalind Russell stars in this successful musical comedy, based on Ruth McKenny's play *My Sister Eileen.* The book is by Joseph Fields and Jerome Chodorov, score by Leonard Bernstein, lyrics by Betty Comden and Adolph Green. It has 559 performances. The musical premieres in the West End at the Prince's on Feb 24, 1955, with Shani Wallis and Pat Kirkwood. Londoners go 207 times.

March 11 *My Three Angels* (NY—Morosco—Comedy). Sam and Bella Spewack adapt Albert Husson's play *La Cuisine des Anges,* with Walter Slezak as the leader of a lovable trio of Devil's Island convicts. It runs 44 weeks. The farce opens

TEA AND SYMPATHY

at London's Lyric on May 12, 1955, with George Rose, Nigel Stock, and Ronald Shiner. It plays four months.

March 19 *Camino Real* (NY—National—Drama). Tennessee William's surreal play about people living on the Camino Real is called " . . . all departure and no point" by the *NY Times* and runs just seven-and-a-half weeks. Jo Van Fleet and Martin Balsam are featured. The show earns 64 performances following its London premiere at the Phoenix on April 8, 1957. Harry Andrews, John Wood, Diana Wynyard, and Denholm Elliott are in the cast.

May 7 *Can-Can* (NY—Shubert—Musical). Abe Burrows stages this story about a young judge (Peter Cookson) who tries to suppress the shocking Can-Can. Cole Porter writes the score which includes such hits as "I Love Paris." Michael Kidd choreographs, and Gwen Verdon dances. This solid hit runs 892 performances. The play comes to London's Coliseum beginning Oct 14, 1954, with Irene Hilda and Edmund Hockridge in the leads. It is shown 375 times.

May 28 *Me and Juliet* (NY—Majestic—Musical). Rodgers and Hammerstein produce their new show, a backstage love story, but it runs only 45 weeks. Isabel Bigley and Bill Hayes head the cast. George Abbott directs. The *N Y Herald-Tribune's* Walter Kerr is not impressed.

Sep 15 *End as a Man* (NY—DeLys—Drama). Calder Willingham turns his novel about a Southern military school into a play. Ben Gazzara plays a major role. Jack Garfein stages. After four weeks Off Broadway, the show transfers to the Vanderbilt for a total of 137 performances.

Sep 30 *Tea and Sympathy* (NY—Barrymore—Drama). Robert Anderson's play depicts a prep school teenager whose sensitivity is misinterpreted as effeminacy. Deborah Kerr, Leif Ericson, and John Kerr play the leads. It wins 712 showings. The headmaster's wife (Kerr) helps the boy (Kerr) realize his manhood. Elia Kazan directs. On April 25, 1957, the play is produced in London at the Comedy as a club theatre venture, owing to censorship.

Oct 2 *Comedy in Music* (NY—Golden—Revue). Pianist-humorist Victor Borge charms critics and public alike with this one-man show and wins 849 performances.

Oct 7 *The Little Hut.* See L premiere, 1950.

Oct 15 *The Teahouse of the August Moon* (NY—Martin Beck—Comedy). The Drama Critics' Circle chooses John Patrick's adaptation of Vern Sneider's novel as Best American Play, and it wins 1,027 showings. David Wayne plays Sakini, the clever Okinawan who orchestrates a meeting between American democracy and Oriental lifestyles during the American postwar occupation. When the show opens at Her Majesty's on April 22, 1954, Eli Wallach has the lead. It earns a run of 964 performances.

Oct 21 *The Ladies of the Corridor* (NY—Longacre—Drama). Dorothy Parker and Arnaud d'Usseau collaborate on this portrait of lonely women living in a New York apartment hotel. Frances Starr, Edna Best, and Betty Field head the cast. Harold Clurman stages.

Nov 3 *The Trip To Bountiful* (NY—Henry Miller—Drama). Lillian Gish plays a widow dominated by her daughter-in-law, in this Horton Foote play. Jo Van Fleet and Eva Marie Saint also appear. Vincent J. Donehue stages. It just meets the 5-week mark.

Nov 4 *Kind Sir* (NY—Alvin—Comedy). Norman Krasna's play about an actress and a philandering diplomat runs almost 21 weeks, thanks largely to the presence of Mary Martin and Charles Boyer. Joshua Logan produces and directs.

Nov 5 *The Solid Gold Cadillac* (NY—Belasco—Comedy). Howard Teichman and George S. Kaufman collaborate on this comedy about a trouble-making small-time lady stockholder (Josephine Hull) who manages to become head of the company. Kaufman stages, and it wins 526 performances.

Nov 11 *Sabrina Fair* (NY—National—Comedy). Joseph Cotton plays the scion of a rich Long Island family, Margaret Sullavan plays his love the chauffeur's daughter, polished by several years in Paris. Samuel Taylor's romantic comedy runs almost 40 weeks. It opens in London at the Palace on Aug 4, 1954, with Ron Randell and Marjorie Steele as the lovers. There are 149 showings.

Dec 3 *Kismet* (NY—Ziegfeld—Musical). There's a newspaper strike, and this lavish version of Otis Skinner's vehicle, with book by Luther Davis and Charles Lederer, wins success by word-of-mouth. Alfred Drake plays the poet and dreamer who marries his daughter (Doretta Morrow) to the Caliph (Richard Kiley). Robert Wright and George Forrest adapt Borodin's music to create a score that includes "Strangers in Paradise." The show opens in London at the Stoll on April 20, 1955, with Drake and Morrow again in the cast. The hit wins 648 performances.

Dec 10 *John Murray Anderson's Almanac* (NY—Imperial—Revue). Anderson has Cyril Ritchard and Donald Saddler stage sketches and dances respectively,

for a company headed by Hermione Gingold, Billy DeWolfe, Harry Belafonte, Polly Bergen, Carleton Carpenter, and Orson Bean. In her American debut, Gingold tells the New York audience how impressed she was to see that huge statue of Judith Anderson standing in the harbor. Jean Kerr contributes sketches, with songs from Richard Adler and Jerry Ross, Harry Belafonte, Bart Howard, and Sheldon Harnick. Anderson revives a *Greenwich Village Follies* Ballet Ballad, *The Nightingale and the Rose*, with a Raoul Pene DuBois setting of silver, pearl, and white. Also in the cast are Larry Kert, Kay Medford, and Monique Van Vooren. The show has 229 performances.

Dec 16 *The Prescott Proposals* (NY—Broadhurst—Drama). Katharine Cornell plays an American delegate to the UN in this drama by Howard Lindsay and Russel Crouse which runs over 15 weeks. Lindsay stages.

Dec 17 *Oh, Men! Oh, Women!* (NY—Henry Miller—Comedy). Edward Chodorov's play about a psychoanalyst (Franchot Tone) who becomes involved in the tangled lives of his patients runs nearly 48 weeks. Betsy von Furstenberg, Larry Blyden, Anne Jackson, and Gig Young are also in the cast. Chodorov stages.

Dec 29 *In the Summer House* (NY—Playhouse—Drama). Jane Bowles' play about a dominating mother (Judith Anderson) has 55 showings. Mildred Dunnock is also in the cast. Jose Quintero directs.

Dec 30 *The Remarkable Mr. Pennypacker* (NY—Coronet—Comedy). Burgess Meredith plays a man who keeps two families, one in Wilmington and one in Philadelphia. There are 221 performances. When the play premieres in London at the New Theatre on May 18, 1955, Nigel Patrick plays the free-thinking Pennypacker. Playwright Liam O'Brien's work has 324 performances.

1953 BRITISH PREMIERES

Jan 20 *Escapade* (L—St. James's—Comedy). Playwright Roger MacDougall constrasts the attitudes of two generations in this comedy, with Nigel Patrick, Phyllis Calvert, and Alec McCowan. John Fernald directs. There are 449 performances.

Feb 11 *Paint Your Wagon.* See NY premiere, 1951.

Feb 28 *The Glorious Days* (L—Palace—Musical). Popular actress Anna Neagle stars as a girl who sees herself in various roles—as Nell Gwyn, Queen Victoria, and as a musical star. James Carney partners her in 357 performances. Robert Nesbitt directs, with music and lyrics by Harold Purcell and Harry Parr-Davies.

April 16 *The Living Room* (L—Wyndham's—Drama). In Graham Greene's ironic new drama, Dorothy Tutin plays a bereaved, frustrated young woman who can find no solace from her narrow, bitter relatives. It has 307 performances. When the show opens at the Henry Miller on Broadway on Nov 17, 1954, Barbara Bel Geddes plays the young woman. Although there are only 22 performances, the play earns "Best Play" status.

April 22 *Airs on a Shoestring* (L—Royal Court—Revue). Devised and staged by Laurier Lister, this popular show wins 777 performances. Denis Quilley, Max Adrian and Moyra Fraser are among the cast. Material by Michael Flanders and Donald Swann is used.

ANASTASIA

May 7 *Over the Moon* (L—Piccadilly—Revue). Popular actress Cicely Courtneidge heads the cast of this revue, devised by Vivian Ellis and staged by Jack Hulbert. It runs 156 performances.

May 14 *The Seven Year Itch.* See NY premiere, 1952.

May 27 *The Uninvited Guest* (L—St. James's—Drama). John Mills stars in his wife Mary Hayley Bell's play about a man returning home unexpectedly after twenty years in a mental institution. Cathleen Nesbitt and Joan Greenwood co-star, but the play has only a dismal 21 performances.

May 28 *Guys and Dolls.* See NY premiere, 1950.

June 11 *The Private Life of Helen* (L—Globe—Comedy). Diana Wynyard and Cecil Parker head the cast in this comedy about Helen of Troy and Menelaus. Adapted from John Erskine's novel by André Roussin, Madeleine Gray and Arthur Macrae, it runs nearly six months.

June 24 *The Bad Samaritan* (L—Criterior—Comedy). George Relph plays a confused Anglican dean with two difficult sons, in William Douglas Home's play which runs 149 performances. Virginia McKenna, Michael Denison, and Ronald Lewis also appear. Murray MacDonald stages.

July 7 *The Moon Is Blue.* See NY premiere, 1951.

July 8 *As Long As They're Happy* (L—Garrick—Comedy). Vernon Sylvaine's farce, with Jack Hulbert and Dorothy Dickson as the harried parents of three daughters, runs 47 weeks. Roy Rich directs.

July 28 *Carrington, V.C.* (L—Westminster—Drama). Dorothy and Campbell Christie's play about an army major (Alec Clunes) who is court-martialled for misappropriation of funds, runs nearly 26 weeks. Charles Hickman stages.

Aug 5 *Anastasia* (L—St. James's—Drama). Guy Bolton adapts Marcelle Maurette's play about the attempt of schemers to pass off a poor, sick girl as the Grand Duchess Anastasia. Mary Kerridge heads the cast. See first on television, the play wins 117 performances. It opens in New York at the Lyceum on Dec 29, 1954, with Viveca Lindfors in the lead. It runs 34 weeks.

Sep 16 *The Confidential Clerk* (L—Lyric—Comedy). T.S. Eliot's wry new play about an aristocratic couple and their not entirely legitimate offspring, has Alan Webb, Paul Rogers, Isabel Jeans, and Margaret Leighton among its cast. It runs eight months. On Feb 11, 1954, the show opens at New York's Morosco where it earns 117 showings. Claude Rains, Douglas Watson, Ina Claire, Joan Greenwood, and Aline MacMahon are in the cast.

Sep 17 *Trial and Error* (L—Vaudeville—Comedy). Kenneth Horne's farce about a young newlywed acquitted of murder, features Naunton Wayne and Constance Cummings. Directed by Roy Rich, it runs 21 weeks.

Sep 17 *Champagne on Ice* (L—Hippodrome—Revue). This popular combined skating show and stage revue runs 214 performances. It is staged by Richard Barstow.

Sep 23 *The Devil's General* (L—Savoy—Drama). Trevor Howard wins praise as a Luftwaffe officer in Carl Zuckmayer's German play, adapted by Robert Gore Browne and Christopher Hassall, but it runs only 77 performances.

Sep 24 *Pardon My French* (L—Prince of Wales's—Revue). This Folies Bergere revue, with pianist Winifred Atwell and comedian Frankie Howerd, runs 758 performances. Dick Hurran stages.

Oct 6 *Birthday Honours* (L—Criterion—Comedy). Paul Jones' comedy of romantic mixups has a cast headed by Moira Lister and Hugh Lattimer. Staged by actor Nigel Patrick, it runs for seven months.

Oct 7 *Fun and the Fair* (L—Palladium—Revue). Comedians Terry Thomas and George Formby head this revue which runs 137 performances. It's staged by Charles Henry.

Oct 8 *The King and I*. See NY premiere, 1951.

Oct 10 *Wish You Were Here*. See NY pre-

miere, 1952.

Oct 28 *Witness for the Prosecution* (L—Winter Garden—Drama). In Agatha Christie's suspenseful courtroom drama, Leonard Vole (Derek Blomfield) is charged with murdering a woman who changed her will in his favor. It has 460 performances. The mystery comes to New York's Henry Miller on Dec 16, 1954, with Robin Craven as the defendant. It runs 645 performances and wins the Drama Critics' Circle Award.

Nov 5 *The Sleeping Prince* (L—Phoenix—Comedy). Laurence Olivier and Vivien Leigh have a 34-week run in Terence Rattigan's comedy about a prince who falls in love with a musical comedy star. Olivier directs.

Nov 9 *The Return* (L—Duchess—Drama). It is admired by critics, but Bridget Boland's new play starring Flora Robson as a nun who leaves her convent, has only 79 performances. Michael MacOwan directs.

Nov 10 *The Love Match* (L—Palace—Comedy). Glenn Melvyn's play about Lancashire football fans stars the popular

comedian Arthur Askey and Thora Hird. It has 593 performances and is staged by Richard Bird.

Nov 25 *Someone Waiting* (L—Globe—Drama). Emlyn Williams' new thriller centers on a father (Williams) who tries to trap the killer of a Swedish girl, a crime for which his son has been hanged. Noel Willman directs. It runs nearly five months.

Nov 26 *A Day by the Sea* (L—Haymarket—Drama). Sybil Thorndike, John Gielgud, Ralph Richardson, Lewis Casson, and Irene Worth animate in N.C. Hunter's family drama. Gielgud directs. The play has 386 performances. In New York, it runs three weeks only, opening at the ANTA on Sep 26, 1955. Hume Cronyn and Jessica Tandy play leads.

Dec 10 *A Question of Fact* (L—Piccadilly—Drama). Paul Scofield, Gladys Cooper, and Pamela Brown head the cast of Wynyard Brown's play about a man who finds out his father was hanged for murder. Staged by Frith Banbury, it has a 30-week run.

1953 REVIVALS/REPERTORIES

Jan 3 O'Neill's *Anna Christie* is revived at the Dublin Gate Theatre. Other plays include Fry's *A Sleep of Prisoners*, Yeats' *The Countess Cathleen*, Romains' *An Apple a Day* (*Dr. Knock*), and Cassella's *Death Takes a Holiday*.

Jan 6 *The Merchant of Venice* is offered by London's Old Vic as its third production in the current season. Hugh Hunt directs. Paul Rogers plays Shylock to the Portia of Irene Worth. Claire Bloom is Jessica. On February 24, Hunt stages *Julius Caesar*. On March 31, director Robert Helpmann revives T.S. Eliot's *Murder in the Cathedral*, with Robert Donat as Thomas Becket. The season concludes with *Henry VIII*, staged by Tyrone Guthrie and lavishly designed by Tanya Moiseiwitch as a kind of Coronation offering on May 6, when the Queen and the Duke of Edinburgh attend. Paul Rogers plays the king.

Jan 20 Paul Vincent Carroll's Irish play, *The Devil Came from Dublin*, directed by Andre van Gyseghem, bows at the Embassy Theatre on January 21. On the 28th, W. Somerset Maugham's *The Breadwinner*, staged by Roy Rich, revives at the Arts Theatre.

Feb 3 Robert Morley directs *The Full Treatment*, a play he's written with Ronald Gow, at the Q Theatre. On the 9th, *The Drunkard*, a 19th century melodrama, is revived at the Irving Theatre. On the 10th, W. Somerset Maugham's story, adapted for the stage as *Rain*, opens at the Embassy Theatre, with Miriam Karlin as Sadie Thompson. On February 17, Terence O'Regan's Irish play, *The Music*

Mountain, is seen at the New Torch Theatre. On the 25th, at the Embassy, the play is Hugh Evans' *Five Philadelphia Physicians*. The next day at the Arts Theatre, Strindberg's *The Father* is revived. On the same day, novelist Doris Lessing has her play, *Before the Deluge*, performed at the Boltons Theatre.

Feb 4 At New York's City Center, director Albert Marre revives *Love's Labour's Lost* for a two-week engagement. On Feb 18, Cyril Ritchard mounts a revival of Bernard Shaw's *Misalliance* which is so well received that it moves to Broadway's Ethel Barrymore Theatre for a total run of 146 performances. The cast includes Roddy McDowell, William Redfield, Jan Farrand, and Tamara Geva. On March 4, Marre revives *The Merchant of Venice*, with Luther Adler as Shylock.

Feb 4 Donald Wolfit opens a London season of classic dramas at the King's Theatre, Hammersmith. He plays Oedipus in Sophocles' two dramas, *Oedipus* and *Oedipus in Exile* (*Oedipus at Colonus*). On the 16th, Wolfit offers *As You Like It*, playing Touchstone. Harold Pinter, the future playwright, is Jacques, with Vivien Merchant as Phoebe. On February 23, *King Lear* has Wolfit in the title-role. *Twelfth Night* follows on the 25th, with Wolfit as Malvolio. On March 9, *The Merchant of Venice* has Vivien Merchant as Jessica and Wolfit as Shylock. He's also Macbeth on the 19th. Pinter is Godfrey on April 6 in E. Temple Thurston's *The Wandering Jew*, with Wolfit in the lead, as he is on April 27 in *The Taming of the Shrew*.

Feb 10 Paul Osborn's play, *On Borrowed*

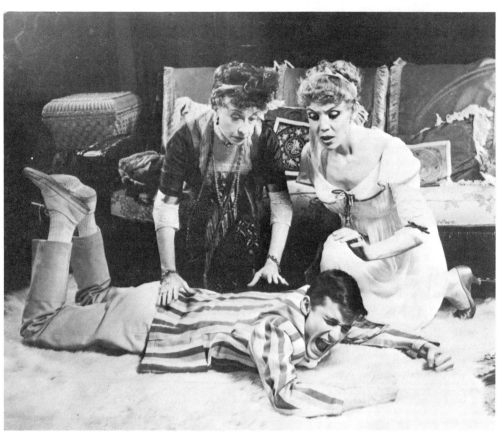

MISALLIANCE

Time, is revived on Broadway at the 48th Street Theatre for a ten-week run. Leo G. Carroll plays Mr. Brink, the incarnation of Death.

Feb 12 Oscar Wilde's *A Woman of No Importance* is given a handsome Edwardian period revival at London's Savoy Theatre. Loudon Sainthill designs, with direction by Michael Benthall. Isabel Jeans, Clive Brook, and Nora Swinburne are in the cast.

Feb 14 Paul Gregory offers 65 performances of Stephen Vincent Benet's poetic epic on the Civil War, *John Brown's Body,* at Broadway's New Century Theatre. The stars are Tyrone Power, Judith Anderson, and Raymond Massey. Charles Laughton stages the poem.

Feb 19 At the Lyric, Hammersmith, John Gielgud stages a London revival of Congreve's *The Way of the World.* Gielgud is Mirabell to the Millament of Pamela Brown. Among the cast are Margaret Rutherford, Eileen Herlie, Paul Scofield, and Eric Porter.

March 10 Blevins Davis and Robert Breen revive the Gershwin/Heyward folk-opera, *Porgy and Bess,* at New York's Ziegfeld Theatre for a run of 38 weeks. Leontyne Price is Bess.

March 17 This year's season of Shakespeare productions at the Memorial Theatre in Stratford-upon-Avon begins with *The Merchant of Venice,* with Michael Redgrave as Shylock and Peggy Ashcroft

as Portia. Marius Goring is the king in *Richard III,* staged by Glen Byam shaw, co-director of the festival. He also stages *Antony and Cleopatra,* with Redgrave and Ashcroft in the title roles. George Devine directs Redgrave in *King Lear* and casts Yvonne Mitchell as Katharina in *The Taming of the Shrew.*

April 14 Richard Buckle's play, *Gossip Column,* opens at the Q Theatre in London, staged by Jordan Lawrence. Adrianne Allen and Gladys Henson are among the cast. On the same night, at the Players' Theatre Club, Sandy Wilson tries out his parody musical, based on 1920's shows, *The Boy Friend.* Vida Hope stages, as she will for the musical's long West End run and for Broadway. Among the lively cast are Larry Drew, Malcolm Goddard, and Ann Rogers. On April 23 at the Arts Theatre, Checkhov's *The Seagull* is revived, staged by John Fernald. Catherine Lacey plays Mme. Arkadina.

May 4 Bernard Miles and his Mermaid Theatre use London's Royal Exchange for the current production of *As You Like it,* directed by Miles and featuring him as Duke Frederick and William.

May 4 The Comedie Française comes to London's St. James's Theatre, opening with Molière's *Tartuffe.* On May 11, the classic is *Brittanicus,* followed on May 18 by *Le Jeu de l'Amour et du Hasard* and *On ne Saurait Penser a Tout.*

May 6 *In the Lap of the Gods,* a revue, opens at the New Lindsey Theatre in Lon-

don. Among the ensemble are Malcolm Goddard and Fenella Fielding. On May 8, the Irving Theatre offers the *Rush Hour Revue.* On May 20, at the Arts Theatre, the play is N. Richard Nash's *Second Best Bed,* with Alan MacNaughton as Will Shakespeare. At the Embassy Theatre on the same day, George Coulouris plays Malvolio in *Twelfth night,* staged by Laurence Payne. On May 26, *Hamlet* bows at the Embassy, with Payne as the Dane. On this day at the New Torch Theatre, Diana Maugham's *Snow* opens.

May 7 Noel Coward plays King Magnus in a lavish Coronation production of Shaw's *The Apple Cart* at London's Haymarket. Designed by Loudon Sainthill and staged by Michael MacOwan, it also stars Margaret Leighton. There are 100 performances.

May 12 Eleanor and Herbert Farjeon's 1936 "Victorian musical," *The Two Bouquets,* is revived at London's St. Martin's Theatre. Willard Stoker directs. A mix-up in the bouqets provides plot complications for Kate and Laura (Sara Gregory and Sonia Williams). The show has 228 performances including those after it transfers to the Piccadilly Theatre.

May 15 Peter Brook stages a revival of Thomas Otway's *Venice Preserved* at London's Lyric, Hammersmith, with John Gielgud, Eileen Herlie, Pamela Brown, Paul Scofield, and Herbert Lomas.

May 27 London's annual summer season of classics in the Open Air Theatre in Regent's Park gets underway with *Twelfth Night,* staged by the Robert Atkins, who also plays Sir Toby Belch. On June 29, *Love's Labour's Lost* opens, staged by Hugh Goldie.

Summer *Val Balfour's Original American Version of The Oberammergau Passion Play* is an adaptation of the life of Jesus from the Oberammergau Passion Play in Bavaria. It plays in the Passion Play Amphitheatre in Strasburg, Virginia.

June 4 Sacha Guitry and his Paris company open at London's Winter Garden with Guitry's play, *Écoutez Bien, Messieurs.*

June 8 London's Arts Theatre summer program begins with Cilli Wang, the dancer and mime artist. On June 25, Bernard Shaw's *Arms and the Man* is revived by Alec Clunes, who plays Bluntschli. This day Wolf Mankowitz's *The Bespoke Overcoat* is also offered by Clunes, with Alfie Bass and David Kossoff. On July 22, director Judith Furse revives James Bridie's *Tobias and the Angel.* On August 11, the Ulster Theatre Group plays Michael Murphy's *Dust Under Our Feet.*

June 9 London's coronation summer is made more amusing with several revues in the smaller theatres. At the New Watergate, the show is *Set To Music.* On July 1 at the Irving Theatre, *Talk of the Night* opens, devised and directed by Peter Croft;

Rachel Roberts is in the company. On the 7th, the show at the Wimbledon Theatre is *The Domino Revue*, featuring such talents as Miriam Karlin, Evelyn Laye, and Ron Moody.

June 10 Bernard Miles' Mermaid Theatre offers *Eastward Ho!*, by Jonson, Chapman, and Marston, at London's Royal Exchange. Joan Swinstead directs, with Miles as Slitgut. On July 1, the play is *Macbeth*, with Miles in the title-role.

June 10 *Out of the Whirlwind*, by Christopher Hassall, is played today in Westminster Abbey, where Queen Elizabeth II has been crowned only eight days ago. This Morality play, staged by Hugh Miller, has Fay Compton in its cast.

June 22 At London's Sadler's Wells Theatre, the D'Oyly Carte Opera Company opens a repertory run of *Iolanthe*, *Cox and Box* and *H. M. S. Pinafore*, *The Mikado*, *The Yeomen of the Guard*, *Patience*, *The Pirates of Penzance*, *The Gondoliers*, and *Ruddigore*.

June 27 *Florida Aflame* opens today in Lake Wales, Florida. Written by John Caldwell, it's an historical drama about the Seminole Indians.

June 29 At London's Westminster Theatre, the Elizabethan Theatre Company offers *Julius Caesar*, staged by Michael MacOwan. Peter Jeffrey plays the title-role, with Toby Robertson as Mark Antony. On July 9, the company presents *Henry V*, with Colin George as the king. John Barton directs.

June 30 The Bristol Old Vic Company comes to London's Old Vic to play *Henry V*. Denis Carey directs a cast including John Neville and Patrick McGoohan. On July 13, the Birmingham Repertory troupe follows with *Henry VI, Part 1*. *Part 2* opens the next evening. *Part 3* is played on July 15. Douglas Seale directs, with Jack May as the king. Richard Pasco and Kenneth Williams are also in the ensemble.

July 13 Alec Guinness plays the title-role in Shakespeare's *Richard III*, the premiere production of the newly established Stratford Shakespeare Festival, in Stratford, Ontario, Canada. The production, designed by Tanya Moiseiwitsch, is staged by Tyrone Guthrie, artistic director of the festival, with music and fanfares by Louis Applebaum. Members of the inaugural ensemble include Douglas Campbell, and Irene Worth. One critic calls it "the most exciting night in the history of Canadian theatre."

July 14 Tonight is the second night of the new Stratford Shakespeare Festival in Canada. Irene Worth and Alec Guinness play the leads in *All's Well That Ends Well*. Tyrone Guthrie directs, with the designs of Tanya Moiseiwitsch. Music is composed by Louis Applebaum.

Aug 1 In Ashland, the Oregon Shakespeare Festival opens with *Coriolanus*, staged by Allen Fletcher. Richard Graham follows with *The Merchant of Venice*, then comes James Sandoe's production of *Henry VI, Part 1* and Philip Hanson's *The Taming of the Shrew*.

Aug 6 A London summer revival of Frederick Lonsdale's vintage comedy, *Aren't We All?*, staged by Roland Culver, with a cast including Marie Löhr and Ronald Squire runs nearly four months.

Aug 23 Britain's Edinburgh International Festival opens. The Old Vic Company presents Hamlet, staged by Michael Benthall and designed by Kenneth Rowell. Richard Burton plays the lead, with Claire Bloom as Ophelia. T. S. Eliot's new play, *The Confidential Clerk*, has its premiere, staged by E. Martin Browne and designed by Hutchinson Scott. Among the players are Paul Rogers, Alan Webb, Margaret Leighton, and Denholm Elliott. The Glasgow Citis' production of *The Highland Fair* returns from last season. Jean Vilar brings his Theatre National Populaire (T. N. P.) from Paris with Moliére's *L'Avare* and Shakespeare's *Richard II*. Vilar stages and plays both leads. Marcel Marceau also comes from Paris with his mime impressions.

Aug 24 Donald Wolfit returns to London's King's Theatre with his repertory of classics. Tonight, it's Baliol Holloway's staging of Sheridan's *The School for Scandal*, with Wolfit and his wife, Rosalind Iden, as Sir Peter and Lady Teazle. On September 14, *Henry IV, Part 1* is offered, with Wolfit as Falstaff. On the 28th, the play is *Macbeth*, with the Wolfits in the central roles. On the 30th, *As You Like It* opens, staged by Wolfit, who plays Touchstone. *Volpone* takes the stage on October 12, with Wolfit in the title-role. Nugent Monk directs him in *King Lear* on October 22. The next day, *Twelfth Night* with Wolfit in the role of Malvolio. Massinger's *A New Way To Pay Old Debts* returns on November 2, followed on the 17th, by the Garrick-Colman *The Clandestine Marriage*.

Aug 31 Rodgers and Hammerstein revive their musical, *Oklahoma!*, at the New York City Center for five weeks at popular prices. Ridge Bond and Florence Henderson are Curly and Laurey. On November 11, José Ferrer revives Rostand's *Cyrano de Bergerac*, starring and staging, with Arlene Dahl. This has a two-week run as does Joseph Kramm's *The Shrike*, revived on November 25, with Ferrer and Judith Evelyn repeating their Broadway roles.

Sep 8 Sandy Wilson, creator of *The Boy Friend*, tries out his musical, *The Buccaneer* in London at the New Watergate Theatre. Rachel Roberts and Enid Lorimer are in the company, directed by Lloyd Lamble. At the Lyric, Hammersmith, Ibsen's *A Doll's House* is revived by director Peter Ashmore on the same night. On the 10th, at the Arts Theatre, W. Somerset Maugham's *Penelope* opens.

Sep 14 The Old Vic ensemble opens its season in London with *Hamlet*, played by Richard Burton and staged by Michael Benthall. Claire Bloom is Ophelia, Fay Compton, Gertrude. On the 15th, *All's Well That Ends Well*, also staged by Benthall, opens. John Neville is Bertram. On October 27, George Devine's staging of *King John* opens. Michael Hordern plays the title-role.

Sep 28 Peter Ustinov's *The Love of Four Colonels* opens the 25th season of the Dublin Gate Theatre, staged as usual by Hilton Edwards, with Michael O'Herlihy and Micheal macLiammoir designing. Other plays include O'Neill's *Anna Christie* and Bernard Shaw's *Saint Joan*.

Oct 15 At the New Watergate Theatre, Georges Simenon's *The Snow Was Black*, adapted by Kitty Black, opens in a Norman Marshall staging. On October 21 at the Arts, Lennox Robinson's Irish comedy, *Drama at Inish*, is presented. In 1933, it was known as *Is Life Worth Living?* In the cast are Lally Bowers and Binnie Hale. On October 25, Luigi Pirandello's *You'd Better Think It Over, Giacomo*, opens, staged by Victor Rietti. Ferenc Molnar's *Olympia* is shown at the Portcullis on the same day, staged by Ann Jellicoe. On October 26, at the Boltons Theatre, Tennessee Williams' *This Property Is Condemned* is paired with Moliére's *George Dandin*, both staged by Frank Marcus.

Nov 4 The Shakespeare Memorial Theatre Company presents *Antony and Cleopatra* at London's Prince's Theatre, staged by Glen Byam Shaw. Peggy Ashcroft plays Cleopatra, Michael Redgrave is Antony.

Nov 10 Enid Bagnold's play, *Little Idiot*, is presented at London's Q Theatre. On November 13 at the Chepstow Theatre, the drama is George Shiels' Irish play, *The Rugged Path*, with an Irish cast. On November 25 at the New Watergate *The Pleasure of Your Company* opens. At the Wimbledon Theatre, audiences are being offered *The Big Knife*, by Clifford Odets, on November 30. Sam Wanamaker directs and stars with Renée Asherson.

Nov 19 Bernard Shaw's *Pygmalion* is revived at London's St. James's Theatre, with Kay Hammond as Eliza, and her actor-director husband, John Clements, as Henry Higgins. It earns a run of 155 performances.

Nov 19 At Broadway's Broadhurst Theatre, producers Blanco and Pozo present the Spanish Theatre Repertory Company for four weeks. The program includes classics such as Calderon's *El Alcalde de Zalamea* and *La Vida Es Sueno*, Rostand's *Cyrano de Bergerac*, and Benevente's modern drama, *La Otra Honra*. Alejandro Ulloa stages and leads the company.

Nov 24 At Joan Littlewood's Theatre Royal, in London's Stratford East, Ewan MacColl's *The Traveller* opens, with MacColl as Pavel Laurentz. Littlewood directs.

THE LITTLE HUT

Dec 1 The late Sidney Howard's play *Madam, Will You Walk* (1939), premieres finally at Off-Broadway's Phoenix Theatre. Hume Cronyn and Jessica Tandy lead the cast.

Dec 1 Revues are in vogue at London's smaller theatres, such as the Irving, which tonight offers *Saints and Sinners*, staged by Cyril Curtis. On December 11, the Irving offers *On With the New*, featuring the new face of Anthony Newley. On the 22nd, the New Watergate presents *Oddly Enough*. On the 23rd at the Lyric, Hammersmith, *At the Lyric* features Hermione Baddeley, Dora Bryan, Rachel Roberts, and Ian Carmichael, among others. Dilys Lay and Ron Moody are in the New Lindsey's *More Intimacy at Eight* on December 31.

Dec 9 At the New York City Center, Jean Dalrymple supervises the production of *Richard III*, with José Ferrer as Richard and a cast including Vincent Price, Maureen Stapleton and Jessie Royce Landis. Margaret Webster stages this two-week venture. On December 22, Ferrer revives *Charley's Aunt*, directing and starring. Peggy Wood plays the real aunt. This is also a popular-price two-week engagement.

Dec 22 London's holiday season opens with *Cinderella* at the Players' Theatre Club. Don Gemmell directs the show, adapted by Hattie Jacques. On the 23rd, Pat Kirkwood is Peter in the Scala Theatre's *Peter Pan* revival. *Beauty and the Beast* opens at the Embassy Theatre, and the Q Theatre offers *Alice in Wonderland and Through the Looking Glass*. On December 24th, the Palladium opens its own version of *Cinderella* with Julie Andrews.

1953   BIRTHS/DEATHS/DEBUTS

March 19 Actress and vocalist Irene Bordoni (b. 1895) dies in New York. Bordoni's various roles included Colette in *Little Miss Bluebeard*, the Duchess of Tann in *The Improper Duchess,* and Madame Bordelaise in *Louisiana Purchase.*

June 5 Stage and screen actor William Farnum (b. 1876) dies in Hollywood. His first stage success in New York was as Ben Hur in 1900. His film career began in 1915.

June 5 English actor Roland Young (b. 1887) is dead in New York. In 1912 Young played in *Improper Peter* in London and in *Hindle Wakes* in New York. Young became a naturalized American citizen in 1918.

Sept 15 Stage and screen actor Ben Gazzara makes his New York debut as Jocko de Paris in Calder Willingham's *End as a Man* at the Theatre de Lys.

Sep 19 American playwright Percival Wilde (B. 1887) dies in New York. When his first short story was published in 1912, Wilde received so many requests for dramatic rights that he turned to playwriting. He is the author of *The Reckoning, Catesby, The Devil's Booth,* and several plays for children.

Oct 7 English actor-director-playwright Roland Culver makes his first appearance on Broadway as Philip in André Roussin's comedy, *The Little Hut,* adapted by Nancy Mitford, at the Coronet Theatre.

Nov 27 Eugene O'Neill, regarded by many as America's greatest playwright, dies today after a lengthy illness. He won the Nobel Prize for Literature in 1936 and the Pulitzer Prize for Beyond the Horizon (1920), Anna Christie (1922), Strange Interlude (1928), and Long Day's Journey Into Night (1957). Other memorable O'Neill plays are: Desire Under the Elms, Mourning Becomes Electra, and The Great God Brown.

tains and drops by means of an electrically controlled winch.

Feb Joan Littlewood takes over London's Theatre Royal (1884), Stratford East, for her Theatre Workshop, "A British People's Theatre," founded in 1945.

April 16 The Lord Chamberlain has seen to it that the London theatre public will not be offended by hearing the off-stage sound of a toilet flushing in Graham Greene's *The Living Room*. This, despite the fact that in many West End theatres, it is possible for portions of the audience to hear real toilets flushing through the auditorium walls.

May 6 When tonight's production of *Henry VIII* has run its course, some 308,050 patrons will have attended London's Old Vic during this Coronation season of 1952-53.

May 30 Tonight is the final performance of *Come Back, Little Sheba* at New York's Empire Theatre (1893). Charles Frohman's handsome theatre is to be demolished.

June 1 Louis Kronenberger, new editor of the annual *Best Plays* series, selects Broadway's ten best shows for the 1952-1953 season. They are Laurents' *The Time of the Cuckoo*, Chase's *Bernardine*, Knott's *Dial "M" for Murder*, Hart's *The Climate of Eden*, Ustinov's *The Love of Four Colonels*, Miller's *The Crucible*, Tabori's *The Emperor's New Clothes*, Inge's *Picnic*, Fields-Chodorov-Comden-Green's *Wonderful Town*, and the Spewacks' *My Three Angels*. Inge's *Picnic* wins both the Pulitzer Prize and the Drama Critics' Circle Award for "Best American Play." Ustinov's is "Best Foreign Play." *Pal Joey* is the "Best Musical Production."

July 13 As a result of an inspiration by Tom Patterson, a Canadian journalist, born in Stratford, Ontario, tonight the dream of a Canadian Shakespearean Festival becomes reality in a temporary tent-theatre in that Western Ontario town. As envisioned by artistic director Tyrone Guthrie and designed by Tanya Moiseiwitsch, the stage is an innovative open playing-space. The original five-week season has to be extended to six, owing to the large numbers of festival visitors.

Oct 31 More than a thousand donors have contributed a total of $157,000 by the close of the fiscal year to make the first Stratford Shakespeare Festival possible in Canada's province of Ontario. The following year, an additional $141,000 will be raised to provide working capital and make changes in the festival's tent-theatre.

Dec 1 T. Edward Hambleton and Norris Houghton open the Phoenix Theatre on Second Avenue, New York in the midst of the city's first newspaper strike. Their partnership in the Phoenix is to last ten seasons, after which Hambleton is to continue the operation in several guises and with various partners, such as the APA.

1953   THEATERS/PRODUCTIONS

1953 Among the patents granted this year in Britain is one to A. M. Low and T. C. Arnold for producing color effects by projecting light through a fluid film or a body formed by colored liquids. This concept will be widely used in the 1960's in "psychedelic" light shows accompanying rock concerts.

Jan 20 Paul M. Fischer obtains an American patent for a device for moving curtains and drops by means of an electrically controlled winch.

Jan 6 *Mademoiselle Colombe*. See L premiere *(Colombe)*, 1951.

Jan 20 *The Caine Mutiny Court-Martial* (NY—Plymouth—Drama). Charles Laughton directs Lloyd Nolan, Henry Fonda, and John Hodiak in Herman Wouk's adaptation of his novel *The Caine Mutiny*. It has 415 performances. The play opens in London at the Hippodrome on June 13, 1956, with Nolan, David Knight, and Nigel Stock in the cast. The production lasts four months.

Feb 8 *The Immoralist* (NY—Royale—Drama). James Dean plays a homosexual Arab boy who tries to blackmail a married archaeologist (Louis Jourdan), uncertain of his own sexuality. Geraldine Page plays the wife. Ruth and Augustus Goetz' adaptation of Andre Gide's novel runs three months. Daniel Mann directs.

Feb 9 *The Girl on the Via Flaminia* (NY—Circle-in-the-Square—Drama). Jose Quintero stages Alfred Hayes' adaptation of his novel about a poor Italian girl (Betty Miller) who marries a GI (Leo Penn). After 43 performances the play transfers to Broadway's 48th Street Theatre for a total run of 111 performances.

Feb 11 *The Confidential Clerk*. See L premiere, 1953.

Feb 18 *Ondine* (NY—46th Street—Drama). Audrey Hepburn plays a water-spirit who longs to marry a mortal (Mel Ferrer) in Maurice Valency's adaptation of Jean Giraudoux's drama. It runs nearly 20 weeks. On Jan 12, 1961, the Royal Shakespeare company premieres the play at the Aldwych with Leslie Caron and Richard Johnson.

March 5 *The Girl in the Pink Tights* (NY—Mark Hellinger—Musical). Jeanmaire's dancing, choreographed by Agnes de Mille, is the highlight of a musical within this musical, directed by Shepard Traube. The score is by Sigmund Romberg (his last), with book by Jerome Chodorov and Joseph Fields. It has 115 showings.

March 11 *The Golden Apple* (NY—Phoenix—Musical).This show wins the Drama Critics' Circle best musical citation and moves to Broadway's Alvin Theatre for a total of 125 performances. Kaye Ballard and Jonathan Lucas head the company in John LaTouche's retelling of the Judgment of Paris myth. The score is by Jerome Moross. Hanya Holm choreographs.

April 1 *King of Hearts* (NY—Lyceum—Comedy). Walter Kerr directs a cast that includes Cloris Leachman and Jackie Cooper in this Jean Kerr-Eleanor Brooke farce about a cartoonist (Donald Cook) with artistic pretensions. It runs nearly 29 weeks.

April 7 *Anniversary Waltz* (NY—Broadhurst—Comedy). Unexpected revelations at a fifteenth wedding anniversary party cause complications in Jerome Chodorov and Joseph Field's popular comedy, staged by Moss Hart. It has 615 showings. The cast includes Kitty Carlisle, Macdonald Carey, and Warren Berlinger.

April 8 *By the Beautiful Sea* (NY—Majestic—Musical). Shirley Booth charms audiences as the keeper of a theatrical boarding-house in Coney Island in this musical that runs for 270 performances. The book is by Herbert and Dorothy Fields, score by Arthur Schwartz. Wilbur Evans co-stars.

April 9 *The Magic and the Loss* (NY—Booth—Drama). Although Julian Funt's play, about the personal and professional crises of a female advertising executive (Uta Hagen), runs only 27 performances, it's chosen as one of the season's best. Robert Preston and Charles Taylor also appear. Staging is by Michael Gordon.

May 13 *The Pajama Game* (NY—St. James—Musical). Harold Prince's first production wins 1,063 performances. Based on Richard Bissell's novel *7½ Cents*, with book by Bissell and George Abbott, who also stages, it tells of a pajama-factory manager (John Raitt) in love with the head of the union grievance committee (Janis Paige). Songs are by Richard Adler and Jerry Ross. Jerome Robbins co-directs and Bob Fosse creates such dances as "Steam Heat" for Carol Haney. Shirley MacLaine is one of the dancers. The musical opens at London's Coliseum on Oct 13, 1955, with Max Wall and Joy Nichols among the cast. There are 588 performances.

Sep 15 *Dear Charles*. See L premiere, 1952.

Sep 23 *All Summer Long* (NY—Coronet—Drama). Robert Anderson bases this family drama about an insecure 12-year-old (Clay Hall) on a novel by Donald Wetzel. John Kerr, Ed Begley, June Walker, and Carroll Baker are in the cast. The Alan Scheider staging runs nearly eight weeks, produced by the Playwrights' Company.

Sep 30 *The Boy Friend*. See L premiere, 1954.

Oct 7 *Reclining Figure* (NY—Lyceum—Comedy). Harry Kurnitz's farce about New York art dealers foisting forgeries on a gullible public runs 116 performances. Abe Burrows stages. Percy Waram plays an eccentric art lover.

Oct 13 *The Tender Trap* (NY—Longacre—Comedy). Charlie Reader (Ronny Graham) is surrounded by adoring females until the trap is sprung in this Max Shulman and Robert Paul Smith farce. Robert Preston and Kim Hunter are in the cast. It runs 13 weeks. On May 3, 1955, the play opens in the West End at the Saville with a cast including Brian Reece and Geraldine McEwen. It has only 22 performances.

Oct 20 *Peter Pan* (NY—Winter Garden—Musical). James Barrie's play becomes a musical vehicle for Mary Martin and runs for 19 weeks. Martin's husband Richard Halliday produces; Jerome Robbins stages

DEAR CHARLES

HIPPO DANCING

and choreographs. There are songs by Mark Charlap, Carolyn Leigh, and Jule Styne among others.

Oct 28 *The Rainmaker* (NY—Cort—Comedy). Geraldine Page is "fresher than the play and equally funny," says the NY Times of this "Western" tale of a plain and plain-spoken girl whose marriage chances seem dim until she meets conman Bill Starbuck (Darren McGavin). There are 125 showings. Page repeats her role in the London production which opens on May 31, 1956, at the St. Martin's. Here it has 228 performances.

Nov 3 *Quadrille.* See L premiere, 1952.

Nov 4 *Fanny* (NY—Majestic—Musical). There are 888 performances of this musical about the pregnant Fanny (Florence Henderson) who gets married off by her father (Ezio Pinza) to the kindly Panisse (Walter Slezak). S.N. Behrman and Joshua Logan have based it on a Marcel Pagnol film trilogy. It has songs by Harold Rome and ballets by Helen Tamiris. Janet Pavek is Fanny in the London production which premieres at the Drury Lane on Nov 15, 1956. Kevin Scott and Robert Morley are also in the cast. The show earns 347 performances.

Nov 17 *The Living Room.* See L premiere, 1953.

Dec 1 *Mrs. Patterson* (NY—National—Drama). Eartha Kitt plays a girl who longs to be like her mother's wealthy white employer, but is also attracted by the idea of being a lively black high-steppin' hellion. She also sings in this Charles Sebree and Greer Johnson play which runs 101 performances.

Dec 8 *The Bad Seed* (NY—46th Street—Drama). Maxwell Anderson's disturbing play, later a film, deals with a child killer (Patty McCormack) who looks like an angel. Nancy Kelly and Eileen Heckart are in the cast. It runs 42 weeks. The play opens in London at the Aldwych on April 14, 1955, with Carol Wolveridge and Diana Wynyard in the leads. It is presented 196 times.

Dec 13 *Lunatics and Lovers* (NY—Broadhurst—Comedy). Sidney Kingsley's knockabout farce, set in a hotel suite crammed with raffish characters from Manhattan's West Side, stars Buddy Hackett and Arthur O'Connell. It runs 42 weeks.

Dec 16 *Witness for the Prosecution.* See L premiere, 1953.

Dec 27 *The Saint of Bleecker Street* (NY—Broadway—Opera). The Drama Critics' Circle votes this Gian-Carlo Menotti tale, about a girl from New York's Little Italy who is regarded as a saint by her simple, devout neighbors, the Best Musical Production. Menotti stages. There are 92 performances.

Dec 28 *The Flowering Peach* (NY—Belasco—Drama). Clifford Odets' retells and stages the story of Noah in a show that runs 17 weeks. Menasha Skulnik, Barbara Baxley, Janice Rule, and Martin Ritt head the cast.

Dec 29 *Anastasia.* See L premiere, 1953.

Dec 30 *House of Flowers* (NY—Alvin—Musical). Truman Capote provides the book and Harold Arlen the score for this musical about two madams with rival bordellos, set in the West Indies. Pearl Bailey, Juanita Hall, and Diahann Carroll head the large cast. Peter Brook stages. Herbert Ross choreographs. It runs nearly 21 weeks.

1954   BRITISH PREMIERES

Jan 1 *The Big Knife.* See NY premiere, 1949.

Jan 14 *The Boy Friend* (L—Wyndham's—Musical). Sandy Wilson's affectionate spoof of 1920's musicals wins a long run of 2,084 performances. The show, developed at the Players' Theatre Club, features Anne Rogers, Anthony Hayes, and Joan Sterndale Bennett. The show opens at Broadway's Royale on Sep 30, with Julie Andrews in the lead. There are 485 showings.

Feb 11 *Angels in Love* (L—Savoy—Comedy). Hugh Mills satirizes what might have happened to little Lord Fauntleroy in later life. Bernard Braden directs Peter Hammond, Barbara Kelly, and Maxine Audley. It runs 25 weeks.

Feb 18 *The Burning Glass* (L—Apollo—Drama). There are 123 performances for Charles Morgan's play about an English scientist abducted by enemy agents. The company includes Michael Goodliffe as Christopher Terriford. The play arrives at New York's Longacre on March 4 with Walter Matthau and Cedric Hardwicke. It runs less than four weeks.

Feb 24 *The Fifth Season.* See NY premiere, 1953.

Feb 25 *You'll Be Lucky* (L—Adelphi—Revue). This show runs 432 performances. Staged by Alec Shanks and Joan Davis, it numbers Al Read and Lauri Lupino Lane among its cast.

March 12 *I Am a Camera.* See NY premiere, 1951.

April 3 *Wedding in Paris* (L—Hippodrome—Musical). Vera Caspary's plot concerns a Canadian girl who sets off to marry her boyfriend, working in Paris. Charles Hickman stages. There are 411 performances, with Evelyn Laye and An-ton Walbrook. Songs are by Hans May, lyrics by Sonny Miller.

April 7 *Hippo Dancing* (L—Lyric—Comedy). Robert Morley plays a suburban tyrant who gets his comeuppance, in his own version of a farce by André Roussin. Peter Ashmore stages a cast including Wilfrid Hyde White and Mona Washbourne. It runs 43 weeks.

April 8 *Marching Song* (L—St. Martin's—Drama). John Whiting's play about a general sentenced for war crimes has only 43 performances but is admired by some critics. Frith Banbury stages.

April 14 *The Prisoner* (L—Globe—Drama). Suggested by real events in Hungary, Bridget Boland's play concerns an imprisoned Cardinal (Alec Guinness) faced by an implacable Interrogator (Noel Willman). Peter Glenville directs. There are 60 performances.

April 21 *Waiting for Gillian* (L—St. James's—Drama). Ronald Millar's play, about a wife sent to prison for manslaughter after a car accident, is based on Nigel Balchin's novel *A Way Through the Wood.* It stars the popular husband-and-wife team Googie Withers and John McCallum. Michael MacOwan directs. It runs 101 performances.

April 22 *The Teahouse of the August Moon.* See NY premiere, 1953.

April 28 *The Manor of Northstead* (L—Duchess—Comedy). William Douglas Home's play satirizes the local political situation in Scotland's Western Isles and runs just over 38 weeks. Veteran actor A.E. Matthews plays an earl with Marie Löhr as his countess. Wallace Douglas directs.

April 29 *Intimacy at 8:30* (L—Criterion—Revue). A revised version of a show produced at the New Lindsey Theatre in December, this earns 552 performances. The cast includes comedian Ron Moody, Joan Sims, Joan Heal, and Dilys Lay.

April 30 *The Dark is Light Enough* (L—Aldwych—Drama). Edith Evans plays a resourceful countess who shields a fugitive during Hungary's 1848 revolution in Christopher Fry's poetic drama. It runs 242 performances. The play opens on Feb 23, 1955, at New York's ANTA with Katharine Cornell and Tyrone Power in the leads. There are only 69 showings.

May 31 *Cockles and Champagne* (L—Saville—Revue). Cecil Landau stages a cast that includes Patricia Burke, Elizabeth Seal, Miriam Karlin, and Renee Houston. It runs four months.

June 2 *Joyce Grenfell Requests the Pleasure* (L—Fortune—Revue). Joyce Grenfell's character sketches win a run of 275 performances. Richard Addinsell provides the music. The revue opens in New York at the Bijou on Oct 10, 1955, with staging by Laurier Lister.

June 3 *It's Never Too Late* (L—Westminster—Comedy). Celia Johnson stars as a housewife who writes a best-seller in Felicity Douglas' play, staged by Joan Swinstead. During the six-month run, Phyllis Calvert replaces Johnson.

June 9 *Both Ends Meet* (L—Apollo—Comedy). Peter Brook directs Arthur Macrae's comedy about a playwright, desperate to make some money and get married, who runs into tax difficulties. Macrae and Brenda Bruce head the cast. It runs almost 36 weeks.

June 10 *After the Ball* (L—Globe—Musical). Noel Coward turns Oscar Wilde's *Lady Windermere's Fan* into a musical, staged by Robert Helpmann. Vanessa Lee, Peter Graves, and Mary Ellis head the cast. It runs almost 24 weeks.

July 22 *Murder Story* (L—Cambridge—Drama). Ludovic Kennedy bases his drama on a recent murder case and makes a protest against capital punishment. Staged by John McKelvey, it has a 2-month run.

Aug 3 *Relations Are Best Apart* (L—Garrick—Comedy). Dermot Walsh, Hazel Court, and Leslie Henson head the cast in this working-class family comedy. Martin Landau directs the 230 performances.

Aug 4 *Sabrina Fair*. See NY premiere, 1953.

Aug 5 *Salad Days* (L—Vaudeville—Musical). A smash run of 2,282 performances for a charming Julian Slade and Dorothy Reynolds musical that is part revue, part story of two university graduates who plan to marry. Julian Slade's music is widely praised. Denis Cary directs this production which is presented by the Bristol Old Vic Company.

Aug 31 *Dry Rot* (L—Whitehall—Comedy). This long-running farce (1,475 performances) by John Chapman centers on the planning of a racetrack swindle. Brian Rix, John Slater, and Basil Lord head the cast. Wallace Douglas directs.

Sep 9 *All for Mary* (L—Duke of York's—Comedy). There are 315 performances of Harold Brooke and Kay Bannerman's farce set in the rustic Hotel Splendide in the French Alps. Kathleen Harrison and David Tomlinson head the cast. It is staged by Jack Williams.

Sep 22 *Separate Tables* (L—St. James's—Drama). Terence Rattigan's double-bill consists of *Table by the Window* and *Table Number Seven*, both set in an English seaside hotel dining-room. Eric Portman and Margaret Leighton play opposite in both plays. The production has 726 performances. It comes to New York's Music Box on Oct 25, 1956, with Portman and Leighton. There are 332 showings.

Sep 23 *The Party Spirit* (L—Piccadilly—Comedy). Veteran comedians Robertson Hare and Ralph Lynn play the only "Free Whigs" in Parliament in Peter Jones's and John Howett's farce, which runs 130 performances. Charles Hickman directs.

Oct 5 *Bell, Book, and Candle*. See NY premiere, 1950.

Oct 14 *Can-Can*. See NY premiere, 1953.

Oct 21 *Book of the Month* (L—Cambridge—Comedy). An M. P.'s 17-year-old daughter (Jane Griffiths) writes a sexy best-seller in this Basil Thomas farce, much to her father's (Hugh Williams) consternation. Pauline Grant directs; there is a seven-month run.

Nov 4 *The Matchmaker* (L—Haymarket—Comedy). Ruth Gordon plays Dolly Levi in Thornton Wilder's reworking of his *The Merchant of Yonkers* (1938), itself an adaptation of a Viennese farce. The show runs over 34 weeks. On Dec 5, 1955, Gordon again leads the cast in the New York premiere at the Royale. There are 486 performances.

Nov 17 *The Talk of the Town* (L—Adelphi—Revue). Comedians Jimmy Edwards, Tony Hancock, and Joan Turner head this popular revue staged by Alec Shanks and Joan Davis. It has 656 performances.

Nov 24 *An Evening with Beatrice Lillie*. See NY premiere, 1952.

Dec 2 *Time Remembered* (L—Lyric—Comedy). Paul Scofield plays Prince Albert, with Mary Ure as Amanda, who vanquishes the memory of Leocadia to win his heart in this William Chapell staging of Jean Anouilh's *Leocadia*, as adapted by Patricia Moyes. The comedy comes to Broadway at the Morosco on Nov 12, 1957. Richard Burton, Helen Hayes, and Susan Strasberg head the cast. The play runs 31 weeks.

Dec 13 *Spider's Web* (L—Savoy—Drama). Along with *The Mousetrap* and *Witness for the Prosecution*, Agatha Christie now has three successful thrillers running simultaneously in the West End. Margaret Lockwood stars in this one, and it wins a run of 577 performances. Wallace Douglas directs.

Dec 16 *Jokers Wild* (L—Victoria Palace—Revue). The Crazy Gang (Flanagan, Nervo, Knox, Naughton, and Gold) wisecracks its way through 814 performances of sketches, songs, and antics in this revue, directed by Alec Shanks and Charles Henry.

1954   REVIVALS/REPERTORIES

Jan 6 *Twelfth Night*, directed by Denis Carey, is the new production at London's Old Vic. The cast includes John Neville, Claire Bloom, and Richard Burton. On February 23, the company presents *Coriolanus*, staged by Michael Benthall. Burton plays the title-role, with Fay Compton as his mother. Leslie Hurry provides the sets and costumes on April 13 for *The Tempest*, staged by Robert Helpmann. Michael Hordern is Prospero.

Jan 13 At London's Arts Theatre, the play is Gaston Baty's version of Dostoevsky's *Crime and Punishment*, staged by John Fernald. At the Embassy on the same night, Wolf Mankowitz's *The Boychick* and *The Bespoke Overcoat* open.

Jan 19 At the Off-Broadway Phoenix Theatre, Shakespeare's *Coriolanus* has a six-week run with Robert Ryan in the title-role and Mildren Natwick as his dominating mother. John Houseman directs the company.

Feb 2 Joan Littlewood stages Anthony Nicholson's *Van Call* at London's Theatre Royal, Stratford East. Nicholson and Avis Bunnage are in the cast. On February 23, she directs John Marston's *The Dutch Courtesan*. On March 30, Littlewood offers audiences Charles Fenn's *The Fire Eaters*. Using Jean Giraudoux's *Amphytrion 38* as a base, she stages *Jupiter's Night Out* on April 13.

Feb 3 At the Arts Theatre in London, Charles Hawtrey's *The Private Secretary* is revived, staged by Hugh Miller. On the 15th at the Embassy Theatre, Karel Capek's *The Mother* is revived, staged by Anthony Hawtrey.

Feb 10 Staged by John Gielgud, with lavish decors by Motley, Brandon Thomas' classic British comedy, *Charley's Aunt*, is revived in London at the New Theatre. John Mills and Gwen Ffrangcon-Davies play leads. This show runs nearly four months.

Feb 16 Continuing its 25th season, the Dublin Gate Theatre presents a revival of

Maura Laverty's *Tolka Row*.

March 3 Garcia Lorca's *Blood Wedding* is staged by Peter Hall, for London's Arts Theatre. At the Irving Theatre on March 10, Ellen Pollock stages a program of five Grand Guignol plays. On March 11 at the New Watergate, Beryl Reid appears in a revue, *First Edition*, staged by Ronnie Hill.

March 10 At the Off-Broadway Theatre DeLys, in an adaptation by Marc Blitzstein, Bertolt Brecht and Kurt Weill's *The Threepenny Opera*, is revived for 96 performances. Brooks Atkinson, the NY Times drama critic, repeatedly calls for its return. On September 20, 1955, it re-opens at the DeLys for a marathon run, totalling 2,611 showings, with Lotte Lenya recreating her role as Jenny.

March 16 At Stratford-upon-Avon, *Othello* opens the annual season at the Shakespeare Memorial Theatre. The festival's co-director, Anthony Quayle stages and plays Othello to Barbara Jefford's Desdemona. George Devine stages *A Midsummer Night's Dream*, with Keith Michell. Devine's *Shrew* is revived from last season. Quayle's co-director of the festival, Glen Byam Shaw directs *Romeo and Juliet*, with Laurence Harvey and Zena Walker. Shaw also stages *Troilus and Cressida*, with Harvey and Muriel Pavlov.

April 1 At London's Arts Theatre, Jean Giraudoux's *The Enchanted*—as adapted by Maurice Valency—is staged by John Fernald. On the 13th, Joan Littlewood opens her version of Giraudoux's *Amphytrion 38* at the Theatre Royal, Stratford East. On the 27th, at the New Lindsey, the play is *In the Train*, by Frank O'Connor and Hugh Hunt. Milo O'Shea is in the cast.

May 5 At the New York City Center, Julius Rudel conducts a two-week revival of Jerome Kern's *Show Boat*, with Burl Ives as Captain Andy. On May 19, it is followed by a two week revival of Strauss's *Die Fledermaus*, with Donald Gramm.

May 11 Off-Broadway at the Phoenix Theatre, Norris Houghton stages a revival of Chekhov's *The Sea Gull*, with Mira Rostova and Montgomery Clift. Rostova, Clift, and Kevin McCarthy have made the adaptation. The production runs for five weeks.

May 16 Today in the Mountain Theatre in Mount Tamalpais State Park, California, Shakespeare's *The Tempest* opens. Beginning in 1913, every third Sunday in May has been "show-day" in this outdoor amphitheatre in the redwoods, with a breathtaking vista 2,000 feet above sea-level. During the war years, productions were abandoned. Other offerings have included *Twelfth Night* and *Alice in Wonderland*.

May 25 Wilkie Collins' novel, *The Woman in White*, comes to the stage of the Q Theatre in Dan Sutherland's adaptation. On the 26th, Goldoni's *The Impresario from Smyrna* is revived, in a Peter Hall staging, with a cast including Prunella Scales and Donald Pleasance.

May 21 John Gielgud adapts and stages Chekhov's *The Cherry Orchard* at London's Lyric, Hammersmith, Theatre with Gwen Ffrangcon-Davies and Trevor Howard.

May 28 *The Book of Job*, arranged from the King James Version of the Bible, by Orlin Corey, who is the drama's director, is presented at Pineville, Kentucky throughout the summer.

June 2 At the New York City Center, Rodgers and Hammerstein's *Carousel* wins a run of ten weeks in a revival staged by William Hammerstein. In the cast are Barbara Cook and Jo Sullivan. On December 22, James Barrie's *What Every Woman Knows*, with Helen Hayes, opens for a two-week revival.

June 8 At London's Theatre Royal, Stratford East, Joan Littlewood directs Molière's *The Flying Doctor*, playing Marinette. She also stages Ewan MacColl's *Johnny Noble*, with MacColl.

June 28 Under the artistic direction of Cecil Clarke, Canada's Stratford Shakespeare Festival opens with Clarke's staging of *Measure for Measure*, designed by Tanya Moiseiwitsch. Two other plays are offered: *The Taming of the Shrew*, and *Oedipus Rex*, both directed by Guthrie and designed by Moiseiwitsch. James Mason is Oedipus. The company performs in a temporary tent-theatre.

July 20 Jean-Paul Sartre's *The Respectable Prostitute* and Oscar Wilde's *Salome* are revived on a double-bill at London's St. Martin's Theatre, after a brief try-out at the Q Theatre. Frederick Farley stages. There are only 22 performances.

July 28 Richard Brinsley Sheridan's *The Duenna*, a comic operetta, is revived in London at the Westminster Theatre, with a new score by Julian Slade. Lionel Harris stages. Joan Plowright and Joyce Carey are in the company.

Aug 1 Festival founder Angus Bowmer stages *Hamlet* for the Oregon Shakespeare Festival in Ashland. H. Paul Kliss follows with *The Winter's Tale*. Allen Fletcher directs *The Merry Wives of Windsor*, after which James Sandoe's production of *Henry VI, Part 2* opens.

Aug 22 Britain's Edinburgh International Festival opens. Thornton Wilder's *The Matchmaker*, staged by Tyrone Guthrie and designed by Tanya Moiseiwitsch, has a cast including Ruth Gordon, Arthur Hill, Alec McCowen, and Prunella Scales. The Old Vic Company offers *Macbeth*, staged by Michael Benthall. This is an Assembly Hall production. At the Royal Lyceum, the Comedie Francaise presents Molière's *Le Bourgeois Gentilhomme*, staged by Jean Mayer and designed by Suzanne Lalique.

LIONEL BARRYMORE

Sep 8 Ibsen's *Hedda Gabler* is revived by director Peter Ashmore with Peggy Ashcroft in the title-role at the Lyric, Hammersmith.

Sep 9 At London's Old Vic Theatre, the season opens with a revival of *Macbeth*, staged by Michael Benthall and designed by Audrey Cruddas. Paul Rogers is Macbeth, with Ann Todd as Lady Macbeth. Others in the cast include John Neville, Alan Dobie and Rachel Roberts. On October 19, the production is *Love's Labour's Lost*, staged by Frith Banbury and designed by Cecil Beaton. Among the cast are Paul Daneman and Virginia McKenna. *The Taming of the Shrew* opens on November 30, staged by Denis Carey, with Kenneth Powell's designs and Julian Slade's music. Todd and Rogers play Katharina and Petruchio.

Sep 13 The D'Oyly Carte Opera Company returns to its traditional London home, the Savoy Theatre, for a season of Gilbert & Sullivan repertory, opening with *The Mikado*. On September 20, *The Yeomen of the Guard* is presented, followed by *Princess Ida*, *Trial by Jury* and *The Pirates of Penzance*, *Iolanthe*, *The Gondoliers*, *Ruddigore*, and *Cox and Box* and *H. M. S. Pinafore*.

Sep 21 At New York's Metropolitan Opera, London's Old Vic production of *A Midsummer Night's Dream* premieres, under the auspices of Sol Hurok, assisted by the Arts Council of Great Britain. Michael Benthall stages. Robert Helpmann choreographs, for there is also a *corps de ballet*. The principal players include Moira Shearer, Anthony Nicholls, Stanley Holloway, and Robert Helpmann. There are

29 performances.

Sep 28 Joan Littlewood stages *Arden of Faversham*, by George Lillo and Dr. Hoadley, at London's Theatre Royal, Stratford East. Maxwell Shaw plays Thomas Arden. On October 19, Littlewood stages her adaptation of Balzac's *Pére Goriot*, with Howard Goorney as Goriot. The title is now *The Cruel Daughters*. On November 9, she directs Ewan MacColl's adaptation of Jaroslav Hasek's Czech novel, *The Good Soldier Schweik*. On the 30th, the play is *The Chimes*, Littlewood's adaptation of Charles Dickens' story, which she stages. In the cast is a newcomer, Michael Caine. The Theatre Royal's Christmas treat for children is the adaptation of Mark Twain's *The Prince and the Pauper* she and MacColl make, opening on December 27.

Sep 29 Bernard Shaw's *Saint Joan* is revived at London's Arts Theatre directed by John Fernald. Siobhan McKenna plays the Maid, Kenneth Williams plays the Dauphin. On October 20, at the Stoll Theatre, Ingrid Bergman appears as the Maid in *Joan of Arc at the Stake*, with Paul Claudel's text and Arthur Honegger's score. Roberto Rossellini directs.

Oct 4 The English Opera Group comes to London's Sadler's Wells Theatre with Benjamin Britten's version of John Gay's *The Beggar's Opera*. Michael Langham directs a cast including Marjorie Thomas, and James Johnston. On October 10, the Repertory Players take over the Strand Theatre for a performance of Tobias Smollett's *The Adventures of Peregrine Pickle*. Alfred Hayes' American play, *The Girl on the Via Flaminia*, opens on October 12 at the New Lindsey Theatre.

Oct 11 George Abbott revives *On Your Toes*, the 1936 musical he created with Rodgers and Hammerstein, on Broadway at the 46th Street Theatre. The run is a scant eight weeks. In the cast are Vera Zorina, Bobby Van and Elaine Stritch.

Oct 14 *Sing Me No Lullaby*, Robert Ardrey's play about the reunion of some disillusioned friends, is produced by T. Edward Hambleton and Norris Houghton

at Off-Broadway Phoenix Theatre. Players include Beatrice Straight, Richard Kiley, Jessie Royce Landis, and Jack Warden. There are 30 performances.

Nov 2 Armand Salacrou's *The Unknown Woman of Arras* is staged by Robin Rook at the New Lindsey Theatre in London. On the next day at the Arts Theatre, André Gide's *The Immoralist* opens, in the Ruth and Augustus Goetz adaptation. Peter Hall stages, with Yvonne Mitchell and Michael Gough. On Noverber 4, Ronnie Hill's *Autumn Revue* opens at the New Watergate Theatre, with Beryl Reid. On November 29, Ralph Reader presents his annual Boy Scout show, *The Gang Show of 1954* at the Golders Green Hippodrome.

Nov 22 Now in its 26th season, the Dublin Gate Theatre presents a revival of Elmer Rice's *Not for Children*. Co-founder Micheal macLiammoir writes the holiday show, *A Slipper for the Moon*, which is staged by Hilton Edwards.

Nov 23 Earl Robinson and Waldo Salt's *Sandhog* opens at New York's Phoenix Theatre. The musical is based on a Theodore Dreiser story. In the ensemble are Jack Cassidy and Alice Ghostly. The show runs six weeks, staged by Howard DaSilva.

Dec 15 London's first holiday pantomime is *Arabian Nightmare*, at the New Watergate Theatre. Julian More describes his text as a "pantomime for parents." At the Fortune Theatre on December 20, *The Marvellous Story of Puss in Boots* is told. On the 21st, it's a revue, *Pay the Piper*, at the Saville Theatre, devised by Michael Flanders and Nancy Hamilton. At the Players' Theatre J. R. Planche's *The Sleeping Beauty in the Wood* comes to life. *Happy Holiday* opens at the Palace Theatre on December 22, while, at the Q Theatre, the play is *The House in the Wood*, with Julia Lockwood as Goldilocks. *Mother Goose* is at the Palladium, with Peter Sellers and Max Bygraves. Barbara Kelly is Peter at the Scala Theatre in *Peter Pan*. *Toad of Toad Hall* is at the Prince's. *Where the Rainbow Ends* is at the Festival Hall.

1920's, he was also librettist of *The Maid of the Mountains*, *Madame Pompadour*, and other musical comedies.

April 17 Russian producer, director, designer, and author Theodore Komisarjevsky (b. 1882) dies in Darien, Connecticut. A naturalized British subject, he was responsible for a number of controversial Shakespearean productions at Stratford-upon-Avon. Two of his best known books are *The Costume of the Theatre* and *The Actor and the Theory of Stanislavsky*.

April 17 Actor-director Larry Blyden is wed to actress-dancer Carol Haney. Born Ivan Lawrence Blieden in Houston, Texas, in 1925, Blyden made his New York City debut succeeding Rufus Smith as the Southern Shore Patrol Officer in *Mr. Roberts* at the Alvin Theatre in 1948.

June 30 American playwright Lynn Riggs (b. 1899) dies in New York. Riggs is the author of the 1931 play, *Green Grow the Lilacs*, which is the basis of the Rodgers and Hammerstein musical, *Oklahoma!* Among his other works are *Roadside*, and *Laughter from a Cloud*.

Aug 6 English stage and screen actor Arthur Riscoe (b. 1896) is dead. Riscoe's first London appearance was in 1920 in *French Leave*. He toured extensively in the 1930s in such plays as *Irene*, *No, No, Nanette*, and *Sitting Pretty*.

Sep 21 Actor-singer Stanley Holloway makes his New York debut as Bottom in the Old Vic's production of Shakespeare's *A Midsummer Night's Dream* at the Metropolitan Opera House.

Sep 25 Actress Audrey Hepburn marries actor Mel Ferrer. Miss Hepburn, of *Gigi* and *Ondine* fame, made her first stage appearance behind locked doors, giving underground concerts to raise funds for the Dutch resistance during World War II.

Sep 27 American scene-designer Nat Karson is dead at age 46. Karson's Broadway career began with *Waltz in Fire* in 1934. He designed the sets for the Negro production of *Macbeth* and was art director for Radio City Music Hall.

Oct 9 Aged 74, the English producer Clare Tree Major dies in New York.

Nov 15 Stage and screen actor Lionel Barrymore (b. 1878) dies in Chatsworth, California. The eldest of the Barrymores, he made his stage debut at fifteen. After a series of successful roles on Broadway in *Peter Ibbetson*, *The Jest*, and *The Copperhead*, he turned to film acting. His autobiography, *We Barrymores*, was published in 1951.

Nov 26 American designer and director Robert Edmond Jones (b. 1887) dies in Milton, N. H. From 1925, Jones was associated with Kenneth MacGowan and Eugene O'Neill in the Provincetown Players productions in New York's Greenwich Village. With MacGowan he wrote *Continental Stagecraft*. Jones was

---

1954   BIRTHS/DEATHS/DEBUTS

Jan 18 Stage and screen actor Sydney Greenstreet (b. 1879) dies in Hollywood.

Jan 30 Producer-director John Murray Anderson (b. 1886) dies in New York. Anderson's first production was *The Greenwich Follies* in New York in 1919. Between 1925 and 1929 he wrote and staged masques and pageants, and over 50 miniature revues.

Feb 20 Augustin Duncan, the American actor-director-producer (b. 1873), dies in Astoria, New York.

March 8 American playwright John Lloyd

Balderston (b. 1889) dies in Beverly Hills. His dramatic works include *A Morality Play for the Leisure Class*, *Berkeley Square*, *Dracula*, and *Red Planet*.

March 24 Swedish-born actress Viveca Lindfors makes her London debut as Sophia in J. B. Priestley and Jacquetta Hawkes' *The White Countess* at the Saville Theatre.

April 4 English dramatist Frederick Lonsdale (b. 1881) dies in London. Best known for his plays *Spring Cleaning* and *The Last of Mrs. Cheyney*, written in the

also instrumental in the development of technicolor in films.

Nov 29 English actor and comedian George Robey (b. 1869) is dead. Robey was one of the most successful comedians on the variety stage, and in 1926 organized his own revue company. Robey was created a Commander of the British Empire in 1919.

Dec 8 American stage and screen actress Gladys George (b. 1904) dies in Hollywood. George's first appearance on the New York stage was in 1918 as Jalline in *The Betrothal*. She played leading parts in numerous stock engagements.

1954   THEATERS/PRODUCTIONS

U. S. patents granted this year include a theatre-related one awarded to Lorimer Brooks for his simulated fireplace flame, in which an irregular reflecting surface revolves behind fake logs, illuminated with colored light.

Radio, screen, and television writers, formerly members of—or affiliated with—the Dramatists Guild, form their own organization to protect their rights and interests: The Writers Guild of America.

Le Conservatoire d'Art Dramatique de la Province de Québec is founded in Montreal, Canada, by Jan Doat, a French actor who has studied with Jean-Louis Barrault and Jean Vilar at the school of Charles Dullin.

Jan 5 This is the opening night of the Crest Theatre, Toronto, Canada. Murray and Donald Davis and their sister Barbara Chilcott have turned an old movie-house into a home for a professional stock company for an annual 40-week season, September to June. Their aim is to produce popular plays at popular prices on a fortnightly basis. The first production is Gordon Daviot's *Richard of Bordeaux*.

Jan 19 The O'Keefe Brewing Company of Toronto, Canada, offers to build a $12 million civic auditorium to be run by a charitable foundation. Local clergymen, headed by Dr. J. Mutchmor, warn against building a civic center "on beer kegs and beer bottles," considering their association with drunkenness and highway injury.

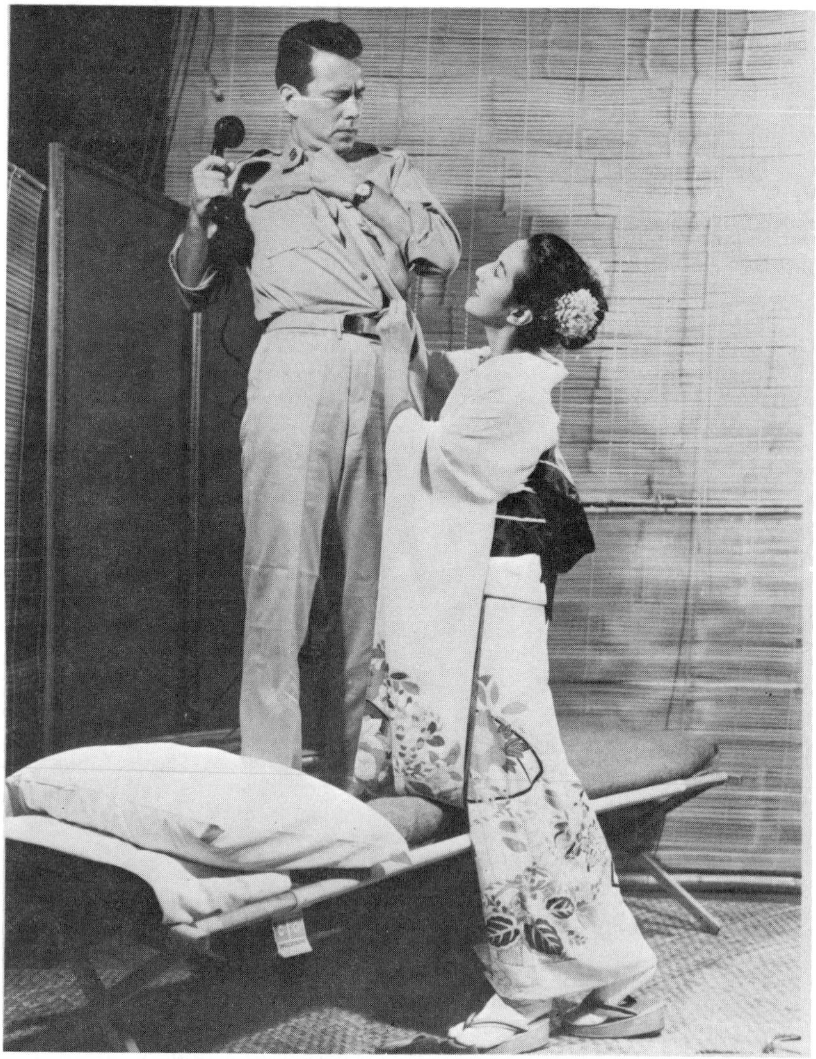

March The Living Theatre, founded by Julian Beck and Judith Malina, finds a performance lane at Manhattan's 100th St. and Broadway. It remains here until 1956.

Summer Joseph Papp inaugurates his first summer program of free Shakespeare for New York City residents, with a production of *As You Like It*, staged in Emmanuel Presbyterian Church (729 East 6th Street). Actors wear street-clothes and work without pay. The Fesitval later moves to the East River amphitheatre, then in 1959 to Central Park.

June 1 Louis Kronenberger, at the close of the 1953–1954 Broadway season, chooses the annual ten "Best Plays." They include Wouk's *The Caine Mutiny Court-Martial*, Bowles' *In the Summer House*, Peterson's *Take a Giant Step*, Patrick's *The Teahouse of the August Moon*, The Goetzes' *The Immoralist*, Anderson's *Tea and Sympathy*, Hayes' *The Girl on the Via Flaminia*, LaTouche and Moross' *The Golden Apple*, and Funt's *The Magic and the Loss*. Both the Pulitzer Prize and the Drama Critics' Circle Award go to *The Teahouse of the August Moon*, the "Best American Play. *The Golden Apple* is "Best Musical Production," and *Ondine* is "Best Foreign Play."

Aug The United States Post Office Department locks up as "obscene, lewd and lascivious" the book of Aristophanes classic comedy, *Lysistrata*, illustrated by Norman Lindsay.

Oct The *NY Times* rejects artist Al Hirschfield's drawing, intended for an advertisement for the play *Reclining Figure*. Based on a famous painting, the sketch doesn't conceal female breasts or navel. These the *Times* will not reproduce, in accord with its dictum on what's "fit to print."

Nov As the New York run of *Fanny* progresses, belly-dancer Nejla Ates is to discard bits and pieces of her already scanty costume. Finally, producer David Merrick hears from the police; they will close down *Fanny* unless Ates resumes her original costume.

TEAHOUSE OF THE AUGUST MOON

Jan 27 *Plain and Fancy* (NY—Mark Hellinger—Musical). Shirl Conway, Richard Derr, and Gloria Marlowe head the cast in this encounter between New Yorkers and Pennsylvania Amish folk. The libretto is by Joseph Stein and Will Glickman; songs by Albert Hague and Arnold Horwitt. It runs 461 performances. Conway and Derr repeat their roles in the London production which opens at the Drury Lane on Jan 25, 1956. There are 217 showings.

Feb 10 *The Desperate Hours* (NY—Ethel Barrymore—Drama). Paul Newman, Karl Malden, and Nancy Coleman play 212 performances in Joseph Hayes's suspense thriller about a family held hostage by escaped convicts. Hayes's play opens in London at the Hippodrome on April 19, with Bernard Lee, Diana Churchill, and Richard Carlyle among the cast. It runs 167 times.

Feb 17 *The Wayward Saint* (NY—Cort—Comedy). The Devil (Paul Lukas) tries to win the soul of an Irish priest (Liam Redmond) who seems able to work miracles. He fails; so does Paul Vincent Carroll's play, which has only 21 showings.

Feb 23 *The Dark Is Light Enough.* See L premiere, 1954.

Feb 24 *Silk Stockings* (NY—Imperial—Musical). *Ninotchka* becomes a musical with songs by Cole Porter ("All of You"). Hildegarde Neff and Don Ameche take the leads in this story by George S. Kaufman, Leueen MacGrath Kaufman, and Abe Burrows. Cy Feuer stages the 478 performances.

Feb 28 *Ben Bagley's Shoestring Revue* (NY—President—Revue). Chita Rivera, Arte Johnson, and Beatrice Arthur head the cast.

March 2 *Bus Stop* (NY—Music Box—Comedy). Kim Stanley, Albert Salmi, and Elaine Stritch give a "glorious performance," says the *New York Times*. William Inge's new play depicts snow-bound passengers forced to take refuge at a bus-stop cafe. Harold Clurman stages.

March 24 *Cat on a Hot Tin Roof* (NY—Morosco—Drama). Barbara Bel Geddes is Maggie; Ben Gazzara is Brick, in Tennessee Williams's drama about family and sexual tensions. The play runs 694 performances and wins the Critics' Circle Award for Best American Play. On Jan 20, 1958, the show opens at the Comedy in London with Kim Stanley and Paul Massie in the leads. The show runs four months.

April 6 *3 For Tonight* (NY—Plymouth—Revue). Harry Belafonte's songs, Marge and Gower Champion's dancing, and Hiram Sherman's comedy routines, give this revue an 11-week run.

April 18 *Ankles Away* (NY—Mark Hellinger—Musical). This melange of songs, girls, broad jokes, and colorful sets and costumes, runs 22 weeks. The book is by Guy Bolton and Eddie Davis, music by Sammy Fain and Dan Shapiro.

April 19 *All in One* (NY—Playhouse—Musical/Dance/Drama). This is a revue that includes Leonard Bernstein's short opera *Trouble in Tahiti*, dance routines by Paul Draper, and a staging of Tennessee Williams' *27 Wagons Full of Cotton* (later filmed as *Baby Doll*). with Maureen Stapleton and Myron McCormick. With designs by Eldon Elder, it runs 6 weeks.

April 21 *Inherit the Wind* (NY—National—Drama). There are 806 performances of Jerome Lawrence and Robert E. Lee's play based on the famed Scopes "Monkey Trial." Ed Begley and Paul Muni head the cast. The drama opens in London at the St. Martin's on March 16, 1960, where it wins critical acclaim but poor audience response. It has only 69 performances.

May 5 *Damn Yankees* (NY—46th Street—Musical). Baseball and ballet make a successful mix in George Abbott and Douglass Wallop's adaptation of Wallop's book *The Year the Yankees Lost the Pennant*. The show runs 1,019 performances. Songs are by Richard Adler and Jerry Rose; choreography is by Bob Fosse. Gwen Verdon scores a personal hit as Lola, the charming lady who intends to seduce the baseball star. On March 28, 1957, the show comes to London's Coliseum with Belita and Ivor Emmanuel in the leads. It runs 861 performances.

Sep 26 *A Day by the Sea.* See L premiere, 1953.

Sept 29 *A View from the Bridge* (NY—Coronet—Drama). An Arthur Miller double-bill opens with *A Memory of Two Mondays* and concludes with *A View From the Bridge*. The latter, in which a simple longshoreman (Van Heflin) breaks the Sicilian code of honor, gets mixed reviews, and the plays runs only 19 weeks. Martin Ritt directs. On Oct 11, 1956, the play is presented in closed club theatre performances—220 of them—at London's Comedy Theatre.

Oct 3 *Tiger at the Gates.* See L premiere, 1955.

Oct 4 *Island of Goats* (NY—Fulton—Drama). Ugo Betti's symbolic drama in which an outsider is left to drown has a mere seven showings, despite a cast that includes Uta Hagen, Laurence Harvey, and Ruth Ford. Peter Glenville directs.

Oct 5 *The Diary of Anne Frank* (NY—Cort—Drama). Susan Strasberg gets rave reviews as the sensitive Anne, maturing in the dark confinement of an attic as she

THE DARK IS LIGHT ENOUGH

and her Jewish family hide from the Nazis. Frances Goodrich and Albert Hackett's dramatization of Anne's journal wins the Pulitzer Prize and the Drama Critics' Circle Award. It runs for 717 performances. Perlita Neilson plays Anne when the drama premieres in London at the Phoenix on Nov 29, 1956. It has only 141 performances here.

Oct 10 *The Reluctant Debutante.* See L premiere, 1955.

Oct 10 *Joyce Grenfell Requests the Pleasure.* See L premiere, 1954.

Oct 13 *Will Success Spoil Rock Hunter?* (NY—Belasco—Comedy). George Axelrod's play about a Hollywood scriptwriter (Orson Bean) who makes a bargain with the Devil and wins jobs, women, fame, and an Oscar, runs 444 performances. Jayne Mansfield, Walter Matthau, Tina Louise, and Martin Gabel also appear.

Oct 20 *No Time For Sergeants* (NY—Alvin—Comedy). Andy Griffith's portrayal of an innocent good-natured hillbilly, who can't seem to adjust to the very special logic of air force routine, wins 796 performances in Ira Levin's adaptation of Mac Hyman's novel. Barry Nelson is featured in the London production which opens at Her Majesty's on Aug 23, 1956. It runs 411 performances.

Oct 24 *The Desk Set* (NY—Broadhurst—Comedy). Shirley Booth appears for 37 weeks in William Marchant's comedy about an electronic computer that threatens to take over an office. Joseph Fields stages.

Oct 26 *The Chalk Garden* (NY—Ethel Barrymore—Drama). Gladys Cooper, Siobhan McKenna, and Betsy von Furstenberg have a run of nearly 23 weeks in Enid Bagnold's well-received play about a patrician woman unable to cope with her disturbed granddaughter. The play opens at London's Haymarket on April 11, 1956, with Edith Evans, Peggy Ashcroft, and Judith Stott in the cast. It runs 663 performances.

Nov 9 *A Hatful of Rain* (NY—Lyceum—Drama). Ben Gazzara, Anthony Franciosa, and Shelley Winters head the cast of Michael V. Gazzo's play about drug addiction. Frank Corsaro directs. There's a 50-week run. The melodrama opens at London's Prince's on March 7, 1957, with Bonar Colleano and Sam Wanamaker among the cast. It has 92 performances.

Nov 10 *The Vamp* (NY—Winter Garden—Musical). Despite a cast headed by Carol Channing, this musical about the early days of the cinema industry musters only 60 showings.

Nov 17 *The Lark.* See L premiere, 1955.

Nov 24 *Janus* (NY—Plymouth—Comedy). Carolyn Green's romantic farce with Robert Preston, Margaret Sullavan, and Claude Dauphin wins 251 performances. Reginald Denham directs.

Nov 30 *Pipe Dream* (NY—Shubert—Musical). Helen Traubel comes from the Metropolitan Opera to play the madam of a brothel in Rodgers and Hammerstein's version of John Steinbeck's novel about the denizens of Cannery Row, *Sweet Thursday.* Harold Clurman stages for a 31-week run.

Dec 5 *The Matchmaker.* See L premiere, 1954.

Dec 28 *Red Roses for Me.* See L premiere, 1946.

1955 BRITISH PREMIERES

Jan 12 *The Night of the Ball* (L—New—Drama). Joseph Losey stages this play by Michael Burn, with a cast that includes Wendy Hiller, Jill Bennett, and Gladys Cooper. It has 93 performances.

Feb 16 *Sailor, Beware!* (L—Strand—Comedy). Peggy Mount plays a domineering mother in Philip King and Falkland Cary's domestic comedy. It earns 1,082 performances. Melville Gillam stages.

Feb 24 *Wonderful Town.* See NY premiere, 1953.

April 9 *Paris by Night* (L—Prince of Wales's—Revue). Comedian Benny Hill is the main attraction in this Folies Bergere show, staged by Dick Hurran. It runs for 890 performances.

April 14 *The Bad Seed.* See NY premiere, 1954.

April 19 *The Desperate Hours.* See NY premiere, 1955.

April 20 *Kismet.* See NY premiere, 1953.

May 3 *The Tender Trap.* See NY premiere, 1954.

May 11 *The Lark* (L—Lyric—Drama). Christophere Fry translates Jean Anouilh's drama about St. Joan. Peter Brook stages. Dorothy Tutin plays Joan, with Donald Pleasance as the Dauphin. On Nov 17, it opens at New York's Longacre in a translation by Lillian Hellman. Julie Harris heads the cast. It has 229 performances.

May 12 *My Three Angels.* See NY premiere, 1953.

May 18 *The Remarkable Mr. Pennypacker.* See NY premiere, 1953.

May 24 *The Reluctant Debutante* (L—Cambridge—Comedy). Celia Johnson and Wilfrid Hyde White play the anxious parents of a spirited debutante (Anna Massey) in William Douglas Home's successful play about "coming out" in London society. There are 752 performances. The following year, on Oct 10, the comedy opens on Broadway at the Henry Miller. Massey and White again lead the cast. The show runs nearly 17 weeks.

May 31 In *Dylan Thomas Growing Up* at London's Globe Theatre, Emlyn Williams uses only a chair and screen as props, as he recreates the world of the Welsh poet for 11 weeks.

June 2 *Tiger at the Gates* (L—Apollo—Drama). Christopher Fry translates Jean Giraudoux's *La Guerre de Troi n'aura pas Lieu,* about the Trojan hero, Hector, who is determined to avoid a disastrous war with Greece. Michael Redgrave leads the cast. The production runs just over 13

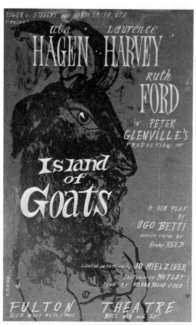

ISLAND OF GOATS

weeks. Five months later, on Oct 3, it opens at New York's Plymouth with Redgrave again in the lead. Voted the "Best Foreign Play" by the Drama Critics' Circle, it runs 27 weeks.

June 16 *Moby Dick* (L—Duke of York's—Drama). There are only 25 performances as Orson Welles directs and plays in his adaptation of Herman Melville's classic. Joan Plowright, Patrick McGoohan, and Kenneth Williams are on deck.

July 7 *The Shadow of a Doubt* (L—Saville—Drama). John Clements plays an atomic scientist who has served a prison sentence for disclosing secrets in Norman King's play. Jane Baxter is also in the cast. Allan Davis stages. There are 188 performances.

Aug 18 *Painting the Town* (L—Palladium—Revue). Comedian Norman Wisdom and singer Ruby Murray head the cast. Dick Hurran stages. The revue has 373 performances.

Aug 24 *Dead on Nine* (L—Westminster—Drama). A melodramatic murder mystery, Jack Poppelwell's play runs almost 23 weeks. Andrew Cruikshank, Hy Hazell, and Griffith Jones head the cast. Geoffrey Wardel directs.

Aug 31 *The Water Gipsies* (L—Winter Garden—Musical). Life and love among the Thames' houseboat dwellers is the theme of A.P. Herbert's book, staged by Charles Hickman, with Vivian Ellis' score. The cast includes Dora Bryan and Wallas Eaton. It runs for 739 performances.

Sep 1 *Mr. Kettle and Mrs. Moon* (L—Duchess—Comedy). J.B. Priestley's play about a bank manager who decides to liven up his life, runs 27 weeks. Clive Morton and Frances Rowe are directed by Tony Richardson.

Sep 14 *Lucky Strike* (L—Apollo—Comedy). Michael Brett's comedy, about a factory owner (Ambrosine Phillpotts) who has her own forceful way of dealing with labor problems, runs 25 weeks. Jack Minster stages.

Oct 11 *The Whole Truth* (L—Aldwych—Drama). Philip Mackie's murder thriller, with Leslie Phillips and Faith Brook, runs 145 performances. Leslie Linder stages.

Oct 12 *Small Hotel* (L—St. Martin's—Comedy). Rex Frost's play, with Gordon Harker and Gladys Henson, explores the plight of an old head-waiter who is to be replaced by an efficient young lady. Murray MacDonald directs. It has 126 performances.

Oct 13 *The Pajama Game.* See NY premiere, 1954.

Oct 26 *The Queen and the Rebels* (L—Haymarket—Drama). Ugo Betti's drama of revolution in an unspecified land, has a cast headed by Irene Worth, Patrick Magee, and Leo McKern. It runs three months and is staged by Frank Hauser.

Nov 3 *La Plume de Ma Tante* (L—Garrick—Revue). This French revue is staged by Alec Shanks. Ross Parker provides English lyrics. Music for the songs is the work of Gerard Calvi. Among the cast are Robert Dhery, Pierre Olaf, and Jacques Legras. It runs 994 performances. The show opens on Broadway at the Royale on Nov 11, 1958, for a long stay of 835 performances.

Nov 4 *Meet Me on the Corner* (L—Hippodrome—Revue). Val Parnell directs comedian Max Bygraves in this revue which runs 38 weeks.

Nov 9 *Summertime* (L—Apollo—Comedy). Peter Hall stages the third Ugo Betti play of the season, with a cast including Geraldine McEwan and Dirk Bogarde. A light comedy of romantic mixups, it runs 119 performances.

Dec 14 *Such Is Life* (L—Adelphi—Re-

vue). Singer Shirley Bassey and comedian Al Read play 548 performances in this revue staged by Alec Shanks and Joan Davis.

Dec 14 *Morning's at Seven* (L—Comedy—Comedy). Paul Osborne's play about the loves and lives of four sisters in a midwestern small town, though alien to British life, wins a run of 157 performances. The sisters are played by Mona Washbourne, Margaret Vines, Marda Vanne, and Nan Munro.

Dec 15 *A Girl Called Jo* (L—Piccadilly—Musical). Denis Quilley and Joan Heal are in the cast of this musical version of Louisa May Alcott's *Little Women* and *Good Wives*, staged by Denis Carey. Adapted by Peter Myers, Alec Grahame, and David Climie, with a score by John Pritchett, it has 141 showings.

1955   REVIVALS/REPERTORIES

Jan 5 Jessica Tandy and Hume Cronyn repeat their roles in Jan DeHartog's *The Four Poster* for two weeks in a revival at the New York City Center. José Ferrer stages. On January 19, Sanford Meisner stages a two-week revival of William Saroyan's *The Time of Your Life*, with a cast including Gloria Vanderbilt and Franchot Tone. On February 2, John Stix directs a revival of the Logan/Chekhov *The Wisteria Trees*, with Helen Hayes and Walter Matthau; On April 20, the revival is *Guys and Dolls;* On May 4, *South Pacific;* on May 18, *Finan's Rainbow.*

Jan 11 Off-Broadway at the Phoenix Theatre, Sidney Lumet stages a 6-week revival of Shaw's *The Doctor's Dilemma.* Geraldine Page heads the cast. On March 1, Ibsen's *The Master Builder* gets a five-week run, staged by and featuring Oscar Homolka.

Jan 11 Sam Wanamaker stages *The World of Sholom Aleichem,* adapted by Arnold Perl from Aleichem stories at London's Embassy Theatre, with a cast including David Kossoff, Miriam Karlin, and America's Minerva Pious. At the Arts Theatre on January 13, Luigi Pirandello's *The Rules of the Game* is shown, staged by John Fernald. Donald Pleasance heads the cast.

Jan 18 London's Old Vic Company continues its season with *Richard II,* staged by Michael Benthall, with John Neville and Virginia McKenna. On March 1, *As You Like It* is staged by Robert Helpmann. Neville plays Orlando, Paul Rogers and Rachel Roberts are Touchstone and Audrey. On April 27, *Henry IV, Part 1* takes the stage, followed by *Part 2* the next night. Douglas Seale directs. Eric Porter is the king.

Feb 9 The Arts Theatre revival of Bernard Shaw's *Saint Joan* transfers to St. Martin's Theatre in the West End. Siobhan

McKenna continues as the Maid. John Fernald has staged; Paul Mayo and Michael Ellis have designed. There are 126 performances.

Feb 15 Joan Littlewood stages Ewan MacColl's *The Other Animals* at London's Theatre Royal, Stratford East. Both she and MacColl are in the cast. On March 3, she stages and appears in Jonson's *Volpone,* using modern dress. Julia Hay's *The Midwife* opens on April 19, also directed by Littlewood. She's again in the cast, with Avis Bunnage and others. On June 3, B. Traven's story becomes Ted Allan's play, *The Legend of Pepito,* which Littlewood also stages.

March 1 The Dublin Gate Theatre revives Laverty's *Liffey Lane,* followed by Pirandello's *Henry IV.* Following a tour, the Olympia Theatre in Dublin is the scene of the Gate's two final productions of the season, Laverty's *Tolka Row* (revival) and Giraudoux's *The Madwoman of Chaillot.*

March 7 In London at the Chelsea Palace, Wilson Barrett's old melodrama, *The Sign of the Cross,* is revived in a new version. J. Grant Anderson directs and plays Nero. At the Irving Theatre on March 8, the revue on view is *Airs and Graces.* On the 9th at the Q Theatre, the play is Eugene O'Neill's *Desire Under the Elms,* staged by Joan Kemp-Welch. Peter Hall stages Eugene Ionesco's *The Lesson* at the Arts Theatre on the same day, on a double-bill with André Obey's *Sacrifice to the Winds,* adapted by John Whiting. On March 30, Hall directs Julien Green's *South,* with a cast including Bessie Love, Denholm Elliott, and André Morrell.

April 12 John Gielgud stages *Twelfth Night* for the opening of the Shakespeare Memorial Theatre's season in Stratford-upon-Avon. Laurence Olivier and Vivien Leigh play Malvolio and Viola. Malcolm Pride designs. *All's Well That Ends Well* has

Noel Willman for its director, with Joyce Redman as Helena. Festival co-director Glen Byam Shaw stages *Macbeth,* starring Olivier and Leigh and designed by Roger Furse. With Motley's designs, he mounts *The Merry Wives of Windsor,* using his co-director, Anthony Quayle, as Falstaff. Peter Brook stages *Titus Andronicus* with Olivier and Quayle. Isamu Noguchi designs the sets for *King Lear,* as staged by George Devine for an end-of-season run (November 28—December 6), with John Gielgud as Lear.

April 23 *Phoenix '55,* an off-Broadway revue at the Phoenix, has sketches by Ira Wallach and a cast including Nancy Walker and Harvey Lembeck. It runs for 97 performances. The evening is largely Walker's; she satirizes the Method school of acting. Marc Daniels directs.

May 3 Voices from the past resound at London's Palace Theatre as Franz Lehar's *The Merry Widow* is revived. Jan Kiepura and Marta Eggerth head the cast. Horst Reday directs.

June 1 At London's Regent's Park Open Air Theatre David William stages *The Tempest,* with Robert Eddison and Robert Atkins. On June 24, Atkins stages *A Midsummer Night's Dream,* playing Bottom. On August 9, William and Atkins co-direct Edmond Rostand's *The Romanticks.*

June 9 At London's Arts Theatre, Eugene O'Neill's *Mourning Becomes Electra* is revived, staged by Peter Hall. Mary Ellis and Mary Morris play the leads. *Light Fantastic,* produced by the Boltons Theatre Company, moves to the Fortune Theatre on June 21. The next day at the Irving Theatre, Margaret Morris and George Edge's revue, *Soho So What!* opens, staged by Joan Swinstead. *From Here and There* is the revue staged by Laurier Lister for the Royal Court Theatre on June 29.

June 27 Canada's Stratford Shakespeare Festival opens, again under the artistic direction of Tyrone Guthrie. The much admired production of Sophocles' *King Oedipus* is revived from last season. Other productions are *The Merchant of Venice,* directed by Guthrie and designed by Tanya Moiseiwitsch; and *Julius Caesar,* directed by Michael Langham and designed by Moiseiwitsch. Among the company are such players as William Hutt, Helen Burns, Loyd Bochner, Frederick Volk, and Lorne Greene. Music is also saluted with a production of *A Soldier's Tale,* by D. F. Ramuz, with score by Igor Stravinsky. Directed by Campbell and designed by Clarence Wilson, the production features Marcel Marceau in his first appearance in North America.

June 29 Berea College in Berea, Kentucky, is celebrating its centennial, commissioning Paul Green to write *Wilderness Road,* "a parable for modern times," produced in an amphitheatre owned by the college.

THE BAD SEED

July 11 Far from the West End, in Wimbledon, Rex Harrison stages *Nina*, adapted by Arthur Macrae from André Roussin's farce. Billie Hill and Michael Hordern head the cast. On July 27, it moves to the Haymarket, where it has only 45 performances.

July 12 Working with John Houseman, Lawrence Langner, founder of the Theatre Guild, establishes the American Shakespeare Festival in Stratford, Connecticut. Edwin Howard designs the Festival Theatre in native woods. Houseman and Jack Landau are the artistic directors, but Dennis Carey of the Bristol Old Vic actually mounts the first season, opening today. He directs *The Tempest* and *Julius Caesar*. The designers are Horace Armistead (sets), Robert Fletcher (costumes), and Jean Rosenthal (lighting). The cast includes Hurd Hatfield and Christopher Plummer, among others.

July 21 At London's Palace Theatre, the Shakespeare Memorial Theatre Company from Stratford present *Much Ado About Nothing*. with Peggy Ashcroft and John Gielgud, who also directs. On July 26, the troupe offers *King Lear*, staged by Devine, with Gielgud, Helen Cherry, Moira Lister and Claire Bloom.

July 22 The San Diego National Shakespeare Festival opens today. The season is projected to run through September 4, with B. Iden Payne staging *Measure for Measure*, Allan Fletcher directing *Hamlet*, and festival founder Craig Noel mounting *The Taming of the Shrew*.

Aug 1 *A Midsummer Night's Dream*, directed by James Sandoe, opens this summer's Oregon Shakespearean Festival in Ashland. H. Paul Kliss stages *Macbeth*, followed by Robert Loper's mounting of *All's Well That Ends Well*. Sandoe then stages *Henry VI, Part 3*, and Loper directs *Timon of Athens*. The plays are performed uncut and without intermissions

in the outdoor Elizabethan Theatre.

Aug 3 Peter Hall stages Samuel Beckett's *Waiting for Godot* at London's Arts Theatre, with Paul Daneman and Peter Woodthorpe.

Aug 17 ANTA, with Robert Whitehead as producer, brings its revival of Thornton Wilder's *The Skin of Our Teeth* to the ANTA Theatre on Broadway for a limited three-week run. This show has been on a European tour, with a cast including George Abbott, Helen Hayes, and Mary Martin.

Aug 21 Britain's Edinburgh International Festival opens. The Old Vic Company shows its production of *Julius Caesar*, staged by Michael Benthall with Rosemary Harris, Wendy Hiller, Paul Rogers, and John Neville. In the Assembly Hall, Tyrone Guthrie stages Thornton Wilder's *A Life in the Sun*, designed by Tanya Moiseiwitsch. Irene Worth takes the lead. Edwige Feuillere and her ensemble come from Paris to present her staging of Dumas fils' *La Dame aux Camélias*, in which she naturally stars. On Sep 13, she opens it in London.

Sep 7 London's Old Vic Company opens the season with *Julius Caesar*, directed by Michael Benthall, with Gerald Cross, Paul Rogers, John Neville, Rosemary Harris and Wendy Hiller. On September 27, Douglas Seale's staging of *The Merry Wives of Windsor* opens, with Rogers, Margaret Rawlings, Hiller, and Rachel Roberts. On November 1, *The Winter's Tale* has Hiller as Hermione and Rogers as Leontes. Benthall stages Benthall also stages *Henry V*, which opens on December 13, with Richard Burton and Zena Walker.

Sep 7 At the New York City Center, the Theatre Company, under Jean Dalrymple's direction, revives *Othello* for a two-week engagement. Jerome Kilty is Iago to William Marshall's Moor. John Stix stages. The production is the work of Kilty's Brattle Shakespeare Players. On September 21, with Kilty directing, the troupe presents *Henry IV, Part 1*, Thayer David plays the King.

Sep 9 Ugo Betti's *The Burnt Flower Bed*, staged by Peter Hall, opens at London's Arts Theatre. The cast includes Yvonne Mitchell and Alexander Knox.

Sep 20 Off-Broadway's Phoenix Theatre imports the famed French mime, Marcel Marceau. On October 4, the four-week engagement is transferred to the Ethel Barrymore Theatre on Broadway. On February 1, 1956, Marceau performs his program at the City Center for two weeks.

Sep 27 From Britain, comes the D'Oyly Carte Opera Company with its repertoire of expertly produced Gilbert & Sullivan works. There are 72 performances of such shows as *Iolanthe*, *The Mikado*, and *Princess Ida* at Broadway's Shubert Theatre.

Sep 27 At Joan Littlewood's Theatre Royal, in London's Stratford East, Lope de Vega's Spanish classic, *The Sheep Well*

opens, in a Littlewood staging. On November 22, she stages *An Italian Straw Hat* by Labiche and Marc-Michel, in a new version by Theodore Hoffman. Alan Lomax's *The Big Rock Candy Mountain* is offered on December 26, also staged by Littlewood.

Oct 5 Leslie French directs and plays Richard, Duke of Glucester, in *The Sun of York*, by O. and I. Wigram, at London's Royal Court Theatre. On October 12, Henry Irving's old vehicle, *The Bells* is revived as a musical to commemorate the 50th anniversary of Irving's death. On October 31, Honoria Plesch and collaborators offer a revue, *Blueprint*. Both these shows are presented at the Irving Theatre.

Oct 25 Imported by Sol Hurok, with the cooperation of the Government of the French Republic, the *Comédie Francaise* comes to the Broadway *Le Bourgeois Gentilhomme*, complete with ballets; Beaumarchais' *Le Barbier de Seville*, Marivaux' *Arlequin Poli par l'Amour* and *Le Jeu de l'Armour et du Hasard*, and de Musset's *Un Caprice*.

Oct 31 The Dublin Gate Theatre is enjoying its 27th season. Jean Anouilh's *The Lark* opens, staged by Hilton Edwards and designed by Molly MacEwan and Micheal macLiammoír. Other plays produced are revivals of Aeschylus' *Oedipus Rex*, Bernard Shaw's *The Man of Destiny*, Shakespeare's *The Merchant of Venice*, and Anouilh's *Ring Round the Moon*.

Nov 10 Flora Robson directs and appears in a revival of *Suspect*, by Reginald Denham and Edward Percy, at London's Royal Court Theatre.

Dec 8 Paul Scofield plays the Dane, in Peter Brook's staging of *Hamlet*, opening at London's Phoenix Theatre. Mary Ure is Ophelia. Alec Clunes, Diana Wynyard are among the cast. The production has been shown in Moscow previously, launching an exchange of performing arts productions. Here at the Phoenix, it begins a Scofield-Brook season of plays.

Dec 19 At the New Watergate Theatre, choreographer John Cranko opens an innovative revue he's devised and staged. Called *Cranks* it features Marcia Ashton and Anthony Newley, among others.

Dec 20 London's Players' Theatre Club gets the holiday season started with J. R. Planché's "fairy extravaganza," *Beauty and the Beast*, staged by Don Gemmell. Sonia Graham and Anthony Newlands play the title roles. On the 21st at the Palace Theatre, *Cinderella* opens. On the 22nd at the Globe Theatre, the show is *Charley's Aunt*. At the Prince's, *Noddy In Toyland*, by Enid Blyton, is on view. (Blyton's adventure play, *The Famous Five*, opens at the Prince's on the next day.) Peggy Cummins is Peter in the Scala Theatre's *Peter Pan* revival. At the Fortune Theatre, the pantomime is *The Marvellous Story of Puss in Boots*. Other shows include *Puss in Boots* (Wimbledon), *Aladdin* (Golders Green Hippodrome), *Alice Through the Looking Glass* (Chelsea Palace), *Where the Rainbow Ends* (Royal Festival Hall), and *Babes in the Wood* (Streatham Hill).

Dec 21 Ibsen's *The Wild Duck* is revived at London's Saville Theatre, staged by Murray Macdonald. Emlyn Williams, Angela Baddeley, and Dorothy Tutin head the cast. The production lasts two months.

1955 BIRTHS/DEATHS/DEBUTS

Jan 11 Sidney Lumet makes his debut as a director with the Phoenix Theatre's production of Shaw's *The Doctor's Dilemma*.

Jan 11 Playwright Anne Crawford Flexner (b. 1874) dies in Providence, Rhode Island. Flexner's most popular play is *Mrs. Wiggs of the Cabbage Patch*, produced in 1903. Her romantic drama, *Aged 26*, is based on the life of John Keats.

Jan 21 English actor-producer Maurice Browne (b. 1881) dies in Torquay, Devon, England. As manager of the Savoy Theatre, Browne produced *Journey's End* in 1929. He also wrote several plays, including *Wings Over Europe* with Robert Nichols. His most notable performance was in *The Unknown Warrior* in 1928.

Feb 16 Theodore Bikel makes his New York City debut as Inspector Massoubre in the symbolic melodrama, *Tonight in Samarkand*, at the Morosco Theatre. He first appeared on stage as an apprentice with the Habimah Theatre in Tel Aviv, Israel in 1943.

Feb 27 American actress Ethel Levey (b. 1880) is dead. She became associated with George M. Cohan in 1901 and appeared in all his productions until 1907 when their marriage was dissolved. In later years Levey appeared in shows and variety theatres.

March 2 Tammy Grimes replaces Kim Stanley in the role of Cherie in William Inge's *Bus Stop* for two weeks. This is her New York City debut.

June 11 American actor-manager Walter Hampden (b. 1879) dies in Hollywood. Hampden made his stage debut in England in 1901 and performed in London until 1907, when he made his New York debut in *The Comtesse Coquette*. In 1925 he leased the Colonial Theatre which he renamed Hampden's Theatre and played in and produced revivals of Ibsen and Shakespeare. Cyrano de Bergerac was his most memorable role.

June 17 American producer and playwright John Golden (b. 1874) dies in Bayside, New York. Originally an actor, Golden later turned author and wrote many plays, including several musical comedies for which he composed the music. He produced *The First Year*, and *Seventh Heaven*, among others.

July 25 American director and producer Margo Jones (b. 1913) dies in Dallas, Texas. Founder of her own theatre, she described her work in *Theatre-in-the-Round*, published in 1951. Jones and Eddie Dowling directed the Broadway production of *The Glass Menagerie* in 1945.

Sep 20 Only 24, the stage and screen actor James Dean today dies in an auto collision near Paso Robles, California.

more critical and audience interest than in the past. At the close of the 1954–1955 season, in *Best Plays*, Garrison Sherwood, singles out such off-Broadway theatres as the Phoenix and Circle-in-the-Square, as well as Proscenium Productions at the Cherry Lane, the Players Theatre at the Provincetown, the Blackfriars' Guild, the Shakespearewrights at the Jan Hus, various producing groups at the Theatre DeLys, Equity Library Theatre, and David Ross' two highly praised revivals—*The Dybbuk* and *The Three Sisters*—at his tiny Fourth Street Theatre. Ben Bagley's *Shoestring Revue* put together on virtually a shoestring, wins Sherwood's admiration as well.

July 12 With *Julius Caesar* as its inaugural production, the American Shakespeare Festival Theatre, designed by Edward Howard, opens in Stratford, Connecticut. The handsome new playhouse seats 1,465. In the initial season, 65,000 see the productions. Despite generous grants from individuals, corporations, and foundations, the Festival experiences financial problems from first.

Oct 18 The League of Off-Broadway Theatres and Producers is formed. Its principal function is negotiating wage and working-condition contracts with the unions and guilds whose members work in Off-Broadway productions.

Oct 25 Leslie Cheek has helped found the community theatre known as the Virginia Museum Theatre which now opens its first production, *High Tor*, by Maxwell Anderson, starring a Richmond favorite, Fred Haseltine.

Nov 21 The Fulton Theatre, at 210 West 46th Street in New York, is renamed the Helen Hayes Theatre to celebrate Miss Hayes' 50 years on the stage. June 1982, the theatre is destroyed to make way for the new multi-story Portman Hotel.

Dec 14 After massive re-modeling and enlargement the Comedy Theatre re-opens off London's Haymarket with *Morning's at Seven*. The new design was supervised by Cecil Masey, and the capacity is now 820.

1955 THEATERS/PRODUCTIONS

March 24 Designer Jo Mielziner uses a zoom lens in conjunction with projections to create a growing, swirling nebula in *Cat on a Hot Tin Roof* at the Morosco Theatre in New York.

June 1 The 1954–1955 Broadway season comes to a close, and Louis Kronenberger picks the ten "Best Plays" for the annual Burns Mantle series. His choices are Wilson's *The Boy Friend*, Greene's *The Living Room*, Christie's *Witness for the Prosecution*, Anderson's *Bad Seed*, Odets' *The Flowering Peach*, Hayes' *The Desperate Hours*, Fry's *The Dark Is Light Enough*, Inge's *Bus Stop*, Williams' *Cat on a Hot Tin Roof*, and Lawrence and Lee's *Inherit the Wind*. Four out the ten are British. *Cat on a Hot Tin Roof* wins both major drama awards, the Pulitzer Prize and the New York Drama Critics' Circle Award for "Best American Play," with Circle Awards also for Gian-Carlo Merotti's and

Christie's works.

June 1 In the past few years, Off-Broadway productions have been exciting much

HELEN HAYES THEATER

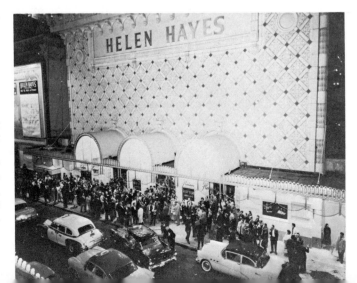

Jan 4 *The Great Sebastians* (NY—ANTA—Comedy). Lynn Fontanne and Alfred Lunt star as a pair of fraudulent performers with a mind-reading act in Howard Lindsay and Russel Crouse's play, which runs nearly 22 weeks. Bretaigne Windust stages.

Jan 24 *Time Limit!* (NY—Booth—Drama). A military officer is subjected to brainwashing techniques and turns traitor in Henry Denker and Ralph Berkey's play, staged by Windsor Lewis. Arthur Kennedy is in the cast. It runs 16 weeks.

Feb 8 *Middle of the Night* (NY—ANTA—Drama). Edward G. Robinson and Gena Rowlands chalk up 477 performances in Paddy Chayevsky's "love story" about a widower and a younger woman. Family and friends are played by Martin Balsam and Anne Jackson, among others. Joshua Logan stages.

Feb 16 *The Ponder Heart* (NY—Music Box—Comedy). David Wayne plays the eccentric Uncle Daniel Ponder, accused of murdering his young wife, in Joseph Fields and Jerome Chodorov's adaptation of Eudora Welty's story. "The plot wears thin . . ." says the *N Y Journal-American*; the play runs 19 weeks.

March 15 *My Fair Lady* (NY—Mark Hellinger—Musical). Rex Harrison, Julie Andrews, Stanley Holloway, and Cathleen Nesbitt play leading roles in Moss Hart's staging of Alan Jay Lerner and Frederick Loewe's adaptation of George Bernard Shaw's *Pygmalion*. Among the hits in the score are "I Could Have Danced All Night." Cecil Beaton designs the costumes; Oliver Smith the sets. The show wins 2,717 performances. The smash hit opens in London at the Drury Lane on April 30, 1958, for a long run of 2,281 performances. Harrison and Andrews again lead the cast.

March 22 *Mr. Wonderful* (NY—Broadway—Musical). Sammy Davis, Jr., and Chita Rivera head the cast in this show conceived by Jule Styne, written by Joseph Stein and Will Glickman, and staged by Jack Donohue. With songs by Jerry Bock, George Weiss and Larry Holofcener, it runs 48 weeks.

March 29 *Mister Johnson* (NY—Martin Beck—Drama). Norman Rosten adapts Joyce Cary's novel about a Nigerian ill-at-ease with his adopted British culture, but it runs only 44 performances. Earle Hyman plays the title role.

April 19 *Waiting for Godot* (NY—Golden—Drama). Samuel Beckett's mystical metaphor for the bleak destiny of the human race runs only 59 performances, but is chosen as a "Best Play." Bert Lahr and E. G. Marshall play leading roles in Herbert Berghof's staging.

May 3 *The Most Happy Fella* (NY—Imperial—Musical). Frank Loesser adapts Sidney Howard's *They Knew What They Wanted*, about a Napa Valley farmer whose mail-order bride becomes pregnant by another man. He also composes the score for this musical which has 676 showings. Robert Weede and Jo Sullivan play the leading roles. The *New York Daily Mirror* calls it "a masterpiece." Loesser's musical runs nine months in London following its premiere at the Coliseum on April 21, 1960. Ina Wiata, Helena Scott and Art Lund head the cast.

June 14 *New Faces of 1956* (NY—Ethel Barrymore—Revue). Jane Connell, T.C. Jones, and Maggie Smith are among the cast in Leonard Sillman's new revue which has 220 showings.

Oct 25 *Separate Tables.* See L premiere, 1954.

Oct 26 *The Best House in Naples* (NY—Lyceum—Comedy). Eduardo de Filippo's play, translated by F. Hugh Herbert, has a mere three performances. Katy Jurado plays the mistress who tricks her lover into marriage. (In the late 1970's Joan Plowright will have a success in the same play, retitled *Filumena*.)

Oct 31 *Auntie Mame* (NY—Broadhurst—Comedy). Rosalind Russell's performance as the madcap sophisticated Mame, who adopts her nephew, is called "a bravura comic portrait," by the *New York Post* and wins 639 showings. Jerome Lawrence and Robert E. Lee adapt Patrick Dennis's novel. On Sep 10, 1958, the show opens at the Adelphi in the West End for 301 performances. Beatrice Lillie has the title role.

Nov 7 *Long Day's Journey Into Night* (NY—Helen Hayes—Drama). Eugene O'Neill's epic drama of a day in the lives of the Tyrone family wins the Pulitzer Prize and the Drama Critics' Circle Award for Best American Play. Fredric March plays the disappointed actor-father, based on O'Neill's own father; Florence Eldridge his drug-addicted wife. Jason Robards, Jr. and Bradford Dillman are also in the cast. Jose Quintero stages, for a 49-week run. Two years later, on Sep 24, 1958, the play opens at the Globe Theatre in London with Anthony Quayle in the lead. The production has already been hailed at the Edinburgh Festival. In the West End, there are 108 performances.

Nov 13 *Child of Fortune* (NY—Royale—Drama). Jed Harris produces and directs Guy Bolton's attempt to adapt Henry James' novel *Wings of the Dove* for the stage. It runs just three weeks.

Nov 15 *Li'l Abner* (NY—St. James—Musical). Al Capp's comic-strip is brought to life on stage and has 694 showings. Adapted by Melvin Frank and Norman Panama, with songs by Johnny Mercer and Gene dePaul, it has a large cast which includes Peter Palmer, Edith Adams, Tina

THE GREAT SEBASTIANS

Louise, and Stubby Kaye. Michael Kidd choreographs and stages.

Nov 20 *The Happiest Millionaire* (NY—Lyceum—Comedy). Walter Pidgeon takes the lead in Kyle Crichton's adaptation of the book he has written with Cordelia Drexel Biddle about her eccentric wealthy father. The comedy runs 34 weeks. Robert Beatty is the title character in the London production which opens at the Cambridge on Nov 15, 1957. There are 147 performances.

Nov 29 *The Bells Are Ringing* (NY—Shubert—Musical). Judy Holliday stars as an answering-service operator who keeps getting involved in the lives of her clients in this popular musical which runs 924 performances. Sidney Chaplin co-stars. The book is by Betty Comden and Adolph Green. Jule Styne composes the score, Bob Fosse choreographs, and Jerome Robbins stages. The show opens at the Coliseum in London on Nov 14, 1957, with Janet Blair in the lead. It runs nine months.

Dec 1 *Candide* (NY—Martin Beck—Musical). Despite a lilting score by Leonard Bernstein, this version of Voltaire's satire on optimism runs only nine weeks. Lillian Hellman adapts; Tyrone Guthrie stages. The show opens at London's Saville on April 30, 1959, where it earns only 60 performances.

Dec 6 *Happy Hunting* (NY—Majestic—Musical). Ethel Merman wins 412 performances as a Philadelphia Main Line mother out to catch a title for her daughter in this Howard Lindsay/Russel Crouse book. Fernando Lamas co-stars.

Dec 20 *Uncle Willie* (NY—Golden—Comedy). Menasha Skulnik plays a Jewish Mr. Fix-it who brings peace to Jewish and Irish families living in a two-family residence just after the turn of the century. It runs almost 18 weeks.

Jan 25 *Plain and Fancy*. See NY premiere, 1955.

Jan 26 *Fresh Airs* (L—Comedy—Revue). Michael Flanders and Donald Swann are the writing duo behind this successor to the popular *Airs on a Shoestring*, but it only runs 21 weeks. Moyra Fraser is among the cast, staged by Max Adrian and Laurier Lister.

Feb 14 *Ring for Catty* (L—Lyric—Comedy). A realistic comedy about life, love, and death in a T.B. sanitorium, Patrick Cargill and Jack Beale's play runs 119 performances. Mary Mackenzie plays Nurse Cattry. Henry Kendall stages.

Feb 16 *Summer Song* (L—Prince's—Musical). In this musical dealing with Anton Dvorak's stay in America, Dvorak's music is arranged by Bernard Grun for the book Eric Machwitz and Hy Kraft have concocted. Charles Hickman stages. The show runs almost 19 weeks. Laurence Naismith and Sally Ann Howes are in the cast.

Feb 22 *The Buccaneer* (L—Apollo—Musical). In Sandy Wilson's show, actor-comedian Kenneth Williams plays a precocious schoolboy who gets his doting mother to buy a boy's paper and save it from becoming an American horror comic-book. William Chappell stages. There are 203 performances.

March 22 *A Likely Tale* (L—Globe—Comedy). Robert Morley plays both father and son in Gerald Savory's family comedy which runs almost 34 weeks. Margaret Rutherford and Violet Farebrother also appear.

April 4 *The Good Sailor*. See NY premiere *(Billy Budd)*, 1951.

April 11 *The Chalk Garden*. See NY premiere, 1955.

April 25 *South Sea Bubble* (L—Lyric—Comedy). Noel Coward's light comedy stars Vivien Leigh as the wife of the British Governor of a tropical island, who bewitches the son of a local leader. William Chappell directs the show, which has 276 performances.

May 8 *Look Back in Anger* (L—Royal Court—Drama). John Osborne's play about an Angry Young Man (Kenneth Haigh), who rages against Britain's complacency and uses his wife (Mary Ure) and friend (Alan Bates) as verbal punching bags, causes a sensation and marks a new phase in British drama. Tony Richardson directs. On Oct 1, 1957, the play opens on Broadway at the Lyceum with Haigh repeating his role. It wins a Critics' Circle Award as "Best Foreign Play" and a run of 51 weeks.

May 9 *The House by the Lake* (L—Duke of York's—Drama). Flora Robson plays a woman saved from suicide by her husband (Andrew Cruickshank) years before through hypnosis. Now, he plans to bring her to commit the act, again through hypnosis. Hugh Mills' thriller, directed by John Fernald, draws audiences for 928 performances.

May 17 *Romanoff and Juliet* (L—Piccadilly—Comedy). Peter Ustinov writes and is featured in this comedy about a general in the smallest state in Europe who furthers the romance between the American Juliet and the Russian Igor. It runs 47 weeks. In New York, the show opens at the Plymouth on Oct 10, 1957, with Ustinov again in the lead. A hit, it runs nearly 49 weeks.

May 17 *Rocking the Town* (L—Palladium—Revue). Robert Nesbitt stages this review which mixes rock-and-roll and comedy. Beryl Reid and Harry Secombe head the cast. The show runs almost 50 weeks.

May 23 *Gigi*. See NY premiere, 1951.

May 31 *The Rainmaker*. See NY premiere, 1954.

June 5 *For Amusement Only* (L—Apollo—Revue). Music parody, and sketches, add up to a run of 709 performances for this show devised by Peter Myers, and staged by Michael Charnley. Among the cast are Ron Moody and Dilys Lay.

June 13 *The Caine Mutiny Court-Martial*. See NY premiere, 1954.

June 26 *Cards of Identity* (L—Royal Court—Drama). Joan Greenwood, Kenneth Haigh, Alan Bates, and Joan Plowright head the cast of Nigel Dennis' satire about a conspiracy. Tony Richardson directs.

June 29 *Night of the Fourth* (L—Westminster—Drama). Hugh Sinclair plays a Scotland Yard detective accused of murder in Jack Roffey and Gordon Harbord's thriller. It has 139 performances.

July 30 *Doctor in the House* (L—Victoria Palace—Comedy). Richard Gordon's novel about medical students is adapted for the stage by Ted Willis and earns a run of 252 performances. Edward Woodward is in the cast.

Aug 23 *No Time for Sergeants*. See NY premiere, 1955.

Sep 4 *Towards Zero* (L—St. James's—Drama). An Agatha Christie mystery, based on the book by Christie and Gerald Verner, the play expires after a 6-month run. Murray MacDonald stages.

Sep 20 *Under Milk Wood* (L—New—Drama). Dylan Thomas's poetic evocation of daily life in a Welsh village has a run of 252 performances. The production has been seen shortly before at the Edinburgh Festival. The show comes to New York's Henry Miller on Oct 15, 1957, following a premiere at the 92nd Street YWHA. It runs five weeks on Broadway.

Oct 12 *Plaintiff in a Pretty Hat* (L—Duchess—Comedy). Hugh and Margaret Williams' romantic comedy about an impoverished earl and his dallying son, has 313 performances. Jack Minster directs a cast which includes Williams, Richard Johnson, and Andree Melly.

Nov 1 *The Dave King Show* (L—Hippodrome-Revue). Singing star Dave King heads this revue which has a run of 388 performances.

Nov 7 *Nude With a Violin* (L—Globe—Comedy). Noel Coward co-directs his new play with John Gielgud. Gielgud also plays the lead, as a suave valet who saves the situation when some modern art masterpieces are discovered to be by amateurs. Kathleen Harrison and Joyce Carey are in the cast. It runs for 617 performances. The comedy opens in New York at the Belasco on Nov 14, 1957, with Coward in the lead. Because the play isn't doing very well, Coward revives *Present Laughter* on Jan 31, 1958, and alternates that six times with this production, which has 86 showings.

AUNTIE MAME

Nov 14 *Double Image* (L—Savoy—Drama). Richard Attenborough plays twin brothers, one of whom is a killer, in this murder thriller. Attenborough's wife Sheila Sim is in the cast. Murray MacDonald directs the 22-week run.

Nov 15 *Fanny*. See NY premiere, 1954.

Nov 28 *Grab Me a Gondola* (L—Lyric—Musical). A spoof on Mediterranean film festivals and the aggressive promotion of attractive starlets, this show by Julian More and James Gilbert earns 687 performances. Denis Quilley and Joan Heal are among the troupe.

Nov 29 *The Diary of Anne Frank.* See NY premiere, 1955.

Dec 18 *These Foolish Kings* (L—Victoria Palace—Revue). The popular Crazy Gang (Nervo and Knox, Naughton and Gold, and Flanagan) head this long-running revue. There are 895 performances. Alec Shanks stages.

Dec 19 *The Bride and the Bachelor* (L—Duchess—Comedy). Cicely Courtneidge, the musical comedy star, plays her first nonsinging role as a mother driven frantic on the eve of her daughter's wedding by the bride's sudden reluctance to wed. Ronald Millar earns a run of 709 performances with his comedy.

1956   REVIVALS/REPERTORIES

Jan 10 Oscar Wilde's *The Picture of Dorian Gray* continues the season at the Dublin Gate Theatre.

Jan 12 At the New York City Center, Orson Welles, who has also directed, plays King Lear in a wheelchair, owing to an accident. Under Jean Dalyrmple's supervision, the production has 21 performances. On Feb 15, Tennessee Williams' *A Streetcar Named Desire* is revived for two weeks with Tallulah Bankhead and Gerald O'Loughlin.

Jan 17 Not a success at its 1927 Broadway premiere (36 performances), Noel Coward's farce, *Fallen Angels,* does much better in this revival at the Playhouse—239 performances. Nancy Walker and Margaret Phillips are among the cast. Charles Bowden directs.

Jan 19 Tyrone Guthrie brings this Stratford, Ontario, revival of Marlowe's *Tamburlaine the Great* to the Winter Garden Theatre on Broadway.

Jan 22 John Houseman and Jack Landau, of Connecticut's American Shakespeare Festival and Academy, bring their production of Shakespeare's *Measure for Measure* to the Off-Broadway Phoenix Theatre for a four-week run. Virgil Thomson composes incidental music. On Feb 20, the Shakespeare Festival *Taming of the Shrew* begins its 23 performance run.

Jan 24 At London's Haymarket Theatre, Donald Wolfitt plays Alfonso Fernandez in this revival of Fritz Hochwalder's *The Strong Are Lonely.* The production runs for 11 weeks.

Feb 4 *Voice In The Wind* opens today in Tampa, Florida. Kermit Hunter's historical drama portrays Andrew Jackson dealing with the Seminole Indians.

Feb 8 George Bernard Shaw's *Misalliance* is revived at the Lyric, Hammersmith with Ursula Jeans, Alan Webb, Roger Livesey and Donald Pleasance.

Feb 9 Bertolt Brecht and Kurt Weill's *The Threepenny Opera* opens in London at the Royal Court Theatre, staged by Sam Wanamaker. Bill Owen is Mack the Knife. In March the production transfers to the Aldwych Theatre. There are 140 performances.

Feb 18 The Bristol Old Vic Company celebrates its tenth anniversary with a performance of *King Lear* at the historic 1766 Theatre Royal.

Feb 21 At London's Old Vic, the season continues with *Othello,* played by Richard Burton (the Moor) and John Neville (Iago). Tomorrow night they will reverse the roles. On April 3, director Tyrone Guthrie unveils his innovative production of *Troilus and Cressida,* in which

designer Frederick Crooke sets the play in Central Europe in the late 19th century. Neville is Troilus and Rosemary Harris Cressida. On May 22, *Macbeth* is offered with Paul Rogers in the title role.

Feb 21 At the Phoenix, Off-Broadway, Strindberg's *Miss Julie* and *The Stronger* are revived for four weeks. Viveca Lindfors Tabori is Miss Julie. On April 3, Turgeniev's *A Month in the Country,* adapted by Emlyn Williams, has a six-week revival, staged by Michael Redgrave, with Uta Hagen. On May 22, the show is *The Littlest Revue,* conceived by Ben Bagley for a four-week run. Joel Gray and Tammy Grimes are in the cast. Most songs are by Odgen Nash and Vernon Duke.

Feb 23 Sheridan's 18th century comedy, *The Rivals,* opens at London's Saville Theatre. William Chappell directs a cast including John Clements, Kay Hammond, Laurence Harvey, and Athene Seyler.

Feb 24 *The Waltz of the Toreodors,* Lucienne Hill's translation of Jean Anouilh's wry comedy opens in London at the Arts Theatre. Peter Hall directs Hugh Griffith as the gruff General St. Pé, bedeviled by his bed-ridden harridan of a wife (Beatrix Lehmann). On March 27, the play moves to the Criterion for a long run of 700 performances. It opens in New York at the Coronet on Jan 17, 1957, staged by Harold Clurman. Ralph Richardson and Mildred Natwick have the leading roles. The Drama Critics' Circle votes this the Best Foreign Play. There are 132 performances.

March 1 John Cranko's revue *Cranks* moves from the modest New Watergate Theatre in London to St. Martin's Theatre, where it begins a run of 223 performances, continued in May at the Duchess Theatre. With John Addison's music, John Piper's strikingly modern decors, and Michael Northern's lights complementing Cranko's own originality, the show is viewed as a new departure in the intimate British revue. Anthony Newley and Annie Ross, are the cast.

March 15 Joan Littlewood brings her Theatre Workshop production of *The Good Soldier Schweik* to the West End's Duke of York's Theatre, where it has a run of only 28 performances. Ewan MacColl has adapted Jaroslav Hasek's Czech classic.

March 28 At London's Arts Theatre, *The Comedy of Errors* is presented as a comic operetta, with a score by Julian Slade, composer of *Salad Days.*

April 2 Under the artistic direction of actor-director George Devine, the English Stage Company begins what will be a long and impressive record of theatre experiments at London's Royal Court Theatre. A resident company is to produce a repertory of modern plays and encourage development of playwrights. Angus Wilson's *The Mulberry Bush,* revised since

THE DIARY OF ANNE FRANK

its Bristol Old Vic production, opens the initial season, but it's found wanting. Gwen Ffrangcon-Davies, Alan Bates and Kenneth Haigh are in the cast. On April 9, Devine directs Arthur Miller's *The Crucible*, with Michael Gwynn, Mary Ure, Joan Plowright, Haigh, and Bates. On May 15, Devine directs a double-bill: Ronald Duncan's *Don Juan* and *The Death of Satan*. In the casts are such players as Nigel Davenport, Keith Michell, Plowright, Rachel Kempson, and John Osborne.

April 5 *The Power and the Glory* is the second production in the Peter Brook-Paul Scofield season at London's Phoenix Theatre. Scofield plays the priest; Brook stages. There are 68 performances of the Graham Greene story. On June 7, *The Family Reunion*, T. S. Eliot's poetic drama, is revived by Brook and Scofield at the Phoenix. Scofield and Sybil Thorndike take the leads. The production is shown 100 times.

April 10 At Stratford-upon Avon, the annual Shakespeare Memorial Theatre season opens with Michael Langham's production of *Hamlet*, with Alan Badel as the prince. Anthony Quayle, who is to retire as festival co-director, directs *Measure for Measure*, with Emlyn Williams as Angelo. Williams is Shylock in Margaret Webster's production of *The Merchant of Venice*, designed by Alan Tagg. Glen Byam Shaw, to be full director of the festival, directs *Othello*, with Harry Andrews. Peter Hall directs *Love's Labour's Lost*, with Badel.

April 16 Peter Daubeny launches an International Season at London's Palace Theatre with France's Theatre Nationale Populaire in Marivaux's *Le Triomphe de l'Amour*, staged by artistic director Jean Vilar. In the next two decades, these international visits, promoted by Daubeny, will be an important part of the London theatre-scene. Vilar also offers Moliere's *Don Juan* and Hugo's *Marie Tudor*.

April 18 Rodgers and Hammerstein's *The King and I*, with Zachary Scott and Jan Clayton, opens for a three-week revival at the New York City Center. On May 9, Cole Porter's *Kiss Me, Kate* is revived. David Atkinson and Kitty Carlisle are in the leads. On May 31, *Carmen Jones* bows with Reri Grist, Glory Van Scott, and Muriel Smith.

April 19 Joan Littlewood's Theatre Workshop at London's Theatre Royal, Stratford East, offers Marlowe's *Edward the Second*. On May 24, the play is Brendan Behan's *The Quare Fellow*, with Behan himself playing a prisoner. On July 24, the production moves to the Comedy Theatre in the West End, but it has only a ten-week run.

May 2 George Feydeau's *Hotel Paradiso* is revived at London's Winter Garden Theatre, in Peter Glenville's translation. He also stages. The show runs 27 weeks,

with Alec Guinness in his first role as a farceur.

May 28 The Shakespeare season in London's Regent's Park, opens with *As You Like It*, staged by Robert Atkins, with Belinda Lee as Rosalind. On June 25, director Atkins offers Edmund Rostand's *The Romanticks*. *Twelfth Night* is presented on July 23, co-directed by Atkins and Andrew Leigh.

Summer Joseph Papp presents his Shakespear Theatre Workshop in its first free summer outdoor performances at New York's East River Amphitheatre. Papp and his players win an Obie. Colleen Dewhurst and J.D. Cannon play the leads in *The Taming of the Shrew*.

June 5 German director Peter Zadek stages Jean Genet's *The Maids (Les Bonnes)*, translated by Bernard Frechtman, in London at the New Lindsey Theatre.

June 12 London's Old Vic opens a new staging of *Romeo and Juliet*, directed by Robert Helpmann. John Neville and Claire Bloom are the young lovers. On July 3, the company revives its *Richard II*, with Neville as the king.

June 18 The major productions of this season's Stratford Shakespeare Festival in Ontario are *Henry V*, *The Merry Wives of Windsor*, and *The Rape of Lucretia*, by Benjamin Britten. Le Theatre du Nouveau Monde presents three farces by Moliere.

June 26 Today is the official opening of the second season of the American Shakespeare Festival in Stratford, Connecticut. *King John* is the initial production, staged by the festival's co-directors, John Houseman and Jack Landau, who also directs *Measure for Measure*. Norman Lloyd directs *The Taming of the Shrew*.

July 4 Alan Schneider directs Horton Foote's American play, *The Trip To Bountiful*, for London's Arts Theatre. Margaret Vines plays Carrie Watts, with John Glen as Ludie Watts, and Mavis Villiers as Jessie Mae Watts.

July 16 At London's Old Vic, it's Shaw Festival time, with the Bristol Old Vic production of *Major Barbara*. Moira Shearer and Peter O'Toole lead the cast. On July 30, the play is *Caesar and Cleopatra*, produced by the Birmingham Repertory Company.

July 20 The eighth season of the San Diego National Shakespeare Festival begins. Among plays presented are *A Midsummer Night's Dream*, staged by Peter Bucknell; *Richard II*, directed by Phillip Hanson; and Ben Jonson's *Volpone*, directed by Craig Noel, the festival's founder.

Aug 1 In Ashland, the Oregon Shakespeare Festival opens with *Richard III* in Allen Fletcher's staging. Fletcher also stages *Love's Labour's Lost*. Hal J. Todd directs *Romeo and Juliet*. B. Iden Payne

TAMBURLAINE THE GREAT

mounts *Cymbeline*, with Todd directing *Titus Andronicus*.

Aug 2 Chekhov's *The Seagull*, translated by David Magarshack, is revived at the Saville Theatre in London, staged by Michael MacOwan, with Diana Wynyard.

Aug 6 At the Gaiety Theatre in Dublin, Micheal macLiammoir's designs for *Gateway To Gaiety* are noted. This will be the 28th season of the Dublin Gate Theatre troupe, which also offers Carroll's *The Wayward Saint* and *Cinderella*, a Christmas pantomime.

Aug 19 Britain's Edinburgh International Festival opens. James Bridie's *The Anatomist* is presented by the local Gateway Company. James Gibson directs. Dylan Thomas' *Under Milk Wood* is staged by Douglas Cleverdon. Piccolo Teatro comes from Milan with Goldoni's *Arlecchino: the Servant of Two Masters* and Luigi Pirandello's *Questa Sera Si Recita a Soggetto*. Producer Henry Sherek offers a Bernard Shaw double-bill of *Village Wooing*, staged by Roy Rich, and *Fanny's First Play*, directed by Douglas Seale. From Canada's Stratford Shakespeare Festival, comes the ensemble with Tyrone Guthrie's staging of *Oedipus Rex*. Michael Langham stages *Henry V*.

Aug 27 Peter Daubeny brings East Berlin's Berliner Ensemble to London and the Palace Theatre. The troupe opens tonight with Brecht's *Mother Courage*, staged by Erich Engel and Brecht. On Aug 29, the play is the Ensemble's adaptation of Farquhar's *The Recruiting Officer*, called *Trumpets and Drums*. On Aug 30, Brecht's *The Caucasian Chalk Circle* is presented.

Aug 30 James Bridie's *Mr. Bolfry* is revived at the Aldwych Theatre in London, with Alastair Sim in the title-role. There are 108 performances.

Sep 5 London's Old Vic opens its new season with *Timon of Athens*. Ralph Richardson has the title role. On Sep 11, *Cymbeline* is offered with Derek Francis as the king. Barbara Jefford and Keith Michell are in *Much Ado About Nothing*, offered on Oct 23. *The Merchant of Venice* opens on Dec 11, with Robert Helpmann as Shylock.

Sep 11 Off-Broadway at the Phoenix Theatre, Shaw's *Saint Joan* is revived. After a limited engagement, it's returned by the Phoenix, then moved to the Coronet on Broadway, for a total of 77 performances. The cast includes Siobhan McKenna and Peter Falk.

Sep 19 Lillian Hellman's *The Children's Hour* is revived by director Graham Evans at the Arts Theatre in London, with Clare Austin, Margot van der Burgh and Bessie Love among the cast.

Oct 4 A revival of George Bernard Shaw's *The Doctor's Dilemma*, staged by Julian Amyes, opens at the Saville Theatre in London. It runs two months, with a cast including Paul Daneman and Ann Todd.

Oct 11 *A View from the Bridge*, Arthur Miller's 1955 play, staged by Peter Brook, is a presentation of the New Watergate Theatre Club, moved from their former premises and operating at London's Comedy as a private club, to be able to produce plays banned by the Lord Chamberlain's office. Anthony Quayle plays the Brooklyn dock-worker, Eddie Carbone. Brian Bedford palys Rodolpho. Mary Ure plays Catherine, Eddie's beloved niece; Megs Jenkins is Beatrice. There are 220 performances of this production.

Oct 18 *The Apple Cart*, George Bernard Shaw's comedy about the place of monarchy in a democracy runs for nearly 16 weeks at New York's Plymouth Theatre. George Schaefer stages a cast that includes Maurice Evans and Katherine Hynes.

Oct 23 London's Old Vic Company comes to Broadway for 95 performances of a repertory including *Richard II*, *Macbeth*, *Romeo and Juliet*, and *Troilus and Cressida*. The company includes John Neville, Claire Bloom, Paul Rogers, and Coral Browne. *Richard II* and *Macbeth* show the staging of Michael Benthall. Robert Helpmann directs *Romeo and Juliet*. Tyrone Guthrie's mounts *Troilus and Cressida*.

Oct 30 On Broadway at the Martin Beck Theatre, Shaw's *Major Barbara* revives, with Glynis Johns, Charles Laughton, Cornelia Otis Skinner, Eli Wallach and Burgess Meredith. The revival runs 29 weeks.

Oct 31 George Devine stages Bertolt Brecht's *The Good Woman of Setzuan*, at London's Royal Court Theatre. Among the cast members are Peggy Ashcroft and Joan Plowright.

Nov 5 The Royal Court's production of John Osborne's *Look Back in Anger* opens at the Lyric, Hammersmith, with Richard Pasco replacing Kenneth Haigh as Jimmy Porter.

Nov 6 At the Arts Theatre in London, Peter Wood stages two plays by Eugene Ionesco: *The Bald Prima Donna* and *The New Tenant*. Michael Bryant and Jill Bennett are among the performers.

Nov 8 This is the Shaw Centenary Year, and *The Devil's Disciple*, which opens tonight in London at the Winter Garden, is the fifth Shaw play to be revived for the celebration. Staged by Noel Willman, the production is shown 36 times. Tyrone Power plays the lead.

Nov 8 Jean Dalrymple revives John Patrick's *The Teahouse of the August Moon* at New York's City Center. On Nov 21, Tennessee Williams' *The Glass Menagerie* has a revival with Helen Hayes. On Dec 5, the show is the Thomas Heggan-Joshua Logan *Mister Roberts*, with Charlton Heston.

Nov 12 At London's Palace Theatre, distinguished foreign troupes continue to show their outstanding productions. Tonight it's the Compagnie Madeleine Renaud—Jean-Louis Barrault, with *Le Chien du Jardinier*, adapted from the Lope de Vega Spanish classic by Georges Neveux. Barrault directs. On the 14th, the troupe offers Molière's *Le Misanthrope*. On Nov 16, the players perform Georges Feydeau's *Occupe-Toi d'Amelie*. On the 19th, Paul Claudel's *Christophe Colomb* is played. Jean Giraudoux's *Intermezzo* opens on the 22nd.

Dec 3 The D'Oyly Carte Opera Company

returns to London for a short season. At the Prince's Theatre, the troupe opens with *Ruddigore*, followed with *The Gondoliers*, *Iolanthe* *The Mikado*, and *The Yeomen of the Guard*, the New Year's Eve treat.

Dec 6 Actor-director John Clements revives Congreve's *The Way of the World* as part of his season of classics at the Saville Theatre in London. Clements, Kay Hammond, and Margaret Rutherford are in the cast. The production runs just over two months.

Dec 12 George Devine stages William Wycherley's *The Country Wife*, at London's Royal Court Theatre. Laurence Harvey, Joan Plowright, and Alan Bates are in the cast.

Dec 18 Playwright Bertolt Brecht provides Uta Hagen with a chance to play both a woman and a man in *The Good Woman of Setzuan* at New York's Phoenix. This parable of human foibles is staged by translator-critic Eric Bentley. The run is limited to three weeks.

Dec 19 *Dick Whittington* opens in London at the Palace, beginning the holiday season of pantomimes, revues, and revivals. On the 20th, *The Famous Five* is at the Hippodrome; *Family Fun* is at the Adelphi Theatre, and *The Ticket-of-Leave Man* is at the Arts Theatre. On Dec 21, *Peter Pan* returns to the Scala Theatre. Other attractions on succeeding days are *Noddy in Toyland* at the Stoll Theatre, *The Wonderful Lamp* (Palladium), *Goody Two—Shoes* (Streatham Hill), *Humpty Dumpty* (Golders Green Hippodrome), *Aladdin* (Wimbledon), *Where the Rainbow Ends* (Coliseum), *The Marvellous Story of Puss in Boots* (Lyric, Hammersmith), *The Princess and the Swineherd* (Arts), and *Alice in Wonderland* (Chelsea Palace).

1956 BIRTHS/DEATHS/DEBUTS

Jan 10 Author and editor Edith J. R. Isaacs (b. 1878) dies in White Plains, N. Y. Isaacs was editor of *Theatre Arts* from 1919 to 1945. She wrote *Architecture for the New Theatre* (1935) and *The Negro in the American Theatre* (1947).

Feb 26 American actress, mimic, and author Elsie Janis (b. 1889) dies in Beverly Hills. Janis first appeared on the New York stage in vaudeville. She is the author of the shows *A Star for the Night*, *It's All Wrong*, *Puzzles of 1925*, in all of which she played and of a movie, *Close Harmony*.

March 8 American actor, playwright, and director John Emerson (b. 1874) dies in Pasadena, California. Emerson was stage director for the Shuberts and for Charles Frohman. He collaborated with his wife,

Anita Loos, on the book, *Breaking Into the Movies*, as well as on plays.

March 12 American actress Grace La Rue (b. 1882) is dead in Burlingame, California. La Rue played in vaudeville, musical comedy and extravaganza.

April 21 Pennsylvania-born playwright Charles MacArthur (b. 1895) dies in New York City. MacArthur's plays include *Lulu Belle* written with Edward Sheldon, *Salvation* with Sidney Howard, and *The Front Page* and *Twentieth Century* with Ben Hecht. He was married to actress Helen Hayes.

April 26 American actor Edward Arnold (b. 1890) dies in Encino, California. Arnold began his film career in 1917. His last New York stage appearance was in 1931 in *The Third Little Show*.

MARGARET WYCHERLEY

May 12 American actor Louis Calhern (b. 1895) dies in Nara, Japan. *Jacobowsky and the Colonel*, *The Magnificent Yankee*, and *King Lear*, were among his outstanding stage credits. His film career began in 1919.

May 20 Drama critic and caricaturist Sir Max Beerbohm (b. 1872) dies in Rapallo, Italy. Beerbohm, half-brother of Sir Herbert Tree, was dramatic critic of the *Saturday Review* from 1898 to 1910. His one-act play, *The Happy Hypocrite*, was produced in 1900 by Mrs. Patrick Campbell.

June 6 Actress Margaret Wycherly (b. 1881) dies in New York. Wycherly made her first appearance on stage in 1898 in *What Dreams May Come*. In 1953 she played the role of the Dowager Duchess of York in *Richard III* at New York's City Center.

June 23 English author and playwright Michael Arlen (b. 1895) dies in New York. He wrote the plays *Dear Father, The Green Hat, The Zoo* with Winchell Smith, and *Good Losers* with Walter Hackett.

Aug 14 German playwright Bertolt Brecht (b. 1898) dies in Eàst Germany. His first success was *Die Dreigroschenoper* in 1928, followed by such works as *Galileo*. He was founder of the Berliner Ensemble.

Aug 16 Actor Bela Lugosi (b. 1884) dies in Los Angeles. By 1913 Lugosi was the leading actor in Budapest. He made his first appearance on the American stage at the Greenwich Village Theatre in 1922. Count Dracula and Jonathan Brewster in *Arsenic and Old Lace* are his two most memorable roles.

Aug 31 American playwright Percy Mackaye (b. 1875) dies in Cornish, New Hampshire. Among his plays are *The Canterbury Pilgrims, Jeanne d'Arc,* and *The Scarecrow*. He was the son of theatre designer and dramatist Steele Mackaye.

Oct 1 Composer, performer, and song publisher Albert Von Tilzer (b. 1878) dies in Los Angeles. Von Tilzer's more notable Broadway stage scores include *Honey Girl, The Gingham Girl, Adrienne,* and *Bye Bye Bonnie*.

Oct 9 Actress Marie Doro (b. 1882) dies in New York.

Oct 14 American playwright Owen Davis (b. 1874) dies in New York. Davis wrote the moving drama, *The Detour* in 1921— a "Best Play" of the season. His autobiography *I'd Like to Do It Again* was published in 1931. In 1923 he won the Pulitzer Prize - for *Icebound*.

Dec 17 English actor Whitford Kane (b. 1881) is dead. Kane played in numerous Broadway productions and toured extensively in America. His volume of reminiscences, *Are We All Met?*, was published in 1931.

Dec 30 American monologist Ruth Draper (b. 1884) dies in New York. Draper's first professional appearance was in London in 1920. Although she was immensely popular in England, her longest runs were primarily in New York.

nenberger selects the annual ten "Best Plays." They include Miller's *A View From the Bridge*, Giraudoux's *Tiger at the Gates*, Goodrich and Hackett's *The Diary of Anne Frank*, Levin's *No Time for Sergeants*, Bagnold's *The Chalk Garden*, Anouilh's *The Lark*, Wilder's *The Matchmaker*, Fields and Chodorov's *The Ponder Heart*, Lerner and Loewe's *My Fair Lady*, and Beckett's *Waiting for Godot*. *The Diary of Anne Frank* wins both major drama awards, the Pulitzer Prize and the Drama Critics' Award for "Best American Play." *My Fair Lady* is the Circle's "Best Musical Production," with *Tiger at the Gates* "Best Foreign Play."

June 22 The Academy Theatre is founded by Frank Wittow in Atlanta, Georgia, and opens with *The Misunderstanding*, by Albert Camus. It is currently located in a 50-year-old opera house, seating 535 people. It has a proscenium stage with a semi-thrust.

Autumn In order to build a permanent theatre for Canada's Stratford Shakespeare Festival, a nation-wide funding drive is organized, producing a total of $1,500,000. By the time the theatre is completed, costs have risen an additional $650,000.

Oct Scottish Television buys the Theatre Royal, Glasgow, a masterpiece of Victorian theatre design, created by the architect Charles John Phipps. Television planners hope to turn the venerable theatre into a complex of studios. In 1975, however, the completely restored theatre will become the home of the Scottish Opera.

Nov Zelda Fichhandler and her co-workers in Washington, D. C. take over an old brewery, which they call the Old Vat. They open with the American premiere of the full-length version of Arthur Miller's *A View from the Bridge*. The Old Vat will be replaced in 1961 by the handsome new Arena Theatre, at Sixth and M Streets, South West.

Dec 8 Today marks the 50th Jubilee of Edinburgh's handsome Edwardian playhouse, the King's Theatre. In the recent renovation of the theatre, the original three balcony levels have been reduced to two, to make better sight-lines and spectator-comfort possible.

1956   THEATERS/PRODUCTIONS

March 31 Tonight marks the closing of the 172-seat Turnabout Theatre in Los Angeles. Founded by puppet-master Harry Burnett, lyricist Forman Brown, and manager Richard Brandon, the theatre has stages at either end, with the audience seated in reversible streetcar seats. Shows have mixed puppets with live sketches. For nine years, guest star Elsa Lanchester didn't miss a performance; occasionally her husband, Charles Laughton, has also performed.

April The English Stage Company, under the artistic direction of George Devine, takes over the management of London's Court Theatre.

June 1 Garrison Sherwood, surveying the 1955–1956 Off-Broadway season for the *Best Plays* annual, notes there have been over 90 productions. About half have been revivals, classics, or semi-classics.

June 1 With the 1955-1956 Broadway season now over, drama critic Louis Kro-

Jan 3 *Small War on Murray Hill* (NY—Ethel Barrymore—Comedy). There are just 12 performances of this Robert E. Sherwood play about an incident during the Revolutionary War, despite direction by Garson Kanin and a cast that includes Leo Genn, Jan Sterling, and Daniel Massey.

Jan 17 *The Waltz of the Toreodors.* See L premiere, 1956.

Jan 29 *The Potting Shed* (NY—Bijou—Drama). Graham Greene's play, about a miracle of faith which brings a boy back to life, has a cast that includes Sybil Thorndike, Robert Fleming, and Carol Lynley. It runs 18 weeks. The drama opens at London's Globe on Feb 5, 1958, with Walter Hudd, Irene Worth, Gwen Ffrangcon-Davies, and John Gielgud. The production has only 101 showings.

Jan 30 *Eugenia* (NY—Ambassador—Drama). "Miss Tallulah Bankhead is an irresistible force," says Walter Kerr," but in 'Eugenia' she has flatly, finally, and irrevocably met an immovable object." Randolph Carter's adaptation of Henry James' novel *The Europeans*, staged by Herbert Machiz, has just 12 performances.

Feb 7 *Visit to a Small Planet* (NY—Booth—Comedy). Gore Vidal's satiric comedy about a visitor from outer space (Cyril Ritchard) runs 388 performances. In London, it has only 12 performances following its premiere at the Westminster on Feb 25, 1960.

Feb 13 *The Tunnel of Love* (NY—Royale—Comedy). Joseph Fields stages and helps adapt Peter De Vries's novel about wandering husbands and pregnant women, wed and unwed. It wins 417 performances. Tom Ewell, Nancy Olson, Darren McGavin, and others help animate the jokes. Ian Carmichael scores a personal success in the London production which premieres at Her Majesty's on Dec 3, Barbara Murray, William Franklyn, and Barbara Hicks are in the cast. The show runs 563 performances.

March 1 *Ziegfeld Follies* (NY—Winter Garden—Revue). A Golden Jubilee edition of the original *Follies*, with Beatrice Lillie and Billy DeWolfe among others. This doesn't please the critics and runs just over 15 weeks.

March 5 *The Glass Cage* (Toronto—Crest—Drama). On a trip to Canada, J.B. Priestley has met the brother-sister acting family of Donald and Murray Davis and Barbara Chilcott. Struck by their unusual appearance—the Davises and Chilcott have Romany blood—Priestly writes *The Glass Cage* expressly for them. The play is set in the Toronto of 1906, and the trio play "black sheep" of the McBane family who come to town to claim an inherit-

ance. After its run at the Crest Theatre, the play opens at the Piccadilly in London, on April 26, for four weeks followed by a provincial tour. W.A. Darlington writes in the *Daily Telegraph* of the London premiere: "In Canada, I have long been led to believe, there is no native professional theatre. I believe it no more." This is the first entirely Canadian troupe to perform in Britain.

March 21 *Orpheus Descending* (NY—Martin Beck—Drama). Cliff Robertson plays a drifter who comes to a small southern town where outsiders aren't much appreciated, in Tennessee Williams' new play. Maureen Stapleton co-stars. Harold Clurman stages. There are 68 showings.

April 13 *Shinbone Alley* (NY—Broadway—Musical). Eartha Kitt plays a very kittenish Mehitabel in this Mel Brooks and Joe Darion adaptation of Don Marquis' "archy and mehitabel" tales. The score is by George Kleinsinger. Eddie Bracken is cast as Archie, the cockroach who adores this alleycat. Rod Alexander stages the dances, with sets by Eldon Elder, costumes by Motley, and lights by Tharon Musser. The show lasts six weeks, but "Toujours Gai" lingers on.

May 2 *A Moon for the Misbegotten* (NY—Bijou—Drama). Franchot Tone and Wendy Hiller get good notices, but Eugene O'Neill's play, about an alcoholic and the girl who loves him, does not. Carmen Capalbo stages the 68 performances.

May 14 *New Girl in Town* (NY—46th Street—Musical). Thelma Ritter and Gwen Verdon, as actress, singer, and dancer, illuminate this musical version of Eugene O'Neill's *Anna Christie*. Directed and adapted by George Abbott, with songs by Robert Merrill, and choreography by Bob Fosse, it has 431 performances.

Sep 26 *West Side Story* (NY—Winter Garden—Musical). Two New York teenage gangs are pitted against each other in this modern-day *Romeo and Juliet* which scores 732 performances. The cast includes Larry Kert, Carol Lawrence, and Chita Rivera. The book is by Arthur Larents, score by Leonard Bernstein, lyrics by Stephen Sondheim, with conception, staging, and choreography by Jerome Robbins. The show has an even longer run in London following its Dec 12, 1958, premiere at Her Majesty's. There it runs 1,039 performances, with George Chakiris, Marlys Watters, and Ken Le Roy heading the cast.

Sep 29 *I Knock at the Door* (NY—Belasco—Reading). Adaptor Paul Shyre has a six-week run with actors reading from Sean O'Casey's first volume of autobiography.

Oct 1 *Look Back in Anger.* See L pre-

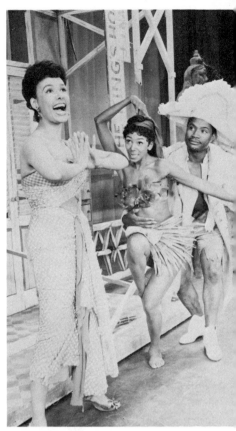

JAMAICA

miere, 1956.

Oct 10 *Romanoff and Juliet.* See L premiere, 1956.

Oct 15 *Under Milk Wood.* See L premiere, 1956.

Oct 19 *The Cave Dwellers* (NY—Bijou—Drama). William Saroyan's down-trodden characters act out their dreams and traumas in an abandoned theatre. This drama runs three months. Carmen Capalbo directs a cast including Wayne Morris and Eugenie Leontovich.

Oct 24 *Compulsion* (NY—Ambassador—Drama). Meyer Levin adapts his book, based on the Leopold and Loeb murder-for-thrills case. Alex Segal stages. Dean Stockwell, Roddy McDowall, and Suzanne Pleshette are in the cast. It has 140 performances.

Oct 31 *Jamaica* (NY—Imperial—Musical). Lena Horne and Ricardo Montalban head the cast in this musical, set on a mythical island off Jamaica, which has 555 performances. David Merrick produces. Robert Lewis stages the book by E.Y. Harburg and Fred Saidy. Harburg and Harold Arlen provide the songs.

Nov 12 *Time Remembered.* See L premiere, 1954.

Nov 14 *Nude With a Violin.* See L premiere, 1956.

Nov 20 *The Rope Dancers* (NY—Cort—Drama). Peter Hall directs Siobhan McKenna, Art Carney, Joan Blondell, and Theodore Bikel in Morton Wishengrad's drama about a New York tenement family at the turn of the century. It runs nearly 24 weeks.

Nov 28 *Look Homeward Angel* (NY—Ethel Barrymore—Drama). Dramatist Ketti Frings wins the Pulitzer Prize and the Drama Critics' Circle Award for her adaptation of Thomas Wolfe's autobiographical novel of a young man's family conflicts. Anthony Perkins, Jo Van Fleet, and Arthur Hill play 564 performances.

Dec 5 *The Dark at the Top of the Stairs* (NY—Music Box—Drama). Elia Kazan directs Pat Hingle, Teresa Wright, and Eileen Heckart in William Inge's moving family drama about a smalltown traveling salesman. "Magnificent performances," says the *NY Daily Mirror*, and the play has 468 showings.

Dec 19 *The Music Man* (NY—Majestic—Musical). Robert Preston delights audiences and critics as a con-man reformed by love. The show wins 1,375 performances, plus the Drama Critics' Circle Award for "Best Musical." Meredith Willson concocts the book, lyrics, and score from a story he and Franklin Lacey have devised. The Broadway hit opens at the Adelphi in the West End on March 16, 1961, with Van Johnson and Patricia Lambert in the leads. It runs almost 50 weeks.

1957 BRITISH PREMIERES

Jan 24 *At the Drop of a Hat* (L—Fortune—Revue). Michael Flanders and Donald Swann win 733 performances with their witty songs and sketches. They bring the revue to Broadway's Golden on Oct 8, 1959, where it runs 27 weeks.

March 7 *A Hatful of Rain.* See NY premiere, 1955.

March 28 *Damn Yankees.* See NY premiere, 1955.

April 8 *Camino Real.* See NY premiere, 1953.

April 10 *The Entertainer* (L—Royal Court—Drama). Laurence Olivier plays the title-role, as a shabby, failed song-and-dance man who won't give up, in John Osborne's play which has difficulties with the censor. The show comes to New York's Royale on Feb 12, 1958, with Olivier repeating his role. There are only 97 showings.

April 11 *Zuleika* (L—Saville—Musical). James Ferman adapts Max Berebohm's satiric classic *Zuleika Dobson*, about a girl (Mildred Mayne) who creates a stir at Oxford University. It has a run of 124 performances.

April 20 *The Lovebirds* (L—Adelphi—Comedy). Dora Bryan and Ronald Shiner play newly-weds whose pet budgerigar becomes possessed by the spirit of the heroine's late husband in Basil Thomas's comedy. There are 516 performances.

April 20 *Plaisirs de Paris* (L—Prince of Wales's—Revue). Comedian Dickie Henderson heads the cast of Robert Nesbitt's new music and comedy revue. It has 850 performances.

April 30 *Summer of the Seventeenth Doll* (L—New—Drama). Australian Ray Lawler's play, performed by an Australian company, wins 254 performances. It centers on the male-female relationships formed in a small township when some Queensland cane-cutters arrive after the harvest. The show opens on Broadway at the Coronet on Jan 22, 1958, where it has only 29 showings.

May 30 *Dead Secret* (L—Piccadilly—Drama). Paul Scofield plays a landlord who poisons a tenant for her money, in Ronald Ackland's play based on a real-life murder. It runs nearly 27 weeks.

June 5 *Dear Delinquent* (L—Westminister—Comedy). Anna Massey plays a teenage burglar, caught by a highly susceptible bachelor (David Tomlinson) in his flat, in this comedy staged by Jack Minster. It has 444 performances, transferring to the Aldwych Theatre in December.

June 6 *Free as Air* (L—Savoy—Musical). Julian Slade, composer of *Salad Days*, has a run of 410 performances with this Dorothy Reynolds collaboration about a runaway heiress (Gillian Lewis).

June 22 *We're Having a Ball* (L—Palladium—Revue). Comedian Max Bygraves heads the troupe in Robert Nesbitt's revue which runs 38 weeks.

July 16 *Odd Man In* (L—St. Martin's—Comedy). Robin Maugham adapts a French farce by Claude Magnier about a love tangle, which runs nearly 30 weeks. Donald Sinden heads the cast.

Aug 21 *Share My Lettuce* (L—Lyric, Hammersmith—Revue). Maggie Smith and Kenneth Williams head the cast of this Bamber Gascoigne revue, with score by Keith Statham and Patrick Gowers. The show earns 285 performances, transferring to the Comedy and then the Garrick Theatre.

Sep 9 *Saturday Night at the Crown* (L—Garrick—Comedy). Comic actress Thora Hird plays a local busybody who passes on gossip at the Crown, a public house, in Walter Greenwood's comedy. It runs seven months.

Sep 26 *Roar Like a Dove* (L—Phoenix—Comedy). Lesley Storm's comedy about a Scottish laird, who wants a male heir from his American wife, who has already born him six daughters, wins 1,019 performances. John McCallum and Evelyn Varden head the cast.

Nov 14 *The Bells Are Ringing.* See NY premiere, 1956.

Nov 15 *The Happiest Millionaire.* See NY premiere, 1956.

Nov 21 *Flowering Cherry* (L—Haymarket—Drama). Ralph Richardson and Celia Johnson head the cast in this Robert Bolt drama about a failed man who takes refuge in dreams and lies. It runs one year. Bolt's play opens at the Lyceum on Broadway on Oct 21, 1959, with Eric Portman in the lead. The play is seen only five times.

Dec 3 *The Tunnel of Love.* See NY premiere, 1957.

Dec 10 *Diner With the Family* (L—New—Comedy). John Justin plays a love-stricken married man who rents a mansion and hires actors to impersonate his family in order to impress a young woman (Jill Bennett) in this Jean Anouilh comedy, translated by Edward Owen Marsh. Frank Hauser stages. The run lasts nearly six-months.

Dec 12 *The Rape of the Belt* (L—Piccadilly—Comedy). Benn W. Levy retells the tale of Theseus and Heracles, and the production runs 37 weeks. John Clements stages, and stars with his wife, Kay Hammond.

THE ROPE DANCERS

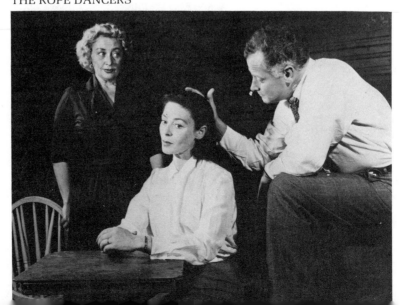

Jan 7 The D'Oyly Carte Opera Company continues its season in London at the Prince's Theatre with *Trial by Jury* and *The Pirates of Penzance*. On Jan 14, the troupe presents another double-bill: *Cox & Box* and *H. M. S. Pinafore*. *Patience* is shown on Jan 28.

Jan 14 Dublin's Irish Players come to the Lyric Hammersmith with a double-bill of Theresa Deevey's *Light Falling* and Sean O'Casey's *Shadow of a Gunman*. Jack MacGowran directs the first play; John Gibson, the second.

Jan 21 An all-black cast gives six performances of Beckett's *Waiting for Godot* on Broadway at the Ethel Barrymore Theatre. Mantan Moreland, Earle Hyman and Geoffrey Holder are in the cast.

Jan 22 At London's Old Vic, the season continues with *The Two Gentlemen of Verona*, staged by Michael Langham. Richard Gale, Keith Michell, Barbara Jefford and Robert Helpmann head the cast. Loudon Sainthill designs *Antony and Cleopatra* for director Helpmann, shown on March 5, with Michell and Margaret Whiting. On April 23, John Barton's versions of *The Tragedy of Titus Andronicus* and *The Comedy of Errors* are presented as a double-bill, staged by Walter Hudd. In *Comedy*, Michell, John Humphrey, John Fraser and Dudley Jones take the leads. On May 29, Robert Helpmann plays the lead in *Richard III*, staged by Douglas Seale.

Jan 22 The American Shakespeare Festival of Stratford, Conncecticut, comes to New York for a four-week season at the Phoenix Theatre. Last summer's *Measure for Measure* and *The Taming of the Shrew* are performed.

Jan 24 At the Arts Theatre in London, Armand Salacrou's *No Laughing Matter* opens. Among the cast' are Alec McCowen and Brenda Bruce.

Jan 30 Madeleine Renaud and Jean-Louis Barrault bring their repertory company from Paris to Broadway's Winter Garden for a limited run. In the repertory are Claudel's *Christophe Colomb*, Jonson's *Volpone*, Molière's *Le Misanthrope*, Salacrou's *Les Nuits de la Colère*, Feydeau's *Feu la Mere de Madame*, Giraudoux' *Intermezzo*, Neveaux/de Vega's *Le Chien du Jardinier*, and *Les Adieux*, a program of songs and sketches.

Feb 4 The Royal Court production of Wycherley's *The Country Wife* opens in the West End at the Adelphi Theatre for a run of 172 performances. Later, it will tour to New York. Tomorrow Carson McCuller's *The Member of the Wedding* (1950), opens at the Royal Court, with Geraldine McEwan as Frankie.

Feb 25 *Julius Caesar AD 1957* is staged in modern-dress by the Dublin Gate Theatre. Other offerings are MacDonagh's *Step-in-the-Hollow*, Maurette/Bolton's *Anastasia*, macLiammoír's *Pageant of Saint Patrick*, and Johnston's *The Old Lady Says "No!"*

March 4 Edwige Feuillere brings her own company to London from Paris for a repertory of French drama. She opens, staging and starring herself, with *La Dame aux Camèlias*, by Dumas, fils. On March 8, she offers Henri Becque's *La Parisienne*, followed by Prosper Merimee's *Le Carrosse du Saint-Sacrement*. On March 18, the play is Racine's *Phèdre*.

March 13 At the New York City Center, John Gay's *The Beggar's Opera* is revived with Jack Cassidy and Shirley Jones. On March 27, *Brigadoon* plays for 47 performances, with Scott McKay and others. On April 10, Jean Dalrymple revives *The Merry Widow*. On April 24, the revival is *South Pacific*. On May 15, *The Pajama Game* is revived.

March 19 Off-Broadway at the Phoenix Theatre, John Webster's *The Duchess of Malfi*, is revived with Jacqueline Brookes. The run is three weeks.

March 25 At London's Winter Garden, The Polish State Jewish Theatre opens an engagement. The company is led by Ida Kaminska, who has adapted—in Yiddish—and directed the initial production, *Meir Ezofowicz*. On the 28th, she plays the title-role in Jacob Gordin's Yiddish drama, *Mirele Efros*. On April 1, *Tevie der Milchiger*, adapted from Sholem Aleichem's stories, is played. On June 6, The Polish State Theatre opens at London's Scala Theatre with *Maz i Zona (Husband and Wife)*, by Aleksander Fredro. The following evening the play is *Dom Kobiet (The House of Women)*, by Zofia Naikowska.

April 2 With Glen Byam Shaw in charge, the Shakespeare Memorial Theatre in Stratford-upon-Avon opens its season with his staging of *As You Like It*, with Peggy Ashcroft as Rosalind. Robert Harris plays the title role in *King John*. Alec Clunes is Brutus in *Julius Caesar*. Ashcroft is Imogen in *Cymbeline*. Peter Brook directs, designs, and composes the score for *The Tempest*, with John Gielgud as Prospero.

April 2 At London's Royal Court Theatre, Samuel Beckett's *Fin de Partie (End Game)* is produced in French by director Roger Blin, who also plays Hamm. The English Stage Company cannot yet offer the play in English, owing to censor's objections. It is followed by Beckett's *Acte sans Paroles*. On May 14, Ronald Duncan's adaptation of Jean Giraudoux's play, *The Apollo of Bellac*, opens, with a cast including Alan Bates and Richard Pasco. It is followed by Donald Watson's translation of Eugene Ionesco's *The Chairs*. Tony Richardson directs George Devine, Joan Plowright, and Richard Pasco.

April 11 Peter Glenville adapts and stages Georges Feydeau's farce *Hotel Paradiso* at New York's Henry Miller Theatre, with Osbert Lancaster's designs from the London production. Bert Lahr and Angela Lansbury head the cast for the 108 showings.

April 25 Although Robert Anderson's American hit, *Tea and Sympathy*, is referred to by some as "the *Young Woodley* of the present," it's too strong for the Lord Chamberlain's Office, dealing as it does with the suggestion of homosexuality at a boys' school. So the play, directed by John Fernald, is presented as a club production of Watergate Presentations, Ltd., at London's Comedy Theatre. Those who join the club may see the play; the general public must be protected from it—as it now stands. Elizabeth Sellers plays Laura, the sympathetic headmaster's wife, who helps Tom Lee (Tim Seely) affirm his masculinity with something more than sympathy.

June 17 At Sadler's Wells Theatre in London, Peter Daubeny has imported Berlin's Kurfurstendamm Theatre Company. The troupe opens with Buechner's *Leonce and Lena*, followed by his *Wozzeck*. On June 19, Lessing's *Philotas* is paired with von Kleist's *The Broken Jug*. On June 21, the production is Strindberg's *The Dream Play*. Maximilian Schell in the company.

June 22 Opening with *Othello*, the American Shakespeare Festival of Stratford, Connecticut, begins its third season. Earle Hyman plays the title-role, with Alfred Drake as Iago. John Houseman directs. Jack Landau stages *The Merchant Venice* with Morris Carnovsky as Shylock and Katharine Hepburn as Portia. Houseman and Landau co-direct *Much Ado About Nothing*, with Hepburn and Drake.

June 25 *The Making of Moo*, Nigel Dennis's satire on religion arouses controversy. Tony Richardson directs George Devine and Joan Plowright, among others in this Royal Court production.

July 1 At London's Stoll Theatre, the company from the Shakespeare Memorial Theatre at Stratford-upon-Avon presents its 1955 production of *Titus Andronicus*, staged by Peter Brook. Laurence Olivier plays the title-role. The production is also toured on the continent.

July 1 Michael Langham, as artistic director of Canada's Stratford Shakespeare Festival, has scheduled three productions for the season, which opens today. Langham stages *Hamlet*. Tyrone Guthrie directs *Twelfth Night*. The English Opera Group stages the North American premiere of Benjamin Britten's opera *The Turn of the Screw*, directed by Basil Coleman with Britten conducting. In this season's ensemble are such talents as Siobhan McKenna, Douglas Campbell, and

THE FLOWERING CHERRY

Christopher Plummer.

July 19 The San Diego National Shakespeare Festival opens today with a program of three plays. Allen Fletcher directs *King Lear*; B. Iden Payne stages *The Tempest*; and Beaumont and Fletcher's *The Knight of the Burning Pestle* is directed by Craig Noel.

July 21 After last summer's success with Shakespeare in the East River Amphitheatre, producer Joseph Papp returns with his newly-christened New York Shakespeare Festival. It now opens a long season touring the city's parks. Performances are free, and the festival's Mobile Theatre keeps moving until Nov 25. Stuart Vaughan directs three plays for Papp: *Richard III*, *The Two Gentlemen of Verona*, and *Macbeth*.

Aug 1 Angus Bowmer directs *As You Like It* for the opening of the Oregon Shakespearean Festival in Ashland. James Sandoe stages the next two plays: *Othello* and *The Two Gentlemen of Verona*. Robert Loper directs *Henry VIII* and *Pericles*.

Aug 18 Britain's Edinburgh International Festival opens. This is Robert Ponsonby's first season as Artistic Director and he's invited Anna Russell, the musical parodist, to spoof the Festival. The Edinburgh Gateway Company offers Robert McLellan's *The Flouers O Edinburgh*. The English Stage Society presents Jean-Paul Sartre's *Nekrassov*. In the Assembly Hall, Jonathan Griffin's *The Hidden King* is staged by Christopher West. Producer Henry Sherek presents Walter Hasenclever's *Man of Distinction* at the Royal Lyceum. Madeliene Renaud and Jean-Louis Barrault bring their ensemble from Paris to perform Jean Anouilh's *Le Repetition, ou L'Amour Puni (The Rehearsal)*. Barrault also offers an anthology of writings by Paul Claudel,

Connaissance de Claudel. There is opera from Milan, with Maria Callas in Bellini's *La Sonnambula*, and Strehler's production of Cimarosa's *Il Matrimonio Segreto.*

Sep 11 At New York City Center, Jean Dalrymple revives Rodgers and Hammerstein's *Carousel*, with Howard Keel and Barbara Cook.

Sep 17 At London's Royal Court, Robert Helpmann plays a clever swindler in Sylvia and Georgia Leeson's translation of Jean-Paul Satre *Nekrassov*, a satire on political corruption. On Oct 19, John Arden's *The Waters of Babylon* is shown, staged without decor by Graham Evans. On Nov 26, William Faulkner's *Requiem for a Nun* is staged by Tony Richardson with the American actors Ruth Ford and Zachary Scott. On Dec 1, William Gaskill produces N.F. Simpson's *A Resounding Tinkle*. On Dec 27, Aristophanes' *Lysistrata* is staged by Mines Volonakis. Joan Greenwood plays the title-role.

Sep 18 At London's Old Vic Theatre, the company opens the season with *Hamlet*, featuring John Neville. This season completes the five-year-plan (begun in 1953) to stage the complete canon of Shakespeare's plays. On Oct 16, Douglas Seale

stages *Henry VI, Parts 1 and 2*, followed on the 17th by *Part 3*. Paul Daneman plays the king. On Nov 19, Margaret Webster shows her staging of *Measure for Measure*. The company has Michael Benthall stage *A Midsummer Night's Dream*, opening on Dec 23.

Oct 7 Emlyn Williams opens at New York's Longacre Theatre in *A Boy Growing Up*, a selection of excerpts from Dylan Thomas' works to evoke a childhood in Wales. It runs for two weeks and is later toured.

Oct 8 Off-Broadway at the Phoenix Theatre, Tyrone Guthrie stages a revival of Schiller's *Mary Stuart*, with Irene Worth and Eva LeGallienne. The production runs seven weeks. On Dec 3, Guthrie offers his translation and staging of Karel Capek's *The Makropoulos Secret*, with Eileen Herlie. The show runs four weeks.

Oct 9 At Joan Littlewood's Theatre Royal, in London's Stratford East, the show is Henry Chapman's *You Won,'t Always Be On Top*. On Nov 13, Littlewood stages *And the Wind Blew*, by Edward da Roche Miranda.

Nov 27 From London to Broadway comes George Devine's English Stage Company revival of Wycherley's *The Country Wife*, with Laurence Harvey, Pamela Brown, Colleen Dewhurst, and Julie Harris among the cast. It runs nearly six weeks.

Dec 5 Peter Brook's Stratford-upon-Avon production of *The Tempest* opens at the Drury Lane Theatre, London. Brook directs, helps design, and provides *musique concrète* of his own invention. John Gielgud plays Prospero. Alec Clunes is Caliban. The engagement is set for seven weeks.

Dec 18 Christmas entertainments get underway at the Lyric, Hammersmith, with a puppet show, *The Water Babies*. *New Clothes for the Emperor* opens the next day at the Arts Theatre, followed on the 20th by *Peter Pan* at the Scala Theatre. On Dec 23, several shows open: *Noddy in Toyland* at the Prince's Theatre, *A Midsummer Night's Dream* at the Old Vic, and *Robinson Crusoe* at the Palladium. Other shows are *Cinderella* (Wimbledon), *Puss in Boots* (Streatham Hill), and *Goody Two Shoes* (Golder's Green Hippodrome).

1957 BIRTHS/DEATHS/DEBUTS

Feb 26 American historian and drama critic Walter Prichard Eaton (b. 1878) dies in Chapel Hill, North Carolina. His works include *The American Stage of Today*, *Plays and Players*, *The Actor's Heritage*, and *The Theatre Guild: The First Ten Years*.

March 5 Actor Donald Davis and his brother and sister, Murray Davis and Barbara Chilcott, from a well-to-do old To-

ronto family, have a local success tonight with *The Glass Cage*. They first produced plays at their summer home, and, in 1948, founded the Straw Hat Players, a successful summer company in Ontario's "cottage country." In 1954, they fulfilled a dream and opened the Crest Theatre in Toronto. Never quite managing to make money, the Crest will close in 1966, but the three actors will do well individually on London and New York stages. Donald Davis will go on to win an Obie for creating the role of the old man in Beckett's *Krapp's Last Tape* (1960).

March 12 Actress Josephine Hull (b. 1886) dies in the Bronx. She appeared in *Arsenic and Old Lace*, *Harvey* and *The Solid Gold Cadillac* among other plays.

March 31 Canadian-born actor Gene Lockhart (b. 1891) dies in Santa Monica. Lockhart's appeared in Broadway in such plays as *The Little Father of the Wilderness*, and *Uncle Tom's Cabin*. He is the author of *Heigh-Ho*, *The Bunk of 1926*, and *How's Your Code*.

May 16 English actor Gerald Lawrence (b. 1873) is dead. Lawrence first appeared with the Bensonians in 1893. Hamlet, Romeo and Orlando were his main Shakespearean roles. Lawrence was married to actress Lilian Braithwaite.

Sep 1 English actress Helen Haye (b. 1874) dies in London. Haye made her first stage appearance in 1898, and her last as the Dowager Empress of Russia in *Anastasia* in 1953.

Sep 30 American playwright Augustus Goetz is dead in New York at age 56. Goetz, in collaboration with Ruth Goetz, wrote *The Heiress*, a stage and screen adaptation of Henry James's *Washington Square*.

Nov 17 Actress Cora Witherspoon (b. 1890) dies in Las Cruces, New Mexico.

Nov 20 Actor Art Carney makes his New York City debut as James Hyland in Morton Wishengrad's *The Rope Dancers* at the Cort Theatre.

Dec 19 English playwright-director John van Druten (b. 1901) dies in Indio, California. Van Druten, is author of *The Voice of the Turtle; Bell, Book, and Candle,* and *I've Got Sixpence*. He also adapted *I Remember Mama* and *I Am a Camera*.

O'Neill's *A Moon for the Misbegotten*. Both the Pulitzer Prize and the Drama Critics' Circle Award go to O'Neill's *Long Day's Journey into Night*.

June 1 Surveying the Off-Broadway 1956–1957 season, Garrison Sherwood notes in *Best Plays* that it is becoming more difficult to draw the line between Broadway and Off-Broadway in terms of professionalism. Theatre-goers must, he says, look to Off-Broadway for the classics and plays which are "difficult" or "highbrow." Quality is expensive, however, and budgets are rising. In 1953, a production could cost $500. Today, $7,000 to $15,000 is common. The breakeven point has risen from 35% to 50% of capacity. Weekly theatre rentals used to be $125; now they've risen to $575. Nonetheless, the season has been notable for Circle-in-the-Square's *Long Day's Journey into Night*, moved to Broadway, and the premiere of George Bernard Shaw's 18-year-old *In Good King Charles' Golden Days*.

July 1 With the opening of the current eason of Canada's Stratford Shakespeare estival, audiences experience for the first time the new, permanent Festival Theatre. No spectator is farther than 65 feet from the open stage, in the amphitheatre-style seating (1,404 in the orchestra; 858 in the balcony).

July 27 The curtain falls for the last time at London's St. James's Theatre. The theatre will be demolished to create a site for an office block.

Aug 4 In London, the Stoll Theatre closes after performances of the Shakespeare Memorial Theatre's production of *Titus Andronicus*, with Laurence Olivier and Vivien Leigh. The theatre will soon be demolished.

1957 THEATERS/PRODUCTIONS

Among the patents granted this year in Britain is one to I. S. de Ferran for a conjuring device which allows two objects to move toward each other on intersecting paths and appear to pass through each other.

The British Theatre Museum Association (BTMA) is founded. Its purpose is to establish a theatre museum and guard British interests in rare material.

Jan 26 Vincent Massey, Governor-General of Canada, lays the foundation stone in the foyer wall of Ontario's Stratford Festival Theatre. Designed by Robert Fairfield, incorporating stage-designer

Tanya Moiseiwitsch's thrust stage, the theatre complex is to win the Massey Gold Medal for Architecture in 1958.

June 1 With the Broadway season of 1956–1957 just completed, drama critic Louis Kronenberger chooses the ten "Best Plays." They are: Rattigan's *Separate Tables*, O'Neill's *Long Day's Journey into Night*, Aurthur's *A Very Special Baby*, Hellman, Wilbur, Latouche, Parker, and Bernstein's *Candide*, Laurents' *A Clearing in the Woods*, Anouilh's *The Waltz of the Toreadors*, Greene's *The Potting Shed*, Vidal's *Visit to a Small Planet*, Williams' *Orpheus Descending*, and

Oct Police issue a summons against founder-producer Joan Littlewood and her Theatre Workshop for violations of the Lord Chamberlain's license for *You Won't Always Be On Top*. Departures from the approved text are judged "vulgar and not in good taste." Fines and costs are about £17. The Queen's cousin, Lord Harewood, assists in the appeal to protect the theatre and its work.

The Canada Council is created by an Act of Parliament to promote the arts in Canada. In addition, a $50 million endowment is made to fund the Council. Yearly appropriations are added. The Touring Office, for example, provides subsidies and technical assistance for shows to tour the country. Canada Council makes annual grants to organizations in dance, music, theatre, visual arts, and publishing.

SEPARATE TABLES

Jan 7 *Garden District* (NY—York—Drama). Tennessee Williams' plays *Something Unspoken* and *Suddenly Last Summer* are produced Off Broadway for a limited run. On Sep 16, they are produced in London at the Arts Theatre, staged by Herbert Machiz, with Beatrix Lehmann and Beryl Meason in the cast.

Jan 16 *Two for the Seesaw* (NY—Booth—Comedy). Henry Fonda and Anne Bancroft win a run of 750 performances in William Gibson's two-character play about a married man and a young New York woman who helps him find himself. The play opens at London's Haymarket on Dec 17, with Gerry Judd and Peter Finch. There are 140 performances.

Jan 22 *Summer of the Seventeenth Doll.* See L premiere, 1957.

Jan 30 *Sunrise at Campobello* (NY—Cort—Drama). Ralph Bellamy plays Franklin Delano Roosevelt, Ann Seymour plays his mother, and Mary Pickett plays Eleanor in Dore Schary's dramatization of FDR's return to political life after he is stricken with polio. Vincent J. Donehue stages the 556 performances.

Feb 4 *Oh Captain!* (NY—Alvin—Musical). José Ferrer directs Tony Randall as a sailor with a wife in London and a mistress in Paris. It runs 192 performances. Songs are by Jay Livingston and Ray Evans.

Feb 12 *The Entertainer.* See L premiere, 1957.

Feb 27 *Blue Denim* (NY—Playhouse—Drama). James Leo Herlihy and William Noble collaborate on a drama about a teenager who gets his girlfriend pregnant. Burt Brinckerhoff and Carol Lynley play the leads. Joshua Logan stages. There's a 21-week run.

March 3 *Who Was That Lady I Saw You With* (NY—Martin Beck—Comedy). Peter Lind Hayes is a university professor who, through a farcical chain of events, finds himself involved with the FBI in Norman Krasna's comedy which runs 26 weeks.

April 3 *Say, Darling* (NY—ANTA—Musical). This musical within a musical, showing how Richard Bissell's novel *7 1/2 Cents* was turned into *The Pajama Game*, has 332 showings. Abe Burrows and the Bissells adapt the novel; Jule Styne writes the score; Betty Comden and Adolph Green create the lyrics. Vivian Blaine, Elliott Gould, David Wayne, and Johnny Desmond head the cast.

April 30 *The Firstborn.* See L premiere, 1952.

May 1 *Jane Eyre* (NY—Belasco—Drama). A & P heir Huntington Hartford dramatizes Charlotte Bronte's novel, but it has only 52 showings. Eric Portman's Rochester is thought by some reviewers to have

Tallulah Bankhead overtones. Jan Brooks is Jane.

May 5 *The Visit* (NY—Lunt-Fontanne—Drama). Lynn Fontanne and Alfred Lunt " . . . give an unforgettable performance" *(NY Times)* in Friedrich Duerrenmatt's Swiss drama *The Visit of the Old Lady*, adapted by Maurice Valency. It shows a woman's revenge on a man who ruined her life years before. The drama is judged Best Foreign Play by the Drama Critics' Circle and wins a nearly six-month run. On June 23, 1960, the play opens in London at the Royalty for 148 performances. The Lunts again star. Peter Brook stages.

Oct 2 *A Touch of the Poet* (NY—Helen Hayes—Drama). Helen Hayes, Eric Portman, and Kim Stanley head the cast of Eugene O'Neill's play about an Irish tavern-keeper who lives on flamboyant memories. Harold Clurman directs the 284 performances.

Oct 11 *Goldilocks* (NY—Lunt-Fontanne—Musical). Don Ameche, Elaine Stritch, Pat Stanley, and others have a run of only 161 performances in this Walter and Jean Kerr book based on the early days of movie-making in New Jersey. Agnes de Mille choreographs.

Oct 14 *The World of Susie Wong* (NY—Broadhurst—Drama). Joshua Logan directs France Nuyen as Susie, the whore who's a good girl at heart, in this Paul Osborn adaptation of Richard Mason's novel. William Shatner co-stars. There are 508 showings. The play opens in the West End at the Prince of Wales's on Nov 17, 1959, with Tsai Chin and Gary Raymond. It runs 823 performances.

Oct 21 *Once More, With Feeling* (NY—National—Comedy). Joseph Cotton and Walter Matthau play an egotistical conductor and a venal concert manager in Harry Kurnitz's satire, which runs 33 weeks. Arlene Francis is also in the cast.

Oct 22 *The Pleasure of His Company* (NY—Longacre—Comedy). Cornelia Otis Skinner gives playwright Samuel Taylor a helping hand with this comedy about a charming rascal (Cyril Ritchard) who shows up for the wedding of a daughter he hasn't seen in years. Dolores Hart and George Peppard play the engaged pair. Ritchard directs the 474 showings. The Haymarket is the scene of the London premiere on April 23, 1959. Nigel Patrick, Judith Stott, and Coral Browne are in the cast. The production lasts nearly 51 weeks.

Oct 23 *Make a Million* (NY—Playhouse—Comedy). Sam Levene takes the lead in Norman Barasch and Carroll Moore's comedy about a quiz-show winner. Jerome Chodorov stages. There are 308 performances.

Oct 29 *The Marriage-Go-Round* (NY—

SUNRISE AT CAMPOBELLO

Plymouth—Comedy). Claudette Colbert and Charles Boyer have a run of 431 performances as an academic husband-and-wife team who lecture on sexual relationships. Meanwhile off the lecture platform, Boyer is tempted by a Swedish lovely (Julie Newmar). Joseph Anthony stages Leslie Stevens' comedy. The show opens at the Piccadilly on Oct 29, 1959, with John Clements and Kay Hammond heading the cast. It has 210 performances.

Nov 4 *Epitaph for George Dillon.* See L premiere, 1958.

Nov 5 *Maria Golovin* (NY—Martin Beck—Opera). Gian-Carlo Menotti stages his own musical drama about a woman who remains faithful to her prisoner-of-war husband. It has just five performances.

Nov 11 *La Plume de Ma Tante.* See L premiere, 1955.

Nov 25 *Cue for Passion* (NY—Henry Miller—Drama). Elmer Rice's modern adaptation of *Hamlet* is laced with heavy doses of psychology and runs just five weeks. Diana Wynyard and John Kerr are in the company.

Dec 1 *Flower Drum Song* (NY—St. James—Musical). Critic Kenneth Tynan, deploring the bogus orientalism of this Richard Rodgers and Oscar Hammerstein II show, based on C.Y. Lee's novel, calls it "the world of woozy song." But this San Francisco story of the conflict between old Asian tradition and modern American ways runs 600 performances. Larry Blyden and Pat Suzuki are in the cast. It opens at the Palace in London on March 24, 1960.

Dec 3 *The Disenchanted* (NY—Coronet—Drama). Jason Robards, Jr. and Rosemary Harris take the leads in Budd Schulberg and Harvey Breit's adaptation of Schulberg's novel about the crack-up of F. Scott

Fitzgerald. It runs nearly six months.

Dec 8 *The Cold Wind and the Warm* (NY—Morosco—Drama). S.N. Behrman's drama about Jewish life in Massachusetts, with Eli Wallach and Maureen Stapleton, runs 15 weeks. Harold Clurman stages.

Dec 10 In New York at the Phoenix, Graham Greene's novel, *The Power and the Glory*, comes to the stage in Denis Cannan and Pierre Bost's adaptation, staged by Stuart Vaughan and designed by Will Steven Armstrong and Klaus Holm. It runs nine weeks, with a company including Eric Berry, Betty Hinritze, Dana Elcar, Fritz Weaver, Betty Miller, Patricia Falkenhain, Jerry Stiller, Jane White, Tom Bos-

ley, and Leonardo Cimino.

Dec 11 *J.B.* (NY—ANTA—Drama). Archibald MacLeish's dramatic parable of good and evil—inspired by the Book of Job—has 364 performances. Raymond Massey, Christopher Plummer, and Pat Hingle head the cast. It opens in London at the Phoenix on March 25, 1961, with Paul Rogers, John Clements, and Donald Sinden. There it has only 101 showings.

Dec 23 *A Party With Betty Comden and Adolph Green* (NY—Golden—Revue). The entertainers and lyricists offer sketches and songs from shows they've worked on, including *On the Town*. It runs nearly five weeks, followed by six weeks in April.

FLOWER DRUM SONG

1958   BRITISH PREMIERES

Jan 20 *Cat on a Hot Tin Roof.* See NY premiere, 1955.

Jan 31 *A Touch of the Sun* (L—Saville—Drama). Father and daughter Michael and Vanessa Redgrave, and Diana Wynyard, head the cast in N.C. Hunter's family drama about an idealistic schoolmaster. It has 203 performances.

Feb 5 *The Potting Shed.* See NY premiere, 1957.

Feb 11 *Epitaph for George Dillon* (L—Royal Court—Drama). Robert Stephens plays the title-role in John Osborne's play, written with Anthony Creighton. Dillon is a failed playwright eager to share his self-pity with others. In May the production moves to the Comedy Theatre for 52 performances. On Nov 4, it opens on Broadway at the Golden with Stephens in the lead. It runs three weeks and is revived in January for six weeks.

Feb 20 *Where's Charley?* See NY premiere, 1948.

March 19 *Simple Spymen* (L—Whitehall—Comedy). John Chapman's farce about two street musicians (Brian Rix and Leo Franklyn), mistaken by MI5 as secret agents, has 1,403 performances.

March 26 *Breath of Spring* (L—Cambridge—Comedy). Athene Seyler plays the ringleader of a bunch of aristocratic burglars in Peter Coke's comedy which has a run of 10 months.

March 29 *The Iceman Cometh.* See NY premiere, 1946.

April 2 *Not in the Book* (L—Criterion—Drama). Wilfred Hyde White and Sidney Tafler head the cast in Arthur Watkyn's thriller about a man threatened with blackmail. Actor Nigel Patrick stages; there are 507 performances.

April 9 *The Dock Brief/What Shall We Tell Caroline?* (L—Lyric, Hammersmith—Comedy). John Mortimer's double-bill is staged by Stuart Burge. In the first play, Michael Hordern plays an unsuccessful barrister. In the second, Brenda

Bruce and Maurice Denham play a bickering married couple, with Hordern as the wife's longtime lover.

April 10 *Any Other Business* (L—Westminster—Drama). George Ross and Campbell Singer's thriller concerns a traitor on a board of directors who is passing secrets to a rival company. It runs 22 weeks.

April 17 *The Brass Butterfly* (L—Strand—Comedy). Alastair Sim plays only 36 performances in William Golding's comedy about a Roman emperor who distrusts innovation. Sim also directs.

April 23 *Expresso Bongo* (L—Saville—Musical). In his first musical, Paul Scofield impresses as a small-time agent who makes a Teddy Boy (James Kenney) into a rock star. Elizabeth Ashley is also in the cast of Wolf Mankowitz's and Julian More's show. William Campbell directs and choreographs. The show earns 313 performances.

April 24 *Duel of Angels* (L—Apollo—Drama). Vivien Leigh and Claire Bloom play characters who symbolize vice and virtue in Christopher Fry's adaptation of Jean Giraudoux's play *Pour Lucrece*. Jean–Louis Barrault directs. There are 252 performances.

April 30 *My Fair Lady.* See NY premiere, 1956.

May 8 *Variation on a Theme* (L—Globe—Drama). Terence Rattigan plunders *La Dame aux Camélias* for this tale of a ballet dancer (Jeremy Brett) who falls in love with a glamorous lady (Margaret Leighton) dying of tuberculosis. John Gielgud directs. There are 132 performances.

May 19 *The Birthday Party* (L—Lyric, Hammersmith—Drama). Harold Pinter's play about a man strangely menaced by mysterious visitors to a boarding house, is staged by Peter Wood. Richard Pearson and Beatrix Lehmann head the cast.

May 23 *Large as Life* (L—Palladium—Revue). Comedians Harry Secombe, Terry-

Thomas, Hattie Jacques, and Eric Sykes, head the cast of Robert Nesbitt's new revue which earns a run of 383 performances.

May 28 *The Party* (L—New—Drama). Charles Laughton returns to the London stage after an absence of 22 years in Jane Arden's play about an alcoholic, which he also directs. Albert Finney, Joyce Redman, and Ann Lynn are also in the cast. There are 197 performances.

June 25 *For Adults Only* (L—Strand—Revue). Comic actors Hugh Paddick, Miriam Karlin, and Ron Moody head the cast of this revue, devised by Peter Myers and Alec Grahame. Michael Charnley stages. It wins 293 performances.

July 10 *Living for Pleasure* (L—Garrick—Revue). Sketches, songs, and spoofs, performed by Dora Bryan, Daniel Massey, and Patience Collier, among others, win this revue a run of 379 performances. It is staged by William Chappell, with music by Richard Addinsell, and sketches and lyrics by Arthur Macrae.

July 15 *The Hamlet of Stepney Green* (L—Lyric, Hammersmith—Drama). Bernard Kops' suburban London tragedy, inspired by Shakespeare, is staged by Frank Hauser. John Fraser and Thelma Ruby are in the cast.

July 17 *Irma La Douce* (L—Lyric—Musical). Peter Brook directs this tale of the charming Irma (Elizabeth Seal), who makes love for a living. The French score is by Margaret Monnot and the book and lyrics by Alexandre Breffort. The show has a long run of 1,512 performances. Two years later it opens at New York's Plymouth on Sep 29, 1960. There are 524 performances.

July 17 *Five Finger Exercise* (L—Comedy—Drama). John Gielgud stages Peter Shaffer's play about a tragic failure in communication between a sensitive son (Brian Bedford) and his business-oriented father (Roland Culver). There are 602 performances. Shaffer's London success opens at New York's Music Box, on Dec 2, 1959, where it wins a 42-week run. The Drama Critics' Circle votes this the "Best Foreign Play."

Aug 12 *The Unexpected Guest* (L—Duchess—Drama). Agatha Christie's new murder thriller has a run of 614 performances. Nigel Stock and Renée Asherson head the cast.

Aug 27 *Brouhaha* (L—Aldwych—Comedy). Peter Sellers makes his debut in legitimate theatre as a Sultan, eager to make his obscure nation a leading trouble-spot and so attract foreign aid, in this George Tabori satire. Peter Hall directs.

Sep 10 *Auntie Mame.* See NY premiere, 1956.

Sep 24 *Long Day's Journey into Night.* See NY premiere, 1956.

Sep 28 *The Elder Statesman* (L—Cambridge—Drama). From the Edinburgh Festival comes T.S. Eliot's new play about a man of stainless reputation who is suddenly confronted by some youthful follies he'd sooner forget. Paul Rogers, Alec McCowen, and Anna Massey head the cast in this E. Martin Browne staging, which has only 92 performances.

Oct 2 *Valmouth* (L—Lyric, Hammersmith—Musical). Sandy Wilson adapts

some Ronald Firbank tales as the basis of this musical staged by Vida Hope and Harry Naughton. Beatrice Reading (later replaced by Cleo Laine) and Fenella Fielding are in the cast. Transferring to the Saville Theatre in January, it has 186 performances. It is a rapid Off-Broadway failure at the York Theatre, opening on Oct 6, 1960.

Oct 7 *Shadow of Heroes* (L—Piccadilly—Drama). Robert Ardrey's play of the 1956 Hungarian people's uprising features Emlyn Williams, Alan Webb, Mogens Wieth, and Peggy Ashcroft. It earns only 47 performances. On Dec 5, 1961, the drama opens at New York's York. Henry Hewes selects it as one of the season's "Best Plays," but it has only 20 performances.

Nov 19 *Hook, Line, and Sinker* (L—Piccadilly—Comedy). Robert Morley plays a husband who's nearly done in by his charming but greedy wife (Joan Plowright), in his adaptation of an André Roussin farce. It has 149 performances.

Dec 2 *The Grass is Greener* (L—St. Martin's—Comedy). Celia Johnson, Hugh Williams, Joan Greenwood, and Edward Underdown play 493 performances in Hugh and Margaret Williams's comedy about an earl who opens his stately home to the public.

Dec 12 *West Side Story.* See NY premiere, 1957.

Dec 17 *Two for the Seesaw.* See NY premiere, 1958.

March 26 On Broadway at the Ambassador Theatre, Arnold Moss offers a highly condensed two-act version of Shaw's *Back to Methuselah*, produced by the Theatre Guild. Moss plays Shaw, with Tyrone Power and Faye Emerson as Adam and Eve. It closes after 29 showings.

April 8 At Stratford-upon-Avon, festival director Glen Byam Shaw casts Richard Johnson and Dorothy Tutin as *Romeo and Juliet* at the Shakespeare Memorial Theatre. *Hamlet* follows with Michael Redgrave, and Tutin as Ophelia. Peter Hall stages *Twelfth Night*, with Geraldine McEwan as Olivia. Tony Richardson directs *Pericles*, with Johnson and Zoe Caldwell. Googie Withers and Redgrave are Beatrice and Benedick in *Much Ado About Nothing*, staged by Douglas Seale.

May 15 The Moscow Art Theatre company comes to London, opening tonight at the Sadler's Wells Theatre with Chekhov's *The Cherry Orchard*, staged by Victor Y. Stanitsyn. On the 16th, Chekhov's *The Three Sisters* is presented, staged at Yosif M. Raevski. On May 20, Chekhov's *Uncle Vanya* is offered, staged by M. M. Kedrov. Vassily Orlov plays the title-role. The repertory is rounded out on May 21 with a contemporary Russian play, *The Troubled Past*, by Leonid Rakhmanov. N. M. Gorchakov directs.

June 2 At the Open Air Theatre in London's Regent's Park, Robert Atkins opens the traditional summer Shakespeare season with *Much Ado About Nothing*. On June 23, Leslie French stages *The Taming of the Shrew*. *As You Like It* opens on July 14.

June 10 The Dublin Gate Theatre presents a revival of George S. Kaufman and Moss Hart's *The Man Who Came To Dinner*.

1958 REVIVALS/REPERTORIES

Jan 8 At Joan Littlewood's Theatre Workshop at London's Theatre Royal, Stratford East, Luigi Pirandello's *Man, Beast, and Virtue* is presented. On Feb 21, Littlewood stages the Spanish classic by de Rojas, *Celestina*. On April 15, John Bury directs and designs a Shaw double-bill, *Love and Lectures*—selected from the letters between Shaw and Ellen Terry—and *The Man of Destiny*. Littlewood and Bury team up to offer on April 29, a double-bill of Paul Green's *Unto Such Glory* and Jean-Paul Sartre's *The Respectable Prostitute*. On May 27, Shelagh Delaney's *A Taste of Honey* opens.

Jan 20 At the Sadler's Wells Theatre in London, Franz Lehar's operetta, *The Merry Widow*, is revived, staged by Charles Hickman. It breaks all records at the Wells.

Jan 21 Marcel Marceau returns to New York's City Center. On Feb 19, Jean Dalrymple revives Irving Berlin's *Annie Get Your Gun*. On March 5, the revival is *Wonderful Town*. On March 19, *Oklahoma!* returns.

Feb 3 Off-Broadway at the Phoenix Theatre, Jean Cocteau's *The Infernal Machine*, adapted by Albert Bermel, wins a

five-week run. On March 18, Michael Langham stages *Two Gentlemen of Verona*, imported from Canada's Stratford Festival. On April 1, von Kleist's *The Broken Jug*, also from Canada and staged by Langham, is offered. On April 29, for two weeks, Montreal's French-Canadian troupe, Le Theatre du Nouveau Monde, arrive with three Molière farces and his *Le Malade Imaginaire*.

Feb 19 At London's Old Vic Theatre, *King Lear* is presented in Douglas Seale's staging. Paul Rogers plays Lear. On April 1, *Twelfth Night* opens. Michael Benthall stages. Barbara Jefford, Paul Daneman and John Neville head the cast. On May 13, Benthall stages *Henry VIII*. Harry Andrews plays the king; Edith Evans is Katharine of Aragon. John Gielgud plays Cardinal Wolsey.

Feb 25 At London's Royal Court, the play is Ann Jellicoe's *The Sport of My Mad Mother*, directed by Jellicoe and George Devine. John Dexter stages Doris Lessing's *Each His Own Wilderness* on March 23. On April 2, William Gaskill directs N. F. Simpson's *A Resounding Tinkle* and *The Hole*. Tony Richardson directs Barry Reckord's *Flesh To a Tiger* on May 21.

HOOK, LINE AND SINKER

This is followed by a revival of Joseph Kesselring's *Arsenic and Old Lace*. In November, Liam O'Flaherty's *The Informer* will be staged by Hilton Edwards.

June 18 At London's Royal Court Theatre, the English Stage Society brings back its popular Tony Richardson production of Ionesco's *The Chairs*, preceding it with Eugene Ionesco's *The Lesson*, translated by Donald Watson. Edgar Wreford and Joan Plowright play the leads.

June 19 In Stratford, Connecticut, the American Shakespeare Festival launches its fourth season with Fritz Weaver, playing the title-role in *Hamlet*, staged by John Houseman. Houseman's festival co-director, Jack Landau, stages *A Midsummer Night's Dream*. Landau and Houseman both direct *The Winter's Tale*. George Balanchine choreographs the last two shows.

June 23 The company of Canada's Stratford Shakespeare Festival opens its new season, under the direction of Michael Langham. Langham directs *Henry IV, Part 1*, Douglas Campbell stages *The Winter's Tale*. Langham directs *Much Ado About Nothing*. John Gay's *The Beggar's Opera* is staged by Tom Brown. Marcel Marceau performs his mime creations; the New York Pro Musica is on hand, and Le Theatre du Nouveau Monde offers Molière's *Le Malade Imaginaire*.

July 2 Producer Joseph Papp opens his first free season in Central Park. His New York Shakespeare Festival offers *Othello*, staged by Stuart Vaughan, with William Marshall in the title-role. Papp directs *Twelfth Night*. Later, the new festival receives a Tony Award for its "distinguished services to the theatre."

July 2 Giorgio Strehler, the distinguished Italian director, brings his Piccolo Teatro Della Citta di Milano to London for an engagement at the Sadler's Wells Theatre, where they perform Goldoni's *The Servant of Two Masters*.

July 2 *The Confederacy*, Paul Green's drama about Robert E. Lee's role in the War Between the States, opens today in Viriginia Beach, Virginia. It plays two summers.

July 7 From Glasgow to London's Royal Court Theatre comes the ensemble of the Citizens' Theatre to perform George Munro's tragi-comedy, *Gay Landscape*, directed by Peter Duguid. On July 14, the Court welcomes the Coventry Belgrade Theatre Company, with Arnold Wesker's *Chicken Soup With Barley*. The Salisbury Arts Theatre Company follows on July 21 with Thomas Wiseman's *The Private Prosecutor*. On July 28, the play is Alison Macleod's *Dear Augustine*, produced by the Leatherhead Repertory Company.

July 18 The San Diego National Shakespeare Festival opens today. There are three plays in the repertory: *Much Ado*

NORMAN BELGEDDES

About Nothing, *Antony and Cleopatra*, and *Macbeth*.

July 28 In Ashland, the Oregon Shakespeare Festival opens with *Much Ado About Nothing*, staged by Robert Loper, who also directs *King Lear*. James Sandoe directs the remaining two plays: *The Merchant of Venice* and *Troilus and Cressida*.

Aug 2 Today is the opening of the Colorado Shakespeare Festival's first season, produced on the campus of the University of Colorado, in Boulder. J. H. Crouch stages *Hamlet*, Hal J. Todd directs *Julius Caesar*, and Gerald Kahan stages *The Taming of the Shrew*. The festival's venue is the Mary Rippon Outdoor Theatre, named for the university's first woman teacher. There are 1,000 seats, flanked by classroom buildings.

Aug 24 Britain's Edinburgh International Festival opens. T. S. Eliot's new play, *The Elder Statesman*, had its world premiere here. The Edinburgh Gateway Theatre offers R. J. B. Sellar's *Weir of Hermiston*. Michael Benthall's Old Vic production of *Twelfth Night* is shown in the Assembly Hall, as is Peter Wood's Vic production of Schiller's *Mary Stuart*. Margaret D'Arcy and Colin Blakely are in the cast of *The Bonefire* (sic), staged by Tyrone Guthrie for the Ulster Group Theatre. From London comes the New Watergate Theatre Club's production of O'Neill's *Long Day's Journey into Night*. The Apollo Society offers a special program, *Portraits of Women: From Chaucer to Dylan Thomas*, with Peggy Aschroft and Edith Evans.

Aug 28 Bernard Shaw's *Major Barbara* is revived by George Devine at London's Royal Court Theatre. Joan Plowright is Barbara, with Vanessa Redgrave as sister Sarah. On Sep 30, the English Stage Company gives John Arden's *Live Like Pigs* a production, directed by George Devine and Anthony Page. On Oct 27, Samuel Beckett offers his a one-character play, *Krapp's Last Tape*. It's performed by Patrick Magee and staged by Donald McWhinnie. George Devine directs *End-Game*. Devine and Jack MacGowran play

Hamm and Clov. Both plays staged are British premieres. On Dec 4, the New Watergate's production of Errol John's *Moon on a Rainbow Shawl* opens, staged by Frith Banbury, with Earl Hyman.

Sep 17 At the Old Vic in London, the fall season opens with Schiller's *Mary Stuart*, in the Stephen Spender translation Irene Worth and Catherine Lacey play the rival queens, Mary and Elizabeth. On Oct 7, Douglas Seale directs *Julius Caesar*, with Jack May and Michael Hordern. John Fernald stages Ibsen's *Ghosts* on Nov 12, with Flora Robson and Hordern. On Dec 17, Seale stages *Macbeth*, with Hordern and Beatrix Lehmann.

Oct 4 At Joan Littlewood's Theatre Workshop, at London's Theatre Royal, Stratford East, Brendan Behan's *The Hostage* opens, staged by Littlewood and designed by Sean Kenny. Murray Melvin plays the British soldier held hostage. The production will move to the West End and continue its success with a Broadway staging. On Dec 16, Littlewood has a change of pace, staging her adaptation of Charles Dickens' *A Christmas Carol*.

Oct 14 France's Theatre National Populaire (TNP), directed by Jean Vilar, comes to Broadway for three weeks. In the repertory are five plays. Vilar stages Marivaux' *Le Triomph de l'Amour*, Hugo's *Marie Tudor*, Moliere's *Don Juan*, and Corneille's *Le Cid*. Gerard Philipe directs de Musset's *Lorenzaccio*.

Oct 20 Off-Broadway the Phoenix Theatre offers a four-week American professional premiere of T. S. Eliot's poetic play *The Family Reunion*. Among the company are Lillian Gish and Dorothy Sands.

Nov 20 *Shadow of a Gunman*, Sean O'Casey's play set in Dublin in 1920, with the Irish eager to be free of Britain, has 52 performances at New York's Bijou Theatre. Jack Garfein directs Bruce Dern, Susan Strasberg, and others.

Dec 9 London's Old Vic Company brings a repertory of *Twelfth Night*, *Hamlet*, and *Henry V*, all staged by Michael Benthall, to the Broadway Theatre for five-weeks.

Laurence Harvey plays Henry V; John Neville is Hamlet, with Barbara Jefford as Ophelia and also Viola in *Twelfth Night*.

Dec 15 The D'Oyly Carte Opera Company opens its brief season in London at the Prince's Theatre with *The Gondoliers*, *The Mikado*, and *The Yeomen of the Guard*.

Dec 18 The big pantomime production this year is the Rodgers and Hammerstein *Cinderella* at the London Coliseum. Tommy Steele, the popular Rock star, makes his West End debut as Buttons, with Kenneth Williams and Ted Durante in drag as the unkind step-sisters. This show has been preceded by Joan Littlewood's *A Christmas Carol* (Theatre Royal, Stratford East) and *King Charming* (Lyric,

Hammersmith). It is followed by *Dick Whittington* (Golder's Green Hippodrome), *The Sleeping Beauty* (Palladium), *Peter Pan* (Scala), *Noddy in Toyland* (Victoria Palace), *The Silver King* (Players'), *Where the Rainbow Ends* (New Victoria), *Radio Rescue* (Arts), and *Billy Bunter's Mystery Christmas* (Palace).

Dec 28 John Gielgud interprets sonnets, soliloquies, and scenes from Shakespeare, in *Ages of Man* at New York's 46th Street Theatre. The program is based on George Rylands' *Shakespeare Anthology* and is performed without setting. The engagement is for five weeks; Gielgud also tours the program.

1958   BIRTHS/DEATHS/DEBUTS

Jan 6 Anne Bancroft makes her New York City debut as Gittel Mosca in William Gibson's *Two for the Seesaw* at the Booth Theatre.

Jan 7 Canadian-born actress Margaret Anglin (b. 1876) dies in Toronto. Anglin had her first success as Roxanne in *Cyrano de Bergerac* in 1898. She also played Shakespearean and Greek classical roles.

June 9 English stage and screen actor Robert Donat (b. 1905) dies in London. During his early career, Donat played a number of Shakespearean roles. His last stage appearance was at the Old Vic in 1953 when he played Becket in T. S. Eliot's *Murder in the Cathedral*.

April 8 American drama critic George Jean Nathan (b. 1882) dies in New York City. Nathan championed the dramatic works of O'Neill, O'Casey, Saroyan, and a host of others. He wrote over 30 books on the theatre, including *Testament of Critic*.

April 22 Australian actress Zoe Caldwell, makes her debut in England with the Royal Shakespeare Company in Stratford-upon-Avon in walk-on roles in *Twelfth Night*.

May 3 American scene designer and producer Norman Bel Geddes (b. 1893) dies in New York City. Bel Geddes won in-

stant recognition in 1923 with his designs for Max Reinhardt's production of *The Miracle*. He was very active in the theatre during the 1930s.

July 11 Actress Evelyn Varden (b. 1895) dies in New York. She made her first New York appearance in 1910 in *The Nest Egg*. Later she appeared in *Our Town*, *Present Laughter*, and *She Stoops to Conquer*.

Aug 16 Drama critic and playwright Wolcott Gibbs dies in Ocean Beach, Fire Island, at age 56. Gibb's replaced Robert Benchley as drama critic of *The New Yorker* in 1939. He was the author of the play *Season in the Sun*.

Sep 5 American actress and singer Lulu Glaser (b. 1874) dies in Norwalk, Conn. She became a Broadway star in 1900 when she played the title role in *Sweet Ann Page*.

Sep 22 American author and playwright Mary Roberts Rinehart (b. 1876) dies in New York City. Rinehart is the author of *The Double Life*, *The Avenger*, and *The Breaking Point*. She co-authored, with Avery Hopwood, *Seven Days*, *Spanish Love*, *The Bat*, and *A Thief in the Night*.

Oct 14 Irish playwright and director Lennox Robinson is dead. Among his plays produced at the Abbey Theatre were *The Cross Roads*, *Patriots*, and *The White Headed Boy*. His autobiography, *Three Homes*, was published in 1938.

Dec 20 English stage and screen actress Elizabeth Risdon is dead at age 71. Born in London, Risdon made her first New York appearance in 1912 in *Fanny's First Play*. In 1933 she played the role of Eliza Harris in The Players Classic Revival of *Uncle Tom's Cabin*.

1958   THEATERS/PRODUCTIONS

London's current Lord Chamberlain, the Earl of Scarborough, announces a change in censorship policies regarding homosexual themes in plays, explaining, "This subject is now so widely debated, written about and talked over that its complete exclusion from the stage can no longer be regarded as justifiable."

May The Lunt-Fontanne Theatre (1,550 seats) opens in New York City on West 46th Street and Broadway. The theatre was previously known as the Globe.

June 1 The ten "Best Plays" of the 1957–1958 Broadway season just completed include Osborne's *Look Back in Anger* and *The Entertainer*, Duerren-

matt's *The Visit*, Thomas' *Under Milk Wood*, Anouilh's *Time Remembered*, Lawler's *Summer of the 17th Doll*, Wishengrad's *The Rope Dancers*, Schary's *Sunrise at Campobello*, Inge's *The Dark at the Top of the Stairs*, and Fring's *Look Homeward, Angel*, which wins both the Pulitzer Prize and the Drama Critics' Circle Award for "Best American Play." Other Circle Awards go to *The Music Man* and *Look Back in Anger*.

June 1 Garrison Sherwood, reporting at the close of the 1957–1958 Off-Broadway season, notes that there are now more than 40 Off-Broadway theatres. In the past season, there have been over a hundred productions. Off-Broadway has recently produced, successfully, plays which have been effective failures on Braodway. A few are *Summer and Smoke*, *The Crucible*, *Ardele*, and *The Iceman Cometh*.

July 31 In Ashland, the Oregon Shakespeare Festival completes the production cycle of Shakespeare's entire canon of dramas with the opening today of *Troilus and Cressida*.

Sep 2 President Dwight D. Eisenhower signs a bill passed by Congress to establish in Washington, D.C., a National Capital Center for the Performing Arts. Later, the Center will be named the John F. Kennedy Center for the Performing Arts.

LUNT-FONTANNE THEATRE

Jan 27 *Rashomon* (NY—Music Box—Drama). Claire Bloom, Rod Steiger, and Oscar Homolka have a 20-week run in Fay and Michael Kanin's dramatization of the Japanese film *Rashomon*, in which different versions of a murder are told by the participants. Peter Glenville directs. Sets and costumes by Oliver Messel.

Jan 29 *Tall Story* (NY—Belasco—Comedy). Marc Connelly and Hans Conried play two professors in Howard Lindsay and Russel Crouse's adaptation of Howard Nemerov's novel about an academically weak basketball star. Herman Shumlin stages. It has 108 performances.

Jan 30 *Requiem for a Nun* (NY—Golden—Drama). For those who want more of the adventures of Temple Drake, first met in William Faulkner's *Sanctuary* and continued in this tale, Ruth Ford plays Temple. Bertice Reading plays Nancy, who has found God even though she's killed Temple's child, to keep Temple from deserting her husband. Scott McKay and Zachary Scott play Gowan and Gavin Stevens. Tony Richardson directed this production, designed by Motley, at London's Royal Court Theatre in 1957. It has 43 performances on Broadway.

Feb 5 *Redhead* (NY—46th Street—Musical). Dancer Gwen Verdon is the intended victim of a Jack-the-Ripper character in this book by Dorothy Fields, Herbert Fields, Sidney Sheldon and David Shaw. Richard Kiley co-stars. Albert Hague writes the music. Bob Fosse directs and choreographs. It wins 452 performances.

Feb 16 *A Majority of One* (NY—Shubert—Comedy). Gertrude Berg plays a nice Jewish mother who charms a reserved Japanese widower (Cedric Hardwicke) in this East-meets-West play by Leonard Spigelgass. It has 556 performances. Molly Picon and Robert Morley lead the cast in the London version of the play premiered at the Phoenix on March 9, 1960. It runs nearly 29 weeks.

March 3 *Look After Lulu* (NY—Henry Miller—Comedy). Noel Coward gets only a five-week run from his version of Feydeau's *Occupe-toi d'Amelie*. Tammy Grimes is featured. The English Stage Company premieres the comedy at London's Royal Court on July 29, with Vivien Leigh in the lead. On Sep 8, the show transfers to the New Theatre for a run of 165 performances.

March 10 *Sweet Bird of Youth* (NY—Martin Beck—Drama). Elia Kazan stages Tennessee Williams' play about an aging actress, her paid stud, and the girl he left behind, with Geraldine Page, Paul Newman, Diana Hyland, Rip Torn, and Sidney Blackmer. Page is "fabulous;" Newman "the perfect companion-piece," says

Brooks Atkinson. The play has 375 performances.

March 11 *A Raisin in the Sun* (NY—Ethel Barrymore—Drama). Sidney Poitier and Claudia McNeil head the cast in Lorraine Hansberry's black family drama which raises questions about matriarchy, manhood, and self-fulfillment. Lloyd Richards directs; there are 530 performances. It wins the Drama Critics' Circle Award for Best American Play. On Aug 4, the drama premieres in London at the Adelphi with Kim Hamilton, Earle Hyman, and Juanita Moore. Here it has only 78 performances.

March 19 *First Impressions* (NY—Alvin—Musical). Abe Burrows stages and adapts Jane Austen's *Pride and Prejudice* but critics find it wooden. Hermione Gingold, Polly Bergen, and Farley Granger head the cast. It has 92 performances.

April 23 *Destry Rides Again* (NY—Imperial—Musical). Andy Griffith is the gentle, law-abiding sheriff; Dolores Gray is the dance-hall girl who comes to love him, in Leonard Gershe's adaptation of Max Brand's story. It has 472 showings. Harold Rome writes the score; Michael Kidd stages and choreographs.

May 21 *Gypsy* (NY—Broadway—Musical). Ethel Merman earns 702 performances as the ambitious stage mother in Arthur Laurents' book based on the memoirs of Gypsy Rose Lee. Sandra Church and Lane Bradbury play her daughters. Jerome Robbins stages, with score by Jule Styne and lyrics by Stephen Sondheim.

July 15 *The Connection* (NY—Living Theatre—Drama). Jack Gelber's play about heroin addiction earns 722 performances. Among the cast are Carl Lee and Warren Finnerty. Judith Malina directs. Julian Beck designs.

Oct 1 *The Gang's All Here* (NY—Ambassador—Drama). Jerome Lawrence and Robert E. Lee's play examines a corrupt presidency and has Melvyn Douglas, Jean Dixon, and E.G. Marshall among the cast. George Roy Hill stages. There are 132 performances.

Oct 8 *At the Drop of a Hat*. See L premiere, 1957.

Oct 12 *Cheri* (NY—Morosco—Drama). Anita Loos adapts two Colette novels and comes up with a drama about a gigolo (Horst Bucholz), in love with an aging cocotte (Kim Stanley), who kills himself. The play dies after seven weeks. Robert Lewis stages.

Oct 19 *The Miracle Worker* (NY—Playhouse—Drama). Anne Bancroft is the teacher trying to communicate with the young deaf and blind Helen Keller (Patty Duke) in William Gibson's much admired play, which has 700 performances.

MAJORITY OF ONE — GERTRUDE BER[G]

Patricia Neal is also in the cast. There is a run of nearly 34 weeks following the London premiere at the Royalty on March 9, 1961. Janina Faye and Anna Massey lead the cast.

Oct 21 *Flowering Cherry*. See L premiere, 1957.

Oct 22 *Take Me Along* (NY—Shubert—Musical). Jackie Gleason plays the bibulous Uncle Sid in this musical version of O'Neill's *Ah, Wilderness* which runs for 448 performances. Walter Pidgeon is also in the cast. Peter Glenville stages this Joseph Stein and Robert Russell adaptation, with songs by Robert Merrill.

Nov 5 *The Tenth Man* (NY—Booth—Drama). Paddy Chayevsky's play about a modern Jewish exorcism is staged by Tyrone Guthrie and has 623 performances. Lou Jacobi, Jack Gilford, and Gene Saks are among the cast. This rewriting of *The Dybbuk* runs 132 performances following its premiere at London's Comedy on April 13, 1961.

Nov 16 *The Sound of Music* (NY—Lunt-Fontanne—Musical). Mary Martin plays the governess who finds a ready-made family and stern but loving husband (Theodore Bikel) in Howard Lindsay and Russel Crouse's adaptation of Baroness Maria von Trapp's book. The score by Richard Rodgers and Oscar Hammerstein II includes such hits as "Climb Every Mountain." There are 1,443 performances. The show opens at London's Palace on May 18, 1961, where it wins 2,386 performances, nearly twice the New York run. Jean Bayless and Roger Dann lead the cast.

ov 18 *Little Mary Sunshine* (NY—Orheum—Musical). Rick Besoyan spoofs perettas in this love story set in the ockies. He wins 1,143 performances. Ei-en Brennan and William Graham head he company. Ray Harrison stages.

ov 23 *Fiorello!* (NY—Broadhurst—Musical). The saga of New York's Mayor aGuardia, written and staged by Jerome eidman and George Abbott, has 795 erformances and wins the Drama Crit-:s' Circle Award for Best Musical Production. Tom Bosley plays the mayor; Jerry rock and Sheldon Harnick provide mu-.c and lyrics; Peter Gennaro choreo-:aphs.

ov 28 *A Loss of Roses* (NY—O'Neill—rama). Warren Beatty, Betty Field, and arol Haney have only 25 performances William Inge's play about a young man ho seeks escape from his possessive other through marriage. Daniel Mann irects.

ec 2 *Five Finger Exercise.* See L pre-iere, 1958.

ec 3 *Silent Night, Lonely Night* (NY—1orosco—Drama). Henry Fonda and Bar-bara Bel Geddes play unhappily married strangers who have a brief encounter on Christmas Eve in Robert Anderson's play, which has 124 performances. Peter Glenville directs.

Dec 8 *The Fighting Cock* (NY—ANTA—Comedy). Jean Anouilh's angry general in unwilling retirement, waiting to be recalled by a fickle France, is like Charles DeGaulle in his post-war withdrawal. Rex Harrison is the cocky general. Peter Brook stages. This play runs 11 weeks.

Dec 16 *Goodbye, Charlie* (NY—Lyceum—Comedy). A notorious womanizer, recently deceased, returns in the body of a beautiful woman (Lauren Bacall), and his best friend (Sidney Chaplin) now finds his former buddy very attractive. George Axelrod stages his own play, which has 109 showings.

Dec 29 *The Andersonville Trial* (NY—Henry Miller—Drama). Saul Levitt's play, based on the trial of the commandant of the infamous Civil War prison, Andersonville, is staged by Jose Ferrer and has 179 performances. Herbert Berghof and Russell Hardie head the cast.

---

959   BRITISH PREMIERES

an 8 *Eighty in the Shade* (L—Globe—rama). Sybil Thorndike plays a retired :tress with a nagging daughter (Valerie aylor) and a loving but unsuccessful son Robert Flemyng) in Clemence Dane's lay, which has 180 performances. Lio-el Harris stages.

an 15 *The Rose Tattoo.* See NY pre-iere, 1951.

larch 5 *Clown Jewels* (L—Victoria Pal-:e—Revue). The Crazy Gang (Bud Flan-ngan, Teddy Knox, Jimmy Nervo, Char-e Naughtonl and Jimmy Gold) head the ast and have a run of 818 performances.

pril 2 *Fool's Paradise* (L—Apollo—omedy). Cicely Courtneidge and Nora winburne play impoverished widows, :rmer wives of the same man, forced to is will to share the same house, in Peter oke's farce. Staged by Allan Davis, it has 57 performances.

pril 22 *How Say You?* (L—Aldwych—omedy). Ann Firbank plays a female arrister seeking to establish the marriage f Mrs. Pudney (Kathleen Harrison) whose :cords have been destroyed by a bomb, John Counsell's staging of Harold rooke and Kay Bannerman's play. It has 09 performances.

pril 23 *The Pleasure of His Company.* ee NY premiere, 1958.

pril 30 *Candide.* See NY premiere, 1956.

lay 5 *The World of Paul Slickey* (L—alace—Musical). John Osborne writes nd directs his first musical, about a de-structive gossip columnist (Dennis Lotis), but it has only 47 performances. The score is by Christopher Whelan.

May 6 *Let Them Eat Cake* (L—Cambridge—Comedy). Frederick Lonsdale's comedy, previously produced in the suburbs as *Half A Loaf*, has only 117 performances. Dulcie Gray and Michael Denison head the cast. Wallace Douglas directs.

May 29 *Swinging Down the Lane* (L—Palladium—Revue). Comedian-singer Max Bygraves heads the cast in Robert Nesbitt's new revue, which has 328 performances.

June 5 *Farewell, Farewell, Eugene* (L—Garrick—Comedy). Peggy Mount and Margaret Rutherford play two elderly sisters who have pinned all their fading hopes on the talents of the unseen Eugene, for whom they are saving money. Eugene proves not worth waiting for in John Vari's play, adapted by Rodney Ackland. William Chappell directs. The play runs nearly nine months, a sharp contrast with its later rapid failure on Broadway.

June 13 *The French Mistress* (L—Adelphi—Comedy). Robert Monro (pseudonym for Sonnie Hale) has a run of 23 weeks with this comedy headed by Marie-Claire Verlene. Joan Riley directs.

June 18 *The Complaisant Lover* (L—Globe—Comedy). Ralph Richardson plays a kindly but failed husband who indulges his wife's (Phyllis Calvert) liaison with a bookseller (Paul Scofield) in Graham Greene's new play. It has a 50-week run. On Nov 1, 1961, it opens at the Ethel Barrymore in New York with a cast including Michael Redgrave, Sandy Dennis, Googie Withers, Gene Wilder and Richard Johnson.

July 16 *Ring of Truth* (L—Savoy—Comedy). Wynyard Browne's domestic comedy centers on the complications which arise when a wife (Margaret Johnston) loses her engagement ring. David Tomlinson plays the husband. Frith Banbury directs. It runs 31 weeks.

Aug 4 *A Raisin in the Sun.* See NY premiere, 1959.

Aug 5 *The Sound of Murder* (L—Aldwych—Drama). Peter Cushing, Patricia Jessel and Elizabeth Sellars head the cast of William Fairchild's thriller which attracts audiences for 229 showings. Fred Sadoff stages.

Aug 6 *Fine Fettle* (L—Palace—Revue). Comedian Benny Hill stars in this revue he's devised with Dave Freeman. There are 181 performances.

Aug 12 *The Aspern Papers* (L—Queen's—Comedy). Michael Redgrave adapts Henry James' novel and heads the cast as Aspern, the American poet. Beatrix Lehmann plays his aging mistress; Flora Robson is her niece. Basil Dean directs. It has 370 performances.

Sep 8 *Look After Lulu.* See NY premiere, 1959.

Sep 10 *The Crooked Mile* (L—Cambridge—Musical). There are 164 showings of Peter Wildblood's musical about two Soho street gangs. Millicent Martin and Elizabeth Welch are in the cast. Jean Meyer directs, with a score by Peter Greenwell.

Sep 15 *The Ginger Man* (L—Fortune—Drama). Richard Harris, Ronald Fraser, Wendy Craig, and Isabel Dean have only 23 performances in J.P. Donleavy's play. Philip Wiseman directs.

Sep 23 *Pieces of Eight* (L—Apollo—Revue). Peter Cook, Harold Pinter, and Sandy Wilson are among the contributors to this revue which has a run of 430 performances. Kenneth Williams and Fenella Fielding head the cast. Paddy Stone stages, with music by Laurie Johnson, and designs by Tony Walton.

Oct 6 *One More River* (L—Duke of York's—Drama). Paul Rogers and Robert Shaw are among the cast of Beverly Cross' play about men under stress in wartime, but it has only 70 performances. Guy Hamilton directs.

Oct 27 *Rollo* (L—Strand—Comedy). Marcel Achard's wry tale of friendship, adapted by Felicity Douglas, has 127 performances. Leo McKern and Freddy Mayne play the friends in this Frank Hauser staging.

Oct 29 *The Marriage-Go-Round.* See NY premiere, 1958.

Nov 17 *The World of Susie Wong.* See NY premiere, 1958.

Dec 9 *The Amorous Prawn* (L—Saville—Comedy). Evelyn Laye heads the cast of Anthony Kimmin's comedy and has 448 performances as a general's wife who turns her official residence into a private hotel while her husband is off on assignment. Murray MacDonald stages.

Dec 13 *A Clean Kill* (L—Criterion—Drama). Alastair Sim directs Peter Copley and Rachel Roberts in Michael Gilbert's thriller about a pharmacist who plans a murder. It has 142 performances.

Dec 26 *When in Rome* (L—Adelphi—Musical). Comedian Dickie Henderson plays a suspicious newlywed who can't believe his wife's best-selling novel about a virile hero is based only on fantasy, in this Italian musical with a score by Kramer, and libretto by Garinei and Giovanni. Harold French stages. It runs 37 weeks.

1959   REVIVALS/REPERTORIES

Jan 5 The D'Oyly Carte's Gilbert & Sullivan season at London's Prince's Theatre continues with *Pricess Ida*, *Trial by Jury* and *The Pirates of Penzance*, and *Iolanthe*.

Jan 7 *The Long and the Short and the Tall,* by Willis Hall, is presented at London's Royal Court Theatre, staged by Clifford Williams. A British patrol in Japanese-occupied Maylaya is cut off from its battalion. Peter O'Toole, and Alfred Lynch are among the cast. Lindsay Anderson directs. The play has been first seen at the Edinburgh Festival, as *The Disciplines of War.* It will transfer to the New Theatre. On Feb 8, director Lindsay Anderson stages Alun Owen's *Progress to the Park* without decor. Donal Donnelly and Margaret Tyzack are in the cast. On April 9, Donald Howarth's *Lady on the Barometer* returns with decor and with a new title, *Sugar in the Morning.* William Gaskill directs; Sean Kenny designs. On April 26, Anderson directs Christopher Logue's "News-play," *The Trial of Cob and Leach.* On May 14, Tennessee Williams' *Orpheus Descending* is staged by Tony Richardson. Among the cast are Diane Cilento, and Bessie Love. On May 17, Victor Rietti stages his translation of Luigi Pirandello's *The Shameless Professor,* playing the lead.

Jan 21 At Joan Littlewood's Theatre Workshop at London's Theatre Royal, Stratford East, Shelagh Delaney's *A Taste of Honey* is revived, with Clifton Jones as the black sailor. *Fings Ain't Wot They Used T' Be,* with songs by Lionel Bart and book by Frank Norman, opens Feb 17. Littlewood directs. Playwright Delaney and Richard Harris are in the cast. On April 24, Littlewood revives John Marston's Jacobean drama, *The Dutch Courtesan.* In the cast are Harris, Yootha Joyce, Rachel Roberts, and others. On May 14, Behan's *The Hostage* is revived.

Jan 27 At London's Lyric, Hammersmith, *Danton's Death,* by George Buechner, is presented and directed by Caspar Wrede. This drama of the French Revolution is now receiving its first professional British production. It's also the opening production of the 59 Theatre Company. Patrick Wymark and the play's translator, James Maxwell, are in the cast. On March 3, Wrede and his 59 Theatre Company resident at the Lyric, Hammersmith present Michael Meyer's translation of Strindberg's *Creditors,* staged by Wrede. Also on the bill is Thomas Otway's version of Molière's farce, *The Cheats of Scapin,* directed by Peter Dews. Mai Zetterling is in the Strindberg drama. On April 8, Meyer's translation of Ibsen's *Brand* is staged by Michael Elliott, with Patrick McGoohan and Patrick Wymark. On June 1, Wrede stages Alun Owen's *The Rough and Ready Lot,* Among the cast is Alan Dobie.

Jan 29 At London's Arts Theatre, John Whiting's translations of Jean Anouilh's *Madame de . . .* and *Traveller Without Luggage* are offered by director Peter Hall. Elizabeth Sellars plays Madame de. She's also in the latter play, as are Denholm Elliott, Joyce Carey, and others. On March 12, Toby Robertson stages Kenneth Jupp's *The Buskers.*

Feb 10 Shelagh Delaney's *A Taste of Honey* moves from Joan Littlewood's Theatre Royal, Stratford East, to London's West End. At Wyndham's Theatre it wins a run of 350 performances.

Feb 10 Jean Dalrymple revives Frank Loesser's *The Most Happy Fella* at the New York City Center. On February 25, the show revived is *Say, Darling,* with Robert Morse repeating his Broadway role of brash young producer. *Lute Song* is brought back on March 12.

Feb 11 Continuing its London season at the Old Vic Theatre the company offers a double-bill of Moliere comedies: *Sganarelle* and *Tartuffe,* both translated by Miles Malleson. Malleson plays the lead in the first play. Douglas Seale stages. On March 18, Arthur Wing Pinero's now classic comedy, *The Magistrate,* is revived, also directed by Seale, with Michael Hordern. On April 29, Shelley's *The Cenci* is revived, staged by Michael Benthall. Hugh Griffith and Barbara Jefford lead the cast.

Feb 24 At the Phoenix Theatre Off-Broadway, Farquhar's *The Beaux' Stratagem* gets a two-week revival, staged by Stuart Vaughan, with a cast including Barbara Barrie and June Havoc. On May 11, the Phoenix produces *Once Upon a Mattress* with a score by Mary Rodgers, Richard Rodgers' daughter. Jay Thompson, Marshall Barer, and Dean Fuller base the book on the old tale of the princess who was so sensitive she could feel a pea beneath a mattress. Carol Burnett is Princess Winnifred. The show has 460 performances moving to Broadway.

March 16 Peter Daubeny continues his work of importing major foreign troupes to the London stage. Tonight the Comedie Francaise opens at the Prince's Theatre with Feydau's *Le Dindon,* staged by Jean Meyer. On March 23, Meyer mounts Molière's *Les Femmes Savantes.* On March 31, the bill is De Musset's *Un Caprice* and Molière's *Les Fourberies de Scapin.* The latter, a triumph of farce in the company's repertoire, is the personal success of Robert Hirsch, who plays Scapin and also designs, directed by Jacques Charon.

April The Dublin Gate Theatre produces Brecht's *Mother Courage,* staged by Hilton Edwards. Bernard Shaw's *Saint Joan* is revived in May. Denis Johnston's *Dreaming Dust* has a revival in September.

April 7 This is Glen Byam Shaw's last season as director of the Shakespeare Memorial Theatre in Stratford-upon-Avon. It is also the 100th anniversary season. Tony Richardson's production of *Othello* opens, with Paul Robeson as the Moor, Sam Wanamaker as Iago, Albert Finney as Cassio, and Mary Ure as Desdemona. Tyrone Guthrie stages *All's Well That Ends Well,* with Edith Evans and Zoe Caldwell. Peter Hall's *A Midsummer Night's Dream* features Charles Laughton as Bottom and Vanessa Redgrave as Helena. Hall has Boris Aronson design sets for *Coriolanus* with Laurence Olivier in the title role and Evans as his mother. Laughton plays the lead in *King Lear,* staged by Glen Byam Shaw.

April 15 *Triple Play* opens at New York's Playhouse Theatre. The Theatre Guild and Dore Schary co-produce this program consisting of Tennessee Williams' *Portrait of a Madonna,* Chekhov's *The Harmful Effects of Tobacco,* and O'Casey's *A Pound on Demand* and *Bedtime Story.* Hume Cronyn stages and acts, joined by Jessica Tandy, among others. There are 37 showings.

April 16 *Die Fledermaus,* Johann Strauss operetta, produced by the Sadler's Well's Opera Company, opens at the London Coliseum after critical acclaim and a good run at the Wells.

May 4 From Malmo in Sweden, the Municipal Theatre Company comes to London's Prince's Theatre to present its acclaimed production of Goethe's *Urfaust,* in the Swedish version of Bertil Malmberg. The play's director is Ingmar Bergman. His Faust is Max Von Sydow.

SOUND OF MUSIC

May 21 At London's Arts Theatre, American actor-director Burgess Meredith stages *Ulysses in Nighttown*, Marjorie Barkentin's adaptation of portions of James Joyce's *Ulysses*. Zero Mostel plays Leopold Bloom, with Alan Badel as Stephen Dedalus.

May 28 *Lock Up Your Daughters* opens Bernard Miles' new Mermaid Theatre in the City of London. This is Miles' musical adaptation of Henry Fielding's *Rape on Rape*, with lyrics by Lionel Bart and music by Laurie Johnson. Directed by Peter Coe and designed by Sean Kenny, with choreography by Gilbert Vernon, the show rapidly becomes a popular favorite. Kenny's talents as a designer, using a revolving stage and ingenious lighting, are singled out for praise. Stephanie Voss, Richard Wordsworth and Hy Hazell are in the cast.

June 6 Today the American Shakespeare Festival in Stratford, Connecticut, opens its fifth season. The three new productions are *The Merry Wives of Windsor*, *All's Well That Ends Well*, and *Romeo and Juliet*.

June 9 The London Old Vic ensemble celebrates the tercentenary of English composer Henry Purcell's birth with a revival of *The Tempest, or The Enchanted Island*, John Dryden and William Davenant's adaptation of Shakespeare's play, with a score by Purcell. Douglas Seale directs, with choreography by Peter Wright. John Phillips, Natasha Pam and Joss Ackland head the cast.

June 11 From its initial success at Joan Littlewood's Theatre Workshop at London's Theatre Royal, Stratford East, Brendan Behan's Irish musical tragi-comedy, *The Hostage*, transfers to Wyndham's Theatre in the West End. This new production will have a run of 422 performances. Later, the play will be seen both on and Off Broadway.

June 16 In London's Regent's Park it's time for summer Shakespeare in the Open Air Theatre. Robert Atkins offers *Twelfth Night* and his accustomed role of Sir Toby Belch. On July 13, the production is *A Midsummer Night's Dream*, with Atkins

in his perennial role of Bottom. He has also staged.

June 23 Producers Lee Henry and Jean Arnold launch a San Francisco Shakespeare Festival with *The Tempest*, *Macbeth*, and *Much Ado About Nothing*. Rolf Forsberg is director.

June 26 The Stephen Foster Drama Association presents *The Stephen Foster Story*, a drama of the life and music of the great American composer by Paul Green. It is produced in My Old Kentucky Home State Park in Bardstown, Kentucky.

June 27 Kermit Hunter's *The Golden Crucible* is presented in the Pittsburgh Bicentennial Amphitheatre in Pennsylvania, during the summer. The play is in two acts, taking place in Western Pennsylvania, in what is now Allegheny County. The time of action is from 1753 to 1946.

June 29 Canada's Stratford Shakespeare Festival gets underway, guided by artistic director Michael Langham. Jean Gascon and George McCowan co-direct *Othello*. *As You Like It* comes to life under the care of director Peter Wood. Tom Brown stages Offenbach's *Orpheus in the Underworld*. Louis Applebaum, Stratford's major composer, conducts. The operetta is performed by singers John McCollum and Martial Singher, among others. *Shakespeare and Music* is a musical diversion. Norman Jewison stages a revue, *After Hours*. The Festival company includes Irene Worth, Roberta Maxwell, William Hutt, and Douglas Campbell.

June 30 At London's Royal Court Theatre, the English Stage Company presents Arnold Wesker's *Roots*. John Dexter directs a cast including Joan Plowright and Alan Howard. The play has been previously produced in the city of Coventry. On July 30, *Roots* transfers to the Duke of York's Theatre for 52 performances.

July 9 At London's Arts Theatre, Morton Wishengrad's American play, *The Rope Dancers*, opens, staged by Peter Cotes. Another American play, Harry Kurnitz' *Once More, With Feeling*, opens the same

evening at the New Theatre, but it lasts just 52 performances, even with Robert Morley staging and Dorothy Tutin and John Neville in the cast.

July 9 Franz Lehar's *The Land of Smiles*, another successful operetta revival by the Sadler's Wells Opera Company transfers from the Wells to the West End's Coliseum.

July 28 *Twelfth Night*, directed by festival founder Angus Bowmer, opens the Oregon Shakespeare Festival in Ashland. Richard Risso stages *King John*, followed by *Measure for Measure* and *Antony and Cleopatra*. Jerry Turner stages *The Maske of the New World*. All plays are performed uncut and without intermission in the open-air Elizabethan Theatre.

Aug 4 At the Queen's Theatre in London's West End, The National Youth Theatre present Shakespeare's *Hamlet*, directed by Michael Croft.

Aug 23 Britain's Edinburgh International Festival opens. Tyrone Guthrie's admired production of *The Thrie Estaites*, a 16th century Scots play, is revived at the Assembly Hall. The Perth Theatre Company offers Eric Linklater's *Breakspear in Gascony*, staged by Julian Herington, with Christopher Burgess. The Old Vic Company presents Michael Benthall's staging of Congreve's *The Double-Dealer*. Maggie Smith, Judi Dench, Alec McCowen, and others are in the cast. The Birmingham Repertory Company arrives with *Gammer Gurton's Needle* and *Fratricide Punished*, staged by Bernard Hepton. Bernard Shaw's *Candida* is the Dundee Repertory Theatre's contribution. It's staged by Raymond Westwell. James Bridie's *The Baikie Charivari*, directed by Peter Duguid is presented by the Glasgow Citizens' Theatre. Sean O'Casey's *Cock-A-Doodle-Dandy*, staged by George Devine and designed by Sean Kenny, is the offering of the English Stage Company. Patrick Magee is among the cast. Michael Flanders and Donald Swann share their intimate, two-man revue, *At the Drop of a Hat*.

Sep 3 London's Old Vic Company opens its fall season with *As You Like It*, staged by Wendy Toye. Barbara Jefford is Rosalind, with Maggie Smith as Celia. Others include Alec McCowen and Judi Dench. On September 7, Congreve's *The Double-Dealer* is presented, staged by Michael Benthall. Donald Houston is in the title-role. On October 13, Wilde's *The Importance of Being Earnest* is staged by Benthall with McCowen and Fay Compton. Val May stages *Richard II* with the Vic ensemble, opening on November 17. John Justin plays the king. On December 22, the troupe offers a holiday treat, written to please Queen Elizabeth I, *The Merry Wives of Windsor*, staged by John Hale.

Sep 17 John Gielgud and Margaret Leighton play Benedick and Beatrice in the Cambridge Drama Festival revival of

Shakespeare's *Much Ado About Nothing*, imported to Broadway from Britain. It runs seven weeks, directed by Gielgud.

Sep 17 At London's Royal Court, the English Stage Company presents the London opening of Sean O'Casey's *Cock-A-Doodle-Dandy*, written over a decade ago but just premiered at the Edinburgh Festival. George Devine directs, with designs by Sean Kenny. Patrick Magee, Colin Blakely, and Pauline Flanagan appear. On Sep 6, Arnold Wesker's *The Kitchen* opens, based on his experiences as a pastry-cook. John Dexter directs the production without decor. Alan Howard, Nigel Davenport, and Robert Stephens are in the large cast. On Oct 22, John Arden's searing drama, *Serjeant Musgrave's Dance*, is staged by Lindsay Anderson. Dudley Moore provides music. Ian Bannen, Donal Donnelly, Alan Dobie, Frank Finlay, and others are in the cast. On Nov 18, Henrik Ibsen's *Rosmersholm*, in a translation by Ann Jellicoe, is revived by director George Devine. Peggy Ashcroft, Eric Porter, and Patrick Magee head the cast. On November 22, John Bird stages a production without decor, Frederick Bland's *The Naming of Murderer's Rock*. On Dec 22, *One Way Pendulum*, N. F. Simpson's rollicking surreal excursion into working-class family-life opens prior to a February transfer to the West End's Criterion Theatre. William Gaskill stages.

Sep 30 At London's Arts Theatre, Friedrich Duerrenmatt's Swiss satire, *The Marriage of Mr. Mississippi*, is staged by Clifford Williams.

Oct 6 Off-Broadway, the Phoenix Theatre revives Eugene O'Neill's mask-play, *The Great God Brown* for a four-week run, staged by Stuart Vaughan. In the cast are Fritz Weaver and John Heffernan, among others. On November 24, Jean Gascon stages a revival of Aristophanes' *Lysistrata*, with Nan Martin in the title role, for three weeks. Will Steven Armstrong designs. On December 26, Paul Shyre's reading version of O'Casey's *Pictures in the Hallway*, staged by Vaughan, is revived.

Oct 18 Maurice Evans plays Captain Shotover and co-produces this revival of Shaw's *Heartbreak House*, which has a 14-week Broadway run, staged by Harold

Clurman. Among the cast are Diane Cilento, Pamela Brown, and Diana Wynyard.

Oct 19 Joan Littlewood stages Wolf Mankowitz's musical, *Make Me an Offer*, with music by Monty Norman and David Heneker, at her Theatre Workshop at London's Theatre Royal, Stratford East. Among the cast are Daniel Massey, Sheila Hancock and Dilys Lay. This production transfers to the New Theatre in the West End for 211 performances. On December 22, Littlewood again presents *Fings Ain't Wot They Used T' Be*.

Dec 10 At London's Lyric, Hammersmith, Colin Graham stages a musical version of *Sweeney Todd, the Demon Barber of Fleet Street*, now called *The Demon Barber*, with book by Donald Cotton and score by Brian Burke. Disley Jones designs.

Dec 14 At his new Mermaid Theatre, Bernard Miles welcomes the holiday season early with his version of Robert Louis Stevenson's *Treasure Island*, staged by Peter Coe and designed by Sean Kenny. Miles plays Long John Silver. On December 17, *Aladdin* opens at the Coliseum, staged by Robert Helpmann, with Loudon Sainthill's designs. On the 18th, the Scala opens *Peter Pan*, followed on the 22nd at the Victoria Palace by *Billy Bunter Flies East*. On the 23rd, the Palladium has *Humpty Dumpty* (Harry Secombe) on view, with *Noddy in Toyland* at the Prince's Theatre, and *Beauty and the Beast* at the Arts. On the 26th, *Alice in Wonderland* opens at the Winter Garden and *The Princess and the Swineherd* at the Theatre Royal, Stratford East.

Dec 18 Tonight's opening night of Toronto Workshop Productions in Çanada. A double-bill of Chekhov's *The Boor* and Garcia Lorca's *Don Perlimplin* is presented under the direction of founder George Luscombe. The company is to work on the principles of Joan Littlewood's group theatre in London, and will often present political works in a highly entertaining way.

Dec 29 The Dallas Theatre Center formally opens with Eugene McKinney's adaptation of the Thomas Wolfe classic, *Of Time and the River*. Paul Baker, the artistic director and founder of the Center, does the staging.

City debut in the Off-Broadway production of Nathaniel Banks' *Season of Choice* at the Barbizon-Plaza Theatre.

May 4 Ashley Dukes (b. 1885) has been a producer, drama critic, and playwright (*Man With a Load of Mischief*). He dies in London.

June 18 Stage and screen actress Ethel Barrymore (b. 1879) dies in Beverly Hills. Daughter of Maurice and Georgiana Drew Barrymore, she scored her first success in *Captain Jinks of the Horse Marines* in 1901. She also appeared as Ophelia, Juliet, Portia, and Camille. In 1928 she opened New York's Ethel Barrymore Theatre playing in *The Kingdom of God*.

EIGHTY IN THE SHADE

Aug 6 Actor-producer Clarence Derwent (b. 1884) dies in New York. Born in London, Derwent began his long career on Broadway in 1915. Author of several plays, he instituted the annual Clarence Derwent Awards for the best supporting male and female performances.

Aug 18 American producer Theresa Helburn (b. 1889) dies in Norwalk, Connecticut. Helburn, a former actress, and drama critic of *The Nation*, became administrative director of the Theatre Guild in 1933.

Sep 6 British stage and screen actor Edmund Gwenn (b. 1875) dies in Woodland Hills, California. Gwenn made his London debut in 1899. He later became famous for his portrayal of lower middle class characters in such plays as *The Twelve Pound Look* and *Laburnum Grove*.

Sep 11 Stage and screen actor Paul Douglas (b. 1907) dies in Hollywood.

1959 BIRTHS/DEATHS/DEBUTS

Jan 1 English author and dramatist Laurence Housman (b. 1865) dies in Somerset. Housman had his first play, *Bethlehem*, produced in 1902. *Victoria Regina* is his most successful play. Housman's memoir, *The Unexpected Years*, was published in 1937.

Feb 28 Playwright Maxwell Anderson (b. 1888) dies in Stamford, Connecticut. Anderson co-authored the popular *What*

Price Glory? with Laurence Stallings in 1924. Among his works are *Elizabeth the Queen, Night Over Taos, Mary of Scotland, Valley Forge,* and *The Wingless Victory*. Recent successes include *Anne of the Thousand Days* and *The Bad Seed*.

April 12 American actor, playwright, and producer James Gleason (b. 1886) dies in Woodland Hills, California.

April 13 Keir Dullea makes his New York

Sep 28 Playwright-director-producer Edward Albee's first produced play, *The Zoo Story*, premieres in Berlin at the Schiller Theatre Werkstatt.

Oct 19 Patty Duke makes her stage debut at age eight as Helen Keller in William Gibson's *The Miracle Worker* at the Playhouse Theatre.

Nov 18 Eileen Brennan makes her New York City debut in the title role of Rick Besoyan's *Little Mary Sunshine* at the Orpheum Theatre, winning the Newspaper Guild Page One Award, the *Theatre World* Award, the *Village Voice* Obie Award, and the Kit-Kat Artists and Models Award.

Dec 4 Actress Rosemary Harris is wed to director-actor Ellis Rabb. After a series of roles in England since 1946, Harris made her New York debut as Mable in Moss Hart's *The Climate of Eden* at the Martin Beck Theatre in 1952.

Dec 14 American actress Edna Wallace Hopper (b. 1864) dies in New York. Hopper made her New York debut in *The Club Friend* in 1891. She played musical comedy with De Wolf Hopper, and later became associated with the Lew Fields Company.

1959   THEATERS/PRODUCTIONS

Jan 1 Sir Alec Guinness is created a Knight Bachelor by Queen Elizabeth at the New Years Honours. A Commander of the British Empire (C.B.E.) was conferred upon him in the Birthday Honours of 1955.

March 12 Leslie Evershed-Martin meets Dr. Tyrone Guthrie in Stratford-upon-Avon to discuss his idea for a thrust-stage festival theatre in England's Chichester. Chichester has not had a professional theatre since 1847.

Mar 23 The Circle in the Square, one of Off-Broadway's most admired producing groups, opens its first show, Wilder's *Our Town*, in its new home at 159 Bleecker Street, a theatre-space vacated by the Amato Opera Company. The 299-seat house has a thrust stage with seating on three sides.

April 1 Letters Patent are issued to the Canadian Theatre Centre/Centre du Théâtre Canadien. CTC now becomes the Canadian representative in the International Theatre Institute. Like ITI, CTC is a clearinghouse for theatre information. In its first full year, CTC sponsors a national survey of theatres in Canada and a "blueprint" for the National Theatre School. CTC is funded through the Canada Council.

Apr 4 Century Lighting (U.S.) introduces the Theatron control system, a remote control lighting system with presetting, mastering, and proportional cross-fading standardized into a "building-block" or modular system, which permits quick delivery and lower costs.

May 5 Before John Osborne's *The World of Paul Slickey* can open on London stage, the playwright has had the customary difficulties with the Lord Chamberlain, the official play-censor. Among the Lord Chamberlain's objections are the use of such words as "crumpet," "queer," and "fairy." Suggested substitutions for each are "muffin," "swishy," and "queen." Answering a letter from the Lord Chamberlain's Office—written by Sir Norman Gwatkin and received at the final dress-rehearsal of *The World of Paul Slickey*—playwright Osborne not only responds to suggestions for changes in the text but says, among other things, " . . . I am one of the few serious artists working in the English theatre, with a serious reputation in almost every civilized country . . . And yet your office seems intent on treating me as if I were the producer of a third-rate nude revue."

May 28 London's new Mermaid Theatre opens with *Lock Up Your Daughters*, a musical based on Henry Fielding's *Rape Upon Rape*. Michael Stringer and C. Walter Hodges are the designers of the 498-seat Elizabethan-style theatre, situated in Blackfriars.

June 1 Drama critic Louis Kronenberger chooses the ten "Best Plays" for the 1958–1959 Broadway season. They are O'Neill's *A Touch of the Poet*, Taylor's *The Pleasure of His Company*, Osborne and Creighton's *Epitaph for George Dillon*, Schulberg and Breit's *The Disenchanted*, Behrman's *The Cold Wind and the Warm*, MacLeish's *J. B.*, Faulkner and Ford's *Requiem for a Nun*, Williams' *Sweet Bird of Youth*, Hansberry's *A Raisin in the Sun*, and Wincelberg's *Kataki*. *J. B.* wins the Pulitzer Prize, while the Drama Critics' Circle Award goes to *A Raisin in the Sun* as "Best American Play," with other Circle Awards for *The Visit* and *La Plume de Ma Tante*.

June 1 Henry Hewes, drama critic for the *Saturday Review*, summarizes Off-Broadway activity during the 1958–1959 season for the *Best Plays* annual. Among his favorites are William Ball's staging of Chekhov's *Ivanov*, Behan's *The Quare Fellow*, Hal Holbrook in *Mark Twain Tonight*, Williams' *I Rise in Flames Cried the Phoenix*, (W. C.) Williams' *Many Loves*, Stavis' *The Man Who Never Died*, Anderson's *The Golden Six*, Joyce's *Ulysses in Nighttown*—with Zero Mostel, Dennis' *The Making of Moo*, Kops' *The Hamlet of Stepney Green*, Ionesco's *Jack* and *The Bald Soprano*, Genet's *Deathwatch*, the medieval *The Play of Daniel*, and Sophocles and Gide's *Philoctetes*. Off-Broadway directors, says Hewes, continue to restage Broadway plays with frequently better results.

June 16 The Legislature of the State of Pennsylvania today votes the Bucks County Playhouse in New Hope as the "Official State Theatre of Pennsylvania."

June 24 After Parks Commissioner Robert Moses' demand for $20,000 to cover costs of erosion to the grass on the site of the New York Shakespeare Festival in Central Park is met, the season opens with *Julius Caesar*. Moses' previous demand that founder-director Joseph Papp charge admission to pay for possible park damage has been rejected by State Supreme Court Justice James B. McNally, who terms Moses' demands "arbitrary, capricious, and unreasonable."

July 8 John Gielgud re-opens London's Queen's Theatre—damaged in World War II bombing—with his one-man show, *Ages of Man*, based on George Rylands' Shakespeare Anthonolgy. Hugh Canon's interiors preserve the Edwardian atmosphere of the old theatre.

July 28 Today the Oregon Shakespeare Festival opens its annual season in Ashland in a new Elizabethan theatre, designed by the festival's resident designer, Richard L. Hay. It has 1,173 seats. It's based on the known dimensions of the Fortune Theatre in London during Shakespeare's day, but is not presented as an authentic reconstruction. *Twelfth Night* inaugurates the new stage.

Sep 30 *The New York Times* announces Tyrone Guthrie's proposal for a regional repertory theatre, to be located in Minneapolis, Minnesota.

Oct 17 After a 26-year run of 9,477 performances, *The Drunkard*, a 19th century melodrama, ends its epic run in Los Angeles, where it opened on July 6, 1933 at the Theatre Mart.

Dec 5 The day after Rosemary Harris has married actor-director Ellis Rabb, he founds the Association of Producing Artists, or APA. In January, he invites 78 theatre-people whose work he admires to join him in the project. More than fifty turn out for initial meetings.

Dec 27 The Dallas Theatre Center, designed by Frank Lloyd Wright, for some dedicated Dallas theatre-lovers, has its official opening. Paul Baker, of Baylor University, is director of the combination school and theatre—called the Kalita Humphreys Theatre. Wright has avoided right-angles in his cantilevered construction, basically a concrete shell. The central stage area—a 40' circle, enclosing a 32' turntable—gives the effect of an Elizabethan stage jutting into the audience area, which seats 404 people. Not properly understanding the traditions of theatre production, Wright has designed a scene-changing system that doesn't work. He has provided virtually no backstage in this $1 million-plus playhouse. A specially designed fly gallery with Izenour synchronous winches helps solve the problem.

Jan 14 *The Zoo Story* (NY—Provincetown—Drama). Edward Albee's first produced play features a curious combat between the cautious, sophisticated Peter (William Daniels) and the rough, menacing Jerry (George Maharis). Samuel Beckett's *Krapp's Last Tape*, featuring Donald Davis, opens the program. There are 582 performances. On Aug 25, Albee's play is presented at London's Arts Theatre along with Tennessee Williams's *This Property is Condemned*.

Feb 11 *The Prodigal* (NY—Downtown—Drama). Jack Richardson's reworking of the Electra/Orestes legend opens a 21-week Off-Broadway run with Carole Macho and Dino Narizzano in the leads. Josephine Nichols is praised for her interpretation of the doomed seeress Cassandra.

Feb 16 *Caligula* (NY—54th Street—Drama). Albert Camus' vision of the Roman emperor is directed by Sidney Lumet, with music by David Amram. Chosen as "Best Play," it nevertheless has only 38 performances.

Feb 24 *The Tumbler* (NY—Helen Hayes—Drama). Benn W. Levy's play is staged by Laurence Olivier and features Rosemary Harris, Charlton Heston, Martha Scott, William Mervyn, and Donald Moffat. It has only five performances.

Feb 25 *Toys in the Attic* (NY—Hudson—Drama). Lillian Hellman's play shows two spinsters obsessed with regaining control of their newly married brother. It wins the Drama Critics' Circle Award and 556 performances. Jason Robards, Jr., Maureen Stapleton, Anne Revere, Irene Worth, and Rochelle Oliver are in the cast. The play fails when it comes to London's Picadilly beginning Nov 10. With Wendy Hiller, Diana Wynyard, and Coral Browne in the cast, it garners only 84 showings.

Feb 26 *A Thurber Carnival* (NY—ANTA—Revue). Burgess Meredith stages this collage of James Thurber sketches, in words and cartoons. With a cast including Paul Ford, Peggy Cass, John McGiver, Alice Ghostley, and Tom Ewell, it runs 16 weeks and is re-opened on Sep 5 for an additional 12 weeks. The revue premieres in London at the Savoy on April 11, 1962, where there are just 27 performances.

March 2 *The Good Soup* (NY—Plymouth—Comedy). Ruth Gordon plays a hard-headed *demi-mondaine* who does very well for herself, until she makes a mistake out of compassion. Garson Kanin adapts and stages Felicien Marceau's Paris hit. There are only 21 performances. On Oct 23, 1961, the play opens at London's Comedy as *Bonne Soupe* with Coral Browne in the lead. Translated by Kitty Black, it earns 286 performances, transferring to Wyndham's in February.

March 3 *The Balcony* (NY—Circle-in-the-

A THURBER CARNIVAL

Square—Drama). Jean Genet's parable of the powerful of the world reduced to sexual supplicants in Madame Irma's brothel earns 672 performances. The cast includes Nancy Marchand, Sylvia Miles, Salome Jens, Betty Miller, Roy Poole, and William Goodwin. Jose Quintero directs.

March 17 *Dear Liar* (NY—Billy Rose—Comedy). Jerome Kilty, the adaptor-director, calls this a "Comedy of Letters." George Bernard Shaw and Mrs. Patrick Campbell bring their witty correspondance to life, impersonated by Brain Aherne and Katharine Cornell. There are only 52 performances, but with tours, revivals, and foreign productions, it becomes one of the most popular small theatre pieces of the decade. It opens at London's Criterion on June 14, where it gets only 54 showings.

March 31 *The Best Man* (NY—Morosco—Comedy). Gore Vidal's salute to election year features characters resembling Harry Truman, Adlai Stevenson, Richard Nixon. Melvyn Douglas takes part in this Joseph Anthony staging, which runs 520 performances.

April 14 *Bye Bye, Birdie* (NY—Martin Beck—Musical). Army service looms for Conrad Birdie, Presleyesque teen idol. Michael Stewart's parody, with songs by Charles Strouse and Lee Adams, has 607 performances. Gower Champion directs. On June 15, 1961, the musical opens at Her Majesty's in London with Marty Wilde, Peter Marshall, Angela Baddeley, and Chita Rivera. It has 268 performances.

April 19 *Duel of Angels* (NY—Helen Hayes—Drama). Christopher Fry has adapted Jean Giradoux's variation of the Rape of Lucrece. Vivien Leigh, Mary Ure, and others play for just 51 performances.

May 3 *The Fantasticks* (NY—Sullivan Street—Musical). This adaptation of a play by Edmond Rostand, with book and lyrics by Tom Jones and score by Harvey Schmidt, is to become New York's equivalent of London's long-running *The Mousetrap*. The theatre is intimate; the audience endless; the songs, charming. A simple *Commedia dell'Arte* story of two fathers plotting their children's wedding, the play features Jerry Orbach, Rita Gardner, and Kenneth Nelson. The show is a failure in London. It has only 44 performances following the opening at the Apollo on Sep 7, 1961.

Sep 14 *The World of Carl Sandburg* (NY—Henry Miller—Reading). Bette Davis and Leif Ericson interpret the prose and poetry of America's Sage of the Prairies. This earns 29 performances and tours.

Sep 20 *The Hostage* (NY—Cort—Drama). Brendan Behan's Irish tragicomedy, with music-hall overtones, tells of a British soldier held hostage in a mad lodging house in contemporary Dublin. It wins a 16-week run. Alfred Lynch plays the soldier.

Sep 29 *Irma La Douce.* See L premiere, 1958.

Oct 4 *A Taste of Honey* (NY—Lyceum—Drama). Shelagh Delaney writes of an unhappy teenager in Lancashire who meets

a black sailor. Joan Plowright and Angela Lansbury are featured. Tony Richardson and George Devine share directing credits and producer David Merrick is pleased by the show's 47-week run.

Oct 5 *Becket* (NY—St. James—Drama). Jean Anouilh's retelling of the clash between Thomas à Becket and Henry II features Laurence Olivier and Anthony Quinn. It runs 24 weeks. The Royal Shakespeare Company presents the play at London's Aldwych beginning July 11, 1961. Christopher Plummer and Eric Porter play the leads.

Oct 8 *An Evening with Mike Nichols and Elaine May* (NY—Golden—Revue). The comedians score with a variety of contemporary satirical targets. Arthur Penn stages for producer Alexander Cohen; the show runs 306 performances and is recorded.

Oct 11 *The Wall* (NY—Billy Rose—Drama). Morton DaCosta stages Millard Lampell's dramatization of John Hersey's Holocaust novel about the Warsaw Ghetto. With a cast of talents including Marian Seldes, Vincent Gardenia, and George C. Scott, the play runs 21 weeks.

Oct 17 *Tenderloin* (NY—46th Street—Musical). Maurice Evans stars as the crusading minister who cleans up New York's Tenderloin District in the late 19th century. George Abbott and Jerome Weidman's book and Jerry Bock and Sheldon Harnick's songs give this production a 27-week run.

Oct 28 *U.S.A.* (NY—Martinique—Drama). Paul Shyre adapts John Dos Passos's collage of fact and fiction about the United States and its people in the past century for Reader's Theatre. Sada Thompson memorably recreates the life and death of Isadora Duncan. The production runs 32 weeks.

Nov 3 *The Unsinkable Molly Brown* (NY—Winter Garden—Musical). Tammy Grimes dominates Meredith Willson's score as Molly, a rich, rough woman from a poor background who cuts a social swath through Europe. Harve Presnell plays her long-suffering husband. Richard Morris devises the book for this Theatre Guild production which runs 532 performances.

Nov 10 *Period of Adjustment* (NY—Helen Hayes—Comedy). Tennessee Williams orchestrates a confrontation of the newly married Haversticks and the more experienced but unsuccessful Bates. Barbara Baxley, Robert Webber, James Daly, and Rosemary Murphy are the two couples. There are 132 performances.

Nov 16 *Under the Yum-Yum Tree* (NY—Henry Miller—Comedy). Lawrence Roman's titillating sex-triangle (Sandra Church, Gig Young, Dean Jones) has 173 showings on Broadway and becomes a favorite of stock, dinner, and community theatres. Joseph Anthony directs.

Nov 17 *Advise and Consent* (NY—Cort—Drama). Allen Drury's political best-seller, adapted for the stage by Loring Mandel, is not an attractive picture of professional Washington. It draws audiences for 212 performances. Franklin Schaffner directs a cast including Ed Begley, Richard Kiley, Kevin McCarthy, and Barnard Hughes.

Nov 30 *All the Way Home* (NY—Belasco—Drama). Tad Mosel adapts James Agee's novel, *A Death in the Family*. Arthur Hill and Colleen Dewhurst head a cast which also includes Lillian Gish. The play wins both the Pulitzer Prize and the Drama Critics' Circle Best Play Award, but there are only 33 performances.

Dec 3 *Camelot* (NY—Majestic—Musical). Richard Burton is Arthur opposite Julie Andrews as Guenevere in Alan Jay Lerner's adaptation of T.H. White's *The Once and Future King*. The score is by Frederick Loewe. The critics aren't ecstatic, but it runs 873 performances. On Aug 19, 1964, it opens in London at the Drury Lane with Laurence Harvey as Arthur and Elizabeth Larner as Guenevere. There are 518 performances.

Dec 14 *Critic's Choice* (NY—Ethel Barrymore—Comedy). Otto Preminger produces and stages Ira Levin's play about a critic who must review his wife's play or send the second-string critic. Henry Fonda heads the cast. The show runs nearly six months. It opens in London at the Vaudeville on Dec 6, 1961, with Ian Carmichael in the lead. Here it also has a six-month run.

Dec 16 *Wildcat* (NY—Alvin—Musical). Lucille Ball drills for oil in a 1912 border town. Michael Kidd produces, stages, and choreographs the N. Richard Nash book, with music and lyrics by Cy Coleman and Carolyn Leigh. The show has only 171 performances, closing when Ball leaves.

Dec 20 *In the Jungle of Cities* (NY—Living Theatre—Drama). Bertolt Brecht's early parable of eaters and eaten is staged by Judith Malina and Julian Beck, founders of the Living Theatre. There are 66 performances.

Dec 26 *Do Re Mi* (NY—St. James—Musical). Nancy Walker and Phil Silvers are featured in this show, with Jule Styne score and Betty Comden-Adolph Green lyrics. Garson Kanin provides the book about a small-time schemer who tries to become rich in the jukebox business. There are 400 performances. The show opens at London's Prince of Wales's on Oct 12, 1961, with Max Bygraves and Maggie Fitzgibbon.

1960 BRITISH PREMIERES

Feb 3 *The Wrong Side of the Park* (L—Cambridge—Drama). Set in a run-down house in London, John Mortimer's play features Margaret Leighton as a neurotic wife who torments her husband (Richard Johnson) with a fantasy of her first spouse, now deceased. Staged by Peter Hall, the play runs nearly 22 weeks.

Feb 11 *Fings Ain't Wot They Used T'Be* (L—Garrick—Musical). Joan Littlewood's hugely successful production of this Cockney musical by Frank Norman with songs by Lionel Bart moves from the Theatre Royal Stratford East to the West End, where it runs 897 performances.

Feb 24 *Watch It, Sailor!* (L—Aldwych—Comedy). Shirley Hornett and her would-be groom, sailor Albert Tufnell are pre-

THE FANTASTICKS (AUTHORS)

THE UNSINKABLE MOLLY BROWN

vented from marrying throughout this sequel to *Sailor, Beware!*, and possibly thereafter. Falkland Cary and Philip King's play features Ian Curry and Josephine Massey. It runs 604 performances.

March 9 *A Majority of One.* See NY premiere, 1959.

March 16 *Inherit the Wind.* See NY premiere, 1955.

March 17 *Follow That Girl!* (L—Vaudeville—Musical). Julian Slade composes and creates the book, with the aid of Dorothy Reynolds, for this show of thwarted love and marriage. Staged by Denis Carey, it features Peter Gilmore and Susan Hampshire and runs 221 performances.

March 24 *Flower Drum Song.* See NY premiere, 1958.

March 29 *The Gazebo* (L—Savoy—Comedy). This murder thriller by Alec Coppel is made an evening of comedy with Ian Carmichael as a TV mystery writer involved with a corpse, a blackmailer, and a gazebo. Anthony Sharp stages. The show has 479 performances.

April 20 *A Passage to India* (L—Comedy—Drama). Santha Rama Rau's adaptation of E.M. Forster's novel is brought from the Oxford Playhouse to the West End by director Frank Hauser. There are 261 performances. It opens on Broadway at the Ambassador on Jan 31, 1963 where it earns 109 showings.

April 21 *The Most Happy Fella.* See NY premiere, 1956.

April 27 *The Caretaker* (L—Arts—Drama). Harold Pinter's new play is staged by Donald McWhinnie with Donald Pleasance, Alan Bates, and Peter Woodthorpe. On Oct 4, 1961 it opens on Broadway with Pleasance, Bates, and Robert Shaw in the three roles. It wins critical admiration but only 165 performances.

April 28 *Rhinoceros* (L—Royal Court—Comedy). Derek Prouse's translation of Eugene Ionesco's Absurdist satire features Laurence Olivier, Duncan Macrae, and Joan Plowright. There are 105 performances. The comedy opens in New York at the Longacre on Jan 9, 1961. Zero Mostel wins admiration his transformation into a rhinoceros by suggestion rather than makeup. Eli Wallach, Anne Jackson, Jean Stapleton, and Morris Carnovsky play 30 weeks under Joseph Anthony's direction.

May 12 *Ross* (L—Haymarket—Drama). Terence Rattigan's play about Lawrence of Arabia stars Alec Guinness. Glen Byam Shaw directs this production which has 762 performances. On Dec 26, 1961, the play opens in New York at the O'Neill with John Mills in the lead. Not as popular on this side of the Atlantic, the drama has only 159 performances.

June 25 *The Visit.* See NY premiere, 1958.

June 30 *Oliver!* (L—New—Musical). Lionel Bart crafts a smash hit from Charles Dickens' novel, *Oliver Twist.* Keith Hampshire plays the young Oliver, with Ron Moody as Fagin. There are 2,618 performances, with later revivals and matching international success. On Jan 6, 1963, the show opens in New York at the Imperial with Bruce Prochnik as Oliver and Clive Revill as Fagin. There are 774 performances.

July 1 *A Man for All Seasons* (L—Globe—Drama). Robert Bolt's portrait of Thomas More features Paul Scofield as the Lord Chancellor and Richard Leech as Henry VIII. The production has 315 performances and eventually becomes a popular classic for rep and college troupes. On Nov 22, 1961, it opens at New York's ANTA with Scofield again in the lead. It wins the Drama Critics' Circle Award as the Best Foreign Play and earns 637 performances.

July 14 *Joie de Vivre* (L—Queen's—Musical). Terence Rattigan adapts his early comic success, *French Without Tears* as a musical. Robert Stolz provides the score, with lyrics by Paul Dehn. It has only a brief run.

Aug 24 *The Tiger and the Horse* (L—Queen's—Drama). Robert Bolt earns 228 performances with his play about an aloof university professor's family discord. Michael Redgrave, Catherine Lacey, and Vanessa Redgrave are directed by Frith Banbury.

Sep 7 *Waiting in the Wings* (L—Duke of York's—Comedy). Noel Coward provides work for a number of beloved older ladies of the stage, notably Sybil Thorndike, in this tale of life in a retirement home for actresses. There are 191 performances.

Sep 13 *Billy Liar* (L—Cambridge—Comedy). Albert Finney plays Billy, who daydreams of a better life than he can achieve, in Keith Waterhouse and Willis Hall's adaptation of Waterhouse's novel, staged by Lindsay Anderson. With a cast including Mona Washbourne and Ethel Griffies, there are 582 performances.

Oct 19 *Settled Out of Court* (L—Strand—Comedy). William Saroyan and Henry Cecil have adapted this thriller from Cecil's novel. Staged by and featuring Nigel Patrick, it runs 221 performances.

Nov 3 *Chin-Chin* (L—Wyndham's—Drama). Celia Johnson and Anthony Quayle are featured in this adaptation of Francois Billetdoux's play by Willis Hall. Director Howard Sackler's staging runs 164 performances. On Oct 25, 1962, the show opens in New York at the Plymouth with a slightly different spelling of the title—*Tchin-Tchin*. Margaret Leighton and Anthony Quinn lead the cast. There are 222 performances.

Nov 10 *Toys in the Attic.* See NY premiere, 1960.

Dec 21 *Young in Heart* (L—Victoria Palace—Revue). The announced last appearance together by the beloved Crazy Gang runs 826 performances. The company (Nervo and Knox, Gold and Naughton, Eddie Gray and Bud Flanagan) are directed by Alec Shanks and Charles Henry.

1960 REVIVALS/REPERTORIES

Jan 12 Ibsen's difficult dramatic poem *Peer Gynt* is staged at the Phoenix Theatre for four weeks, featuring Fritz Weaver. On March 1, Phoenix revives *Henry IV, Part 1,* and Weaver is king for 65 performances. *Part 2* is offered on April 18 and plays 31 times.

Jan 24 At the Royal Court Theatre in London, the production is *Christopher Sly.* On Jan 27, a musical, *The Lily White Boys,* opens with Albert Finney under Lindsay Anderson's direction. On March 2, a double bill of Harold Pinter's *The Dumbwaiter* and *The Room* is produced. In the casts are Nicholas Selby and George Tovey, Vivien Merchant, and Michael Caine. On March 20, Edward Bond performs in a "Production Without Decor" of Albert Bermel's *One Leg Over the Wall.* On March 30, Colin Blakely appears in Frederick Bland's *The Naming of Murderer's Rock,* and on April 10, Ron Fraser's *Eleven Plus* is staged by Keith Johnstone. On June 7, the Court opens a trilogy of Arnold Wesker plays which show three aspects of socialism: *Chicken Soup with Barley*, *Roots* on June 28, and *I'm Talking About Jerusalem* on July 27. (*Roots* opens at New York's Mayfair on March 6, 1961, for a nine-week run.) On July 10, Lloyd Reckford directs two dramas by Trinidadian poet Derek Walcott: *Sea at Dauphin* and *Six in the Rain*. On Aug 7, Graham Crowden stages Gwyn Thomas's *The Keep*, with a largely Welsh cast.

Feb 9 London's Old Vic Theatre ensemble continues its revival of George Bernard Shaw's *Saint Joan* with Barbara Jefford and Alec McCowen. James Barrie's centenary is honored with his *What Every Woman Knows* on April 12. Maggie Smith heads the cast. On May 31 *Henry V* opens.

Feb 23 Orson Welles directs his adaptation of Shakespeare and Holinshead, which he calls *Chimes at Midnight*, for the Dublin Gate. In May, the melodrama, *The Drunkard*, is revived.

Feb 23 Milan's Piccolo Teatro plays Goldoni's *The Servant of Two Masters* for two weeks at New York's City Center. The Lunts play *The Visit* for two weeks starting March 8, and a revival of *Finian's Rainbow* opens for 27 performances on April 27. Three weeks of *The King and I* with Barbara Cook and Farley Granger begin May 11.

Feb 25 At Bernard Miles' Mermaid Theatre in London, *Henry V* is staged by Julius Gellner. On April 13, Frow's adaptation of Charles Dickens' *Great Expectations* is staged by Sally Miles.

March 7 The Compagnie Marie Bell plays Racine's *Phedre* at the Savoy in London. On March 10, Racine's *Berenice* and on March 15 his *Britannicus* are staged. Bell heads the cast in all three.

March 8 The Belgrade Theatre of Coventry brings John Wiles' *Never Had It so Good* to the Theatre Royal, Stratford East. On April 6, William Saroyan stages his *Sam, the Highest Jumper of Them All*. The New Negro Theatre Company performs Saroyan's *Hello, Out There!* on April 24. Joan Littlewood stages American James Clancy's *Ned Kelly* on May 23.

April 5 Peter Hall directs the 101st season of the Memorial Theatre at Stratford-upon-Avon. The season includes *Merchant of Venice*, *Twelfth Night*, *The Taming of the Shrew*, *Troilus and Cressida* and Peter Wood's staging of *A Winter's Tale*. Peter O'Toole, Peggy Ashcroft, and Max Adrian are in the company.

April 27 Producers Robert Griffith and Harold Prince revive *West Side Story* at Broadway's Winter Garden for a run of 31 weeks.

May 5 In *A Country Scandal*, Off-Broadway at the Greenwich Mews Theatre Chekhov's tragi-comic Platonov (Mark Lenard) is brought to the stage by adaptor Alex Szogyi. Others in the company which enjoys a 203-performance run, include Carol Teitel, Crystal Field, and Conrad Bain.

June 3 The American Shakespeare Festival at Stratford Connecticut opens with *Antony and Cleopatra*. *Twelfth Night* and *The Tempest* will also play this season. Katharine Hepburn and Robert Ryan are featured.

June 11 *The Third Frontier*, by Kermit Hunter, opens today at New Bern, North Carolina. This historical drama is produced by the 250th Anniversary Committee, founded by the city fathers.

June 13 A handsome revival of George Bernard Shaw's *Candida* is staged by Frank Hauser at London's Piccadilly Theatre for a run of 160 performances. Among the players are Dulcie Gray, Michael Denison, and Jeremy Spenser.

June 16 Charles Laughton's adaptation of Bertolt Brecht's *The Life of Galileo*, previously performed in Los Angeles and New York in close collaboration with the author, opens in London at the Mermaid Theatre.

June 25 Earl Hobson writes an historical drama of the frontier, *The Daniel Boone Story*. It is played at the Indian Fort Theatre in Berea College Forest, Berea, Kentucky.

June 27 Canada's Stratford Shakespeare Festival opens under Michael Langham. *King John*, *A Midsummer Night's Dream* and *Romeo and Juliet* are presented, as is Tyrone Guthrie's staging of *H.M.S. Pinafore*. The company includes Julie Harris and Christopher Plummer.

June 29 The New York Shakespeare Festival opens its season of free productions in Central Park. *The Taming of the Shrew*, *Measure for Measure*, and *Henry V* are mounted, the last by founder Joseph Papp. Among the company are Kathleen Widdoes and James Ray.

July 4 At the Theatre Royal, Stratford East, Joan Littlewood's Theatre Workshop productions are Ben Jonson's *Every Man in His Humour* and Stephen Lewis's Cockney show, *Sparrers Can't Sing*. The latter opens on Aug 24.

July 5 The twelfth season of the San Diego National Shapespeare Festival opens in Balboa Park. The repertory consists of *Julius Caesar*, directed by William Ball; *As You Like It*, and *Hamlet*, both directed by Allen Fletcher.

July 19 In Regent's Park in the Open Air Theatre, James Bridie's *Tobias and the Angel* is revived by Robert Atkins.

July 25 In Ashland, in the outdoor Elizabethan Theatre, the Oregon Shakespearean Festival opens its season of *The Taming of the Shrew*, *Julius Caesar*, *The Tempest*, *Richard II*, and John Webster's *Duchess of Malfi*.

Aug 21 Britain's Edinburgh International

JOIE DE VIVRE

Festival includes Chekhov's *The Seagull* with Judith Anderson. Hal Holbrook performs *Mark Twain Tonight!* Sydney Smith's *The Wallace* is presented as is Friedrich Dürrenmatt's *Romulus the Great*, Dumas fils' *Les Trois Mousquetaires*, Bjoernson's *Mary Stuart in Scotland*, and Bernard Kops's *The Dream of Peter Mann*. *Beyond the Fringe*, devised and performed by Jonathan Miller, Peter Cook, Dudley Moore, and Allan Bennett is an instant success.

Sep 1 The 47th annual season of the Old Vic honors Chekhov's centenary with *The Seagull*. On Oct 4, Franco Zefferelli's production of *Romeo and Juliet* plays. On Nov 8, *She Stoops to Conquer* is given. Shakespeare's *A Midsummer Night's Dream* opens on Dec 20.

Sep 7 The Phoenix Theatre Off-Broadway offers Tyrone Guthrie's interpretation of *H.M.S. Pinafore* for 55 performances. Thirty-one performances of Oliver Goldsmith's *She Stoops to Conquer* commence on Nov 1, and Sean O'Casey's *The Plough and the Stars* plays 32 times beginning Dec 6.

Sep 14 John Arden's *The Happy Haven* is staged at London's Royal Court Theatre. Chekhov's centenary is noted with *Platonov*, featuring Rex Harrison on Oct 13. On Nov 23, Mary Ure has the title role in *Antigone*. *Trials by Logue* and *Cob and Leach* are also presented. Shelagh Delaney's *The Lion in Love* opens on Dec 29.

Sep 15 Micheal macLiammoir impersonates Oscar Wilde in his mono-drama *The Importance of Being Oscar* at the Dublin Gate Theatre. Donagh MacDonagh's *God Gentry* is revived this fall as well. On Oct 31, macLiammoir Opens his Wilde impersonation for a limited London run at the Apollo Theatre.

Oct 6 Bernard Miles's Mermaid Theatre offers Gerald Frow's *Mr. Burke, M.P.* (Can an ape be elected to the House of Commons?). The Mermaid's Christmas treat: *Emil and the Detectives*, with music by Eric Lunney, opens on Dec 15.

Oct 12 The Dublin Festival Company brings Synge's *The Playboy of the Western World* to the Piccadilly Theatre for 141 performances. Donal Donnelly and Siobhan McKenna have the leads.

Nov 9 David Ross continues his revivals of Ibsen and Chekhov in his unusual and intimate Fourth Street Theatre. *Hedda Gabler*, with Anne Meacham, enjoys 340 performances.

Nov 22 Improvisation based on audience suggestion gives Theodore J. Flicker and troupe a success with *The Premise*. It runs 1,255 performances in New York.

Dec 15 London's Aldwych Theatre becomes the West End home of the Stratford-upon-Avon Memorial Theatre company. A stellar cast, including Peggy Ashcroft, inaugurates the house with Webster's *The Duchess of Malfi*.

Dec 16 Julia Lockwood, following mother Margaret, is now playing Peter Pan in the annual revival of Barrie's fantasy, shown at London's Scala Theatre as a holiday treat. Shakespeare helps the holiday mood with *Twelfth Night* at the Aldwych and *A Midsummer Night's Dream* at the Old Vic. On Dec 20, *Toad of Toad Hall* is

THE PREMISE

revived at the Westminster Theatre. Other holiday offerings include *Riquet with the Tuft* (Players'), *Hooray for Daisy* (Lyric, Hammersmith), *The Imperial Nightingale* (Arts), *Turn Again Whittington* (Palladium—with Norman Wisdom as Dick), *Cinderella* (Adelphi), and *Billy Bunter's Swiss Roll* (Victoria Palace).

Dec 19 Peter Hall's production of *Twelfth Night*, previously shown at Stratford-upon-Avon, is performed at London's Aldwych. Last winter it played Leningrad and Moscow.

thews excelled in farce, from the plays of Pinero to his creation of the Earl of Lister in *The Chiltern Hundreds*, and *The Manor of Northstead*. He was awarded the O. B. E. in 1951. *Matty*, his autobiography, was published in 1953.

July 25 English actor Dennis Hoey (b. 1893) is dead. Hoey made his first New York appearance in 1924 as Masrur in *Hassan*. He played Horatio in the all-star 1931 production at London's Haymarket Theatre.

July 29 Actress Leonora Corbett dies today in the Netherlands. She is only 52, remembered in New York for her work in *Blithe Spirit*.

Aug 23 Lyricist and librettist Oscar Hammerstein II (b. 1895) dies in Doylestown, Pennsylvania. Grandson of impresario Oscar Hammerstein I, the second Oscar first came into prominence with *Wildflower* in 1923, followed by *Rose Marie*, *Show Boat*, *The Desert Song*, *Music in the Air*, and others. It was in 1943 that he began his successful collaboration with Richard Rodgers.

Sep 6 Musical comedian Jimmy Savo dies in Italy at age 64. He won praise for his role in *The Boys from Syracuse*. Even after losing a leg, he continued to appear on stage.

Sep 11 Actress Queenie Vassar is dead in West Los Angeles at age 89.

Oct 15 At age 70, actress Clara Kimball Young dies in Woodland Hills, California.

Oct 16 The distinguished American theatre scholar and critic, Arthur Hobson Quinn (b. 1875), dies in Philadelphia.

Nov 4 Walter Catlett made his debut in San Francisco at 13, playing some 104 roles in comic operas in a two-year span. He made his New York debut in 1911, followed by a British debut in *Baby Bunting*. He was also known for his films. To-

1960 BIRTHS/DEATHS/DEBUTS

Jan 1 Remembered for her roles in *The Voice of the Turtle* and *The Deep Blue Sea*, Margaret Sullavan dies in New Haven, Connecticut, at 48.

Jan 10 Gilmore Brown, founder in 1917 of the Pasadena Playhouse, dies in Palm Springs at 73.

Jan 25 John Barrymore's daughter Diana (b. 1921) a stage and screen actress, dies in New York.

Feb 12 American actor Bobby Clark (b. 1888) dies in New York. Clark appeared in minstrel shows, circuses, vaudeville, and burlesque. His Broadway credits include the *Ziegfeld Follies of 1936* and *Mexican Hayride*.

Feb 18 Actress and artist, Gertrude Vanderbilt dies in New York at age 72.

March 18 Director-actor Bretaigne Windust dies in New York at 54.

March 26 American actor Ian Keith (b. 1899) is dead. Keith first appeared with the Washington Square Players in 1917.

April 5 American actress Alma Kruger is dead in Seattle, Washington, at age 88. Kruger played in the Sothern-Marlowe and Civic Repertory companies and toured

with Ben Greet, Robert B. Mantell, Annie Russell, and Blanche Walsh.

April 15 In London, Lillah McCarthy, for whom Bernard Shaw wrote *Fanny's First Play*, dies at age 84. At one time, she was married to Harley Granville Barker.

April 24 English stage and screen actor George Relph (b. 1888) is dead in London. Relph made his American debut in 1911 as Kafur in *Kismet* at New York's Knickerbocker Theatre. In 1913 he was engaged by Sir Herbert Tree to play Joseph in *Joseph and His Brethren*. During the 1940's Relph toured with the Old Vic Company.

May 10 Maurice Schwartz, founder of New York's Yiddish Art Theatre, dies in Israel at 69.

July 12 Actress Judith Anderson is created Dame Commander of the Most Excellent Order of the British Empire (D.B.E.) in the Queen's Birthday Honours. Dame Judith made her stage debut in Sydney, Australia, in 1915, as Stephanie in *A Royal Divorce* at the Theatre Royal.

July 25 English actor Albert Edward Matthews (b. 1869) dies in London. Mat-

day he dies in Los Angeles at 71.

Nov 16 Stage and screen star Clark Gable dies in Hollywood.

Dec 13 John Charles Thomas, early a musical comedy star and later a leading singer at the Metropolitan Opera, dies today in Apple Valley, California, aged 69.

Dec 14 Russian-born stage and screen actor Gregory Ratoff (b. 1893) is dead in Switzerland. Ratoff first appeared on stage at the Imperial Theatre in Moscow. He made his first appearance in New York in 1922 in *Revue Russe*. Ratoff directed the New York productions of *Nina* in 1951, *The Fifth Season* in 1953, and *Black-Eyed Susan* in 1954.

1960 THEATERS/PRODUCTIONS

A patent is granted in Britain to A. I. Cohen for a complex apparatus to produce light shows and optical effects, using various mechanical, electronic and hydraulic means.

Jan 9 The Circle in the Square's new home at 159 Bleecker Street is inaugurated with a revival of Thornton Wilder's *Our Town*. David Hayes has re-worked the Amato Opera Company's space as a 299-seat, tiered house with thrust stage.

Jan 19 In an effort to bring serious theatre to Los Angeles, Robert Ryan heads the cast in T.S. Eliot's *Murder in the Cathedral* on the UCLA campus in Westwood. Artistic Director John Houseman will also bring Chekhov's *Three Sisters* to life with Nina Foch, Betty Harford, and Gloria Grahame. The Theatre Group ceases after 42 productions in 1966.

May 31 With the closing of the London season, Frances Stephens, editor of the *Theatre World Annual*, notes a landslide of West End failures, most deserved. Better fare is being provided by the English Stage Company at the Royal Court Theatre and by Joan Littlewood's Theatre Workshop, he says.

June 1 The 1959–1960 Broadway season has just closed. The ten "Best Plays," selected by editor-drama critic Louis Kro-

nenberger, are Chayefsky's *The Tenth Man*, Shaffer's *Five Finger Exercise*, Levitt's *The Andersonville Trial*, Dürrenmatt and Yaffe's *The Deadly Game*, Camus' *Caligula*, Hellman's *Toys in the Attic*, Vidal's *The Best Man*, Giraudoux's *Duel of Angels*, Thurber's *A Thurber Carnival*, and Weidman and Abbott's *Fiorello!* *Toys in the Attic* wins the Drama Critics' Circle "Best American Play" Award. The Pulitzer Prize goes to *Fiorello!*, which is "Best Musical production" for the Critics' Circle. *Five Finger Exercise* wins the "Best Foreign Play" citation.

June 1 Surveying the Off-Broadway season just past, Henry Hewes, critic for the *Saturday Review*, notes premieres by three impressive new playwrights, Edward Albee, with *The Zoo Story*; Jack Richardson, with *The Prodigal*, and, as Hewes says, "At the top of this list was Jack Gelber, whose play *The Connection* established itself as the most original piece of new American Theatre writing in a long, long time." He also lists debuts of new playwrights who, by 1980, were with their plays forgotten. Broadway playwrights show unproduced works Off-Broadway instead of on, such as the Spewacks, with *Under the Sycamore Tree*, William Gibson, with *Dinny and the Witches*, and George Tabori, with *Brouhaha*. Revivals

of classics and Broadway failures continue. Important contemporary foreign plays are also seen Off-Broadway, because Broadway cannot afford the risk, fearing small audiences for such dramas.

June 24 The Royalty Theatre on Portugal Street just off Kingsway, opens to the public with *The Visit*. The 997-seat theatre is managed by H.M. Tennent Ltd. and Two Arts Ltd.

June 28 The Synchronous Winch System is patented in the United States by George C. Izenour. It is an electrically-controlled winch system for the raising and lowering of drops and curtains.

Fall This season, members of Actors' Equity who are cast will receive a minimum wage of $112.50 weekly. Important players may receive $1,500. Some are guaranteed as much as $5,050. Those contracted with guarantees or percentages of the gross receipts will make even more in solid hits.

Sep 12 The Mansfield Theatre on New York's West 47th Street is re-opened and renamed for New York drama critic, Brooks Atkinson. *Vintage '60*, produced by David Merrick, inaugurates.

Oct 1 This is the opening night of the 3,200-seat O'Keefe Centre, Toronto, Canada. *Camelot* is staged in a pre-Broadway tryout on the 140-foot apron stage, starring Richard Burton, Julie Andrews, and Canadian Robert Goulet. 18,500 season subscriptions are sold, and the first season will net $2.7 million at the box office.

Oct 10 In Cincinnati, the Playhouse in the Park, a 227-seat theatre made possible by community members and Gerald Covell, opens tonight with Meyer Levin's *Compulsion*.

Oct 15 At Harvard University, where drama is still not an academic discipline, authorities permit the opening of the new Loeb Drama Center, with a performance of *Troilus and Cressida*, presented by Harvard and Radcliffe students.

Nov 2 The National Theatre School of Canada/L'Ecole National de Théâtre du Canada opens in Montreal. Funded by the Canada Council ($40,000) and the province of Quebec ($50,000) the School offers training in all aspects of professional theatre in both English and French. The School is conceived and planned through the Canadian Theatre Centre in consultation with Michel St. Denis, founder and director of the Old Vic Theatre School and the Centre de l'Est in Strasbourg. The first Artistic Director is Jean Gascon. Actor Powys Thomas heads the English Section of the School.

Dec 15 The Royal Shakespeare Company has invested £25,000 to adapt London's Aldwych Theatre for transfers from Stratford-upon-Avon. Producer Prince Littler has donated £50,000. The new house, though smaller, has a reproduction of Stratford's apron and raked stage.

RODGERS AND HAMMERSTEIN

Jan 9 *Rhinoceros.* See L premiere, 1960.

Jan 12 *Show Girl* (NY—O'Neill—Revue). Carol Channing and Jules Munshin are the leads in Charles Gaynor's show. There are only 100 performances.

Jan 24 *The American Dream* (NY—York—Comedy). Edward Albee's satire on marriage and family life, staged by Alan Schneider, wins 370 performances. The cast includes Jane Hoffman, John C. Becher, Sudie Bond, Nancy Cushman, and Ben Piazza.

Feb 1 *Midgie Purvis* (NY—Martin Beck—Comedy). Author Mary Chase has a failure with this play about a society matron who disguises herself as a frump to enjoy life with some children. Despite the presence of Tallulah Bankhead in the lead, there are only 21 performances.

Feb 22 *Come Blow Your Horn* (NY—Brooks Atkinson—Comedy). Neil Simon's first full-length Broadway play tells the story of a Jewish manufacturer whose two sons are more interested in girls than in helping with the business. Lou Jacobi, Hal March, and Warren Berlinger are in the cast. Critics don't rave, but there are 677 performances. On Feb 27, 1962, the show opens at the Prince of Wales's in the West End. Bob Monkhouse, Michael Crawford, David Kossoff, and Libby Morris have the leads. There are 592 showings.

March 8 *Mary, Mary* (NY—Helen Hayes—Comedy). Barbara Bel Geddes plays the basically insecure Mary in Jean Kerr's play about a woman who might lose her husband to another. Barry Nelson and Betsy von Furstenberg are also in the cast. The show wins 1,572 performances, followed by tours, revivals, and amateur productions. It opens at London's Queen's Theatre on Feb 27, 1963, with Maggie Smith in the title role. A success, it has 588 showings.

March 9 *The Devil's Advocate* (NY—Billy Rose—Drama). Dore Schary adapts and directs Morris West's novel for 116 performances. Leo Genn leads the cast.

March 13 *Big Fish, Little Fish* (NY—ANTA—Drama). Hugh Wheeler makes a playwright's debut with this tale of a once influential editor (Jason Robards, Jr.), surrounded by nervous nonentities who feed on his attention. There are 101 performances. On Sep 18, 1962, the drama opens at the Duke of York's in the West End. Even with Hume Cronyn and Jessica Tandy in the cast, there are only 14 performances.

April 4 *A Far Country* (NY—Music Box—Drama). Steven Hill impersonates Sigmund Freud in Henry Denker's documentary of Freud's family life and the birth of psychoanalysis. The play runs 34 weeks.

CARNIVAL

April 13 *Carnival!* (NY—Imperial—Musical). Michael Stewart bases his book on the film, *Lili,* and song writer Bob Merrill produces an attractive new score. Gower Champion stages Anna Maria Alberghetti, James Mitchell, and Jerry Orbach, winning 719 performances.

May 4 *The Blacks* (NY—St. Marks Playhouse—Drama). There are 1,408 performances for Jean Genet's vivid satire, in which some black actors sham whiteness, and one, a man, pretends to be a white woman, raped by a black. The company includes James Earl Jones and Cicely Tyson. Critics respond warmly but with varying interpretations of the text.

June 12 *The Red Eye of Love* (NY—Living Theatre—Comedy). Arnold Weinstein's satiric/parodic treatment of American ideals and practices runs 169 performances.

Sep 17 *Happy Days* (NY—Cherry Lane—Comedy). Samuel Beckett's sardonic spoof on the unceasing optimism of man is staged by Alan Schneider and animated by Ruth White. This plays in repertory with Edward Albee's *The American Dream* for 28 times.

Sep 18 *One Way Pendulum* (NY—East 47th Street—Comedy). N. F. Simpson's British absurdist play runs five weeks, with Anna Russell directed by Douglas Seale. Peter Harvey designs.

Sep 26 *From the Second City* (NY—Royale—Revue). Chicago's Compass Theatre offers a program of satires on midstream culture and socio-political topics. Alan Arkin, Barbara Harris, and Paul Sand are among the cast. It runs for 11 weeks.

Sep 28 *Purlie Victorious* (NY—Cort—Comedy). Ossie Davis plays the cartoon hero in his play. Ruby Dee, Sorrell Book, Alan Alda, and Godfrey Cambridge are also in the cast, staged by Howard Da Silva. The show runs 33 weeks and later becomes the musical *Purlie.*

Oct 3 *Sail Away* (NY—Broadhurst—Musical). Elaine Stritch is a hard-working ocean-cruise hostess, determined that the passengers should have fun. Despite the fact that Noel Coward has written book, lyrics, and score, and even staged the production, it runs only 21 performances. It fares far better in London, where it premieres on June 21, 1962. There it has 252 showings.

Oct 4 *The Caretaker.* See L premiere, 1960.

Oct 10 *Milk and Honey* (NY—Martin Beck—Musical). Jerry Herman provides the music and lyrics for Don Appell's celebration of Israel. Molly Picon heads the cast. Audiences flock to the 543 performances.

Oct 14 *How To Succeed in Business Without Really Trying* (NY—46th Street—Musical). Robert Morse's manic perfornance as an opportunistic corporate climber delights critics and audiences. The show earns 1,416 performances. Also playing are Rudy Vallee, Virginia Martin, and Charles Nelson Reilly. The show wins both the Pulitzer Prize and Drama Critics' Circle "Best Musical" Award. Bob Fosse choreographs. Frank Loesser provides the score and Abe Burrows the book. Warren Berlinger and Billy De Wolfe lead the cast when the show premieres in London at the Shaftesbury on March 28, 1963. It runs 520 performances.

Oct 18 *A Shot in the Dark* (NY—Booth—Drama). Harry Kurnitz adapts Marcel Achard's French play, focusing on the question of whether Josefa (Julie Harris) will be tried for murder. The show wins 389 performances. It has only 44 showings in London when it opens on May 16, 1963, at the Lyric.

Oct 25 *Look: We've Come Through* (NY—Hudson—Drama). Hugh Wheeler's play deals with confusing sexual experiences. The cast includes Burt Reynolds and Colin Wilcox. Jose Quintero directs. There are just five performances, but there are admirers and later revivals.

Oct 26 *Write Me a Murder* (NY—Belasco—Drama). Frederick Knott's thriller about an author and her lover plotting murder features Ethel Griffies, Kim Hunter, Torin Thatcher, and Denholm Elliott among others. It runs nearly 25 weeks. The play comes to London's Lyric on March 28, 1962, with Brian Bedford and Judith Stott as the couple. It runs over 22 weeks.

Nov 22 *A Man for All Seasons.* See L premiere, 1960.

Nov 1 *The Complaisant Lover.* See L premiere, 1959.

Nov 4 *Time, Gentlemen, Please* (NY—Strollers Theatre-Club—Revue). From London's Players Theatre Club comes this Victorian music-hall nostalgia, with Fred Stone as Chairman. There are 336 performances of various period treats.

Nov 9 *Gideon* (NY—Plymouth—Comedy). Douglas Campbell is privileged to debate God in the image of an angel (Frederic March). Tyrone Guthrie stages Paddy Chayefsky's work for 236 performances.

Nov 29 *Sunday in New York* (NY—Cort—Comedy). David Merrick produces. Gardon Kanin directs Norman Krasna's tale of seduction in Manhattan. 188 performances are played by Conrad Janis, Pat Stanley, Sondra Lee, and Robert Redford.

Dec 5 *Shadow of Heroes.* See L premiere, 1958.

Dec 7 *The Apple* (NY—Living Theatre—Comedy). Jack Gelber provides a zany script in which Living Theatre actors indulge themselves. Julian Beck and Judith Malina design and direct, respectively. Beck, James Earl Jones, and Marilyn Chris perform for two months.

Dec 11 *Black Nativity* (NY—41st Street—Musical). Vinnette Carroll directs Langston Hughes' Christmas "song-play." It runs seven weeks. The drama has 55 performances following its London premiere at the Criterion on Aug 14, 1962. Carroll, Cristyne Lawson, and Ronald Frazier are among the cast.

Dec 21 *Take Her, She's Mine* (NY—Biltmore—Comedy). Harold Prince produces Phoebe and Henry Ephron's comic tale of a loving father who has to adjust to his daughter's growing up and going away to college. Art Carney, Elizabeth Ashley, and Phyllis Thaxter are in the cast. The show has 404 performances.

Dec 26 *Ross.* See L premiere, 1960.

Dec 27 *Subways Are for Sleeping* (NY—St. James—Musical). David Merrick presents Betty Comden and Adolph Green's reworking of Edmund Love's book about the poor and eccentric who sleep on New York's subways. Jule Styne creates the score. Sydney Chaplin, Carol Lawrence, Orson Bean, and Phyllis Newman lead a cast that also includes Michael Bennett. There are 316 performances.

Dec 28 *The Night of the Iguana* (NY—Royale—Drama). Tennessee Williams's tale of a defrocked divine who's no match for the proprietress of a Mexican resort wins the Drama Critics' Circle Award. Patrick O'Neal, Bette Davis, and Margaret Leighton head the cast. Frank Corsaro stages for 316 performances. It is played only 76 times following its London premiere at the Savoy on March 24, 1965.

1961   BRITISH PREMIERES

Jan 12 *Ondine.* See NY premiere, 1954.

Feb 20 *The Devils* (L—Aldwych—Drama). John Whiting's play, based on Aldous Huxley's study of true events in a French convent, features Dorothy Tutin, Max Adrian, Diana Rigg, and Roy Dotrice. The Royal Shakespeare Company's production is under the direction of Peter Wood. The drama opens on Nov 16, 1965, at New York's Broadway with Anne Bancroft in the lead. It has only 63 performances.

Feb 22 *The Connection.* See NY premiere, 1959.

Feb 25 *King Kong* (L—Prince's—Musical). Todd Matshikiza writes jazz to lyrics by Pat Williams and Ralph Treewhela; book by Harry Bloom. The 201 performances are staged by Leon Gluckman. A black cast is highly praised for this tale of a South African boxer.

March 9 *The Miracle Worker.* See NY premiere, 1959.

March 16 *The Music Man.* See NY premiere, 1957.

March 25 *J. B.* See NY premiere, 1958.

HOW TO SUCCEED IN BUSINESS WITHOUT REALLY TRYING

J.B.

April 5 *One Over the Eight* (L—Duke of York's—Revue). This is a sequel to *Pieces of Eight*. Paddy Stone stages the ensemble, which includes Kenneth Williams, Sheila Hancock, and Irving Davies. Sketches are credited to Peter Cook. Additional material is from Lionel Bart, among others. The show runs a year.

April 6 *The Rehearsal* (L—Globe—Comedy). Jean Anouilh's wry comedy about a count pursuing his affair during rehearsals of an annual theatrical at his chateau features Robert Hardy, Diana Churchill, and Phyllis Calvert. First shown at the Bristol Old Vic, there is a 43 week run. The play comes to New York on Sep 23, 1962, where it opens at the Royale. With a British cast including Jennifer Hilary, Adrienne Corri, and Coral Browne, it runs nearly 14 weeks.

April 11 *The Irregular Verb To Love* (L—Criterion—Comedy). Hugh and Margaret Williams create a vehicle for his acting talents. He plays a long-suffering husband, a curator in the zoo, whose dedicated but eccentric wife has served a prison term for trying to blow up a furrier's shop. Joan Greenwood plays the wife. The show runs 45 weeks.

April 13 *The Tenth Man.* See NY premiere, 1959.

May 10 *Beyond the Fringe* (L—Fortune—Revue). After its Edinburgh Festival success last summer, this revue, with its creators Peter Cook, Dudley Moore, Jonathan Miller and Alan Bennett, runs 1,184 performances in the West End. They bring their show to New York's Golden Theatre beginning Oct 27, 1962. It wins 667 performances and gets a special citation from the Drama Critics' Circle.

May 18 *The Sound of Music.* See NY premiere, 1959.

May 31 *The Bird of Time* (L—Savoy—Drama). Gladys Cooper and Clive Morton play British who won't leave Kashmir despite threats of Chinese attacks. Allen Davis directs Peter Mayne's play for 197 performances.

June 15 *Bye Bye, Birdie.* See NY premiere, 1960.

July 11 *Becket.* See NY premiere, 1960.

July 18 *Goodnight, Mrs. Puffin* (L—Strand—Comedy). Irene Handl has a success as a perky Cockney precognitive: she amazes a Hampstead family, delights audiences, and plays for 691 performances. Alexander Dore stages.

July 20 *Stop the World—I Want to Get Off* (L—Queen's—Musical). Anthony Newley is the center of interest in this show, for which he has written book, lyrics, and music, in collaboration with Leslie Bricusse. This story of a man's life from cradle to grave has 485 performances. It opens in New York at the Shubert on Oct 3, 1962, with Newley again in the lead. It achieves 555 performances on Broadway and a national tour.

July 27 *Luther* (L—Royal Court—Drama). John Osborne's play is staged by Tony Richardson for the English Stage Company. Albert Finney plays the title role, with Peter Bull's assistance as a papal agent. Successfully performed at the Edinburgh Festival, it earns 239 performances before being seen on Broadway,

where it has 211 showings. It opens on Sep 25, 1963, with Finney.

Aug 2 *One for the Pot* (L—Whitehall—Comedy). There are 1,223 performances of Ray Cooney and Tony Hilton's popular Whitehall farce about an inheritance. Brian Rix is starred.

Aug 17 *Guilty Party* (L—St. Martin's—Drama). George Ross and Campbell Singer's thriller has Donald Sinden falsely accused of embezzlement for 380 performances. Anthony Sharp stages.

Aug 23 *The Lord Chamberlain Regrets . . . !* (L—Saville—Revue). The title suggests material banned by play examiners, but Peter Myers and Ronald Cass's show is not condemned by anyone at all. It runs for 220 performances. Among the players are Joan Sims, Millicent Martin, Barry Godney, Gordon Clyde, and Josephine Gordon.

Sep 21 *The Affair* (L—Strand—Drama). Ronald Millar adapts C. P. Snow's novel about a Cambridge fellow who is dismissed for his communist ideas and abrasive personality. Donald Howard and Dorothy Alison are featured. There are 379 performances. On Sep 20, 1962, the drama opens on Broadway at the Henry Miller with Christopher Hewett, Brewster Mason, Brenda Vaccaro, Kenneth Mars, and Donald Moffat in the cast. It plays 116 times.

Oct 12 *Do Re Mi.* See NY premiere, 1960.

Oct 23 *Bonne Soup.* See NY premiere (*The Good Soup*), 1960.

Nov 25 *The Bride Comes Back* (L—Vaudeville—Comedy). Ronald Millar writes a sequel to *The Bride and the Bachelor*. It brings Cicely Courtneidge and Jack Hulbert together in a non-musical for the first time. 267 performances result.

Dec 6 *Critic's Choice.* See NY premiere, 1960.

1961   REVIVALS/REPERTORIES

Jan 23 At the Theatre Royal, Stratford East, Joan Littlewood's Theatre Workshop presents *We're Not Just Practical*, book by Marvin Kane with songs by Ronnie Franklin and John Junkin. On April 3, the musical is *Glory Be!*, with book and lyrics by Fergus Lineham and music by Aideen Kinlen and Paddy Murray. Milo O'Shea leads a largely Irish cast. On June 28, Littlewood stages American James Goldman's *They Might Be Giants*. On Sep 11, Edward Burnham directs Thomas Murphy's *A Whistle in the Dark*. On Oct 23, the Workshop offers Alan Seymour's *The One Day of the Year*. On Nov 28, it's Henry Livings' *Big, Soft Nellie*.

Jan 27 Dion Boucicault's *The Octoroon* is revived Off-Broadway at the Phoenix Theatre for 45 performances. Juliet Randall plays the title character and Stuart Vaughn stages. On March 16, *Hamlet* is staged. It wins 103 performances. Donald Madden is the Dane and Joyce Ebert is Ophelia.

Feb 7 Hamburg's *Deutsches Schauspielhaus* brings Gustaf Grundgens' famed production of Goethe's *Faust, Part I* to New York City Center for two weeks. On Feb 21, following the Germans into the City Center are the *Societiares* of the Comedie Francaise who play for three weeks with a repertory including Moliere's *Tartuffe*, *L'Impromptu de Versailles* and *Les Fourberies de Scapin*. Robert Hirsch repeats his celebrated, hilarious, and acrobatic Scapin.

Feb 14 London's Old Vic season continues with *Henry IV, Part 1*, featuring Robert Harris as the king and Douglas Campbell as Falstaff. *Twelfth Night* opens April 18 with Alec McCowen and Tom Courtenay, Joss Ackland, and Barbara Jefford. On May 30, Robert Harris plays Shylock with Barbara Leigh-Hunt as Portia in *The Merchant of Venice*.

Feb 16 Henrik Ibsen's *John Gabriel Borkman* is revived at the Mermaid Theatre with an ingenious set by Michael Stringer. Julius Gellner directs. April 5 brings 18 of the *Wakefield Mystery Plays*, staged by Colin Ellis and Sally Miles. *Take a Life*, a melodrama with words by Sebastian Shaw and music by Humphrey Searle opens on April 9. On June 6, Saul Leavitt's American play, *The Andersonville Trial*, is staged by Bernard Miles, with John Woodvine and Maurice Denham. On July 26, the London premiere of Sean O'Casey's *The Bishop's Bonfire* is staged by Frank Dunlop with Paul Farrell. On Aug 29, a revival of John Ford's *'Tis Pity She's a Whore* is directed by David Thompson. Patience Collier plays Putana. On Oct 3, a Shaw double-bill, *The Shewing Up of Blanco Posnet* and *Androcles and the Lion*, is directed by Frank Dunlop. On Nov 7, R. C. Sherriff's *The Long Sunset* is staged.

Feb 20 Micheal macLiammoir's *The Importance of Being Oscar* is revived by the Dublin Gate, first at the Gaiety and then on Broadway on March 14. It will be revived in the fall with Bertolt Brecht's *Saint Joan of the Stockyards*.

Feb 21 Middleton and Rowley's Jacobean classic, *The Changeling*, is revived at London's Royal Court Theatre, for the first professional production since the 17th century. Tony Richardson stages Robert Shaw, Mary Ure, and Zoe Caldwell. On March 22, Eugene Ionesco's *Jacques* is staged by R. D. Smith. Jean-Paul Sartre's *Altona* opens on April 19 and Jean Genet's *The Blacks* on May 30.

March 15 Henrik Ibsen's *The Lady from the Sea* is revived by director Glen Byam Shaw at London's Queen's Theatre for two months with Margaret Leighton in the title-role.

March 19 *The Hollow Crown*, John Barton's anthology of the lives of England's anointed monarchs, staged by Barton with Dorothy Tutin, Max Adrian, Barton, and Richard Johnson, opens at the Royal Shakespeare's London home, the Aldwych Theatre.

March 29 Dylan Thomas's *Under Milk Wood* is imaginatively staged by William Ball. It has a run of 202 performances Off-Broadway at the Circle-in-the-Square. The play is produced by Jose Quintero and Ted Mann.

April 4 In Stratford-upon-Avon, the Royal Shakespeare Company opens its season with Michael Langham's production of *Much Ado About Nothing*. Geraldine McEwan and Christopher Plummer are Beatrice and Benedick. Ian Bannen plays Hamlet, in Peter Wood's staging of the play. William Gaskill stages *Richard III*, with Plummer as the king and Edith Evans as Queen Margaret. Vanessa Redgrave is Rosalind in Michael Elliott's production of *As You Like It*. Brian Murray and Dorothy Tutin are the lovers in *Romeo and Juliet*. John Gielgud plays the title role in *Othello*, staged by Franco Zeffirelli.

April 12 Jean Dalrymple revives Jerome Kern's *Show Boat* at New York's City Center for a two-week run. Hollywood's big-mouthed comic, Joe E. Brown, is Captain Andy. On April 26, Rodgers and Hammerstein's *South Pacific* is the revival. *Porgy and Bess* makes its appearance on May 17. On May 31, *Pal Joey* returns with Bob Fosse as Joey.

June 5 Jean-Paul Sartre's *Altona* moves from London's Royal Court to the Saville Theatre where it runs 77 performances. Kenneth Haigh, Basil Sydney, and Claire Bloom are among those directed by John Berry.

June 6 In Connecticut's Stratford, the American Shakespeare Festival performs three plays in repertory for 112 performances: *As You Like It*, staged by Word Baker, with Kim Hunter and Carrie Nye; *Macbeth*, staged by Jack Landau, with Pat Hingle and Jessica Tandy; *Troilus and Cressida*, also staged by Landau, with Ted van Griethuysen and Nye.

June 19 The Stratford Shakespeare Festival of Canada opens its new season, still under Michael Langham's artistic direction. He stages *Coriolanus*, played by Paul Scofield, and George McCowan directs *Henry VIII*. The new Canadian play, *The Canvas Barricade*, by Donald Jack is presented, and Tyrone Guthrie stages Gilbert and Sullivan's *The Pirates of Penzance*.

June 24 Ashland's Oregon Shakespearean Festival produces *Hamlet*, *A Midsummer Night's Dream*, *All's Well That Ends Well*, and *Henry IV, Part 1*. Ben Jonson's *The Alchemist* is also played. The traditional Elizabethan stage sees a total of 42 performances.

June 25 Kermit Hunter's *Honey in The Rock*, a drama about the Civil War and West Virginia's secession from Virginia, is presented in Beckley, West Virginia, to celebrate the state's centennial.

June 25 Jean Genet's one-act play, *Deathwatch*, is paired with Georges Neveux's *The Splits* at London's Arts Theatre. An entertainment based on Tolstoy's *The Kreutzer Sonata* opens July 10, and *Lady Chatterley*, an adaptation from D. H. Lawrence by John Hart, is staged by Alan Cooke on Aug 16.

June 27 *Twelfth Night*, staged by William Ball, and *The Merchant of Venice*, and *Richard III*, both staged by Allen Fletcher, are presented at the Old Globe Theatre in Balboa Park by the San Diego National Shakespeare Festival.

July Vivien Leigh heads the Old Vic's tour of Australasia, and performs Shakespeare scenes in repertory with *Twelfth Night* and Dumas fils' *The Lady of the Camellias*, under Robert Helpmann's direction. Eight South American cities see the same in the spring of 1962.

July 3 *Bound for Kentucky!* opens in Louisville, Kentucky. Written by Kermit Hunter, it deals with George Rogers Clark and the early days of Louisville.

July 5 In Central Park's Wollman Skating Rink, Joseph Papp's New York Shakespeare Festival offers three productions, not in repertory, for a total of 46 performances: *Much Ado About Nothing* is staged by Papp; *A Midsummer Night's Dream*, with James Earl Jones and Kathleen Widdoes; and *Richard III*, staged by Gladys Vaughn.

July 6 At the Lyric, Hammersmith, Arthur Kopit's American absurdist comedy, *Oh, Dad, Poor Dad, Mama's Hung You in the Closet, and I'm Feeling So Sad*, is staged by Frank Corsaro, with Andrew Ray and Stella Adler in the cast.

Aug 9 The National Youth Theatre presents Shakespeare's *Richard II* at London's Apollo Theatre. Michael Croft directs this and *Henry IV, Part 2*, which opens Aug 22.

Aug 20 Britain's Edinburgh International Festival opens with a new artistic director, Lord Harewood. The Old Vic presents Marlowe's *Doctor Faustus*; the English Stage Company produces John Osborne's *Luther*; the Bristol Old Vic performs Lawrence Durrell's *Sappho*; the Edinburgh Gateway Company mounts Robert Kemp's *Let Wives Tak' Tent*. L'Association Francaise d'Action Artistique stages Moliere's *Le Misanthrope*, and Marcel Achard's *Jean de la Lune*. In the final week, the English Stage Company presents Nigel Dennis' *August for the People*, and the Old Vic offers *King John*.

Sep 13 *The Taming of the Shrew*, with Vanessa Redgrave and Derek Godfrey, brings Stratford production values to London's Aldwych. Maurice Daniels directs.

Sep 14 The Old Vic plays Christopher Marlowe's *Doctor Faustus* at its historic home in London's Waterloo Road. A touring compano is playing Franco Zeffirelli's *Romeo and Juliet* in Venice and Turin. On Sep 19, *King John* opens in London, and on Oct 2, *Twelfth Night* is offered. On Nov 7, Aeschylus' *Oresteia* opens for 15 performances at London's Old Vic Theatre in a translation by Edith Hamilton and Minos Volanakis, who also directs. On Nov 21, Eugene O'Neill's *Mourning Becomes Electra* opens for 23 performances, directed by Val May, and featuring Barbara Jefford. Oliver Neville's direction of *Macbeth* opens on Dec 19th with Maurice Denham and Maxine Audley.

Sep 21 Hendrik Ibsen's *Ghosts* wins a 27-week run, staged by David Ross at his 4th Street Theatre. Carrie Nye, Leueen MacGrath, and Staats Cotsworth appear.

Oct 24 Edward Albee's *The Death of Bessie Smith* and *The American Dream* are staged by Peter Yates at London's Royal Court Theatre. On Nov 13, Henry Chapman's *That's Us* is staged; on the 22nd, Gwyn Thomas' *The Keep* is revived. Fernando Arrabal's *Orison* and *Fando and Lis* open on the 26th, and Derek Marlowe's *The Scarecrow*, based on Leonid Andreyev's *The Seven Who Were Hanged* opens Dec 3, directed by Corin Redgrave. Max Frisch's *The Fire Eaters* is staged by Lindsay Anderson on the 21st.

Nov 1 George Bernard Shaw's *Heartbreak House* is revived at Wyndham's Theatre by Frank Hauser. It runs 117 performances. Roger Livesey and Dulcie Gray play major roles.

Nov 27 Producer Stella Holt revives Sean O'Casey's *Red Roses for Me* for a run of 176 performances at the Off-Broadway Greenwich Mews.

Dec 11 The D'Oyly Carte Opera Company opens its season at London's Savoy with a Gilbert and Sullivan repertory including *Trial by Jury*, *H.M.S. Pinafore*, *Cox and Box*, *Pirates of Penzance*, *Patience*, *Iolanthe*, and *Princess Ida*.

Dec 12 Brendan Behan's *The Hostage* is revived Off-Broadway for 545 performances at One Sheridan Square. Geoff Garland plays the title role.

Dec 13 Holiday productions begin to open. Today, it's the Mermaid's *Treasure Island*. On the 15th, *Peter Pan* returns to the Scala Theatre. On the 19th, *Cinderella* opens at the Players' Theatre Club. *Little Old King Cole* follows at the Palladium, with Charlie Drake as the king. Other holiday shows include *Through the Looking Glass* (Lyric, Hammersmith), *The Circus Adventure* (Arts), *Toad of Toad Hall* (Saville), *Billy Bunter Shipwrecked* (Victoria Palace), *Mother Goose* (Wimbledon), *Jack and Jill* (Streatham Hill), *Cinderella* (Golder's Green Hippodrome), and *The Marvellous Story of Puss in Boots* (Theatre Royal, Stratford East).

Dec 14 Royal Shakespeare's Aldwych sees a revival of Chekhov's *The Cherry Orchard* in an English version by John Gielgud. He plays Gaev, with Peggy Ashcroft as Ranevskaya. Judi Dench, Dorothy Tutin and Roy Dotrice are also in the cast.

1961   BIRTHS/DEATHS/DEBUTS

Jan 4 Actor Barry Fitzgerald (b. 1888) dies in Dublin. His first appearance with the Abbey Players was in the role of Capt. Jack Boyle in *Juno and the Paycock*. His successful film career began in 1937.

Jan 13 American actress and singer Blanche Ring (b. 1876) dies in Santa Monica. Her career began with James Herne, Nat Goodwin, and Chauncey Olcott. In 1908 she toured with Joe Weber in burlesques. Nanette in *No, No Nanette*, Mrs. Draper in *Strike Up the Band*, and Aunt Min in *Her Master's Voice* were among her successful roles.

Jan 14 Harry Pilcer, composer and inventor of "The Gaby Glide" (for Gaby Deslys), dies in Cannes, France, at 75. He was a leading show dancer for a number of years, partnering Mistinguett for a decade.

Feb 1 English stage and screen actor J. H. Roberts (b. 1884) is dead. He was one of the original members of the Liverpool Repertory Company.

Feb 17 Born Nonna Dooley, the stage and screen actress Nita Naldi dies at 63 in New York.

March 27 Beloved comedienne of Dublin's Abbey Theatre, Maureen Delaney dies in London at 73.

April 3 Impressario and playwright Sir Barry Vincent Jackson (b. 1879) dies in Birmingham. He was founder of the Birmingham Repertory Theatre and the Malvern Festival, and director of the Memorial Theatre at Stratford-upon-Avon from 1945 to 1948. Sir Barry was knighted in 1925.

May 17 English actress Viola Roache (b. 1885) dies in Hollywood. Her favorite roles were Eliza Doolittle in *Pygmalion* and Mrs. Malaprop in *The Rivals*.

May 19 American stage actress Grace George (b. 1879) dies in New York. Her first important appearance was in 1898 as Juliette in *The Turtle*. She was married to producer William Brady.

May 19 Joe Howard, vaudeville star and composer of such musicals as *The Time, the Place, and The Girl* and *A Stubborn Cinderella*, dies in Chicago at 93.

June 2 American playwright George S. Kaufman (b. 1889) dies in New York City. Kaufman wrote many of his plays in collaboration; *Beggar on Horseback* with Marc Connelly, *The Royal Family* with Edna Ferber, *Strike Up the Band* with Morrie Ryskind, and *You Can't Take It With You* (among others) with Moss Hart. He is the sole author of *The Butter and Egg Man* and *Cocoanuts*.

Aug 17 The distinguished British stage actress Violet Kemble Cooper passes on.

Aug 30 American actor-producer Charles Coburn (b. 1877) dies in New York. Coburn and his wife, Ivah Wills, organized the Coburn Shakespearean Players in 1906.

Sep 10 Leo Carillo, experienced both on Broadway and in films, dies at the age of 81.

Sep 22 Stage and screen actress Marion Davies (b. 1897) dies in Los Angeles. Her career was materially advanced by William Randolph Hearst, her great admirer.

Sep 25 Actor Frank Fay (b. 1897) dies in Santa Monica. An extra in Henry Irving's *The Merchant of Venice*, a vaudevillian ("Dyer and Fay"), his great stage success was as Elwood P. Dowd in *Harvey* in 1944. *How to be Poor*, his reminiscences, was published in 1945.

Oct 1 American actor Donald Cook dies.

Oct 5 Percy Waram dies in Huntington, New York, at age 80. Born in Kent, England, he worked and toured with Ben Greet, and in 1941 played Father in *Life With Father*.

Oct 11 Chico, one of the stage and screen comedy team of the Marx Brothers, dies today at the age of 70.

Oct 29 Producer Guthrie McClintic, husband of Katharine Cornell, whom he also directed on stage, dies at 68.

Nov 1 Musical comedy actress Joan McCracken is only 38 when she dies.

Nov 2 *New Yorker* humorist James Thurber, whose comic sketches and characters have been seen on stage in such shows as *The Thurber Carnival*, dies today at 66.

Nov 7 Bijou Fernandez dies in New York City at 84. She appeared as Prince Arthur in *King John* with Edwin Booth and had been acclaimed in the early 1900's for performance in *As You Like It*, *The Climbers*, and *The Frisky Mrs. Johnson*. She took control of her mother's theatrical agency in 1909.

Nov 13 A beloved British actress, Madge Titheradge passes on at age 74.

Nov 15 Actress Elsie Ferguson (b. 1883) dies in New London, Connecticut. In addition to silent films, her Broadway roles included Portia in *The Merchant of Venice* with Sir Herbert Tree, Kate Hardcastle in *She Stoops to Conquer*, and Crystal Grainger in *Outrageous Fortune*.

Nov 18 Al Carmines, minister, director, playwright and composer, presents a double bill (*The Great American Desert* and *The Breasts of Teresius*) at New York's Judson Memorial Church in an effort to bring together artistic creativity and religious worship.

Nov 19 American playwright Dorothy Heyward (b. 1880) is dead. Author of *Porgy* and *Mamba's Daughters* with Du Bose Heyward, her husband, she had collaborated with Moss Hart on *Jonica*.

Nov 22 English actor Keith Baxter debuts in New York as Henry VIII in Bolt's *A Man for All Seasons* at the ANTA Theatre.

Nov 24 Ruth Chatterton, a beloved actress, dies at 67.

Dec 20 American playwright and director Moss Hart (b. 1904) is dead in Palm Springs. Hart collaborated with George S. Kaufman on *Merrily We Roll Along, You Can't Take It With You,* and *The Man Who Came to Dinner.* On his own he wrote *Lady in the Dark, Winged Victory,* and others. *My Fair Lady* and *Camelot* were two of his productions. His autobiography, *Act One,* was published in 1959. He was married to actress Kitty Carlisle.

1961 THEATERS/PRODUCTIONS

U.S. patents include one better suited to films than the stage: James Avery's flaming-car illusion, in which a series of pipes mounted on the car feed fuel which can be suddenly ignited.

Chicago's old Grand Opera House is razed. It seated 1,700 and had been remodeled in 1880 by Adler and Sullivan. The Daley Civic Center and Plaza will rise on its site.

Chicago's Great Northern Theatre is demolished. It opened in 1896, designed by'D. H. Burnham, with a capacity of 1,385 seats. It has also been known as the Lyric and the Hippodrome.

Jan In 1931, Broadway boasted 63 theatres; this year finds only 33. Eighteen are Shubert theatres and most of the remainder are mortgaged.

Feb 6 The major interest of *Magic Lantern* at London's Saville is the combination of live performers with filmed sequences also featuring them. It's devised by Czech designer Josef Svoboda; Milos Forman is also involved.

March Playwright John Osborne, confronted with the Lord Chamberlain's list of 14 cuts required in his new drama *Luther,* initially refuses to comply, preferring to postpone a British premiere in-definitely. After negotiations, objections are reduced to use of "convent piss," "monk's piss," "piss-scared," "crap," and "balls of the Medici." Osborne notes that even Shakespeare has used the word "piss." The censors offer "testicles" as an acceptable substitute for "balls."

March 15 The formation of the Theatre Communications Group, a national service organization for the nonprofit professional theatre in the United States, is announced.

March 19 Queen Elizabeth II commands that the Shakespeare Memorial Theatre in Stratford-upon-Avon be known as the Royal Shakespeare Theatre.

May 10 Even though *Beyond the Fringe* mocks the Prime Minister, the Lord Chamberlain has not censored the show, and he will see it with the Prime Minister as part of the Queen's theatre-party.

May 24 Members of the Dramatists Guild, meaning to ease the financial crisis of the New York theatre, agree to take royalty cuts if other personnel will also take cuts in compensation.

Summer The Marin Shakespeare Festival is founded by John and Ann Brebner as a non-profit tax-exempt corporation to bring Shakespearian plays to the San Francisco Bay area. It leases Forest Meadows Theatre, seating 598, from Dominican College in San Rafael.

June 1 Louis Kronenberger, in his role as editor of the Burns Mantle theatre yearbook, *Best Plays,* chooses his ten best candidates for the 1960–1961 Broadway season just closed. They are Brendan Behan's *The Hostage,* Shelagh Delaney's *A Taste of Honey,* Jean Anouilh's *Becket,* Eugene Ionesco's *Rhinoceros,* Tennessee Williams' *Period of Adjustment,* Tad Mosel's *All the Way Home,* Jean Kerr's *Mary, Mary,* Dore Schary's *The Devil's Advocate,* Hugh Wheeler's *Big Fish, Little Fish,* and Henry Denker's *A Far Country. All the Way Home* wins both the Pulitzer Prize and the Drama Critics' Circle Awards, with *A Taste of Honey* judged by the Circle to be the Best Foreign Play. *Carnival* is Best Musical Production.

June 5 Writing in the *NY Times,* Arthur Gelb reports very considerable financial losses for the past season. "Of the 46 shows this season—a record low—only six to eight are expected to return their investment."

June 6 Writing in the *NY Times,* A. H. Raskin reports Broadway producers' charges of "featherbedding," with stage-unions' denials.

Fall Top stage-directors this Broadway season can expect a directing fee of $5,000, plus 2 percent of the gross until the show has paid off its costs, with beginner's fees as low as $500 or $1,000.

Oct 18 Ellen Stewart pays $55 to rent the basement at 321 East 9th Street in New York for the first home of her La Mama Experimental Theatre Club. She will have continuing difficulties with local residents and city officials.

Oct 30 Harry Weese designed the Arena Theatre in Washington, D.C., which opens today. Seating for 811 is in tiered rows along the sides of a rectangular acting arena, a design evolved from earlier arena-stagings by the ensemble.

Dec Producer David Merrick, annoyed with negative critics, has located people with the critics' names and now publishes their raves for his new show in a *Herald Tribune* full-page ad. Readers may perceive the truth through small accompanying photos, but the ethics of this maneuver are hotly debated.

Dec 31 The last of the Gilbert & Sullivan copyrights expire. Bridget D'Oyly Carte, whose company has preserved the traditional stagings, forms a trust.

GEORGE KAUFMAN/MOSS HART

Jan 3 *Brecht on Brecht* (NY—Theatre deLys—Reading). George Tabori translates and adapts a sampler of Brecht's prose, poetry, songs, and drama. Lotte Lenya, Viveca Lindfors, Dane Clark, Anne Jackson, George Voskovec, and Michael Wager play 424 performances.

Jan 8 *The Egg* (NY—Cort—Comedy). Felicien Marceau's satire is chosen by Henry Hewes as a "Best Play," yet it runs only a week, despite its success at Washington's Arena Stage last season.

Jan 10 *Romulus* (NY—Music Box—Comedy). Friedrich Duerrenmatt's satire on the end of the Roman Empire is adapted by Gore Vidal, yet something incisive in the original is lost. Cyril Ritchard plays the last emperor for the 69 performances.

Jan 11 *Plays for Bleecker Street* (NY—Circle-in-the-Square—Drama). Thornton Wilder's *Infancy*, *Childhood*, and *Someone from Assisi* are staged by Jose Quintero.

Jan 15 *Moon on a Rainbow Shawl* (NY—East 11th Street—Drama). Errol John's tale of a Trinidadian who won't let life discourage him features James Earl Jones, Cicely Tyson and Vinnette Carroll. It runs for 13 weeks.

Jan 31 *A Passage to India*. See L premiere, 1960.

Feb 7 *The Aspern Papers*. See L premiere, 1959.

Feb 26 *Oh Dad, Poor Dad, Mamma's Hung You in the Closet and I'm Feelin' So Sad* (NY—Phoenix—Comedy). Arthur Kopit's Absurdist parody, staged by Jerome Robbins, is chosen as a "Best Play" and receives 454 performances. Austin Pendleton plays Jonathan, the mother dominated boy with remarkable collections of coins and stamps, and a dead father hanging in the hotel closet. It's shown at the Piccadilly Theatre in London on Oct 6, 1965. Hermione Gingold is the mother.

March 1 *This Was Burlesque* (NY—Casino East—Revue). Ann Corio stars in this sampler of a virtually lost art-form. This first edition plays nearly 900 times. The show also has a long life on tour. A second will play Off-Broadway for 609 performances, then opening on Broadway on March 16, 1965.

March 15 *No Strings* (NY—54th Street—Musical). Richard Rodgers becomes his own lyricist for this show. He also uses, as the title indicates, no strings in his score. Richard Kiley plays an American novelist abroad, in love with a stunning Parisian model (Diahann Carroll). There are 580 performances. The show premieres in London on Dec 30, 1963, with Art Lund and Beverly Todd. There are only 151 showings.

March 22 *I Can Get It For You Wholesale* (NY—Shubert—Musical). Barbra Streisand wins her first Broadway praise in Jerome Weidman's adaptation of his own book, with songs by Harold Rome. Elliott Gould also appears in Arthur Laurents' staging, and David Merrick produces for 300 performances.

April 5 *A Thousand Clowns* (NY—Eugene O'Neill—Comedy). Jason Robards, Jr., is the non-conformist caring for a young nephew and investigated by the Welfare Department in Herb Gardner's play. There are 428 performances. It fails in London. Following its premiere at the Comedy on June 2, 1964, there are only 46 performances.

May 8 *A Funny Thing Happened on the Way to the Forum* (NY—Alvin—Musical). Stephen Sondheim creates music and lyrics for Larry Gelbart and Burt Shevelove's mingling of plot and characters from Plautus. Zero Mostel heads the cast. Harold Prince produces the 964 performances. Popular comic Frankie Howerd is the clever slave in the successful London production (763 performances) which opens on Oct 3, 1963 at the Strand.

July 2 In Dawson City, in the Yukon, producers Robert Whitehead and Stanley Gilky open *Foxy*, a musical about the Klondike Gold Rush, based on Ben Jonson's *Volpone*. There are 43 performances at the Palace Grand Theatre, with songs by Robert Emmett Dolan and Johnny Mercer. The book's by Ring Lardner, Jr., and Ian McLellan Hunter. On Feb 6, 1964, the show is staged in New York at the Ziegfeld Theatre, with Bert Lahr in the title role—his last. It runs only nine weeks, even with a cast including Cathryn Damon, Larry Blyden, Gerald Hiken, David Rounds, and John Davidson. Robert Lewis directs.

Sep 17 *The Days and Nights of Beebee Fenstermacher* (NY—Sheridan Square—Drama). Rose Gregorio plays Beebee, a girl who comes to the city in search of success and love, in William Snyder's play. Robert Duvall is also in the cast. The play wins 304 performances.

Sep 20 *The Affair*. See L premiere, 1961.

Sep 23 *The Rehearsal*. See L premiere, 1961.

Oct 1 *Whisper into My Good Ear/Mrs. Dally Has a Lover* (NY—Cherry Lane—Drama). William Hanley's two one-act plays have a six-week run Off-Broadway. Roberts Blossom and Boris Tumarin, in the first, play two old men with a suicide pact. In the second, Estelle Parsons, as Mrs. Dally, is an older woman having an affair with a young man (Robert Drivas).

Oct 3 *Stop the World—I Want To Get Off*. See L premiere, 1961.

Oct 13 *Who's Afraid of Virginia Woolf?* (NY—Billy Rose—Drama). Edward Albee's story about two couples who lay bare their personal secrets, features Uta Hagen, Arthur Hill, Melinda Dillon, and George Grizzard. Directed by Alan Schneider, there are 664 performances. The play wins the Critics' Circle Award. Two years later, on Feb 6, 1964, it opens in the West End at the Piccadilly with Hagen, Hill, Richard Easton, and Beverlee McKinsey. There are 428 showings.

Oct 18 *Dime a Dozen* (NY—Plaza 9—Revue). Julius Monk's revue wins 728 performances for Mary Louise Wilson, Rex Robbins, Susan Browning, and Gerry Matthews, among others. Frank Wagner stages.

Oct 20 *Mr. President* (NY—St. James—Musical). Irving Berlin writes the songs for this Howard Lindsay and Russel Crouse book about a president who has lost a reelection campaign. Robert Ryan has the lead. The show runs eight months.

Oct 25 *Tchin-Tchin*. See L premiere (*Chin-Chin*), 1960.

Oct 27 *Beyond the Fringe*. See L premiere, 1961.

Oct 31 *Calculated Risk* (NY—Ambassador—Drama). Someone on the corporate board has sold out in Joseph Hayes' script. Joseph Cotton, Russell Collins, John Beal, and Patricia Medina are in the cast directed by Robert Montgomery. The play lasts 221 performances.

Nov 17 *Little Me* (NY—Lunt-Fontanne—Musical). Neil Simon adapts Patrick Dennis's parody of an ambitious poor girl's memoirs. Songs are by Cy Coleman and Carolyn Leigh. Sid Caesar plays a wide range of roles, with Virginia Martin and Nancy Andrews also in the cast. Choreography is by Bob Fosse. There are 257 performances. The musical opens in London at the Cambridge on Nov 18, 1964, with Bruce Forsyth, Eileen Gourlay, Avril Angers, and Swen Swenson in the cast. It has 406 performances.

Nov 19 *Lord Pengo* (NY—Royale—Comedy). S. N. Behrman adapts this vehicle for Charles Boyer from his *The Days of Duveen*. Brian Bedford, Agnes Moorehead, Henry Daniell, Lee Richardson, and Ruth White are in the cast. Vincent J. Donehue directs. There are 175 performances.

Nov 26 *The Dumbwaiter/The Collection* (NY—Cherry Lane—Drama). Harold Pinter's ambiguities attract audiences for 578 performances. Alan Schneider stages, with Dana Elcar and John C. Becher as two thugs awaiting orders in the first play: they get orders for food. In the second, sets of sexual relationships are called into question with an allegation of adultery. This cast includes Henderson Forsythe,

LITTLE ME

Patricia Roe, James Ray, and James Paterson.

Nov 26 *The Coach with the Six Insides* (NY—Village South—Drama). Choreographer-dancer Jean Erdman stages James Joyce's classic and interprets Anna Livia Plurabelle herself in this collage of mime, dance, song, and speech. The production runs over 14 weeks and tours college campuses.

Nov 27 *Never Too Late* (NY—Playhouse—Comedy). A middleaged couple discover they are to have a baby. Maureen O'Sullivan and Paul Ford are featured with Orson Bean, House Jameson, and Leona Maricle. George Abbott stages Sumner Arthur Long's play for 1,007 showings. The play earns 191 showings in London after its Sep 24, 1963, opening at the Prince of Wales's Theatre.

Nov 28 *Moby Dick* (NY—Ethel Barrymore—Drama). Orson Welle's adaptation of the Melville novel is staged by Douglas

Campbell and features Rod Steiger. The production lasts just two weeks.

Dec 12 *Riverwind* (NY—Actors Playhouse—Musical). John Jennings' plot requires a middle-aged couple to return to a rundown tourist spot where they once honeymooned. Adrian Hall directs a company including Lovelady Powell, Brooks Morton, and Elizabeth Parrish. Robert Soule and Jules Fisher design. The show runs for 433 performances.

Dec 22 *Tiger, Tiger, Burning Bright* (NY—Booth—Drama). Dancer Alvin Ailey plays Clarence Morris in Peter Feibleman's adaptation of his novel, *A Place Without Twilight*. Joshua Logan stages the production which runs only four weeks.

Dec 26 *The Beauty Part* (NY—Music Box—Comedy). S. J. Perelman's satire on contemporary artistic striving is staged by Noel Willman and runs nearly 11 weeks. Bert Lahr is the star, with Sean Garrison and Alice Ghostley among the cast.

1962 BRITISH PREMIERES

Feb 9 *Signpost to Murder* (L—Cambridge—Drama). Monte Doyle's thriller about a convicted murderer who tries to

prove his innocence features Derek Farr and Margaret Lockwood. There are 419 performances.

Feb 20 *Boeing-Boeing* (L—Apollo—Comedy). Patrick Cargill plays a clever Frenchman who's carrying on affairs with an American, a French, and a German stewardess. Beverley Cross's adaptation of Mark Camoletti's French farce runs 2,035 performances. On Feb 2, 1965, the comedy opens in New York at the Cort with Ian Carmichael in the lead. There are just 23 showings.

Feb 27 *Come Blow Your Horn*. See NY premiere, 1961.

March 27 *The Knack* (L—Royal Court—Comedy). Ann Jellico assists Keith Johnstone in directing her play about the pangs of adolescent love. Rita Tushingham and Philip Locke play leads. The play, seen first at the Arts Theatre, is quite a success. On May 27, 1964, it opens at Broadway's New Theatre with Brian Bedford, Roddy Maude-Roxby, Alexandra Berlin, and George Segal. Staged by Mike Nichols, it wins 426 performances.

April 3 *Look Homeward Angel*. See NY premiere, 1957.

April 4 *Two Stars for Comfort* (L—Garrick—Drama). Trevor Howard plays Sam Turner, proprietor of a riverside hotel, who manages to charm the girls each Regatta season, to the despair of his wife, who this summer leaves him for good. John Mortimer's play has a run of 188 performances.

April 25 *Photo Finish* (L—Saville—Comedy). Peter Ustinov writes, directs, and has the lead in this comedy about an 80-year-old actor looking back on his life. The production runs nearly eight months. Ustinov is again featured when the play opens on Broadway at the Brooks Atkinson on Feb 12, 1963. It plays 159 times.

April 27 *Chips with Everything* (L—Royal Court—Drama). Arnold Wesker's drama of young men being drilled into obedience in an RAF training unit features Frank Finlay and Ronald Lacey. Moving to the Vaudeville, it has a run of 318 performances. The show opens at New York's Plymouth on Oct 1, 1963, with John Dexter directing Alan Dobie, Gary Bond, John Noakes, and Corin Redgrave, among others. It runs over 18 weeks.

May 8 *Blitz!* (L—Adelphi—Musical). With 567 performances, Lionel Bart's new show is remarkable for Sean Kenny's settings. Joan Maitland has collaborated with Bart on the book, evoking the brave Cockney spirit during the Blitz. Amelia Bayntun heads the cast.

May 10 *The Private Earl/The Public Eye* (L—Globe—Comedy). Peter Shaffer's double-bill plays 549 performances. The first play, dealing with a classic triangle, features Maggie Smith, Terry Scully, and Douglas Livingston. The second, about a woman who finds a new way of viewing life—from the detective her husband has hired to shadow her—features Smith and Kenneth Williams. On Oct 9, the show premieres on Broadway at the Morosco where it runs over 20 weeks. The cast includes Brian Bedford, Geraldine McEwan, and Barry Foster.

May 17 *Little Mary Sunshine*. See NY premiere, 1959.

May 25 *The Black and White Minstrel Show* (L—Victoria Palace—Revue). Although minstrel shows of any description are an embarassment in America now, this show has a long run. George Inns has devised it and Larry Gordon choreographs. Margo Henderson, Tony Mercer, Leslie Crowther, and George Chisholm are among the opening cast.

June 20 *Judith* (L—Her Majesty's—Drama). Sean Connery plays Holofernes in Christopher Fry's translation of Jean Giradoux's play. Ruth Meyer plays the title role. It runs only 29 performances. Harold Clurman stages.

June 21 *Sail Away*. See NY premiere, 1961.

June 28 *The Genius and the Goddess* (L—Comedy—Drama). Frank Hauser directs Constance Cummings and Paul Massie, among others, in this play by Aldous Huxley and Beth Wendel. Designers are Pauline Whitehouse and Philip Prowse.

July 19 *Plays for England* (L—Royal Court—Comedy). Two plays by John Osborne open: *The Blood of the Bambergs* (directed by John Dexter) and *Under Plain Cover* (directed by Jonathan Miller). In the first is a royal wedding, and in the second a slightly kinky and oddly-paired couple.

Aug 20 *Gentlemen Prefer Blondes* (L—Prince's—Musical). Anita Loos and Joseph Fields have fashioned the show-book from her now classic spoof. Leo Rabin and Jule Styne have created songs that made this a Broadway success. It plays 223 West End performances with Dora Bryan as Lorelei.

Sep 12 *Miss Pell Is Missing* (L—Criterion—Comedy). Leonard Gershe's American play stars Wilfrid Hyde White, Amanda Reiss and Richard Briers and is staged by Murray MacDonald. It plays 157 performances.

Sep 19 *Rattle of a Simple Man* (L—Garrick—Comedy). Charles Dyer's play about the relationship between an awkward prostitute and a simple sports fan features Sheila Hancock and Edward Woodward. (The rattle is a soccer fan's noisemaker.) There are 369 performances. The comedy arrives in New York at the Booth on April 17, 1963, with Woodward and Tammy Grimes in the leads. Although there are only 94 performances, Henry Hewes chooses it as one of his ten "Best Plays."

Nov 8 *Out of Bounds* (L—Wyndham's—Comedy). Michael Redgrave plays an unworldly headmaster who is asked by the government to break a spy ring. The play runs nearly 31 weeks.

Nov 27 *Vanity Fair* (L—Queen's—Musical). Robin Miller and Alan Pryce-Jones collaborate on this musicalization of Thackeray's novel. Julian Slade scores. Sybil Thorndike at 80 appears in her first musical, which runs for 78 performances.

Nov 29 *The Tulip Tree* (L—Haymarket—Drama). N. C. Hunter's play about marital problems features John Clements, Colin Elliot, and Celia Johnson. There are 140 performances.

Dec 5 *Semi-Detached* (L—Saville—Comedy). Laurence Olivier plays Fred Midway, ambitious and pretentious beyond his capabilities and understanding. Mona Washbourne is his wife, Hilda, eager to marry off daughter Eileen (Eileen Atkins). Tony Richardson directs. Loudon Sainthill designs. There are 133 performances.

Dec 20 *Rule of Three* (L—Duchess—Drama). These are three one-act plays by Agatha Christie: *The Rats, Afternoon at the Seaside*, and *The Patient*. Hubert Gregg directs. They run nearly three months.

1962 REVIVALS/REPERTORIES

Jan 1 At London's Savoy Theatre, the D'Oyly Carte Opera Company continues its season with *The Mikado*, followed by *Ruddigore, The Yeoman of the Guard*, and *The Gondoliers*.

Jan 10 The Royal Shakespeare Company's London season at the Aldwych will present *As You Like It*, an "entertainment" by John Barton based on *Les Liasons Dangereuses*, Bertolt Brecht's *The Caucasian Chalk Circle*, and August Strindberg's *Dance of Death*.

Jan 17 The Old Vic Theatre's season continues with *Twelfth Night*, to be followed by *Richard III, Julius Caesar*, and *The Tempest*. The casts include Paul Daneman, Eileen Atkins, Maurice Good, John Gregson, and Alastair Sim (as Prospero).

Jan 24 At the Royal Court Theatre in London's Sloane Square, Tony Richardson stages *A Midsummer Night's Dream*, with Corin Redgrave, Robert Lang, Colin Blakely, Rita Tushingham, Lynn Redgrave, Samantha Eggar, Alfred Lynch, and Nicol Williamson. On Feb 18, George Devine stages them in *Twelfth Night*—without decor.

Jan 24 Gilbert & Sullivan's *Iolanthe* is given a new production by the Oxford Playhouse's director, Frank Hauser, at the Sadler's Wells Theatre. Tyrone Guthrie beings his *H.M.S. Pinafore* from Canada's Stratford, and later his *Pirates of Penzance*, to Her Majesty's where they will play in repertory.

Feb 6 London's Old Vic comes to the New York City Center for six weeks, bringing *Macbeth, Romeo and Juliet*, and George Bernard Shaw's *Saint Joan*. Productions are staged by Michael Benthall, Franco Zefirelli, and Douglas Seale. John Clements, John Stride, Joanna Dunham, and Barbara Jefford, respectively, have the title roles.

Feb 14 At London's Mermaid Theatre, Mayakovsky's *The Bed Bug* opens. George Bernard Shaw's *Arms and the Man*, Fred Hoyle's *Rockets in Ursa Major*, and Miles's musical, *Lock Up Your Daughters*, which opened the new theatre, will all be played this season.

Feb 19 Marie Bell brings her company from Paris to London's Piccadilly Theatre for a season of repertory including Francoise Sagan's *Les Violons Parfois*, Moliere's *Le Misanthrope*, Marcel Achard's *Jean de la Lune*, Jean Anouilh's *L'Invitation au Chateau* and Paul Claudel's *L'Annonce Faite a Marie*.

March 13 The Royal Shakespeare Company opens a second London home as a center for experimental plays and productions. It is the New Arts—formerly the Arts Theatre Club. Giles Cooper's *Everything in the Garden* is the first offering, transferring to the Duke of York's on May 16. On April 12, Henry Livings' *Nil Carborundum* is presented. On May 9, Toby Robertson stages Gorki's *The Lower Depths*.

March 17 Off-Broadway, at the Folksbiene Playhouse, Ellis Rabb and his APA Repertory Company play 38 performances of *The School for Scandal, The Seagull*, and Cohan's *The Tavern*. Rosemary Harris and George Grizzard are among others in the company.

April 5 John Gielgud directs an elegant period revival of *The School for Scandal*, with Anthony Powell designing. Ralph Richardson and Anna Massey appear with John Neville, Daniel Massey, Margaret Rutherford and Merial Forbes. The show runs eight months.

April 10 The Royal Shakespeare Company's Stratford-upon-Avon season opens with *Measure for Measure*. Later, Peter Hall will direct *A Midsummer Night's Dream*. The 1960 *Taming of the Shrew* is restaged. *Macbeth, Cymbeline* and *King Lear* (with Paul Scofield) will appear. *The Comedy of Errors* completes the repertory.

April 11 David Ross stages Henrik Ibsen's *Rosmersholm* for 119 performances at his Fourth Street Theatre. Nancy Wickwire is Rebecca West and Donald Woods is Rosmer.

April 19 Dublin Gate Theatre co-founders, Hilton Edwards and Micheal macLiammoir, stage and design their new production of *Rashomon*. Other offerings this year include macLiammoir's *Talking About Yeats* and a revival, *Philadelphia, Here I Come!*

May 16 At New York City Center, Jean Dalrymple begins a program of musical revivals, opening today with *Can-Can*. *Brigadoon* is scheduled for May 30 and *Fiorello!* for June 13.

May 30 At the Sadler's Wells Theatre, Gilbert & Sullivan's *The Mikado* is revived, but not in a D'Oyly Carte staging. This one is the work of Craig Douglas, with designs by Peter Rice.

Summer The Utah Shakespeare Festival begins annual summer presentation of Shakespeare's plays on the campus of Southern Utah State College in Cedar City.

June 4 The traditional summer Shakespeare season in the Open Air Theatre in London's Regent's Park opens with David William's staging of *A Midsummer Night's Dream*, with Patrick Wymark as Bottom. *Twelfth Night* and *Love's Labour's Lost*, both featuring Michael Blakemore, will also be presented.

June 12 The American Shakespeare Festival at Stratford, Connecticut, will total 113 performances of *Henry IV, Part 1*, and *Richard II*. A sampler, *Shakespeare Revisited*, starring Helen Hayes and Maurice Evans, will play 34 times and tour nationally.

June 12 San Diego's National Shakespeare Festival offers 95 repertory performances of *The Taming of the Shrew*, *Henry IV, Part 2*, and *Othello*. The company includes director William Ball, Ed Flanders, Victor Buono, and Ellen Geer.

June 14 The Bristol Old Vic comes to London's Old Vic with an adaptation of Tolstoy's *War and Peace*, staged by Val May. Moved to the Phoenix June 27, it runs 44 performances.

June 18 Canada's Stratford Shakespeare Festival opens under Michael Langham. The repertory is *Macbeth*, *The Taming of the Shrew*, *The Tempest*, Rostand's *Cyrano de Begerac* and Gilbert & Sullivan's *The Gondoliers*.

June 18 August Strindberg's *Playing with Fire* precedes Pinter's new play, *The Collection*, staged at the Royal Shakespeare's Aldwych Theater. John Blatchley directs the Strindberg; Pinter and Peter Hall stage the second, with Michael Hordern, Kenneth Haigh, Barbara Murray, and John Ronane in the cast. On Aug 1, the company presents a revival of John Whiting's *A Penny for a Song* at the Aldwych. Director Colin Graham casts Marius Goring, Newton Blick, Gwen Ffrangcon-Davies, and Judi Dench.

June 19 Joseph Papp's New York Shakespeare Festival will offer 53 performances in Central Park's Delacorte Theatre this season. The plays are *Merchant of Venice*, with George C. Scott as Shylock; *The Tempest*, with James Earl Jones as Caliban, and *King Lear*, played by Frank

Silvera.

June 29 The Shaw Festival in Canada's Niagara-on-the-Lake opens with *Don Juan in Hell*, followed by *Candida*. Maynard Burgess directs 10 unpaid actors for this inaugural season, which runs weekends until Aug 11.

July 3 Laurence Olivier stages all three productions at this season's Chichester Festival. John Fletcher's *The Chances* opens; John Ford's Jacobean drama *The Broken Heart* is the second offering, and Chekhov's *Uncle Vanya* is the final and most most successful production. The season runs nine weeks.

July 4 The Jacobean tragedy, *Women Beware Women*, is revived by the Royal Shakespeare Company at its experimental center, the New Arts. Boris Vian's *The Empire Builders* opens on the 31st, and Fred Watson's *Infanticide in the House of Fred Ginger* is presented on Aug 29.

July 10 Tennessee Williams' *Period of Adjustment* plays 164 performances at Wyndham's Theatre when it moves from its Royal Court Theatre premiere.

July 21 Oregon's Shakespearean Festival in Ashland plays 51 performances of four by the Bard: *The Comedy of Errors*, *Henry IV, Part 2*, *As You Like It*, and *Coriolanus*. Stacy Keach, Ric Murphy, Michael Addison, founder Angus Bowmer, Hugh Evans, and Richard Ramos are in the ensemble.

Aug 15 *Purple Dust* inaugurates an O'Casey Festival at London's Mermaid Theatre. *The Plough and the Stars* and

Red Roses for Me follow. *Pictures in the Hallway*, an adaptation of the playwright's biography by Paul Shyre, completes the season.

Aug 16 Bernard Miles' Mermaid Theatre production of *Lock Up Your Daughters*, with lyrics by Lionel Bart and music by Laurie Johnson, opens at Her Majesty's Theatre, where it achieves 885 performances.

Aug 19 This year's Edinburgh Festival features the music of Shostakovitch and the Royal Shakespeare Company in *Troilus and Cressida*, John Whiting's *The Devils*, Christopher Fry's *Curtmantle*, Dylan Thomas's *The Doctor and the Devils*, Robert McLellan's *Young Auchinleck*, and the innovation of the "Happening."

Aug 27 The National Youth Theatre, directed by Michael Croft, offers *Henry V* at London's Sadler's Wells, followed on Aug 30 by a modern-dress *Julius Caesar*.

Sep 11 *Brecht on Brecht* opens at the Royal Court Theatre with Lotte Lenya in the cast. Samuel Beckett's *Happy Days*, with Brenda Bruce, opens on Nov 1. Dec 18 brings a double-bill by Keith Waterhouse and Willis Hall, *Squat Betty* and *The Sponge Room*, directed by John Dexter.

Sep 18 Two versions of Bertolt Brecht's *Man Is Man* are staged in New York. For the Living Theatre, Julian Beck directs the Gerhard Nellhaus version. Eric Bentley's *A Man's a Man* is mounted by John Hancock. Each earns 175 performances.

Sep 24 The Dublin Gate Theatre revives

CHAS. LAUGHTON

its *Othello*, which subsequently tours Belgium and Holland. In December, Micheal macLiammoir revives *The Importance of Being Oscar*.

Sep 26 The Old Vic Theatre Company's season begins with Henrik Ibsen's *Peer Gynt*. On Oct 17, *The Merchant of Venice* plays. Both are staged by Michael Elliott. Ben Jonson's *The Alchemist* is revived by Tyrone Guthrie on Oct 8, in modern-dress.

Oct 2 At The New Arts Theatre in London, Muriel Spark's *Doctors of Philosophy* opens, staged by Donald McWhinnie. A late night entertainment opens on the 16th with Jack MacGowran appearing in Samuel Beckett's *End of Day*, also staged by McWhinnie. Edna O'Brien's *A Cheap Bunch of Flowers*, with Susannah York, opens on Nov 20th.

Oct 4 William Saroyan's *Talking To You* and *Across the Board on Tomorrow Morning* are revived briefly by American director Arthur Storch at London's Duke of York's Theatre. There are 12 performances.

Oct 9 Christopher Fry's *Curtmantle*, about Henry II, seen at the Edinburgh Festival, now opens at the Aldwych Theatre in London, staged by Stuart Burge for the Royal Shakespeare Company. On Oct 15, *Troilus and Cressida*, seen in Stratford and in Edinburgh, opens. Peter Hall stages. On Nov 18, John Whiting's *The Devils*, a 1961 production, is revived. On Dec 12, Peter Brook's Stratford staging of *King Lear*

comes to the Aldwych, to critical acclaim. Paul Scofield and Alec McCowen are in the cast, with Irene Worth and Diana Rigg. On the 19th, *Comedy of Errors* is offered for the Christmas season, with McCowen and Ian Richardson.

Oct 17 London's Mermaid Theatre sees a revival of the Jacobean farce, *Eastward, Ho!*, first performed for the Coronation in 1953. *The Witch of Edmonton*, a Jacobean melodrama is staged on Nov 21, and the holiday brings Fred Hoyle's *Rockets in Ursa Major*, on Dec 26.

Nov 14 David Ross achieves a run of 61 performances for his revival of Chekhov's *The Cherry Orchard*, with Marian Winters. It is given in his new Theatre Four in a remodeled Manhattan church.

Dec 17 The holiday season is at hand. At the Garrick Theatre, Caryl Brahms and Ned Sherrin concoct *Cindy-Ella, or I Gotta Shoe*, staged by Colin Graham and designed by Tony Walton. Cleo Laine, Cy Grant, Elizabeth Welch, and George Brown are cast. Other seasonal shows are *Toad of Toad Hall* (Comedy), *Puss in Boots* (Palladium—with Jimmy Edwards and Frankie Vaughan), *Amelia's African Adventure* (New Arts), *The Pied Piper* (Theatre Royal, Stratford East), *Space Is So Startling* (Westminster), *Emil and the Detectives* (Her Majesty's), *Noddy in Toyland* (Scala), *Cinderella* (Wimbledon), *Billy Bunter's Christmas Circus* (Queen's), *The Blue Bird* (Lyric, Hammersmith), and *Let's Make an Opera* (Vaudeville).

Lupino traced his descent from a line of Italian puppet-masters.

Oct 2 Actor Frank Lovejoy (b. 1914) dies in New York.

Oct 10 Vivian Beaumont Allen, a New York philanthropist, dies at 70. Her public memorial will be the Vivian Beaumont Theatre in Lincoln Center.

Nov 9 Actress Carroll McComas is dead at 76 years of age. She created the role of Miss Lulu Bett.

Nov 18 English dramatist Clifford Bax (b. 1886) dies in London. Bax was one of the founders of the Phoenix Society. His plays include *Polly*, *Midsummer Madness*, *The Immortal Lady*, and *April in August*.

Nov 27 Actress Gerry Jedd is only 37 when she dies.

Nov 30 English stage and screen actor Evelyn Roberts (b. 1886) dies. Roberts made his first stage appearance in 1918 with Lena Ashwell's repertory company. In 1919 he joined Sir Frank Benson's company. Roberts' roles included Captain Hardy in *Journey's End*, Charles Dupont in *Tovarich*, Admiral Carlisle in *Lady Frederick*, and the Earl of Avalon in *Family Tree*.

Dec 1 American drama critic Thomas H. Wenning is dead at age 59 in New York. In 1955 he was appointed theatre editor for *Newsweek*.

Dec 10 American novelist-playwright John Steinbeck is awarded the Nobel Prize for Literature.

Dec 15 English actor Charles Laughton (b. 1899) dies in Hollywood. Laughton made his stage debut in *The Government Inspector* in 1926. An actor of character roles, he also appeared in such classics as *Macbeth*, *Love for Love*, and *Measure for Measure*. Laughton, husband of actress Elsa Lanchester, achieved immediate fame in films.

Dec 17 Thomas Mitchell, popular early in his career as an actor-playwright, later became best known for screen roles in films such as *Gone With The Wind*. He dies at 70.

Dec 24 British actress Jean Forbes-Robertson is dead at 57.

Dec 26 Producer and attorney Lawrence Langer (b. 1890) dies in New York City. Langner helped to organize the Washington Square Players in 1914, which led to the formation of the Theatre Guild. He also founded the American Shakespeare Festival in Stratford, Connecticut.

1962 BIRTHS/DEATHS/DEBUTS

Jan 20 Poet-playwright Robinson Jeffers (*Medea, Tower Beyond Tragedy*) dies aged 75.

Feb 19 Stage and screen actor James Barton, praised for his role in *Paint Your Wagon*, dies at 71.

Feb 25 Remembered for his crazy fun in *Hellzapoppin'*, comic Harold (Chic) Johnson dies at 66. He was long a partner of Ole Olsen.

April 12 English actor Brian Reece (b. 1913) is dead. Reece first appeared in London in 1938 as the Judge in *But For the Grace*. Among his roles were Thomas Trout in *Bless The Bride* and Richard in *The Seven Year Itch*.

June 3 122 of Atlanta's leading advocates of culture are killed at Paris' Orly Field when their Air France charter crashes.

June 24 Canadian-born stage and screen actress Lucile Watson (b. 1879) dies in New York. Watson made her first appearance in New York in *The Wisdom of the Wise*. She was Fanny Farrelly in *Watch on the Rhine*, a role she repeated in the film version.

June 29 English actress and vocalist Ella

Retford is dead in London at age 76. Retford made her first appearance on stage as a dancer in 1900, but later took up singing.

July 23 Famed musical comedy funnyman Victor Moore passes on at age 86.

Aug 24 Long a champion of Shakespeare production, touring Britain with his ensemble, Anew McMaster today dies at 72.

Sep 9 Irish comedian and singer Pat Rooney is dead at 82.

Sep 24 The author of *Gaslight/Angel Street* is dead. Patrick Hamilton was 58.

Sep 26 English comedian Barry Lupino (b. 1884) dies in Brighton. Lupino, stock comedian at the Britannia Theatre for many years, toured extensively, and was seen in pantomime and musical comedy.

1962 THEATERS/PRODUCTIONS

Dingle Foot introduces in Parliament a bill to implement the 1909 proposals on theatre censorship made by a joint committee of both houses. After brief debate,

the bill is defeated, 134 to 77.

Jan The Guthrie Theatre in Minneapolis engages 42 actors, including Hume

DELACORTE THEATER

Cronym, Jessica Tandy, Zoe Caldwell, and George Grizzard, for the premiere season.

Jan Century Lighting introduces a punch-card lighting control system with infinite preset possibilities, using IBM cards to store information. Because of the time needed to punch cards, this American system will not be generally used.

April 11 Peter Hall, the Director of the Royal Shakesepare Company, today announces a new management triumvirate: himself, Michel Saint-Denis, and Peter Brook.

June 1 Henry Hewes, new editor of the Burns Mantle *Best Plays* annual, chooses the "ten best" of the 1961–62 season: Harold Pinter's *The Caretaker*, Robert Bolt's *A Man for All Seasons*, Tennessee Williams' *The Night of the Iguana*, Paddy Chayevsky's *Gideon*, Graham Greene's *The Complaisant Lover*, Frank Loesser's *How To Succeed in Business Without Really Trying*, Felicien Marceau's *The Egg*, Herb Gardner's *A Thousand Clowns*, Robert Ardrey's *Stone and Star*, and Arthur Kopit's *Oh Dad, Poor Dad, Mamma's Hung You in the Closet and I'm Feeling So Sad*. Loesser's musical wins the Pulitzer Prize and the Critics' Circle Award for Best Musical.

June 18 Free Shakespeare in Central Park begins this summer with the inauguration of the Delacorte Theatre. Nearly half the $400,000 needed to build the theatre has been donated by George Delacorte of Dell Publishing. George C. Scott opens with *Merchant of Venice*.

June 28 The constitution and by-laws are ratified for the Neptune Theatre Foundation in Halifax, Nova Scotia, Canada, with Leon Major as Artistic Director. The Old Garrick Theatre, built in 1909 as the Strand and later renovated as a movie house, is again renovated as a 525-seat theatre. The new name, Neptune, honors the first theatre in Canada, at Port Royal, Marc Lescarbot's Théâtre de Neptune, 1606.

June 29 The first Shaw Festival, at Niagara-on-the-Lake in Canada, opens in the 19th-century Court House turned into a theatre by locally donated funds. Two hundred enthusiasts attend.

July 3 The Chichester Festival Theatre is completed and licensed just in time for its festive opening. Inside, it is a modified Greek theatre. It had been budgeted for a £95,064 and finally cost £105,000, with an added £18,000 for the stage lighting system.

July 23 Portions of *Macbeth* from Canada's Stratford are broadcast for the first intercontinental transmission via Telestar satellite. The Canadian Broadcasting Company broadcasts simultaneously to North America and Europe.

July 26 *The Premise*, an evening of improvisation by young Americans at the Comedy Theatre, plays for four months before the Lord Chamberlain discovers what they are doing: breaking an 1843

Act which gives him power as theatre censor. They are ordered to stop; they refuse to comply. They are not closed down.

Aug 13 The Society of Stage Directors and Choreographers is recognized by the League of New York Theatre and Producers, and its minimum basic agreement signed.

Oct 21 The Ford Foundation's program director, W. McNeil Lowry, announces $6,100,000 in grants to professional ensembles to achieve and maintain new levels of excellence. The recipients include San Francisco's Actor's Workshop ($197,000), Houston's Alley Theatre ($2,100,000), part of it for a new theatre; the American Shakespeare Festival Theatre and Academy ($503,000), Washington's Arena Stage ($863,000), Milwaukee's Fred Miller Theatre ($100,000), Oklahoma City's Mummers Theatre ($1,250,000), partly for a new theatre which will close shortly after it is opened, with the demise of the Mummers; UCLA's Theatre Group ($337,000), and Minneapolis' Tyrone Guthrie Theatre ($337,000).

Nov 3 The Prince's Theatre on Shaftesbury Avenue closes for reconstruction, and *Gentlemen Prefer Blondes* must move to the Strand. The theatre will reopen in March as the Shaftesbury Theatre, with *How To Succeed in Business*.

Nov 25 Today marks the tenth anniversary of Agatha Christie's suspense drama, *The Mousetrap*, now a London perenniel.

Dec 7 A newspaper strike in New York, which will run 114 days, does damage to the theatre season, and radio and TV reviews and advertising assume new importance.

Dec 26 The Prince Charles Theatre, off London's Leicester Square, opens with a Canadian revue, *Clap Hands*. It plays 113 performances in this 420-seat house.

337

Jan 6 *Oliver!* See L premiere, 1960.

Jan 16 *The Milk Train Doesn't Stop Here Anymore* (NY—Morosco—Drama). Tennessee Williams's new play has Hermione Baddeley as a rich, aging woman intrigued with a handsome young wastrel poet (Paul Roebling). The play lasts just 69 performances but is chosen as "Best Play." Next season's revival will star Tallulah Bankhead. It opens on Jan 1, 1964.

Jan 23 *Graham Crackers* (NY—Upstairs at the Downstairs—Revue). Ronny Graham directs his sketches for 286 performances. David Shire arranges and conducts; Lee Becker choreographs. Pat Stanley, Anita Darian, and Bill McCutcheon are in the company.

Jan 29 *The Hollow Crown.* See L premiere, 1961.

Feb 4 *The Typists/The Tiger* (NY—Orpheum—Comedy). Murray Schisgal's plays are animated by Eli Wallach and Anne Jackson. In the one, a rape is thwarted; in the other, endless address-typing helps reveal the characters to each other. There are 200 performances. The plays open at London's Globe on May 25, 1964, with Wallach and Jackson again in the leads. There are only 38 showings.

Feb 9 *Andorra* (NY—Biltmore—Drama). Max Frisch's allegory of Nazi persecution of the Jews has only nine performances. Michael Langham directs Horst Buchholz, Barbara Mattes, and Hugh Griffith. The National Theatre presents the drama at London's Old Vic on Jan 28, 1964.

Feb 12 *Photo Finish.* See L premiere, 1962.

March 13 *Enter Laughing* (NY—Henry Miller—Comedy). Carl Reiner's novel, adapted by Joseph Stein, gives Alan Arkin a field day as a stage-struck delivery boy from the Bronx who has a chance to play in a Yiddish theatre troupe. There are 419 performances.

March 18 *Tovarich* (NY—Broadway—Musical). David Shaw's book is based on the 1937 play by Robert E. Sherwood and Jacques Deval, with songs by Lee Pockriss and Anne Crosswell. Peter Glenville directs Vivian Leigh and Jean-Pierre Aumont. There are 264 performances.

April 4 *To the Water Tower* (NY—Square East—Revue). This is the fourth edition of the Second City Revue. Paul Sills stages, and Tom O'Horgan, an innovative young musician, composes and plays. There are 210 performances.

April 13 *She Loves Me* (NY—O'Neill—Musical). Based on Miklos Lazslo's play *Parfumerie*, this book is by Joe Masteroff, with songs by Jerry Bock and Sheldon Harnick. Jack Cassidy and Barbara Cook head the cast. The show runs nine months. It has 189 performances following its London premiere at the Lyric on April

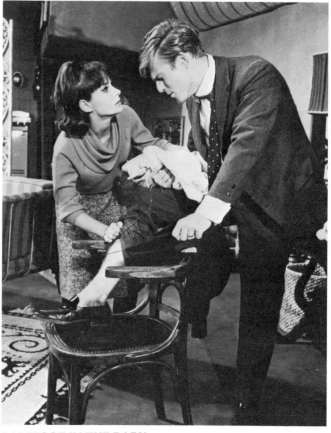

BAREFOOT IN THE PARK

29, 1964. Anne Rogers, Gary Raymond, and Rita Moreno are in the cast.

April 17 *Battle of a Simple Man.* See L premiere, 1962.

May 15 *The Brig* (NY—Living Theatre—Drama). Author Kenneth H. Brown shows 24 hours of vivid interaction between brutal Marines and their prisoners. Judith Malina stages for 177 performances.

June 6 *The World of Kurt Weill in Song* (NY—One Sheridan Square—Revue). Martha Schlamme and Will Holt win 245 performances of this Weill sampler, selected and directed by Holt. They earn 61 performances in London at the Vaudeville when they open on Aug 5, 1964.

June 13 *Cages* (NY—York—Drama). Lewis John Carlino's two one-act plays, *Snowangel* and *Epiphany*, are about people trapped in roles. Shelley Winters and Jack Warden head the cast. The bill runs for 22 weeks, under Howard De Silva's direction.

Sep 25 *Luther.* See L premiere, 1961.

Sep 29 *Spoon River Anthology* (NY—Booth—Reading). Edgar Lee Masters' verses are brought to life for 111 performances by Betty Garrett, Joyce Van Patten, and Charles Aidman, among others. The show tours, and becomes an amateur favorite.

Oct 1 *Chips With Everything.* See L premiere, 1962.

Oct 3 *Here's Love* (NY—Shubert—Musical). Meredith Willson borrows from *Miracle on 34th Street.* The cast includes Laurence Naismith, Valerie Lee, Janis Paige, and Craig Stevens. Producer Stuart Ostrow directs. The show runs nearly 42 weeks.

Oct 8 *Corruption in the Palace of Justice* (NY—Cherry Lane—Drama). Ugo Betti's play wins 103 performances for the producers of Theatre 1964: Richard Barr, Clinton Wilder, and Edward Albee. Richard Altman directs.

Oct 9 *The Private Ear /The Public Eye.* See L premiere, 1962.

Oct 10 *A Case of Libel* (NY—Longacre—Drama). A court case from Louis Nizer's book *My Life in Court*, dramatized by Henry Denker, runs over 30 weeks with Van Heflin directed by Sam Wanamaker.

Oct 17 *Jennie* (NY—Majestic—Musical). Mary Martin stars in this adaptation of Laurette Taylor's biography. With songs by Howard Dietz and Arthur Schwarz and book by Arnold Schulman, the show plays only 82 performances.

Oct 23 *Barefoot in the Park* (NY—Biltmore—Comedy). Neil Simon's play about newlyweds has Robert Redford and Eliz-beth Ashley in the leads. Mildred Dunnock and Kurt Kazsnar also appear in Mike Nichols's staging. There are 251 performances. On Nov 24, 1965, it opens at London's Piccadilly with Daniel Massey and Marlo Thomas as the couple.

Oct 24 *110 in the Shade* (NY—Broadhurst—Musical). N. Richard Nash adapts his *The Rainmaker* for Harvey Schmidt's music and Tom Jones's lyrics. Robert Horton leads the cast. Agnes de Mille choreographs. David Merrick's production wins 330 performances. There are only 52 showings, following the musical's opening in London at the Palace on Feb 8, 1967.

Oct 30 *The Ballad of the Sad Cafe* (NY—Martin Beck—Drama). Edward Albee's inspiration is Carson McCullers' story of the Amazonian Amelia Evans (Colleen Dewhurst), the dwarf Cousin Lymon (Michael Dunn), and the reformed rascal Marvin Macy (Lou Antonio). Alan Schneider directs. There are 123 performances.

Oct 31 *In White America* (NY—Sheridan Square—Reading). Martin Duberman's chronology of American views on the black "problem" plays 493 performances. It reopens in May 1965, tours, and has foreign productions. London's New Arts Theatre presents it on Nov 16, 1964.

Nov 11 *Arturo Ui* (NY—Lunt-Fontanne—Comedy). Bertolt Brecht's satire on Hitler runs just one week. It is adapted by George Tabori. Christopher Plummer has the title role.

Nov 13 *One Flew Over the Cuckoo's Nest* (NY—Cort—Drama). Kirk Douglas stars, with Joan Tetzel as Nurse Ratched, in Dale Wasserman's adaptation of Ken Kesey's novel. The play runs over ten weeks, but has an extended run Off-Broadway in a revival.

Nov 21 *The Ginger·Man.* See L premiere, 1959.

Dec 8 *The Girl Who Came to Supper* (NY—Broadway—Musical). Terence Rattigan's *The Sleeping Prince* gets musical treatment from Harry Kurnitz (book) and Noel Coward (music and lyrics). Florence Henderson and Jose Ferrer head the cast; Tessis O'Shea steals the show. The show runs just 14 weeks.

Dec 19 *Nobody Loves an Albatross* (NY—Lyceum—Comedy). Robert Preston is featured in Ronald Alexander's play about a Hollywood television writer-producer who uses tricks and slickness to cover up his lack of ideas and talent. There are 212 performances.

Dec 21 *Trumpets of the Lord* (NY—Astor Place—Musical). Vinnette Carroll adapts James Weldon Johnson's *God's Trombones* for Donald McKayle to stage. Al Freeman, Jr., and Cicely Tyson are in the show, which runs 20 weeks.

Dec 22 *Marathon '33* (NY—ANTA—Drama). June Havoc stages her play about Depression dance marathons for the Actors Studio. Julie Harris leads the cast. Under Lee Strasberg's supervision, the show lasts six weeks.

Murray and Alexandra Berlin are the newly-weds. There are only 44 showings.

March 19 *Oh What a Lovely War* (L—Theatre Royal, Stratford East—Revue). Devised by Joan Littlewood and her company—including Murray Melvin, Victor Spinetti, and Barbara Windsor—from materials gathered by Ted Allen, the show transfers on June 20 to Wyndham's Theatre in the West End for a run of 501 performances. On Sep 30, 1964, it opens on Broadway at the Broadhurst for nearly 16 weeks, the songs and events of World War I being presented in a circus-like but bitter atmosphere.

March 21 *Half-a-Sixpence* (L—Cambridge—Musical). Beverley Cross adapts H. G. Well's novel, *Kipps*, for the stage. Songs are by David Heneker. Tommy Steel is Kipps, an ambitious shop boy who inherits money and then loses it but finds happiness. The show has 677 performances. On April 25, 1965, the play opens on Broadway at the Broadhurst with Steele again in the lead. It wins 511 showings.

March 28 *How To Succeed in Business Without Really Trying.* See NY premiere, 1961.

April 2 *Who'll Save the Plowboy?* (L—Haymarket—Drama). Frank D. Gilroy's American play has only 37 performances. Donal Donnelly is seen in John Barry's staging.

April 10 *Virtue in Danger* (L—Mermaid—Musical). This adaptation of Vanbrugh's *The Relapse* will move to the Strand for 120 performances on June 3. It features John Moffatt, Patricia Routledge, and Alan Howard in a witty staging by Wendy Toye.

May 16 *A Shot in the Dark.* See NY premiere, 1961.

May 29 *The Masters* (L—Savoy—Drama). Ronald Millar's third adaptation of a C. P. Snow novel is directed by John Clements, who also heads the cast. There is an eight-month run.

May 30 *On the Town* (L—Prince of Wales's—Musical). Bernstein's score, wedded to book and lyrics by Comden and Green, has been inspired by Jerome Robbins' ballet, *Fancy Free*. Popular in America, the show has only 53 performances in the West End.

June 19 *Alfie* (L—Mermaid—Comedy). John Neville and Glenda Jackson lead the cast in Bill Naughton's play about a consummate heel. They are directed by Donald McWhinnie. Transferred to the Duchess Theatre, the play runs 189 performances. The play fails in New York where it premieres on Dec 17, 1964, at the Morosco. There are only 20 performances.

June 27 *A Severed Head* (L—Criterion—Drama). J. B. Priestley and Iris Murdoch have based this play on Murdoch's novel about the lives of London sophisticates.

1963 BRITISH PREMIERES

Jan 9 *The Physicists* (L—Aldwych—Drama). Friedrich Duerrenmatt's play about a physicist hiding in an insane asylum proves a success for Peter Brook and the Royal Shakespeare Company. Cyril Cusack and Irene Worth head the cast. The play comes to New York on Oct 13, 1964, where it opens at the Martin Beck. Hume Cronyn, George Voskovec, Robert Shaw, and Jessica Tandy are in the cast. Although successful in London, the play has only 55 performances.

Jan 23 *Nest Time I'll Sing To You* (L—New Arts—Drama). James Saunders' play exploring the nature of life features Denys Graham, Michael Caine, Liz Fraser, and Peter McEnery. It opens in New York at the Phoenix on Nov 27, 1963, with Estelle Parsons and James Earl Jones in the leads. Peter Coe stages.

Jan 24 *An Evening of British Rubbish* (L—Comedy—Revue). Ivor Cutler, Joyce Grant, and The Alberts perform their mockery of British traditions for 139 performances. Gordon Fleming directs.

Jan 31 *The Bedsitting Room* (L—Mermaid—Revue). John Antrobus and Spike Milligan stage their absurdist romp, with

Milligan and Valentine Dyall in the cast. It moves to the Duke of York's on March 20 for 399 performances.

Feb 8 *Carnival* (L—Lyric—Musical). The Broadway hit plays only 34 performances, starring Sally Logan as Lili.

Feb 12 *Stephen D.* (L—St. Martin's—Drama). James Joyce's *Portrait of the Artist* and *Stephen Hero* are adapted by Hugh Leonard. Norman Rodway plays Stephen in this 1962 Dublin Festival production, which now earns 117 performances.

Feb 27 *Mary, Mary.* See NY premiere, 1961.

March 6 *All in Good Time* (L—Mermaid—Comedy). Opening at Bernard Miles' theatre for a limited run, Bill Naughton's play about a young working class newly-wed couple, living with the groom's parents, wins plaudits, with Miles and Marjorie Rhodes as the parents and John Pickles and Lois Daine as the couple. After a transfer on April 18 to the Phoenix in the West End, it has a total run of 156 performances. On Feb 18, 1965, it opens in New York at the Royale Theatre. Donald Wolfit is now the father. Brian

Val May has first staged this for the Briston Old Vic before bringing it to the West End. It opens in New York at the Royale on Oct 28, 1964, where it plays only 29 times.

July 4 *Pickwick* (L—Saville—Musical). Wolf Mankowitz has adapted Charles Dickens' novel, with lyrics by Leslie Bricusse and score by Cyril Ornadel. Peter Coe directs Harry Secombe in the title role. There are 695 repetitions. The show opens at New York's 46th Street on Oct 4, 1965, with Secombe in the cast. It has only 55 performances.

Aug 8 *The Ides of March* (L—Haymarket—Drama). Thornton Wilder's novel is adapted for the stage by Jerome Kilty, who co-directs with John Gielgud—who also stars as Julius Caesar. A skilled cast, a simple and elegant production, but a short run: 60 performances.

Sep 4 *Man and Boy* (L—Queen's—Drama). Charles Boyer and Barry Justice play in Terence Rattigan's tale about a ruthless magnate who cannot be deterred, even by his son. There are 69 performances prior to a Broadway engagement which begins on Nov 12 at the Brooks Atkinson. Boyer again plays the tycoon. The show runs seven weeks.

Sep 12 *Exit the King* (L—Royal Court—Drama). Alec Guinness is the ineffective king in a decaying world in Eugene Ionesco's play. George Devine stages.

Sep 24 *Never Too Late.* See NY premiere, 1962.

Sep 25 *The Representative* (L—Aldwych—Drama). Rolf Hochhuth's German script, *Der Stellvertreter,* is eight hours long on paper. Adapted for this Royal Shakespeare production, it shows the alleged indifference of Pope Pius XII to Jewish sufferings under the Nazis. Clifford Williams stages. Among the cast are Alec McCowen, Alan Webb, and Michael Williams. On Feb 26, 1964, it opens in New York at the Brooks Atkinson—with picket-lines protesting its production—under the title of *The Deputy.* Emlyn Williams plays the Pope. There are 316 performances.

Sep 26 *Six of One* (L—Adelphi—Musical). Dora Bryan is the heroine of this show, built around her stage career. William Chappell directs. Her ensemble includes Richard Wattis, Dennis Lotis, John Hewer, Amanda Barrie, Sheila O'Neill, and Hilda Campbell. There are 354 performances.

Oct 2 *At the Drop of Another Hat* (L—Haymarket—Revue). Michael Flanders and Donald Swann's sequel to their popular *At the Drop of a Hat* begins a run of 174 performances, staged by Peter Fern. It opens at New York's Booth Theatre on Dec 27, 1966, where it plays 104 times.

Oct 3 *A Funny Thing Happened on the Way To the Forum.* See NY premiere, 1961.

Nov 21 *Difference of Opinion* (L—Garrick—Drama). John Gregson heads the cast in George Ross and Campbell Singer's play about a managing director removed from his job by a campaign of suspicion. There are 489 performances.

Dec 3 *The Wings of the Dove* (L—Lyric—Drama). Henry James' novel is adapted by Christopher Taylor and staged by Frith Banbury. Susannah York, Gene Anderson, and James Donald are in the cast. The show has 324 performances.

Dec 30 *No Strings.* See NY premiere, 1962.

4, Diane Cilento's translation of Luigi Pirandello's *Naked* opens, with Cilento in the central role. On April 7, without decor, Barry Reckford's *Skyvers* opens, staged by Ann Jellicoe. Also without decor is Frank Wedekind's *Spring Awakening,* staged by Desmond O'Donovan for an April 21 opening. On May 14, Frank Hilton's *Day of the Prince* opens.

Jan 8 Off-Broadway at the Circle in the Square, Jose Quintero revives Eugene O'Neill's *Desire Under the Elms,* with George C. Scott and Colleen Dewhurst. The production runs 380 performances.

Jan 21 The Phoenix Theatre, playing at New York's Anderson, revives Robert E. Sherwood's *Abe Lincoln in Illinois* for five weeks, with Hal Holbrook. *The Taming of the Shrew* is played for five weeks beginning March 6. There are four weeks of Eugene Schwartz's Russian allegory, *The Dragon* beginning on April 9.

Jan 30 London's Old Vic Company presents *Othello,* with Errol John and Leo McKern. *Measure for Measure* will be revived on April 3, as the last production of the company.

Feb 2 David and Carmel Ross produce her adaptation of Henrik Ibsen's *A Doll's House* Off-Broadway at Theatre Four. Astrid Wilsrud is Nora to Paxton Whitehead's Torvald Helmer. There are 66 performances.

Feb 20 London's New Arts Theatre's season includes Athol Fugard's *The Blood Knot, Divorce a la Carte* (this is Sardou-Najac's farce *Divorcons-Nous*), Schisgal's *Luv,* Elizabeth Hart's adaptation of E. M. Forster's *Where Angels Fear To Tread,* and Riccardo Aragno's adaptation of Anthony Powell's *Afternoon Men.*

Feb 25 *So Who's Afraid of Edward Albee?,* David Starkweather's fantasy of lust, sex, and incipient literary criticism plays for two weeks now and two more beginning March 24 at New York's Caffe Cino.

March 8 William Ball stages Pirandello's *Six Characters in Search of an Author* Off-Broadway at the Martinique for 515 performances. Richard Dysart and Jacqueline Brookes head the cast.

March 11 On Broadway at the Hudson Theatre, Eugene O'Neill's *Strange Interlude* is revived for 97 performances, Jose Quintero stages for the Actors Studio.

March 12 Broadway's 54th Street Theatre sees a revival of George Bernard Shaw's *Too True to Be Good,* with Cyril Ritchard, Lillian Gish, Cedric Hardwicke, Robert Preston, Eileen Heckart, Glynis Johns, David Wayne, and Ray Middleton.

March 18 The Comedie Francaise comes to London's Piccadilly Theatre with Beaumarchais' *Le Mariage de Figaro.* Their repertory also includes *Naives Hirondelles, Amadee, L'Avenir est dans les Oeufs, Le Systeme Ribadier,* and *Un Caprice.*

1963   REVIVALS/REPERTORIES

Jan 1 Marcel Marceau returns to New York City Center for four weeks. On Jan 30, *Brigadoon* returns. On Feb 13, Jean Dalrymple revives *Wonderful Town.* On Feb 27, the show revived is *Oklahoma!.* On May 29, Dalyrmple revives *Pal Joey,* with Bob Fossé as Joey and Viveca Lindfors as Vera Simpson.

Jan 2 Edinburgh's Traverse Theatre opens its season with Terry Lane's stagings of Arrabal's *Orison* and Sartre's *Huis Clos.* Lane, as artistic director, stages virtually all the plays, which include Gibson's *Two for the See-Saw,* Donleavy's *Fairy Tales of New York,* Arrabal's *Picnic on the Battlefield* and *Fando and Lis,* Shaw's *Don Juan,* Jarry's *Ubu Roi,* Ibsen's *A Doll's House,* Ionesco's *The Lesson,* Genet's *The Maids,* Coward's *Private Lives,* Faulkner's *Requiem for a Nun,* Eveling's *The Balachites,* Grabbe's *Comedy, Satire, Irony and Deeper Meaning,* Saunders' *Next Time I'll Sing To You,* Snyder's *The Days and Nights of Beebee Fenstermaker,* Shaw's *Candida,* Mishima's *The Lady Aoi, Hanjo,* and *The Damask Drum,* and Betti's *Crime on Goat Island.* Just two days before the opening of the 1964 season, Lane is replaced as artistic director by Jim Haynes.

Jan 8 London's Royal Court Theatre welcomes Frank Hauser's Oxford Playhouse production of Bernard Shaw's *Misalliance,* designed by Desmond Heeley. The production transfers to the Criterion Theatre on Jan 28. Gwyn Thomas's *Jackie the Jumper* follows on Feb 1. The title-role, played by Ronald Lewis, is a Welsh mill-worker to whom his fellows look for leadership in their struggles with mill-owners. This is a ballad-drama, set in Wales of the 1830's. John Dexter stages, with designs by Michael Annals. On March 7, director Lindsay Anderson and actor Richard Harris collaborate on presenting Gogol's *The Diary of a Madman.* On April

March 20 Terence McNally adapts Giles Cooper's adaptation of the Dumas, fils, classic, *The Lady of the Camellias*. Zeffirelli stages Susan Strasberg and John Stride, at New York's Winter Garden. There is music by Ned Rorem. It runs two weeks.

March 28 An established modern classic, Bertolt Brecht's *Mother Courage and Her Children* opens on Broadway at the Martin Beck. It soon closes after less than seven weeks. Anne Bancroft plays Courage. The cast includes Gene Wilder and Barbara Harris.

April 2 At Stratford-upon-Avon, the annual season of the Royal Shakespeare Company opens with *The Tempest*, staged by Clifford Willians and Peter Brook. John Blatchley stages *Julius Caesar. The Comedy of Errors* is revived from last season. Most impressive is *The Wars of the Roses*, compounded of *Henry VI, Parts 1, 2, & 3*, and *Richard III*, divided into three parts: *Henry VI, Edward IV*, and *Richard III*. Peter Hall, John Barton, and Frank Evans direct.

April 2 Danny Daniels stages newcomer Liza Minelli in a revival of *Best Foot Forward* Off-Broadway at Stage 73. There are 224 performances.

April 15 Micheal macLiammoir presents his mono-drama, called *I Must Be Talking To My Friends*. This is staged by Hilton Edwards. Also produced this year are Thompson's *The Evangelist*, Farrington's *The Last P. M.*, Redgrave's *The Aspern Papers*, and Paterson's *The Roses Are Real* for Dublin Gate Theatre audiences. On April 21, macLiammoir comes from Eire to London's Aldwych with *The Importance of Being Oscar*, and on May 2, he presents *I Must Be Talking to My Friends*, based on the lives and works of distinguished Irish poets and patriots.

April 15 Off-Broadway at Theatre Four, *The Boys from Syracuse* is revived for 469 performances. Christopher Hewett stages.

April 18 In Greenwich Village at The Premise, a *New Show* of improvisations opens with Thomas Aldredge, Joan Darling, James Frawley, and Theodore J. Flicker. Since its founding in 1960, the troupe has had 1,225 performances.

May 7 The Guthrie Theatre in Minneapolis presents its first production, an exquisite and highly controversial staging of *Hamlet*, directed by Tyrone Guthrie.

May 21 *The Heroes*, an examination of heroes from Aeschylus to Danilo Dolci, is directed, narrated, and played by Vittorio Gassman and a largely Italian cast at London's Aldwych Theatre.

May 23 George Bernard Shaw's *The Doctor's Dilemma* is revived at London's Haymarket, staged by Donald McWhinnie. James Donald, Brian Bedford, and Anna Massey play 84 performances.

May 31 In Stratford, Connecticut, the American Shakespeare Festival offers 152 performances of its season's repertory: George Bernard Shaw's *Caesar and Cleopatra, Henry V, King Lear* with Morris Carnovsky, and *The Comedy of Errors*.

June 10 The Shaw Festival opens its second season in Niagara-on-the-Lake in Canada's Ontario Province. The 300 seat theatre is the scene of *You Never Can Tell, How He Lied to Her Husband, The Man of Destiny*, and *Androcles and the Lion*.

June 10 Summer Shakespeare in London's Regent's Park begins in the Open Air Theatre with *Much Ado About Nothing*. On July 17, *A Midsummer Night's Dream* is offered. David William directs both.

June 13 The New York Shakespeare Festival presents three plays this season in Central Park at the Delacorte: *Antony and Cleopatra*, with Michael Higgins and Colleen Dewhurst; *As You Like It*, with Paula Prentiss and Richard Benjamin, and *The Winter's Tale*, with James Earl Jones.

June 15 After its last performance of *Measure for Measure*, the Old Vic company ceases to be. It will be replaced by the National Theatre Company in October.

June 17 Canada's Stratford Festival gives 168 performances of its summer repertory: *Troilus and Cressida, The Comedy of Errors, Timon of Athens*, Rostand's *Cyrano de Begerac*, and Gilbert & Sullivan's *The Mikado*.

June 17 London's new May Fair Theatre opens with Pirandello's *Six Characters in Search of an Author*, which director William Ball has staged successfully in New York. It has a run of 37 weeks.

June 18 San Diego's National Shakespeare Festival offers 101 performances of three by the Bard: *A Midsummer Night's Dream, The Winter's Tale*, and *Antony and Cleopatra*.

June 22 *Stars In My Crown*, Kermit Hunter's play about the founding of the TVA, is presented at the Kenlake Amphitheatre in Murray, Kentucky.

June 24 The second annual Chichester Festival opens with three plays, the premiere being George Bernard Shaw's *Saint Joan*, with Joan Plowright. Chekhov's *Uncle Vanya*, with Artistic Director Laurence Olivier as Vanya is the second, and the third is John Arden's *The Workhouse Donkey*.

June 29 Robert Emmett McDowell's *Home Is The Hunter*, which dramatises the settlement of the Kentucky frontier, is produced in Harrodsburg, Kentucky.

July 3 Noel Coward's *Private Lives* opens at the Duke of York's Theatre, following a revival at the Hampstead Theatre Club in April. James Roose-Evans has directed Rosemary Martin and Edward de Souza, with Sarah Harter and Roger Booth. The production runs 27 weeks.

July 16 The Royal Shakespeare Company presents John Gay's *The Beggar's Opera* at the Aldwych Theatre. Peter Wood directs.

July 18 Bertolt Brecht's *Life of Galileo* is revived at London's Mermaid Theatre, where it played in 1960. Joss Ackland has the title-role.

July 24 At London's Vaudeville Theatre, John Vanbrugh's *The Provok'd Wife* is revived, with Trevor Martin and Eileen Atkins. Toby Robertson directs for a brief run of 45 performances.

July 24 The Oregon Shakespearean Festival offers 46 showings of four plays: *The Merry Wives of Windsor, Romeo and Juliet, Love's Labour's Lost*, and *Henry V*. In the company are Elizabeth Huddle, Robert Benson, Hugh Evans, and Stacy Keach.

July 29 Joan Littlewood's Theatre Workshop performs a Festival of Irish Comedy, featuring J. M. Synge's *The Tinker's Wedding* and *In the Shadow of the Glen* and Brendan Behan's *The Big House*. M. J. Molloy's *The Wood of the Whispering* and Hugh Leonard's *Madigan's Lock* follow in August.

Aug 18 The Edinburgh Festival opens. Martha Graham brings her company. The Chichester Festival's production of George Bernard Shaw's *Saint Joan*, Ray Lawler's *The Unshaven Cheek*, Roddy MacMillan's *All in Good Faith*, Martin Walser's *The Rabbit Race* and Henrik Ibsen's *Little Eyolf* are the season's offerings.

Aug 21 Frank Dunlop has directed Bertolt

TYRONE GUTHRIE

Brecht's *Schweyk in the Second World War*, which now opens at London's Mermaid Theatre. Bernard Miles, the theatre's director, plays Schweyk in William Rowlinson's translation. On Sep 24, Miles, Anthony Hopkins, and Fritz Spegl devise an evening of music and verse called *The Buxom Muse*. On Oct 23, Albert Camus's *The Possessed* opens, staged by Julius Gellner. Barrie Ingham is Nicholas Stavrogin in Justin O'Brien's English adaptation.

Sep 2 The National Youth Theatre makes its annual end-of-summer appearance in London: Michael Croft presents *Hamlet* and *Julius Caesar* at the Scala Theatre.

Sep 18 Harold Pinter's double-bill of *The Lover* and *The Dwarfs* opens at the New Arts in London. Pinter directs Vivien Merchant (his wife) in the first and John Hurt in the latter.

Oct 7 For the Board of Education, Joseph Papp and the New York Shakespeare Festival produce 73 performances of *Twelfth Night* at the Hecksher Theatre on upper Fifth Avenue. Karen Black and Charles Durning head the cast.

Oct 20 Sol Hurok has imported the Companie Marie Bell for two weeks at New York's Brooks Atkinson, with two plays by Racine, *Phedre* and *Berenice*.

Oct 22 London's Old Vic Theatre gleams after refurbishment for the inauguration of the new National Theatre in its temporary home. Artistic Director Laurence Olivier presents his production of *Hamlet*, with Peter O'Toole in the role. On Oct 30, Olivier offers George Bernard Shaw's *Saint Joan*, with Joan Plowright. John Dexter directs. This production has just been at the Chichester Festival, which Olivier also directs. On Nov 19, the National presents Chekhov's *Uncle Vanya*, directed by Olivier, who also performs.

On Dec 10, Farquhar's *The Recruiting Officer* is staged by William Gaskill, with Maggie Smith leading the cast.

Oct 29 Off-Broadway at the Maidman Playhouse, Dion Boucicault's *The Streets of New York* becomes a musical with libretto by Barry Alan Grael and score by Richard Chodosh. It wins 318 performances.

Nov 7 *The Boys from Syracuse*, a vintage Broadway success, attracts Londoners for only 100 performances at the Drury Lane.

Dec 11 To celebrate Shakespeare's 400th anniversary, the Royal Shakespeare Company revives *Comedy of Errors*, which will go on extended tour with Peter Brook's *King Lear*. Europe and North America are visited, and the RSC is warmly received in Eastern Europe and the USSR.

Dec 13 Alastair Sim plays Captain Hook in the revival of Barrie's *Peter Pan* which launches the holiday season at the Scala Theatre in London. Other children's shows include *Merry Roosters Panto*, written by Peter Shaffer (Wyndham's), *Pinocchio* (Lyceum), *The Sleeping Beauty in the Wood* (Players'), *Treasure Island* (Mermaid), *The Panther and the Unicorn* and *Mango-Leaf Magic* (New Arts), *The Man in the Moon* (Palladium), *Billy Bunter Meets Magic* (Shaftesbury), *Toad of Toad Hall* (Comedy), *Cindy-Ella* (New Arts), *Aladdin* (Wimbledon, Golder's Green Hippodrome), *New Clothes for the Emperor* (Theatre Royal, Stratford East), and *The Singing Dolphin* (Hampstead Theatre Club).

Dec 23 Michael Cacoyannis stages Edith Hamilton's *The Trojan Women* Off-Broadway at the Circle-in-the-Square, for a run of 600 performances. Mildred Dunnock, Joyce Ebert, Carrie Nye, and Jane White are among the cast.

1963 BIRTHS/DEATHS/DEBUTS

Jan 6 German-born musical star Lina Abarbanell (b. 1880) is dead in New York. Abarbanell made her American debut in 1905 at the Irving Place Theatre. Her best known roles were Gretel in Humperdinck's opera, *Hansel and Gretel*, Yvonne in *Madame Sherry*, and Sonia in *The Merry Widow*.

Jan 6 American playwright, author, and critic Stark Young (b. 1881) dies in Fairfield, Connecticut. Young is considered one of the best drama critics of his time. He also wrote and translated several plays.

Jan 24 American Librettist-lyricist Otto Harbach (b. 1873) dies in New York City. Harbach's major musicals include *No, No, Nanette*, *The Desert Song*, and *Roberta*.

Jan 26 John (Ole) Olson dies at 71. His longtime musical comedy and revue partner Harold (Chic) Johnson has died in 1962. *Hellzapoppin'* was their greatest success.

Feb 2 Actor William Gaxton (b. 1893) dies in New York.

Feb 4 Irish dramatist and novelist Brinsley MacNamara, drama critic of the *Irish Times*, is dead in Dublin at 72. He joined the Abbey Theatre in 1891, and his play *The Rebellion at Ballycullen* was staged there in 1917.

Feb 12 American playwright Morton Wishengrad (*The Rope Dancers*) dies.

Feb 12 Drama critic Garrison P. Sherwood dies at 60. He is well remembered for compiling, with Burns Mantle, the indispensable record of Broadway theatre productions from 1899 to 1919.

April 4 In Sherman Oaks, California, the American actor Jason Robards, Sr., dies at 70.

April 26 Roland Pertwee, the British author of lively farces, dies at age 79.

April 27 American author, historian, and film producer Kenneth MacGowan is dead at age 74. Born in 1888, MacGowan was editor of *Theatre Arts Magazine* from 1919 to 1925. From 1923 to 1925, he was associated with Eugene O'Neill and Robert Edmond Jones at the Provincetown Playhouse. MacGowan's several books include *A Theatre of Tomorrow* and *Footlights Across America*.

May 6 In Albany, New York, actor-director Monty Woolley (b. 1888) is dead at age 74. He is best remembered as the irascible Sheridan Whiteside, in *The Man Who Came To Dinner*.

June 16 John Whiting, English author of *The Devils* and other plays, dies at 45.

June 17 English dramatist Sutton Vane is dead at 74 in Hastings, England. He performed for the troops during World War I. His play, *Outward Bound*, was written in 1923.

July 9 Actor Frank Mayo is dead at 74.

Aug 14 American playwright Clifford Odets first came to critical attention as an actor in the Group Theatre ensemble, followed rapidly by praise for such plays as *Awake and Sing*. Now he is dead at age 57.

Sep 3 Irish-born poet and dramatist Louis MacNiece (b. 1907) dies in London. MacNiece was associated with W. H. Auden and Christopher Isherwood during the 1930's. He is the author of the verse play, *Out of the Picture*.

Sep 18 Dave Stamper, composer of a number of Broadway musicals and hit songs, dies at age 79.

Sep 20 British actor Allan Jeayes dies at age 78.

Sep 25 English actor Albert Finney makes his Broadway debut as John Osborne's *Luther* at the St. James.

Oct 1 English director John Dexter's American debut is Arnold Wesker's *Chips With Everything* at New York's Plymouth Theatre. He began his career as a BBC radio and television actor.

Oct 30 Henry Daniell, stage and screen actor, dies at age 69. Daniell became well known for the portrayal of handsome, cold, suave villains.

Nov 29 American actress Gertrude Quinlan (b. 1875) is dead in New York. Quinlan made her first stage appearance at the Castle Square Theatre in Boston in 1895.

Dec 1 Phil Baker, star of American variety and revues, dies at age 67.

Dec 23 Vida Hope, the British director of Sandy Wilson's *The Boy Friend*, is dead at 43.

Dec 26 Broadway producer and theatre-magnate J. J. Shubert is dead at 86.

British patents this year include one to M. A. Bourbonnais for a theatre structure with floor and ceiling constructed of prism-shaped elements which can be moved to change the shape and volume of the theatre-space.

U.S. patents this year include one for Ralph Alswang for a system of quick-dissolve scenic illusions for the theatre, involving rapidly shifted cinema screens.

A Community Arts Committee in Baltimore, Maryland, founds the Center Stage in a second floor walk-up, a remodeled gymnausium.

Chicago's Garrick Theatre is demolished. It opened in 1892 as the Schiller Theatre, designed by Adler and Sullivan, who also designed the Auditorium Theatre.

London's Drama Centre is founded to train actors in techniques of Stanislavsky (acting), Rudolf Laban (dance), and Jacques LeCoq (mime). The Earl of Harewood is the Centre's president.

The London Academy of Music and Dramatic Arts opens its versatile new experimental theatre, which permits directors to use any stage-space they wish.

Jan The Institute of Outdoor Drama is founded in Chapel Hill, to serve equally as a source of stimulation, advice, and information to North Carolina and to the nation.

Jan 1 Due to New York's newspaper strike, the emergency weekly *Firstnite* appears to make critics' comments available. Walter Kerr, who is broadcasting his for CBS, contributes.

Jan 2 Edinburgh's Traverse Theatre, which is to win acclaim as a center for experiment and production of important new plays, offers its first formal production.

Feb 28 $720,000 is raised to improve the Avon Theatre, which has been acquired by the Stratford Shakespeare Festival of Canada. The 1901 western Ontario landmark is being returned to its original use after years as a cinema.

Spring John Gassner and John Mason Brown resign as advisors to the Trustees of Columbia University, who have overlooked their nominee, *Who's Afraid of Virginia Woolf*, for the Pulitzer Prize.

May 7 In Minneapolis, Minnesota, Tyrone Guthrie's namesake theatre, designed by Ralph Rapson, opens. The complex has cost $2.5 million to construct and outfit.

June 1 Henry Hewes, as editor of the Burns Mantle *Best Plays* annual, makes his selection of the ten best from the 1962–1963 Broadway season just concluded. They are Bricusse and Newley's *Stop the World—I Want to Get Off*, Albee's *Who's Afraid of Virginia Woolf?*, Michael's

Tchin-Tchin, Rayfiel's *P. S. 193*, Pinter's *The Collection*, Williams' *The Milk Train Doesn't Stop Here Anymore*, Frisch's *Andorra*, Brecht's *Mother Courage and Her Children*, Dyer's *Rattle of a Simple Man*, and Masteroff, Bock, and Harnick's *She Loves Me*. Albee's play wins the Drama Critics' Circle Award, but there is no Pulitzer Prize for drama this year.

June 1 Editor Henry Hewes notes that three-fourths of the past Broadway season have come from abroad, mainly Britain. Broadway's production costs are now five times those of London.

June 5 The Lord Chamberlain permits use of Strindberg's own epithet—"Merde"—in a performance version of *Miss Julie*, translated by Michael Meyer. (Performances of this play had been banned until 1939.)

June 15 London's Old Vic Theatre Company ceases to exist. The house will be the temporary home of Laurence Olivier's National Theatre until a new complex can be designed and built.

June 17 The May Fair Theatre opens in the Candlelight Room of Berkeley Square's May Fair Hotel. Home of Big Band Broadcasting in the '30's, it has been completely reconstructed for stage-audience flexibility.

July 16 Sean Kenny's set for the Royal Shakespeare Company's production of *The Beggar's Opera* is a Piranesi-like debtors' prison, which at the finale astonishes by becoming a ship on which the cast appears to sail to the New World.

Fall The opening season of the Playhouse Theatre in Vancouver, in the new Queen Elizabeth Playhouse, commences. The theatre was built by the city at a cost of $3 million and seats 647.

Sep The first electronic lighting control system is permanently installed in a professional New York theatre, the Vivian Beaumont.

Sep New York Attorney General Louis Lefkowitz begins investigation of payoffs for good seats to hit shows, known as "ice," or "incidental campaign expenses," and of producers who have lined their pockets at the expense of "angels" and employees.

Sep 9 The Royal Alexandra Theatre in Toronto re-opens after restoration to its original Edwardian elegance. The play is *Never Too Late*, featuring William Bendix and Nancy Carroll.

Sep 11–Dec 29 The Quebec government gives exclusive jurisdiction over performers at Place des Arts to the UDA, chiefly a union of French-speaking performers. Actor's Equity bans its members from the Place, thus delaying its opening.

LIVING THEATER

Eventual agreement holds that UDA may charge performance fee to any foreign performer, except Canadian and American Equity members.

Sept 21 Place des Arts in Montreal opens with a concert in the 3,000 seat Salle Wilfred Pelletier. The complex, designed by Raymond Affleck, took ten years and $37 million to build. Cost is split among the Province of Quebec, the city of Montreal, and the private sector.

Oct 15 Phillip Meister founds the National Shakespeare Company as a nonprofit ensemble. His first production is *Taming of the Shrew*. In future years, audiences in 120 cities will total one-quarter million or more.

Oct 18 The Living Theatre of Julian Beck and Judith Malina is served an eviction notice. The *NY Times* reports the Theatre's tax difficulties as well.

Oct 22 Laurence Olivier's National Theatre Company takes over the Old Vic and opens with *Hamlet*, played by Peter O'Toole.

Nov 13 The Seattle Repertory Theatre opens its first season at the Seattle Center Playhouse with a critically-acclaimed production of *King Lear*.

Dec 20 The establishment of the National Arts Foundation is approved by a vote in the U.S. Senate today.

Jan 2 *The Chinese Prime Minister* (NY—Royale—Comedy). Margaret Leighton plays an aged actress savoring retirement in Enid Bagnold's play. It has 108 performances. On May 20, 1965, the show opens in the West End at the Globe with Edith Evans in the lead.

Jan 16 *Hello, Dolly!* (NY—St. James—Musical). Carol Channing triumphs as Mrs. Dolly Levi in Michael Stewart's adaptation of Thornton Wilder's play, *The Matchmaker*. Music and lyrics are by Jerry Herman. Gower Champion directs and choreographs. There are 2,844 performances. It opens at London's Drury Lane on Dec 2, 1965, with Mary Martin in the lead. Here, it plays 794 times.

Jan 18 *Dylan* (NY—Plymouth—Drama). Alec Guinness plays poet Dylan Thomas, with Kate Reid as his wife, in this play by Sidney Michaels. Peter Glenville stages the production which runs 34 weeks.

Jan 23 *After the Fall* (NY—ANTA Washington Square—Drama). Arthur Miller's new play seems strongly autobiographical, with Jason Robards, Jr., and Barbara Loden. Staged by Elia Kazan, there are 208 performances in repertory.

Feb 6 *Foxy*. See Yukon premiere, 1962.

Feb 11 *The Passion of Josef D.* (NY—Ethel Barrymore—Drama). Paddy Chayevsky writes and directs this story of Josef Stalin and his major battles. Peter Falk is Stalin for the two-week run. Henry Hewes chooses it as a "Best Play."

Feb 18 *Any Wednesday* (NY—Music Box—Comedy). Don Porter plays a smug, pompous businessman who keeps a mistress on the side. Sandy Dennis, Rosemary Murphy, and Gene Hackman are in the cast. Muriel Resnik's comedy runs 982 performances. It opens in London on Aug 4, 1965, staged by Frank Dunlop. The cast is Dennis Price, Amanda Barrie, Moira Lister, and John Fraser.

Feb 26 *The Deputy*. See L premiere *(The Representative)*, 1963.

Feb 27 *What Makes Sammy Run?* (NY—54th Street—Musical). Steve Lawrence plays an opportunist clawing his way to fame and fortune in Hollywood in Budd and Stuart Schulberg's adaptation of the former's novel. Songs are by Ervin Drake. There are 540 performances.

March 1 *The Blood Knot* (NY—Cricket—Drama). Athol Fugard's tale of two brothers in South Africa wins a 30-week run. J. D. Cannon and James Earl Jones are directed by John Berry.

March 12 *But for Whom Charlie* (NY—ANTA Washington Square—Comedy). S. N. Behrman's play about a man trying to free himself from a domineering father features Ralph Meeker as Charles. The play, for the Repertory Theatre of Lincoln Center, has 47 performances.

March 19 *Cindy* (NY—Gate—Musical). This tale of Cinderella, set in a New York delicatessen, wins 318 performances. Songs are by Johnny Brandon and book by Joe Sauter and Mike Sawyer. Marvin Gordon directs Joe Masiell and Jacqueline Mayro.

March 26 *Funny Girl* (NY—Winter Garden—Musical). Barbra Streisand is Fanny Brice in Isobel Lennard's story of her rise to stardom. Bob Merrill and Jule Styne provide the songs which include "People." There are 1,348 performances. On April 13, 1966, the musical opens in London at the Prince of Wales's. Despite Streisand in the lead, the show does not last long.

April 4 *Anyone Can Whistle* (NY—Majestic—Musical). Stephen Sondheim creates the songs for this show, with a book by Arthur Laurents. It is about a Mayoress who helps revive her town with a fake miracle. There are only nine performances, but the show becomes a cult favorite.

April 7 *High Spirits* (NY—Alvin—Musical). Hugh Martin and Timothy Gray base this show on Noel Coward's *Blithe Spirit*. Beatrice Lillie is featured. Coward stages Tammy Grimes and Louise Troy for 375 performances. In London, where the show opens on Nov 3, at the Savoy, Cicely Courtneidge plays Madam Arcati, with Denis Quilley as the husband with two wives—one of them a ghost.

April 23 *Blues for Mister Charlie* (NY—ANTA—Drama). James Baldwin's tale of a northern black murdered by a white southern shopkeeper is staged by Burgess Meredith for the Actors Studio. Rip Torn and Al Freeman, Jr., are in the cast. There are 148 performances.

May 21 *Roar Like a Dove*. See L premiere, 1957.

May 25 *The Subject Was Roses* (NY—Royale—Drama). Martin Sheen plays Timmy Cleary, returned from the service, and pulled back and forth between father (Jack Albertson) and mother (Irene Dailey) in their efforts to earn his respect and affection. Frank D. Gilroy's play gets 425 performances, winning both the Pulitzer Prize and the Critics' Circle Award for the following season.

May 26 *Fade Out—Fade In* (NY—Mark Hellinger—Musical). Carol Burnett parodies Shirley Temple in this Betty Comden-Adolph Green-Jule Styne show. Dick Patterson and Lou Jacobi also are directed by George Abbott. It plays 271 performances, closes for repairs, and reopens.

May 27 *The Knack*. See L premiere, 1962.

Sep 21 *Absence of a Cello* (NY—Ambassador—Comedy). Fred Clark plays a rumpled but brilliant scientist who plays a cello. He is facing a corporate interview. James Hammerstein directs this Ira Wallach play. It premieres in London on Oct 15, 1968 at St. Martin's under the title *Out of the Question* with a cast including Michael Denison, Andrew Pilgrim, and Gladys Cooper. There are 315 performances.

Sep 22 *Fiddler on the Roof* (NY—Imperial—Musical). Zero Mostel brings Sholom Aleichem's optimistic milkman, Tevya, to life in this long-running show (3,242 performances) by Joseph Stein (book), Jerry Bock (music), and Sheldon Harnick (lyrics). Among the beloved songs are "Sunrise, Sunset" and "Tradition." Jerome Robbins stages and choreographs. Topol plays Tevye in the London production which opens at Her Majesty's on Feb 16, 1967. There are 2,030 performances.

Sep 30 *Oh What a Lovely War*. See L premiere, 1963.

Oct 1 *The Last Analysis* (NY—Belasco—Comedy). Saul Bellow's wildly satiric play about neuroses and traumas baffles for only 28 performances. Sam Levene heads a cast including Lucille Patton and Tony Roberts.

Oct 6 *Bits and Pieces* (NY—Plaza 9—Revue). Julius Monk's cabaret show wins 426 performances at the Hotel Plaza. It is directed and choreographed by Frank Wagner.

Oct 13 *The Physicists*. See L premiere, 1963.

Oct 15 *The Sign in Sidney Brustein's Window* (NY—Longacre—Comedy). Lorraine Hansberry's play depicts a liberal skirmishing with reality in contemporary Greenwich Village. Gabriel Dell and Rita Moreno are also cast for 101 performances.

Oct 20 *Golden Boy* (NY—Majestic—Musical). Sammy Davis, Jr., stars. Clifford Odets has died before completing the libretto adapted from his 1938 play of the same title. The show previews on Broadway for weeks while the work is completed by William Gibson. Also involved are director Arthur Penn, producer Hillard Elkins, composer Charles Strouse, and lyricist Lee Adams. There are 568 performances.

Oct 27 *Ben Franklin in Paris* (NY—Lunt-Fontanne—Musical). Robert Preston plays Franklin in Sidney Michaels's libretto with a score by Mark Sandrich, Jr. The show has a 27-week run.

Nov 11 *Luv* (NY—Booth—Comedy). Murray Schisgal's raffish satire on *angst* has had a London tryout and now wins a run of 901 performances, with Alan Arkin, Eli Wallach, and Anne Jackson in the

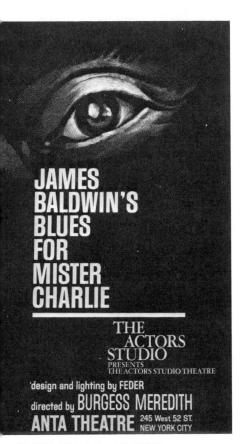

JAMES BALDWIN'S BLUES FOR MISTER CHARLIE

THE ACTORS STUDIO PRESENTS THE ACTORS STUDIO THEATRE

design and lighting by FEDER

directed by BURGESS MEREDITH

ANTA THEATRE 245 West 52 ST. NEW YORK CITY

BLUES FOR MR. CHARLIE

cast. Mike Nichols stages with panache.

Nov 18 *The Owl and the Pussycat* (NY—ANTA—Comedy). Bill Manhoff's lively farce about a studious young writer and the prostitute who moves in with him features Alan Alda and Diana Sands. It runs 427 performances. On March 2, 1966, the play opens in London at the Criterion with Anton Rogers and Sands in the cast.

Nov 23 *Bajour* (NY—Shubert—Musical). A *bajour* (gypsy swindle) is worked by Chita Rivera to win the Gypsy King's son for spouse. Joseph Mitchell's stories of alert, urban gypsies is the basis for Ernest Kinoy's book, with a score by Walter Marks.

Nov 30 *Slow Dance on the Killing Ground* (NY—Plymouth—Drama). Hume Cronyn co-produces William Hanley's play about individuals associated with murder and death features George Rose. Joseph Anthony stages the 11-week run, and the drama is chosen a "Best Play."

Dec 2 *Poor Richard* (NY—Helen Hayes—Comedy). Jean Kerr gets only 118 performances from this script, but she does have Alan Bates as a British poet who cuts a swath on a Manhattan visit.

Dec 3 *Incident at Vichy* (NY—ANTA Washington Square—Drama). Arthur Miller examines the motives and actions of a group of prisoners detained by Nazis in Vichy and faced with deportation to concentration camps. The cast includes Hal Holbrook, David Wayne, and Paul Mann. There are 99 performances. On Jan

26, 1966, the drama opens at London's Phoenix with Alec Guinness and Anthony Quayle among the players. It has 96 performances.

Dec 9 *Tiny Alice* (NY—Billy Rose—Drama). Edward Albee's enigmatic drama of a lay brother called to catalogue a library in a mansion with a replica of itself in the foyer features John Gielgud and Irene Worth. Alan Schneider directs. It fascinates for 21 weeks. The show is presented by the Royal Shakespeare Company at London's Aldwych beginning Jan 15, 1970. Worth and David Warner are in the cast.

Dec 9 *The Room* and *A Slight Ache* (NY—Writers Stage—Drama). Word Baker directs to heighten the implicit but ambiguous menace in these Harold Pinter plays. Frances Sternhagen, Henderson Forsythe, Margaret Linn, and Ralph Drischell are in the casts. The double-bill wins

343 performances.

Dec 15 *I Had a Ball* (NY—Martin Beck—Musical). Is it a good time or a *crystal* ball? Ask boardwalk seer Buddy Hackett, whose burlesque and vaudeville are the real comedy here. Richard Kiley and Karen Morrow sing songs by Jack Lawrence and Stan Freeman for director Lloyd Richards. 199 performances result.

Dec 16 *The Slave/The Toilet* (NY—St. Marks Playhouse—Drama). LeRoi Jones creates menace in a high school boys' toilet and harassment for a white woman and her professor husband by her black revolutionary ex-spouse. The plays run 19 weeks.

Dec 22 *Hughie* (NY—Royale—Drama). Jason Robards, Jr., brags about his adventures to a hotel night-clerk in this Broadway premiere for the Eugene O'Neill play. Jose Quintero directs. There are 51 performances.

1964   BRITISH PREMIERES

Jan 6 *Poor Bitos* (L—Duke of York's—Comedy). Jean Anouilh's comedy of a man who has risen above his station is adapted by Lucienne Hill. Previously seen at the New Arts on Nov 13, 1963, it now runs 335 performances. On Nov 14, 1964, it opens at New York's Cort with Donald Pleasance again in the title-role. It plays only 17 times.

Jan 15 *The Reluctant Peer* (L—Duchess—Comedy). Naunton Wayne plays Lord Lister, willing to renounce his title to become Prime Minister, in William Douglas Home's new play. Sybil Thorndike plays the Dowager Countess of Lister. Charles Hickman directs, and the show wins 475 performances.

Feb 6 *Who's Afraid of Virginia Woolf?* See NY premiere, 1962.

March 28 *Round About Piccadilly* (L—Prince of Wales—Revue). Dick Hurran devises and stages this show, starring Max Bygraves. It runs for 318 performances.

April 29 *She Loves Me.* See NY premiere, 1963.

May 6 *Entertaining Mr. Sloane* (L—New Arts—Comedy). Joe Orton's play about a homicidal drifter (Dudley Sutton) taken in by a businessman (Peter Vaughn) and his sluttish sister (Madge Ryan) is staged by Patrick Dromgoole. It earns 152 performances when it transfers to Wyndham's Theatre in the West End opening June 29. It has only 13 performances on Broadway, opening at the Lyceum on Oct 12, 1965.

May 28 *The Right Honourable Gentleman* (L—Her Majesty's—Drama). Anthony Quayle plays Sir Charles Dilke, M. P., whose political career is scuttled by his moral lapses. Glen Byam Shaw stages Michael Dyne's play, which runs

17 months. It opens on Oct 19, 1965 in New York, at the Billy Rose Theatre, for only 118 performances. Charles D. Gray plays Dilke.

June 24 *Past Imperfect* (L—St. Martin's—Comedy). Hugh and Margaret Williams again collaborate. He is also featured as the Earl of Flint, who falls in love with a temporary secretary who spies a little (Susan Hampshire). Nigel Patrick stages and the show has 301 performances.

July 9 *12 Angry Men* (L—Queen's—Drama). Reginald Rose's American hit has only 99 performances in the West End. Leo Genn plays Juror No. 8, unwilling to vote with the other eleven that the accused is guilty as charged. Margaret Webster directs.

July 15 *Chase Me, Comrade* (L—Whitehall—Comedy). Ray Cooney's new farce has Brian Rix as Gerry Buss, helping a young Russian ballet dancer who is seeking asylum in Britain when his company is on tour to escape from Soviet Russia. Kerry Gardner plays the dancer, Petrovyan. There are 773 performances.

Aug 19 *Camelot.* See NY premiere, 1960.

Aug 20 *The Persecution and Assassination of Marat as Performed by the Inmates of the Asylum of Charenton under the Direction of the Marquis de Sade* (L—Aldwych—Drama). Peter Weiss's play, in which Marat's (Ian Richardson) murder by Charlotte Corday (Glenda Jackson) is re-enacted in a French insane asylum is brilliantly staged for the Royal Shakespeare Company by Peter Brook. The production opens for a limited run (144 performances) at New York's Martin Beck beginning Dec 27, 1965. Glenda Jackson and Patrick Magee (de Sade) again lead the cast.

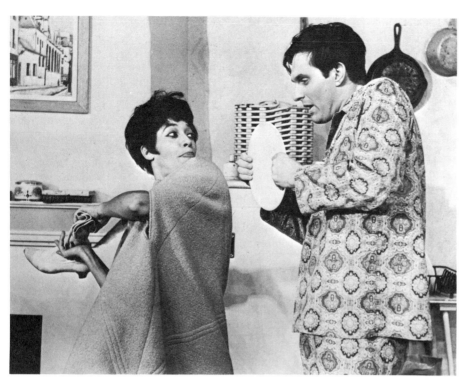

THE OWL AND THE PUSSYCAT

Sep 9 *Inadmissible Evidence* (L—Royal Court—Drama). Nicol Williamson is the burned-out lawyer in John Osborne's new play, staged by Anthony Page. The show moves to Wyndham's Theatre on March 17, 1965, where it runs for 252 performances. On Nov 30, 1965, it opens at New York's Belasco with Williamson repeating his London success. The show runs nearly 21 weeks and is chosen as a "Best Play."

Sep 17 *Carving a Statue* (L—Haymarket—Drama). Graham Greene's play has Ralph Richardson as the father and Dennis Waterman as the son. Peter Wood stages, but this is not to be a high point of the season.

Sep 22 *Maggie May* (L—Adelphi—Musical). Lionel Bart creates music and lyrics for Alun Owen's story of a lively Lime Street prostitute (Rachel Roberts) in Liverpool's dock area. Kenneth Haigh is her childhood sweetheart. Ted Kotcheff stages. There are 501 performances.

Sep 30 *A Scent of Flowers* (L—Duke of York's—Drama). Jennifer Hilary plays a suicide who looks back on her life from beyond the grave in James Saunders' drama. There are only 77 performances, but the play is widely produced on the continent. It opens in New York at the Martinique on Oct 20, 1969, with Katharine Houghton in the lead.

Oct 6 *Oblomov* (L—New Lyric, Hammersmith—Comedy). Goncharov's novel has been adapted for the stage by Riccardo Aragno and staged by Frank Dunlop. Joan Greenwood plays Olga, with zany Spike Milligan in the title role. On Dec 2, it moves to the Comedy Theatre as *Son of*

Oblomov.

Oct 20 *Robert and Elizabeth* (L—Lyric—Musical). This is based on Rudolf Besier's *The Barretts of Wimpole Street* by Ronald Millar (book and lyrics) and Ron Grainer (score). Wendy Toye stages Keith Michell

and June Bronhill in the title roles. There are 948 performances.

Oct 29 *Eh?* (L—Aldwych—Comedy). David Warner is the rebellious and half-witted Valentine Brose in Henry Livings's play, presented by the Royal Shakespeare Company. It opens in New York at the Circle-in-the Square on Oct 16, 1966, with Dustin Hoffman in the lead. There are 233 performances.

Nov 4 *Hostile Witness* (L—Haymarket—Drama). Jack Roffey's play has Michael Denison as an important barrister, accused of murdering a noted judge. It runs 444 performances. On Feb 17, 1966, the thriller opens in New York at the Music Box with Ray Milland in the lead. It plays 156 times.

Nov 18 *Little Me*. See NY premiere, 1962.

Dec 8 *The Royal Hunt of the Sun* (L—Old Vic—Drama). The National Theatre opens a restaging of its recent Chichester Festival success. Colin Blakely, Robert Lang, and Robert Stephens are in the cast of Peter Shaffer's tale of the conquest of Peru. The drama opens in New York at the ANTA on Oct 26, 1965, with Christopher Plummer and David Carridine heading the cast. Chosen as a "Best Play," it runs 31 weeks.

Dec 9 *Divorce Me, Darling* (L—Players'—Musical). Sandy Wilson tries out his sequel to *The Boy Friend*, staged by Steven Vinaver. Transferred to the Globe Theatre, it runs only 71 performances.

1964   REVIVALS/REPERTORIES

Jan 2 The D'Oyly Carte Opera Company continues its London season at the Savoy Theatre with Gilbert & Sullivan's *Patience, The Gondoliers, The Yeomen of the Guard, The Mikado, Princess Ida,* and *Ruddigore.*

Jan 4 Off-Broadway at the Cherry Lane Theatre, Alan Schneider stages Samuel Beckett's *Play,* with Frances Sternhagen, Marian Reardon, and Michael Lipton as three faces peering out of urns to tell their versions of a love-triangle. In Harold Pinter's *The Lover,* Hilda Brawner and Lipton play a couple who each pretend to have an outside amour. There are 89 showings of the latter, *Play* continuing on a later triple bill.

Jan 7 At the Old Vic, the National Theatre opens its production of Harold Brighouse's *Hobson's Choice,* directed by John Dexter. Joan Plowright and Michael Redgrave head the cast. On April 7, National presents Samuel Beckett's *Play* and Sophocles' *Philoctetes.* George Devine directs the first; William Gaskill, the second. Rosemary Harris and Colin Blakely are in the company. On April 21, at the Old Vic, the Shakespeare Quatercentenary opens with *Othello,* featuring Laur-

ence Olivier in the title role. Maggie Smith is his Desdemona and Frank Finley Iago. John Dexter directs. On June 9, the National presents Emlyn Williams's adaptation of Henrik Ibsen's *The Master Builder.* Michael Redgrave and Maggie Smith are directed by Peter Wood. Celia Johnson is also cast.

Jan 11 To salute the Shakespeare Quatercentenary, the Royal Shakespeare Company brings its three-part *Wars of the Roses* to London's Aldwych. John Barton has edited *Henry VI* and *Richard III* to create *Edward IV. Henry VI* plays in the morning, *Edward IV* in the afternoon, and *Richard III* in the evening.

Jan 12 The Royal Shakespeare Company explores the *Theatre of Cruelty* at the London Academy of Music and Dramatic Arts (LAMDA). Director Peter Brook has been inspired by the writings of Antonin Artaud *(The Theatre and Its Double).*

Jan 14 Trevor Howard plays the Captain in August Strindberg's *The Father,* revived by director Caspar Wrede at London's Piccadilly Theatre. Joyce Redman plays Laura. There are 63 performances.

Jan 15 At the Phoenix Theatre Off-Broadway, Burt Shevelove adapts and stages a revival of William Gillette's *Too Much Johnson* for three weeks. John McMartin, Dom DeLuise, and Charles Durning are among the cast.

Jan 21 Under the artistic direction of Jim Haynes, Edinburgh's adventurous Traverse Theatre opens its new year with Strindberg's *The Stronger* and *Playing with Fire*, staged by Callum Mill. Other plays include Pinter's *The Caretaker*, staged by Michael Geliot; *An Evening of Farce with Chekhov*, O'Neill's *Hughie*, Albee's *Zoo Story*, Pinget's *Dead Letter*, Walser's *The Detour*, de Ghelderode's *Escorial* and *Red Magic*, Richardson's *Gallows Humor*, staged by Charles Marowitz; the Brecht/Weill *Happy End*, staged for the Edinburgh Festival by Geliot; Frisch's *Philipp Hotz's Fury*, Mrozek's *The Party* and *The Enchanted Night*, McGough's *Birds, Marriages, and Deaths*, Bermel's *The Work Out* and *The Recovery*, Ionesco's *The Motor Show*, Pinget's *The Old Tune* Pinter's *The Lover*, Antrobus' *You'll Come To Love Your Sperm Test*, Calder's *The Voice*, Conn's *Birds in a Wilderness*, and the Lindsay Kemp mime version of Thomas' *A Child's Christmas in Wales*.

Jan 27 Robert Bolt's *A Man for All Seasons* is revived at New York City Center with William Roderick as Thomas Moore. On Feb 25, Jean-Louis Barrault and Madeleine Renaud bring their Theatre de France to New York for three weeks. Gilbert & Sullivan, *West Side Story*, *Porgy and Bess* and *My Fair Lady* will complete City Center's season.

Feb 3 At Broadway's Little Theatre, the National Theatre of Israel, the Habimah, offers 55 performances of a three-play repertory: S. Ansky's *The Dybbuk*, Ben-Zio Tomer's *Children of the Shadows*, and Hanoch Bartov's *Each Had Six Wings*.

Feb 4 Josephine Baker presents her revue of songs and dances at the Brooks Atkinson Theatre for two weeks. Geoffrey Holder dances. On March 31, after touring, she offers three more weeks at Henry Miller's Theatre.

Feb 5 Bernard Miles' production of Euripides' *The Bacchae* opens at London's Mermaid Theatre in a new translation by Kenneth Cavander. Josephine Wilson, Barrie Ingham, and John Woodvine are in the cast. On March 11, the show is *The Royal Commission Revue*, a spoof of current events and private quirks, devised and directed by John Antrobus and Spike Milligan. On April 22, *Macbeth* opens as the first in a series of Elizabethan and Jacobean plays to celebrate the Bard's 400th anniversary. The life of Shakespeare's time is dramatized by *The Canker and the Rose*, a compilation by Philip Collins and Ronald Draper from Elizabethan sources. On June 2, Beaumont and Fletcher's *The Maid's Tragedy* opens. On July 24, *The Shoemaker's Holiday*, by Thomas Dekker, is presented to continue

the series of Jacobean dramas.

Feb 12 At London's New Arts Theatre, Henrik Ibsen's *Hedda Gabler* is revived, with Joan Greenwood as Hedda and Maurice Good as Lovborg. Minos Volanakis stages. On March 2, it transfers to St. Martin's Theatre for 89 performances.

Feb 20 In Greenwich Village's ANTA Washington Square Theatre, Eugene O'Neill's *Marco Millions* is revived by the Repertory Theatre of Lincoln Center for 49 performances. Jose Quintero directs Hal Holbrook, David Wayne, and Zohra Lampert.

Feb 27 *Fielding's Music Hall* was not a success last month at London's Comedy, but William Chappell revises it and stages it at the Prince Charles with noted performers: Donald Wolfit, Cicely Courtneidge, Billy Russell, and Joyce Grant.

March 4 Ellis Rabb's Association of Producing Artists offers a repertory of five plays for over 17 weeks in New York at the Phoenix Theatre. They include Pirandello's *Right You Are*, Cohan's *The Tavern*, Moliere's *Scapin* and *The Impromptu at Versailles*, and Gorky's *The Lower Depths*.

March 10 Joan Littlewood stages *A Kayf Up West* at the Theatre Royal, Stratford East. Frank Norman's characters are impersonated by Richard Curnock, Barry Humphries, Roy Barnett, and Howard Goorney, among others. On May 20, Herbert Wise stages *The Man Who Let It Rain*, by Marc Brandel.

March 12 A London revival of Chekhov's *The Seagull* in a new translation by Ann Jellicoe is staged by Tony Richardson. Vanessa Redgrave and Peggy Ashcroft are in the cast. The production has 93 performances.

March 15 Shakespeare's 400th anniversary is honored at New York's Philharmonic Hall with *Homage to Shakespeare*, staged by William Ball. Edith Evans, John Gielgud, and Margaret Leighton interpret selections from the Bard's works.

March 17 Seven famed foreign troupes play the Aldwych while the Royal Shakespeare Company is on tour: the Comedie Francaise, Berlin's Schiller Theatre, de Filippo's Italian Theatre Company, Dublin's Abbey Theatre, the Polish Contemporary Theatre, Koun's Greek Art Theatre and the Moscow Art Theatre. This becomes an annual event, The World Theatre Festival.

March 23 To the Alan Schneider staging of Beckett's *Play* are added Fernando Arrabal's *The Two Executioners* and LeRoi Jones's *Dutchman*, both staged by Edward Parone Off-Broadway at the Cherry Lane Theatre. *Dutchman* has 366 performances; the Arrabal only 32. It is replaced by Edward Albee's *The American Dream*. Jones' play is animated by Robert Hooks as a black who is propositioned on a subway by a white girl (Jennifer West),

who then insults him and finally stabs him.

April 5 At Broadway's Belasco Theatre, the National Repertory Theatre offers two plays for four weeks. Eva LeGallienne plays in Chekhov's *The Seagull* with Farley Granger. Granger also plays John Proctor in Arthur Miller's *The Crucible*.

April 8 Arthur Wing Pinero's *The Schoolmistress* is revived at London's Savoy Theatre, staged by John Fernald. Megs Jenkins and Nigel Patrick appear for 85 performances.

Apr 9 After a two-year run in Johannesburg, South Africa, the revue *Wait a Minim* opens in London at the Fortune for a run of 656 performances.

April 9 On Broadway at the Lunt-Fontanne Theatre, Alexander Cohen produces John Gielgud's staging of *Hamlet* in rehearsal dress. Richard Burton plays Hamlet. Alfred Drake, Eileen Herlie, Hume Cronyn, and Linda Marsh are also in the cast.

April 15 The Royal Shakespeare Company opens its annual season in Stratford with *Richard II*, staged by Peter Hall. *The Wars of the Roses* is revived, and both parts of *Henry IV* and *Henry V* are also in the repertory.

May 18 The new New York State Theatre, at Lincoln Center, opens with Peter Brook's Royal Shakespeare production of *King Lear*, with Paul Scofield. There are immediate complaints of inaudibility in the 2,729 seat theatre, which has cost over $17 million. *Lear* plays 12 times, as does *The Comedy of Errors*.

May 30 The American Shakespeare Festival in Stratford, Connecticut, offers a 118 performance season of three plays: *Richard III*, *Hamlet*, and *Much Ado About Nothing*. Allen Fletcher stages all three.

June 2 The *Folies Bergere* wins 191 performances at the Broadway Theatre, even without nude chorus girls. The show is a sampler of Folies programming, supported by 15 tons of scenery and 1,200 costumes.

June 5 In London's Regent's Park, the Open Air Theatre has *Henry V* with Dinsdale Landen. On July 15, Landen plays Petruchio to Sheila Ballantine's Katherina in *The Taming of the Shrew*.

June 9 The National Shakespeare Festival, at San Diego's Old Globe, offers 110 performances of a three-play repertory: *Much Ado About Nothing*, *Macbeth*, and *Measure for Measure*. Charles Macauley and Patricia Morrill play Macbeth and his lady.

June 11 Siobhan McKenna plays Joan Dark, the title role in Bertolt Brecht's *Saint Joan of the Stockyards* at the Queen's Theatre in London. Tony Richardson stages Brecht's parable of worker-owner confrontation in Chicago, which runs only 20 performances.

347

June 15 At Canada's Stratford Shakespeare Festival, the fare this season will include *Richard II* and *King Lear*. Michael Langham, artistic director, has programmed the rest of the season to include Moliere's *Le Bourgeois Gentilhomme*, Wycherley's *The Country Wife*, and Mozart's *The Marriage of Figaro*, with musical direction by Richard Bonynge.

June 16 Central Park's Delacorte Theatre sees the New York Shakespeare Festival's productions of *Hamlet, Othello,* and Sophocles' *Electra*.

June 18 Harold Pinter's *The Birthday Party* is revived at London's Aldwych. The playwright's staging is praised. Bryan Pringle plays Stanley, fussed over by his landlady Meg (Doris Hare) at her seaside rooming-house. On June 25, the Royal Shakespeare Company opens David Rudkin's *Afore Night Come* at the Aldwych. The play has been first produced by the RSC in 1962 at the New Arts Theatre. Clifford Williams directs. John Bury designs. It will provoke the "dirty play" controversy at the RSC, drawing complaints from board member Prince Littler.

June 22 The Actors Studio revives Chekhov's *The Three Sisters* on Broadway in a version by Randall Jarrell, for 119 performances. Lee Strasberg directs Kim Stanley, Geraldine Page and Shirley Knight as the sisters.

June 23 At Canada's Shaw Festival in Niagara-on-the-Lake, the third season opens with *Heartbreak House*, staged by Andrew Allan. *Village Wooing* and *Dark Lady of the Sonnets* follow. *John Bull's Other Island* completes the season.

July 1 This year is Christopher Marlowe's Quatercentenary as well as Shakespeare's, and his *Edward the Second* is revived at the New Arts in London. The production, staged by Clive Perry and featuring Richard Perry, comes from Leicester's Phoenix Theatre. Anthony Hopkins plays several roles.

July 2 At London's Aldwych Theatre, the Royal Shakespeare Company presents an exploratory program of plays by Arrabal, Saunders, Tardieu, Whiting, and Beckett under the general rubric of *Expeditions One*. The plays include Saunders' *The Pedagogue* and Arrabal's *Picnic on the Battlefield*, both staged by Robin Midgley; Whiting's *No Why*, staged by John Schlesigner, later to gain attention as a film-director; Beckett's *Act Without Words II*, directed by Elsa Bolam, and Tardieu's *The Keyhole*, staged by Garry O'Connor. On July 9, Samuel Beckett's *Endgame* is offered. On Aug 5, at the Aldwych, Roger Vitrac's precursor of Black Comedy, *Victor, or The Children Take Over*. Written in 1928, it shows a precocious sub-teen committing various social outrages.

July 6 A revival of Richard Rodgers and Oscar Hammerstein II's *The King and I* is presented at the State Theatre in New York, with Darren McGavin and Rise Stevens in the title roles. There are 40 showings. Lehar's *The Merry Widow*, with Patrice Munsel, opens on Aug 17.

July 7 The Chichester Festival opens with the premiere of Peter Shaffer's *The Royal Hunt of the Sun*, an epic-theatre treatment of the conquest of Peru, directed by John Dexter with Robert Stephens and Colin Blakely. *The Dutch Courtesan* by John Marston and *Othello* will also be played this season.

July 7 The Missouri Repertory Theatre's first production is *The Corn Is Green*, staged by founder and director Patricia McIlrath at the University of Missouri in Kansas City.

July 11 The Oregon Shakespearean Festival offers 55 performances in repertory of *The Merchant of Venice, King Lear, Twelfth Night,* and *Henry IV, Part 1*.

Aug 3 At Carnegie Hall, there are 28 performances of *Laterna Magika*, a Czech entertainment which mixes live actors with their images on film. Also today, at Philharmonic Hall, the Black Theatre of Prague, a pantomime theatre with blacklight effects, opens for two weeks.

Aug 9 Earl Hobson Smith has adapted the novel of John Fox, Jr., *The Trail of the Lonesome Pine*, for the Lonesome Pine Arts and Crafts Association at June Tolliver Playhouse in Big Stone Gap, Virginia.

Aug 16 Britain's Edinburgh International Festival opens. Joan Littlewood brings her Theatre Workshop production of *Henry IV*. James Bridie's *The Golden Legend of Shults* is the offering of the Edinburgh Gateway Company. Lennox Milne's one-woman show, *The Heart Is a Highland*, written for her by Robert Kemp, is also on view. John Wilson's play *Hamp* is staged by John Gibson. Val May of the Bristol Old Vic directs the company in *Love's Labour's Lost*. The Bristol ensemble also plays *Henry V*, directed by Stuart Burge and designed by Graham Barlow. Marlene Dietrich performs as do Guinea's *Les Ballets Africaines*.

Aug 18 At London's Queen's Theatre, Michael Croft's National Youth Theatre presents his staging of *Coriolanus*. Paul Hill's staging of *A Midsummer Night's Dream* follows on Aug 31.

Aug 23 Pirandello's *Lazarus* is staged by Robert Gillespie at the Mermaid Theatre. On Sep 2, New York's Living Theatre opens its production of Kenneth H. Brown's *The Brig*, showing brutalization of prisoners and guards in a U.S. Marine jail. On Sep 28, the play is Ray Mathew's *A Spring Song*, staged by Michael Rudman and designed by Martin Lees. On Oct 21, T. J. Feely's *Don't Let Summer Come* is staged by Bernard Miles and designed by Trewin Copplestone and Brenda Bishop. Miles revives *Treasure Island* for the holiday season on Dec 23.

Sep 7 The Bristol Old Vic opens at London's Old Vic with *Love's Labour's Lost*, staged by Val May. On Sep 11, they present *Henry V*. On Sep 15, Italy's Proclemer-Albertazzi Company presents *Amleto (Hamlet)* in Franco Zeffirelli's staging.

Sep 18 Joan Littlewood's Theatre Royal, Stratford East, becomes Stage Sixty for David Thompson and Adrian Rendle. (She wants to create a Fun Palace for the masses.) Max Frisch's *Edge of Reason*, their first production, will feature Maxwell Shaw as a public prosecutor who launches a revolution.

Sep 21 The Sanskrit classic, *The Little Clay Cart*, is revived by James Roose-Evans at the Hampstead Theatre Club. Emlyn Williams' *The Corn Is Green* is revived on Oct 19, and Leonid Andreyev's *He Who Gets Slapped* is produced on Nov 19.

Sep 28 The Dublin Gate uses the Gaiety Theatre for Brian Friel's *Philadelphia, Here I Come!*, staged by Hilton Edwards. Shaw's *You Never Can Tell*, macLiammoir's *I Must Be Talking to My Friends* and Fletcher's *The Bernard Shaw Story* will be the fall's other shows.

Oct 1 For Marlowe's 400th anniversary, the Royal Shakespeare Company stages his *Jew of Malta* at the Aldwych. Clifford Williams directs a large cast, including Derek Godfrey, Michele Dotrice, Ian Richardson, and Glenda Jackson. On Dec 17, the Royal Shakespeare presents their holiday treat, *The Merry Wives of Windsor*, brought from Stratford. John Blatchley has directed Ian Richardson, Patsy Byren, Brenda Bruce, Clive Swift, and Doris Hare.

ARTHUR MILLER

Oct 5 New York's Phoenix Theatre revives Christopher Marlowe's *Doctor Faustus* for an eight week run, staged by Word Baker. Lou Antonio, James Ray and William Devane are in the cast.

Oct 13 The National Theatre revives John Marston's *The Dutch Courtesan* at the Old Vic. On the 27th, Noel Coward directs a revival of his *Hay Fever*, with Edith Evans.

Oct 21 Euripides' *Electra* opens at the Theatre Royal, Stratford East. On the 27th, *Iphigenia in Aulis* and on Nov 2, *The Trojan Women* complete the Euripides season. All are directed by David Thompson.

Oct 22 Ben Traver's *A Cuckoo in the Nest* is revived at London's Royal Court, staged by Anthony Page. Playwright John Osborne, Nicol Williamson, and Beatrix Lehman are in the cast. On Nov 26, *Julius Caesar* is revived, staged by Lindsay Anderson.

Oct 29 At the ANTA Washington Square Theatre, the Repertory Theatre of Lincoln Center opens its season with the American premiere of Middleton and Rowley's Jacobean *The Changeling* for 32 performances. Arthur Miller's *After the Fall*, held over from last season, is presented.

Nov 1 At St. Clement's Church, near but not on Broadway, the American Place Theatre opens its premiere season with Robert Lowell's one-act plays, based on American novellas: *Benito Cereno* (Melville) and *My Kinsman, Major Molineux* (Hawthorne). Jonathan Miller stages, with designs by Will Steven Armstrong and Willa Kim. Under the title, *The Old Glory*, these plays and a third from Hawthorne have been read at the APT last March. Now they have 36 performances. *Benito Cereno* moves to the Theatre deLys for 11 weeks on January 14, 1965. In this original company, Frank Langella plays Cereno, with Roscoe Lee Brown as the insidious, menacing Babu.

Nov 8 Leonard Bernstein is consultant for Howard Da Silva's revival of *The Cradle Will Rock*, which runs over ten weeks Off-Broadway at Theatre Four.

Nov 16 A musical version of the 19th century temperance melodrama, *The Drunkard*, called *The Wayward Way*, opens at the New Lyric, Hammersmith. Jim Dale is in the cast.

Nov 17 London's D'Oyly Carte Opera Company offers five weeks of Gilbert & Sullivan at New York's City Center. On Dec 23, Jean Dalrymple revives *Brigadoon* for two weeks.

Nov 24 Berlin's prestigious Schiller Theatre comes to the New York State Theatre for two weeks, opening with Friedrich Schiller's *Don Carlos*, followed by Carl Zuckmayer's 1931 *Der Hauptmann von Koepenick*.

Dec 6 Off-Broadway, at the Phoenix Theatre, Ellis Rabb's APA troupe opens three plays in repertory: Shaw's *Man and Superman*, the Tolstoy/Piscator *War and Peace*, and Giraudoux's *Judith*.

Dec 9 *Give a Dog a Bone* is the pantomime at London's Westminster Theatre, launching the holiday season of special entertainments. Dawn Addams is Peter in the Scala Theatre's revival of *Peter Pan* on Dec 18. Thackeray's "Fireside Pantomime," *The Rose and The Ring*, is staged on the 21st at the Theatre Royal, Stratford East. Other holiday shows include *The Tingalary Bird* (New Arts), *Toad of Toad Hall* (Queen's), *Aladdin* (Palladium, with Cliff Richard as Aladdin), *Treasure Island* (Mermaid), *Dick Whittington* (Golder's Green Hippodrome), *The Three Wishes* (New Lyric, Hammersmith), *Let's Make an Opera* (Vaudeville), *Pinocchio* (Apollo), *The Puppet Prince* (Hampstead Theatre Club), and the more-adult treats of *Lady Audley's Secret* (New Arts), *The Importance of Being Oscar* (Queen's), and *Waiting for Godot*—hardly a holiday play, with Alfred Lynch and Nicol Williamson as Gogo and Didi at the Royal Court Theatre.

Dec 14 *Late Joys*, a Victorian Music Hall production, is transferred to London's Prince Charles from the Players' Theatre Club, where it has long delighted members and guests. Don Gemmel directs the 83 performances.

Dec 16 The D'Oyly Carte Opera Company's annual season at the Savoy opens with Gilbert and Sullivan's *Trial by Jury* and *H.M.S. Pinafore*. On the 23rd, the bill is *Cox and Box* and *The Pirates of Penzance*, followed on Dec 30 by *Iolanthe*.

1964   BIRTHS/DEATHS/DEBUTS

Jan 4 Ralph Dumke, an American musical comedy actor, dies at 64.

Jan 22 Composer-playwright Marc Blitzstein (b. 1905) is murdered on Martinique, West Indies, at age 58. Composer-librettist of *The Cradle Will Rock* in 1937, he also composed the incidental music for the Orson Welles production of *Julius Caesar* at the Mercury Theatre the same year. His adaptation of Bertolt Brecht's *The Threepenny Opera* was a long running hit at New York's Theatre de Lys in 1955. He also composed scores for films and television.

March 20 Irish playwright Brendan Behan (b. 1923) is dead at 41. Behan's first play, *The Quare Fellow*, was initially produced in London in 1956 and in New York two years later at the Circle in the Square. This was followed by *The Hostage*.

March 21 Glenn Hughes, a noted American professor of theatre, dies at 69. At the University of Washington in Seattle, Hughes has instituted several innovative theatres and programs, including a showboat.

March 23 In Hollywood, actor Peter Lorre (b. 1904) passes on.

April 18 American author and dramatist Ben Hecht (b. 1894) dies in New York. Hecht began his career as a journalist. Among his better known plays are his collaborations with Charles MacArthur: *The Front Page*, *Jumbo*, and *Ladies and Gentlemen*. He also wrote the popular *Twentieth Century*.

May 10 The dancer-choreographer Carol Haney (b. 1924) dies young in New York. She is remembered for her dynamic dancing in Broadway musicals such as *Pajama Game*, in which she performed "Steam Heat."

May 13 English actress Diana Wynyard dies at age 58 in London. Wynyard made her first appearance on the professional stage in London in 1925. Her New York debut was made at the Selwyn Theatre in *The Devil Passes* (1932). She also appeared with the Shakespeare Memorial Theatre Company.

June 21 British actress Diana Beaumont dies at age 55.

July 7 At age 87, actress Elaine Inescourt dies.

July 27 American actress Winifred Lenihan is dead in Sea Cliff, New York, at 66. Lenihan was acclaimed for her role as Joan in the American premiere of George Bernard Shaw's *Saint Joan* in 1924.

Aug 6 Actor-director Sir Cedric Hardwicke (b. 1893) dies in New York. Among

SIR CEDRIC HARDWICK

Hardwicke's major roles were King Magnus in *The Apple Cart*, Edward Moulton Barrett in *The Barretts of Wimpole Street*, and Dr. Haggett in *The Late Christopher Bean*. He wrote two volumes of reminiscences, *Let's Pretend* (1932) and *A Victorian in Orbit* (1961). He was knighted in 1934.

Aug 28 Lumsden Hare, the British actor, dies today at 89.

Sep 19 In Dublin, the Abbey Theatre closes, out of respect for playwright Sean O'Casey, who has died in Devon on the previous day. Among O'Casey's plays are *The Plough and the Stars* and *Juno and the Paycock*.

Sep 28 Harpo Marx, the silent, harp-playing member of the Marx Brothers, dies today at age 75.

Oct 10 Cole Porter, the American composer of so many Broadway hit musicals, dies today at age 71. *Kiss Me, Kate*, based on Shakespeare's *The Taming of the Shrew*, will remain popular in revivals.

Oct 10 Actor-comedian Eddie Cantor (b. 1892) dies in Hollywood. Born Edward Israel Iskowitz, Cantor appeared first on stage in *Amateur Night* at Winer's Bowery in New York and made his vaudeville debut at New York's Clinton Music Hall in 1907. His writings include sketches for the *Ziegfeld Follies* and *Earl Carroll's Sketch Book*, his 1928 autobiography *My Life is in Your Hands*, and his 1963 work, *As I Remember Them*.

1964 THEATERS/PRODUCTIONS

Richard Block and Ewel Cornett, as founders, open the Actors Theatre of Louisville (ATL) in a converted loft, formerly a tea-room, with a seating capacity of only 100, in Louisville, Kentucky.

Jan 10 Congress passes Public Law 88-260 whereby Washington, D.C.'s sole memorial to martyred president John F. Kennedy will be the new Center for the Performing Arts.

Jan 19 Producer Robert Whitehead notes, in the *NY Times Magazine*, that producing a play on Broadway in 1941 cost $20,000, and today it costs from $100,000 to $150,000. Ticket prices haven't kept pace: a $3.30 ticket in 1941 costs only $6.90 today.

Jan 23 The Lincoln Center Repertory Theatre opens in its temporary home off Greenwich Village's Washington Square. The ANTA Washington Square theatre seats 1,137 and cost $540,000. It is basically a Greek theatre inside, and is to approximate the auditorium of their future home, the Vivian Beaumont at Lincoln Center.

Feb The last issue of *Theatre Arts* magazine is printed and bound, but never distributed. Founded in 1916 by Sheldon Cheney, it was edited by Edith J. R. Isaacs for nearly three decades.

Feb 3 Moss Hart's *Light Up The Sky* opens at the Arts Theatre Club in Vancouver. The theatre, creation of Yvonne Firkins, will receive its first Canada Council Grant ($5,000) in 1973 under Artistic Director Bill Millerd.

April 1 Jacques Cartier has founded the Hartford Stage Company and now directs its premiere production, *Othello*. An abandoned warehouse, drugstore, and supermarket complex has been renovated into a 225-seat theatre.

April 6–25 Canada's Stratford Shakespeare Festival Company journeys to Britain to honor the Bard's 400th anniversary with productions of *Timon of Athens* and *Love's Labour's Lost* at the Chichester Festival Theatre.

April 23 James Baldwin's *Blues for Mister Charlie* causes critical controversies in New York for its depiction of, in critic Tom Driver's words, "racial warfare between black people and white people rooted in their separate ways of seeing life . . ." Rev. Sidney Lanier heads 75 people who raise money to keep it running.

April 24 Shakespeare's 400th anniversary is honored in America at all festivals dedicated to him and his works. Louis Marder, editor of the *Shakespeare Newsletter*, notes 433 productions of 31 of the 37 plays. *Midsummer Night's Dream*, *Twelfth Night*, and *Taming of the Shrew* are the most popular.

May Confederation Centre, the home of the summer Charlottetown Festival which sponsors Canadian musical theatre, opens. The $5.6 million complex is funded jointly by the 10 provinces (15¢ per capita) and by matching grants from the federal government. The theatre seats 900.

June 1 Henry Hewes, editor of *Best Plays*, summarizes the statistics for the Broadway season of 1963–1964, including the New York State Theatre and the ANTA Washington Square Theatre, both new playhouses. There have been 37 new plays, 14 new musicals, eight revivals, three readings, two puppet shows, 1½ revues, one "evening with," and five foreign-language plays, not counting five given at the City Center by the Theatre de France. He cites a *NY Times* estimate of Broadway losses through May 31 as $5,746,500 and profits as $873,000. Crystal-gazing, the *Times* sees an eventual $21 million profit in the season's three hit plays, six hit musicals, and one hit revival. Off-Broadway, there have been 38 new plays, eight new musicals, 23 revivals, and 10 revues.

June 1 At the close of the 1963–1964 Broadway season, Henry Hewes chooses the annual ten "Best Plays." His selections include Anouilh's *The Rehearsal*, Osborne's *Luther*, Wesker's *Chips with Everything*, Simon's *Barefoot in the Park*, Saunders' *Next Time I'll Sing To You*, Stewart and Herman's *Hello, Dolly!*, Michaels' *Dylan*, Miller's *After the Fall*, Chayevsky's *The Passion of Josef D.*, and Hochhuth's *The Deputy*. Drama Critics' Circle Awards go to *Luther* and *Hello, Dolly!* Again this season there is no Pulitzer Prize awarded.

June 7 Actors Equity stages a one-day strike to further its negotiations for a new four-year contract. The weekly actor minimum rises to $125 for Broadway and $60 Off-Broadway.

June 12 *Time* reports that A&P heir Huntington Hartford has poured $6 million into *Show* magazine during its three-year life, and that even though subscriptions and ad revenues have improved, each issue is losing $100,000.

Sep 21 The Playhouse opens in Fredericton, New Brunswick, Canada. Lord Beaverbrook has given $1 million toward its cost and a provincial grant of $500,000 has been awarded. Beaverbrook also gives $100,000 for production costs.

Oct 1 The Dramatists Guild (DG), born out of earlier organizations and attempts to secure just dealings for playwrights, it begins to function as a separate corporation from the parent organization, the Authors League of America.

Oct 14 The Trinity Square Repertory Company opens its first home in the Trinity United Methodist Church in Providence, Rhode Island, with *The Dark of the Moon*.

Oct 31 The Windmill Theatre, London, closes down after being sold to the Compton Cinema Group.

Nov 1 The American Place Theatre opens as a forum for living American writers with the production of Robert Lowell's *The Old Glory*. Founders Sidney Lanier, Myrna Loy, Wynn Handman, and Michael Tolan wish to create an atmosphere free of Broadway pressures for writers to create for the theatre.

Dec 6 The Dorothy Chandler Pavilion opens. It is the first completed unit of the projected Music Center of Los Angeles, being built in a rundown section of the city's downtown. The Mark Taper Forum and the Ahmanson Theatres are not yet finished.

Feb 6 *Kelly* (NY—Broadhurst—Musical). There is just one performance of this very costly show about a man, very much like Steve Brodie, who also jumps off the Brooklyn Bridge. Investors lose $650,000. Walter Kerr appraises the production: "A bad idea gone wrong."

Feb 10 *Diamond Orchid* (NY—Henry Miller's—Drama). There are only five performances of this play which very much resembles the career of Eva Peron. Jerome Lawrence and Robert E. Lee are the playwrights; Jose Quintero stages.

Feb 16 *Baker Street* (NY—Broadway—Musical). Fritz Weaver sings as Sherlock Holmes comes to Broadway in this show by Jerome Coopersmith (book) and Marian Grudeff and Raymond Jessel (music and lyrics). Inga Swenson plays Irene Adler, who asks Holmes to recover some letters and comes to love him. Harold Prince directs.

Feb 18 *All in Good Time.* See L premiere, 1963.

March 10 *The Odd Couple* (NY—Plymouth—Comedy). Neil Simon's play, inspired by the contrast in personal habits between himself and his writer-brother, offers the spectacle of Walter Matthau as the genial, sloppy Oscar, and Art Carney as the neat, fussy Felix, sharing an apartment and trying to charm two sisters (Carole Shelley and Monica Evans). There are 964 performances, a successful film, and a television series. The show has 406 performances following its London opening at the Queen's on Oct 12, 1966. Jack Klugman and Victor Spinetti have the leading roles.

March 16 *This Was Burlesque* (NY—Hudson—Revue). Ann Corio's nostalgic revue moves to Broadway, after a running Off-Broadway in two editions and touring. This engagement plays 124 performances.

March 17 *Harry, Noon and Night* (NY—American Place—Comedy). Dustin Hoffman and Joel Gray play a peculiar German and an alienated American painter in post-war Munich. Ronald Ribman's play excites much interest and it moves Off-Broadway on May 5, but only runs a week there.

March 18 *Do I Hear a Waltz?* (NY—46th Street—Musical). Composer Richard Rodgers collaborates with lyricist Stephen Sondheim for Arthur Laurent's adaptation of his play, *The Time of the Cuckoo.* Elizabeth Allen is Leona Smith, the American spinster eager for love, who finds it briefly with a married man (Sergio Franchi). John Dexter directs. There are only 220 performances.

March 30 *The Decline and Fall of the Entire World as Seen Through the Eyes*

HALF A SIXPENCE

of Cole Porter Revisited (NY—Square East—Revue). Ben Bagley presents some Porter works that are not done frequently. Kay Ballard, Harold Lang, William Hickey, and Carmen Alvarez are in the company. There are 273 performances. The revue opens in London at the Criterion on Aug 27, 1966, with Joan Heal, Bill Oddie, and Rod McLennan in the cast.

April 15 *The Amen Corner* (NY—Ethel Barrymore—Drama). James Baldwin writes about a woman preacher who learns that God is also served by caring for one's family. The play has been produced at Howard University in 1953 and in Los Angeles in 1964. There are 84 performances of this production, which is seen at the Edinburgh Festival in August 1965. The play opens in the West End at the Saville on Oct 12.

April 25 *Half-a-Sixpence.* See L premiere, 1963.

April 26 *And Things That Go Bump in the Night* (NY—Royale—Drama). Ruby (Eileen Heckart) and her bizarre children wait for the nuclear holocaust in Terence McNally's apocalyptic vision. The show runs only two weeks, in spite of a $1 seat policy adopted to keep it running. Michael Cacoyannis stages.

May 11 *Flora, the Red Menace* (NY—Alvin—Musical). Liza Minelli is the fledgling fashion designer who joins the Communist Party during the Depression. George Abbott (who directs) and Robert Russell have written the book based on Lester Atwell's novel, *Love is Just Around the Corner.* Songs are by John Kander and Fred Ebb. It runs 87 performances.

May 16 *The Roar of the Greasepaint—The Smell of the Crowd* (NY—Shubert—Musical). Leslie Bricusse and Anthony Newley's show gets 231 performances, staged by and starring Newley, with Cyril Ritchard. An allegory of power games,

the show offers Ritchard as Sir, holding the reins of power, and Newley as Cocky, willing to challenge authority, often with comic results. Other types are The Kid (Sally Smith), The Girl (Joyce Jillson), The Negro (Gilbert Price), and The Bully (Murray Tannenbaum). Gillian Lynne choreographs. Sean Kenny and Freddy Wittop design. "What Kind of Fool Am I?" becomes popular. This is the world premiere, but it's not followed by a London showing.

Oct 4 *Pickwick.* See L premiere, 1963.

Oct 6 *Generation* (NY—Morosco—Comedy). Henry Fonda plays an advertising man whose Bohemian daughter (Holly Turner) and her husband (Richard Jordan) plan to have their first child without benefit of hospital or doctor. Gene Saks stages for 299 performances. It is chosen as a "Best Play."

Oct 12 *Entertaining Mr. Sloane.* See L premiere, 1964.

Oct 13 *The Impossible Years* (NY—Playhouse—Comedy). Alan King plays an eminent alienist, famed for his good advice about raising children, but harried and baffled at home by his teen-age daughter and her chums. Authors Bob Fisher and Arthur Marx are rewarded by a run of 33 weeks. The comedy garners only 84 showings in London following its Nov 24, 1966, premiere at the Cambridge.

Oct 14 *Pick a Number XV* (NY—Plaza 9—Revue). Julius Monk's new show opens with Bill Hinnant, Rex Robbins, and Elizabeth Wilson. It has a long run of 400 performances.

Oct 17 *On a Clear Day You Can See Forever* (NY—Mark Hellinger—Musical). Librettist Alan Jay Lerner and composer Burton Lane's show about a modern woman who remembers her 18th century life runs eight months. Barbara Harris and

MAN OF LA MANCHA

John Cullum have the leads; Robert Lewis directs.

Oct 19 *The Right Honourable Gentleman.* See L premiere, 1964.

Oct 26 *The Royal Hunt of the Sun.* See L premiere, 1964.

Nov 11 *Hogan's Goat* (NY—American Place—Drama). Harvard Professor William Alfred's play about the Irish in Brooklyn in 1890 opens tonight with Ralph Waite and Faye Dunaway, among others, directed by Frederick Rolf. Selected as a "Best Play," it has 56 performances here and an extended run at the East 74th Street Theatre.

Nov 13 *Skyscraper* (NY—Lunt-Fontanne—Musical). Julie Harris plays Georgina, whose home and shop are threatened by builders of a skyscraper. Peter Stone has adapted Elmer Rice's *Dream Girl*, with lyrics by Sammy Kahn and music by James Van Heusen. Cy Feur directs, and the production lasts seven months.

Nov 16 *Happy Ending/Day of Absence* (NY—St. Marks—Comedy). Douglas Turner Ward's scripts, the first showing two shrewd maids revealing how well they've done with what they've brought home, and the second with blacks as Southern whites whose blacks have disappeared, run 504 performances.

Nov 16 *The Devils.* See L premiere, 1961.

Nov 22 *Man of La Mancha* (NY—ANTA Washington Square—Musical). Richard Kiley is starred in Dale Wasserman's adaptation of *Don Quixote* by Cervantes. Mitch Leigh provides the score and Joe Darion the lyrics. "The Quest" wins tremendous popularity. The production moves to Broadway for an extended run, achieving a total of 2,328 performances. The musical opens in London at the Piccadilly on April 24, 1968, with Keith Michell in the lead. There are only 253 showings.

Nov 30 *Inadmissible Evidence.* See L premiere, 1964.

Dec 8 *Cactus Flower* (NY—Royale—Comedy). Abe Burrows directs the play he's adapted from *Fleur de Cactus*, by Pierre Barillet and Jean-Pierre Gredy. Lauren Bacall enjoys a great personal success as a clever nurse of an attractive, unmarried dentist (Barry Nelson). The show has 1,234 performances and is chosen as a "Best Play." The comedy comes to London's Lyric on March 6, 1967, with Margaret Leighton in the lead.

Dec 27 *Marat/Sade.* See L premiere, 1964.

May 18 *A Heritage—and Its History* (L—Phoenix—Drama). Ivy Compton Burnett's novel is adapted by Julien Mitchell. Robert Morris, Dilys Hamlett, and James Cairncross are directed by Frank Hauser, who previously staged the play at his Oxford Playhouse.

May 20 *The Chinese Prime Minister.* See NY premiere, 1964.

June 3 *The Homecoming* (L—Aldwych—Drama). The Royal Shakespeare Company premieres Harold Pinter's curious new play, with Michael Bryant as an emigre professor at an American college, who's returned to visit his all-male London family, leaving behind his wife Ruth, (Vivian Merchant), a former prostitute, who will return to former ways in service of the family. Peter Hall directs. On Jan 5, 1967, the play opens in New York at the Music Box Theatre for a run of 324 performances. Merchant, Paul Rogers, Ian Holm, and others are in the cast.

June 17 *The Killing of Sister George* (L—Duke of York's—Comedy). Frank Marcus's play about a lesbian relationship features Beryl Reid and Eileen Atkins. Seen first at the Theatre Royal in Bristol, the production is directed by Val May of the Bristol Old Vic. There are 620 performances. It opens in New York at the Belasco on Oct 5, 1966, with Atkins and Reid repeating their roles. The play has 205 performances and is named a "Best Play."

June 24 *Ride a Cock Horse* (L—Piccadilly—Drama). David Mercer's play, directed by Gordon Flemyng, features Peter O'Toole, with Barbara Jefford, Sian Phillips, Judy Wilson, and Wendy Craig.

June 30 *A Patriot for Me* (L—Royal Court—Drama). John Osborne writes this story of a young Austrian officer whose career is compromised by his vulnerability through being homosexual. Maximilian Schell has the lead. The play opens on Broadway at the Imperial on Oct 4, 1969, with Schell again in the lead. There are only 49 showings.

July 15 *The Creeper* (L—St. Martin's—Drama). Eric Portman plays Edward Kimberley in Pauline Macaulay's play, seen initially at the Nottingham Playhouse. Donald McWhinnie directs. Kimberley prizes a garden creeper which has killed the tree it lives on. His fatal mistake is to engage a human creeper, the last of a succession of young men he hires as companions until he is bored with them.

Aug 4 *Any Wednesday.* See NY premiere, 1964.

Aug 5 *Alibi for a Judge* (L—Savoy—Drama). Henry Cecil's novel comes to the stage in his adaptation with Felicity Douglas, for a run of 704 performances. It is directed by Hugh Goldie and features Andrew Cruickshank.

Sep 21 *The Four Seasons* (L—Saville—Drama). Arnold Wesker directs his play

---

1965   BRITISH PREMIERES

March 24 *The Night of the Iguana.* See NY premiere, 1961.

April 8 *Travelling Light* (L—Prince of Wales—Comedy). Leonard Kingston's play, the *Edgware Road Blues*, first seen at the Royal Court, is re-titled and wins him the Charles Henry Foyle Play Award. Michael Crawford plays an eccentric, sharing a room with a door-to-door salesman (Harry H. Corbett). Julia Foster is caught between them.

April 16 *Anne of Green Gables* (L—New—Musical). Presented in the summers at the Charlottetown Festival in Canada, this show is based on L. M. Montgomery's beloved children's book about the orphan girl who changed the lives of those who took her in. Polly James plays Anne Shirley. Donald Harron has adapted the book, with lyrics by Harron and Norman Campbell, who provides the score.

May 4 *The Solid Gold Cadillac* (L—Saville—Comedy). Howard Teichmann and George S. Kaufman's American play is staged by Arthur Lewis. Margaret Rutherford plays the Josephine Hull role of Laura Partridge, a holder of 12 shares in a major corporation. Sidney James co-stars with Rutherford; he's Ed McKeever, desperately trying to keep her from interfering with the company.

May 6 *Portrait of a Queen* (L—Vaudeville—Drama). Dorothy Tutin delights as Queen Victoria in William Francis's entertainment from the monarch's diaries, letters and comments. There are 274 performances. The show opens at Broadway's Henry Miller's on Feb 28, 1968 with Tutin again in the lead. It garners only 61 showings.

about a couple (Alan Bates and Diane Cilento) whose love grows from winter silence through spring opening, summer blossoming, to fall decay.

Oct 14 *Say Who You Are* (L—Her Majesty's—Comedy). Ian Carmichael, Jan Holden, Patrick Cargill and Dilys Lave are cast in Keith Waterhouse and Willis Hall's play, staged by Shirley Butler. The farce springs from a wife's desire to let a girl friend use the apartment on Friday evenings to romp with a married man.

Oct 19 *The Investigation* (L—Aldwych—Drama). The Royal Shakespeare Company presents Peter Weiss's inquest-like drama on the atrocities of Auschwitz in a version prepared by Peter Brook and David Jones. Roy Dotrice and Glenda Jackson are among the cast. The play is presented at New York's Ambassador beginning Oct 4, 1966. There are 103 performances.

Nov 3 *Saved* (L—Royal Court—Drama). William Gaskill stages Edward Bond's brutally direct drama about youthful boredom and, the murder of a child. The play opens Off-Broadway at the Cherry Lane on Nov 13, 1970, following a production at the Brooklyn Academy of Music by the Chelsea Theatre Center. Among the cast are Kevin Conway, Dorrie Kavanagh, James Woods, and Lynn Ann Leveridge. There are only 29 performances.

Nov 11 *The Cavern* (L—Strand—Comedy). Jean Anouilh's play has Alec McCowen, Griffith Jones, Sally Home, and Siobhan McKenna in Donald McWhinnie's cast.

Nov 24 *Barefoot in the Park.* See NY premiere, 1963.

Dec 2 *Hello, Dolly!* See NY premiere, 1964.

Dec 15 *Charlie Girl* (L—Adelphi—Musical). Anna Neagle stars in this popular British musical, with book by Hugh and Margaret Williams and Ray Cooney, based on a story by Ross Taylor. Music and lyrics are by David Heneker and John Taylor. There are 2,202 performances.

1965 REVIVALS/REPERTORIES

Jan 2 In Edinburgh at the Traverse Theatre, Lindsay Kemp's *All Seats Fourpence* opens. This year some 28 productions—some of more than one play or dance—are to be presented, including Tom Wright's *There Was a Man,* Slawomir Mrozek's *Charlie,* Peter Barnes's *Sclerosis,* Murray Schisgal's *The Tiger,* Paul Ableman's *Dialogues,* C. P. Taylor's *Happy Days Are Here Again,* and Guenter Grass's *Onkel, Onkel.*

Jan 5 The Polish Mime Theatre comes to New York City Center for a two-week engagement.

Jan 14 William Ball stages the Richard Wilbur translation of Moliere's *Tartuffe* for the Repertory Theatre of Lincoln Center at their ANTA Washington Square Theatre. Michael O'Sullivan, plays the lead for 74 performances.

Jan 18 John Antrobus's *You'll Come to Love Your Sperm Count* plays the Hampstead Theatre Club, out of reach of the Lord Chamberlain's censorship. The playwright directs and appears, with Salubrious Lane and others. On March 3, Euripides's *Hippolytus,* in a translation by Kenneth Cavender, opens at the Club. Ian Messiter's *The Platinum People* is staged on March 30, and George Bernard Shaw's *Mrs. Warren's Profession* is revived on April 22. On May 17, John Moffatt devises a *Victorian Music Hall.*

Jan 19 The National Theatre produces Arthur Miller's *The Crucible* at London's Old Vic. Colin Blakely and Joyce Redman are directed by Laurence Olivier in this tale of the Salem witchcraft hysteria. On Feb 16, the National opens Franco Zefirelli's production of *Much Ado About Nothing,* with music by Nino Rota. Robert Stephens is Benedick and Maggie Smith, Beatrice. On May 12, the National produces Eric Bentley's translation of Bertolt Brecht's *Mother Courage,* with Madge Ryan as Courage. Lynn Redgrave, Mike Gambon and George Innes are her children. Colin Blakely and Frank Finlay also appear.

Jan 28 Off-Broadway at the Sheridan Square Playhouse, Ulu Grosbard revives Arthur Miller's *A View from the Bridge* for 780 performances. Robert Duvall plays Eddie, with Jon Voight as Rodolpho.

Feb 2 At London's Mermaid Theatre, Julius Gellner stages *The Marriage Brokers,* based on Gogol. On March 16, Pirandello's *Right You Are (If You Say So)* is given. On April 6, last season's revival of 15 of *The Wakefield Mystery Plays* is repeated, and on May 11, Sophocles' *Oedipus the King* and *Oedipus at Colonus* open.

Feb 4 At London's Aldwych, the Royal Shakespeare Company opens *Expeditions Two: Home and Colonial* an experimental program of short plays, given only five performances. David Jones directs.

Feb 4 The famed Moscow Art Theatre opens its first Broadway engagement since 1923 at New York City Center. The four-week run will see *Dead Souls,* adapted from Gogol, Chekhov's *The Cherry Orchard* and *The Three Sisters,* and Pogodin's *Kremlin Chimes.*

Feb 8 The season at the Theatre Royal, Stratford East, includes Edward Albee's *The Zoo Story,* Moliere's *George Dandin,* George Bernard Shaw's *Widowers' Houses,* Henrik Ibsen's *Ghosts* and John Whiting's *Saint's Day.*

Feb 10 At the Cherry Lane Theatre in Greenwich Village, the first New Playwrights program offers: Sam Shepard's *Up To Thursday,* Paul Foster's *Balls,* and Lanford Wilson's *Home Free.* New talents Stephanie Gordon, Harvey Keitel, Shirley Stoler, and Kevin O'Connor are in the casts. On March 3, the second series of New Playwrights begins with Lawrence Osgood's *Pigeons* and Frank Gagliano's *Concerico Was Here to Stay.* Geraldine Fitzgerald is in the first; Jaime Sanchez performs in the second.

Feb 28 At London's Royal Court Theatre, the play is Peter Gill's *The Sleeper Den,* staged by Desmond O'Donovan. Other productions this season include Bertolt Brecht/Kurt Weill's *Happy End,* Frank Wedekind's *Spring Awakening,* David Cregan's *Minatures,* and Charles Wood's *Meals on Wheels.*

March 22 The second World Theatre Season at London's Aldwych presents Jean-Louis Barrault's stagings of Racine's *Andromaque,* Eugene Ionesco's *Le Pieton de l'Air,* Feydeau's *Ne Te Promene donc pas Toute Nue,* and Paul Claudel's *Le Soulier de Satin.* Roger Blin stages Samuel Beckett's *Oh Les Beaux Jours.* The Compagnia die Giovani from Rome offers Diego Fabbri's *La Bugiarda* and Pirandello's *Six Characters in Search of an Author.* Karolos Koun stages Aristophanes' *The Birds* and the Greek Art Theatre Company's production of Aeschylus's *The Persians.* From Israel comes the Habimah Troupe to present Ansky's *The Dybbuk.* The season concludes with two productions of New York's Actors Studio Theatre Company: James Baldwin's *Blues for Mister Charlie* and Chekhov's *The Three Sisters.*

April 5 Le Treteau de Paris imports a French-language production of Paul Claudel's *L'Annonce Faite a Marie.* Daniele Dolorme plays Violaine, whose compassion is an imitation of Christ's. There are 18 performances at New York's Barbizon-Plaza Theatre and the company tours.

April 7 The Royal Shakespeare Company's Stratford season opens with John Barton's production of *Love's Labour's Lost.* Also to be presented this season are Marlowe's *The Jew of Malta,* *The Merchant of Venice,* *The Comedy of Errors,* *Timon of Athens,* and *Hamlet,* with David Warner.

April 7 The Trinity Square Repertory Company in Providence, Rhode Island, presents its first world premiere, *All to Hell Laughing,* in its initial season.

April 12 Noel Coward's *Present Laughter* is revived at London's Queen's Theatre, with director Nigel Patrick as Garry Essendine and Phyllis Calvert as Liz.

April 28 Jean Dalrymple's season of musical revivals at New York City Center opens with Frank Loesser's *Guys and Dolls,* with Alan King, Jerry Orbach, Anita Gillette, and Sheila MacRae. *Kiss Me Kate* follows on May 12. *South Pacific* and *The Music Man* complete the program in June.

May 4 At the Brooks Atkinson Theatre, the revival of Tennessee Williams's *The Glass Menagerie* features Maureen Stapleton, George Grizzard, and Piper Laurie. There are 175 performances.

May 27 At London's Aldwych, the Royal Shakespeare Company opens its Stratford *Henry V*, directed by John Barton and Trevor Nunn. Ian Holm and Michele Dotrice play leads. On July 15, Bertolt Brecht's *Squire Puntila and His Servant Matti* opens. Michel Saint-Denis directs Roy Dotrice as the blustering mini-capitalist, proud of his prosperity and local influence. Patrick Magee is his valet-chauffeur.

June 2 Honoring a beloved British actress, the Yvonne Arnaud Theatre opens tonight in Guildford, south of London, with Emlyn Williams' version of Turgenev's *A Month in the Country*, staged by Michael Redgrave, who plays opposite Ingrid Bergman.

June 8 Samuel Beckett's *Krapp's Last Tape* and Edward Albee's *The Zoo Story* are revived at New York's Cherry Lane, with Alan Schneider staging. George Bartenieff and Ben Piazza perform for 21 weeks.

June 9 In Central Park's Delacorte Theatre, the New York Shakespeare Festival offers three productions for 69 performances: *Love's Labour's Lost*, *Coriolanus*, and *Troilus and Cressida*.

June 10 The Open Air Theatre in London's Regent's Park offers *As You Like It*, staged by Harold Lang. Edward Atienza plays Touchstone.

June 14 Ontario's Stratford Shakespeare Festival stages *Henry IV, Part 1* and *Part 2*, renamed *Falstaff*. Their season also includes *Julius Caesar*, Chekhov's *The Cherry Orchard*, and musical produc-

NIGHT OF THE IGUANA

tions *The Marriage of Figaro* and Bertolt Brecht/Kurt Weill's *The Rise and Fall of the City of Mahagonny*.

June 14 W. Somerset Maugham's *The Circle* is revived at London's Savoy Theatre, with Evelyn Laye as Lady Catherine Champion-Cheney. Charles Hickman directs.

June 15 San Diego's National Shakespeare Festival offers 90 performances of a three-play repertory. They are: *The Merry Wives of Windsor*, *Henry VIII*, and *Coriolanus*.

June 15 The Corporation of London has commissioned John Arden's *Left-Handed Liberty* to commemorate the 750th anniversary of the signing of the Magna Carta. It opens tonight at the Mermaid Theatre. On July 8, Bernard Miles' adaptation of Dryden's *Amphitryon* opens as a musical. Arthur Wing Pinero's *Dandy Dick* opens on Aug 18.

June 19 The American Shakespeare Festival offers 112 performances of four plays in Stratford, Connecticut: *Coriolanus*, *Romeo and Juliet*, *The Taming of the Shrew* and *King Lear*.

June 22 At the New York State Theatre, the Music Theatre of Lincoln Center revives *Kismet* for six weeks, with Alfred Drake and Lee Venora. On Aug 10, *Carousel* is revived for six weeks, starring John Raitt and Eileen Christy.

June 27 *Cross and Sword*, the story of the settlement of St. Augustine by the Spanish in the 16th century, is produced by the St. Augustine 400th Anniversary, Inc., from 1965 to 1967. Paul Green's work becomes Florida's State Play in 1968.

June 29 The fourth season of the Shaw Festival in Niagara-on-the-Lake, Canada, opens with *Pygmalion*. *The Millionairess* and Sean O'Casey's *The Shadow of a Gunman* will fill the season.

July *Reynard the Fox*, a fable set in medieval Europe, written by Arthur Fauquez, is presented by the Everyman Players in Murray, Kentucky at the Kenlake Amphitheatre. It has previously toured Europe.

July 6 Britain's Chichester Festival opens its annual season with John Arden's *Armstrong's Last Goodnight*, featuring Albert Finney. Arthur Wing Pinero's *Trelawny of the "Wells"* will be played this season, as will a double-bill of August Strindberg's *Miss Julie* and Peter Shaffer's new *Black Comedy*.

July 6 In New Haven, Connecticut, founders of the new Long Wharf Theatre, Jon Jory and Harlan Kleiman, open their inaugural production of Arthur Miller's *The Crucible* on the Main Stage, a 484-seat stage built into a warehouse.

July 26 The Oregon Shakespearean Festival offers 45 performances in repertory of *Much Ado About Nothing*, *Macbeth*, *The Winter's Tale*, and *Henry IV, Part 2*.

In the company are Nagle Jackson, Laird Williamson, Douglas Richardson, Gretchen Corbett, and Rick Hamilton.

Aug 3 Ben Travers' *Thark* is revived at London's Garrick Theatre, with staging by Ray Cooney. Amanda Reiss is Cherry Buck, with Alec McCowen as Ronald Gamble.

Aug 9–12 The Berliner Ensemble, Bertolt Brecht's own troupe, bring four of his plays to London's Old Vic. They are *The Resistible Rise of Alberto Ui*, *Coriolanus*, *The Threepenny Opera*, and *The Days of the Commune*.

Aug 22 The Edinburgh Festival opens. On the program is James Baldwin's *The Amen Corner*. The Traverse Theatre plays *Macbeth*. Genoa's Il Teatro Stabile plays Goldoni's *I Due Gemelli Veneziani*. The Edinburgh Gateway presents Ada Kay's *The Man from Thermopylae*, and Peter Bridge produces a revival of George Bernard Shaw's *Too True to Be Good*.

Sep 6 Michel Croft's National Youth Theatre presents *Antony and Cleopatra* at the Old Vic. On Sep 13, the youthful actors play *Troilus and Cressida*.

Sep 14 Madeleine Renaud plays Samuel Beckett's *Happy Days* in the original French for 14 performances at the Cherry Lane Theatre. On the 28th, Ruth White plays the drama in English.

Sep 14 A Commonwealth Arts Festival brings the Nigerian drama, *The Road*, to the Theatre Royal, Stratford East. On the 16th, the East Nigerian Theatre Company presents *Song of the Goat* and *The Masquerade* at the Scala, and on the 23rd, Canada's Le Theatre du Nouveau Monde offers Moliere's *L'Ecole des Femmes* and later, a musical, *Klondyke*.

Sep 20 The talented Scotsman Robert David Macdonald shows his staging of Friedrich Duerrenmatt's *The Marriage of Mr. Mississippi* at London's Hampstead Theatre Club.

Sep 22 George Bernard Shaw's *Too True to Be Good* is revived by director Frank Dunlop at the London's Strand Theatre. Dora Bryan, Kenneth Haigh and Alastair Sim are in the cast. The following night, Turgenev's *A Month in the Country*, directed by Michael Redgrave, opens at the Cambridge Theatre.

Sep 29 At London's Mermaid Theatre, George Bernard Shaw's *Fanny's First Play* is revived, with Robert Eddison and Denise Coffee in leading roles. On Nov 10, Bill Naughton's new play, *Spring and Port Wine* opens. It's well received and earns a transfer. On Sep 27, 1967, it opens on Broadway under the title of *Keep It in the Family*, echoing Naughton's earlier *All in the Family*. In the cast are Karen Black, Patrick Magee, and Maureen O'Sullivan, among others. Unfortunately, its locale has been changed from Yorkshire to Boston and it doesn't have a long run.

Sep 30 John Gielgud adapts, directs, and

stars in Chekhov's *Ivanov* at London's Phoenix Theatre. The production opens in New York at the Shubert on May 3, 1966.

Oct *Fortune and Men's Eyes*, by John Herbert, plays at a workshop in Stratford Ontario, Canada. The play tells of a young man's rites of passage in a brutal reformatory setting.

Oct 1 Equity Library Theatre opens its New York season with a revival of *A Thurber Carnival*. Other shows to be produced include *Come Back, Little Sheba, Say, Darling, The Firebrand, Arms and the Man, The Boy Friend, Witness for the Prosecution, The Beaux' Strategem, A Tree Grows in Brooklyn*, and *Here Come the Clowns*.

Oct 12 At the Old Vic, the National Theatre presents John Arden's *Armstrong's Last Goodnight*, first seen in Chichester. Albert Finney plays the contentious borderer who is ordered hanged by Scotland's James V for endangering an uneasy peace with England. On Oct 20, a revival of Congreve's *Love for Love* has Laurence Olivier as Tattle, the would-be fop and seducer. Peter Wood stages a cast including John Stride, Joyce Redman, Lynn Redgrave and Madge Ryan. On Nov 17, the National presents a handsome period revival of Arthur Wing Pinero's *Trelawny of the "Wells,"* with Louise Purnell as Rose and Michael York as Arthur Gower. Desmond O'Donovan's staging has been shown at the Chichester Festival.

Oct 21 The first offering of the Repertory Theatre of Lincoln Center at the Vivian Beaumont is a re-translation of Georg Buechner's *Danton's Death* by one of its new directors, Herbert Blau. There are 46 performances. On Dec 9, William Wycherley's Restoration comedy, *The Country Wife*, staged by Robert Symonds, opens as the second production. Stacy Keach plays Mr. Horner to Elizabeth Huddle's Mrs. Pinchwife. There are 54 performances.

Nov 23 Moss Hart and George S. Kaufman's *You Can't Take It With You* wins a run of 217 performances in this New York revival by the APA-Phoenix Repertory Company, under artistic director Ellis Rabb, at the Lyceum Theatre.

Nov 28 Robinson Jeffers's version of Euripides' *Medea*, with Gloria Foster in the title role, is revived Off-Broadway at the Martinique Theatre for 77 showings.

Dec 1 Vivian Matalon directs this revival of Tennessee William's *The Glass Menagerie* at London's Haymarket Theatre. Gwen Ffrangcon-Davies plays Amanda, with Anna Massey as Laura and Ian McShane as Tom.

Dec 6 Jack Landau stages John Webster's Jacobean *The White Devil* at New York's Circle-in-the-Square. Carrie Nye plays Vittoria Corombona, with Frank Langella as Flamineo. It runs 19 weeks.

AMERICAN SHAKESPEARE THEATRE — STRATFORD, CONN.

Dec 6 The D'Oyly Carte Opera Company plays London's Saville Theatre, opening with *Ruddigore*. Also to be offered are *The Mikado, Iolanthe, Princess Ida*, and a double-bill of *Cox and Box* and *The Pirates of Penzance*.

Dec 9 The holiday season begins early at London's Westminster Theatre with a revival of Peter Howard and George Fraser's musical, *Give a Dog a Bone*. On Dec 11, Robert Bolt's play for children, *The Thwarting of Baron Bolligrew*, is presented at the Aldwych by the RSC, with Trevor Nunn directing and Leo McKern as the baron. Sylvia Syms plays Peter at the Scala Theatre in Barrie's *Peter Pan* on Dec 17. Other seasonal treats include *Beauty and the Beast* (Hampstead The-

atre Club), *Treasure Island* (Mermaid), *Babes in the Wood* (Palladium, with Frank Ifield as Robin Hood), *The Curse of the Daleks* (Wyndham's), *The Wappy Water Bus* (New Arts), *Clowning* (Royal Court—a clown and mask show), *Ali Baba* (Players'), *Cinderella* (Golder's Green Hippodrome), and *Toad of Toad Hall* (Comedy).

Dec 16 Oscar Wilde's *An Ideal Husband* is stylishly revived in London at the Strand by director James Roose-Evans. Roger Livesey, Dulcie Gray, Ursula Jeans, Perlita Neilson, and Margaret Lockwood are among the talents on stage.

Dec 22 Peter Hall's Royal Shakespeare Company production of *Hamlet* opens at the Aldwych, with David Warner and Janet Suzman.

1965 BIRTHS/DEATHS/DEBUTS

Jan 4 T. S. Eliot (b. 1888) is dead in London. Credited with the revival of poetic drama by writing *Murder in the Cathedral* for production in Canterbury in 1935, his later plays include *The Cocktail Party, The Family Reunion*, and *The Confidential Clerk*.

Jan 12 American playwright Lorraine Hansberry (b. 1930) dies in New York. Her *A Raisin in the Sun* was successfully produced on Broadway in 1959. Her second production was *The Sign in Sidney Brustein's Window*.

Jan 14 Musical star Jeannette MacDonald dies at age 57.

Jan 19 American actor-director Frank Reicher (b. 1875) is dead. He played Quince in Reinhardt's 1934 Hollywood production of *A Midsummer Night's Dream* and later became director for the Theatre Guild.

Feb 7 Nance O'Neil, the venerable American actress, dies now at age 90.

March 28 The British novelist-playwright Clemence Dane dies at 77 years of age.

June 7 American actress Judy Holliday (b. 1922) dies in New York City. As Judith Tuvim, she appeared for some years with

a nightclub act, *The Revuers*. Her great success was as Billie Dawn in *Born Yesterday*, her portrayal of which on screen won an Academy Award.

June 12 Actor-director John Neville is awarded the O. B. E. in the Queen's Birthday Honours List. Born in 1925, Neville attended the Royal Academy of Dramatic Arts and made his stage debut as a walk-on in an Old Vic production of *Richard II* at the New Theatre in London in 1947.

June 23 Actress Mary Boland (b. 1885) dies in New York after more than 60 years on stage and screen.

July 24 Stage and screen actress Constance Bennett (b. 1904) dies at Fort Dix, New Jersey. Daughter of actor-producer Richard Bennett, she made her stage debut as Amanda in a touring production of Noel Coward's *Easy Virtue* in 1939. From 1949 to 1951, she was director, producer, and coordinator of productions flown to Europe for the Berlin Airlift, appearing in and producing Ruth Gordon's *Over 21*, among others.

July 28 American actor Minor Watson (b. 1889) dies in Alton, Illinois. Having first appeared at Brooklyn's Montauk Theatre in 1911, he played with numerous stock companies and, in 1945, appeared in *State* *of the Union.*

July 31 Stage and screen actor James Rennie dies in New York. Born in 1890, Rennie's career began in 1919 as Tod Musgrave in *Moonlight and Honeysuckle*, and included Jay Gatsby, Marcus Antonius, and others. In 1952, he played Benjamin Goodman in *Remains To Be Seen*.

Aug 29 Actress Renee Kelly has died at 77 years of age.

Oct 24 The distinguished American stage designer Cleon Throckmorton dies today aged 68.

Nov 16 John Emery, the American actor, dies in New York at age 59.

Dec 10 Local color dialect comic Percy Kilbride dies at age 76.

Dec 16 British playwright and novelist, W. Somerset Maugham (b. 1874) dies. Among Maugham's plays are *The Circle*, *The Constant Wife*, and other social comedies. His stories, such as *Rain*, have been adapted for the stage and screen.

Dec 22 One of the comic Ritz Brothers, Al Ritz today dies at 62.

1965 THEATERS/PRODUCTIONS

Since 1945, the Lord Chamberlain's office has surveyed, censored, and licensed plays for public performance. 397 plays have been "inspected" during performance since then. 125 have earned warnings, and 33 have been prosecuted for violations.

El Teatro Campesino, a theatre company of farm-workers and strong unionists, is born out of the Great Delano Grape Strike in California. Led by Luis Valdez, it will be praised by New York and Los Angeles critics, both for its productions and its special vitality.

The Center Stage of Baltimore, Maryland, leases and renovates the old Oriole Cafeteria on North Avenue into a 296-seat thrust stage theatre.

The League of Resident Theatres is established by 26 leading professional American companies. Tyrone Guthrie is chosen its first president. By season's end, they will number 33 in 30 cities and will have performed more than 200 plays this season.

MARY BOLAND

Jules Irving and Herbert Blau, former directors of San Francisco's Actors Workshop, officially assume duties as co-directors of the Repertory Theatre of Lincoln Center.

March 30 The London borough of Watford sees the re-opening of the historic and beautiful Edwardian playhouse, the Watford Palace Theatre (1908), under management of Giles Havergal for the Watford Civic Theatre Trust.

April After 40 years of non-theatre usage, the Theatre Royal, Bury St. Edmunds re-opens as a playhouse. Its restoration is a compromise between its initial 1819 appearance and its 1906 "refurbishing."

April 19 Long after its composition, Frank Wedekind's drama, *Spring Awakening*, is finally given a license for public performance by the Lord Chamberlain and is staged at London's Royal Court Theatre.

May 3 Tonight marks the fifth anniversary of the long-running Off-Broadway musical, *The Fantasticks*.

May 10 William Ball and others found the American Conservatory Theatre in Pittsburgh, with *Tartuffe* as the premiere production. In 1967, the troupe will become San Francisco's resident repertory theatre.

May 14 The East-West Players come into existence in Los Angeles to "truthfully express Asian Pacific American thought and depict on stage Asian Pacific American life . . ." The first performance is *Rashomon*.

June President Lyndon Johnson signs a bill creating the National Foundation for the Arts and Humanities.

June The Lord Chamberlain is offended by two scenes in Edward Bond's *Saved*, one of which shows a group of young men stoning to death a baby in its pram. The play becomes a *cause celebre*.

June 1 Otis L. Guernsey, Jr., the new editor of the Burns Mantle yearbook, *Best Plays*, selects the best of '64–'65. They include: *The Subject Was Roses*, *Fiddler on the Roof*, *The Physicists*, *Luv*, *The Odd Couple*, *Poor Bitos*, *Slow Dance on the Killing Ground*, *Incident at Vichy*, *The Toilet*, and *Tiny Alice*. *Roses* wins the Pulitzer Price and the Drama Critics' Circle Award, and *Fiddler* is the Drama Critics' Circle's "Best Musical" with its notably long run of 3,242 performances.

June 1 This Broadway season, there is a record total gross of $56,462,765. There have been 1,250 playing weeks. $9.90 is new top for best seats on best nights. *Kelly*, a one-night flop, lost $650,000, and the beautiful *Baker Street* has a record weekly gross of $103,210.

July 1 The Loretto-Hilton Theatre, funds for which have been raised or donated in part by Conrad Hilton, opens tonight in Webster Grove, Missouri. Of necessity very flexible, it can seat as few as 500 or as many as 1,000.

July 9 A Contemporary Theatre (ACT), Seattle's first professional theatre, opens with Arthur Kopit's *Oh, Dad, Poor Dad*, directed by Gregory A. Falls, the founder and artistic director.

Sep 16 Several New York newspapers are struck, preventing their critics from reviewing the new Broadway season. The strike hampers reviewers and advertisers for 24 days.

Sep 29 The National Endowment for the Arts becomes a reality in Washington, D.C. Its government grants will prove of great value to the development of regional theatres and to the avant-garde ensembles as well.

Oct The Kennedy Center, opening in Washington, D.C., is a five-theatre complex designed by Edward Stone. It contains an opera house, a music hall, a proscenium theatre, a cinema, and a multiform studio theatre.

Oct The Alley Theatre in Houston opens its new home. Architect Ulrich Franzen and theatre engineer George Izenour have designed a complex with two theatres: a 300-seat arena, and an 800-seat "multi-space."

Oct 7 The Studio Arena Theatre has grown out of the Community Theatre School, and founder Neal Du Brock opens the season with Eugene O'Neill's *A Moon for the Misbegotten*, in Buffalo, New York.

Oct 21 The Vivian Beaumont Theatre (1,140 seats) opens in New York's Lincoln Center. The theatre has both a thrust stage and a proscenium. Jo Mielziner and Eero Sarinen have designed the theatre.

Nov 8 Canada's smallest regional theatre, the home of the Citadel Theatre Company, is created by Joseph Shoctor in Edmonton, Alberta. Formerly a Salvation Army Hall, built in 1927, it seats 277 people within 47 feet of the stage.

Nov 9 A power failure causes a massive blackout of the New York metropolitan area. The theatres also go dark, but most return to regular performances tomorrow night.

Jan 10 *The Mad Show* (NY—New—Revue). Based on *Mad Magazine*, these satires on popular culture and American life earn a run of 871 performances. Linda Lavin, Paul Sand, and Jo Anne Worley are among the cast, directed by Steven Vinaver, with book by Larry Siegel and Stan Hart, and music by Mary Rodgers.

Jan 11 *Malcolm* (NY—Shubert—Drama). Edward Albee dramatizes James Purdy's novel, which despite his best efforts and director Alan Schneider's talents, fails to come into focus. There are only seven performances. Matthew Cowles, Estelle Parsons, Henderson Forsythe, and Ruth White are in the cast.

Jan 29 *Sweet Charity* (NY—Palace—Musical). Neil Simon adapts the Federico Fellini film, *Nights of Cabiria*, with a score by Cy Coleman and lyrics by Dorothy Fields. Bob Fosse takes credit for conception, direction, and choreography. Gwen Verdon plays Charity, a tart with a heart of gold. The show earns 608 performances. Juliet Prowse has the lead in the London production which premieres at the Prince of Wales's on Oct 11, 1967. There are 476 performances.

Feb 2 *Wait Until Dark* (NY—Barrymore—Drama). Frederick Knott's thriller involves the blind Susy Hendrix (Lee Remick) with some crooks who think she possesses a doll concealing a cache of heroin. Robert Duvall is also in the cast. The play runs 373 performances. It has 683 repetitions following its London premiere at the Strand on July 27. Honor Blackman and Michael Griffiths are featured.

Feb 3 *The Condemned of Altona* (NY—Vivian Beaumont—Drama). The American premiere of Jean-Paul Sartre's play is directed by Herbert Blau, with Tom Rosqui as a former Nazi who voluntarily imprisons himself in his wealthy industrialist family's mansion to expiate his guilt.

Feb 16 *Philadelphia, Here I Come!* (NY—Helen Hayes—Drama). Playwright Brian Friel's hero is preparing to emigrate from Ireland to America. Patrick Bedford and Donal Donnelly are featured in this show which has only 119 performances but becomes a favorite with amateur theatre groups. It is also chosen as a "Best Play." It fails in London (61 performances) following its premiere at the Lyric on Sep 20, 1967.

Feb 17 *Hostile Witness*. See L premiere, 1964.

Feb 22 *Slapstick Tragedy* (NY—Longacre—Drama). Tennessee Williams earns only seven performances for his two one-act plays. *The Mutilated* features Kate Reid and Margaret Leighton and deals with the abrasive friendship of two shopworn women. In *The Gnadiges Fraulein,*

Leighton plays a pathetic ex-performer who must fight with birds for meals of dead fish. Alan Schneider directs.

March 3 *The Lion in Winter* (NY—Ambassador—Drama). Robert Preston and Rosemary Harris play the royal couple in James Goldman's historical drama about Henry II and Eleanor of Aquitaine. Noel Willman stages the play for 92 performances. It is selected as a "Best Play."

March 8 *Sarjeant Musgrave's Dance* (NY—Theatre DeLys—Drama). John Colicos plays the deserting sergeant, who comes to a small town in the north of England with some followers and the skeleton of a soldier killed in action abroad. John Arden's anti-war play, set in the 19th century, has a run of 135 performances. Stuart Burge stages. The cast includes Paul Hecht, Jeanne Hepple, David Doyle, and Roy Scheider.

March 13 *You Know I Can't Hear You When the Water's Running* (NY—Ambassador—Comedy). Alan Schneider stages these four short comedies by Robert Anderson for a run of 755 performances. The playlets are *The Shock of Recognition, The Footsteps of Doves, I'll Be Home for Christmas,* and *I'm Herbert.* The show is a failure in London (37 performances), following its premiere at the New Theatre on June 26, 1968.

March 29 *"It's a Bird It's a Plane It's SUPERMAN"* (NY—Alvin—Musical). Michael O'Sullivan plays a mad scientist; Bob Holiday plays Superman; and Patricia Morand plays Lois Lane for only 75 performances of David Newman and Robert Benton's book and Lee Adams and Charles Strouse's songs. Harold Prince directs. It is chosen a "Best Play."

April 21 *The Journey of the Fifth Horse* (NY—American Place—Drama). Ronald Ribman's play, based on Turgenev's *Diary of a Superfluous Man,* opens briefly at St. Clement's Church in Manhattan, with Dustin Hoffman as the neurotic, useless anti-hero.

May 24 *Mame* (NY—Winter Garden—Musical). Patrick Dennis's parodic novel about an orphan boy whose life is made wonderful by a madcap aunt (Angela Lansbury) opens for a run of 1,508 performances. The book is by Jerome Lawrence and Robert E. Lee; the music and lyrics are the work of Jerry Herman. Ginger Rogers has the title role in the London production, which premieres on Feb 20, 1969. There are 443 performances.

June 7 British playwright John Arden's *Live Like Pigs* opens Off-Broadway at the Actors' Playhouse, with David Wheeler staging this story of a working-class family who won't conform to conventional living-standards in council housing. There are 128 showings.

WAIT UNTIL DARK

June 13 *The Kitchen* (NY—81st Street—Drama). Arnold Wesker's British tour de force, in which the cast recreates the hectic atmosphere of popular restaurant's kitchen at the dinner-hour, has a run of 137 performances, staged by playwright Jack Gelber. Among the cast members are Rip Torn, Constance Clarke, Conrad Bain, and Sylvia Miles.

Sep 22 *A Delicate Balance* (NY—Martin Beck—Drama). Hume Cronyn and Jessica Tandy are featured as a couple confronted with the needs of desperate friends and a daughter in Edward Albee's play. It earns 132 performances, is designated a "Best Play," and wins a Tony Award and a Pulitzer Prize. The Royal Shakespeare Company presents the play at its Aldwych Theatre on Jan 14, 1969. Peggy Ashcroft and Michael Hordern are the central characters.

Oct 4 *The Investigation*. See L premiere, 1965.

Oct 5 *The Killing of Sister George*. See L premiere, 1965.

Oct 11 *A Whitman Portrait* (NY—Gramercy Arts—Drama). Alexander Scourby impersonates the poet in Paul Shyre's show. It runs nine weeks.

Oct 12 *Who's Got His Own* (NY—American Place—Drama). Ron Milner's play opens at St. Clement's Church, staged by Lloyd Richards. Barbara Ann Teer, Glynn Turman, and others are in the cast.

Oct 16 *Eh?* See L premiere, 1964.

Oct 18 *The Apple Tree* (NY—Shubert—Musical). Jerry Bock and Sheldon Harnick have devised songs and drafted the script, with Jerome Coopersmith, for these three fables based on popular stories: Mark Twain's *The Diary of Adam and Eve,* Frank Stockton's *The Lady or the Tiger?* and Jules Feiffer's *Passionella.* Barbara Harris, Alan Alda, and Larry Blyden are supported by Robert Klein and others under Mike Nichols direction. There are 463 performances.

Oct 19 *Mixed Doubles* (NY—Upstairs at the Downstairs—Revue). Rod Warren's cabaret will run 428 performances with Madeline Kahn and Janie Sell in the troupe.

Nov 6 *America Hurrah* (NY—Pocket—Drama). Shown first at La Mama E. T. C., this was originally the title of *Motel,* one of three short satires on American life by Jean-Claude van Itallie. The others are *TV* and *Interview,* the latter staged by Joseph Chaikin, with Jacques Levy directing the other two. Among the cast are Ronnie Gilbert, Bill Macy, Joyce Aaron, Ruth White, and Cynthia Harris. There are 634 showings. On Aug 2, 1967, the troupe performs them in London at the Royal Court. They are widely produced in America and abroad.

Nov 6 *Man With a Load of Mischief* (NY—Jan Hus—Musical). Ben Tarver adapts Ashley Dukes's play to a score by John Clifton. The two collaborate on the lyrics. Reid Shelton and Virginia Vestoff are featured in this story of a woman who flees her travelling companion to join another man. There are 241 performances. It opens at London's Comedy on Dec 9, 1968, with Roberta d'Esti, Valentine Palmer, and Paul Dawkins.

Nov 10 *Viet Rock* (NY—Martinique—Drama). Megan Terry's Vietnam war protest is animated by a cast including Shami Chaikin, Seth Allen, and Sharon Gans. The author stages for 62 showings.

Nov 17 *Don't Drink the Water* (NY—Morosco—Comedy). Woody Allen's play about an American from Newark suspected of spying in Eastern Europe runs 598 performances. Lou Jacobi, Kay Medford, and Anita Gillette are in Stanley Prager's cast.

Nov 20 *Cabaret* (NY—Broadhurst—Musical). Joe Masteroff adapts Christopher Isherwood's Berlin stories and *I Am a Camera,* with a score by John Kander and lyrics by Fred Ebb. Joel Gray plays a suggestive master of ceremonies in a Berlin nightclub in the days before the Nazi takeover. The show runs 1,165 performances and is selected a "Best Play." On Feb 28, 1968, it opens at London's Palace with Barry Dennen. There are only 336 showings.

Nov 26 *Walking Happy* (NY—Lunt-Fontanne—Musical). Norman Wisdom stars

CABARET

in the adaptation of *Hobson's Choice* made by Roger Hirson and Ketti Frings, with songs by James Van Heusen and Sammy Kahn. Cy Feuer directs Louise Troy as Maggie and George Rose as her tyrannical father. The show plays 161 performances.

Dec 5 *I Do! I Do!* (NY—46th Street—Musical). Playwright Tom Jones and composer Harvey Schmidt adapt Jan de Hartog's comedy, *The Fourposter.* Mary Martin and Robert Preston play the couple in this saga of loving married life. The show wins 560 performances and many other productions. Gower Champion stages. Anne Rogers and Ian Carmichael are featured in the London production, which opens at the Lyric on May 16, 1968.

Dec 19 *The Ox Cart* (NY—Greenwich Mews—Drama). Rene Marques shows the contrast between poverty in Puerto Rico and worse poverty in New York. Lloyd Richards directs Miriam Colon, Raul Julia, and Carla Pinza, among others. There are 83 performances.

Dec 21 *The Star-Spangled Girl* (NY—Plymouth—Comedy). Neil Simon's new show has Connie Stevens as a young conservative in San Francisco, distracting radical journalists Anthony Perkins and Richard Benjamin. George Axelrod directs the 261 performance run.

Dec 29 *The Displaced Person* (NY—American Place—Drama). Cecil Dawkins has adapted Flannery O'Connor short stories. The play is directed by Edward Parone, with Frances Sternhagen, Dixie Marquis, William Jordan, and Woodie King, Jr., in the ensemble.

1966 BRITISH PREMIERES

Jan 26 *Incident at Vichy.* See NY premiere, 1964.

March 2 *The Owl and the Pussycat.* See NY premiere, 1964.

April 13 *Funny Girl.* See NY premiere, 1964.

April 14 *Suite in Three Keys* (L—Queen's—Drama). Noel Coward has written three plays—at least—which he now offers under the suite title. Tonight, Vivian Matalon shows his staging of *A Song at Twilight,* with Irene Worth as Hilde Latymer and Coward as her husband, Hugo, in the sunset of a marriage of convenience. Lilli Palmer plays Carlotta Gray. On April 25, *Shadows of the Evening* and *Come into the Garden Maud* are presented.

April 19 *On the Level* (L—Saville—Musical). Ronald Millar's book and lyrics make fun of schools, exams, and student anxiety. Ron Grainer composes. Wendy Toye directs a large cast, with Gary Bond, Eileen Wells, and Barrie Ingham.

May 5 *The Prime of Miss Jean Brodie* (L—Wyndham's—Comedy). Jay Presson Allen adapts Muriel Spark's novel about a Scottish schoolmistress who mixes romance, subtle tyranny, and some teaching for her class of adoring girls. Vanessa Redgrave stars. The show plays 588 times. It opens in New York at the Helen Hayes on Jan 16, 1968, for a 47-week run. Zoe Caldwell has the lead.

May 6 *London Laughs* (L—Palladium—Revue). This "musical spectacular" has Harry Secombe heading a cast of Thora Hird, Jimmy Tarbuck, Anita Harris, Nicky Henson, and Russ Conway. There are 407 performances.

May 19 *Their Very Own and Golden City* (L—Royal Court—Drama). Arnold Wesker's interesting and lengthy play shows the frustrations encountered by an architect who wants to build fine homes for workers, but finds his vision unwanted. William Gaskill directs Ian McKellan and Gertrude Martell, among others.

May 26 *Come Spy With Me* (L—Whitehall—Musical). Bryan Blackburn has concocted book, lyrics, and music for this show, and Ned Sherrin stages for a run of 484 performances. Female impersonator Danny LaRue appears, as does Richard Wattis.

June 15 *There's a Girl in My Soup* (L—Globe—Comedy). Terence Frisby has a success with the comedy about a lover of fine cookery who finds a lively, trendy young woman more than he can handle. Donald Sinden is featured. There are 2,547 showings. This farce has only 321 performances in New York, following its premiere at the Music Box on Oct 18, 1967. Gig Young has the lead.

July 20 *The King's Mare* (L—Garrick—Comedy). Anita Loos adapts Jean Canolle's play about Henry VIII's reaction to Anne of Cleves: He called her a "Flanders brood-mare." Glynis Johns and Keith Michell are featured. The show has 164 performances, directed by Peter Coe.

July 28 *The Meteor* (L—Aldwych—Drama). The Royal Shakespeare Company presents Friedrich Duerrenmatt's play, a satiric view of the life and death of a great man, played by Patrick Magee. Other cast members, directed by Clifford Williams, are Patience Collier, Nicholas Selby, and Charles Kay.

Sep 22 *Jorrocks* (L—New—Musical). David Heneker's words and music complement Beverley Cross's book, based on a novel about fox-hunting by R. S. Surtees. Val May directs Joss Ackland, Thelma Ruby, and Cheryl Kennedy. The show has 180 performances.

Sep 27 *Loot* (L—Jeannetta Cochrane—Comedy). Joe Orton's black comedy about two friends who hide stolen money in the coffin recently occupied by the dead mother of one of them features Kenneth Cranham and Simon Ward. The show premieres on Broadway at the Biltmore on March 18, 1968, where it has just 22 performances.

Oct 12 *The Odd Couple*. See NY premiere, 1965.

Oct 13 *U S* (L—Aldwych—Drama). Peter Brook and his ensemble, working with Mike Stott and Michael Kustow on Denis Cannan's text, devise this indictment of American involvement in Vietnam. Adrian Mitchell provides lyrics for Richard Peaslee's music. The show provokes lively controversy.

Oct 17 *Big, Bad Mouse* (L—Shaftesbury—Comedy). Jimmy Edwards plays Mr. Price-Hargreaves in this play by Philip King and Falkland Cary. Alexander Dore directs; there are 634 performances.

Oct 25 *The Fighting Cock* (L—Duke of York's—Comedy). Jean Anouilh's play is a portrait of a French general in idleness, waiting for an ungrateful nation to recall him to service. John Clements plays the testy general, as he has at the recently concluded Chichester Festival. There are 118 performances.

Nov 3 *Way Out in Piccadilly* (L—Prince of Wales's—Revue). There are 395 performances of this Bernard Delfont production, staged by Maurice Fournier, with a cast led by Frankie Howerd and Cilla Black.

1966   REVIVALS/REPERTORIES

Jan 6 Works by George Bernard Shaw in London this month include *Man and Superman* at the Vaudeville; *You Never Can Tell*, staged by Glen Byam Shaw at the Haymarket, with Ralph Richardson, for 284 performances, and *The Philanderer* at the Mermaid, with Derek Godfrey staged by Don Taylor.

Jan 10 Feydeau's farce, *The Birdwatcher*, is revived at London's Hampstead Theatre club, with Prunella Scales, John Brown, and Michael Bates. On Feb 7, Howard Sackler's *The Pastime of Monsieur Robert* opens, with Julian Glover in the title role. On March 7, *Adventures in the Skin Trade*, based on Dylan Thomas's book, features David Hemmings, directed by James Roose-Evans. On March 13, the poetry and prose of Thomas and others is presented as *Flashing into the Dark*.

Jan 13 Middleton's *A Chaste Maid in Cheapside*, with Sebastian Shaw and Ronald Pickup, opens at the Royal Court Theatre. Feb 6 sees Keith Johnstone's *Instant Theatre*. *The Knack* is revived on the 17th. On March 3, Keith Johnstone helps William Gaskill stage his play *The Performing Giant*, with music by Marc Wilkinson. Bernard Gallagher plays the giant. On March 27, Leonard Pluta's *Little Guy, Napoleon* and Heathcote Williams' *The Local Stigmatic* are given without decor. On April 11, Harley Granville Barker's *The Voysey Inheritance* is revived. Jane Howell directs. Sebastian Shaw and Gwen Nelson are Mr. and Mrs. Voysey. On June 5, Christopher Hampton's play, *When Did You Last See My Mother*, surprises some viewers when a teenage boy, very fond of his chum, makes an approach to the young man's mother, which leads to her untimely demise. This is a production without decor, staged by Robert Kidd. Victor Henry plays the wily, potent lad. On June 26, Herman Melville's *Bartleby* comes to life, also without decor, paired with Heathcote Williams's *The Local Stigmatic*.

Jan 18 Edinburgh's Traverse Theatre opens its season with *A Moral Evening*. Some of the 32 programs presented this year will be: Peter Weiss's *The Investigation*, Harold Pinter's *The Dwarfs*, Brian Way's *Mirror Man*, David Mercer's *Ride a Cock Horse*, David Cregan's *The Dancers*, and a double-bill of Edward Albee's *The Sandbox* and T. S. Eliot's *The Wasteland*.

Jan 19 Peter Hall's Royal Shakespeare production of Gogol's *The Government Inspector* opens at London's Aldwych. Paul Rogers plays the pompous mayor, and Paul Scofield is the impoverished Khlestakov, who's mistaken for the official. On May 25, Trevor Nunn stages and performs in the Polish satire, *Tango*, by Slawomir Mrozek, adapted by Tom Stoppard.

Feb 8 Feydeau's *A Flea in Her Ear* opens at London's Old Vic, staged for the National Theatre by Jacques Charon of the Comedie Francaise. Among the cast are Albert Finney, Edward Hardwicke, and Geraldine McEwan. On March 8, Peter Shaffer's new play, *Black Comedy*, premiered at Chichester, opens paired with August Strindberg's *Miss Julie*. On April 26, Laurence Olivier stages a revival of Sean O'Casey's *Juno and the Paycock*, with Joyce Redman as Juno and Colin Blakely as her husband. On June 6, John Osborne's *A Bond Honoured* replaces *Miss Julie* on the Shaffer bill.

Feb 8 The Comedie Francaise comes from Paris to New York City Center with four plays: Moliere's *L'Avare*, Corneille's *Le Cid*, Henri de Montherlant's *La Reine Morte*, and Feydeau's *Un Fil a la Patte*. The visit lasts three weeks.

Feb 10 Racine's classic, *Phedre*, in a new translation by William Packard, opens at New York's Greenwich Mews for 100 performances. Paul-Emile Deiber of the Comedie Francaise directs Beatrice Straight in the title-role and Mildred Dunnock as her nurse.

Feb 23 Sybil Thorndike and Athene Seyler play the kindly poisoners in Joseph Kesselring's *Arsenic and Old Lace*, revived at London's Vaudeville Theatre.

March 3 Gerhart Hauptman's comedy, *The Beaver Coat*, opens at the Mermaid Theatre, with Peggy Mount and John Moffatt. On April 20, Moliere's *The Imaginary Invalid* is coupled with *The Miser*, both directed by Julius Gellner. On June 2, Feydeau's *Divorcons-nous* is revived, staged by Robin Midgley. Hugh Paddick and Fenella Fielding play the couple with marital troubles. This English version, *Let's Get a Divorce*, is the work of Robert Goldsby and Angela Patton. The show will play 414 performances in the West End beginning on July 26. On July 29, Bill Naughton's *He Was Gone When They Got*

There is staged by David William. A revue by David Wood and John Gould, *Four Degrees Over*, opens on July 31. On Aug 30, Paul Shyre's adaptation of Sean O'Casey's autobiographical work, *Pictures in the Hallway*, opens.

March 15 Japan's Bunraku puppet-theatre comes to New York City Center for two weeks.

March 21 At the Aldwych Theatre in London, the World Theatre Season opens with the Czech National Theatre of Prague presenting Karel and Josef Capek's *The Insect Play*. Italy's Compagnia die Giovani then appears with two plays by Pirandello, *The Rules of the Game* and *Six Characters in Search of an Author*. On April 12, the National Theatre of Greece offers Euripides' *Hecuba*. Katina Paxinou plays the title role with her husband Alexis Minotis as Talthybius. She has composed music; he directs. On the 14th, Sophocles' *Oedipus Rex* opens, and, on the 18th, *Oedipus at Colonus*. On April 25, the season continues at the Aldwych with the arrival of the Polish Popular Theatre. They will play Stanislaw Wyspianski's *The Wedding*, Dostoievsky's *Crime and Punishment*, and an adaptation of Roman Bratny's *The Columbus Boys*. On May 9, the Leningrad Gorki Theatre offers *The Idiot* of Dostoievsky and, on May 12, a play from Soviet Georgia called *Grandma, Uncle Iliko, Hilarion, and I.*

Mar 23 Hal Holbrook opens on Broadway at the Longacre Theatre in his one-man impersonation, *Mark Twain Tonight!*, which he has widely toured since it was first seen Off Broadway in 1959. The engagement runs for nine weeks.

Mar 24 Eric Bentley's translation of Bertolt Brecht's *The Caucasian Chalk Circle* opens at the Vivian Beaumont Theatre in Lincoln Center. Directed by Jules Irving, it is to prove the most popular of this season's four productions, with 77 performances.

April 5 From Munich's *Residenz Theater* comes the ensemble of the Bavarian State Theatre with a repertory of three plays: Goethe's *Die Mitschuldigen*, Georg Buechner's *Woyzeck*, and Gerhart Hauptmann's *Die Ratten*. The last is directed by Helmut Henrichs. They have a two-week visit to New York's City Center.

April 6 John Barton, Trevor Nunn and Clifford Williams collaborate on productions of *Henry IV, Parts 1 and 2* to open the Royal Shakespeare Company's Stratford-upon-Avon season. Peter Hall's *Hamlet* returns from last season, with David Warner. *Twelfth Night*, *Henry V*, and Tourneur's *The Revenger's Tragedy* will also be seen.

April 11 *Six from La Mama*, two programs of three, open tonight and tomorrow at New York's Martinique: William Hoffman's *Thank You, Miss Victoria*,

Lanford Wilson's *This Is the Rill Speaking*, Leonard Melfi's *Birdbath*, Jean-Claude van Itallie's *War*, Paul Foster's *The Recluse*, and Sam Shepard's *Chicago*. There are 16 performances.

April 20 Jean Dalrymple offers four Frank Loesser revivals this spring at New York City Center: *How to Succeed in Business Without Really Trying*, *The Most Happy Fella*, *Where's Charley?* and *Guys and Dolls*.

April 28 At London's Jeannetta Cochrane Theatre, Michael Geliot stages *A Moral Evening*, really two one-act plays, *The Gaiety of Nations* by Alan Seymour, and *Allergy* by Cecil Taylor. On May 5, Anthony Ainley will play *Hamlet*, and on May 26, there will be three plays by Saul Bellow: *Out from Under*, *Orange Souffle*, and *A Wen*.

PHEDRE

May 19 The classical Chinese drama, *The Butterfly Dream*, plays 10 performances at the Greenwich Mews Theatre. Hu Hung-Yen stages, using the traditions of his native theatre as mastered by American actors in New York workshops of the Institute of Advanced Studies in Theatre Arts (IASTA).

June 1 The Chichester Festival, under artistic director John Clements, offers a season of four plays: the Colman-Garrick *The Clandestine Marriage*, Anouilh's *The Fighting Cock*, Chekhov's *The Cherry Orchard*, and *Macbeth*. The casts include Margaret Rutherford, Alistair Sim, John Standing, Tom Courtenay, Celia Johnson, Hugh Williams, and Clements.

June 2 George Bernard Shaw's *The Doctor's Dilemma*, recently revived in London, is back. Eleanor Bron and Barry Justice play 36 performances at the Comedy Theatre.

June 6 Charles Nolte's play *Do Not Pass Go* is staged by Frith Banbury at London's Hampstead Theatre Club. Two African dramas will play later this season: *The Trials of Brother Jero*, by Wole Soyinka, and *The Blood Knot*, written and staged by Athol Fugard.

June 6 Canada's Stratford Shakespeare Festival opens, still under Michael Langham's direction. To be presented this year are: *Henry V*, *Henry VI*, *Twelfth Night*, Michael Bawtree's *The Last of the Czars*, August Strindberg's *The Dance of Death*, Mozart's *Don Giovanni*, and the world premiere of *Rose LaTulippe*, choreographed by Brian Macdonald and danced by the Royal Winnipeg Ballet.

June 6 In the Open Air Theatre in Regent's Park, London, the summer offering is Michael Meacham's staging of *A Midsummer Night's Dream*, with Edgar Wreford and Louise Breslein as the fairy royalty.

June 9 *Days in the Trees*, a play by the French novelist Marguerite Duras, opens in London at the Royal Shakespeare's Aldwych Theatre, in Sonia Orwell's translation. It's staged by John Schlesinger. Peggy Ashcroft plays the mother, whose indulgence has ruined the character of her son (George Baker).

June 14 The National Shakespeare Festival in San Diego offers three plays: *Romeo and Juliet*, with Jon Voight and Lauri Peters, *The Tempest*, with Will Geer, Anthony Zerbe, and Voight, and *Two Gentlemen of Verona*, with Richard Lupino and Zerbe.

June 14 James Liggat and Robert Sheaf's adaptation of Jane Austen's *Pride and Prejudice* is briefly staged at London's New Arts Theatre, by David Phethean. Arthur Wing Pinero's *The Thunderbolt* is revived on Aug 3, with staging by Jordan Lawrence.

June 15 The Delacorte Theatre in Central Park is the site of the New York Shakespeare Festival's summer program: *All's Well That Ends Well*, *Measure for Measure*, and *Richard III*. The company includes Barbara Barrie, Richard Jordan, Christopher Walken, and Joseph Bova.

June 18 The American Shakespeare Festival in Stratford, Connecticut, offers *Henry IV*, rechristened as *Falstaff*, *Twelfth Night*, *Julius Caesar*, and T. S. Eliot's *Murder in the Cathedral*.

June 28 The Ypsilanti Greek Theatre opens its first and only season, under artistic director Alexis Solomos. Richmond Lattimore's translation of Aeschylus' *Oresteia* is played by Judith Anderson, Donald Davis, and Ruby Dee. Aristophanes' *The Birds* will also play, with Bert Lahr as the comic hero.

July 1 Paul Green's *Texas*, a musical romance of Panhandle history, is presented in the 1,644-seat Palo Duro Canyon Pioneer Amphitheatre in Canyon, Texas, by the Texas Panhandle Heritage Foundation.

July 19 The Music Theatre of Lincoln Center opens *Show Boat* for a run of 63 performances. Lawrence Kasha directs David Wayne, Barbara Cook, and Constance Towers. Ron Field choreographs.

July 19 The fifth season of the Shaw Festival at Niagara-on-the-Lake opens with *Man and Superman*, directed by Barry Morse. He will also stage *Misalliance*, while Edward Gilbert stages *The Apple Cart*.

July 21 Alfred Jarry's *Ubu Roi* opens at the Royal Court Theatre, staged by Iain Cuthbertson and designed by David Hockney. Popular comic Max Wall plays Ubu outrageously. The cast includes Bernard Gallagher, Elspeth MacNaughton, and Janet Chappell. John Sheperd is Mere Ubu, whose breasts light up when fondled. On Aug 21, Joe Orton's first play, *The Ruffian on the Stair*, a one-act black comedy of menace and murder, is given a performance without decor. Howard Brenton's *It's My Criminal* is also staged. On Aug 30, the National Youth Theatre plays Ben Jonson's *Bartholomew Fair* and, at the Scala Theatre, *Antony and Cleopatra*. On Sep 12, the youths perform David Halliwell's *Little Malcolm* at the Court. On Oct 20, Alec Guiness plays Macbeth, with Simone Signoret as his consort, William Gaskill directing. On the 30th, Peter Gill gives *A Provincial Life*, based on Chekhov's *My Life*. *The Lion and the Jewel*, by Nigeria's Wole Soyinka, is seen on Dec 12, staged by Desmond O'Donovan.

July 23 The Oregon Shakespeare Festival in Ashland offers five productions this year. They are *A Midsummer Night's Dream*, *Othello*, *Two Gentlemen of Verona*, *Henry VI, Part 3* and John Gay's *The Beggar's Opera*.

Aug 21 The Edinburgh International Festival opens. This season's offerings include Douglas Young's adaptation of Aristophanes' *The Birds* (which he calls *The Burdies*), *The Winter's Tale*, *An Evening with G.B.S.* and, from Greece's Piraikon Theatre, Sophocles' *Electra* and Euripides' *Medea*. Pop Theatre offers Euripides' *The Trojan Women*. For children there is Nicholas Stuart Gray's *The Wrong Side of the Moon*. Sergei Obraztsov and his Moscow Puppets are for everyone. Sholem Aleichem's *The Little Men* is also staged, as is John Hailstone's *A Present from the Past*. In addition, Bettina Jonic's *Lorca* is presented. Alban Berg is a featured composer, with the Stuttgart Opera presenting both *Wozzeck* and *Lulu*.

Sep 1 At London's Hampstead Theatre Club, Vivian Matalon stages John Bowen's dramatization of his novel, *After the Rain*. Alec McCowen plays Arthur Henderson, who sets himself up as leader after the second world-engulfing flood. This transfers and even opens on Broadway,

on Oct 9, 1967, at the John Golden Theatre. It runs only eight weeks, with McCowen in the lead, but it's chosen as a "Best Play." On Sep 21, at the Hampstead Theatre, the play is *Letters from an Eastern Front*, based on real missives from the German Sixth Batallion before it was annihilated at Stalingrad. This transfers to the West End at the Duchess Theatre in Jan 1967 for 46 performances. It's also briefly seen on Broadway as *Letters from Stalingrad*.

Sep 4 *The Fire of London*, Peter and Kitty Black's work about the Great Fire of 1666, opens at the Mermaid Theatre, directed by Joseph Lawrence. On Sep 14, George Bernard Shaw's *The Man of Destiny* opens with *O'Flaherty, V.C.*

Sep 6 Thornton Wilder is saluted at New York's Cherry Lane Theatre by Richard Barr, Clinton Wilder, and Edward Albee. Michael Kahn directs three of his one-acts: *The Long Christmas Dinner*, *Queens of France*, and *The Happy Journey to Trenton and Camden*. The show runs nine weeks.

Sep 27 George S. Kaufman and Edna Ferber's *Dinner at Eight* is revived at the Alvin Theatre, with Tyrone Guthrie staging. The cast includes Walter Pidgeon, June Havoc, Ruth Ford, Arlene Francis, and Darren McGavin. There are 127 performances.

Sep 29 Jean Dalrymple offers three revivals in the American Playwrights Series at New York City Center. Clifford Odets' *The Country Girl*, Tennessee William's *The Rose Tatoo* on Oct 20, and Maxwell Anderson's *Elizabeth the Queen* on Nov 3.

Sep 30 Direct from the Edinburgh Festival to London's Young Vic comes the Frank Dunlop production of Shakespeare's *The Winter's Tale*, in which Jim Dale scores a hit as Autolycus, the singing, rascally peddler. Dale has composed the music.

Oct 6 The West End sees another revival: Sheridan's *The Rivals*, directed by Glen Byam Shaw. Ralph Richardson is Sir Anthony Absolute and Margaret Rutherford is Mrs. Malaprop. This show runs beyond the season's end. On Oct 13, there's a handsome staging of Oscar Wilde's *Lady Windemere's Fan* at the Phoenix Theatre. On Dec 13, Wilde's *An Ideal Husband* is brought to the Garrick Theatre.

Oct 13 Jules Irving opens the new season of the Repertory Theatre of Lincoln Center at the Vivian Beaumont with Ben Jonson's *The Alchemist*. On Dec 8, Garcia Lorca's *Yerma* opens. The former has 52 performances; the latter, 60.

Oct 17 *In the Matter of J. Robert Oppenheimer*, German playwright Heinar Kipphardt's docu-drama about the attacks on Oppenheimer, when he was reluctant to pursue research which would develop an H-Bomb, comes to life in London at the Hampstead Theatre Club, with Robert

HAROLD PINTER

Harris as the atomic scientist. On Nov 28, the production moves to the Fortune Theatre. On Nov 23, the club and director Peter Coe present another kind of docu-drama, Michael Hasting's *The Silence of Lee Harvey Oswald*.

Oct 18 The National Theatre presents Doris Lessing's adaptation of Alexander Ostrovsky's Russian classic, *The Storm*, directed by John Dexter at the Old Vic. In the company are Beatrix Lehmann, John Stride, Jill Bennett, Ronald Pickup, Frank Finlay, and Sheila Reid.

Oct 21 The Equity Library Theatre in New York opens a season of revivals, highlighted by *You Never Can Tell*, *All the King's Men*, *The Night of the Iguana*, and *The Wood Demon*.

Oct 27 The Stockholm Marionette Theatre, created and operated by Michael Meschke, comes to Broadway with Bertolt Brecht's *The Threepenny Opera* for a limited engagement at the Billy Rose Theatre.

Nov 2 At the Royal Shakespeare's London home, the Aldwych Theatre, Peter Hall stages Charles Dyer's *Staircase*. Patrick Magee and Paul Scofield play two homosexuals, confronting problems of jealousy, aging, and British laws and attitudes. (On Jan 10, 1968, the play opens on Broadway at the Biltmore Theatre, staged by Barry Morse, with Milo O'Shea and Eli Wallach. It's chosen as a "Best Play," but it doesn't last quite eight weeks.) On Nov 17, David Waller plays Harry Belcher in *Belcher's Luck*, by David Mercer, staged for the RSC by David Jones.

Nov 15 The D'Oyly Carte Opera Company comes to New York City Center with *The Pirates of Penzance, The Mikado, Ruddigore, H.M.S. Pinafore,* and *Patience.*

Nov 16 The Apparition Theatre of Prague arrives at New York's Cort Theatre for 21 performances. They are internationally known as the Black Theatre of Prague, since performers dress in black, on a black stage with black drapes, as they manipulate props to act out stories and jokes. Les Ballets Africains also opens tonight, for over ten weeks at the Ethel Barrymore Theatre.

Nov 21 At New York's Lyceum Theatre, the Association of Producing Artists and the Phoenix Theatre open their fall season with Sheridan's *The Rivals,* with Helen Hayes and Rosemary Harris directed by Ellis Rabb. To come are Pirandello's *Right You Are* and a plundering of Walt Whitman's writings, *We Comrades Three.*

Dec 15 Frederick Lonsdale's vintage comedy, *On Approval,* opens at St. Martin's Theatre in the West End. Dulcie Gray, Polly Adams, Michael Denison, and Robert Flemyng are directed by Murray MacDonald. There are 142 performances.

Dec 16 At London's Scala Theatre, the annual revival of Barrie's *Peter Pan,* with Julia Lockwood in the title-role, launches the holiday season of children's productions and pantomimes. Among the fare this year are the Mermaid's *Treasure Island* revival and the Palladium's *Cinderella,* with Pippa Steel as Cinders and pop singer Cliff Richard as Buttons. Other shows are *The Thwarting of Baron Bolligrew* (Aldwych), *Whittington Junior and*

FLORENCE VANDAMM

His Sensational Cat (Players'), *Circus Adventure* (Hampstead Theatre Club), James Thurber's *The Thirteen Clocks* (New Arts), *Robinson Crusoe* (Golder's Green Hippodrome), *Toad of Toad Hall* (Comedy), and *Babes in the Wood* (Wimbledon).

matic Soundings.

April 3 The American playwright Russel Crouse has died at age 72. Working with actor-author Howard Lindsay, he wrote a number of hit Broadway comedies and musicals.

April 29 Paula Strasberg, a founder with Lee Strasberg of the Actors Studio and also a drama coach, dies today at age 55.

June 19 In Beverly Hills, Ed Wynn is dead at 80. In addition to his appearances on the Orpheum-Keith-Albee vaudeville circuit from 1903 to 1913, he was the first actor to broadcast an entire Broadway show, his own musical review, *The Perfect Fool,* on WJZ, New York, June 12, 1922.

June 25 Stage designer Raymond Sovey is dead at 72.

July 9 Sir Fordham Flower is dead at 62. He has been Chairman of the Royal Shakespeare Company, based at Stratford-upon-Avon.

July 23 Actor Montgomery Clift (b. 1920) dies in New York. Clift made his first professional appearance as Harmen Masters in Dorothy Bennett and Irving White's comedy *Fly Away Home* at the Berkshire Playhouse in 1934, followed by the Broadway production in 1935. He also appeared with the Lunts in Robert E. Sherwood's *There Shall Be No Night* both on Broadway and on tour. His film credits are many.

July 29 Designer, director, actor, and writer

1966 BIRTHS/DEATHS/DEBUTS

Jan 20 Actor-director George Devine, a founder of the English Stage Company at London's Royal Court Theatre, today dies at age 55.

Jan 21 English actor Herbert Marshall (b. 1890) dies in Beverly Hills. He won recognition in *Aren't We All?, The Pelican, Tomorrow and Tomorrow,* and *There's Always Juliet.* A successful film career began in 1927. Marshall married and divorced Edna Best.

Feb 3 Actress June Walker (b. 1899) dies in Los Angeles. Her New York debut was in the 1918 *Hitchy-Koo.* Later roles included Mrs. Gordon in *Ladies of the Corridor,* Paulina in *The Seagull,* and Jessie Bartley in *Blue Denim.*

Feb 9 Singer-entertainer Sophie Tucker dies at 82.

Feb 10 The diminutive but dynamic Broadway impressario Billy Rose has died at age 66. He is remembered for such spectacles as *Jumbo,* the 1939 World's Fair Aquacade, and ownership of the Ziegfeld

Theatre.

March 15 Noted theatrical photographer Florence Vandam dies in New York at 83.

March 28 American actress Helen Menken is dead, aged 64.

March 30 At 72, Erwin Pisactor is dead. An innovative German theatre director, Piscator helped playwright Bertolt Brecht develop productions suitable to his concept of Epic Theatre. During the Nazi period, Piscator had a theatre workshop in New York at the New School.

April 2 The distinguished American theatre critic and scholar John Gassner dies at age 64. He was influential in bringing important European plays to the Broadway stage, as head of the Theatre Guild's play department, where he also helped the careers of such writers as Arthur Miller and Tennessee Williams. Author of many books on drama and theatre, Gassner had for some years been teaching playwriting at the Yale School of Drama. His last book, published posthumously, is to be *Dra-*

Edward Gordon Craig (b. 1872) dies in Vence, France. Craig's early years were spent on the stage with Henry Irving. Among his production designs were Venice Preserved in Berlin, Rosmersholm for Eleanor Duse, and Hamlet at the Moscow Art Theatre. In 1908 he founded and edited The Mask, a journal of theatre art. Among his prolific writings is Index to the Story of My Days, 1872–1907.

Aug 14 Alfred Kreymborg (b. 1883) dies in Milford, Connecticut. His poetic dramas include Plays for Poem-Mimes and Puppet Plays, many of which were presented at the Provincetown Players. He was also active in Federal Theatre.

Aug 19 Jeanne de Casalis, the British actress-author, dies at age 70.

Sep 14 Gertrude Berg dies in New York at 67. She was born Gertrude Edelstein. Her Broadway debut was as Molly in Me and Molly at the Belasco in 1948. She was awarded the Tony in 1959 and the Sarah Siddons Award in 1961 for her performance as Mrs. Jacoby in A Majority of One.

Sep 25 English Actress Ada Reeve (b. 1874) is dead. She was one of the principal light comedy artistes in 1890's music halls and toured extensively in Australia, South Africa, and America in such plays as Three Little Maids, Murder on the Second Floor, and Let Us Be Gay.

Oct 13 Clifton Webb (b. 1893) dies in Beverly Hills. Born Webb Parmelee Hollenbeck in Indianapolis, he began his career in grand opera and appeared in Broadway musicals such as Very Good, Eddie and Sunny. In 1941, he played Charles Condomine in Blithe Spirit. After 1946, he appeared only in films.

Dec 7 Drama critic Ward Morehouse dies at 67. He has reviewed Broadway for the Newhouse newspaper chain.

Dec 8 Hungarian-born John Hirsch makes his U.S. directorial debut with the Repertory Company of Lincoln Center's production of Lorca's Yerma at the Vivian Beaumont Theatre.

Dec 14 Actor, director, producer, and designer Richard Whorf (b. 1906) dies in Santa Monica. Whorf toured with the Lunts in Idiot's Delight, The Seagull, and The Taming of the Shrew in the 1938–39 season. He designed the costumes for the 1954 Broadway production of Ondine.

1966 THEATERS/PRODUCTIONS

U.S. patents granted this year include that given Candirus de Scranage for a stage snowfall machine with a perforated cylinder which revolves slowly, allowing the "snow" to fall in a leisurely, natural manner.

Jan 1 New York City's transit employees strike. This hurts the theatre industry, since many of the audience depend on public transportation to reach Broadway and Off-Broadway theatres.

Jan 15 Barry Morse is appointed Artistic Director of Canada's Shaw Festival at Niagara-on-the-Lake. He is to serve two years.

Jan 29 New York's Palace Theatre, at 1564 Broadway, presents its first legitimate attraction, Sweet Charity. The space had been the "Valhalla of Vaudeville" and is later remembered for Judy Garland's "come-back" engagement in the late 50's.

Feb 1 In Victoria, British Columbia, the McPherson Playhouse opens. The Pantages Theatre (c. 1913) is renovated at a cost of $750,000 through a legacy from Thomas McPherson, and will become the home of the Bastion Theatre company.

Feb 15 NY Times' new drama critic, Stanley Kauffman, arrives for the final preview of Brian Friel's Philadelphia, Here I Come! at the Helen Hayes. The performance is cancelled when the lights suddenly go out. Producer David Merrick blames "a rat in the generator."

March Michael Foot attempts to introduce in Parliament a bill to abolish stage censorship. No positive action is taken.

March The English Stage Company is served with 18 summonses this month as a result of William Gaskill's decision to produce Edward Bond's controversial Saved without the changes demanded by the Lord Chamberlain. Although luminaries testify on their behalf, the company and Bond are ordered to pay costs.

March 18 The League of Resident Theatres (LORT) is founded. It will promote community interests, raise funds, and renegotiate with labor unions every three years for America's regional professional theatres. Peter Zeisler, of the Minnesota Theatre Company, is the first director.

April 24 New York's second newspaper strike of the season is called against the World-Journal-Tribune. It lasts through the season, leaving the critics of the Times, Post, and News to provide reviews.

May National Endowment for the Arts chairman Roger Stevens announces $660,000 in awards to American professional regional theatres. Nearly $3 million in NEA grants aids American theatres in the coming season.

May The Crest Theatre, Toronto, Canada, closes its doors with a $33,000 deficit after a 12-year life. By December, it will revert to a movie house.

May 31 This is technically the end of the Broadway season and Variety judges the following to be hits: Pickwick, Generation, The Impossible Years, You Can't Take It With You, Inadmissable Evidence, Marat/Sade, Wait Until Dark, Cactus Flower, Mark Twain Tonight, and The World of Charles Aznavour.

Summer After many decades, the Lord Chamberlain lifts the ban on representation of Jesus Christ on the British stage. The modern Passion Play, A Man Dies, is performed.

June 1 The total of shows produced on Broadway this season is 76, compared with 81 last year. Otis Guernsey, Jr., editor of Best Plays, breaks down the total thus: 25 plays, 11 musicals, 16 revivals, 14 foreign plays in English, four specialties, and six productions by foreign language troupes. Variety estimates the season's gross at $53,862,187. Five musical flops lost over $2 million. The musical Superman had a top ticket price of $12. Guernsey, Jr., chooses Broadway's annual ten "Best Plays." They are Goodhart's Generation, Shaffer's The Royal Hunt of the Sun, Alfred's Hogan's Goat, Wasserman/Darion/Leigh's Man of La Mancha, Osborne's Inadmissible Evidence, Benton/Newman/Adams/Strouse's Superman, Burrows' Cactus Flower, Weiss's Marat/Sade, Friel's Philadelphia, Here I Come!, and Goldman's The Lion in Winter.

July 18 Tonight, the President of Eire, Eammon de Valera, opens the newly completed Abbey Theatre, replacing the historic one damaged by fire in 1951.

July 28 Puppeteers Bil and Cora Baird open their own Bil Baird Theatre in Greenwich Village with a series of free matinees for children in Operation Headstart.

Aug The Globe Theatre in Regina, Saskatchewan, is founded by Ken and Sue Kramer as a touring company to promote creative drama in provincial schools.

Nov 2 The $1 million Theatre Atlanta opens in Georgia. None of the 775 seats is more than 38 feet from the Greek-theatre style stage. The theatre's first director is Jay Broad, who has given up acting by "popular demand."

Dec 8 After extensive renovation, the Westminster Theatre in London re-opens with a Christmas attraction, Give a Dog a Bone.

Jan 5 *The Homecoming.* See L premiere, 1965.

Feb 1 *The Deer Park* (NY—Theatre de Lys—Drama). Norman Mailer had adapted his novel for the stage, and it runs 128 performances with Rip Torn, Gene Lindsey, and Marsha Mason, directed by Leo Garen.

Feb 12 *Black Comedy* (NY—Ethel Barrymore—Comedy). Dark is light in Peter Shaffer's London success, with *White Lies* as a curtainraiser. In *Black Comedy,* Michael Crawford plays the manic, knockabout hero. Lynn Redgrave is his girl and Peter Bull her father, whom he's trying to impress. The show has 337 performances. The two plays (with *White Lies* now called *The White Liars*) open at London's Lyric on Feb 21, 1968. Ian McKellen and Dorothy Reynolds are in the cast.

Feb 22 *MacBird!* (NY—Village Gate—Comedy). Following an old theatre tradition, Barbara Garson parodies *Macbeth* and satirizes Lyndon Johnson as president as well. There are 386 performances. Among the performers are Stacy Keach and Rue McClanahan. On April 10, Joan Littlewood stages the show in London at her Theatre Workshop at the Theatre Royal, Stratford East.

Feb 23 *Fortune and Men's Eyes* (NY—Actors Playhouse—Drama). John Herbert shows the violence that confronts young offenders in prison in his forthright play which has already been seen in Canada. Bill Moor and Robert Christian are in the cast. The show has 382 performances. It comes to London's Comedy Theatre on Oct 17, 1968. Charles Marowitz stages for the Open Space Theatre.

Feb 28 *A Hole in the Head* (NY—Plymouth—Comedy). Arnold Shulman offers Jewish family humor to leaven this story of an opportunist father with few opportunities and a motherless child to raise. Garson Kanin directs Kay Medford, Lee Grant, Paul Douglas, and others. There are 156 performances.

March 7 *You're a Good Man, Charlie Brown* (NY—Theatre 80 St. Marks—Musical). Cartoonist Charles Schultz's popular comic-strip characters come to life in Clark Gessner's musical which has 1,597 performances. It is also a "Best Play." The show runs only four months following its London premiere on Feb 1, 1968, at the Fortune.

March 9 *Hamp* (NY—Renata—Drama). This is chosen as a "Best Play" and it has a run of 101 performances. John Wilson has adapted a portion of J. L. Hodson's novel, dealing with the trial and execution of a pathetic British soldier (Robert Salvio), who has deserted after three years in action.

April 11 *Illya Darling* (NY—Mark Hellinger—Musical). Melina Mercouri plays the title role in Jules Dassin's adaptation of *Never on Sunday.* Joe Darion provides lyrics for Manos Hadjidakis' music. Dassin directs. There are 318 performances.

April 24 *Gorilla Queen* (NY—Martinique—Comedy). Ron Tavel's parody of Tarzan films has a run of 64 performances, with George Harris II as Brute, an effeminate gorilla.

April 25 *Little Murders* (NY—Broadhurst—Comedy). Jules Feiffer presents his black comedy in which the streets of New York are not safe. The cast includes Barbara Cook, Elliott Gould, Heywood Hale Broun, and Ruth White. It last only seven performances but is revived Off-Broadway at the Circle in the Square on Jan 5, 1969, for 400 showings. The Royal Shakespeare Company produces the comedy at London's Aldwych beginning July 3, 1967. Brenda Bruce, Barbara Jefford, and Derek Godfrey are in the cast.

April 26 *Hallelujah, Baby!* (NY—Martin Beck—Musical). Leslie Uggams plays Georgina, who doesn't grow old throughout her saga from poverty to celebrity. Arthur Laurents provides the book; Betty Comden and Adolph Green, the lyrics, and Jule Styne, the music. Burt Shevelove stages. The run is 293 performances.

July 6 *The Unknown Soldier and His Wife* (NY—Vivian Beaumont—Drama). Peter Ustinov writes this parable of a common soldier who dies over and over again in centuries of wars, until he refuses to fight anymore. Christopher Walken and Melissa Murphy are in the cast. The show runs nearly 19 weeks, transferring to the George Abbott Theatre in September. It opens in the West End at the New London on Jan 11, 1973, with Miles Anderson and Tamara Ustinov. The production continues into the next season.

Sep 26 *Now Is the Time for All Good Men* (NY—Theatre de Lys—Musical). Gretchen Cryer writes book and lyrics for Nancy Ford's score. David Cryer co-produces and plays Mike Butler, rallying draft resistance in the Midwest. Word Baker stages, and the show runs 14 weeks.

Oct 1 *The Niggerlovers* (NY—Orpheum—Drama). George Tabori's play has only 25 performances, with Gene Frankel directing Morgan Freeman, Viveca Lindford, and Stacy Keach.

Oct 3 *The Birthday Party* (NY—Booth—Drama). Harold Pinter's deliberately ambiguous play, seen earlier in London, has a run of almost four months in this Alan Schneider staging. James Patterson plays Stanley, an unkempt and insecure lodger, staying with Meg and Petey (Ruth White and Henderson Forsythe). Two mysteri-

THE BIRTHDAY PARTY

ous and menacing " friends" turn up on the pretext that they have come to help Stanley celebrate his birthday. William Ritman and Tharon Musser design.

Oct 8 *Johnny No-Trump* (NY—Cort—Drama). Mary Mercier's play about a teenager coming to terms with himself, his father, and his uncle has only this premiere performance, staged by Joseph Hardy. Don Scardino plays the boy, with Sada Thompson and James Broderick as his parents. The play is later called a "Beautiful Loser."

Oct 9 *After the Rain.* See L listing, 1966.

Oct 10 *Scuba Duba* (NY—New—Comedy). Bruce Jay Friedman's manic script about a desperate white husband whose wife deserts him for a black skin-diver has a long run of 692 performances, directed by Jacques Levy. Jerry Orbach, Conrad Bain, Judd Hirsch, Jennifer Warren, and Cleavon Little are cast. It is chosen a "Best Play."

Oct 18 *There's a Girl in My Soup.* See L premiere, 1966.

Oct 29 *Hair* (NY—Public—Musical). Gerome Ragni and James Rado write the book and Galt MacDermot the music for this rock musical about young people rebelling against authority and seeking nonviolence, love, and hope. Among the hits are "Aquarius" and "Good Morning Sunshine." The show moves on to the Cheetah and thence to Broadway on April 29, 1968, where it is reworked and restaged by Tom O'Horgan. The show wins 1,844 performances Off and on Broadway. It premieres in London at the Shaftesbury on Sep 27, 1968, for a run of 1,997 performances.

Oct 31 *More Stately Mansions* (NY—

Broadhurst—Drama). Eugene O'Neill's drama follows the action of *A Touch of the Poet*, and the saga of the Melody family continues, with Colleen Dewhurst as Sara and Arthur Hill as Simon. Ingrid Bergman plays his mother. Jose Quintero directs. The play runs almost 18 weeks.

Nov 5 *In Circles* (NY—Cherry Lane—Musical-. The Rev. Al Carmines's musical adaptation of Gertrude Stein texts is staged by Lawrence Kornfield, and has a run of 222 performances. Carmines, Theo Barnes, Elaine Summers, and Nancy Zala are in the cast.

Nov 5 *The Trial of Lee Harvey Oswald* (NY—ANTA—Drama). There are only nine performances of this mock trial of John F. Kennedy's alleged slayer, written by Amram Ducovny and Leon Friedman. Peter Masterson plays Oswald.

Nov 7 *Halfway Up the Tree* (NY—Brooks Atkinson—Comedy). Peter Ustinov's attempt to wring some amusement from the current generation gap consciousness features Anthony Quayle. It runs only eight weeks. On Nov 23, it opens in London at the Queen's with Robert Morley. The production plays 443 times.

Nov 9 *The Trials of Brother Jero/The Strong Breed* (NY—Greenwich Mews—Drama). Nigerian playwright Wole Soyinka's plays are staged by Cynthia Belgrave, with Harold Scott and Afolabi Ajayi. There are 115 performances.

Nov 22 *Curley McDimple* (NY—Bert Wheeler—Musical). This Shirley Temple-film parody, devised by Robert Dahdah and Mary Boylan has a run of 931 performances, with Bayn Johnson in the title role.

Nov 23 *The Ecstasy of Rita Joe* (Vancouver—Playhouse—Drama). A young Indian woman becomes symbolic of her race when she arrives in a white community and is raped by white men. Frances Hyland is featured in George Ryga's play.

Nov 29 *Everything in the Garden* (NY—Plymouth—Drama). Edward Albee makes changes in Giles Cooper's play, in which some housewives turn to prostitution to provide the extras their husbands can't. Barry Nelson and Barbara Bel Geddes are featured with Beatrice Straight. Peter Glenville directs. There are only 84 performances.

Dec 7 *How Now, Dow Jones* (NY—Lunt-Fontanne—Musical). An original musical about the day on Wall Street when the Dow Jones average breaks 1,000, this show—with book by Max Shulman, lyrics by Carolyn Leigh, and music by Elmer Bernstein—is directed by George Abbott. It lasts nearly seven months.

Dec 12 *The Great White Hope* (DC—Arena—Drama). Howard Sackler's play about a black American boxing champion, harried by white envy, is animated by actor James Earl Jones, with Jane Alexander playing the white woman he loves. Director Edwin Sherin stages this world premiere in the Arena Stage's award-winning new 827-seat theatre, designed by Harry Weese for its directors, Zelda and Thomas Fichhandler. After this Washington production, the play will open on Broadway on Oct 3, 1968, for a run of 556 performances at the Alvin Theatre. It's chosen as a "Best Play." It also wins a Tony and the Pulitzer Prize.

Dec 18 *Brief Lives* (NY—John Golden—Comedy). Roy Dotrice recreates the 17th century diarist and biographer John Aubrey in this show by Patrick Garland. It has first been seen in London at the Hampstead Theatre Club in January. On Feb 25, 1969, the show opens at London's Criterion with Dotrice for 213 performances.

rick—Comedy). Wallace Douglas directs Brian Rix in this farce by Anthony Marriott and Alistair Foot. It runs for 482 performances.

June 7 *The Ruffian on the Stair/The Erpingham Camp* (L—Royal Court—Comedy). Joe Orton has a double bill of black comedies. *The Ruffian on the Stair* has been seen before, but *The Erpingham Camp*, a parody of Billy Butlin's holiday camps, has been written to pair with the first. The plays come to New York on Oct 26, 1969, at the Astor Place. Entitled *Crimes of Passion*, the program lasts only nine performances.

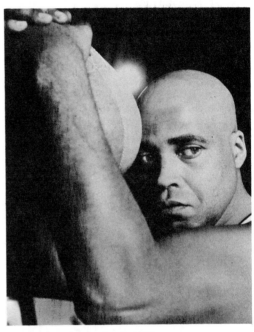

THE GREAT WHITE HOPE

July 19 *Let Sleeping Wives Lie* (L—Garrick—Comedy). Brian Rix produces and plays Jack for director Wallace Douglas. Harold Brooke and Kaye Bannerman's play about the British take-over of an American corporation runs 647 performances.

July 20 *A Day in the Death of Joe Egg* (L—Comedy—Drama). Peter Nichols's tale shows a couple trying to joke about their retarded child, whom they call "Joe Egg." Joe Melia and Zena Walker are featured in the play which has already been seen at Glasgow Citizens' Theatre. In London there are 148 performances. The show opens at New York's Brooks Atkinson on Feb 1, 1968, for a run of 154 performances. Albert Finney and Walker are the couple. Nichols's work is chosen a "Best Play."

July 27 *The Man in the Glass Booth* (L—St. Martin's—Drama). Harold Pinter directs Robert Shaw's play in which Donald Pleasance is Arthur Goldman, seemingly a Nazi war criminal in an Israeli trial resembling that of Adolf Eichmann. The play opens at New York's Royale on

1967 BRITISH PREMIERES

Jan 17 *The Promise* (L—Fortune—Drama). Aleksei Arbuzov's successful Russian play about the personal lives of three young people who've survived the seige of Leningrad is animated by Judi Dench, Ian McShane, and Ian McKellen. Frank Hauser has first staged this at his Oxford Playhouse. There are 289 performances. It earns only 23 showings following the New York premiere on Nov 14, at the Henry Miller Theatre.

Feb 16 *Fiddler on the Roof*. See NY premiere, 1964.

Feb 28 *Howard's End* (L—New—Drama). E. M. Forster's novel is adapted by Lance Sieveking in collaboration with Richard Cottrell. Frith Banbury directs Gemma Jones, Joyce Carey, Gwen Watford, and Andrew Ray, among others. The play runs almost five weeks.

March 6 *Cactus Flower*. See NY premiere, 1965.

March 29 *Relatively Speaking* (L—Duke of York's—Comedy). Alan Ayckbourn's domestic comedy wins 355 performances, staged by Nigel Patrick. Richard Briers, Jennifer Hilary, Michael Hordern, and Celia Johnson appear.

April 11 *Rosencrantz and Guildenstern Are Dead* (L—Old Vic—Comedy). The National Theatre produces Tom Stoppard's play in which the audience sees the two characters in all the scenes Shakespeare kept off-stage in *Hamlet*. John Stride and Edward Petherbridge have the leads. There are 420 performances following the New York premiere on Oct 16 at the Alvin. Brian Murray and John Wood are featured.

April 20 *Uproar in the House* (L—Gar-

Sep 26, 1968, with Pleasance again in the lead. The production runs nearly 34 weeks. Shaw's work is selected as a "Best Play."

Aug 1 *The Flip Side* (L—Apollo—Comedy). Hugh and Margaret Williams have written a play in which wife-swapping is contemplated. Anna Massey, Toby Robins, Patrick Allen, and Ronald Lewis are in the cast. The production runs through the season. It has only four performances following the New York premiere on Oct 10, 1968, at the Booth.

Aug 29 *Black New World* (L—Strand—Revue). Donald McKayle has devised and staged this show, with music by Dorothea Freitag and Howard A. Roberts. Charles Berry, Miriam Burton, Jerry Grimes, Sally Neal, and Trina Parks are in the cast.

Sep 14 *According to the Evidence* (L—Savoy—Drama). Henry Cecil's book, adapted by Cecil and Felicity Douglas, is staged by Hugh Goldie, with Michael Dawson, Muriel Pavlow, and Naunton Wayne for a run of 259 performances.

Sep 21 *Mrs. Wilson's Diary* (L—Theatre Royal Stratford East—Comedy). A feature of London's *Private Eye* magazine of satire and gossip comes to life at Joan Littlewood's hands. Myfanwy Jenn and Bill Wallis play Gladys and Harold Wilson. Jeremy Taylor has written music for John Well's lyrics. The show earns a run of 254 performances after transfer to the Criterion.

The Criminals (L—Aldwych—Drama). The Royal Shakespeare Company presents this adaptation by Adrian Mitchell of Jose Triana's work. Brenda Bruce, Susan Fleetwood, and Barrie Ingham perform for director Terry Hands.

Oct 4 *Let's All Go Down the Strand* (L—Phoenix—Comedy). Hugh and Margaret Williams' offering is staged by Murray MacDonald. James Craig is played by Williams, with Jill Johnson as Caroline Cobbold. The show runs beyond the season.

Oct 10 *Wise Child* (L—Wyndham's—Comedy). Alec Guinness stars in Simon Gray's black comedy about a man trying to evade the law and a hotel-keeper. It runs four months. The show has only five performances following its New York premiere on Jan 27, 1972. Donald Pleasance has the lead.

Oct 11 *Sweet Charity*. See NY premiere, 1966.

Oct 17 *Tom Paine* (L—Vaudeville—Drama). Tom O'Horgan stages the La Mama production of Paul Foster's view of the American radical. It has been seen earlier at the Edinburgh Festival. Kevin O'Connor has the title role for this four-week run. On March 25, 1968, it opens Off-Broadway for 295 performances.

Dec 5 *The Four Musketeers* (L—Drury Lane—Musical). Peter Coe directs Harry Secombe as D'Artagnan, with Aubrey Woods as as Richelieu, for 462 performances of this comedy musical with book by Michael Pertwee and songs by Laurie Johnson and critic Herbert Kretzmer.

ham's *An Expedition to Pick Mushrooms*, Conn's *The King*, Taylor's *Grounds for Marriage*, O'Neill's *Mourning Becomes Electra*, *The Still Life Story*, Eveling's *Come and Be Killed*, Aeschylus' *The Persians*, "Mini-Plays," Owens' *Futz*, Melfi's *Times Square*, *Contratype III*, Shepard's *Melodrama Play*, Wilson's *Untitled Play*, Head's *Sanctity*, Brecht's *The Messingkauf Dialogues*, Jarry's *Ubu in Chains*, Foster's *Tom Paine*, Hooker's *Season in Hell*, "New Bill of Mini-Plays," MacDiarmid's *A Drunk Man Looks at the Thistle*, Wilson's *Ludlow Fair*, and Beckett's *Waiting for Godot*.

Jan 19 The 1942 Rodgers and Hart musical *By Jupiter* is revived Off-Broadway at Theatre Four, staged by Christopher Hewett. It runs 118 performances.

Jan 21 William Ball's production of Moliere's *Tartuffe* opens the first season of the American Conservatory Theatre in San Francisco. The ensemble will play repertory in two theatres: the 1,449-seat Geary and the 640-seat Marines Memorial.

Jan 31 Ben Jonson's *Volpone* opens at London's Garrick Theatre, with Leo McKern and Zia Mohyeddin. Frank Hauser directs.

Jan 31 At London's Mermaid Theatrem Robert Chetwyn stages *Trifles and Tomfooleries*, three one-act plays by Bernard Shaw: *Augustus Does His Bit*, *Press Cuttings*, and *Passion, Poison, and Petrifaction*. On Feb 13, Dedwydd Jones's *Drink from an Amethyst Cup* is staged by Peter Oyston. Robert Lowell's *Benito Cereno* opens on March 8. On April 5, it's an O'Casey double-bill of *A Pound on Demand* and *The Shadow of a Gunman*. On May 17, director Bernard Miles stages *The Trojan Wars*. Jack Lindsay has translated a sequence of four plays by Euripides. Tonight *Iphigenia in Aulis* and *Hecuba* are played. On the 30th, *Electra* and *Orestes* are offered.

Feb 2 A revival of W. Somerset Maugham's *The Sacred Flame* is brought to London's Duke of York's Theatre from Guildford's Yvonne Arnaud Theatre. Murray MacDonald directs Gladys Cooper, Leo Genn, Wendy Hiller, and Jack Gwillim. There are only 52 performances.

Feb 9 Leo Lehman's *The East Wind* is premiered at the Vivian Beaumont Theatre. It has 60 performances. There are 56 showings for Bertolt Brecht's *Galileo*, which follows. Anthony Quayle has the title role.

Feb 14 Bristol Old Vic comes to New York City Center with *Measure for Measure*, *Hamlet*, and *Romeo and Juliet*. Tyrone Guthrie stages the first and Val May, the others. Barbara Leigh-Hunt, Richard Pasco, Madge Ryan, Gawn Grainger, and Jane Asher are in the company.

Feb 21 At the Old Vic, the National Theatre presents August Strindberg's *The Dance of Death*, staged by Glen Byam Shaw. Laurence Olivier, Geraldine

1967   REVIVALS/REPERTORIES

Jan 3 At London's Saville Theatre, the D'Oyly Carte Opera Company opens with *Yeomen of the Guard*. The stint also includes *Trial by Jury*, *H.M.S. Pinafore*, *The Gondoliers* and *Patience*.

Jan 4 Bertolt Brecht's *The Caucasian Chalk Circle* opens as the Meadow Brook Theatre's first production, directed by founding artistic director John Fernland, at Oakland University, Rochester, Michigan.

Jan 11 The APA-Phoenix repertory season continues at New York's Lyceum Theatre with Henrik Ibsen's *The Wild Duck*, translated by Eva LeGallienne. Stephen Porter directs Rosemary Harris and Betty Miller, among others. Last season's successful Kaufman and Hart *You Can't Take It With You* is revived on Feb 10, and Erwin Piscator's version of *War and Peace* opens on March 21.

Jan 11 London's Royal Court Theatre audiences this spring will see Thomas Otway's *The Soldier's Fortune*, Arnold Wesker's *Roots*, Pratap Sharma's *A Touch of Brightness*, D. H. Lawrence's *The Daughter-in-Law*, and James Clancy's A

View to the Common. On April 18, Glenda Jackson, Avril Elgar, and Marianne Faithfull are Chekhov's *Three Sisters* in the Royal Court revival, staged by William Gaskill.

Jan 16 Roy Dotrice plays John Aubrey, a 17th century diarist, in the one-man show, *Brief Lives*, now at the Hampstead Theatre Club. Patrick Garland directs, with decor by Julia Trevelyan Oman. On April 6, Frank Marcus' play, *Studies of the Nude*, opens. On May 8, James Saunders' *Neighbours* is paired with LeRoi Jones' *Dutchman*.

Jan 17 Edinburgh's Traverse Theatre starts another year with D. H. Lawrence's *The Daughter-in-Law*, followed by such fare as *The Denning Report on the Profumo Affair*, Foster's *The Recluse Balls*, Hurrah for the Bridge, and *The Hessian Corporal*, Pinner's *Fanghorn*, Marowitz's "Happening" *Come*, McGough's *The Commission*, Wright/Wood's *A Life in Bedrooms*, Lewsen's *How Pleasant to Know Mr. Lear*, Dürrenmatt's *Sunset in Late Autumn*, Olusola's *Morning, Noon, and Night*, Bundi's *The Suitcase*, Gra-

McEwan, and Robert Stephens are in the cast. On July 4, Olivier directs Chekhov's *The Three Sisters*. Joan Plowright, Jeanne Watts, and Louise Purnell are the sisters. On Oct 3, the National Theatre presents its all-male *As You Like It*, with an all-white set designed by Ralph Koltai, at the Old Vic. Ronald Pickup, Jeremy Brett, Anthony Hopkins, and Derek Jacobi are in the cast. Clifford Williams directs. On Nov 21, Moliere's *Tartuffe*, in Richard Wilbur's translation, is staged by Tyrone Guthrie. Robert Stephens is in the title role, with Joan Plowright as Dorine and John Gielgud as Orgon.

March 4 Sam Shepard's *La Turista* is staged by Jacques Levy for subscribers only at the American Place Theatre in New York. On May 11, Niccolo Tucci's *Posterity for Sale* is presented.

April 3 The World Theatre Season at the Aldwych Theatre in London begins with the Comedy Francaise presenting three plays: Corneille's *Le Cid*, Marivaux's *Le Jeu de l'Amour et du Hasard* and Feydeau's *Feu la Mere de Madame*. On April 10, The Noh Theatre of Japan begins two programs of traditional productions. The Bremen Theatre Company follows with Frank Wedekind's *Spring Awakening* and Thomas Valentin and Robert Muller's *Die Unberatenen*. On May 1, Israel's Cameri Theatre offers an Israeli musical, *King Solomon and the Cobbler*. The Greek Art Theatre Company returns on May 8 with two plays by Aristophanes: *The Frogs* and *The Birds*. It also offers Aeschylus' *The Persians*. On May 22, Milan's Piccolo Theatre presents Goldoni's *The Servant of Two Masters*. The season concludes with the Czechoslovakia's Theatre on the Balustrade production of Kafka's *The Trial*.

April 4 Noel Coward's comedy, *Fallen Angels*, is revived at London's Vaudeville Theatre. Philip Wiseman directs Joan Greenwood and Constance Cummings, the two wives who drink themselves silly while waiting for an old flame.

April 5 In the Royal Shakespeare Theatre in Stratford-upon-Avon, the stage takes on the character of a gray box for this season's productions. The first play is *The Taming of the Shrew*, staged by Trevor Nunn and designed by Christopher Morley. John Barton casts Ian Richardson as Coriolanus. Nunn's production of *The Revenger's Tragedy* is revived from last season. Barton stages *All's Well That Ends Well*. Timothy O'Brien designs *As You Like It* for director David Jones. Peter Hall directs *Macbeth*. Greek director Karolos Koun stages *Romeo and Juliet*.

April 5 At New York City Center, spring musical revivals are *Finian's Rainbow*, *The Sound of Music* (with Constance Towers), and *Wonderful Town*.

April 19 George Bernard Shaw's *Getting Married* is revived at London's Strand Theatre in a Frank Dunlop staging.

April 20 Los Angeles' Mark Taper Forum opens with John Whiting's *The Devils*, staged by Gordon Davidson. The 750-seat theatre is part of the Los Angeles Music Center complex.

May 1 The National Repertory Theatre comes to Broadway's ANTA Theatre with Moliere's *The Imaginary Invalid*, Eugene O'Neill's *A Touch of the Poet*, and Noel Coward's *Tonight at 8:30*.

May 13 Joan Davis directs a revival of Sigmund Romberg's *The Desert Song* at London's Palace Theatre.

May 17 At Circle-in-the-Square, Theodore Mann and Paul Libin present Bertolt Brecht's *Drums in the Night*, with Joanna Miles, Hector Elizondo, Ralph Waite, and Michael Egan.

May 24 At the Theatre Royal Stratford East, Joan Littlewood stages *Intrigues and Amours*, based on Vanbrugh's Restoration play, *The Provoked Wife*. On June 26, Paul Ableman's *Green Julia*, staged by Frank Coda, opens with Pat Tull and Johnny Lyons.

May 30 Four plays are offered visitors to Britain's Chichester Festival, opening with *The Farmer's Wife*, by Eden Phillpotts. Farquhar's *The Beaux' Stratagem* is directed by William Chappell. Shaw's *Heartbreak House* is mounted by John Clements. The Labiche/Marc-Michel *Italian Straw Hat's* staged by Peter Coe.

June 5 London's Regent's Park's Open Air Theatre sees *A Midsummer Night's Dream*, staged by Michael Meacham. Rostand's *Cyrano de Bergerac* opens July 12, with David Buck in the title role and Christopher Gable as Christian.

June 6 *Song of Norway* is presented by the Song of Norway Festival in the 900-seat Tyrol Basin Amphitheatre near Mount Horeb, Wisconsin. The lyrics and adaptation of the life and music of Edvard Grieg are by Robert Wright and George Forrest, with a book by Milton Lazarus.

June 7 The New York Shakespeare Festival launches a three-play season in Central Park: *The Comedy of Errors*, *King John*, and *Titus Andronicus*. Gerald Freedman and founder Joseph Papp direct a company including David Birney, Joe Bova, Harris Yulin, Cavada Humphrey, Jack Hollander, Moses Gunn, and Raul Julia.

June 12 This is Michael Langham's last season as artistic director of Canada's Stratford Shakespeare Festival. His valedictory production is *Antony and Cleopatra*. He also stages Gogol's *The Government Inspector*. *Richard III's* staged by John Hirsch. David William stages *The Merry Wives of Windsor*. James Reaney's *Colours in the Dark*, a new Canadian play, is directed by Hirsch. Desmond Heeley designs Jean Gascon's production of Mozart's *Cosi fan Tutte*. Leslie Hurry designs William's staging of Britten's *Albert Herring*.

June 12 *South Pacific* opens at the New York State Theatre for 13 weeks. Florence

IPHIGENIA IN AULIS

Henderson and Giorgio Tozzi play the leads for director Joe Layton in this Music Theatre of Lincoln Center production.

June 13 In San Diego, the National Shakespeare Festival offers three plays in repertory: *Twelfth Night*, *All's Well That Ends Well*, and *Othello*.

June 13 The Birmingham Repertory Theatre Company brings its production of *As You Like It* to London's Vaudeville Theatre, directed by Peter Dews. The production runs nearly nine weeks.

June 14 Henrik Ibsen's *Ghosts* is revived by the Royal Shakespeare Company at the Aldwych Theatre. Alan Bridges directs Peggy Ashcroft, David Waller, and Chloe Ashcroft. On July 19, the Royal Shakespeare presents David Jones' staging of *As You Like It*, with Dorothy Tutin and Janet Suzman. On Aug 3, Trevor Nunn's production of *The Taming of the Shrew*, opens, with Suzman and John Kane, and on the 17th, his production of Vanbrugh's *The Relapse* features Susan Fleetwood and Charles Thomas.

June 17 The American Shakespeare Festival in Stratford, Connecticut, opens its season today. *A Midsummer Night's Dream*, Jean Anouilh's *Antigone*, and *The Merchant of Venice* will be directed by Cyril Ritchard, Jerome Kilty, and Michael Kahn, respectively. Ritchard will play both Bottom and Oberon, and Moris Carnovsky will appear as Creon and Shylock.

June 20 Peter Terson's *The Mighty Reservoy* is presented in London at the Jeanetta Cochran Theatre, staged for the Barge Theatre by Ronald Hayman. On Aug 21, Terson's *Zigger Zagger* is staged with members of the National Youth Theatre, who will also play *The Tempest* and *Henry IV, Part 1* in September.

June 21 The Shaw Festival at Niagara-on-the-Lake opens its nine-week season with *Arms and the Man*. *Major Barbara* will be next, both staged by Edward Gilbert. Paxton Whitehead will then direct *The Circle*, by Shaw's contemporary, W. Somerset Maugham.

June 22 At Greenwich Village's Sheridan Square Playhouse, George Bernard Shaw's *Arms and the Man* opens for 189 performances, staged by Philip Minor. John Heffernan and Pamela Burrell head the cast.

June 27 Eugene O'Neill's *Mourning Becomes Electra* opens in London at the Arts Theatre, as played by Edinburgh's Traverse Theatre Club. Valeria Sarruf and Judy Campbell play Lavinia and Christine Mannon.

June 28 Keith Dewhurst's new play, *Rafferty's Chant*, is staged at London's Mermaid Theatre by Robin Midgley. On July 3, Martin Beech's *You've Had Your War* opens, staged by Peter Oyston. On Aug 9, Midgley's staging of D. H. Lawrence's *The Fight for Barbara* is presented. On Sep 13, there's a revival of G. E. Lessing's *Nathan the Wise*, staged by Julius Gellner, with Maurice Denham. On Oct 18, Henry James's *The High Bid* is staged by Bernard Miles, with Billy Russell, Edward Woodward, and Fenella Fielding. On Nov 23, Frank Dunlop stages Vincent Longhi's *Climb the Greased Pole*, with Bernard Miles.

June 29 John Hancock repeats his San Francisco Actor's Workshop staging of *A Midsummer Night's Dream* at New York's Theatre de Lys. Alvin Epstein plays Theseus and Oberon to Gloria Foster's Hippolyta and Titania. Robert Benson is a tall, manly Helena. There are 28 performances.

July This month the Dublin Gate Theatre produces Brian Friels' *Lovers*, staged by Hilton Edwards. It will be seen in London at The Fortune on Aug 25, 1969.

July 4 At London's Royal Court Theatre, David Storey's *The Restoration of Arnold Middleton*, directed by Robert Kidd, opens on the July 4 with John Shepherd and Eileen Atkins. Don Howarth directs his play *Ogodiveleftthegason* beginning July 24. The Open Theatre of New York presents a three-play bill called *America Hurrah* on Aug. 2. On Oct 8, Ronald Ribman's American *The Journey of the Fifth Horse* is played at the Royal Court, in Bill Bryden's staging. On Oct 19, Isaac Babel's *Marya* is staged by Robert Kidd, and on Nov 15, *Dingo*, by Charles Wood, bows, with Tom Kempinski in the title role. Yevgeny Schwartz' Russian play, *The Dragon*, opens on Dec 7.

July 8 Playwright Frank Brink and composer Willard Straight collaborate on *Tovon of Alaska*, a story of the settlement of Russian America. The show is presented in Anchorage, then Juneau and Fairbanks. It is not repeated the following season.

July 13 Frederick Lonsdale's comedy, *The Last of Mrs Cheyney*, is revived at London's Phoenix Theatre. Charles Hickman directs Vanessa Lee in the title role.

July 22 The Oregon Shakespeare Festival, in Ashland, offers four plays by the Bard, Pericles, Antony and Cleopatra, The Taming of the Shrew, and Richard III. The 18th century comic opera, *The Maid of the Mill*, by Bickerstaffe, is also in the repertory.

July 23 The birth and growth of the Mormon movement is dramatized in the *Mormon Miracle Pageant*, by Grace Johnson, at the Sanpete County Fairgrounds. Next year it will move to the Manti Temple Hill in Manti, Utah.

Aug 20 Britain's EDinburgh International Festival opens, Director Peter Diamond presents for the first time the Scottish Opera, with productions of Stravinsky's *The Rake's Progress* and *The Soldier's Tale*. Tom O'Horgan directs Paul Foster's *Tom Paine*. Frank Dunlop's Pop Theatre offers *A Midsummer Night's Dream*. Dunlop also directs Molière's *The Tricks of Scapin*. Carl Toms designs this show and Ionesco's *The Lesson* as a Pop Theatre double-bill. The Voyage Theatre offers Harold Lang as actor, director, and author, with *Macbeth in Camera* and *Man Speaking*. Michael Meschke's Stockholm Marionette Theatre presents *The Wizard of Oz* and *Ubu Roi*. James Earl Jones plays the title-role in Eugene O'Neill's *The Emperor Jones*. The Hampstead Theatre Club offers Barry Bermange's *Nathan and Tabileth*. James Roose-Evans stages this and Bermange's *Oldenberg*. Olwen Wymark's *Triple Image* is presented by the Close Theatre Club. Prospect Productions present two plays, Chekhov's *The Cherry Orchard* and *A Room With a View*, by Lance Sieveking and Richard Cottrell, who directs both.

Sep 7 Ralph Richardson plays Shylock in Glen Byam Shaw's revival of *The Merchant of Venice* at London's Haymarket Theatre. Angela Thorne plays Portia.

Sep 26 Frank Dunlop's Edinburgh Festival production of *A Midsummer Night's Dream* comes to London's Saville Theatre for 38 performances. Cleo Laine plays Hippolyta; her busband, Johnny Dankworth, composes music. David Baxter is Puck; Jim Dale, Bottom.

Oct 5 From the Cambridge Festival, Richard Cottrell's staging of Chekhov's *The Cherry Orchard* comes to London's Queen's Theatre. Lila Kedrova, Patrick Wymark, and Hazel Hughes are among the cast.

Oct 19 The Jewish State Theatre of Poland comes to Broadway's Billy Rose Theatre with Jacob Gordin's *Mirele Efros* and Bertolt Brecht's *Mother Courage*, both played in Yiddish. Ida Kaminska has adapted, staged and heads the cast. There are 53 performances.

Oct 19 Jean Dalrymple's play revivals at New York City Center are Howard Lindsay and Russel Crouse's *Life with Father* and, on Nov 8, Paddy Chayevsky's *The Tenth Man*. On Dec 13, Dalrymple revives *Brigadoon* at City Center, with Ed-

ward Villela as Harry Beaton, Karen Morrow as Meg, and Margot Moster as Fiona. Gus Schirmer stages.

Oct 26 Mike Nichols stages Lillian Hellman's *The Little Foxes* to open the Repertory Theatre of Lincoln Center's season at the Vivian Beaumont. Anne Bancroft, Margaret Leighton, Austin Pendleton, and E. G. Marshall are among the cast. There will be 60 showings, a move to the Ethel Barrymore Theatre and 40 more performances. On Nov 10, a Mayo Simon double-bill, *Walking to Waldheim* and *Happiness*, is presented beneath the Vivian Beaumont in the Forum Theatre by the Repertory Theatre.

Oct 26 The Equity Library Theatre opens its season with *Babes in Arms*. Their plays at the Master Theatre on New York's Riverside Drive will also include *He Who Gets Slapped*, *Under the Gaslight*, *Redhead*, *An Enemy of the People*, *Lost in the Stars*, and *The Visit*.

Oct 28 The American Place Theatre in Manhattan's St. Clement's Church opens its season with *Father Uxbridge Wants to Marry*, by Frank Gagliano.

Nov 9 George Bernard Shaw's *Heartbreak House* comes to London's Lyric Theatre from Chichester. John Clements directs and plays Captain Shotover. Irene Worth, Doris Hare, Sarah Badel, and Diana Churchill are in the cast. The show runs nearly 15 weeks.

Nov 21 Michael Cacoyannis revives Euripides' *Iphigenia in Aulis* for 29 weeks at the Circle-in-the-Square. Jenny Leigh plays the title role, with Frank Langella as Achilles and Irene Papas as Clytemnestra.

Nov 25 *The Marie Lloyd Story* is told by Daniel Farson and Harry Moore with some of the music hall's artiste's own songs. Joan Littlewood directs this at her Theatre Workshop at the Theatre Royal Stratford East. Avis Bunnage plays Lloyd.

Nov 28 Oscar Wilde's *A Woman of No Importance* is stylishly revived by Malcolm Farquhar at the West End's Vaudeville Theatre, with a distinguished cast. Sandy Wilson's *The Boy Friend* is staged by Wilson on the 29th, with Polly Brown. The show runs beyond the season's end at the Comedy.

Nov 30 The APA in association with the Phoenix Theatre, opens its season at New York's Lyceum Theatre with Michel de Ghelderode's *Pantagleize*, followed on Dec 5 with George Kelly's *The Show-Off*. Ellis Rabb plays Pantagleize and co-directs with John Houseman. Stephen Porter stages the Kelly play.

Dec 7 Dodie Smith's comedy, *Dear Octopus*, is revived at London's Haymarket Theatre. Popular musical comedy stars Jack Hulbert and Cicely Courtneidge play Charles and Dora Randolph. The play runs beyond the end of the season.

Dec 12 Tennessee William's *The Two-Character Play* opens at London's Hampstead Theatre Club, with Peter Wyngarde and Mary Ure. James Roose-Evans directs.

Dec 14 At London's Westminster Theatre, the holiday season is noted by the revival of the musical, *Give A Dog a Bone*. On the 15th at the Scala Theatre, the annual revival of Barrie's *Peter Pan* has Millicent Martin as Peter, wires and all. On the 18th, Bernard Miles revives *Treasure Island* at the Mermaid Theatre. Other holiday shows include *The Snow Queen* (Arts), *Robinson Crusoe* (Palladium), with the pop singer Engelbert Humperdinck as Crusoe and comedian Arthur Askey as Aunt Martha, a drag-role), *Little Women* (Jeannetta Cochrane), *Babes in the Wood*

(Players'), *Toad of Toad Hall* (Fortune), *Aladdin* (Wimbledon), *The Sleeping Beauty* (Golder's Green Hippodrome), and at the Royal Court Theatre, New York's innovative Paper Bag Players in *Group Soup*, with Judith Martin, Betty Osgood, Gary Maxwell, Don Ashwander, and Irving Burton.

Dec 18 Traditional Gilbert and Sullivan returns to London's Saville Theatre as the D'Oyly Carte Opera Company presents its season of *Cox and Box, Iolanthe*, and H.M.S. Pinafore with the curtain-raiser *Trial by Jury*.

Dec 26 Joseph Papp stages an unorthodox *Hamlet* at his Public Theatre. in Greenwich Village. Martin Sheen plays the title-role, with April Shawan as Ophelia. There are 56 performances.

1967 BIRTHS/DEATHS/DEBUTS

Jan 18 Evelyn Nesbit Thaw, the "Girl in the Red Velvet Swing," a Broadway showgirl, is dead at 82. Her husband, the jealous Harry K. Thaw, shot architect Stanford White during a roof-garden theatre performance, convinced that White had debauched his wife.

Jan 21 Rollo Peters, an actor, director, producer, and designer, has died at 74. He was a founder of the Theatre Guild.

Jan 23 The distinguished American stage designer, Lee Simonson, author of *The Stage Is Set* and other books on theatre, dies today at age 78.

Feb 18 Swedish actress Ingrid Thulin makes her Broadway debut in English in *Of Love Remembered* at the ANTA Theatre. Burgess Meredith directs this Arnold Sundgaard tale of Norwegians in Minnesota. There are only nine performances.

March 2 The British stage comedian Gordon Harker dies at age 81.

March 16 American director, producer, and designer Jack Landau (b. 1925) is dead in Boston. Landau joined the American Shakespeare Festival Theatre and Academy in Stratford, Connecticut in 1956 to become associate director with John Houseman.

May 1 George Freedley, founding curator of the Theatre Collection of the New York Public Library retires. He is succeeded by Paul Myers.

May 3 John McClain, drama critic for the *NY Journal-American*, dies at age 63.

May 7 American actress Judith Evelyn (b. 1913) dies in New York.

May 8 American playwright and director Elmer Rice (b. 1892) dies in Southampton, England. Among his notable works are *The Adding Machine*, the 1929 Pulitzer Prize-winning *Street Scene, Coun-*

sellor-at-Law, Dream Girl, and *Cue for Passion*.

May 12 English Poet Laureate John Masefield (b. 1878) dies in Berkshire, England. His plays include *The Faithful, Good Friday, The Tragedy of Nan*, and *The Witch*.

May 22 American playwright and poet Langston Hughes (b. 1902) dies in New York City. Hughes wrote two full-length plays; the first, *Mulatto*, was based on his poem, *Cross*. This in turn was produced in a musical version titled *The Barrier* in 1950. *Troubled Island* was his second play. An autobiography, *The Big Sea*, was published in 1940.

May 30 London-born Claude Rains (b. 1889) is dead. He toured the United States with Granville Barker in 1914, and appeared for the Theatre Guild in 1928 as Volpone. *Marco Millions, The Apple Cart*, and *Darkness at Noon* were his outstanding plays. His film career began in 1933.

June 2 Irish-born Tony Quinn (b. 1899) is dead. Quinn studied at the Abbey School of Acting and made his first appearance at the Abbey Theatre as Patrick in *The Mineral Workers* in 1919.

June 16 English actor Reginald Denny (b. 1891) dies in Richmond, England. He made his New York debut in 1911 in *The Quaker Girl*. In 1958 he succeeded Robert Coote as Colonel Pickering on Broadway in *My Fair Lady*. Denny also appeared in films and on American television.

June 25 English actor Leon Quartermaine (b. 1876) dies in Salisbury, England. Quartermaine made his first appearance on the West End stage under the management of Sir Johnston Forbes-Robertson in 1901. In 1944 and 1945 he appeared with the Gielgud Repertory Company.

June 29 Irish playwright and actor Percy Robinson (b. 1889) is dead. His major appearances were in *Ghosts, Abraham Lincoln*, and *Romeo and Juliet*. His dramatic works include *The Last Rose of Summer, Con o' the Hills, For None Can Tell*, and *The Unseen Menace*.

July 8 Vivien Leigh (b. 1913) dies in London. Second wife of Laurence Olivier, she played Blanche DuBois in *Streetcar Named Desire*. Leigh sang and danced on stage for the first time in 1963 in the musical version of *Tovarich*.

July 21 English actor Basil Rathbone (b. 1892) dies in New York. Rathbone arrived in America in 1913, appearing in *Romeo and Juliet, The Merry Wives of Windsor*, and *As You Like It*. In the 1930's he played Romeo to Katharine Cornell's Juliet.

Aug 9 Britain's blackly comic playwright, Joe Orton, is dead at 34, murdered by his roommate. Orton's satires have at first shocked some critics, but plays such as *Entertaining Mr. Sloane* and *Loot* are winning international attention.

ELMER RICE

Aug 9 Anton Walbrook dies at age 66. He began his career in Germany, acting in films and on stage, but left for England when the Nazis took over, changing his name for the British stage.

Aug 25 Stage and screen actor Paul Muni dies. He began his career as Muni Weisenfrend in the Yiddish theatre in New York.

Sep 11 Theatre historian and curator George Freedley (b. 1901) dies in Bay Shore, New York. Founder and director of the Theatre Collection of the New York Public Library and a founder of the Theatre Library Association and Equity Library Theatre, he wrote and lectured extensively on American theatre.

Sep 26 Actress Jean Cadell dies at age 83.

Sep 29 Actor-teacher Ludwig Donath (b. 1907) is dead in New York. Donath's career began in Austria in 1924. He made his New York debut in Joseph Kesselring's *Four Twelves Are 48* in 1951. He also appeared on television and radio.

Oct 2 Choreographer Albertina Rasch has died at 76.

Oct 4 David T. Nederlander, president of the Nederlander Theatrical Corporation, dies at 81.

Oct 5 May Davenport Seymour, an American actress who was for many years curator of the Theatre Collection of the Museum of the City of New York, has died, aged 83.

Nov 1 English Actress Benita Hume is dead in Egerton, England, at 61. She played Robina Hill in *Easy Money* at Wyndham's Theatre in 1927 and made her Broadway debut in 1930. She was married to actor Ronald Colman.

Nov 5 Playwright Joseph Kesselring (b. 1902) dies in Kingston, N.Y. An actor, writer and producer of vaudeville from 1925 to 1933, his plays include *Aggie Applyby, Maker of Men*, and *Arsenic and Old Lace*.

Nov 9 Jack Carter, remembered for his work in Orson Wells-John Houseman productions in the Depression, dies now at age 65.

Nov 21 Actress Florence Reed (b. 1883) dies in East Islip, New York. Acclaimed as Mother Goddam in *The Shanghai Gesture*, she toured for the Theatre Guild as Christine in *Mourning Becomes Electra* and played the same role in New York in 1932. She appeared as Amy in T. S. Eliot's *The Family Reunion* in 1958.

Dec 4 Actor-comedian Bert Lahr (b. 1895) dies in New York City. After early years in vaudeville and burlesque, his Broadway appearances included *George White's Scandals, Du Barry Was a Lady, Seven Lively Arts*, and *Waiting for Godot*.

Dec 6 Puppeteer-actress Cora Baird (b. 1912) dies in New York City. She appeared as Cora Burlar in Maxwell Anderson's *Valley Forge* in 1934 at the Guild Theatre. With her husband, she formed the "Bil and Cora Baird Marionettes."

Dec 27 Playwright Martin Flavin (b. 1883) dies in Carmel, California. His first produced play, *Children of the Moon*, appeared in 1923, and was followed by *Lady of the Rose*, Service for Two, Broken Dishes, Achilles Had a Heel, and *Amaco*.

This Broadway season's ten "Best Plays," selected by Otis Guernsey, Jr., include Albee's *A Delicate Balance*, Marcus' *The Killing of Sister George*, Wilson's *Hamp*, Masteroff/Ebb/Kander's *Cabaret*, Bock/Harnick's *The Apple Tree*, Van Itallie's *America Hurrah*, Pinter's *The Homecoming*, Shaffer's *Black Comedy*, Gessner's *You're a Good Man Charlie Brown*, and Anderson's *You Know I Can't Hear You When the Water's Running*.

Jun 11 Carol Channing has been touring America in Jerry Herman's *Hello, Dolly!* since Nov 18, 1963. It closes today, after 1,272 performances, with a total gross of $17,015,018.

July 7 Renovations at the Avon Theatre, owned by Canada's Stratford Shakespeare Festival are completed. The enlarged stage facilities, more attractive auditorium, and new facade and foyer are inaugurated with Mozart's *Cosi fan tutte*.

July 23 The Abbey Theatre's new Peacock Theatre is formally opened in Dublin.

July 23 The Mormon Miracle Pageant has its initial performance in Manti, Utah. 2,000 witness the saga of the Mormon pioneers, with two narrators and a 300-voice chorus.

Aug 2 *America Hurrah* is permitted to run in a private club in London's Royal Court Theatre. A transfer to the Vaudeville Theatre is banned by the Lord Chamberlain, who objects to rude words written on a piece of scenery and to offensive mockery of President Lyndon Johnson.

Sep The Lord Chamberlain moves to protect the feelings of the Churchill family by banning performance of Rolf Hochhuth's *Soldiers*, which insists that Winston Churchill arranged the death of the leader of the Free Polish Forces in World War II. Laurence Olivier has sought to present the work at the National Theatre.

Oct 7 The Public Theatre, housed in New York's renovated Astor Library Building, built by John Astor in 1948, opens with Gerome Ragni and James Rado's *Hair*, with music by Galt MacDermott.

Oct 28 Paxton Whitehead is appointed artistic director of the Shaw Festival at Niagara-on-the-Lake, a post he will hold for ten years.

Oct 31 Chicago's famed Adler and Sullivan Auditorium Theatre has its thorough restoration completed today. It opened on Dec 9, 1889.

Nov Canada's Stratford Shakespeare Festival establishes its Archives, the first of its kind attached to any producing theatre in North America.

Nov 25 This is the 15th anniversary of *The Mousetrap*, Agatha Christie's long-running West End mystery-play.

1967   THEATERS/PRODUCTIONS

U.S. patents this year include one to George C. Izenour for improvements on his Synchronous Winch System.

Feb–March The Stratford Shakespeare Festival makes its first coast-to-coast Canadian tour, with *Twelfth Night* and *The Government Inspector*, as part of the Centennial celebrations.

April 9 The Mark Taper Forum opens in Los Angeles, part of the Music Center Complex. With no curtain or proscenium arch, it seats 750 in 14 steeply tiered rows, bordering the pentagonal thrust stage. The artistic director is Gordon Davidson.

April 12 The Ahmanson Theatre, the third and final theatre in Los Angeles' Music Center Complex, opens. The auditorium seats 2,100 with a bowed, archless stage-playing area 40' wide by 45' deep.

May 31 This is the last day of the current Broadway season and the six hits, in Variety's estimation, are: *At the Drop of Another Hat, A Delicate Balance, The Killing of Sister George, The Star-Spangled Girl, The Investigation*, and *You Know I Can't Hear You When the Water's Running*.

June 1 With the 1966–67 Broadway season just concluded, the tallies are a total of 76 productions, 19 of them plays, 8 musicals, 4 specialties, 10 foreign plays in English, 5 foreign-language productions, and 32 revivals. The season's gross is estimated by *Variety* at $55 million. Shows on tour grossed over $43 million. Playwright Neil Simon, with four hit shows running simultaneously on Broadway, tops $200,000 gross in the best week for his productions. *Hello, Dolly!* is reported to have made more than $30 million gross in productions around the world. David Merrick's production of *Breakfast at Tiffany's* has closed in previews for a loss of $425,000. Off-Broadway, there are a total of 69 productions, 29 of them plays, 8 musicals, 5 revues, 8 foreign plays in English, 6 specialty shows, 10 revivals, and three plays in foreign languages. Off-off-Broadway, some 300 new plays have been produced.

1968 AMERICAN PREMIERES

Jan 10 *Staircase.* See London premiere, 1966.

Jan 13 *Your Own Thing* (NY—Orpheum—Musical). This version of *Twelfth Night* features Tom Ligon, and Leland Palmer. Director Donald Driver has adapted Shakespeare's play and developed the multi-media conception. Hal Hester and Danny Apolinar provide the music and lyrics. It runs 933 performances and is chosen a "Best Play." The Off-Broadway musical opens in the West End at the Comedy on Feb 6, 1969, for only 59 showings.

Jan 16 *The Prime of Miss Jean Brodie.* See L premiere, 1966.

Jan 17 *The Indian Wants the Bronx* (NY—Astor Place—Drama). John Cazale plays a Hindu in New York, tormented by two toughs (Al Pacino and Matthew Cowles) in the first play of an Israel Horowitz double-bill. Marsha Mason is in the cast of the second, *It's Called the Sugar Plum.* There are 204 performances. James Hammerstein stages.

Jan 18 *The Happy Time* (NY—Broadway—Musical). Robert Goulet and David Wayne head the cast of N. Richard Nash's adaptation of Robert Fontaine's book about family life in a Canadian town. Gower Champion directs and choreographs. There are 285 performances.

Jan 22 *Jacques Brel Is Alive and Well and Living in Paris* (NY—Village Gate—Revue). Jacques Brel's songs, with English lyrics and Brel's own comments to give a narrative thread, are the meat of this show devised by Eric Blau and Mort Shuman. Shawn Elliott, Elly Stone, Alice Whitefield, and Shuman are in the cast. It has 1,847 performances. There are only 22 performances following a premiere at the Duchess on July 9 in London.

Jan 25 *I Never Sang for My Father* (NY—Longacre—Drama). Robert Anderson's drama about a stiff father-son relationship is selected as a "Best Play," though this production runs only 15 weeks. Lillian Gish, Hal Holbrook, and Alan Webb head the cast. Alan Schneider directs. The play opens at London's Duke of York's on May 27, 1970, with George Baker, Gene Garrison, Raymond Massey and Catherine Lacey.

Feb 1 *A Day in the Death of Joe Egg.* See L premiere, 1967.

Feb 4 *Golden Rainbow* (NY—Shubert—Musical). Singers Steve Lawrence and Eydie Gorme have a 48-week run in Ernest Kinoy's musical adaptation of Arnold Schulman's play *A Hole in the Head.* Walter Marks writes the songs, Arthur Storch directs.

Feb 14 *Plaza Suite* (NY—Plymouth—Comedy). Playwright Neil Simon's triple-bill of comedies, all set in the same suite of the Plaza Hotel on Central Park, earns 1,097 performances. George C. Scott and Maureen Stapleton star in all three. The plays are *Visitor from Mamaroneck, Visitor from Hollywood,* and *Visitor from Forest Hills.* Mike Nichols directs. It is chosen a "Best Play." There are only 294 showings following the London premiere at the Lyric on Feb 18, 1969. Paul Rogers, Rosemary Harris, and Gillian Lewis are in the cast.

Feb 17 *The Price* (NY—Morosco—Drama). Arthur Miller's new script is a confrontation between two brothers, one (Pat Hingle) a seemingly unsuccessful policeman who believes he's sacrificed a career to look after his late—and ungrateful—father. The other (Arthur Kennedy) is a prosperous doctor whose life is not satisfying. There are 429 performances. It is chosen a "Best Play." The drama opens at London's Duke of York's on March 4, 1969, with Albert Salmi and Shepperd Strudwick as the brothers. It runs beyond the season.

March 3 *Summertree* (NY—Forum—Drama). David Birney plays a youth who will die in Vietnam. Blythe Danner plays the girl who loves him, in Ron Cowen's play which has a run of 127 performances. David Pressman directs.

March 18 *Loot.* See L premiere, 1966.

March 25 *Tom Paine.* See L listing, 1967.

March 27 *The Seven Descents of Myrtle* (NY—Ethel Barrymore—Drama). Tennessee Williams's fable about the conflict between two brothers (Brian Bedford and Harry Guardino) has only 27 performances, but there is a film sale. Estelle Parsons is also in the cast. Jose Quintero stages.

April 10 *George M!* (NY—Palace—Musical). Joel Grey plays Broadway's song-and-dance man George M. Cohan, in this Michael Stewart and John and Fran Pascal show based on Cohan's career. Mary Cohan revises Cohan's music and lyrics. Joe Layton directs and choreographs. There are 427 performances.

April 15 *The Boys in the Band* (NY—Theatre Four—Drama). Playwright Mart Crowley's script about a group of homosexuals at a birthday party features Leonard Frey, Kenneth Nelson, and Robert La Tourneaux. The show has 1,000 performances and becomes a film. It is also chosen a "Best Play." On Feb 11, 1969, it opens at Wyndham's Theatre in London with an American cast. It has 380 showings.

May 1 *Soldiers* (NY—Billy Rose—Drama). Rolf Hochhuth's German quasi-documentary drama alleges that Winston Churchill, to placate Joseph Stalin, con-

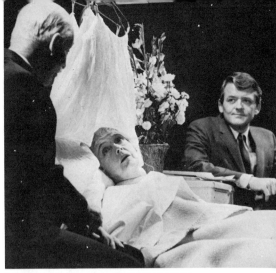

I NEVER SANG FOR MY FATHER

nived in the death of the leader of the Free Polish forces in World War II. Initially not welcomed in London, it has only 22 performances on Broadway. The show is finally performed in the West End on Dec 12. It plays 116 times at the New Theatre.

June 13 *Futz!* (NY—Theatre de Lys—Drama). Rochelle Owens's controversial play tells of a farmer in love with a female pig. John Bakos plays the farmer and Sally Kirkland narrates in this Tom O'Horgan staging. It runs 29 weeks.

Sep 26 *The Man in the Glass Booth.* See L premiere, 1967.

Oct 15 *Tea Party/The Basement* (NY—Eastside Playhouse—Drama). Harold Pinter's two one-act plays have their world stage premiere and run for nearly 19 weeks. James Hammerstein directs. Under the title *Pinter Plays,* they are presented at London's Duchess beginning Sep 17, 1970, for a 10-week run.

Oct 16 *We Bombed in New Haven* (NY—Ambassador—Comedy). Jason Robards, Jr. is among the cast of Joseph Heller's peculiar play about airmen involved in wartime bombings. John Hirsch directs. There are 85 performances.

Oct 20 *Her First Roman* (NY—Lunt Fontanne—Musical). Richard Kiley and Leslie Uggams have only 17 performances in Ervin Drake's musical adaptation of George Bernard Shaw's *Caesar and Cleopatra.* Derek Goldby directs.

Nov 17 *Zorbá* (NY—Imperial—Musical). Joseph Stein adapts Nikos Kazantzakis's novel *Zorbá the Greek,* with music by John Kander and lyrics by Fred Ebb. The show has a nine-month run. Harold Prince directs. Herschel Bernardi plays Zorba.

Nov 21 *Sweet Eros/Witness* (NY—Gramercy Arts—Drama). Robert Drivas plays a rapist; Sally Kirkland plays his victim, in the first play of this Terrence McNally double-bill. James Coco is in the second play. There is a 10-week run. Larry Arrick stages.

Nov 28 *Morning, Noon, and Night* (NY—

371

Henry Miller—Comedy). This program of three avant-garde plays, by Israel Horovitz, Terrence McNally, and Leonard Melfi respectively, has only 52 performances. Robert Klein and Sorrell Booke are among the cast of all three plays, which Theodore Mann directs.

Dec 1 *Promises, Promises* (NY—Shubert—Musical). Neil Simon's book is based on Billy Wilder and I.A.L. Diamond's screenplay for *The Apartment*, in which the hero loans out his apartment to business associates for liaisons, hoping for advancement and esteem in return. Burt Bacharach composes the score, and Hal David provides the lyrics. Jerry Orbach leads the cast. It wins a run of 1,281 performances. The show plays 570 times, following its London premiere at the Prince of Wales's on Oct 2, 1969. Tony Roberts is featured.

Dec 8 *Big Time Buck White* (NY—Village South—Comedy). Dick Williams plays Buck White, an expansive black power figure, in Joseph Dolan Tuotti's comedy

which runs for nearly four months. Williams stages. The show transfers to Broadway briefly.

Dec 20 *Dames at Sea* (NY—Bouwerie Lane—Musical). First animated on a miniscule stage at the Caffe Cino, George Haimsohn and Robin Miller's book and lyrics good-naturedly spoof old Dick Powell-Ruby Keeler films. Jim Wise creates the score. Bernadette Peters, Tamara Long, and David Christmas are in the cast. The show has a run of 575 performances and is revived at the Plaza Musical Hall beginning Sep 23, 1970, for a run of nearly 22 weeks. The parody has 117 performances in London following its premiere at the Duchess on Aug 27, 1969.

Dec 26 *Forty Carats* (NY—Morosco—Comedy). Julie Harris plays a woman of 40 in love with a younger man (Marco St. John) in Abe Burrows' adaptation of a Parisian farce, which has 780 performances and is chosen as a "Best Play." Burrows directs.

staging of *The Audition*, by Sean Patrick Vincent. There are 200 performances.

July 4 *Indians* (L—Aldwych—Drama). Arthur Kopit's satirical fantasy, with extracts from actual speeches of notable American Indian leaders, features Barrie Ingham as Buffalo Bill and Michael Jayston as General Custer. The drama opens in New York at the Brooks Atkinson on Oct 13, 1969, for only three months, having been produced at the Arena Theatre in Washington, D.C. It is chosen a "Best Play."

July 4 *The Man Most Likely To . . .* (L—Vaudeville—Comedy). Joyce Rayburn's comedy, about a father and son interested in the same young woman, has 768 performances. Leslie Phillips and Dermont Walsh are in the cast, which Phillips directs.

Aug 28 *Oh, Clarence* (L—Lyric—Comedy). Naunton Wayne, Peggy Mount, and Robertson Hare head the cast of John Chapman's comedy, which he bases on some of P. G. Wodehouse's Lord Emsworth stories. Charles Hickman stages. It runs nearly six months. (In July the play ran at Manchester's Opera House under the title *Blanding's Castle*.)

Sep 16 *The Latent Heterosexual* (L—Aldwych—Comedy). Paddy Chayevsky's bitter American comedy is produced by the Royal Shakespeare Company as part of their fall season. Lee Montague heads the cast. Terry Hands stages.

Sep 19 *A Boston Story* (L—Duchess—Drama). Henry James's novel *Watch and Ward* is the basic for Ronald Gow's play, staged by Malcolm Farquhar. First seen at Birmingham's Repertory Theatre in 1966, it now has a run of 220 performances.

Sep 27 *Hair.* See NY premiere, 1967.

Oct 15 *Out of the Question.* See NY premiere (*Absence of a Cello*), 1964.

Oct 16 *The Secretary Bird* (L—Savoy—Comedy). Kenneth More and Jane Downs head the cast of William Douglas Home's love triangle, which has a long run of 1,463 performances. Philip Dudley stages.

Oct 23 *God Bless* (L—Aldwych—Comedy). Jules Feiffer's American satire on religion and politics is produced as part of the Royal Shakespeare Company's fall season. Geoffrey Reeves stages.

Oct 31 *Forty Years On* (L—Apollo—Comedy). John Gielgud plays the headmaster in Alan Bennett's comedy, which includes a schoolboy pageant based on recent British history. It has a run of 444 performances. Patrick Garland stages.

1968 BRITISH PREMIERES

Feb 1 *The Italian Girl* (L—Wyndham's—Drama). With James Saunders, Iris Murdoch adapts her popular novel for the stage, and it earns a run of 315 performances. Richard Pasco and Elizabeth Sellars head the cast. Val May stages.

Feb 1 *You're a Good Man, Charlie Brown.* See NY premiere, 1967.

Feb 21 *White Liars/Black Comedy.* See NY listings, 1967.

Feb 26 *Little Boxes*, John Bowen's two plays about "boxed-in" people, *The Coffee Lace* and *Trevor*, are staged for London's Hampstead Theatre Club. David Cook is featured. On April 1, the production opens at the Duchess Theatre and runs beyond the season. Bowen's plays last only two weeks following the Broadway premiere at the New Theatre on Dec 3, 1969.

Feb 28 *Cabaret.* See NY premiere, 1966.

March 21 *Canterbury Tales* (L—Phoenix—Musical). This colorful, bawdy musical adaptation of selected tales from Chaucer achieves a run of 2,082 performances. The book is by Nevill Coghill and Martin Starkie, with Coghill's lyrics and music by Richard Hill and John Hawkins. The hit proves a failure on Broadway following its premiere at the Eugene O'Neill on Feb 3, 1969. It runs only 15 weeks.

March 28 *Enter a Free Man* (L—St. Martin's—Drama). Tom Stoppard's play about a would-be inventor earns only 44 performances, despite having a cast headed by Michael Hordern. Frith Banbury stages.

April 18 *Hadrian the Seventh* (L—Mermaid—Drama). Alec McCowen has a

triumph in Peter Luke's play about a bitter, poverty-stricken man, rejected for the priesthood, fantasizing that he is elected pope. The show transfers to the West End and is also popular on Broadway, where it premieres at the Helen Hayes on Jan 8, 1969. McCowen is again in the lead. In New York the production runs 359 performances and is chosen a "Best Play."

April 24 *Man of La Mancha.* See NY premiere, 1965.

May 15 *Mrs. Mouse, Are You Within?* (L—Duke of York's—Drama). Barbara Leigh-Hunt and Peter Whitbread are among the cast of Frank Marcus' wry drama, which is staged by Val May after a previous run at Bristol's Theatre Royal.

May 16 *I Do! I Do!* See NY premiere, 1966.

June 12 *Not Now, Darling* (L—Strand—Comedy). Ray Cooney and John Chapman's farce about romantic mix-ups earns a run of 669 performances. Donald Sinden and Bernard Cribbens head the cast. Patrick Cargill stages. There are only 21 performances following the New York premiere at the Brooks Atkinson on Oct 29, 1970.

June 17 *The Real Inspector Hound* (L—Criterion—Comedy). Tom Stoppard's one-act farce spoofs Agatha Christie murder mysteries. Robert Chetwyn directs. The play is preceded by David Calderisi's

1968 REVIVALS/REPERTORIES

Jan 1 Ronald Ribman's *Ceremony of Innocence* continues the season of the American Place Theatre at St. Clements

Church in Manhattan. Sandy Duncan and William Devane are among the cast. Arthur Seidelman directs. On March 6, Ed

Bullins's *The Electronic Nigger and Others* opens, staged by Robert Macbeth. The others are *A Son, Come Home* and *Clara's Ole Man*. On May 7, Robert Lowell's *Endecott and the Red Cross*, based on two Hawthorne stories, makes a bow, directed by John Hancock, with a cast including Kenneth Haigh.

Jan 1 The D'Oyly Carte Company continues its London season at the Saville Theatre with *The Yeomen of the Guard*, *Ruddigore*, *Patience*, *Princess Ida*, *The Mikado*, and *The Gondoliers*.

Jan 2 The Negro Ensemble Company launches its first season Off-Broadway at the St. Marks Playhouse with Peter Weiss's *Song of the Lusitanian Bogey*, staged by Michael Schultz. Ray Lawler's Australian *Summer of the 17th Doll* follows on Feb 20, staged by Edmund Cambridge. Wole Soyinka's *Kongi's Harvest* opens on April 14, directed by Schultz. *Daddy Goodness* closes the season, bowing on June 4, in a staging by Douglas Turner Ward.

Jan 4 The RSC offers *Macbeth* at its London home, the Aldwych Theatre. Peter Hall directs a cast including Paul Scofield and Vivien Merchant. On Jan 17, *All's Well That Ends Well*, is staged by John Barton, with Catherine Lacey. On March 4, Terry Hands stages Dylan Thomas' dramatic poem, *Under Milk Wood*. This is the Theatregoround's touring show, with Emrys James and Sheila Allen among others.

Jan 4 George Bernard Shaw's *Saint Joan* is revived by Lincoln Center Repertory Theatre. John Hirsch stages the drama at the Vivian Beaumont Theatre, with Diana Sands and Edward Zang among the cast. On Feb 29, the third seasonal offering of the Repertory Theatre of Lincoln Center is Christopher Fry's adaptation of Jean Giraudoux's *Tiger at the Gates*. Diana Sands plays Cassandra. Anthony Quayle directs the show. There are 44 performances. On April 25, Edmond Rostand's *Cyrano de Bergerac*, in a new translation by James Forsyth, opens. Carl Weber stages, with Robert Symonds and Suzanne Grossmann. The production lasts 42 performances on the Vivian Beaumont stage.

Jan 6 In Edinburgh at the Traverse Theatre, a revue, *Please Renew Your Membership*, opens the year. There are some 23 productions. Among the offerings are Ranald Graham's *Aberfan*, David Wright's *Would You Look at Them Smashing All the Lovely Windows*, David Benedictus's *Angels (Over Your Graves) and Geese (Over Mine)*, Megan Terry's *Comings and Goings*, David Mowat's *Anna-Luise*, Rosalyn Drexler's *The Line of Least Existence*, and several editions of *The People Show*.

Jan 9 The APA-Phoenix Company continues its repertory season at New York's Lyceum Theatre with Eugene Ionesco's *Exit the King*, staged by Ellis Rabb, with Richard Easton, Eva LeGallienne and Patricia Connolly. Anton Chekhov's *The Cherry Orchard* is revived on March 19, in LeGallienne's translation. She also stages the drama, with Uta Hagen and Nancy Walker.

Jan 16 At London's Old Vic, the National Theatre presents a revival of Ben Jonson's *Volpone*, with Colin Blakely as the fox. On March 19, Seneca's *Oedipus* opens, with John Gielgud and Irene Worth. Director Peter Brook designs this production as a "Happening." On April 30, Marlowe's *Edward the Second* opens with John Stride, Geraldine McEwen and Derek Jacobi. Frank Dunlop stages. On June 18, the National Theatre presents a triple-bill of Henry Fielding's *The Covent Garden Tragedy*, John Maddison Morton's *A Most Unwarrantable Intrusion*, and *In His Own Write*, based on Beatle John Lennon's short parodies, *A Spaniard in the Works* and *In His Own Write*.

Jan 23 The Dublin Gate Theatre opens the new year with a revival of *The Importance of Being Oscar*, with Micheal macLiammoir, followed by a revival of Brian Friel's *Philadelphia, Here I Come!* In November, the troupe will produced Friel's new play, *Crystal and Fox*.

Jan 31 At London's Royal Court Theatre, *Twelfth Night* is revived, staged by Jane Howell, with Malcolm McDowell in the cast. On Feb 11, Michael Rosen's decorless *Backbone* has a tryout, staged by Bill Bryden. On Feb 29, D. H. Lawrence season gets underway at the Court with Peter Gill's staging of *A Collier's Friday Night*. On March 7, the play is Lawrence's *The Daughter-in-Law*, and on March 14, *The Widowing of Mrs. Holroyd* opens.

Feb 7 At London's Mermaid Theatre, George Bernard Shaw's *The Adventures of a Black Girl in her Search for God* and *Aerial Football: a New Game* are paired by director Basil Ashmore as a "public reading." Among his readers is Edith Evans. On March 14, the entertainment is a play, *Open on Sunday*, by Michael Landy and Ron Pember. Pember stages.

Feb 8 Oscar Wilde's *The Importance of Being Earnest* is revived by Robert Chetwyn at London's Haymarket Theatre. Daniel Massey, John Standing, Isabel Jeans, and Flora Robson head the cast.

Feb 14 Murray MacDonald directs the revival of Noel Coward's *Hay Fever* now opening at the Duke of York's Theatre in the West End. Motley designs. Roland Culver and Celia Johnson play the Blisses. It runs nearly nine weeks.

March 3 At Joseph Papp's Public Theatre, Jakov Lind's play *Ergo*, based on his novel, opens for a run of 49 performances, Gerald Freedman stages a cast including Jack Hollander, Sam Waterston, and Cliff Gorman. On May 5, Vaclav Havel's Czech satire, *The Memorandum* bows. Papp directs; the show has 49 performances.

March 19 Vienna's famed *Burgtheater*, the Austrian National Theatre, comes to New York City Center for a limited engagement of four plays: Arthur Schnitzler's *Professor Bernhardi* (with Ernst Deutsch), Hermann Bahr's *Das Konzert*, Friedrich Schiller's *Maria Stuart*, and Johann Nestroy's *Einen Jux will er sich machen* (starring Austria's beloved comic, Josef Meinrad). The last play has been Thornton Wilder's source for *The Merchant of Yonkers* and *The Matchmaker*, which makes it the grandfather of *Hello, Dolly!* The shows are directed, respectively, by Kurt Meisel, Meinrad, Rudolf Steinbock, and Axel von Ambesser. Among the Burg's distinguished players are Ewald Balser, Sebastian Fischer, and Adrienne Gessner. There are six performances of each play in German.

April 3 At Stratford-upon-Avon, the Royal Shakespeare Company again has a basic "gray box" for its stage-space as it did last season. John Barton's production of *Julius Caesar* opens the season, with Brewster Mason. Eric Porter plays Lear in Trevor Nunn's production of *King Lear*. Tim O'Brien and Tazeena Firth design a much admired Terry Hands production of *The Merry Wives of Windsor*, with Mason, Ian Richardson, Brenda Bruce, and Elizabeth Spriggs. *As You Like It* is revived from last season. Marlowe's *Doctor Faustus*, with Porter as Faustus, has staging by Clifford Williams. Barton stages *Troilus and Cressida*, with Michael Williams and Helen Mirren. Nunn directs *Much Ado About Nothing*, with Alan Howard and Janet Suzman.

April 7 London's Royal Court Theatre, interested in helping Edward Bond develop as a writer, shows his *Early Morning*, which has Queen Victoria involved in an affair with Florence Nightingale. This is a private performance for critics and friends. The play is not the sort to please the Lord Chamberlain's censors. William Gaskill directs Moira Redmond and Marianne Faithfull among others.

April 15 It's World Theatre Season again at London's Aldwych Theatre. It begins with Ladislav Fialka and his Balustrade Mime Group from Prague, playing *The Clowns*, followed on April 18 by *The Fools*. On April 25, the Balustrade's Drama Group presents Jarry's *King Ubu*, staged by Jan Grossman. On April 29, The Theatre de France opens with Paul Claudel's *Partage de Midi*, directed and performed by Jean-Louis Barrault, with Edwige Feuillere among the cast. On May 6, Barrault presents Francois Billetdoux's *Il Faut Passer par les Nuages*, with Madeleine Renaud among the cast. On May 9, Barrault offers Beaumarchais's *Le Barbier de Seville*, with Dominique Paturel as Figaro. Rome's Stabile Theatre Company opens on May 13, with Raffaele Viviani's *Naples By Night, Naples by Day*, directed by Giuseppie Patroni Griffi. Dublin's Abbey Theatre opens on May 20, with Boucicault's *The Shaughran*, staged by Hugh Hunt. Cyril Cusak heads the cast. On June 3, the Royal Dramatic Theatre of Stockholm opens with Henrik Ibsen's *Hedda Gabler*. Ingmar Bergman stages. Japan's Bunraku National Theatre opens next, on June 10, with puppet performances of *Kanadehon Chushingura*, *Tsubosaka*, *Kannon Reigenki*, and *Tsuri Onna*. On June 17, the troupe offers a second program.

April 16 Two American plays by Lanford Wilson are staged at London's Mercury Theatre: *Home Free* and *The Madness of Lady Bright*. Marshal W. Mason, directs and designs. There are 19 performances.

April 25 At New York City Center, the Center's Gilbert & Sullivan Company presents a repertory of five G & S shows: *The Pirates of Penzance*, *H. M. S. Pinafore*, *The Mikado*, *The Yeomen of the Guard*, and *Patience*. Allen Fletcher and others direct.

April 28 Adrienne Kennedy's American plays *A Lesson in a Dead Language* and *Funnyhouse of a Negro*, directed by Rob Knights, open in London at the Royal Court Theatre. On May 8, Michel Rosen's *Backbone*, staged by Bill Bryden, opens. On May 23, there is a major event when John Osborne's new play, *Time Present* opens, staged by Anthony Page. Jill Bennett—Mrs. Osborne—is in the cast. On July 3, another new Osborne script is premiered, *The Hotel in Amsterdam*. Among the cast members are Paul Scofield and Isabel Dean. Again, Anthony Page stages.

April 28 John Guare's *Muzeeka* and Sam Shepard's *Red Cross*, seen earlier Off-off-Broadway, open Off-Broadway at the Provincetown Playhouse for a run of 65 performances. Melvin Bernhardt and Jacques Levy direct, respectively.

May 1 Molière's *The Imaginary Invalid*, complete with *Commedia* interludes, is staged by Janos Nyiri at London's Vaudeville Theatre.

May 8 At New York's Cafe Au Go Go, producers Lyn Austin, Hale Matthews, and Oliver Smith present *Collision Course*, a program of 11 avant-garde one-act plays, staged by Edward Parone. There are 80 performances of the bill, featuring the talents of Lanford Wilson (*Wandering*), Leonard Melfi (*Stars and Stripes*), Jack Larson (*Chuck*), Rosalyn Drexler (*Skywriting*), Harvey Perr (*Jew!*), Jean-Claude van Itallie and Sharon Thie (*Thoughts on the Instant of Greeting a Friend on the Street*), Terrence McNally (*Tour*), Robert Patrick (*Camera Obscura*), Martin Duberman (*Metaphors*), Jules Feiffer (*The Unexpurgated Memoirs of Bernard Mergendeiler*), and Israel Horovitz (*Rats*).

May 8 Terence Rattigan's *The Sleeping Prince* is revived at London's St. Martin's Theatre, staged by George Baker. Susan Hampshire plays the ingenue.

May 22 John Clements presents four plays in the annual Chichester Festival in Southern England. Peter Ustinov's *The Unknown Soldier and His Wife* premieres, with Ustinov staging and starring. T. S. Eliot's *The Cocktail Party* is staged by Alec Guinness, who plays the leading role. David Jones directs Shakespeare's *The Tempest*, with Clements as Prospero. Thornton Wilder's *The Skin of Our Teeth*, directed by Peter Coe, is the final production, with Millicent Martin in the cast.

May 23 Michael Kermoyan is the king, with Constance Towers as Anna, in this New York City Center revival of Richard Rodgers and Oscar Hammerstein II's *The King and I*, staged by John Fearnley. Jerome Robbins's choreography is reproduced by Yuriko. It runs three weeks. On June 13, Alan Lerner and Frederick Loewe's *My Fair Lady* returns to City Center for 22 showings, staged by Samuel Liff. Inga Swenson is Eliza and Fritz Weaver is Higgins.

May 28 To New York comes Genoa's *Teatro Stabile di Genova*, with its much-admired production of Carlo Goldoni's 18th century comedy, *I Due Gemelli Veneziani (The Venetian Twins)*. The company performs in Italian for four weeks. Luigi Squarzina directs.

June 4 In London's Regent's Park, Shakespeare's *The Merry Wives of Windsor* is presented in the Open Air Theatre. Richard Digby Day stages. On July 17, Day opens *Two Gentlemen of Verona*, with Bernard Bresslaw, Gemma Jones, and Peter Egan.

June 6 Ivor Novello's big success, *Dancing Years*, is revived in London at the Saville Theatre, with Joan Davis staging. On June 8, at the Cambridge Theatre, the musical revival is *The Student Prince*, staged by Leslie Branch. On July 25, George Gershwin's *Lady Be Good* opens in revival at the Saville Theatre. Hugh Goldie stages.

June 10 Jean Gascon begins his tenure as artistic director of Canada's Stratford Shakespeare Festival, scheduling a program including opera—Rossini's *Cinderella (La Cenerentola)*, staged by Douglas Campbell—and ballet—The Royal Winnipeg Ballet. *Romeo and Juliet*, is staged by Campbell. John Hirsch stages *A Midsummer Night's Dream*. Gascon stages Molière's *Tartuffe*. Hirsch directs *The Three Musketeers*. Gascon directs Chekov's *The Seagull*, designed by Brian Jackson. He also designs Beckett's *Waiting for Godot*, directed by William Hutt. Hutt, Martha Henry and Max Helpmann, are familiar faces in the Festival ensemble. Christopher Walken is new.

June 11 The San Diego National Shakespeare Festival, performing in the Old Globe Theatre in Balboa Park, opens with *Hamlet*, staged by Ellis Rabb. Robert Moss directs *As You Like It*, with producing director Craig Noel staging *King John*.

June 11 The New York Shakespeare Festival presents a program of three plays in its Central Park Delacorte Theatre, with tonight's opening performance rained out during its progress: *Henry IV, Parts 1 and 2*, staged by Gerald Freedman; with James Ray, Sam Waterston, and Stacy Keach. *Romeo and Juliet*, staged by festival founder Joseph Papp; with Martin Sheen and Susan McArthur.

June 12 Eugene O'Neill's *A Moon for the Misbegotten* features Salome Jens and Mitchell Ryan. Theodore Mann stages this Circle in the Square revival, which runs 25 weeks.

June 22 The American Shakespeare Festival in Stratford, Connecticut, opens its public season with a repertory of four plays: *Richard II*, staged by Michael Kahn, with a cast including Donald Madden and Richard Mathews. *As You Like It*, staged by Stephen Porter, with Stefan Gierasch and Marian Hailey among others. *Androcles and the Lion*, by George Bernard Shaw, staged by Nikos Psacharopoulos with Gene Troobnick and Jan Miner among others. *Love's Labour's Lost*, staged by Kahn with Charles Siebert among others.

June 24 At Lincoln Center's New York State Theatre, Richard Rodgers, as producing director of the Music Theatre revivals, offers Leonard Bernstein's *West Side Story* for a run of 11 weeks.

June 25 Roger Planchon brings his Compagnie du Théâtre de la Cité de Villeurbanne to the Vivian Beaumont Theatre for the Lincoln Center Festival, opening with his adaptation of *The Three Musketeers*, followed by Molière's *George Dandin* and *Tartuffe*. There are 19 performances in French.

In the Forum Theatre, beneath the Vivian Beaumont Theatre, the Serbo-Croat *Atelje 212* presents a four-play repertory as part of the Lincoln Center Festival. The plays are *The Progress of Bora, the Tailor*, *Ubu Roi*, *Who's Afraid of Virginia Woolf?*, and *Victor, or the Children Take Over*. This is a three-week engagement.

June 27 Kermit Hunter's *The Liberty Tree*, about the American Revolution in South Carolina, is presented in the University of South Carolina Outdoor Theatre, in Columbia. It is sponsored and produced by the Palmetto Outdoor Historical Drama Association.

July 14 *The Great Passion Play* is Robert A. Hyde's adaptation from the Bible of the last few weeks of Jesus' life. It is presented in Eureka Springs, Arkansas, at Mount Oberammergau.

July 15 Terry Hands' production of *The Merry Wives of Windsor*, with Timothy O'Brien's decors, comes to the RSC's London house, the Aldwych Theatre, following its presentation at Stratford-upon-Avon. On Aug 15, Vanburgh's Restoration comedy *The Relapse* is revived. Trevor Nunn stages.

July 20 In Ashland, the annual Oregon Shakespearean Festival opens with *Cymbeline*, staged by James Sandoe. There are four plays by Shakespeare and one musical in the repertory this summer. *Hamlet* is directed by Patrick Hines; *As You Like it*, by William Kinsolving, and *Henry VIII*, by Richard Risso. Bernard Miles' adaptation of *Rape Upon Rape*, the musical *Lock Up Your Daughters*, is staged by Carl Ritchie.

July 21 In Canada, the Shaw Festival at Niagara-on-the-Lake opens its nine-week season with *Heartbreak House*, directed by Val Gielgud. Micheal macLiammoir performs his one-man show, *The Importance of Being Oscar*. Paxton Whitehead directs Feydeau's *La Main Passe*, translated by Suzanne Grossman as *The Chemmy Circle*.

July 25 Brian Friel's *Lovers* opens at New York's Vivian Beaumont. Made up of two one-act plays, *Winners* and *Losers*, it comes to Lincoln Center from the Dublin Gate Theatre, staged here as there by Hilton Edwards. Art Carney narrates the first play, and plays a role in the second. The production is well received and moves to Broadway's Music Box Theatre for a total of 148 performances. This is a "Best Play." It opens in London at the Fortune Theatre on Aug 25, 1969, for only 27 performances.

Aug 9 Frank Cranford has written *From This Day Forward*, a play telling the story of the Waldenses who came from the Cottian Alps to the foothills of North Carolina. It is presented in the Old Colony Amphitheatre in Valdese by the Old Colony Players.

Aug 18 Britain's Edinburgh International Festival opens. The 69 Theatre Company offers *Hamlet*, staged by Caspar Wrede and designed by Malcolm Pride. Tom Courtenay plays the prince. Also staged in the Assembly Hall is the troupe's production of Ibsen's *When We Dead Awaken*, staged by Michael Elliott. From Rhode Island comes Adrian Hall with his Trinity Square Repertory Company in Norman Holland's *Years of the Locust*. The Traverse Theatre Club offers Eugene O'Neill's *Mourning Becomes Electra*. From Wroclaw in Poland comes Jerzy Grotowski with his "Poor Theatre" and his production of *Acropolis*. Dublin's Abbey Theatre contributes a revival of Synge's *The Playboy of the Western World*, staged by Thomas MacAnna. Michael Blakemore stages Bertolt Brecht's *The Resistible Rise of Arturo Ui* for Glasgow's Citizens' Theatre.

Aug 19 London's National Youth Theatre again offers its end-of-summer productions. Peter Terson's *The Apprentices*, staged by the theatre's director, Michael Croft, opens in the Jeannetta Cochrane Theatre. On Sep 4, the troupe performs *Richard the Second* at the Collegiate Theatre, with Paul Hill directing.

HOUSE OF ATREUS

Aug 28 Michel Tremblay's first major play *Les Belles Soeurs* opens at Montreal's Rideau Vert Theatre. About a woman who wins a million trading stamps in a lottery, it is the first Quebec play to be written entirely in *joual*, the everyday language of Quebec. It will be named Best Foreign Play of the Year in Paris in 1973.

Sep 3 At Broadway's Lyceum Theatre, the APA-Phoenix ensemble revives of two of its recent productions: de Ghelderode's *Pantagleize*, staged by John Houseman and Ellis Rabb, and Kelly's *The Show-Off*, directed by Stephen Porter. There are 28 performances. On Oct 7, the APA ensemble opens its production of T. S. Eliot's *The Cocktail Party*. Molière's *The Misanthrope* follows. Sean O'Casey's *Cock-A-Doodle Dandy* comes next. *Hamlet*, staged by Ellis Rabb, who also gloomily acts the prince, is the last production, ringing the death-knell of the APA. The ensemble includes Brian Bedford and Barry Bostwick.

Sep 11 At London's Royal Court Theatre, *Total Eclipse*, by Christopher Hampton, deals with the destructive affair between Arthur Rimbaud and Paul Verlaine. Robert Kidd stages. On Oct 2, David Cregan's *The Houses by the Green* opens, directed by Jane Howell. On the 13th, Barry Hanson shows his staging of *The Tutor*, by Jakob Lenz. On the 29th, John Osborne's *Look Back in Anger* is revived. On Nov 4, Michael McClure's San Francisco sensation of absurdist playwriting, *The Beard*, opens at the Court as a late-night production. John Hopkins' *This Story of Yours*, opens on Dec 11.

Sep 12 Richard Pilbrow and Harold Prince co-produce Toby Robertson's new staging of John Gay's *The Beggar's Opera*. London's Apollo Theatre is the venue, but only for 68 performances.

Sep 24 At London's Old Vic, the National Theatre presents *The Advertisement*, a play by Natalia Ginzburg, translated by Henry Reed. Laurence Olivier and Donald MacKechnie co-direct. Joan Plo-

wright plays the lead. On Oct 8, Frank Dunlop's revival of W. Somerset Maugham's *Home and Beauty* opens, with Geraldine McEwan and Robert Stephens. Olivier directs *Love's Labour's Lost*, opening on Dec 19, with Plowright and Jeremy Brett.

Sep 30 At the Billy Rose Theatre on Broadway, Edward Albee and Richard Barr, producers of Theatre 1969, present a Playwrights' Repertory of plays usually seen Off-Broadway. Tonight is the New York premiere of Albee's *Box*, in which the voice of Ruth White is heard on an empty stage, followed by *Quotations from Chairman Mao*. Albee's *The Death of Bessie Smith*, *The American Dream*, and *The Zoo Story* are also performed, as are Beckett's *Krapp's Last Tape* and *Happy Days*.

Oct 2 After a voluntary exile in Europe, Julian Beck and Judith Malina's Living Theatre has returned to the United States. Tonight they open a program of their recent works at the Brooklyn Academy of Music (BAM). *Frankenstein* is this evening's piece. On Oct 9, *Mysteries and Smaller Pieces* is played, followed on the 10th by *The Antigone of Sophokles*, a Malina adaptation of Brecht's adaptation. On Oct 14, in *Paradise Now*, company members move through the audience, disrobing and inviting the audience to do the same and join them on the stage. Drama critic and cultist Richard Schechner promptly joins in, appalling some and amusing others around him.

Oct 17 At St. Clement's Church in midtown Manhattan, the American Place Theatre presents a new season of four programs. Tonight the play is George Tabori's *Cannibals*. Martin Fried stages. On Dec 12, a triple-bill opens, featuring David Trainer's *The Acquisition*, Philip Hayes Dean's *The Bird of Dawning Singeth All Night Long*, and Werner Liepolt's *The Young Master Dante*. The first production has 40 performances; the second, 44.

Oct 18 This season at the Master Theatre

on Riverside Drive, the Equity Library Theatre (ELT) presents the following works in revival: *Of Thee I Sing*, *All My Sons*, *As You Like It*, *Five Finger Exercise*, *Sacco-Vanzetti!*, *Purlie Victorious*, *Night Must Fall*, *She Loves Me*, and *Accent on Youth*.

Oct 29 The D'Oyly Carte Opera Company returns to New York, opening at the City Center with *H. M. S. Pinafore*. The rest of its Gilbert & Sullivan repertory consists of *Patience*, *The Mikado*, *The Pirates of Penzance*, and *Iolanthe* on this visit.

Oct 29 At London's Mermaid Theatre, *The Goblet Game*, by Rex Edwards, is the new play. Rom Pember stages. On Dec 18, Bernard Miles has a new holiday show, Sean Kenny's version of *Gulliver's Travels*, directed and designed by Kenny.

Oct 30 At London's Haymarket Theatre, Jean Anouilh's *Ring Round the Moon* is revived, staged by Noel Willman. This is the Christopher Fry translation, with music by Richard Addinsell. John Standing, Isabel Jeans and Flora Robson are in the cast. The production runs for three months.

Nov 6 T. S. Eliot's *The Cocktail Party*, revived initially for the Chichester Festival by Alec Guinness, now opens in the West End at Wyndham's Theatre. Guinness takes the lead. On the 19th, Cicely Courtneidge is featured in the Duke of York's revival of *Dear Charles*, Alan Melville's adaptation of a French play, staged by Alexander Doré. The production runs nearly 19 weeks.

Nov 7 At the Vivian Beaumont Theatre, the Repertory Theatre of Lincoln Center opens its new season with *King Lear*, staged by Gerald Freedman and featuring Lee J. Cobb. On Nov 14, William Gibson's *A Cry of Players* opens, to play in repertory with *Lear*. Frank Langella plays Will Shakespeare, Anne Bancroft is Anne Hathaway. Each production has 72 performances.

Nov 12 Gotthold Ephraim Lessing's *Minna von Barnhelm* opens in New York at the Barbizon-Plaza Theatre, the first of two German-language productions by Germany's *Die Bruecke*. Max Brod's adaptation of Franz Kafka's *The Castle* follows in this two-week engagement.

Nov 29 Brewster Mason plays the title-role in John Barton's staging of *Julius Caesar*, opening now at the RSC's Aldwych Theatre in London.

Dec 5 The Repertory Theatre of Lincoln Center opens a season of experimental plays in the Forum Theatre. Tonight, John White's *Bananas* is staged by Robert Symonds. On Dec 29, the bill is called *An Evening for Merlin Finch*, composed of that play and *A Great Career*, both by Charles Dizenzo. George Sherman directs. Sada Thompson and Philip Bosco are among the actors.

Dec 12 It's that time of year, and at the Westminster Theatre in London, it's also that old children's show again, *Give a Dog a Bone*. The next day, Barrie's *Peter Pan* is revived at the Scala Theatre. On December 16, the Arts Theatre presents *The Prince, The Wolf, and The Firebird*. Other entertainments include *Jack and the Beanstalk* (Palladium), *The Servant of Two Masters* (Queen's). *Gulliver's Travels* (Mermaid), *Cinderella* (Players'), *Toad of Toad Hall* (Duke of York's), and *Queen Passionella and the Sleeping Beauty*, staged at the Saville Theatre with a notably long run for Christmas pantomime, largely owing to the presence in the cast of the glamorous female-impersonater, Danny LaRue.

Dec 17 The Minnesota Theatre Company comes to Broadway and the Billy Rose Theatre with two productions: *The House of Atreus*, adapted by John Lewin from Aeschylus' *Oresteia*, and Bertolt Brecht's *The Resistible Rise of Arturo Ui*. Tyrone Guthrie stages the first, which has 17 showings; Edward Payson Call directs the Brecht, which plays 14 times. Among the company are Len Cariou and Douglas Campbell.

Dec 17 The Negro Ensemble Company at the St. Marks Playhouse in Greenwich Village opens a new season of four plays with Ray McIver's *God is a (Guess What?)*, with music by Coleride-Taylor Perkinson. Lynching and minstrelsy are intertwined. Michael Schultz directs, with Louis Johnson choreographing. This runs for four weeks.

1968   BIRTHS/DEATHS/DEBUTS

Jan 10 British actor Basil Sydney has died, aged 73.

Jan 16 Veteran actor Guy Bates is dead at 92.

Jan 18 Stage and screen actor Bert Wheeler (b. 1895) dies in New York. Wheeler made his 1923 Broadway debut in the *Ziegfeld Follies*. He appeared in vaudeville, stock, and films.

Feb 11 American actor, dramatist, and producer Howard Lindsay (b. 1889) dies in New York. Lindsay collaborated with Russel Crouse on the dramatization of Clarence Day's *Life With Father* in 1939, in which Lindsay starred; *The Sound of Music*; and the Pulitzer Prize-winning *State of the Union*.

Feb 17 English actor-manager Sir Donald Wolfit (b. 1902) dies in London. Sir Donald was best known for the many Shakespeare productions he directed and appeared in. He was knighted in 1957 and wrote an autobiography, *First Interval*.

Feb 28 Remembered for her role as Bloody Mary in *South Pacific*, actress Juanita Hall is dead at 66.

March 20 British actor Derek Oldham has died, aged 75.

April 16 Author Edna Ferber (b. 1887) dies in New York. Ferber collaborated with George S. Kaufman on such plays as *Dinner at Eight* and *Stage Door*. Her novel, *Show Boat*, was adapted for the musical stage by Jerome Kern and Oscar Hammerstein II. She wrote two autobiographies, *A Peculiar Treasure* and *A Kind of Magic*.

April 16 Stage and screen actress Fay Bainter (b. 1892) dies in Beverly Hills. Her notable Broadway roles included Lady Mary Lasenby in *The Admirable Crichton*.

May 5 Stage and screen actor Albert Dekker (b. 1905) dies in Hollywood. His portrayal of the Duke of Norfolk in Robert Bolt's *A Man for All Seasons* at the ANTA Theatre in 1961 was praised.

May 7 British actress Olga Lindo is dead.

May 9 American actress Marian Lorne (b. 1888) dies in New York. She appeared on the New York and London stages, and was known for her portrayals of fluffy-minded women in such plays as *Other Men's Wives*, *Park Lane*, and *Hyde Park Corner*.

May 9 Veteran British stage and screen actor Finlay Currie dies, aged 90.

June 4 American stage and screen actress Dorothy Gish (b. 1898) dies in Rapallo, Italy. Gish made her first appearance on the stage in 1902. Her first New York role was in *East Lynne* in 1903. Gish played juvenile parts until 1912 when she turned to films. She resumed her stage career in 1928.

June 7 Stage and screen actor Dan Duryea (b. 1907) dies today in Hollywood.

June 8 English actress Patricia Jessel (b. 1920) dies in London. Jessel's first stage appearance was as Wendy in *Peter Pan*, in 1933. She was known for her role as Romaine in *Witness for the Prosecution* and for many Shakespearean roles in actor-manager Donald Wolfit's touring company.

Aug 26 American actress Kay Francis dies.

Oct 11 Canadian-born dancer, producer, and director George White is dead at 78 in Hollywood. White appeared in the *Ziegfeld Follies of 1915*. He produced and acted in the *Scandals of 1919*, which became known as *George White's Scandals*.

Sep 18 American stage and screen actor Franchot Tone, long with the Theatre Guild, dies at 63.

Oct 18 American actor Lee Tracy dies, aged 70.

Oct 20 Bud Flanagan, of London's beloved Crazy Gang, dies today at age 72.

Oct 30 American stage and screen actress Pert Kelton is dead at age 61. *The Music Man*, *Greenwillow*, and *Come Blow Your Horn* were among her more recent Broadway appearances.

Dec 12 Vibrant stage and screen star Tallulah Bankhead (b. 1903) is dead at 65 in New York. She was the daughter of former Speaker of the House of Representatives, William Brockman Bankhead. Her two most notable stage roles were Regina in *The Little Foxes* and Sabina in *The Skin of Our Teeth*. Her autobiography, *Tallulah*, was published in 1952.

1968   THEATERS/PRODUCTIONS

U.S. patents granted this year include one to Howard Wolfe for his theatre structure which has audience seating around a central stage. The stage can be raised up into an attic for scenery changes.

Theatre Passe Muraille—literally, "Theatre Without Walls"—begins as a drama project at Rochdale College, Toronto, Canada, with the aim of bringing theatre and community closer together. Managing directors Jim Garrard (1968–69) and Martin Kinch (1970) move the theatre "outside the walls of Rochdale," and Paul Thompson becomes the catalyst for this unique group. They perform collective works such as *The Farm Show* (1972), which is created out of the company's experience living in the farming community of Clinton, Ontario, where the show premieres.

Jan 30 It is announced that in June Trevor Nunn will become chief of the Royal Shakespeare Company and its activities in Stratford-upon-Avon and in London at the Aldwych Theatre.

April 8 Ed Berman writes and directs *Super Santa*, for the Ambiance Lunch-Hour Theatre Club, which he has just founded in London. In 1972, he will change the name to The Almost Free Theatre. Among the new playwrights represented is John Arden.

May 31 At the official end of the Broadway season, those shows which have paid off their production costs qualify for *Variety's* list of hits. Successful shows this season include: *Rosencrantz and Guildenstern Are Dead*, *There's a Girl in My Soup*, *Marlene Dietrich*, *The Only Game in Town*, *The Price*, *Everything in the Garden*, *Plaza Suite*, *More Stately Mansions*, *The Little Foxes*, *The Prime of Miss Jean Brodie*, *A Day in the Death of Joe Egg*, and *The Seven Descents of Myrtle*.

Summer Walter Learning stages four plays at the Playhouse Auditorium in Fredericton, New Brunswick, Canada, on a $5,000 provincial grant. 5,883 people attend. In the fall, Learning proposes a winter schedule and tour of other provincial centres, and Theatre New Brunswick is born.

Summer The O'Keefe Brewing Company of Toronto, Canada, complaining of $1000-a-day taxes, donates the 3200-seat O'Keefe Centre to the City of Toronto, retaining title to the land underneath it.

June 1 At the close of the current Broadway season, there have been 84 shows, 25 of them new American plays and 10 of them musicals. The balance includes 16 revivals, 1 revue, 6 specialties, 17 foreign plays in English, and 9 foreign-language productions. According to *Variety*, the seasonal gross is nearly $59 million. Road company grosses raise that figure to over $140 million. Broadway musical failures have lost over $3 million. Producer David Merrick's *Mata Hari* closed out of town with a half-million loss. Off-Broadway productions number 72 at the close of the current season. In America's regional or "resident theatres" there have been 291 productions of 214 plays, mounted by 37 groups in 44 theatres. Shakespeare leads the pack of playwrights.

This Broadway season's ten "Best Plays," as chosen by editor Otis Guernsey, Jr., are Bowen's *After the Rain*, Freedman's *Scuba Duba*, Stoppard's *Rosencrantz and Guildenstern Are Dead*, Dyer's *Staircase*, Driver/Hester/Apolinar's *Your Own Thing*, Nichols' *A Day in the Death of Joe Egg*, Miller's *The Price*, Anderson's *I Never Sang For My Father*, Crowley's *The Boys in the Band*, and Simon's *Plaza Suite*.

June 17 Members of New York Actors Equity go out on strike, closing 19 Broadway shows. The Equity contract has expired on June 2, and new contract negotiations are snagged over minimums and the irritating issue of hiring foreign—especially British—actors for roles unemployed American actors could be playing. On June 19, in an all-night meeting at Gracie Mansion with Mayor Lindsay, the issues are resolved. The minimum rises from $130 to $155 a week; chorus members can't be fired after 20 weeks with a show, and no aliens can replace American actors in a show. Appearances of foreigners in new productions will be subject to arbitration. During the strike, producers close three shows permanently. The strike costs actors $80,000 in wages; producers lose $400,000 in gross receipts.

July In front of the imposing white Latter Day Saints Temple in Manti, Utah, the Mormon Miracle Pageant opens for its second summer of performance. It will, by the late 1970's, have eight performances a summer.

July 18 Today the Robert S. Mark Theatre opens in Cincinnati, the second theatre in the Playhouse in the Park complex. Hugh Hardy, has designed the 672-seat theatre with its irregular thrust stage at the center of the steeply tiered rows. Costing $900,000, the theatre is baptised with Tennessee Williams's *Camino Real*.

Aug 21 The London Coliseum re-opens as the new home of the Sadler's Wells Opera Company. (In 1974, the company will be renamed the English National Opera.)

Sep 26 Today the Act of Parliament abolishing the function of censor of plays, exercised by the Lord Chamberlain (since 1737) takes effect. Producers and playwrights will no longer have to submit scripts to the Chamberlain's office. The London premiere of *Hair* has been planned to take place after the office ceases operations.

Oct 23 Theatre Calgary, Alberta, Canada, opens with Neil Simon's *The Odd Couple*, under artistic director Christopher Newton, in the 493-seat Allied Arts Theatre, a converted tractor warehouse.

Oct 29 Six years ago, 122 prominent Atlantans were killed in an air crash in Paris as they sought to widen their cultural horizons. Today, the Georgia metropolis opens the cultural complex constructed in their memory: the Atlanta Memorial Arts Center, costing over $13 million. The building and operations are supervised by the Atlanta Arts Alliance, which now has under one roof the Atlanta Symphony, the Atlanta Repertory Theatre Company, the Atlanta Ballet, the Atlanta Opera, the Atlanta School of Art, and the High Museum of Art. Robert Shaw directs the Symphony, performing in its 1,900-seat theatre. Blanche Thebom directs the Opera. Michael Howard directs the theatre activity, in the 800-seat Alliance Theatre. A central galleria, 230' long by 50' wide, links the various elements of the complex.

Nov 28 Nina Vance's Alley Theatre opens in Houston, Texas, designed by Ulrich Franzen, in consultation with Paul Owen. Dedicated to open-stagings, the Alley has two theatres.

Dec 14 The Chelsea Theater Center, now the resident theatre company of the Brooklyn Academy of Music (BAM), opens with *Christophe*, by John Gay, directed by founder Robert Kalfin. In October 1973, the Chelsea expands its operation into Manhattan taking a lease on a renovated church at 407 West 43rd Street, which it calls the Westside Theater. In 1978 Chelsea's association with BAM ends. The Westside Theater becomes the Chelsea Theater Center, and the building is renovated to include three performance spaces.

Jan 2 *To Be Young, Gifted, and Black* (NY—Cherry Lane—Revue). Robert Nemiroff salutes the memory of black playwright-novelist Lorraine Hansberry with a collage of her work, staged by Gene Frankel. Barbara Bazley and Cicely Tyson are among the cast. There are 380 performances.

Jan 5 *Little Murders*. See NY premiere, 1967.

Jan 8 *Hadrian the Seventh*. See L premiere, 1968.

Jan 12 *Geese* (NY—Players—Drama). Gus Weill's two one-act plays, *Geese* and *Parents and Children*, about lesbianism and homosexuality respectively, have 336 performances. Among the players are Kenneth Carr and Dan Halleck. Philip Osterman stages.

Jan 18 *Tango* (NY—Pocket—Drama). Slawomir Mrozek's Polish absurdist drama runs two months Off-Broadway, in a Heinz Engels staging. Among the cast are David Margulies and Stefan Schnabel.

Jan 22 *Celebration* (NY—Ambassador—Musical). There are only 109 performances, but Tom Jones's fable of young love menaced by corruption is selected as a "Best Play." Jones stages, with music by Harvey Schmidt. Susan Watson is the girl, and Ted Thurston plays old Mr. Rich.

Jan 26 *Red, White and Maddox* (NY—Cort—Musical). Co-author and director Jay Broad's satire on Georgia's governor Lester Maddox and his racist policies, has only a 5-week run. Jay Garner plays Maddox. Broad's collaborator, Don Tucker, also provides the music.

Feb 6 *Dear World* (NY—Mark Hellinger—Musical). Angela Lansbury and Milo O'Shea head the cast, but Jean Giraudoux's *The Madwoman of Chaillot*, adapted as a musical by Jerome Lawrence and Robert E. Lee, has only 132 performances. Jerry Herman writes the score; Joe Layton directs and choreographs.

Feb 10 *Adaptation/Next* (NY—Greenwich Mews—Comedy). Elaine May and Terrence McNally are the respective authors of this double-bill which has 707 showings, and is chosen as a "Best Play." Gabe Dell plays a contestant in a television game in *Adaptation*. In *Next* James Coco plays an overweight potential draftee. May stages.

Feb 12 *Play It Again, Sam* (NY—Broadhurst—Comedy). Woody Allen and Diane Keaton head the cast in Allen's fantasy about a failed husband who believes he can achieve a rich romantic life by modeling himself on Humphrey Bogart. Joseph Hardy directs the 453 performances. On September 11, Hardy also directs the London production at the Globe Theatre, with Dudley Moore. It has 355 showings.

March 16 *1776* (NY—46th Street—Musical). Peter Stone's book, about the personal enmities and regional differences that lay behind the signing of the Declaration of Independence, is selected as a "Best Play," wins the Drama Critics' Circle Award for Best Musical, and earns 1,217 performances. Howard Da Silva and William Daniels are among the large cast. Peter Hunt directs and Sherman Edwards writes the music. There are 168 performances of the musical in London following its premiere at the New Theatre on June 16, 1970.

April 23 *The Gingham Dog* (NY—John Golden—Drama). Later in his career Lanford Wilson will win the Pulitzer Prize, but this drama about an interracial marriage (Diana Sands and George Grizzard) has only five performances on Broadway.

May 11 *In the Bar of a Tokyo Hotel* (NY—Eastside—Drama). Tennessee Williams's play about a failed marriage has just 25 performances. Herbert Machiz directs Donald Madden and Anne Meacham.

June 4 *Promenade* (NY—Promenade—Musical). Ty McConnell and Gilbert Price play a pair of jailbirds in Maria Irene Fornes's fey libretto, with music by the Rev. Al Carmines. It has an eight-month run. Lawrence Kornfeld directs.

June 17 *Oh! Calcutta!* (NY—Eden—Revue). Clive Barnes (*NY Times*) calls it "a silly little diversion," but Kenneth Tynan's erotic revue moves from Second Avenue to Broadway for a run of 1,314 performances. Samuel Beckett, John Lennon, and Jules Feiffer are among the show's contributors; Margo Sappington provides the choreography; The Open Window provides music and lyrics. Jacques Levy directs. The show premieres in London at the Round House on July 27, 1970. Later, it returns to Broadway for an extended run with 2,410 showings on June 16, 1982.

July 30 *A Black Quartet* (NY—Tambellini's Gate—Drama). The Chelsea Theatre Center and Woody King Associates present a program of four black plays: Ben Caldwell's *Prayer Meeting or The First Militant Minister*, Ronald Milner's *The Warning—A Theme for Linda*, Ed Bullins's *The Gentleman Caller*, and LeRoi Jones's *Great Goodness of Life*. There are 111 performances.

Sep 4 *The Reckoning* (NY—St. Mark's Playhouse—Drama). Actor-author Douglas Turner Ward's play, about a white governor (Lester Rawlins) and his confrontation with a black pimp, runs for nearly three months. Michael Schultz stages.

Sep 29 *Salvation* (NY—Jan Hus—Musical). Peter Link and C. C. Courtney create and appear in this rock revue which has a run of 30 weeks.

1776

Oct 20 *A Scent of Flowers*. See L premiere, 1964.

Oct 21 *Butterflies Are Free* (NY—Booth—Comedy). Keir Dullea plays a young blind man trying to make a life on his own, in Leonard Gershe's play which has 1,128 performances. Eileen Heckart plays his interfering mother. Blythe Danner acts the girl he falls in love with. It is chosen one of the season's ten "Best Plays." The comedy runs only five weeks following its London premiere at the Apollo on Nov 4, 1970.

Dec 18 *Coco* (NY—Mark Hellinger—Musical). Katharine Hepburn stars and sings in Alan Jay Lerner's book about Coco Chanel, the French fashion designer, which has 332 performances. Lerner also provides the lyrics for Andre Previn's score. Michael Bennett choreographs, and Cecil Beaton creates the costumes and setting.

Dec 28 *Last of the Red Hot Lovers* (NY—Eugene O'Neill—Comedy). James Coco plays a chubby married man who fears the sexual revolution is passing him by in Neil Simon's three playlets. Chosen as a "Best Play," it has 706 performances.

1969 BRITISH PREMIERES

Jan 14 *A Delicate Balance.* See NY premiere, 1966.

Feb 11 *The Boys in the Band.* See NY premiere, 1968.

Feb 18 *Plaza Suite.* See NY premiere, 1968.

Feb 20 *Mame.* See NY premiere, 1966.

Feb 26 *The Ruling Class* (L—Piccadilly—Comedy). Derek Godfrey's performance in Peter Barnes's play about an eccentric, non-conformist earl, is called "extraordinary," but the comedy runs for only 11 weeks. Stuart Burge stages. (The play was originally performed in November 1968, at the Nottingham Playhouse.)

March 4 *The Price.* See NY premiere, 1968.

March 5 *What the Butler Saw* (L—Queen's—Comedy). Ralph Richardson, Stanley Baxter, and Coral Browne head the cast of Joe Orton's black comedy which, among other things, provides an unorthodox view of British medical practice. It has 101 performances. Orton's play opens at New York's McAlpin Rooftop on May 4, 1970. It runs for 224 performances and is chosen a "Best Play."

March 26 *Dutch Uncle* (L—Aldwych—Comedy). Peter Hall directs Simon Gray's play about the misadventures of a would-be wife-killer as part of the Royal Shakespeare Company's spring season. Warren Mitchell heads the cast.

April 17 *Ann Veronica* (L—Cambridge—Musical). Mary Miller plays the lead in Frank Wells and Ronald Gow's book, based on H. G. Wells's novel. Cyril Ornadel composes the score. David Croft directs and provides the lyrics.(It was first seen in February at Coventry's Belgrade Theatre.)

April 23 *The Au Pair Man* (L—Duchess—Comedy). Joan Greenwood and Donal McCann head the cast of Hugh Leonard's comedy, first seen at the Oxford Playhouse. Ted Kotcheff stages.

April 30 *Belle Starr* (L—Palace—Musical). Betty Grable stars in this Warren Douglas book about the 19th century female desperado Belle Starr. American TV personality Steve Allen composes the score, and with Douglas and director Jerry Schafer devises the lyrics. It doesn't last long.

July 2 *Landscape/Silence* (L—Aldwych—Drama). Peggy Ashcroft and David Waller appear in *Landscape*, the first part of Harold Pinter's new double-bill, directed by Peter Hall as part of the Royal Shakespeare Company's London season.

July 10 *Conduct Unbecoming* (L—Queen's—Drama). Barry England's play about British officers in India, who cover-up a sexual assault by one of their men, has 682 performances. Maxine Audley and Michael Barrington play major roles. Val May stages the play, which was first produced by the Bristol Old Vic Company. The drama comes to Broadway's Ethel Barrymore on Oct 12, 1970, for a run of 18 weeks. Paul Jones and Jeremy Clyde again play the newly posted young lieutenants who have to learn the rules of conduct. It is chosen a "Best Play."

Aug 27 *Dames at Sea.* See NY premiere, 1968.

Sep 22 *Pyjama Tops* (L—Whitehall—Comedy). One of the Whitehall's famous long-running farces (2,498 performances), this is Mawby Green's adaptation of Jean de Letraz's French comedy *Moumou.* Alexander Dore stages.

Oct 2 *Promises, Promises.* See NY premiere, 1968.

1969 REVIVALS/REPERTORIES

Jan 4 At Joseph Papp's Public Theatre in Greenwich Village, the season continues with *Cities in Bezique*, a program of two one-act plays by Adrienne Kennedy. They are staged by Gerald Freedman. Joan Harris, Cynthia Belgrave, and others are in the cast. On March 8, Vladimir Nabokov's *Invitation to a Beheading*, adapted by Russell McGrath, opens for 67 performances, the same number achieved by the previous bill. Freedman directs. Among the cast are Charles Durning and John Heffernan. On May 4, Charles Gordone's *No Place to Be Somebody* opens, staged by Ted Cornell. Nick Lewis plays a gangster who tyrannizes a black bar-keeper and some of his customers. The play is much admired and achieves a long life.

Jan 13 At London's Royal Court Theatre, *Life Price*, by Michael O'Neill and Jeremy Seabrook, opens in Peter Gill's staging. Jocelyn Herbert designs. On Feb 7, Edward Bond's *Saved* is revived. On the 19th, Bond's new play, *Narrow Road to the Deep North*, inspired by the life and poems of a Japanese, opens with Peter Needham. Jane Howell directs. The play has been first produced in Coventry at the Belgrade Theatre. On Feb 24, in the Upstairs theatre, the show is *A Comedy of the Changing Years*, by David Cregan. On the 27th New York's Paper Bag Players offer *Dandelion* Upstairs. On March 13, Edward Bond's *Early Morning*, previously given a special performance at the Court, now has fully staged performanced, directed by William Gaskill.

Moira Redmond and Shirley Ann Field play Queen Victoria and Florence Nightingale in this fantasy, which presumes the pair had a lesbian affair. On March 18, Sam Shepard's *La Turista*—set in Mexico—opens Upstairs, at the Court staged by Roger Hendricks-Simon. On April 22, David Storey's *In Celebration* shows three sons arriving to fete their aged parents. Lindsay Anderson stages. Alan Bates, James Bolam, and Brian Cox play the quite different sons. On July 6, John Antrobus offers his play, *Captain Oates' Left Sock*, tried out with no decor and staged by Barry Hanson. Michael Gough and Yvonne Antrobus are among the players. On the 15th, Peter Tegel has his play, *Blim at School*, done Upstairs at the Court, followed by *Poet of the Anemones*. On July 22, William Gaskill directs a revival of William Congreve's *The Double Dealer*. On Aug 6, director Peter Gill stages his own play, *Over Gardens Out*, Upstairs. On Sep 2, Howard Brenton's *Revenge* is seen Upstairs, in Chris Parr's staging. On Sep 17, Stanley Eveling's *Dear Janet Rosenberg, Dear Mr. Kooning* has an Upstairs opening, staged by Max Stafford-Clark. In the main theatre on the 25th, Madeleine Renaud plays in Marguerite Duras' *L'Amante Anglais*, staged by Claude Regy. On the 29th, she plays in Samuel Beckett's *Oh! Les Beaux Jours*, staged by Roger Blin. On Nov 9, Thomas Murphy's Irish play, *Famine*, opens in Clifford Williams's staging. On the 19th, Peter Gill stages his play, *The Sleeper's Den*, with Eileen Atkins. On Dec 1, the play is Frank Norman's *Insideout*, staged by Ken Campbell.

Jan 27 Aristophane's anti-war comedy *Peace* is updated as a musical by Tim Reynolds, at New York's Astor Place Theatre, with a score by the Rev. Al Carmines. Lawrence Kornfeld stages. The show has a run of 192 performances.

Jan 28 In Edinburgh at the Traverse Theatre, Stewart Conn's *Broche*, from the Edinburgh University Dramatic Society, opens the new year, which is to see some 27 productions. Among them are editions of *The People Show*, as well as Harold Pinter's *The Lover*, Carey Harrison's *In a Cottage Hospital*, David Hare's *How Brophy Made Good*, C. P. Taylor's *Lies About Vietnam*, John Heilpern's *The Man Who Almost Knew Eammon Andrews*, and Michael Almaz' *Monsieur Artaud*.

Feb 4 Frank Marcus's *The Window* opens the new year's season at Ed Berman's Ambiance Lunch-Hour Theater Club in London. Among the playwrights represented are Henry Livings and James Saunders. Directors include Berman, and Chris Parr. Actors include Richard Pasco, and Margaret Nolan. The plays include *Dog Accident, Strip-Stease*, and *A Who's Who of Flapland.*

Feb 4 Lonne Elder III offers his *Ceremonies in Dark Old Men* (a "Best Play") at the Negro Ensemble Company's St. Marks Playhouse in Greenwich Village. Douglas Turner (Ward), artistic director of the NEC, plays a former show-dancer who's trying to save his children from the consequences of folly in a big city. Edmund Cambridge directs. The show has a five-week run and is later shown Off-Broadway at the Pocket Theatre for another five. Subsequently it is widely produced around the U.S. and abroad. On March 25, the NEC opens *An Evening of One-Acts*, composed of Alice Childress' *String*, Ted Shine's *Contribution*, and Derek Walcott's *Malcochon*. Cambridge and Ward direct. There is a four-week run.

Feb 8 The National Theatre tries out *Macrune's Guevara*, an "experimental production," at the Jeannetta Cochrane Theatre in London. On Feb 11, John Plowright and Donald McKechnie direct *An Evasion of Women* for the National. This is a program of short plays by women writers, including Sheena Mackay's *Nurse Macateer*, Gillian Freeman's *Pursuit*, Margaret Drabble's *Bird of Paradise*, and Margaret Duffy's *Rites*. On the 17th, mime expert Claude Chagrin stages *Scrabble*.

Feb 14 The American Place Theatre continues its season of experimental plays in midtown Manhattan at St. Clement's Church. Ronald Tavel's *Boy on the Straight-Back Chair* opens tonight. Staged by Lee Von Rhau, the play suggests the career of Charles Starkweather, the hitch-hiking murderer. There are 38 performances. On April 17, Kenneth Cameron's *Papp* is unveiled. This production has a five-week run.

Feb 18 The Dublin Gate Theatre revives *Talking About Yeats*, followed by Stoppard's *Rosencrantz and Guildenstern Are Dead*. Other shows this year include Aleksei Arbuzov's *The Promise*, Micheal macLiammoir's *Ill Met by Moonlight* and *The Liar*, and Conor Cruise O'Brien's *King Herod Explains*. In October, the Gate will close for reconstruction, not to re-open until March 1971.

Feb 19 At London's Cambridge Theatre, Franz Lehar's *The Merry Widow* is revived, with Lizbeth Webb.

Feb 24 *The National Theatre of the Deaf* opens a two-week run in New York at the Longacre Theatre, offering programs including *The Tale of Kasane*, *On the Harmfulness of Tobacco*, *Gianni Schicchi*, *The Critic*, *Tyger! Tyger! And Other Burnings*, and *Blueprints: Projections and Perspectives*.

March 6 Gordon Davidson, artistic director of the Mark Taper Forum in Los Angles, comes to the Vivian Beaumont Theatre to restage Heinar Kipphardt's *In the Matter of J. Robert Oppenheimer*, seen first in America at the Taper. This is the third play in the season of the Repertory Theatre of Lincoln Center, directed by Jules Irving. Joseph Wiseman plays Oppenheimer. The script is chosen as a "Best

THE INNER JOURNEY

Play"; there are 64 performances. On May 8, Molière's *The Miser* is revived, staged by Carl Weber and designed by David Hays, James Hart Stearns, and John Gleason. It has 27 showings, with Robert Symonds in the title-role.

March 20 James Hanley's *The Inner Journey* continues the experimental play season in the Forum Theatre of the Lincoln Center Repertory ensemble. On May 22, John Ford Noonan's *The Year Boston Won the Pennant* opens.

March 31 Bernard Miles revives his musical *Lock Up Your Daughters* at the Mermaid Theatre in London. On June 11, Ken Campbell's *Anything You Say Will Be Twisted* is staged by the author and designed by Sean Kenny. On Aug 7, Bernard Miles stages Henry James' *The Other House*.

April 2 The Royal Shakespeare Company opens its annual Stratford-upon-Avon season with *Pericles*, staged by Terry Hands. Ian Richardson plays the title role. Hands's production of *The Merry Wives of Windsor* is revived from last season. Barrie Ingham and Judi Dench play in Trevor Nunn's staging of *The Winter's Tale*. Hands stages *Women Beware Women*, with Richard Pasco and Dench. John Barton directs *Twelfth Night*, with Donald Sinden. John Bury designs Nunn's production of *Henry VIII*. Sinden plays the king, with Peggy Ashcroft as Katharine.

April 14 The World Theatre Season, produced annually by Peter Daubeny in association with the Royal Shakespeare Company, opens at London's Aldwych Theatre. Racine's *Berenice*, presented by Roger Planchon's Theatre de la Cite, is

the first offering followed by Molière's *Georges Dandin*, which opens on the 17th. Chekhov's *The Three Sisters* is presented on April 28 by Czechoslovakia's Theatre Behind the Gate. On May 1, the troupe plays Johann Nestroy's *The Single-Ended Rope*, in Czech. On May 3, they offer a double-bill of Josef Topol's *An Hour of Love* and Arthur Schnitzler's *The Green Cockatoo*. All of the plays are staged by the theatre's director, Otomar Krejca. On May 5, New York's Negro Ensemble Company opens with Peter Weiss' documentary, *Song of the Lusitanian Bogey*, translated by Lee Baxendall. Michael A. Schultz directs. On May 8, the troupe offers Ray McIver's *God Is a (Guess What?)*. In the company are such performers as Samuel Blue, Jr., William Jay, and Esther Rolle. On May 19, Karolos Koun's Greek Art Theatre Company opens with Aristophanes' *Lysistrata*. On May 22, Sophocles' *Oedipus Rex* is performed. On June 2, Anna Magnani brings her company from Rome to perform *La Lupa*, by Giovanni Verga. The production has been re-rehearsed from Franco Zeffirelli's original.

April 15 *Cat Among the Pigeons*, Georges Feydeau's French farce, staged by Jacques Charon of the Comedie Francaise opens at London's Prince of Wales's Theatre. Richard Briers, Elizabeth Seal, and Victor Spinetti head the cast.

April 22 Off-Broadway at the Sheridan Square Playhouse, a triple-bill of plays by Luigi Pirandello opens: *The Man with the Flower in His Mouth*, *The License*, and *The Jar*. Michael Simone directs a cast including Mitchell Jason and Danny De Vito. The show has 80 performances.

May 1 Nicol Williamson proves a temeramental prince in this British revival of *Hamlet*, staged by Tony Richardson at Broadway's Lunt-Fontanne Theatre. It survives only 4 weeks.

May 1 At London's Old Vic, the National Theatre presents Congreve's Restoration comedy, *The Way of the World*, staged by Michael Langham. Geraldine McEwan, Robert Lang and Jane Lapotaire are in the cast. On May 27, there is a double-bill: *Macrune's Guevara* and *Rites*. On July 31, the National presents *Part I* of its two-part production of Bernard Shaw's *Back to Methuselah*, staged by Clifford Williams and Donald McKechnie. Derek Jacobi and Louise Purnell play Adam and Eve, with Judy Wilson as the Serpent. Joan Plowright is the Voice of Lilith, heard in *Part II*, opening on August 1.

May 7 Lighting-designer Richard Pilbrow produces Goldsmith's *She Stoops to Conquer* in this revival at the Garrick Theatre in London. Braham Murray stages, with Tom Courtenay, Trevor Peacock, and Juliet Mills.

May 10 Ben Hecht and Charles MacArthur's *The Front Page* opens in this revival staged by Harold Kennedy at New York's Ethel Barrymore Theatre. Robert Ryan plays the manipulative newspaper editor, with Bert Convy as his star investigative reporter. The show has a run of 64 performances, with a further 158 when it re-opens on Oct 18.

May 12 Tonight the Off-Broadway titillation is provided by the opening of *DeSade Illustrated*, adapted by Josef Bush from *Philosphy in the Boudoir*, one of the Marquis de Sade's more startling works. This production bows at the Bouwerie Lane Theatre. On May 21, the Gramercy Arts Theatre hosts the opening of *Philosphy in the Boudoir*, by Eric Kahane, adapted from de Sade. The original Paris production was stopped after 7 performances.

May 14 In Southern England, the Chichester Festival opens with Bertolt Brecht's *The Caucasian Chalk Circle*, staged by Peter Coe. Arthur Wing Pinero's *The Magistrate* is mounted by Artistic Director John Clements. William Wycherley's *The Country Wife*, with Maggie Smith, is directed by Robert Chetwyn. Shakespeare's *Antony and Cleopatra* is staged by Peter Dews.

May 26 Another Stratford Shakespeare Festival opens in Ontario, Canada, under the direction of Jean Gascon. John Hirsch stages *Hamlet*. Gascon directs Jonson's *The Alchemist*. *Measure for Measure* is directed by David Giles. Gascon's production of *Tartuffe* is revived from last season. Gascon also stages Peter Luke's *Hadrian VII*. The Festival company includes Jason Robards and Donald Sutherland. Petronius' *Satyricon*, as adapted by Tom Hendry, with Stanley Silverman's score, is staged by Hirsch.

May 31 In San Francisco, at the traditional end of the current theatre season, the city's resident professional repertory company, the ACT has presented 25 productions. They include *The Misanthrope*, *Tartuffe*, *Twelfth Night*, *A Streetcar Named Desire*, *Long Day's Journey into Night*, *Tiny Alice*, *The Crucible*, *Hamlet*, *A Flea in Her Ear*—staged by Gower Champion, *The Devil's Disciple*, *Three Sisters*, and *Rosencrantz and Guildenstern Are Dead*.

June 2 It's Shakespeare time in the Open Air Theatre in London's Regent's Park. Director Richard Digby presents *Two Gentlemen of Verona*, with Bernard Breslaw and Richard Monette, a Canadian. On July 9, Day unveils his staging of *The Merchant of Venice*. Perlita Neilson and William Russell head the cast.

June 10 This is the 20th season for the San Diego National Shakespeare Festival in Balboa Park's Old Globe Theatre. Producing director Craig Noel programs *Julius Caesar*, *The Comedy of Errors*, and *Macbeth*, with Richard Easton, Ellis Rabb, and Jack O'Brien as his stage directors. Among the cast are Sada Thompson and Christopher Walken.

June 18 In Stratford, Connecticut, the American Shakespeare Festival opens with a program of four productions: *Much Ado About Nothing*, staged by Peter Gill with Roberta Maxwell, Tony van Bridge, and Patricia Elliott; *Hamlet*, staged by John Dexter, with Brian Bedford among others; *Henry V*, staged by Michael Kahn, with Len Cariou and Michael McGuire among others; *Three Sisters*, staged by Kahn, with Marian Seldes, and Bedford in the cast.

June 19 The Royal Shakespeare Company in London at the Aldwych Theatre opens its Stratford-upon-Avon production of *Troilus and Cressida*, staged by John Barton, with Hildegard Neil and Helen Mirren among the cast. On July 29, Trevor Nunn's Stratford production of *Much Ado About Nothing* comes to the Aldwych. Alan Howard, Janet Suzman and Helen Mirren head the cast.

June 23 Richard Rodgers has chosen *Oklahoma!* as this summer's revival for the Music Theatre of Lincoln Center, staged by John Kennedy at the New York State Theatre for a run of 11 weeks.

June 23 Artistic Director Paxton·Whitehead opens the Shaw Festival's first ten-week season at Niagara-on-the-Lake, Ontario, Canada, with *The Doctor's Dilemma*, staged by Dillon Evans. Marigold Charlesworth directs *Back to Methuselah, Part 1*. John Horton and Patrick Boxill play in *Five Variations for Corno di Bassetto*, complete with musicians and soprano. Stephen Porter stages Ferenc Molnar's *The Guardsman*, with Lila Kedrova and Whitehead. Others in the ensemble this season include Frances Hyland, and Robert Flemyng.

June 24 Peter Schumann's American troupe, the Bread and Puppet Theatre, open an engagement at London's Royal Court Theatre with *The Cry of the People for Meat*. At the close of the performances, audiences receive bread baked by Schumann. Critic Harold Hobson notes that the bread is stale, suggesting that's not all that's stale.

June 26 Heinar Kipphardt's *In the Matter of J. Robert Oppenheimer*, a recent success, is revived for a run of over 13 weeks at the Vivian Beaumont Theatre in New York's Lincoln Center.

June 29 *The Trail of Tears*, by Kermit Hunter, a play about the relocation of the Cherokees, is presented by the Cherokee National History Society in the 1,800-seat theatre in Tahlequah, Oklahoma.

June 29 America's La Mama-Plexus II troupe, directed by Joel Zwick, opens at London's Arts Theatre in Andy Robinson's *The Last Chance Saloon*. The troupe also performs Buechner's *Woyzeck*, translated by Ted Hoffman, on July 8. Robinson, John Bottoms, Diane Callum, and others are in the cast.

July 1 Bertolt Brecht's *The Resistible Rise of Arturo Ui*, previously produced by the Glasgow Citizens' Theatre in 1968, now opens at London's Saville Theatre. Michael Blakemore directs, Leonard Rossiter plays Ui, a Hitler parody. There are 148 performances.

July 8 Joseph Papp's New York Shakespeare Festival gets underway with its customary free performances in Central Park's Delacorte Theatre. Henrik Ibsen's *Peer Gynt* opens the season, directed by Gerald Freedman. Stacy Keach plays Peer, with Estelle Parsons as Aase and folksinger Judy Collins as Solveig. The second and final production is *Twelfth Night*, staged by Papp. Sasha von Scherler and Ralph Waite are among the cast.

July 12 Kermit Hunter has written *Walk Toward the Sunset*, a drama about the Melungeons of East Tennessee. It is shown in a 500-seat amphitheatre in Sneedville, Tennessee.

July 19 In Ashland, Angus Bowmer's Oregon Shakespearean Festival opens with *The Tempest*, staged by Richard Risso, followed by *Romeo and Juliet*, directed by Patrick Hines. Also programmed are *Twelfth Night*, directed by Hugh Evans, and *King John*, staged by Edward Brubaker. This summer's musical is *Virtue in Danger*, staged by Carl Ritchie. The company includes Dorothy French, Carol London, and Jose Carillo.

Aug 12 At the Open Space Theatre in London, Mike Weller's double-bill opens. It's *And Now There's Just the Three of Us*, followed by *The Body Builders*. Roland Rees directs. On Aug 25, director Walter Donohue stages two American plays by Israel Horovitz, *The Indian Wants the Bronx* and *Rats*. On Sep 2, two Amer-

RICHARD II

ican plays by Leonard Melfi are staged by Rees. They are *Birdbath*, with Mari Gorman, and *Halloween*, with Megs Jenkins.

Aug 18 Brazilian playwright Agusto Boal stages *Arena Conta Zumbi*, which he and Gianfrancesco Guarnieri have written in Portuguese, for TOLA (Theatre of Latin America) in New York at St. Clement's Church.

Aug 24 The Edinburgh Festival opens with its customary mixture of theatre, dance, music, and opera. Theatre offerings include the Scottish Actors Company, with Ibsen's *The Wild Duck*, staged by Fulton Mackay; the Prospect Theatre Company, with Shakespeare's *Richard II*, directed by Richard Cottrell and Marlowe's *Edward II*, staged by Toby Robertson; Prague's Theatre on the Balustrade, with Ladislav Fialka's *The Fools*. Also on the program: Kevin Laffan's *Zoo Zoo Widdershins Zoo*, presented by Bridge Productions and staged by Frank Dunlop; the Nottingham Playhouse Company, with John Arden and Margaretta D'Arcy's *The Hero Rises Up* and George Bernard Shaw's *Widowers' Houses*, and the Stables Theatre Company, with Barry Davis' staging of David Wright's *Would you look at them smashing all the lovely windows*.

Aug 25 The National Youth Theatre, as is customary at the end of summer when its young actors will be going back to school, presents its productions in London, with Peter Terson's *Fuzz*, directed by Michael Croft, opening at the Jeannetta Cochrane Theatre. David Weston directs *Macbeth*, at the Roundhouse on Sep 9.

Sep 3 At the Mermaid Theatre in the City

of London, the play is Keith Waterhouse and Willis Hall's *Children's Day*, staged by Clive Perry. Among the company are Prunella Scales and Dilys Lay. On the 24th, Marlowe's *Edward the Second* is performed by the Prospect Theatre, which has brought this production from the Assembly Hall and the Edinburgh Festival. Toby Robertson directs. Ian McKellen is the king. Also from Edinburgh and by the Prospect is the Richard Cottrell staging of Shakespeare's *Richard II*. McKellen also plays this unfortunate king. This production is seen on the 25th.

Sep 10 At London's Aldwych Theatre, the Royal Shakespeare Company presents Sean O'Casey's *The Silver Tassie*, an attack on the senselessness of war. David Jones directs. David Waller, Patience Collier and Helen Mirren are among the cast. On Oct 30, Ben Jonson's *Bartholomew Fair* is revived, with Terry Hands staging. On Nov 27, Cyril Tourneur's *The Revenger's Tragedy* is revived, edited by John Barton and directed by Trevor Nunn.

Sep 10 Japan's Grand Kabuki ensemble comes to New York City Center with a program of four classic productions, opening with *Chushingura*, followed by *Kagami-Jishi*, *Kumagai Jinya*, and *Momiji-Gari*. There are 18 performances.

Sep 18 From the Chichester Festival comes the successful production of Arthur Wing Pinero's *The Magistrate*, opening in London at the Cambridge Theatre. John Clements directs. Alastair Sim plays the title-role. The show runs beyond season's end.

Sep 24 At the Old Vic, the Compagnie Renaud-Barrault presents Jean-Louis Barrault's "dramatic game," *Rabelais*, with Barrault directing and starring.

Sep 29 At New York's ANTA Theatre, what is planned as a festival of performances from America's resident professional theatres opens with Edward Albee's *Tiny Alice*, one of three productions imported by San Francisco's ACT. William Ball stages this play. Also on the bill are Gower Champion's production of Feydeau's *A Flea in Her Ear* and Chekhov's *Three Sisters*, directed by Ball. This is to be a four-week engagement. Manhattan critics are not enthusiastic, causing some previously scheduled resident theatres to reconsider and cancel, crippling the season. On Nov 10, Michael Kahn's production of *Henry V* comes to the ANTA Theatre from the American Shakespeare Festival in Stratford, Connecticut. Len Cariou is the king, with Roberta Maxwell as his French princess. There are 16 performances. On Nov 27, producer Alfred de Liagre, Jr., brings the Plumstead Playhouse production of Wilder's *Our Town* to Broadway's ANTA Theatre. Donald Driver directs, with a cast that includes Henry Fonda, Mildred Natwick, and Ed Begley. There are 36 per-

formances. On Dec 30, the festival of American regional theatres continues with *No Place To Be Somebody*, by Charles Gordone. This production is imported for two weeks from Joseph Papp's Public Theatre in Greenwich Village.

Oct 8 Arvin Brown stages Thomas Murphy's Irish play, *A Whistle in the Dark*, at New York's Mercury Theatre. His cast includes Roberta Maxwell and Charles Cioffi. Previously produced in London, the play has a run here of 100 performances.

Oct 11 At the American Place Theatre in St. Clement's Church in midtown Manhattan, Anne Sexton's *Mercy Street* opens the new season of experimental plays by American authors and poets and has 46 performances. This is followed by Charlie Russell's *Five on the Black Hand Side* on Dec 10. Charles Maryan stages the first production, with Marian Seldes, William Prince, and others in the company. Barbara Ann Teer directs the second, with a cast including Clarice Taylor and Jonelle Allen. There are 62 performances of Russell's play.

Oct 16 George Abbott stages the revival of the play he and John Cecil Holm premiered on Broadway in 1935, *Three Men on a Horse*. Opening at the Lyceum Theatre in New York, it earns 100 performances. Butterfly McQueen, Sam Levene and Jack Gilford are among the cast. On Oct 18, last season's *The Front Page* returns for a an additional run of nearly five months at the Ethel Barrymore Theatre.

Oct 16 At London's Old Vic, the National Theatre stages Peter Nichols' novel comedy, *The National Health, or, Nurse Norton's Affair*. Jim Dale is praised for his work as Barnet, an orderly who functions as a comic narrator. Michael Blakemore directs. On Nov 13, the National Theatre presents John Webster's Jacobean melodrama, *The White Devil*, staged by Frank Dunlop, with Geraldine McEwan, Derek Godfrey, and Jane Lapotaire among the cast. On Dec 18, James Saunders' *The Travails of Sancho Panza* opens, staged by Donald MacKechnie and Joan Plowright. Tony Walton designs this reworking of *Don Quixote*. Godfrey plays the Don, with Roy Kinnear as Sancho.

Oct 16 From Wroclaw, Poland, comes the innovative director Jerzy Grotowski with his Actor's Research Laboratory Theatre and its techniques of "Poor Theatre." The opening production at New York's Washington Square Methodist Church is Calderon's *The Constant Prince*, devised by Grotowsky, with Riszard Cieslak. There are 24 showings. On Nov 4, *Acropolis* opens, based on a text by Stanislaw Wyspianki, for a run of 12 performances. On the 18th, the show is *Apocalypsis Cum Figurus*, developed by Grotowsky and his actors from texts of T. S. Eliot, the Bible, Simone Weil, and Feodor Dostoevsky. This has 15 performances.

Oct 16 At the Master Theatre on Riverside Drive, New York's Equity Library Theatre opens its new season of revivals with *Lend an Ear*, followed by *The Lower Depths*, *Romeo and Jeannette*, *Getting Married*, *Little Mary Sunshine*, *Barefoot in the Park*, *Hatful of Rain*, and *Me and Juliet*.

Oct 18 At the Chelsea Theatre Center in the Brooklyn Academy of Music (BAM), LeRoi Jones' *Slave Ship* opens, with spectators seated on narrow benches surrounding a rectangular wooden construction—designed by Eugene Lee—representing a slave ship, bringing blacks to the New World in bondage. Gilbert Moses stages this historical survey of slavery. Later, the production, which will have 56 performances here, moves Off-Broadway, but a strike and a fire limit it to four performances only.

Oct 21 London's Greenwich Theatre opens with Ewan Hooper's play, *Martin Luther King*. Bari Jonson plays Dr. King. Jumoke Debayo plays Coretta King. Alan Vaughan-Williams directs. On Nov 18, the play is John Hale's *Spithead*, a naval drama, staged by Hale. Esmond Knight leads the cast.

Nov 4 Hugh Walpole's story *The Old Ladies*, dramatized by Rodney Ackland, is revived by director Peter Cotes, at London's Westminster Theatre. His cast is Joyce Carey, Joan Miller, and Flora Robson. There are 100 performances.

Nov 6 Artistic Director Jules Irving opens the new Vivian Beaumont season of the Repertory Theatre of Lincoln Center with a revival of William Saroyan's *The Time of Your Life*, staged by John Hirsh. Among the large cast are James Broderick, Philip Bosco, and Biff McGuire. There are 52 performances.

Nov 16 At the New York Shakespeare Festival's winter home, the Public Theatre, producer Joseph Papp presents *Stomp*, a protest rock musical using mul-timedia techniques and developed by The Combine, former University of Texas students. The show has a total of 161 performances. On Dec 12, Ron Steward and Neil Tate's musical, *Sambo*, opens, staged by Gerald Freedman. This is described as a "black opera with white spots." This runs almost five weeks.

Dec 3 It's holiday season again and today *You're a Good Man, Charlie Brown* is revived in London at the MayFair Theatre. On the 11th, the Westminster Theatre revives *Give a Dog a Bone*. Other pantomimes, revivals, and children's plays include *The New Adventures of Noah's Ark* (Greenwich), *The Owl and The Pussy Cat Went To See . . .* (Jeannetta Cochrane), *Treasure Island* (Mermaid), *Aladdin* (Players'), *The Three Musketeers Ride Again* (Royal Court), *Peter Pan* (New Victoria, with Hayley Mills as Peter), and *Dick Whittington* (Palladium, with Tommy Steele as Dick).

Dec 4 Brian Bedford and Tammy Grimes lead the cast in a revival of Noel Coward's *Private Lives*, directed by Stephen Porter, at New York's Billy Rose Theatre. It runs nearly 26 weeks.

Dec 4 At Lincoln Center in the Forum Theatre Vaclav Havel's Czech drama, *The Increased Difficulty of Concentration*, opens for 28 showings.

Dec 30 At the Negro Ensemble Company's St. Marks Playhouse in Greenwich Village, the new season opens with Joseph Walker's *The Harangues*. Israel Hicks stages a cast including Robert Hooks and Rosalind Cash. It runs 7 weeks.

1969 BIRTHS/DEATHS/DEBUTS

Jan 1 British actor Ian Fleming, aged 80, dies today.

Jan 2 The American producer-director Gilbert Miller, who has worked on both sides of the Atlantic, today dies at age 84. He was the son of Henry Miller, the American actor.

Jan 15 Shakespearean scholar John Dover Wilson (b. 1881) dies in Scotland. Among his books are *What Happens in Hamlet* and *Shakespeare's Happy Comedies*.

Jan 17 Broadway composer Vernon Duke dies, aged 65.

Jan 19 American stage and screen actor Charles Winninger (b. 1884) dies in Palm Springs, California. Winninger played Cap'n Andy in the 1927 Broadway production of *Showboat*, and its 1932 New York revival.

Jan 25 Dancer-actress Irene Castle, once the toast of the 1920's with her partner Vernon Castle, dies in Eureka Springs, Arkansas, aged 77.

Feb 2 Actor Boris Karloff (b. 1887) dies in Sussex, England. Karloff made his first appearance on stage in 1910. His great success came in *Arsenic and Old Lace* in 1941 at New York's Fulton Theatre.

March 15 English actor and dramatist Miles Malleson (b. 1888) dies in London. Malleson was known for his Shakespearean and Restoration comedy roles. Apart from his Moliére adaptations, his best-known play is *The Fanatics*.

March 16 Drama critic and lecturer John Mason Brown is dead in New York at age 68. Brown's published works include *The Modern Theatre in Revolt*, *Two on the Aisle*, and *Dramatis Personae*. He edited, with Montrose Moses, the classic *The American Theatre as Seen by Its Critics*. He served as critic for the *Saturday Review of Literature*, and the *New York Post*, among other publications.

May 1 Scottish-born actress and singer Ella Logan (b. 1913) is dead. She played on Broadway in *George White's Scandals*, *Show Time*, and *Finian's Rainbow*.

May 1 Jean Rosenthal, the noted American lighting designer, dies at age 57.

May 16 Sir Lewis Casson, actor-director-producer and husband of actress Dame Sybil Thorndike, dies at the age of 93.

May 23 Jimmy McHugh, Broadway musical songsmith, dies at 74.

May 28 Welsh stage and screen actor Rhys Williams dies at 71.

June 5 Manager-producer Vinton Freedley (b. 1891) dies in New York City. With Alex Aarons, Freedley built the Alvin Theatre and opened it with their production of *Funny Face* in 1927. Under his own management, Freedley produced *Anything Goes*, *Red, Hot and Blue!*, and *Liliom*.

June 9 Stage designer Loudon Sainthill

GRAND KABUKI

HALLIE FLANAGAN

dies at 50.

June 13 English actress Martita Hunt (b. 1900) dies in London. She made her first American appearance in 1948 in *The Madwoman of Chaillot.* Hunt's film career began in 1933.

July 23 Director, educator, and author Hallie Flanagan Davis (b. 1890) dies in Old Tappan, New Jersey. Davis was national director of the Federal Theatre Project from 1935 to 1939—a milestone in the American theatre which she duly recorded in her book, *Arena.* She also wrote *Dynamo: the Story of the Vassar Theatre.*

July 28 American composer and lyricist Frank Loesser (b. 1910) dies in New York City. Loesser composed the music and wrote the lyrics for *Where's Charley?, Guys and Dolls, The Most Happy Fella, Greenwillow,* and the 1961 Pulitzer Prize-winning *How to Succeed in Business Without Really Trying.*

Sep 27 At age 81, the British actress Violet Farebrother passes on.

Oct 18 English composer and conductor Alfred Reynolds (b. 1884) is dead. He composed the musical setting for the 1930's productions of *1066 and All That* and *The Swiss Family Robinson,* and the 1947 production of *Alice in Wonderland.*

Oct 27 Erik Maschwitz, author of many British musical comedy librettos, dies at age 68.

Nov 9 Stewart Cheney, distinguished American stage designer and theatre theorist, dies aged 59.

Nov 24 British theatre critic and historian Maurice Wilson Disher dies, aged 76.

Dec 3 American stage and screen actress Ruth White dies in her birthplace of Perth Amboy, New Jersey at 55. White made her New York City debut in *The Ponder Heart* in 1956. Her role as Winnie in Beckett's *Happy Days* was acclaimed by critics.

Dec 7 British actor Eric Portman, aged 66, dies.

Dec 10 Irish-born playwright Samuel Beckett is awarded the Nobel Prize for Literature.

1969　THEATERS/PRODUCTIONS

U.S. patents granted this year include one to Tibor Rudas for a cinema screen made of flat, parallel, stretchable strips, which permit an actor to squeeze through one one of the resulting slits, without disturbing the projected film-sequence, in which he may also appear.

Feb 17 The Round House officially opens as a new London theatre with the Free Theatre's production of *Hamlet,* with Nicol Williamson in the title role. This old railway building has been preserved because of architectural and historical importance. The architects Bickerdale, Allen, Rich & Partners have designed this theatre with a flexible capacity of 400–600.

March 5 Rochelle Owens' play *Futz* about a farmer in love with his prize sow is staged at the Central Library Theatre, Toronto, Canada, by Theatre Passe Muraille. The Toronto Police Morality Squad issues summonses to the cast and crew for participating in an obscene performance and get a conviction. This is overturned a year later.

Spring Albert Millaire becomes Artistic Director of Théâtre Populaire du Québec

in Canada. It performs mostly the classics—Musset, Racine, Corneille—but Millaire takes it in a new direction with highly political modern Quebec plays and collective creations.

Apr 15 Peter Foy obtains a U.S. patent for a flying apparatus in which both the vertical and lateral motion of the performer can be controlled.

April 24 The $21 million Krannert Center for the Performing Arts opens at the University of Illinois in Urbana. The complex contains three theatres, a large auditorium, and an open-air amphitheatre. Max Abramowitz is the architect.

May 20 La Corporation du Grand Théâtre de Québec is founded to promote arts and letters in Quebec City, Canada. The building has a large 1800-seat theatre for opera, concerts, and drama; a small 300–600-seat flexible room for plays, and a music conservatory for the 250–350 students.

May 31 A two-week arts festival opens the new National Arts Centre in Ottawa, Canada, designed by Fred Lebensold. The $46.4 million complex is totally funded

by the federal government. There are three theatres with simultaneous translation facilities: a 2,300-seat opera house-concert hall; an 800-seat conventional theatre; and a 300-seat studio theatre.

May 31 For 1968–69, *Variety* offers the following list of financial hits, based on the criterion of paying back their investment: *Lovers, Marlene Dietrich, The Great White Hope, The Front Page, Hadrian VII, Play It Again, Sam, Promises, Promises, Jimmy Shine,* and *Forty Carats.*

June 1 On the first day of the new theatre season, the tally of Broadway productions during the last stands at 76, 24 of them new American plays and 12, new musicals. Other categories are specialties (5), revues (1), revivals (23), foreign plays in English (6), and foreign-language productions (5). The Broadway season grosses nearly $58 million, with almost $43 million earned by Broadway touring shows. For *Promises, Promises,* the weekend top price has risen to $15, with $12.50 standard. Legitimate plays command a top of $9.50, with Off-Broadway hits asking a $10 top. It now costs half a million dollars to mount a musical, with straight plays costing as much as $150,000. Over $3 million is lost on six musical flops this season. Produced Off-Broadway for $20,000, *The Boys in the Band* shows a net profit of $210,000. There have been 102 Off-Broadway productions, 55 of them plays and 11, musicals.

Otis Guernsey, Jr., editor of the annual "Best Play's," chooses ten from the season just completed: Friel's *Lover's,* Shaw's *The Man in the Glass Booth,* Sackler's *The Great White Hope,* Kipphardt's *In the Matter of J. Robert Oppenheimer,* Burrows' *Forty Carats,* Luke's *Hadrian VII,* Jones/Schmidt's *Celebration,* Stone's *1776,* Gordone's *No Place To Be Somebody,* and May/McNally's *Adaptation/Next.*

June 1 Beyond Broadway, America's professional regional—or resident—theatres have produced 279 plays in the season just closed. These represent the work of 37 groups in 49 theatres in 35 cities. Of the plays, 153 are by American authors, 32 have been world premieres and 9 others American premieres.

Oct 21 The Greenwich Theatre, Crooms Hill, Greenwich, opens with *Martin Luther King.* The 426-seat theatre has been designed by Brian Meeking and is managed by the Greenwich Theatre Trust.

Oct 28 The new Centaur Theatre opens in Montreal, Canada, with a production of Muriel Spark's *The Prime of Miss Jean Brodie.* Under the artistic direction of Maurice Podbrey, Centaur will become the principal English-language theatre in Quebec, performing in the old Montreal Stock Exchange.

Jan 26 *The Last Sweet Days of Isaac* (NY—East Side Playhouse—Musical). Gretchen Cryer and Nancy Ford's rock musical wins 485 performances. Austin Pendleton plays the title role, jailed for making political protests. Word Baker stages.

Feb 14 *Gantry* (NY—George Abbott—Musical). Robert Shaw opens and closes in one night in this musical version of Sinclair Lewis' novel *Elmer Gantry*. Onna White directs.

Feb 17 *Child's Play* (NY—Royale—Drama). Named a "Best Play," Robert Marasco's drama is set in a Catholic boys' school where pupils appear to become possessed. Pat Hingle plays a lead during the 43-week run. Joseph Hardy directs both the Broadway and London productions. The latter, starring Lawrence Harvey, opens on March 16, 1971 at the Queen's Theatre and continues into next season.

Feb 18 *The White House Murder Case* (NY—Circle in the Square—Comedy). In Jules Feiffer's "Best Play," the First Lady has been murdered and suspicion is thrown on cabinet secretaries. Alan Arkin directs. It runs almost 15 weeks.

Feb 19 *Norman, Is That You?* (NY—Lyceum—Comedy). Maureen Stapleton and Lou Jacobi play distraught parents who discover their son is gay, in this Ron Clark and Sam Bobrick farce, directed by George Abbott. It has only 12 performances on Broadway, and the London production, which opens on April 16, 1975, at the Phoenix Theatre, has 58 showings.

March 15 *Purlie* (NY—Broadway—Musical). Ossie Davis' play *Purlie Victorious*, which parodies black-white relationships in an unreconstructed South, becomes a musical. Melba Moore, Cleavon Little, and Novella Nelson are among the cast. Philip Rose directs; there are 688 performances.

March 26 *Minnie's Boys* (NY—Imperial—Musical). Shelley Winters plays mother Minnie Marx in this Robert Fisher and Arthur Marx show about the Marx Brothers. Lewis Stadlen impersonates Groucho. There are only 76 performances.

March 30 *Applause* (NY—Palace—Musical). Lauren Bacall is "a sensation," says Clive Barnes (*NY Times*), in Betty Comden and Adolph Green's adaptation of the film *All About Eve*, with Penny Fuller as the scheming Eve Harrington. The show, which Ron Field directs and choreographs, has 896 performances, is chosen a "Best Play," and wins a Tony Award as Best Musical. Lauren Bacall repeats her role when the show opens at London's Her Majesty's Theatre on Nov 16, 1972. It has 382 showings.

APPLAUSE

March 31 *Borstal Boy* (NY—Lyceum—Drama). Dublin's Abbey Theatre is co-producer of this Frank McMahon adaptation of Brendan Behan's autobiographical book about his experiences in a British reformatory. Niall Toibin of the Abbey plays Behan. Tomas MacAnna directs the 18-week run.

April 7 *The Effect of Gamma Rays on Man-in-the-Moon Marigolds* (NY—Mercer–O'Casey—Drama). Paul Zindel's play, about a beleaguered mother (Sada Thompson) who doesn't know how to cope with life and two fatherless daughters (Pamela Payton-Wright and Amy Levitt), is chosen as one of the season's ten "Best Plays" and, next year, wins the Pulitzer Prize. It has 819 performances. Melvin Bernhardt stages.

April 26 *Company* (NY—Alvin—Musical). Stephen Sondheim gets raves for the music and lyrics he creates for this George Furth book about the problems of modern love-affairs. It has 705 performances and is chosen a "Best Play." Harold Prince stages, with choreography by Michael Bennett. Elaine Stritch repeats her leading role in the London production which opens Jan 18, 1972, at Her Majesty's Theatre and continues into the next season.

May 4 *What the Butler Saw.* See L premiere, 1969.

May 6 *Colette* (NY—Ellen Stewart—Musical). Tom Jones and Harvey Schmidt provide the songs for Elinor Jones's adaptation of *Earthly Paradise*, an anthology of Colette's memoirs. Zoe Caldwell plays Colette. It has 101 performances.

May 18 *The Me Nobody Knows* (NY—Orpheum—Musical). Stephen Joseph adapts the book of the same name, written by New York's ghetto children, with songs by Will Holt and Gary William Friedman. Robert Livingstone stages. On Dec 18, the show opens at Broadway's Helen Hayes Theatre for a combined run of 586 performances.

June 18 *The Cage* (NY—Playhouse—Drama). Ex-convict Rick Cluchey's play about prison life, seen earlier in San Francisco, runs almost four months. Cluchey plays the lead, Kenneth Kitch stages.

June 22 *Boesman and Lena* (NY—Circle in the Square—Drama). James Earl Jones and Ruby Dee play two blacks trying to survive in modern South Africa, in Athol Fugard's "Best Play" which runs almost 26 weeks. John Berry directs.

June 27 *The Dirtiest Show in Town* (NY—Astor Place—Comedy). From the La Mama Experimental Theatre Club Off-off-Broadway, Tom Eyen's carnival of sex-sketches and environmental jibes transfers to Off-Broadway for a run of 509 performances. On May 11, 1971, a London production opens at the Duchess Theatre. Madeleine Le Roux repeats her leading role.

June 30 *Steambath* (NY—Truck and Warehouse—Comedy). Tony Perkins di-

"A BEAUTIFUL AND ENTHRALLING EXPERIENCE!"
—William Glover, Associated Press

ZOE CALDWELL in COLETTE

"A SPLENDID EVENING IN THE THEATRE!"
—Clive Barnes, New York Times

AIR-CONDITIONED
ELLEN STEWART
THEATRE
240 E. 3rd St. N.Y.C.
477-4400

COLETTE

rects and plays a leading role in Bruce Jay Friedman's satiric comedy about the customers—all of whom are dead—who frequent a steambath. Chosen as a "Best Play," it runs 16 weeks.

July 21 *The Golden Bat* (NY—Sheridan Square Playhouse—Musical). Seen earlier at La Mama E.T.C., this show about East and West is the creation of the Tokyo Kid Brothers, the Japanese La Mama troupe. It runs 19 weeks. Yutaka Higashi directs and provides the libretto.

Sep 24 *Bob and Ray the Two and Only* (NY—John Golden—Revue). This radio team has a run of almost five months in a program of their satiric sketches. Joseph Hardy directs.

Oct 7 *Happy Birthday, Wanda June* (NY—Theatre de Lys—Comedy). Kurt Vonnegut, Jr. reworks the Ulysses legend, and

Marsha Mason plays a latter-day Penelope. Michael Kane stages. On Dec 22, the show moves to Broadway's Edison Theatre. It has a total run of 143 performances.

Oct 12 *Conduct Unbecoming.* See L premiere, 1969.

Oct 19 *The Rothschilds* (NY—Lunt-Fontanne—Musical). Sherman Yellen's musical, based on Frederic Morton's book *The Rothschilds*, is called "lead-footed and overstuffed" by one critic, but it earns 507 performances. Michael Kidd directs and choreographs. Jerry Bock and Sheldon Harnick write the songs. Hal Linden plays the lead.

Nov 8 *Touch* (NY—Village Arena—Musical). There are 422 performances of Jim Crozier and Kenn Long's musical about young commune-dwellers eager to "get in touch with their feelings."

Nov 10 *Two by Two* (NY—Imperial—Musical). Danny Kaye plays Noah in Peter Stone's book, based on Clifford Odets's *Flowering Peach*. Richard Rodgers writes the music; Martin Charnin provides the lyrics. Joe Layton conceives and directs the show, which has 351 performances.

Nov 13 *Saved.* See L premiere, 1965.

Dec 13 *The Gingerbread Lady* (NY—Plymouth—Drama). Maureen Stapleton plays a singer with drinking problems whose career is sliding downhill, in Neil Simon's first serious drama. Robert Moore stages. A "Best Play," it has only 193 performances. On Oct 23, 1974, Elaine Stritch heads the cast in a London production at the Phoenix Theatre which has 189 showings.

Dec 22 *A Place Without Doors* (NY—Stairway—Drama). Mildred Dunnock plays a French housewife who has committed a grisly murder in this version of Marguerite Duras' play *L'Amante Anglaise*. Brian Murray directs. It has a "limited" contract and runs for 30 performances.

Dec 28 *Lovely Ladies, Kind Gentlemen* (NY—Majestic—Musical). John Patrick's musical adaptation of his play, based on Vern Schneider's novel *The Teahouse of the August Moon*, closes after just two weeks. Lawrence Kasha directs.

Anthony Quayle and Keith Baxter head the cast in Anthony Shaffer's hit thriller, which has 2,359 performances. Clifford Williams stages this duel of wits between a mystery writer and the brash young man who's taken away his wife. Quayle and Baxter repeat their roles in the Broadway Music Box production which opens on Nov 12. It has 1,222 performances and is named a "Best Play."

March 11 *The Happy Apple* (L—Apollo—Comedy). Paul Rogers and Pauline Collins head the cast of Jack Pulman's play about the excesses committed by the advertising industry. James Roose-Evans directs.

April 9 *At the Palace* (L—Palace—Revue). Danny LaRue, glamorous female impersonator, and comedian Roy Hudd head the cast of this Barry Cryer and Dick Vosburgh revue. There are 811 performances.

April 22 *Carol Channing With Her Ten Stout-Hearted Men* (L—Drury Lane—Revue). Joe Layton conceives and directs what he calls a "musical frappe" for Channing.

May 5 *Flint* (L—Criterion—Drama). Michael Hordern plays an unorthodox pastor doing battle with his church in David Mercer's often bizarre play. Vivien Merchant, Moira Redmond, and Julia Foster are also in the cast, directed by Christopher Morahan.

May 19 *Abelard and Heloise* (L—Wyndham's—Drama). Keith Michell and Diana Rigg play the famous lovers in Ronald Millar's drama, which has a run of 706 performances. Robin Phillips directs. On March 10, 1971, the same cast appears in the Broadway production at the Brooks Atkinson, after previews at Los Angeles's Ahmanson Theatre, but the run is a mere seven weeks.

June 16 *1776.* See NY premiere, 1969.

June 17 *Home* (L—Royal Court—Drama). John Gielgud, Ralph Richardson, Dandy Nichols, and Mona Washbourne head the cast of David Storey's ambiguous new play about the residents of a home. On July 29, it transfers to London's Apollo Theatre, and on Nov 17 the cast opens at New York's Morosco Theatre for a limited run of 110 performances. It is chosen as a "Best Play." Lindsay Anderson stages.

July 16 *The Heretic* (L—Duke of York's—Drama). Morris West's play about an unorthodox astronomer in the time of the Inquisition is staged by West and Joseph O'Conner. Leonard Rossiter plays the title-role.

Aug 5 *How the Other Half Loves* (L—Lyric—Comedy). Alan Ayckbourne's farce about marital infidelity has a run of 869 performances. Robert Morley and Joan Tetzel head the cast. Robin Midgley directs and Alan Tagg designs an ingenious set. On March 29, 1971, the play opens at New York's Royale Theatre, with a cast

1970   BRITISH PREMIERES

Jan 15 *Tiny Alice.* See NY premiere, 1964.

Jan 21 *It's A Two Foot Six Inches Above The Ground World.* (L—Wyndham's—Comedy). Kevin Laffan's play, first seen in November at Bristol's Theatre Royal, offers a satirical view of Catholic ideas on family planning. Prunella Scales is in the cast, directed by Val May. It runs for almost four months.

Jan 27 *Come As You Are* (L—New—Comedy). Allan Davis stages four short

plays by John Mortimer: *Mill Hill, Bermondsey, Gloucester Road,* and *Marble Arch*—all of the names being stops on London's Underground. There are 277 performances.

Feb 5 *The Battle of Shrivings* (L—Lyric—Drama). John Gielgud and Wendy Hiller are in the cast of Peter Shaffer's new play about ethical values, but it has only 73 performances. Peter Hall directs.

Feb 12 *Sleuth* (L—St. Martin's—Drama).

including Phil Silvers and Sandy Dennis. It has a run of only 13 weeks.

Sep 23 *A Bequest to the Nation* (L—Haymarket—Drama). Peter Glenville directs Terence Rattigan's play about the love affair between Lord Nelson (Ian Holm) and Lady Emma Hamilton (Zoe Caldwell). There are 125 performances.

Sep 30 *The Jockey Club Stakes* (L—Vaudeville—Comedy). Alastair Sim plays a marquis, whose club is embroiled in a scandal over a possible race horse scam. William Douglas Home's play has 396 performances. On Jan 24, 1973, Wilfrid Hyde White opens at New York's Cort Theatre in a production initially shown at the J. F. Kennedy Center in Washington, D.C. It has barely a nine-week run.

Oct 8 *Vivat! Vivat Regina!* (L—Piccadilly—Drama). Robert Bolt's historical drama, premiered at the Chichester Festival, deals with the conflict between Mary Stuart (Sarah Miles) and Queen Elizabeth I (Eileen Atkins). It has 442 performances. Peter Dews directs. On Jan 20, 1972, the play opens at New York's Broadhurst Theatre with Atkins, and Claire Bloom as Mary Stuart. Although chosen as a "Best Play," it has only 116 performances.

1970 REVIVALS/REPERTORIES

Jan 8 At the Vivian Beaumont Theatre, the season continues with a revival of Tennessee Williams's *Camino Real*. The show has 52 performances, followed by an equal number for Sam Shepard's *Operation Sidewinder*. The final production is a musical version of the Kaufman and Connelly *Beggar on Horseback*. There are 22 performances only.

Jan 9 In Edinburgh, Lindsay Kemp's troupe opens the year, at the Traverse Theatre, with *The Turquoise Pantomime*. There will be nearly forty programs presented this year. Among the productions are Arnold Wesker's *The Four Seasons* and Bertolt Brecht's *Drums in the Night*. Sam Shepard's *Cowboys No. 2*, David Halliwell's *A Who's Who of Flapland*, David Kranes' *Drive-In*, Martin Sherman's *The Night Before Paris*, Syd Cheadle's *Straight Up*, Howard Brenton's *Fruit*, David Snodin's *A Game Called Arthur*, Annie Stainer's *Trolls*, some editions of *The People Show*, and *Christ Was a Peace Freak*. At the end of April, Michael Rudman takes over as Artistic Director.

Jan 12 At Broadway's ANTA Theatre, the festival of American regional theatres goes forward, this evening with The National Theatre of the Deaf offering a double-bill in pantomime and words of Molière's *Sganarelle* and Dylan Thomas's *Songs from Milk Wood*. The engagement lasts a week. On Jan 21, Philip Magdalany's double-bill *Watercolor* and *Criss-Crossing* opens. The playlets have been workshop experiments of the Playwrights Unit, Greenwich Village, sponsored by producers Richard Barr, Edward Albee, and Charles Woodward. There are five sparsely attended performances.

Jan 22 At London's Mermaid Theatre, Bernard Kops's *Enter Solly Gold* opens, staged by Ron Pember. George Bernard Shaw's *The Apple Cart* is revived on March 5. On April 23, director Pember's *Part 1* of *Henry IV* opens, followed on May 6 by *Part 2*.

Jan 26 *Three*, staged in London at the Fortune Theatre by Ray Cooney, is a George Bernard Shaw triple-bill, consisting of *How He Lied To Her Husband*, *Village Wooing*, and *Press Cuttings*. The cast includes Dulcie Gray and Michael Denison. There are 64 performances.

Jan 28 At London's Royal Court Theatre, Donald Howarth's *Three Months Gone* opens, with Jill Bennett and Diana Dors. Feb 24, Anthony Page directs Christopher Hampton's new version of Chekhov's *Uncle Vanya*. On April 1, Theatre Upstairs has *Beckett 3* ready; it's *Come and Go*, *Cascando*, and *Play*. On April 14, Bernard Shaw's *Widowers' Houses* is revived. On May 14, Heathcote Williams' *AC/DC* opens.

Jan 29 Continuing its experimental season in the Forum Theatre, the Repertory Theatre of Lincoln Center opens Jeff Wanshel's *The Disintegration of James Cherry*. On April 2, Harold Pinter's double-bill *Landscape* and *Silence* opens, staged by Peter Gill. On May 28, Peter Hacks' East German version of *Amphitryon* is unveiled in Ralph Manheim's translation. There are 28 showings.

Feb 3 At London's Round House, Jean Genet's *The Blacks* is presented, staged by Minos Volanakis. On March 24, the play is Alan Sillitoe's *This Foreign Field*, staged by William Martin. Arnold Wesker has staged his *The Friends* for the opening on May 19, with Ian Holm, in

DANNY LA RUE

the cast.

Feb 3 France's Comèdie Française opens at New York City Center in a brief engagement, presenting four Molière programs in repertory; the first is *La Troupe du Roi*—made up of scenes from Molière's comedies—paired with *Amphitryon*. This is followed by *Don Juan*, *Les Femmes Savanates*, and *Le Malade Imagininaire*.

On Feb 4, Julie Bovasso's *Gloria and Esperanza* opens in a staging at Ellen Stewart's La Mama Experimental Theatre Club of New York City. Bovasso takes the lead. There are only 13 performances.

Feb 9 At London's Old Vic, the Nottingham Playhouse Company offers its revival of Jonson's *The Alchemist*, directed by Stuart Burge. On Feb 10, the company presents *King Lear*, as staged by Jonathan Miller. Michael Hordern plays Lear.

Feb 11 Former burlesque queen Ann Corio returns to New York with *This Was Burlesque*, seen first in the metropolis in 1962 and on tour ever since. At the Hudson West Theatre, she earns a run of 106 performances.

Feb 16 N. F. Simpson's *How Are Your Handles?* is the first production of the new year at Ed Berman's Ambiance Lunch-Hour Theatre Club in London. Among the plays are Tom Stoppard's *After Magritte*, LeRoi Jones's *The Baptism*, and Howard Brenton's *The Education of Skinny Spew*.

Feb 18 *Sing a Rude Song*, a musical by Caryl Brahms and Ned Sherrin, opens at the Greenwich Theatre. Sherrin stages. On March 17, there's another musical; this time it's that old melodrama, *The Corsican Brothers*, reworked by John Bowen, using music from Gounod and others. John Cox directs. On April 14, Euripides' *Medea* has Katharine Blake in the title-role. On May 12, Ewan Hooper stages Alexander Reid's *What a Mouth*, with Tom Conti.

Feb 19 *The Drexler Plays*—by Rosalyn Drexler—are performed in London at the Open Space Theatre, with Charles Marowitz directing. The plays are *Hot Buttered Rolls* and *The Investigation*. On March 1, there's a revue, *New Victoria Line*. On the 16th, *Bleak Moments* is Mike Leigh's improvised play, aptly named. On May 12, John Hopkins's *Find Your Way Home* deals with the attraction a married man finds he has for a young man. The cast includes Anthony Bate, and Margaret Tyzack.

Feb 24 The National Theatre presents a Young Vic Season at the Jeannetta Cochrane Theatre in London, offering Frank Dunlop's inventive staging of Molière's *The Cheats of Scapin*, with comic-singer Jim Dale and Jane Lapotaire. Dale also composes the music. Eventually, the show will evolve into *Scapino*, starring Dale on Broadway.

Feb 26 At the Aldwych Theatre in London, the Royal Shakespeare Company stages David Mercer's *After Haggerty*, directed by David Jones. Frank Finlay heads the cast. Mercer's anti-hero is a drama critic, hampered by feelings of sexual and class inadequacy.

March 9 *Two Times One* continues the experimental play season at New York's American Place Theatre in St. Clement's Church. It's a double-bill of Charles Dizenzo's *The Last Straw* and David Scott Milton's *Duet for Solo Voice*. On April 29, Ed Bullins' *The Pig Pen* opens, staged by Dick Williams.

March 10 The NEC's artistic director, Douglas Turner Ward revives his playlet, *Day of Absence*, pairing it with a premiere, *Brotherhood*, in which a white couple open their home to a black couple, only to uncover racial antagonisms. This bill is to run two months at the company's St. Marks Playhouse in Greenwich Village. *Akokawe*, Afolabi Ajayi's collection of African texts, songs, and rituals, opens on May 19 for a run of 44 performances, staged by Ajayi.

April 1 At Stratford-upon-Avon, the Royal Shakespeare Company opens its season with John Barton's staging of *Measure for Measure*, with Ian Richardson and Estelle Kohler. Terry Hands stages *Richard III*, with Norman Rodway and Helen Mirren. Trevor Nunn directs *Hamlet*, with Alan Howard as the prince. Robin Phillips stages *Two Gentlemen of Verona*, with Richardson and Peter Egan. Peter Brook's celebrated "white box" production of *A Midsummer Night's Dream*, designed by Sally Jacobs, features Alan Howard, Sara Kestleman, and John Kane. (It opens on Aug 27.) *The Tempest* has Barton for its director. Richardson is Prospero. The touring Theatre-Go-Round offers *Doctor Faustus* and *King John*.

April 8 Returned from its successful visit to Los Angeles, the National Theatre now shows Farquhar's *The Beaux' Stratagem*—which has had its premiere in Los Angeles—at London's Old Vic. William Gaskill directs. Maggie Smith, Ronald Pickup, and Robert Stephens head the cast. On April 28, the National offers Jonathan Miller's staging of *The Merchant of Venice*, with Laurence Olivier as Shylock, dressed in prosperous late Victorian style. Julia Trevelyan Oman carries the Victorian motif throughout the settings and costumes. Joan Plowright, Jane Lapotaire, and Jim Dale are also in the cast. On July 15, Josef Svoboda, the Czech wizard of stage-design and theatre-technology, creates the settings for Simon Gray's adaptation of Dostoievsky's *The Idiot*. Unfortunately, the scenery doesn't work too well; Svoboda later blames the inefficiency of British craftsmen. Anthony Quayle directs.

April 13 At the Aldwych Theatre, the RSC again helps sponsor London's World Theatre Season, produced by Peter Daubeny. It opens with *Mandragola* a Renaissance Italian sex-farce by Machiavelli now performed in Czech by the Cinoherni Klub of Prague. Jiri Menzel directs. On April 16, Alena Vostra's *Whose Turn Next* is performed by the troupe, in Jan Kacer's staging. On May 25, the Moscow Art Theatre comes to the Aldwych for its World Theatre performances of Chekhov's *The Seagull*, staged by B. N. Livanov.

April 13 There must be a lesson in this evening's Off-Broadway premiere. The venerable musical melodrama, *The Drunkard*, has been running for years here at the 13th Street Theatre to audiences of young people, with steins of beer and boos for the villainous Lawyer Cribbs (Christopher Cable). The theatre has been refurbished and the show reworked for review by professional critics—with music by Barry Manilow. The play closes in six weeks.

April 14 Sandy Wilson's parody of a 1920's British musical, *The Boy Friend*, opens in a New York revival staged by Gus Schirmer. It runs 15 weeks. Judy Carne and Sandy Duncan are in the cast.

April 24 Joseph Papp continues the season at his Public Theatre in Greenwich Village with *Mod Donna*, a musical by Myrna Lamb (libretto) and Susan Bingham (score). It has a run of seven weeks.

April 28 For years, Kurt Weill and Bertolt Brecht fans have been waiting for a fully staged production of their satire on mindless capitalism, *Mahagonny*. Carmen Capalbo's staging at the Anderson Theatre on New York's Second Avenue has just eight performances, even with a cast including Estelle Parsons and Barbara Harris.

May 6 After a long lapse, this season's program of regional residential theatre company productions at New York's ANTA Theatre briefly resumes with five performances of Chekhov's *The Cherry Orchard*, staged by John Fernald, artistic director of the Meadow Brook Theatre in Rochester, Michigan. On May 26 *Wilson in the Promised Land* is offered. This is Adrian Hall's production for the Trinity Square Repertory Company of Providence, Rhode Island. There are only seven performances.

May 13 The Chichester Festival, under the direction of John Clements, opens its summer season of four plays in Southern England. Henrik Ibsen's *Peer Gynt* is staged by Peter Coe and designed by Sean Kenny. Robert Bolt's *Vivat! Vivat Regina!* premieres, staged by Peter Dews. George Bernard Shaw's *Arms and the Man* is directed by Clements. Jonson's *The Alchemist* is staged by Dews.

May 22 Artistic director Angus Bowmer opens the Oregon Shakespeare Festival with his staging of *The Merchant of Ven-*

ice. Other productions in the outdoor Elizabethan Theatre are Stoppard's *Rosencrantz and Guildenstern Are Dead*, Molière's *The Imaginary Invalid*, and the Bard's *Julius Caesar*, *Richard II*, and *The Comedy of Errors*.

May 25 The Cafe La Mama Company from New York opens at the Royal Court Theatre in London with a double-bill: Leonard Melfi's *Cinque* and Adrienne Kennedy's *Rats Mass*. On June 1, the troupe offers Alfred Jarry's *Ubu Roi*, followed by *Arden of Faversham*.

May 26 Joseph Chaikin's Open Theatre uses New York's Washington Square Methodist Church to produce a program of three company works: *Terminal*, *The Serpent: A Ceremony*, and *Endgame*. Yankowitz, van Itallie, and Beckett are the respective authors, whose texts have been enlarged upon by the improvisatory techniques of Chaikin's troupe. There are 18 performances. *The Serpent* becomes a "Best Play."

June In San Diego, the National Shakespeare Festival gets underway. Plays chosen by producing director Craig Noel include *Cymbeline*, *Much Ado About Nothing*, and *Richard II*, all staged in the festival's Old Globe Theatre in Balboa Park. Nearby is the new Carter Theatre, where Brandon Thomas's *Charley's Aunt* is on view.

June 2 Time for summer Shakespeare in London again. *A Midsummer Night's Dream* opens the season in the Open Air Theatre at Regent's Park. Richard Digby Day stages. Trevor Peacock plays Bottom. On July 14, *Much Ado About Nothing* opens, staged by David Conville. On Aug 4, Day presents *The Lord Byron Show*, which he's devised from the poet's works and life. Gary Bond is Byron.

June 7 Jean Gascon opens another season of Canada's Stratford Festival, directing *The Merchant of Venice*. Michael Langham, former festival director, returns to stage Sheridan's *The School for Scandal*. Peter Gill stages Ibsen's *Hedda Gabler*, in Christopher Hampton's version. Gascon directs *Cymbeline*, designed by Tanya Moiseiwitsch. Arrabal's *The Architect and the Emperor of Assyria* has Chattie Salaman as its director. Kurt Reis stages Arnold Wesker's *The Friends*. Slawomir Mrozek's *Vatzlav* is directed by Colin George. Powys Thomas stages Patrick Crean's one-man show, *The Sun Never Sets*. Marcel Marceau presents his mime characters.

June 11 At London's Greenwich Theatre, Brendan Behan's *The Hostage* is revived, staged by Alan Vaughan Williams.

June 15 At London's Mermaid Theatre, Jonathan Miller directs *The Tempest*, with Graham Crowden and Angela Pleasance.

June 16 In Stratford, Connecticut, the American Shakespeare Festival opens with three productions: *All's Well That Ends Well*, staged by Michael Kahn; *Othello*, staged by Kahn; and *The Devil's Disciple*, by George Bernard Shaw, staged by Cyril Ritchard.

June 20 At London's Royal Court Theatre, Barry Hines's *Billy's Last Stand* is performed in the Theatre Upstairs, staged by Michael Wearing. Ian McKellen plays Darkly. On Aug 3, Christopher Hampton's play, *The Philanthropist*, opens, with Alec McCowen in the leading role. Robert Kidd directs. On Aug 11, Hampton's *When Did You Last See My Mother?* is revived.

June 20 Theatre Arts of West Virginia presents *The Hatfields and the McCoys*, a drama by Billy Ed Wheeler on the feud between the two mountaineer families during and after the Civil War. It is shown in the 1,500-seat Cliffside Amphitheatre in Beckley, West Virginia.

June 22 Canada's Shaw Festival at Niagara-on-the-Lake opens with *Candida*, staged by Harris Yulin. This production has already previewed in Ottawa and Kingston. Tony Van Bridge has compiled and arranged *G. K. C.*, which he now plays as "The Wit and Wisdom of Gilbert Keith Chesterton." Artistic Director Paxton Whitehead stages Alan Bennett's *Forty Years On*.

June 23 Dion Boucicault's forgotten 19th century comedy, *London Assurance*, adapted and staged by Ronald Eyre, opens at London's Aldwych Theatre, with a Royal Shakespeare cast including Donald Sinden, Judi Dench, and Elizabeth Spriggs. It remains a repertory favorite, opening on April 5, 1972 at the New Theatre in the West End. It tallies 390 performances and later moves to Broadway's Palace Theatre, which is too large for the production to be effective. On July 2, the RSC presents its 1969 Stratford staging of *The Winter's Tale*, followed on July 21 with Gunter Grass' *The Plebeians Rehearse the Uprising*, an indictment of Bertolt Brecht's failure to support fellow East Berliners in their uprising against Russian oppression. On Aug 6, the Stratford *Twelfth Night* (1969) opens, with Sinden, Dench, Spriggs, and Richard Pasco as Orsino.

June 23 In Central Park's Delacorte Theatre, Joseph Papp's New York Shakespeare Festival offers a sequence of three plays under the title *The Wars of the Roses*, a concept pioneered by the Royal Shakespeare Company. Stuart Vaughan stages. The plays are *The Chronicles of King Henry VI, Part 1*, *The Chronicles of King Henry VI, Part 2*, and *Richard III*.

June 24 W. Somerset Maugham's *Lady Frederick* is revived in London at the Vaudeville Theatre. Malcolm Farquhar stages. Margaret Lockwood plays the title-role in this production, seen first at the Yvonne Arnaud Theatre in Guildford. There are 104 performances.

June 29 The much-admired Ingmar Bergman production of Henrik Ibsen's *Hedda Gabler*, shown at the World Theatre Festival by Stockholm's Royal Dramatic Theatre in 1968, is now reproduced in English, and staged by Bergman. Maggie Smith is Hedda. Robert Stephens and Jeremy Brett are also in the cast.

July 3 Paul Green's *Trumpet In The Land* opens in the Schoenbrunn Amphitheatre in Philadelphia, Ohio. It tells the story of Ohio's first settlement in 1772.

July 4 In Monmouth, Maine, the first season of summer Shakespeare begins, produced by "The Theatre at Monmouth." Robert Joyce and Richard Sewall are the directors, offering *Twelfth Night*, *Romeo and Juliet*, and Christopher Fry's *The Lady's Not for Burning*.

July 9 At London's Drury Lane Theatre, *The Great Waltz* opens, based on the compositions of Johann Strauss, with lyrics by Robert Wright and George Forrest. In Wendy Toye's staging, with choreography by Edmund Balin, the production earns a run of 706 performances.

July 23 Noel Coward's *Blithe Spirit* is revived in London at the Globe Theatre. Staged by Nigel Patrick, the play's cast includes Beryl Reid, Patrick Cargill, Phyllis Calvert, and Amanda Reiss.

Aug 3 Dublin's Abbey Theatre Company comes to London's Old Vic with a double-bill of *The Dandy Dolls*, by George Fitzmaurice, and *The Well of the Saints*, by John Millington Synge. Hugh Hunt directs.

Aug 19–Sept 6 The Festival of Underground Theatre is held at St. Lawrence Centre, Toronto, Canada. Participants include Toronto's fledgling Factory Lab Theatre, Theatre Passe Muraille, New York's Bread and Puppet Theatre, the Living Theatre, and, from Paris, Théâtre de la Grande Panique.

Aug 23 The Edinburgh Festival opens with theatre productions prominent among the offerings of music, dance, opera, and drama. Among foreign guests are the Deutsches Theater, with Aristophanes' *Peace*; Productions d'Aujourdui, with Jean Rougerie's staging of Ionesco's *Inedits*, and Rome's Teatro Libero, with Luca Ronconi's staging of Ariosto's *Orlando Furioso*. From Britain come the Leeds Playhouse troupe, with Bill Hays' production of Pirandello's *Henry IV*; The Combine create *Stomp*; the Royal Shakespeare Company presents Terry Hands' collage, *Pleasure and Repentance*, with Janet Suzman and others. The Prospect Theatre, bred in Edinburgh, presents Shakespeare's *Much Ado About Nothing* and Boswell's *Life of Johnson*, both staged by Toby Robertson. Edinburgh's Royal Lyceum ensemble plays Middleton and Rowley's *The Changeling* and John McGrath's *Random Happenings in the Hebrides*.

Sep 1 At London's Greenwich Theatre, John Hale stages his own play, *Lorna and*

Ted, with Rita Tushingham and Ray McAnally in the title-roles. On the 29th, Iris Murdoch's *The Servants and the Snow* is presented, staged by Alan Vaughan Williams. Adrienne Corri, Tom Conti, and Maxine Audley are among this cast. Ewan Hooper stages his play, *Down the Arches*, on Oct 29. John Mortimer's *A Voyage Round My Father* opens, later to transfer to the West End.

Sep 3 George Bernard Shaw's *Saint Joan*, with Angela Pleasance as the Maid, opens in revival at London's Mermaid Theatre. Bernard Miles directs. On Nov 12, Harold Pinter directs James Joyce's *Exiles*, with John Wood and Vivien Merchant. Ron Pember stages *Dick Turpin*, a holiday treat about the notorious highwayman, on Dec 17.

Sep 4 In Glasgow at the Citizens' Theatre, now under Giles Havergal's artistic direction, a triumvirate including director-playwright Robert David MacDonald and designer-director Philip Prowse, is established. The season opens with *Hamlet*, followed by Tom Stoppard's *Rosencrantz and Guildenstern Are Dead, Mother Courage, Saint Joan, A Taste of Honey,* and *Aladdin*. At the Close Theatre, the Cits' second stage, the productions are *Landscape and Silence, Stop You're Killing Me, What the Butler Saw, The Madman and the Nun, 'Tis Pity She's a Whore,* and *Private Lives*.

Sep 10 At London's Royal Court Theatre, the Upstairs show is Howard Barker's *Cheek*, directed by William Gaskill. On Sep 14, Michael Weller's *Cancer*—called *Moonchildren* in New York—has its premiere, staged by Roger Hendricks Simon. Seth Allen and Davis Hall play Flower Children who sell out to the Establishment. Howard Brenton's *Fruit* is performed Upstairs on Sep 28, staged by David Hare. The next day Hare's *What Happened to Blake* is offered, staged by Tony Bicat.

Sep 11 The new Young Vic Theatre, located near London's Old Vic, opens with Frank Dunlop's innovative production of Molière's *The Cheats of Scapin*, with Jim Dale as Scapino. On the 24th, the company acts Sophocles' *Oedipus* in the W. B. Yeats translation. Ronald Pickup plays the king. On the 28th, Stravinsky's *The Soldier's Tale* opens, with an English text by Michael Flanders and Kitty Black. Wendy Toye stages. Nicky Henson plays the soldier. On Nov 18, Dale and Jane Lapotaire play in Shakespeare's *The Taming of the Shrew*, staged by Frank Dunlop. Carl Toms designs the show so that some spectators will be seated on bleachers in the stage area, where the play is performed as an entertainment for Christopher Sly—with an updating, making Sly into a modern football rooter. This production will be toured to the Holland Festival and to New York, among other centers. On Dec 10, Peter James stages

CAMINO REAL

some plays from The Wakefield Mystery Play Cycle, *The Wakefield Nativity*. On the 22nd, Gozzi's 18th century fantasy, *King Stag*, opens.

Oct 4 In Greenwich Village at Joseph Papp's Public Theatre, Dennis Reardon's *The Happiness Cage* opens the new season for a four-week run, staged by Tom Aldridge. Next comes a revival of *Trelawny of the "Wells"* for a six-week engagement, staged by Robert Ronan, beginning Oct 11. On Nov 19, Jack MacGowran offers his one-man show of Samuel Beckett works for 67 performances.

Oct 6 Joan Littlewood directs *Forward, Up Your End*, a play by Kenneth Hill, with music by Len Newberry, for her Theatre Workshop at London's Theatre Royal, Stratford East. On Dec 1, Littlewood stages *The Projector*, by William Rufus Chetwood.

Oct 8 André Gregory and his Manhattan Project ensemble adapt Lewis Carroll's *Alice in Wonderland* with psychedelic overtones and improvisational theatre techniques. The show has a run of 119 performances at the Extension in New York.

Oct 15 Equity Library Theatre opens its new season of revivals on New York's Riverside Drive at the Master Theatre with Ben Bagley's *Shoestring Revues*, followed by *Johnny No-Trump, Greenwillow, Present Laughter, Heloise, Ruddigore, The False Confessions,* and *Now Is the Time for All Good Men*.

Oct 16 At the American Place Theatre in St. Clement's Church in midtown Manhattan, Joyce Carol Oates' *Sunday Dinner* opens, staged by Curt Dempster. Steven Tesich's *The Carpenters* follows on Dec 10, in a staging by Eugene Lesser. The cast includes Vincent Gardenia and Alice Drummond.

Oct 19 George Bernard Shaw's *Major Barbara* is revived by the RSC at its Aldwych Theatre in London, with Clifford Williams staging. Judi Dench is Barbara. Richard Pasco, Brewster Mason and Elizabeth Spriggs are also in the cast. On Dec 17, Trevor Nunn's mounting of *King Henry the Eighth* opens with Donald Sinden as the king. On the 22nd, the play is *The Two Gentlemen of Verona*, featuring Peter Egan and Ian Richardson, directed by Robin Phillips.

Oct 21 At London's Royal Court Theatre, a Festival of New Work, titled *Come Together*, begins. It will last until Nov 9. Later in the decade, such ensembles and shows will be called "Alternative Theatre." Some of the current fare includes The People Show, Cartoon Archetypal Slogan Theatre, Ken Campbell's Road Show, Theatre Machine, Bruce Lacey and the Alberts, and the Freehold in *Antigone*, the Other Company in *The Journey*, the Pip Simmons Theatre Group in *The Pardoner's Tale*, the Brighton Combination in *The NAB Show*, and *A Celebration for Due Process*.

Oct 26 *Paul Sills' Story Theatre* opens in New York at the Ambassador Theatre, staged by Sills and animated by an ensemble including Hamilton Camp, and Valerie Harper. The troupe acts out old children stories, with a minimum of de-

or or props. There are 278 performances.

Oct 27 The National Theatre opens its production of Rostand's *Cyrano*, in the West End at the Cambridge Theatre, with Edward Woodward in the title-role. Patrick Garland has adapted and directed. On Dec 30, the National offers George Bernard Shaw's *Mrs. Warren's Profession* at the Old Vic, in Ron Eyre's staging. Sarah Badel and Coral Browne head the cast.

Nov 3 In London at the Round House, the Royal Shakespeare's traveling Theatre-ground troupe stages a festival of its productions: *When Thou Art King* opens, followed on the 5th by *Arden of Faversham*, and on the 9th by *King John*. On Nov 23, *Doctor Faustus* is presented, followed on the 26th by *The Elizabethans*.

Nov 4 A big bubble-tent, inflated with air, in New York's Bryant Park, is tonight's venue for *Orlando Furioso*, an Italian-language production brought from Italy by the Teatro Libero di Roma. Ludovico Ariosto's 16th-century poem has been adapted by Eduardo Sanguineti. Using avant-garde techniques and giant moving set-pieces, the company plays scenes throughout the tent, often simultaneously, requiring the standing audience to keep on the move. This production has a four-week run.

Nov 5 The Repertory Theatre of Lincoln Center opens its new season in the Vivian Beaumont Theatre with Bertolt Brecht's *The Good Woman of Setzuan*, staged by Robert Symonds. It has a six-week run, with Colleen Dewhurst in the lead.

Nov 5 Terence Rattigan's *The Winslow Boy*, staged by Frith Banbury, is revived at London's New Theatre. Steven Pacey plays Ronnie Winslow, wrongly accused of theft and dismissed from the Naval Academy. Kenneth More is the barrister, who wins the case for him. The production runs on into the next season.

Nov 10 Ibsen's *The Wild Duck*, is revived at London's Criterion, with Dulcie Gray, and Michael Denison and Hayley Mills. Glen Byam Shaw stages. On Nov 17, J. B. Priestley's *When We Are Married* is revived at the Strand Theatre, having originated at the Yvonne Arnaud Theatre in Guildford. Robert Chetwyn directs.

Nov 17 The Negro Ensemble Company begins its new season in Greenwich Village at the St. Marks Playhouse, under the direction of Douglas Turner Ward. *Ododo* opens the season, a musical play by Joseph Walker with a score by Dorothy Dinroe. Walker directs. The show runs six weeks.

Nov 18 At London's Royal Court Theatre, Upstairs, Howard Barker's *No One Was Saved* opens, in Pam Brighton's staging. On Dec 8, Peter Barnes's adaptation of Frank Wedekind's *Erdgeist* and *Die Buchse Pandoras*, called *Lulu*, opens with Julia Foster in the title-role. Barnes and Stuart Burge direct, with choreography by Eleanor Fazan. The production, with some cast changes, has been first seen at the Nottingham Playhouse in October.

Dec 8 The holiday season, that time of pantomimes, spectacles, and revivals for children of various ages, now opens with the Young Vic's *Wakefield Nativity*, followed on the 10th by *Give a Dog a Bone*, at the Westminster Theatre. Other shows include *Isabel's a Jezebel* (Duchess), *The Owl and the Pussy Cat Went to See . . .* (Jeannetta Cochrane), *Robinson Crusoe* (Players'), *Dick Turpin* (Mermaid), *Winnie the Pooh* (Phoenix), *Toad of Toad Hall* (Duke of York's), *Aladdin* (Palladium, with Cilla Black), *King Stag* (Young Vic), and *The Watched Pot* (Mermaid).

Dec 17 Avant-garde theatre theorist and practitioner Richard Schechner stages *Commune* in New York's Soho district at the Performing Garage. The world of Charles Manson and the murder of Sharon Tate are explored, among other contemporary events. The show runs for eight weeks.

Dec 21 At London's Hampstead Theatre Club, Noel Coward's one-acts, *Tonight at Eight*, as it's now called, opens in Gillian Lynne's staging. The plays are *We Were Dancing*, *Red Peppers*, and *Family Album*.

Dec 24 The Sadler's Wells Opera Company opens at the London Coliseum in Cole Porter's *Kiss Me, Kate*, staged by Peter Coe. Ann Howard and Emile Belcourt play the leading roles.

1970 BIRTHS/DEATHS/DEBUTS

Jan 30 English actor Malcolm Keen (b. 1887) is dead. He appeared in *The Skin Game*, *R.U.R.*, and *Rain*, among other plays. In 1936 he was Claudius in John Gielgud's Broadway *Hamlet*.

March 13 Playwright-composer-actor Rick Besoyan (b. 1924) dies in Sayville, New York. Besoyan made his New York debut as producer and director of Cole Porter's *Out of this World* in 1957. His *Little Mary Sunshine* earned him the Drama Desk's Vernon Rice Award in 1960.

April 26 American actress and author Gypsy Rose Lee (b. 1914) dies in Los Angeles. Lee appeared on stage at age six in vaudeville with her sister, June Havoc. She was later noted for her "strip-tease" act.

April 29 Actor Ed Begley (b. 1901) dies in Los Angeles. His Broadway debut was in *Land of Fame* at the Belasco Theatre in 1943. Begley received the Donaldson Award in 1955 for his performance in *Inherit the Wind*.

May 14 Actress Billie Burke (b. 1886) dies in Los Angeles. Burke first appeared on stage in the musical, *The School Girl*, in London in 1903. She made her Broadway debut in *My Wife* in 1907. She married producer Florenz Ziegfeld in 1914.

May 22 American drama critic Joseph Wood Krutch (b. 1893) dies in Tucson, Arizona. From 1924 he was critic of *The Nation*. His *American Drama Since 1918* is a standard source on American theatre between the two world wars.

May 23 American actress Nydia Westman (b. 1902) dies in Burbank, California. Westman first appeared on stage in 1915 at the Bronx Opera House as part of The Westman Family. Her film career began in 1932.

June 4 The popular American performer, Menasha Skulnik, who for years was a mainstay of Yiddish theatre, now dies, aged 79.

June 11 American actor Frank Silvera dies, aged 56.

June 12 Sir Laurence Olivier is named a life peer. He is the first actor in British history to be seated in the House of Lords. Lord Olivier is currently appearing as Shylock in the National Theatre production of *The Merchant of Venice*.

July 7 American actress Marjorie Rambeau (b. 1889) is dead. Rambeau spent several years in stock companies, notably at the Burbank and Belasco Theatres in Los Angeles. She made her first appearance in New York in 1913 in *Kick In*.

Aug 10 Actor Leo Ciceri dies at age 46.

Sep 29 Edward Everett Horton dies at 83. *Springtime for Henry* was a role he often played.

Nov 17 Nauton Wayne, the British actor, has died, aged 69.

Nov 21 Actress Carlotta Monterey, widow of playwright Eugene O'Neill, dies at 82.

Dec 7 Actress Lenore Ulric dies at 78.

Dec 27 Playwright William Archibald is dead at 53. *The Innocents* was his most successful work.

1970 THEATERS/PRODUCTIONS

U.S. patents granted this year include a theatre-related one for Herman Neilsen and Stephen Valiant's fireplace noise-simulator.

Feb 26 The new Saint Lawrence Centre, which houses an 830-seat thrust stage theatre and a 487-seat concert hall, opens in Toronto, Canada. *Man, Inc.*, by Montrealer Jacques Languirand, is the premiere production, with music by Norman Symonds.

March 21 The Angus Bowmer Theatre is dedicated in Ashland. It is a new indoor end-stage performance-space for the Oregon Shakespearean Festival, founded in 1935 by Angus Bowmer.

Spring Douglas Bankson and Sheila Neville form the New Play Centre in Vancouver, British Columbia, Canada, to develop new Canadian plays.

April 2 The Royalty Theatre in London re-opens, after ten years as a cinema, with *Birds of a Feather*, an all-male revue.

April 10 In Boston, the producers of *Hair* temporarily close the show, rather than remove the nudity which has offended the Massachusetts Supreme Court. A federal panel finds in favor of *Hair*, supported on May 22 by the U.S. Supreme Court.

May The Factory Theatre Lab opens in Toronto, Canada, in a disused factory. Founder-playwright Ken Gass produces only Canadian plays, and gives a start to new playwrights such as David Freeman and Larry Fineberg.

May 3 Tonight marks the 10th anniversary of the Off-Broadway musical, *The Fantasticks*.

May 31 On this last day of the current 1969–1970 Broadway season, there are only a handful of shows which have paid off their investment, technically making them hits in *Variety's* estimation. They are *Butterflies Are Free*, *Last of the Red Hot Lovers*, *Child's Play*, *Charles Azna-*

vour, and *The Front Page.*

June 1 Economically, the Broadway season, which officially ended yesterday, has been disappointing. *Variety* estimates a seven percent drop in gross income over last season. From $59 million in 1968, the gross has declined to $53 million. $48 million gross is earned by Broadway roadshows, however. On Broadway, there have been 68 productions, 21 of them new American plays, with 14 musicals. There have been 18 revivals, four specialties, three foreign plays in English, and eight foreign-language productions, according to Otis Guernsey, Jr. Off-Broadway, 33 productions have lasted only two weeks or less; seven of them had only one showing. But there have been 64 new plays Off-Broadway, 53 of them by American playwrights. Also on view: 16 musicals, 10 revues, 13 revivals, five specialties, and 11 each of foreign plays in English and foreign plays in their original languages.

New York's ten "Best Plays," in the judgment of Guernsey, Jr., have been Kopit's *Indians*, Gershe's *Butterflies Are Free*, Simon's *The Last of the Red Hot Lovers*, Marasco's *Child's Play*, Zindel's *The Effect of Gamma Rays on Man-in-the-Moon Marigolds*, Furth/Sondheim's *Company*, Comden/Green/Adams/Strouse's *Applause*, Feiffer's *The White House Murder Case*, Orton's *What the Butler Saw*, and Jean-Claude Van Itallie's *The Serpent.*

June 1 In America's professional resident theatres, there have been, by season's close, 302 productions, offered by 37 troupes in 52 theatres in 36 cities, ac-

cording to Ella Malin, in *Best Play* American scripts account for 157 of t productions, with 114 of the total pla produced given fully staged production Of the total, 56 are world premiere Shakespeare is the most popular pla wright. Shaw, Chekhov, Molière, Kau man, and Williams follow in that orde

July Concerned about the on-going f nancing of Canada's Stratford Festival, th Province of Ontario retires 54% of th festival's accumulated deficit with a on time grant. The Canada Council pays th first of five annual installments to retir the balance. No deficits will be permitte in the future.

Sep 5 The Glasgow Citizens' Theatre open a second stage, The Close Theatre, as venue for experimental productions.

Sep 11 London's Young Vic Theatre open with *The Cheats of Scapin* (a.k.a. *Sca pino*), presented by the National Theatre

Sep 25 Philadelphia grants a buildin permit for the restoration and renovatio of the Walnut Street Theatre. In 1969, i has been named a National Historica Landmark, the first step in saving an restoring it.

Nov 16 Actors Equity members strike Off Broadway theatres, closing 17 shows, ove demands for salary, welfare, and pen sions. The strike ends Dec 16. Only 13 o the struck shows re-open Off-Broadway. Two move to Broadway and "middle" theatres. Equity minimums now are $75–$150, depending on the show's weekly gross. Arbitration awards Equity $100–$175, rising in 1971 to $125–$175.

Nov 29 In Washington, D.C., a second playhouse, The Kreeger Theatre, is added to Zelda Fichhandler's prestigious Arena Theatre. The designer of the 500-seat fanshaped auditorium is Harry Weese.

Dec 2 Today in Oklahoma City, the Mummers Theatre, directed by Mack Scism, opens. Scism's troupe has been performing in various guises and venues since 1949. The theatre, a strikingly modernistfunctionalist complex, has been eight years in planning, with David Hays as stage designer and John Johansen as architect. There are two theatre-spaces—a 592-seat open-thrust, with seating bordering the stage in a 270° arc, and a 240-seat arena stage. Not long after the theatre's opening, because of awkward financial arrangements and some political machinations, the Mummers are through as an ensemble, and the theatre is closed.

Dec 17 In Norwich, England, the Theatre Royal reopens after extensive improvements. The London Festival Ballet offers *The Nutcracker* at the opening gala. In the mid-1970's, the theatre will become one of the most profitable civic theatres in Britain and Europe.

Dec 22 The cinemas ABC 1 and ABC 2 open in London's reconstructed Saville Theatre, which opened in 1931.

MARCEL MARCEAU

Jan 3 *Stag Movie* (NY—Gate—Musical). Touted as the first nude stage musical, this show has a run of 11 weeks, directed by Bernard Barrow. About the making of a porn film, it outrages some Gay Liberationists.

Feb 7 *The Trial of the Catonsville Nine* (NY—Good Shepherd Faith Church—Drama). Saul Levitt and Daniel Berrigan's play about the Berrigan brothers' trial for antiwar protests, is a "Best Play." Ed Flanders and Michael Kane play the brothers. After a run of 130 performances, it moves to the Lyceum Theatre for 29 more showings.

Feb 10 *The House of Blue Leaves* (NY—Truck and Warehouse—Comedy). John Guare's antic play, about a New York Catholic family preparing for a Pope's visit to the city, is chosen as a "Best Play." It has a run of 42 weeks. Katherine Helmond and Harold Gould are among the cast. Mel Shapiro stages.

Feb 25 *And Miss Reardon Drinks a Little* (NY—Morosco—Drama). Julie Harris plays a spinster school-teacher, living a life of quiet desperation, who turns to alcohol to sustain her in Paul Zindel's play. A "Best Play," it has a run of 108 performances. Nancy Marchand and Estelle Parsons are also in the cast. Melvin Bernhardt directs.

March 15 *The Philanthropist* (NY—Ethel Barrymore—Comedy). Alec McCowen and Jane Asher head the cast of this Ibsen comedy, translated by Christopher Hampton. A success in London, it runs only nine weeks but is selected as a "Best Play." Robert Kidd stages.

March 24 *The Proposition* (NY—Gramercy Arts—Revue). Josh Mostel and Karen Welles are among the company of comic improvisers who build sketches from ideas suggested by the audience. There are 1,109 performances.

March 28 *All Over* (NY—Martin Beck—Drama). In Edward Albee's play, a man lies dying and his family, mistress, doctor, and friend review their relationships with him. Despite a cast headed by Colleen Dewhurst and Jessica Tandy, and staging by John Gielgud, it is all over after 42 performances. On Jan 31, 1972, however, Peter Hall directs a new Royal Shakespeare Company production at London's Aldwych Theatre. Peggy Ashcroft and Angela Lansbury appear.

April 4 *Follies* (NY—Winter Garden—Musical). Harold Prince conceives, produces, and directs this musical about Follies girls, basing it on James Goldman's play *The Girls Upstairs*. It has a run of 521 performances, is named a "Best Play," and wins the New York Drama Critics' Circle Best Musical citation. Stephen Sondheim writes the songs, and Michael

TRIAL OF THE CATONSVILLE NINE

Bennett choreographs. Alexis Smith heads the cast.

May 17 *Godspell* (NY—Cherry Lane—Musical). Seen first at La Mama E.T.C., John-Michael Tebelak's musical adaptation of the Gospel of St. Matthew, with songs by Stephen Schwartz, has the third-longest Off-Broadway run in history—2,124 performances. On June 22, 1976, it opens on Broadway at the Broadhurst Theatre for 527 performances.

May 26 *Lenny* (NY—Brooks Atkinson—Drama). Cliff Gorman plays satirist Lenny Bruce, in Julian Barry's script, built from incidents in Bruce's life and extracts from his writings. Tom O'Horgan directs; there are 455 performances. On April 14, 1975, Marty Brill opens as Lenny in the London production at the Criterion Theatre for 58 performances.

June 16 *Black Girl* (NY—Theatre de Lys—Drama). After a debut at the New Federal Theatre, J. E. Franklin's tale of a black family living in a small Texas town, transfers Off-Broadway for a 29-week run. Shauneille Perry stages a cast including Kishasha and Minnie Gentry.

Oct 6 *Look Me Up* (NY—Plaza 9—Revue). There are 406 performances of this cabaret featuring popular songs of the past decades. Laurence Taylor conceives the show; Costas Omero stages. Zan Charisse and Kevin Christopher are among the performers.

Oct 7 *Where Has Tommy Flowers Gone?* (NY—Eastside—Comedy). Terrence McNally's play about a man who has his own ways of getting along in a big unfriendly city is selected as a "Best Play." Seen previously at the Yale Repertory Theatre and the Berkshire Festival, it has a 10-week run, staged by Jacques Levy. Robert Drivas plays the lead.

Oct 12 *Jesus Christ Superstar* (NY—Mark Hellinger—Musical). Andrew Lloyd Webber creates the music; Tim Rice writes the lyrics, and Tom O'Horgan stages this phenomenally successful mod-rock version of Jesus' life. Jeff Fenholt and Yvonne Elliman play the leading roles. It has 720 performances, tours, has a return Broadway engagement, and on Aug 9, 1972, opens at London's Palace Theatre, with Jim Sharman directing. By Jan 1, 1980, there had been 3,085 London performances.

Oct 20 *Ain't Supposed to Die a Natural Death* (NY—Ethel Barrymore—Musical). Melvin Van Peebles writes the book (chosen as a "Best Play"), music, and lyrics for this collection of sketches about black experiences in contemporary America. Previously seen in California, it has a 10-month run, staged by Gilbert Moses. Dick Williams and Joe Fields are in the cast.

Nov 3 *Love Me, Love My Children* (NY—Mercer-O'Casey—Musical). Seen first in Toronto, this Robert Swerdlow show has a six-month run. Paul Aaron stages a cast including Mark Baker and Jacqueline Britt.

Nov 11 *The Prisoner of Second Avenue* (NY—Eugene O'Neill—Comedy). Neil Simon's comedy, staged by Mike Nichols, has 780 performances and is selected as a "Best Play." Peter Falk plays a New Yorker who loses his job, can't find another, and has a breakdown. Lee Grant plays his wife.

Nov 14 *Twigs* (NY—Broadhurst—Comedy). Sada Thompson plays four quite different women in George Furth's four playlets, *Emily, Celia, Dorothy,* and *Ma.* Michael Bennett directs the nine-month run.

Dec 19 *Inner City* (NY—Ethel Barry-more—Musical). Tom O'Horgan conceives and directs this show, based on Eve Merriam's *The Inner City Mother Goose,* a satire on growing up in the ghettos of an American city. It has a three-month run. Merriam provides lyrics.

Dec 20 *Murderous Angels* (NY—Playhouse—Drama). Conor Cruise O'Brien, former special emissary to the U. N. Secretary General in Africa, speculates about what may have happened to Dag Hammarskjöld (Jean-Pierre Aumont) and Patrice Lumumba (Lou Gossett) in their final hours, in this play which runs only three weeks. Gordon Davidson stages.

1971 BRITISH PREMIERES

Jan 18 *Company.* See NY premiere, 1970.

Jan 28 *Kean* (L—Globe—Drama). Alan Badel plays the British actor Edmund Kean in Jean-Paul Sartre's adaptation of Dumas' play. Frank Hauser, who's first shown the production at the Oxford Playhouse in Sep 1970, directs. It runs into the next season.

Feb 24 *Spoiled* (L—Haymarket—Drama). There are only 38 showings of Simon Gray's new play about a student who disrupts the homelife of a married teacher. Anna Massey, Jeremy Kemp, and Simon Ward head the cast. Stephen Hollis directs.

March 17 *Move Over Mrs. Markham* (L—Vaudeville—Comedy). Ray Cooney and John Chapman's farce, a sexual wild goose chase, has 785 performances. Moira Lister, Cicely Courtneidge, and Tony Britton head the cast. Cooney stages.

May 11 *The Dirtiest Show in Town.* See NY premiere, 1970.

June 1 *Old Times* (L—Aldwych—Drama). Peter Hall directs the Royal Shakespeare Company's production of Harold Pinter's play about the ambiguous relationships between a man and two women, one his wife, the other her friend. Colin Blakely, Vivien Merchant, and Dorothy Tutin appear. There are 70 performances in repertory. On Nov 16, 1971, the play opens at Broadway's Billy Rose Theatre, with Robert Shaw, Mary Ure, and Rosemary Harris. It is chosen as a "Best Play" but has only a 15-week run.

June 3 *No Sex Please—We're British* (L—Strand—Comedy). Anthony Marriott and Alistair Foot's farce about a family man mistakenly inundated with shipments of pornography, has 3,571 performances by Jan 1, 1980. Allan Davis stages with Anthony Valentine, Michael Crawford, and Evelyn Laye. On Feb 20, 1973, an American production opens at New York's Ritz with Maureen O'Sullivan and Stephen Collins. It barely lasts two weeks.

June 17 *The Patrick Pearse Motel* (L—Queen's—Comedy). First seen at the Dublin Theatre Festival in March, Hugh Leonard's Irish fable about a wife (Moira Redmond) who decides to see an old beau, has 84 performances. James Grout directs.

July 14 *Butley* (L—Criterion—Drama). Alan Bates plays a self-destructive teacher whose sarcasm and cruelty are alienating both his wife and lover, in Simon Gray's play. Harold Pinter directs. There are 464 performances. Bates repeats his role when the play opens at Broadway's Morosco Theatre on Oct 31, 1972. It runs just 17 weeks.

Aug 4 *A Voyage Round My Father* (L—Haymarket—Drama). Alec Guinness has the lead in John Mortimer's well-received play about a man coming to terms with himself and with his father. It has 498 performances. The play has previously been seen at the Greenwich Theatre in 1970.

Sep 15 *Don't Just Lie There, Say Something!* (L—Garrick—Comedy). There are 612 performances of this Michael Pertwee farce about members of parliament, presented by "The Brian Rix Theatre of Laughter." Rix and Alfred Marks head the cast. Wallace Douglas directs.

Sep 30 . . . *Suddenly at Home* (L—Fortune—Drama). 715 performances reward Francis Durbridge's mystery thriller, in which a husband (Gerald Harper) plans the murder of his rich wife (Penelope Keith). Basil Coleman directs.

Oct 6 *West of Suez* (L—Cambridge—Drama). Ralph Richardson and Jill Bennett head the cast of John Osborne's new play, about the death-throes of colonialism. It has 206 performances. It was first seen at the Royal Court Theatre in August.

Oct 14 *Getting On* (L—Queen's—Comedy). Kenneth More and Gemma Jones animate Alan Bennett's comedy about an M.P. who feels trapped between the foolishness of the young and the materialism of the mature. Patrick Garland directs. There are 227 performances.

Oct 19 *Ambassador* (L—Her Majesty's—Musical). Howard Keel is featured in this American musical adaptation of Henry James's novel *The Ambassadors.* It has only 86 performances. Stone Widney directs. Hal Hackaday, Don Ettlinger, and Don Gohman are the creators.

Nov 9 *The Changing Room* (L—Royal Court—Drama). David Storey's naturalistic play about a football team and the camaraderie among the players, involves the cast in total nudity. Lindsay Anderson directs. On March 6, 1973, the play opens at Broadway's Morosco Theatre. It has a run of six months and is chosen as a "Best Play." John Lithgow wins a Tony Award as Best Supporting Actor.

Nov 16 *Applause.* See NY premiere, 1970.

1971 REVIVALS/REPERTORIES

Jan 6 At the Young Vic in London, Misha Williams' *Byron—The Naked Peacock* opens, in a Donald MacKechnie staging. Samuel Beckett's *Endgame* is revived on Feb 2. Peter James directs.

Jan 7 Sean O'Casey's *The Playboy of the Western World* opens at New York's Vivian Beaumont Theatre, continuing the current season. There are 52 showings, followed by 54 of Arthur Miller's re-working of Ibsen's *An Enemy of the People,* staged by Jules Irving on March 11. On May 13, Sophocles' *Antigone* opens for 46 performances with Martha Henry.

Jan 7 In Edinburgh at the Traverse Theatre, *Sweet Alice* and *Oh Starlings,* by Stanley Eveling, open the new year. Some 42 productions will be offered: the Pip Simmons Theatre Group's production of *Superman,* Victor Revis' *Boots,* Snoo Wilson's *Pignight,* Alisdair Skinner's *The One To One,* and Stephen Poliakoff's *A Day With My Sister.*

Jan 9 Today is the last day of Edward Bond's *Black Mass* in London at Ed Berman's Ambiance Lunch-Hour Theatre Club. It's been playing with Michael Stevens' *Have You Met Our Rabbit* since the holiday season began. In the coming year, plays will be performed by such talents as Prunella Scales, Patrick Barlow, and Corin Redgrave. Directors will include Berman, Jim Hiley, and Roland Rees. Among the playwrights are James Saunders, Tom Stoppard, and Bernard Pomerance.

Jan 11 Alan Bates plays *Hamlet* in the Nottingham Playhouse production, opening tonight at the Cambridge Theatre, London. Anthony Page stages.

Jan 12 The Negro Ensemble Company's

New York season continues with the opening of a double-bill: *Perry's Mission*, by Clarence Young III, and *Rosalee Pritchett*, by Carlton and Barbara Molette. There are 44 showings, followed by Derek Walcott's *The Dream on Monkey Mountain*. This runs six weeks. John Scott's *Ride a Black Horse* is the final offering, on May 25, for a run of four weeks. Ward directs.

Jan 13 Producer Hillard Elkins gives his wife, Claire Bloom, the opportunity to play leads in two Ibsen masterpieces in repertory. Tonight *A Doll's House* opens, followed on Feb 17 by *Hedda Gabler*. Britain's Christopher Hampton translates. Patrick Garland stages both plays at the Playhouse Theatre. There are 111 showings of the first production and 56 of the second.

Jan 18 At London's Royal Court Theatre. Judy Parfitt plays the lead in John Webster's *The Duchess of Malfi*, staged by Peter Gill. On Jan 22 in the Theatre Upstairs, Michael Smith's *Captain Jack's Revenge* is played. Bill Bryden directs Bertolt Brecht's *The Baby Elephant* Upstairs for a Feb 9 opening, followed on Feb 23 by David Snodin's *A Game Called Arthur*, directed by Michael Rudman for the Traverse Theatre of Edinburgh. William Gaskill directs Brecht's *Man Is Man* on March 1, with Georgia Brown as Widow Begbick. E. A. Whitehead's *The Foursome* opens Upstairs on the 17th, followed on May 4 by a transfer to the Fortune Theatre. Edward Bond's *Passion* is a Court production on April 11, but it's played at the Alexandra Park Racecourse. Dennis Cannan's *One at Night* opens on the 13th, with Michael Almaz's *Anarchist* on the 28th. May 19, Bill Bryden stages *Corunna!*, a ballad musical. On May 24, David Hare's *Slag* opens, with Anna Massey and Lynn Redgrave in the cast.

Jan 19 *No, No, Nanette* is a new but nostalgic revival of the 1925 hit musical. Staged on Broadway at the 46th Street Theatre by Burt Shevelove, supervising credit is given to Busby Berkeley. Ruby Keeler returns to Broadway to dance again as Sue Smith. The show wins 861 performances. It opens at London's Drury Lane on May 15, 1973 for 277 performances.

Jan 20 The highly praised Peter Brook production of Shakespeare's *A Midsummer Night's Dream*, staged for the Royal Shakespeare Company, opens on Broadway at the Billy Rose Theatre for a limited run of 62 showings, after which it plays two weeks more at the Brooklyn Academy of Music. Sally Jacobs has designed an empty "White Box" for Brook's players, who wear elements of clown costumes and use bits and pieces of circus juggling props. Oberon and Puck, played by Alan Howard and John Kane, are seen aloft on trapezes. Others in the ensemble include Sara Kestleman, David Waller,

and Frances de la Tour. On June 10, the production returns to London's Aldwych Theatre.

Jan 25 At London's Hampstead Theatre Club, Vivian Matalon stages Frank Marcus' *Formation Dancers*, with a cast including Barbara Leigh-Hunt, and Anton Rodgers. On March 1, Peter Ransley's *Ellen* is presented. On April 5, Tom Fleming performs *Vincent*, W. Gordon Smith's portrait of Van Gogh. Robin Midgley directs. Ransley's *Disabled* is directed by Matalon on May 10.

GODSPELL

Feb 3 At the Old Vic, the National Theatre presents Fernando Arrabal's *The Architect and the Emperor of Assyria*, with Jim Dale and Anthony Hopkins, Victor Garcia staging. Frank Dunlop directs Carl Zuckmayer's German comedy, *The Captain from Koepenick*, opening on March 9. Paul Scofield plays the title role. John Dexter stages Thomas Heywood's *A Woman Killed with Kindness*. Opening April 7, it features Joan Plowright and Hopkins. On May 6, the ensemble mounts a Brechtian staging of *Coriolanus*, with direction by Manfred Wekwerth and Joachim Tenschert. Hopkins, Denis Quilley, and Constance Cummings play the leading roles.

Feb 3 Director Alan Schneider revives Samuel Beckett's fable, *Waiting for Godot*, at the Sheridan Square Playhouse in Greenwich Village. It is to run nearly 35 weeks, with Paul Price and Henderson Forsythe.

Feb 5 The Repertory Theatre of Lincoln Center opens a season of intimate dramas in the Forum Theatre. The plays are: Har-

old Pinter's *The Birthday Party*, *Landscape*, and *Silence*; A. R. Gurney's *Scenes From American Life*; Paul Shyre's O'Casey adaptation, *Pictures in the Hallway*, and Friedrich Duerrenmatt's *Play Strindberg*.

Feb 12 At New Haven's Long Wharf Theatre, artistic director Arvin Brown stages the world premiere of Robert Anderson's double-bill, *Solitaire/Double Solitaire*, with a cast including Richard Venture, Joyce Ebert, Ruth Nelson, and William Swetland. The production is invited to the Edinburgh International Festival and opens on Broadway Sep 30 for a 36 performance run.

Feb 14 Robert Montgomery's *Subject to Fits* opens in New York at Joseph Papp's Public Theatre. Other plays to be shown at the Theatre this season are: David Hare's *Slag*, Siobhan McKenna's *Here Are Ladies*, Doug Dyer's *Blood*, and David Rabe's *The Basic Training of Pavlo Hummel*.

Feb 15 Israel Horovitz's double-bill, *Acrobats* and *Line*, opens in Greenwich Village at the Theatre de Lys, staged by James Hammerstein for a four-week run.

Feb 15 At London's Mermaid Theatre, Huntly Harding's *The Licentious Fly* is staged by Philip Grout. On April 1, Josephine Wilson stages *Hanky Park*. On May 13, Bernard Shaw's *John Bull's Other Island* opens, staged by Alan Strachan.

Feb 16 Molière's *School for Wives* is revived on Broadway at the Lyceum Theatre by Phoenix Theatre producer T. Edward Hambleton. Stephen Porter stages, with Brian Bedford in the cast. The production has a 15-week run.

Feb 18 At London's Greenwich Theatre, *Macbeth* is performed, with Alan Dobie in the title-role. On April 1, Peter Nichols's *Forget-Me-Not Lane* has its premiere in a Michael Blakemore staging. On April 29, Ibsen's *The Lady from the Sea* is revived, staged by Kenneth Ives with Ann Lynn and Robert Powell. On May 27, Tennessee Williams' *The Glass Menagerie* is revived, staged by Alan Vaughan Williams.

Feb 18 George Bernard Shaw's *Captain Brassbound's Conversion* is revived in London at the Cambridge Theatre, with Ingrid Bergman, Kenneth Williams, and Joss Ackland. This production runs on into the following season.

Feb 22 *Pinkville*, George Tabori's anti-Vietnam War exercise, opens in St. Clement's Church, produced by the American Place Theatre, under the direction of Wynn Handman. Michael Douglas is in the cast. The production has 42 performances, followed, on April 29, by Sam Shepard's *Back Bog Beast Bait*, a workshop production.

Feb 23 The Chelsea Theatre Center in Brooklyn at BAM opens Heathcote Williams' bizarre parable of modern life, *AC/DC*. John Hirsch stages. The play has been premiered in London at the Royal Court

Theatre. On March 4, the Chelsea Theatre's fall production of the musical *Tarot* transfers Off-Broadway to the Circle in the Square for 38 showings.

March 15 Closed for nearly a year-and-a-half while undergoing reconstruction, the Dublin Gate Theatre now re-opens with Anouilh's *It's Later Than You Think (Ornifle)*, staged by Hilton Edwards. Other shows this year include *Soft Morning City*, Gallacher's *Mr. Joyce Is Leaving Paris*, Bernard Shaw's *Heartbreak House*, macLiammoir's *The Importance of Being Oscar*, Wilde's *The Importance of Being Earnest*, Shakespeare's *Romeo and Juliet*, Phelan's *The Signalman's Apprentice*, Hanley's *Slow Dance on the Killing Ground*, *Talking About Yeats*, and Good's *John Synge Comes Next*.

March 18 Jean-Louis Barrault opens his production of *Rabelais* at London's Round House, staging it with a British cast that includes Bernard Bresslaw. On May 5, Coventry's Belgrade Theatre imports its production of Hans Keuls's *Confrontation*, staged by Warren Jenkins.

March 19 In Ashland, the Oregon Shakespearean Festival inaugurates its new indoor playhouse, the Angus Bowmer Theatre, named in honor of the festival's founder, with a production of *A Midsummer Night's Dream*, staged by Raye Birk. Other shows offered in repertory are *Under Milk Wood*, *Arsenic and Old Lace*, and *A Man for All Seasons*.

March 23 Ken Kesey's novel, *One Flew Over the Cuckoo's Nest*, a failure on Broadway with Kirk Douglas, comes to life again in Dale Wasserman's adaptation, newly revised, at the Mercer-Hansberry Theatre in Greenwich Village. Lee D. Sankowich stages, with William Devane in the leading role. The show has 1,025 performances.

March 24 It's the opening of another World Theatre Season at London's Aldwych Theatre, produced by Peter Daubeny. The Theatre Michel of Paris presents Henri de Montherlant's *La Ville dont le Prince est un Enfant*, staged by Jean Meyer. On April 10, the Royal Dramatic Theatre of Sweden presents Strindberg's *The Dream Play*, staged by Ingmar Bergman. On April 26, Berlin's Schiller Theatre offers Witold Gombrowicz's *Yvonne, Princess of Burgundy*. On April 29, the Schiller company presents Beckett's *Krapp's Last Tape* and *Endgame*, both staged by the author. On May 3, Genoa's Stabile Theatre offers Goldoni's classic, *The Venetian Twins*. On May 10, *A Tale of Istanbul*, a musical play by Erol Gunayadin, is the Dormen Theatre's Turkish contribution. On May 17, Jean Genet's *The Maids* is produced by the Nuria Espert Company of Spain.

March 30 The Royal Shakespeare Company opens its annual Stratford-upon-Avon season with *The Merchant of Venice*, staged by Terry Hands. Emrys James is Shylock. Richard Pasco and Judi Dench are in John Barton's staging of *Twelfth Night*. Derek Godfrey and Elizabeth Spriggs play in *Much Ado About Nothing*, staged by Ronald Eyre. Farrah designs John Webster's *The Duchess of Malfi*. Director Clifford Williams casts Dench as the duchess. Barton has Julia Trevelyan Oman design his production of *Othello* and Brewster Mason play the title role. For the RSC's touring ensemble, the Theatre-Go-Round, Barton stages *Richard II*, with Pasco and *Henry V*, with Michael Williams.

April 5 Shakespeare's *Hamlet*, as staged by Jonathan Miller for the Oxford and Cambridge Theatre Company, opens in London at the Fortune Theatre. This production has toured the United States.

April 14 Madeleine Renaud opens at New York's Barbizon-Plaza Theatre as the enigmatic murderess in Marguerite Duras' play, *L'Amante Anglaise*, produced by Le Treteau de Paris in French. It plays two weeks, staged by Claude Régy.

April 17 Ingrid Bergman stars in this touring revival of George Bernard Shaw's *Captain Brassbound's Conversion*, opening now at the Ethel Barrymore Theatre in Manhattan for a run of two weeks.

April 21 Arvin Brown revives Eugene O'Neill's *Long Day's Journey into Night* Off-Broadway at the Promenade Theatre for a run of 15 weeks. The cast includes Robert Ryan, Geraldine Fitzgerald and Stacy Keach.

April 26 *Two Gentlemen of Verona*, the American musical by John Guare and Mel Shapiro, with score by Galt MacDermot, opens in London at the Phoenix Theatre.

May 5 The Chichester Festival opens with Sheridan's *The Rivals*. Other plays to be presented this summer are Jean Anouilh's *Dear Antoine*, George Bernard Shaw's *Caesar and Cleopatra* and Robert Sherwood's *Reunion in Vienna*.

June 2 Summer brings Shakespeare to London's Open Air Theatre in Regent's Park. *Romeo and Juliet* with Maureen Pryor as the nurse is staged by Richard Digby Day. Day also stages *A Midsummer Night's Dream* on July 14.

June 2 Already seen in Edinburgh at the Traverse Theatre, Stanley Eveling's *Our Sunday Times* is shown in London at the Royal Court Theatre's Upstairs venue. On June 24, the play Upstairs is Barry Reckord's *Skyvers*. Downstairs on July 6, Marguerite Duras's *The Lovers of Viorne* is presented. On the 19th, Athol Fugard's *Boesman and Lena* opens Upstairs. Yvonne Bryceland is Lena, with Zakes Mokae as Boesman. On Aug 17, John Osborne's *West of Suez* has its premiere downstairs.

June 8 Canada's Stratford Festival opens. The plays to be presented include *Much Ado About Nothing*, *Macbeth*, John Webster's *The Duchess of Malfi*, Ben Jonson's *Volpone*, Labiche and Marc-Michel's *An Italian Straw Hat*, Feydeau's *There's One in Every Marriage*, and Enrique Buenaventura's *The Red Convertible*. Adrian Pecknold's Canadian Mime Theatre offers *Shapes and Shadows*.

June 8 In Balboa Park, the San Diego National Shakespeare Festival opens in the Old Globe Theatre with a program of *Antony and Cleopatra*, *A Midsummer Night's Dream*, and *The Taming of the Shrew*. In the neighboring Carter Theatre, the play is Woody Allen's *Play It Again, Sam*.

June 12 In Stratford, Connecticut, the American Shakespeare Festival opens with a repertory of three productions, *The Merry Wives of Windsor*, *The Tempest*, and *Mourning Becomes Electra*.

June 14 This is the first time Canada's Shaw Festival at Niagara-on-the-Lake has offered a 12-week season. It opens with *The Philanderer*. Romain Weingarten's *Summer Days* is staged by Michael Bawtree. Eric House directs Noel Coward's *Tonight at 8:30*. Patrick Boxill and Paxton Whitehead share direction tasks with *War, Women, and Other Trivia*, consisting of Max Beerbohm's *A Social Success*, Shaw's *O'Flaherty, V. C.*, and his *Press Cuttings*.

June 15 The National Theatre opens its production of Luigi Pirandello's *The Rules of the Game* at London's New Theatre. Paul Scofield and Joan Plowright lead the cast. On June 23, Giraudoux's *Amphitryon 38* opens at the New, staged by Laurence Olivier, with Christopher Plummer, Geraldine McEwan, and Constance Cummings. On July 20, *Tyger* opens, Adrian Mitchell's "celebration of William Blake." Michael Blakemore and John Dexter stage. On Aug 3, Jonathan Miller stages Buechner's *Danton's Death* at the New for the National, with Christopher Plummer.

June 19 The Oregon Shakespearean Festival in Ashland opens its summer season with *Henry IV, Part 1*. Other productions in the repertory include *Much Ado About Nothing*, *Macbeth*, and *A Midsummer Night's Dream*. *The Glass Menagerie* and *A Man for All Seasons* are also played. Among company members are Fredi Olster and Shirley Patton.

June 24 At London's Mermaid Theatre, Robert Lowell's adaptation of Aeschylus' *Prometheus Bound* is shown, directed by Jonathan Miller. On July 29, Michael Redgrave appears in William Trevor's *The Old Boys*.

June 25 In the Delacorte Theatre in Central Park, Joseph Papp opens the six week season of his New York Shakespeare Festival with *Timon of Athens*. This is followed by *Two Gentlemen of Verona* and *The Tale of Cymbeline*.

July 22 Maxim Gorky's *Enemies* is staged by David Jones for the Royal Shakespeare Company at its London home, the Aldwych. John Wood, Alan Howard, and

JAMES JOYCE MEMORIAL THEATER

Brenda Bruce are in the cast. On Sep 13, Terry Hands directs the revival of George Etherege's Restoration comedy, *The Man of Mode*, with Wood as Sir Fopling Flutter. James Joyce's *Exiles*, staged by Harold Pinter, opens on Oct 7, animated by Wood and Vivien Merchant. Jean Genet's *The Balcony* is also a Hands staging, with Helen Mirren and Frances de la Tour, among others, opening on Nov 25. The Stratford production of *Much Ado About Nothing* opens on Dec 15.

July 29 Wendy Toye stages and choreographs Jerome Kern's *Showboat* for the London revival at the Adelphi Theatre. It earns 917 performances.

Aug 5 Ian McKellen plays the Dane in the Prospect Theatre Company production of *Hamlet*, now opening at the Cambridge Theatre in London.

Aug 22 Another Edinburgh Festival opens. Among the many events of music, dance, and theatre are performances by two American troupes. New Haven's Long Wharf Theatre presents the British premiere of two Robert Anderson plays: *Solitaire/Double Solitaire*, staged by Arvin Brown. He also directs the Kaufman-Hart comedy, *You Can't Take It With You*. Also from America is The Manhattan Project with the André Gregory production of *Alice in Wonderland*. From Bucharest comes the Bulandra Theatre, with I. L. Caragiale's *Carnival Scenes*. Frank Dunlop

brings his Young Vic production of Shakespeare's *The Comedy of Errors*. Closer to home are Edinburgh's own Royal Lyceum troupe, with James Hogg's *Confessions of a Justified Sinner*, staged by Richard Eyre, and the Prospect Theatre Company, with Toby Robertson's staging of Shakespeare's *King Lear*.

Aug 23 London's National Youth Theatre has its customary end-of-summer shows on view. Peter Terson's *Good Lads at Heart* opens at the Jeannetta Cochrane Theatre. On Aug 25, at the Shaw Theatre, the young players present Thomas Dekker's *The Shoemaker's Holiday*.

Aug 24 At London's Old Vic Theatre, the Octagon Theatre of Bolton opens a "summer guest season" with Strindberg's *The Father*. On Sep 6, the production is from the Theatre Royal York, a British mounting of the American mini-musical, *The Last Sweet Days of Isaac*, by Gretchen Cryer (libretto) and Nancy Ford (music). On the 16th, the Belgian National Theatre presents de Ghelderode's *Pantagleize*. Dario Fo's *The Seventh Commandment* is offered the following day.

Sep 14 At London's Royal Court Theatre Upstairs, the Traverse Theatre presents Mustapha Matura's *As Time Goes By*, staged by Roland Rees. On the 26th, Snoo Wilson directs the Portable Theatre in *Lay By*, done without decor but with the help of a number of authors, including How-

ard Brenton, David Hare, and Trevor Griffiths. On Sep 29, Edward Bond's stark view of an English king, *Lear*, opens.

Sep 16 At London's Greenwich Theatre, Michael Frayn's *The Sandboy* opens. On Oct 14, Sophocles' *Antigone* is presented. Euripides's *Electra* opens on Oct 28. Barry Reckord's *A Liberated Woman* opens Nov 11. Author Peter Nichols stages a revival of his play, *A Day in the Death of Joe Egg*, with Ray Brooks.

Sep 16 *Othello* is revived at London's Mermaid Theatre, with Bruce Purchase. On Nov 4, George Bernard Shaw's *Geneva* is revived.

Sep 22 The Dolphin Theatre Company opens a season of plays in London at the Shaw Theatre, beginning with *The Samaritan*, by Peter Terson and Mike Butler. On Oct 12, Terson's *Slip Road Wedding* is played.

Sep 27 Patience Collier heads the cast in director Vivian Matalon's revival of Clifford Odets's *Awake and Sing* at the Hampstead Theatre Club in London. Tom Mallin's *The Novelist* opens on Nov 1. On Dec 20, Sandy Wilson's adaptation of John Collier's novel, *His Monkey Wife*, makes its debut.

Oct 4 Brother Jonathan (Ringkamp) and Geraldine Fitzgerald have devised a rock opera, *Everyman and Roach*, for their Everyman Street Theatre Company. They now perform it at New York's Ethical Culture Society. John Orlando has created the score.

Oct 5 Tonight's the opening night of Tarragon Theatre, Toronto, Canada. Founder Bill Glassco directs David Freeman's *Creeps*. About the physical and psychological difficulties of handicapped people, the play, has first been produced at the Factory Lab Theatre as a work-in-progress. The Tarragon production will win the Chalmers Award for best Canadian play. *Creeps* will tour to the Folger Theatre, Washington, D.C.; the Playhouse 2, New York, in Dec 1973 where it will be chosen as a "Best Play"; and will win a prize at the 1979 Edinburgh Fringe Festival.

Oct 11 On the main floor of New York's Solomon R. Guggenheim Museum, spectators divest themselves of as much clothing as they wish and are then conducted into the bowels of the building by members of the James Joyce Memorial Liquid Theatre. They are supposed to keep their eyes closed as they are led through a maze, cuddled, kissed, and tantalized by the performers. Theatre-games, random nudity, and other current devices supposedly designed to increase people's sensual awareness are part of the liquidity of the evening. This entertainment has come from Los Angeles, courtesy of the Company Theatre. It runs nearly six months.

Oct 12 Ariane Mnouchkine shows her Le Theatre du Soleil production of *1798—*

GLADYS COOPER

The French Revolution Year One in London at the Round House. On Nov 17, the American musical, *Godspell*, opens, with book by John-Michael Tebelak and songs by Stephen Schwartz. Tebelak stages. Transferring to the West End, the show will have a long run.

Oct 13 At The Place, the Royal Shakespeare opens a London series of experimental productions with Trevor Griffiths's *Occupations*. Robert Montgomery's American play, *Subject To Fits*, opens on the 21st. Sara Kestelman and Julian Glover head the cast. Robin Phillips stages Strindberg's *Miss Julie* on Oct 27.

Oct 15 Théâtre du Trident opens its first full season in Quebec City with a Québécois adaptation of George Bernard Shaw's *Pygmalion*. Instead of humble English background, Eliza is of humble French-Canadian background.

Oct 21 New York's Equity Library Theatre's (ELT) season of revivals begins in the Master Theatre with *June Moon*, followed by *Park*, *Middle of the Night*, *Oedipus at Colonos*, *No Strings*, *The Servant of Two Masters*, and *Du Barry Was a Lady*.

Nov 3 John Clements, the Artistic Director of the Chichester Festival, comes to London's Piccadilly Theatre, starring in Jean Anouilh's *Dear Antoine*, seen at the Festival the past summer. There are 45 showings.

Nov 7 At Joseph Papp's Public Theatre in Greenwich Village, the fall season begins with David Rabe's anti-Vietnam War play, *Sticks and Bones*. The production has 121 performances before moving to Broadway's John Golden Theatre on March 1, 1972, for a run of 245 performances. It is chosen as a "Best Play." Also given at the Public Theatre this season are Peter Link, Gretchen Cryer, and Doug Dyer's *The Wedding of Iphigenia* and

Iphigenia in Concert.

Nov 11 The Repertory Theatre of New York's Lincoln Center opens its season in the Vivian Beaumont Theatre with Schiller's *Mary Stuart*, in Stephen Spender's translation. There are 44 performances.

Nov 15 Robert Shaw's play, *Cato Street*, opens at London's Young Vic Theatre, staged by Peter Gill. Vanessa Redgrave heads the cast.

Nov 16 The Negro Ensemble Company begins its season in Greenwich Village at the St. Marks Playhouse with Philip Hayes Dean's *The Sty of the Blind Pig* about a black family with generation-gap problems. This runs eight weeks.

Nov 18 New York's Repertory Theatre of Lincoln Center opens its program of experimental plays in the Forum Theatre with Athol Fugard's *People Are Living There*, with Estelle Parsons and Leonard Frey, among others. John Berry stages.

Nov 30 At the Chelsea Theatre Center in the Brooklyn Academy of Music (BAM), Jean Genet's *The Screens* opens, staged by Minos Volanakis. This long, difficult play has a run of 28 performances, exciting critical praise for the inventiveness of the staging. It is chosen as a "Best Play."

Dec 1 Joseph Papp's summer Central Park production of *Two Gentlemen of Verona*, staged by Mel Shapiro, who has adapted the original text with John Guare, opens on Broadway at the St. James Theatre for a run of 627 performances. The score is the invention of Galt MacDermot, composer of *Hair*. Clifton Davis and Raul Julia play the title-roles.

Dec 6 It's long been a holiday tradition for London theatres to offer a Christmas pantomime, a musical, or a revival of a popular comedy. Brandon Thomas's *Charley's Aunt* with Tom Courtenay opens today at the Apollo Theatre, followed on the 9th by *The Owl and the Pussycat Went to See . . . .* Also on the 9th, Peter Howard and George Fraser's *Give a Dog a Bone* is revived at the Westminster Theatre. Other entertainments include *Pinocchio* (Jeannetta Cochrane), *Pirates* (Royal Court), *Dick Turpin* (Mermaid), *The Sleeping Beauty* (Players'), *The Plotters of Cabbage Patch Corner* (Shaw), *Winnie the Pooh* (Phoenix), *Toad of Toad Hall* (Duke of York's), *Dandelion* (Young Vic), and *Cinderella* (Palladium).

Dec 9 At London's Old Vic, the National Theatre revives Oliver Goldsmith's play, *The Good-Natured Man*, staged by John Dexter.

Dec 21 Laurence Olivier plays James Tyrone in the National Theatre's revival of Eugene O'Neill's *Long Day's Journey into Night*, opening at the New Theatre.

1971   BIRTHS/DEATHS/DEBUTS

Jan 7 American actor-producer Richard Kollmar (b. 1910) dies in New York City. He first appeared on stage in New York in *Knickerbocker Holiday* in 1938. Some of his productions were *By Jupiter*, *Plain and Fancy*, and *The Body Beautiful*.

Jan 24 Irish playwright and critic St. John Ervine (b. 1883) dies in London. Ervine's numerous plays include *Mixed Marriage*, *Jane Clegg*, and *People of Our Class*.

March 12 In Philadelphia, just after his major number in the second act of *70, Girls, 70*, the popular comedian David Burns dies in the wings of a heart attack.

March 19 Producer Leland Hayward dies at age 68.

April 19 British playwright N. C. Hunter dies at 62. He wrote *Waters of the Moon*.

May 1 Stage and screen actress Glenda Farrell (b. 1904) dies in New York. Farrell made her New York debut in Aurania Rouverol's *Skidding* in 1928. She made Broadway appearances in *Home is the Hero* and *Masquerade*.

May 15 English director and producer Sir Tyrone Guthrie (b. 1900) dies in Dublin, Ireland. Guthrie was director at the Old Vic in the 1930's. From 1953 to 1957, he headed the Stratford Festival, in Ontario, Canada, which was largely his creation. In 1963, the Guthrie Theatre in Minne-apolis was named in his honor. He wrote *A Life in the Theatre* and was knighted in 1961.

May 21 Actor and singer Dennis King (b. 1897) dies in New York. King was a great success in New York in *The Vagabond King* in 1925. His later Broadway credits include *Portrait of a Queen* and *A Patriot for Me*.

June 6 Flournoy Miller, of the black musical comedy team of Miller and Lyles, dies today at 84.

June 7 J. I. Rodale, founder-publisher of *Theatre Crafts* magazine and cautionary playwright, dies at age 72, while being interviewed on the Dick Cavett Show.

June 16 Ellaline Terris, the distinguished British actress, dies today at age 100.

June 19 American stage and screen actor Thomas Gomez (b. 1905) dies in Santa Monica, California.

July 23 American stage and screen actor Van Heflin (b. 1910) dies. His first regular engagement in New York was at the Lyceum Theatre in 1933 as an understudy in *Sailor Beware!* In the late 1930s and the early 1940s, Heflin commuted between Broadway and Hollywood.

Aug 15 Hungarian-born actor Paul Lukas (b. 1894) dies in Tangier, Morocco. He made his first New York appearance in *A Doll's House* in 1937. His role as Kurt Müller in *Watch on the Rhine* in 1941 brought him immediate success.

Aug 25 Band-leader and entertainer Ted Lewis (b. 1891) dies in New York. His customary audience salute was: "Is everybody happy?"

Sep 25 American actress Muriel Kirkland (b. 1903) dies in New York City. On Broadway she appeared as Mary Todd in *Abe Lincoln in Illinois* and *The Legend of Lizzie*, among others.

Oct 13 Phoebe Ephron, the American playwright (b. 1916), dies in New York.

Oct 14 Prolific playwright Samuel Spewack, most often working with his wife Bella, dies today at 72.

Oct 28 An unknown young player, Sylvester Stallone, is Mike in *Score*, Jerry Douglas' show about male and female sexual antics, complete with nudity. It has a three-week run.

Nov 4 Ann Pennington, long a dancing star of the *George White's Scandals*, dies at age 77.

Nov 8 British actress Ivy St. Helier is dead.

Nov 17 English actress Gladys Cooper (b. 1889) dies in England. She made her Broadway debut in *The Shining Hour* at the Booth Theatre in 1934. In addition to her film credits, she published two autobiographies, *Gladys Cooper* (1931) and *Without Veils* (1953).

Dec 7 British actor-director Milton Rosmer dies today at age 89. He was known for his work with Shakespeare's plays.

Its membership is over 6,500.

Sep 8 The John F. Kennedy Center for the Performing Arts opens in Washington, D.C. Designed by Edward Durrell Stone, it contains a concert hall, an opera house, a theatre for plays and dance, and a cinema to be used by the American Film Institute.

Sep 14 The Guthrie Theatre in Minneapolis receives a $75,000 NEA Grant, and goes on its first five-state tour with *Fables Then and Now*.

Oct 12 Even before the opening of the Broadway production of *Jesus Christ Superstar*, already popular with young audiences owing to an LP recording of the work, there has been controversy about the depiction of Jesus and those around him. With the show now visible as well as audible, even stronger objections will be made. The Anti-Defamation League of B'nai B'rith and the American Jewish Committee will protest the portrayal of Caiaphas, the high priest, and other Orthodox Jews abetting him, on the ground that this lays the primary responsibility for Jesus' torture and execution on the Jewish priests. Some Christian groups will also protest the depiction of Christ and his mother, Mary.

Oct 15 Helen Hayes is in the audience as Philadelphia's historic 1808 Walnut Street Theatre reopens with its Greek Revival facade restored and seating for 1,054. Architect F. Bryan Loving's remodelling has cost $4 million. This venerable playhouse is regarded as the oldest in America in continuous use. Reviewing the restoration after the opening, Clive Barnes of the *NY Times* says in part: "The result is sadly like a debilitated movie house . . . ."

Nov 19 Today is the official opening of Playwrights Horizons, at the Clark Center for the Performing Arts in New York, celebrated with a staged reading of Margaret Power's *Victims Anonymous*. Robert Moss is the founder and producing director of this venture, which aims to support and encourage new American playwrights. Later Moss will move Playwrights Horizons to a shabby old porn theatre on West 42nd, which he and his colleagues will transform, eventually turning the entire block, by example, into Theatre Row.

Nov 23 The Theatre Upstairs opens in the upstairs room at London's Royal Court Theatre. The 80-seat theatre is to be used for experimental productions.

Nov 27 Tonight marks the 100th anniversary of Dublin's Gaiety Theatre.

Dec 22 The American Place Theatre moves into its new theatre at 111 West 46th Street. This is a 290-seat space four levels below ground, designed by Frank Trotter with architect Richard D. Kaplan. Ronald Ribman's *Fingernails Blue as Flowers* and Steve Tesich's *Lake of the Woods* are the opening double-bill.

1971   THEATERS/PRODUCTIONS

The Black Theatre Alliance (BTA) is founded to solve common problems, share information and resources, and to create an instrument to validate Black Theatre and dance companies as community institutions.

Jan 4 Tonight, all Broadway shows begin at 7:00 p.m., changing from the traditional 8:30 curtain, to help theatre-goers who previously have had over three hours to kill after work. At season's end, a 17 percent increase in ticket-sales will be noted.

May 31 On the last day of the current Broadway season, only a few shows have repaid their initial investment. According to *Variety's* estimates, they are *Oh! Calcutta!*, *Sleuth*, *Home*, and *And Miss Reardon Drinks a Little*.

June 1 With the 1970–1971 Broadway season closed, there have been only 56 productions, a dramatic decline from 84 three seasons ago. 14 of these are "middle theatre" contract productions, rather than straight Broadway stagings. Of the total, 15 are revivals; 14 are new American plays; 11 are musicals; four are specialties; four are foreign plays in English; and four are plays in foreign tongues, as tallied by Otis Guernsey, Jr., editor of the *Best Plays* series. The Broadway gross this past season is almost $55 million, with some $50 million grossed from touring productions. A new musical, *Lolita*, closes in Boston with a $900,000 loss. *Hello, Dolly!* finally ends its marathon run with 2,844 showings, and a return of $9 million net profit on an initial $350,000 investment. The average cost for mounting a Broadway show is now $300,000, with $47,000 Off-Broadway. In addition to Off-Broadway's 39 new plays, productions include 13 musicals, 20 revivals, seven specialties, six revues, six foreign plays in translation, and four in foreign languages. In America's regional profes-

sional theatres, there have been 323 productions by 39 groups in 53 theatres in 37 cities. 141 of these were American plays, 112 of them fully produced. 57 of the productions have been world premieres. As usual, Shakespeare is the most produced playwright, with 38 mountings of 15 of his plays.

With the New York season just concluded, the ten "Best Plays" chosen by Guernsey, Jr., include Fugard's *Boesman and Lena*, Freedman's *Steambath*, England's *Conduct Unbecoming*, Shaffer's *Sleuth*, Berrigan's *The Trial of the Catonsville Nine*, Storey's *Home*, Simon's *The Gingerbread Lady*, Guare's *The House of Blue Leaves*, Hampton's *The Philanthropist*, and Goldman/Sondheim's *Follies*.

July 1 Canada's Stratford Festival opens a third stage, the Casino on River Drive, to be used primarily as a workshop theatre for Canadian plays, developmental productions, and chamber operas. The inaugural production is the premiere of Enrique Buenaventura's *The Red Convertible*.

July 5 The Shaw Theatre opens in London with *The Devil's Disciple*, presented by the National Youth Theatre—Dolphin Theatre Company.

Aug 15 Formerly the American Educational Theatre Association, the American Theatre Association (ATA) is formed. The ATA includes persons and institutions interested in noncommercial theatre. Currently it is composed of the American Community Theatre Association (ACTA), the Army Theatre Arts Association (ATAA), the National Association of Schools of Theatre (NAST), the National Children's Theatre Association (NCTA), the University and College Theatre Association (UCTA), the University Resident Theatre Association (URTA), and the American Theatre Student League (ATSL).

Jan 20 *Vivat! Vivat! Regina!* See L premiere, 1970.

Feb 14 *Grease* (NY—Eden—Musical). Jim Jacobs and Warren Casey collaborate on this exercise in 1950's nostalgia, which features Barry Bostwick and Carole Demas. The show moves to Broadway and the Broadhurst Theatre for a long run of 3,388 performances. There are only 258 performances following the London premiere on June 26, 1973, at the New London.

Feb 21 *Moonchildren* (NY—Royale—Comedy). Michael Weller's picture of American college students as Flower Children, already seen in London and Washington, will close on Broadway after only two weeks, to reopen successfully on Nov 4, 1973, at the Theatre de Lys. Alan Schneider directs. It is chosen as a "Best Play."

Feb 28 *Night Watch* (NY—Morosco—Drama). Lucille Fletcher's murder thriller features Joan Hackett as a woman terrorized by her husband, played by Len Cariou. Fred Coe directs. It has a 15-week run.

April 2 *Small Craft Warnings* (NY—Truck and Warehouse—Drama). Tennessee Williams' play (a "Best Play") is set in a run-down bar, filled with philosophical, beaten people. Richard Altman directs for a run of 200 performances, two of which feature the playwright.

April 5 *Elizabeth I* (NY—Lyceum—Drama). Playwright Paul Foster's absurdist treatment of the Virgin Queen, staged by John-Michael Tebelak, plays only five performances.

April 9 *Sugar* (NY—Majestic—Musical). Peter Stone has adapted the film, *Some Like It Hot*, for the stage. Songs are by Jule Styne and Bob Merrill, with staging by Gower Champion. It runs 505 performances.

April 19 *Don't Bother Me, I Can't Cope* (NY—Playhouse—Musical). Directed by Vinnette Carroll, Micki Grant's show, successful in Washington, D.C., and Off-off Broadway, wins a run of 1,065 performances.

April 30 *An Evening with Richard Nixon and . . .* (NY—Shubert—Comedy). Gore Vidal's satire on the President is based on public statements and shows him as a revengeful opportunist. Nixon-haters can keep the show open for only two weeks. Ed Sherin directs. George S. Irving impersonates the President.

May 7 *Anna K.* (NY—Actors Playhouse—Drama). Actress-teacher Eugenie Leontovich stages actors rehearsing a play about Anna Karenina. She also appears, with Catherine Ellis as Anna. It runs 25 weeks.

May 11 *The Silent Partner* (NY—Actors

GREASE

Studio—Drama). Clifford Odets' 1937 play, previously unproduced, is given 12 performances, directed by Martin Freid.

May 16 *Don't Play Us Cheap!* (NY—Ethel Barrymore—Musical). Melvin Peebles has directed and produced his modern Harlem fairy-tale, with Avon Long and Esther Rolle. It runs almost 21 weeks.

June 15 *The Sunshine Train* (NY—Abbey—Musical). William Hunt stages his "Gospel Musical," which runs seven months with Mary Johnson, Clara Walker, Peggie Henry, and the Carl Murray Singers supporting.

June 19 *Joan* (NY—Circle in the Square—Musical). Al Carmines's modern version of the story of St. Joan runs two months, He accompanies a cast including Lee Guilliat, Essie Borden, Julie Kurnitz, Ira Siff, and Sandy Padilla.

Oct 1 *Berlin to Broadway with Kurt Weill* (NY—Theatre de Lys—Revue). Weill's theatre music, with lyrics by a number of poets, has a run of 19 weeks, under Donald Sadler's direction.

Oct 4 *Oh Coward!* (NY—New—Revue). Roderick Cook has devised this Noel Coward revue, which he performs supported by Jamie Ross and Barbara Carson. It runs nearly 37 weeks. On June 5, 1975, the show opens at London's Criterion.

Oct 9 *Dude* (NY—Broadway—Musical). Jerome Ragni and Galt MacDermot's show costs $900,000 and runs for only two weeks. Tom O'Horgan directs William Redfield, Rae Allen, Nell Carter, Ralph Carter, and Nat Morris.

Oct 17 *6 Rms Riv Vu* (NY—Helen Hayes—

Comedy). Rob Randall's work, chosen as a "Best Play," features Jane Alexander and Jerry Orbach, apartment seekers who fall in love. Edwin Sherin stages. It runs 51 weeks.

Oct 23 *Pippin* (NY—Imperial—Musical). Bob Fosse directs and choreographs this show about Charlemagne's supposed son, Pippin. John Rubinstein plays the title-role of a picaresque youth, sampling all of life's experiences and at last settling for marriage and children. Roger O. Hirson concocts the book, with songs by Stephen Schwartz. The show runs 1,944 performances. A flop in London, it has only 86 showings following the premiere on Oct 30, 1973, at Her Majesty's.

Oct 30 *The Lincoln Mask* (NY—Plymouth—Drama). Eva Marie Saint plays Mary Todd to Fred Gwynne's Lincoln in V. J. Longhi's drama. Gene Frankel directs. The show runs just one week.

Oct 31 *Butley.* See L premiere, 1971.

Nov 23 *Dr. Selavy's Magic Theatre* (NY—Mercer–O'Casey—Musical). This Richard Foreman creation, about a five-day mental therapy program, runs 18 weeks, with George McGrath in the title role. Stanley Silverman writes the score and Tom Hendry the lyrics.

Nov 28 *Via Galactica* (NY—Uris—Musical). An expensive new Broadway theatre opens with a major musical, which costs $900,000 and lasts seven performances. Peter Hall directs, Galt McDermot provides the score.

Nov 30 *The Creation of the World and Other Business* (NY—Shubert—Comedy). Arthur Miller retells the Adam and Eve story with Bob Dishy and Zoe Caldwell. The show has only 20 repetitions under director Gerald Freedman.

Dec 5 *The River Niger* (NY—St. Marks—Drama). The Negro Ensemble opens Joseph Walker's protest play of a black poet and housepainter buffeted by a white world. It transfers to Broadway for a long run and is chosen as a "Best Play."

Dec 12 *The Last of Mrs. Lincoln* (NY—ANTA—Drama). This, the second play this season to feature Mary Todd Lincoln, has only 63 performances. Julie Harris wins a Tony for her performance in James Prideaux's drama, directed by George Schaefer. So does Leora Dana.

Dec 20 *The Sunshine Boys* (NY—Broadhurst—Comedy). Neil Simon provides Jack Albertson and Sam Levene with the roles of two retired vaudevillians who have a reunion, in spite of a long feud. The script is chosen as a "Best Play," and the show has a run of 538 performances. Alfred Marks and Jimmy Jewel are featured in the London production, which opens at the Piccadilly on May 7, 1975.

1972 BRITISH PREMIERES

Jan 18 *Company.* See NY premiere, 1970.

Feb 2 *Jumpers* (L—Old Vic—Comedy). Tom Stoppard's farce of word-play and mystification features Diana Rigg and Michael Hordern. This London success opens at New York's Billy Rose on April 22, 1974, with Jill Clayburgh and Brian Bedford. It is chosen a "Best Play," although it runs only six weeks.

March 23 *Notes on a Love Affair* (L—Globe—Drama). Irene Worth, Nigel Davenport, and Julia Foster animate Frank Marcus' play, staged by Robin Phillips.

May 3 *Gone With the Wind* (L—Drury Lane—Musical). Initially staged in Japan, this reworking of Margaret Mitchell's novel, with songs by Harold Rome, features June Ritchie and Harve Presnell. Joe Layton directs and choreographs for 397 performances.

May 9 *Tom Brown's Schooldays* (L—Cambridge—Musical). This children's classic is adapted by Joan and Jack Maitland, with Chris Andrews' score. Peter Coe directs Adam Walton and Roy Dotrice, among others.

June 14 *The Mating Game* (L—Apollo—Comedy). Robin Hawdon's play, about a youthful TV personality who is very popular with women, wins a run of 427 performances for co-producer/director Ray Cooney.

July 4 *Lloyd George Knew My Father* (L—Savoy—Comedy). Peggy Ashcroft and Ralph Richardson appear in William Douglas Home's script. She plays a woman who threatens suicide if a roadway is built through her grounds. It earns a run of 637 performances, directed by Robin Midgley.

July 10 *Cowardy Custard* (L—Mermaid—Revue). Wendy Toye's cast includes Una Stubbs, Patricia Routledge, and John Moffatt, in this show created from Noel Coward's words and music.

July 11 *I Claudius* (L—Queen's—Drama). Robert Graves' historical fictions are adapted by John Mortimer and staged by Tony Richardson. David Warner plays the title-role, with Freda Jackson as Livia and Charles Lloyd Pack as Augustus. There are 71 performances.

Aug 9 *Jesus Christ Superstar.* See NY premiere, 1971.

Aug 16 *Time and Time Again* (L—Comedy—Comedy). Alan Ayckbourn's play of flirtations between families of boss and employee has Tom Courtenay and Cheryl Kennedy in the cast and Eric Thompson directing. There are 229 performances.

Oct 4 *The Day after the Fair* (L—Lyric—Drama). Thomas Hardy's story is adapted by Frank Harvey, directed by Frith Banbury, and features Deborah Kerr, Avice Landon, and Duncan Lamont for 245 showings.

Oct 19 *Crown Matrimonial* (L—Haymarket—Drama). Royce Ryton recreates the events surrounding Edward VIII's abdication. Wendy Hiller and Peter Barkworth head the cast. The show runs into next season. On Oct 2, 1973, the play opens in New York at the Helen Hayes with Eileen Herlie and George Grizzard. It remains only 10 weeks.

Nov 6 *I and Albert* (L—Piccadilly—Musical). An American show about Queen Victoria and Prince Albert has been crafted by Jay Presson Allen (book) and Charles Strouse and Lee Adams (songs). John Schlesinger directs the ambitious show, which spans years and requires a large cast. It has only 120 performances.

Nov 21 *Behind the Fridge* (L—Cambridge—Revue). Peter Cook and Dudley Moore are authors, co-directors, and performers in their show, bringing the same kind of humor they used in *Beyond the Fringe* to its 318 performance run. It has 438 performances in New York, opening at the Plymouth Theatre on Nov 14, 1973, titled *Good Evening.*

Dec 5 *The Island of the Mighty* (L—Aldwych—Drama). The Royal Shakespeare Company unveils John Arden and Margaretta D'Arcy's curious play, staged by David Jones. Patrick Allen plays King Arthur, and Emrys James is Merlin.

Dec 6 *My Fat Friend* (L—Globe—Comedy). Jennie Linden is cast as Vicky, chubby and wanting to be loved, but despairing until a handsome engineer finds her attractive. Charles Laurence's play continues into the following season. On March 31, 1974, the show opens in New York at the Brooks Atkinson with Lynn Redgrave as Vicky. It runs nine months.

Dec 20 *The Good Old Bad Old Days* (L—Prince of Wales's—Musical). Anthony Newley stars in his collaboration with Leslie Bricusse, and also directs the show, which runs for 309 performances.

1972 REVIVALS/REPERTORIES

Jan 6 Edward Bond's *Narrow Road to the Deep North* opens at the Vivian Beaumont Theatre, continuing the season of the Repertory Theatre of Lincoln Center. On March 2, the company offers *Twelfth Night*, in an Ellis Rabb staging. Arthur Miller's *The Crucible* is the final offering of the season, opening on April 27.

Jan 9 An eight week program of rotating repertory, consisting of *Gertrude*, *Demon*, *Carmilla*, and *The Only Jealousy of Emer*, opens at New York's La Mama. It is the work of Wilford Leach and John Braswell.

Jan 11 In Edinburgh at the Traverse Theatre, Snoo Wilson's *Reason the Sun King* and John Grillo's *Will the King Leave the Teapot?* open the new year, along with a revival of *Moby Dick*. There are some 32 programs. A number of the productions are given by visiting troupes. Among the shows are Howard Brenton's *Hilter Dances*, Tom Buchan's *Tell Charlie Thanks for the Truss*, John Melville's *Khartoum 1971*, Charles Marowitz's *Marowitz Hamlet* and *Ham-Omlet*, Trevor Griffiths' *Occupations*, Howard Barker's *Private Parts*, Lord Byron's *The Deformed Transformed*, Stanley Eveling's *Caravaggio Buddy*, Jack Gelber's *Sleep*, Richard Crane's *The Blood Stream*, Lindsay Kemp's *Sideshow*, and *Sandy Wilson Thanks the Ladies*, a one-man show by Wilson.

Jan 13 Carl Weber, formerly a director with Bertolt Brecht at the Berliner Ensemble, brings his central European sensibilities to bear on the linguistic abstractions in Peter Handke's *The Ride Across Lake Constance*, which has 20 showings in the Forum Theatre of the Repertory Theatre of Lincoln Center. This is followed by Ed Bullins' *The Duplex*, moved from the New Lafayette Theatre in Harlem. On May 4, *Suggs*, by David Wiltse, opens for 20 showings.

Jan 26 The season at London's Royal Court through Nov 13 includes: E. A. Whitehead's *Alpha Beta*, John Arden's *Live Like Pigs*, Roy Kift's *Mary, Mary*, Charles Wood's *Veterans*, Harald Mueller's *Big Wolf*, John Antrobus's *Crete and Sergeant Pepper*, Howard Brenton's *Hitler Dances*, Ibsen's *Hedda Gabler*, N. F. Simpson's *Was He Anyone?* and Arnold Wesker's *The Old Ones*. Brendan Behan's *Richard's Cork Leg*, Tom MacIntyre's *Eye Winker, Tom Tinker*, Edna O'Brien's *A Pagan Place*, David Edgar's *State of Emergency*, and John Osborne's *A Sense of Detachment* are also seen.

Jan 27 Albert Camus's *The Price of Justice*, staged by Bernard Miles, opens at London's Mermaid Theatre. Harold Pinter's *The Caretaker* is revived on March 2. On May 18, R. C. Sherriff's *Journey's End* is revived.

Jan 28 At Glasgow's Citizens' Theatre, the season includes *The Relapse*, *The Crucible*, *In the Jungle of Cities*, *Antony and Cleopatra*, *Tamburlaine*, *The Threepenny Opera*, *Venice Preserved*, *Tartuffe* and *Puss in Boots*. At the Close Theatre, the Cits' second stage, the plays are *The Foursome*, *AC/DC*, *The Architect and the Emperor of Assyria*, *Timon of Athens*, *Marat/Sade*, *Lear*, and *Dracula*.

Jan 29 The CSC Repertory offers Off-

Broadway *Titus Andronicus, Marat/Sade* and *Julius Caesar* this season, in stagings by its chief, Christopher Martin.

Feb 1 London's Dolphin Theatre Company presents *Romeo and Juliet* at the Shaw Theatre, staged by Michael Croft. On May 16, Michael Bakewell stages *Twelfth Night*, with Vanessa Redgrave.

Feb 1 Allen Ginsberg's poetry about his mother becomes *Kaddish* at the Chelsea Theatre Center, in Brooklyn which also sees a revival of John Gay's *The Beggar's Opera* on March 21. On May 9, the Polish surrealistic satire, *The Water Hen*, is presented. On Oct 17, *Lady Day: A Musical Tragedy* will open, followed by Peter Handke's *Kaspar*.

Feb 3 Oliver Goldsmith's *She Stoops to Conquer* is revived in London by the Young Vic, staged by Wendy Toye. Kathleen Harrison and Gavin Reed appear. Sean O'Casey's *Shadow of a Gunman* is revived on July 4, and *Julius Caesar*, on Aug 17. John Osborne and Anthony Creighton's *Epitaph for George Dillon* and Osborne's *Look Back in Anger* will play in December.

Feb 10 At the American Place Theatre's new Manhattan home Jack Gelber's *Sleep*, Frank Chin's prize-winning *The Chickencoop Chinaman*, Robert Coover's *The Kid*, Phillip Hayes Dean's *Freeman*, Rochelle Owen's *The Karl Marx Play*, and Steve Tesich's *Baba Goya*, all play between now and December.

Feb 10 Bertolt Brecht and Kurt Weill's *The Threepenny Opera* opens in London at the Prince of Wales's Theatre, directed by Tony Richardson, It will continue into the following season.

Feb 17 Robert E. Sherwood's *Reunion in Vienna* comes to London for only 20 showings, with Nigel Patrick and Margaret Leighton. Frith Banbury directs.

Feb 20 Marshall W. Mason stages Berilla Kerr's *The Elephant in the House* in repertory with August Strindberg's *Ghost Sonata* on upper Broadway for the Circle Theatre Company. In October, a triple-bill by resident playwright Lanford Wilson will be seen, followed by Wilson's *Hot l Baltimore*, Henrik Ibsen's *When We Dead Awaken*, and Ron Wilcox's *The Tragedy of Thomas Andros*.

March 6 Alberta Theatre Projects, Calgary, Alberta, presents its first production, *The History Show*, a play for young people about the history of Calgary and Southern Alberta. Through government funding, director-manager Douglas Riske and playwright Paddy Campbell are able to tour their show throughout the province.

March 7 The Negro Ensemble's New York season continues at the St. Marks with Lennox Brown's *A Ballet Behind the Bridge* and, on May 9, *Frederick Douglas . . . Through His Own Words* opens for 26 performances.

THAT CHAMPIONSHIP SEASON

March 10 The Oregon Shakespearean Festival opens its second spring season in the indoor Angus Bowmer Theatre in Ashland. Laird Williamson's staging of John Murray and Allen Boretz's *Room Service* is joined the next day in repertory by Synge's *The Playboy of the Western World* and Chekhov's *Uncle Vanya*. The following day, Miller's *The Crucible* opens.

March 14 The Dublin Gate Theatre presents Desmond Forristal's new play, *The True Story of the Horrid Popish Plot*, staged by Hilton Edwards. Other shows this year include Wolf Mankowitz's *The Samson Riddle* and Oscar Wilde's *An Ideal Husband*.

March 15 Clifford Odets' *The Country Girl*, staged by John Houseman for the Kennedy Center, comes to New York's Billy Rose Theatre for almost two months. Jason Robards and Maureen Stapleton head the cast.

March 27 Joan Littlewood stages *The Londoners* at the Theatre Royal, Stratford East. Lionel Bart has turned Stephen Lewis's *Sparrers Can't Sing* into a musical. On May 30, Littlewood revives Brendan Behan's *The Hostage*.

March 29 At the Old Vic, the National Theatre presents Ronald Pickup as *Richard III*, directed by David William. The season will also include Sheridan's *School for Scandal*, Ben Hecht and Charles MacArthur's *The Front Page*, and, in November, *Macbeth*, with Anthony Hopkins and Diana Rigg.

March 30 Phil Silvers is featured in *A Funny Thing Happened on the Way to the Forum* in New York at the Lunt-Fontanne, now revived for almost five months.

April 3 London's Aldwych sees another World Theatre Season, beginning with Welcome Msomi's black *Macbeth, Umabatha*, played by the Natal Theatre Workshop. Spaniard Nuria Espert's production of Lorca's *Yerma* follows. The Greek National Theatre brings Aeschylus' *Oresteia* and Il Teatro di Eduardo plays Filippo's *Napoli Milionaria*. Cracow's Stary Theatre Company completes the season with Andrzj Wajda's *The Possessed* on May 29.

April 11 At Stratford-upon-Avon, the Royal Shakespeare Company begins its season with *Coriolanus. Julius Caesar, Antony and Cleopatra, The Comedy of Errors,* and *Titus Andronicus* will also be seen.

April 17 Ingrid Bergman stars in this touring revival of George Bernard Shaw's *Captain Brassbound's Conversion*, opening now at the Ethel Barrymore Theatre in Manhattan for a run of two weeks.

April 18 Brock Peters plays Stephen Kumalo in a New York revival of Maxwell Anderson and Kurt Weill's *Lost in the Stars* at the Imperial Theatre for five weeks. Gene Frankel stages.

April 21 Fernando Arrabal directs his protest play, *And They Put Handcuffs on the Flowers*, translated by Charles Marowitz, for a run of 172 performances Off-Broadway at the Mercer-O'Casey Theatre.

April 29 Producer Emile Littler revises and directs this revival of *The Maid of the Mountains* at London's Palace Theatre. Comedian Jimmy Edwards plays General Malona.

May 2 Jason Miller's *That Championship Season* opens at the Public Theatre, staged by A. J. Antoon, for a run of 144 performances. In September it will move to Broadway's Booth Theatre for 844 more. It will win both the Tony Award and the Pulitzer Prize.

May 3 This year's Chichester Festival includes John Gay's *The Beggar's Opera*, George Bernard Shaw's *The Doctor's Di-*

lemma, Christopher Fry's *The Lady's Not for Burning*, and Shakespeare's *The Taming of the Shrew*.

May 30 Summer Shakespeare is on view in the Open Air Theatre in Regent's Park in London. Richard Digby Day has prepared *The Tempest*. Wayne Sleep is Ariel. On July 13, *Twelfth Night* opens, directed by David Conville.

June 5 The twentieth season opens in Ontario at the Stratford Festival of Canada. *As You Like It, King Lear*, Alfred de Musset's *Lorenzaccio*, Oliver Goldsmith's *She Stoops To Conquer*, Bertolt Brecht and Kurt Weill's *Threepenny Opera*, Roch Carrier's *La Guerre, Yes Sir!*, Betty Jane Wylie's *Mark*, Carlo Collodi's *Pinocchio*, Gabriel Charpentier's *Orpheus* and R. Murray Schafer's *Patria II: Requiems for the Party Girl* are offered.

June 6 This year the San Diego National Shakespeare Festival presents *The Merry Wives of Windsor, Love's Labour's Lost* and *Richard III*. In addition, it offers the British revue, *Beyond the Fringe*.

June 7 The Prospect Theatre presents *King Lear* at London's Aldwych, with Toby Robertson's staging. Timothy West is Lear.

June 8 Charles Marowitz's play "after Shakespeare," *An Othello*, is staged at London's Open Space Theatre, directed by the creator. Sam Shepard's *The Tooth of Crime* provides a change of pace on July 17, staged by Marowitz and Walter Donohue.

June 12 The Shaw Festival at Niagara-on-the-Lake in Canada is 13 weeks long this summer, opening with *The Royal Family*, by George S. Kaufman and Edna Ferber. *Getting Married* is staged by Paxton Whitehead, as is *Misalliance*.

June 20 The New York Shakespeare Festival's summer Central Park season includes *Hamlet*, with Stacy Keach; Derek Walcott's *Ti-Jean and His Brothers*, and *Much Ado About Nothing*. This last play will move to Broadway in November and will be televised, with Kathleen Widdoes and Sam Waterston.

June 22 The Royal Shakespeare Company brings two of its Stratford-upon-Avon productions to London's Aldwych: *Merchant of Venice*, staged by Terry Hands with Susan Fleetwood and Emrys James, and *Othello*, directed by John Barton, with Brewster Mason and Lisa Harrow. Gorki's *The Lower Depths* and T. S. Eliot's *Murder in the Cathedral* will also be seen this month.

June 22 In Stratford Connecticut, the American Shakespeare Festival opens a new season with *Julius Caesar* and *Antony and Cleopatra*, staged by Michael Kahn, and George Bernard Shaw's *Major Barbara*, staged by Edwin Sherin.

June 24 The Oregon Shakespeare Festival in Ashland opens today with Robert Benedetti's staging of *The Taming of the Shrew* in the outdoor Elizabethan Theatre. This is followed by Laird Williamson's mounting of *Love's Labour's Lost*, and William Roberts' staging of *Henry IV, Part 2*. On July 1, in the indoor Angus Bowmer Theatre, *Troilus and Cressida* opens, staged by Jerry Turner. It's followed by two productions shown in the new spring season, Miller's *The Crucible* and Chekhov's *Uncle Vanya*.

June 27 The Bristol Old Vic brings London *Trelawny*, a musical based on Arthur Wing Pinero's *Trelawny of the "Wells,"* by Julian Slade, Aubrey Woods, and George Rowell. Val May directs Ian Richardson and Gemma Craven.

July 3 Today the improvised Bankside Globe Playhouse opens, under the artistic direction of actor-director-producer Sam Wanamaker, who dreams of rebuilding Shakespeare's Globe Theatre here on the South Bank of the Thames, near the site of the original. Dekker's *The Shoemaker's Holiday* inaugurates the open-air theatre. On July 23, the RSC's Theatregoround troupe present Terry Hands's *Pleasure and Repentance*. On the 24, Campbell offers his staging of Robert Bolt's *A Man for All Seasons*. On Aug 10, Peter Coe stages *Hamlet* with Keith Michell in the title-role.

July 13 Mia Farrow plays James Barrie's *Mary Rose* at London's Shaw Theatre. Braham Murray directs for the 69 Theatre Company.

July 20 The Manhattan Theatre Club's season opens with Margie Appleman's *The Best Is Yet To Be*. To come are Joanna Glass's *Canadian Gothic/American Modern*, Michael McGuire's *Off The Wall*, Albert Innaurato and Christopher Durang's *I Don't Generally Like Poetry But Have You Read Trees?* and Jeff Wanshel's *Auto-Destruct*.

Aug 14 The National Youth Theatre's London end-of-summer shows include three by Peter Terson, *The Apprentices, Zigger Zagger*, and *Good Lads at Heart*, all directed by Michael Croft, and *Measure for Measure*, staged by Paul Hill.

Aug 20 Festival time again in Edinburgh, the Scottish capital, which now welcomes Tokyo's Hosho Noh Theatre, playing two bills of traditional Noh drama. From Rome comes the Gruppo Sperimentazione Teatrale with Mario Ricci's version of Melville's *Moby Dick*. Among the festival mix of music, theatre, dance, and opera are also programmed the Glasgow Citizens' Theatre productions of Marlowe's *Tamburlaine the Great*, staged by Keith Hack, and Shakespeare's *Twelfth Night*, staged by Giles Havergal. The Actors Company present Feydeau's *Ruling the Roost* and Ford's *'Tis Pity She's a Whore*, representing the Cambridge Theatre. The Young Vic's director, Frank Dunlop offers two shows: *Bible One*, including *Joseph and the Amazing Tech-*

nicolor Dreamcoat (lyrics by Tim Rice, score by Andrew Lloyd Webber), and Shakespeare's *The Comedy of Errors*.

Sep 4 Julia Jones' *TheGarden* is the new show at London's Hampstead Theatre Club, to be followed on Oct 9 by James Roose-Evans reworking of Sophocles: *Oedipus Now*, and on Nov 13 by the American play, *The Effect of Gamma Rays on Man-in-the-Moon Marigolds* by Paul Zindel. Terence Rattigan's *While the Sun Shines* is revived on Dec 18.

Sep 7 Peter Schuman's Bread and Puppet Theatre comes to Joseph Papp's Public Theatre with *Revenge of the Law, Hallelujah*, and *Harvey McLeod*.

Sep 7 Ellen Stewart's La Mama Experimental Theatre Club opens with the Everyman Street Theatre. Also offered are *Tramp, Luna Park, Fuente Ovejuna, Pompeii, Audition, Sissy, Thoughts, City of Light, The White Whore and the Bit Player*, and *Blood Wedding*.

Sep 14 T. W. Robertson's *Caste* is revived at London's Greenwich Theatre, staged by Robert Cushman. On Nov 1, Henrik Ibsen's *A Doll House* opens with Susan Hampshire. Peter Dews directs Ian Curteis's *The Inferno*, opening on Nov 30.

Sep 21 Maggie Smith is Amanda to Robert Stephen's Elyot in Noel Coward's *Private Lives*, directed by John Gielgud, There are 517 performances at London's Queen's Theatre.

Sep 26 Joseph Papp's Public Theatre begins its new season with Alice Childress' *Wedding Band*, with Ruby Dee. On Nov 28, Michael McGuire's *The Children* opens, and on Dec 7, Anton Chekhov's *The Cherry Orchard* is revived with an all black cast.

Sep 27 John Houseman's young troupe of

HAPPY DAYS — JESSICA TANDY

403

KRAPP'S LAST TAPE

actors, trained at the Juilliard School, call themselves the City Center Acting Company, but this brief New York season is staged at the Good Shepherd-Faith Church near Lincoln Center. It opens with *The School for Scandal*, staged by Gerald Freedman, followed by *U. S. A.*, directed by Anne McNaughton; *The Hostage*, staged by Gene Lesser; *Women Beware Women*, mounted by Michael Kahn; *Next Time I'll Sing To You*, staged by Marian Seldes, and *The Lower Depths*, directed by Boris Tumarin.

Oct 5 Joan Littlewood directs an entertainment by Lionel Bart, Frank Norman, and Alan Klein, entitled *Costa Packet*, at the Theatre Royal, Stratford East. Avis Bunnage will stage a holiday show on Dec 21, *The Big Rock Candy Mountain*, based on songs of Woody Guthrie.

Oct 19 Equity Library Theatre's season of revivals includes *The Maid's Tragedy*, *How to Succeed in Business*, *In White America*, *Walter Mitty*, *Thunder Rock*, *Out of This World*, *Summer Brave*, and *Riverwind*.

Nov 9 At New York's Vivian Beaumont Theatre, *Enemies*, Maxim Gorky's play is staged by Ellis Rabb as the first play in artistic director Jules Irving's last and best season with the Repertory Company of Lincoln Center. Joseph Wiseman, Frances Sternhagen, Barbara Cook and Christopher Walken, among others, perform for 44 performances.

Nov 15 Theodore Mann and Paul Libin

move the Circle in the Square uptown to the Uris Building with *Mourning Becomes Electra*. Colleen Dewhurst and Pamela Payton-Wright are featured.

Nov 16 Frank Dunlop and London's Young Vic present Andrew Lloyd Webber and Tim Rice's *Bible One: Joseph and the Amazing Technicolor Dreamcoat*, which will later be staged at New York's Brooklyn Academy of Music for three weeks beginning Dec 30, 1976.

Nov 20 A Samuel Beckett festival opens the Forum Theatre season of the Repertory Theatre of Lincoln Center. *Happy Days*, *Act Without Words*, *Krapp's Last Tape* and *Not I* (a world premiere) are staged by Alan Schneider, with Jessica Tandy, Hume Cronyn, and Henderson Forsythe.

Dec 6 Holiday theatre treats begin today with *The Plotters of Cabbage Patch Corner*, revived in London at the Shaw Theatre. On Dec 18 at the Royalty Theatre, *The Rupert Christmas Show* opens, followed on the 19th by *Treasure Island* at the Mermaid. Other shows include *Babes in the Wood* (Palladium), *The Wizard of Oz* (Victoria Palace), and *Peter Pan* (Coliseum, with Dorothy Tutin as Peter).

Dec 10 The New Phoenix Theatre Company opens a New York season of two revivals with Eugene O'Neill's *The Great God Brown*, staged by Harold Prince and, tomorrow, Moliere's *Don Juan*, staged by Stephen Porter.

1972   BIRTHS/DEATHS/DEBUTS

Jan 1 Maurice Chevalier (b. 1888), who made his debut in Paris in 1900, dies in Paris. The world-famous entertainer had performed on stage, in music halls, and

films.

Jan 6 Alice Lewisohn, who with her sister Irene built and endowed New York's Neighborhood Playhouse, at 466 Grand

Street, is dead in Zurich at age 88.

Jan 19 Drama Critic John Chapman die at 71. He had been critic for the *New Yor Post*.

Feb 2 American actress Jessie Royce Landis (b. 1906) dies in Danbury, Connecticut. She debuted in New York in 1926 and her many roles included Janet Archer in *Kiss and Tell* and Hermione in *The Winter's Tale*.

Feb 9 Briton Robert Atkins, long know for his dedication to Shakespeare, both as an actor and a director, passes today at age 85.

April 3 Actress Mary Ure (b. 1933) die in London. After her first stage appearance as the Virgin Mary in the *York Mystery Play* in 1949, she debuted in husband John Osborne's *Look Back In Anger* in New York in 1957.

April 27 Bobby Howes, long a star of British musicals, dies at 76.

May 18 Playwright Arthur Arent (b. 1904 dies in New York. His Federal Theatre Project productions included the Living Newspaper Play, *It's Up to You*. In 1937 he co-authored the ILGWU's revue, *Pins and Needles*.

May 22 Margaret Rutherford, beloved British actress in both stage and cinema comedies, dies today at age 80.

May 31 Producer-director-actor-teacher Jasper Deeter (b. 1893) dies. He was producer and director, as well as actor, for his Hedgerow Theatre in Moylan, Pennsylvania.

July 6 Actor Brandon de Wilde (b. 1942) dies in Lakewood, California. He made his debut at seven in Carson McCuller's *The Member of the Wedding*, for which he became the youngest actor to receive the Donaldson Award.

July 24 Only 37, the flamboyantly comic actor Michael O'Sullivan dies.

Aug 19 British stage designer Roger Furse, known for his lavish and handsome decors, today dies, aged 68.

Oct 9 Miriam Hopkins (b. 1902) dies in New York. She danced in the 1921 *Music Box Revue* and played in numerous works on Broadway, including *Excess Baggage*, *Lysistrata*, and *Jezebel*. Her film career began in 1930.

Oct 16 Leo G. Carroll dies in Hollywood at 80. The English-born actor made his Broadway debut in *Rutherford and Son* in 1912.

Nov 6 Tod Andrews, actor-singer, dies today at age 51. He is remembered for his role in *Lost in the Stars*.

Nov 7 British actor Russell Thorndike dies at 87.

Nov 12 Rudolf Friml (b. 1879) is dead in Los Angeles. The Bohemian pianist and composer is best known for light operas, among which are *The Firefly*, *Rose Marie*, and *The Vagabond King*.

Nov 13 Margaret Webster (b. 1905) dies in London. Daughter of Ben Webster and Dame May Whitty, she made an outstanding reputation as a Shakespearean director in America and wrote *Shakespeare Without Tears* in 1942.

1972 THEATERS/PRODUCTIONS

Daniel Seltzer helps form the McCarter Theatre Company in Princeton, New Jersey, with aid from the Rockefeller Foundation and the Mellon Foundation.

Margaret Booker founds the Intiman Theatre Company in Seattle, Washington. Henrik Ibsen's *Rosmersholm* opens the premiere season.

Jan 1 The American Playwrights Theatre circuit's option of Jerome Lawrence and Robert E. Lee's *The Night Thoreau Spent in Jail* expires. The authors are not distressed: the play has received 141 separate productions across the nation, many in college communities.

Jan 21 Playwright's Co-op opens in Toronto, with a $24,000 federal grant. This year, it will publish 70 Canadian scripts and set up reading-rooms in eight major Canadian cities. New scripts are evaluated and, within two years, 150 plays are published from 86 member playwrights.

April A "writers' theatre" is founded in the dining room of London's Bush Hotel at Shepherds Green. The Bush Theatre provides flexible, intimate staging. Its drama discoveries will win productions, awards, and foreign tours. It will be the Alternative Theatre Company in 1975. John Fowles' *The Collector* is the initial production.

April 2 The rock musical *Hair* is banned in Chattanooga, Tennessee, sight unseen. Use of the civic auditorium is denied on the show's reputation alone.

May 25 The Manhattan Theatre Club, on the upper East Side, opens with Anthony Scully's *All Through the House*. Originally incorporated by A. E. Jeffcoat and a group of businessmen, it will offer American premieres of David Rudkin's *Ashes*, Milan Stitt's *The Runner Stumbles*, and Richard Maltby's *Ain't Misbehavin'*.

May 31 This season on Broadway, the revival of *Captain Brassbound's Conversion* is the only show which has paid off its initial investment and can therefore be labeled a hit by *Variety*. *Jesus Christ Superstar* and *The Prisoner of Second Avenue* are labeled imminent hits.

June Daryl Wedwick notes that from 1916 to 1970, 135 patents have been granted for scenic devices and effects. 68 are British and 67 American, valid for 16 and 17 years respectively. 86 have been granted for scene-shifting devices.

June Over 50 new Canadian plays have been premiered this season in Toronto, where there are four companies which perform only Canadian works.

June 1 With the 1971–1972 Broadway season now completed, the production tally stands at 56 productions. 19 have been plays, 13 musicals, 12 revivals, two revues, nine foreign plays in English, and one a specialty. At one point in April, all the Broadway houses have been booked. *Variety* sets the Broadway gross as $52.3 million, with $49.7 million earned on the road. Average production costs for a musical now stand at $534,000, with straight plays averaging $141,000 on Broadway. Off-Broadway, musicals cost $100,000, with $40,000 average for plays. The top ticket-price for a musical is now $15, with $9 for plays. Off-Broadway, popular shows can charge as much as $7.50. Off-Broadway end-of-season tallies are 43 productions of plays, 10 of musicals, 12 revivals, six specialties, 11 foreign scripts in English, three revues, and two foreign-language productions. Ella Malin's annual tally of regional theatre productions notes 325 of them, staged by 38 groups in 56 theatres in 36 cities—five of which are Canadian.

Otis Guernsey, Jr., thoughtful editor of the "*Best Play's*" series, picks the ten best of the season just over. They are McNally's *Where Has Tommy Flowers Gone*, Genet's *The Screens*, Miller's *That Championship Season*, Van Peebles' *Ain't Supposed To Die a Natural Death*, Rabe's *Sticks and Bones*, Simon's *The Prisoner of Second Avenue*, Pinter's *Old Times*, Bolt's *Vivat! Vivat! Regina!*, Weller's *Moonchildren*, and Williams' *Small Craft Warnings*.

June 19 The Off-off-Broadway Alliance is established to promote recognition of Off-off Broadway as a significant cultural force in New York City and the nation, and to help its members achieve their artistic goals.

June 20 The Toronto Free Theatre, which will present all Canadian plays and all world premieres, opens with founder Tom Hendry's *How Are Things With The Walking Wounded*. The Consumer's Gasworks has been renovated as a 100-seat theatre, and, thanks to government funding, there is no admission charged. Martin Kinch and John Palmer are the other co-founders.

July 2 *Fiddler on the Roof* closes today after 3,242 performances, making it the longest running Broadway show to date. The net profit to investors is $8,347,500.

July 3 John Houseman and Margot Harley form the City Center Acting Company in order to keep the first graduating class of the Juilliard School's Drama Program together as an ensemble. It gives its first performance at the Saratoga Performing Arts Festival.

July 8–Aug 19 Festival Lennoxville has its first season at Bishop's University, Lennoxville, Quebec. Artistic director William Davis operates on federal monies, a small city grant, and private donations. The Festival produces Canadian plays, either in premieres or revivals.

Oct The Mummers Troupe of Newfoundland is formed in St. John's. This Christmas, they will perform the traditional folkplay, *Newfoundland Night*, at 49 homes. The troupe also creates collective pieces, usually political, and gains support from trade unions and small communities throughout the province.

Oct Artistic director Jules Irving decides to resign from the Lincoln Center Repertory Company at the end of the Beaumont season. Financial and technical burdens have caused endless and futile struggles for the company.

Oct 26 The Circle in the Square moves from the Village to midtown Manhattan, to the new Joseph E. Levine Theatre in the sub-basement of the Uris Building. The first production is Eugene O'Neill's *Mourning Becomes Electra*, directed by Theodore Mann.

Nov 25 Today, Agatha Christie's *The Moustrap*, London's longest running drama, is 20 years old.

Nov 28 The Uris Theatre in New York opens with the musical, *Via Galactica*, set in 2977. The theatre, owned by the Nederlander Organization and Gerard Oestreicher, costs approximately $12.5 million and took $4^1/2$ years to complete.

MAURICE CHEVALIER

Jan 7 *Look Away* (NY—Playhouse—Drama). The season's third play about Mary Todd Lincoln features Geraldine Page as the mentally unstable widow of the martyr president. Maya Angelou supports her in Jerome Kilty's play, directed by Rip Torn. The show opens and closes the same night.

Jan 25 *National Lampoon's Lemmings* (NY—Village Gate—Revue). The magazine *National Lampoon* opens its own revue with such performers as John Belushi and Chevy Chase. It has an 11-month run. Tony Hendra stages.

Feb 8 *Finishing Touches* (NY—Plymouth—Comedy). Jean Kerr's comedy about a professor's mid-life crisis, and its effect on his family, is chosen as a "Best Play." Joseph Anthony directs Barbara Bel Geddes and James Woods for a five-month run. On Sep 4, a London production opens at the Apollo Theatre, for the 47 showings Nigel Patrick directs.

Feb 13 *El Grande de Coca Cola* (NY—Mercer Arts—Revue). Ron House plays a Honduran night-club owner who foists his family on the paying customers, pretending they are famous stars. It has 1,114 performances—all in fractured Spanish. The Low Moan Spectacular has shown it previously in England and on the Continent.

Feb 25 *A Little Night Music* (NY—Shubert—Musical). Glynis Johns, Len Cariou, and Hermione Gingold head the cast of this Hal Prince and Hugh Wheeler musical based on Ingmar Bergman's film *Smiles of a Summer Night,* with music and lyrics by Stephen Sondheim. It wins the Tony Award for Best Musical, is chosen as a "Best Play," and has a run of 600 performances. Prince directs. He also directs the London production at the Adelphi Theatre, which opens on April 15, 1975, with Jean Simmons in the lead. It has 299 performances.

March 1 *Out Cry* (NY—Lyceum—Drama). Tennessee Williams' ambiguous new play about a brother and sister (Michael York and Cara Duff-MacCormick) has only 12 performances. Previously seen in London, Chicago, and elsewhere, as The Two-Character Play, it is directed by Peter Glenville.

March 6 *The Changing Room.* See L premiere, 1971.

March 7 *The Tooth of Crime* (NY—Performing Garage—Drama). Sam Shepard's play about a rock star past his best and a driving young musician, has a 15-week run. Richard Schechner directs Timothy Shelton and Spalding Gray, among others.

March 13 *Irene* (NY—Minskoff—Musical). Debbie Reynolds plays the title-role in this reworking of the musical about a fashion designer. Songs are by Harry Tierney and Joseph McCarthy. Hugh Wheeler and Joseph Stein have revamped the book with some new lyrics from Charles Gaynore and Otis Clements. It runs 604 performances. On June 15, 1976, a West End production opens at the Adelphi Theatre, with Julie Anthony in the lead. It has 974 performances.

March 18 *Seesaw* (NY—Uris—Musical). Director-choreographer Michael Bennett adapts William Gibson's play *Two for the Seesaw* as a musical, with songs by Cy Coleman and Dorothy Fields. Ken Howard and Michele Lee play the duo. It runs for 37 weeks.

March 22 *The Hot l Baltimore* (NY—Circle in the Square—Drama). Lanford Wilson's drama about the inhabitants of a not-so-grand hotel, waiting for the wreckers who will change their lives, is selected as a "Best Play." Marshall Mason directs for a run of 1,166 performances with a cast that includes Judd Hirsch and Trish Hawkins. (The Circle Theatre Company first produced it in a hotel lobby on upper Broadway.)

March 27 *The River Niger* (NY—Brooks Atkinson—Drama). Joseph Walker's melodrama of protest and confrontation shows an angry Harlem black family in crisis. This Negro Ensemble Company production has a run of 400 performances on Broadway.

June 18 *The Faggot* (NY—Truck and Warehouse—Revue). Al Carmines directs this show about homosexuals, which runs for almost 23 weeks. It was first seen at Judson Memorial Church's Judson Poets Theatre.

Oct 18 *Raisin* (NY—46th Street—Musical). Robert Nemiroff and Charlotte Zaltzberg adapt Lorraine Hansberry's play *A Raisin in the Sun* and win 847 performances and the Tony Award for Best Musical. Donald McKayle directs and choreographs a cast including Ernestine Jackson, Ralph Carter, and Joe Horton. Music is by Judd Woldin, with lyrics by Robert Brittan.

Nov 13 *Gigi* (NY—Uris—Musical). The film *Gigi* and Colette's story inspire this less-than-inspired adaptation, with book and lyrics by Alan Jay Lerner and music by Frederick Loewe. It runs for only 13 weeks. Karin Wolfe, Agnes Moorehead, Alfred Drake, and Daniel Massey are in the cast. Joseph Hardy stages.

Nov 14 *Good Evening.* See L premiere (*Behind the Fridge*), 1972.

Nov 27 *The Good Doctor* (NY—Eugene O'Neill—Drama). Chosen as a "Best Play," Neil Simon's adaptation of various works by Anton Chekhov has a cast headed by Marsha Mason and Christopher Plummer. It runs 26 weeks. A.J. Antoon directs.

1973 BRITISH PREMIERES

Jan 11 *The Unknown Soldier and His Wife.* See NY premiere, 1967.

March 27 *The Man from the East* (L—Piccadilly—Musical). The Red Buddha Theatre has 94 performances with its rock musical which surveys Japan's past. Stomu Yamash'ta stages. On Oct 23, 1973, the troupe has a week's engagement at New York's Brooklyn Academy of Music.

May 10 *Habeas Corpus* (L—Lyric—Comedy). Alec Guinness plays a physician enduring a mid-life crisis in Alan Bennett's comedy which has a run of 523 performances. Ronald Eyre directs. On Nov 25, 1975, Donald Sinden plays the lead in a New York production at the Martin Beck Theatre. Celeste Holm, June Havoc, and Rachel Roberts are also among the cast. Frank Dunlop stages the three-month run.

May 23 *Dear Love* (L—Comedy—Drama). Keith Michell and Geraldine McEwan play Robert Browning and Elizabeth Barrett in this drama, devised by Jerome Kilty from the Browning/Barrett letters. Peter Wood directs.

June 26 *Grease.* See NY premiere, 1972.

July 4 *Absurd Person Singular* (L—Criterion—Comedy). Alan Ayckbourn's comedy, which shows three families at three successive Christmas parties, with the lower-class Hopcrafts obviously on their way up the social ladder and the others in decline, has 973 showings. Sheila Hancock and Richard Briers head the cast, directed by Erik Thompson. A New York production, with Geraldine Page and Sandy Dennis, among others, opens at the Music Box Theatre on Oct 8, 1974. It has 592 performances.

July 24 *The Card* (L—Queen's—Musical). Jim Dale, Millicent Martin, and Eleanor Bron head the cast in this Keith Waterhouse and Willis Hall adaptation of Arnold Bennett's novel. Val May directs. Tony Hatch and Jackie Trent provide the songs.

July 26 *Equus* (L—Old Vic—Drama). Alec McCowen plays a psychiatrist dealing with the sexually related neurosis of a young patient (Peter Firth) in Peter Shaffer's play. John Dexter directs this National Theatre production which has 60 performances in repertory. On April 20, 1976, it has a revival of 482 performances at London's Albery Theatre. A New York production at the Plymouth Theatre, which opens Oct 24, 1974, has a run of 1,209 performances and is chosen as a "Best Play." Anthony Hopkins plays the psychiatrist, with Richard Burton making some guest appearances. Burton is to star in the film version.

Aug 30 *Two and Two Make Sex* (L—Cambridge—Comedy). First seen at the Richmond Theatre a year ago, Richard Harris and Leslie Darbon's comedy about an insecure middle-aged man (Patrick Cargill) who has an affair with a girl in her twenties, has 430 performances. Jan Butlin stages.

Sep 27 *In Praise of Love* (L—Duchess—Comedy). Terence Rattigan's double-bill *Before Dawn* and *After Lydia* has a run of 123 performances in John Dexter's staging. Donald Sinden plays a crusty, opinionated man whose wife (Joan Greenwood) is dying of cancer in the second play. On Dec 4, 1974, Rex Harrison and Julie Harris play the same roles in a Broadway production at the Morosco Theatre. It has a six-month run.

Oct 3 *At the End of the Day* (L—Savoy—Comedy). John Mills, Dulcie Gray, and Michael Denison head the cast of William Douglas Home's play about a prime minister's family life during election time. Robert Chetwyn directs. There are 205 performances.

Oct 4 *Carry On London!* (L—Victoria Palace—Revue). Once London seasons were filled with new revues. Now this genre is the exception. Heading the cast are Barbara Windsor, Bernard Bresslaw, Sidney James, Kenneth Connor, and others. This continues into next season.

Oct 31 *Saturday, Sunday, and Monday* (L—Old Vic—Comedy). Laurence Olivier and Joan Plowright head the cast in the National Theatre's production of Eduardo de Filippo's Neapolitan comedy about a family upset caused by a hus-

THE CHANGING ROOM

band's failure to compliment his wife's cooking. On Oct 8, 1974, there is a revival in the West End at the Queen's Theatre. It has 260 performances. Franco Zeffirelli stages it, as well as the New York production at the Martin Beck Theatre, which opens on Nov 21, 1974, and closes 12 days later. Sada Thompson and Eli Wallach head the cast.

Dec 12 *Cockie* (L—Vaudeville—Musical). William Chappel stages scenes from the musical career of Charles (C.B.) Cochrane, one of London's most successful producers. Max Wall and Avril Angers head the cast. There are 85 performances.

Dec 13 *Why Not Stay for Breakfast?* (L—Apollo—Comedy). A bachelor takes pity on a unmarried mother in this Ray Cooney and Gene Stone farce, which has 510 performances. Derek Nimmo heads the cast. Cooney directs.

1973   REVIVALS/REPERTORIES

Jan 2 In Edinburgh at the Traverse Theatre, the new year begins with *The People Show No. 48*. On Jan 21, the Traverse company is at the King's Theatre in Edinburgh with its *10th Anniversary Gala Programme*. Among the year's nearly 30 productions are Edvardo Manet's *The Nuns*, David Halliwell's *Janitress Thrilled by Prehensile Penis*, Michael McClure's *The Beard*, Hugh Hastings's *The Boy*, Peter Handke's *Kaspar*, Brian Comport's *Plat du Jour*, Archie Hind's *I Am a Cabaret*, Tom Mallin's *Mrs. Argent*, Lindsay Kemp's *Legends*, and Reg Bolton's *Son, Son, Get the Gun*.

Jan 4 At the Vivian Beaumont Theatre, the Lincoln Center Repertory Theatre continues its season with a revival of Sean O'Casey's *The Plough and the Stars*. *The Merchant of Venice* follows on March 1. On April 26, Tennessee Williams' *A Streetcar Named Desire* opens for 110 performances, followed by a Broadway engagement.

Jan 9 Dennis Reardon's *Siamese Connections* opens at Joseph Papp's Public Theatre in Greenwich Village for a two-month run. David Rabe's *The Orphan* opens on March 30, for a run of almost seven weeks.

Jan 15 George Bernard Shaw's *Don Juan in Hell* is revived for three weeks on Broadway at the Palace Theatre. John Houseman directs a cast composed of Paul Heinreid, Ricardo Montalban, Edward Mulhare, and Agnes Moorehead.

Jan 16 At London's Royal Court Theatre Samuel Beckett's *Krapp's Last Tape* is revived. On Feb 27, Brian Friel's play about the agonies of Northern Ireland, *The Freedom of the City*, opens. Sam Shepard's *The Unseen Hand* is given on March 12. One month later, on April 12, Christopher Hampton's *Savages* is offered. Edward Bond's *The Sea* opens on May 22.

Jan 17 Bill Bryden's *Willie Rough*, staged by Bryden with the ensemble of Edinburgh's Royal Lyceum Theatre, opens in London at the Shaw Theatre. The Dolphin Theatre Company presents Barrie Keeffe's *Only a Game* on March 20, with direction by Michael Croft. On May 29, the American mini-musical, based on children's writings, *The Me Nobody Knows*, opens in a production also staged by Croft for the Dolphin.

Jan 17 The Circle in the Square continues its season in its new home, the Joseph E. Levine Theatre. Minos Volanakis adapts and stages Euripides' *Medea*, with Irene Papas in the title-role. This runs nine weeks. It's followed by a return to New York of Siobhan McKenna in her one-woman program, *Here Are Ladies*, opening March 29, for a run of five weeks. The final production is Chekhov's *Uncle Vanya*, produced on June 4. Mike Nichols stages a cast including Lillian Gish, Nicol Williamson, and others.

Jan 18 George Bernard Shaw's *The Man*

of Destiny is revived at the Open Space in London, with David Schofield and Diana Quick. On Feb 19, Charles Marowitz stages his adaptation of Buechner's *Woyzeck.*

Jan 22 At Glasgow's Citizens' Theatre, the new year opens with a premiere of Gogol's *The Government Inspector,* followed by *Troilus and Cressida, Happy End, The Devils,* and *Dick Whittington.* At the Close Theatre, the Cits' second stage, the productions are *The Father* and *The Connection.* When the Close Theatre burns, three Harold Pinter productions already prepared are presented on the main stage of the Citizens' Theatre. They are *Old Times, The Collection,* and *A Slight Ache.*

Jan 25 Robin Phillips directs this revival of Chekhov's *The Three Sisters* for London's Greenwich Theatre. The season continues with Saunder's *Hans Kohlhass,* Garcia Lorca's *The House of Bernarda Alba,* Kanin's *Born Yesterday,* and Ibsen's *Rosmersholm.*

Jan 29 At the Hampstead Theatre Club in London, Tennessee Williams' *Small Craft Warnings* bows. It transfers to the Comedy Theatre on March 13. Alexander Buzo's *Rooted* begins on March 2. On April 16, Charles Dyer stages his *Mother Adam.* Eric Chappell's *The Banana Box* opens on May 17.

Jan 29 At the Young Vic Theatre, Bernard Goss stages a revival of Harold Brighouse's *Hobson's Choice.*

Feb 5 Tom Eyen's *The White Whore and the Bit Player,* seen in 1964 at Café La Mama, opens in mid-Manhattan at St. Clement's Church, staged by Manuel Martin for a run of 18 performances. The play is alternately offered in English and Spanish.

Feb 14 At the Theatre Royal, in London's Stratford East, Ken Hill directs the play he's written with Tony Macaulay, *Is Your Doctor Really Necessary?* Avis Bunnage plays the Misister of Health. On May 2, C. G. Bond's new version of the 19th century melodrama, *Sweeney Todd,* opens, staged by Shaw. Brain Murphy plays the Demon Barber, Todd.

Feb 20 At London's Criterion Theatre Henrik Ibsen's *A Doll's House* opens, with Claire Bloom, Colin Blakely, and Anton Rodgers. Patrick Garland directs this production, which has been seen in New York at the Playhouse Theatre in 1971.

Feb 22 At London's Old Vic, the National Theatre presents a revival of Molière's *The Misanthrope,* staged by John Dexter. Alec McCowen and Diana Rigg play the leading roles. On May 24, the National produces Chekhov's *The Cherry Orchard,* in Ronald Hingley's translation, with Constance Cummings, Michael Hordern, and Denis Quilley.

Feb 22 Ayn Rand's thriller, the *Night of January 16th,* is revived, as *Penthouse*

THREE SISTERS AT GREENWICH

Legend at New York's McAlpin Rooftop. At each performance a jury of audience members is impaneled to decide the case on trial. Rand has provided two endings so that the play will work out as she wishes, no matter what the jury does. There are 30 showings.

March The Dublin Gate Theatre this month offers Goldoni's *The Servant of Two Masters,* staged by Hilton Edwards. Other productions this year will include White's *After Sunset,* Strindberg's *The Stronger,* Shaw's *Don Juan in Hell,* macLiammoir's *The Importance of Being Oscar,* O'Donnell's *Noone,* macLiammoir's *Prelude in Kazbek Street,* and Wilde's *Lady Windermere's Fan.*

March 26 It's time again for London's World Theatre Season at the Aldwych Theatre. West Germany's Bochum Schauspielhaus opens with *Little Man—What Now?,* based on Hans Fallada's novel, by Tankred Dorst and director Peter Zadek. On April 9, Vienna's Burgtheatre offers Arthur Schnitzler's *Liebelei.* The Comedie Française arrives on the 16th with Molière's *Le Malade Ima-*

ginaire and *Le Medicin Volant. Richard III* is played by the Comedie on April 23. From Italy comes Peppino De Filippo and his troupe, opening on the 30th with *The Metamorphoses of a Wandering Minstrel.* On May 14, Belgium's Le Rideau de Bruxelles opens its production of Guillaume Apollinaire's 'Enchanteur Pourrissant. Pierre Laroche stages. On June 4 the Umewaka Noh Troupe, directed by Manzaburo Umewaka, opens with Zeami's *Sagi* and *Kiyotsune* and a Kyogen play, *FutariDaimyo.* On the 9th and the 11th, two other programs of traditional Noh plays are presented. On June 18, the Zulu *Macbeth, Umabatha,* returns to London in Welcome Msomi's staging.

March 28 Pirandello's Italian drama of paradoxes, *Enrico IV,* is revived on Broadway at the Ethel Barrymore Theatre as *Emperor Henry IV,* starring Rex Harrison as the make-believe monarch. Clifford Williams directs. There are only 37 performances, but the show has been touring and has recouped its investment. On Feb 20, 1974, Harrison opens in the play at Her Majesty's Theatre.

March 28 England's Royal Shakespeare Company opens its season in Stratford-upon-Avon with *Romeo and Juliet. As You Like It, Love's Labour's Lost,* and *The Taming of the Shrew* are seen later.

April 18 At London's Mermaid Theatre, Shaw's *Misalliance* has a revival.

April 19 *What'a A Nice Country Like You Doing in a State Like This?* is a satiric cabaret revue which opens on the Upstage at Jimmy's in New York. Miriam Ford stages the show, with a cast including Barry Michlin and Priscilla Lopez. Songs are by Cary Hoffman and Ira Gasman. The show has a run of 543 performances.

April 25 Clare Boothe Luce's play, *The Women,* is revived on Broadway at the 46th Street Theatre, staged by Morton Da Costa, with a roster of stars including Alexis Smith, Kim Hunter, Myrna Loy, and Rhonda Fleming. The revival has a run of only two months, having lost the shock-value it once had.

May 7 Ferenc Molnar's *The Play's the Thing,* seen in this revival earlier Off-Broadway at the Roundabout Theatre, now opens on Broadway at the intimate Bijou Theatre, with a cast including David Dukes and Elizabeth Owens. Gene Feist stages the show for an 11-week run.

May 9 The Chichester Festival gets underway with Jean Anouilh's *The Director of the Opera.* Chekhov's *The Seagull,* Peter Ustinov's *Romanov and Juliet,* and Arthur Wing Pinero's *Dandy Dick* will also be seen.

May 10 *Hosanna* at Montreal's Théâtre de Quat'Sous tells of a transvestite who wants to be Elizabeth Taylor in the movie *Cleopatra.* After a successful run in Montreal, Michel Tremblay's play moves to a 10-week run in Toronto, in English translation, in May 1974. It has a three-week run in New York and returns to a national tour in Canada.

May 29 The American musical *Gypsy* is revived at the Piccadilly Theatre in London for 300 performances. Angela Lansbury is in the lead. The show returns to Broadway on Sep 23, 1974 for 15 weeks.

June 1 In Stratford, Connecticut, the American Shakespeare Festival opens with Wycherley's *The Country Wife. Measure for Measure, Macbeth,* and *Julius Caesar* are also seen during the season.

June 1 At the Open Air Theatre in Regent's Park in London, it's time for summer Shakespeare. Robert Lang stages *Twelfth Night,* with Ronald Radd and John Justin. On July 18, *As You Like It* opens, staged by Richard Digby Day.

June 4 In Ontario, Canada's Stratford Festival opens with *The Taming of the Shrew.* Other plays to be presented are *Othello, Pericles,* Goldsmith's *She Stoops to Conquer,* Turgeniev's *A Month in the Country,* Gogol's *The Marriage Brokers,* Michael Ondaatje's *The Collected Works of Billy the Kid,* Henry Beissel's *Inook and the Sun,* and Raymond and Beverly Panell's *Exiles.*

June 5 The National Shakespeare Festival in the Old Globe Theatre in San Diego's Balboa Park opens today with *The Merchant of Venice.* Other productions are *Two Gentlemen of Verona* and *King Lear.* In the nearby Carter Theatre, *Private Lives* and *I Do! I Do!* are on view.

June 11 David Rudkin's *Ashes* is revived at the Young Vic, staged by Ron Daniels. On Aug 18, the Young Vic presents the Bush Theatre production of Bertolt Brecht's adaptation of Christopher Marlowe's Elizabethan tragedy, titled by Brecht *The Life of Edward the Second of England,* in Ralph Manheim's translation.

June 12 This summer the Shaw Festival at Niagara-on-the-Lake presents *You Never Can Tell, Fanny's First Play,* William Golding's *The Brass Butterfly,* and Leonard Cohen's *Sisters of Mercy.*

June 14 Vanbrugh's *The Provok'd Wife* is revived by director Frederick Proud at London's Greenwich Theatre with Fenella Fielding.

June 19 *The Rocky Horror Show* opens in the Theatre Upstairs at London's Royal Court, with Tim Curry as the transvestite Dr. Frank N. Furter. Richard O'Brien's rock musical, set in a camp parody of Frankenstein's castle, is directed by Jim Sharman. A huge hit, it transfers to the King's Road Theatre on Nov 3, then on April 6, 1979, to the West End's Comedy Theatre. By Jan 1, 1980, the show will have had 2,599 performances. A New York production at the Belasco Theatre opens on March 10, 1975, with Tim Curry in the lead. It lasts just four weeks.

June 21 In the Delacorte Theatre in Central Park, the New York Shakespeare Festival opens its summer season with *As You Like It.* On July 26 *King Lear* begins, followed by *Two Gentlemen of Verona.*

June 23 The Oregon Shakespearean Festival in Ashland opens its season with *As You Like It. The Merry Wives of Windsor, Henry V, Othello,* August Strindberg's *The Dance of Death* and Ben Jonson's *The Alchemist* will also be shown.

June 28 Howard Brenton's *Magnificence,* staged by Max Stafford-Clark, opens at London's Royal Court Theatre. On July 19, David Williamson's *The Removalist* is shown, staged by Jim Sharman. Stephen Frears stages Michael Abbensett's *Sweet Talk* in the Upstairs Theatre on July 31. On the main stage on Aug 15, Albert Finney heads the cast in David Storey's *Cromwell.* Anthony Page stages.

June 29 Robert Temple has adapted *Smoky Mountain Passion Play* from the Bible. It is presented today in the 2,000-seat Passion Play Amphitheatre in Townsend, Tennessee.

June 30 The Scioto Society presents *Tecumseh!,* a play by Allan W. Eckert, about the Indian leader. Ohio's Sugarloaf Mountain. Amphitheatre, in Chillicothe, is the production site.

July 2 At the Round House in London, Steve Gooch's translation of Bertolt Brecht's *The Mother* is presented, staged by Jonathan Chadwick. On Aug 14, *Decameron '73* opens, a musical devised by Peter Coe with songs by Joe Griffiths. On Aug 27, The Prospect Theatre Company presents a revival of Peter Shaffer's *The Royal Hunt of the Sun* followed, on the 29th, by Shakespeare's *Pericles.* On Sep 5, *Twelfth Night* is seen.

July 2 Sean Kenny designs and directs the Sean O'Casey revival at the Mermaid Theatre, *Juno and the Paycock,* with Siobhan McKenna and Niall Buggy. Bernard Miles directs the revival of J. B. Priestley's *An Inspector Calls,* opening on Aug 29.

July 3 At the Hampstead Theatre Club in London, Friedrich Duerrenmatt's *Play Strindberg,* based on the Swedish playwright's *The Dance of Death,* opens. On Aug 13, the play is *Mad Dog,* by Nicholas Salaman. Patrick Garland stages.

July 7 *Antony and Cleopatra,* produced by the Royal Shakespeare Company at Stratford-upon-Avon nearly a year ago, opens now in London at the Aldwych Theatre as part of a trio of Roman plays staged by Trevor Nunn. Richard Johnson is Antony to Janet Suzman's Cleopatra. On July 21, *Julius Caesar* opens, with Mark Dignam and John Wood. On Aug 4, *Titus Andronicus* opens with Colin Blakely and Judy Geeson.

July 18 At Sam Wanamaker's Bankside Globe Theatre in London, Charles Marowitz stages his adaptation of Eugene Ionesco's *Macbett,* based on a Shakespearean model, with Harry H. Corbett, Victor Spinetti, and Frances Cuka. Tony Richardson stages *Antony and Cleopatra* on Aug 9 with Vanessa Redgrave, and Julian Glover.

Aug 2 At London's Old Vic, the National Theatre offers Euripides' *The Bacchae* in the version of Wole Soyinka, the Nigerian playwright. Constance Cummings and Martin Shaw head the cast.

Aug 16 London's National Youth Theatre shows an end-of-summer show, *The Petticoat Rebellion,* by D. Emyr Edwards and Gareth Thomas at the Shaw Theatre. On Sep 6, Barrie Rutter's staging of *Geordie's March,* by Peter Terson, opens.

Aug 19 The annual Edinburgh Festival opens today with four British theatre companies providing productions. Edinburgh's own Royal Lyceum Theatre offers *The Thrie Estaites,* by David Lindsay of the Mount, staged by Bill Bryden, and Ian

Brown's *The Knife*, directed by John David. The adjunct ensemble, the Young Lyceum, presents Georg Buechner's *Woyzeck* in a production mounted by the Roumanian director, Radu Peniculescu. The Actors Company provides four productions: *Knots*, based on R. D. Laing's book; Gabriel Josipovici's *Flow*; Chekhov's *The Wood Demon*, and Congreve's *The Way of the World*. The Prospect Theatre troupe offers *Don Juan in Love*, devised and directed by Kenny McBain, and Shakespeare's *Pericles*, staged by Toby Robertson.

Sep 4 Noel Coward's *Relative Values*, staged by Charles Hickman, is revived in London at the Westminster Theatre with Margaret Lockwood.

Sep 5 Sigmund Romberg's 1926 musical, *The Desert Song*, opens in revival on Broadway at the new Uris Theatre. It has only 15 showings, losing some $200,000.

Sep 11 At the Hampstead Theatre Club in London, Bertolt Brecht's *Drums in the Night*, adapted by C. P. Taylor, opens in Roland Rees' staging. Nicholas Wood's *Country Life* is seen on Oct 8, staged by Chris Parr. On Nov 12, Peter Handke's *The Ride Across Lake Constance* opens, Michael Rudman directing Michael Roloff's translation. The production moves to the May Fair Theatre in the West End on Dec 12. On Dec 17, the Club presents Stanley Eveling's *Union Jack and Bonzo*, staged by Mike Ockrent.

Sep 12 Fernando Arrabal's *And They Put Handcuffs on the Flowers*, as translated by Charles Marowitz, is staged by Arrabal and Petrika Ionescu at London's Open Space. On Nov 14, Robert Stephens directs and plays Apollon in *Apropos of Falling Sleet*, based on Dostoievsky's *Notes from the Underground*, by Alan Brown and Kyra Dietz.

Sep 13 The Circle in the Square opens its season with Jean Anouilh's *The Waltz of the Toreadors*, staged by Brian Murray. This runs almost 11 weeks, as does Eugene O'Neill's *The Iceman Cometh*, which opens on Dec 13, staged by Theodore Mann.

Sep 19 W. Somerset Maugham's *The Constant Wife* is revived at the Albery Theatre in the West End. As staged by John Gielgud, it has a run of 260 performances. Ingrid Bergman leads the cast.

Sep 20 Athol Fugard's *Sizwe Banzi Is Dead* is performed by the African actors John Kani and Winston Ntshona, who have helped Fugard devise it, for the Royal Court's Theatre Upstairs in London. On the 26th on the main stage, the play is David Storey's *The Farm*. On Nov 1, the production moves to the May Fair Theatre in the West End. On Nov 7, Peter Gill unveils his production of D. H. Lawrence's *The Merry-Go-Round*. Snoo Wilson's *The Pleasure Principle* opens Upstairs on Nov 26.

Sep 20 Geraldine McEwan plays Zoe in *Not Drowning but Waving*, by Leonard Webb, now opening at London's Greenwich Theatre. Robin Phillips directs. On Oct 29, Phillips presents Istvan Orkeny's modern Hungarian success, *Catsplay*. The American musical, *Zorba*, with songs by John Kander and Fred Ebb, opens on Nov 27, staged by Phillips.

Oct 2 At the Manhattan Theatre Club a busy season begins with Adam Le Fevre's *Yucca Flats*. Among the other plays presented are Joyce Carol Oates' *Miracle Play*, Mark Medoff's *The Wager*, Kenneth Brown's *The Cretan Bull*, Cecil Taylor's *Allergy*, Leonard Melfi's *Birdbath*, Israel Horovitz's *Our Father's Failing*, Tennessee Williams's *Suddenly Last Summer*, Garson Kanin's *Born Yesterday*, Richard Wesley's *The Sirens*, and Thomas Murphy's *Morning After Optimism*.

Oct 4 The Royal Shakespeare Company launches a season of new plays in London at The Place, with David Rudkin's *Cries from Casement*. Philip Magdalany's *Section Nine* opens on Oct 11. On Oct 18, Athol Fugard's *Hello and Goodby*, seen first at the King's Head Theatre Club, is presented. On Oct 20, *Sylvia Plath*, a dramatization of the poet's writings, is staged. John Wiles' *A Lesson in Blood and Roses* opens on Nov 6.

Oct 10 Peter Wyngarde plays the King in this revival of *The King and I* at London's Adelphi Theatre. Sally Ann Howes plays Anna. It has a run of 260 performances.

Oct 17 Produced the past summer at the Chichester Festival, John Clements's production of Arthur Wing Pinero's *Dandy Dick* opens in the West End at the Garrick Theatre. Alastair Sim repeats his success as the Very Rev. Augustine Jedd. There are 165 performances.

Oct 18 Joseph Papp's Public Theatre in Greenwich Village opens its season with Robert Montgomery's *Lotta*. On Nov 21, *More Than You Deserve* is given, with words by Michael Weller and music by Jim Steinman. On Dec 18, Jack Gelber presents his adaptation of Norman Mailer's novel, *Barbary Shore*.

Oct 18 The Equity Library Theatre season opens in the Master Theatre near Riverside Drive in Manhattan with a revival of *Broadway*, followed by *Call Me Madam*, *Rashomon*, *Look: We've Come Through*, *Carousel*, *Oh, Lady! Lady!*, *Bloomers*, and *Man With a Load of Mischief*.

Oct 22 The RSC brings its Stratford-upon-Avon production of *Coriolanus* to London's Aldwych Theatre. Nicol Williamson and Margaret Tyzack head the cast. Trevor Nunn directs assisted by Buzz Goodbody and Euan Smith.

Oct 23 Frank Hauser brings his Oxford Playhouse production of Ferenc Molnar's *The Wolf* to the Apollo Theatre in the West End. Judi Dench, Leo McKern, and Edward Woodward play 239 perfor-

mances in this comedy about jealousy.

Oct 25 Michael McClure's San Francisco sensation, *The Beard*, featuring Billy the Kid and Jean Harlow in Heaven, both wearing paper beards, opens at Richard Schechner's Performing Garage in New York's Soho district.

Nov 5 Marshall Mason heads New York's Circle Repertory Theatre Company, a collective of actors, designers, directors, and playwrights. Their new season opens with Mark Medoff's *When You Comin' Back, Red Ryder?* Richard Lortz's *Prodigal* follows on Dec 16 and Roy London's *The Amazing Activity of Charley Contrare and the Ninety-Eighth Street Gang* on Jan 20. Edward Moore's *The Sea Horse* is given on March 3 and Aeschylus's *The Persians* on May 19.

Nov 10 Joseph Papp has reversed Jules Irving's policy for the Lincoln Center Beaumont and Forum Theatres. Formerly, classics occupied the large Beaumont stage, with experiments confined to the Forum downstairs. Now Papp is presenting experiments such as David Rabe's *The Boom Boom Room* upstairs, using the renamed downstairs theatre, now the Mitzi E. Newhouse, as the home for his stock-in-trade, Shakespeare. *Troilus and Cressida* is his first venture with the Bard here, staged by David Schweizer. It has 57 performances, rude reviews, and a truncated run. Christopher Walken, Madeleine Le Roux, and Leonard Frey are in the cast.

Nov 21 Vanessa Redgrave stars in a revival of Noel Coward's *Design for Living* at London's Phoenix Theatre, staged by Michael Blakemore. The production runs on into the following season.

Nov 25 Friedrich Duerrenmatt's *The Visit* opens the season of New York's New Phoenix Repertory Company. Georges Feydeau's *Chemin de Fer* follows on Nov 26, and Philip Barry's *Holiday* on Dec 26.

Nov 27 Eric Bentley's *Are You Now Or Have You Ever Been*, a reworking of the hearings of the House Un-American Activity Committee, under Chairman J. Parnell Thomas, opens at the Theatre of the Riverside Church in New York. Jay Broad stages, with a cast including Joseph Leon and Anne Francine.

Dec 11 The Chelsea Theatre Center opens the revised version of Leonard Bernstein's *Candide* in its rebuilt theatre-space at New York's Brooklyn Academy of Music. Hugh Wheeler has provided a new book to replace Lillian Hellman's original. Lyrics are by John LaTouche, Richard Wilbur, and Stephen Sondheim. The show runs for six weeks and on March 10, 1974, transfers to the Broadway Theatre where it has 740 performances.

Dec 15 Tonight Robert Wilson's marathon theatre-dance-opera piece, *The Life and Times of Joseph Stalin*, opens at the Brooklyn Academy of Music. It begins at

7 p.m., with long intermissions between acts, and ends with a stage full of dancing ostriches at 7 a.m. There is a cast of 144. There are threads of Stalin's life in this amazing spectacle of the terrain of dreams. It will be repeated tomorrow night.

Dec 17 It's holiday time again, and where there once were a score of Christmas pantomimes, musicals, and comedy revivals in and around London, this season there are only three. Bernard Miles's *Treasure Island* is revived at the Mermaid Theatre today, followed tomorrow by the Palladium's lavish staging of *Jack and the Beanstalk*, with comedian Frankie Howerd. Albert Knight stages. On Dec 19 at the Prince of Wales *The Danny La Rue Show* opens, starring the popular female impersonator Danny La Rue, directed by Freddie Carpenter. It has 515 performances.

Dec 19 The City Center Acting Company opens a repertory of five revivals at the Billy Rose Theatre, beginning with Chekhov's *Three Sisters*, staged by Boris Tumarin, followed by Gay's *The Beggar's Opera*, staged by Gene Lesser; *Measure for Measure*, directed by John Houseman; *Scapin*, mounted by Pierre Lefevre, and *Next Time I'll Sing To You*, staged by Marian Seldes. The engagement lasts three weeks.

Dec 20 At London's Old Vic, the National Theatre presents Trevor Griffiths' *The Party*, staged by John Dexter. Laurence Olivier, Denis Quilley, and Frank Finlay head the cast. The play is about a Scottish Trotskyite labor leader.

Dec 29 Eugene O'Neill's *A Moon for the Misbegotten*, staged by Jose Quintero, is revived at the Morosco Theatre on Broadway for a run of 39 weeks. Colleen Dewhurst and Jason Robards head the cast.

Top of the Stairs, and *A Loss of Roses* were also produced on Broadway.

June 11 Sean Kenny, the innovative stage designer whose work was so often praised by London critics, dies, only 40 years old. His moving scenery for *Blitz* and *Pickwick* was especially admired.

June 26 Actress Fanny Bradshaw dies, aged 76.

June 27 Ernest Truex, the actor, is dead today, aged 82.

July 6 Wide-mouthed comedian Joe E. Brown passes on, aged 82.

July 11 Cinema and stage actor Robert Ryan dies, aged 63.

July 18 English actor Jack Hawkins (b. 1910) dies in London. Hawkins made his first New York appearance in 1929 in *Journey's End*. In addition to his many Shakespearean roles, he received critical acclaim in *The Importance of Being Earnest*, *Candida*, *Thor With Angels*, and *The Apple Cart*. Hawkins's film career began in 1932.

Aug 1 Stage and screen actor Frederick Worlock (b. 1886) dies in Woodland Hills, California. Worlock became a member of the Benson Shakespeare Company in 1905. His Broadway credits include Zoe Akins' *The Greeks Had a Word for It*, Dumas' *Camille*, and Sydney Howard's *Dodsworth*.

Sep 9 Playwright S. N. (Samuel Nathaniel) Behrman (b. 1893) dies in New York. Behrman's first play to be produced was *The Second Man*. *Biography*, *Amphitryon 38*, *No Time for Comedy*, *Jacobowsky and the Colonel*, and *Fanny* (with Joshua Logan) are a few of his memorable plays.

Sep 13 Actress Betty Field (b. 1918) dies

1973   BIRTHS/DEATHS/DEBUTS

Jan 19 Actor-director Max Adrian (b. 1903) dies in Surrey, England. He appeared with the Northampton Repertory Company, the Old Vic, and the British National Theatre. His first New York appearance was in 1934.

Jan 26 Stage and screen star Edward G. Robinson is dead, aged 79.

Feb 22 The "First Lady" of the Greek National Theatre, Katina Paxinou, is dead at 72. During the Nazi occupation of Greece in World War II, Paxinou acted in American plays and films. In later years she was especially proud of her American citizenship, returning to play, with her director-actor husband Alexis Minotis, in Greek classics in modern Greek.

March 3 American theatrical producer Richard Halliday (b. 1905) dies in Brazil. Halliday was co-producer of the Broadway productions of *Peter Pan*, *The Sound of Music*, and *Jennie*, all starring his wife Mary Martin.

March 22 British producer Hugh Beaumont is dead at age 64.

March 26 English playwright, composer, and actor Noel Coward (b. 1899) dies in Jamaica. Coward made his Broadway debut in *The Vortex*, which he wrote and directed. In association with the Lunts, he produced and acted in *Design for Living*. Author of such plays as *Private Lives* and *Hay Fever*, he also wrote *Present Indicative* and *Future Indefinite*.

March 29 Actor Melville Cooper (b. 1896) dies in Hollywood. Cooper made his London debut in 1924 in George Bernard Shaw's *Back to Methuselah*. His New York debut was in 1935 in J. B. Priestley's *Laburnum Grove*. In 1959, he joined the cast of *My Fair Lady* as Colonel Pickering.

April 21 English actress Ursula Jeans (b. 1906) dies in London. Among the plays in which she appeared are *Escape*, *The Fanatics*, *The First Mrs. Fraser*, and *Grand Hotel*.

April 26 Actress Irene Ryan dies at age 70.

May 10 Lyricist, writer, and *Variety* editor Abel Green (b. 1900) dies in New York. Among his books are *Inside Stuff* and *How to Write Popular Songs*.

June 10 American playwright William Inge (b. 1913) dies in Hollywood. Inge was awarded the Pulitzer Prize for *Picnic* in 1953. He had previously scored a success with *Come Back, Little Sheba*, with Shirley Booth. His *Bus Stop*, *The Dark at the*

TKTS BOOTH

in Hyannis, Massachusetts. Her Broadway credits include *Three Men on a Horse, Boy Meets Girl, Dream Girl,* and *The Ladies of the Corridor.* Two of her notable films are *Of Mice and Men* and *The Great Gatsby.*

Sep 21 Actress Diana Sands is dead at 39.

Sep 28 Mantan Moreland, the popular black comedian, dies at age 72.

Sep 28 Playwright and poet W. H. Auden (b. 1907) is dead. Auden's first produced work was the verse drama, *The Dance of Death,* in 1933. He is the author, with Christopher Isherwood, of *The Dog Beneath the Skin, The Ascent of F6,* and *On the Frontier.* He also wrote opera librettos with Chester Kallman.

Oct 5 Actor-producer-director Sidney Blackmer (b. 1895) dies in New York. His performance as Doc in William Inge's *Come Back, Little Sheba,* earned him the Donaldson Award for best actor of the 1949–50 season and the Tony Award in 1950. He also appeared in films and television.

Nov 25 Joseph Verner Reed (b. 1902), producer of Broadway shows and a founder and longtime patron of the American Shakespeare Festival in Stratford, Connecticut, dies in New York.

Nov 26 English stage and screen actor Laurence Harvey (b. 1928) dies in London. Harvey first appeared with the Johannesburg Repertory Theatre in 1943. Later he appeared with the Shakespeare Memorial Theatre and the Old Vic company. Harvey made his New York debut in 1955 in *The Island of the Goats.*

Dec 7 English playwright and director Benn W. Levy (b. 1900) dies in Oxford, England. Levy wrote a number of light comedies including *Mrs. Moonlight, The Devil, Accent on Youth,* and *Springtime for Henry.*

designed by architect R. J. Thom.

June 21 The United States Supreme Court hands down two rulings which set new standards in obscenity cases. In the future, films can be banned only if they have "no redeeming value." And the determination of what is obscene is now to be set by local community standards, not by national standards. Implications for judging possibly offensive plays and dramatic productions are seen in these two rulings.

June 25 TKTS, the Times Square Theatre Center booth set up by the Theatre Development Fund (TDF), opens at Broadway and 47th Street to provide theatregoers with half-price tickets to Broadway and Off-Broadway attractions. Patrons stand in line before matinee and evening performances in the hope of obtaining good seats at bargain prices. By the end of 1974, *Variety* will estimate that the new ticket-booth, has sold 409,886 tickets, representing a gross of $1,860,568. This is four per cent of the total Broadway gross in that period.

August Without warning, the historic Broadway Central Hotel collapses, making the various theatre premises in the integral and adjoining Mercer Arts Center untenable and dangerous. They all must be abandoned and the ruined structure is torn down.

Sep 22 A 30-day Opening Festival inaugurates the 2,183-seat Great Hall and 400-seat Studio Theatre of the Hamilton Place arts complex in Hamilton, Ontario, Canada. The $10 million complex is designed by Trevor Garwood-Jones.

Dec Six graduates of Memorial University in St. John's, Newfoundland, Canada, borrow $300 "seed" money from Paul Thompson, Artistic Director of Theatre Passe Muraille in Toronto and stage a satirical revue, *Cod on a Stick,* to wildly enthusiastic audiences. Thenceforth known as "Codco," the group stages several more revues, hitting home with topics of local veneration like the Catholic Church, Irish folksingers, and the annual seal hunt. They will have a very successful run at the Walnut Street Theatre in Philadelphia (Oct 28, 1975) and play to large audiences across Canada.

1973   THEATERS/PRODUCTIONS

Jan Director Christopher Wootten founds the Vancouver East Cultural Centre in British Columbia, Canada, on a Local Initiatives Program grant. He renovates an old church. In the next eight months, there are 227 events: 113 theatrical performances, 24 concerts, 26 dance programs, 29 film evenings, 25 children's events, and a 10-day crafts fair for a total audience of 40,000.

Jan 1 The New Theatre in London's St. Martin's Lane is renamed the Albery Theatre.

Jan 10 The New London Theatre opens off Drury Lane, on the site of the former Winter Garden Theatre, with *The Unknown Soldier and His Wife.*

Jan 15 The first Chalmers Award for Outstanding Canadian Play is given to David Freeman's *Creeps.*

Jan 24 Canada's Stratford Festival company travels to Europe to show its work in such cities as Copenhagen, Utrecht, The Hague, Warsaw, Krakow, Moscow, and Leningrad. This is the first European tour by an English-speaking Canadian ensemble. The troupe's repertory includes *King Lear* and *The Taming of the Shrew.*

March 7 Joseph Papp today announces that he and his New York Shakespeare Festival management will take over the operation of Lincoln Center's Vivian Beaumont Theatre and the Forum Theatre at the close of the current season.

March 13 The Minskoff Theatre, at 200 West 45th Street, in New York, opens with the musical, *Irene,* starring Debbie Reynolds. The theatre is housed in a striking 54-story glass office-tower.

May 31 On this last day of the current Broadway season, the following productions have recouped their initial investments, which in *Variety's* estimation technically makes them hits: *Butley, That Championship Season, The Sunshine Boys, Pippin, A Little Night Music, Jacques Brel, The Changing Room, Man of La Mancha, Irene,* and *Emperor Henry IV.*

June 1 With the close of the Broadway season of 1972–1973 yesterday, new productions have totaled 54, in contrast to the 84 mounted in the 1967–68 season. Of the total, some shows have been opened on "limited" or "middle" theatre contracts. Otis Guernsey, Jr. tallies the offerings thus: 16 plays, 13 musicals, two revues, three specialties, two foreign plays in English, two in foreign tongues, and 16 revivals. *Variety* will report a Broadway gross of $45 million, with the road gross about $55.5 million. Production tallies for Off-Broadway include 28 plays, 16 musicals, seven revues, eight specialties, 19 revivals, nine foreign plays in English, and eight foreign-language shows. In regional theatres, there have been 341 productions of 354 plays by 40 groups in 59 playhouses in 36 cities—five of them in Canada. Shakespeare has had 31 productions of 21 of his plays.

The ten "Best Plays" of the New York season just past, picked by Guernsey, Jr., include Randall's *6 Rms Riv Vu,* Gray's *Butley,* Ableman's *Green Julia,* Miller's *The Creation of the World and Other Business,* Walker's *The River Niger,* Simon's *The Sunshine Boys,* Kerr's *Finishing Touches,* Storey's *The Changing Room,* Wilson's *The Hot l Baltimore,* and Wheeler/Soundheim's *A Little Night Music.*

June 12 Canada's new Shaw Festival Theatre at Niagara-on-the-Lake opens,

Jan 2 *Find Your Way Home* (NY—Brooks Atkinson—Drama). John Hopkins' play about a married man (Lee Richardson) who becomes involved with a homosexual hustler (Michael Moriarty), is named a "Best Play." Staged by Edwin Sherin, it runs for 17 weeks.

Jan 8 *Let My People Come* (NY—Village Gate—Revue). Earl Wilson, Jr.'s, celebration of nudity and sexual liberation has 1,327 showings. A London production opens on Aug 19 at the Regent Theatre, under the direction of Philip Oesterman, and earns 1,245 performances.

Jan 20 *The Ritz* (NY—Longacre—Comedy). Rita Moreno and Jack Weston head the cast in Terrence McNally's comedy, set in a Turkish bath known for its homosexual clientele. Chosen as a "Best Play," it has 400 performances. It was first seen at Robert Brustein's Yale Repertory in New Haven.

Jan 27 *Lorelei* (NY—Palace—Musical). Carol Channing stars in this Kenny Solms and Gail Parent musical, inspired by an earlier show, *Gentlemen Prefer Blondes.* Jule Styne, Betty Comden, and Adolph Green write the songs. Robert Moore directs.

Feb 4 *Bad Habits* (NY—Astor Place—Comedy). Terrence McNally's double-bill, black comedies on mental illness, runs until May 5, then transfers to Broadway's Booth Theatre for a 34-week run. It is chosen as a "Best Play." Robert Drivas stages a cast that includes F. Murray Abraham and Emory Bass.

Feb 28 *Noel Coward in Two Keys* (NY—Ethel Barrymore—Drama). Hume Cronyn, Jessica Tandy, and Anne Baxter appear in this Coward double-bill. In London it was called *Suite in Three Keys*—with one more play. *A Song at Twilight* and *Come into the Garden Maud* are the plays shown here for nearly 18 weeks. They get "Best Play" status.

March 6 *Over Here!* (NY—Shubert—Musical). Maxene and Patty Andrews, of the Andrews Sisters trio, Treat Williams, and John Travolta are in the cast of this Will Holt musical set in America during World War II. Tom Moore directs.

March 31 *My Fat Friend.* See L premiere, 1972.

April 15 *The Sea Horse* (NY—Westside—Drama). Selected as a "Best Play," Edward J. Moore's drama about a lonely barmaid (Conchata Ferrell) and the man who wants to marry her (played by Moore) has a run of four months. Marshall Mason directs. It has previously been produced by Circle Repertory Company.

April 16 *Words and Music* (NY—John Golden—Revue). Sammy Cahn stars in a revue made up of his songs and lyrics.

FIND YOUR WAY HOME

Jerry Adler directs the four-month run. On Sep 11 the show opens at London's New London Theatre under the title *Sammy Cahn's Songbook.*

May 6 *Will Rogers' U.S.A.* (NY—Helen Hayes—Revue). James Whitmore is a one-man show as Will Rogers, in Paul Shyre's revue based on Rogers' writings and routines. It has a week's run but has toured successfully.

May 28 *The Magic Show* (NY—Cort—Musical). There are 1,920 performances of this Rob Randall musical about a young nightclub magician (Doug Henning) and a broken-down trickster (David Odgen Stiers). Grover Dale directs and choreographs. Stephen Schwartz provides the songs.

June 11 *The World of Lenny Bruce* (NY—Players—Revue). Frank Spieser's one-man show, in which he impersonates the satirist Lenny Bruce, runs for 17 weeks.

July 1 *Why Hanna's Skirt Won't Stay Down* (NY—Top of the Village Gate—Comedy). Tom Eyen's play about a girl who loves to let the air-jet at Coney Island's funhouse lift her skirts has 139 performances. Neil Flanagan and Eyen direct.

Oct 6 *Mack and Mabel* (NY—Majestic—Musical). Despite a cast that includes Robert Preston and Bernadette Peters, songs by Jerry Herman, and staging by Gower Champion, this Michael Stewart book about the silent film era wins only 65 performances.

Oct 8 *Absurd Person Singular.* See L premiere, 1973.

Oct 14 *Hosanna* (NY—Bijou—Drama). Michel Tremblay's French-Canadian play about social outcasts, a transvestite (Richard Monette) and his leather-clad lover (Richard Donat), has a three-week run. Previously seen at the Tarragon Theatre in Toronto, it is directed by Bill Glassco.

Oct 21 *The Wager* (NY—Eastside Playhouse—Drama). Anthony Perkins stages Mark Medoff's drama, which is chosen as a "Best Play." Kristoffer Tabori is among the cast. It has 104 performances.

Oct 24 *Equus.* See L premiere, 1973.

Nov 13 *Sizwe Banzi Is Dead* and *The Island* (NY—Edison—Drama). Devised by South African playwright Athol Fugard, and by John Kani and Winston Ntshona, the two black actors who appear in them, these dramas of life in South Africa have 159 and 52 performances respectively. *Newsweek* calls them "remarkable." Seen originally in South Africa, the plays have also been performed at London's Royal Court Theatre and New Haven's Long Wharf Theatre.

Nov 17 *Sgt. Pepper's Lonely Hearts Club*

Band on the Road (NY—Beacon—Musical). Director Tom O'Horgan and designer Robin Wagner animate the Beatles' *Sgt. Pepper* album, adding a further 17 Lennon-McCartney songs. It has a two-month run.

Dec 4 *In Praise of Love.* See L premiere, 1973.

Dec 11 *God's Favorite* (NY—Eugene O'Neill—Comedy). Neil Simon's comedy is about Joe Benjamin, a modern Jewish Job. Vincent Gardenia, Laura Esterman, and Charles Nelson Reilly are in the cast. Michael Bennett directs, for 119 performances, in which the Devil's emissary is allowed to test Benjamin's steadfastness.

Dec 29 *All Over Town* (NY—Booth—Comedy). Dustin Hoffman directs Murray Schisgal's sex farce about mistaken identity. It is chosen as a "Best Play." Cleavon Little heads the cast. There are 233 performances.

1974 BRITISH PREMIERES

Feb 6 *Chez Nous* (L—Globe—Drama). Albert Finney, Denholm Elliott, and Geraldine McEwan head the cast of Peter Nichols' play about changing sexual mores, which continues its run into the next season. Robert Chetwyn directs.

Feb 26 *Monty Python's First Farewell Tour* (L—Drury Lane—Revue). John Cleese, Graham Chapman, and other members of the satiric TV team have a five-week run in this revue. On April 14, 1976, they open a three-week run at New York's City Center 56th Street Theatre in *Monty Python Live!*

March 4 *Knuckle* (L—Comedy—Drama). Edward Fox and Kate Nelligan head the cast of David Hare's play about a gun-runner, which continues into the next season. Michael Blakemore stages.

March 10 *Candide.* See NY listing, 1973.

March 13 *Snap* (L—Vaudeville—Comedy). Maggie Smith heads the cast of Charles Laurence's comedy about a smart liberated set who become distinctly unsettled by an outbreak of venereal disease. William Gaskill stages the production, which continues into next season.

April 25 *A Ghost on Tiptoe* (L—Savoy—Comedy). Robert Morley plays a man who's given only 18 months to live and decides to go out with flying colors, in this comedy he's written with Rosemary Ann Sisson. Jan Butlin directs the 372 performances.

May 1 *Billy* (L—Drury Lane—Musical). Michael Crawford heads the cast as daydreaming Billy, who's offered a chance to escape from his provincial boredom, in this Dick Clement and Ian Le Frenais musical adaptation of Keith Waterhouse and Willis Hall's play *Billy Liar*. There are 904 performances. Patrick Garland stages.

June 10 *Travesties* (L—Aldwych—Drama). James Joyce, Lenin, and Tristan Tzara are among the leading characters in Tom Stoppard's play set in Zurich in 1917. Tom Bell and John Hurt are among the cast of this Royal Shakespeare Company repertory production, staged by Peter Wood. On Oct 30, 1975, the play opens on Broadway at the Ethel Barrymore, with a different RSC cast which includes Tim Curry. It is chosen as a "Best Play" and wins the Tony Award for Best Play of the Season, but there are only 155 showings.

July 2 *Cole* (L—Mermaid—Revue). Benny Green and Alan Strachen stage an entertainment based on Cole Porter's songs that has 326 performances. Una Stubbs and Julia McKenzie are among the cast.

July 10 *Bloomsbury* (L—Phoenix—Drama). Peter Luke evokes the manners and mores of Bloomsbury's literary set in this drama which has 53 performances. Richard Cottrell directs Yvonne Mitchell as Virginia Woolf and Daniel Massey as Lytton Strachey.

July 11 *The Good Companions* (L—Her Majesty's—Musical). John Mills and Judi Dench head the cast of Ronald Harwood's musical adaptation of J.B. Priestley's novel about a concert party tour. Johnny Mercer and Andre Previn provide the songs. Braham Murray stages; there are 261 performances.

Aug 1 *The Norman Conquests* (L—Globe—Comedy). First seen at the Greenwich Theatre in May, this Alan Ayckbourn trilogy about a weekend house party has 672 performances. The three plays, *Table Manners, Living Together,* and *Round and Round the Garden,* all set at different times during the weekend, are shown in rotation. On Dec 7, 1975, as Norman, bent on seducing three women, Richard Benjamin opens in the New York production at the Morosco Theatre. Chosen collectively as a "Best Play," the plays have a total run of 228 performances.

Aug 15 *John, Paul, George, Ringo . . . And Bert* (L—Lyric—Musical). Willy Russell's musical about the Beatles, first seen at the Everyman in Liverpool, has 418 performances. Alan Dossor stages.

Sep 2 *Let's Get Laid* (L—Windmill—Comedy). Long identified with suggestive revues and unclad girls, the Windmill now offers Paul Raymond's production of Sam Cree's play, staged by Victor Spinetti. It has 468 performances.

Sep 17 *Jack the Ripper* (L—Ambassadors'—Musical). Ron Pember and Denis Demarne's book, an imitation Victorian melodrama, with a music-hall setting, in which the real identity of the Ripper is unmasked, has 251 performances. Seen first at the Players' Theatre in June, it is directed and designed by Reginald Woolley.

Oct 7 *There Goes the Bride* (L—Criterion—Comedy). Peggy Mount, Bill Pertwee, and Bernard Cribbins head the cast of this Ray Cooney and John Chapman farce about the sexual generation gap. Jan Butlin directs the production, which continues into the next season.

Oct 17 *The Dame of Sark* (L—Wyndham's—Drama). Although the Channel Island of Sark has been invaded by the Nazis, its redoubtable Dame (Celia Johnson) is equal to any challenge in William Douglas Home's play, first seen at the Oxford Playhouse. Charles Hickman directs. There are 281 performances.

Oct 22 *Kennedy's Children* (L—King's Head—Drama). Robert Patrick's American play about the burnt-out dreams of the 1960's, is staged by Clive Donner. It continues into the next season and, on April 17, 1975, transfers to the Arts Theatre for an extended run. A Broadway production, at the John Golden Theatre, opens on Nov 3, 1975, but runs only nine weeks. Shirley Knight wins a Tony Award as Best Featured Actress. Clive Donner again directs.

Oct 23 *The Gingerbread Lady.* See NY premiere, 1970.

1974 REVIVALS/REPERTORIES

Jan 1 *Sherlock Holmes,* by William Gillette and Arthur Conan Doyle, is revived by the Royal Shakespeare Company in Frank Dunlop's staging at London's Aldwych Theatre. John Wood plays the fictional sleuth, with Tim Piggot-Smith his Dr. Watson. On Nov 12, the production opens on Broadway at the Broadhurst Theatre. The show runs for 471 performances.

Jan 2 *Flowers,* a Lindsay Kemp pantomime based on Jean Genet's *Notre Dame des Fleurs,* opens at London's intimate Bush Theatre. On March 27, it transfers to the new Regent Theatre in the West End. On October 7, there is a three-week run at Broadway's Biltmore Theatre.

Jan 2 At London's Royal Court Theatre, John Kani and Winston Ntshona, black actors from South Africa, improvise *The Island,* working with author-director Athol Fugard. On the 8th, they add *Sizwe Banzi Is Dead,* seen earlier. On the 22nd, Fugard directs his play, *Statements After an Arrest Under the Immorality Act,* with Yvonne Bryceland as a white woman in love with a South African black. On March 11, Peter Ransley's *Runaway*, staged by Alfred Lynch, opens. David Storey's *Life Class* opens on April 9, with Ian Bates as a despairing art teacher. Lindsay Anderson stages. It transfers to the Duke of York's Theatre on June 4. On April 25, David Lan's *Bird Child* is on view Upstairs, followed on the 28th with a Sunday night performance of Robert Thornton's *Johnny*, staged by John Tydeman. On May 12, Peggy Ashcroft, and John Gielgud, are in the cast of Clifford Williams' *A Salute to the Chile of Pablo Neruda*, an Actors' Equity show for the International Federation of Actors. On May 14 Upstairs, Stanley Eveling's *Shivvers* is the attraction, staged by Max Stafford-Clark.

Jan 9 Peter McEnery and Lynn Farleigh play a couple desperate to have a child in David Rudkin's *Ashes*, which bows at London's Open Space. Pam Brighton stages.

Jan 9 The Royal Shakespeare Company comes to the Brooklyn Academy of Music with its production of *Richard II*, in which Ian Richardson and Richard Pasco alternate roles of Richard and Bolingbroke. There are 22 showings of this production, with 14 of *Sylvia Plath*, an intimate dramatization of the writings of the American poet.

Jan 15 In Edinburgh at the Traverse Theatre, the new year begins with David Edgar's *Operation Iskra*, followed by Rainer Werner Fassbinder's *Bremen Coffee*. There are around 40 programs this year, some presented by visiting troupes. Among the shows are Annie Stainer's *Don Quixote*, Stanley Eveling's *Shivvers*, C. P. Taylor's *Schippel*, Pam Gems' *After Birthday* and *My Warren*, Edgar Allan Poe's *The Fall of the House of Usher*, Cary Harrison's *26 Efforts at Pornography*, Mike Stott's *Hard Slog*, Rick Cluchey's *The Cage* (from San Quentin Prison's Drama Workshop), Franz Xaver Kroetz's *Request Program*, Harold Pinter's *Monologue*, and Thomas Murphy's *On the Outside*.

Jan 17 At London's Greenwich Theatre Henrik Ibsen's *Ghosts* is revived. Chekhov's *The Seagull* is given on Jan 21, followed by Jean Genet's *The Maids* on Feb 14. *Hamlet* opens on March 14, with Peter Eyre as the prince. Eric Thompson stages Alan Ayckbourn's *The Norman Conquests* on May 9 and 12, and June 6.

Jan 18 At Glasgow's Citizens' Theatre, the new year opens with *Arden of Faversham*. Other plays to be shown are *The Taming of the Shrew*, *Macbeth*, *The Collection*, *A Slight Ache*, *Camille*, *Early Morning*, *St. Joan of the Stockyards*, *Coriolanus*, *Indians*, *Camino Real*, *Kennedy's Children* and *Jack and the Beanstalk*.

Jan 23 At London's Aldwych Theatre, the Royal Shakespeare Company opens *Section Nine*, a bizarre spoof on American

intelligence operations, written by the young American Philip Magdalany. (It's later produced in New Jersey at Princeton's McCarter Theatre). David Mercer's *Duck Song*, also an unusual vision, opens on Feb 5, staged by David Jones, with a cast including David Waller and Elizabeth Spriggs. Even more bizarre is Peter Barnes' carnival of cruelty, power struggles, and religious superstition in the Spanish Court of Philip IV, *Bewitched*. Mark Dignam is the king; Spriggs, the queen. Terry Hands directs.

Jan 26 Shakespeare's *The Tempest* is Joseph Papp's second production in the Mitzi E. Newhouse Theatre under the Vivian Beaumont in Lincoln Center. This production runs ten weeks.

Jan 29 The Actors Company arrives from Britain to play in Brooklyn at BAM, opening with Chekhov's *The Wood Demon*, staged by David Giles. Edward Petherbridge's adaptation and staging of R. D. Laing's *Knots*; *King Lear*, staged by David William, and Congreve's *The Way of the World*, also staged by William follow.

Jan 29 At London's Round House, the show is *From Moses to Mao*, with Jerome Savary and his Grand Magic Circus. The show has been first seen in Nov 1973 at the Strasbourg National Theatre, and is described as "an historic operetta." On May 29, Pierre Cardin presents *Les Veuves*, a puppet-play by Francois Billetdoux.

Feb 7 Charles Ludlam brings his Ridiculous Theatrical Company to Greenwich Village's Evergreen Theatre with *Hot Ice*. Boundaries of theatre freedom are broken when a character in the play urinates in full view of the audience. Ludlam directs his play for a three-month run. It is followed by two weeks of Ludlam's *Camille*, in revival.

Feb 11 At London's Mermaid Theatre, director Ronald Eyre turns author with *Something's Burning*, staged by Eyre and Euan Smith. On April 8, A. R. Gurney's American play, *Children*, opens, staged by Alan Strachan. Beverly Cross's *The Great Society*, about the time of Richard II, is staged by Bernard Miles and Julius Gellner.

Feb 12 The Negro Ensemble Company belatedly opens its season in Greenwich Village at the St. Marks Playhouse, after the success of its *The River Niger* on Broadway and on tour. Paul Carter Harrison's *The Great Macdaddy* is presented, followed by A. I. Davis's *Black Sunlight*, Herman Johnson's *Nowhere to Run, Nowhere to Hide*, Steve Carter's *Terraces*, and J. E. Gaines's *Heaven and Hell's Agreement*. On June 4, Charles Fuller's *In the Deepest Part of Sleep* opens.

Feb 14 Joseph Papp continues his new season of plays at Lincoln Center's Vivian Beaumont Theatre, opening Ron Milner's *What the Wine-Sellers Buy*. On April 4, Strindberg's *The Dance of Death* is re-

vived. On May 23, Miguel Pinero's prison drama *Short Eyes*, a "Best Play," opens. This has been seen at the Theatre of the Riverside Church, and has had 54 showings at the Public Theatre.

Feb 14 Jean Anouilh's *The Waltz of the Toreodors* is revived in London at the Haymarket Theatre. Peter Dews directs Trevor Howard and Coral Browne. The production continues into the next season.

Feb 18 Anna Cora Mowatt Ritchie's 19th century American comedy, *Fashion*, is revived Off-Broadway in a musical version by Anthony Stimac, with songs by Donald Pippin and Steve Brown. There are 94 performances. The cast includes Mary Jo Catlett, and Henrietta Valor.

Feb 21 At Joseph Papp's Public Theatre, Edgar White's *Les Femmes Noires* opens, staged by Novella Nelson. On Feb 28 Miguel Pinero's *Short Eyes* is offered. Jay Broad's *The Killdeer* opens on March 12, staged by Melvin Bernhardt.

Feb 23 Christopher Hampton's *Total Eclipse* opens at the Chelsea Theatre Center in Brooklyn. The play has been shown earlier in London at the Royal Court Theatre and in Washington at the Folger Theatre. The show runs four weeks, followed by *The Wild Stunt Show*, played by the Madhouse Company, a London-based troupe evolved from the Ken Campbell Show, a street and pub theatre group.

March 5 John Gielgud is Prospero in this National Theatre revival, directed by Peter Hall at the Old Vic in London. Denis Quilley is Caliban. On April 4, as an 80th birthday salute to playwright J. B. Priestley, his drama *Eden End* is revived by director Laurence Olivier, with his wife, Joan Plowright, in the cast. Harold Pinter stages John Hopkins' *Next of Kin* on May 2, with decors by Timothy O'Brien and Tazeena Firth. On May 28, Edward Bond's translation of Frank Wedekind's *Spring Awakening* opens, with a cast including Peter Firth, Beryl Reid, and Jenny Agguter. Bill Bryden directs.

March 6 London's Young Vic Theatre comes to the Brooklyn Academy of Music with *The Taming of the Shrew*, played in repertory with *Scapino*, adapted from Moliere by director Frank Dunlop and star Jim Dale. Terence Rattigan's *French Without Tears* is also given. On April 20, the production of *Scapino*, opens on Broadway at the Circle in the Square (121 performances), moving later to the Ambassador Theatre for 22 weeks.

March 10 Zero Mostel returns to Broadway in this revival of *Ulysses in Nighttown*, adapted by Marjorie Barkentin from James Joyce's *Ulysses*. There are 69 showings at the Winter Garden Theatre.

March 12 At London's Wimbledon Theatre, the Actors' Company offers a revival of Chekhov's *The Wood Demon*. On March 21, *King Lear* opens with Robert Eddison in the title-role. Ford's *'Tis Pity She's a Whore* is given on March 26. Feydeau's *Ruling the Roost* opens on April 16.

March 13 Shakespeare's *The Taming of the Shrew* opens at the Dublin Gate Theatre, staged by Hilton Edwards. Other productions this year include Forristal's *Black Man's Country*, Manning's *The Voice of Shem*, and Goldsmith's *The Good-Natured Man*.

March 14 *A Streetcar Named Desire*, the Tennessee Williams classic, is revived in London at the Piccadilly Theatre, staged by American director Edwin Sherin. Claire Bloom plays Blanche, with Martin Shaw as Stanley. The play continues its run in the following season.

March 20 At Stratford-upon-Avon, the Royal Shakespeare Company opens its annual season with *King John*. *Richard II*, *Cymbeline*, *Twelfth Night*, *Measure for Measure*, and *Macbeth* follow.

March 30 *Mummenschanz*, an inventive Swiss pantomime troupe, seen earlier in New York and around the U.S. in concert bookings, now opens on Broadway at the intimate Bijou Theatre for a run of 1,326 performances.

April 10 The Other Place is inaugurated by the Royal Shakespeare Company in Stratford-upon-Avon as a flexible theatre-space for developing new scripts and experimental productions of classics. This season the plays are: Shakespeare's *Lear*, John Downie's *I Was Shakespeare's Double*, Mike Leigh's *Babies Grow Old*, Shakespeare's *The Tempest*, David Rudkin's *Afore Night Come*, and Anton Chekhov's *Uncle Vanya*.

April 20 Murray Schisgal's *An American Millionaire* continues the current season of the Circle in the Square on Broadway, staged by Theodore Mann. With 17 performances, it is not a success.

April 26 In Association with the du Maurier Council for the Performing Arts, the New Play Centre of Vancouver, British Columbia, Canada, presents the first Du Maurier Festival of One-act Plays. The annual event brings together works by playwrights from across Canada.

May 13 Canada's Shaw Festival at Niagara-on-the-Lake opens with *The Devil's Disciple*, followed by *The Admirable Bashville* and *Too True To Be Good*. During the season, Brandon Thomas's *Charley's Aunt* and Henrik Ibsen's *Rosmersholm* are also staged.

May 15 The annual summer season of Britain's Chichester Festival opens with Pirandello's *Tonight We Improvise*. Vanbrugh's *The Confederacy*, Sophocles' *Oedipus Tyrannus*, and Turgenev's *A Month in the Country* are presented later.

May 15 Bernard Shaw's *Pygmalion* is revived at London's Albery Theatre, staged by John Dexter. Diana Rigg is Eliza, Alec McCowen is Higgins.

MEDIUM

May 27 At Her Majesty's Theatre in London, Shakespeare's *Pericles* is presented by the Prospect Theatre Company, with Toby Robertson staging. Derek Jacobi plays the title role.

May 30 London's summer Shakespeare opens in Regent's Park's Open Air Theatre with *A Midsummer Night's Dream*, staged by David Conville. Nicky Henson is Bottom. Mervyn Willis stages *The Two Noble Kinsmen* on July 31, using Richard Digby Day's version of this play, by John Fletcher and Shakespeare.

June At the Manhattan Theatre Club, artistic director Lynne Meadow gets the new season off to a prompt start with *Naomi Court*, followed by *This Property Is Condemned*, *A Touch of the Poet*, *Night Must Fall*, *The Caretaker*, *One Sunday Afternoon*, *Blues for Mister Charlie*, *The Subject was Roses*, *The Prime of Miss Jean Brodie*, *An Evening of Cole Porter*, *Look Back in Anger*, *The Philadelphia Story*, *End of Summer*, *The Runner Stumbles*, *Look Homeward, Angel*, *The Seagull*, *Bus Stop*, *Valentine's Day*, *The Sea*, *Staircase* and *East Lynne*, among other plays.

June In Greenwich Village, Ellen Stewart's La Mama E. T. C. opens an adaptation of Herman Melville's *Pierre or the Ambiguities*. This is followed by *The Big

Broadcast on East 53rd Street*, *Julia Caesar*, Andrei Serban's *Fragments of a Trilogy—Medea*, *Electra*, and the *Trojan Women*, *The 20th Century Limited*, *Big Mother*, *A Midsummer Night's Dream*, *Measure for Measure*, *The Good Woman of Setzuan*, *The Mystic Writings of Paul Revere*, *Hotel Paradiso*, *The Revenger's Tragedy*, *Lazarus*, and *Spring Rites*, among others.

June 3 Canada's Stratford Festival opens with Moliere's *The Imaginary Invalid*. *Love's Labour's Lost*, *King John*, *Pericles*, Offenbach's *La Vie Parisienne*, Sharon Pollock's *Walsh*, and Sandra Jones's *Ready Steady Go* are offered later in the season.

June 4 San Diego's National Shakespeare Festival opens in the Old Globe Theatre with *Twelfth Night*. *Romeo and Juliet*, *Henry IV, Part 2*, and Driver/Apolinar's *Your Own Thing* are presented later in the season.

June 5 Sam Shepard's *The Tooth of Crime*, staged by Jim Sharman, is on view at London's Royal Court Theatre, followed on June 11 by an Upstairs production of Paul Bailey's *A Worthy Guest*, staged by Ann Jellicoe. On July 11 the Upstairs fare is E. A. Whitehead's *The Sea Anchor*, staged by Jonathan Hales. On the main stage on the 16th, the play is Mustapha Matura's

Play Mas, directed by Donald Howarth. Edward Bond's *Bingo* opens on Aug 14, showing Shakespeare's declining years in Stratford as a time of bitterness and concern only for money and property. John Gielgud plays the Bard, with Gillian Martell as his daughter Judith. Jane Howell and John Dove direct. Hayden Griffin and Chelton design. Barry Reckord's *X* opens on Aug 16.

June 11 In New York, the Circle Repertory Company begins a season of experiments to "make the action of the play become the experience of the audience." A triple-bill opens: Robert Patrick's *One Person*, Bill Hoffman's *XXX's*, and Lance Belville's *When Everything Becomes the City's Music*. On June 18th, Elaine May's *Not Enough Rope* and Sheila Quitten's *Busy Dyin'* are premiered. On Oct 27, Tennessee Williams's *Battle of Angels* is revived, staged by Mason. John Heuer's *Innocent Thoughts, Harmless Intentions* is shown on Dec 4, followed by *Fire in the Mind House*, by Arnold Borget and Lance Mulcahy.

June 15 The American Shakespeare Festival opens in Stratford, Connecticut, with *Twelfth Night*. *Romeo and Juliet* and Tennessee Williams's *Cat on a Hot Tin Roof* are also offered during the season.

June 20 In the Delacorte Theatre in Central Park, Joseph Papp's annual summer New York Shakespeare Festival opens with *Pericles, Prince of Tyre*, directed by Edward Berkeley for a three-week run. *The Merry Wives of Windsor* follows for three weeks, directed by David Margulies.

June 21 In Ashland, the Oregon Shakespearean Festival opens its summer season with *Twelfth Night*. *Titus Andronicus* and *Hamlet* follow. The indoor Angus Bowmer Theatre is also the scene of three productions: *The Two Gentlemen of Verona*, Samuel Beckett's *Waiting for Godot*, and William Saroyan's *The Time of Your Life*.

June 25 *Hair*, the salute to the 1960's by Gerome Ragni and James Rado, comes back to life at the Queen's Theatre in London. There are 110 performances this time around.

July 9 *The Marriage of Figaro*—Beaumarchais's play, not the Mozart-Da Ponte opera—opens today in London at the Old Vic. Jonathan Miller directs the John Wells translation for the National Theatre. Derek Godfrey and Gemma Jones are the Count and Countess Almaviva. On Aug 28, Peter Firth and Veronica Quilligan play *Romeo and Juliet*, in a Bill Bryden staging. Beryl Reid is the Nurse. Peter Nichols' new play, *The Freeway*, has 30 repertory showings, opening on Oct 1 in a Miller staging. Among the cast are Paul Rogers, Irene Handl, and Rachel Kempson. Michael Blakemore directs A. E. Ellis' *Grand Manouvres*, dealing with the infamous Dreyfuss Affair in France. It

opens on Dec 3, with Alan MacNaughton as the Jewish officer who is unjustly disgraced.

Aug 18 The Edinburgh Festival gets underway with productions of seven plays among the many attractions. They are Sophocles' *King Oedipus* presented by Dublin's Abbey Theatre; August Strindberg's *Gustav III* given by Sweden's Gothenberg City Theatre; Sam Shepard's *The Tooth of Crime* offered by New York's Performance Group; Sean McCarthy's *The Fantastical Feats of Finn MacCool* by Edinburg's Young Lyceum Company; Christopher Marlowe's *Dr. Faustus* presented by The Royal Shakespeare Company; and Euripides' *The Bacchae* and Moliere's *Tartuffe* offered by the Actors Company.

Aug 20 The National Youth Theatre is again ready to show its summer work, opening at London's Shaw Theatre with *Magnyficence*, a play by John Skelton, adapted and directed by John Duncan. On the 26th, at the Cockpit Theatre, the Youth Theatre offers Paul Thompson's *The Children's Crusade*. Ron Daniels stages. On Sep 9 at the Cockpit, the troupe offers Paul Thompson's *By Common Consent*, staged by Daniels.

Aug 27 Maxim Gorky's *Summerfolk* opens at the Royal Shakespeare's London home, the Aldwych, directed by David Jones, with a cast including Estelle Kohler, Tony Church, and Margaret Tyzack. Ian McKellen plays Marlowe's *Doctor Faustus* on Sep 5, directed by John Barton. Michael Annals designs. On Sep 18, Richard Pasco and Ian Richardson begin alternating leading roles in *Richard II*, seen initially at Stratford and last February in Brooklyn at BAM. This is another Barton staging. On Nov 19, Frank Wedekind's *The Marquis of Keith*, translated by Ronald Eyre and Alan Best, opens in Eyre's staging. McKellen is the Marquis, supported by such players as Sara Kestleman, Mike Gwilym, and Richardson. On Dec 19, *Cymbeline* opens, a Stratford production staged by a committee of Barton, Barry Kyle, and Clifford Williams. Sebastian Shaw plays the title role.

Fall Christopher Martin's CSC Repertory Theatre, in the Off-Broadway Abbey Theatre in New York, opens a season of classics and modern plays, beginning with Marlowe's *Edward II*. Other plays are Ibsen's *Hedda Gabler*, Shakespeare's *The Tempest*, Robin Maugham's *The Servant*, Jean Genet's *The Maids*, Harold Pinter's *The Dwarfs*, Christopher Fry's *The Lady's Not for Burning*, Jean Anouilh's *Antigone*, and Georg Buechner's *Woyzeck*.

Sep 9 At the Round House in London, the Prospect Theatre Company presents *Henry IV, Part 1. Part 2* opens on the following day. On Nov 12, Schiller's *The Robbers* opens under the title of *The Highwaymen*, translated by Gail Rademacher. On the 27th, the Prospect players

present *Henry V*.

Sep 9 Jack Gelber's *The Connection* is revived at the Hampstead Theatre Club in London, with Michael Rudman directing. On Oct 14, the show is *The Looneys*, by John Antrobus, with a cast including Leonard Rossiter. Rudman again directs. Stephen Poliakoff's *Clever Soldiers* opens on Nov 25, staged by Vivian Matalon.

Sep 17 At the Royal Court's Theatre Upstairs, Sam Shepard's *Action* is offered to London audiences, in Nancy Meckler's staging. Ken Campbell's *The Great Caper* is on the main stage on Oct 9. Colin Bennett's *Fourth Day Like Four Long Months of Absence* opens Upstairs on Nov 6, staged by Max Stafford-Clark. The Tokyo Kid Brothers Company arrive on the 12th with their production of *The City*, a rock musical. On Nov 26, Perri St. Claire and George Logan appear in drag in *An Evening With Hinge and Bracket*. This moves to the May Fair in the West End on Dec 10. On Dec 13, the Upstairs offering is Heathcote Williams's revue, *Remember the Truth Dentist*.

Sep 19 At London's Greenwich Theatre, Eugene O'Neill's *More Stately Mansions* opens, with Frances Cuka in the cast. David Giles stages. John Whiting's *Marching Song* is revived by director Ewan Hooper on Oct 24, with Kenneth Haigh. On Nov 28, John Osborne's *The Entertainer* is revived, with Osborne directing Max Wall as Archie Rice. E. Nesbit's *Harding's Luck*, adapted by Peter Nichols, opens Dec 26. John Cox directs.

Sep 23 *Gypsy*. See L revival, 1973.

Sep 24 Tennessee Williams's *Cat on a Hot Tin Roof*, recently revived in Connecticut at the American Shakespeare Festival, comes back to Broadway, winning a run of 160 performances at the ANTA Theatre. Michael Kahn directs Elizabeth Ashley and Keir Dullea in the leads.

Oct 4 The Dolphin Company, ensconced in London's Shaw Theatre, revives *The Taming of the Shrew*, staged by James Roose-Evans, with Susan Hampshire as Katharina and Nicky Henson as Petruchio.

Oct 5 At Joseph Papp's Public Theatre in Greenwich Village, the season begins with John Ford Noonan's *Where Do We Go From Here?*, staged by David Margulies, followed on Oct 22, by Ronald Tavel's *The Last Days of British Honduras*, David Rabe's *The Boom Boom Room* opens on Nov 20.

Oct 10 Strindberg's *Comrades* is presented by the Royal Shakespeare Company at The Place, its London experimental stage. Barry Kyle stages. Susan Fleetwood and Brenda Bruce are among the cast members. Director Buzz Goodbody presents on the 22nd, her abbreviated version of *King Lear*, called *Lear* with

Tony Church and Sheila Allen. Snoo Wilson's *The Beast* is shown on Nov 18, staged by Howard Davies. Richard Pasco is in the cast.

Oct 10 At the Circle in the Square on Broadway, the season opens with Peter Nichols's *The National Health* for a run of nearly seven weeks. Arvin Brown has staged this in New Haven at the Long Wharf. Transferring to Manhattan, it has a cast including Rita Moreno and Leonard Frey. On Dec 20, a revival of *Where's Charley?* opens for a run of almost ten weeks. Theodore Mann stages, with Raul Julia as Charley.

Oct 11 At London's Young Vic, Wendy Toye stages Nina and Jimmy Thompson's entertainment, *The Englishman Amused*. On Nov 20, Denise Coffey stages John Antrobus' *Crete and Sergeant Pepper*. Henry Fielding's *Tom Thumb the Great* is the Christmas treat on Dec 23, with Bernard Gross directing.

Oct 15 The Chelsea Theatre Center of Brooklyn opens its season at BAM with Megan Terry's play, *Hothouse*. Rae Allen stages. The show runs for four weeks, followed on Dec 17 by *Yentl the Yeshiva Boy*, based on an Isaac Bashevis Singer story, and staged by Robert Kalfin. Tovah Feldshuh plays Yentl, a girl who disguises herself as a boy to get an education. The production moves to Broadway, after six weeks at the Chelsea.

Oct 16 André Roussin's *The Little Hut* is revived in the West End at the Duke of York's Theatre, with Geraldine McEwan. Crutwell directs. This production has come from the New Theatre, Oxford.

Oct 17 Equity Library Theatre, playing in the Master Theatre on New York's Upper West Side, opens its season of revivals with Shaw's *Arms and the Man*, followed by Wilson's *The Boy Friend*. Other shows include Hayes's *The Desperate Hours*, Merrill and Abbott's *New Girl in Town*, Inge's *Bus Stop*, Laurents, Rodgers, and Sondheim's *Do I Hear a Waltz?*, Gorky's *The Zykovs*, and Friml's *The Three Musketeers*.

Oct 18 At the Judson Memorial Church in Greenwich Village, the Judson Poets Theatre opens its season with Gertrude Stein's *Listen To Me*, with music by Al Carmines.

Oct 20 At Lincoln Center's Mitzi E. Newhouse Theatre, Joseph Papp opens Shakespeare's *Richard III*, staged by Mel Shapiro, for a run of 90 performances. Michael Moriarty and Marsha Mason are in the cast.

Oct 23 At the American Place Theatre in midtown Manhattan, S. J. Perelman's *The Beauty Part* is revived for 36 showings, staged by James Hammerstein. Later in the season, the APT mounts two Sam Shepard plays, *Killer's Head* and *Action*. These run for 34 performances, with 145 for Jonathan Reynolds's two one-act plays,

Rubbers and *Yanks 3 Detroit 0 Top of the Seventh*, which open on May 16. Alan Arkin directs the latter plays.

Oct 30 Joseph Papp opens his new season in the Vivian Beaumont at Lincoln Center with Anne Burr's *Mert & Phil*. It runs for five weeks, staged by Papp. Title roles are played by Estelle Parsons and Michael Lombard.

Nov 11 Harold Prince stages the New Phoenix Repertory Company's revival of Congreve's *Love for Love* at the Helen Hayes Theatre for 24 performances. On Dec 12, Pirandello's *The Rules of the Game* opens for 12 performances, staged by Stephen Porter.

Nov 28 Dorothy Tutin plays Maggie Wylie in this revival of James Barrie's *What Every Woman Knows*, staged by Clifford Williams for the Albery Theatre in London. There are 212 performances.

Dec 5 The Royal Shakespeare's production of Dion Boucucault's *London Assurance* opens on Broadway at the huge Palace Theatre, which is entirely too large for this witty, handsome period-piece. Donald Sinden heads the cast. There are only 46 performances.

Dec 6 Playwright-lyricist Tom Jones and his collaborator, composer Harvey Schmidt *(The Fantasticks)*, present the *Portfolio Revue* at their newly established Portfolio Studio in New York.

Dec 8 In Greenwich Village at the Evergreen Theatre, the Ridiculous Theatrical Company opens *Stage Blood* for a run of

45 performances. Charles Ludlam, the founder, stages and plays the lead. On April 18, he offers his version of *Bluebeard*. This has a four-week run.

Dec 17 The holiday season opens with Frank Loesser's musical *Hans Andersen*, which has a run of 383 performances at the London Palladium. Tommy Steele is Andersen. At the Casino Theatre, Frank Hauser's *Cinderella* opens on the 18th. Susan Hampshire plays Peter in Barrie's *Peter Pan*, revived at the London Coliseum. Other shows primarily for young audiences are the Young Vic's *Tom Thumb the Great* and the Greenwich Theatre's *Harding's Luck*. At the New London, there is *Deja Revue*, a revue staged by Victor Spinetti and animated by Sheila Hancock and George Cole, among others.

Dec 18 John Steinbeck's *Of Mice and Men* opens in this Edwin Sherin–directed revival on Broadway at the Brooks Atkinson Theatre. Kevin Conway and James Earl Jones head the cast. The show runs nearly two months.

Dec 19 Leonard Bernstein's *West Side Story* is revived in London at the Shaftesbury Theatre. Roger Finch reproduces the Jerome Robbins choreography and plays Riff. Bill Kenwright directs. The production runs on into the next season.

Dec 21 David Mamet, Patricia Cox, Steven Schachter and W. H. Macy found the St. Nicholas Theatre in Chicago, Illinois, opening with the world premiere production of Mamet's *American Buffalo*.

1974 BIRTHS/DEATHS/DEBUTS

Feb 17 Jack Cole, the innovative choreographer who brought together Oriental, African, and native dance movements in his Broadway, cinema, and cabaret work, dies today at age 60.

March 5 Actor Billy DeWolfe (b. 1907) dies in Los Angeles. DeWolfe first appeared as a dancer in vaudeville, later touring with his own act, DeWolfe and Kindler. He received the Donaldson Award in 1954 for his performance in *John Murray Anderson's Almanac*. DeWolfe also appeared in films and made night club appearances.

March 5 Russian-born impresario Sol Hurok (b. 1888) dies in New York City. Author of two autobiographical works, *Impresario*, and *Sol Hurok Presents*, Hurok estimated that he had presented over 4,000 artists and companies during his career.

March 28 Lyricist-librettist Dorothy Fields (b. 1905) dies in New York City. Fields first served as lyricist for *Blackbirds of 1928*. She collaborated with her brother Herbert on five Broadway musicals: *Let's Face It, Something for the Boys, Mexican Hayride, Up in Central Park,* and *Annie*

Get Your Gun. She was awarded a Tony for *Redhead* in 1959.

April 10 Patricia Collinge, the actress, dies at 81.

April 17 Actress-entertainer Blossom Seeley is dead at 82.

April 22 The distinguished British drama critic and historian, Ivor Brown, dies at age 82.

June 5 Actress Blanche Yurka dies in New York at age 86. Yurka made her stage debut in *Parsifal* in 1905. She directed and acted in *The Wild Duck, Hedda Gabler,* and *Lysistrata*. Her most notable screen role was Mme. De Farge in *A Tale of Two Cities*. Her autobiography, *Bohemian Girl*, was published in 1970.

June 9 Actress Katharine Cornell (b. 1898) dies at Vineyard Haven, Massachusetts. Cornell made her New York City debut in 1916. She toured for the American troops in *The Barretts of Wimpole Street* in 1944–45, having played the same role on Broadway. She wrote two volumes of autobiography: *I Wanted to be an Actress* (1939) and *Curtain Going Up* (1943).

June 18 The American playwright George

elly dies aged 87. Among his comedies
nd dramas are *Craig's Wife*, *The Torch-
earers*, and *The Show-Off*.

ıly 10 American actress Nancy Wick-
ire (b. 1925) dies in San Francisco.
Vickwire appeared with both the New
ork Shakespeare and American Shake-
peare Festivals. She appeared in the 1964
roadway production of Jean Anouilh's
raveller Without Luggage.

uly 24 British actor Ernest Milton dies
t 84.

ep 6 American actor Otto Kruger (b. 1885)
dies in Los Angeles. Kruger made his first
New York appearance in *The Natural Law*
in 1915. Some of his later roles were in
Laura, *Old Heidelberg*, and *The Straw*.

Sep 6 Michael Benthall, the accom-
plished British director, dies at age 55.

Sep 19 English actress Edna Best (b. 1900)
dies in Geneva, Switzerland. Best made
her London debut in *Charley's Aunt* in
1917. Her 1925 New York debut was in
Michael Arlen's *These Charming People*.
She also appeared in films, television, and
radio.

1974   THEATERS/PRODUCTIONS

an 10 The Jesuits of Maryland Province
ffer the 119-year-old Loyola College
omplex in Baltimore to Center Stage, af-
er its theatre burns down. The City of
Baltimore "purchases" the building from
he Jesuits for $200,000 and donates the
noney to Center Stage. The city then sells
he property to Center Stage for five dol-
ars.

Feb–April Canada's noted Stratford Fes-
ival has its first tour of Australia. Jean
Gascon's production of Molière's *The
maginary Invalid* is played.

March 27 The Regent Street Theatre in

London opens with *Flowers*. Formerly it
was the Polytechnic Theatre.

Mar 29 A Ford Foundation grant of $2
million enables the American Conservatory Theatre to purchase the Geary Theatre for its permanent San Francisco home.
The grant also provides funds for a four-
year support plan and cash reserves.

May 31 This is the last day of the
1973–1974 Broadway season. Only *Good
Evening* and *Will Rogers' U. S. A.* have
paid off their initial investments by season's end.

June 1 At the end of the current Broadway season, there have been only 54 productions, including those in "middle"
theatres such as the Bijou and the Little
Theatre. Otis Guernsey, Jr., tallies the
shows thus: 10 plays, nine musicals, one
revue, seven specialties, 19 revivals, and
eight foreign plays in English. Broadway's gross is more than $46 million, with
the road grossing $45.3 million, a drop
of more than $10 million. *Variety* reports
losses on failed musicals this season at
$2 million, with *Molly* losing $600,000
and *Rachel Lily Rosenbloom* losing half
a million dollars. David Rabe's *Boom
Boom Room* at the Vivian Beaumont is
said to have cost producer Joseph Papp
$250,000. Off-Broadway there have been
76 productions, tallied as follows: 27
plays, six musicals, three revues, eight
foreign plays in English, two plays in foreign tongues, eight specialties, and 22 revivals. In regional resident theatres, there
have been 370 productions of 336 plays
by 39 troupes in 61 theatres in 40 cities,
four of them in Canada. These figures are
tallied by Ella Malin for *Best Plays* each
season.

This season's ten "Best Plays" in New
York, as selected by Guernsey, editor of
the *Best Plays* annual, are Storey's *The
Contractor*, McNally's *Bad Habits*, John
Hopkins' *Find Your Way Home*, Pinero's
Short Eyes, Freeman's *Creeps*, Coward's
Noel Coward in Two Keys, Stoppard's
Jumpers, Simon/Chekhov's *The Good
Doctor*, Medoff's *When You Comin' Back,
Red Ryder?*, and Moore's *The Sea Horse*.

June 5 This month the Folly Theatre in
Kansas City, Missouri, is placed on the
National Register of Historic Places. After
restoration, it will re-open on November
10, 1981.

Aug The American Theatre Critics Asso.
is formed due to the rapid growth of
regional professional theatre. Previously,
critics' groups have been limited to New
York and a few other major American cities. Henry Hewes is Executive Secretary.
Others elected to guide the new organization include Elliot Norton (Boston), Dan
Sullivan (Los Angeles), Clara Hierony-
mus (Nashville), and Ernest Schier (Philadelphia).

Nov 3 The Circle Repertory presents its
first production in its new space at 99
Seventh Avenue South in New York: *Battle of Angels*, by Tennessee Williams.

Nov 25 Agatha Christie's suspense drama,
The Mousetrap, is 22 years old today,
which makes it London's longest-running drama ever.

SOL HUROK

Jan 5 *The Wiz* (NY—Majestic—Musical). Based on *The Wizard of Oz*, William Brown's book and Charlie Smalls' songs are staged by Geoffrey Holder. Stephanie Mills is Dorothy, with Mabel King as Evillene. Andre de Shields plays The Wiz. There are 1,672 performances.

Jan 7 *Shenandoah* (NY—Alvin—Musical). John Cullum is featured as a pacifist farmer during the Civil War. James Lee Barrett helps adapt his screenplay for Peter Udell's lyrics and Gary Geld's score. Philip Rose directs. There are 1,050 performances.

Jan 14 *Diamond Studs* (NY—Westside—Musical). The life of Jesse James is produced by the Chelsea Theatre and directed by John Haber. Written by Jim Wand and Bland Simpson, the show plays for 29 weeks.

Jan 15 *I Love You Baby Blue* (Toronto—Passe Muraille—Comedy). A collective creation, this show satirizes sex in Toronto. It is briefly closed by the Morality Squad and re-opens with the support of local politicians and clergymen against censorship. The show runs 12 weeks.

Jan 23 *Dance With Me* (NY—Mayfair—Musical). Seen first at La Mama and the Public Theatre, Greg Atonacci's play runs almost 50 weeks. Joel Zwick directs the show, whose hero is trying to avoid the realities of present failures by recalling the past.

Jan 26 *Seascape* (NY—Shubert—Drama). Frank Langella and Maureen Anderman impersonate two giant lizards in this new Edward Albee play. They confront a middle-aged and middle-class couple (Deborah Kerr and Barry Nelson) in a two month run, directed by the author. Chosen as a "Best Play," this wins the Pulitzer Prize.

March 2 *The National Lampoon Show* (NY—Palladium—Revue). Martin Charnin directs this college-humor collage, with Paul Jacobs' music. Gilda Radner, John Belushi, and Bill Murray are among the cast. The show runs almost 23 weeks.

March 13 *Same Time, Next Year* (NY—Brooks Atkinson—Comedy). Ellen Burstyn and Charles Grodin are the twosome in Bernard Slade's play about annual fleeting adultery. Chosen a "Best Play," it runs 1,453 performances. The comedy plays 39 weeks following its London premiere at the Prince of Wales's on Sep 23, 1976.

March 22 *A Letter for Queen Victoria* (NY—ANTA—Musical). Robert Wilson's avant-garde work, described variously as an opera, a play, and a dance presentation, is dominated by his dreamland imagery. On May 9, Wilson and protege Christopher Knowles will present *The $

Value of Man for eight performances at the Brooklyn Academy of Music.

April 17 *Bette Midler's Clams on the Half Shell Revue* (NY—Minskoff—Revue). Joe Layton directs and choreographs this Midler show-case, in which she's supported by the Harlettes. There are 67 performances.

June 3 *Chicago* (NY—46th Street—Musical). Bob Fosse and Fred Ebb adapt the play by Maurine Dallas Watkins, with songs by Ebb and John Kander. Gwen Verdon is Roxy Hart, the center of a scandalous murder case, defended by Billy Flynn (Jerry Orbach). Chosen a "Best Play," it runs 898 performances. On April 10, 1979, the musical opens in the West End at the Cambridge for a run that continues into the next decade.

June 18 *The Red Devil Battery Sign* (Boston—Shubert—Drama). Tennessee Williams' new play, with Claire Bloom and Anthony Quinn, deals with a bandleader's problems with American society, poisoned by the Kennedy assassination. Producer David Merrick closes the show before it reaches Broadway.

July 25 *A Chorus Line* (NY—Shubert—Musical). Successful at the Public Theatre, Michael Bennett's show comes to Broadway for a very long run, which extends into the next decade. Presented as an audition in which dancers reveal their lives and are weeded out, it wins the Tony Award for Best Musical and the Pulitzer Prize. On July 22, 1976, the musical opens in London at the Drury Lane for a run of 903 performances.

Sep 3 *The Nature and Purpose of the Universe* (NY—Direct—Drama). The first of Christopher Durang's fierce satires on Roman Catholic beliefs and practices to play Manhattan, this is an "After-Theatre" production at the Direct Theatre on West 43rd Street.

Sep 17 *Boy Meets Boy* (NY—Actors Playhouse—Musical). Billy Solly has created the songs and the book (with the aid of Donald Ward) for this story of like attracting like. Ron Troutman directs Joe Barrett, David Gallegly, and Raymond Wood for 463 performances.

Oct 17 *Jesse and the Bandit Queen* (NY—Public—Drama). David Freeman's play is staged by Gordon Stewart, with Kevin O'Connor and Pamela Payton-Wright. There are 155 performances.

Oct 21 *Treemonisha* (NY—Palace—Musical). Scott Joplin's 1907 folk-opera, never fully staged in New York, now comes to Broadway. Carmen Balthrop plays a girl, born under a tree, who strives for a better life for herself and other blacks. It runs two months.

Oct 22 *Me and Bessie Smith* (NY—Am-

CHICAGO

bassador—Revue). Linda Hopkins plays a singer identifying with Bessie Smith in this show she and Will Holt have devised. Having first played Los Angeles's Mark Taper Forum, it plays 453 performances here.

Oct 23 *Yentl* (NY—Eugene O'Neill—Drama). Tovah Feldshuh plays the lead in this play by Leah Napolin and Isaac Bashevis Singer. It runs seven months under director Robert Kalfin.

Oct 24 *Gorky* (NY—American Place—Drama). Steve Tesich's play has Philip Baker Hall as the Russian poet-playwright for 44 performances.

Oct 30 *Travesties.* See L premiere, 1974.

Nov 3 *Kennedy's Children.* See L premiere, 1974.

Nov 13 *A Musical Jubilee* (NY—St. James—Musical). This celebration of the Broadway musical, featuring Lillian Gish, Tammy Grimes, Larry Kert, Patrice Munsel, John Raitt, Cyril Ritchard, and Dick Shawn, is directed by Morton DaCosta. It runs nearly three months.

Nov 18 *Ice Age* (NY—Brooklyn Academy—Drama). The Chelsea Theatre Center opens Tankred Dorst's play, suggested by the later life of Norwegian novelist Knut Hamsun, for a four week run. Arne Zaslove directs Roberts Blossom in the lead.

Nov 25 *Habeas Corpus.* See L premiere, 1973.

Dec 1 *Tuscaloosa's Calling Me . . . But I'm

Not Going! (NY—Top of the Gate—Revue). James Hammerstein and Gui Andrisano co-direct this salute to New York in songs and sketches. It runs 429 performances.

Dec 7 *The Norman Conquests.* See L premiere, 1974.

1975 BRITISH PREMIERES

Feb 3 *Aspects of Max Wall* (L—Garrick—Revue). The popular variety and stage comedian, Max Wall, shows his range in this show, seen first at the Greenwich Theatre.

March 10 *The Case in Question* (L—Haymarket—Drama). John Clements, Margaret Courtenay, and Charles Lloyd Pack appear in Ronald Millar's adaptation of C.P. Snow's novel, *In Their Wisdom.* Staged by Clements, it plays 254 performances.

March 12 *Murderer* (L—Garrick—Drama). *Sleuth* author Anthony Shaffer tries again. This time the main character is urged by his mistress to dispose of his wife. Clifford Williams directs, and the show runs into the next season.

April 10 *A Family and a Fortune* (L—Apollo—Drama). Julian Mitchell's adaptation of the Ivy Compton-Burnett novel features a distinguished cast under director Alan Strachan. Alec Guinness plays the very correct head of an Edwardian family who is extremely cruel to others. The production continues into the next season.

April 15 *A Little Night Music.* See NY premiere, 1973.

April 22 *Jeeves* (L—Her Majesty's—Musical). Andrew Lloyd Webber collaborates with Alan Ayckbourn on this entertainment based on P.G. Wodehouse characters. Eric Thompson directs David Hemmings and Michael Aldridge. The show runs only six weeks.

April 23 *No Man's Land* (L—Old Vic—Drama). The National Theatre produces Harold Pinter's ambiguous tale of a poor man who may have once had an affair with a rich man's wife. It transfers to Wyndham's Theatre on July 15, and comes to the Longacre on Broadway on Nov 9, 1976. In New York, there is a limited run of six weeks.

May 7 *The Sunshine Boys.* See NY premiere, 1972.

May 13 *A Touch of Spring* (L—Comedy—Comedy). Samuel Taylor's American play, called *Avanti* on Broadway, wins 300 performances with Hayley Mills and Peter Donat. He plays a married American who falls in love with the daughter of his late father's mistress. Allan Davis directs.

June 5 *Oh Coward!* See NY premiere, 1972.

July 16 *Clarence Darrow* (L—Piccadilly—Drama). Henry Fonda is Darrow in this one-man play by David W. Rintels, based on Irving Stone's book, *Clarence Darrow for the Defense.* John Houseman directs.

July 22 *Trantara! Tarantara!* (L—Westminster—Musical). Ian Taylor's musical play about the collaboration of Gilbert & Sullivan has Christopher Scoular and Timothy Knightley among others directed by David Horlock.

July 23 *Absent Friends* (L—Garrick—Comedy). Alan Ayckbourn's wry picture of British middle-class home-life features Richard Briers and is staged by Eric Thompson. There are 316 performances.

July 30 *Otherwise Engaged* (L—Queen's—Drama). Simon Gray's play about a cultivated Londoner who keeps both friends and family at a distance features Alan Bates. Harold Pinter directs. Later transferred to the Comedy Theatre, the show will have a total run of 1,029 performances. It opens in New York at the Plymouth on Feb 2, 1977, with Tom Courtenay in the lead. Chosen a "Best Play," it runs almost 39 weeks.

July 31 *Hinge and Bracket at the Ambassadors'* (L—Ambassadors'—Revue). Ray Cooney produces this two-man revue, with George Logan and Patrick Fyffe, whose drag appearances have developed a cult following among British audiences.

Aug 19 *Jingo* (L—Aldwych—Drama). Charles Wood's play is staged for the Royal Shakespeare Company by Richard Eyre, with Anna Massey and John Standing.

Sep 10 *Happy as a Sandbag* (L—Ambassadors'—Musical). Ken Lee has compiled this show, staged by Philip Hedley. The ensemble includes David Ashton, Martin Duncan, Lesley Duff, Geraldine Wright, and Julian Hough. There will be 508 performances and a transfer to the Westminster.

Sep 25 *The Comedians* (L—Old Vic—Drama). Trevor Griffiths's play, in which an old pro teaches aspiring stand-up comedians, is a vision of Britain's social insecurities. Jonathan Pryce is admired as Gethin Price, and will play the role on Broadway. Richard Eyre directs.

Oct 2 *Dad's Army* (L—Shaftesbury—Comedy). Jimmy Perry and David Croft base this show on their BBC-TV series, with staging credited to Roger Redfarn. Arthur Loew and Jen LeMesurier appear, with Bill Pertwee.

Oct 8 *The Plumber's Progress* (L—Prince of Wales's—Comedy). C.P. Taylor has adapted Carl Sternheim's *Burger Schippel.* Already seen in Edinburgh, the London production has Harry Secombe in the title role, with Simon Callow. It is directed by Mike Ockrent.

Oct 9 *City Sugar* (L—Bush—Drama). Stephen Poliakoff's play is staged by Hugh Thomas, and features John Schrapnel as the carelessly cruel, self-loathing disc-jockey, Leonard Brazil.

Nov 5 *Double Edge* (L—Vaudeville—Drama). Margaret Lockwood, Barrie Ingham and Paul Daneman animate Leslie Darbon and Peter Whelan's thriller for 252 performances. It is directed by Anthony Sharp.

Nov 19 *Ipi Tombi* (L—Her Majesty's—Musical). South African tribal life and daily experience is celebrated in this musical with a native cast, scripted by Bertha Egnos, with lyrics by Gail Lakier. Moving several times during its run, the show plays 1,879 performances in London. The musical is picketed by American blacks when it premieres at New York's Harkness Theatre on Jan 12, 1977. There are only 39 performances.

Dec 4 *The Return of A.J. Raffles* (L—Aldwych—Drama). David Jones directs the Royal Shakespeare Company in Graham Greene's work, with Denholm Elliott as the gentleman-thief. Peter Blythe plays Lord Alfred Douglas, with Norman Tyrell as the Marquis of Queensbury.

Dec 30 *The Runner Stumbles* (Stamford—Hartman—Drama). Milan Stitt's play about the doomed affection of a lonely priest and a loving nun has its world premiere. (Next May 18, it will open in New York at the Little for 191 performances.) Austin Pendleton directs Stephen Joyce and Nancy Donohue.

1975 REVIVALS/REPERTORIES

Jan 2 The season at the Royal Court Theatre opens with Caryl Churchill's *Objections to Sex and Violence,* staged by John Tydeman. Highlights of the season will be Joe Orton's *Entertaining Mr. Sloane* on April 17 (moving to the Duke of York's), David Hare's satire on rock music stars, *Teeth 'n Smiles* on Sep 2, and Edward Bond's *The Fool* on Nov 18.

Jan 6 The Lincoln Center season at the Vivian Beaumont continues with Bill Gunn's *Black Picture Show* for 41 performances. Ibsen's *A Doll's House* follows on March 5 with Liv Ullmann. Anthony Scully's *Little Black Sheep* opens for four weeks on May 17. On Oct 15, *Trelawny of the "Wells"* opens, followed by Sam Waterston's *Hamlet,* on Dec 17.

Jan 8 Andre Gregory's Manhattan Project brings Chekhov's *The Sea Gull* to the Public Theatre for 42 performances in repertory with Wallace Shawn's *Our Late*

Night. Alice in Wonderland opens on April 15 and Samuel Beckett's *Endgame* on April 29. The Public will also have Thomas Babe's *Kid Champion*, beginning Jan 28, Michael Weller's *Fishing*, beginning Feb 1, and *A Chorus Line*, opening April 15.

Jan 8 Harold Pinter's *The Birthday Party* is revived at the Shaw Theatre in London by the Dolphin Theatre Company. Kevin Billington stages.

Jan 9 The Aldwych will be the house for these RSC productions seen at Stratford-upon-Avon: *King John* (opening tonight), *Twelfth Night, Macbeth,* and *Love's Labour's Lost.* Other revivals will be Henrik Ibsen's *Hedda Gabler,* Harley Granville Barker's *The Marrying of Ann Leete* and George Bernard Shaw's *Too True To Be Good.*

Jan 9 In Edinburgh at the Traverse Theatre, Sam Shepard's *Action* starts the new year off, a year of some 26 programs. Some programs are presented by visiting troupes with goals similar to the experiments of the Traverse. Among the shows are Leonard Maguire's *An Evening of Scottish Horrors,* René Marques' *The Fanlights,* Lars Forsell's *Sunday Promenade,* Istvan Orkeny's *God Bless the Major,* Ray Hassett's *Wild Animals from Memory,* Annie Stainer's *Moon,* Alan Bryce's *The Trouble with Ants,* Michael Almaz's *Masoch,* and *A Waste of Time III,* created by the Will Spoor Mime Company. The Salakta Balloon Band also offer *Snow White and the Chicken* at holiday time.

Jan 16 The Greenwich Theatre in London shows John Osborne's *The End of Me Old Cigar* tonight, and later will present two plays by Oscar Wilde, *The Picture of Dorian Gray* and *The Importance of Being Earnest.* Noel Coward's *The Vortex* will open on Oct 2.

Jan 19 Joseph Papp continues his season at Lincoln Center with *A Midsummer Night's Dream* at the Mitzi E. Newhouse Theatre, staged by Edward Berkeley. On May 4, Gilbert Moses will direct Ed Bullins' *The Taking of Miss Janie,* with Hilary Jane Beane in the title-role.

Jan 20 Circle Repertory Company, in its Off-Broadway Sheridan Square home, premieres Lanford Wilson's *The Mound Builders* tonight. On March 23, Julie Bovasso's *Down by the River Where the Waterlilies are Disfigured Every Day* opens, and on April 16, Harvey Perr's *Scandalous Marriages* and *Afternoon Tea* debut. May 11 sees Corinne Jacker's *Harry Outside.*

Jan 20 At Glasgow's Citizens' Theatre, the new year opens with *The Government Inspector,* followed by *The Duchess of Malfi, Romeo and Juliet, De Sade Show, Hamlet, Sailor Beware, Thyestes,* and *Aladdin.*

Jan 28 At the Old Vic, the National Theatre offers Henrik Ibsen's *John Gabriel*

Borkman. The season will also include George Bernard Shaw's *Heartbreak House,* Samuel Beckett's *Happy Days,* W.S. Gilbert's *Engaged,* Tony Harrison's *Phaedra Britannica,* John Millington Synge's *The Playboy of the Western World,* and *Hamlet,* with Albert Finney in the lead.

Feb 5 The Royal Shakespeare Company comes to the Brooklyn Academy of Music with a four-production repertory, opening with Maxim Gorky's *Summerfolk,* staged by David Jones. Jones also stages *Love's Labour's Lost,* opening on the 13th. The other offerings are director Buzz Goodbody's truncation of *King Lear,* and Ian Richardson's recital of Shakespearean extracts, *He That Plays the King.*

Feb 6 Maggie Smith and John Standing bring John Gielgud's revival of Noel Coward's *Private Lives* to Broadway, for a stay of almost three months. Remak Ramsay and Niki Flacks play the unfortunates, Victor and Sybil.

Feb 20 The Leeds Playhouse production of *The Tempest* opens in London at Wyndham's Theatre, with Paul Scofield as Prospero. John Harrison stages.

Feb 27 The Chelsea Theatre Center plays Allan Knee's *Santa Anita '42* at Brooklyn's Academy of Music for four weeks. John Gay's sequel to *The Beggar's Opera,* the seldom produced *Polly,* appears on April 29.

March 2 The Negro Ensemble Company opens its season at New York's St. Marks Playhouse with Leslie Lee's *The First Breeze of Summer.* On May 18, Silas Jones' *Waiting for Mongo* opens for four weeks. Both are directed by Douglas Turner Ward.

March 12 The National Theatre of Great Britain brings its admired production of Moliere's *The Misanthrope* to Broadway, with Alec McGowan and Diana Rigg directed by John Dexter. Previously seen at the Kennedy Center, the show runs nearly three months.

March 20 The Circle in the Square's season continues with Eugene O'Neill's *All God Chillun' Got Wings* for 53 performances, followed on June 19 by Arthur Miller's *Death of a Salesman.* George C. Scott stages both productions, and also plays Willy Loman. O'Neill's *Ah, Wilderness!* and Tennessee Williams's *The Glass Menagerie* will open the season in the fall.

March 27 London's adventurous Bush Theatre sees the Alternative Theatre Company's productions of Stephen Poliakoff's *Hitting Town,* followed by his *City Sugar,* on Oct 8. Both will be televised, and the latter will also be produced in New York.

March 31 Andrzej Wajda returns to the Aldwych Theatre in London with *November Night,* the World Theatre Season's initial offering, presented by Cracow's Stary Theatre. The play is by Stanislaw Wyspianski, with music by

Zygmunt Konieczny. On April 7, Gothenburg's City Theatre presents Strindberg's *Gustav III.* April 14 sees the opening of *Regeneration,* by Italo Svevo, staged by Edmo Fenoglio for Italy's Compagnia di Prosa Tino Buazelli. The same company offers Ibsen's *An Enemy of the People* on April 18. On the 21st, the play is Robert Serumaga's *Renga Moi,* directed by the author for Uganda's Abafumi Company of Kampala.

March 31 At the Dublin Gate Theatre Hilton Edwards stages Strindberg's *Miss Julie.* Other productions this year include Forristal's *The True Story of the Horrid Popish Plot,* Somerville/Ross's *The Real Charlotte,* macLiammoir's *The Importance of Being Oscar,* and Anouilh's *Ring Round the Moon.*

April 8 *Henry V,* staged by Terry Hands, opens the Royal Shakespeare Company's annual season in Stratford-upon-Avon. Hands also stages *Henry IV, Parts 1 & 2.* Hands's production of *The Merry Wives of Windsor,* so admired in 1968, is revived but doesn't fare well with the critics this time.

April 8 At the Royal Shakespeare's Other Place in Stratford-upon-Avon, the new season of experimental productions, together with their directors, is comprised of *Hamlet,* Buzz Goodbody; *The Mouth Organ,* Ralph Koltai/Clifford Williams; John Ford's *Perkin Warbeck,* Barry Kyle/ John Barton; Bertolt Brecht's *Man Is Man,* Howard Davies; *Richard III,* Kyle.

April 8 Adam Mickiewicz's *Forefathers' Eve* is presented by Cracow's Stary Theatre in Southwark Cathedral as part of London's World Theatre Season. Konrad Swinarski directs.

April 9 At London's Prince of Wales's Theatre, Anthony Quayle directs a revival of Mary Chase's *Harvey,* with Jimmy Stewart as Elwood P. Dowd.

April 14 W. Somerset Maugham's *The Constant Wife* is revived on Broadway for four weeks at the Shubert. John Gielgud directs Ingrid Bergman in the title role.

April 21 London's Mermaid Theatre is the venue of a revival of George Bernard Shaw's *The Doctor's Dilemma.* The *Merry Wives of Windsor* (with Paul Scofield as Falstaff), *Spike Milligan and Musical Friends,* Shaw's *On the Rocks,* and a revue based on musicals once devised by Herbert and Eleanor Farjeon, called *Farjeon Reviewed,* will be given during the year.

April 24 An adaptation of Gilbert & Sullivan's *The Mikado, The Black Mikado,* by Eddie Quansan, George Larnyoh and Janos Bajala, is offered Londoners for 472 performances.

April 29 At London's Savoy, Ian McKellan directs the revival of the Colman-Garrick 18th century classic comedy, *The Clandestine Marriage.*

May 6 Canada's Shaw Festival at Niagara-

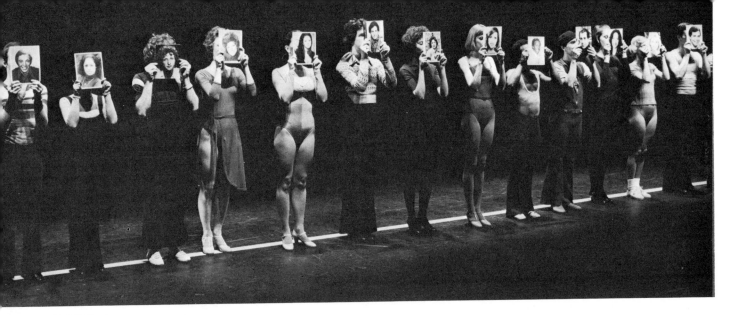

A CHORUS LINE

on-the-Lake begins its season with *Pygmalion*. Robertson Davies's *Leaven of Malice*, George Bernard Shaw's *Caesar and Cleopatra*, Richard Huggett's *The First Night of Pygmalion*, and Tony Van Bridge's *G. K. C.* are later offered. The season ends on Oct 5.

May 14 Britain's Chichester Festival opens its annual summer season with Edmond Rostand's *Cyrano de Bergerac*. Henrik Ibsen's *An Enemy of the People*, Andrew Sach's *Made in Heaven* and *Othello* will follow.

June 2 Tonight, the Royal Court Theatre revival of Joe Orton's *Entertaining Mr. Sloane* moves to the Duke of York's in the West End, and Orton's *Loot* is revived by Albert Finney at the theatre in Sloane Square. On July 16, another Orton revival opens: *What the Butler Saw*, directed by Lindsay Anderson.

June 3 In Balboa Park, the San Diego National Shakespeare Festival opens in the Old Globe Theatre with *The Tempest*, followed by *Much Ado About Nothing* and *Measure for Measure*. In the neighboring Carter Theatre, the show is the Tebelak/Schwartz *Godspell*.

June 3 The New Shakespeare Company presents *The Taming of the Shrew* in London at the Round House, with Sam Wanamaker's daughter, Zoe, as Katharina and Jeremy Irons as Petruchio. The company is later to be seen in Regent's Park in the Open Air Theatre in other productions.

June 9 The Stratford Festival in Ontario opens today. The season's schedule includes George Bernard Shaw's *Saint Joan*, *Twelfth Night*, Bertolt Brecht's *Trumpets and Drums*, *The Comedy of Errors*, *Two Gentlemen of Verona*, Arthur Miller's *The Crucible*, Michael Tait's *Fellowship*, Maxim Mazumdar's *Oscar Remembered*, Robert Patrick's *Kennedy's Children*, Oscar Wilde's *The Importance of Being Earnest*, Harry Somers's *The Fool*,

Jean Vallerand's *Le Magicien* and Richard Strauss' opera, *Ariadne auf Naxos*.

June 9 The Actors' Company opens its London season at the Wimbledon with David Giles' version of Gaston Leroux's novel, *The Phantom of the Opera*, staged by Giles. Kerry Lee Crabbe's *The Last Romantic* opens June 1. Richard Wilbur's version of Moliere's *Tartuffe* is shown on June 23, and Euripides' *The Bacchae* and Edward Petherbridge's *The Beanstalk* are given on July 8.

June 16 *The Gay Lord Quex*, by Arthur Wing Pinero, is revived at London's Albery Theatre, directed by John Gielgud, with Daniel Massey as the Marquis known for his *joie de vivre*.

June 18 In Central Park's Delacorte Theatre, Joseph Papp opens this summer's New York Shakespeare Festival with *Hamlet*. Sam Waterston is in the title role. Four weeks later, *The Comedy of Errors* is offered.

June 18 At the Sundown Theatre in Livingston, Texas, the Alabama-Coushatta Indian tribes present Kermit Hunter's *Beyond the Sundown*, the story of their difficult times when Texas rebelled against Mexico.

June 18 Jean Anouilh's *Ardele* is revived in London at the Queen's Theatre, staged by Frith Banbury, with Vincent Price and Coral Browne.

June 20 The Oregon Shakespearean Festival opens in Ashland with *All's Well That Ends Well*. Other productions in the Elizabethan Theatre include *Henry VI, Part 1* and *Romeo and Juliet*. In the Angus Bowmer Theatre, the productions are Eugene O'Neill's *Long Day's Journey into Night*, *The Winter's Tale*, and Brandon Thomas's *Charley's Aunt*.

June 21 The American Shakespeare Festival in Stratford, Connecticut, opens its new season with *King Lear*. Thornton Wilder's *Our Town* and *The Winter's Tale* will also be seen.

Summer *Where Free Man Shall Stand*, a drama by Revis Frye, about the ending of British recruitment in South Carolina, is played by the Pendleton District Historical and Recreational Commission.

July 16 In the Open Air Theatre of Regent's Park, the New Shakespeare Company offers *A Midsummer Night's Dream*, directed by David Conville. On Sep 1, the troupe offers Richard Digby Day's anthology, *Sweet Mr. Shakespeare*, staged by Day.

July 28 Agatha Christie's *Murder at the Vicarage* is revived at London's Savoy Theatre in Moie Charles and Barbara Toy's adaptation, directed by Donald Bodley. Miss Marple solves the crime for 1,776 performances.

Aug 18 The National Youth Theatre opens at London's Shaw Theatre with *The Lord of Misrule*, by Allan Swift and Bob Tomson. Barrie Keeffe's *A Sight of Glory* is staged by Michael Croft on the 20th at the Cockpit Theatre. Back at the Shaw on Sep 3, the youths revive Peter Terson's *Zigger Zagger*, staged by Kenneth Macdonald. On the 17th, the troupe presents *Henry IV, Part 1*, staged by Croft.

Aug 24 The Edinburgh Festival opens with a variety of attractions in the performing arts. Among the plays to be presented are *Cantilena* by the Nuova Compagnia di Canto Popolare, Aristophanes' *Utopia*, played by the company of the Cooperativa Tuscolano; Athol Fugard's *Dimetos*, presented by The Space/The Company; *As You Like It* offered by the Nottingham Playhouse; *Pilgrim*, a musical adaptation of *Pilgrim's Progress*, produced by the Prospect Theatre Company, and John Morris's *How Mad Tulloch Was Taken Away*, played by Edinburgh's Royal Lyceum Company.

Sep 9 Jose Quintero stages Thornton Wilder's *The Skin of Our Teeth* at Broadway's Mark Hellinger Theatre. Elizabeth Ashley is Sabina, with Alfred Drake and

Martha Scott as the Antrobuses. The revival comes from the Kennedy Center in Washington. The show has only seven performances.

Sep 22 London's Hampstead Theatre presents George Ryga's *The Ecstasy of Rita Joe* with Toby Robins tonight. Scheduled this fall are the Welsh Drama Company's production of Bertolt Brecht's *The Good Woman of Setzuan*, followed by his *A Man's A Man*, Franz Xaver Kroetz's *Morecambe*, and Roger McGough's *Wordplay*.

Oct 1 *Othello* is staged for the Young Vic by Alfred Lynch, with David Burke as the Moor. A musical based on writings of John Lennon, *All Walks of Leg*, is offered by Denise Coffey. Frank Dunlop's unusual *Macbeth* (with three Macbeths and two Lady Macbeths) appears Nov 4. Coffey stages *Charley's Aunt* on Dec 15.

Oct 2 Craig Anderson's Hudson Guild Theatre on New York's West Side offers Lonne Elder III's *Ceremonies in Dark Old Men*, Oliver Hailey's *Who's Happy Now*, and Jeff Wanshel's *The Disintegration of James Cherry*, among its showcase productions.

Oct 7 The Acting Company opens on Broadway at the Harkness Theatre with a musical, *The Robber Bridegroom*, based on a tale by Eudora Welty. On the 12th, Marlowe's *Edward II* opens, staged by Ellis Rabb. Saroyan's *The Time of Your Life*, directed by Jack O'Brien, opens on Oct 28, followed by Chekhov's *Three Sisters* on Nov 4, staged by Boris Tumarin.

Oct 16 Equity Library Theatre opens its annual season of revivals at New York's Master Theatre. Armina Marshall and Lawrence Langner's *The Pursuit of Happiness* is the initial offering. It's followed by the Harnick/Bock musical *Tenderloin*, Rose Franken's *Another Language*, Cole Porter's *Panama Hattie*, E. B. Ginty's *Missouri Legend*, the forgotten musical *Maggie Flynn*, Lanford Wilson's *The Rimers of Eldritch*, and Stephen Sondheim's *Follies*.

Oct 20 Ellen Stewart's season at her La Mama E.T.C. in the East Village includes *C.O.R.F.A.X. (Don't Ask)* by Wilfred Leach, *Cotton Club Gala*, Andre Serban's *Fragments of a Trilogy*, the Swados/Serban *Good Woman of Setzuan*, Adrienne Kennedy's *A Rat's Mass*, the opera *Carmilla*, Meredith Monk's *Quarry*, *Dr. Jekyll and Mr. Hyde* and Tom O'Horgan's production of Fernando Arrabal's *The Architect and the Emperor of Assyria*.

Oct 28 Chekhov's *The Sea Gull*, with Joan Plowright and Helen Mirren, is revived at the Lyric Theatre in London. On Dec 9, Ben Travers' farce, *The Bed Before Yesterday*, is played by the same actresses and John Moffatt, among others.

Nov 1 The Manhattan Theatre Club offer Gardner McKay's *Sea Marks*. Also to be seen are Pinter's *A Slight Ache* and The

Basement, Shepard's *Geography of a Horse Dreamer*, Ketron's *Patrick Henry Lake Liquors*, Van Druten's *The Voice of the Turtle*, Sexton/Sousa's *Transformations*, Odets' *Golden Boy*, Storey's *Life Class*, Fugard's *Blood Knot*, Bullins' *In the Wine Time*, Rome's *Pins and Needles*, and *Sholom Aleichem*.

Nov 5 The Light Opera of Manhattan (LOOM) opens its season of revivals with Gilbert & Sullivan's *Iolanthe*. Other G&S pieces in the repertory are *The Mikado*, *The Pirates of Penzance*, *H.M.S. Pinafore*, *The Gondoliers* and *Patience*. Victor Herbert's *Naughty Marietta*, Rudolf Frimls' *The Vagabond King*, and Sigmund Romberg's *The Student Prince* complete the season.

Nov 6 Pearl Bailey brings *Hello, Dolly!* back to Broadway at the Minskoff Theatre for 51 performances. Lucia Victor stages, and Billy Daniels is her Horace Vandergelder.

Dec 3 The holiday season in London's theatreland opens early with Willis Hall's *Kidnapped at Christmas*, presented by the Dolphin Theatre Company at the Shaw Theatre. On Dec 15 at the Mermaid Theatre, *Gulliver's Travels* opens, with the Mermaid's production of *Treasure Island* being revived at the New London Theatre. *Charley's Aunt* is at the Young Vic. Danny LaRue opens in *The Exciting Ad-*

ventures of Queen Daniella, a Bryan Blackburn pantomime on Dec 18 at the Casino Theatre. On Dec 23, Charles Marowitz offers a stripped-down Shakespeare, *The Shrew*, at the Open Space.

Dec 3 Tennessee Williams's *Sweet Bird of Youth* opens at the Brooklyn Academy of Music, followed by George S. Kaufman and Edna Ferber's *The Royal Family*. Both will open on Broadway later this month, the latter for 29 weeks.

Dec 16 Frederick Lonsdale's venerable comedy, *On Approval*, is revived at London's Haymarket Theatre, directed by Frank Hauser. Geraldine McEwan plays Maria Wislack.

Dec 17 Charles Marowitz offers his *Artaud at Rodez* at the Open Space in London. Clive Merrison plays Artaud.

Dec 18 *Rhoda in Potatoland* opens Off-Off Broadway in New York, conceived and directed by Richard Foreman and his Ontological-Hysteric Theatre. Kate Manheim plays Rhoda.

Dec 21 At Broadway's Booth Theatre, Jerome Kern's *Very Good Eddie* is revived for 38 weeks. Guy Bolton has revised his 1915 book for director Bill Gile. Charles Repole and Spring Fairbank play a badly matched couple who sort themselves out with song. The show opens in London for 411 performances, beginning March 23, 1976.

1975   BIRTHS/DEATHS/DEBUTS

Jan 21 Popular British actress Marie Lohr dies at age 84.

Jan 27 Actress Julia Sanderson, age 87, dies today.

Feb 8 Martyn Green (b. 1899) dies in New York. His career was devoted primarily to Gilbert & Sullivan. He joined the D'Oyly Carte Opera Company in 1922 as a chorister and understudy.

Feb 14 British author P. G. Wodehouse, who often collaborated with Guy Bolton on musical books, dies at age 93.

March 8 Actress Francine Larrimore (b. 1898) dies in New York City. The niece of Yiddish actor Jacob P. Adler, her more memorable roles included Roxie Hart in *Chicago*, Kitty Brown in *Let Us Be Gay*, and Kate Colman in *What Every Woman Wants*.

Apr 12 The American actress-singer Josephine Baker (b. 1906) dies at age 68. For many years, she has lived and worked in France, making occasional visits to the United States for performances.

April 12 Buzz Goodbody, a talented director with the Royal Shakespeare, dies today. She was only 28.

April 14 Frederic March (b. 1897) dies in Los Angeles. Billed as Fred Bickel, he made his stage debut in Belasco's pro-

duction of *Deburau* in Baltimore in 1920. He appeared on Broadway in 1956 as James Tyrone in Eugene O'Neill's *A Long Day's Journey into Night*.

June 6 Larry Blyden (b. 1925) dies suddenly in Morocco. His debut was in 1949 in *Mr. Roberts* at the Alvin Theatre, and he played in *Oh, Men! Oh, Women!*, *The Flower Drum Song* and *Foxy*.

June 21 The distinguished Broadway scenic designer Donald Oenslager dies. He was 73.

July 2 The actor James Robertson Justice dies at 70.

Aug 6 Peter Daubeny, the London-based producer responsible for the World Theatre seasons at the Aldwych, dies at 54.

Sep 9 Ethel Griffies (b. 1878) dies. She toured the provinces in the 1890's, before making her London debut in 1901. Her favorite roles included Paula Tanqueray, Viola, Fanny Cavendish, and Mrs. White in *Druid Circle*.

Sep 18 British actress Pamela Brown dies, aged 58.

Nov 13 Robert C. Sherriff, author of the successful play about World War I, *Journey's End*, at 79 years comes to the end of his own journey.

Nov 16 Harold Lang (b. 1931) is dead in

Cairo, Egypt. He made his Broadway debut as a solo dancer in *Mr. Strauss Goes to Boston*. In 1962, he played in *I Can Get It for You Wholesale*.

Dec 7 Thornton Wilder (b. 1897) dies in New Haven, Connecticut. *Our Town*, *The Skin of Our Teeth*, and *The Matchmaker* are among his most successful and often produced plays.

Dec 24 Tilly Losch (b. 1907) dies in New York City. She was associated with Max Reinhardt and came to America with his company in 1927, when she appeared as the First Fairy in *A Midsummer Night's Dream*.

Dec 27 British actress Winifred Ward dies, age 95.

Canada. 175 of the plays are American. Shakespeare is most often produced, with 44 productions of 22 plays. *Hamlet* gets five regional productions.

New York's season is now over, and Guernsey, Jr., picks the annual ten "Best Plays." But they are—as must be the case in recent years—by no means all Broadway productions, since so many interesting scripts can only be done Off or Off-Off Broadway. The list includes Shaffer's *Equus*, Fugard's *The Island*, Schisgal's *All Over Town*, McNally's *The Ritz*, Albee's *Seascape*, Slade's *Same Time, Next Year*, Kirkwood/Dante/Kleban/Hamlish's *Chorus Line*, Bullins' *The Taking of Miss Janie*, Nichols' *The National Health*, and Medoff's *The Wager*.

1975   THEATERS/PRODUCTIONS

Jan The Persephone Theatre in Saskatoon, Saskatchewan, opens its first season with *Cruel Tears*, a country and western opera based on *Othello*, with music by Humphrey and the Dumptrucks. This will be very popular on its cross-country tour. Brian Richmond is artistic director.

Jan 30 Playwrights Horizons opens its 65-seat Manhattan Studio Theatre with a production of Dennis Hackin's comedy, *Carcass Chrome*, staged by Jake Arnett. The decay of the West 42nd Street block is arrested, as other theatre groups come, and it becomes known as Theatre Row.

March 10 In London, *The Rocky Horror Show* has enjoyed continued success in an old cinema, marked for demolition. Attempts to re-create this atmosphere when the show comes to New York do considerable damage to the Belasco Theatre.

May 3 Tonight marks the 15th anniversary of the long-running Off-Broadway musical, *The Fantasticks*. It is the longest running musical in the world.

May 23 The historic Theatre Royal in Bury St. Edmunds (built in 1819, William Williams as architect) is today officially placed in the care of the National Trust.

May 31 *Variety* designates the following shows of the Broadway season closing today as hits: *Same Time, Next Year*, *Equus*, *Absurd Person Singular*, *In Praise of Love*, *Scapino*, *Gypsy*, *Sherlock Holmes*, *Private Lives* and *The Constant Wife*. The annual gross revenue from ticket sales is approximately $57 million.

June 1 This past Broadway season, which closed yesterday, has seen 62 productions, compared with 54 last season. Otis Guernsey, Jr., tabulates the shows thus: 18 plays, nine musicals, three revues, three specialties, 18 revivals, three return engagements, and eight foreign dramas in English. *Variety* estimates the Broadway gross at $57 + million, with $51 million earned on the road. Harry Rigby's Broadway revival of *Good News* has lost $1.5 million, with *Goodtime Charley* a million-dollar loser. Off-Broadway records a total of 81 productions. Plays account for 30; there are 12 musicals, five revues, 17 revivals, 11 specialties, three return engagements, and three foreign plays in English. Some shows now cost $8.50 a ticket Off-Broadway. Ella Malin's tabulation of regional theatre work shows 378 productions of 327 plays by 41 groups in 68 theatres in 39 cities, five of them in

June 7 Daphne Dare, resident designer of Canada's Stratford Festival, sees her innovative redesigning of the stage and auditorium for the Avon Theatre opened to the public.

Aug 23 As the curtain rises on *The Dame of Sark* at the Theatre Royal, Bath, some cast members swear they see the ghost of the Lady in Grey in an upper circle box. Said to have killed herself after her husband killed her lover, she trails a scent of jasmine between the theatre and Garrick's Head pub.

Aug 25 Actors vote to recommend to Actors' Equity Council that a proposed Off-Off Broadway showcase production code be tabled. They fear curtailed activity because the new code would require payment to actors in the initial showcase from royalties of future productions.

Sep 12 From today, all seats in Glasgow's Citizens' Theatre, located in an extremely poor area of the city, will cost only 50 pence. Many local people attend, regardless of the complexity of the plays because it's too good a bargain to miss.

Sep 18 Broadway musicians' union Local 802 strikes for higher wages and other improvements in contracts. When ended on Oct 12, the strike will have cost $1 million per day in lost income for the city. The musicians' minimum of $290 is increased to $350–$380 per week.

Sep 28 Tonight's Gala at the Perth Theatre in Scotland will celebrate the theatre's 40th anniversary. There is a staged reading of the history of theatre in Perth and tributes from leading Scottish actors.

Oct The New Drama Forum is founded in New York to provide occasions for the exchange of ideas among people interested and actively involved in the theatre.

Nov 5 In Stamford, Connecticut, the Palace Theatre, an old vaudeville house, has been saved from demolition by the Hartman Foundation. The Hartman Theatre Company opens the renovated house with Nicolai Gogol's *The Inspector General*, staged by Byron Ringland.

KID CHAMPION

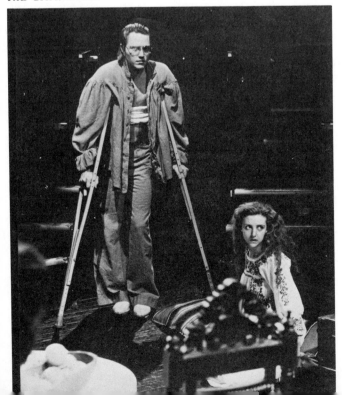

Jan 11 *Pacific Overtures* (NY—Winter Garden—Musical). John Weidman's book, about U.S. trade and influence in Japan, is produced and directed by Harold Prince, with songs by Stephen Sondheim. It is chosen as a "Best Play," but runs for only six months.

Feb 3 *A Matter of Gravity* (NY—Broadhurst—Comedy). Katharine Hepburn stars in Enid Bagnold's English comedy about an elderly lady and her troublesome grandson (Christopher Reeve), but there are only 79 performances. Noel Willman stages.

Feb 24 *Knock Knock* (NY—Biltmore—Drama). In Jules Feiffer's absurdist drama, chosen as a "Best Play," Joan of Arc appears to two lonely old men. It has first been seen at Greenwich Village's Circle Repertory Theatre. After it opens, it gets a new director, Jose Quintero, and a new cast including Lynn Redgrave and Leonard Frey, it has 192 performances.

March 2 *Bubbling Brown Sugar* (NY—ANTA—Revue). A musical look at Harlem of the 1920's through the 1940's, this Loften Mitchell book has a run of 766 performances. Rosetta LeNoire, who's developed the concept, has shown the work Off-Off Broadway at her AMAS Repertory Theatre. Robert Cooper directs. On Sep 28, 1977, a London production opens at the Royalty Theatre, with staging and choreography by Billy Wilson. It has 784 showings.

March 22 *Vanities* (NY—Chelsea—Comedy). Jack Heifner's play traces the lives of three girlhood chums through high school, college, and maturity. First showcased by Playwrights' Horizons, it is a phenomenal success and in 1980 is still running. Garland Wright directs.

April 28 *The Belle of Amherst* (NY—Longacre—Monodrama). Julie Harris plays Emily Dickinson in William Luce's one-woman show based on the poet's life and works. After a tour, Harris has a 15-week run on Broadway, followed on Sep 14, 1977 by an engagement at London's Phoenix Theatre.

May 4 *1600 Pennsylvania Avenue* (NY—Mark Hellinger—Musical). There are just seven performances of Alan Jay Lerner's musical about former U.S. presidents and their wives. Leonard Bernstein composes the score.

May 6 *Rebel Women* (NY—Public—Drama). Thomas Babe's play, about three women resisters during the Civil War, is directed by Jack Hofsiss. Leora Dana, Kathryn Walker, and Mandy Patinkin are among the cast.

May 17 *For Colored Girls Who Have Considered Suicide/When the Rainbow Is Enuf* (NY—Public—Drama). Author Ntozake

FOR COLORED GIRLS…

Shange also acts in her "choreopoem" about black women's problems. Oz Scott directs the cast of seven, working with the show first at the Henry Street Settlement House. On Sep 15, producer Joseph Papp transfers it to Broadway's Booth Theatre. It has a run of 742 performances. A London production, which opens on Oct 10, 1979 at the Royalty Theatre, has only a five-week run.

June 10 *California Suite* (NY—Eugene O'Neill—Comedy). Tammy Grimes and Jack Weston are among the cast of Neil Simon's comedy—four short plays set in the Beverly Hills Hotel. Chosen as a "Best Play," it has 445 performances. Gene Saks directs.

June 16 *Sexual Perversity in Chicago* and *Duck Variations* (NY—Cherry Lane—Drama). David Mamet's two one-act plays, seen earlier at Chicago's Organic Theatre and in New York at St. Clement's, where they won an Obie Award, have a 34-week run. Albert Takazauckas stages. On Dec 1, 1977, the plays open at London's Re-

gent Theatre.

Sep 21 *A Texas Trilogy* (NY—Broadhurst—Drama). Two of Preston Jones' three plays, *The Last Meeting of the Knights of the White Magnolia* and *The Oldest Living Graduate*, are chosen as "Best Plays" but the trilogy, played in repertory, has only 60 showings. Alan Schneider directs. First seen in Dallas and later in Washington, D.C., at the Kennedy Center, the trilogy will also have a short run at London's Hampstead Theatre in February 1977.

Oct 14 *The Club* (NY—Circle in the Square Downtown—Revue). Tommy Tune directs this Eve Merriam show in which Victorian dandies are portrayed by women in smart male attire. There are 674 performances. On May 15, 1978, the show opens a six-week run at London's Regent Theatre. Tony Tanner stages.

Oct 20 *Poor Murderer* (NY—Ethel Barrymore—Drama). Laurence Luckinbill plays an actor being treated in an asylum in Pavel Kohout's Czech drama, which runs for 11 weeks. Herbert Berghof translates and directs.

Nov 9 *No Man's Land.* See L premiere, 1975.

Nov 23 *The Eccentricities of a Nightingale* (NY—Morosco—Drama). Tennessee Williams' *Summer and Smoke* appears under a new guise, but it has only a three-week run. Betsy Palmer and Shepperd Strudwick are in the cast, directed by Edwin Sherin.

Dec 14 *Sly Fox* (NY—Broadhurst—Comedy). George C. Scott stars as a confidence man in Victorian San Francisco, in Larry Gelbart's adaptation of Ben Jonson's *Volpone.* The show earns 495 performances. Arthur Penn stages. It is chosen as a "Best Play."

Dec 22 *Your Arms Too Short To Box With God* (NY—Lyceum—Musical). Vinnette Carroll's Urban Arts production, based on the Book of Matthew, has 429 performances. Created for Italy's Spoleto Festival of Two Worlds in 1975, it has also been seen at the Ford Theatre, Washington, D.C. Songs are by Alex Bradford and Micki Grant.

1976 BRITISH PREMIERES

Jan 22 *Funny Peculiar* (L—Mermaid—Comedy). Mike Stott's play about a young husband (Richard Beckinsale) eager to try the promised delights of sexual liberation, transfers to the West End's Garrick Theatre on April 28. It has a total run of 618 performances. Alan Dossor directs.

Jan 26 *Come Into My Bed* (L—Whitehall—Comedy). Fiona Richmond is in the cast of Andre Launay's sex comedy. Paul Raymond, well-known for shows designed to titillate the tired businessman, produces.

Jan 27 *Comedians* (L—Wyndham's—Drama). Trevor Griffiths' play, about comedians auditioning for a working-class club, has previously been seen at the Nottingham Playhouse in 1975, and later at London's Old Vic. Richard Eyre stages. A New York production opens at the Music Box Theatre on Nov 28, with Jonathan Pryce and Milo O'Shea in the cast. It runs 18 weeks.

Feb 5 *Treats* (L—Royal Court—Drama). Christopher Hampton's play deals with a woman who dominates two men in her life. Jane Asher is featured. On May 9, the play moves to the May Fair Theatre.

Feb 24 *Watch It Come Down* (L—Old Vic—Drama). John Osborne writes this play about a couple living in a remodeled railroad station, railing at the disintegration of traditions and expectations. Jill Bennett and Frank Finlay are featured.

March 10 *The Chairman* (L—Globe—Comedy). Tony Britton heads the cast of Philip Mackie's comedy, set in the frenetic public relations department of a huge international company. Gareth Davies directs.

March 11 *Sons of Light* (Newcastle—University—Drama). David Rudkin's monumental play is produced by the Tyneside Theatre Company. Themes of guilt, redemption, sexuality, and religious repression are dealt with in the play.

March 16 *Housewife-Superstar!!* (L—Apollo—Comedy). From Australia comes Barry Humphries with his alter-ego Dame Edna Everage—Humphries in drag as a formidable middle-class Australian housewife. Well-received in London, moving to the Globe in May, the show will be less popular in New York, opening on Oct 19, 1977 at Theatre Four.

April 8 *A Bedfull of Foreigners* (L—Victoria Palace—Comedy). Julia Sutton and June Whitfield are in the cast of Dave Freeman's farce about English on vacation in France. Staged by Roger Redfarn, it has 475 performances.

May 4 *Side by Side by Sondheim* (L—ermaid—Revue). Narrator-director Ned Sherrin devises this collage of songs, entirely by Stephen Sondheim. Millicent Martin, Julia McKenzie, and David Kernan complete the cast. The show transfers to Wyndham's in the West End for a total of 781 performances. The same team opens at New York's Music Box Theatre on April 18, 1977, and plays 384 performances.

May 19 *Confusions* (L—Apollo—Comedy). Pauline Collins and John Alderton head the cast of Alan Ayckbourn's comedy, made up of five short plays. It runs for nearly 34 weeks. Alan Strachan directs.

May 24 *Dimetos* (L—Comedy—Drama). Athol Fugard's South African play, seen at the Edinburgh Festival in 1975 and the Nottingham Playhouse last month, moves to the West End with Paul Scofield in the title role.

May 26 *Teeth 'n' Smiles* (L—Wyndham's—Musical). Helen Mirren and comedian Dave King are in the cast of David Hare's musical, first shown in 1975 at the Royal Court Theatre. Hare directs.

June 5 *The Family Dance* (L—Criterion—Drama). While their children hold a dance, parents gather together for a drink and play out their own antagonisms in Felicity Brown's play, which features Alec McCowen. Jonathan Hales stages.

June 8 *Liza of Lambeth* (L—Shaftesbury—Musical). William Rushton and Berny Stringle adapt W. Somerset Maugham's novel as a musical, with Cliff Adams providing the music. Stringle directs a cast including Angela Richards.

June 16 *Dirty Linen/New-Found-Land* (L—Arts—Comedy). Tom Stoppard's two plays, the first a spoof on Parliamentary sex scandals, the second a backhanded salute to the American Bicentennial, have a run of 1,667 performances. They have been previously seen in April at the Almost Free Theatre. Ed Berman stages. On Jan 11, 1977, the plays open a five-month run at New York's John Golden Theatre.

June 23 *Signed and Sealed* (L—Comedy—Comedy). Comedians Kenneth Williams and Peggy Mount play in Christopher Hampton's translation of the Feydeau Deguallieres comedy *Le Mariage de Barillon.* Patrick Garland stages.

July 7 *The Pleasure of His Company* (L—Phoenix—Comedy). Douglas Fairbanks, Jr., plays a wealthy jet-setter in Samuel Taylor's American play. Wilfrid Hyde White is also in the cast. Peter Dews directs.

July 15 *Donkey's Years* (L—Globe—Comedy). Penelope Keith and Peter Barkworth head the cast of Michael Frayn's comedy, which has 668 performances. Michael Rudman stages.

July 22 *A Chorus Line.* See NY premiere, 1975.

Sep 23 *Same Time, Next Year.* See NY premiere, 1975.

Sep 30 *Carte Blanche* (L—Phoenix—Revue). Kenneth Tynan's erotic revue, with sketches by such writers as Eugene Ionesco and Keith Waterhouse, has 320 performances. Clifford Williams directs.

Oct 6 *Yahoo* (L—Queen's—Revue). Alec Guinness and director Alan Strachan devise this revue, based on the life and writings of Jonathan Swift. Nicola Paget is also among the cast.

Oct 7 *Old World* (L—Aldwych—Comedy). Peggy Ashcroft and Anthony Quayle head the cast of the Royal Shakespeare Company's repertory production of Aleksei Arbusov's Russian play about two people looking back over their pasts. Terry Hands directs. On Jan 9, 1978, Mary Martin and Anthony Quayle open at New York's 46th Street Theatre, after showings at Washington, D.C.'s Kennedy Center. The play, retitled *Do You Turn Somersaults?* lasts only two weeks.

Oct 20 *Dear Daddy* (L—Ambassadors'—Comedy). Phyllis Calvert and Nigel Patrick are featured in Denis Cannan's play, first seen last month at the Oxford Playhouse. David William directs; there's a 33-week run.

Oct 21 *Out on a Limb* (L—Vaudeville—Comedy). Ian Carmichael heads the cast of Joyce Rayburn's play about a married man's attempts to keep an extra-marital affair secret from his wife. James Grout stages.

Jan 6 In Edinburgh, at the Traverse Theatre, the new year begins with David Pownall's *Ladybird, Ladybird*. This year there are some 25 programs. Among the shows are Tom Gallacher's *The Sea Change*, Tom McGrath's *Laurel and Hardy*, Snoo Wilson's *The Everest Hotel*, Donald Campbell's *The Jesuit*, Ian Brown's *The Fork*, John Morris' *Messages in Bottles*, David Edgar's *Saigon Rose*, Richard Crane's *Nero and the Golden House*, Howard Barker's *Wax*, and Caryl Churchill's *Light Shining in Buckinghamshire*.

Jan 14 At the Old Vic, the National Theatre revives Ben Travers' farce *Plunder*, in a staging by Michael Blakemore.

Jan 15 At the Citizens' Theatre in Glasgow, the new year begins with a reprise of the *DeSade Show* of Robert David MacDonald, followed by *Mirandolina*, *The Changeling*, *Woyzeck*, *Maskerade*, *The Seven Deadly Sins of the Lower Middle Class*, *What the Butler Saw*, *Elizabeth I*, and *Cinderella*.

Jan 15 Peter Brook and his Paris-based troupe come to London to the Round House to show *The Ik*, based on anthropologist Colin Turnbull's book about an African tribe, deprived of their lands and reduced to starvation.

Jan 18 In Greenwich Village, the Circle Repertory Company continues its season with the opening of Jules Feiffer's *Knock Knock*. This runs five weeks and later transfers to Broadway. On March 10, A.R. Gurney's *Who Killed Richard Cory?* opens. Lanford Wilson's *Serenading Louie* is offered on May 2.

Jan 20 The Royal Shakespeare Company brings its highly praised production of *Henry V* from Stratford to its London home, the Aldwych. On Jan 29 *Henry IV, Parts 1 and 2* open. On March 26 they are followed by *The Merry Wives of Windsor*.

Jan 21 Istvan Orkeny's Hungarian satire, *The Tot Family*, has its American premiere at the Arena Stage's Kreeger Theatre in Washington, D.C. Edward Payson Call directs.

Jan 22 At Lincoln Center in the Mitzi E. Newhouse Theatre, producer Joseph Papp offers Michael Dorn Moody's *The Shortchanged Review*. On April 21, David Rabe's *Streamers* opens. There are 478 performances. Set in an army barracks in Virginia, the play touches on such themes as the Vietnam war, homosexuality and racial tensions. First seen in January at New Haven's Long Wharf Theatre, it's selected as a "Best Play."

Jan 26 The Phoenix Theatre presents two repertory programs in midtown Manhattan, opening with a double-bill of Williams' *27 Wagons Full of Cotton* and Miller's *A Memory of Two Mondays*, both staged by Arvin Brown for 33 performances. They alternate with Howard's *They Knew What They Wanted*, staged by Stephen Porter for 30 showings, opening the following day. On April 12 and 13, a second rep program opens: Gillette's *The Secret Service*, staged by Daniel Freudenberger for 13 performances, and Bella and Sam Spewack's *Boy Meets Girl*, directed by John Lithgow for ten performances.

Jan 27 At London's Greenwich Theatre, John Hale stages his *Love's Old Sweet Song*. Leopold Lewis's *The Bells* is revived on March 2. Colin Morris's *Reluctant Heroes* opens on March 31, and August Strindberg's *Miss Julie* is given on April 29. John Mortimer's two plays, *The Fear of Heaven* and *The Prince of Darkness*, open on May 28 as *Heaven and Hell*.

Jan 28 Eugene O'Neill's *Long Day's Journey into Night* opens at the Brooklyn Academy of Music. Jason Robards directs and plays the role of James Tyrone, supported by Zoe Caldwell. There are 11 performances.

Jan 29 Anthony Quayle appears at the John F. Kennedy Center in Washington, D.C., in a Bicentennial revival of Dion Boucicault's drama, *Rip Van Winkle*. Joshua Logan directs the show, first seen at the Clarence Brown Theatre in Knoxville, Tennessee. There are 30 performances.

Jan 30 Edward Bond's play, *Bingo: Scenes of Death and Money*, about Shakespeare's bitter life in retirement in Stratford, has its American premiere at Yale's New Haven Repertory Theatre. Ron Daniels directs.

Feb 10 Bernard Shaw's *The Doctor's Dilemma* opens at the Dublin Gate Theatre, directed by Christopher Casson. Other shows this year include Forristal's *The Seventh Sin*, Kelly's *In My Father's Time*, and macLiammoir's *Home for Christmas*.

Feb 11 Frank Marcus adapts Schnitzler's *Anatol*, now staged by Charles Marowitz in London at the Open Sace. *Love Us and Leave Us*, by Peter Terson and Paul Joyce, opens on May 26.

Feb 12 *Apple Pie*, by Myrna Lamb and Nicholas Meyers, opens at the Public Theatre in Greenwich Village. Joseph Papp continues his season with John Guare's *Rich and Famous* on Feb 19. Neil Harris's *So Nice They Named It Twice* is given on May 26. On June 3, Thomas Babe's *Rebel Women* is offered. Ntozake Shange's *For Colored Girls Who Have Considered Suicide/When the Rainbow Is Enuf* opens June 1. It has 120 performances and then moves to Broadway for an extended run.

Feb 12 At the Bush Theatre in London, Wolfgang Bauer's Austrian play, *Magic Afternoon*, opens, with Barbara Markham directing. Andy Smith's *Winter Visitors* opens on March 2. Snoo Wilson's *Soul of the White Ant* opens on March 29. David Pownall's *Ladybird, Ladybird* is given on April 20. On May 11, Franz Xaver Kroetz's Bavarian play, *Geisterbahn*, is offered.

Feb 18 George Bernard Shaw's *Mrs. Warren's Profession* continues the Vivian Beaumont season in Lincoln Center. On May 1, Bertolt Brecht's *Threepenny Opera* opens in a new translation by Ralph Manheim.

Feb 28 As its farewell salute to London's Old Vic, prior to moving to its new home on the South Bank of the Thames, the National Theatre Company honors Vic founder Lilian Bayliss with *Tribute to a Lady*, a recreation of Bayliss's life and work.

March 3 The Off-Broadway season of the Negro Ensemble Company presents Steve Carter's *Eden*, which later transfers to the Theatre de Lys for a total run of 181 performances. On April 6, the NEC begins a program of four week-long productions: *The Trap Play*, *A Love Play*, *A Fictional Account of the Lives of Richard and Sarah Allen*, *Sunshine*, *Moonbeam*, and *Kingdom*. On June 1, Judi Ann Mason's *Livin' Fat* opens for a run of 61 performances.

March 4 In Brooklyn, at the Brooklyn Academy of Music, the Chelsea Theatre revives Edward Sheldon's *The Boss*, as a Bicentennial event. It runs three weeks.

March 4 In London at the Comedy, pop singer Adam Faith plays a sadistic disc jockey in Stephen Poliakoff's *City Sugar*, first seen at the Bush Theatre. It is later staged in New York by the Phoenix Theatre. Hugh Thomas directs.

March 15 *Spokesong*, by Stewart Parker, continues the Circle in the Square's Broadway season in the Joseph E. Levine Theatre. It has 77 performances. The production is an import from New Haven's Long Wharf Theatre, but the play—set in Northern Ireland—has already been seen in Dublin and London. Kenneth Frankel stages.

March 16 Albert Finney plays the prince in *Hamlet*, presented in London on the Lytlleton stage of the National Theatre.

March 17 At London's Phoenix Theatre, Glynis Johns and Louis Jourdan are featured in George Feydeau's *13 Rue de l'Amour*.

March 18 Ibsen's *The Lady from the Sea* opens at the Circle in the Square in midtown Manhattan, continuing the current season of revivals. It runs nearly ten weeks. It is followed on June 28 by a revival of *Pal Joey*.

March 23 *Very Good Eddie*. See NY revival, 1975.

March 23 At the Bristol Old Vic's Theatre

Royal, three plays by the Russian dramatist, Aleksei Arbusov, open for nearly a month's run. *Evening Light*, *The Promise*, and *Once Upon a Time* are staged by Richard Cottrell.

March 24 Patrick Hamilton's thriller, *Gaslight*, opens in a West End revival at the Criterion Theatre, with Anton Rodgers and Nicola Pagett. Robert Young directs.

March 25 *My Fair Lady* comes back to Broadway at the St. James Theatre for a run of 377 performances, staged by Jerry Adler. Ian Richardson plays Henry Higgins, Christine Andreas is Eliza.

March 29 Samuel Beckett has staged his play *Waiting for Godot*, in German with actors of Berlin's Schiller Theatre. They come to the Brooklyn Academy of Music. On April 2, the same production opens in London at the Royal Court.

March 31 At the Royal Shakespeare's Other Place in Stratford-upon-Avon, the season of experimental productions opens with Bertolt Brecht's *Schweyk in the Second World War*, Charles Wood's *Dingo*, Shakespeare's *Macbeth*, David Edgar's *Destiny*, and Edward Bond's *Bingo*. The directors, in respective order, are Howard Davies, Barry Kyle, Trevor Nunn, Ron Daniels, and Davies.

April 1 Edward Albee's *Who's Afraid of Virginia Woolf?* returns to Broadway at the Music Box Theatre for a run of 141 showings. Albee directs Colleen Dewhurst and Ben Gazzara.

April 1 This season at the Royal Shakespeare Theatre at Stratford-upon-Avon opens with Trevor Nunn's staging of *Romeo and Juliet*. *Much Ado About Nothing*, *The Winter's Tale*, *Troilus and Cressida*, *The Comedy of Errors*, and *King Lear* will also be seen.

April 14 Julian Slade's musical, *Salad Days*, gets a revival at London's Duke of York's Theatre, staged by David Conville.

April 15 Charles Ludlam's Ridiculous Theatrical Company opens *Caprice*, a zany, camp expose of the world of fashion design. Ludlam directs and stars.

April 18 The Royal Shakespeare Company's production of John O'Keeffe's *Wild Oats*, so successful at London's Aldwych Theatre, moves now to the Piccadilly Theatre for a total run of 324 performances.

April 20 Peter Shaffer's *Equus* is revived in London at the Albery for 482 performances.

April 20 The John F. Kennedy Center's revival of *The Heiress*, the Ruth and Augustus Goetz dramatization of Henry James' novel *Washington Square*, opens on Broadway at the Broadhurst Theatre. In George Keathley's staging, it has a run of three weeks, with Jane Alexander and Richard Kiley among the cast.

April 21 At George Murcell's St. George's

STREAMERS

Elizabethan Theatre in North London, Frank Hauser directs *Twelfth Night*. On June 2 Murcell stages *Romeo and Juliet* with Sarah Badel and Peter McEnery. Murcell presents *Richard III*, staged by Douglas Campbell, with Alan Badel in the title-role.

April 22 The Royal Shakespeare Company opens its stripped-down production of *Henry V* at the Brooklyn Academy of Music for a three-week run. Terry Hands directs. Two performances are also given of the RSC's anthology-show, *The Hollow Crown*.

April 26 On the same night as the French transvestite revue, *La Grande Eugene*, opens at the Round House, an American ensemble of black-leather transvestites, calling themselves *Cycle Sluts*, bows at the Broadway Theatre in Kilburn. The company comes to London from Los Angeles' Roxy Theatre.

April 26 Canada's Shaw Festival at Niagara-on-the-Lake, opens with Barry Morse's staging of J. M. Barrie's *The Admirable Crichton*. Leslie Yeo directs *Mrs. Warren's Profession. Arms and the Man* is staged by Paxton Whitehead. Noel Willman directs *The Apple Cart*.

April 28 At the RSC's Aldwych Theatre, in London, Maxim Gorky's *The Zykovs* is directed by David Jones. Paul Rogers and Mia Farrow are among the cast. On May 25, Eugene O'Neill's *The Iceman Cometh* is staged by Howard Davies. On

July 13, Bernard Shaw's tale of the American Revolution, *The Devil's Disciple*, becomes a Bicentennial salute from the Royal Shakespeare Company. Jack Gold directs a cast including Tom Conti, Patience Collier, and John Wood. On Sep 8 Wood and Mia Farrow are among the players in Chekhov's *Ivanov*. David Jones directs.

May 5 The D'Oyly Carte Opera Company returns to New York, opening at the Uris Theatre with Gilbert & Sullivan's *The Mikado*. *The Pirates of Penzance* and *H.M.S. Pinafore* are also in the repertory.

May 6 Madeleine Renaud and Jean-Pierre Aumont play a limited run in Margaret Duras's *Des Journees Entieres dans les Arbres* at New York's Ambassador Theatre. It is performed in French.

May 6 At London's Royal Court Theatre, Donald McWhinnie stages Beckett's *Endgame*, with Patrick Magee and Stephen Rea. Beckett's *Play and Other Plays* opens on May 20, staged by McWhinnie and the author, with a cast including Anna Massey, and Billie Whitelaw.

May 10 Christopher Durang, a young playwright-parodist from the Yale School of Drama, has his disaster-spoof *Titanic* and his mock-Brecht cabaret, *Das Lusitania Songspiel* presented at the Van Dam Theatre in New York's Soho. Both shows have been seen earlier in workshop at the Direct Theatre. *Songspiel* will later appear again as an entire evening's entertainment.

May 12 William Inge's *Bus Stop* gets a revival in the West End, staged by Vivian Matalon at the Phoenix Theatre. Lee Remick heads the cast.

May 18 Britain's Chichester Festival opens with a production of Andre Obey's *Noah*. *Twelfth Night*, Maugham's *The Circle* and the Labiche-Martin *Monsieur Perrichon's Travels* are also seen during the season.

May 30 On the banks of the Thames, in Hammersmith, the Riverside Studios open with Shakespeare's *As You Like It*, staged by Peter Gill. Jane Lapotaire and Zoe Wanamaker are among the cast.

June 1 California's San Diego National Shakespeare Festival gets underway in Balboa Park with *As You Like It*, staged by Jack O'Brien. It is followed by Dan Sullivan's staging of *Othello* and Edward Payson Call's mounting of *Troilus and Cressida*. Wayne Bryan directs a revue, *Rodgers and Hart* in the nearby Carter Theatre.

June 3 Off-off Broadway at Playwrights' Horizons, directed by Robert Moss, work continues with a production of Steven Shea's *Paradise*. On September 29, Philip Magdalany's *Boo Hoo* opens; this is later shown at the Queens Theatre in the Park, also operated by Moss's group. Other major productions include Martin Sherman's *Rio Grande*, Albert Innaurato's *Gemini*, Karen Malpede's *Rebeccah*, Marsha Sheiness' *Stop the Parade*, Magdalany and Pressman's *Fair Weather Friends*, Oliver Hailey's *For the Use of the Hall*, Sally Ordway's *S. W. A. K.*, and Innaurato's *Earthworms*. Four of these also go to Queens to the former World's Fairgrounds.

June 7 The Stratford Festival in Canada opens with William Hutt's staging of *Hamlet*. *The Tempest*, Congreve's *The Way of the World*, *The Merchant of Venice*, *Antony and Cleopatra*, *Measure for Measure*, *A Midsummer Night's Dream*, Wilde's *The Importance of Being Earnest*, Larry Fineberg's *Eve*, and Chekhov's *The Three Sisters* will also be seen.

June 8 At London's I C A Theatre, Edward Bond's *Stone* is presented, staged by Gerald Chapman.

June 8 The American Shakespeare Festival, in Stratford, Connecticut, opens with last season's production of *The Winter's Tale*. *As You Like It* and Arthur Miller's *The Crucible* are also scheduled.

June 9 At the Open Air Theatre in Regent's Park, summer Shakespeare begins with *Othello*. On July 21, *Love's Labour's Lost* is given.

June 12 Off-off Broadway at the Hudson Guild Theatre, artistic director Craig Anderson programs a variety of shows, some of which he also stages. They include *The Diary of Anne Frank*, *The Wobblies*, *The Admirable Crichton*, *The Stronger*, *Creditors*, *Miss Julie*, *Savages*, and *Dance on a Country Grave*. Gordon Davidson of Los Angeles' Mark Taper Forum stages Christopher Hampton's *Savages*. The last production is a musical version of Thomas Hardy's *Return of the Native*.

June 14 At Ellen Stewart's La Mama E. T. C., in New York's East Village, the season opens with *Signals* followed by such shows as *Heaven Grand in Amber Orbit*, *Godsong*, *A-Non*, *Festoons*, *The Architect and the Emperor of Assyria*, *Good Sex!*, *The Caucasian Chalk Circle*, *Lament for Rastafari*, *Hellbent for Heaven*, *The Flying Doctor*, and *Macbeth*.

June 15 *Irene*. See NY premiere, 1973.

June 17 At London's Young Vic Theatre, the National Theatre presents *Troilus and Cressida*. On July 5 the play is Slawomir Mrozek's *Emigres*. On July 26, the Hull Truck Company offers Mike Bradwell's *Bridget's House*. On Aug 5, Gawn Grainger's play, *Four To One*, has a workshop staging. Mustapha Matura's *Bread* is staged on Aug 20.

June 18 *Much Ado About Nothing*, staged by James Edmondson, opens this summer's Oregon Shakespearean Festival in Ashland's open-air Elizabethan Theatre. *Henry VI, Part 2*, staged by Jerry Turner, and *King Lear*, staged by Pat Patton, complete the three-play repertory. Indoors in the Angus Bowmer Theatre, the productions played at matinees are Hellman's *The Little Foxes*, directed by James Moll; Shaw's *The Devil's Disciple*, staged by

Michael Leibert, and *The Comedy of Errors*, directed by Will Huddleston. Delaney's *A Taste of Honey* opens in the new Black Swan Theatre, with Edmondson staging.

June 21 At London's Windmill Theatre, Paul Raymond produces *Rip Off*, described as "an erotic experience."

June 22 *Godspell*. See NY listing, 1971.

June 23 Chekhov's *Three Sisters* has a revival in the West End at the Cambridge Theatre. Director Jonathan Miller has previously tried the production out at the Yvonne Arnaud Theatre in Guildford. Janet Suzman and Angela Down are among the cast.

June 24 London's National Theatre presents a revival of Noel Coward's *Blithe Spirit* in the Lyttleton Theatre, with Harold Pinter directing. Richard Johnson and Elizabeth Spriggs are in the cast.

June 24 Joseph Papp's New York Shakespeare Festival opens in Central Park with *Henry V*, staged by Papp. Paul Rudd and Meryl Streep are in the cast. This has 28 performances, followed with 27 for John Pasquin's staging of *Measure for Measure*, with a cast including Sam Waterston, John Cazale, and Streep.

June 29 David Edgar's play, *Blood Sports*, opens at the Bush Theatre in London, staged by Dusty Hughes. Simon Callow is in the cast. Callow performs *Juvenalia*, Richard Quick's adaptation of Juvenal's writings on July 28.

June 30 At London's New End Theatre, Rainer Werner Fassbinder's *The Bitter Tears of Petra Von Kant* opens, in a translation by Robert Walker, who also directs. On Aug 17, *An Evening With Quentin Crisp* opens, with Crisp relating his experiences as a "naked civil servant."

July 1 Charles Marowitz stages Andrew Carr's *Hanratty in Hell* at the Open Space in London.

July 5 Seen first in the West End at the Savoy Theatre, the Agatha Christie mystery thriller, *Murder in the Vicarage*, now opens at the Fortune Theatre. Its total run will be 1,776 performances.

July 9 At London's Mermaid Theatre, Irish playwright Hugh Leonard presents his adaptation of plot by Eugene Labiche, *Some of My Best Friends Are Husbands*, staged by Hugh Grout. On Sep 24, Paul Copley is Hamp in this London revival of John Wilson's *For King and Country* at the Mermaid Theatre. Bernard Miles and Ron Pember direct.

July 9 *Daniel Shays Rebellion* is presented in the Pines Amphitheatre in Look Memorial Park, Northhampton, Massachusetts. Kermit Hunter is the author of this play about Western Massachusetts' revolt against the Commonweath of Massachusetts in 1786.

July 11 *Mister Lincoln*, a drama of the life of Abraham Lincoln, is directed by Don

Patterson. It is presented in the Hodgenville Amphitheatre, near Lincoln's birthplace in Kentucky.

July 14 In the Lyttleton Theatre at London's National Theatre complex, Howard Brenton's *Weapons of Happiness* is premiered. David Hare directs a cast including Frank Finlay, Michael Medwin, and Julie Covington.

July 19 Ben Travers's farce, *Banana Ridge*, is revived in the West End at the Savoy Theatre, with Robert Morley. It has 447 performances. Val May directs.

July 21 Frank Loesser's musical, *Guys and Dolls*, is revived on Broadway at the Broadway Theatre for a run of 30 weeks, staged by Billy Wilson. The entirely black cast features such performers as Ken Page and Robert Guillaume.

July 29 Randolph Umberger's drama, *The Liberty Cart*, about the development of eastern North Carolina, opens at the William R. Kenan, Jr. Memorial Amphitheatre in Kenansville, N.C.

Aug 11 Chekhov's *The Seagull* opens in revival at London's Duke of York's Theatre. Mark Woolgar directs.

Aug 16 The National Youth Theatre presents Barrie Keeffe's *Here Comes the Sun* at the Jeannetta Cochrane Theatre. Willis Hall's *Stag Night* opens on Aug 31. (The young troupe also plays at the Shaw Theatre, opening on the 18th with Peter Terson's *The Bread and Butter Trade*.)

Aug 22 This year's Edinburgh Festival welcomes New York's La Mama troupe with the Andrei Serban production of Bertolt Brecht's *The Good Woman of Setzuan*, plus two parts of Serban's admired *Trilogy*, his version of *Electra* and of *The Trojan Women*. Also programmed among the festival's mix of dance, opera, drama, and concerts are two bills of Bunraku Puppets from Japan and Rome's Gruppo Teatro Libero, with Armondo Pugliese's staging of *Masaniello*, adapted by Elvio Porta and Pugliese. Carlo and Alberto Colombaion present *The Clowns* at the Royal Lyceum Theatre. In the Assembly Hall of the Church of Scotland, Stuart Burge directs Shakespeare's *Measure for Measure* as a special Festival offering, plus Ben Jonson's *The Devil Is an Ass*. London's English Stage Company brings David Storey's *Night* to the North, with Robert Kidd directing.

Sep 9 New York's Roundabout Theatre opens its new season with Bernard Shaw's *The Philanderer*, staged by Stephen Hollis. This runs for six weeks, followed by 12 weeks of Anouilh's *The Rehearsal*, opening on Oct 14. On Dec 30, Gene Feist's production of Ibsen's *John Gabriel Borkman* opens for a run of over five weeks.

Sep 10 At the Young Vic Theatre in London, Peter Handke's *They Are Dying Out* is offered as a National Theatre workshop production. Robert Bolt's *A Man for All Seasons* is revived on Oct 21. Two Tom

Stoppard plays, *If You're Glad, I'll Be Frank* and *The Real Inspector Hound* open on Nov 23. Brandon Thomas's *Charley's Aunt* opens on Dec 30.

Sep 11 At London's Riverside Studios, Tadeusz Kantor and his Polish Circot 2 Theatre troupe present *The Dead Class*, recently seen at the Edinburgh Festival.

Sep 14 At the King's Head in London, Stewart Parker's play about the troubles in Northern Ireland, *Spokesong, or The Common Wheel*, opens almost a year after it's been seen at the Dublin Festival. Robert Gillespie stages. This will be produced later in New York at Circle in the Square.

Sep 15 Michael Weller's *Fishing* opens in London at the New End Theatre. Robert Walker plays Bill and also directs this study of what happened to the rebel youth of the 1960's.

Sep 19 In East Haddam, Connecticut, the Goodspeed Opera House is a summer haven for revivals of vintage American musicals. Its production of *Going Up*, based on James Montgomery's play *The Aviator* (seen on Broadway in 1910), with music by Louis Hirsch, opens now on Broadway at the John Golden Theatre, staged by Bill Gile. It runs only six weeks.

Sep 22 David Storey's new play *Mother's Day* opens at London's Royal Court. Staged by Robert Kidd, the cast includes Betty Marsden.

Sep 22 *Anastasia*, Marcelle Maurette's play adapted by Guy Bolton, has a revival at London's Cambridge Theatre. Nyree Dawn Porter plays the lead.

Sep 24 Kenneth Tynan's successful sex-revue, *Oh! Calcutta!* comes back to Broadway, arriving at the Edison Theatre, a "middle" playhouse, where it alternates with *Me and Bessie* until December when it displaces that show entirely. It has already been on Broadway in 1971 and after, for 610 performances. The current engagement is to prove a very long one. Only three weeks ago, the League of New York Theatres and Producers has passed a resolution condemning sex-oriented activities in the Broadway district, threatening expulsion from the League for producing such shows. On June 16, 1982, the show has its 2,410[th] performance. In the past 13 years, over 80 million admissions have been recorded.

Sep 25 George Gershwin's *Porgy and Bess*, newly staged for the Houston Grand Opera, has a Broadway opening at the Uris Theatre. There are 122 performances.

Sep 26 On Broadway, the Circle in the Square opens its new season with Stephen Porter's staging of Marguerite Duras's *Days in the Trees*, with Mildred Dunnock. On Dec 16, Tennessee Williams' *The Night of the Iguana* opens with a cast including Richard Chamberlain, Sylvia Miles, and Dorothy McGuire.

Sep 27 At the Royal Court Theatre in Lon-

don, Caryl Churchill's *Light Shining in Buckinghamshire* opens in the Theatre Upstairs, staged by Max Stafford-Clark. On Oct 20, the Upstairs show is Billy Connolly's *An' Me Wi' a Bad Leg, Tae*, staged by Stuart Mitchell.

Oct 1 In Greenwich Village at the Abbey Theatre, the Classic Stage Company (CSC) opens its season with Shaw's *Heartbreak House*, revived for three weeks and staged by Christopher Martin. He also stages the rest of the repertory, which includes Pinter's *The Homecoming*, Bond's *Bingo*, Molière's *Tartuffe*, and Genet's *The Balcony*.

Oct 4 At London's National Theatre the new open-stage Olivier Theatre opens with Marlowe's *Tamburlaine the Great, Parts 1 and 2*. Albert Finney plays the title-role, directed by the National's chief, Peter Hall.

Oct 7 Barrie Keeffe's *Scribes*, staged by Keith Hack, opens in London at the Greenwich Theatre. On Nov 4, Goldoni's *The Artful Widow* is revived, with Diane Cilento. David Thompson's translation of Moliere's *Tartuffe* opens on Dec 9, staged by Thompson. On the 27th, Max Wall animates the revue, *The Great Wall*, staged by John Link.

Oct 9 *The Robber Bridegroom*, shown on Broadway by The Acting Company in 1975, returns now, opening at the Biltmore Theatre in this John Houseman production, staged by Gerald Freedman. Barry Bostwick heads the cast. It runs for 18 weeks.

Oct 10 At their Sheridan Square Theatre, members of the Circle Repertory Company launch the new season with David Storey's *The Farm*, staged by Marshal Mason. On Nov 28, Arthur Whitney's *A Tribue to Lili Lamont* opens, directed by Mason.

Oct 13 W. Somerset Maugham's *The Circle* is revived in London at the Theatre Royal, Haymarket, for a run of 418 performances. Peter Dews directs a company including Susan Hampshire, John McCallum, and Googie Withers.

Oct 14 In New York, the Equity Library Theatre opens its season of revivals at the Master Theatre with the musical *Fiorello!* Other shows include Shaw's *Heartbreak House*, the musical *The Boys from Syracuse*, Shakespeare's *Twelfth Night*, Inge's *Come Back, Little Sheba*, the musical *Wonderful Town*, Kesselring's *Arsenic and Old Lace*, and the musical *Silk Stockings*.

Oct 19 The Chelsea Theatre Center opens its new season, divided between the Brooklyn Academy of Music and its Manhattan Westside Theatre, with Von Kleist's *The Prince of Homburg*, with Frank Langella in the title-role, directed by Robert Kalfin. On Nov 30, Saul Levitt's *Lincoln* opens in Brooklyn, directed by Carl Weber, with Fritz Weaver as the president.

Oct 20 At the Manhattan Theatre Club, Lynne Meadow has programmed a busy season, beginning with *Children*, by A. R. Gurney, Jr. Other offerings include David Rudkin's *Ashes*, Howard Barker's *Claw*, Michael Neville's *Ballymurphy*, Athol Fugard's *Boesman and Lena*, Thomas Babe's *Billy Irish*, Larry Ketron's *Quail Southwest*, Edna O'Brien's *The Gathering*, Jane Bowles' *In the Summerhouse*, and Richard Wesley's *The Last Street Play*. Musical shows include the Comden and Green Revue.

Oct 26 At London's Olivier Theatre in the National Theatre complex, the new production is Goldoni's 18th century play, *Il Campiello*, staged by Bill Bryden, who has adapted it with Susanna Graham-Jones. Comic actresses Beryl Reid and Peggy Mount are in the cast.

Oct 28 At the Marymount Manhattan Theatre, T. Edward Hambleton's Phoenix Theatre opens its season with Kevin O'Morrison's *Ladyhouse Blues*. On Nov 25, the offering is a double-bill of Joanna Glass's *Canadian Gothic* and *American Modern*, staged by Daniel Freudenberger. Jonathan Levy's *Marco Polo* opens on Dec 26, staged by Lynne Meadow.

Nov 3 Mustapha Matura's Caribbean drama, *Rum an' Coca-Cola*, opens in London at the Royal Court Theatre, staged by Donald Howarth.

Nov 5 In New York, the Off-off Broadway Mabou Mines troupe offers Samuel Beckett's *Cascando*, staged by JoAnne Akalaitis.

Nov 8 At London's Hampstead Theatre, Adrian Mitchell's dramatization of John Berger's *A Seventh Man* has its premiere, in a staging by Roland Rees. On Dec 2, Nancy Meckler offers her staging of Pam Gems' feminist play, *Dusa, Fish, Stas and Vi*.

Nov 9 Thomas Bernard's German text for *Force of Habit* is translated by Neville and Stephen Plaice and staged by Elijah Moshinksy for the Lyttleton stage of London's National Theatre.

Nov 12 The National Theatre of Greece, under the artistic direction of Alexis Minotis, comes to New York's City Center with a repertory of two classics in modern Greek: Sophocles's *Oedipus at Colonus* and Aristophanes's *The Knights*. Minotis plays Oedipus and stages. Alexis Solomos directs the comedy.

Nov 16 Eire's Abbey Theatre comes to the Brooklyn Academy of Music for two weeks with its production of Sean O'Casey's *The Plough and the Stars*, staged by Tomas MacAnna. There are also eight performances of *In My Father's Time*, a one-man show by Eamon Kelly.

Nov 17 France's Theatre National Populaire presents Roger Planchon's production of Molière's *Tartuffe* on the Lyttleton stage of London's National Theatre. Planchon plays the title-role. Patrice

Chereau's staging of Marivaux's *La Dispute* opens on the 23rd.

Nov 18 *The Ghost Train*, Arnold Ridley's vintage thriller, is revived at London's Old Vic Theatre. Bill Hays directs.

Nov 20 The Prospect Theatre Company offers its revival of Turgenev's *A Month in the Country* in London at the Albery Theatre. Toby Robertson directs Dorothy Tutin, Derek Jacobi, and Jane Lapotaire among others. On the 27th, directors Robertson and Tim West show E. M. Forster's *A Room with a View*, adapted from the novel by Richard Cottrell and Lance Sieveking.

Dec 5 At the Theatre de Lys, the Negro Ensemble Company opens its New York season with Charles Fuller's *The Brownsville Raid*, which has a run of 112 performances. Israel Hicks directs a cast including Douglas Turner Ward.

Dec 6 Edward Albee's *Counting the Ways*, a "vaudeville" seen first at the Hartford Stage, Connecticut, now opens in London in the Olivier Theatre of the National Theatre complex. Bill Bryden directs the cast of two: Michael Gough and Beryl Reid.

Dec 7 At London's Royal Court Theatre, the Pip Simmons Theatre Group presents their musical production of Bram Stoker's *Dracula*. Simmons stages. The show has had its premiere in Rotterdam at the Piccolo Theatre in 1974.

Dec 9 John O'Keeffe's 18th century tale, *Wild Oats*, is revived in London at the RSC's Aldwych Theatre, with Alan Howard. Clifford Williams stages this popular revival.

Dec 13 It is the traditional time for Christmas pantomimes in London. Today, the Theatre Royal, Stratford East, leads off with *Old King Cole*. Ken Campbell has devised this entertainment, staged by Clare Venables. On Dec 15 at the *Criterion*, Ned Sherin and Caryl Brahms offer their version of the Cinderella story, *I Gotta Shoe*. At the Mermaid, the show is a musical, *The Point*, opening on the 16th. On the 18th, Lindsay Kemp presents *Mr. Punch's Pantomime* at the Round House. On the same day, Rod Hull's *Emu in Pantoland* opens at the Shaftesbury Theatre, with Irene Handl in the cast. At Her Majesty's Theatre on the 20th, *Toad of Toad Hall* opens. *Cinderella* opens on Dec 21 at the London Palladium. On Dec 27, at the Greenwich, the show is *The Great Wall*, a revue with Max Wall. The holiday favorite, Brandon Thomas's *Charley's Aunt*, is revived on the 30th at the Young Vic Theatre.

Dec 28 The musical *Fiddler on the Roof* is revived at New York's Winter Garden with Zero Mostel recreating his role as Tevye.

PAUL ROBESON

standing in comedy roles but also appeared in classics and modern dramas at the Old Vic, and Stratford-on-Avon, as well as in the West End.

March 16 Scenic designer and theatre architecture consultant Jo Mielziner (b. 1901) dies. Winner of 5 Tonys, Mielziner designed for scores of Broadway shows, including such successes as *Death of a Salesman* and *The King and I*. He wrote *Designing for the Theatre* (1965) and *The Shapes of our Theatre* (1970).

April 2 Actor Paul Ford (b. 1901) dies. Ford was known chiefly for comic roles (*Thurber Carnival*) but he was also a capable serious actor, playing Charlie in *Death of a Salesman*. He was frequently seen in films and on television.

April 17 Allardyce Nicoll, theatre historian specializing in British drama, dies at 81. A professor at various universities, including Yale, Nicoll edited *Shakespeare Survey* from its first issue until 1965. Among his works are *Masks, Mimes, and Miracles* and *A History of English Drama* (6 vols.). Nicoll was a lifetime Trustee of the Shakespeare Birthplace, among other honors.

May Denise Pelletier (b. 1928) dies. One of the rare bilingual actresses in Canada, she acted with all the major Quebec theatre companies and at the Stratford Shakespeare Festival of Canada. In 1967 she was awarded the Medal of Confederation and in 1970 the Order of Canada.

May 2 Alfred Harbage, distinguished Shakespeare scholar, dies at 74. A professor of English literature at Harvard, Dr. Harbage edited *The Pelican Shakespeare* and wrote such works as *As They Liked It* and *Theatre for Shakespeare*.

1976 BIRTHS/DEATHS/DEBUTS

Jan 12 Dame Agatha Christie, the prolific writer of mystery novels and plays, is dead at age 85, but her drama, *The Mousetrap*, is still the longest-running play in theatre history.

Jan 13 English actress Margaret Leighton (b. 1922), O. B. E., dies at 53. She played many Shakespearean roles at the Old Vic, Stratford-upon-Avon, and the Chichester Festival. She was also popular with West End and Broadway audiences. In 1962, she won a Tony for her portrayal of Hannah Jelkes in Tennessee Williams' *The Night of the Iguana*.

Jan 23 Actor-singer Paul Robeson (b. 1898) dies. He won acclaim in serious roles such as Jones in Eugene O'Neill's *The Emperor Jones*. His interpretation of *Othello*, with 295 performances, had the longest run of any American Shakespeare production. A spokesman for equal rights for all disenfranchised peoples, Robeson's public statements were criticized during the McCarthy Era in the early 1950's. In 1952, he won the Stalin Peace Prize.

Feb 3 Actor Roger Livesey (b. 1906) dies. He played in the West End, on Broadway, and on tour. He was also well known as a film and TV actor, Colonel Blimp being one of his most memorable characterizations.

Feb 5 Actress Ethel Shutta (b. 1896) dies. She made her debut at five doing a cakewalk at the Academy of Music. Performing in revues such as *The Passing Show* and *Ziegfeld Follies*, she also toured as a band vocalist, a dancer, and cabaret artist. She appeared in *Follies* in 1971.

Feb 11 Actor Lee J. Cobb (b. 1911) dies. His portrayal of Willy Loman in Arthur Miller's *Death of a Salesman* in the 1948-1949 Broadway season was a high point in his career. In later years, he worked mostly on the West Coast in films and television. He played *King Lear* at Lincoln Center in the Vivian Beaumont Theatre in the 1960's.

Feb 12 Actor Sal Mineo, 37, is murdered in Los Angeles.

Feb 18 Actor-director-producer Eddie Dowling (b. 1894) dies. A veteran of vaudeville, revues, and musicals, he wrote music, lyrics, and show-books. In 1945 he produced, directed and acted in *The Glass Menagerie*. He was president of the USO in World War II.

Feb 21 Actress Frieda Inescourt (b. 1901) dies. After a British debut, she appeared in several sophisticated comedies on Broadway. In 1935, she began a career in motion-pictures.

Feb 22 Actress Angela Baddeley (b. 1904) dies. Holder of the C. B. E., she was out-

May 27 Actress Ruth McDevitt (b. 1895) dies. A favorite in comedy roles, she appeared in several productions of *Arsenic and Old Lace* and *Harvey*. She was often seen in films and on TV.

June 6 Dame Sybil Thorndike (b. 1882) dies. Made a Dame of the British Empire in 1931, she was created Companion of Honor in 1970. She made her debut in 1904. She later toured the U.S. with Shakespearean repertory. In a long career of major roles, she appeared often at the Old Vic, toured as far as Australia, and when possible played opposite her husband, Sir Lewis Casson.

June 14 The British actress, Margaret Bannerman, dies at age 83.

Aug 17 American actor William Redfield (b. 1927) dies in New York.

Aug 19 At age 75, Alistair Sim passes on, having won fame on the English stage and in films.

Sep 24 Actor Romney Brent dies at 74.

Oct 14 The distinguished British actress, Dame Edith Evans, dies at 88.

Dec 10 American novelist-playwright Saul Bellow is awarded the Nobel Prize for Literature.

August The Berkshire Playhouse is placed on America's National Register of Historic Places. Designed by Stanford White in 1887 as the Stockbridge Casino, the building was spared demolition in 1928 when it was moved to land donated by sculptor Daniel Chester French—after being purchased for $1—and opened by Eva LeGallienne.

Aug 31 The League of New York Theatres and Producers passes a resolution threatening dismissal to any member who produces a play that "shall be antithetical to the programs of the League seeking to upgrade the physical appearance of the theatrical district . . ." The resolution also reaffirms the League's determination to stamp out sex-related businesses in the district, such as massage parlors, topless bars, and pornographic cinemas. Despite this, *Let My People Come* has opened already on Broadway at the Morosco Theatre, and *Oh! Calcutta!* will open at the Edison Theatre, with no League action taken.

Sep 29 The Brooklyn Academy of Music (BAM) Theatre Company is incorporated. Frank Dunlop is to be the artistic director.

Oct The touring company of Peter Shaffer's drama *Equus* has been having difficulties finding a theatre in Dallas because authorities will not permit performance of the play's nude scene. Finally, Fort Worth's Will Rogers Auditorium is made available to the production.

1976   THEATERS/PRODUCTIONS

Jan 4 This week Broadway records its first $2 million gross at the box-office.

Jan 4 *Home Sweet Homer* becomes a one-night failure on Broadway, after an original production at Washington, D.C.'s Kennedy Center, and a tour, and loses its $1.2 million investment.

Feb 7 In Philadelphia, the newly refurbished Shubert Theatre, acquired in 1972 by the Academy of Music, re-opens with a revival of *My Fair Lady*.

Feb 21 London's Apollo Theatre celebrates its 75th anniversary.

March 16 After many delays, the first of three theatres—the Lyttleton—opens in the new National Theatre complex on the South Bank of London's Thames. Designed by Sir Denys Lasdun, with special technology by Theatre Projects, it is an intimate, conventional proscenium theatre. *Hamlet* is the inaugural production.

April 10 In a time of high production costs, necessitating long runs to recoup the initial investment, *A Matter of Gravity* has done very well at the close of its Broadway run. With an investment of $160,000, the show has cleared a profit of $350,000. This is more a tribue to the drawing-power of its star, Katharine Hepburn, than to the show's text, by Enid Bagnold.

May 17 The Al Ringling Theatre, a Rapp-designed playhouse in Baraboo, Wisconsin, is placed on the National Register of Historic Places. Designed to reproduce at 1/3 scale the historic opera house in the Palace at Versailles, the theatre will be restored to its handsome original appearance during 1978–1980.

May 31 On the last day of the current Broadway season, some productions have repaid their initial investment, qualifying them as hits by *Variety's* financial rule-of-thumb. *A Chorus Line*, *Travesties*, *A Matter of Gravity*, and *Very Good Eddie* are the fortunate four.

June 1 With the 1975-76 Broadway season now closed, the tally of productions stands at 65. Otis Guernsey, Jr., lists 10 plays, three specialties, 13 musicals, three revues, 28 revivals, seven foreign plays in English, and one play in a foreign tongue. The Broadway gross is nearly $71 million, contrasted with a previous high mark of $59 million in 1967-68. Touring companies have grossed $52.6 million. Top ticket price for a Broadway musical is now $17.50. Off-Broadway there have been 76 productions, among them 26 plays, 29 revivals, three revues, six musicals, seven specialties, three foreign plays in English, and one in a foreign language. Ella Malin's annual summary of regional productions lists 453 stagings of 368 plays offered by 46 groups in 79 venues in 44 cities, five of them in Canada; 217 have been American plays, with 181 in full production. Shakespeare remains the most popular playwright, with 39 stagings of 22 plays.

Guernsey, Jr., picks the ten "Best Plays." This year they include Freeman's *Jesse and the Bandit Queen*, Weidman/Sondheim's *Pacific Overtures*, Fosse/Ebb/Kander's *Chicago*, Stoppard's *Travesties*, Ayckbourn's *The Norman Conquests*, Feiffer's *Knock Knock*, Rabe's *Streamers*, Wilson's *Serenading Louie*, Babe's *Rebel Women*, and Stitt's *The Runner Stumbles*.

June 28 New York producer David Merrick and investors are estimated to have lost $360,000 on *The Red Devil Battery Sign*.

Oct 25 Queen Elizabeth II formally opens the new National Theatre complex on the South Bank of the Thames in London. Sir Denys Lasdun is the architect. There are three theatres in the complex, the Lyttleton (proscenium arch stage, with 890 seats); the Olivier (open-stage, with 1,160 seats in amphitheatre conformation); and the Cottesloe (flexible rectangular room, with two tiers of galleries on three sides and possible for as many as 400 seats).

Nov 13 The new Citadel Theatre complex in Edmonton, Alberta, Canada opens with Artistic Director John Neville's production of *Romeo and Juliet*. The new $6.5 million complex includes the 684-seat Shoctor Theatre, the 208-seat Rice Theatre, and the 270-seat Zeidler Hall (a movie-theatre).

BROOKLYN ACADEMY OF MUSIC EXTERIOR

Jan 9 *Nightclub Cantata* (NY—Top of the Gate—Revue). Elizabeth Swados creates, directs, and plays in this musical revue which earns 145 performances.

Jan 11 *Dirty Linen/New Found Land.* See L premiere, 1976.

Feb 2 *Otherwise Engaged.* See L premiere, 1975.

Feb 10 *A Party With Betty Comden and Adolph Green* (NY—Morosco—Revue). Comden and Green perform songs they've written for hit shows in this intimate revue which runs for three months. A similar revue with the same title was seen in the 1958–1959 season.

Feb 16 *American Buffalo* (NY—Ethel Barrymore—Drama). Robert Duvall, Kenneth McMillan, and John Savage play a gang of inept thieves in David Mamet's drama. Although chosen as a "Best Play," it has only 135 performances. It's been previously seen in Chicago and at New York's St. Clement's Theatre on Jan 26, 1976. It will be produced in London on June 28, 1978, on the National Theatre's Cottesloe stage.

March 24 *Lily Tomlin in "Appearing Nitely"* (NY—Biltmore—Revue). The popular TV and film character actress presents her one-woman show of sketches and impressions for 84 performances.

March 27 *Cold Storage* (NY—American Place—Drama). Martin Balsam and Paul Sparer play cancer victims, each trying to accept fate in different ways, in Ronald Ribman's play, which plays for six weeks. On Dec 29, it opens at Broadway's Lyceum Theatre and runs for nearly 23 weeks. In this cast, Balsam and Len Cariou are directed by Frank Corsaro.

April 17 *I Love My Wife* (NY—Ethel Barrymore—Musical). There are 872 performances of this Michael Stewart musical, based on a French farce about wife-swapping. Cy Coleman writes the score. Gene Saks directs a cast including Lenny Baker and Joanna Gleason. Saks also directs a different cast in a London production at the Prince of Wales's Theatre which opens on Oct 6. It has 410 performances.

April 18 *Side by Side by Sondheim.* See L premiere, 1976.

April 21 *Annie* (NY—Alvin—Musical). Andrea McArdle plays Annie, the young orphan adopted by rich Daddy Warbucks (Reid Shelton) in Thomas Meehan's "Best Play" book based on Harold Gray's comic-strip, *Little Orphan Annie.* Dorothy Loudon plays Miss Hannigan. Martin Charnin stages and writes the lyrics, with score by Charles Strouse. The show runs into the 1980's. McArdle repeats her role in the London production at the Victoria Palace, which opens on May 3, 1978. By January 1, 1980, it had run for 695 performances.

May 11 *Vieux Carré* (NY—St. James—Drama). There are only seven performances of Tennessee Williams's new play, set in New Orleans. Sylvia Sidney plays an inquisitive landlady. Arthur Allan Seidelman stages. Sidney repeats her role in a Nottingham Playhouse production that opens at London's Piccadilly Theatre on Aug 15, 1978. It has 118 performances.

May 21 *Gemini* (NY—Little—Drama). Robert Picardo plays a young Harvard student unsure of his sexual orientation in Albert Innaurato's play, which has 1,789 performances. Peter Mark Schifter stages. Transferring from the Circle Repertory, the play has previously been seen at Playwrights' Horizons and the PAF Playhouse, Long Island.

May 31 *Beatlemania* (NY—Winter Garden—Revue). Randy Clark, Reed Kailing, P. M. Howard, and Bobby Taylor recreate the music of the Beatles in this rock concert which has 920 performances. Jules Fisher stages. A different cast, directed by Robert Mitchell, opens in a London production at the Astoria on Oct 18, 1979.

Sep 27 *Miss Margarida's Way* (NY—Ambassador—Drama). Estelle Parsons is in the cast of Roberto Athayde's play about a sexually repressed schoolteacher. It has 98 performances. Athayde directs. It has been previously seen at the Public Theatre; it tours, and it will be given other productions in many countries.

Sep 28 *The Passion of Dracula* (NY—Cherry Lane—Drama). Bob Hall and David Richmond have based their new play on Bram Stoker's old thriller. It's been seen initially at the George Street Playhouse in New Brunswick, New Jersey. Off-Broadway, staged by Peter Bennett, it proves a rapid cult-success running for 714 performances, providing an inexpensive alternative to Frank Langella's Broadway *Dracula.* Christopher Bernau plays the Transylvanian vampire count. Designers of the modest show are Hall, Allen Cornell, and Jane Tschetter. In London it opens at the Queen's Theatre on Aug 23, 1978, staged by Clifford Williams. American film-actor George Chakiris plays Dracula, with Roy Dotrice as Ven Helsing, scourge of vampires. There are 165 performances.

Oct 6 *The Gin Game* (NY—John Golden—Drama). D. L. Coburn wins the Pulitzer Prize, a "Best Play" citation, and 517 performances for this two-handed drama about the lonely inhabitants of a senior citizens' home. Mike Nichols directs the play, previously seen at regional theatres in California, Kentucky, and Connecticut. Jessica Tandy and Hume Cronyn repeat their roles in the London Lyric Theatre production which opens July 21, 1979.

THE GIN GAME

It runs for only eight weeks.

Oct 13 *The Night of the Tribades* (NY—Helen Hayes—Drama). Max Von Sydow, Bibi Anderson, and Eileen Atkins have only 12 performances in Per Olov Enquist's tense drama, a conflict between Swedish dramatist August Strindberg and his first wife. Michael Kahn directs. The play has been previously shown at Princeton's McCarter Theatre.

Oct 20 *A Life in the Theatre* (NY—Theatre de Lys—Comedy). David Mamet's "Best Play" about a rising young actor (Peter Evans) and a failing star (Ellis Rabb) runs for nine months. Gerald Gutierrez stages. It has been previously seen at Chicago's Goodman Theatre.

Oct 29 *The Act* (NY—Majestic—Revue). Liza Minelli wins 240 performances in this concert-type musical, which presents her as a Las Vegas star reliving some of her struggles to reach the top. The book is by George Furth; songs, by John Kander and Fred Ebb; staging, by Martin Scorsese.

Nov 14 *Golda* (NY—Morosco—Drama). Anne Bancroft plays Golda Meir, in William Gibson's documentary drama about Israel's former prime minister. Arthur Penn directs the 13-week run.

Nov 16 *The Merchant* (NY—Plymouth—Drama). There are just five performances for this world premiere of Arnold Wesker's new play, a modern-day view of Shakespeare's Shylock, in *The Merchant of Venice.* John Clements, Joe Leon, and Roberta Maxwell head the cast. John Dexter directs.

Dec 4 *Chapter Two* (NY—Imperial—Drama). Neil Simon's play, about a widower's painful adjustment to a new love, has 857 performances. Herbert Ross directs a cast including Judd Hirsch, Anita Gillette, and Cliff Gorman. It is chosen as a "Best Play."

Feb 22 *Privates on Parade* (L—Aldwych—Drama). Denis Quilley impersonates Marlene Dietrich in his role as leader of a British entertainment unit sent to divert the troops in wartime in Southeast Asia, in Peter Nichols's play. Michael Blakemore directs. On Feb 8, 1978, it transfers to the West End's Piccadilly Theatre, earning 208 performances. Jim Dale will play Dietrich when New Haven's Long Wharf produces the show later.

March 16 *Bedroom Farce* (L—Lyttleton—Comedy). Peter Hall directs Alan Ayckbourn's farce about the sexual havoc created by one couple among their married friends. On Nov 7, 1978, it moves to the Prince of Wales's Theatre in the West End for a run of 370 performances. The cast, which includes Michael Gough and Joan Hickson, opens at Broadway's Brooks Atkinson on March 29, 1979, for 278 performances. It is chosen as a "Best Play."

March 23 *Stevie* (L—Vaudeville—Drama). Glenda Jackson plays Stevie Smith in Hugh Whitemore's play based on the poet's life with her aunt (Mona Washbourne). Clifford Williams directs.

March 25 *In the Red* (L—Whitehall—Comedy). William Douglas Home's domestic comedy is directed by Allan Davis. Dinah Sheridan and Gerald Harper are among the cast.

April 13 *Sextet* (L—Criterion—Comedy). Julia Lockwood and Leslie Phillips head the cast of Michael Pertwee's new comedy, staged by Robin Midgley.

April 20 *Just Between Ourselves* (L—Queen's—Comedy). Two wives are driven to distraction by their husbands' passion for cars in Alan Ayckbourn's family comedy, directed by Alan Strachan. Colin Blakely and Rosemary Leach are among the cast.

May 4 *The Kingfisher* (L—Lyric—Comedy). Alan Webb plays a tart butler, too attached to his aging employer (Ralph Richardson) to suffer his twilight flirtation with an old love (Celia Johnson), in William Douglas Home's play. Lindsay Anderson directs both the London and the New York production, which opens Dec 6, 1978 at the Biltmore. Rex Harrison and Claudette Colbert have a 23-week run.

May 11 *Rolls Hyphen Royce* (L—Shaftesbury—Comedy). William Douglas Home's third play to bow in the West End this season has a cast including Wilfrid Hyde White and Peter Egan. Allan Davis directs.

May 16 *Lionel!* (L—New London—Musical). The life and music of composer Lionel Bart (*Oliver!*) is brought to the stage, with Todd Carty as Li and Avis Bunnage as Ma. John Wells writes the book; Gillian Gregory stages.

May 18 *State of Revolution* (L—Lyttelton—Drama). Robert Bolt's new play shows the Bolsheviks planning establishment of the new Soviet state. Michael Bryant plays Lenin; Sara Kestelman, Kollontai; Terence Rigby, Stalin. Christopher Morahan stages. Ralph Koltai and David Hersey design.

June 22 *Women Behind Bars* (L—Whitehall—Comedy). Tom Eyen's Off-off-Broadway parody of Grade B films about women in prison is staged by Ron Link, with the American female impersonator Divine as Matron.

July 4 *Cause Celebre* (L—Her Majesty's—Drama). Glynis Johns plays a woman who murders her husband with the help of her lover, in Terence Rattigan's play based on a real-life trial. First seen at the Haymarket, Leicester, it has a run of 277 performances. Robin Midgley directs.

July 27 *The Bells of Hell* (L—Garrick—Comedy). Tony Britton heads the cast of John Mortimer's new play, directed by John Tydeman.

Aug 10 *Once a Catholic* (L—Royal Court—Comedy). Mary O'Malley's play about life in a Catholic girls' school opens in Sloane Square, then on Oct 4 transfers to Wyndham's Theatre in the West End where it has 851 performances. On Oct 10, 1979, it opens at Broadway's Helen Hayes Theatre, but despite a cast headed by Rachel Roberts it has only six performances.

Sep 7 *The Old Country* (L—Queen's—Comedy). Alec Guinness and Rachel Kempson play the leading roles in Alan Bennett's comedy, which has 371 performances. Clifford Williams directs.

Sep 21 *A Murder is Announced* (L—Vaudeville—Drama). Dulcie Gray plays the spinster sleuth Miss Marple, in Leslie Darbon's adaptation of Agatha Christie's mystery thriller. It earns 429 performances. Robert Chetwyn directs.

Sep 28 *Bubbling Brown Sugar.* See NY premiere, 1976.

Oct 12 *Maggie* (L—Shaftesbury—Musical). Anna Neagle, Anna Sharkey (Maggie), and Peter Gale (John) head the cast of Michael Wild's musical adaptation of James Barrie's *What Every Woman Knows*, about a political aspirant and the clever woman behind him. Tom Hawkes directs.

Nov 2 *Filumena* (L—Lyric—Comedy). Joan Plowright plays the long-time mistress of Soriano (Colin Blakely), who longs for the respectability of marriage and a father for her three sons, in Keith Waterhouse and Willis Hall's adaptation of Eduardo De Filippo's Neapolitan comedy. It has 711 performances. Franco Zeffirelli directs.

Nov 15 *Shut Your Eyes and Think of England* (L—Apollo—Comedy). The title of Anthony Marriott and John Chapman's comedy offers traditional Victorian advice to young English brides, faced with their husband's marital demands. Patrick Garland directs a cast including Donald Sinden. There are 525 performances.

Nov 28 *Elvis* (L—Astoria—Musical). Ray Cooney presents this multi-media entertainment he's devised with Jack Good, P. J. Proby, Shakin' Stevens, and Timothy Whitnall.

1977   REVIVALS/REPERTORIES

Jan 4 In Edinburgh at the Traverse Theatre, *The Art of the Clown*, by Annie Stainer and Reg Bolton, launches the new year of productions, some of them by visiting troupes. There are 35 programs. Among the shows are Michael Almaz's *Letters from K*, Marcella Evaristi's *Dorothy and the Bitch*, David Pownall's *Motocar*, John Anderson's *Hag*, Drew Griffiths's *Age of Consent*, George Byatt's *Kong Lives*, Ian Brown's *New Reekie*, Pete Atkin's *A & R*, Billy Connolly's *When Hair Was Long and Time Was Short*, C. P. Taylor's *Peter Pan and Emily*, and Barry Keeffe's *A Mad World My Masters.*

Jan 5 At the Royal Court's Theatre Upstairs, in London, Joannesburg's Workshop '71 presents *Uhlanga (The Reed)*, with James Mthoba. On Jan 13, John Kani and Winston Ntshona appear in Athol Fugard's *Sizwe Bansi Is Dead*. On the 27th, Caryl Churchill's *Traps* bows, in a staging by John Ashford. Tunde Ikoli's *Short Sleeves in the Summer* opens on Feb 23, staged by Michael Joyce. On April 4, Anna Calder-Marshall performs in *For All Those Who Get Despondent*, a Brecht-Wedekind cabaret. Tim Fywell and John Chapman devise and direct *I Made It, Ma—Top of the World!*, opening on April 14. Michael Hastings's *For the West* opens on May 11. Nicholas Wright directs. On June 15, *The Winter Dancers*, by David Lan, has Ian Kellgren for director. Nigel Baldwin's *Sudlow's Dawn* bows on Aug 17, staged by Tim Fywell. Amy Cesaire's monologue, *Return To My Native Land*, performed by Cy Grant, opens on Oct 31, followed by Heathcote Williams's *Playpen* on Nov 22, in a Gerald Chapman staging. Peter Farago directs *The Kreutzer Sonata*, based on Tolstoi's tale, on Dec 31.

Jan 12 At his Greenwich Village Public

Theatre, producer Joseph Papp opens John Guare's *Marco Polo Sings a Solo*, staged by Mel Shapiro. On Jan 25, David Rudkin's *Ashes* opens. This runs 21 weeks and is chosen as a "Best Play." On March 8, Ernest Joselovitz's *Hagar's Children* begins a run of ten weeks, staged by Robert Graham Small. This has been seen earlier in Denver and San Francisco. David Langston Smyrl's musical, *On the Lock-In*, staged by Robert Macbeth of the New Lafayette Theatre in Harlem, opens on April 14 for a run of two months. On the 15th, a Strindberg double-bill of *Creditors* and *The Stronger* opens for a run of seven weeks. On Sep 27, an ambitious program of 14 productions opens with Roberto Athayde's *Miss Margarida's Way*, starring Estelle Parsons for 30 performances. This will move to Broadway. John Guare's *Landscape of the Body* has a two-month run, staged by John Pasquin, with a cast including Shirley Knight. Molière's *The Misanthrope*, set to music, also runs for two months, staged by Bill Gile. This opens Oct 5, followed on Nov 18 by Paul Sills's improvisations on *Tales of the Hasidim*, which runs for 20 performances. On Dec 6, Wallace Shawn's version of Machiavelli's *The Mandrake* opens for a five-month run, staged by Wilford Leach. On Dec 1, Ntozake Shange's *A Photograph* begins its 62 performances, staged by Oz Scott. Joseph Chaikin's staging of S. Ansky's *The Dybbuk* opens on Dec 6 also for 62 showings. David Mamet's *The Water Engine* opens on Dec 20, staged by Steven Schachter. It bows briefly on Broadway. On Dec 27, Thomas Babe's *A Prayer for My Daughter* opens, staged by Robert Allan Ackerman. This is selected as a "Best Play." It runs for four months.

Jan 13 At the Marymount Manhattan Theatre, the Phoenix Theatre's season continues with Peter Handke's *A Sorrow Beyond Dreams*, translated by Ralph Manheim and adapted and staged by Daniel Freudenberger. Len Cariou plays Handke. This has 30 performances, followed on April 7 by 12 for David Berry's *G. R. Point*, a Vietnam tragedy. Tony Giordano stages. Barrie Keeffe's *Scribes* opens on May 26 for 12 performances, staged by Keith Hack.

Jan 14 At the Yale Repertory Theatre in New Haven, Christopher Durang's parody of David Rabe's anti-Vietnam War plays, *The Vietnamization of New Jersey: an American Tragedy*, has its world premiere, staged by Walt Jones. On the 28th, Yale presents *The Durango Flash* by William Hauptman. On April 15, Poland's distinguished director, Andrzej Wajda, stages the American premiere of Tadeusz Rosewicz's *White Marriage*.

Jan 17 Terence Rattigan's *Separate Tables* is revived in London at the Apollo Theatre. Michael Blakemore directs a cast including John Mills and Jill Bennett.

Jan 18 At the Brooklyn Academy of Music, the Chelsea Theatre Center opens S. I. Witkiewicz's *The Crazy Locomotive* for 29 performances, split between BAM and the troupe's Manhattan theatre. Des McAnuff directs. On March 8, Michael Feingold's adaptation of the Brecht-Weill-Lane *Happy End* opens for a seven-week run before transferring to Broadway, at the Martin Beck Theatre. Michael Posnick and Patricia Birch stage the work. The run is just over nine weeks.

Jan 22 Continuing under the artistic direction of Giles Havergal, the Glasgow Citizens' Theatre begins its new year with *The Country Wife*, followed by *The Importance of Being Earnest*, *Figaro*, *Chinchilla*, *Semi-Monde*, *Vautrin*, *Loot*, and *Mother Goose*.

Jan 23 *My Life*, Corrine Jacker's new play, opens on Sheridan Square in Circle Repertory's Greenwich Village theatre, staged by Marshall Mason for a four-week run. In the cast are Christopher Reeve and William Hurt, among others. This is followed with 63 showings of Albert Innaurato's *Gemini*, a production just played on Long Island at the PAF Playhouse. Staged by Peter Mark Schifter, it transfers to Broadway's Little Theatre for an extended run. On May 10, James Joyce's *Exiles* is revived for 36 performances, directed by Rob Thirkield. Patrick Meyers's *Feedlot* opens on Oct 13, in a Terry Schreiber mounting. It runs six weeks as does Innaurato's *Ulysses in Traction*, opening Dec 8 in a Mason staging.

Jan 25 Jeff Wanshel's *Isadora Duncan Sleeps with the Russian Navy* continues the New York season of the American Place Theatre. It has a four-week run, staged by Tom Haas. On Feb 14, Jules Feiffer's satiric revue, *Jules Feiffer's Hold Me!*, opens for a run of 100 performances, at the Chelsea Westside Cabaret Theatre.

Jan 25 *German Skerries*, a play by Robert Holman, opens at London's Bush Theatre, staged by Chris Parr. Snoo Wilson's *Vampire* strikes on March 10, staged by Dusty Hughes. On April 12, the play is *Blisters*, devised by Sarah Pia Anderson and Sheila Kelley. Tina Brown's *Happy Yellow* opens on May 19.

Jan 26 Ödön von Horvath's play, *Tales From the Vienna Woods*, translated by Christopher Hampton, opens on the Olivier stage of the National Theatre in a staging by Maximilian Schell. Stephen Rea and Paul Rogers are among the cast. On March 22, John Gielgud plays Caesar in the National's revival of *Julius Caesar*. Cinema director John Schlesinger stages. On April 26, the play is Jonson's *Volpone*, revived by director Peter Hall, with Paul Scofield and Gielgud in the leading roles. William Gaskill directs a revival of Harley Granville Barker's *The Madras House*, on June 22. Ronald Pickup, Paul Scofield, Rogers, and Elspeth March head the cast. Sean O'Casey's *The Plough and*

the *Stars* opens on Sep 20, staged by Bill Bryden. Susan Fleetwood and Cyril Cusak are among the cast. Wycherley's Restoration comedy, *The Country Wife*, is staged by Peter Hall and Stewart Trotter on Nov 16. Albert Finney plays the lead.

Feb 1 Barrie Keeffe's *Gimme Shelter*, composed of three one-act plays, *Gem*, *Gotcha!*, and *Getaway*, opens in London at the Soho Poly Theatre, staged by Keith Washington. On Dec 10, 1978, it has a two-week run at the Brooklyn Academy of Music, staged by Des McAnuff.

Feb 3 At the Greenwich Theatre in London, *The Sons of Oedipus*, David Thompson's translation of Euripides' drama, opens with Siobhan McKenna as Jocasta. Thompson directs. *Twelfth Night* follows on March 10. Mike Ockrent stages a revival of Barrie's *The Admirable Crichton* on April 14. Thompson stages John Willet's translation of Bertolt Brecht's *The Good Person of Szechwan* on May 23. On June 23 John Bowen's *Singles* opens. On Sep 29, Barrie Keeffe's *Barbarians* is staged by Keith Hack. Paul Joyce directs Harold Pinter's *The Caretaker* on Oct 20, with Max Wall in the title-role. Keith Hack stages Strindberg's *The Father* on Nov 17, with Patrick Allen and Vivien Merchant. John Tydeman directs Richard O'Keefe's *Pinch-Me-Not* on Dec 14.

Feb 16 George Bernard Shaw's *The Devil's Disciple* is a belated tribute by the Dublin Gate Theatre to the American Bicentennial, celebrated in 1976. Other shows produced this year include Shakespeare's *The Merchant of Venice*, Shaffer's *Equus*, and Shaw's *Major Barbara*.

Feb 17 In the Vivian Beaumont Theatre in New York's Lincoln Center, Joseph Papp opens a revival of Chekhov's *The Cherry Orchard*, in staging by Andrei Serban. Irene Worth is Ranevskaya, supported by a cast including Raul Julia and Meryl Streep. The production runs for two months. It is revived on June 29 for a six-week run. On May 18, Serban and Elizabeth Swados rework Aeschylus's *Agamemnon* in Greek and English as a primitive ritual. It runs five weeks.

Feb 23 At the Young Vic in London, the National Youth Theatre offers its production of *Romeo and Juliet*. On March 4, Denise Coffey stages a revival of James Bridie's *Tobias and the Angel*. Barrie Keeffe's *A Mad World My Masters* opens on May 1, staged by Max Stafford-Clark and William Gaskill. On May 31, Tom Stoppard's *Rosencrantz and Guildenstern* is revived, followed by the return of a Stoppard double-bill of *The Real Inspector Hound* and *If You're Glad, I'll Be Frank* on June 4. On Sep 30, Ken Campbell's *Henry Pilk's Awesome World* opens, followed on Oct 4 by Denise Coffey's staging of *Romeo and Juliet*, with Paul Jones and Natasha Pyne. On Oct 13, Frank Dunlop offers the extended version of Molière's *Scapin*. On Nov 3, Dunlop opens his production of *The Taming of the Shrew*. Coffey directs a revival of Wilde's *The Importance of Being Earnest* for a Dec 22 opening. Just seven days before, the Actors' Company has opened its production of the play at the Round House.

Feb 24 At the Royal Court Theatre, Tony Bicat's *Devil's Island* bows on the main stage, directed by David Hare. Last month, the show has been played in Cardiff, Wales. Simon Callow is among the cast. On March 22, Barrie Keeffe's *Gimme Shelter*, presented at the Soho Poly, moves to the Court. Sam Shepard's *Curse of the Starving Class* opens on April 21, staged by Nancy Meckler. Also on the Court's main stage is Howard Barker's *Fair Slaughter*, opening on June 13, staged by Stuart Burge, with Max Wall. On Aug 10, Mary O'Malley's *Once a Catholic* bows, directed by Mike Ockrent. It transfers to the West End for a long run on Oct 4, though its life on Broadway, opening Oct 10, 1979, will be brief. On Sep 12, a new musical, seen Upstairs in a workshop, opens: C. P. Lee's *Sleak*.

Feb 24 Rex Harrison and Elizabeth Ashley open at the Palace Theatre on Broadway in a revival of George Bernard Shaw's *Caesar and Cleopatra*, seen earlier at the John F. Kennedy Center in Washington, D. C. Ellis Rabb stages. It has just 12 performances.

March 2 At London's Mermaid Theatre, the new play is Terence Frisby's *It's All Right If I Do It*, with John Stride and Prunella Scales. Robert Chetwyn directs. The play has been produced in Leicester at the Haymarket Theatre. On April 27, Cole Porter's songs are saluted in *Oh! Mr. Porter*, devised by Benny Green and staged by Wendy Toye. Among the performers are Kenneth Nelson and Una Stubbs. On Sep 12, Willy Russell's *Breezeblock Park* is directed by Alan Dossor, with a cast including Wendy Craig. This play has been produced in 1975 at the Everyman Theatre in Liverpool, and it later transfers to the West End. On Oct 13 Bernard Miles directs the translation he's made with Vivian Cox of Henri de Montherlant's *La Ville dont le Prince est un Enfant*. They call it *The Fire That Consumes*. Nigel Hawthorne and David William play two abbés.

March 3 Maxim Gorky's *Summerfolk*, adapted by Peter Stein and Botho Strauss, comes from Berlin's Schaubühne am Halleschen Ufer to the Lyttelton stage of London's National Theatre.

March 4 In Richmond, Virginia, at the Virginia Museum Theatre, Keith Fowler stages the world premiere of Romulus Linney's play about Lord Byron, and his daughter: *Childe Byron*. It will later be seen Off-Broadway at Circle Repertory.

March 4 The Cottesloe Theatre, the newest and smallest of the National Theatre's three stages, is inaugurated with *Illumi-*

natus, adapted by Ken Campbell and Chris Langham from the book by Robert Shea and Robert Anton Wilson. The production is the work of the Science Fiction Theatre of Liverpool. On April 5, the play is Stephen Poliakoff's *Strawberry Fields*, staged by Michael Apted with Jane Asher. On the 21st, *The Passion*, a selection of plays from the York Cycle of mystery plays, is offered, staged by Bill Bryden and Sebastian Graham-Jones. On May 9, the life of Ramsay MacDonald is turned into a musical called *Sell-Out*, by Tom Kempinski and Roger Smith. David Scase directs. On June 9, director Michael Kustow unveils *To Those Born Later*, a collage of Bertolt Brecht's songs and poems, animated by Asher and Gawn Grainger, among others. On July 16, Bill Bryden directs his own script, *Old Movies*, with E. G. Marshall. On July 11, Chris Harris performs his one-man show, *Kemp's Jig*. Ben Kingsley performs Barry Collins' monologue, *Judgement*, on Aug 11. On Aug 14, Michael Hastings' *For the West* opens. On Aug 25, Shane Connaughton's *Sir Is Winning* opens in a staging by Christopher Morahan. On Nov 10, John MacKendrick's *Lavender Blue* opens with Susan Fleetwood and Derek Thompson. Sebastian Graham-Jones directs. On the 17th, Julian Mitchell's *Half-Life* is presented in Waris Hussein's production, with Paul Rogers and John Gielgud. On Dec 5, David Pownall's double-bill of *Motocar* and *Richard III, Part Two* opens, staged by Bettina Reeves.

March 7 *Starting Here, Starting Now*, a revue with music by David Shire and lyrics by Richard Maltby, Jr., opens at New York's Barbarann Theatre restaurant. It runs for 15 weeks.

March 10 Adela Holzer, producer of *Hair* and other Broadway successes, presents *Monsters* Off-Broadway at the Astor Place Theatre. This is a double-bill of William Dews' *Side Show* and Albert Innaurato's *The Transfiguration of Benno Blimpie*, staged by Robert Drivas. James Coco plays the blimp-fat Benno, with Rosemary DeAngelis as his mother. The show runs two months.

March 11 *A History of the American Film* opens at Connecticut's Hartford Stage. Christopher Durang's parody of American film and image-making has a cast including Jeff Brooks and Jerry Zaks. Paul Weidner stages. The Mark Taper Forum in Los Angeles and the Arena Stage in Washington, D. C. also produce the play this season. Later it will be briefly seen on Broadway at the ANTA.

March 15 The Roundabout Theatre continues its current New York season with Samuel Beckett's *Endgame*, staged by producing director Gene Feist. It has a ten-week run. Kilty's *Dear Liar*, staged by the adaptor, opens on April 28 for a run of 55 performances. Kilty plays Bernard Shaw, with Deann Mears as Mrs. Patrick

CHAPTER II

Campbell.

March 17 On Broadway, the Circle-in-the-Square offers a revival of *Romeo and Juliet*, staged by Theodore Mann, with Paul Rudd and Pamela Payton-Wright. It runs nearly ten weeks, followed on June 16 by Wilde's *The Importance of Being Earnest*, which lasts for more than 13 weeks, staged by Stephen Porter. On Sep 6, a new season of four revivals opens with Stephen Porter's staging of Molière's *Tartuffe*, with John Wood in the title-role. The show runs 11 weeks, followed on Dec 15 by a three-month run for George Bernard Shaw's *Saint Joan*, staged by John Clark, with Lynn Redgrave.

March 18 *Paper Wheat* opens at the 25th Street House in Sintaluta, Saskatchewan. A collective creation, it tours other provincial towns before a cross-country tour financed by Canada Council.

March 18 Harvey Lichtenstein, director of the Brooklyn Academy of Music, has asked Frank Dunlop to form a BAM Theatre Company. The brief inaugural season opens with revivals of Langdon Mitchell's 1906 social comedy, *The New York Idea*, and Chekhov's *Three Sisters*. The shows have 28 and 24 performances, respectively. Both are staged by Dunlop. Among the ensemble members are Rosemary Harris, Ellen Burstyn, Blythe Danner, and Denholm Elliott.

April 12 At Stratford-upon-Avon, the Royal Shakespeare Company season opens with Trevor Nunn's production of *Macbeth* with Ian McKellen and Judi Dench. John Napier designs, as he does for *A Midsummer Night's Dream*, staged by John Barton and Gillian Lynne. In Terry Hands' productions of *Henry VI, Parts 1, 2, & 3* and *Henry V*, Alan Howard plays both King Henrys. Nunn stages *As You Like It*, with Peter McEnery and Kate Nelligan. Hands directs *Coriolanus*, with Howard.

437

April 14 Eugene O'Neill's *Anna Christie* is revived at the Imperial Theatre on Broadway for a run of almost four months. Liv Ullmann plays the title-role. Jose Quintero directs.

April 20 Le Treteau de Paris brings a French production of Jean Giraudoux's *La Guerre de Troie N'Aura Pas Lieu (Tiger at the Gates)* to New York's City Center for a limited two-week run. Jean-Pierre Aumont plays Ulysse.

April 22 At the Open Space in London, Robert Walker directs the play he's adapted from a Nathaniel West story, *A Cool Million*. On May 17, the new Open Space is opened, with Charles Marowitz's *Variations on the Merchant of Venice*, staged by Marowitz.

April 24 David Rabe's *The Basic Training of Pavlo Hummel* is revived on Broadway at the Longacre Theatre. Al Pacino plays the title-role in this production first mounted by the Theatre Company of Boston. David Wheeler directs. The show lasts more than 13 weeks.

April 27 Charles Ludlam and his Ridiculous Theatrical Company tackle Richard Wagner's *Ring* cycle Off-Broadway at the Truck and Warehouse Theatre. Called *Der Ring Gott Farblonjet*, the musical is both a summary of the narrative and a collage of sexual shocks and modern clichés. It has a run of ten weeks.

May 2 The Royal Shakespeare Company begins a revival of several productions first seen at Stratford-upon-Avon in 1976 at its London home, the Aldwych Theatre. Trevor Nunn's staging of *King Lear* with Donald Sinden is the first production. On June 21, *The Comedy of Errors* is shown. Roger Rees and Judi Dench are among the cast directed by Nunn. *A Midsummer Night's Dream*, staged by John Barton and Gillian Lynne, follows on June 25. John Barton's staging of *Much Ado About Nothing* opens on the 29th. Judi Dench is Beatrice, with Donald Sinden as Benedick. On July 5, Nunn's staging of *Romeo and Juliet* opens, with Ian McKellen and Francesca Annis. On Sep 15, there's a Stratford production of *Troilus and Cressida* staged by Barry Kyle. Mike Gwylim and Francesca Annis play the title-roles.

May 2 Yul Brynner returns to Broadway in Rodgers and Hammerstein's *The King and I*, opening at the Uris Theatre for a run of 696 performances. Constance Towers plays Anna.

May 2 Peter Barnes adapts Ben Jonson's comedy, *The Devil Is an Ass*, for the Birmingham Repertory Theatre, which now presents it on the Lyttelton stage of the National Theatre in London. Stuart Burge directs, with the aid of Barnes. Among the players are Anna Calder-Marshall and Derek Godfrey. On May 5, the Lyttelton revives Shakespeare's *Measure for Measure* in a staging by Stuart Burge with the visiting Birmingham Repertory Com-

pany.

May 4 At London's Old Vic Theatre, the Prospect Theatre Company revives George Bernard Shaw's *Saint Joan*, with Eileen Atkins as the Maid. John Dove directs. On May 25, *War Music*, based on Homer's *Iliad* by Christopher Logue, opens. Barbara Jefford is Thetis, with Timothy West as the Storyteller. Toby Robertson directs. On the 27th, the company offers *Hamlet*, also staged by Robertson, with Derek Jacobi. On July 4, there's a revival of John Dryden's poetic tragedy, *All for Love, or, The World Well Lost*, with John Turner and Barbara Jefford as Antony and Cleopatra. Frank Hauser directs. On July 11, Welcome Msomi's *Umabatha*, from South Africa, is presented. On Sep 12, the State Theatre of Northern Greece opens with Euripides' *Medea*, translated by Minos Volonakis. This is followed on the 14th by a revue called *Buster*, a Prospect Theatre production, staged by Toby Robertson, featuring Max Wall and Jan Waters. On the 19th, the Nottingham Playhouse imports its production of Adrian Mitchell's musical, *White Suit Blues*. Richard Eyre directs. On Nov 16, the Prospect Theatre Company reclaims the stage with Shakespeare's *Antony and Cleopatra*, staged by Toby Robertson. Alec McCowen and Dorothy Tutin play the title-roles. Derek Jacobi is Octavius Caesar.

May 9 St. George's Elizabethan Theatre, in North London, offers Shakespeare's *The Merchant of Venice*, staged by Joseph O'Conor. On June 8, Don Taylor directs *Measure for Measure*. Alan Dobie is Angelo. On July 6, the theatre's artistic director, George Murcell, plays Claudius to Dobie's Hamlet. Dobie directs *The Merry Wives of Windsor*, on Aug 2.

May 10 At the Chichester Festival, the annual summer season is launched with N. C. Hunter's *Waters of the Moon*, featuring Ingrid Bergman, Wendy Hiller, and Paul Hardwick. John Clements directs. Shaw's *The Apple Cart* is staged by Patrick Garland. Keith Michell, the festival's artistic director, plays King Magnus. Peter Dews directs *Julius Caesar*. A revue, *In Order of Appearance*, offers a pageant of British royalty to salute the Queen's Jubilee. Michell directs, having compiled the material with Wally K. Daly.

May 12 David Edgar's drama, *Destiny*, opens in London at the Aldwych Theatre, a presentation of the Royal Shakespeare Company. Ron Daniels stages. This has been shown first in Stratford at The Other Place. On Aug 1, John Barton stages Ibsen's *Pillars of the Community* with Ian McKellen and Judi Dench among the cast. Bertolt Brecht's *The Days of the Commune* is revived on Nov 4. Howard Davies directs. Among the players are Mike Gwylim and McKellen. Finally, on Dec 14, Peter Barnes adapts Ben Jonson's comedy *The Alchemist*. Trevor Nunn directs. Roger Rees is Ananias. This production also comes from The Other Place.

May 13 *Man and Superman* opens the Shaw Festival at Canada's Niagara-on-the-Lake. Tony Van Bridge directs. Michael Meacham stages *The Millionairess*. Heath Lamberts directs *The Great Catherine*. Ben Travers' *Thark* is a Meacham staging.

May 19 At the Royal Shakespeare Company's Other Place in Stratford-upon-Avon the season of experimental productions opens with Ben Jonson's *The Alchemist*. John Ford's *'Tis Pity She's a Whore*, Paul Thompson's *The Lorenzaccio Story*, Pam Gems' *Queen Christina*, and David Rudkin's *The Sons of Light* follow.

May 19 Joseph Kesselring's classic American comedy, *Arsenic and Old Lace*, is revived in London at the Whitehall Theatre, with Barbara Mullen and Joyce Heron.

May 22 Robert Wilson's new conceptual-theatre work, *I Was Sitting on My Patio This Guy Appeared I Thought I was Hallucinating*, opens Off-Broadway at the Cherry Lane Theatre for a limited engagement of nine performances. Wilson directs with his co-performer Lucinda Childs. On June 5, 1978, the piece opens at London's Royal Court Theatre.

May 30 The Shakespeare season opens in London's Regent's Park at the Open Air Theatre. Today, it's *Love's Labour's Lost*, staged by David Conville. On June 15, Coville presents *Henry V*.

May 31 In San Diego at the Old Globe Theatre, producing director Craig Noel presents another season of the National Shakespeare Festival, opening with *Hamlet*, staged by Jack O'Brien. It plays in repertory with *The Taming of the Shrew*, directed by Laird Williamson, and *Timon of Athens*, staged by Eric Christmas. In the nearby Carter Center Stage venue, the festival offers Wayne Brian's staging of Brandon Thomas's *Charley's Aunt*, which runs for 11 weeks.

June 2 *The 2nd Greatest Entertainer in the Whole Wide World*, Dick Shawn's one-man show as a seedy performer determined not to give up, opens at New York's Promenade. It has a ten-week run.

June 2 At Ellen Stewart's La Mama E. T. C. in New York's East Village, production continues into the new season with Wilford Leach's *Between the Wars*, performed by the Manhattan Project. The same night, Ken Bernard's *The Sixty Minute Queer Show* opens, staged by John Vaccaro. On June 4, Tom O'Horgan stages Camus's *Caligula*. On Oct 6, Tisa Chang's Pan Asian Repertory offers *The Legend of Wu Chang*. Spiderwoman Theatre presents *The Lysistrata Numbah!* on Oct 20. Tsao Yu's *Thunderstorm* opens on Nov 3. On Dec 9, *The Seven Deadly Elements* is presented.

June 6 Canada's Stratford Festival opens under the artistic direction of Robin Phillips. His production of *A Midsummer Night's Dream* from last season is revived. *All's Well That Ends Well* is staged by David Jones. Phillips directs *Richard III*, with Brian Bedford. Marigold Charlesworth directs *Much Ado About Nothing*. Phillips's production of *As You Like It* stars Maggie Smith. *Romeo and Juliet* is staged by David William. Arif Hasnain stages Ibsen's *Ghosts*. Strindberg's *Miss Julie* is directed by Eric Steiner. Phillips directs Molnar's *The Guardsman*, with Bedford and Smith. Noel Coward's *Hay Fever* is also a Phillips staging.

June 7 At London's Bush Theatre, Eric Bentley's *Are You Now Or Have You Ever Been . . . ?*, a docu-drama of American HUAC hearings, opens in Anton Rodgers's staging. Kurt Vonnegut, Jr., the American author, is represented on June 28 with *Happy Birthday, Wanda June*, seen first in Greenwich Village. Dusty Hughes directs.

June 8 Keith Baxter repeats his role of King, first played by him in Vienna's English Theatre, in Tennessee Williams's *The Red Devil Battery Sign* at London's Roundhouse. Baxter co-directs with David Leland. This transfers to the Phoenix Theater. The Joint Stock Company offers Howard Brenton's *Epsom Downs* on Aug 4, staged by Max Starford-Clark. Simon Callow is in the ensemble. The National Youth Theatre presents Peter Terson's double-bill, *Family Ties: Wrong First Time* and *Never Right, Yet Again*. It opens Aug 18, staged by Derek Seaton.

June 13 Tennessee Williams's *The Glass Menagerie*, produced by the Cambridge Theatre Company, opens in London at the Shaw Theatre with Maxine Audley. Jonathan Lynn directs. The National Youth Theatre presents Barrie Keeffe's *Up the Truncheon* on Aug 17.

June 13 Nuria Espert brings her company from Spain to the Lyttelton stage of London's National Theatre. They present the Valle Inclan drama, *Divinas Palabras*, staged by Victor Garcia.

June 15 Henrik Ibsen's *Hedda Gabler* is given new life by Janet Suzman in the title-role, directed by Keith Hack in this revival in London at the Duke of York's Theatre.

June 16 At Playwrights' Horizons on Theatre Row on New York's West 42nd Street, artistic director Robert Moss presents a program of new plays. Martin Sherman's *Cracks* leads off the new season. Larry Carpenter directs. Len Jenkin's *Gogol* follows, staged by David Schweizer. Sam Shepard's *Angel City* is next, directed by Marty Kapell. Ann Commire's *Shay* is staged by Elinor Renfield, followed by Ted Tally's *Hooters*, directed by Gary Pearle.

June 17 In Ashland, the Oregon Shakespearean Festival opens with Michael Addison's staging of *The Merchant of Venice* in the open-air Elizabethan Theatre, followed by *Henry VI, Part 3*, staged by Pat Patton, and *Antony and Cleopatra*, directed by Robert Loper, each production having 33 performances. Indoors in the Angus Bowmer Theatre, the productions are Williams's *A Streetcar Named Desire*, *Measure for Measure*, and Sheridan's *The Rivals*. The ensemble includes James Edmondson and Christine Healy.

June 23 George Bernard Shaw's *Candida* is revived at the Albery Theatre in the West End. Michael Blakemore directs, with Deborah Kerr in the title-role. A revival of Frederick Lonsdale's *On Approval*, with Kenneth More, directed by Frith Banbury, opens June 28 at the Vaudeville Theatre.

June 28 Financially pressed for a summer season, the New York Shakespeare Festival revives two recent Vivian Beaumont Theatre successes at the Delacorte in Central Park. The Brecht-Weill *Threepenny Opera* opens this non-Shakespearean season, in Richard Foreman's staging. It has 27 performances, followed by Aeschylus' *Agamemnon*, staged by Andrei Serban for a run of three weeks.

July 19 Hugh Leonard's *Da* opens in London at the King's Head Theatre, with Eamonn Kelly as Da and Tony Doyle as Charlie Now. Robert Gillespie directs. This Irish nostalgia excites little attention. Only after its 1978 New York Hudson Guild showcase will it become a "Best Play" and a Broadway hit. Its world premiere was in 1973, unheralded in Olney, Maryland.

July 28 To match the Stratford experimental theatre, The Other Place, the Royal Shakespeare Company now opens a London performance space, the Warehouse, Covent Garden, with Howard Barker's *That Good Between Us*, directed by Barry Kyle. On Aug 3, the play is *Bandits*, by C. P. Taylor, staged by Howard Davies. On Aug 9, the troupe opens Edward Bond's *Bingo*, produced first at The Other Place. Davies directs this vision of Shakespeare's last bitter years in Stratford. Bertolt Brecht's *Schweyck in the Second World War* opens on Aug 12, also staged by Davies. On Sep 13, Trevor Nunn's production of *Macbeth*, premiered in Stratford at The Other Place in 1976, opens. Ian McKellen and Judi Dench are the Macbeths. James Robson's *Factory Birds* opens on Nov 1, staged by Bill Alexander. Howard Davies directs Edward Bond's play, *The Bundle*, on Dec 13. Barry Keeffe's *Frozen Assets* opens on Dec 20, staged by Barry Kyle.

Aug 16 George Bernard Shaw's *Man and Superman* is revived in London at the Savoy Theatre, in a Clifford Williams staging. The cast includes Richard Pasco and Susan Hampshire.

Aug 21 This is the thirtieth annual Edinburgh Festival, with an impressive program of dance, opera, drama, and concerts scheduled. Among the theatre troupes and productions is the Stuttgart State Theatre, with Heinrich von Kleist's *Das Kaetchen von Heilbronn*, staged by Claus Peymann. Minos Volanakis stages Euripides' *Medea* with the ensemble of the State Theatre of Northern Greece. Comedian Max Wall appears in *Buster*, a mini-musical about Buster Keaton, staged by Toby Robertson, who also directs several productions for the Prospect Theatre Company: Shakespeare's *Hamlet* with Derek Jacobi, *Antony and Cleopatra* with Alec McCowen and Dorothy Tutin, and *War Music*—Christopher Logue's version of Homer's *Iliad*. Frank Hauser's production of John Dryden's *All for Love* has Barbara Jefford in the cast. Richard Eyre directs two shows for the Nottingham Playhouse Company: Adrian Mitchell's *White Suit Blues* and Stephen Lowe's *Touched*. Trevor Peacock plays Mark Twain in the first drama. Julie Harris repeats her American success as Emily Dickinson, in William Luce's *The Belle of Amherst*, also presented under Nottingham's banner.

Sep 6 The tiny Off-off Broadway Quaigh Theatre in midtown Manhattan opens a revival of Elmer Rice's *Counsellor-at-Law*. Will Lieberson directs. It runs two months.

Sep 13 At London's Hampstead Theatre Club, Mark Long presents his one-man show, *Pictorial Smash*. On Oct 3, the play is an American script by Jonathan Ringkamp called *The Dog Ran Away*. Michael Rudman directs Denis Lawson, Manning Redwood, and Robert Flemyng in the roles of three religious brothers. American playwright Bernard Pomerance's play, written in Britain, *The Elephant Man*, opens on Nov 7, staged by Roland Rees. David Schofield plays John Merrick. The play later receives a noteworthy New York workshop production, culminating in a long run on Broadway.

Sep 15 *Man of La Mancha* returns to Broadway at the Palace Theatre for a run of almost four months. Richard Kiley recreates his roles of Don Quixote and Cervantes.

Sep 19 Lawrence Taubman stages three American plays at London's New End. Corinne Jacker's *Harry Outside* opens the run. Tom Cole's *Medal of Honor Rag* follows on Nov 1. Terrence McNally's *And Things That Go Bump in the Night* opens Dec 6.

Sep 19 Samuel Beckett's *Happy Days*, with Peggy Ashcroft, is revived at London's Lyttelton Theatre on Sep 19. Peter Hall directs. This is followed on Oct 18 by John Mortimer's translation of Georges Feydeau's farce, here called *The Lady from Maxim's*, in a staging by Christopher Morahan. The large cast includes Michael Bryant and Sara Kestleman. On Dec 8, the new production is an animation of a 14th century poem, *Sir Gawain and the Green Knight*, staged by Michael Bogdanov.

Oct 4 Mabou Mines, an alternative, mixed-media performance group, presents Samuel Beckett's tale, *The Lost Ones*, at Joseph Papp's Public Theatre in Greenwich Village. Lee Breuer adapts and directs. Thom Cathcart creates a miniature city of cliff-dwellings with tiny figures which will be used to narrate the story. Binoculars are loaned to the audience, the better to observe the mini-drama. Philip Glass composes and performs a musical score for the performance. David Warrilow and Lynn Spano help animate the show. Three days before this premiere, the troupe's *Dressed Like an Egg*, devised by JoAnne Akalaitis, has had its opening at the Public Theatre. It is based on writings of the French novelist Colette. On Nov 19, the troupe presents *The Shaggy Dog Animation*, devised by Breuer and animated by Ruth Maleczech, Clover Breuer, Linda Wolfe, Terry O'Reilly, and others.

Oct 5 Tom O'Horgan restages his 1968 production of *Hair* for this Broadway revival at the Biltmore Theatre. It runs just over five weeks.

Oct 5 Craig Anderson, artistic director of the Off-off Broadway Hudson Guild Theatre, opens the new season with Christopher Hampton's British play, *Treats*, for a three-week run. Michael Montel stages this American premiere with a cast including John Glover and Suzanne Lederer. On Nov 23, Anderson directs the world premiere of George Sibbald's *The Dodge Boys*, which also has a three-week limited run.

Oct 6 This is the 25th anniversary of New York's Phoenix Theatre. To celebrate, the season is opened with a musical by Jim Wann and Bland Simpson, *Hot Grog*. Edward Berkeley directs the three-week run. On Nov 17, an O'Neill Center script, Wendy Wasserstein's *Uncommon Women and Others*, opens for a 22-performance run, directed by Steven Robman. Jack Gilhooley's *The Elusive Angel* opens on Dec 22, staged by Robman. This has a three-week run. The shows are all produced at the Marymount Manhattan Theatre.

Oct 13 At the Performing Garage in New York's Soho, Richard Schechner's Performance Group opens its new environmental production of Seneca's *Oedipus*, adapted by Ted Hughes. Audiences sit in steeply tiered seats, like a miniature medical operating theatre. In the center of the arena is a mound of dirt, in which players mold faces, dig holes, and even bury themselves. Schechner directs. The production runs two months.

Oct 13 New York's Off-off Broadway actors' showcase, the Equity Library Theatre (ELT), opens its season of revivals with Edward Mabley's *Glad Tidings*, followed by the musical *Carnival*, Arthur Miller's *The Crucible*, the musical *Allegro*, Ted Tiller's *Count Dracula*, the musical *Gay Divorce*, Shakespeare's *The*

Taming of the Shrew, and the musical *Company*.

Oct 17 Sam Shepard's American play, *Suicide in B Flat*, opens at London's Open Space, produced by the Wakefield Tricycle Company. Kenneth Chubb directs. Colin Bucksey stages Howard Schuman's *Censored Scenes from King Kong* on Nov 28.

Oct 18 At the Brooklyn Academy of Music (BAM), the Chelsea Theatre Center opens its season—split between Brooklyn and its Manhattan Westside Theatre—with Mustapha Matura's Trinidadian drama, *Rum an' Coca Cola*, staged by Donald Howarth for a five-week run. Robert Montgomery and Mel Marvin write a musical, *Green Pond*, which opens on Nov 22 for a run of four weeks. David Chambers directs.

Oct 19 Henrik Ibsen's *Rosmersholm* is revived in this Clifford Williams production, opening at the Haymarket, London. Claire Bloom and Daniel Massey head the cast.

Oct 20 Bram Stoker's *Dracula*, in the Hamilton Deane-John Balderston dramatization, returns to the Broadway stage in a haunting design concept devised by Edward Gorey. Frank Langella achieves a major success as Dracula. This production has been seen on much smaller scale in Nantucket, Massachusetts. Dennis Rosa directs. The show has a run of 925 performances. The production sparks a spate of Dracula films and parodies.

Oct 26 The Manhattan Theatre Club opens its new season with Peter Nichols's *Chez Nous*, staged by artistic director Lynne Meadow, with a cast including Sam Waterston and Christina Pickles. It has 28 performances. Samuel Beckett's *Play and Other Plays* has a four-week run. Alan Schneider stages.

Oct 27 At the Duke of York's Theatre in London, director Hugh Goldie revives J. B. Priestly's *Laburnam Grove*.

Nov 7 George Bernard Shaw's *The Apple Cart* is revived in London at the Phoenix Theatre, with Keith Michell and Penelope Keith. Patrick Garland directs. This is last summer's Chichester Festival production.

Nov 22 Dublin's Abbey Theatre comes to London's Royal Court Theatre with Patrick Mason's staging of Thomas Kilroy's *Talbot's Box*, seen earlier at the Dublin Theatre Festival this year.

Nov 23 *Jesus Christ Superstar*, the rock musical by Tim Rice and Andrew Lloyd Webber, returns to Broadway at the Longacre Theatre, in a road-show production for a three-month run. William Daniel Grey, who plays Jesus, directs.

Nov 25 In their new quarters on Theatre Row on West 42nd Street, the Lion Theatre presents *K*, a visually striking adaptation of Franz Kafka's *The Trial*. Garland Wright directs and designs, with John

ZERO MOSTEL

Arnone and David James co-designing.

Nov 26 At New York's St. Mark's Playhouse, the Negro Ensemble Company opens its new season with Gus Edwards' *The Offering*, directed by Douglas Turner Ward, who also plays the lead. It has a broken run of 59 performances, followed by Edwards' *Black Body Blues*, also staged by Ward and with Ward in the cast. This show has 40 performances, opening in repertory with the first drama on Jan 19, 1978.

Nov 30 At London's Round House, the Actors' Company presents Edward Petherbridge's *Do You Love Me?*, drawn from the writings of R. D. Laing. Petherbridge directs.

Nov 30 The Dolphin Theatre Company gets an early start on London's holiday theatre business with *A Right Christmas Caper*, Willis Hall's play for children, at the Shaw Theatre, staged by Brian Rawlinson. On Dec 15, the Theatre Royal, Stratford East, offers Martin Duncan's *The Amusing Spectacle of Cinderella and Her Naughty-Naughty Sisters*. On the same day, at the Round House, the Actors' Company opens Wilde's *The Importance of Being Earnest*, also produced at the Young Vic, opening there on the 22nd. On Dec 19, the Cambridge Theatre presents *Toad of Toad Hall*, and *Hans Andersen* opens at the London Palladium, with rock star Tommy Steele. At the Royal Court on Dec 20, the show is John McGrath's *The Trembling Giant*. On the 21st, Barrie's *Peter Pan* is revived at the London Casino; Susannah York is Peter. At the Mermaid, *The Point*, based on a TV program, is the holiday treat.

Dec 21 Lionel Bart's internationally successful musical, *Oliver!*, based on Charles Dickens's novel, *Oliver Twist*, is revived in the West End at the Albery Theatre, with Roy Hudd as Fagin. Robin Midgley and Larry Oaks direct. By Jan 1, 1980, the show will have had 846 performances and still be running.

Dec 21 Richard Foreman's Ontological-Hysteric Theatre, an Off-off Broadway ensemble, presents the new production, written, designed, and directed by Foreman. It runs for 11 weeks, with the title of *Blvd. de Paris (I've Got the Shakes)* or *Torture on a Train (Brain-Mechanisms of the Redistributed French Virgin)* or *Certainly Not (A Tortuous Train of Thought)*.

Dec 28 Eugene O'Neill's *A Touch of the Poet* is revived on Broadway at the Helen Hayes Theatre, staged by Jose Quintero, with a cast including Jason Robards, Milo O'Shea, and Geraldine Fitzgerald. It runs nearly 18 weeks.

1977 BIRTHS/DEATHS/DEBUTS

March 8 The American actor Henry Hull dies at 86.

May 22 Actress-singer Ethel Barrymore Colt (b. 1912) is dead. Daughter of Ethel Barrymore, Colt made her professional debut in *Scarlet Sister Mary* at the Ethel Barrymore Theatre in 1930. In recent years she had gained recognition in her one-woman show, *Curtains Up.*

Aug 3 Actor-director Alfred Lunt (b. 1892) is dead. With his wife, actress Lynn Fontanne, Lunt appeared in *Reunion in Vienna, Design for Living, Amphitryon 38,* and *O Mistress Mine,* among many others. The Lunts' last stage appearance was in Friedrich Duerrenmatt's *The Visit.*

Aug 14 George Oppenheimer, drama critic for Long Island's *Newsday* in recent years, dies today at 77. He also wrote for the stage and for films.

Sep 1 Ethel Waters, dynamic American musical star, dies today at age 80. She's remembered for her work in *Cabin in the Sky* and *A Member of the Wedding.*

Sep 8 Stage and screen actor Zero Mostel (b. 1915) dies on tour. Mostel made his Broadway debut in a vaudeville production of *Keep 'Em Laughing* in 1942. He is best remembered for his roles as Leopold Bloom in *Ulysses in Nighttown,* Prologus in *A Funny Thing Happened on the Way to the Forum,* and Tevye in *Fiddler on the Roof.*

Sep 24 The American stage-lighting designer H. R. Poindexter dies at 41.

Sep 25 British actress Phyllis Neilson-Terry dies at 84.

Dec 18 Comic actor and director Cyril Ritchard, known to both British and American audiences, dies at 79.

Dec 25 The famed stage and cinema comedian Charles Chaplin dies now at 88 years in Switzerland.

1977 THEATERS/PRODUCTIONS

Feb 12 In Ashland, the Oregon Shakespeare Festival opens its third theatre, the Black Swan, designed by festival designer Richard L. Hay. The theatre is intended for experimental and intimate productions. *A Taste of Honey,* staged by James Edmondson, is the premiere production.

Feb 22 Results of Dr. William Baumol's survey, made during the Fall 1975 strike of Broadway musicians, are published today by the League of New York Theatres and Producers as *The Impact of the Broadway Theatre on the Economy of New York City.* In the season preceding the strike, for instance, gross annual revenue for the commercial theatre was $57 million. The theatres themselves pay out $43 million directly in salaries, materials, services, and rents. In addition, those who visit the theatres spend $45 million annually on restaurants, $10.3 million on taxis, $4.3 million on parking, and $2.5 million on hotels, shopping, etc., for those on theatre tours. New York City receives direct tax payments from this activity amounting to at least $5.7 million. Baumol notes that a dollar spent on theatre or related activity in New York can mean 90 cents injected into the economy outside the city. Theatre's direct contribution to New York is $104 million annually at present. With ancillary expenditures, the total is $168 million. Direct theatre contributions to the U.S. economy are $110 million, with a total contribution of $275 million.

March 20 Fifty playwrights form the Guild of Canadian Playwrights to encourage standardization of contract rights across Canada.

April 14 Tonight, after a year-long restoration, the Empire Theatre (1911) reopens in Richmond, Virginia. The theatre has been purchased, rehabilitated, and made available to the community by a private developer.

May 26 This is opening night for *Scribes.* It's also the last time that the NY *Times's* scribe, drama critic Clive Barnes, will be reviewing a play for that newspaper. He is to be succeeded by Richard Eder. Walter Kerr remains as Sunday NY *Times* drama critic. Barnes moves on to the NY *Post.*

May 31 This is the last day of the 1976–1977 Broadway season. New productions which have paid off their initial investments include *California Suite, Sly Fox, Godspell, I Love My Wife, Annie, Your Arms Too Short To Box With God, No Man's Land, Dirty Linen & New-Found-Land, Otherwise Engaged, Porgy and Bess, Fiddler on the Roof, Anna Christie, The King and I, The Basic Training of Pavlo Hummel,* and *Mark Twain Tonight!* Fiddler has now returned 1,308 percent on its original investment.

June There is to be no American Shakespeare Festival in Stratford, Connecticut.

June 1 Today marks the opening of the new theatre season in New York. In that just closed, there have been on Broadway 65 new productions, including 17 plays, two revues, six musicals, 17 revivals, 11 specialties, eight foreign plays in English, and four in foreign tongues. *Variety* reports the Broadway gross as more than $93 million, nearly 32% higher than last year's record. Road shows have earned nearly $83 million, for a total of $176 million. *Fiddler on the Roof* top ticket price is now $20, but the increased revenue comes largely from increased audiences, up nearly 23% over last season. The Duffy Square TKTS booth has shown 3/4 million cut-rate tickets this season. Two big-budget musicals, *The Baker's Wife* and *Hellzapoppin,* have closed before reaching Broadway, both with losses over $1 million. Off-Broadway there have been 87 productions, including 22 plays, five revues, nine musicals, three specialties, 34 revivals, 11 foreign plays in English, and three in foreign tongues. For American regional theatres, Ella Malin's compilation of statistics reveals 517 productions of 387 plays by 55 groups in 85 theatres in 49 cities, eight of them in Canada. Shakespeare is the most popular playwright, with 46 productions.

The ten "Best Plays" are Gelbart's *Sly Fox,* Rudkin's *Ashes,* Meehan/Charnin/Strouse's *Annie,* Simon's *California Suite,* Jones' *The Last Meeting of the Knights of the White Magnolia* and *The Oldest Living Graduate,* Griffiths' *Comedians,* Gray's *Otherwise Engaged,* Mamet's *American Buffalo,* and Cristofer's *The Shadow Box.*

July 19 Tonight is the official opening of the renovated 1926 Orpheum Theatre on Market Street in San Francisco.

Sept Young People's Theatre in Toronto, Canada, opens its new home in a Victorian building. $1.8 million has been spent on renovation.

Nov 9 *Variety* publishes a report on a Broadway controversy under the headline: "Liza's Lip-Synch in *The Act* Shocks Purists." Liza Minelli does sing most of her songs live, but the act of miming to pre-recorded singing is especially galling to those theatregoers who object to paying the $25 top ticket price this show is charging.

Nov 25 Breaking records for length of run for a drama, Agatha Christie's *The Mousetrap* today has its 25th birthday in London.

Jan 18 *My Astonishing Self* (NY—Astor Place—Reading). Michael Voysey's adaptation from the writings of George Bernard Shaw features Donal Donnelly in this one-man show, which runs six weeks.

Jan 19 *Paul Robeson* (NY—Lunt-Fontanne—Drama). James Earl Jones is Robeson in this one-man show by Phillip Hayes Dean. There are 45 performances before it moves to the Booth, playing in repertory with *For Colored Girls* until April 30. In London, there are only 28 showings, following its premiere at her Majesty's on July 27. Jones again plays Robeson.

Feb 1 *By Strouse* (NY—Ballroom—Revue). The music is by Charles Strouse; the lyrics are by Lee Adams and Martin Charnin. Gary Beach and Gail Nelson are among the cast of this intimate Soho cabaret, which runs nearly five months.

Feb 19 *On the Twentieth Century* (NY—St. James—Musical). Betty Comden and Adolph Green have devised lyrics and a book, based on earlier plays by Bruce Milholland, Ben Hecht, and Charles MacArthur. Madeline Kahn is featured as a glamorous star conned by an impressario into one of his production schemes. There are 453 performances.

Feb 26 *Deathtrap* (NY—Music Box—Drama). Ira Levin's thriller about a playwright who does away with his wife is chosen a "Best Play" and closes on June 13, 1982. With 1,793 performances, it becomes Broadway's fourth-longest running play. John Wood and Marian Seldes are in the first cast. On Oct 26, the show opens in London at the Garrick, where it plays 492 times.

March 1 *Timbuktu!* (NY—Mark Hellinger—Musical). Although the cast is black, directed, choreographed, and costumed by Geoffrey Holder, this show is really *Kismet*, transposed from an Arabian Nights setting to Africa. Among the cast are Eartha Kitt, Melba Moore, Gilbert Price, and Ira Hawkins. The play runs for 25 weeks.

March 9 *Moliere in Spite of Himself* (NY—Colonnades Theatre Lab—Drama). Michael Lessac adapts and stages Bulgakov's *A Cabal of Hypocrites*. It plays 100 times and wins for Lessac the Rosamund Gilder Award.

March 27 *Dancin'* (NY—Broadhurst—Revue). This Bob Fosse creation offers a glittering showcase for Fosse's dance vocabulary and inventive fantasy. It runs into the next decade.

March 30 *A History of the American Film* (NY—ANTA—Comedy). Christopher Durang's cinema parody also is a chronolgy of American hopes and dreams. It has only 21 performances, although major regional theatre productions have al-

ON THE 20TH CENTURY

ready been mounted in Hartford, Los Angeles, and Washington, D.C.

April 9 *Ain't Misbehavin'* (NY—Longacre—Revue). This show started as an intimate cabaret production performed in very cramped quarters at the Manhattan Theatre Club. It evokes the work and style of "Fats" Waller. The revue runs into the next decade. There are 196 performances following its premiere in London at Her Majesty's on March 22, 1979.

April 12 *Family Business* (NY—Astor Place—Drama). Dick Goldberg's tale of a family quarrel between two brothers after the demise of their father is chosen as a "Best Play." It runs 438 performances.

April 17 *The Best Little Whorehouse in Texas* (NY—Entermedia—Musical). Larry King and Peter Masterson write this tale of the closing of a brothel. Carol Hall creates the songs. Seen first in an Actors' Studio workshop production, it moves to Broadway's 46th Street Theatre on June 19. It is chosen as a "Best Play" and runs into the next decade.

May 13 *Runaways* (NY—Plymouth—Musical). Elizabeth Swados's show, which she's written, composed, and staged, has already had a ten-week run at the Public Theatre. It supposedly depicts the effects of big city evils on children growing up in disintegrating families. There are 267 performances.

May 14 *Working* (NY—46th Street—Musical). Stephen Schwartz adapts and creates songs for characters originally interviewed by Studs Terkel, talking about their workaday lives. The run is only three weeks long.

May 17 *The Biko Inquest* (NY—Theatre Four—Drama). Norman Fenton and Jon Blair have based this drama on actual events. The production runs nearly four

weeks.

June 22 *Crimes Against Nature* (NY—Actors' Playhouse—Revue). This creation of San Francisco's Gay Men's Theatre Collective deals with current events and personal instances of concern to them. It runs 10 weeks.

July 1 *Tribute* (NY—Brooks Atkinson—Drama). Jack Lemmon stars in Bernard Slade's play about a terminally ill writer. It is chosen a "Best Play" and runs almost 27 weeks.

Sep 20 *Eubie!* (NY—Ambassador—Revue). Eubie Blake's music is saluted in this show, conceived and staged by Julianne Boyd. Performers include Gregory and Maurice Hines, Ethel Beatty, and Alaina Reed. There are 439 performances.

Sep 28 *Crucifer of Blood* (NY—Helen Hayes—Drama). Paxton Whitehead plays a young Sherlock Holmes in this thriller by Paul Giovanni. The play runs nearly 29 weeks and is later popular with regional, college, and amateur theatres. It opens in London at the Haymarket on March 21, 1979, for a run of 398 performances. Keith Michell is Holmes.

Oct 3 *First Monday in October* (NY—Majestic—Drama). Jane Alexander plays a fictional first woman to sit on the U.S. Supreme Court in Jerome Lawrence and Robert E. Lee's play. Henry Fonda is her liberal opponent on the Court. Chosen a "Best Play," it runs ten weeks, opening on the first Monday.

Oct 4 *End of the War* (NY—Ensemble Studio—Drama). *NY Times* film critic Vincent Canby offers this story of men aboard ship in wartime in a showcase production.

Oct 15 *Are You Now or Have You Ever Been* (NY—Promenade—Drama). Eric

Bentley's play, based on his account of the House Un-American Activities Committee's hearings of artists suspected of Communist ties, runs for 129 performances. The show has been tried out at the Theatre of the Riverside Church.

Oct 19 *Getting Out* (NY—Marymount Manhattan—Drama). Marsha Norman's play shows a young woman in and out of prison. Pamela Reed and Susan Kingsley play her two selves. The play wins the American Theatre Critics Association award as an outstanding new play in regional theatre, is chosen a "Best Play," and wins the John Gassner Award of the Outer Critics Circle. The show moves to the Theatre de Lys, after a lapse of half-a-year.

Oct 30 *Gorey Stories* (NY—Booth—Revues). Illustrator of ghoulish tales, Edward Gorey, has his weird world brought to Broadway after a successful showcase Off-off Broadway. There is only one performance.

Nov 3 *Billy Bishop Goes to War* (Vancouver—Vancouver East Cultural Centre—Drama) This is the true story of Billy Bishop, the most decorated Allied pilot of World War I. Written and directed by John Gray, he also composes the music and plays the piano onstage. Actor Eric Peterson plays Billy Bishop and the other

16 characters in the play. Originally funded as a workshop by Toronto's Theatre Passe Muraille, the play tours Canada, and plays New York's Morosco Theater and Theatre de Lys (June 1980), the Edinburgh Festival (Aug 1980) and London's Comedy Theatre (June 1981).

Nov 28 *Porno Stars at Home* (NY—Courtyard Playhouse—Comedy). Leonard Melfi's play about a birthday party with imaginary luminaries of the blue-movie world has already been seen at Caffe Cino and La Mama. It runs two months Off Broadway.

Dec 5 *Buried Child* (NY—Theatre de Lys—Drama). Sam Shepard's enigmatic play, echoing old myths and modern fears, runs 152 performances after a critically admired premiere Off-off Broadway. It wins the Pulitzer Prize. The show is revived at Circle Repertory on Sheridan Square on June 29, 1979.

Dec 6 *The Kingfisher.* See L premiere, 1977.

Dec 14 *Ballroom* (NY—Majestic—Musical). Jerome Kass adapts his TV play, *Queen of the Stardust Ballroom,* for the stage. Dorothy Louden is featured in this show directed and choreographed by Michael Bennett. It has only 116 performances.

1978 BRITISH PREMIERES

Jan 25 *Laughter!* (L—Royal Court—Drama). Peter Barnes's bitterly black play features Timothy West, Frances de la Tour, and Roger Kemp.

Feb 7 *The Elocution of Benjamin Franklin* (L—May Fair—Drama). Gordon Chater is the sole performer in this Australian play about a speech teacher who comes to grief through community intolerance. The production runs until mid-June. The show opens in New York at Theatre Four on March 20, 1979, for a run of almost four weeks, with *Franklin* dropped from its title.

Feb 22 *The Rear Column* (L—Globe—Drama). Simon Gray's drama of British soldiers on a special mission in the heart of Africa features Simon Ward and Jeremy Irons. Harold Pinter directs. There are only 44 performances. In New York, it is mounted briefly at the Manhattan Theatre Club on Nov 19.

March 2 *Half-Life* (L—Duke of York's—Drama). Julian Mitchell's play, seen first in London at the Cottesloe Theatre, opens in the West End, with John Gielgud in the lead.

March 6 *Whose Life It It, Anyway?* (L—Mermaid—Drama). Brian Clark's play opens with Tom Conti as a sculptor paralyzed from the neck down and eager to end his life. The production transfers to

the Savoy on June 13, for a total of 672 performances in London. It opens in New York at the Trafalger on April 17, 1979, with Conti again in the lead, for 223 performances. Toward the end of the New York run, the script is reworked to permit TV star Mary Tyler Moore to play Conti's role. It is chosen a "Best Play" and is later made into a movie.

March 28 *The Travelling Music Show* (L—Her Majesty's—Musical). Bruce Forsyth plays Fred Limelight in this show by Leslie Bricusse and Anthony Newley. Bert Shevelove stages.

March 29 *Let the Good Stones Roll* (L—Ambassadors'—Musical). This Rolling Stone musical, concocted by Rayner Bourton, has 106 performances.

April 4 *Class Enemy* (L—Royal Court—Drama). Nigel Williams' play shows a classroom of disruptive students no teacher wants to handle. The drama has already been tried out at the Court in the Theatre Upstairs. The play comes to New York's Players on Nov 19, 1979, for a run of 23 weeks.

April 5 *Ten Times Table* (L—Globe—Comedy). Alan Ayckbourn stages his own play, featuring Paul Eddington and Julia McKenzie. It runs 380 performances.

April 12 *Plenty* (L—Lyttelton—Comedy). On the Lyttelton stage of the National

Theatre, David Hare's play comes to life with music by Nick Bicat. Kate Nelligan and Julie Covington are among the cast.

April 13 *The Unvarnished Truth* (L—Phoenix—Comedy). Royce Ryton is featured in Bill Carlisle's black farce about love, produced by the Cambridge Theatre Company. There are 236 performances.

May 3 *Annie.* See NY premiere, 1977.

June 21 *Evita* (L—Prince Edward—Musical). Harold Prince directs this new show by Andrew Lloyd Webber (score) and Tim Rice (lyrics), based on the life of Eva Peron. Elaine Paige has the title-role. The show runs into the next decade. It opens in New York at the Broadway Theatre on Sep 25, 1979, with Patti LuPone in the lead. Here, too, it runs into the 1980's.

July 6 *A Family* (L—Haymarket—Drama). Ronald Harwood's play has a cast including Paul Scofield. Casper Wrede directs. There are 100 performances.

July 26 *The Women–Pirates Ann Bonney and Mary Read* (L—Aldwych—Drama). Steve Gooch's feminist play features Diana Quick and Charlotte Cornwell. Ron Daniels directs.

Aug 10 *The Woman* (L—Olivier—Drama). Edward Bond's look at prehistoric Greece and its values is staged by Bond with Susan Fleetwood, Yvonne Bryceland, and Dinah Stabb in the cast.

Aug 15 *Vieux Carré.* See NY premiere, 1977.

Aug 23 *The Passion of Dracula.* See NY premiere, 1977.

Sep 20 *Cousin Vladimir* (L—Aldwych—Drama). David Mercer's play features Mark Dignam, Susan Engel, and Julian Glover. Jane Howell stages.

Oct 18 *Who Killed "Agatha" Christie?* (L—Ambassadors'—Drama). Tudor Gates' melodrama has been seen on the fringe already. John Dove directs James Bolam, Gerald Flood, Hugh Janes, and Juliette Kaplan. There are 170 performances.

Nov 1 *Clouds* (L—Duke of York's—Comedy). Seen first at the Hampstead Theatre Club in 1976, Michael Frayn's play now opens for a run of 287 performances, with a cast including of Tom Courteney and Felicity Kendal, among others. Michael Rudman directs.

Nov 7 *Gloo Joo* (L—Criterion—Comedy). Michael Hastings's play has been seen in September at the Hampstead Theatre Club. This production, directed by Michael Rudman, now opens in the West End. There are 195 performances.

Nov 8 *Night and Day* (L—Phoenix—Drama). Tom Stoppard's tale of British and native unrest in the heart of Africa opens with Diana Rigg as an attractive Englishwoman in the center of things. There are 477 performances. With Maggie Smith, the show plays three months in New York following its opening at the ANTA on Nov 27, 1979.

Nov 9 *Beyond the Rainbow* (L—Adelphi—Musical). Roy Kinnear, Johnny Dorelli, and Dorothy Vernon are featured in this musical, by Iaia Fiastri and Armando Trovailoi, based on David Forrest's novel, *After Me, the Deluge*. English lyrics are by Leslie Bricusse. There are 158 performances.

Nov 15 *Betrayal* (L—Lyttelton—Drama). Harold Pinter's play traces a marriage and a friendship from breakup to beginnings. Peter Hall stages. Michael Gambon, Penelope Wilton, and Daniel Massey are in the cast. This will later be seen on Broadway.

cess, and from thence to Broadway, where its star, Jane Lapotaire, wins a Tony as Best Actress.

Jan 24 At the RSC's experimental stage in London, the Warehouse, Covent Garden, Charles Wood's *Dingo* opens, imported from Stratford and The Other Place. On April 10, Ron Daniels stages *The Lorenzaccio Story*, based on Alfred De Musset's drama by adaptor Paul Thompson. On April 12, the RSC opens John Ford's *'Tis Pity She's a Whore*, also staged by Daniels. David Rudkin's epic drama, *The Sons of Light*, staged by Daniels, has its London premiere on May 30. This is also from The Other Place in Stratford-Upon-Avon. On June 13, *The Jail Diary of Albie Sachs* opens. David Edgar's play about injustice in South Africa is staged by Howard Davies.

1978   REVIVALS/REPERTORIES

Jan 3 Christopher Martin's East 13th Street CSC repertory season continues in New York with the production of Genet's *The Maids*, staged by Martin, followed by a new play about the American Revolution by actress Karen Sunde, *The Running of the Deer*, on Feb 2. On March 2, Giraudoux's *The Madwoman of Chaillot* makes its bow, with Sunde in the title-role.

Jan 8 Alec McCowen reads the St. Mark's Gospel at the Riverside Studios in Hammersmith. Athol Fugard's *Hello and Goodbye* opens at the Studios on Feb 28, followed on April 11 by Shuji Terayama's *Directions to Servants*. The Pip Simmons Theatre Group offers *The Tempest* on May 9.

Jan 10 In Edinburgh at the Traverse Theatre, Michael Almaz opens the new year directing his own play, *Diary of a Rat*, performed by the Artaud Company. There are some 40 programs this year, with a number of them having more than one play. Among the shows are Donald Mackenzie's *Fighting Mac*, Tom Gallacher's *Mr Joyce Is Leaving Paris*, Brian Miller's *Work and Other Dear Green Fables*, C. P. Taylor's *Withdrawal Symptoms*, John Byrne's *The Slab Boys*, John Bett's *Street Fighting Man*, Steve Wilmer's *Scenes from Soweto*, Tom McGrath's *The Android Circuit*, Robert Holman's *Rooting*, Oddur Bjornsson's *Yolk Life*, Albert Camus's *The Just*, and Marcella Evaristi's *Scotia's Darlings*.

Jan 11 Simon Gray's *Molly*, with Tammy Grimes in the title role, opens in an Off-off Broadway showcase at the Hudson Guild Theatre, directed by Stephen Hollis. It has 30 performances in a limited run. In London on Oct 25, the play earns

RUNAWAYS

only 45, opening at the Comedy Theatre with Billie Whitelaw, directed by Hollis. Bored in her marriage to an older man, Molly has an affair with the young gardner. He's serious and murders the husband, leaving Molly more lonely than before, with neither husband nor lover.

Jan 12 Continuing its 25th anniversary celebrations, the Phoenix Theatre at the Marymount Manhattan Theatre offers David French's *One Crack Out*, staged by Daniel Freudenberger. Stephen Poliakoff's *City Sugar*, follows on June 1, staged by Freudenberger.

Jan 16 At the Old Vic, the Prospect Theatre Company revives its *Hamlet* of last season. George Bernard Shaw's *Saint Joan* is given on Feb 9, and *Antony and Cleopatra* on Feb 20. *Twelfth Night* enters the repertory on April 24. On June 11, the show is *Great English Eccentrics*, a series of three entertainments devised by Jane Smith. Christopher Fry's *The Lady's Not for Burning* is presented on July 3; Ariadne Nicolaeff's version of Chekhov's *Ivanov* opens on Aug 14; Sheridan's *The Rivals* is given on Sep 4, and *King Lear* is offered on Oct 24, with Anthony Quayle in the title role.

Jan 22 In Glasgow, the Citizens' Theatre opens its new year with *Summit Conference*, followed by *No Orchids for Miss Blandish*, *Painter's Palace of Pleasure*, *The Threepenny Opera*, *The Spanish Tragedy*, *The Seagull* and *Dick Whittington*.

Jan 22 At the Almost Free Theatre in London, founded by Ed Berman, the founder stages Wolf Mankowitz's *The Irish Hebrew Lesson*. Other plays include Robert Patrick's *My Cup Ranneth Over*, Harold Pinter's *The Examination*, Alan Sillitoe's *The Interview*, and the Vonnegut/Saunders', *Player Piano*.

Jan 24 At the Royal Shakespeare's Other Place in Stratford-upon-Avon, the season of experimental productions (with their directors) opens with August Strindberg's *The Dance of Death*, John Caird; Shakespeare's *The Merchant of Venice*, John Barton; Howard Brenton's *The Shakespeare Play*, Barry Kyle; Pam Gems' *Piaf*, Howard Davies; David Rudkin/Euripides' *The Judgement on Hippolytus*, and 'Ron Daniels' *The Shepherds' Play*, Barton. Gems' *Piaf* moves from Stratford to London, where it has a West End suc-

Jan 26 The Chichester Festival revival of N. C. Hunter's *Waters of the Moon* arrives in London at the Haymarket. Ingrid Bergman and Wendy Hiller repeat their roles. There are 180 performances.

Jan 27 At London's Aldwych, the Royal Shakespeare Company revives Congreve's *The Way of the World*, staged by John Barton. Shakespeare's *Henry VI, Part 1* opens on April 6, with Parts 2 and 3 opening on the 8th and 10th. On April 20, *Henry V* is offered. *Coriolanus* is presented on May 31, staged by Terry Hands. On June 13, Strindberg's *The Dance of Death* opens. Trevor Nunn and John Caird mount *As You Like It*, which opens on Sep 5. Middleton and Rowley's *The Changeling* is given on Oct 11 and Bronson Howard's *Saratoga* is presented on Dec 13.

Jan 31 Ferenc Molnar's *The Guardsman*, in a version by Frank Marcus, opens on the Lyttelton stage of London's National Theatre. Peter Wood directs. On May 31, Ben Travers's "Aldwych" farce, *Plunder*, is shown with Peggy Mount and Dinsdale Landen. George Bernard Shaw's *The Philanderer* opens on Sep 7, directed by Christopher Morahan.

Jan 31 In London at the New End Theatre, David Rabe's American play about the aftermath of Vietnam for an American soldier, *Sticks and Bones*, opens in a Lawrence Taubman staging.

Feb 1 Lynne Meadow, artistic director of the Manhattan Theatre Club, continues her season with Athol Fugard's *Statements After an Arrest Under the Immorality Act* and Steve Wilmer's *Scenes from Soweto*. An Appalachian troupe, the Roadside Theatre, presents its *Red Fox/Second Hangin'* on March 1. Istvan Orkeny's *Catsplay* opens on April 5 and later transfers to the Promenade. Stephen Poliakoff's *Strawberry Fields Forever* is given on May 24. Simon Gray's *The Rear Column* is given on Nov 7, and Eduardo de Filippo's *Grand Magic* is offered on Dec 28.

Feb 2 At London's Greenwich Theatre,

Oscar Wilde's *An Ideal Husband* is staged by Robert Kidd. Moliere's *Don Juan* is presented on March 14, George Bernard Shaw's *Arms and the Man* is revived on April 13, and Don Taylor's *The Achurch Letters* opens on May 18. On June 14, five Irish plays are offered as part of the "Miss Horniman Season." They are Lady Gregory's *The Rising of the Moon*, W. B. Yeats's *The Cat and the Moon*, *Purgatory*, and *The Pot of Broth*, and J.M. Synge's *Riders to the Sea*. On June 29 Stanley Houghton's *Hindle Wakes* is revived.

Feb 2 At Ellen Stewart's La Mama E.T.C., located just off the Bowery, Harvey Fierstein presents his fantasy, *International Stud*, followed by Tom O'Horgan's staging of *The Tempest* on Feb 14. On Feb 23, the show is the musical *The Coolest Cat in Town*. Ping Chong and the Fiji Company present *Humboldt's Current* on March 30. On June 1 Stewart's company offers William Hoffman's *The Book of Etiquette*. Among other plays this season are Artau's *Contradictions*, Tomioka's *Ningyo Shimai* and Mandel and Sachs' *Gulliver's Travels*.

Feb 7 At the Public Theatre, Greenwich Village home of Joseph Papp's New York Shakespeare Festival, the season continues with the opening of Tina Howe's *Museum*. On Feb 14, Sam Shepard's *The Curse of the Starving Class* is presented. Elizabeth Swados's musical, *Runaways*, is given for ten weeks beginning Feb 21. It later transfers to Broadway. Gretchen Cryer and Nancy Ford's *I'm Getting My Act Together and Taking It on the Road* opens for a long run, followed by an Off-Broadway transfer and tour. Jessica Hagedorn's *Mango Tango* opens on May 28. On June 7, two programs premiered in New Haven at the Yale Repertory Theatre arrive. The first is a group of four farces by Moliere, translated by Albert Bermel. They are *The Flying Doctor*, *The Forced Marriage*, *Sganarelle* and *A Dumb Show*. Arthur Kopit's *Wings* is staged by John Madden. This production moves to Broadway and is named a "Best Play." Mikhail Bulgakov's *The Master and Margarita* opens on Nov 10. Swados' musical version of Lewis Carroll's two great children's classics, *Wonderland in Concert*, is given on Dec 27.

Feb 8 Frank Dunlop's new BAM Theatre Company opens at the Brooklyn Academy of Music with George Bernard Shaw's *The Devil's Disciple*. Molnar's *The Play's the Thing* is given on Feb 26; *Julius Caesar* is presented on April 7, and Samuel Beckett's *Waiting for Godot* is played on May 31.

Feb 8 The Royal Shakespeare production of Peter Nichols' *Privates on Parade* opens in the West End at the Piccadilly for a run of 208 performances.

Feb 9 Frank Wedekind's *Lulu* makes its debut in Greenwich Village at the Circle Repertory Theatre, staged by Rob Thir-

kield. Among the other plays offered this year are Lanford Wilson's *The 5th of July*, beginning April 27; Patrick Meyer's *Glorious Morning*, presented Oct 22, and James Farrell's *In the Recovery Lounge*, given on Dec 3. Wilson's play has 159 performances before moving to Broadway for a run of 511 performances.

Feb 14 At London's National Theatre on the Olivier stage, Michael Frayn's translation of Chekhov's *The Cherry Orchard* opens with Albert Finney and Ralph Richardson. On April 25, Henrik Ibsen's *Brand* is given, staged by Christopher Morahan. Finney has the lead in *Macbeth*, which opens on June 6. Congreve's *The Double Dealer* is presented on Sep 27, and Galsworthy's *Strife* is offered beginning Nov 30.

Feb 15 On the Cottesloe stage of London's National Theatre, Arnold Wesker's *Love Letters on Blue Paper* is presented. *Lark Rise*, adapted from Flora Thompson's novel by Keith Dewhurst, opens on March 29. Odon von Horvath's *Don Juan Comes Back from War* is given beginning April 18. Wilson John Haire's *Lost Worlds* is played beginning May 25, and David Mamet's *American Buffalo* opens on June 28. On Aug 9 *The Passion*, drawn from the York Cycle of Mystery Plays, returns. On Nov 2 the show is Dewhurst's *The World Turned Upside Down*. Charles Wood's *Has "Washington" Legs?* is offered on Nov 29, and Paul Mills' *Herod* is presented on Dec 11.

Feb 20 James Saunders's *Bodies* is played at London's Hampstead Theatre Club, with Dinsdale Landen and Gwen Watford in the cast. Per Olov Enquist's *The Tribades* bows on May 16, staged by Michael Rudman.

Feb 21 At London's Round House, the Liverpool Playhouse production of David Rabe's American drama, *Streamers*, opens staged by Leslie Lawton.

March 1 At London's Young Vic Theatre, Nancy Meckler directs *Twelfth Night*. On April 4, *Macbeth* opens, and on June 22 Ben Jonson's *Bartholomew Fair* is revived. On July 26 Michael Burrell performs his one-man show, *Hess*, based on the career of Nazi leader Rudolf Hess. Michael Bogdanov stages *Richard III*, presented Oct 17. Philip Bowen plays the prince in *Hamlet* on Oct 19, and Bill Wallis is Prospero in *The Tempest*, opening on Nov 28. On Dec 20, the show is *Canterbury Tales*.

March 5 As Broadway retreats from the risk of mounting new, untried musicals—with production costs of at least $1 million a show—revivals are increasingly popular. Tonight the treat is a recreation of the Michael Stewart/Jerry Herman show, *Hello, Dolly!*, with its original star, Carol Channing. It runs 18 weeks.

March 7 Anthony Shaffer's thriller, *Sleuth*, gets a revival in London at the Savoy. It

has 181 performances after a transfer to the Ambassadors' Theatre.

March 8 Hugh Leonard's Irish play, *Da*, opens in a showcase Off-off Broadway at the Hudson Guild, with Barnard Hughes in the title role. Melvin Bernhardt directs. After moving on May 1 to Broadway's Morosco Theatre, the show has a long run and wins a Tony. On May 5, Phyllis Newman opens her one-woman show, *My Mother Was a Fortune Teller*, staged by playwright Arthur Laurents. It opens later in a small Broadway theatre as *The Madwoman of Central Park West*.

March 8 In the Theatre Upstairs at the Royal Court, Nigel Williams's *Class Enemy* is offered, followed on April 4 with a main stage production. Under the direction of Mike Alfreds, the Shared Experience Theatre presents Charles Dickens's *Bleak House* in four installments on April 4. On July 12 Nigel Baldwin's *Irish Eyes and English Tears* is staged by Ian Kellgren. Thomas Babe's American play, *A Prayer for My Daughter:* opens on Aug 24. The Traverse Theatre offers John Byrne's Scottish play, *The Slab Boys* on Oct 17. Edgar White's *Masada* is produced on Nov 27.

March 8 At the Circle in the Square on Broadway, the season continues with Feydeau's *13 Rue de l'Amour*. On June 15 George S. Kaufman and Moss Hart's *Once in a Lifetime* opens for a run of almost 11 weeks. On Sep 21 the new season begins with Gogol's *The Inspector General*, followed on Dec 14 by George Bernard Shaw's *Man and Superman*.

March 9 Encompass Theatre, an Off-off Broadway group which specializes in production of operas and new plays launches a series of plays titled *Hear Their Voices: Women Founders of the American Theatre, 1910–1945*, with Zona Gale's *Miss Lulu Bett*. Other plays include Hallie Flanagan's *Can You Hear Their Voices*, Rachel Crothers' *Expressin' Willie*, Zoe Akins' *The Old Maid*, Susan Glaspell's *Alison's House*, and Sophie Treadwell's *Machinal*.

March 16 Next door to the Performing Garage in Soho, Richard Schechner's Performance group has set up a coffee-shop in complete, operational detail, wrapping the audience around on two sides, for this production of Terry Curtis Fox's *Cops*, with its raw naturalism in action, speech, and environment. Including open rehearsals, this runs nearly seven weeks.

March 21 Lacking a surplus of good new plays and musicals, the West End welcomes another revival: Wright and Forrest's musical *Kismet*, staged by the American director Albert Marre for the Shaftesbury Theatre.

March 22 James Kirkwood's *P. S. Your Cat Is Dead* opens Off Broadway at the Promenade Theatre for a run of 301 performances. Seen on Broadway in 1975, it

BRAND

ran only two weeks. Kirkwood has reduced the cast from seven to four and made other improvements. Robert Nigro stages the new production.

April 5 John Houseman's The Acting Company comes to the American Place Theatre in midtown Manhattan for a three-week engagement, playing a repertory of Bertolt Brecht's *Mother Courage and Her Children*, staged by Alan Schneider; Shakespeare's *King Lear*, directed by Houseman, and David Mamet's *Duck Variations*, staged by Gerald Gutierrez.

April 19 At Stratford-upon-Avon, the Royal Shakespeare Company opens its annual season with *The Taming of the Shrew*, staged by Michael Bogdanov. *The Tempest*, staged by Clifford Williams; *Measure for Measure*, directed by Barry Kyle; *Love's Labour's Lost*, staged by John Barton, and *Antony and Cleopatra* directed by Peter Brook are also seen during the season.

May In San Diego, the National Shakespeare Festival opens its summer season. Four plays will be presented: *Henry V, A Midsummer Night's Dream, The Winter's Tale*, and Alan Ayckbourn's *How the Other Half Loves*.

May 1 Harold Pinter's *The Homecoming* is revived in London at the Garrick Theatre, with Timothy West, Michael Kitchen, and Charles Kay among the cast. Kevin Billington directs. There are 200 performances.

May 8 Britain's Chichester Festival gets underway with a production of Wilde's *A Woman of No Importance*. Marivaux's *The Inconsistant Couple*, Michael Redgrave's adaptation of Henry James' *The Aspern Papers*, and Noel Coward's *Look After Lulu* are also seen during the season.

May 9 The American Shakespeare Festival, in Stratford, Connecticut, shows some renewed signs of life as William Woodman imports his staging of *Much Ado About Nothing*, created at Chicago's Goodman Theatre. On July 12, Gerald Freedman's production of *Twelfth Night* is offered.

May 11 The Shaw Festival at Niagara-on-the-Lake opens with Henrik Ibsen's *John*

Gabriel Borkman, Heartbreak House, Major Barbara and *Lady Audley's Secret* will also be seen before the season ends on Oct 1.

May 22 *We Can't Pay? We Won't Pay*, Dario Fo's Italian play about outraged housewives features Frances de la Tour and Patti Love at London's Half Moon Theatre. The show later achieves a West End success.

May 22 At London's Old Vic, Jean Marais is featured in Jean Cocteau's *Les Parents Terribles*. Seven days later the International Turkish Players offer *The Turkish Clogs*.

May 24 Charles Ludlams Ridiculous Theatrical Company opens an Off-off-Broadway season of three plays at New York's Sheridan Square: *Stage Blood, The Ventriloquist's Wife*, and *Camille*. On July 17, Ludlam's *Bluebeard* joins the repertory.

June 5 It's the 25th anniversary of the Stratford Festival of Canada, so a Gala Shakespeare Revel opens the season. Among the plays to be offered are *The Merry Wives of Windsor, Macbeth, The Winter's Tale, As You Like It, Julius Caesar*, and *Titus Andronicus*. John Whiting's *The Devils*, Chekhov's *Uncle Vanya*, Barry Collins's *Judgement*, *Heloise and Abelard: Love Letters from the Middle Ages*, Noel Coward's *Private Lives*, Leonard Bernstein's *Candide*, Sheldon Rosen's *Ned and Jack*, Larry Fineberg's *Medea*, and Tom Cone's *Stargazing* are also given.

June 5 Summer Shakespeare begins in the Open Air Theatre in London's Regent's Park with *A Midsummer Night's Dream*. On July 17 a double bill by George Bernard Shaw begins: *The Man of Destiny* and *The Dark Lady of the Sonnets*.

June 7 The Light Opera of Manhattan (LOOM) opens the new season with Victor Herbert's *Mlle. Modiste*, the first of a reportory of 16 operetta revivals at its Eastside Playhouse. Other revivals include Gilbert & Sullivan's *The Grand Duke*, Lehar's *The Merry Widow*, G & S's *H. M. S. Pinafore* and *The Pirates of Penzance*, followed by Romberg's *The Student Prince* and Herbert's *Babes in Toyland*.

June 7 The Watford Palace Theatre, in a London suburb, revives *Rain*, based on a story by W. Somerset Maugham. The Hollywood film actress, Gloria Grahame plays Sadie Thompson.

June 14 Tom Stoppard's *Every Good Boy Deserves Favour*, a musical fable about repression in Eastern Europe, is revived in London at the Mermaid Theatre. The run ends on Sep 30, when the theatre closes for rebuilding and enlargement.

June 14 The American Dance Machine, directed by Lee Theodore, opens on Broadway at the Century Theatre for a three-month run, with a varied program

of theatre dances, reconstructed and preserved by the company, which is a "living archive" of often forgotten Broadway show dances. Among the dances are: "June is Bustin' Out All Over" (*Carousel*), "Charleston" (*The Boy Friend*), "All Aboard for Broadway" (*George M*), "Rich Kid's Rag" (*Little Me*), "Come To Me, Bend To Me" (*Brigadoon*), and "Clog Dance" (*Walking Happy*).

June 16 The Oregon Shakespearean Festival opens in its outdoor Elizabethan Theatre in Ashland with *The Taming of the Shrew, The Tempest* and *Richard II* will also be offered. In the indoor Angus Bowmer Theatre, Jerry Turner stages *Timon of Athens*. Moliere's *Tartuffe*, Bertolt Brecht's *Mother Courage*, and August Strindberg's *Miss Julie* are also given. In the Black Swan Theatre, William Glover directs Zindel's *The Effect of Gamma Rays on Man-in-the-Moon Marigolds*, followed by Turner's staging of Enquist's *The Night of the Tribades*.

Summer The Los Pobres Bilingual Theatre presents *Viva! El Paso!*, a drama of the El Paso Southwest in McKelligon Canyon Ampitheatre, El Paso, Texas. It has been written by the Los Pobres staff.

June 26 Dylan Thomas' dramatic poem, *Under Milk Wood*, is revived in London at the May Fair Theatre, staged by Malcolm Taylor. There are 256 performances.

June 29 In the open-air Delacorte Theatre in Central Park, Joseph Papp's New York Shakespeare Festival opens with Wilford Leach's staging of *All's Well That Ends Well*. On Aug 3, *The Taming of the Shrew* opens, also staged by Leach.

July 3 At the Royal Shakespeare's London experimental theatre, the Warehouse, Covent Garden, John Caird directs Peter Flannery's *Savage Amusement*. On July 25, the play is Pete Atkin's *A & R*, staged by Walter Donohue. Stephen Poliakoff's *Shout Across the River* opens on Sep 9, staged by Bill Alexander. On Nov 2, the play is Mary O'Malley's *Look Out . . . Here Comes Trouble*, directed by Caird. Howard Barker's *The Hang of the Gaol* has Alexander as director on Dec 12. On the 20th, the show is *The Adventures of Awful Knawful*, a Christmas treat.

July 7 The recent Liviu Ciulei staging of Frank Wedekind's *Spring Awakening*, translated by Edward Bond and presented at the Juilliard School by the drama students, has been so well received that Joseph Papp now opens it at his Public Theatre. There are 28 performances.

July 17 Britain's D'Oyly Carte Opera Company opens a repertory of four Gilbert & Sullivan revivals with *Iolanthe*, followed by *The Mikado, H. M. S. Pinafore*, and *The Pirates of Penzance*, in the New York State Theatre at Lincoln Center. On Aug 3, there is a revival of Leslie Bricusse and Anthony Newley's *Stop the*

World—I Want to Get Off, with Sammy Davis, Jr., in the Newley role of Littlechap.

July 20 Roger Rees devises an anthology-show for the Royal Shakespeare Company to perform in the Merchant Taylor's Hall in the City of London. It's called *And Is There Honey Still for Tea?*

July 27 Philip Magdalany's play, *Boo Hoo*, staged by Charles Marlowitz, opens in London at the Open Space. On Oct 18, Samuel Beckett's *Krapp's Last Tape* and *Endgame* open, followed on Dec 12, by Bertolt Brecht's *A Respectable Wedding*.

Aug 2 At London's Royal Court, Leigh Jackson's *Eclipse*, features Paul Rogers and Leonard Fenton, among others. Stuart Burge directs. On Sep 13, John Osborne's *Inadmissible Evidence*, with Nicol Williamson as Bill Maitland, returns to the Court for 60 performances. On Nov 13, Thomas Babe's American play, *A Prayer for My Daughter*, seen in the Theatre Upstairs, now opens on the mainstage.

Aug 17 The National Youth Theatre presents Peter Terson's *England My Own* at the Shaw Theatre in London. Michael Croft and Graham Chinn direct. On Aug 22, Terson's *Soldier Boy* is shown at the Jeannetta Cochrane Theatre.

Aug 20 In Edinburgh's historic Assembly Hall, this year's Edinburgh Festival opens with *The Tempest*, staged by David Giles, who also directs *A Midsummer Night's Dream*. The Royal Shakespeare Company brings its Jon Amiel staging of *Twelfth Night* and Trevor Nunn's mounting of Chekhov's *Three Sisters*. The Moscow Drama Theatre presents Gogol's *The Marriage* and Turgenev's *A Month in the Country*. The Prospect Theatre troupe offers Chekhov's *Ivanov*.

Aug 25 Off-off Broadway at the Bouwerie Lane Theatre, the Jean Cocteau Repertory, under Eve Adamson's artistic direction, opens its season with Thomas Middleton's *A Mad World. My Masters*, followed by MacKaye's *The Scarecrow*, Ionesco's *Exit the King*, Corneille's *The Cid*, Shakespeare's *As You Like It*, Williams' *In the Bar of a Tokyo Hotel*, Middleton and Rowley's *The Changeling*, and Shakespeare's *Hamlet*.

Sep 7 Off Broadway at the Marymount Manhattan Theatre, Alec McCowen appears in his one-man interpretation of *St. Mark's Gospel*. This is a two-week run, followed by a Broadway engagement at the Playhouse beginning Oct 24.

Sep 13 At the Hudson Theatre Guild on Manhattan's West Side, the season of new plays opens with Ernest Thompson's *On Golden Pond*, later to win many productions and even a filming. There are 30 performances, as there are for Lee Kalcheim's *Winning Isn't Everything* which opens on Nov 8.

Sep 13 *Dracula*. See NY revival, 1977.

Sep 14 The season of revivals presented regularly by Equity Library Theatre in New York at the Masters Theatre opens now with Rodgers and Hammerstein's *Oklahoma!*, followed by *A Midsummer Night's Dream*, the musical *Can-Can*, Gibson's *The Miracle Worker*, Schnitzler's *La Ronde*—adapted by Eric Bentley, the musical *Mary*, and Wilde's *The Importance of Being Earnest*.

Oct 2 At London's Bush Theatre, Albert Innaurato's *The Transformation of Benno Blimpie* is presented, staged by Simon Stokes. Snoo Wilson's *A Greenish Man* opens on Nov 15.

Oct 3 Celebrating its Golden Jubilee, the Dublin Gate Theatre opens its fall season with Benedict Kiely's *Proxopera*, adapted by Peter Luke, and staged by Hilton Edwards, who co-founded the theatre in 1928 with the late Micheál macLiammóir, whose design style is recreated by Robert Heade for this production. Other shows include Hugh Carr's *Encounter in the Wilderness* and a revival of macLiammóir's *Where Stars Walk*, which opens on Dec 28 and runs until March 31, 1979.

Oct 9 Noel Coward's adaptation of a Feydeau farce, *Occupe-toi d'Amalie*, known as *Look After Lulu*, opens in a revival at London's Haymarket Theatre. The show runs nine weeks.

Dec 7 The Negro Ensemble Company (NEC) opens its season with Steve Carter's *Nevis Mountain Dew*, chosen as a "Best Play." Horacena J. Taylor stages. On Dec 20, Judi Ann Mason's *Daughters of the Mock* opens, staged by Glenda Dickerson.

Dec 14 George Bernard Shaw's *The Millionaress* returns to the West End, at the Theatre Royal, Haymarket, staged by Michael Lindsay-Hogg. There are 192 performances.

Dec 18 The holiday season is at hand, as *Toad of Toad Hall* opens in the West End at the Piccadilly Theatre. On Dec 20, Jane Asher plays Peter in Barrie's *Peter Pan* at the Shaftesbury Theatre, with Nigel Patrick as Captain Hook. At the RSC's Warehouse, Covent Garden, the show is Peter Flannery and Mick Ford's *The Adventures of Awful Knawful*. At the Young Vic, *Canterbury Tales* is an adaptation of Chaucer's lively stories.

1978 BIRTHS/DEATHS/DEBUTS

Jan 18 American actress Charlotte Greenwood (b. 1893) is dead. Greenwood made her birthday debut as a chorus girl in *The White Cat*. She toured extensively in the United States and Australia, playing in vaudeville and musical comedy. In 1950 she appeared as Juno in *Out of This World* in New York. Her reminiscences, *Just for Kicks*, was published in 1947.

Jan 26 At 72 years, the suave British actor Leo Genn dies.

Feb 15 Actress-author Ilka Chase dies at age 72. Daughter of hotel manager Francis Chase and former *Vogue* editor Edna Woolman, Chase made her professional Broadway debut in *The Red Falcon* in 1924.

March 6 Micheal macLiammoir, founder with Hilton Edwards of Dublin's prestigious Gate Theatre, dies in the year of that theatre's Golden Jubilee. Remembered as an actor, director, designer, and playwright, his one-man shows, *The Importance of Being Oscar* and *I Must Be Talking to My Friends* have been popular both in America and Britain.

March 18 Peggy Wood, popular musical comedy star, dies at the age of 86.

April 22 The distinguished British director Basil Dean dies at 89. His productions of *Hassan* and *Young Woodley* are remembered.

April 22 American actor Will Geer (b. 1909) is dead. Geer's first professional engagement was with the Sothern-Marlowe Shakespeare Repertory Company in Chicago in 1920. Prior to his film and television commitments, he appeared on Broadway. Geer also established the Theatricum Botanicum near his California home where Shakespearean productions were presented.

July 13 Oliver Messel, the distinguished British stage designer, dies aged 74.

Aug 26 Stage and screen star Charles Boyer dies at age 78.

Aug 26 Robert Shaw (56) the dynamic British stage and screen actor, dies. He was also a playwright, with *The Man in the Glass Booth* produced both in London and New York.

Sep 24 Former *Follies* star Ruth Etting dies at 81.

Nov 2 American producer Max Gordon (b. 1892) is dead. Gordon made his debut as an advance man for the touring Behman Show in 1910. His notable Broadway productions include *My Sister Eileen*, *Hollywood Pinafore*, *Born Yesterday*, and *The Solid Gold Cadillac*. Gordon collaborated with Lewis Funke on his autobiography, *Max Gordon Presents*, in 1963.

Nov 20 British stage and costume designer Leslie Hurry dies, aged 69.

Dec 12 English actress Fay Compton (b. 1894) is dead. Compton made her debut in 1911 in *The Follies*, produced by her first husband, H. G. Pelissier. Among her later successes were the title role in James Barrie's *Mary Rose*, written specially for her, and Phoebe in *Quality Street*. She also played Ophelia to the Hamlets of John Barrymore and of John Gielgud. In 1926 she published a volume of reminiscences titled *Rosemary*.

1978　THEATERS/PRODUCTIONS

Jan 12 On the bank of the Thames in Hammersmith, the Riverside Studios formally opens its theatre with Chekhov's *The Cherry Orchard*, staged by its director, Peter Gill. The intimate house, with tiered seating set in metal scaffolding, has a thrust performance area. The space was formerly a television studio.

Jan 19 Even before the opening of Phillip Hayes Dean's *Paul Robeson*, a self-appointed committee has been denouncing the play for Dean's interpretation of some events in Robeson's difficult struggle to survive as an artist. Some of the committee members have not read the play or seen it in performance. The Dramatists Guild comes to the playwright's defense, with 33 leading playwrights signing an open letter, emphasizing the dangers of group censorship, which violates the writer's First Amendment rights, especially when such censorship attempts to prejudge a play for potential theatre-goers.

March In San Diego's Balboa Park, the Old Globe Theatre, built for performances of scenes from Shakespeare's plays during an exposition in the early 1930's, is destroyed by fire. The San Diego National Shakespeare Festival's coming productions will have to be presented outdoors on a wooden stage designed by Richard Hay, who has also designed the Shakespeare stages in Ashland, Oregon. This temporary stage will be so successful that it will be retained for summer stagings in future seasons.

THE TAMING OF THE SHREW

March-April Harvey Lichtenstein, President of the Brooklyn Academy of Music (BAM), has asked Michael David, former Executive Director of the new BAM-based Chelsea Theatre—which is leaving BAM—to create a new experimental theatre at BAM. With author-director Des McAnnuf, Edward Strong, and Sherman Warner, he is able to evolve The Dodger Theatre, a name suggested by the baseball-team, once known as the "Brooklyn Trolley Dodgers." A law-suit by the Los Angeles Dodgers is settled out of court when the BAM Dodgers change their logo, which has suggested a tie with baseball. The first season will open this coming December, with Barrie Keeffe's *Gimme Shelter*, with two other productions following. After a second season at BAM, the company will move to Joseph Papp's Public Theatre.

April 1 In the Canadian Rockies, The Banff Centre, once a summer school in arts and theatre, is today made autonomous.

May 31 On the last day of the 1977–78 season, some Broadway plays have recouped their initial investment—or soon will. By *Variety's* measure, this qualifies them as hits. Among the fortunate productions are *The Gin Game, Chapter Two, Deathtrap, Man of La Mancha,* and *A Touch of the Poet*.

Summer In Philadelphia, the Forrest Theatre is undergoing a million-dollar restoration. This will increase its seating capacity to 1,889, give it a symphony-sized orchestra pit, and otherwise enhance its appearance.

June 1 At the beginning of a new Broadway season, the one just past has had only 41 productions. Otis Guernsey, Jr., divides them thusly: 13 plays, five musicals, four revues, 14 revivals, five specialties, four foreign plays in English, and one in a foreign tongue. Most of the best plays have been developed away from Broadway in America's regional theatres or Off-off Broadway. The Broadway gross has increased 11 per cent over last season, climbing to almost $104 million, with a total of $209.5 million, counting road show grosses. *A Chorus Line* has been earning a weekly gross of $475,000 from two touring companies and the Broadway production. Surging activity Off-off Broadway blurs lines between it and Off-Broadway, but there seem to have been some 107 Off-Broadway productions this past season, broken down into 28 plays, 45 revivals, 13 specialties, six musicals, six revues, and nine foreign plays in English. Ella Malin's annual summary of regional theatre activity cites 585 produc-

tions of 426 plays produced by 61 groups in 105 theatres in 57 cities, seven of them in Canada. 242 have been American plays, 59 of them world premieres and 164 in full production, the rest in workshop stagings. New Equity weekly minimums negotiated this past season are $355, rising to $400 in the third year of the new contract, with road minimums from $547.50 to $645 per week, expenses included.

Guernsey, Jr., selects the ten "Best Plays" from the productions of the New York season just over. They are Coburn's *The Gin Game*, Mamet's *A Life in the Theatre*, Simon's *Chapter Two*, Babe's *A Prayer for My Daughter*, Levin's *Deathtrap*, Goldberg's *Family Business*, Wilson's *The Fifth of July*, King/Masterson's *The Best Little Whorehouse in Texas*, Slade's *Tribute*, and Leonard's *DA*.

June 9 The Chelsea Theatre, with its producer-founder, Robert Kalfin, officially leaves the Brooklyn Academy of Music (BAM), where it has achieved a distinguished record of producing new scripts and difficult plays with great style and imagination. The operation relocates in Manhattan at the Chelsea Westside Theatre.

June 17 With the opening production of *Timon of Athens*, the Oregon Shakespearean Festival accomplishes the unique feat of having produced two complete cycles of all of the Bard's plays. The first cycle of the complete canon was achieved in 1958. The festival's resident designer, Richard L. Hay, who has designed all the productions in the current canon cycle is, it's believed, the first designer in history to have designed productions of all of Shakespeare's plays—some of them several times.

Aug 9 New York's daily newspapers are struck today. Using television advertising and TV reviews, among other media alternatives, Broadway producers are to insist that the stoppage hasn't seriously hurt even new shows.

September This month demolition begins on Philadelphia's Erlanger Theatre, opened in 1927 and constructed at a cost of $2.5 million. The demolition permit has been issued in April, but attempts to save the theatre have delayed action until now.

Sep 27 The Brooklyn Academy of Music (BAM) Theatre Company Incorporated is dissolved. Frank Dunlop has been responsible for the direction of the ill-fated ensemble.

Nov 22 Theatre London in Ontario reopens after $5.4 million renovations, designed by Peter Smith. Only the inner shell remains of the old Grand Theatre which served the city from 1901 until 1977. The 1,102-seat theatre saw opera, vaudeville, and movies before being sold to the London Little Theatre, precursor of Theatre London in 1945.

Jan 28 *Wings* (NY—Lyceum—Drama). Written originally for radio, Arthur Kopit's saga of a brave woman stroke-victim, fighting her way back to competence, has been expanded for the stage. Shown first at the Yale Repertory, that production has visited New York's Public Theatre on June 21, 1978, it is to have a later production in London at the National Theatre's Cottesloe, on Aug 15 of this year. John Madden directs Constance Cummings for the Broadway production. There are 117 performances, and it's named a "Best Play."

Feb 11 *They're Playing Our Song* (NY—Imperial—Musical). Neil Simon dramatizes the conflicts between a male composer and a female lyricist, suggesting to some in the audience a possible parallel with the show's composer Marvin Hamlisch and the lyricist Carole Bayer Sager. Robert Klein plays the tunesmith, with Lucie Arnaz, as the rhymesmith. Robert Moore directs, with choreography by Patricia Birch. The show has a run of 1,082 performances; it's named a "Best Play."

Feb 28 *On Golden Pond* (NY—Apollo—Drama). Ernest Thompson's play about old age opens the newly refurbished Apollo, an initial step in cleaning up the 42nd Street "Theatre Block." Showcased at the Hudson Guild, the play now earns 156 performances, directed and produced by Craig Anderson, of the Guild. Frances Sternhagen and Tom Aldredge play an aging couple, faced with the limits of mortality on their annual summer visit to a cabin in Maine. On Sep 12, it's revived at the Century Theatre in midtown Manhattan for a run of nearly eight months. It's chosen a "Best Play." In 1981, it becomes a film with Katharine Hepburn, Jane Fonda, and Henry Fonda, who wins an Oscar for his role as the crusty Norman, whose strength and memory are failing.

March 1 *Sweeney Todd, the Demon Barber of Fleet Street* (NY—Uris—Musical). George Dibdin-Pitt's 1847 British melodrama about a mad barber, who slices the throats of customers who seek a shave, has been adapted by Hugh Wheeler from a 1973 Christopher Bond version, to suggest the influence of the immorality of the powerful on the actions of working-class people such as Todd. Stephen Sondheim provides score and lyrics of such quality some critics see the show as verging on opera. Harold Prince stages. Len Cariou plays the title-role, with Angela Lansbury as Mrs. Lovett, who makes meat-pies from his victims. This is selected as a "Best Play" and is judged the best musical by the Tony Awards jury as well as by the New York Drama Critics' Circle and the Outer Critics' Circle. It has 558 performances, followed by a U.S. tour. In London at the large Drury Lane Theatre, it is

SWEENEY TODD

a rapid failure.

March 25 *Zoot Suit* (NY—Winter Garden—Drama). The Shubert Organization imports Gordon Davidson's Mark Taper Forum production from Los Angeles. The book, by Luiz Valdez, is based on the Sleepy Lagoon murder case in 1942 and later Zoot Suit riots. Edward James Olmos, moves in and out of the play as El Pachuco, commentator on the action. Valdez directs. The show lasts only five weeks; local hispanics don't respond; Chicano slang, for one thing, is alien to them.

March 29 *Bedroom Farce.* See L premiere, 1977.

Apr 17 *Whose Life Is It Anyway?* See L premiere, 1978.

April 19 *Elephant Man* (NY—Booth—Drama). Bernard Pomerance's play depicts John Merrick, mis-shapen through incurable disease. This has been briefly seen in London at the Hampstead Theatre on Nov 7, 1977. On Jan 14, 1979, it has been showcased in Manhattan at the Theatre of St. Peter's Church. It has 907 performances on Broadway. Jack Hofsiss directs a cast including Carole Shelley, Philip Anglim (Merrick), and Kevin Conway. It's chosen a "Best Play." It wins the same award from both the Drama Critics' Circle and Outer Critics' Circle, and it receives the Tony Award.

April 29 *Break a Leg* (NY—Palace—Comedy). Ira Levin's new play makes fun of a drama critic. It's set in Central Europe, but some detect an attack on the vitriolic John Simon. Jack Weston plays Dietrich Merkenschrift, with René Auberjonois as Johann Schiml. Comedian Charles

Nelson Reilly directs. The show closes on opening night. Drama critics have the last say about the play.

May 3 *Bosoms and Neglect* (NY—Longacre—Comedy). Paul Rudd plays Scooper in John Guare's play; Kate Reid plays his mother, Henny, dying of cancer. Marian Mercer plays his wife, Dierdre. Some critics and audiences find the subject-matter lugubrious. Others view the play with tempered respect. Mel Shapiro directs; there are only four performances.

May 6 *Knockout* (NY—Helen Hayes—Drama). Danny Aiello is admired as a former fighter who returns to the ring in a realistic, gruelling fight sequence in Louis La Russo II's play. Frank Corsaro directs. The show runs for 154 performances.

June 6 *The Days Between* (NY—Park Royal—Drama). Robert Anderson's 1965 play, widely produced in regional theatres through the American Playwrights Theatre, now has its New York professional premiere Off Broadway. Kent Paul directs. It runs three weeks.

June 6 *Loose Ends* (NY—Circle in the Square—Drama). Alan Schneider stages Michael Weller's play for a run of almost nine months. This is chosen a "Best Play" and, last season, has been designated an outstanding play by the American Theatre Critics Association. The break-up of a modern marriage is the focus of the drama, with Kevin Kline as Paul and Roxanne Hart as Susan at the Joseph Levine Theatre.

June 11 *Scrambled Feet* (NY—Village Gate Upstairs—Revue). Hermione is a live goose who joins the cast of Evalyn Baron, Roger Neil, and creators John Driver and Jeffrey

Haddow in this comic sequence of songs and sketches, many of them about the theatre. Driver directs.

July 30 *Every Good Boy Deserves Favour* (NY—Metropolitan Opera—Drama). Tom Stoppard created this in collaboration with Andre Previn. It opens for a week at the Metropolitan, after being seen in Washington at the Kennedy Center. It has been first shown in London at the Mermaid Theatre. Stoppard stages. The play, inspired by East European methods of controlling dissent, involves inmates of a mental hospital, as well as a symphony orchestra, which one of them thinks he can conduct.

Sep 25 *Evita.* See L premiere, 1978.

Oct 7 *The 1940's Radio Hour* (NY—St. James—Musical). Director Walton Jones has recreated a vintage live-broadcast from the Hotel Astor in New York, recapturing the fashions, fads, and fears of wartime 1942. Among the cast are Jeff Keller, Joe Grifasi, Dee Dee Bridgewater, and Josef Somer. The show runs 13 weeks.

Oct 8 *Sugar Babies* (NY—Mark Hellinger—Musical). Ann Miller dazzles audiences with her dancing and comedic flair. Mickey Rooney, making his Broadway debut, delights them with his clowning. Ralph G. Allen, a collector of burlesque routines, has written the sketches, based on famous acts. Harry Rigby, a co-producer helps develop the concept. The show runs into the 1980s. Ernest Flatt directs and choreographs, suggesting routines of Gypsy Rose Lee, Sally Rand, and other noted strippers. It's chosen a "Best Play." NY *Daily News* critic Douglas Watt says, " . . . burlesque is dead, dead, dead, and it is the misfortune of 'Sugar Babies' that it insists on showing us why."

Oct 10 *Once a Catholic.* See L premiere, 1977.

Oct 22 *One Mo' Time* (NY—Village Gate Downstairs—Revue). Director Vernel Bagneris recreates an old-time black vaudeville show on the Toba circuit (Tough on black actors), with a vital cast con-

THE 1940'S RADIO HOUR

sisting of Bagneris, Thais Clark, Topsy Chapman, Sylvia Williams, and John Stell as the white theatre owner. Seen first in New Orleans, the production is successful, with a long run, and other productions at home and abroad.

Nov 8 *Romantic Comedy* (NY—Ethel Barrymore—Comedy). Bernard Slade's play is just what its title says: a romantic comedy, in which Anthony Perkins plays Jason Carmichael, a difficult playwright who takes years to realize he is very fond of his collaborator. Mia Farrow is Phoebe Craddock. Joseph Hardy stages. The production has 396 performances.

Nov 11 *Modigliani* (NY—Astor Place—Drama). Seen first at the Direct Theatre, Dennis McIntyre's script, depicting the self-destructiveness of the painter in his last months, has a run of 15 weeks, staged by Allen R. Belknap. Jeffrey De Munn plays the title-role.

Nov 19 *Class Enemy.* See L premiere, 1978.

Nov 27 *Night and Day.* See L premiere, 1978.

1979 BRITISH PREMIERES

Jan 10 *Mary Barnes* (L—Royal Court—Drama). David Edgar's dramatization of the book about her "Journey Through Madness," by Barnes and Joseph Berke, is staged by Peter Farago. Patti Love plays the title-role, with Simon Callow as Eddie and David Gant as Simon. The play has been premiered by the Birmingham Repertory Studio Theatre in August 1978. There are 40 performances.

Feb 6 *Tommy* (L—Queen's—Musical). Already well known in recordings, this musical by Pete Townshend and The Who is staged by Paul Tomlinson and John Hole. Allan Love plays Tommy, with Lor-

elei Lynn as Sally Simpson. Tudor Davies choreographs. The show plays 118 times.

March 7 *Joking Apart* (L—Globe—Comedy). Alan Ayckbourn's play has Diane Bull as Melody, Mandy, and Mo. Christopher Cazenove and Alison Steadman are Richard and Anthea. This show is seen 141 times.

March 21 *Crucifer of Blood.* See NY premiere, 1978.

March 22 *Ain't Misbehavin'.* See NY premiere, 1978.

March 28 *A Day in Hollywood/A Night in the Ukraine* (L—May Fair—Musical).

The Marx Brothers are remembered in the second of these sketches by Dick Vosburgh, recalling old films. Frank Lazarus provides the score. This is the same cast as that at the New End Theatre in January. The show will be a Broadway success as well. It plays 175 times.

March 29 *Cloud Nine* (L—Royal Court—Comedy). Caryl Churchill's wry comedy of sexual repression in a British family, seen first in 19th century India and much later but not much older in modern Britain, is presented by the Joint Stock Company, directed by Max Stafford-Clark. Performers shift sexes and roles from Part One to Part Two. Among the cast are Julie Covington, Antony Sher, and Carole Hayman. The show is also to win favor in New York at the Theatre de Lys. At the Court, there are 24 performances.

April 10 *Chicago.* See NY premiere, 1975.

April 18 *Happy Birthday* (L—Apollo—Comedy). Marc Camoletti's play, adapted by Beverley Cross, has a run of 308 performances, with a cast including Elizabeth Counsel and Ian Lavender. Roger Redfarn directs.

April 23 *Bodies* (L—Ambassadors'—Comedy). James Saunders' play has already been seen in London on the fringe. Now, in Robin Lefevre's staging, it earns a run of 346 performances. Dinsdale Landen, Gwen Watford, Angela Down, and David Burke are in the cast.

May 3 *Bent* (L—Royal Court—Drama). Martin Sherman's American play about Nazi persecution of homosexuals has been showcased in Manhattan at Playwright's Horizons. Now it has a professional London production, staged by Robert Chetwyn, with Ian McKellan as Max, a spoiled young man accustomed to taking advantage of others, who learns the meaning of caring about others in a concentration camp. It transfers to the Criterion Theatre on July 4. There are 33 showings at the Court; 134 at the Criterion. On Dec 2, the play opens in New York at the Apollo, with Richard Gere as Max and David Dukes as a fellow internee. Robert Allan Ackerman directs. There are 240 performances, and it's chosen a "Best Play."

May 24 *Close of Play* (L—Lyttelton—Drama). Simon Gray's vision of a bickering English family is staged by Harold Pinter. Michael Redgrave plays Jasper, the ailing head of the clan, now incapable of responding to their angry, impatient questions. Among the cast are Anna Massey, Zena Walker, Michael Gambon, and John Standing.

June 14 *Flowers for Algernon* (L—Queen's—Musical). Charles Strouse creates the score for David Rodgers's book, based on the novel by Daniel Keyes. Michael Crawford plays Charlie Gordon, retarded and withdrawn, with a mouse (Algernon) as his friend. Cheryl Kennedy plays Alice Kinnian, who befriends him as doctors dramatically increase his intelligence in lab sessions. only to have him slip back to his former stupor. Peter Coe directs. There are only 28 performances. The show will later be a failure on Broadway.

June 20 *Undiscovered Country* (L—Olivier—Drama). Tom Stoppard adapts Arthur Schnitzler's drama of frustrated Viennese sexuality and cruelty, staged by Peter Wood. John Wood plays Friedrich Hofreiter, a rich, powerful man, who encourages his wife to have an affair, then kills her young officer in a duel. Dorothy Tutin plays his suffering wife, Gina.

July 16 *Dogg's Hamlet/Cahoot's Macbeth* (L—Collegiate—Drama). Tom Stoppard revises the first Shakespearian classic as a schoolboys' production. The second is presented as an homage to the private-home productions of plays by Czech playwright Pavel Kohout and fellow dissenters have been giving. This is a production of the British-American Repertory Theatre (BART). In the troupe are Stephen D. Newman, Alan Thompson, and Ruth Hunt, among others. On Oct 3, the shows open in New York at the 22 Steps and later tour.

July 21 *The Gin Game.* See NY premiere, 1977.

Sep 13 *The Case of the Oily Levantine* (L—Her Majesty's—Drama). Anthony Shaffer, author of the mystery thriller *Sleuth*, tries to repeat his earlier West End success. It is not so fated. In his cast, directed by Patrick Dromgoole, are Anna Quayle, Hywel Bennett, and Gwen Nelson, among others. It is seen only 60 times.

Oct 18 *Beatlemania.* See NY premiere, 1977.

Nov 2 *Amadeus* (L—Olivier—Drama). Peter Shaffer's new play shows an aged, dying Salieri repeating his claim that he poisoned Mozart, the musical genius he

so envied when he, Salieri, was powerful in Vienna's music life but not able to compose such sublime music. Paul Scofield slips in and out of age and youth as Salieri. Simon Callow plays the oafish, outspoken, scatalogical Mozart. Felicity Kendal is Constanze Mozart. Peter Hall directs. John Bury designs. It opens at the Broadhurst on Dec 17, 1980.

Nov 13 *Last of the Red Hot Lovers* (L—Criterion—Comedy). Lee Montague plays Barney Cashman, a love-lorn man who thinks he's missing out on the sexual revolution. In Neil Simon's Broadway play, he tries his luck with three different women (Susan Engel, Georgina Hale, and Bridget Turner). It's a disaster every time. Eric Thompson stages. The play has had its British premiere in April in Manchester at the Royal Exchange Theatre.

Nov 21 *Stage Struck* (L—Vaudeville—Comedy). Simon Gray's play, staged by Stephen Hollis, is animated by Alan Bates, Andrew Sharp, Sheila Ballantine, and Nigel Stock. In this comedy-thriller, Robert Simon, an ex-stage manager, has been keeping house for his successful actress-wife while having sexual adventures on the side. A psychiatrist upsets all this, leading Simon to plan an ingenious, stage-managed revenge on wife and shrink.

Nov 22 *Waiting for the Parade* (L—Lyric, Hammersmith—Drama). John Murrell's Canadian play is the second production in the restored Lyric Theatre. It deals with five women—played by Frances Cuka, Beth Morris, Deborah Norton, Fiona Reid, and June Watson—all trying to survive the tensions of life on the home-front in World War II. Richard Cottrell stages.

Dec 28 *Piaf* (L—Aldwych—Drama). Pam Gems's drama about the French chanteuse is a Royal Shakespeare production seen first at the Warehouse last June. Jane Lapotaire plays Edith Piaf. This show will be seen on Broadway, starring Lapotaire.

of *Albie Sachs*, opening on Nov 6.

Jan 4 At London's Round House, the show is a revue, *It's Nothing Serious*. On Jan 22, Michel de Ghelderode's *Pantagleize* is on view. Evelyn Waugh's novel, *The Ordeal of Gilbert Pinfold*, in an adaptation by Ronald Harwood, comes to life on Feb 14. Michael Hordern plays Pinfold. Michael Elliott directs. Director Andrew Carr, Altom Kumalo, and Peter Rodda devise *Mister Biko*, with Kumalo as the South African black, Stephen Biko, who died in prison. This opens on March 7. On April 10, Strindberg's *Miss Julie* opens, directed by Eric Hillyard. Manchester's Royal Exchange Theatre returns on April 18 with T. S. Eliot's *The Family Reunion*. Elliott directs. Ibsen's *The Lady from the Sea* is another Manchester production, staged by Elliott, opening on May 16. Vanessa Redgrave plays Elida, with Terence Stamp as the Stranger. New York's Living Theatre troupe present *Prometheus*, with Julian Beck as Zeus and Lenin. His wife, Judith Malina, is Io and Emma Goldman. Josef Szajna opens his Warsaw Teatr Studio production of *Dante*, September 4. The National Youth Theatre mounts *A Midsummer Night's Dream* on September 18, with David Weston directing. Tennessee Williams' *The Glass Menagerie*, opening on November 20, has screen star Gloria Grahame as Amanda Wingfield.

Jan 11 Ellen Stewart's La Mama E. T. C. continues its hectic program on East 4th Street in New York. John Morrow's *Frank & Ruby* is followed by Harvey Fierstein's *Fugue in a Nursery*, part of a trilogy dealing with homosexual sensibilities. Other shows include *Man and Artifact* and the striking Polish production of Tadeusz Kantor's Cricot Two Theatre, *The Dead Class*, followed by *Re-Arrangements*, Winston Tong's *Bound Feet/Nijinsky*, *Beowulf, a Pageant*, Viera's *Dreams of a Mischievous Heart Shipwrecked on Illusion*, Kobo Abe's *The Little Elephant Is Dead*, Jeff Weiss's *And That's How the Rent Gets Paid*. Liviu Ciulei's Bulandra Theatre ensemble from Bucharest, Roumania, plays Paul Foster's *Elizabeth I* and Ion Caragiale's *The Lost Letter*. Other shows include Rosalyn Drexler's *Vulgar Lives*, Harvey Fierstein's *Widows and Children First*, Meredith Monk's *Recent Ruins*, and Ronald Tavel's *The Nutcracker in the Land of Nuts*.

Jan 11 The Phoenix Theatre continues its season at the Marymount Manhattan Theatre with Corinne Jacker's *Later*, staged by Daniel Freudenberger. Steve Robman directs Ron Hutchinson's *Says I, Says He*, opening on Feb 19, followed by the March 27 premiere of Botho Strauss's German drama, *Big and Little*, in a Freudenberger mounting. Director Philip Prowse recreates his Glasgow Citizens' Theatre production—which he designed—of Robert David MacDonald's *Chinchilla*, a parable about creating art, based on Serge Di-

1979 REVIVALS/REPERTORIES

Jan 3 In Edinburgh at the Traverse Theatre, the new year begins with Reg Bolton's *Robinson Crusoe*. There are some 31 programs, some by visiting troupes. Among the shows are Flann O'Brien's *The Dalkey Archive*, Neil Hornick's *Loaded Questions*, Michael Wilcox's *Rents*, Andrew Dallmeyer's *A Big Treatise in Store*, Caryl Churchill's *Cloud Nine*—in 1981 an Off-Broadway hit, Michael Burrell's *Hess*, John Byrne's *The Loveliest Night of the Year*, Alan Williams' *The Cockroach That Ate Cincinnati*, Elizabeth Bond's *The Black Stuffer*, Donald Campbell's *The Widows of Clyth*, and Tom McGrath's *Animal*, programmed as part of the Edinburgh Festival.

Jan 3 At the Manhattan Theatre Club, David Rush's *Beethoven/Karl* opens with

George Voskovec as the aged composer. On Feb 7, Roberta Maxwell plays the British poetess Stevie Smith in *Stevie*, by Hugh Whitemore, directed by Brian Murray. On Feb 13, Joanna Glass's *Artichoke*, a Canadian comedy, is staged by the MTC's director, Lynne Meadow, with a cast including Patricia Elliott, Rex Robbins, James Greene, and Daniel Keyes. John Hopkins's *Losing Time* opens on March 28, with Edwin Sherin directing a cast including Shirley Knight and Jane Alexander. Ödön von Hörvath's *Don Juan Comes Back from War*, in a Stephen Pascal staging, opens on April 3, with Peter Evans as the Don. Nigel Baldwin's *Just a Little Bit Less Than-Normal* bows on May 9. *Losing Time* returns on Sep 11, shorter but not better, for a six-week run, the same time given David Edgar's *The Jail Diary*

aghilev. Michael Cristofer plays the title role, a nickname. The fall season opens on Oct 18 with David Lan's *The Winter Dancers*, in Keith Hack's staging. *Shout Across the River*, by Stephen Poliakoff, opens on Dec 27, directed by Robert Woodruff, done in London by the Royal Shakespeare in 1978 at the Warehouse.

Jan 11 Hugh Leonard's *Da* is shown in London at the Greenwich Theatre, staged by Robert Gillespie, with Eamon Kelly as Da. On Feb 28, David Turner's *Semi-Detached* is revived in Leonard Rossiter's staging. Jonathan Miller directs George Etherege's Restoration comedy *She Would If She Could*, opening on April 5 with Margaret Courtenay as Lady Cockwood. Ferenc Molnar's *The Play's the Thing* is revived by director Alan Strachan on May 17. On June 28, Pirandello's *Six Characters in Search of an Author* has a revival, staged by Phil Young. On Aug 6, Alan Ayckbourn's *Ten Times Table* has staging by Tenniel Evans. Trevor Baxter's *The Undertaking* opens on Aug 29, with Kenneth Williams. On Sep 20, the play is Anne Valery's *The Passing-Out Parade*, followed on Nov 1 by Bernice Rubens' *I Sent a Letter To My Love*, staged by Strachan. Patrick Mason directs the revival of Oliver Goldsmith's *She Stoops To Conquer* opening Dec 13, with Paul Hardwick and Ursula Jeans.

Jan 14 In Greenwich Village, playwright Milan Stitt is currently dramaturg of the Circle Repertory Theatre. His drama, *The Runner Stumbles*, is revived tonight for a run of 35 showings. On March 4, John Bishop's *Winter Signs* opens, staged by Marshall Mason. The season closes with Judd Hirsch and Trish Hawkins in Lanford Wilson's *Talley's Folly*, staged by Mason. Opening on May 3, the play will transfer to Broadway and win Wilson a Pulitzer Prize. The fall season begins on Oct 18 with *Reunion*, three short plays by David Mamet: *The Sanctity of Marriage*, *Dark Pony*, and the title play. Mamet stages. On Dec 12 and 13, the Circle begins repertory performances of Shakespeare's *Hamlet* and Schiller's *Mary Stuart*. There will be a total of 77 performances.

Jan 17 Tennessee Williams's *A Lovely Sunday for Creve Coeur* is staged by Keith Hack at the Hudson Guild Theatre. On March 7, David Mercer's *Ride a Cock Horse* opens, staged by Geoffrey Sherman. Abe Polsky's tale of a trial after the deadly ordeal of the Donner Party in the High Sierras, *Devour the Snow*, opens on May 2, winning critical praise which encourages producers to move it to Broadway, where it rapidly dies. Terry Schreiber stages.

Jan 17 Jerome Savary brings his Grand Magic Circus from Paris to the West End, where they take over the Shaftesbury Theatre, presenting *1001 Nights*, Savaroy's musical fantasy, with Michael Dus-

sarrat as Sinbad and Maxime Lobard as Aladdin. Gail Gatterburg is Sheherazade. There are 43 performances.

Jan 18 Richard Nelson's *Vienna Notes* opens at Playwrights' Horizons on West 42nd Street in New York. Andre Ernotte stages. On Feb 21, William Finn's *In Trousers* opens, with Chip Zien as the youthful hero, Marvin. Finn stages the show with minimal setting and maximum energy. On March 21, James Lapine's *Table Settings* opens, staged by the author. On April 19, the play is *The Terrorists*, by Dallas Murphy, Jr.

Jan 21 The Citizens' Theatre in Glasgow, directed by Giles Havergal, opens the new year with *Orpheus*, followed by *Macbeth*, *Country Life*, *Chinchilla*, *The Good-Humoured Ladies*, *Pygmalion*, *The Maid's Tragedy*, and *Puss in Boots*.

Jan 25 At the New York Shakespeare Festival's Public Theatre in the Village, Joseph Papp conceives a Black and Hispanic Acting Ensemble, bowing tonight with *Julius Caesar*, staged by Michael Langham, who also mounts *Coriolanus* for the troupe, opening on March 14. There are 42 and 13 performances, respectively. On Feb 1, Papp opens a musical, *The Umbrellas of Cherbourg*, based on the French film. Andrei Serban directs, and the show later tours on the West Coast. Thomas Babe's *Taken in Marriage*, staged by Robert Allan Ackerman, opens on Feb 22. A musical, *Sanchocho*, has a one-week run, beginning March 28. Elizabeth Swado's *Dispatches* bows on April 18. On April 25, David Mamet's *The Woods* is on view in one of the Public's several theatres. *Wake Up, It's Time To Go To Bed* opens on May 16, staged by author Carson Kievman. There is also an active program of workshop productions.

Feb 1 At London's Young Vic Theatre, John Labanowski plays Jimmy Porter in Mel Smith's staging of John Osborne's *Look Back in Anger*. The Oxford Playhouse troupe presents Nigel Williams's *Class Enemy*, on Feb 28. Nicolas Kent directs. On June 1, Joe Orton's *What the Butler Saw* gets a revival from director Michael Attenborough. On July 4, *Faust!*, a new rock musical is staged by Michael Bogdanov. On Sep 20, Antony Milner plays the Dane in *Hamlet*, staged by Bogdanov. Tom Stoppard's *Rosencrantz and Guildenstern Are Dead* opens on Oct 16. On Oct 29, Ivor Dembina's *1917* tells four stories of the Russian Revolution, staged by Sarah Harding. Nov 20, *The Merchant of Venice* opens, directed by Attenborough. On Nov 28, *The Ancient Mariner* appears, adapted and staged by Bogdanov from Coleridge's poem. On Dec 10, John Edward Adams presents his staging of Elizabeth Bond's *The Messiah of Ismir*. Bogdanov directs Ken Hill's adaptation of Victor Hugo's *The Hunchback of Notre Dame*, opening on Dec 19.

Feb 2 Sam Shepard's *Seduced* opens at

the American Place Theatre in mid-town Manhattan, staged by playwright Jack Gelber. Rip Torn plays an aging recluse, rather like Howard Hughes. On April 22, Jonathan Reynold's *Tunnel Fever, or The Sheep Is Out* confounds audiences in the Marshall Oglesby staging.

Feb 7 *Brimstone and Treacle* by Dennis Potter opens at London's Open Space. Robert Chetwyn directs. Leopold Von Sacher-Masoch's *Venus in Furs*, adapted by Philip Oxman, opens on Mar 22, staged by Geoff Moore. James Kirkwood's Broadway play *P.S. Your Cat Is Dead!*, has an April 19 opening. Christopher Gable plays Jimmy. On July 18, the play is David Mamet's American backstage comedy, *A Life in the Theatre*, with Freddie Jones and Patrick Ryecart. Nikolas Simmonds stages Bertolt Brecht's *Private Life of the Third Reich*, opening on Sep 12. On Nov 8, Denholm Elliott plays the Captain in Strindberg's *The Father*, staged by Charles Marowitz, with Diane Cilento as Laura.

Feb 8 On the Olivier stage of London's National Theatre, William Gaskill directs this revival of Middleton and Rowley's *A Fair Quarrel*, with Nicky Henson and Margery Yates. On March 8, Leo Tolstoy's *The Fruits of Enlightenment* bows in Christopher Morahan's staging. Ralph Richardson and Joyce Redman play Master and Mistress. *As You Like It* is revived in John Dexter's staging on Aug 1. Sara Kestelman and Simon Callow are Rosalind and Orland. Morahan directs John Wood in *Richard III*, revived on Oct 4. Ibsen's *The Wild Duck*, in a new Christopher Hampton version, opens on Dec 13, staged again by Morahan. Richardson, Michael Bryant, and Yvonne Bryceland are among the cast.

Feb 14 Charles Repole plays the Eddie Cantor role in this revival of the 1928 musical *Whoopee!* on Broadway at the ANTA Theatre. It's William Anthony McGuire's adaptation of Owen Davis's *The Nervous Wreck*, with some updating. Seen first in East Haddam, Connecticut, at the historic Goodspeed Opera House, the show is staged by Frank Corsaro. There are 204 performances.

Feb 15 At New York's Theatre of the Open Eye on the Upper East Side, Jean Erdman revives her adaptation of James Joyce's *Finnegan's Wake*, called *The Coach with the Six Insides*, for 31 performances.

Feb 20 Four Eugene O'Neill sea plays are offered in London in the National Theatre's Cottesloe Theatre, staged by Bill Bryden. They are: *The Moon of the Caribbees*, *Bound East for Cardiff*, *In the Zone*, and *The Long Voyage Home*. Bryden stages his version of Michael Herr's Vietnam reporting, *Dispatches*, on June 6. Arthur Kopit's *Wings*, so successful in New York, opens on Aug 15 with Constance Cummings repeating her Broadway role. John

Madden stages. *Lark Rise*, as adapted by Keith Dewhurst, opens on Oct 15, staged by Bryden and Sebastian Graham-Jones. On Nov 7, *Candlefords*, a companion to *Lark Rise*, opens with the same credits.

March 14 The Royal Shakespeare Company offers Alan Howard in the title role of *Coriolanus*, opening now in London at the Aldwych, directed by Terry Hands. John Barton's Stratford production of *Love's Labour's Lost* opens on April 11, designed by Ralph Koltai and Nick Chelton. On April 24, Michael Bogdanov's Stratford staging of *The Taming of the Shrew* joins the repertory, with Jonathan Pryce and Paola Dionisotti in the leads. Mikhail Bulgakov's *The White Guard* bows on May 29, directed by Barry Kyle. Glenda Jackson appears with Howard in *Antony and Cleopatra*, Peter Brook's Stratford staging, on July 6. On Sep 4, Moss Hart and George S. Kaufman's *Once in a Lifetime* is revived, directed by Trevor Nunn and Walter Donohue. Hands stages Maxim Gorky's *Children of the Sun* opening on Oct. 9, followed on Nov 6 by Kyle's mounting of *Measure for Measure*.

March 15 Joyce Carey plays Miss Marple in this revival of Agatha Christie's *A Murder is Announced*, staged by Charles Hickman for the Vaudeville Theatre in London. It runs ten weeks.

March 20 In Islington at St. George's Theatre, *Beowulf*, adapted by Lawrence Butler, is played with puppets as part of the Puppet Theatre '79 Festival. On April 25, *Julius Caesar* is revived on the Elizabethan stage, Don Taylor directing. George Murcell, the theatre's founder, directs *Richard II* for a May 23 opening. *As You Like It* opens on June 20, in Murcell's staging.

March 24 At the Brooklyn Academy of Music, the Goodspeed Opera House revival of the Bolton/Thompson/Gershwin musical, *Tip-Toes*, opens, staged by Sue Lawless. On March 27, Peter Terson's *Good Lads at Heart* opens for a two-week run, a guest appearance of the National Youth Theatre of Britain, directed by Michael Croft.

March 28 The Royal Shakespeare Company opens its annual season on Stratford-upon-Avon with *The Merry Wives of Windsor*, staged by Trevor Nunn and John Caird. John Woodvine is Falstaff. David Jones directs *Cymbeline*. Judi Dench is Imogen, with Roger Rees as Posthumus. Napier designs *Twelfth Night* for director Terry Hands. Donald Sinden plays the title role in Ronald Eyre's production of *Othello*. Barry Kyle stages *Julius Caesar*. Ben Kingsley is Brutus; David Threlfall, Mark Antony.

March 28 At the Royal Shakespeare's Other Place in Stratford-upon-Avon, the season of experimental productions, with their directors, opens with Shakespeare's *Pericles* (Ron Daniels); David Edgar's The

Jail Diary of Albie Sachs (Howard Davies); Nikolai Erdmann's *The Suicide* (Daniels); Bert Brecht's *Baal* (David Jones); Eugene O'Neill's *Anna Christie* (Jonathan Lynn); Anton Chekhov's *The Three Sisters* (Trevor Nunn).

April 4 The Golden Jubilee season continues at the Dublin Gate Theatre with the opening of Ruth and Augustus Goetz's *The Heiress*. The singer Brendan O'Dowda then presents his one-man show, *The World of Percy French*.

April 5 In Manhattan at its Westside Theatre, the Chelsea Theatre Center has its first season not divided between this space and the Brooklyn Academy of Music. Max Frisch's *Biography* opens; Arne Zaslove directs. On May 31, *Strider: The Story of a Horse* opens to admiring reviews which encourage its later transfer to Broadway. Robert Kalfin, has adapted the Russian dramatization of Leo Tolstoy's story, *Kholstomer: The Story of a Horse.*

April 19 Arthur Miller's *The Price* is revived Off Broadway at the Harold Clurman Theatre on 42nd Street's Theatre Row. John Stix directs. Mitchell Ryan and Scotty Bloch play Victor and Esther Franz, with Fritz Weaver as Walter Franz, and Joseph Buloff as Solomons, the furniture-buyer. Moving to the Playhouse on Broadway, opening June 19, it earns an 18 week run.

April 20 At the Royal Shakespeare's London experimental stage, the Warehouse, Covent Garden, Howard Brenton's *The Churchill Play* is on view, brought up from Stratford-upon-Avon. Barry Kyle directs. Another Stratford import is *The Merchant of Venice*, bowing on May 2 in John Barton's production. On May 24, Howard Davies' staging of Tom McGrath's *The Innocent* opens. On June 15, Pam Gems's *Piaf* opens, with Jane Lapotaire in the title-role, directed by Howard Davies. This show comes from Stratford's Other Place as does David Rudkin's version of Euripides' *Hippolytus*, opening on June 27.

April 24 At the Shaftesbury Theatre in the West End, the musical *Canterbury Tales* is revived. Martin Starkie, who has adapted the show from Chaucer with Nevill Coghill, does the directing. There are 149 performances.

May 1 W. Somerset Maugham's *For Services Rendered* comes back to fitful life on the Lyttelton stage of the National Theatre. Michael Rudman directs this melodrama of World War I veterans who cannot adjust to postwar life. On Sep 20, Arthur Miller's *Death of a Salesman* opens, rapidly acclaimed by critics and public; values are discovered in this revival which were not so apparent in its London premiere. Warren Mitchell plays Willy Loman, with Doreen Mantle as Linda. Michael Rudman directs. On Dec 12, J. B. Priestley's *When We Are Married* is revived, directed by Robin Lefevre.

UNDISCOVERED COUNTRY

Among the cast are Harold Innocent, Joan Sanderson, Peter Jeffrey, Leslie Sands, Mary Maddox, and John Quayle.

May 7 The Comedie Francaise comes to the Brooklyn Academy of Music with two productions from its celebrated repretory. Molière's *Le Misanthrope*, staged by Pierre Dux, and Feydeau's *La Puce a l'Oreille (A Flea in Her Ear)*, directed by Jean-Laurent Cochet.

May 8 Opening the annual Chichester Festival is Shaw's *The Devil's Disciple*, with John Clements as General Burgoyne. Festival Director Peter Dews stages. Kaufman and Hart's *The Man Who Came To Dinner* has Charles Gray as Sheridan Whiteside. Patrick Lau directs. Wilde's *The Importance of Being Earnest* has Hayley Mills and Mel Martin as Gwendolen and Cecily, with Ian Ogilvy as Earnest. Dews directs Cocteau's *The Eagle Has Two Heads*, staged by David William, features Jill Bennett as the Queen.

May 22 The Shaw Festival opens at Canada's Niagara-on-the-Lake, running until Sep 30, with a total audience of 140,655. Tony Van Bridge directs the premiere show, *You Never Can Tell. Village Wooing* is staged by Scott Swan. *Captain Brassbound's Conversion* is directed by Douglas Campbell. Campbell stages Jerome Kilty's *Dear Liar*. Donal Donnelly plays Shaw in *My Astonishing Self*, by Michael Voysey. Emlyn Williams's *The Corn Is Green* is directed by Leslie Yeo. Yeo's staging of Noel Coward's *Blithe Spirit* has an extensive post-season tour of cities and towns in New York and Canada in the Ontario area.

May 29 At Gene Feist's Roundabout Theatre Off Broadway, a program of six revivals opens with Dick Goldberg's *Family Business*, with 32 performances, staged by John Stix. Ibsen's *Little Eyolf*, directed by Feist, opens on June 29. On Nov 29,

TAKEN IN MARRIAGE

Stix's production of Inge's *The Dark at the Top of the Stairs* opens for a run of 62 performances.

May 29 A play about Mark Twain and the immortal characters he created, called *The Reflections of Mark Twain*, is presented in the Clemens Amphitheatre in Hannibal, Missouri, where Twain was born.

June 1 At Joseph Papp's New York Public Theatre, Irene Worth and George Voskovec revive Samuel Beckett's *Happy Days* for a run of three months. Andrei Serban directs them. On June 7, at the Royal Court Theatre in London, Billie Whitelaw plays Winnie in *Happy Days*, with the playwright directing her. Leonard Fenton is Willie.

June 4 At the Open Air Theatre in Regent's Park in London, *A Midsummer Night's Dream* is staged by David Weston. On July 3, *Twelfth Night* opens, followed on Aug 13 by a double-bill of *Overruled* and *O'Flaherty V.C.* by George Bernard Shaw.

June 5 Canada's Stratford Festival opens another season in its western Ontario home, under the artistic direction of Robin Phillips. Phillips and Urjo Kareda team up to direct *Love's Labour's Lost*, designed by Daphne Dare. Peter Moss stages both parts of *Henry IV*. *Othello* is directed by Frances Hyland. Last season's *Ned and Jack* returns. Zoe Caldwell directs *Richard II*, with Dare designing. Wilde's *The Importance of Being Earnest* returns. Philip Barry's *Holiday*, outfitted with Cole Porter's music, becomes *Happy New Year*, staged by Burt Shevelove and choreographed by Donald Saddler. Edward Bond's *The Woman* is co-directed by Moss and Kareda. *King Lear* is a Phillips-Dare production. Pamela Hawthorn stages *The Taming of the Shrew*, Kathryn Shaw does the same for Steve Petch's play, *Victoria*. Lorca's *Yerma* is the basis of an improvisation, *barren/Yerma*, directed by

Pam Brighton.

June 12 The San Diego National Shakespeare Festival opens with *Julius Caesar*, staged by Jerome Kilty, followed by *The Comedy of Errors*, directed by Ken Ruta, and *Macbeth*, staged by Nagle Jackson. On June 26 at the nearby Carter Center Stage, Alan Ayckbourn's *The Norman Conquests* has a total of 77 performances for this trilogy. Producing director Craig Noel stages.

June 12 Rodgers and Hammerstein's *The King and I* returns to the London stage, opening at the Palladium with Yul Brynner and Virginia McKenna. Yuriko directs the revival, recreating Jerome Robbins' choreography.

June 14 Al Pacino opens on Broadway at the Cort Theatre in Shakespeare's *Richard III*, playing Richard of Gloucester. David Wheeler directs. This vanity production runs four weeks. *Newsweek's* Jack Kroll says, "It's not that Pacino gives a bad performance—bad is not the word; impossible would be closer. Pacino tries to enlist the audience in an anti-highbrow conspiracy; he stalks about the stage as the malevolent, deformed Duke, crumpled beneath his hunchback, flashing the audience looks as if to say, 'Come on, let's cut all this Shakespeare bull. You and I know this is just good old Godfather stuff, decked out in highfalutin language, so let's have fun.' But Pacino's lowfalutin approach destroys both the fun and the art in Shakespeare."

June 15 The Oregon Shakespeare Festival in Ashland opens its annual summer season with Dennis Bigelow's production of *A Midsummer Night's Dream*, followed by Marlowe's *The Tragical History of Doctor Faustus*, directed by Jerry Turner. The final outdoor production, playing in rep, is *As You Like It*, staged by Audrey Stanley. Indoors, in the Angus Bowmer Theatre, the productions are Kanin's *Born Yesterday*, opening on June 2, staged by

James Moels. On the 3rd, Pat Patton staging of *Macbeth* opens, followed b Molnar's *The Play's the Thing* on the 6t staged by Bigelow. Turner stages Ibsen *The Wild Duck* on July 26. In the Blac Swan Theatre, Hailey's *Who's Happ Now?*, directed by Michael Leibert, ope on June 1, followed on the 3rd by Robe Symonds' direction of Machiavelli's *Ro of the Mandrake* and John Orlock's *I dulgences in the Louisville Harem*, stage by Michael Kevin. Among the ensemb are Fredi Olster, Ronald Edmundso Woods, Mimi Carr, Richard Rossi, an Joan Stuart-Morris.

June 19 T. S. Eliot's verse-drama, *Th Family Reunion*, based on Aeschylu *Oresteia*, has a revival in London at th Vaudeville Theatre. It transfers from th Round House but has originated in Man chester with the Royal Exchange Com pany. There are 174 performances.

June 19 Brandon Thomas' vintage farce *Charley's Aunt*, comes back to the Wes End, opening at the Adelphi Theatre i Bill Robertson's staging. John Inman play Lord Fancourt Babberley, with Heler Cherry as Donna Lucia.

June 21 Oliver Hailey's *Father's Day* i revived at the American Place Theatre fo a run of almost 13 weeks, staged by Rae Allen. The three divorced women are played by Susan Tyrell, Marybeth Hurt, and Tammy Grimes.

June 22 In Stratford, Connecticut, Gerald Freedman is artistic director of the American Shakespeare Festival, recovering from financial and artistic difficulties of recent summers. He stages all three Shakespearean plays, opening with *Julius Caesar*, followed by *Twelfth Night*, and *The Tempest*. Among his actors are Kenneth Haigh, Robert Burr, Ellen Tobie, Anne Kerry, and Harris Yulin. Designers include Robin Wagner, Ming Cho Lee, Jeanne Button, Ray Diffen, and Martin Aronstein.

June 22 In Central Park's Delacorte Theatre, Joseph Papp opens the annual summer New York Shakespeare Festival with *Coriolanus*, staged by Wilford Leach, who also stages *Othello* on June 27. The *Coriolanus* cast is Papp's Black and Hispanic Acting Ensemble. In *Othello*, Raul Julia plays the Moor. Richard Dreyfuss is Iago. Starting August 17, the Festival's Mobile Theatre begins touring New York boroughs with Richard Wesley's *The Mighty Gents*, staged by Ntozake Shange.

June 23 *The Legend Of Tom Dooley*, by Thomas Fuller, about Tom Dula, a Civil War hero, opens today in Wilkesboro's Lakeside Amphitheatre, which seats 1500. This is another North Carolina historical drama.

July 13 Wallace Shawn's *Marie and Bruce* seen first in New York at Joseph Papp's Public Theatre opens at the Royal Court in London at the Theatre Upstairs. Michael Hastings' *Carnival War a Go Hot* opens on August 17. Richard Crane performs his monologue, *Gogol*, on September 19. Barrie Keeffe's *Sus* opens on October 5. On the 31st, David Mowat's *The Guise* comes alive in Roland Rees' staging. Edward Bond's *The Worlds* opens on November 21, directed by Bond and designed by Eamon D'Arcy and Andy Phillips.

July 15 At Joseph Papp's Public Theatre in Greenwich Village, Ntozake Shange's play, *Spell #7* opens for a run of 175 performances, staged by Oz Scott. On Oct 25, Beckett's *Mercier & Camier* opens. On Nov 15, Joseph Chaikin performs *Tongues*, a collaboration with Sam Shepard, composed of *Tongues* and *Savage/Love*. Tina Howe's *The Art of Dining* opens on Dec 6, staged by A. J. Antoon. This is followed on the 11th by Peter Parnell's *Sorrows of Stephen*, with John Shea as Stephen, under the influence of Goethe's *Sorrows of Werther*. This runs 21 weeks, staged by Sheldon Larry.

Aug 1 In London, *Hamlet* is this evening's Old Vic Company production, staged by Toby Robertson. Derek Jacobi plays the melancholy prince. On August 17, Robertson offers his staging of *Romeo and Juliet*. Barbara Jefford plays Nurse, with Ian Richardson as Mercutio. On Sep 3, Gogol's *The Government Inspector* opens, staged by Robertson and Christopher Selbie. Richardson plays the imposter, Klestakov. On the 27th, the Old Vic Company offers *Miss in Her Teens* and *The Padlock*, directed respectively by John Dove and Robertson. On Oct 22, Joe Orton's black comedy, *What the Butler Saw*, gets a revival, staged by John Dobe. On Nov 25, *The Trial of Queen Caroline* is staged by Robertson. Prunella Scales plays the humiliated queen, repudiated by King George IV. Others in the cast include Barbara Leigh-Hunt and Timothy West.

Aug 19 At the Edinburgh Festival this summer, the impressario of the Ballet Russe de Monte Carlo, Sergei Diaghilev, is being honored in exhibitions, dance events, and in some theatre offerings. From the Clydeside comes the troupe of the Glasgow Citizens' Theatre with two salutes: Robert David MacDonald's *Chinchilla* is loosely based on events and personalities in Diaghilev's life. MacDonald's *The Good-Humoured Ladies* is a reworking of Carlo Goldoni's comic satire, with decors inspired by Leon Bakst's sets for the Ballet Russe. Edinburgh's Traverse Theatre Company presents Billy Connolly's *The Red Runner* and Tom McGrath's *The Animal*, with actors impersonating jungle simians. The Bristol Old Vic Company brings Shakespeare's *Troilus and Cressida*, and George Farquhar's *The Recruiting Officer*. Both are staged by Richard Cottrell. Russia's Rustavelli Company present Shakespeare's *Richard III*

and Bertolt Brecht's *The Caucasian Chalk Circle*. This Georgian ensemble from Tbilisi is directed by R. Sturua.

Aug 28 Howard Brenton's *Sore Throats* opens at the Warehouse, Covent Garden, the Royal Shakespeare's experimental stage. Barry Kyle directs. Nigel Baldwin's *Men's Beano* opens on September 17, directed by Bill Alexander. On November 5, the play is Peter Whelan's *Captain Swing*, directed by Alexander.

Sep 4 The National Youth Theatre offers *The Merchant of Venice* in London at the Jeannetta Cochrane Theatre. Michael Croft and Paul Hill have done the staging. The troupe also performs *A Midsummer Night's Dream* on the 18th, at the Round House, in a David Weston staging.

Sep 6 The musical version of James Barrie's *Peter Pan* is revived on Broadway at the Lunt-Fontanne Theatre, starring Sandy Duncan as Peter, with George Rose as Captain Hook. Rob Iscove stages and choreographs. The show earns a run of 550 performances, followed by an extended national tour.

Sep 20 The Equity Library Theatre (ELT) opens its season of revivals in Manhattan at the Masters Theatre with *The Sound of Music*, followed by Mosel's *All the Way Home*, the musical *Canterbury Tales*, *Romeo and Juliet*, Laurent's *Time of the Cuckoo*, the musical *Plain and Fancy*, Kaufman and Connelly's *Merton of the Movies*, and the Berlin musical, *Annie Get Your Gun*.

Sep 25 At the Theatre Royal, Drury Lane, London audiences can see the Michael Stewart/Jerry Herman *Hello, Dolly!* again. Carol Channing is Mrs. Dolly Levi. Lucia Victor directs, from Gower Champion's original. The American actor Eddie Bracken plays Horace Vandergelder.

Oct 1 At London's Shaftesbury Theatre, the Questors Theatre production, *The Coarse Acting Show 2*, seen at Edinburgh at the Fringe Festival, now opens with parodies entitled *Moby Dick*, *Last Call for Breakfast (Dernier Appel au Petit Déjeuner)*, *The Cherry Sisters*, and *Henry the Tenth (Part Seven)*. Michael Green, coauthor of three of the sketches and an authority on Coarse Acting, directs the shows. On the 2nd, *The Cambridge Revue*, also from Edinburgh, opens, followed on the 5th by another Edinburgh production, *Instant Sunshine*.

Oct 6 Charles Ludlam's Ridiculous Theatrical Company offer his vintage space-fantasy of drag queens and other oddities: *Conquest of the Universe, Or When Queens Collide*. On December 1, the troupe revives its quaint staging of Dickens' *A Christmas Carol*, adapted and directed by Ludlam, who also stars as Scrooge.

Oct 10 The Dublin Gate Theatre's contribution to the Dublin Theatre Festival is this production of Desmond Forristal's

Captive Audience, staged by Hilton Edwards. The only other production presented this fall is Tom Stoppard's *Enter a Free Man*.

Oct 14 Christopher Martin's Classic Stage Company (CSC) opens a repertory season of five programs, beginning with William Butler Yeats' five-play cycle, *Cuchulain the Warrior King*, including *At The Hawk's Well*, *The Green Helmet*, *On Baile's Strand*, *The Only Jealousy of Emer*, and *The Death of Cuchulain*. Martin stages all the plays. Jean Anouilh's *The Cavern* opens on October 28, followed on December 16 by Marlowe's *Doctor Faustus*.

Oct 18 At Radio City Music Hall, recently threatened with destruction, owing to steadily decreasing audiences for sporadic and disappointing productions, a new producing policy is in force, lead by Robert F. Jani, a former Walt Disney executive. Joe Cook's stage adaptation of *Snow White and the Seven Dwarfs*, directed and choreographed by Frank Wagner, opens the house, completely refurbished to its 1931 Art Deco brilliance. Mary Jo Salerno is Snow White, with Anne Francine as the evil queen. The show has 106 performances, its run interrupted by the annual holiday show, called this year *The Magnificent Christmas Spectacular*, opening on November 25.

Oct 18 Bernard Shaw's *You Never Can Tell*, staged by David Giles, opens the newly restored Lyric Theatre, Hammersmith. Paul Rogers plays the Waiter, with Lynsey Baxter and Peter Egan as Dolly and Valentine.

Oct 19 Marc Blitzstein's opera, *Regina*, based on Lillian Hellman's *The Little Foxes*, is revived Off-off Broadway by the Encompass Theatre, staged by Nancy Rhodes. Other productions include Jeff Sweet's play, *Porch*; Howard Richardson and E. G. Kasakoff's *A Thread of Scarlet*; a program of short operas, *Fantasies Take Flight*, and Carl Orff's opera, *The Wise Woman (Die Kluge)*.

Oct 25 At London's Adelphi Theatre, the Lerner and Loewe musical, *My Fair Lady*, is revived. Tony Britton and Liz Robertson play Henry Higgins and Eliza Doolittle. Robin Midgley stages. Anna Neagle graces the production as Higgins' mother.

Oct 29 *Tin Pan Ali* is briefly seen at London's Shaftesbury. Jeremy James Taylor, once with the Young Vic troupe under Frank Dunlop, has directed this musical he's written—music by David Nield—with young schoolboys playing all the roles, male and female. It's a spoof which mingles images of American gangsterism and the popular song industry. Seen at the Edinburgh Festival on the Fringe, the show cannot have a run for the boys must go back to school. An earlier Taylor show, *Helen Come Home, or, Achilles, the Heel*, based on the *Iliad*, has been shown on national television after the fringe.

Nov 15 Ray Cooney revives his play—written with John Chapman—*Not Now Darling* for London's Savoy Theatre. He directs a cast including Leslie Phillips, Amanda Holmes, and June Whitfield.

Nov 16 The Negro Ensemble Company (NEC) opens its season at St. Mark's Playhouse on Second Avenue in New York with Dan Owen's *The Michigan*, with Dean Irby directing. *Home*, by Samm-Art Williams, opens on December 14 for an interrupted run and later Broadway transfer. Irby again directs.

Nov 17 At New York's Metropolitan Opera House, Bertolt Brecht and Kurt Weill's musical, *The Rise and Fall of the City of Mahagonny*, opens as part of the repertory season. John Dexter stages; Jocelyn Herbert designs, and James Levine conducts.

Nov 20 The Birmingham Repertory Theatre production of Ben Travers' vintage farce, *Rookery Nook*, opens at Her Majesty's Theatre in the West End. Frank Dunlop directs. Among the players are Dora Bryan, Terence Frisby, Nicky Henson, and Nina Thomas.

Nov 21 The Chelsea Theatre Center's *Strider*, seen first on May 31, comes to Broadway and the Helen Hayes Theatre for a run of 27 weeks, with Gerald Hiken playing the horse Strider, based on a story by Tolstoy.

Nov 27 A popular musical of the recent past, *Irma La Douce*, comes back to London and the Shaftesbury Theatre in a revival seen first in Guildford at the Yvonne Arnaud Theatre. The show lasts 3 weeks only.

Dec 13 Rodgers and Hammerstein's *Oklahoma!* comes back to Broadway and opens at the Palace Theatre for a run of 293 performances. Laurence Guittard is Curly, with Christine Andreas as Laurey.

Dec 18 London's holiday season is underway. At the Royalty Theatre, the show is David Wood's *The Gingerbread Man*, staged by Jonathan Lynn. Bernard Cribbins is Herr Von Cuckoo. At the Young Vic on the 19th, the play is Ken Hill's version of *The Hunchback of Notre Dame*. Barrie's *Peter Pan* opens the next day at the Shaftesbury Theatre. On December 21, Sandy Wilson's *Aladdin* opens at the Lyric, Hammersmith, staged by David Giles. *Toad of Toad Hall* opens at the Old Vic on Christmas Eve.

its new Vivian Beaumont Theatre opened. Later, he lead the theatre alone and finally resigned after a series of financial crises, not of his making.

Sep 2 Britain's beloved character actor, Felix Aylmer, dies at 90.

Sep 5 Playwright Guy Bolton, responsible for memorable musicals at the Princess Theatre on Broadway, dies now, aged 96. He often collaborated with British humorist P. G. Wodehouse.

Sep 19 Preston Jones, the promising playwright of *The Texas Trilogy*, shown briefly on Broadway, dies today at 43.

Sep 25 Stage and screen actress Joan Blondell (b. 1909) dies. Blondell made her debut at age three in her parent's vaudeville act in Sydney, Australia. New York's Cort Theatre saw her Broadway debut in 1929 in George Kelly's *Maggie the Magnificent*. Her screen credits are numerous.

Oct 13 Andre van Gyseghem, long active in London theatre life, dies now at 73.

Nov 30 English actress and author Joyce Grenfell (b. 1910) is dead. Grenfell made her London debut appearing in her own monologues titled *The Little Revue*. She has presented a series of monologues and songs in her one-woman shows throughout the world, her latest being *An Evening With Joyce Grenfell*.

Dec 15 American producer-director Jed Harris (b. 1900) is dead. During the 1920's, Harris produced *The Royal Family*, *The Front Page*, and *Serena Blandish*. *A Doll's House* and *Our Town* were two of his major productions in the 1930's. He directed *The Crucible* at the Martin Beck Theatre in 1953.

1979 BIRTHS/DEATHS/DEBUTS

Jan 24 Mabel Taliaferro, a veteran of the stage, dies today at 91.

Jan 28 Boris Tumarin, who both acted and directed in the New York theatre dies now at age 68.

Feb 9 Alice Delysia, once the toast of London's West End theatre, dies today at 90.

Feb 15 The American stage designer and theatre consultant Ralph Alswang dies. He was instrumental in the design of the Uris Theatre on Broadway.

April 9 Actor Staats Cotsworth (b. 1908) dies in New York. Among his Broadway credits was *Inherit the Wind*.

May 15 Dora Mavor Moore dies in Toronto, Canada, at 91. She was the first Canadian to graduate from RADA in London and the first to play at the Old Vic. She also toured with the Ben Greet Players. From 1926–46, she taught and directed numerous amateur and university groups in Toronto, where she founded the Village Players. In 1946, she founded the New Play Society, an important training-centre for young professionals.

May 25 The noted British critic, W. A. Darlington, dies at age 89.

June 4 Herman Shumlin, the distinguished Broadway producer, who first helped Lillian Hellman's plays to win an audience, dies now at age 80.

July 9 Cornelia Otis Skinner, of a distinguished American theatre family, dies today at age 78. She was noted for her inventive character sketches.

July 28 American actor-director-producer Jules Irving dies at 54. With Hebert Blau he founded the San Francisco Actors Workshop. On the basis of that work, they were invited to be co-directors of the Repertory Theatre of Lincoln Center when

1979 THEATERS/PRODUCTIONS

Jan 3 *Variety* reports that the Manhattan Theatre Club is to receive a $230,000 five-year grant for operating funds, from the Ford Foundation.

Feb 28 The New Apollo Theatre is new only in the sense that its owner, the Brandt Corporation has restored it attractively for use as a legitimate theatre. Since the Depression, it has served as a home for burlesque and films. Its restoration is seen as a first step in the campaign to clean up 42nd Street. The facades of both the Apollo and the Lyric have been thoroughly cleaned, encouraging the managers of the *NY Times*, across the street, to clean their sooty building.

March The Theatre Royal, Bath, is purchased by a non-profit trust, headed by Jeremy Fry, with the object of continuing the career of this playhouse, built in 1805 and rebuilt after a disastrous 1862 fire. Many of Britain's most famed performers have trod its boards, among them Sarah Siddons, "Joey" Grimaldi, and Peggy Ashcroft.

March As a result of concerted community action, Britain's Hereford is able to open its new Nell Gwynne Theatre, set up in a converted swimming pool. There are 362 seats and a proscenium arch stage.

March 16 The stage staff of London's National Theatre goes on strike, seriously hampering, but not stopping production. The strike is ended on May 13.

April 8 Renovation work begins on the Indiana Repertory's redesigned Indiana Theatre, which used to be a 3,000-seat movie theatre. Architect Evans Woollen's new design for IRT gives the 1927 structure a modified proscenium theatre called the Mainstage, seating 583. There are also the Upperstage, seating 250, and Theatre 3 (on third floor), seating 100.

April 17 The Billy Rose Theatre, on West 41st Street in New York, reopens as the

Trafalgar Theatre. *Whose Life Is It Anyway?* is the opening production. The theatre is owned by Joseph and James Nederlander, in association with the Cooney-Marsh Group. Other theatres currently owned or controlled by the Nederlanders in New York are: the Alvin, the Brooks Atkinson, the Lunt-Fontanne, the Mark Hellinger, the Palace, and the Uris.

April 23 The Prospect Theatre Company changes its name to The Old Vic Company, in honor of the theatre which is to be the troupe's permanent home.

May 3 Tonight marks the 19th anniversary of the Off Broadway musical, *The Fantasticks*. This show is the longest-running musical in the world.

May 31 Today is the last day of the current 1978–79 Broadway season. *Variety* will shortly list those shows which have repaid their initial investment, qualifying them—financially, at least—as hits. Among the fortunate shows are *First Monday in October*, *The Kingfisher*, *They're Playing Our Song*, and *The Best Little Whorehouse in Texas*.

Summer At Glasgow's famed Citizens' Theatre, extensive front-of-house renovations are finished, including a repainting of foyers and auditorium, which now gleams in gold, Chinese red, black and silver, highlighting the theatre's elaborate Victorian decor.

June David Wood organizes a national touring children's theatre for Britain, to be called the Whirligig Theatre Company.

June 1 With the Broadway season officially over, there have been 54 productions. Otis Guernsey, Jr., counts 15 plays, 13 musicals, 2 revues, one foreign-language play, five specialties, and 11 revivals. Tickets can now cost $25 for musicals, with a $20 top for a straight play, *First Monday in October*. The Broadway gross has been a record $128 million-plus, with 9.1 million admissions. On the road, the gross has been $143 million. Expensive musical flops include *Ballroom*, costing $2,400,000. *A Chorus Line* has earned a profit of $22 million over costs, not including a $5,500,000-plus film sale. *Annie* has made $2.5 million on an investment of $800,000. Before bowing on Broadway, *A Matter of Gravity* has made a tour profit of more than $1 million. *Fiddler on the Roof* has returned 1,378 percent on its initial investment. *Hello, Dolly!* is close, with 1,307 per cent. Off-Broadway, there have been at least 111 productions, sorted out as follows: 38 plays, seven specialties, 11 musicals, 35 revivals, four plays in a foreign tongue, 15 foreign plays in English, and one revue. Ella Malin's annual regional theatre statistics show 642 productions of 490 plays staged by 60 groups in 115 theatres in 58 cities, seven of them in Canada. There have been 14 productions of Dickens' *A Christmas Carol*, variously adapted, making this the theatre's holiday answer to ballet's *Nutcracker* and opera's *Hansel and Gretel*. *Shadow Box* has had eight productions. Shakespeare remains the most popular dramatist, with 37 productions of 22 of his plays.

The ten "Best Plays" of the New York season now ended are chosen by Guerney, Jr. He picks Lawrence and Lee's *The First Monday in October*, Kopit's *Wings*, Thompson's *On Golden Pond*, Pomerance's *The Elephant Man*, Wheeler/Bond/Sondheim's *Sweeney Todd*, Norman's *Getting Out*, Ayckbourn's *Bedroom Farce*, Carter's *Nevis Mountain Dew*, Keeffe's *Gimme Shelter*, and Clark's *Whose Life Is It Anyway?*

July 30 Handsomely restored to the elegance of its inauguration in May 1903, the Buxton Opera House, designed by architect Frank Matcham for this spa-town near Birmingham, re-opens as the home of the new Buxton Festival. The initial production is an opera, *Lucia Di Lammermoor*.

Fall In Chicago the passing of eight decades has seen also the passing of a number of legitimate theatres. These are the playhouses still operating: the Shubert, the Blackstone, the Studebaker, the Aire Crown, the Civic Opera House, the Auditorium, the Civic, and the Goodman.

Sep 19 In Britain, in Ipswich, the Wolsey Theatre opens, designed by Roderick Ham and Partners. Seating 400, the theatre has a thrust stage and rear stage.

Oct 14 The Helen F. Spencer Theatre (733 seats in proscenium, and 631 seats in thrust) is dedicated in the $11.4 million Kansas City Performing Arts Center in Missouri. It is designed by Kivett and Myers.

Oct 18 Tonight, after months of reconstruction, the fussily handsome Victorian auditorium of the Lyric Theatre, Hammersmith, opens again. The theatre was razed some seasons ago, but the interior plasterwork was dismantled and saved. Now it has been re-assembled and restored, not in an old theatre-shell, but inside a new concrete office and shop complex, owned by the borough authorities. To fit the new space, some rows of seats have had to be eliminated. The stage is completely modern.

Nov This month the first issue of a new British theatre magazine, *Platform*, appears. Founded by Malcolm Hay, Cathy Itzin, Roger Howard, Steve Gooch, and others, its emphasis is to be on Alternative Theatre.

Nov 22 This is the official opening night of the Adelaide Court/Cour Adelaide. The old York County Courthouse (1952, Toronto, Canada) has been renovated at a cost of $2.3 million for use as a theatre complex. The complex includes the 280-seat Adelaide Theatre, the 150-seat Court Theatre, a Victorian-style bar, and a bistro. Three Toronto theatre companies share the space: Open Circle (founded 1972), New Theatre (also 1972), and Théâtre du P'tit Bonheur (1967). The building is leased to the non-profit theatre corporation for $1 a year.

Nov 25 Agatha Christie's *The Mousetrap*, the longest-running commercial production of a drama in history, celebrates its 28th anniversary today in London.

Dec 27 The renovated Golden Gate Theatre re-opens officially tonight on San Francisco's Market Street. Designed in 1922 for films and vaudeville by G. Albert Lansburgh—who designed the Martin Beck in New York—it's now to be programmed for touring musicals and plays. It seats 2,339.

JED HARRIS

BIBLIOGRAPHY

AMERICAN

1900

Dithmar, Edw. A. *John Drew* (NY, Stokes Co.)
Fyles, Franklin. *The Theatre and Its People* (NY, Doubleday, Page & Co.)
Robins, Edw. *Twelve Great Actors* (Boston, Page & Co.)
Strang, Lewis C. *Famous Actors of the Day in America* (Boston, Page)
Strang, Lewis C. *Primadonnas and Soubrettes of Light Opera and Musical Comedy in America* (Boston, Page)

1901

Copeland, Chas. Townsend. *Edwin Booth* (Boston, Small, Maynard)
Edgett, Edwin Francis. *Edward Loomis Davenport: A Biography* (NY, Dunlap Soc. Pub.)
Hapgood, Norman. *The Stage in America; 1897–1900* (NY, Macmillan)
Keese, Wm. L. *A Group of Comedians* (NY, Dunlap Soc. Pub.)
Morris, Clara. *Life on the Stage; my personal experiences and recollections* (NY, McClure, Phillips)

1902

Clapp, Henry Austin. *Reminiscences of a Drama Critic* (Boston, Houghton Mifflin)
Hamm, Margherita A. *Eminent Actors and Their Homes* (NY, Potts)
Morris, Clara. *Stage Confidences: Talks about Players and Play-acting* (Boston, Lothrop)
Schelling, Felix. *The English Chronicle Play* (NY, Macmillan)
Stoddart, James Henry. *Recollections of a Player* (NY, Century)

1903

Brown, T. Allston. *History of the New York Stage, from the first performance in 1732 to 1901*, 3 vols. (NY, Dodd, Mead)
Kobbe, Gustave. *Famous Actors and Actresses in Their Homes* (Boston, Little, Brown)
Strang, Lewis C. *Plays and Players of the Last Quarter Century*, 2 vols. (Boston, Page)
Thompson, E.N. *The Controversy Between the Puritans and the Stage* (NY, McClure, Phillips)
Waller, A.R., and Glover, Arnold; eds. *The Collected Works of William Hazlitt*, 12 vols. (NY, McClure, Phillips)

1904

Adams, W. Davenport, *A Dictionary of the Drama*, Vol. 1, A–G (Phila., Lippincott)
Baker, H. Barton. *History of the London Stage and Its Famous Players, 1576–1903* (NY, Dutton)
Matthews, Brander. *The Development of the Drama* (NY, C. Scribner's Sons)
Rennert, Hugo A. *The Life of Lope de Vega* (Phila., Campion & Co., and Glasgow, Gowans & Gray, Ltd.)
Rolfe, Wm. James. *A Life of William Shakespeare* (Boston, Estes)

1905

Eytinge, Rose. *The Memories of Rose Eytinge: being recollections and observations of men, women, and events, during half a century* (NY, Stokes Co.)
Huneker, James G. *Iconoclasts: A Book of Dramatists* (NY, Scribner's)
Jenks, Tudor. *In the Days of Shakespeare* (NY, Barnes & Co.)
Matthews, Brander. *French Dramatists of the Nineteenth Century* (NY, Scribner's)
Young, James. *Making Up* (Chicago & NY, Witmark & Sons)

1906

Browne, Walter, and Austin, F.A., eds. *Who's Who on the Stage* (NY, Browne & Austin)
Egan, Maurice F. *The Ghost in Hamlet, and other essays in comparative literature* (Chicago, McClurg & Co.)
Moses, Montrose J. *Famous Actor-Families in America* (NY, Crowell)
Nicholson, Watson. *The Struggle for a Free Stage in London* (Boston, NY, Houghton Mifflin)
Wilson, Francis. *Joseph Jefferson; Reminiscences of a Fellow Player* (NY, Scribner's)

1907

Briscoe, Johnson. *The Actor's Birthday Book* (NY, Moffat, Yard & Co.)
Lancaster, Henry C. *The French Tragi-Comedy, Its Origin and Development from 1552 to 1628* (Baltimore, Furst Co)
Paget, Violet. *Studies of the Eighteenth Century in Italy* (Chicago, McClurg)
Ristori, Adelaide; Mantellini, G., trans. *Memoirs and Artistic Studies of Adelaide Ristori* (NY, Doubleday, Page & Co.)
Tunison, Joseph Salathiel. *Dramatic Traditions of the Dark Ages* (Ill., Univ. of Chicago Press)

1908

Eaton, Walter Prichard. *The American Stage of Today* (Boston, Small, Maynard)
McKenney, Marie M. *Studies of Shakespeare's Women* (St. Paul, Minn., McGill-Warner)
O'Connor, John Bartholomew. *Chapters in the History of Actors and Acting in Ancient Greece* (Ill., Univ. of Chicago Press)
Schelling, Emmanuel, *Elizabethan Drama 1558–1642* (Boston, Houghton Mifflin)
Thorndike, Ashley. *Tragedy* (Boston, Houghton Mifflin)

1909

Hartt, Rollin Lynde. *The People at Play; Excursions in the Humor and Philosophy of Popular Entertainments* (Boston & NY, Houghton Mifflin)
Johnson, Chas. F. *Shakespeare and His Critics* (Boston & NY, Houghton Mifflin)
MacKaye, Percy. *The Playhouse and the Play, and other addresses concerning theatre and democracy in America* (NY, Macmillan)
Rennert, Hugo A. *The Spanish Stage in the Time of Lope de Vega* (NY, The Hispanic Society of America)

1910

Bradley, Will. *The American Stage of Today* (NY, P.F. Collier & Son)
Matthews, Brander. *A Study of the Drama* (Boston, NY, Houghton Mifflin)
Miles, Dudley Howe. *The Influence of Moliere on Restoration Comedy* (NY, Columbia Univ. Press)
Ranous, Dora Knowlton. *Diary of a Daly Debutante, being passages from the journal of a member of Augustin Daly's famous company of players* (NY, Duffield)
Winter, William. *Life and Art of Richard Mansfield, with selections from his letters*, 2 vols. (NY, Moffat, Yard)

1911

Brooke, C.E. Tucker. *The Tudor Drama; a history of English national drama to the retirement of Shakespeare* (Boston & NY, Houghton Mifflin)
Frohman, Daniel. *Daniel Frohman: Memories of a Manager; Reminiscences of the old Lyceum and some players of the last quarter century* (NY, Doubleday, Page)
Jenkins, Stephen. *The Greatest Street in the World—Broadway* (NY, G. P. Putnam's Sons)
Pollock, Channing. *The Footlights, Fore and Aft* (Boston, R.G. Badger)
Winter, William. *Shakespeare on the Stage* (NY, Moffat, Yard)

1912

Archer, Wm. *Play-Making, A Manual of Craftsmanship* (Boston, Small, Maynard)
Griffith, Frank Carlos. *Mrs. Fiske* (NY, Neale)
Hedgcock, Frank A. *A Cosmopolitan Actor, David Garrick and His French Friends* (NY, Duffield & Co.)
Kerr, Mina. *Influence of Ben Jonson on English Comedy, 1598–1642* (NY, D. Appleton & Co.)
Smith, Winifred. *The Commedia dell'Arte* (NY, Columbia Univ. Press)

1913

Crawford, Mary Caroline. *The Romance of the American Theatre* (Boston, Little, Brown)
Dimmick, Ruth Crowby. *Our Theatre Today and Yesterday* (NY, H. K. Fly Co.)
Hart, Jerome A. *Sardou and the Sardou Plays* (Phila. & London, Lippincott)
Henderson, Archibald. *European Dramatists* (Cincinnati, Stewart & Kidd Co.)
Sullivan, Mary A. *Court Masques of James I; their influence on Shakespeare and the public theatres* (NY, Putnam's Sons)

1914

Burton, Richard. *How to See a Play* (NY, Macmillan)
Campbell, Oscar James, Jr. *The Comedies of Holberg* (Cambridge, Mass., Harvard Univ. Press)
Chandler, Frank Wadleigh. *Aspects of Modern Drama* (NY, Macmillan)
Cheney, Sheldon. *The New Movement in the Theatre* (NY, Kennerley)
Goldman, Emma. *The Social Significance of the Modern Drama* (Boston, Badger)

1915

Bernbaum, Ernest. *The Drama of Sensibility; a sketch of the history of English sentimental comedy and domestic tragedy, 1696–1780* (Boston, Ginn & Co.)
Clark, Barrett H. *The British and American Drama of To-day* (NY, Holt & Co.)
Clark, Barrett H. *Contemporary French Dramatists; studies on the Theatre Libre, Curel, Brieux, Porto-Riche, etc.* (Cincinnati, Stewart & Kidd Co.)
Thomas P.V. *The Plays of Eugene Brieux* (Boston, J.W. Luce & Co.)
Walsh, Townsend. *The Career of Dion Boucicault* (NY, Dunlap Soc. Pub.)

1916

Eaton, Walter Prichard. *Plays and Players, Leaves from a Critic's Notebook* (Cincinnati, Stewart & Kidd Co.)
Marcosson, Isaac F., and Frohman, Daniel. *Charles Frohman: Manager and Man* (NY, Harper & Row)
Sothern, Edw. H. *The Melancholy Tale of "Me:" My Remembrances* (NY, Scribner's)
Thorndike, Ashley H. *Shakespeare's Theatre* (NY, Macmillan)
Towse, John Ranken. *Sixty Years of the Theatre; An Old Critic's Memories* (NY, Funk & Wagnalls)

1917

Adams, Jos. Quincy. *Shakespearean Playhouses: A History of the English Theatres from the Beginning to the Restoration* (NY, Boston, Houghton Mifflin)
Austin, Stephen F. *Principles of Drama-Therapy* (NY, Sopherim)
Mackay, Constance D'Arcy. *The Little Theatre in the United States* (NY, Holt & Co.)
Scheifley, Wm. H. *Brieux and Contemporary French Society* (NY, Putnam's Sons)
Woollcott, Alexander, recorder. *Mrs. Fiske; Her Views on the Stage* (NY, Century Co.)

1918

Calvert, Louis. *Problems of the Actor* (NY, Holt)
Clark, Barrett H. *European Theories of the Drama* (Cincinnati, Stewart & Kidd Co.)
Nathan, George Jean. *The Popular Theatre* (NY, Knopf)
Taylor, Laurette. *The Greatest of These—* (NY, Ceo. H. Doran Co.)
Winter, William. *The Life of David Belasco*, 2 vols. (NY, Moffat, Yard & Co.)

1919

Baker, Geo. Pierce. *Dramatic Technique* (NY, Houghton Mifflin)
Belasco, David; Defoe, Louis, ed. *The Theatre Through Its Stage Door* (NY, Harper & Bros.)
Ford, Jeremiah D. M., and Ford, M. A. *Main Currents of Spanish Literature* (NY, Holt)
Hornblow, Arthur. *A History of the Theatre in America, from its beginning to the present time*, 2 vols. (Phila. & London, Lippincott)
Matthews, Brander. *The Principles of Playmaking, and other discussions of the drama* (NY, Scribner's Sons)

1920

MacClintock, Lander. *The Contemporary Drama of Italy* (Boston, Little, Brown)
Odell, Geo. C.D. *Shakespeare from Betterton to Irving*, 2 vols. (NY, Scribner's)
Pichel, Irving. *On Building a Theatre; Stage Construction and Equipment for Small Theatres, Schools, and Community Buildings* (NY, Theatre Arts, Inc.)
Sayler, Oliver Martin. *The Russian Theatre Under the Revolution* (Boston, Little, Brown)
Warde, Frederick B. *Fifty Years of Make-Believe* (NY, The International Press Syndicate, M. M. Marcy)

1921

Drew, John. *My Years on the Stage* (NY, E. P. Dutton & Co.)
Jourdain, Eleanor F. *Dramatic Theory and Practice in France 1690–1808* (NY, Longmans, Green & Co.)
Lewisohn, Ludwig. *The Modern Drama, An Essay in Interpretation* (NY, B. W. Huebsch, Inc.)
Macgowan, Kenneth. *The Theatre of Tomorrow* (NY, Boni & Liveright)
Norwood, Gilbert. *Euripides and Shaw, with other essays* (Boston, J.W. Luce & Co.)

1922

Campbell, Patrick, Mrs. *My Life and Some Letters* (NY, Dodd, Mead)
Creahan, John. *The Life of Laura Keene, Actress, Manager and Scholar* (Phila., Rodgers Pub. Co.)
Macgowan, Kenneth, and Jones, Robert E. *Continental Stagecraft* (NY, Harcourt, Brace & Co.)
Nathan, George Jean. *Materia Critica* (NY, Knopf)
Woollcott, Alexander. *Shouts and Murmurs; echoes of a thousand and one first nights* (NY, Century Co.)

1923

Adams, Jos. Quincy. *A Life of William Shakespeare* (Boston, NY, Houghton Mifflin)
Quinn, Arthur Hobson. *A History of the American Drama, from the beginning to the Civil War* (NY, Harper & Bros.)
Sayler, Oliver M. *Our American Theatre* (NY, Brentano's)
Young, Stark. *The Flower in Drama; A Book of Papers on the Theatre* (NY, Scribner's Sons)
Wilde, Percival. *Craftsmanship of the One-Act Play* (Boston, Little, Brown)

1924

Arvin, Neil Cole. *Eugene Scribe and the French Theatre, 1815–1860* (Cambridge, Harvard Univ. Press)
Eaton, Walter Prichard. *The Actor's Heritage; scenes from the theatre of yesterday and the day before* (Boston, Atlantic Monthly Press)
Krutch, Jos. Wood. *Comedy and Conscience After the Restoration* (NY, Columbia Univ. Press)
Skinner, Otis. *Footlights and Spotlights; recollections of my life on the stage* (Indianapolis, Bobbs-Merril Co.)
Wilson, Francis. *Francis Wilson's Life of Himself* (Boston, NY, Houghton Mifflin)

1925

Cohan, George M. *Twenty Years on Broadway and the Years It Took to Get There; the true story of a trouper's life* (NY, Harper & Bros.)
Dunkel, Wilbur D. *The Dramatic Technique of Thomas Middleton in His Comedies of London Life* (NY, Russell & Russell)
Smith, Hugh Allison. *Main Currents of Modern French Drama* (NY, Holt & Co.)
Weigand, H.J. *The Modern Ibsen; A Reconsideration* (NY, Dutton)
Zucker, A. E. *The Chinese Theater* (Boston, Little, Brown)

1926

Barrymore, John. *Confessions of an Actor* (Indianapolis, Bobbs-Merrill Co.)
Hillebrand, Harold Newcomb. *The Child Actors; A Chapter in Elizabethan Stage History*, 2 vols. (Urbana, Univ. of Ill. Press)
Quinn, Germain. *Fifty Years Back Stage, Being the Life Story of a Theatrical Stage Mechanic* (Minn., Stage Pub. Co.)
Watson, Ernest Bradlee. *Sheridan to Robson; A Study of the Nineteenth Century London Stage* (Cambridge, Harvard U. Pr.)
Waxman, Samuel Montefiore. *Antoine and the Theatre-Libre* (Cambridge, Harvard U. Pr.)

1927

Allen, James T. *Stage Antiquities of the Greeks and Romans and Their Influence* (NY, Longmans, Green & Co.)
Baldwin, T.W. *The Organization and Personnel of the Shakespearean Company* (Princeton, NJ, Princeton Univ. Press)
Cunliffe, John W. *Modern English Playwrights; a short history of the English drama from 1825* (NY, Harper)
MacKaye, Percy. *Epoch; The Life of Steele MacKaye; genius of the theatre, in relation to his time and contemporaries;*

a memoir by his son (NY, Boni & Liveright)
Page, Will A. *Behind the Curtains of the Broadway Beauty Trust* (NY, Edw. A. Miller Pub. Co.)

1928

Davis, Hallie Flanagan. *Shifting Scenes of the Modern European Theatre* (NY, Coward-McCann)
Foy, Eddie, and Harlow, Alvin F. *Clowning Through Life* (NY, Dutton)
Melcher, Edith. *Stage Realism in France Between Diderot and Antoine* (Penn., Bryn Mawr Univ. Press)
Senior, Dorothy. *The Life and Times of Colley Cibber* (NY, Rae D. Henkle Co.)
Stuart, D. C. *The Development of Dramatic Art* (NY, Appleton-Century-Crofts)

1929

Carter, Huntly. *The New Spirit in the Russian Theatre, 1917–1928; and a sketch of the Russian kinema and radio, showing the new communal relationship between the three* (NY & London, Brentano's)
Cheney, Sheldon. *The Theatre; Three Thousand Years of Drama, Acting and Stagecraft* (NY, McKay Co.)
Eaton, Walter Prichard. *The Theatre Guild; The First Ten Years* (NY, Brentano's)
Harding, Alfred. *The Revolt of the Actors* (NY, Wm. Morrow & Co.)
Lancaster, Henry C. *A History of French Dramatic Literature in the Seventeenth Century*, Vol. 1 (Baltimore, Johns Hopkins Press)

1930

Clark, Barrett H. *Hour of American Drama* (NY, Lippincott)
Komisarjevsky, Theodore. *Myself and the Theatre* (NY, Dutton)
Lanier, Henry Wysham. *The First English Actress, from the initial appearance of women on the stage in 1660 till 1700* (NY, The Players)
Taylor, Jos. Richard. *Story of the Drama: Beginnings of the Commonwealth* (Boston, Expression Co.)
Wittke, Carl F. *Tambo and Bones: A History of the American Minstrel Stage* (Durham, N.C., Duke Univ. Press)

1931

Blankenagel, John C. *The Dramas of Heinrich von Kleist* (Chapel Hill, Univ. of North Carolina Press)
Deutsch, Helen, and Hanau, Stella. *The Provincetown, a story of the theatre* (NY, Farrar & Rinehart)
Gilder, Rosamond. *Enter the Actress; The First Women in the Theatre* (Boston & NY, Houghton Mifflin)
Norwood, Gilbert. *Greek Comedy* (Boston, J. W. Luce & Co.)
Steinberg, Mollie M. *History of the Fourteenth Street Theatre* (NY, Dial)

1932

Bernheim, Alfred L. *The Business of the Theatre* (NY, AEA)
Boswell, Eleanore. *The Resotration Court Stage (1660–1702)* (Howard Univ. Pr.)
Cordell, Richard A. *Henry Arthur Jones and the Modern Drama* (NY, R. Long & R. R. Smith, Inc.)
Kennard, Jos. Spencer. *The Italian Theatre*, 2 vols. (NY, W. R. Rudge)
Robinson, Herbert S. *English Shakespearian Criticism in the Eighteenth Century* (NY, H. W. Wilson Co.)

1933

Clark, Barrett H. *Maxwell Anderson: The Man and His Plays* (NY, Sam'l. French)
Harry, Jos. Edw. *Greek Tragedy; Emendations, Interpretations and Critical Notes* (NY, Columbia Univ. Press)
Nathan, George Jean. *Since Ibsen; a statistical, historical outline of the popular theatre since 1900* (NY, Knopf)
Lancaster, Henry C. *French Tragedy in the Reign of Louis XIV and the Early Years of the French Revolution, 1774–1792.* (Blat., Johns Hopkins Press)
Waitzkin, Leo. *The Witch of Wych Street: A Study of the Theatrical Reforms of Madame Vestris* (Cambridge, Mass., Harvard Univ. Press)

1934

Brasol, Boris. *The Mighty Three—Pushkin, Gogol, Dostoievsky* (NY, Wm. Farquhar Payson)
Cantor, Eddie, and Freedman, David. *Ziegfeld, the Great Glorifier* (NY, King)
Eustis, Morton. *Broadway, Inc.!* (NY, Dodd, Mead)
Hill, Frank Pierce, compiler. *American Plays (Printed 1714–1830)* (Palo Alto, Calif., Stanford Univ. Press)
Moses, Montrose J., and Brown, John Mason. *The American Theatre as Seen by Its Critics, 1752–1934* (NY, Norton)

1935

Allen, Ned Bliss. *The Sources of John Dryden's Comedies* (Ann Arbor, Univ. of Michigan Press)
Barton, Lucy. *Historic Costume for the Stage* (NY, Walter H. Baker Co.)
Kreider, Paul V. *Elizabethan Comic Characters Revealed in the Comedies of George Chapman* (Ann Arbor, Univ. of Mich. Pr.)
Markov, P. A. *The Soviet Theatre* (NY, G. P. Putnam's Sons)
Morrow, Donald. *Where Shakespeare Stood; his part in the crucial struggles of his day* (Milwaukee, The Casanova Press)

1936

Brown, John Mason. *The Art of Playgoing* (NY, Norton)
Farnham, Willard. *The Medieval Heritage of Elizabethan Tragedy* (Berkeley, Univ. of Calif. Press)
Gilder, Rosamond, and Freedley, George. *Theatre Collections in Libraries and Museums, An International Handbook* (NY, Theatre Arts, Inc.)
Houghton, Norris. *Moscow Rehearsals; an account of the methods of production in the Soviet Theatre* (NY, Harcourt, Brace)
Stanislavski, Constantin; Hapgood, Eliz. Reynolds, trans. *An Actor Prepares* (NY, Theatre Arts, Inc.)

1937

Anderson, Maxwell. *The Essence of Tragedy, and other footnotes and papers* (Washington, D.C., Anderson House)
Bodeen, DeWitt. *Ladies of the Footlights* (Pasadena, The Login Printing & Binding Co.)
Brady, Wm. A. *Showman* (NY, E. P. Dutton)
Frohman, Daniel. *Encore* (NY, L. Furman, Inc.)
McCandless, Stanley. *A Syllabus of Stage Lighting* (Ann Arbor, Mich., Edwards Bros.)

1938

Dana, H. W. L. *Handbook on Soviet Drama* (NY, The American-Russian Institute for Cultural Relations with the Soviet Union, Inc.)
Flexner, Eleanor. *American Playwrights, 1918–1938; the theatre retreats from reality* (NY, Simon & Schuster)
Mantle, Burns. *Contemporary American Playwrights* (NY, Dodd, Mead)
Ormsbee, Helen. *Backstage with Actors, from the time of Shakespeare to the present day* (NY, Crowell)
Stein, Elizabeth P. *David Garrick, Dramatist* (NY, The Modern Language Assoc. of America)

1939

Clark, Alexander F. B. *Jean Racine* (Cambridge, Mass., Harvard Univ. Press)
Hartman, John C. *The Development of American Social Comedy from 1787–1936* (Univ. of Penn. Press)
O'Casey, Sean. *I Knock at the Door; swift glances back at the things that made me* (NY, Macmillan)
Powers, James T. *Twinkle, Little Star; Sparkling Memories of Seventy Years* (NY, G. P. Putnam's Sons)
Stockwell, La Tourette. *Dublin Theatre and Theatre Customs (1637–1820)* (Tenn., Kingsport Press)

1940

Bowers, Fredson T. *Elizabethan Revenge Tragedy, 1587–1642* (NJ, Princeton U. Pr.)
Flanagan, Hallie. *Arena; the history of the Federal Theatre* (NY, Duell, Sloane & Pearce)
Gassner, John. *Masters of the Drama* (NY, Random House)
Gilbert, Douglas. *American Vaudeville, Its Life and Times* (NY, McGraw-Hill)
Gorelik, Mordecai. *New Theatres for Old* (NY, Samuel French)

1941

Freedley, George, and Reeves, J. A. *A History of the Theatre* (NY, Crown)
Grube, Georges M. *The Drama of Euripides* (NY,Barnes & Noble)
Houghton, Norris. *Advance from Broadway, 19,000 Miles of the American Theatre* (NY, Harcourt, Brace)
Jones, Robert Edmond. *The Dramatic Imagination* (NY, Duell, Sloane & Pearce)
Power-Waters, Alma. *John Barrymore: The Legend and the Man* (NY, J. Messner)

1942

Adams, John Cranford. *The Globe Playhouse: Its Design and Equipment* (Cambridge, Mass., Harvard Univ. Press)
Bakeless, John E. *The Tragicall History of Christopher Marlowe*, 2 vols. (NY, Wm. Morrow & Co.)
Cocroft, Thoda. *Great Names and How They Are Made* (NY, Chicago, The Dartnell Pr.)
Nathan, George Jean. *The Entertainment of a Nation, or, Three Sheets in the Wind* (NY, Knopf)
Verneuil, Louis; Boyd, Ernest, Trans. *The Fabulous Life of Sarah Bernhardt* (NY & London, Harper & Bros.)

1943

Evans, Marshall B. *The Passion Play of Lucerne; an historical and critical introduction* (NY, Modern Language Assoc. of America)
Irwin, Constance H. *The Dramatic Criticism of George Jean Nathan* (Ithaca, NY, Cornell Univ. Press)
Morehouse, Ward. *George M. Cohan, Prince of the American Theatre* (Phila., NY, Lippincott)
Ottemiller, John Henry. *Index to Plays in Collections; an author and title index to plays appearing in collections published between 1900 and 1942* (NY, Wilson)
Spencer, Theodore. *Shakespeare and the Nature of Man* (NY, Macmillan)

1944

Fowler, Gene. *Good Night, Sweet Prince* (NY, Viking Press)
Hayden, Therese, ed. *Players Guide* (NY, Actors' Equity Assoc.)
Honig, Edwin. *Garcia Lorca* (Norfolk, Conn., New Directions Books)
Kernodle, George R. *From Art to Theatre* (Univ. of Chicago Press)
Morosco, Helen M., and Dugger, Leonard P. *Life of Oliver Morosco; The Oracle of Broadway, written from his own notes and comments* (Caldwell, Ind., The Caxton Printers, Ltd.)

1945

Adams, Samuel Hopkins. *Alexander Woollcott, His Life and His World* (NY, Reynal & Hitchcock)
Clurman, Harold. *The Fervent Years; The Story of the Group Theatre and the Thirties* (NY, Knopf)
Lancaster, Henry C. *Sunset, a history of Parisian drama in the last years of Louis XIV, 1701–1715* (Baltimore, Md., Johns Hopkins Press)
Lawrence, Gertrude. *. . . A Star Danced* (NY, Doubleday, Doran & Co.)
Malvern, Gladys. *Good Troupers All, the study of Joseph Jefferson* (Phila., Macrae Smith Co.)

1946

Bentley, Eric. *The Playwright as Thinker; A Study of Drama in Modern Times* (NY, Reynal & Hitchcock)
Bradbrook, Muriel C. *Ibsen the Norwegian; a Re-evaluation* (Conn., Shoe String Pr.)
Gardiner, Harold C. *Mysteries' End: An Investigation of the Last Days of the Medieval Religious Stage* (New Haven, Conn., Yale Univ. Press)
Kocher, Paul H. *Christopher Marlowe, a study of his thought, learning, and character* (Chapel Hill, Univ. of No. Carolina Press)
Seyler, Athene, and Haggard, Stephen. *The Craft of Comedy* (NY, Theatre Arts, Inc.)

1947

Anderson, Maxwell. *Off Broadway; Essays About the Theater* (NY, W. Sloane Associates)
Campbell, Lily. *Shakespeare's "Histories;" Mirrors of Elizabethan Policy* (San Marino, Calif., The Huntington Library)
Clark, Barrett H., and Freedley, George; eds. *A History of the Modern Drama* (NY, D. Appleton—Century)
Gagey, Edmond M. *Revolution in American Drama* (NY, Columbia Univ. Press)
Isaacs, Edith J. R. *The Negro in the American Theatre* (NY, Theatre Arts, Inc.)

1948

Burris-Meyer, Harold, and Cole, Edw. C. *Theatres and Auditoriums* (NY, Reinhold)
James, Henry; Wade, Alan, ed. *The Scenic Art, Notes on acting and the drama 1872–1901* (New Brunswick, NJ, Rutgers Univ. Press)
Samuel Maurice. *Prince of the Ghetto* (NY, Schocken Press)
Thompson, Alan Reynolds. *The Dry Mock, A Study of Irony in Drama* (Berkeley, Univ. Of Calif. Press)
Young, Stark. *Immortal Shadows; A Book of Dramatic Criticism* (NY, C. Scribner's Sons)

1949

Chute, Marchette. *Shakespeare of London* (NY, Dutton)
Cole, Toby, and Chinoy, Helen Krich. *Actors on Acting* (NY, Crown)
Fergusson, Francis. *The Idea of a Theatre, A Study of Ten Plays; the art of drama in changing perspective* (NY, Princeton Univ. Press)
McPharlin, Paul; Batchelder, Marjorie, ed. *The Puppet Theatre in America, with a list of puppeteers, 1524–1948* (NY, Harper)

1950

Adams, Henry Hitch, and Hathaway, Baxter, eds. *Dramatic Essays of the Neoclassic Age* (NY, Columbia Univ. Press)
Davis, Owen. *My First Fifty Years in the Theatre* (Boston, W. H. Baker Co.)
Downer, Alan S. *The British Drama, a handbook and brief chronicle* (NY, Appleton-Century-Crofts)
Lancaster, Henry C. *French Tragedy in the Time of Louis XV and Voltaire, 1715–1774* (Baltimore, Johns Hopkins Press)
Smith, Cecil M. *Musical Comedy in America* (NY, Theatre Arts Books)

1951

Adams, Agatha B.; Walser, Richard, ed. *Paul Green of Chapel Hill* (Chapel Hill, Univ. of No. Carolina Library)
Hughes, Glenn. *A History of the American Theatre, 1700–1950* (NY, Samuel French)
Jones, Margo. *Theatre-in-the-Round* (NY, Rinehart)
MacClintock, Lander. *The Age of Pirandello* (Bloomington, Indiana Univ. Press)
Whitman, Cedric H. *Sophocles; A Study of Heroic Humanism* (Cambridge, Mass., Harvard Univ. Press)

1952

Bowers, Faubion. *Japanese Theatre* (NY, Hermitage House)
Granville, Wilfred. *The Theater Dictionary; British and American Terms in the Drama, Opera, and Ballet* (NY, Philosophical Library)
Levin, Harry. *The Overreacher; A Study of Christopher Marlowe* (Cambridge, Mass., Harvard Univ. Press)
Magarschack, David. *Chekhov; A Life* (NY, Grove Press)
Nagler, A. M. *Sources of Theatrical History* (NY, Theatre Annual)

1953

Altman, George, et al. *Theatre Pictorial; a history of world theatre as recorded in drawings, paintings, engravings and photographs* (Berkeley, Univ. of Calif. Press)
Bentley, Eric. *In Search of Theatre* (NY, Knopf)
le Gallienne, Eva. *With a Quiet Heart; An Autobiography* (NY, Viking Press)
Lynch, James J. *Box, Pit, and Gallery; Stage and Society in Johnson's London* (Berkeley, Univ. of Calif. Press)
Ruggles, Eleanor. *Prince of Players* (NY, Norton)

1954

Bentley, Eric. *The Dramatic Event; An American Chronicle* (NY, Horizon Pr.)
Chiari, Joseph. *THe Poetic Drama of Paul Claudel* (NY, P. J. Kenedy)
Samachson, Dorothy, and Samachson, Joseph. *Let's Meet the Theatre* (NY, Abelard, Schuman)
Sothern, Edward H. (as told to him by Miss Marlowe), Downey, Fairfax, ed. *Julia Marlowe's Story* (NY, Rinehart)
Timberlake, Craig. *David Belasco, Bishop of Broadway* (NY, Library Publishers)

1955

Benchley, Nathaniel. *Robert Benchley, A Biography* (NY, McGraw-Hill)
Bogard, Travis. *The Tragic Satire of John Webster* (Berkeley, Univ. of Calif. Pr.)
Crosland, Margaret. *Jean Cocteau; A Biography* (NY, Knopf)
Kahn, Ely J. *The Merry Partners; The Age of Harrigan and Hart* (NY, Random House)
McGaw, Charles J. *Acting is Believing* (NY, Rinehart)

1956

Bowers, Faubion. *Theatre in the East; a survey of Asian dance and drama* (NY, Nelson)

Felheim, Marvin. *The Theater of Augustin D Daly; an account of the late nineteenth century American stage* (Cambridge, Mass., Harvard Univ. Press)

Hughes, Leo. *A Century of English Farce* (NJ, Princeton Univ. Press)

Purdom, C.B. *Harley Granville Barker; Man of the Theatre, Dramatist, Scholar* (Cambridge, Mass., Harvard Univ. Pr.)

Smith, Grover Cleveland. *T. S. Eliot's Poetry and Plays; A Study in Sources and Meaning* (Chicago, Univ. of Chicago Press)

1957

Gorchakov, Nikolai; Lehrman, Edgar, trans. *The Theater in Soviet Russia* (NY, Columbia Univ. Press)

Lilar, Suzanne; Goris, Jan-Albert, trans. *The Belgian Theatre since 1890* (NY, Belgian Government Information Center)

Oxenhandler, Neal. *Scandal and Parade; The Theater of Jean Cocteau* (New Brunswick, NJ, Rutgers Univ. Press)

Scott, A. C. *The Classical Theatre of China* (NY, Macmillan)

Wardle, Ralph Martin. *Oliver Goldsmith* (Lawrence, Univ. of Kansas Press)

1958

Artaud, Antonin; Richards, Mary C., trans. *The Theater and Its Double* (NY, Grove Press)

Barker, Richard H. *Thomas Middleton* (NY, Columbia Univ. Press)

Harrison, Harry P. *Culture Under Canvas: The Story of Tent Chautauqua* (NY, Hastings House)

Landau, Jacob M. *Studies in the Arab Theatre and Cinema* (Phila., Univ. of Penn. Pr.)

Wilson, John Harold. *All the King's Ladies; Actresses of the Restoration* (Chicago, Univ. of Chicago Press)

1959

Bowen, Croswell, with Shane O'Neill. *The Curse of the Misbegotten: A Tale of the House of O'Neill* (NY, McGraw-Hill)

Crowley, Alice Lewisohn. *The Neighborhood Playhouse* (NY, Theatre Arts)

Guthrie, Tyrone, Sir. *A Life in the Theatre* (NY, McGraw-Hill)

Hart, Moss. *Act One: An Autobiography* (NY, Random House)

Hewitt, Barnard H. *Theatre USA, 1665 to 1957* (NY, McGraw-Hill)

1960

Cole, Toby. *Playwrights on Playwriting; the meaning and making of modern drama from Ibsen to Ionesco* (NY, Hill & Wang)

Fowlie, Wallace. *Dionysus in Paris; a Guide to Contemporary French Theatre* (NY, Meridian Books)

Gassner, John. *Theatre at the Crossroads; plays and playwrights of the mid-century American stage* (NY, Holt, Rinehart & Winston)

Ornstein, Robert. *The Moral Vision of Jacobean Tragedy* (Madison, Univ. of Wisconsin Press)

Wiley, W. L. *The Early Public Theatre in France* (Cambridge, Mass., Harvard Univ. Press)

1961

Caputi, Anthony. *John Marston, Satirist* (Ithaca, NY, Cornell Univ. Press)

Coe, Richard N. *Eugene Ionesco* (NY, Grove Press)

Driver, Tom F. *The Sense of History in Greek and Shakespearean Drama* (NY, Columbia Univ. Press)

Funke, Lewis, and Booth, John E., eds. *Actors Talk About Acting* (NY, Random House)

Gropius, Walter, ed. *The Theatre of the Bauhaus* (Middleton, Conn., Wesleyan Univ. Press)

1962

Churchill, Allen. *The Great White Way: A Re-creation of Broadway's Golden Age of Theatrical Entertainment* (NY, Dutton)

Duerr, Edwin. *The Length and Depth of Acting* (NY, Holt, Rinehart & Winston)

Gelb, Barbara, and Gelb, Arthur. *O'Neill* (NY, Harper)

Harkins, Wm. Edw. *Karel Capek* (NY, Columbia Univ. Press)

Pronko, Leonard C. *Avant Garde: The Experimental Theatre of France* (Berkeley, Univ. of Calif. Press)

1963

Himelstein, Morgan Y. *Drama Was a Weapon: The Left-Wing Theatre in NY 1929–1941* (New Brunswick, NJ, Rutgers Univ. Pr.)

Sartre, Jean Paul; Frechtman, Bernard, trans. *Saint Genet, Actor and Martyr* (NY, G. Braziller)

Ure, Peter. *Yeats, the Playwright; A Commentary on Character and Design in the Major Plays* (NY, Barnes & Noble)

Valency, Maurice. *The Flower and the Castle; an introduction to modern drama* (NY, Macmillan)

Yarrow, Philip J. *Corneille* (NY, St. Martin's Press)

1964

Bentley, Eric. *The Life of the Drama* (NY, Atheneum)

Brecht, Bertolt; Kett, John W., trans. *Brecht on Theatre; The Development of an Aesthetic* (NY, Hill & Wang)

Brustein, Robert. *The Theatre of Revolt* (Boston, Little, Brown)

Freed, Donald. *Freud and Stanislavsky; new directions in the performing arts* (NY, Vantage Press)

Gassner, John, and Allen, Ralph G. *Theatre and Drama in the Making* (Boston, Houghton Mifflin)

1965

Brustein, Robert. *Seasons of Discontent; Dramatic Opinions, 1959–1965* (NY, Simon & Schuster)

Edwards, Christine. *The Stanislavsky Heritage, Its Contribution to the Russian and American Theatre* (NY, New York Univ. Press)

Huftel, Sheila. *Arthur Miller: The Burning Glass* (NY, Citadel)

Lifson, David S. *The Yiddish Theatre in America* (NY, T. Yoseloff)

Roppolo, Joseph P. *Philip Barry* (NY, Twayne)

1966

Campbell, Oscar J., and Quinn, Edw. G., eds. *The Reader's Encyclopedia of Shakespeare* (NY, Crowell)

Clurman, Harold. *The Naked Image; observations on the modern theatre* (NY, Macmillan)

Gargi, Balwant. *Folk Theatre of India* (Seattle, Univ. of Washington Pr.)

Hardison, O. B. *Christian Rite and Christian Drama in the Middle Ages* (Baltimore, Md., Johns Hopkins Univ. Press)

Keene, Donald, *Nō: The Classical Drama of Japan* (Palo Alto, Calif. & Tokyo, Kodansha International)

Kernan, Alvin B. *The Plot of Satire* (Conn., Yale Univ. Press)

1967

Bentley, Eric. *The Theatre of Commitment, and Other Essays on Drama in Our Society* (NY, Atheneum)

Gard, Robert Edw., and Semmes, David. *America's Players* (NY, Seabury Press)

Haberman, Donald *The Plays of Thornton Wilder; a critical study* (Middletown, Conn., Wesleyan Univ. Press)

Hogan, Robert. *After the Irish Renaissance: A Critical History of Irish Drama Since "The Plough and the Stars"* (Minn., Univ. of Minn. Pr.)

Rahill, F. *The World of Melodrama* (University Park, Penn. State Univ. Pr.)

1968

Bauland, Peter. *The Hooded Eagle; Modern German Drama on the New York Stage* (Syracuse, NY, Syracuse Univ. Pr.)

Brockett, Oscar. *History of the Theatre* (Boston, Allyn & Bacon)

Knowles, Dorothy. *French Drama in the Inter-War Years 1918–1939* (NY, Barnes & Noble)

Novick, Julius. *Beyond Broadway* (NY, Hill & Wang)

Segal, Erich. *Roman Laughter: The Comedy of Plautus* (Cambridge, Mass., Harvard Univ. Press)

1969

Carter, Alan. *John Osborne* (NY, Barnes & Noble)

Gassner, John, and Quinn, Edw. eds. *The Reader's Encyclopedia of World Drama* (NY, Crowell)

Goldman, William. *The Season; A Candid Look at Broadway* (NY, Harcourt, Brace & World)

Lahr, John. *Notes on a Cowardly Lion; The Biography of Bert Lahr* (NY, Knopf)

Rutenberg, Michael E. *Edward Albee: Playwright* (NY, DBS Publications)

1970

Atkinson, Brooks. *Broadway* (NY, Macmillan)

Beckerman, Bernard. *Dynamics of Drama: Theory and Method of Analysis* (NY, Knopf)

Durham, Frank. *Elmer Rice* (NY, Twayne)

Harvey, Lawrence E. *Samuel Beckett, Poet and Critic* (NJ, Princeton Univ. Pr.)

Sullivan, Frank. *Frank Sullivan Through the Looking Glass* (NY, Doubleday)

1971

Donohue, Joseph W., Jr., ed. *The Theatrical Manager in England and America* (NJ, Princeton Univ. Press)

Grossman, Manuel L. *Dada: Paradox, Mystification and Ambiguity in European Literature* (Indianapolis, Bobbs-Merrill)

Kerr, Walter. *God on the Gymnasium Floor, and other theatrical adventures* (NY, Simon & Schuster)

Roberts, Vera Mowry. *The Nature of Theatre* (NY, Harper & Row)

Weales, Gerald. *Clifford Odets, Playwright* (NY, Pegasus)

1972

Gruver, Elbert. *The Stage Manager's Handbook* (NY, Drama Book Specialists)

Mabley, Edw. Howe. *Dramatic Construction; An Outline of Basic Principles* (Phila., Chilton Book Co.)

Matlaw, Myron. *Modern World Drama: An Encyclopedia* (NY, Dutton)

Phillips, Julien. *Stars of the Ziegfeld Follies* (Minn., Lerner Pubs. Co.)

Rosenthal, Jean, and Wertenbaker, Lael. *The Magic of Light: The Craft and Career of Jean Rosenthal, Pioneer in Lighting for the Modern Stage* (Boston, Little, Brown)

1973

Bermel, Albert. *Contradictory Characters; an interpretation of the modern theatre* (NY, Dutton)

Corrigan, Robert. *The Theatre in Search of a Fix* (NY, Delacorte Press)

Hagen, Uta, and Frankel, Haskel. *Respect for Acting* (NY, Macmillan)

Tunney, Kieran. *Tallulah: Darling of the Gods* (NY, Dutton)

Zeigler, Jos. W. *Regional Theatre: The Revolutionary Stage* (Minn., Univ. of Minn. Press)

1974

Dukore, Bernard, compiler. *Dramatic Theory and Criticism: Greeks to Grotowski* (NY, Holt, Rinehart & Winston)

Graham-White, Anthony. *The Drama of Black Africa* (NY, Samuel French)

Langley, Stephen. *Theatre Management in America: Principle and Practice* (NY, Drama Book Specialists)

Paolucci, Anne. *Pirandello's Theatre; the Recovery of the Modern Stage for Dramatic Art* (Carbondale, Southern Illinois Univ. Press)

Wharton, John F. *Life Among the Playwrights; Being Mostly the Story of the Playwrights Producing Company, Inc.* (NY, Quadrangle/NY Times Bk. Co.)

1975

Grebanier, Bernard. *Then Came Each Actor* (NY, McKay)

Knapp, Bettina; Amoia, Alba, ed. *Off-Stage Voices: Interviews with Modern French Dramatists* (Troy, NY, Whitson Pub. Co.)

Krawitz, Herman E., and Klein, Howard K. *The Royal American Symphonic Theater, a radical proposal for a subsidized professional theater* (NY, Macmillan)

Loeffler, Donald L. *An Analysis of the Treatment of the Homosexual Character in Dramas Produced in the New York Theatre from 1950 to 1968* (NY, Arno Pr.)

Williams, Tennessee. *Memoirs* (NY, Doubleday)

1976

Gordon, Ruth. *My Side* (NY, Harper)

Kauffman, Stanley. *Persons of the Drama; Theatre Criticisms and Comment* (NY, Harper & Row)

Marshall, Herbert. *A Pictorial History of the Russian Theatre* (NY, Crown)

Shattuck, Charles H. *Shakespeare on the American Stage: from the Hallams to Edwin Booth* (Univ. Press of Virginia)

Smith, Bill. *The Vaudevillians* (NY, Harper)

1977

Blum, Daniel C. *A Pictorial History of the American Theatre 1860–1976* (NY, Crown)

Kotsilibas-Davis, James. *Great Times, Good Times, The Odyssey of Maurice Barrymore* (NY, Doubleday)

Lahoud, John. *Theatre Awakening: A Report on Ford Foundation Assistance to American Drama* (NY, Ford Foundation, Office of Reports)

Rosenfeld, Lulla. *Bright Star of Exile; Jacob Adler and the Yiddish Theatre* (NY, Crowell)

Rowse, A. L. *Shakespeare the Elizabethan* (NY, Putnam)

1978

Gale, Steven H. *Harold Pinter: An Annotated Bibliography* (Boston, G. K. Hall)

Lahr, John. *Prick Up Your Ears: The Biography of Joe Orton* (NY, Knopf)

Laufe, Abe. *The Wicked Stage: A History of Theatre Censorship and Harassment in the United States* (NY, Frederick Ungar Pub. Co.)

Oenslager, Donald. *The Theatre of Donald Oenslager* (Middletown, Conn., Wesleyan Univ. Press)

Seldes, Marian. *The Bright Lights: A Theatre Life* (Boston, Houghton Mifflin)

1979

Goldstein, Malcolm. *George S. Kaufman: His Life, His Theatre* (NY, Oxford Univ. Pr.)

Harris, Jed. *A Dance on the High Wire: Recollections of a Time and a Temperament* (NY, Crown)

Houseman, John. *Front and Center* (NY, Simon & Schuster)

Stone, George Winchester, Jr., and Kahrl, George M. *David Garrick, A Critical Biography* (Carbondale, Southern Illinois Univ. Press)

Tynan, Kenneth. *Show People; Profiles in Entertainment* (NY, Simon & Schuster)

BRITISH

1900

Grein, J. T. *Premieres of the Year* (J. Macqueen).

Lawrence, B., ed. *Celebrities of the Stage* (Newnes).

Martin, Sir Theodore. *Helena Faucit* (Blackwood).

Pemberton, T. Edgar. *The Kendals: A Biography* (C. Arthur Pearson, Ltd.).

Scott, Clement Wm. *Some Notable Hamlets of the Present Time* (Greening & Co., Ltd.).

1901

Boas, F. S. *The Works of Thomas Kyd. with Biography and Critical Introduction.*

Broadbent, R. J. *A History of Pantomime* (Simplin, Marshall, Hamilton, Kent & Co., Ltd.).

Boulton, W. B. *The Amusements of Old London*, 2 vols. (Nimmo).

Plache, Jas. Robinson. *Recollections and Reflections* (Sampson Low).

Sillard, Rob't. M. *Barry Sullivan and His Contemporaries: A Histrionic Record*, 2 vols. (Unwin).

1902

Adams, W. E., ed. *An Actor's Life: The Biography of Jas. Robertson Anderson* (Walter Scott Pub. Co.).

Bond, R. W. *The Complete Works of John Lyly, with Biography and Critical Introduction*, 3 vols.

Brookfield, Chas. H. E. *Random Reminiscences* (Arnold).

Fyfe, H. Hamilton. *Arthur Wing Pinero.*

Grein, J. T. *Dramatic Criticism, 1900–1901* (Greening & Co.).

1903

Andrewes, Amelia. *Little Notes on Shakespeare's England* (Swan, Sonnenschein & Co., Ltd.).

Brereton, Austin. *The Lyceum and Henry Irving* (Lawrence & Bullen, Ltd.).

Chambers, Sir Edmund K. *The Medieval Stage*, 2 vols. (Clarendon Press).

Cunningham, Peter. *The Story of Nell Gwyn* (Bullen).

Maude, Cyril & Maude, Ralph, eds. *The Haymarket Theatre: Some Records and Reminiscences* (Richards)

1904

Baker, Henry Barton. *History of the London Stage and Its Famous Players, 1576–1903* (Routledge & Sons, Ltd.).
Burnand, Sir Francis C. *Records and Reminiscences, Personal and General*, 2 vols. (Methuen & Co.).
Egan, Pierce. *The Life of an Actor* (Methuen).
Fitzgerald, Percy H. *The Garrick Club* (Stock).
Ordish, T. Fairman. *Shakespeare's London* (Dent).
Pemberton, T. Edgar. *Sir Charles Wyndham: A Biography*.

1905

Findon, B. W. *The Playgoer's Club, 1884–1905; Its History and Memories*.
Hatton, Jos. *The Boyhood of Henry Irving*.
Morton, W. H. and Newton, H. C. *Sixty Years' Stage Service, Being a Record of the Life of Charles Morton. "The Father of the Halls"* (Gale & Polden, Ltd.).
Wood, J. Hickory. Dan Leno (Methuen & Co.)

1906

Aria, E. *Costume: Fanciful, Historical and Theatrical* (Macmillan & Co.).
Fyvie, John. *Comedy Queens of the Georgian Era* (Archibald Constable & Co., Ltd.).
Hunt, Bampton, ed. *The Green Room Book; "Who's Who on the Stage"* (Clark).
MacFall, Haldane. *Sir Henry Irving* (Foulds).
Wyndham, Henry Saxe. *The Annals of Covent Garden Theatre from 1732–1897*, 2 vols. (Chatto & Windus).

1907

Archer, Wm., and Granville Barker, Harley. *A National Theatre: Scheme and Estimates* (Duckworth).
Greg, Walter W., ed. *The Henslowe Papers, Being Documents Supplementary to Henslowe's Diary* (Bullen).
MacCarthy, Desmond. *The Court Theatre, 1904–1907; A Commentary and Criticism* (Bullen).
Moore, E. Hamilton. *English Miracle Plays and Moralities* (Sherratt & Hughes).
Stoker, Bram. *Personal Reminiscences of Henry Irving* (Heinemann).

1908

Barrington, Rutland. *Rutland Barrington: A Record of Thirty-Five Years' Experience on the English Stage* (Richards).
Borsa, Mario, translated by Brinton, Selwyn. *The English Stage of Today* (Bodley Head).
Caffin, Chas. H. *The Appreciation of the Drama* (Barker & Taylor).
Schelling, Felix E. *Elizabethan Drama 1558–1642*, 2 vols. (Constable).
Terry, Ellen. *The Story of My Life* (Hutchinson).

1909

Bancroft, Sir Squire and Lady Marie. *Recollections of Sixty Years* (Murray).
Clarence, Reginald, compiler. *"The Stage" Cyclopedia; bibliography of nearly 50,000 plays spanning nearly 500 years* ("The Stage").
Morton, Cavendish. *The Art of Theatrical Makeup* (Black).
Parsons, Florence M. *The Incomparable Siddons* (Methuen & Co.).
Sichel, Walter. *Sheridan*, 2 vols. (Constable & Co., Ltd.).

1910

Chesterton, G. K. *George Bernard Shaw*.
Guilbert, Yvette and Simpson, Harold, ed. *Yvette Guilbert: Struggles and Victories* (Mills & Boon, Ltd.).
Howe, P. P. *The Repertory Theatre: A Record and A Criticism* (M. Secker).
Mackinnon, Alan. *The Oxford Amateurs: A Short History of Theatricals at the University*.
Murray, J. T. *English Dramatic Companies 1558–1642*, 2 vols. (Constable).

1911

Buckley, Reginald R. *The Shakespeare Revival and the Stratford-on-Avon Movement* (G. Allen).
Calvert, Mrs. Charles. *Sixty-Eight Years on the Stage* (Mills & Boon, Ltd.).
Craig, Edward Gordon. *On the Art of the Theatre* (Heinemann).
Henderson, Archibald. *George Bernard Shaw: His Life and Works* (Hurst & Blackett).
Walbrook, H. M. *Nights at the Play* (W. J. Ham-Smith).

1912

Armstrong, Cecil F. *A Century of Great Actors, 1750–1850* (Mills & Boon, Ltd.).
Carter, Huntley. *The New Spirit in Drama and Art* (Frank Palmer).
Craig, Edw. Gordon. *Towards a New Theatre; Forty Designs for Stage Scenes, with critical notes by the inventor* (J. M. Dent & Sons, Ltd.).
Macready, Wm. Chas., Toynbee, W., ed. *Diaries*, 2 vols. (Chapman).
Oliver, D. E. *The English Stage: Its Origins and Modern Developments* (John Ouseley, Ltd.).
Palmer, John Leslie. *The Censor and the Theatres* (Fisher, Unwin).

1913

Archer, Wm. *Playmaking: A Manual of Craftsmanship* (Chapman & Hall).
Craig, Edward Gordon. *Towards a New Theatre* (Dent).
Fowell, Frank, and Palmer, Frank. *Censorship in England* (Palmer).
Jones, Henry Arthur. *The Foundations of a National Drama* (Chapman & Hall).
Palmer, John L. *The Comedy of Manners* (G. Bell & Sons, Ltd.).
Simpson, H. and Braun, C. *A Century of Famous Actresses, 1750–1850* (Mills & Boon, Ltd.).
Tree, Herbert Beerbohm. *Thoughts and Afterthoughts* (Cassell).

1914

Barnes, G. H. *Forty Years on the Stage* (Chapman & Hall).
Boas, Frederick S. *University Drama in the Tudor Age* (The Clarendon Press).
Jerrold, C. *The Story of Dorothy Jordan*.
Jerrold, Walter. *Douglas Jerrold: Dramatist and Wit*, 2 vols.
Parker, John, compiler and editor. *Who's Who in the Theatre; A Biographical Record of the Contemporary Stage* (Sir Isaac Pitman & Sons).

1915

Howe, P. P. *Bernard Shaw: A Critical Study*.
Moderwell, H. K. *The Theatre of Today* (Bodley Head).
Sand, Maurice. *The History of the Harlequinade*, 2 vols. (M. Secker).

1916

Cargill, Alexander. *Shakespeare the Player* (Constable).
Hatcher, O. L. *A Book for Shakespearean Plays and Pageants* (Dent).
Hibbert, H. G. *Fifty Years of a Londoner's Life* (Grant Richards, Ltd.).

1917

Adams, Jos. Quincy. *Shakespearean Playhouses: A History of English Theatres from the Beginnings to the Restoration*.
Agate, Jas. E. *Buzz, Buzz! Essays of the Theatre* (Collins).
Booth, J. *The Old Vic: A Century of Theatrical History 1816–1916*.
Lawson, R. *The Story of the Scots Stage* (Gardner).
Sims, Geo. R. *My Life: Sixty Years' Recollections of Bohemian London*.

1918

Lauder, Sir Harry. *A Minstrel in France*.
Phelps, W. L. *The Twentieth Century Theatre: Observations on the Contemporary English and American Stage*.
Ward, Genevieve and Whiteing, R. *Both Sides of the Curtain* (Cassell).
Watson, A. E. T. *A Sporting and Dramatic Career*.

1919

Boyd, Frank M. *A Pelican's Tale*.
Plowman, Thos. F. *Fifty Years of a Showman's Life*.
Rendle, T. McDonald. *Swings and Roundabouts*.
Scott, M. C. *Old Days in Bohemian London: Recollections of Clement Scott*.

1920

Beerbohm, Max. *Herbert Beerbohm Tree: Some Memories of Him and His Art*.
Hibbert, H. G. *A Playgoer's Memories* (Grant Richards).
Poel, Wm. *What is Wrong with the Stage? Some Notes on the English Theatre from the Earliest Times to the Present Day* (G. Allen & Unwin).

1921

Craig, Edw. Gordon. *The Theatre Advancing* (Constable).
Grein, J. T. *The World of the Theatre: Impressions and Memoirs*.
Langtry, Lillie. *The Days I Knew*.
Littlewood, S. R. *Elizabeth Inchbald and Her Circle* (O'Connor).
Lubbock, Percy. *George Calderon: A Sketch from Memory*.

1922

Campbell, Mrs. Patrick. *My Life and Some Letters* (Hutchinson).
Darlington, W. A. *Through the Fourth Wal* (Chapman & Hall).
Granville Barker, Harley. *The Exemplary Theatre* (Chatto & Windus).
Litton, Sir Henry A. *The Secrets of a Savoyard*.

1923

Agate, Jas. E. *At Half-Past Eight: Essays of the Theatre 1921–1922* (Cape).
Chambers, E. K. *The Elizabethan Stage*, 4 vols. (The Clarendon Press).
Craig, Edw. Gordon. *Scene* (Oxford).
Drinkwater, J. and Rutherston, A. *Claud Lovat Fraser* (Heinemann).
Murray, Gilbert, *Euripides and His Age* (Williams & Norgate).
Nicoll, Allardyce. *A History of English Drama: The Restoration, 1660–1700*. vol. 1.
Pearce, Chas. E. *Madame Vestris and Her Times*.

1924

Bardley, A. C. *Shakespearean Tragedy* (Macmillan).
Craig, Edward Gordon. *Woodcuts and Some Words* (Dent).
Ervine, St. John. *The Organized Theatre: A Plea in Civics* (Allen & Unwin).
Grein, J. T. *The New World of the Theatre 1923–1924* (Martin Hopkinson).
Hawtrey, Sir Chas., and Maugham, W. Somerset, ed. *The Truth At Last* (Butterworth).
Mayer, Sylvain. *Reminiscences of a K. C., Theatrical and Legal* (Selwyn & Blount).
Vernon, Frank. *The Twenthieth Century Theatre* (Harrap).

1925

Bordeaux, Jeanne. *Eleanora Duse: The Story of Her Life* (Hutchinson).
Calthrop, Dion C. *Music Hall Nights* (Bodley Head).
Carter, Huntley. *The New Spirit in European Theatre* (Benn).
Forbes-Robertson, Sir J. *A Player Under Three Reigns*.
Playfair, Nigel. *The Story of the Lyric Theatre, Hammersmith* (Chatto & Windus).
Priestley, J. B. *The English Comic Characters*.
Sherson, Errol. *London's Lost Theatres of the Nineteenth Century: with Notes on the Plays and Players Seen There* (Bodley Head).

1926

Agate, Jas. E. *A Short View of the English Stage 1900–1926* (H. Jenkins).
Hamilton, Cicely and Baylis, Lilian. *The Old Vic* (J. Cape).
Landa, M. J. *The Jew in Drama* (P. S. King).
Russell, C. E. *Julia Marlowe—Her Life and Art* (Appleton).
Yeats, William Butler. *Autobiographies: Reveries over Childhood and Youth and the Trembling of the Veil* (Macmillan).

1927

Albright, Evelyn M. *Dramatic Publication in England 1580–1640: A Study of Conditions Affecting Content and Form of Drama* (Oxford Univ. Press).
Drinkwater, John. *The Gentle Art of Theatre-going* (Robert Holder).
Newton, H. Chance. *Cues and Curtain Calls: Being the Theatrical Reminiscences of H. Chance Newton ("Carados" of The Referee)* (Bodley Head).
Sackville-West, Vita. *The Incomparable Aphra*.
Sheppard, Thos. *Evolution of the Drama in Hull and District* (A. Brown).

1928

Agate, James. *Rachel* (Gerald Howe).
Arliss, Geo. *On the Stage—An Autobiography* (Murray).
Elwin, Malcolm. *The Playgoer's Handbook to Restoration Drama* (Cape).
Reynolds, H. *Minstrel Memories; The Story of Burnt Cork Minstrelsy in Great Britain from 1836–1927* (A. Rivers).
Sheringham, G. and Morrison, R. B. *Robes of Thespis: Costume Designs by Modern Artists* (Benn).

1929

Asche, Oscar. *Oscar Asche: His Life* (Hurst & Blackett).
Collier, Constance. *Harlequinade: The Story of My Life* (John Lane).
Komisarjevsky, Theodore. *Myself and the Theatre* (Heinemann).
Motter, Thos. H. V. *The School Drama in England* (Longmans Green).
Stanton, Sanford E. *Theatre Management* (Appleton).
Thorndike, Russell. *Sybil Thorndike* (Butterworth).

1930

Benson, Francis Robert. *My Memoirs* (Benn).
Craig, Edward Gordon. *Henry Irving* (Dent).
Crauford, Lane. *Acting: Its Theory and Practice* (Constable).
Fyfe, Hamilton. *Sir Arthur Pinero's Plays and Players* (Benn).
Granville-Barker, H. *A National Theatre* (Sidgwick).
Lanier, H. W. *The First English Actresses—from the Initial Appearance of Women on the Stage in 1660 till 1700* (Players).
Palmer, John. *Moliere: His Life and Works* (G. Bell).
Playfair, Sir Nigel. *Hammersmith Hoy!* (Faber).

1931

Craig, Edw. Gordon. *Ellen Terry and Her Secret Self* (Low).
Granville Barker, Harley. *On Dramatic Method* (Sidgwick & Jackson).
Harris, Frank. *Frank Harris on Bernard Shaw* (Gollancz).
Komisarjevsky, Theordore. *The Costume of the Theatre* (G. Bles).
Moussinac, L. *The New Movement in the Theatre: A Survey of Recent Developments in Europe and America* (Batsford).
Nicoll, Allardyce. *Masks, Mimes and Miracles: Studies in the Popular Theatre* (Harrap).
Rose, Enid. *Gordon Craig and the Theatre* (Sampson Low).
Terry, Ellen and Shaw, G. B.; (St. John, C., ed.) *A Correspondence* (Constable).

1932

Agate, Jas. E. *The English Dramatic Critics: An Anthology 1660–1932* (Barker).
Bobbe, Dorothea. *Fanny Kemble* (Elkin Mathews).
Day, M. C. and Trewin, J. C. *The Shakespeare Memorial Theatre* (Dent).
Guthrie, Tyrone. *Theatre Prospect* (Wishart).
Hardwicke, Sir Cedric. *Let's Pretend* (Grayson).
Leverton, W. H. and Booth, J. B. *Through the Box-Office Window: Memories of Fifty Years at The Haymarket* (T. Werner Laurie).

1933

Bishop, G. W. *Barry Jackson and the London Theatre* (A. Barker).
Braybrooke, P. *The Amazing Mr. Noel Coward* (Archer).
Ervine, St. John *The Theatre in My Time* (Rich & Cowan).
Godfrey, Philip. *Back-Stage: A Survey of the Contemporary English Stage from Behind the Scenes* (Harrap).
Harvey, Martin. *The Autobiography of Sir John Martin Harvey* (Sampson Low).
Kendal, Dame Madge; de Cordoba, R., ed. *Dame Madge Kendal* (Murray).
Messel, Oliver. *Stage Designs and Costumes* (Lane).
Murray, Gilbert. *Aristophanes: a Study* (Oxford).
Robey, George. *Looking Back on Life* (Constable).
Terry, Ellen. *Ellen Terry's Memoirs* (Gollancz).

1934

Chisholm, Cecil. *Repertory: An Outline of the Modern Theatre Movement: Production, Plays, Management* (P. Davies).
Du Maurier, Daphne. *Gerald: A Portrait* (Gollancz).
Falk, Bernard. *The Naked Lady: or, Storm over Adah*.
Granville Barker, Harley. *The Study of Drama* (Cambridge).
Lupino, Stanley. *From the Stocks of the Stars* (Hutchinson).
Ould, Herman. *John Galsworthy* (Chapman & Hall).
Wilson, A. E. *Christmas Pantomime: The Story of an English Institution* (Allen & Unwin).

1935

Boardman, Wm. H. ("Billy"). *Vaudeville Days* (Jarrold's).
Fay, Wm. G., and Carswell, C. *The Fays of the Abbey Theatre* (Rich & Cowan).

Goldie, Grace W. *The Liverpool Repertory Theatre 1911–1934* (University Press of Liverpool).
Mason, A. E. W. *Sir George Alexander and the St. James Theatre* (Macmillan).
Spurgeon, Caroline F. E. *Shakespeare's Imagery and What it Tells Us* (Cambridge).
Summers, Montague. *The Playhouse of Pepys* (Kegan Paul).

1936

Arthur, Sir George. *From Phelps to Gielgud: Reminiscences of the Stage through Sixty-five Years* (Chapman & Hall).
Bolitho, Hector. *Marie Tempest: Her Biography* (Cobden-Sanderson).
French, Yvonne. *Mrs. Siddons: Tragic Actress* (Cobden-Sanderson).
Linthicum, M. Channing. *Costume in the Drama of Shakespeare and His Contemporaries* (The Clarendon Press).
Nicoll, Allardyce. *The English Theatre: A Short History* (T. Nelson).
Orme, Michael. *J. T. Grein: The Story of a Pioneer, 1862–1935, by his wife* (Murray).

1937

Booth, J. B. *A Pink 'Un Remembers* (T. Werner Laurie).
Clark, Cumberland. *Shakespeare and Costume* (Mitre Press).
Coward, Noel. *Present Indicative* (Heinemann).
Granville Barker, Harley. *On Poetry in Drama* (Sidgwick & Jackson).
Nicoll, A. *Stuart Masques and the Renaissance Stage* (Harrap).
O'Casey, Sean. *The Flying Wasp* (Macmillan).
Playfair, Giles W. *My Father's Son* (Bles).

1938

Harris, Frank. *Oscar Wilde, His Life and Confessions.*
Lanchester, Elsa. *Charles Laughton and I* (Faber).
Matthews, Mrs. *Memoirs of Charles Matthews*, 4 vols. (Bentley).
Short, Ernest and Compton-Rickett, A. *Ring Up the Curtain: Being a Pegeant of English Entertainment, Covering Half a Century* (Jenkins).
Thorndike, Sybil and Russell. *Lilian Baylis* (Chapman & Hall).

1939

Ellis-Fermor, Una. *The Irish Dramatic Movement* (Methuen).
Gielgud, John. *Early Stages* (Macmillan).
Hicks, Sir Seymour. *Me and My Missus (Fifty Years on the Stage).*
Littlewood, S. R. *Dramatic Criticism* (Pitman).
Playfair, Giles W. *Kean* (G. Bles).
Rosenfeld, Sybil. *Strolling Players and Drama in the Provinces 1660–1765* (Cambridge).
Speaight, R. *Acting: Its Idea and Tradition* (Cassell).

1940

Lang, Matheson. *Mr. Wu Looks Back* (Paul).
Murray, Gilbert. *Aeschylus: The Creator of Tragedy.* (Oxford).
Pertwee, Roland. *Master of None.*
Reynolds, Geo. F. *The Staging of Elizabethan Plays: At the Red Bull Theatre 1605–1625* (Oxford).
Robins, Eliz. *Both Sides of the Curtain* (Heinemann).
St. Denis, Teddie. *Almost a Star.*

1941

Carstairs, John Paddy. *"Bunch": A Biography of Nelson Keys.*
Cochran, C. B. *Cock-A-Doodle-Doo* (Dent).
Fleischer, Nathaniel S. *Reckless Lady: The Life of Adah Isaacs Menken.*
Mackail, Denis. *The Story of J. M. B.* (Sir Jas. M. Barrie) (Peter Davies).

1942

Greene, Graham. *British Dramatists.*
Robinson, Lennox. *Curtain Up.*
Short, Ernest. *Theatrical Cavalcade* (Eyre & Spottiswoode).
Stirling, W. Edw. *Something to Declare: The Story of My English Theatre Abroad* (F. Muller).
Taylor, W. Buchanan. *Shake the Bottle.*

1943

Agate, Jas. E. *These Were Actors.*
Anderson, Jean. *Late Joys at the Player's Theatre* (T. V. Boardman).
Booth, J. B. *The Days We Knew.*
Clarence, O. B. *No Complaints* (Cape).
Tillyard, E. M. W. *The Elizabethan World Picture* (Chatto & Windus).

1944

Agate, Jas. E. *Red Letter Nights—A Survey of the Post-Elizabethan Drama in Actual Performance on the London Stage 1921–1943* (Cape).
British Drama League. *Twenty-Five Years of the British Drama League 1919–1944* (B.D.L.).
Granville Barker, Harley. *The Use of Drama* (Cambridge).
Marks, Edw. Bennett. *They All Had Glamour; from the Swedish Nightingale to the Naked Lady.*
Odell, M. T. *Mr. Trotter of Worthing and the Brighton Theatre: The Theatre Royal 1814–1819.*
Taylor, W. B. *One More Shake.*
Tillyard, E. M. W. *Shakespeare's History Plays* (Chatto & Windus).

1945

Agate, J. E. *Innocent Toys: A Survey of Light Entertainment on the London Stage 1920–1943* (Cape).
Bridie, Jas. *The British Drama* (Craig Wilson).
Burnham, Barbara. *Actors—Let's Talk Shop* (Allen & Unwin).
Dent, Edw. J. *A Theatre for Everybody: The Story of the Old Vic and Sadler's Wells* (T. V. Boardman).
Gibbs, H. *Affectionately Yours, Fanny* (Jarrold's).

1946

MacLiammoir, Micheal. *All for Hecuba* (Methuen).
Nicoll, A. *A History of Late Nineteenth-Century Drama 1850–1900*, 2 vols. (Cambridge).
Pearson, Hesketh. *The Life of Oscar Wilde* (Methuen).
Robinson, Lennox. *Lady Gregory's Journals 1916–1930* (Putnam).
Scott, Harold. *The Early Doors: Origins of the Music Hall* (Nicholson).
Scott, Walter S. *The Georgian Theatre* (Westhouse).
Short, Ernest. *Fifty Years of Vaudeville* (Eyre & Spottiswoode).

1947

Bridges-Adams, W. *Looking at a Play* (Phoenix House).
Costanduros, Mabel. *Shreds and Patches.*
Gibbs, Henry. *Affectionately Yours, Fanny* (Jarrolds).
Marshall, Norman. *The Other Theatre* (J. Lehmann).
Nicoll, Allardyce. *British Drama: An Historical Survey* (Harrap).
Priestley, J. B. *Theatre Outlook* (Nicholson & Watson).

1948

Barton, Margaret. *Garrick* (Faber).
Knight, G. Wilson. *The Crown of Life* (Methuen).
Macqueen-Pope, W. *Haymarket, Theatre of Perfection* (W. H. Allen).
Miles, Sir Bernard. *The British Theatre* (Collins).
Nicoll, Allardyce. *The Development of the Theatre* (Harrap).
Southern, Richard. *The Georgian Playhouse* (Pleiades Books).
Vanbrugb, Dame Irene, *To Tell My Story.*

1949

Baxter, Beverley. *First Nights and Noises Off* (Hutchinson).
Colbourne, Maurice. *The Real Bernard Shaw* (Dent).
Darlington, W. A. *The Actor and His Audience* (Phoenix House).
Disher, Maurice Willson. *Blood and Thunder: Mid-Victorian Melodrama and Its Origins* (F. Muller).
Macqueen-Pope, W. *Gaiety: Theatre of Enchantment* (W. H. Allen).
O'Casey, Sean. *Inishfallen Fare Thee Well* (Macmillan).
Shaw, George Bernard. *Sixteen Self Sketches.*
Sprigge, Elizabeth. *The Strange Life of August Strindberg* (Hamilton).

1950

Disher, M. W. *Mad Genius: A Life of Edmund Kean and the Women who Made and Unmade Him* (Hutchinson).
Forman, Robert. *Scene Painting* (Pitman).
Pearson, Hesketh. *The Last Actor-Managers* (Methuen).
Reynolds, E. *Modern English Drama: A Survey of the Theatre from 1900* (Harrap).
Whistler, Rex. *Designs for the Theatre* (Batsford).

1951

Hartnoll, Phyllis, ed. *The Oxford Companion to the Theatre* (Oxford).
Irving, Laurence. *Henry Irving, The Actor and His World* (Faber).
Joseph, Bernard. *Elizabethan Acting* (Oxford).
Laver, James. *Drama: Its Costume and Decor* (Studio Publications).
Noble, Peter. *Ivor Novell, Man of the Theatre* (Falcon Press).
Trewin, J. C. *The Theatre Since 1900* (A. Dakers).

1952

Daubeny, Peter. *Stage by Stage* (Murray).
Hobson, Harold. *Verdict at Midnight: Sixty Years of Dramatic Criticism* (Longmans, Green).
James, David G. *The Universities and the Theatre* (Allen & Unwin).
Lucey, J. C. *Lovely Peggy* (Hurst & Blackett).
Southern, Richard. *Changeable Scenery—Its Origin and Development in the British Theatre* (Faber).
Mander, Raymond, and Mitchenson, Joe. *Hamlet Through the Ages: A Pictorial Record From 1709* (Rockliff).

1953

Courtneidge, Cicely. *Cicely* (Hutchinson).
Dent, Alan, ed. *Bernard Shaw and Mrs. Patrick Campbell: Their Correspondence* (Gollancz).
Downs, Harold. *The Critic in the Theatre* (Pitman).
D'Oyly Carte, Bridget. *A D'Oyly Carte Album* (A. & C. Black).
Hodges, C. Walter. *The Globe Restored* (Benn).
Landstone, Chas. *Off-Stage: A Personal Record of the First Twelve Years of State-Sponsored Drama in Great Britain* (Elek).
Stokes, S. *Without Veils: An Intimate Biography of Gladys Cooper* (Davies).
Tynan, Kenneth. *Alec Guinness* (Rockliff).

1954

Asquith, Cynthia. *Portrait of Barrie.*
Bridges-Adams, W. *The Lost Leader* (Sidgwick & Johnson).
Lowndes, J. Selby. *The Conti Story* (Collins).
Mander, R. and Mitchenson, J. *Theatrical Companion to Shaw: A Pictorial Record of the First Performances of the Theatrical Works of George Bernard Shaw* (Rockliff).
Trewin, J, C. *Edith Evans* (Rockliff).
Wolfit, Donald. *First Interval* (Odhams).

1955

Brown, Ivor. *Theatre 1954–1955* (Rienhardt).
Craig, Harden. *English Religious Drama of the Middle Ages* (Clarendon).
Downs, H. *Appraising a Play* (H. Jenkins).
Findlater, Richard. *Grimaldi, King of Clowns* (MacGibbon & Kee).
Ivamy, E. R. H. *Show Business and the Law* (Stevens).
Keown, Eric. *Peggy Ashcroft* (Rockliff).
Lockwood, Margaret. *Lucky Star* (Odhams).
Purdom, C. B. *Harley Granville Barker* (Rockliff).
Trewin, J. C. *Mr. Macready: A Nineteenth Century Tragedian.*

1956

Dean, Paul. *The Theatre at War* (Harrap).
Hare, Robertson. *Yours Indubitably* (Hale).
Findlater, R. *Emlyn Williams* (Rockliff).
Keown, E. *Margaret Rutherford* (Rockliff).
Williamson, Audrey. *Contemporary Theatre 1953–1956* (Rockliff).

1957

Barton, J. *The First Stage: A Chronicle of the Development of the English Drama from its Beginnings to the 1580s* (B.B.C.)
Brown, R. Core. *Gay Was the Pit: The Life and Times of Anne Oldfield, Actress, 1683–1730* (Reinhardt).
Pearson, H. Gilbert, *His Life and Strife* (Methuen).
Travers, Ben. *Vale of Laughter, An Autobiography* (G. Bles).

1958

Blakelock, Denys. *Advice to a Player: Letters to a Young Actor* (Heinemann).
Craik, T. W. *The Tudor Interlude: Stage, Costume, and Acting* (Leicester).
Hobson, H. *Ralph Richardson* (Rockliff).
Redgrave, Michael. *Mask or Face* (Heinemann).
Trewin, J. C. *The Gay Twenties: A Decade of the Theatre* (Macdonald).

1959

Macqueen-Pope, W. *The Footlights Flickered* (Jenkins).
More, Kenneth. *Happy Go Lucky* (Hale).
Priestley, J. B. *The Story of Theatre* (Rathbone).
Seed, T. Alec. *The Sheffield Repertory Theatre: A History* (Sheffield Rep).
Wickham, G. *Early English Stages, 1300–1660, Vol 1* (Routledge & Kegan Paul).

1960

Burton, E. J. *The British Theatre: Its Repertory and Practice 1100–1900 A. D.* (H. Jenkins).
Guthrie, Tyrone. *A Life in the Theatre* (Hamish Hamilton).
Hodgkinson, J. L. and Pogson, Rex. *The Early Manchester Theatre* (Blond).
Nathan, Archibald J. *Costumes by Nathan* (Newnes).
Rosenfeld, Sybil. *The Theatre of the London Fairs in the Eighteenth Century* (Cambridge).

1961

Hardwicke, Sir Cedric. *A Victorian in Orbit* (Methuen).
MacLiammoir, Micheal. *Each Actor on His Ass* (Routledge).
Mander, Raymond and Mitchenson, Joe *The Theatres of London* (Hart Davis).
Tynan, Kenneth. *Curtains: Selections from the Drama Criticism and Related Writings* (Longmans, Green).
Williams, Emlyn. *George: An Early Autobiography* (Hamilton).

1962

Bradbrook, Muriel. *The Rise of the Common Player: A Study of Actor and Society in Shakespeare's England* (Chatto & Windus).
Brooke, Iris. *Costume in Greek Classic Drama* (Methuen).
Hunt, Hugh. *The Live Theatre: An Introduction to the History and Practices of the Stage* (Oxford).
Southern, R. *The Seven Ages of the Theatre* (Faber).
Steele, Richard; Loftis, J., ed. *The Theatre 1720* (Clarendon Press).

1963

Burton, E. J. *The Student's Guide to British Theatre and Drama* (H. Jenkins).
Garrick, David. *The Letters of David Garrick*, 3 vols. (Oxford).
Loftis, John. *The Politics of Drama in Augustan England* (Clarendon Press).
Price, Cecil. *Theatre in the Age of Garrick* (Blackwell).
Trewin, J. C. *The Birmingham Repertory Theatre 1913–1963* (Barrie & Rockliff).

1964

Brown, Ivor. *What Is a Play?* (Macdonald).
Clunes, Alic. *The British Theatre* (Cassell).
Mander, Raymond, and Mitchenson, Joe. *Musical Comedy: A Story in Pictures* (P. Davies).
Motley. *Designing and Making Stage Costumes* (Studio Vista).
Stochholm, J. M. *Garrick's Folly: The Shakespeare Jubilee of 1769 at Stratford and Drury Lane* (Methuen).
Trewin, J. C. *Shakespeare on the English Stage: 1900–1964* (Barrie & Rockliff).
Tynan, Kenneth. *Tynan on Theatre* (Penguin).

1965

Belden, K. D. *The Story of the Westminster Theatre* (Westminster).
Booth, M. R. *Drama in Britain 1951–1964* (Longmans, Green).
The Twelve Seasons of the Edinburgh Gateway Company 1953–1965 (St. Giles).
Fothergill, B. *Mrs. Jordan* (Faber).
Mehl, Dieter. *The Elizabethan Dumb Show: The History of a Dramatic Convention* (Methuen).

1966

Barker, Kathleen. *The Theatre Royal. Bristol: Decline and Rebirth 1834–1943* (Bristol Historical Assoc.).
Brown, John Russell. *Shakespearean Plays in Performance* (Arnold).
Kitchin, Laurence. *Drama in the Sixties: Form and Interpretation* (Faber).
Morley, Malcolm. *Margate and Its Theatres: 1730–1965* (Museum).
Morley, Rob't. and Stokes, S. *Robert Morley, "Responsible Gentleman"* (Heinemann).
Williams, P. C. *English Shakespearean Actors* (Regency).

1967

Burton, H., ed. *Great Acting* (B.B.C.).

Findlater, R. *Banned! A Review of Theatrical Censorship in Britain* (Macgibbon & Kee).
Holloway, Stanley. *Wiv a Little Bit O' Luck* (Frewin).
Marowitz, Chas. and Trussler, Simon., eds. *Theatre at Work: Playwrights and Productions in the Modern British Theatre*.
Troubridge, St. Vincent. *The Benefit System in the British Theatre* (Society for Theatre Res.)

1968

Craig, Edw. Anthony. *Gordon Craig—The Story of His Life* (Gollancz).
Fernald, John. *Sense of Direction: The Director and His Actors* (Secker & Warburg).
Hartnoll, Phyllis. *A Concise History of the Theatre* (Thames & Hudson).
Hodges, C. Walter. *The Globe Restored: A Study of the Elizabethan Theatre* (Oxford).
Irving, Gordon. *Great Scot: The Life Story of Sir Harry Lauder, Legendary Laird of the Music Hall* (Frewin).
Morrison, Bradley G. and Fliehr, Kay. *In Search of an Audience*, New York: Pitman.

1969

Grotowski, Jerzy. *Towards a Poor Theatre* (Methuen).
Hayman, Ronald. *Techniques of Acting* (Methuen).
Sweeting, Eliz. *Theatre Administration* (Pitman).
Webster, Margaret. *The Same Only Different: Five Generations of a Great Theatre Family* (Gollancz).

1970

Dean, Basil. *Seven Ages: An Autobiography* (Hutchinson).
Esslin, Martin. *Brief Chronicles: Essays on Modern Theatre* (Temple Smith).
Kostelanetz, Richard. *The Theatre of Mixed Means* (Pitman).
Leyson, Peter. *London Theatres: A Short History and Guide* (Apollo).
Manvell, Roger. *Sarah Siddons* (Heinemann).
Southern, Richard. *The Victorian Theatre: A Pictorial Survey* (David & Charles).
Williams, Clifford. *Theatres and Audiences: A Background to Dramatic Texts* (Longmans).

1971

Daubeny, Peter. *My World of Theatre* (J. Cape).
Evershed-Martin, Leslie. *The Impossible Theatre: The Chichester Festival Theatre Adventure* (Phillimore).
Guthrie, Tyrone. *Tyrone Guthrie on Acting* (Studio Vista).
Harwood, Ronald. *Sir Donald Wolfit: His Life and Work in the Unfashionable Theatre* (Secker & Warburg).
Mander, Raymond, and Mitchenson, Joe. *Revue: A Story in Pictures* (P. Davies).
The Stage Guide: Technical Information on British Theatres (Coulson & Comerford).

1972

Brody, Alan. *The English Mummers and Their Plays* (Routledge & Kegan Paul).
Casson, John. *Lewis and Sybil: A Memoir* (Collins).
Dobbs, Brian. *Drury Lane: Three Centuries of the Theatre Royal 1663–1971* (Cassell).
Gielgud, John. *Distingusihed Company* (Heinemann).
Stokes, John. *Resistible Theatres: Enterprise and Experiment in the Late Nineteenth Century* (Paul Elek).

1973

Billington, Michael. *The Modern Actor* (Hamish Hamilton)
Dean, Basil. *Mind's Eye; An Autobiography, 1927–1972* (Hutchinson)
Hayman, Ronald. *The Set-Up: An Anatomy of the English Theatre Today* (Eyre Methuen)
Hodges, C. Walter. *Shakespeare's Second Globe: The Missing Monument* (Oxford University Press)
Price, Cecil. *Theatre in the Age of Garrick* (Blackwell)

Rosenfeld, Sybil. *A Short History of Scenic Design in Great Britain* (Blackwell)
Sorell, Walter. *The Other Face: The Mask in the Arts* (Thames and Hudson)
Southern, Richard. *The Staging of Plays Before Shakespeare* (Faber)
Williams, Emlyn. *Emlyn: An Early Autobiography, 1927–35* (Bodley Head)

1974

Addenbrooke, David. *The Royal Shakespeare Company: The Peter Hall Years* (W. Kimber).
Cook, Judith. *Directors Theatre* (Harrap).
Johns, Eric. *Dames of the Theatre* (W. H. Allen).
Pertwee, Michael. *Name Dropping: The Autobiography* (Frewin).
Rose, Richard. *Perchance To Dream: The World of Ivor Novello* (Frewin).
Wickham, Glynne. *The Medieval Theatre* (Weidenfeld).

1975

Ansorge, P. *Disrupting the Spectacle: Five Years of Experimental and Fringe Theatre in Britain* (Pitman).
Glasstone, Victor. *Victorian and Edwardian Theatres: An Architectural and Social Survey* (Thames & Hudson).
Findlater, R. *Lilian Baylis: The Lady of the Old Vic* (Allen Lane).
Pisk, Litz. *The Actor and His Body* (Harrap).
Tynan, Kenneth. *A View of the English Stage 1944–1963* (Davis—Poynter).

1976

Bentham, Frederick. *The Act of Stage Lighting* (Pitman).
Bradbrook, Muriel C. *The Living Monument: Shakespeare and the Theatre of His Time* (Cambridge).
Hughes, J. G. *The Greasepaint War: Show Business 1939–1945* (New English Library).
Lesley, Cole. *The Life of Noel Coward* (Cape).
Samuel, Edwin. *See How They Run: The Administration of Venerable Institutions* (Woburn).

1977

Arden, John. *To Present the Pretence: Essays on the Theatre and Its Public* (Eyre Methuen).
Forbes, Bryan. *Ned's Girl: The Authorised Biography of Dame Edith Evans* (Elm Tree).
Grice, Elizabeth. *Rogues and Vagabonds, or, The Actor's Road to Respectability* (T. Dalton).
Nash, Mary. *The Provoked Wife: The Life and Times of Susannah Cibber* (Hutchinson).
Roose-Evans, James. *London Theatre from the Globe to the National* (Phaidon).

1978

Baker, Michael. *The Rise of the Victorian Actor* (Croom).
Fawkes, Richard. *Fighting for a Laugh: Entertaining the British and American Armed Forces 1939–1946* (Macdonald & Evans).
Luke, Peter, ed. *Enter Certain Players: Edwards, MacLiammoir and The Gate, 1928–1978* (Dolmen).
Marowtiz, Chas. *The Act of Being* (Secker & Warburg).
Moffat, Alistair. *The Edinburgh Fringe* (Johnston).

1979

Hayman, Ronald. *Theatre and Anti-Theatre: New Movements Since Beckett* (Secker).
Holland, Peter. *The Ornament of Action: Text and Performance in Restoration Comedy* (Cambridge).
Holroyd, Michael, ed. *The Genius of Shaw: A Symposium* (Hodder).
Morley, Sheridan. *Gladys Cooper: A Biography* (Heinemann).
Parker, Derek and Julia. *The Story and the Song: A Survey of English Musical Plays 1916–1978* (Chappell & Co.).

Compiled by Maryilyn Daljord

INDEX

Aaron, Joyce—358
Aaron, Paul—393
Aarons, Alex—155, 383
Aase—381
Abafumi Company—422
Abarbanell, Lina—78, 106
Abba, Marta—136, 196
Abbensett, Michael—409
Abbey Experimental Theater—209
Abbey School of Acting—369
Abbey Theater (Dublin)—3, 24, 37, 58, 59, 60, 63, 64, 65, 68, 69, 73, 76, 77, 81, 84, 89, 90, 91, 96, 102, 149, 256, 275, 313, 347, 350, 373, 375, 385, 389, 417, 431, 440
Abbey Theatre Irish Players—38, 152, 160, 162, 180, 184, 185, 199, 208, 209, 220, 233, 246
Abbott, Bud—216
Abbott Dancers, The—164
Abbott, George—69, 76, 87, 98, 100, 124, 131, 141, 142, 149, 150, 155, 190, 195, 205, 206, 211, 212, 217, 226, 244, 252, 257, 271, 281, 287, 291, 293, 296, 304, 315, 321, 325, 333, 344, 351, 365, 382, 385
Abbott, Merrill—418
Abdication—260
Abe, Kobo—451
Abelard and Heloise—386
Abeles, Edward—25
Abe Lincoln in Illinois—211, 220, 340, 399
Abel, Walter—111, 121, 131, 132, 150, 200
Aberfan—373
Abie's Irish Rose—28, 111, 124, 238
Abingdon, W.L.—90
Ableman, Paul—353, 367
About Town—30
Abraham, F. Murry—413
Abraham Lincoln—90, 94, 104, 109, 183, 237, 369
Abraham, Paul—177
Abramowitz, Max—384
Abravanel, Maurice—240
Absence of a Cello—344, 372
Absent Friends—421
Absurd Person Singular—406, 413, 425
Abyssinina—30
Acacia Avenue—236
Academy of Music (Toronto)—9
Accent on Youth—191, 199, 376, 412
Accolade—268
According to the Evidence—366
Account Rendered—69
AC/DC—387, 395, 401
Ace of Clubs—268
Achard, Marcel—214, 265, 315, 327, 329, 334
Achilles, The Heel—455
Achurch Letters, The—445
Acis and Galatea—12
Ackerly, J.R.—136, 195
Ackerman, Robert Allan—436, 450, 452
Ackland, Joss—317, 329, 341, 359, 395
Ackland, Rodney—183, 201, 206, 249, 269, 305, 315, 383
Acquisition, The—375
Acres, Harry—171
Acrobats and Line—395
Acropolis—375, 382
Across the Board on Tomorrow Morning—232, 336
Acte sans Paroles—306
Acting company, The—424, 431, 446
Action—417, 418, 422
Actors' Association (London)—91
Actors' Equity Association (AEA)—70, 98, 130, 199, 325, 343, 350, 392, 415
Actor's Equity Council—425

Actors' Fidelity Association—98
Actor's Fidelity League—70
Actor's Heritage, The—307
Actor's Studio, The (N.Y.)—260, 340, 342, 344
Actors Theatre Company (N.Y.)—145, 148
Actors Theater of Louisville (ATL)—350
Actor's Workshop (San Francisco)—280, 337, 356
Act, The—434
Act Without Words—404
Act Without Words II—348
Adair, Jean—186, 217, 226
Adair, Patricia—101
Adair, Tom—262
Adair, Yvonne—258
Adam and Eva—93, 104
Adams, Cliff—427
Adams, Edith—298
Adams, Frank—35
Adams, Frederick B.—91
Adams, Ida—83
Adams, John Edward—452
Adams, Lee—320, 344, 357, 401, 442
Adams, Lionel—23
Adams, Maude—1, 7, 15, 22, 23, 28, 41, 43, 56, 71, 130, 137, 146, 238
Adamson, Eve—447
Adamson, Harold—227
Adam's Opera—160
Adams, Polly—362
Adams, Robert—226
Adams, Stanley—201
Adams, (Walter) Bridges—96, 103, 109, 114, 121, 128, 136, 144, 152, 160, 166, 173, 178, 183, 192, 194, 202
Adaption/Next—378
Addams, Dawn—349
Adding Machine, The—117, 159, 166, 369
Addinsell, Richard—160, 177, 272, 277, 289, 310, 315, 376
Addison, John—300
Addison, Michael—335, 439
Ade, George—10, 11, 14, 19, 20, 25, 47, 51, 52, 55, 73, 82
Adele—66
Adler and Sullivan—343
Adler, Caroll—97
Adler, Celia—103
Adler, Jacob P.—146, 424
Adler, Jerry—429
Adler, John—413
Adler, Julia—115
Adler, Lola—116
Adler, Luther—122, 141, 181, 184, 186, 196, 205, 219, 233, 247, 283
Adler, Richard—282, 287, 293
Adler, Stella—116, 179, 181, 184, 195, 234, 329
Admirable Bashville, The—416
Admirable Critchton, The—12, 60, 103, 115, 237, 376, 429, 430, 436
Admirable Pashville, The—273
Admirals All—192
Adonis—116
Adrea—154
Adrian, Max—191, 219, 227, 253, 263, 268, 272, 282, 299, 323, 327, 329, 411
Adrienne—303
Adrienne Lecouvreur—44
Advanced Vaudeville—40
Advent—109
Adventures in the Skin Trade—359
Adventures of a Black Girl in her Search for God, The—373
Adventures of Peregrine Pickle, The—291
Adventures of Awful Knawful, The—446, 447
Adventure Story—263
Advertisement, The—375

Advise and Consent—321
Aeidl, Lea—177
Aerial Football: a New Game—373
Aeschylus—22, 176, 188, 217, 269, 296, 329, 353, 360, 366, 367, 376, 396, 402, 410, 436, 439, 454
Affairs—154
Affairs of Anatol, The—61
Affairs of State—266, 275, 277
Affair, The—328, 332
Affleck, Raymond—343
Afgar—95, 100
Afore Night Come—348, 416
Africana—148
After All—177
After Birthday and My Warren—415
After Haggerty—388
After Hours—317
After Lydia—407
After Magritte—388
Aftermath—114
After Me, The Deluge—444
Afternoon at the Seaside—334
Afternoon Men—340
After October—201
After Sunset—408
After the Ball—289
After the Dance—218
After the Fall—344, 349, 350
After the Girl—72
After the Rain—361
After Tomorrow—189
Agamemnon—188, 436, 439
Agate, James—256
Agate, May—188
Age of Consent—435
Age of Innocence, The—157
Ager, Milton—156
Ages of Man—313, 319
Agguter, Jenny—415
Aglavaine and Selysette—23
Aherne, Brian—118, 151, 165, 172, 179, 182, 194, 265
"Ah, Sweet Mystery of Life"—52
Ah, Wilderness—186, 194, 201, 203, 233, 314, 422
Aickin, Elinor—21
Aida—280
Aidman, Charles—338
Aiello, Danny—449
Aiken, Caroll—97
Aiken, Elinor—11
Aiken, Frank—7
Ailey, Alvin—333
Ainley, Anthony—360
Ainley, Henry—11, 43, 48, 52, 64, 67, 72, 75, 107, 108, 112, 120, 135, 145, 173, 178, 182, 228
Ain't Misbehavin'—405, 442, 450
Ain't Supposed to Die a Natural Death—393
Airs and Graces—295
Airs on a Shoestring—282, 299
Ajayi, Afolabi—365, 388
Akalaitis, JoAnne—431, 440
Aked, Muriel—241
Akins, Zoe—93, 104, 106, 163, 170, 192, 195, 199, 209, 239, 411, 445
Akokawe—388
Alabama—329
A la Broadway—59
A La Carte—258
Aladdin—29, 38, 50, 64, 85, 145, 174, 179, 184, 189, 193, 203, 208, 220, 224, 229, 249, 250, 269, 275, 297, 302, 318, 330, 342, 349, 391, 422, 452, 456
Albanesi, Meggie—102, 107, 114, 120, 122
Albaugh, John Sr.—50
Albee, Edward Franklin—174, 319, 320, 325, 326, 330, 332, 338, 343, 345, 347, 353, 354, 357, 359, 361, 365, 375, 382, 387, 393, 420, 429, 432
Alberghetti, Anna Maria—326

Albert, Eddie—200, 205, 212, 262
Albert, Ernest—6, 30
Albert Herring—367
Albertson, Jack—272, 344, 400
Albertson, Lillian—41, 61
Alberts, The—339
Albert Theatre—46
Albery, Bronson—137
Albery Theatre—410, 418
Albough, John Jr.—7
Alcalde de Zalamea, El—285
Alcazar Theater (San Francisco)—34, 60
Alchemist, The—185, 254, 259, 329, 336, 361, 381, 388, 409, 438
Alcott, Louisa May—97, 295
Alda, Alan—326, 345, 358
Alda, Robert—267, 270
Alden, Darius Adner—146
Alderton, John—427
Aldington, Margery—144
Aldredge, Thomas—341, 390, 449
Aldrich, Richard—186, 280
Aldridge, Michael—421
Aldwych Theater (London)—29, 34, 143, 177, 325
Aleichem, Sholem—179, 306, 344, 361
Aleko—137
Alexander, Ben—221
Alexander, Bill—439, 446, 455
Alexander, Chris—241
Alexander, Jane—365, 400, 429, 442, 445
Alexander, John—226
Alexander, Katherine—176
Alexander, Muriel—112
Alexander, Rod—257, 304
Alexander, Ronald—339
Alexander, Sir George—2, 3, 7, 11, 12, 16, 21, 27, 32, 50, 53, 57, 58, 68, 75, 83, 90, 109, 199
Alexander, William—5
Alfie—339
Alfreds, Mike—445
Alfred, William—352
Alfs Button—128, 129, 137, 179, 189
Algeria—42
Alhambra Theater (San Francisco)—34
Alias Jimmy Valentine—52
Alias the Deacon—133
Ali Baba—355
Alibi—159
Alibi for a Judge—352
Alice and Thomas and Jane—184, 189
Alice in Wonderland—33, 38, 69, 77, 81, 153, 174, 180, 184, 189, 193, 237, 243, 254, 286, 290, 302, 318, 384, 390, 397, 422
Alice of Old Vincennes—7
Alice-Sit-by-the-Fire—26, 56
Alice Through the Looking-Glass—17, 198, 203, 208, 214, 237, 255, 297
Aliens—89
Alison, Dorothy—328
All Aboard—66
"All Aboard for Broadway"—446
All About Eve—385
Allan, Adrianne—231
Allan, A. Hylton—102
Allan, Andrew—348
Allandale, Fred—94
Allan, Jack—227
Allan, Ted—388
Allardice, James B.—262
All Clear—218
Allegro—252, 261, 440
Allen, Adrianne—172, 190, 245, 254, 278, 279, 284
Allen, Amelia—134
Allen, Austen—182
Allenby, Frank—172

Allen, Elizabeth—351
Allen, Fred—112, 124, 163, 171
Allen, Hilary—222
Allen, H. Marsh—58
Allen, Jay Presson—358, 401
Allen, John—223
Allen, Jonella—382
Allen, Lester—105
Allen, Martha Bryan—131
Allen, Patrick—366, 401, 436
Allen, Rae—400, 418, 454
Allen, Ralph G.—450
Allen, Seth—358, 390
Allen, Sheila—373, 418
Allen, Steve—379
Allen, Ted—339
Allen, Vera—216
Allen, Viola—1, 2, 33, 48, 261
Allen, Vivian Beaumont—336
Allen, Woody—358, 378, 396
Allergy—98, 410
"All Er Nuthin'"—234
Allers, Franz—246
Alley Theatre (Houston)—337, 356
All For a Girl—45
All for All—238
All for Love—114, 435, 438
All for Mary—289
All God's Chillun Got Wings—145, 160, 422
Allgood, Sara—37, 45, 48, 53, 54, 59, 63, 76, 103, 151, 152, 153, 166, 189, 207, 208, 219, 223, 270
All in Good Faith—341
All in Good Time—339, 351
All in One—293
All in the Family—354
Allison's House—174, 180, 182, 186, 218, 220
All My Sons—252, 256, 258, 376
"All of You"—293
All Over—393
All Over Town—414
All Scotch—75
All Seats Four-pence—353
All Summer Long—287
All's Well That Ends Well—80, 109, 114, 115, 184, 197, 224, 285, 295, 296, 317, 329, 360, 367, 389, 373, 423, 438, 446
All the King's Horses—190
All the King's Men—361
"All the Things You Are"—217
All the Way Home—321, 331, 455
All Through the House—405
"All Through the Night"—191
All To Hell Laughing—353
All Walks of Leg—424
Allyson, June—211
Alman, Samuel—63
Almaviva, Count—417
Alma, Where Do You Live?—52
Almaz, Michael—379, 395, 422, 435, 444
Almost a Honeymoon—172
"Almost Like Being in Love"—252
Aloma—143
Alone at Last—74
Along Fifth Avenue—262
Alpha Beta—401
Alshansky, I.—219
Alswang, Ralph—233, 343, 456
Alternative Theatre Company—405, 422, 457
Altman, Richard—338, 400
Alt, Natalie—66
Altona—329
Alton, Robert—200
Alvarez, Carmen—351
Always You—99
Alwyn, William—197
Amadee—340
Amadeus—451
Amasis—32
AMAS Repertory Theatre—426

Amateur Stage—251
Amazing Activity of Charley Contrare, The—410
Amazing Dr. Clitterhouse, The—201, 205
Ambassadors, The—394
Ambiance Lunch-Hour Theatre Club—377, 379, 388, 394
Ambient, Mark—48, 79, 97
Ambrose Applejohn's Adventure—107, 187
Ambush—243
Ameche, Don—293, 309
Amelia's African Adventure—336
Amelia's Suitors—114
Amen Corner, The—351, 354
Amends—114
America—66, 88
Americana—140, 181
American Academy of Arts and Letters—244
American Academy of Dramatic Art—153
American Beauty, An—2
American Broadcasting Company (ABC)—147
American Buffalo—418, 434, 445
American Conservatory Theater (Pittsburgh)—356, 366, 419. (San Francisco)—381, 382
American Critics Association—419
American Dance Machine—446
American Diplomacy—75
American Dramatists Club—45
American Dream, The—188, 326, 330, 347, 375
American Drama Since 1918—391
"American Eagles"—230
American Educational Theatre Association—399
American Federal Theatre Project—209
American Federation of Labor—98
American Federation of Television and Radio Artists (AFTRA)—98
American Film Institute—399
American Guild of Musical Artists (AGMA)—98
American Holiday—202
American Idea, The—42
American Jewish Committee—399
American Laboratory Theatre—159
American Maid, The—66
American Medical Association—221
American Millionaire, An—416
American Modern—431
American National Theatre and Academy—121, 138
American Negro Theatre—240, 246
American Negro Theatre Playhouse—259
American Place Theatre, The—349, 350, 368, 375, 380, 388, 390, 395, 399, 402
American Play Company—189
American Playwrights of Today—261
American Playwrights Theatre—405, 449
American Repertory Theatre—250, 251, 254, 259
American Stage of Today, The—307
American Theatre as Seen by its Critics, The—383
American Theatre Association—399
American Theatre Critics Association—443, 449
American Theatre Student League—399
American Theatre Wing War Service Inc.—232
American Tragedy, An—141, 147, 189
American Way, The—216, 220
American Yiddish Art Theatre Company—198
American Youth Theatre—230
Ames, Florenz—117
Ames, Leon—203

Ames, Robert—117
Ames, Winthrop—61, 62, 65, 67, 70, 72, 88, 105, 108, 144, 145, 209
Amiel, Denys—109
Amiel, Jon—447
Amleto—348
Among the Girls—153
Amorous Prawn, The—316
Amoureuse—23
Amphitryon—38, 114, 208, 215, 267, 274, 290, 354, 387, 388, 396, 411, 441
Amram, David—320
Amusing Spectacle of Cinderella and Her Naughty-Naughty Sisters, The—440
Amyes, Julian—302
Anarchist—395
Anastasia—283, 288, 306, 308, 431
Anathema—121
Anatole—246, 428
Anatomist, The—178, 180, 260, 301
Ancient Mariner, The—452
And All That—182
Anderman, Maureen—420
Andersen, Hans Christian—8, 44, 193
Anders, Glenn—106, 124, 126, 143, 163, 170, 181, 257
Anderson, Alan—271
Anderson, Arthur—67, 84
Anderson, Bibi—434
Anderson, Constance P.—96
Anderson, Craig—424, 430, 440, 449
Anderson, Dallas—88
Anderson, F. Richard—10, 41
Anderson, Garland—132
Anderson, Gene—340
Anderson, Gwen—230
Anderson, J. Grant—295
Anderson, John—435
Anderson, John Lloyd—291
Anderson, John Murray—92, 99, 100, 107, 112, 118, 125, 126, 237, 247, 418
Anderson, Judith—150, 188, 195, 208, 216, 228, 232, 255, 264, 269, 282, 284, 323, 324, 360
Anderson, Lawrence—63, 143, 158
Anderson, Lindsay—316, 318, 322, 330, 340, 349, 379, 386, 394, 415, 423, 435
Anderson, Mary—57, 102, 224
Anderson, Maxwell—125, 132, 138, 148, 155, 157, 163, 171, 180, 181, 186, 189, 193, 194, 195, 199, 200, 204, 205, 209, 210, 211, 215, 217, 221, 224, 225, 226, 230, 233, 238, 243, 247, 251, 256, 258, 262, 265, 271, 280, 288, 297, 318, 319, 402
Anderson, Miles—364
Anderson, Percy—3, 6, 8, 11
Anderson, Robert—270, 281, 287, 292, 301, 315, 357, 371, 395, 397, 449
Anderson, Rona—273
Anderson, Sarah Pia—436
Anderson, Sherwood—229
Andersonville Trial, The—315, 325, 329
Andes, Keith—254
And Is There Honey Still for Tea?—447
And Miss Reardon Drinks a Little—393, 399
And Now There's Just the Three of Us—381
Andorra—338, 343
And Other Burnings—380
And Pastures New—250
Andrea—25
Andreas, Christine—329, 456
Andre Charlot's London Revue of 1924—122
Andre Charlot's Revue of 1924—124
Andrews, Ann—150
Andrews, Bobbie—107
Andrews, Charlton—99
Andrews, Chris—401
Andrews, Harry—281, 301, 311

Andrews, Herbert—221
Andrews, Julie—253, 256, 260, 286, 288, 298, 321, 325
Andrews, Maidie—17, 159, 197, 236
Andrews, Maxene—413
Andrews, Nancy—332
Andrews, Patty—413
Andrews, Robert—134
Andrews Sisters—413
Andrews, Tod—257, 404
Andreyev, Leonid—76, 111, 121, 122, 144, 166, 249, 348
Andreyevna, Lyubov—241
Andrisano, Gui—295
Androcles and the Lion—67, 76, 137, 173, 193, 203, 214, 250, 251, 329, 341, 374
Android Circuit, The—444
Andromaque—16, 253, 260
Andronicus—275
And So To Bed—143, 214, 273
And That's How the Rent Gets Paid—451
And That's the Truth—135
And the Wind Blew—307
And They Put Handcuffs on the Flowers—402, 410
And Things That Go Bump In the Night—351, 439
An Evening of Farce with Chekov—347
An Evening of One Acts—380
An Evening of Scottish Horrors—422
Angela Maria—152
Angel City—439
Angel Face—114
Angel in the Wings—253
Angell, James Rowland—147
Angelou, Maya—406
Angels in Love—288
Angels (Over Your Grave) and Geese (Over Mine)—373
Angel Street—154, 217, 227, 233, 239, 259
Angelus, Muriel—234
Angers, Avril—332, 407
Anglim, Philip—449
Anglin, Margaret—22, 31, 48, 72, 80, 100, 108, 187, 313
Angry Men—345
Angus Bowmer Theatre—423
Anhalt, Lawrence—144
An Ideal Husband—402
Animal—451, 455
Animal Crackers—157, 256
Animal Kingdom, The—181, 185
An Inspector Calls—248, 252
Ankles Away—293
An' Me Wi' a Bad Leg, Tae—431
Anna and the King of Siam—271
Annabella—239, 247
Anna Christie—106, 116, 119, 166, 208, 234, 240, 242, 278, 283, 285, 304, 438, 456
Annajanska—274
Anna K.—400
Anna Karenina—35, 69, 400
Annals, Michael—340, 417
Anna Lucasta—246, 253
Anna-Luse—373
Anne of Green Gables—352
Anne of the Thousand Days—258, 265, 318
Annie—434, 441, 443, 457
Annie Get Your Gun—247, 253, 256, 311, 418, 455
Annis, Francesca—438
Anniversary Waltz—287
Ann Veronica—263
A-Non—430
Another Language—181, 183, 185, 424
Another Love Story—244
Another Part of the Forest—247, 256
Another Way Out—80
Anouilh, Jean—249, 251, 264, 267, 268, 272, 273, 274, 278, 279, 289, 294, 296, 300, 305, 307, 308, 313, 315, 316, 321, 328, 331, 334, 345, 350, 353, 359, 360, 367, 376, 396,

398, 409, 410, 415, 417, 419, 422, 423, 430, 455
Anschluss—218
Ansell, John—95
Ansky, S.—133, 145, 147, 346, 347
Anson, A.E.—75
Anstey, F.—7, 49, 85, 145, 167, 182, 235
Anstruther, Gerald—263
ANTA Washington Square Theater—296, 350, 382, 388, 452
Anthony And Anna—197
Anthony, C.L.—177, 183, 192, 197
Anthony, Hilda—41, 63
Anthony in Wonderland—83
Anthony, Joseph—276, 309, 320, 321, 322, 345, 406
Anthony, Julie—406
Anti-Christ—135
Antick, The—77
Anti-Defamation League of B'nai B'rith—399
Antigone—249, 251, 264, 323, 367, 390, 394, 397, 417
Antigone of Sophokles, The—375
Antonio, Lou—339, 349
Antony and Cleopatra—3, 33, 50, 51, 56, 63, 109, 114, 127, 128, 152, 178, 193, 197, 203, 237, 245, 250, 255, 284, 285, 306, 312, 317, 323, 354, 361, 367, 368, 381, 396, 401, 402, 403, 409, 430, 438, 439, 444, 446, 453
Antoon, A.J.—402, 406, 455
Antrobus, John—339, 347, 353, 379, 401, 417, 418, 424
Antrobus, Yvonne—379
Any Day Now—224
"Any Old Place with You"—92
Anyone Can Whistle—344
Any Other Business—310
Anything Goes—191, 197, 383
Anything You Say Will Be Twisted—380
Any Wednesday—344, 352
Apache, The—150
APA-Phoenix Repertory Company—334, 349, 355, 366, 368, 373, 375
Apartment, The—372
Aphrodite—93
Apocalypsis Cum Figurus—382
Apolinar, Danny—371
Apollo in Mourne—192
Apollo of Bellac, The—306
Apollo Society, The—312
Apollo Theater (London)—9
Apparition Theatre of Prague, The—362
Appearances—132
Appell, Don—326
Applause—385, 394
Apple a Day, An—283
Applebaum, Louis—285, 317
Apple Blossoms—93
Apple Cart, The—165, 170, 198, 249, 284, 302, 361, 369, 387, 411, 429, 438, 440
Appleman, Margie—403
Apple Pie—428
Apple Sauce—227
Apple, The—327
Apple Tree, The—358
Appointment with Death—244
Appollinaire, Guillaume—408
Apprentices, The—403
"April in Paris"—182
"April Showers"—106
Apropos of Falling Sleet—410
Apted, Michael—437
A Quoi Revient les Jeunes Filles—80
A & R—435, 446
Arabian Nightmare—291
Ararbanell, Lina—342
Arbitration, The—249
Arbuckle, Maclyn—35, 121
Arbuzov, Aleksei—365, 380, 427, 429
Arcaro, Flavia—132
Arc de Trimphe—236
Archdupe, The—179

Archer, Corliss—234
Archer, Harry—126
Archer, Janet—404
Archer, John—269
Archer, Osceola—259
Archer, William—8, 44, 58, 68, 105, 110, 129, 251
Archibald, William—266, 270, 391
Archie Andrews' Christmas Party—275
Archie, Will—42, 56
Architect and the Emperor of Assyria, The—389, 395, 401, 424, 430
Architecture for the New Theatre—302
Ardele—272, 313, 423
Arden, Eve—200, 217, 226
Arden, Jane—310
Arden, John—307, 312, 318, 323, 341, 354, 355, 357, 377, 382, 401
Arden of Faversham—136, 291, 389, 391, 415
Ardrey, Robert—214, 219, 228, 249, 273, 291, 311, 337
Arena—384
Arena Conta Zumbi—382
Arena Stage (Washington)—270, 337, 437
Arena Theater (Washington D.C.)—331, 372
Arenski, Anton—137
Arent, Arthur—206, 213, 404
Aren't Men Beasts—201, 232
Aren't We All?—117, 119, 285, 362
Are We All Met?—303
Are We Downhearted—75
Are You A Crook?—70
Are You Now Or Have You Ever Been . . .?—410, 439, 442
Are You With It?—244
Ariadne—131, 134
Ariadne auf Naxos—423
Ariosto—389
Aristocrat, The—83
Aristophanes—137, 173, 204, 250, 292, 307, 318, 353, 360, 361, 367, 379, 380, 389, 423, 431
Arizona—1, 11
Arkell, Reginald—102, 115, 120, 127, 151, 173, 196
Arkin, Alan—326, 338, 344, 418
Arlecchino: the Servant of Two Masters—389
Arlen, Harold—176, 181, 190, 206, 219, 230, 247, 250, 288, 304
Arlen, Michael—132, 135, 147, 177, 303, 419
Arlen, Richard—240
Arlequin—115
Arlequin Poli par l'Amour—296
Arlette—84
Arliss, George—2, 8, 11, 12, 13, 16, 20, 27, 42, 56, 105, 127, 250
Armageddon—75
Armaury—75
Armistead, Horace—296
Armont—58, 89
Arms and the Man—48, 58, 76, 137, 154, 168, 178, 198, 242, 284, 334, 355, 367, 368, 388, 418, 429, 445
Arms and the Girl—161
Armstrong, Anthony—183, 187
Armstrong, Leslie—248
Armstrong, Louis—164, 217
Armstrong, Paul—42, 52, 77
Armstrong's Last Goodnight—354, 355
Armstrong, Thomas—75
Armstrong, Will Steven—258, 310, 318, 349
Army Emergency Relief—230, 238
Army Play-By-Play, The—234
Army Theatre Arts Association—399
Arnaud, Yvonne—63, 72, 85, 94, 113, 134, 138, 143, 159, 177, 192, 253, 258, 273, 278
Arnaux, Germaine—84
Arnaz, Desi—217
Arnaz, Lucie—449

Arnett, Jake—425
Arnim, Elizabeth—53
Arnold, Edward—93, 133, 302
Arnold, Florrie—33
Arnold, Hap—238
Arnold, Jean—317
Arnold, T. C.—286
Arnone, John—440
Aronson, Boris—199, 222, 316
Aronstein, Martin—454
Around the World—56
Around the World in 80 Days—247
Arrabal, Fernando—330, 340, 347, 348, 389, 395, 402, 410, 424
Arrah-Na-Pogue—16
Arren, Charlotte—195
Arrick, Larry—371
Arsene Lupin—47, 108
Arsenic and Old Lace—226, 229, 231, 233, 242, 247, 303, 308, 312, 359, 383, 396, 431, 433, 438
Art and Mrs. Bottle—166
Artaud, Antonin—346
Artaud at Rodez—424
Artaud Company—444
Artef Company—46
Artful Widow, The—431
Arthur—121
Arthur, Beatrice—256, 293
Arthur, Daphne—267
Arthur, Helen—131
Arthur, Jean—184, 268
Arthur, Julia—108
Arthurs, George—43, 83, 84, 172
Artichoke—451
Artistic Director of Theatre Passe Muraille—412
Artists and Models—118, 125, 131, 150, 170
Artist's Model, An—55
Artist, The—95
Art of Dining, The—455
Art of the Clown, The—435
Arts Council of Great Britain—249, 251
Arturo Ui—339
Arundale, Sybil—8, 15, 21, 153, 173
Arundell, Dennis—136, 217
As a Man Thinks—56
Ascarra, Maria—100
Ascendancy—197
Ascent of F.6, The—206, 218, 412
Asche, Oscar—8, 23, 45, 57, 58, 79, 95, 108, 134, 159, 167, 184, 223
Asche, Phyllis—101
Ascherson, Renee—245, 253, 259, 274, 285, 311
Asch, Sholom—113, 116, 198
Ash, Arty—172, 222
Ashcroft, Chloe—367
Ashcroft, Peggy—152, 166, 172, 284, 188, 191, 198, 205, 213, 214, 222, 252, 253, 259, 294, 296, 302, 306, 311, 312, 318, 323, 379, 380, 393, 401, 415, 427, 439, 456
Asher, Jane—366, 393, 427, 437, 447
Asherson, Renee—249, 250
Ashes—140, 143, 405, 409, 415, 431, 436
Ashe, Warren—239
Ashford, Daisy—101
Ashford, John—435
Ash, Gordon—94
Ashley, Elizabeth—310, 327, 339, 417, 423, 437
Ashley, Minnie—10
Ashmore, Basil—278, 373
Ashmore, Peter—259, 263, 272, 273, 285, 288, 290
Ashton, David—421
Ashton, Frederick—255
Ashton, Jr., Herbert—158
Ashton, Marcia—296
As Husbands Go—176, 180
Ashwander, Don—369
Ashwell, Lena—2, 13, 16, 20, 40, 43, 49
Asile de Nuit—75
Ask Beccles—143
Askey, Arthur—236, 255, 259, 276,

369
Ask No Questions and You'll Hear No Stories—57
As Long As They're Happy—283
Aspect of Max Wall—421
Aspern Papers, The—315, 341, 446
Asquith, Anthony—231
Assassin, The—244
Assignation, The; Or, Love in a Nunnery—135
Association of Producing Artists (APA)—319, 347
Association Actors and Artistes of America (AAAA)—98
Astaire, Adele—85, 87, 93, 120, 126, 150, 155, 171, 176, 209
Astaire, Fred—126, 150, 151, 155, 171, 176, 182, 209
As the Girls Go—261, 265
As Thousands Cheer—186
"*As Time Goes By*"—176
As Time Goes By—397
Astonished Heart, The—201
Astonished Ostrich, The—203
Astor, Kay—217
As You Like It—3, 8, 12, 22, 37, 49, 53, 54, 58, 59, 68, 72, 73, 76, 96, 103, 109, 110, 121, 136, 152, 160, 173, 184, 188, 189, 193, 197, 198, 202, 207, 208, 214, 219, 223, 225, 232, 237, 242, 245, 249, 254, 260, 264, 268, 278, 279, 283, 284, 285, 292, 295, 301, 306, 307, 311, 317, 323, 329, 334, 335, 354, 367, 373, 374, 375, 376, 403, 409, 423, 429, 430, 432, 437, 439, 444, 446, 447, 452, 453, 454
As You Were—89, 91, 99
Atalanta in Calydon—58
Atelje 212—374
Ates, Nejla—292
Athayde, Roberto—434, 436
At Home Abroad—195
Atkins, Alfred—191
Atkins, Eileen—334, 341, 352, 368, 379, 387, 434, 438
Atkinson, Brooks—179, 187, 253, 257, 265, 266, 279, 290, 314, 325
Atkinson, David—301
Atkinson, Robert—147
Atkins, Pete—435, 446
Atkins, Robert—80, 109, 121, 167, 183, 184, 193, 208, 214, 219, 223, 224, 228, 232, 237, 242, 245, 246, 249, 254, 260, 264, 269, 279, 284, 295, 301, 311, 317, 323, 404
Atlanta Memorial Arts Center (Georgia)—377
Atlas, Leopold—190, 194
Atlas, Leopold—190, 194
"*At Long Last Love*"—211
At Mrs. Beam's—119, 143
At 9:45—92
Atom Doctor, The—269
Atonacci, Greg—420
Atonement—90
A to Z—108
Atta Boy—88
Attenborough, Michael—452
Attenborough, Richard, 232, 235, 268, 277, 278, 299
Atteridge, Harold—66, 74, 111, 124, 131, 132, 176
At the Barn—62
At the Boar's Head—135
At the Bottom—173
At the Drop of a Hat—305, 314, 317, 340
At the End of the Day—407
At the Gates of the Kingdom—114
At the Hawk's Well—455
At the Lyric—286
At the Mercy of the Mormons—68
At the Palace—386
At the Telephone—114
At the Villa Rose—102
At War with the Army—262
Atwell, Wilfrid—283
Atwill, Lionel—88, 90, 101, 106, 136
Atwood, Alban—37
Aubert, Jeanne—191

Aubjerjonois, Rene—449
Au Coin Joli—76
Auctioneer, The—6, 77
Auden, W. H.—197, 201, 206, 218, 219, 256, 412
Audition, The—372, 403
Audley, Maxine—102, 258, 264, 274, 288, 329, 379, 390, 439
Audrey—11
Auerbach, Arnold—257
Augarde, Adrienne—22, 26
Augarde, Amy—102, 115, 127
Augusta, Lady Gregory—60, 152, 220
August for the People—329
Augustin Daly's Musical Company—10, 180
Augustus Does His Bit—92, 274, 366
Ault, Marie—151, 167, 178
Aumont, Jean Pierre—264, 338, 429, 438
Aureng-Zebe—192
Austen, Edward—17, 23
Austen, Jane—184, 196, 244, 278, 314, 360
Austin, Alfred—107
Austin, Charles—113
Austin, Clare—302
Austin, Frederic—103, 115, 143
Austin, Lyn—374
Australian Summer of the 17th Doll—373
Authors League of America—65, 98, 350
Autier, Paul—76
Auto-Destruct—403
Auto Race, The—36
Autumn—207
Autumn Crocus—177, 181
Autumn Fire—128, 144
Autumn Garden, The—271, 275
"*Autumn in New York*"—191
Autumn Manoeuvres—62
Autumn Revue—291
Avanti—421
Avedon, Doe—264
Avenger, The—313
Avers, Lemuel—234
Avery, James—331
Aviator, The—83, 431
Avril, Suzanne—23
Awake and Sing—195, 199, 232, 397
Awakening of Helena Richie, The—48
Awakening, The—7
Awakening Woman, The—69
Away We Go—234
Awful Truth, The—112, 243
Axelrod, George—257, 276, 293, 315, 358
Ayckbourn, Alan—365, 386, 401, 406, 414, 415, 421, 427, 435, 441, 443, 446, 450, 452, 454
Ayer, Nat—79, 80, 88, 95
Ayer, Nat Jr.—206
Ayers, Catherine—259
Ayers, Lemuel—257
Ayliff, H.K.—143, 159, 165, 184, 223, 245, 259
Aylmer, Felix—77, 113, 120, 151, 166, 192, 263, 456
Aylwin, Jean—43
Aynesworth, Allan—2, 12, 16, 22, 43, 63, 79, 107, 151, 172, 178, 192
Ayrton, Randle—59, 89, 120, 136, 144, 178

Baal—453
Baba Goya—402
Babberley, Fancourt—454
Babel, Isaac—368
Babes in Arms—205, 368
Babes in the Wood—38, 59, 77, 90, 168, 184, 214, 228, 232, 234, 255, 260, 269, 280, 297, 355, 362, 369, 404

Babes in Toyland—15, 59, 128, 129, 161, 167, 446
Babe, Thomas—422, 426, 428, 431, 436, 445, 447, 452
Babies Grow Old—416
Baby Bunting—95
Baby Cyclone—149
Baby Doll—293
Baby Elephant, The—395
Baby Mine—52, 57, 137, 232
Bacac, The—84
Bacall, Lauren—315, 352, 385
Bacchae, The—45, 347, 409, 417, 423
Bacharach, Burt—372
Bachelor Born—211
Bachelor Father, The—166
Bachelor's Baby, The—199
Bachelor's Romance, A—137
Bach, Reginald—127
Back Bog Beast Bait—395
Backbone—373, 374
Back Pay—105
Back To Methuselah—111, 120, 123, 159, 174, 254, 311, 381, 411
Backus, Goerge—92
Bacon, Faith—170, 175
Bacon, Frank—62, 78, 87, 129
Bacon, Mai—107, 114, 213
Bad Before Yesterday, The—424
Baddeley, Angela—128, 134, 137, 141, 143, 151, 182, 183, 188, 192, 197, 241, 249, 260, 273, 297, 258, 286, 320, 432
Baddeley, Hermione—152, 158, 192, 212, 218, 223, 227, 231, 235, 244, 248, 265, 338
Bade, Alan—279
Badel, Alan—268, 274, 279, 301, 317, 394, 429
Badel, Sarah—368, 391, 429
Bad Girl of the Family, The—49
Bad Habits—413
Bad Man, The—99, 110, 119, 180
Bad Samaritan, The—282
Bad Seed, The—288, 294, 297, 318
Baer, Arthur (Bugs)—132
Bafunno, Antonio—88
Bagels and Yox—271
Bagley, Ben—297, 300, 351
Bagneris, Vernel—450
Bagnold, Enid—248, 280, 285, 294, 344, 426, 433
Bahr, Hermann—52, 63, 373
Baikie Charvari, The—317
Bailey, James—279
Bailey, Paul—416
Bailey, Pearl—77, 247, 288, 424
Bain, Conrad—323, 357, 364
Bainter, Fay—87, 88, 124, 132, 134, 144, 183, 190, 376
Baird, Bil—363
Baird, Cora—363, 370
Baird, Dorothea—22, 45, 49, 53
Baird, Ethel—143, 159
Bairnsfather, Bruce—83, 87
Baithwaite, Lillian—206
Bajala, Janos—422
Bajour—345
Baker, Benny—226
Baker, Carroll—287
Baker, Dorothy—241, 279
Baker, Elizabeth—54, 69
Baker, Evelyn—26
Baker, George—3260, 371, 374
Baker, George Pierce—147, 198
Baker, Howard—241, 279
Baker, Iris—184, 190, 201
Baker, Josephine—125, 347, 424
Baker, Kenny—235
Baker, Lee—132
Baker, Lenny—434
Baker, Mark—393
Baker, Melville—118
Baker, Paul—318, 319
Baker, Phil—100, 118, 131, 148, 163, 230, 342
Baker, Stanley—272
Baker Street—356
Baker's Wife, The—441

Baker, Word—329, 345, 349, 364, 385, 351
Bakewell, Michael—402
Bakos, John—371
Bakst, Leon—455
Balachites, The—340
Balalaika—202
Balanchine, George—200, 205, 211, 212, 221, 222, 230, 237, 239, 254, 257, 312
Balchin, Nigel—288
Balcony, The—320, 397, 431
Balderston, John—143, 440
Balderstson/Squire—213, 173, 183, 202, 223, 228
Balde Voleurs, Le—274
Baldwin, James—344, 351, 353, 354
Baldwin, Nigel—435, 445, 451, 455
Balfour, Val—284
Balieff, Nikita—109, 111, 135, 178, 233
Balin, Edmund—389
Balkan Princess, The—53
Ballad of the Sad Cafe, The—339
Ballantine, Sheila—347, 451
Ballard, Frederick—66
Ballard, Kaye—262, 287, 351
Ballet Ballads—257, 261
Ballet Behind the Bridge, A—402
Ballet Caravan—219
Ballet Russe de Monte Carlo—239, 455
Ball, Lucille—321
Ballou, Bill—248
Ballroom—443, 457
Balls—353
Ball, William—319, 323, 329, 335, 340, 341, 347, 353, 356, 366, 382
Ballymurphy—431
Balsam, Martin—260, 271, 281, 298, 434
Balser, Ewald—373
Balthrop, Carmen—420
Balustrade Drama Group—373
Balustrade Mime Group—373
Balzac, Honore—291
Balzer, George—244
"*Bambalina*"—117, 126
Banana Box, The—408
Banana Ridge—212, 430
Bananas—376
Banbury, Frith—222, 272, 273, 283, 288, 290, 312, 315, 322, 360, 365, 372, 394, 401, 402, 423, 439
Banbury Nose, The—241
Bancroft, Anne—309, 313, 314, 327, 341, 368, 376, 434
Bancroft, Marie Effie Wilton—109, 110
Bancroft, Sir Squire—34, 110, 146
Bandana Land—41
Bandits—439
Bandmann, Daniel—28
Bandmann Opera Company—229
Band Wagon, The—176
Bane, Robert—136
Banff Centre for Continuing Education—189, 448
Banff Festival of the Arts—189
Bangs, John Kendrick—23
Banjo Eyes—227
Bankhead, Tallulah—93, 105, 119, 126, 127, 128, 129, 134, 135, 142, 148, 151, 161, 191, 200, 216, 227, 230, 244, 253, 260, 265, 278, 300, 304, 309, 326, 338, 377
Bankhead, William Brockman—377
Bankside Players—207
Banks, Leslie J.—126, 135, 144, 159, 177, 183, 197, 207, 208, 212, 213, 217, 222, 248
Banks, Nathaniel—318
Bankson, Douglas—392
Bannen, Ian—247, 318, 329
Bannerman, Kay—289, 315, 365
Bannerman, Margaret—87, 101, 206, 433
Bantock, Leedham—43
Banville, Theodore de—90

Baptism, The—388
Baptiste—260, 274
Barasch, Norman—309
Bara, Theda—42
Barbara Freitchie—5, 51
Barbaretto, Burrell—67
Barbarians—436
Barbary Shore—410
Barbee, Richard—148
Barber and the Cow, The—144
Barberine—85
Barbour, Joyce—102, 142, 148, 151, 156, 201, 206, 226
Barcena, Catalina—152
Bardelys the Magnificent—57
Bard, William S.—80, 84, 102, 184
Barefoot Boy With Cheek—252
Barefoot in Athens—271, 280
Barefoot in the Park—139, 338, 350, 353, 383
Barer, Marshall—316
Barett, Augustus—8, 107, 108
Barge Theatre, The—367
Bariatinsky, Princess (Lydia Yavorskaya)—50
Barkentin, Marjorie—317, 415
Barker, Albert—202
Barker, Edith—16
Barker, Edwin—202
Barker, Harley Granville—8, 19, 22, 23, 24, 27, 28, 29, 32, 39, 46, 54, 57, 60, 63, 64, 67, 68, 72, 76, 77, 137, 193, 202, 203, 223, 359, 369, 422, 436
Barker, Howard—390, 391, 401, 428, 431, 437, 439, 446
Barker, Irene—93
Barker, Lee—176
Barker, The—148
Barkworth, Peter—401, 427
Barlow, Ann—273
Barlow, Graham—348
Barlow, Patrick—394
Barnabetta—78
Barnes, Barry K. 207
Barnes, Billie—159
Barnes, Clive—378, 385, 399, 441
Barnes, Djuna—144
Barnes, Mae—123
Barnes, Margaret Ayer—157
Barnes, Peter—353, 379, 391, 415, 438, 443
Barnes, Theo—365
Barnes, Will R.—10
Barnes, Winifred—75, 84, 126
Barnett, Roy—347
Barnova, Vera—206
Barnum, P.T.—77, 190
Barnum Was Right—117
Barnwall, John—84
Barrasford, Thomas—24
Barratt, Queenie—272
Barrault, Jean-Louis—260, 280, 302, 306, 307, 310, 347, 353, 373, 382, 396
Barrel Organ, The—232
Barren/Yerma—454
Barrett, Edith—164, 170
Barrett, Edward—90
Barrett, Elizabeth—406
Barrett, George—113
Barrett, James Lee—420
Barrett, Joe—420
Barrett, Lawrence—55, 202
Barretts of Wimpole Street, The—172, 175, 176, 179, 180, 237, 259, 418
Barrett, T.R.—64
Barrett, Wilson—23, 295
Barrie, Amanda—340, 344
Barrie, Barbara—316, 360
Barrier, The—67, 369
Barrie, Sir James Matthew—2, 7, 12, 16, 22, 23, 24, 26, 32, 43, 46, 54, 56, 63, 66, 71, 73, 79, 82, 84, 85, 88, 90, 101, 103, 114, 115, 121, 122, 129, 137, 146, 153, 160, 189, 193, 202, 209, 228, 232, 237, 248, 261, 268, 273, 281, 290, 323, 324, 342, 355, 362, 369, 376, 403, 418,

429, 435, 440, 447, 455, 456
Barrington, Michael—379
Barrington, Rutland—13, 23, 32, 102
Barrison, Mabel—42
Barrow, Bernard—393
Barrow, Henry C.—33
Barrow, P. J.—43
Barr, Richard—215, 259, 338, 361, 375, 387, 373
Barry, Christine—201
Barry Jackson's Repertory Company—128, 130, 144
Barry, Joan—121, 177, 187
Barry, John—339
Barry, Julian—393
Barrymore, Diana—244, 248, 324
Barrymore, Georgiana, Drew—318
Barrymore, John—15, 17, 19, 26, 32, 38, 47, 61, 66, 71, 82, 90, 103, 105, 115, 122, 128, 135, 137, 221, 233, 448
Barrymore, Lionel—1, 10, 15, 26, 82, 87, 99, 106, 108, 291
Barrymore, Maurice—28, 318
Barrymore, Mrs. John—146
Barry, Philip—91, 117, 123, 126, 133, 149, 150, 156, 170, 176, 180, 181, 185, 196, 212, 216, 220, 226, 232, 246, 264, 265, 271, 275, 410, 454
Barry, Shiel—57
Barry, Tom—157
Barsacq, Andre—274
Barstow, Richard—283
Bartels, Louis John—124
Bartenieff, George—354
Bartet, Madame—45
Barthelemess, Richard—200
Bartholomae, Philip—74, 105, 117
Bartholomew Fair—269, 361, 382, 445
Bartlett, Basil—223, 225
Bartlett, Michael—206
Bart, Lionel—316, 317, 321, 322, 328, 333, 335, 346, 404, 435, 440
Barton, Dora—7, 94
Barton, James—105, 125, 171, 247, 272, 285, 306, 336
Barton, John—329, 334, 341, 346, 353, 354, 360, 367, 373, 376, 380, 381, 382, 388, 396, 403, 417, 437, 438, 444, 446, 453
Barton, Lionel—154
Barton, Margaret—236, 241
Barton, Mary—107, 217
Barton Mystery, The—79
Bartrop, Roland—217
Bascomb, A.W.—135
Basehart Richard—244
Basement, The—424
Basic Training of Pavlo Hummel, The—395, 438, 441
Baskette, Jimmie—164
Bass, Alfie—252, 284
Bass, Emory—413
Bassey, Shirley—295
Basso Porto—53
Bastian/Merivale—214
Bataille, Henri—16, 53, 112, 113, 115
"Batavia"—119
Bate, Anthony—388
Bateman, Jessie—21, 49, 105
Batemann-Hunter, Leah—50
Bates, Alan—299, 301, 302, 306, 322, 345, 353, 379, 394, 415
Bates, Blanche—1, 6, 11, 26, 42, 52, 131
Bates, Guy—376
Bates, Michael—359
Bates, Thorpe—126
Bathsheba—256
Batie and Foster—201
Batley, Dorothy—127
Bats in the Belfry—206
Batson, George—239
Bat, The—100, 113, 116, 161, 207,

313
Bat Theatre of Moscow—111
Battle Hymn—202
Battle of Angels—417, 419
Battle of a Simple Man—338
Battle of Shrivings, The—386
Battle of the Butterflies, The—44
Battleship Gertie—199
Battles, James—252
Battles, John—241
Battling Butler—114
Batty, Archibald—182
Baty, Gaston—198, 208, 289
Bauer, Wolfgang—428
Baughan, E. A.—98
Baumer, Marie—203
Baum, L. Frank—14
Baum, Vicki—171, 180, 246
Baumol, William—441
Bawtree, Michael—360, 396
Baxendall, Lee—380
Bax, Hammersmith Clifford—63, 113, 115, 127, 182, 196, 199, 241, 336
Baxter, Alan—197
Baxter, Anne—203, 413
Baxter, Beryl—248
Baxter, David—368
Baxter, George—122
Baxter, Godfrey—188
Baxter, Jane—165, 177, 230, 236, 267, 277, 294
Baxter, Keith—330, 386, 439
Baxter, Lynsey—455
Baxter, Stanley—379
Baxter, Trevor—452
Bayadere (Die Bajadere)—112
Bayes, Nora—41, 46, 47, 62, 74, 83
Bay, Howard—248
Bayless, Jean—314
Bayley, Hilda—103, 107, 126
Baylis, Lillian—73, 76, 80, 90, 103, 109, 114, 121, 180, 209
Bayliss, Lilian—428
Bayntun, Amelia—333
Beach, Gary—442
Beach, Lewis—77
Beach, Rex—35, 67
Beale, Jack—299
Beal, John—181, 200, 226, 332
Beane, Hillary Jane—422
Bean, Orson—282, 293, 327, 333
Beanstalk, The—423
Beard, The—375, 407, 410
Bear-Leaders, The—62
Bear, The—260
Beast, The—418
Beatlemania—434, 451
Beatles—414
Beaton, Cecil—250, 276, 290, 298, 378
Beatrice, in March—44
Beatty, Ethel—442
Beatty, Robert—240, 241, 298
Beatty, Warren—315
Beau Brummell—22, 27, 80, 189
Beaucaire—7, 22, 94
Beau Geste—165
Beaumarchais, Pierre Augustin Caron de—90, 196, 340, 373
Beaumont and Fletcher—23, 96, 108, 136, 183, 307, 347
Beaumont, Diana—192, 201, 349
Beaumont, Hugh—411
Béaumont, Muriel—21, 10
Beautiful People, The—226
Beauty and the Barge—21, 29
Beauty and the Beast—160, 208, 265, 269, 280, 296, 318, 355
Beauty of Bath, The—32, 34
Beauty Part, The—333, 418
Beauty Prize, The—120
Beauty Spot, The—47, 84
Beaux' Stratagem, The—152, 174, 249, 264, 316, 355, 367, 388
Beaverbrook, Lord—350
Beaver Coat, The—359
Becey Sharp—8
Becher, John C.—326, 332
Becker, Lee—338

Becket—27, 313, 321, 328, 331
Beckett 3—387
Becket, Thomas A—197
Beckett, Samuel—296, 298, 306, 308, 312, 320, 326, 335, 336, 346, 347, 348, 353, 354, 366, 374, 375, 378, 379, 384, 389, 390, 394, 395, 396, 404, 407, 417, 422, 429, 431, 437, 439, 440, 445, 447, 454, 455
Beckinsale, Richard—427
Beck, Julian—275, 292, 314, 321, 327, 335, 375, 451
Beck, Martin—130, 224
Beckley, Beatrice—83
Beckworth, Reginald—241
Becque, Henri—23, 85, 237, 269, 306
Bed Bug, The—334
Bedford, Brian—302, 311, 327, 332, 333, 334, 341, 371, 375, 381, 383, 395, 401, 439
Bedford, Patrick—357
Bedful of Foreigners, A—427
Bedroom Farce—435, 449
Bedsitting Room, The—339
Beecher, Janet—157
Beech, Martin—368
Been, Grace—82
Beerbohm, Max—3, 12, 303, 305, 396
Beery, Wallace—35
Beet, Alice—32
Beethoven/Karl—451
Before and After—67
Before Breakfast—144, 166, 192, 275
Before Dawn—407
Before the Deluge—283
Beggar on Horseback—124, 130, 134, 387
Beggar's Bowl, The—187
Beggar's Holiday—247
Beggar's Opera, The—103, 115, 135, 137, 138, 188, 223, 232, 247, 260, 269, 291, 306, 312, 341, 343, 361, 375, 402, 411, 422
"Begin the Beguine"—196
Begley, Ed—252, 287, 293, 321, 382, 391
Begley, Edward—66
Behan, Brendan—301, 312, 316, 317, 319, 320, 330, 331, 341, 349, 385, 389, 401, 402
Behind Red Lights—205
Behind the Fridge—401, 406
Behman Show—447
Behold the Bridegroom—150
Behold, We Live!—183
Behrman, Samuel Nathaniel—148, 163, 168, 177, 182, 194, 200, 204, 208, 214, 215, 216, 253, 265, 270, 280, 288, 310, 319, 332, 344, 411
Beissel, Henry—409
Belafonte, Harry—282, 293
Belasco, David—1, 2, 6, 7, 11, 13, 15, 19, 25, 26, 29, 31, 34, 36, 37, 40, 42, 47, 51, 52, 55, 56, 57, 61, 66, 67, 69, 74, 75, 77, 78, 80, 82, 85, 87, 88, 93, 98, 106, 107, 108, 110, 115, 119, 121, 126, 132, 137, 140, 141, 154, 158, 164, 171, 179, 264, 275
Belasco Trophy—138, 144, 152
Belcher, Ernest—138
Belcher, Marjorie Celeste (Marge Champion)—137
Belcher's Luck—361
Belcourt, Emile—391
Belden, Eileen—159, 223
Bel Geddes, Barbara—282, 293, 315, 326, 365, 406
Bel Geddes, Norman—124, 199, 313
Belgian National Theatre—397
Belgrade Theatre—396
Belgrate Theater of Coventry—323
Belgrave, Cynthia—365, 379
Believe It Or Not—278
Believe Me, Zantipee—66
Belinda—91
Belknap, Allen—450
Bella Donna—58
Bellam, George—151

Bellamy, Franklyn—107, 126
Bellamy, Ralph—234, 244, 262, 309
Bellamy the Magnificent—43
Bell, Book and Candle—267, 275, 289, 308
Bell, C. W.—83
Bell, Digby Valentine—25, 85
Bell, Enid—41
Belle of Amherst, The—426, 439
Belle of Bohemia, The—9
Belle of Brittany, The—43
Belle of Mayfair, The—32
Belle of New York, The—4, 96, 178, 193, 232
Belle of the Barbers' Ball, The—45
Belle's Strategem, The—49
Belle Starr—379
Bellew, Kyrle—7, 27, 35, 60, 89, 102, 107
Bell for Adano, A—240, 245, 246
Bell, Galt—188
Bell, Gorden—248
Bellini, Vincenzo—307
Bell, James—170, 190
Bell, Marie—334
Bell, Marion—252
Bell, Mary Hale—231, 245, 249, 282
Bellow, Saul—344, 360
Bells are Ringing, The—298, 305
Bells of Hell, The—435
Bell, Stanley—206, 1232
Bells, The—17, 50, 84, 188, 268, 296, 428
Bell, Tom—414
Belmont, Mrs. August—119, 155
Belmont Theatre—91, 166
Belmore, Bertha—206
Bel, Norman—116
Belot, A.—8
Belushi, John—406, 420
Belville, Lance—417
Ben-Ami, Jacob—104, 124, 144, 149, 167, 174
Benavente, Jacinto—96, 99, 144, 145, 146, 285
Ben Bagley's Shoestring Revue—293, 390
Benchley, Robert—118, 146, 150, 177, 202, 223, 246, 313
Bendall, Ernest—60, 73
Bending of the Bough of Edward Martyn, The—3
Bendix, Doreen—172
Bendix, Max—71
Bendix, William—343
Benedetti, Robert—403
Benedictus, David—373
Benelli, Sem—54, 104, 154
Benet, Stephen Vincent—219, 284
Benett, Colin—417
Ben Franklin in Paris—344
Ben Greet Repertory, The—53, 456
Ben-Hur—4, 9, 12, 80
Benito Cereno—349, 366
Benjamin, Joe—414
Benjamin, Richard—341, 358, 414
Bennet, Richard—30, 43, 66, 70, 94, 99, 106, 111, 119, 243
Bennett, Allan—323, 328, 372, 389, 394, 406, 435
Bennett, Arnold—49, 58, 62, 67, 89, 90, 99, 154, 246, 274
Bennett, Barbara—243
Bennett, Billy—222
Bennett, Constance—90, 243, 355
Bennett, Dave—150
Bennett, Dorothy—362
Bennett, Hywel—451
Bennett, Jill—253, 274, 294, 302, 305, 361, 374, 387, 394, 427, 436, 453
Bennett, Joan—243, 288
Bennett, Michael—327, 378, 385, 393, 394, 406, 414, 420, 443
Bennett, Peter—434, 341, 368
Bennett, T. P. & Sons—180
Bennett, Vivienne—198, 213, 223, 232, 242, 248, 274
Bennett, Wilda—93, 113
Bennie, G.—64

Benny, Jack—140, 170
Benrimo, J. Harry—25, 31, 62, 82
Benson Company—33
Benson, Constance (Mrs. Frank)—8, 44, 80
Benson, Frank—3, 4, 8, 12, 16, 22, 27, 33, 37, 44, 49, 54, 58, 59, 63, 68, 69, 72, 73, 76, 77, 80, 97, 103, 159, 220
Bensonians—73, 308
Benson Ltd.—60
Benson, Sally—227, 271
Benson Shakespeare Company—411
Bent—450
Benthall, Michael—241, 254, 259, 260, 263, 264, 265, 268, 274, 279, 284, 285, 289, 290, 295, 296, 302, 307, 311, 312, 316, 317, 334, 419
Bentham, Josephine—230
Bentine, Michael—263
Bentley, Dick—268
Bentley, Eric—81, 302, 335, 353, 360, 410, 439, 443, 447
Bently, Irene—10, 32
Benton, Robert—357
Beowulf—453
Beowulf, a Pageant—451
Bequest to the Nation, A—387
Berenice—139, 342
Beresford, Harry—112
Berg, Alban—361
Bergen, Henning—197
Bergen, Polly—282, 314
Bergere, Folies—294
Bergere, Valerie—166
Berger, John—431
Berg, Gertrude—257, 261, 314, 363
Berghof, Herbert—223, 228, 233, 235, 254, 269, 298, 315, 427
Bergman, Hjalmar—89
Bergman, Ingmar—258, 316, 389, 396, 406
Bergman, Ingrid—223, 247, 291, 354, 365, 395, 396, 410, 422, 438, 444
Bergner, Elizabeth—188, 202, 209, 235, 250, 273
Beringer, Esme—12, 21, 41, 72, 159, 215
Berke, Barnes—450
Berke, Joseph—450
Berkeley, Busby—149, 156, 163, 164, 194, 395
Berkeley, Edward—417, 422, 440
Berkeley, Martin—203
Berkeley, Reginald—102, 165
Berkeley Square—141, 143, 173, 183, 202, 213, 223, 224, 228, 237
Berkey, Ralph—298
Berkshire Festival—393
Berle, Milton—45, 181, 216, 234
Berlin, Alexandra—333, 339
Berlin Deutsches Theater—59
Berliner Ensemble—301, 303, 354, 401
Berlinger, Warren—287, 326, 327
Berlin, Irving—55, 71, 74, 78, 83, 87, 92, 99, 106, 110, 118, 112, 126, 133, 142, 148, 181, 186, 247, 256, 262, 266, 311, 332, 455
Berlin Schaubuhne am Halleschen Ufer—437
Berlin to Broadway with Kurt Weill—400
Berlyn, Ivan—107
Berman, Ed—377, 379, 388, 394, 427, 444
Bermange, Barry—368
Bermel, Albert—311, 322, 347, 386, 445
Bernard, Barney—66, 74, 93, 111
Bernard, Dick—36
Bernardi, Herschel—371
Bernardine—276, 286
Bernard, Jean-Jacques—90, 160, 241, 264
Bernard, K.C.—45
Bernard, Ken—438
Bernard, Sam—25, 31, 41, 99, 106
Bernard Shaw in Heaven—279, 348
Bernard, Thomas—431

Bernard, Tristan—32, 45, 66, 75
Bernau, Christopher—434
Bernauer—67
Bernauer and Jacobson—48
Bernays, Edward L.—70
Berney, William—244
Bernhardt, Maurice—80
Bernhardt, Melvin—374, 385, 393, 415, 445
Bernhardt, Sarah—4, 8, 13, 16, 23, 28, 34, 38, 54, 80, 84, 86, 90, 108, 122, 130
Bernice—137, 323, 380
Bernier, Raymond—138
Bernstein, Aline—148, 190, 243
Bernstein, Elmer—365
Bernstein, Henri—35, 42, 50, 67, 68, 90, 102, 106, 201
Bernstein, Leonard—240, 281, 293, 298, 304, 339, 349, 374, 410, 418, 426, 446
Berr, Georges—62, 95, 183
Berrigan Brothers, The—393
Berrigan, Daniel—393
Berry, Charles—366
Berry, David—436
Berry, Eric—206, 208, 217, 269, 310
Berry, John—329, 344, 385, 398
Berry, W. H.—79, 95, 108, 120, 126, 143, 159, 165
Berte, Heinrich—59, 106
Bertha, the Beautiful Sewing Machine Girl—185
Besant, Reginald—67
Besier, Rudolf—49, 62, 102, 114, 172, 179, 180, 237, 259
Besoyan, Rick—315, 319
Bespoke Overcoat, The—284, 289
Bessborough, Governor General Lord—189
Bessie, Alvah—131
Best, Alan—417
Best Bib and Tucker—231
Best, Edna—82, 102, 119, 120, 132, 134, 143, 150, 164, 172, 176, 181, 189, 201, 212, 217, 253, 258, 269, 273, 281, 362, 419
Best Foot Forward—226, 341
Best House in Naples, The—298
Best Is Yet To Be, The—403
Best Little Whorehouse in Texas, The—130, 442, 457
Best Man, The—75, 320, 325
Best of Friends, The—15
Best of Luck, The—79
Best People, The—143
Best Plays—51, 60, 65, 70, 77, 81, 73, 86, 91, 98, 104, 141, 142, 185, 189, 199, 217, 220, 225, 232, 233, 238, 246, 251, 257, 261, 286, 350, 363, 399, 419
Beswick, Harry—62
Bethlehem—13, 318
Betrayal—444
Betrothal, The—88, 107
Betsy Baker—81
Bette Midler's Clams on the Half Shell Revue—420
Better Days—134
Better Half, The—115
Better Late—248
Better 'Ole, The—83, 87
Better Times—112
Better Understanding, The—251
Bettger, Lyle—230
Bettis, Valerie—257
Betti, Ugo—293, 294, 295, 296, 338, 340
Bett, John—444
Betty—75, 93, 107
Betty in Mayfair—135
Between the Devil—206
Between the Wars—438
Between Two Women—76, 191
Bet Your Life—276
Bevan, Donald—271
Beverley, S.—154
Bewitched—415
"Bewitched Bothered and Bewildered"—222

Bewitching Witch, The—280
Beyond—131
Beyond Compre—222
Beyond Human Power—12
Beyond the Fringe—323, 328, 331, 332, 401, 403
Beyond the Horizon—99, 104, 144, 145, 214, 260
Beyond the Rainbow—444
Beyond the Sundown—423
Be Yourself—125
Biberman, Herbert J.—167, 171
Bible One—403
Bible One: Joseph and the Amazing Technicolor Dreamcoat—404
Bible, The—382
Bicat, Nick—443
Bicat, Tony—390, 437
Bickel, Fred—424
Bickerdale, Allen, Rich & Partners—384
Bickford, Charles—157, 214
Biddle, Cordelia Drexel—298
Biddle, Esme—129
Biff, Bing, Bang—86
Big and Little—451
Big, Bad Mouse—359
Big Ben—248
Big Blow, The—214
Big Boy—131, 245
Big Broadcast on East 53rd Street, The—416
Big Business—206
Big Drum, The—75
Bigelow, Charles—30
Bigelow, Dennis—454
Big Fish, Little Fish—326, 331
Bigger, Earl Derr—66, 83
Biggest Thief in Town, The—272
Big House, The—145, 341
Big Knife, The—262, 285, 288
Bigley, Isabel—267, 281
Big Mother—416
Big Rock Candy Mountain, The—296, 404
Big Scene, The—90
Big Sea, The—369
Big Time Buck White—372
Big Top—231
Big Treatise in Store, A—451
Big White Fog—224
Big Wolf—401
Bikel, Theodore—264, 272, 297, 304, 314
Biko Inquest, The—442
Biko, Stephen—451
Billeray, Ferdinand—39
Billetdoux, Francoise—322, 373, 415
Billeted—83
Billington, Kevin—422, 446
Billion Dollar Baby—244
Bill of Divorcement, A—106, 107, 116
Bill, The—69
Billy—414
Billy Bishop Goes to War—443
.Billy Budd—271, 285
Billy Bunter Flies East—318
Billy Bunter Meets Magic—342
Billy Bunter's Christmas Circus—336
Billy Bunter Shipwrecked—330
Billy Bunter's Mystery Christmas—313
Billy Bunter's Swiss Roll—324
Billy Irish—431
Billy Liar—322, 414
Billy's Last Stand—389
Billy's Little Love Affair—16
Billy the Kid—219
Bing Boys Are Here, The—79, 193
Bing Boys on Broadway, The—88
Bingham, Amelia—6, 14, 136
Bingham, Madeleine—248
Bingham, Susan—388
Bingo—417, 429, 431, 439
Bingo: Scene of Death and Money—428
Bing, Rudolph—256
Binney, Constance—124

Binyon, Lawrence—97, 121
Biography—182, 189, 192, 411, 453
Birch, Frank—214
Birch, Patricia—436, 449
Birdbath—360, 382, 410
Bird Child—415
Bird, David—274
Bird in Hand—152, 158, 214, 241, 242
Bird, John—318
Bird of Dawning Singeth All Night Long, The—375
Bird of Paradise, The—61, 70, 380
Bird of Time, The—328
Bird, Richard—126, 227, 235, 244, 248, 258, 259, 263, 276, 278, 283
Birds in a Wilderness—347
Birds, Marriages, and Deaths—347
Birds of a Feather—392
Birds, The—353, 360, 361, 367
Birdwatcher, The—359
Birkett, Viva—85
Birk, Raye—396
Birmingham, George A.—67
Birmingham Repertory Theatre Company—39, 68, 69, 73, 76, 80, 84, 86, 90, 96, 97, 103, 115, 122, 130, 136, 137, 144, 158, 159, 165, 185, 214, 259, 285, 301, 317, 372, 438, 450, 456
Birney, David—367, 371
Birthday Honours—283
Birthday Party, The—310, 348, 364, 395, 422
Birthright—58, 59, 160, 187
Bishop, Alfred—3
Bishop, Brenda—348
Bishop, Harry W.—18
Bishop, John—452
Bishop, Kate—13, 75
Bishop Misbehaves, The—195
Bishop of Broadminster—195
Bishop's Bonfire, The—329
Bishop, Washington Irving—36
Bispham, David—32
Bissell, Richard—287, 309
Bisson, Alexandre—48, 54, 63, 75
Bithell, Jethro—67
Bit of A Test, A—187
Bit of Love, A—131
Bits and Pieces—152, 344
Bitter Oleander—198
Bitter Stream—202
Bitter Sweet—165
Bitter Tears of Petra Von Kant, The—430
Bizet, Alexandre—137
Bizet, George—235
Bjornson, Bjornstjerne—12, 68, 166
Bjornsson, Oddur—323, 444
Blackall, Clarence—73, 147
Black and Hispanic Acting Ensemble—452, 454
Black and White Minstrel Show, The—334
Blackbird Beauty Chorus—192
Blackbirds of (1926)—143, 154 (1928)—156, 418 (1933)—187 (1934)—192 (1936)—201
Black Body Blues—440
Black Boy—141
Blackburn, A. E.—116
Blackburn, Bryan—359, 424
Blackburn, R.—116
Black Chiffon—263, 266
Black, Cilla—359
Black Comedy—348, 354, 359, 364
Black, Dorothy—144
Black-Eyed Susan—268
Blackfriar's Guild—237, 297
Black, George—218, 227, 231, 241
Black Girl—393
Black Hills Passion Play, The—219
Black, Karen—342, 354
Black, Kitty—260, 268, 285, 320, 361, 390
Black Limelight—206
Blackman, Fred J.—114, 121, 134
Blackman, Honor—253, 357
Black Man's Country—416

Black Mask, The—69
Black Mass—394
Blackmer, Sidney—107, 108, 113, 118, 121, 158, 177, 266, 314, 412
Black Mikado, The—422
Black Nativity—327
Black New World—366
Black Oliver—152
Blackouts—231
Black, Pauline—241
Black, Peter—361
Black Picture Show—421
Black Pit—197
Black Quartet, A—378
Black Sheep, A—153
Blacks, The—326, 329, 387
Blackstone Boulevard—232
Black Stuffer, The—451
Black Sunlight—415
Black Swan—441
Black Theatre Alliance, The—399
Black Theatre of Prague—348, 362
Blackton, Jay—257
Black Velvet—218
Blaine, Vivian—309
Blair, Betsy—226
Blair, Janet—298
Blair, John—47
Blair, Jon—442
Blair, Mary—101, 111, 166
Blake, Eubie—105, 120, 125, 143, 171, 182, 442
Blake, Hal—56
Blake, Katharine—388
Blakelock, Denys—151, 207
Blakely, Colin—318, 322, 339, 346, 348, 353, 359, 373, 394, 408, 409, 435
Blakemore, Michael—335, 375, 381, 382, 395, 410, 414, 417, 428, 435, 436, 439
Blake, William—396
Blanche, Ada—15
Blanche, Marie—134
Blanchette—84, 90
Blanco and Pozo—285
Bland, Frederick—318, 322
Blandick, Clara—124
Blanding's Castle—372
Bland, Joyce—183
Blane, Ralph—226
Blaney, Norah—119
Blankfort, Michael—202
Blatchley, John—335, 341, 348
Blatt, Edgar—206
Blau, Eric—371
Blau, Herbert—280, 355, 356, 357, 456
Bleak House—279, 445
Bleak Moments—388
Bleckler, Robert—141
Bledsoe, Jules—142, 150, 201
Bless the Bride—253
Blick, Newton—335
Blight—84
Blim at School—379
Blind, Eric—72
Blind Goddess, The—253
Blind Heart, The—152
Blinn, Holbrook—16, 30, 35, 38, 56, 61, 68, 69, 73, 92, 99, 142, 180
Blin, Roger—306, 353, 379
Bliss and Favel—55, 130
Blisters—436
Blithe Spirit—226, 223, 227, 232, 233, 245, 363, 389, 430, 453
Blitz—227, 333
Blitz and Pickwick—411
Blitzstein, Marc—170, 206, 213, 229, 262, 290, 349, 455
Bloch, Scotty—453
Block, Bertaum—191, 226
Block, Richard—350
Block, Sheridan—47
Blomfield, Derek—273, 283, 304
Blondell, Joan—456
Blonde Sinner, The—140
Blood—395
Blood and Sand—188
Bloodgood, Clara—11, 35

Blood Knot, The—340, 344, 360, 424
Blood of the Bambergs, The—334
Blood Sports—430
Blood Stream, The—401
Blood Wedding—219, 290, 403
Bloom, Claire—230, 279, 283, 285, 289, 296, 301, 302, 310, 314, 315, 329, 387, 395, 408, 416, 420, 440
Bloomer Girl—240
Bloomers—410
Bloomfield et Cie.—75
Bloomgarden, Kermit—280
Bloom, Harry—327
Bloom, Leopold—317, 441
Bloom, Rube—201
Bloomsbury—414
Blore, Eric—102, 114, 163
Blossom, Henry, Jr.—19, 26, 30, 43, 71, 74
Blossom Time—106, 231, 264
Blosson, Roberts—332, 420
Blow, Detmar—39
"Blow, Gabriel, Blow"—191
Blow, Sydney—67, 89, 95
Blow Your Own Trumpet—237
Blue Beard—8
Bluebeard—418, 446
Bluebeard's Eighth Wife—106, 114
Blue Bell—29
Bluebell in Fairyland—8, 28, 97, 122, 137, 153, 198, 203, 209
Blue, Ben—216
Blue Bird, The—53, 126, 137, 336
Bluebird, The—107, 115, 122, 296
Blue Denium—309, 362
Blue Eyes—158, 162
Blue Kitten, The—137
Blue Lagoon, The—101
Blue Mazurka, The—150
"Blue Monday Blues"—112
Blue Moon, The—27
Blue Mouse, The—42
Blue Paradise, The—74
"Blue Room, The"—140
Blue, Samuel Jr.—380
Blues for Mister Charlie—344, 353, 416
"Blue Skies"—142, 151
Blue Train, The—151
Blumenthal and Kadelberg—47
Blunt, Wilfred Scawen—37
Blvd. de Paris (I've Got the Shakes)—441
Blyden, Larry—282, 291, 309, 332, 358, 424
Blythe, Bobby—114
Blythe, Peter—421
Blythe, Violet—95
Blyton, Enid—296
Boal, Agusto—382
Bob and Ray the Two and Only—386
Bobrick, Sam—385
Bob's Your Uncle—258
Boccaccio, Giovanni—113
Bochner, Lloyd—295
Bock, Jerry—98, 298, 321, 338, 343, 344, 358, 386
Bocksgesang—246
Boddington, E. F.—6, 11
Bodies—445, 450
Bodley, Donald—423
Body Beautiful, The—398
Body Builders, The—381
Boeing-Boeing—333
Boesman and Lena—385, 396, 431
Bogarde, Dirk—224, 268, 278, 295
Bogart, Humphrey—17, 132, 181, 195, 378
Bogdanov, Michael—439, 445, 446, 452
Boggie, De Dio—23
Boggis, P. H.—85
Bohemian Girl—418
Bohemos—16
Bohen, Roman—216
Bolam, Elsa—348
Bolam, James—443
Boland, Bridget—283
Boland, Mary—57, 69, 72, 93, 112, 132, 171, 196, 355

Bolden, Harry—186
Boleslavsky, Richard—142, 159
Bolger, Ray—164, 176, 190, 200, 230, 247, 257
Bolitho, William—171, 180
Bolman, James—379
Bolshevik Empress, The—274
Bolshevik Peril, The—96
Bolton, Betty—159
Bolton, Guy—74, 78, 82, 87, 88, 93, 94, 104, 105, 117, 126, 127, 130, 133, 141, 142, 144, 148, 149, 156, 158, 164, 170, 177, 197, 201, 207, 212, 213, 227, 231, 239, 258, 267, 273, 283, 293, 298, 424, 431, 453, 456
Bolton, Reg—407, 435, 451
Bolton, Wodehouse, Lindsay, and Crouse—191
Bolt, Robert—305, 322, 337, 347, 355, 376, 387, 388, 403, 430, 435
Bombo—106
Bonaventure—263
Bond, Christopher G.—408, 449
Bond, Edward—322, 356, 359, 363, 373, 379, 394, 395, 397, 401, 407, 415, 417, 421, 428, 429, 430, 431, 439, 443, 446, 454, 455
Bond, Elizabeth—451
Bond, Gary—333, 358, 389
Bond Honoured, A—359
Bondi, Beulah—138, 148, 156, 181
Bondman, The—32
Bond, Norman Acton—22
Bond, Ridge—285
Bonds of Interest, The—96, 233
Bond, Sudie—326
Bonefire, The—312
"Bongo Bongo Bongo, I don't want to leave the Congo"—253
Bonnell, John S.—246
Bonne Soupe—320, 328
Bonnet Over the Windmill—207
Bonstelle, Jessie—52, 185
Bontemps, Arna—247
Bonynge, Richard—348
Boo Hoo—429, 447
Booker, Margaret—405
Booke, Sorrell—326, 372
Book of Etiquette, The—445
Book of Job, The—95, 290, 310
Book of Tobit—182
Boomerang, The—74, 116
Boone, Daniel—279
Boor, The—318
Booth, Agnes—55
Boothe, Clare—17, 201, 210, 211, 217, 220, 225
Booth, Edwin—55, 85, 104, 137, 179
Booth, Janice B.—7
Booth, John H.—82
Booth, John Wilkes—77
Booth, Junius Brutus Jr.—55
Booth, Roger—341
Booth, Shirley—133, 188, 195, 216, 222, 234, 252, 257, 266, 271, 276, 287, 293, 411
Boots—394
Borde, Andre—83
Borden, Essie—400
Bordoni, Irene—82, 84, 87, 99, 118, 221, 133, 145, 157, 286
Boretz, Allen—205, 402
Borget, Arnold—417
Borge, Victor—281
Borgnine, Ernest—276
Boris, Ruthanna—217
Borned in Texas—269
Born Yesterday—247, 251, 253, 408, 410, 447, 454
Borodin, Alexander—282
Borstal Boy—385
Bosco, Philip—376, 383
Bosler, Virginia—248
Bosley, Tom—310, 315
Bosoms and Neglect—449
Boss, The—56, 448
Bostock, Patricia—68
Boston Herald—179
Boston Museum Stock Company—

116
Boston Opera Company—104
Boston Story, A—372
Boston Times—179
Bost, Pierre—310
Bostwick, Barry—375, 400, 431
Boswell, James—389
Both Ends Meet—289
Both Your Houses—186, 189
Bottoms, John—381
Boubouroche—90, 109
Boucicault, Aubrey—11, 30, 69, 232
Boucicault, Dion—16, 21, 27, 32, 35, 44, 49, 53, 57, 62, 83, 91, 101, 108, 114, 254, 268, 328, 342, 373, 389, 418, 428
Boucicault, Nina—15, 16, 22, 63, 151
Bouedet, Edouard—111, 141, 194
Bought and Paid For—56
Boult, Adrian—130
Bound East for Cardiff—128, 208, 452
Bound Feet/Nijinsky—451
Bound for Kentucky—329
Bourbonnais, M.A.—343
Bourchier, Arthur—12, 15, 21, 34, 49, 54, 58, 63, 67, 83, 102, 103, 107, 127
Bourdelle, Joan—141
Bourget, Paul—50
Bourke, P. J.—76
Bourne, Adeline—58
Bourton, Raynor—443
Bousille et les Justes—259, 261
Boutal, Arthur—138
Boutall, Kathleen—213
Boutal, Pauline—138
Boutet, Frederic—76
Bouyant Billions—263
Bova, Joseph—360, 367
Bovasso, Julie—388, 422
Bovill, C. H.—37, 57, 75, 79, 80
Bow Bells—182
Bowden, Charles—300
Bowen, John—361, 372, 388, 436
Bowen, Philip—445
Bower, Marion—89
Bowers, Alice—102
Bowers, Lally—241, 278, 285
Bowers, Robert Hood—30
Bowes, Major—194
Bowles, Jane—282, 292, 431
Bowles, Paul—221, 226, 247
Bowman, Nellie—12
Bowmeester, Louis—109
Bowmer, Angus—198, 202, 208, 225, 255, 256, 260, 274, 279, 290, 307, 317, 335, 381, 388, 392
Bowyer, Fred—59
Box—375
Boxill, Patrick—381, 396
Box, Muriel—272
Box Office—237
Box o' Tricks—88
Boychick, The—289
Boyd, Julianne—442
Boyd, William—78, 92, 125
Boyer, Charles—275, 282, 309, 332, 340, 447
Boy Friend, The—284, 285, 287, 288, 297, 355, 368, 388, 418, 446
Boy Grows Up, A—307
Boylan, Mary—365
Boyle, William—28, 54, 59, 62, 64, 78
Boy Meets Girl—196, 201, 204, 412, 420, 428
Boyne, Clifton—102
Boyne, Leonard—12, 20
Boy O'Carroll—34
Boy on the Straight-Back Chair—380
Boys and Girls Together—221
Boys From Syracuse, The—212, 341, 342, 431
Boys in Company "B", The—38
Boys in the Band, The—371, 379, 384
Boys of the Bull Dog Breed—75
Boy, The—84, 407

"Boy Wanted"—127
Boy Who Lost His Temper, The—203, 209, 211
Boy With a Cart, The—268, 279
Braatz, A.—9
Bracco, Roberto—35
Bracken, Eddie—211, 217, 304, 455
Bradbury, Lane—314
Braddell, Maurice—187
Braden, Bernard—288
Bradford, Alex—427
Bradford, Billy—143
Bradley, Alice—61
Bradley, June—118
Bradshaw, Fanny—411
Bradwell, Mike—430
Brady, Alice—66, 76, 87, 123, 167, 176, 199
Brady, William A. (Jr.)—275
Brady, William A.—8, 19, 30, 47, 52, 56, 57, 60, 63, 66, 68, 74, 76, 87, 98, 112, 199
Brady, W. J.—71
Bragdon, Claude—98
Braham, Horace—157
Braham, Lionel—82
Braham, Philip—83, 89, 114, 102, 120, 134
Braham, Ronald Jeans-Phillip—119
Brahams, Caryl Braham—336, 388, 432
Brahms, Johannes—112
Brains—144
Braithwaite, Lillian—21, 32, 35, 53, 59, 78, 107, 127, 144, 151, 177, 182, 187, 192, 197, 212, 217, 226, 308
Bramball, Charles—13
Brammer and Gruenwald—134
Bramson, Karen—238, 174
Branbury, Frith—340
Branch, Leslie—374
Brand—64, 147, 202, 316, 445
Brandel, Marc—347
Brand, Max—314
Brand, Millen—217
Brando, Marlon—240, 247, 249, 252
Brandon, Dorothy—124
Brandon, John—151
Brandon, Johnny—344
Brandon, Richard—303
Brandon-Thomas, Amy—159
Brandon-Thomas, Jevan—248
Brandram, Rosina—12, 15, 21, 58
Brandt Corporation—456
Brand, Tita—48
Brandt, Ivan—165
Brangwyn, Frank—185
Bran Pie—95
Brass Ankle, The—182, 224
Brass Bottle, The—49
Brass Butterfly, The—310, 409
Braswell, John—401
Bratny, Roman—360
Brattle Shakespeare Players—296
Brave Women Who Wait—75
Brawner, Hilda—346
Brayton, Lily—8, 23, 45, 57, 58, 159
Brazil, Leonard—421
Bread—430
Bread and Butter Trade, The—430
Bread and Puppet Theatre—381, 403
Breadwinner, The—172, 242
Breadwinners, The—283
Break a Leg—449
Breaking Into the Movies—302
Breaking Point, The—39, 313
Breakspear in Gascony—317
Breath of Spring—310
Brebner, Ann—331
Brebner, John—331
Brecher, Egon—160
Brecht, Bertolt—166, 188, 198, 245, 255, 290, 300, 301, 302, 303, 316, 321, 323, 329, 334, 335, 339, 341, 342, 343, 347, 353, 354, 361, 362, 366, 367, 368, 375, 376, 381, 387, 388, 389, 391, 395, 401, 402, 403, 409, 422, 423, 424, 428, 429, 430, 435, 436, 437, 438, 439, 441, 446,

447, 452, 453, 455, 456
Brecht on Brecht—332, 335
Brecht/Weill—436, 439
Brecht/Weill Happy End—347
Bredschneider, Willy—67
Breen, Robert—212, 279, 284
Breese, Edward—26
Breezeblock Park—437
Breffort, Alexandre—310
Breit, Harvey—309, 319
Brel, Jacques—371
Bremen Coffee—415
Bremen Theatre Company, The—367
Brennan, Eileen—315, 319
Brennan, Frederick—226
Brennan, M. M.—114
Brentano, Lowell—148
Brenton, Howard—361, 379, 387, 388, 390, 397, 401, 409, 430, 439, 453, 455
Brent, Romney—13, 14, 131, 142, 137, 163, 178, 183, 188, 219, 248, 249, 433
Breon, Edmond—68, 141, 142
Br'er Fox and Br'er Rabbit—17
Brer Rabbit and Mr. Fox—72
Breslein, Louise—360
Bresslaw, Bernard—374, 381, 396, 407
Breton, Howard—444
Brett, Jeremy—310, 367, 375, 389
Brett, Michael—294
Breuer, Bessie—260
Breuer, Clover—440
Breuer, Lee—440
Brewer, George—191
Brewster, Jonathan—303
Brewster's Millions—31, 273
Brian, Donald—30, 37, 47, 56, 78, 113, 117
Brian Rix Theatre of Laughter, The—394
Brian, Wayne—438
Brice, Elizabeth—41
Brice, Fanny—126, 141, 171, 190, 200, 275
Brice, Lew—141
Brickert, Carlton—142
Bricusse, Leslie—328, 340, 343, 351, 401, 443, 444, 446
Bride and the Bachelor, The—300
Bride Comes Back, The—328
Bride for the Unicorn, A—188, 197
Bride of Denmark Hill, The—277, 280
Bride of Lammermoor, The—43, 45
Bride, The—69, 178
Bride the Sun Shines On, The—179
Bridges—108
Bridges, Alan—367
Bridges, Ann Preston—150
Bridget's House—430
Bridgewater, Dee Dee—450
Bridie, James—178, 182, 188, 193, 208, 213, 214, 219, 220, 237, 238, 239, 241, 253, 254, 256, 260, 263, 267, 269, 284, 301, 302, 317, 323, 348, 436
Brief Chronicle—256
Brief Lives—365, 366
Brief Moment—177, 185
Brierley, Joan—187
Briers, Richard—334, 365, 380, 406, 421
Brigadier Gerard—32
Brigadoon—252, 256, 263, 268, 306, 335, 340, 349, 368, 446
Brige, Peter—354
Briggs, Hedley—187, 218
Brighouse, Harold—46, 69, 74, 79, 90, 279, 346, 408
Brighter London—119
Bright Honor—203
Brightman, Stanley—114, 171
"Brighton"—97
Brighton Combination—390
Brighton, Pam—391, 415, 454
Brighton Rock—235
Bright Star—196
Brig, The—338, 348

Brill, Marty—393
Brimstone and Treacle—452
Brinckerhoff, Burt—309
Brink, Frank—368
Brinkley, Grace—177
Briquet, Jean—52, 66
Brisson, Carl—121, 134, 150
Brisson, Frederick—174
Brisson, Tilly—134
Bristol Old Vic—251, 259, 264, 269, 279, 285, 296, 300, 301, 329, 335, 348, 379, 403, 455
Britannicus—284, 323
British Actors Equity Association—169, 174, 199, 233
British-American Repertory Theatre—451
British Broadcasting Corp. (BBC)—162
British National Theatre—411
British Poster and Advertising Association—60
British Puppet and Model Theatre Guild (BPMTG)—138
British Theatre Association—98, 102
British Theatre Museum Association—308
Brittan, Robert—406
Britten, Benjamin—217, 246, 250, 269, 291, 301, 306, 367
Britt, Jacqueline—393
Britton, Hutin—103
Britton, Pamela—252
Britton, Tony—394, 427, 435, 455
Broadhurst, George—14, 31, 35, 42, 56, 98
Broad, Jay—363, 378, 410, 415
Broadway—90, 141, 144, 155, 410
Broadway Jones—61
Broadway Theatre, The—175
Broche—379
Brockbank, Harrison—66
Broderick, Helen—181, 186
Broderick, James—364, 383
Brod, Max—376
Brodszky, Nikolaus—206
Brody, Hal—67, 158, 165
Brogden, Gwendoline—101
Broken Dishes—164
Broken Faith—68
Broken Heart, The—23, 335
Broken Jug, The—306, 311
Broken Wing, The—100
Bromberg, J. Edward—160, 181, 186, 272
Bromley, Sidney—222
Bron, Eleanor—360, 406
Bronhill, June—346
Bronson, Percy—36
Bronte, Charlotte—202, 223, 241, 242, 250, 309
Bronte, Emily—207
Brontes, The—259
Bronx Express, The—111
Brook, Clive—97, 244, 254, 271, 284, 301, 307
Brooke, Clifford—82
Brooke, Eleanor—287
Brooke, Emily—94, 102, 107
Brooke, Faith—260, 294
Brooke, G. V.—85
Brooke, Harold—289, 315, 365
Brooke, Sarah—47
Brookes, Jacqueline—306, 340
Brookfield, Charles H. E.—32, 58, 60, 265
Brook, Lesley—244
Brooklyn Academy of Music Theatre Company (BAM)—104, 433, 445, 448
"Brooklyn Cantata"—230
Brook, Neville—135
Brook, Peter—137, 249, 255, 268, 272, 273, 274, 284, 288, 289, 294, 295, 296, 301, 302, 306, 307, 309, 310, 315, 339, 341, 342, 345, 346, 347, 353, 359, 373, 388, 395, 428, 446, 453
Brooks Atkinson Theater, The—325, 354

Brooks, David—252
Brooks, Harry—164
Brooks, Jan—309
Brooks, Jeff—437
Brooks, Joseph—7
Brooks, Lawrence—239
Brooks, Lorimer—292
Brooks, Marjorie—151, 120
Brooks, Mel—304
Brooks, Peter—254
Brooks, Ray—397
Brooks, Shelton—112
Broones, Martin—197
"Brother, Can You Spare a Dime?"—181
Brotherhood—388
Brother Jonathan (Ringkamp)—397
Brother Rat—200
Brothers—158
Brothers Karamazoff, The—122, 152, 249
Brough, Fanny—7, 43
Brough, Lionel—8, 32
Brough, Mary—113, 143, 151, 159, 165, 172
Brough, Sydney—2, 33
Broughton, Rutland—115, 144
Brouhaha—311, 325
Broun, Heywood Campbell—203, 220
Broun, Heywood Hale—364
Brown, Alan—410
Brown, Anne Wiggens—96, 196
Brown, Arthur Jr.—185
Brown, Arvin—382, 395, 396, 397, 418, 428
Brown, Beth—205
Brownbill, Bert—206
Brown, Bubbles—165
Brown Buddies—170
Browne, Coral—208, 217, 222, 250, 264, 266, 274, 302, 309, 320, 328, 379, 391, 415, 423
Browne, E. Martin—208, 214, 217, 246, 249, 259, 264, 285, 311
Browne, Graham—21
Browne, Irene—114, 206
Browne, K. R. G.—192, 206
Browne, Lewis—92
Browne, Louise—207, 213
Browne, Maurice—103, 160, 297
Browne, Pamela—208
Browne, Robert Gore—283
Browne, W. Graham—110, 112, 134, 159, 171
Browne, Wynyard—267, 283, 315
Brown, Felicity—427
Brown, Forman—303
Brown, George—336
Brown, Georgia—395
Brown, George Anderson—104
Brown, George Carlton—239
Brown, Gilmore—86, 129, 138, 324
Brown, Harry J.—256
Brown, Helen—148
Brown, Ian—410, 428, 435
Browning, Elizabeth Barrett—259, 406
Browning, Robert—33, 142, 179, 406
Browning, Susan—332
Browning Version/Harlequinade, The—262
Browning Version, The—258
Brown, Irene—134
Brown, Ivor—418
Brown, Joe E.—106, 132, 329, 411
Brown, John—359
Brown, John Mason—147, 383
Brown, Kenneth H.—338, 348, 410
Brown, Kitty—424
Brown, Larson—248
Brown, Lennox—402
Brown, Lew—131, 140, 149, 157, 163, 170, 176, 181, 194, 216
Brown, Louise—151
Brown, L. P.—103
Brown, Martin—113
Brown, Nacio Herb—182
Brown of Harvard—30
Brown, Pamela—218, 226, 249, 254,

263, 278, 279, 283, 284, 307, 318, 424
Brown, Phil—244
Brown, Polly—368
Brown, Porter Emerson—47, 99
Brown, Ralph—216
Brown, R. Gore—172
Brown, Roscoe Lee—349
Brown, Steve—415
Brown Sugar—102
Brownsville Raid, The—432
Brown, Teddy—218, 227
Brown, Tina—436
Brown, Tom—312, 317
Brown, Vanessa—276
Brown, Velvet—248
Brown, William—420
Brox Sisters—148
Brubaker, Edward—381
Bruce, Brenda—236, 264, 274, 280, 289, 306, 310, 335, 348, 364, 366, 373, 396, 417
Bruce, Carol—249
Bruce, Edgar K.—219
Bruce Lacey and the Alberts—390
Bruce, Lenny—393, 413
Bruce, Nigel—83, 127, 128, 134, 142, 150, 158, 177
Bruce-Potter, Hilda—120, 236
Bruckner, Ferdinand—178, 228
Brule, Andre—108
Brune, Gabrielle—231, 236
Bruning, Albert—30, 50, 93, 111, 115, 145
Bruning, Francesca—186
Bruno, Albert—102
Bruno, Christopher—2
Brunton, Anna—202
Brustein, Robert—413
Bryan, Dora—274, 277, 286, 294, 305, 310, 334, 340, 354, 356
Bryan, Herbert—127
Bryant, Arthur—207
Bryant, Charles—42
Bryant, J. V.—79
Bryant, Michael—302
Bryant, Michael—352, 435, 439, 452
Bryant, Nana—149
Bryan, Wayne—429
Bryce, Alan—422
Bryceland, Yvonne—396, 414, 443, 452
Bryden, Bill—368, 373, 374, 395, 407, 409, 415, 417, 431, 432, 436, 437, 452, 453
Bryer, Vera—172
Brynner, Yul—247, 271, 438, 454
Bryon-The Naked Peacock—394
Bubbles, John R.—196, 235
Bubbling Brown Sugar—426, 435
Bubbly—83
Bucaneer, The—285, 299
Buchanan, Jack—101, 108, 109, 114, 124, 133, 159, 165, 177, 191, 201, 206, 231, 236, 263
Buchan, Tom—401
Buchman, Harold—240
Bucholz, Horst—314, 338
Buck, David—367
Buck, Gene—78, 82, 93, 99, 106, 235
Buckie's Bears—179, 184, 189, 193, 198, 203
"Buckle Down Winsocki"—226
Buckle, Richard—284
Bucknell, Peter—301
Buck, Pearl S.—184
Bucks County Playhouse (New Hope)—319
Bucksey, Colin—440
Buckton, Florence—121
Buechner, Georg—153, 213, 215, 306, 355, 360, 381, 396, 408, 410, 417
Buenaventura, Enrique—396, 399
Buffalo Bill—161
Buggy, Niall—409
Building Fund, The—28, 54, 59, 90
Bulandra Theatre—397
Bulgakov, Leo—173, 197, 214
Bulgakov, Mikhail—442, 445, 453

Bulger, Harry—25
Bull, Diane—450
Bullins, Ed—194, 378, 388, 401, 422, 424
Bull, Peter—328, 364
Buloff, Joseph—234, 281, 453
Bulwer-Lytton, Edward—13, 23, 33, 68, 76, 84, 90, 97
Bunce, Alan—157
Bundle, The—439
Bunk of 1926—140, 147, 308
Bunnage, Avis—279, 289, 295, 368, 404, 408, 435
Bunny Bunting—95
Bunraku Puppets—430
Bunraku Puppet Theatre—360
Bunty Pulls the Strings—57
Bunyan, John—36
Buono, Victor—335
Burbank Theater—28
Burdett, Madge—84
Burdies, The—361
Bureau de Change, The—218
Burger Schippel—421
Burge, Stuart—310, 336, 348, 357, 379, 388, 391, 430, 437, 438, 447
Burgomaster of Stilemonde, The—122
Burgess, Christopher—317
Burgess, Grover—157, 207
Burgess, Maynard—335
Burgess, Neilson—28
Burgtheater—373, 408
Buried Child—443
Burke, Billie—27, 35, 36, 52, 67, 125, 150, 178, 185, 239, 391
Burke, Brian—318
Burke, Marie—150, 177, 248
Burke, Patricia—222, 236, 255, 289
Burke, Tom—117, 136
Burkhardt, Addision—14
Burlesque—148, 161, 250
Burnaby, Davy—89, 159, 167
Burne, Dolly—99
Burnege, Mabel—61
Burnet, Dana—149
Burnett, Carol—316, 344
Burnett, Frances Hodson—15, 69
Burnett, Harry—303
Burnett, Ivy Compton—352
Burnham, Barbara—183, 213
Burnham, D. H.—24, 331
Burnham, Edward—328
Burning Bright—266
Burning Glass, The—288
Burn, Michael—294
Burns, David—206, 398, 424, 450
Burns, Helen—295
Burnside, John R.—23, 30, 35, 36, 42, 52, 82, 99, 100, 106, 112, 123
Burns Mantle Best Play Series—270, 331, 333, 343, 356
Burns, Robert—54
Burnt Flower Bed, The—296
Burr, Aaron—177
Burr, Anne—226, 418
Burr, Courtney—199
Burrell, John—242, 243, 246, 254, 255, 259, 260, 264
Burrell, Michael—445, 451
Burrell, Pamela—368
Burridge, Walter—10, 11, 19, 30
Burroughs, Marie—137
Burrows, Abe—267, 271, 275, 281, 287, 293, 309, 314, 327, 352, 372
Burrows, W. and R. L.—185
Burr, Robert—454
Burstyn, Ellen—420, 437
Burt, Laura—66
Burton, Irving—369
Burton, Langhorne—36
Burton, Miriam—366
Burton, Richard—138, 241, 262, 268, 272, 274, 285, 296, 300, 321, 325, 347, 407
Bury, John—311, 348, 380, 451
Bury, Rosamund—32
Bury the Dead—200, 202
Burzo, Alexander—408
Bushell, Ellen—81

Bush, Josef—381
Bushman, Frank X. (later Francis)—43
Bush Theatre—405, 409
Business Before Pleasure—82
Buskers, The—316
Busley, Jessie—142
Busoni, Ferruccio—67
Buss, Gerry—345
Bus Stop—293, 297, 411, 416, 418, 429
Buster—438, 439
Buster Brown—25
Busy Dyin'—417
Buteaux, L.—75
But for the Grace of God—248
But for Whom Charlie—344
Butler, Etta—6, 104
Butler, Frank—247
Butler, Lawrence—453
Butler, Mike—397
Butler, Shirley—353
Butlery, Herbert—188
Butley—394, 400, 412
Butlin, Billy—365
Butlin, Jan—407, 414
Butt, Alfred—60, 72, 130
Butter and Egg Man, The—132, 147, 153
Butterflies—43
Butterflies are Free—378, 392
Butterfly Dream, The—360
Butterfly on the Wheel, A—57
Butterworth, Charles—141, 157
Button, Guy—193
Button, Jeanne—454
Buttons, Red—252, 255, 313
Button Your Lip—235
Buxom Muse, The—342
Buxton Festival—457
Buxton Opera House, The—18
Buzz-Buzz—89
Buzzell, Eddie—157
Buzz Goobody—422
Byam, John—125
Byatt, George—435
By Candle Light—159
By Common Consent—417
Bye Bye, Birdie—320, 328
Bye Bye Bonnie—303
Byford, Roy—208
Bygraves, Max—278, 291, 295, 305, 315, 321, 345
Byington, Spring—124, 170
By Jupiter—230, 366, 398
Byng, Douglas—134, 143, 151, 165, 182, 231
By Pigeon Post—88
Byren, Patsy—348
Byrne, Cicely—242
Byrne, George—55
Byrne, John—444, 445, 451
Byrne, M. St. Clare—110, 202
Byrnes, James—83
Byron—11, 104, 129
Byron, Arthur—11, 119, 238
Byron, Henry—268
Byron, Kate—238
Byron, Lord George Gordon—135, 401
Byron, Oliver Doud—104, 238
By Strouse—442
By the Beautiful Sea—287
By the Way—133

Cabal of Hypocrites, A—442
Cabaret—272, 358, 372
Cabaret Girl, The—114
Cabell, James Branch—144
Cabin in the Sky—222, 441
Cable, Christopher—388
Cabot, Elliot—140
Cacoyannis, Michael—342, 351, 368
Cactus Flower—352, 363, 365
Cadell, Jean—71, 127, 182, 370
Cadus, Romain—75
Caesar and Cleopatra—31, 37, 67, 69, 136, 138, 184, 197, 220, 228,

265, 274, 301, 341, 371, 396, 423, 437
Caesar, Irving—87, 112, 127, 134, 149, 177, 202
Caesar's Wife—94
Caesar, Sid—257, 332
Cafe La Mama Company—389, 408
Caffe Cino—443
Cage Me a Peacock—258
Cages—338
Cage, The—385, 415
Cagney, James—132, 157, 161, 164, 282
Cahcaster, Osbert—306
Cahill, Hope—171
Cahill, Lily—176
Cahill, Marie—10, 14, 20, 26, 74, 148
Cahn, Sammy—252, 276, 413
Cain—135
Caine, Georgia—16, 66
Caine, Hall—12, 27, 32, 88
Caine, Henry—108
Caine, Michael—322, 339
Caine Mutiny Court-Martial, The—287, 292, 299
Cain, Henri—80
Cain, James M.—200
Caird, John—444, 446, 453
Caird, Laurence—120
Cairdmont, John—444
Cairncross, James—352
Cairo—108
Calculated Risk—332
Caldara, Orme—35, 94
Calderisi, David—372
Calderon de La Barca, Pedro—68, 116, 382
Calderon, George—64
Caldicott, Margery—212
Caldwell, Anne—36, 62, 82, 99, 100, 106, 123
Caldwell, Ben—378
Caldwell, Erskine—187
Caldwell, John—285
Caldwell, Zoe—311, 313, 316, 329, 337, 358, 385, 387, 400, 428, 454
Caleb West—1
Calendar, The—165
Calhern, Louis—133, 163, 247, 239, 269, 303
Calhoun, Eleanor—3, 8
Caliban of the Yellow Sands—78, 81, 245, 307
California Bush Theater (San Francisco)—34
California-Nevada—87
California Suite—426, 441
Caligula—264, 320, 325, 438
Callahan, Carrie McCobb—145
Callas, Maria—307
Called Back—194
Call, Edward Payson—376, 428, 429
Calleia, Joseph—252
Calling All Stars—194
Callister, Christian—89
Call It a Day—197, 200, 204
Call Me Madam—266, 276, 410
Call Me Mister—247
Call of Life, The—132
Callow, Simon—421, 430, 437, 439, 450, 451, 452
Call, The—76
Callum, Diane—381
Calthrop, Donald—84, 94, 101, 122, 127
Calthrop, Dion C.—101, 107
Calthrop, Gladys—216
Calvert, Charles, Mrs.—20, 21
Calvert, Louis—15, 22, 27, 28, 49, 50, 53, 54, 72, 80, 82, 84, 88, 103, 112
Calvert, Phyllis—231, 282, 289, 315, 328, 353, 389, 427
Calvert, William—97
Calvi, Gerard—295
Camain, C. H. A.—209
Cambridge Revue, The—455
Cambridge Drama Festival—317, 368
Cambridge, Edmund—373, 380
Cambridge, Godfrey—326
Cambridge Theatre, The—175, 403,

439, 440, 443
Camelot—321, 325, 345
Camel's Back, The—123
Camel Through the Needle's Eye—163
Camera Obscura—374
Cameri Theatre—367
Cameron, Audrey—101
Cameron, Ine—44
Cameron, Kenneth—380
Cameron, Lord—256
Cameron, Madeline—163
Cameron, Violet—16
Camille—4, 8, 13, 22, 24, 44, 105, 178, 185, 224, 318, 411, 415, 446
Camino Real—281, 305, 377, 387, 415
Camoletti, Mark—333, 450
Campbell, Alan Patrick—45
Campbell, Alexander—196
Campbell, Charles—248
Campbell, Craig—62
Campbell, Donald—428, 451
Campbell, Douglas—274, 285, 306, 312, 317, 329, 333, 374, 376, 429, 453
Campbell, Herbert—4, 17
Campbell, Hilda—340
Campbell, Joseph—63
Campbell, Judy—273, 368
Campbell, Ken—379, 380, 417, 432, 436, 437
Campbell, Marjorie—82
Campbell, Norman—352
Campbell, Paddy—45
Campbell, Patrick—57, 58
Campbell, Patrick (Mrs.)—2, 3, 8, 9, 12, 13, 20, 32, 43, 44, 45, 48, 50, 58, 68, 72, 84, 103, 108, 144, 165, 182, 303, 320, 437
Campbell, Stella Mervyn—96
Campbell, William—310
Campden Wonder, The—37
Camp, Hamilton—390
Campion, Cyril—143
Camp Upton—87
Camus, Albert—264, 303, 320, 325, 342, 401, 438, 444
Canada Council—308, 350, 392, 437
Canadian Broadcasting Company—337
Canadian Gothic/American Modern—403, 431
Canadian Mime Theatre—396
Canadian Theatre Centre/Centre du Theatre Canadien—261, 319, 325
Canary Cottage—85
Canary, The—87
Canby, Vincent—442
Can-Can—281, 289, 335, 447
Cancer—390
Candida—17, 22, 23, 27, 28, 38, 76, 96, 123, 129, 197, 219, 232, 242, 249, 273, 278, 317, 323, 335, 340, 389, 411, 439
Candidate—308
Candide—210, 298, 315, 410, 414, 446
Candlefors—453
Candle in the Wind—226, 233
Caney, R.—5
Canfield, William—131
Canker and the Rose, The—347
Cannan, Dennis—268, 310, 359, 395, 427
Cannan, Gilbert—63
Cannery Row—294
Cannibals—375
Cannon, J. D.—301, 344
Canolle, Jean—359
Canon, Hugh—319
Canova, Judy—200
Cansinos—118
Canterbury Tales—372, 445, 447, 453, 455
Canterbury Pilgrims, The—104, 303
Can the Leopard?—178
Cantilena—423
Cantor, Eddie—84, 87, 119, 130, 148, 157, 227, 350, 452

Canvas Barricade—329
Can You Hear Their Voices—445
Capalbo, Carmen—304, 388
Capek, Josef—112, 116, 237, 260
Capek, Karel—112, 116, 123, 140, 166, 179, 237, 260, 289, 307, 360
Cape Playhouse, The—155
Capon, Eric—245
Caponsacchi—142, 229
Capotaire, Jane—388
Capote, Truman—129, 276, 288
Capp, Al—298
Cappy Ricks—92
Cappy, Ted—271
Capra, Jean—207
Caprice—160, 168, 429
Captain Brassbound's Conversion—32, 37, 65, 77, 167, 237, 260, 269, 273, 395, 396, 405, 453
Captain Drew on Leave—27
Captain from Koepenick, The—395
Captain Jack's Revenge—395
Captain Jinks of the Horse Marines—6, 50, 132, 213, 318
Captain Kettle—12
Captain Kidd, Jr.—78
Captain Oates' Left Sock—379
Captain Swing—455
Captive, The—141, 147
Captive Audience—455
Capuana, Luigi—44
Capus, Albert—27, 63, 95
Caragiale, Ion L.—397, 451
Caravaggio Buddy—401
Caravan Theatre—210
Carb, David—119
Carcass Chrome—425
Cardinal, The—16
Cardinal Hayes—175
Cardin, Pierre—415
Cards of Identity—299
Card, The—406
Careless Rapture—201
Carel, Josef—360
Caretaker, The—322, 326, 337, 347, 401, 436
Carew, James—89
Carey, Denis—235, 255, 278, 279, 285, 289, 290, 295, 296, 322
Carey, Eileen—152
Carey, Joyce—97, 101, 103, 108, 120, 189, 192, 218, 235, 254, 273, 299, 316, 365, 383, 453
Carey, Macdonald—287
Carfax, Bruce—181, 201, 235
Cargill, Patrick—299, 333, 353, 372, 389, 407
Caribbean Rhapsody, A—258
Carillo, Jose—381
Carillo, Leo—78, 82, 330
Cariou, Len—376, 381, 382, 400, 406, 434, 436, 449
Carisma—258
Carle, Richard—1, 27, 74, 171
Carlino, Lewis John—338
Carlisle, Alexandra—27, 43, 44, 47, 52
Carlisle, Bill—443
Carlisle, Elsie—101
Carlisle, Kitty—202, 206, 287, 301
Carlisle, Margaret—178
Carlisle, Peggy—236
Carlisle, Sybil—3, 121
Carlisle, Una—201
Carl Murray Singers—400
Carlos and Inez—107
Carlson, Richard—216
Carlyle, Richard—293
Carmen—28, 44, 235
Carmencita and the Soldier—137
Carmen Jones—235, 245, 246, 301
Carmichael, Hoagey—201
Carmichael, Ian—220, 274, 277, 286, 304, 321, 322, 333, 353, 358, 427
Carmichael, Jason—450
Carmilla—183, 188, 401, 424
Carmines, Rev. Al—330, 365, 378, 379, 400, 406, 418
Carminetta—83
Carnegie, Andrew—34

Carnegie, Hattie—226
Carnegie Institute of Technology—139
Carne, Judy—388
Carney, Art—304, 308, 327, 351, 375
Carney, Frank—232
Carnival—103, 326, 339, 440
Carnival Scenes—397
Carnival War a Go Hot—455
Carnovsky, Morris—113, 116, 145, 152, 170, 186, 196, 221, 306, 322, 341, 367
Carol Channing With Her Ten Stout-Hearted Men—386
Carole, Joseph—221
Carolina Playmakers, The—91, 97, 139
Caroline—60, 79, 91, 117, 144, 264
Caron, Leslie—272, 287
Carousel—154, 244, 264, 267, 290, 307, 354, 410, 446
Caro William—279
Carpenter, C. A.—83
Carpenter, Carleton—282
Carpenter, Constance—33, 149, 182, 212
Carpenter, Edward Childs—78, 166, 181
Carpenter, Freddie—244, 411
Carpenter, Larry—439
Carpenters, The—390
Carpenter, Thelma—257
Carpet Slippers—174
Carradine, David—346
Carradine, John—259
Carr, Alexander—66, 111
Carr, Andrew—430, 451
Carre, Michel—135
Carrere and Hastings—51
Carr, Hugh—447
Carrick, Hartley—72, 74
Carrier, Roch—403
Carrington, V. C.—283
Carrington, Reginald—10, 47
Carr, J. Comyns—27, 45, 46, 53, 61
Carr, Jean—227
Carr, Kenneth—378
Carr, Mimi—454
Carroll, Albert—128, 131, 148, 157, 164
Carroll, Diahann—288, 332
Carroll, Earl—78, 116, 118, 123, 141, 146, 176, 179, 186, 195, 225, 261
Carroll, Joan—222
Carroll, Leo G.—170, 183, 186, 188, 195, 217, 240, 252, 259, 284, 404
Carroll, Lewis—184, 243, 390, 445
Carroll, Madeleine—159, 165, 168, 177, 182, 257
Carroll, Marie—111
Carroll, Nancy—343
Carroll, Paul Vincent—184, 188, 211, 215, 216, 220, 235, 249, 254, 283, 293, 301
Carroll, Sydney W.—189
Carroll, Vinnette—327, 332, 400, 427
Carroll, Walter—259
Carrots—10, 45
Carr, Phillip—17
Carry On London!—407
Carson, Barbara—400
Carson, Charles—145
Carson, Frances—126, 144, 179
Carson, Jack—279
Carson, Jean—277
Carson, Murray—4, 12, 21
Carte Blanche—427
Carten, Audrey—201
Carten, Waveney—201
Carter, Desmond—127, 131, 144, 151, 158, 159, 171, 172, 177, 178, 182, 183, 192, 201, 206
Carter, Hubert—95
Carter, Jack—176, 190, 207, 370
Carter, Jessie—61
Carter, J. L.—81
Carter, Lee—206
Carter, Margaret—120
Carter, Mrs. Leslie—2, 7, 25, 89, 107, 154, 161, 180

Carter, Nell—52, 400
Carter, Ralph—400, 406
Carter, Randolph—304
Carter, Steve—415, 428, 447
Carte, Rupert D'Oyly—97
Cartier, Jacques—350
Cartney and Kevney—152
Carton, R. C.—15, 26, 48, 53, 62, 89
Cartoon Archetypal Slogan Theatre—390
Cartwright, Peggy—178
Carty, Todd—435
Carving A Statue—346
Cary, Falkland—294, 322, 359
Cary, Joyce—298
Caryll and Monckton—8
Caryll, Ivan—2, 6, 10, 16, 26, 31, 36, 37, 48, 56, 61, 66, 82, 87, 94, 95, 100
Casadhan Sugain—3
Casanova—123, 182
Casartelli, Gabrielle—207
Casavant, Louis—82
Cascando—387, 431
Case in Question, The—421
Casella, Alberto—183, 188, 207, 218, 283
Case of Lady Camber, The—75
Case of Libel, A—338
Case of Philip Lawrence, The—208
Case of the Oily Levantine, The—451
Casey at the Bat—199
Casey Jones—214, 249
Casey, Rosemary—263
Casey, Warren—400
Casey, W. F.—68, 85
Cash, Rosalind—383
Casino Girl, The—1
Caspary, Vera—288
Cass, Henry—193, 198, 219, 231, 241
Cassidy, Jack—257, 276, 291, 306, 338
Cassilis Engagement, The—36
Casson, Ann—206
Casson, Christopher—428
Casson, John—264, 269
Casson, Lewis—23, 28, 46, 95, 108, 114, 122, 137, 143, 145, 152, 166, 178, 186, 188, 190, 192, 207, 208, 214, 223, 228, 230, 249, 253, 263, 283, 383, 433
Casson, Mary—183
Cass, Peggy—320
Cass, Ronald—328
Caste—16, 166, 254, 403
Casting-Out of Martin Whelan, The—54, 58
Castle, Irene—71, 82, 383
Castles, Dolly—54
Castles in the Air—60, 141, 263
Castle Spectre, The—278
Castle, The—376
Castle, Vernon—47, 48, 52, 71, 90, 383
Cat Among the Pigeons—380
Cat and the Canary, The—111, 114, 209
Cat and the Fiddle, The—176, 182
Cat and the Moon, The—445
Catch of the Season, The—21, 34
Cathcart, Countess of—143
Cathcart, Thom—440
Catheleen Ni Houlihan—23, 38, 59, 185
Catherine—120
Catherine of Braganza—223
Catherine Was Great—239
Cathleen Listens—121
Catlett, Mary Jo—415
Catlett, Walter—324
Cato, Minto—171
Cat on a Hot Tin Roof—293, 297, 310, 417
Cato Street—298
Catsplay—410, 444
Catto, Max—264
Caubet, Suzanne—142
Caucasian Chalk Circle, The—302, 334, 360, 366, 381, 430, 455
Caught in the Rain—31, 161

Caulfield, Joan—234
Cause Celebre—435
Cause of It All, The—63
Cavalcade—178
Cavalleria Rusticana—44
Cavallini, Mme Margherita—75
Cavanagh, Lilian—177
Cavanagh, Paul—158
Cave Dwellers, The—304
Cavender, Kenneth—347, 353
Cavendish, Fanny—424
Cavern, The—353, 455
Cawthorne, Joseph—15, 42, 78, 87
Cazale, John—371, 430
Cazeneau, Marie—113
Cazenove, Christopher—450
CCC Murder Mystery—204
Ceballos, Larry—135
Cecil, Henry—322, 366
Cecil, John—382
Cecil, Sylvia—159
Celebration—378
Celebration for Due Process, A—390
Celestina—273, 311
Celia—394
Cellier, Antoinette—191
Cellier, Frank—108, 134, 143, 151, 158, 165, 167, 177, 197, 213, 248
Celli, Faith—101, 108, 119, 127, 134
Cenci, The—115, 116, 316
Censored Scenes from King Kong—440
Censorship Committee of the British Poster and Advertising Association—13, 60
Center Opera Company—243
Center Stage—342, 356, 419
Cent Lignes Emues—76
Central Theater (San Francisco)—34
Century Girl, The—78, 82
Century Lighting, Inc.—168, 209, 319, 337
Century Opera Company—51
Century Players, The—22
Century Theater—9, 34
Ceremonies in Dark Old Men—379, 424
Ceremony of Innocence—372
Certainly Not (A Tortuous Train of Thought)—441
Cervantes, Miguel—439
Cervi, Gino—136
Cesaire, Amy—435
Chacun Sa Vie—38
Chadwick, Jonathan—409
Chagrin, Claude—380
Chaikin, Joseph—389, 436, 455
Chaikin, Shami—358
Chains—54
Chairman, The—427
Chairs, The—306, 312
Chakiris, George—304, 434
Chalk Garden, The—293, 299
Challee, William—208
Challenge, The—92
Chalmers Award—397, 412
Chalmers, Thomas—176
Chamberlain, Lord—60, 83, 363, 377
Chamberlain, Richard—431
Chambers, C. Haddon—7, 35, 57, 84
Chambers, David—440
Chameleon, The—116
Champagne on Ice—283
Champion, Gower—216, 257, 258, 271, 293, 320, 326, 344, 358, 371, 381, 382, 400, 413, 455
Champion, Marge—137, 293
Chancellor, F. G. M.—180
Chances, The—335
Chandler, Colin—253
Chandler, Helen—135, 137, 160, 177, 196
Chanel, Coco—378
Chaney, Sheldon—350
Changeling, The—329, 349, 389, 428, 444, 447
Changelings, The—118, 130, 146
Changing Room, The—394, 406, 412
Changing Guard—114
Chanin brothers—130, 139

Channel Island of Sark—414
Channing, Carol—229, 258, 262, 294, 344, 386, 413, 445, 455
Chanticleer—56, 60
Chaperone, The—10, 46
Chapin, Harold—68, 115, 136
Chapin, Katherine Garrison—259
Chaplin, Charles—46, 441
Chaplin, Sidney—298, 315, 327
Chapman, Edyth—179
Chapman, George—285
Chapman, Gerald—430, 435
Chapman, Graham—414
Chapman, Henry—307, 330
Chapman, John—252, 261, 262, 265, 266, 270, 275, 280, 289, 310, 372, 394, 404, 414, 435, 456
Chapman, Robert—271
Chapman, Topsy—450
Chappelle, Frederick—83, 88, 94, 95, 101, 107, 126, 134
Chappell, Eric—408
Chappell, Janet—361
Chappell, William—274, 277, 289, 299, 300, 310, 315, 340, 347, 367, 407
Chapter Two—434, 448
Charell, Erik—202, 217
Charig, Philip—158, 159, 177, 239
Chariot's Revue of 1926—133
Charisse, Zan—393
Charity That Begins at Home, The—33
Charlap, Mark—288
Charlemagne—400
Charles Aznavour—392
Charles B, Cochran's 1930 Revue—172
Charles Frohman Empire Theatre Company—98, 224
Charles I—33, 49
Charles Ludlam's Ridiculous Theatrical Company—455
Charles, Moie—264, 423
Charleston Chronicle, The—179
"Charleston, The"—118, 446
Charlesworth, Marigold—381, 439
Charley's Aunt—33, 69, 90, 97, 109, 115, 122, 128, 145, 160, 167, 174, 189, 193, 214, 224, 255, 257, 261, 265, 269, 286, 289, 296, 389, 398, 416, 419, 423, 424, 431, 432, 438, 454
Charlie—350, 353, 432
Charlie Girl—353
Charlot—159
Charlot, Andre—83, 95, 127, 196, 206, 224
Charlot's Char-A-Bang—196
Charlot's Masquerade—172
Charlot's Revue—127, 135
Charlotte—106
Charm School, The—102
Charnin, Martin—386, 420, 434, 442
Charnley, Michael—299, 310
Charon, Jacques—316, 359, 380
Charpentier, Gabriel—403
Charto, S. M.—280
Chase, Chevy—406
Chase, Francis—447
Chase, Ilka—191, 201, 447
Chase, James Hadley—227, 231
Chase, Mary—38, 65, 240, 246, 276, 280, 286, 326, 422
"Chase Me. Charlie"—268
Chase me Comrade—345
Chase, Pauline—22, 33, 59
Chaste Maid in Cheapside, A—65, 359
Chastening, The—121, 129
Chater, Gordon—443
Chatham, Pitt—115
Chatrian—95
Chatterton—95
Chatterton, Ruth—71, 78, 101, 112, 118, 330
Chatwin, Margaret—111, 115
Chaucer, Geoffrey—372, 453, 447
Chauve-Souris—109, 111, 135, 178, 223

Chayefsky, Paddy—122, 298, 314, 325, 327, 337, 344, 350, 368, 372
Cheap Bunch of Flowers, A—336
Cheatle, Syd—387
Cheats of Scapin, The—316, 388, 390, 392
Cheek—390
Cheek, Leslie—297
Cheep!—83
Cheer Up—82
Chekhov, Anton—58, 63, 72, 76, 77, 103, 121, 122, 136, 137, 144, 145, 160, 167, 173, 184, 188, 202, 213, 220, 232, 237, 241, 245, 259, 260, 264, 268, 273, 274, 278, 284, 290, 301, 311, 318, 319, 323, 325, 330, 335, 336, 341, 342, 347, 348, 353, 354, 355, 360, 361, 366, 367, 368, 373, 374, 380, 382, 387, 388, 392, 402, 403, 406, 407, 408, 409, 410, 411, 415, 416, 421, 424, 429, 430, 436, 437, 444, 445, 446, 447, 448, 453
Chekhov, Michael—228
Chelsea Follies, The—173
Chelsea Theatre Center—377, 378, 383, 395, 396, 398, 410, 415, 418, 420, 422, 428, 431, 436, 440, 448, 453, 456
Chelton, Nick—453
Chemin de Fer—410
Chemist, The—108
Chemmy Circle, The—375
Cheney, Peter—277
Cheney, Steward—384
Chereau, Patrice—432
Cheri—314
Cherokee Indians—269
Cherokee National History Society—381
Cherry, Charles—89, 107, 123, 127
Cherry Girl, The—16
Cherry, Helen—296, 454
Cherry, James—6
Cherry Lane Theatre—353
Cherry, Malcolm—48, 57
Cherry Orchard, The—58, 121, 136, 160, 167, 184, 188, 241, 245, 259, 260, 290, 311, 330, 336, 353, 354, 360, 368, 373, 388, 403, 408, 436, 445, 448
Cherry Sister, The—455
Chesney, Arthur—126
Chester, Betty—101, 126, 144, 167
Chester, George Randolph—52
Chester Mystery Cycle—49, 58, 197
Chesterton, G. K.—136, 197, 389
Chetwood, William Rufus—390
Chetwynd, Sylvia—75
Chetwyn, Robert—366, 372, 373, 381, 391, 407, 414, 435, 437, 450, 452
Chevalier, Albert—102
Chevalier, Maurice—404
Chez Nous—414, 440
Chiarelli, Luigi—127, 188
Chicago—142, 155, 360, 420, 424, 450
Chicago Civic Shakespeare Society—173, 179
Chicago's Civic Theatre—169
Chicago's Civic Opera House—169
Chichester Festival Theatre—319, 335, 337, 341, 346, 348, 350, 355, 362, 367, 374, 376, 381, 382, 387, 388, 396, 398, 402, 409, 410, 416, 423, 429, 432, 438, 440, 444, 446, 453
Chickencoop Chinaman, The—402
Chicken Every Sunday—239
Chicken Feed—130
Chicken Soup With Barley—312, 323
Chilcott, Barbara—292, 304, 307
Childe Byron—437
Childhood—332
Child of Nature, A—44
Child of Fortune—298
Children, The—403, 415, 431
Children's Crusade, The—417
Children in Uniform—183, 192

Children of the Moon—118
Children of the Shadows—347
Children of the Sun, The—44, 453
Children's Hour, The—161, 191, 199, 280, 302
Children's Day—382
Children Take Over, The—348, 374
Children's Theatre—180
Childress, Alice—380, 403
Childs, Lucinda—438
Child's Christmas in Wales, A—347
Child's Play—385, 392
Chiltern Hundreds, The—253, 256, 264
Chimes at Midnight—323
Chimes, The—291
Chinchilla—436, 451, 455
Chinese Honeymoon, A—8, 24, 97
Chinese Love—108
Chinese Nightingale, The—193
Chinese Prime Minister, The—344, 352
Chinese Puzzle, The—89
Chin, Frank—402
Chink in the Armour, The—94
Chinn, Graham—447
Chin, Tsai—309
Chips With Everything—333, 338, 350
Chip Woman's Fortune, The—121
Chisholm, George—334
Chisholm, Robert—150, 188
Chitty, Eric—206, 222, 269
Chloridia—198
Chlumverg, Hans—178
Chocolate Dandies, The—124
Chocolate Soldier, The—47, 53, 58, 154, 167, 183, 224, 254
Chodorov, Edward—195, 234, 239, 243, 282
Chodorov, Jerome—222, 227, 233, 286, 287, 298, 309
Chodosh, Richard—342
Choice, The—95
Choir Rehearsal, The—108
Chong, Ping—445
Chopin, Fredrick—231
Chorus—264
Chorus Line, A—420, 422, 427, 433, 448, 457
Chosen People, The—27
Chris and the Wonderful Lamp—1
Chris, Marilyn—327
Christian, The—128, 261
Christian Pilgrim, The—36
Christian, Robert—364
Christiansen, Lew—219, 226
Christians, Mady—240
Christie, Agatha—201, 236, 244, 248, 264, 272, 278, 283, 289, 297, 299, 311, 334, 337, 372, 405, 419, 423, 430, 432, 435, 441, 453, 457
Christie, Audrey—168, 186, 227, 235, 257
Christie, Campbell—248, 267, 278, 283
Christie, Dorothy—248, 267, 278, 283
Christine, Countess of Longford—183, 188, 192
Christmas Pie—174
Christmas Present, A—57
Christmas Party, The—115, 265
Christmas Carol, A—174, 312, 313, 455, 457
Christmas, David—372
Christmas, Eric—438
Christophe—377
Christopher Sly—322
Christophe Colomb—302, 306
Christopher Blake—256
Christopher, Kevin—393
Christ's Emperor—278
Christ Was a Peace Freak—387
Christy, Eileen—248
Chubb, Kenneth—440
Chu-Chin-Chow—79, 91, 108, 223
Church, Esme—160, 182, 213, 219
Churchill Play, The—453
Churchill, Berton—78, 120, 133

Churchill, Caryl—421, 428, 431, 435, 450, 451
Churchill, Diana—207, 217, 263, 268, 274, 276, 293, 328, 368
Churchill, Lady Randolph—69
Churchill, Randolph—65
Churchill, Winston—11, 65, 69, 371
Church, Sandra—314, 321
Church Street—193
Church, Tony—417, 418
Chushingura—382
Chutes Theater (San Francisco)—13, 264
Ciannelli, Eduardo—157
Ciceri, Leo—391
Cid, The—447
Cieslak, Riszard—382
Cieulei, Liviu—446
Cigarette-Maker's Romance, A—7
Cilento, Diane—316, 318, 340, 353, 431, 452
Cimarosa, Domenico—307
Cimino, Leonardo—310
Cinderella—4, 9, 34, 38, 45, 50, 59, 64, 90, 97, 109, 115, 137, 153, 174, 179, 193, 203, 208, 220, 229, 232, 237, 243, 246, 250, 255, 261, 265, 275, 280, 286, 296, 301, 307, 313, 324, 330, 336, 355, 362, 374, 376, 398, 418, 428, 432
Cinderella Comes of Age—265
Cinderella Man, The—78
Cindy—344
Cindy-Ella or I Gotta Shoe—336, 342
Cinema Star, The—72
Cingalee, The—21
Cinoherni Klub of Prague—388
Cinque—389
Cioffi, Charles—382
Cioquemin, Paul—76
Circle Awards—297, 313, 319
Circle-in-the-Square—297, 308, 319, 325, 340, 404, 405, 407, 410, 422, 428, 431, 437
Circle of Chalk, The—166, 224
Circle Repertory Theatre Company—402, 406, 410, 413, 417, 419, 422, 426, 428, 431, 436, 445, 452
Circle, The—106, 107, 116, 178, 242, 354, 367, 429, 431, 452
Circus Adventure, The—330, 362
Circus Princess, The—148
Cires from Casement—410
Citadel Theatre Company (Alberta, Canada)—356
Cith Theatre—422
Cities in Bezique—379
City Center (New York)—349, 350
City Center Acting Company—404, 405, 411
City of Light—403
City of Perth Theater and Opera House—5
City Sugar—421, 422, 428, 444
City, The—50, 51, 52, 417
City Theatre Company—254, 260, 265
Civic Light Opera—116, 117
Civic Repertory Theatre—145, 146, 147, 152, 159, 160, 166, 167, 173, 174, 178, 180, 184, 189, 191, 198
Civilian Clothes—93
Civil War—87, 420
Clair de Lune—105
Claire, Helen—211
Claire, Ina—50, 67, 78, 82, 93, 106, 112, 135, 182, 191, 211, 150, 283
Claire, Marion—190
Clancy, James—323, 366
Clancy Name, The—58
Clandestine Marriage, The—16, 274, 285, 360, 422
Clansman, The—30, 33
Clap Hands—337
"Clap Yo' Hands"—142
Clara's Ole Man—373
Clare, Frances—218
Clare, Mary—118, 130, 159, 178
Clarence—93, 104

Clarence Darrow for the Defense—421
Clarence, O. B.—62
Clarence, Rene—80
Clare Tree Major Children's Theatre—229
Clarion Call, The—75
Clark, Alfred—134
Clark, Bobby—112, 126, 141, 170, 177, 191, 200, 216, 230, 239, 254, 261, 266, 272, 324
Clark, Brian—443
Clark Center for the Performing Arts—399
Clark, Dane—332
Clarke, Cecil—290
Clarke, Constance—357
Clarke, George—143, 171
Clark, E. Holman—49, 121, 127
Clarke, Jack—172
Clarke, J. I. C.—30
Clarke, John—143, 156
Clarke, Mary—135
Clarke, Richard—191
Clark, Frank—174
Clark, Harry—216
Clark, John—437
Clark, Kenneth—31
Clark, Mae—141
Clark, Marguerite—47
Clark, Randy—434
Clark, Ron—385
Clarkson, Joan—143
Clark, Thais—450
Clash By Night—227
Class Enemy—443, 445, 450, 452
Classic Stage Company (CSC)—401, 417, 431, 455
Class of '29—202
Claudel, Paul—84, 95, 116, 274, 291, 302, 306, 307, 334, 353, 373
Claudia—226, 229, 231
Claudius, The Bee—237
Clavert, Louis—43
Claw, The—106, 431
Clayburgh, Jill—401
Clayton and White—92
Clayton, Bessie—32, 36, 47, 146
Clayton, Herbert—166
Clayton, Jan—244, 249, 301
Clayton, Marjorie—190
Clean Kill, A—316
Clean Slate, A—15, 18
Clear All Wires—181, 187
Clearing in the Woods, A—308
Cleary, M.—5
Cleese, John—414
Clegg, Edith—32
Clemenceau—90
Clemens, Le Roy—143
Clement, Clay—143
Clement, Dick—414
Clements, Colin—234, 257
Clements, Dudley—170
Clements, John—186, 207, 235, 242, 250, 264, 274, 277, 285, 300, 302, 305, 309, 310, 334, 339, 359, 360, 367, 368, 374, 381, 382, 388, 398, 410, 421, 434, 438, 453
Clements, Miriam—2
Clements, Otis—406
Clements, Ryerson—238, 242
Cleopatra—83, 99, 134, 137, 265, 409
Cleveland Play House—85, 154
Cleveland, Phyllis—131
Cleverdon, Douglas—301
Clever Soldiers—417
Cliff, Laddie—101, 126, 151, 158, 165, 167, 172
Clifford, John—226
Clift, Montgomery—230, 239, 241, 244, 290, 362
Clifton, Bernard—151, 222
Clifton, Bertha—68
Clifton, John—358
Climate of Eden, The—276, 286, 319
Climax, The—47
Climbers, The—6, 51
Climb the Greased Pole—368

Climie, David—295
Clinton-Baddeley, V. C.—156, 187
Clive, Colin—172, 191
Clive, Vincent—49
Clod, The—77
"Clog Dance"—446
Close Harmony—302
Close of Play—450
Close Quarters—202
Close Theatre Club—368, 392, 408
Clothes—30, 161
Cloud Nine—450, 451
Clouds—443
Clowes, St. Johns—279
Clowning—355
Clowning Through Life—161
Clown Jewels—315
Clowns in Clover—151
Clowns, The—373, 430
Club Friend, The—319
Club, The—426
Cluchey, Rick—385, 415
Clunes, Alec—134, 206, 223, 232, 241, 246, 249, 254, 259, 260, 264, 269, 276, 279, 283, 284, 296, 306, 307
Clurman, Harold—145, 221, 247, 262, 276, 278, 281, 293, 294, 300, 304, 309, 310, 318
Clutterbuck—248, 262, 270
Clyde, Gordon—328
Clyde, Jeremy—379
Coach with the Six Insides, The—333, 452
Coakley, Marion—100
Coals of Fire—275
Coarse Acting Show 2, The—455
Cobb and Frost—70
Cobb, Lee J.—227, 262, 281, 376, 432
Coburn, Charles—87, 111, 136, 191, 330
Coburn, D. L.—434
Cobweb, The—73
Coca, Imogene—138, 170, 181, 190, 200, 217
Cochet, Jean-Laurent—453
Cochran, Charles B.—79, 81, 91, 106, 107, 114, 116, 177, 210, 224, 251, 407
Cochrane, Frank—158
Cochran's Revue—143, 177
Cock-a-Doodle-Dandy—317, 318, 375
Cockie—407
Cockles and Champagne—289
Cockroach That Ate Cincinnati, The—451
Cock Robin—156, 187
Cocktail Party, The—264, 266, 267, 270, 374, 375, 376
Coco—378
Cocoanuts, The—133
Coco, James—371, 378, 437
Cocteau, Jean—103, 208, 223, 224, 250, 253, 273, 311, 446, 453
Coda, Frank—367
Cod on a Stick—412
Coe, Fred—400
Coe, Peter—317, 318, 339, 340, 359, 361, 366, 367, 374, 381, 388, 391, 401, 403, 409, 451
Coeur de Lilas—108
Coeur de Moineau—108
Coffee Lace, The—372
Coffee, Lenora—216, 220
Coffey, Denise—354, 418, 424, 436, 437
Coffin, C. Hayden—11, 21, 36
Coghill, Nevill—372, 453
Coghill, Patrick—295
Coghlan, Gertrude—82, 194
Coghlan, Rose—82, 194
Cohan and Harris—48
Cohan and Harris Minstrels—45, 51
Cohan, George M.—6, 14, 15, 20, 30, 31, 34, 36, 41, 42, 45, 48, 51, 52, 56, 60, 61, 66, 71, 74, 78, 83, 88, 92, 98, 100, 106, 113, 119, 124, 149, 153, 155, 156, 186, 189, 205,

229, 233, 297, 334, 371
Cohanized Opera Comique—92
Cohan, Jerry J.—6, 14
Cohan, Josephine—6, 14, 19
Cohan, Mary—371
Cohan, Nellie—6, 14
Cohan Revue of 1916, The—78
Cohan Revue of 1918, The—83
Cohen, Alex—230, 239, 321, 325, 347
Cohen, Leonard—409
Cohn, Sidney—206
Coiner, The—90, 193
Coke, Peter—310, 315
Colbert, Claudette—148, 163, 164, 309, 435
Colbron, Grace Isabel—35
Cold Storage—434
Cold Wind and the Warm, The—310, 319
Cole—414
Cole, Bob—20, 35, 47
Coleby, W. T.—67
Cole, George—253, 418
Cole, Harry—107
Cole, Jack—191, 418
Cole, Janet—116
Coleman, Basil—306, 394
Coleman, Cy—321, 332, 357, 406, 434
Coleman, John—3
Coleman, Nancy—226, 293
Coleman, Ronald—105
Coleridge, Ethel—143, 213, 227
Coleridge, Samuel Taylor—452
Cole, Tom—439
Colette—385, 406, 440
Colicos, John—357
Colin, Jean—149, 172
Colins, Arthur—113
Colleano, Bonar—236, 241, 253, 294
Collected Works of Billy the Kid, The—409
Collection, The 99—332, 335, 343, 408, 415
Collector, The—405
College Widow, The—19, 82
Collette—154
Collier, Constance—12, 27, 33, 42, 56, 61, 75, 82, 90, 103, 127, 135, 149, 163, 181
Collier, John—397
Collier, Patience—310, 329, 359, 382, 397, 429
Collier's Friday Night, A—373
Collier, William—6, 19, 31, 42, 78, 106, 148
Collinge, Patricia—43, 115, 131, 181, 216, 418
Collins, Arthur—4, 6, 9, 14, 15, 20, 23, 32, 54, 58, 59, 67, 79, 85, 102, 120
Collins, Barry—437, 446
Collins, Frank—114, 116, 177, 227
Collins, Jose—74, 78, 79, 83, 101, 115, 120, 127, 219
Collins, Judy—381
Collins, Lottie—55
Collins, Pauline—386, 427
Collins, Philip—347
Collins, Russell—200, 230, 332
Collins, Sewell—151
Collins, Stephen—394
Collins, Wilkie—290
Collision Course—374
Collison, Wilson—92, 93, 105, 161, 183, 224, 232
Collis, William R.—219, 228, 232
Collodi, Carlo—403
Colman-Garrick—422
Colman, George—16, 274, 285, 360
Colman, Kate—424
Colombaion, Alberto—430
Colombaion, Carlo—430
Colombe—273
Colombine—114
Colonel Newcome—32
Colonel Satan—177
Colonial Theater (San Francisco)—34

Colon, Miriam—358
Colorado—7
Colours in the Dark—367
Colt, Ethel Barrymore—441
Colton, John—113, 123
Colton, Joseph—277
Columbia Broadcasting System (CBS)—46, 110, 139
Columbia Theater (San francisco)—34
Columbia University Varsity Show—30, 103
Columbus Boys, The—360
Colum, Padraic—28, 54, 114, 179
Comber, Bobby—144, 151, 166
Combermere, Edward—83
Combine, The—383, 389
Combs, Samuel—9
Comden, Betty—240, 241, 244, 271, 281, 286, 298, 309, 327, 339, 344, 364, 385, 413, 434, 442
Comden, The—431
Come Along—92
Come and Be Killed—366
Come and Go—387
Come As You Are—386
Come Back, Little Sheba—266, 270, 286, 355, 411, 412, 431
Come Blow Your Horn—326, 333, 377
Comedians, The—421, 427
Comedie Francaise—38, 115, 122, 218, 245, 260, 296, 316, 340, 347, 362, 367, 380, 388, 408, 453
Comedienne—212
Comedy in Music—281
Comedy of Aideen, The—59
Comedy of Errors, The—27, 72, 73, 80, 96, 193, 208, 212, 214, 219, 225, 264, 300, 306, 334, 335, 336, 341, 342, 347, 353, 367, 381, 389, 397, 402, 403, 423, 429, 430, 438, 454
Comedy of Good and Evil, The—188
Comedy of the Changing Years, A—379
Comedy of the Man Who Married a Dumb Wife, The—84
Comedy Theatre—(London) 39, 302, 337, 408 (New York) 46
Come Home—373
Come Into My Bed—427
Come into the Garden Maud—358, 413
Comelli—120, 126, 134
Come Out of the Kitchen—78, 101
Come Spy With Me—359
Comes the Revelation—233
Come Together—390
Comet, The—36
Comic Artist, The—223
Comings and Goings—373
Command Decision—252, 261
Commedia—374
Comment on Ecrit l'Histoire—122
Commire, Ann—439
Commission, The—366
Committee of Forty, The—70
Common Glory, The—254
Common Wheel, The—431
Commune—391
Community Players—138
Community Theatre Association—399
Community Theatre School (Buffalo, N.Y.)—356
Compagnia de Giovani (Rome)—353, 362
Compagnia di Prosa Tino Buazelli—422
Compagnie des Quine—192
Compagnie du Theatre de la Cite de Villeurbanne—374
Compagnie Marie Bell—323, 342
Compagnie Madeleine Renaud et Jean-Louis Barrault—260, 274, 302, 382
Compagnons de la Chanson—256, 267

Companion of Honor—433
Company—385, 394, 440
Company Theatre—397
Compeau, Jacques—192
Compiegne—75
Complaisant Lover, The—315, 327, 337
Complexe de Philemon, Le—277
Comport, Brian—407
Compton, Betty—141
Compton-Burnett, Ivy—421
Compton Cinema Group—350
Compton, Fay—69, 94, 101, 107, 114, 131, 134, 135, 142, 143, 145, 177, 187, 197, 216, 219, 227, 241, 260, 263, 285, 289, 317, 447
Compton, Juliette—127
Compton, Katherine—15, 26, 53, 62
Compton, Madge—107, 120
Compton, Viola—196
Compulsion—304, 325
Comrades—417
Comstock, Frances Ray—25, 82, 98, 111, 117
Comstock, Howard—170
Comstock, Nanette—30, 47
Comtesse Coquette—35, 297
Comtesse Mitzi—68
Comus—198, 208, 250, 279
Concerico Was Here to Stay—353
Concert, The—52, 55
Conchita—128
Condemned of Altona, The—357
Condon, Carol—381
Conduct Unbecoming—379, 386
Cone, Tom—446
Confederacy, The—23, 312, 416
Confessional of a Justified Sinner—397
Confessions of an Actor—233
Confidential Clerk, The—283, 285, 287
Confrontation—396
Confusions—427
Congreve Restoration—232
Congreve, William—108, 127, 135, 136, 179, 184, 192, 237, 242, 254, 260, 284, 302, 317, 355, 379, 410, 415, 418, 430, 444, 445
Conjur Man Dies—202
Conkle, E. P.—213, 215
Conklin, Peggy—164, 186, 195, 205, 226
Conlin, Terry—227
Connaissance de Claudel—307
Connaughton, Shane—437
Connecticut Yankee, A—149, 161, 237
Connection, The—314, 325, 417
Connell, Jane—298
Connell, Norreys—50
Connelly, Marc—105, 111, 113, 118, 123, 124, 125, 130, 147, 170, 191, 198, 199, 205, 241, 274, 314, 387, 455
Connery, Sean—334
Connolly, Billy—431, 435, 455
Connolly, Patricia—373
Connolly, Sean—81
Connolly, Walter—195
Connor, Harry—43, 97
Connor, Kenneth—407
Connors, Barry—133, 176
Conn, Stewart—347, 366, 379
Con o' the Hills—369
Conqueror, The—27
Conquest of the Universe—455
Conquest, Ida—27
Conrad, Con—135, 141, 151
Conradi—59
Conrad, Joseph—94
Conried, Hans—314
Conroy, Frank—105, 133, 167, 211
Conservatoire d'Art Dramatique, Le—292
Conspiracy, The—45, 55
Conspiracy and Tragedy of Charles, Duke of Byron, The—167
Constanduros, Denis—236
Constanduros, Mabel—236

Constant Lover, The—278
Constant Nymph, The—142, 143, 237
Constant Prince, The—382
Constant Wife, The—142, 155, 250, 410, 422, 425
Constantin Stanislavsky's Moscow Art Theatre Musical Studio—137
Consul, The—266, 272
Consumer's Gasworks—405
Contemporary Theatre, (ACT), A (Seattle)—356
Contemptible Little Army, The—75
Conti, Italia—83, 159
Conti, Tom—388, 390, 429, 443
Contradictions—445
Contratype III—366
Contribution—380
Conversation Piece—191
Conversations of Anatol—57
Convict on the Hearth, The—32
Conville, David—389, 403, 416, 423, 429, 438
Convy, Bert—381
Conway, Curt—230
Conway, John—256
Conway, Kevin—359, 418, 449
Conway, Russ—358
Conway, Shirl—258, 293
Cook, Barbara—275, 307, 323, 338, 361, 364, 404
Cook, David—372
Cook, Donald—217, 244, 287, 330
Cook, Donn—150
Cooke, Alan—329
Cooke, Rosa—43
Cook, George Cram—77, 81, 84
Cook, Joe—118, 125, 156, 170, 455
Cook Jr., Elisha—150, 186
Cook, Madge Carr—6, 19
Cook, Olga—106
Cook, Peter—315, 323, 328, 401
Cook, Roderick—400
Cooksey, Curtis—156
Cookson, Peter—252, 281
Cook, Will A.—113
Cook, Will Marion—2, 14, 19, 30, 41
Coolard, Avalon—8
Coolest Cat in Town, The—445
Coolidge, Philip—243
Cool Million, A—438
Coon Band—114
Cooney-Marsh Group—457
Cooney, Ray—328, 345, 353, 354, 372, 387, 401, 407, 414, 421, 435, 456
Cooperativa Tuscolano—423
Cooper, Doris—127, 158
Cooper, Edward—212
Cooper, Frank Kemble—32, 69, 90
Cooper, Giles—334, 365
Cooper, Gladys—37, 62, 66, 68, 72, 79, 80, 84, 94, 95, 107, 115, 121, 128, 135, 150, 158, 172, 178, 187, 190, 197, 212, 273, 283, 293, 294, 328, 344, 366, 398
Cooper, Jackie—287
Cooper, Lillian Kemble—183
Cooper, Melville—111, 126, 177, 196, 248, 411
Cooper, Robert—426
Coopersmith, Jerome—351, 358
Cooper, Violet Kemble—88, 105, 123, 141, 155, 173, 330
Co-Optimists, The—109, 115, 120, 128, 136, 145, 167
Coote, Henry—31
Coote, Robert—272, 369
Coots, J. Fred—112, 140, 164
Coover, Robert—402
Copeau, Jacques—85, 89, 90, 95, 152
Copland, Aaron—170, 219
Copley, Paul—430
Copley, Peter—316
Coppel, Alec—322
Copperhead, The—87
Copplestone, Trewin—348
Cops—445
Coquelin, Constant—4, 8, 13, 27, 33, 45

Coquette—150
Corbett, Gretchen—354
Corbett, Harry—279, 352, 409
Corbett, Leonora—188, 213, 227, 324
Corbett, Marjorie—183
Corday, Andree—88
Corey, Edward B.—65
Corey, Orlin—290
C.O.R.F.A.X. (Don't Ask)—424
Corio, Ann—332, 351, 388
Coriolanus—8, 37, 54, 63, 76, 96, 103, 144, 145, 188, 213, 214, 219, 259, 278, 285, 289, 316, 329, 335, 348, 354, 395, 402, 410, 415, 437, 444, 452, 453, 454
Corkery, Daniel—96
Cormack, Bartlett—178
Corneille, Pierre—95, 312, 359, 384, 447
Cornelius—196, 224
Cornell, Allen—434
Cornell, Katherine—40, 46, 84, 85, 97, 105, 107, 113, 123, 128, 129, 135, 150, 157, 172, 182, 185, 186, 192, 193, 200, 202, 216, 228, 232, 235, 249, 255, 262, 276, 282, 289, 418
Cornell, Ted—379
Cornett, Ewel—350
Corn Is Green, The—213, 222, 229, 268, 348, 453
Cornish, Joyce—109
Cornwallis-West, Mrs. George—48, 69
Cornwell, Charlotte—443
Coronation Revue—206
Coronbona, Victoria—355
Corporation of London, The—354
Corri, Adrienne—328, 390
Corruption in the Palace of Justice—312
Corsaro, Frank—294, 327, 329, 434, 449, 452
Corsican Brothers, The—45, 388
Cort, Harry—88
Cort, John—65, 83
Corunna!—395
Corwin, H. G.—39
Cory, Bob—161
Cory, Edward Gordon—8, 12, 15, 16,
Cosentino, Nicholas—195
Cosi e se vi Pare—135
Cosi fan Tutte—260, 264, 367
Cosi Sia—123
Costa Packet—404
Costello, Lou—216
Costello, Mary—59
Cotes, Peter—249, 251, 255, 259, 273, 278, 317, 383
Cotsworth, Staats—330, 456
Cottage To Let—222, 228
Cotter, Sinclair—84
Cotton Club Gala—424
Cotton, David—318
Cotton, Joseph—216, 282, 309, 322
Cotton, Will—179
Cottrell, Richard—365, 368, 382, 414, 429, 432, 451, 455
Cottrell, William—225
Couch, L. J.—17
Coulouris, George—152, 168, 181, 216, 226, 259, 260, 264, 284
Council for the Encouragement of Music and the Arts (CEMA)—251
Council of Actor's Equity—256
Counsel, Elizabeth—450
Counsell, John—260, 272, 274, 278, 315
Counsellor-At-Law—176, 192, 233, 369, 439
Count Dracula—303, 440
Counterfeit Presentment, A—104
Countess Cathleen, The—3, 64, 283
Countess Maritza—141
Count Hannibal—58
Counting the Ways—432
Count of Luxembourg, The—57, 167
Count of Monte Cristo, The—104, 180
Country Boy, The—52
Country Dressmaker, The—68

Country Girl, The—10, 11, 37, 44, 178, 267, 275, 276, 361, 402
Country Life—410
Country Mouse, A—10, 11
Country Wife, The—202, 223, 302, 306, 307, 348, 355, 381, 409, 436
"Count Your Blessings"—239
Couper, Barbara—273
Courage—157
Courchier, Arthur—53
Courteline, George—75, 89, 90, 109
Courtenay, Margaret—421, 452
Courtenay, William—22
Court, Hazel—289
Courtleigh, William—112
Courtneidge, Cicely—62, 67, 79, 133, 144, 151, 166, 177, 207, 213, 231, 236, 263, 282, 300, 315, 328, 344, 347, 368, 376, 394
Courtneidge, Robert—32, 36, 57, 61, 62, 72, 107
Courtney, C. C.—378
Courtney, Gordon—178
Courtney, Tom—329, 360, 375, 381, 398, 401, 421, 443
Courtney, W. L.—33
Courtship of Miles Standish, The—179
Court Theatre (London)—96
Courville, Albert—107
Cousin Billy—25
Cousin from Nowhere, The—119
Cousin Kate—16, 18
Cousin Muriel—222
Cousin Vladimir—443
Covell, Gerald—325
Covent Garden Tragedy, The—373
Covent Garden—33
Coventry, Ann—213
Coventry Belgrade Theatre Company—312
Covington, Julie—430, 443, 450
Cowan, Jerome—196
Coward, Noel—79, 82, 84, 89, 97, 102, 115, 120, 127, 133, 134, 142, 143, 148, 150, 151, 152, 158, 165, 172, 176, 177, 178, 183, 186, 189, 191, 195, 201, 212, 216, 227, 232, 233, 235, 242, 245, 248, 251, 253, 254, 260, 265, 268, 273, 277, 278, 284, 289, 299, 300, 314, 322, 326, 339, 340, 341, 349, 353, 358, 367, 373, 383, 389, 391, 396, 401, 403, 410, 411, 413, 422, 430, 439, 441, 446, 447, 453
Cowardy Custard—401
Cowboys No. 2—387
Cowell, Henry—224
Cowen, Laurence—89, 130, 220
Cowen, Ron—371
Cowie, Laura—54, 113, 122, 181, 183
Cowles, Denis—114
Cowles, Matthew—357, 371
Cowley, Hannah—49
Cowl, Jane—31, 36, 37, 47, 61, 94, 112, 121, 128, 133, 148, 161, 189, 196, 212, 222, 270
Cow-Puncher, The—64
Cox and Box—184, 193, 260, 264, 269, 274, 285, 290, 306, 330, 349, 355, 369
Cox, Brian—379
Cox, Constance—250
Coxe, Louis O.—271, 275
Cox, John—388, 417
Cox, Patricia—418
Cox, Vivian—437
Coyne, Joseph—49, 53, 141, 149
Crabbe, Kerry Lee—423
Crabtree, Carlotta—129
Crabtree, Paul—262, 281
Cracks—439
Cracow Stary Theatre Company—402
Craddock, Phoebe—450
Cradle Snatchers—132, 226
Cradle Song, The—152, 155, 167, 193, 241
Cradle Will Rock, The—213, 349
Craig, Edward Gordon—8, 12, 15, 16,

55, 110, 160, 162, 258, 363
Craig, Helen—221
Craig, John—115, 121
Craig, May—84, 135
Craig, Robert—117
Craig, Wendy—315, 352, 437
Crainquebille—50, 90
Crandall, Edward—142
Crane, C. Howard—116, 138
Crane, Jean—62
Crane, Richard—401, 428, 455
Crane, William H.—1, 55, 123, 179
Cranford, Frank—375
Cranham, Kenneth—359
Cranko, John—296, 300
Cranks—296, 300
Craven, A. Scott—62
Craven, Frank—71, 78, 83, 100, 113, 170, 211, 239
Craven, Gemma—403
Craven, Hawes—3
Craven, John—221
Craven, Robert—202
Craven, Robin—283
Crawford, Broderick—205
Crawford, Cheryl—13, 145, 179, 241, 250, 254, 257, 262, 268
Crawford, Clifton—74, 94
Crawford, F. Marion—48
Crawford, Michael—326, 352, 364, 394, 414, 450
Crawford, Mimi—134, 151
Crazy Gang, The—280, 289, 300, 315, 322
Crazy Locomotive, The—436
Creaking Chair, The—127
Creamer, Henry—112
Crean, Patrick—389
Creation of the World and Other Business, The—400
Creditors, The—63, 278, 316, 430, 436
Creeper, The—352
Creeps—397, 412
Cree, Sam—414
Cregan, David—353, 359, 375, 379
Creighton, Anthony—310, 319, 402
Cremieux, Hector—27
Cressall, Maud—59
Creston, Clark—55
Crest of the Wave—207
Crest Theatre (Toronto)—292
Creswell, Peter—237
Cretan Bull, The—410
Crete and Sergeant Pepper—401, 418
Crewe, Bertie—60, 180
Crews, Laura Hope—52, 69, 82, 101, 118, 131, 134, 145, 187
Cribbins, Bernard—372, 414, 456
Crichton, Kyle—197, 298
Crichton, Madge—14
Crick, Monte—206
Cricot Two Theatre—451
Crier, Gordon—268
Crime—108, 148, 202
Crime and Punishment—53, 198, 249, 289, 360
Crime at Blossoms, The—188
Crime in the Whistler Room, The—129
Crime of Margaret Foley, The—253
Crime on Goat Island—340
Crime Passionel—260
Crimes Against Nature—442
Crimes of Passion—365
Criminal at Large—181
Criminal Code, The—164
Criminals, The—228
Criminals, The—366
Crinoline Girl, The—71
Crisham, Walter—217, 231
Crisis, The—11, 45
Crisp, Donald—41
Criss Cross—155
Criss-Crossing—387
Cristofer, Michael—452
Criterion Theater (London)—18
Critic's Choice—321, 328
Critics' Circle Award—293, 299, 337

Critic, The—58, 69, 86, 136, 237, 243, 246, 249, 380
Croesus—67
Croft, Annie—107, 118, 119, 143, 144
Croft, David—379, 421
Croft, Michael—317, 329, 335, 342, 348, 354, 375, 382, 402, 403, 407, 423, 447, 453, 455
Croft, Peter—231, 284
Croker-King, C. H.—53
Cromie, Robert—210
Crompton, William H.—50
Cromwell—409
Cromwell, John—66, 71, 74, 132, 145
Cronin, A. J.—227
Cronin-Wilson, W.—172
Cronyn, Hume—205, 268, 283, 286, 295, 316, 326, 337, 339, 345, 347, 357, 404, 413, 434
Crooked Mile, The—315
Crooke, Frederick—300
Crosby, Emma—101
Crosby, Harry—71
Crosman, Henrietta—12, 15, 36, 56, 118, 144, 160, 161
Cross and Sword—354
Cross, Beverly—315, 333, 359, 415, 450
Cross, Gerald—296
Cross Roads, The—54, 313
Crossways—13
Croswell, Anne—338
Crothers, Rachel—31, 52, 78, 88, 104, 105, 110, 117, 123, 133, 163, 176, 180, 181, 185, 189, 205, 215, 445
Crouch, J. H.—312
Croue, Jean—89, 95, 152
Crouse, Russel—200, 206, 217, 225, 244, 251, 257, 265, 266, 280, 282, 298, 314, 332, 362, 368, 376
Crowden, Graham—323, 389
Crowe, Eileen—145
Crowley, Ann—271
Crowley, Mart—371
Crowley, Matt—230
Crown Matrimonial—401
Crowther, Leslie—334
Crozier, Eric—249
Crozier, Jim—386
Crucible, The—281, 286, 301, 313, 347, 353, 354, 381, 401, 402, 403, 423, 430, 440, 456
Crucifer of Blood—442, 450
Cruddas, Audrey—290
Cruel Daughter, The—291
Cruel Tears—425
Cruikshank, Andrew—219, 294, 299, 352
Cruikshank, W. S., and Company—34
Cruikshanks, Charles—34
Cruishank, A. Steward—34
Cryer, Barry—386
Cryer, David—364
Cryer, Gretchen—364, 385, 397, 398, 445
Cry of Players, A—376
Cry of the People for Meat, The—381
Crystal and Fox—373
Cry, the Beloved Country—262
Cuchulain the Warrior King—455
Cuchulain Cycle—53
Cuckoo in the Nest, A—134, 138, 349
Cue for Passion—309, 369
Cuisine des anges, La—281
Cuka, Frances—409, 417, 451
Cukor, George—140, 163
Culbertson, Ernest—105
Cullen, Countee—247
Cullen, James—92
Cullen, Paddy—185
Cullman, Howard—238
Cullum, John—174, 352, 420
Culver, C. S.—60
Culver, Roland—154, 263, 268, 286, 311, 373
Cumming, Dorothy—88
Cummings, Asa—50
Cummings, Constance—191, 195,

217, 219, 248, 258, 276, 283, 334, 367, 395, 396, 408, 409, 449, 452
Cummings, Robert—33, 186
Cummins, Peggy—296
Cunard, Victor—197
Cunningham, Joseph A.—146
Cunningham, Philip—32
Cunningham, Roland—48
Cupboard Love—114
Cupid and the Styx—64
Cup of Kindness, A—165
Curate of St. Ohad's, The—96
Cure for Love, The—245
Curious Savage, The—266
Curley McDimple—365
Curnock, Richard—347
Curran, Homer—116, 239
Currie, Clive—121, 165, 192
Currie, Finlay—376
Currie, J.—246
Currie, Rob—197
Curry, Ian—322
Curry, Tim—409, 414
Curse It, Foiled Again!—203
Curse of the Country, The—96
Curse of the Daleks, The—355
Curse of the Starving Class—437, 445
Curtain Going Up—418
Curtain Group—103
Curtains Up—441
Curteis, Ian—403
Curti, Alfredo—56
Curtis, Cyril—286
Curtmantle—335, 336
Curzon, Frank—18, 46, 53, 102, 150
Curzon, George—100, 158, 159
Cusak, Cyril—186, 188, 203, 218, 219, 223, 339, 374, 436
Cushing, Catherine Chisholm—56, 78, 126
Cushing, Peter—273, 315
Cushing, Tom—106, 119, 142, 165
Cushman, Charlotte—137
Cushman, Nancy—326
Cushman, Robert—403
Cusley, Gideon—96
Cuthbertson, Iain—361
Cutler, Ben—205
Cutler, Ivor—339
Cutler, John—45
Cutler, Kate—21, 26, 43
Cuvillier, Charles—88, 95, 101, 102
Cycle Sluts—429
Cymbeline—33, 49, 55, 90, 103, 115, 122, 208, 249, 264, 301, 302, 306, 334, 375, 389, 396, 417, 453
Cynara—172, 176, 185
Cyrano—391
Cyrano de Bergerac—3, 13, 45, 90, 96, 122, 184, 199, 243, 250, 251, 285, 297, 313, 335, 341, 367, 373, 423
Cyranose—229
Czardasfurstin—82
Czar Fyodor Ivanovitch—121
Czarina, The—111
Czech National Theatre of Prague —362
Czinner, Paul—235, 250

Da Costa, Morton—73, 259, 265, 269, 275, 321, 409, 420
Daddies—87
Daddy Goodness—373
Daddy Long-Legs—71, 189, 227, 255
Daddy's Gone A-Hunting—105
Dad's Army—421
Daemon in the House, The—102
Dagenham Girl Pipers—241
Dagger and the Rose, The—189
d'Aguzay, Jean—76
Dahdah, Robert—365
Dahl, Arlene—285
Dahl, Magda—41
Dailey, Dan—205
Dailey, Irene—237, 344
Dailey, Peter—19
Daily Mail—146

Daily Telegraph—146, 147, 204
Daine, Lois—339
Dainton, Marie—143, 166
Dainty, Billy—241
Dairymaids, The—32
Dairyworth, Jean—306
Daisy Mayme—142, 155
Daisy, The—145
Dale, Gladys—109
Dale, Grover—413
Dale, James—93, 100, 149, 186
Dale, Jim—349, 361, 368, 382, 388, 390, 395, 406, 415, 435
Dale, Margaret—10, 132
Daley, Arnold—2
Daley Civic Center—331
Dalgarni—275
Dalkey Archive, The—451
Dallas, J. J.—2
Dallas Theatre Centre—318, 319
Dall, Evelyn—222
Dallmeyer, Andrew—451
D'Alroy, Evelyn—48, 58, 67
Dalrymple, Jean—250, 286, 296, 300, 302, 307, 311, 316, 329, 335, 340, 349, 353, 360, 361, 368
Dalton, Charles—41, 44
Dalton, Dorothy—93
Dalton, William—229
Daly, Arnold—13, 15, 17, 19, 27, 38, 58, 80, 100, 109, 145, 146, 183, 225
Daly, Augustin—45, 55, 138, 153, 225
Daly, Blythe—132, 152
Daly Company—215
Daly, Dan—23
Daly, James—321
Daly, John—22
Daly, Orlando—126
Daly, Wally K.—438
Daly, William—120
Damaged Goods—66, 70, 83, 237
Damask Cheek, The—230, 238, 263
Damask Drum, The—340
Dame Nature—53
Dame of Sark, The—414, 425
Damer's Gold—64
Dames at Sea—372, 379
Damita, Lily—164
Damn Yankees—130, 293, 305
Damon, Cathryn—332
Damrosch, Walter—122
Dana, Leora—256, 272, 400, 426
Dan and Van—183
Danbery, Peter—380
Dance, George—6, 8
Dance League—197
Dance Me A Song—270
Dance of Death, The—197, 334, 360, 366, 409, 412, 415, 444
Dance on a Country Grave—430
Dancers, The—119, 359
Dance With Me—360
Dance with Your Gods—194
Dancin'—442
Dancing Around—71
Dancing Girl, The—117
"Dancing in the Dark"—176
Dancing Mistress, The—63
Dancing Mothers—124, 126
Dancing Princess, The—280
Dancing Shadow—228
Dancing Years, The—217, 231, 254, 374
Dandelion—398
Dandelion Upstairs—379
Dandy Dick—354, 409, 410
Dandy Dolls, The—389
Dandy Duck—3
Dane, Clemence—107, 126, 143, 160, 166, 183, 187, 193, 219, 222, 315, 355, 397
Daneman, Paul—290, 296, 302, 307, 311, 334, 421
Danger, Men Working—274
Dangerous Corner—181, 182, 214
Dangerous Maid, A—109
Daniel—108
Daniel Boone Story, The—323

Daniel Frohman Presents—225
Daniell, Henry—105, 128, 142, 171, 190, 195, 332, 342
Daniels, Bebe—227, 245
Daniel Mayer Company—126
Daniels, Billy—424
Daniels, Danny—341
Daniels, Frank—15, 21, 35
Daniels, March—295
Daniels, Maurice—329
Daniels, Ron—409, 417, 428, 429, 438, 443, 444, 453
Daniels, William—320, 378
Danites, The—73
Dankworth, Johnny—368
Danner, Blythe—371, 378, 437
Dann, Roger—314
D'Annunzio, Gabriele—4, 13, 16, 18, 123, 128
Danny La Rue Show, The—411
Dante—16, 17, 451
Dantes, Edmond—104
Dante, the Danish magician—204
Dantine, Helmut—253
Danton's Death—213, 215, 316, 355, 396
Danton's Tod—153
Danvers, Johnny—122
Daphne Laureola—263, 266
Darbon, Leslie—407, 421, 435
D'Arcy, Eamon—455
D'Arcy, Margaretta—382, 401, 454
Dare, Phyllis—34, 57, 62, 113, 127, 144, 201, 227, 263
Darewski, Herman—75, 79, 80, 83, 84, 87, 89, 101, 102, 113, 114, 120
Darewski, Max—75, 83
Dare, Zena—21, 31, 37, 144, 212
Darian, Anita—338
Darion, Joe—304, 352, 364
Dark Angel, The—131
Dark at the Top of the Stairs, The— 305, 313
Dark Eyes—234
"Dark Grows the Sky"—101
Dark Hours, The—209
Dark is Light Enough, The—289, 293, 297
Dark Lady of the Sonnets, The—108, 192, 242, 273, 274, 348, 411, 446, 454
Darkness at Noon—271, 279, 369
Dark of the Moon—244, 275, 350
Dark Pony—452
Dark Potential, The—241
Dark Victory—191
Dark Waters—184
Darley, J. H.—2
D'Arle, Yvonne—141
Darling! I Love You—171
Darling, Joan—341
Darling of the Gods, The—11, 13, 51, 154, 250
Darlington, W. A.—129, 168, 304, 456
Darrell, Maisie—143
Darvas, Lili—153, 228
Das Dreimadlerhaus—106
Das Gupta, K. N.—97
da Silva, Howard—192, 234, 291, 326, 338, 349, 378
Das Kaetchen von Heilbronn—49, 439
Das Konzert—373
Das Lusitania Songspiel—429
Dassin, Jules—364
D'Auban, Ernest—7, 20
Daubeny, Peter—301, 306, 316, 388, 396, 424
Daudet, Alphonse—1, 8, 23, 54, 57
Daughter-in-Law, The—366, 373
Daughter of Belgium, A—75
Daughter of England, A—75
Daughters of Atreus—203, 210
Daughters of the Mock—447
Dauphin, Claude—247, 266, 294
Daussmond, Betty—198
Dave—152
Dave King Show, The—299

Davenant, William—317
Davenport, A. Bromley—166
Davenport, E. L.—1, 30
Davenport, Fanny—146, 185, 215
Davenport, Harry—6, 87, 134, 194
Davenport, Nigel—301, 318, 401
David—152
David Copperfield—122
David, Fred Thompson-Worton—95
David, Hal—372
David Harum—1
David, John—410
David, Michael—448
Davidson, George—394
Davidson, John—207, 332, 367, 380, 430, 449
David, Thayer—296
David, Worton—95, 197
Davies, D. T.—144
Davies, Edna—135, 151, 161
Davies, Gareth—427
Davies, Hilda—218
Davies, Howard—418, 422, 429, 438, 439, 444, 453
Davies, Hubert Henry—16, 27, 43, 63, 264
Davies, Irving—328
Davies, Lillian—115, 133, 157
Davies, Louise—185
Davies, Marion—74, 82, 104, 330
Davies, N. Newnham—22
Davies, Robert—423
Davies, Tudor—135, 450
Daviot, Gordon—183, 192, 208, 292
Davis, Adele—30
Davis, Allan—264, 294, 315, 328, 415, 421, 435, 486, 494
Davis, Barry—382
Davis, Bessie McCoy—92
Davis, Bette—164, 168, 276, 320, 327
Davis, Blevins—284
Davis, Clifton—398
Davis, Donald—184, 200, 204, 292, 304, 307, 308, 320, 360
Davis, Eddie—239, 293
Davis, Edgar B.—142
Davis, Fay—7, 8, 15, 25, 30, 31, 49, 71, 74, 188
Davis, Hallie Flanagan—384
Davis, Harry Parr—248
Davis, Irving Kaye—240
Davis, Jessie Bartlett—28
Davis, J. Frank—142
Davis, Joan—245, 248, 276, 288, 295, 367, 374
Davis, Joe—418
Davis, Luther—244, 282
Davis, Murray—292, 304, 307
Davison, Alec—32
Davis, Ossie—326, 385
Davis, Owen—66, 73, 87, 91, 92, 99, 105, 111, 112, 117, 123, 133, 140, 141, 163, 184, 200, 209, 226, 303, 452
Davis, Reginald—49
Davis, Richard Harding—19, 30, 81
Davis, Sammy Jr.—298, 344, 447
Davis, Stringer—159, 167
Davis, Tom B.—9
Davis, W. Boyd—99
Davis, Wilbur—97
Davis, William—405
Dawkins, Cecil—358
Dawkins, Paul—358
Dawn, Glora—124
Dawn, Hazel—40, 53, 56, 59, 62, 66, 78, 92, 106, 124, 140
Dawn, Pearl—143
Dawson, Basil—279
Dawson, Ivo—16
Dawson, Michael—366
Day Before the Day, The—75
Day Before Spring, The—246
Day by the Sea, A—283, 294
Day, Clarence—217, 376
Day, Edith—83, 84, 93, 117, 125, 142
Day, Edmund—35
Day, Frances—183, 192, 217, 243, 248, 263
Day in Hollywood/A Night in the

Ukraine, A—450
Day in the Death of Joe Egg, A—365, 371, 377, 397
Day, Juliette—82
Day, Marie—52
Day of Absence—352, 352
Day of the Prince—340
Day, Richard Digby—374, 381, 389, 396, 401, 403, 409, 416, 423
Days and Nights of Beebee Fenster-maker—340
Days Between, The—449
Days in the Trees—360, 431
Days of the Commune, The—354, 438
Days Without End—190
Dayton, Katharine—196, 204, 279
Day With My Sister, A—394
Dazey, Frank—141
Dead Class, The—431, 451
Dead End—196, 199, 204
Dead Letter—347
Deadly Game, The—325
Dead Men's Pool—108
Dead on Nine—294
Dead Ride Fast, The—179
Dead Secret—305
Dead Souls—353
Dean, Basil—60, 97, 107, 117, 123, 129, 130, 133, 138, 143, 159, 161, 165, 177, 212, 217, 274, 315, 447
Deane, Hamilton—135, 150, 219, 440
Deane, Tessa—177
De Angelis, Jefferson—36, 47
De Angelis, Rosemary—437
Dean, Isabel—315, 374
Dean, James—287
Dean, Julia—35, 93
Dean of St. Patrick's, The—68
Dean, Philip Hayes—375, 398, 402, 442, 448
Dean, Phyllis—153
Dear Antoine—396, 398
Dear Augustine—312
Dear Brutus—84, 88, 114, 193
Dear Charles—278, 287, 376
Dear Daddy—427
Dear Delinquent—305
Dearden, Harold—150, 158
Dear Departing, The—122
Dearest Enemy—132
Dear Father—303
Dearing, Peter—183
Dear Jane—184
Dear Janet Rosenberg, Dear Mr. Kooning—379
Dear Liar—320, 406, 437, 453
Dear Little Denmark—49
Dear Love—186
Dearmer, Mrs. Percy—72
Dear Miss Phoebe—268
Dear Octopus—213, 216, 224
Dear Ruth—240, 246, 248
Dear World—378
Death of Bessie Smith, The—330, 375
Death of Chopin, The—68
Death of Cuchulain, The—455
Death of Tintagiles, The—69
Death of a Salesman—262, 263, 265, 273, 422, 432, 453
Death of Satan, The—301
Death Takes a Holiday—164, 177, 183, 188, 207, 218, 283
Deathtrap—442, 448
Death Valley—59
Deathwatch—319, 329
de Azertis, Lorenzo—123
de Banville, Theodore—85
de Banzie, Brenda—233, 267
Debayo, Jumoke—383
de Bear, Archibald—142, 147, 167, 173, 177, 196
de Becker, Harold—74
Debenham, Cicely—88, 108, 114, 127, 151
Deborah—70
DeBoudkowsky, N.—104
De Bray, Sybil—67
de Bruxelles, Le Rideau—408

Debt of Honour, A—2
Deburau—101, 108, 110, 424
de Burgh, Aimee—83
Debussy, Claude—112
Decameron '73—409
Decameron Nights—113, 116
de Cappet, Theodosia—42
deCasalis, Jeanne—177, 197, 200, 202, 224, 272, 363
Decision—243
Deckers, Eugene—272
Declaration of Independence—378
Declasse—93, 104
Decline and Fall of the Entire World as Seen Through the Eyes of Cole Porter Revisited, The—351
de Cordoba, Mercedes—121
de Cordoba, Pedro—50, 72, 82, 87, 115, 191
DeCosta, Leon—140
Decour, Pierre—27
de Courville, Albert—79, 83, 88, 94, 95, 101, 119, 126, 134
de Croisset, Francis—47, 71, 102
de Eduardo, Teatro—402
Deep Are the Roots—244, 251, 276
Deep River—141
Deering, Jane—234
Deering, Olvie—205, 221
Deer Park, The—364
Dee, Ruby—259, 326, 360, 385, 403
Dee, Sylvia—252
Deeter, Jaspar—123, 142, 245, 404
Deevey, Theresa—208, 306
Defeat—103
Defence of Queen Caroline, The—59
Defender, The—10
de Ferran, I. S.—308
de Filippo, Eduardo—298, 402, 407, 435, 444
De Filippo, Peppino—347, 408
DeFore, Don—221
de Forest, Marion—97
Deformed Transformed, The—401
de Frece, Lauri—53
DeGaulle, Charles—315
de Ghelderode, Michel—347, 368, 375, 397, 451
Deguallieres, Feydeau—427
de Hartog, Jan—73, 259, 261, 268, 280, 295, 358
De Haven, Carter—43
De Havilland, Olivia—274, 278
Dehn, Paul—272, 322
Deiber, Paul-Emile—359
Deighton, John—258
Deirdre of the Sorrows—54
Deity—102
Deitz, Howard—176
Deja Revue—418
Dekker, Albert—376
Dekker, Thomas—202, 213, 242, 337, 397
DeKoven, Reginald—6, 10, 15, 25, 31, 47, 104
DeKoven, Roger—146
DeKruif, Paul—190
Delacorte, George—337
Delacorte Theatre—337
De Lalonde, C.—138
Deland, Margaret—48
Delaney, Maureen—145, 330
Delaney, Shelagh—311, 316, 320, 323, 331, 430
Delaney, Sholto—187
Delany, Maureen—84, 96
de la Pasture, Henry, Mrs.—32
de la Roche, Mazo—201
de la Torre, Raf—206
de la Tour, Frances—395, 397, 443, 446
deLatraz, Jean—379
Delavigne, Casimir—27, 49, 90
Delfont, Bernard—359
de Liagre, Alfred Jr.—23, 186, 206, 269, 382
Delicate Balance, A—357, 379
Delius, Frederick—120
Deliverer, The—58
Dell,—202

Dellenbaugh, Harriet Otis—22, 31
Dell, Floyd—157
Dell, Gabriel—196, 344, 378
Delmar, Ethel—99
Delmar, Jane—75
Delmar, Kenny—262
Delmar, Vina—281
Delroy, Irene—163
Delubac, Jacqueline—198
Deluge, The—145, 197
De Luise, Dom—347
Del Val, Smuel—28
Delysia, Alice—75, 79, 83, 89, 95, 100, 116, 134, 143, 176, 187, 218, 456
DeMarco, Sally—221, 230, 240
DeMarco, Tony—221, 230, 240
Demarest, William—164, 176
Demarne, Denis—414
deMarney, Derrick—277
deMarney, Terence—236, 244, 253, 277
Demas, Carole—400
de Mattos, Alexander Teixeira—214
Dembina, Ivor—452
de Mendoza, Fernando Diaz—144
de Mille, Agnes—234, 235, 240, 244, 252, 267, 272, 287, 309, 339
DeMille, Cecil B.—7, 31, 36, 41
De Mille, William C.—25, 31, 36, 41, 56, 68
Demi-Virgin, The—106
Demon Barber, The—318
Demon, The—401
de Montherlant, Henri—359, 396, 437
De Mortuis—114
Dempsey, Clifford—92
Dempster, Curt—390
De Munn, Jeffery—450
de Musset, Alfred—45, 77, 80, 85, 90, 218, 296, 312, 316, 403, 444
Dence, Marjorie—199
Dench, Judi—317, 330, 335, 365, 380, 389, 390, 396, 410, 414, 437, 438, 439, 454
Denham, Maurice—310, 329, 368
Denham, Reginald—96, 115, 158, 165, 166, 218, 228, 239, 294, 296
Denise—45
Denison, Michael—263, 268, 282, 315, 344, 362, 391, 407
Denker, Henry—298, 326, 331, 338
Dennee, Charles—10
Dennelly, Donal—453
Dennen, Barry—358
Denning Report on the Profumo Affair, The—366
Dennis, Nigel—299, 319, 329
Dennison, Michael—323, 387
Dennis, Patrick—298, 332, 357
Dennis, Sandy—209, 315, 344, 387, 406
Denniston, Charlotte—141
Denny, Reginald—267, 369
Denny, Rubin—55
Dent, C. H.—91
Denton, Hilda—126
Denvers, Mary—142
dePaul, Gene—298
DePaur, Leonard—238
de Porto-Riche, Georges—264
Depres, Suzanne—45
Depuis Six Mois—75
Deputy Sheriff, The—60
Deputy, The—340, 344, 350
Derby Day—182
Dere, Ann—248
Der Hauptmann von Koepenick—349
Der Liebe Augustin—62
Dern, Bruce—312
Dernier Appel au Petit Dejeuner—455
de Rojas, Fernando—311
DeRosa and Perira—91
DeRosa, Eugene—104, 110
de Rothschild, Henri—63, 67
Derrill, Joanna—248
Der Ring Gott Farblonjet—438

Derr, Richard—293
Der Storm—27
Der Tag—73
Dervall, Paul—263, 272
Der Vetter aus Dingsda—117
Dervorgilla—50
Der Weg zur Holle—44
Derwent, Clarence—54, 64, 67, 72, 119, 135, 140, 163, 181, 235, 244
DeSade Illustrated—381
de Sade, Marquis—381
DeSade Show—422, 428
Desborough, Philip—144
Desclos, Jeanne—50
de Scranage, Candirus—363
Deserter, The—75
Desert Song, The—142, 236, 246, 410
de Severac, Jacqueline—248
deShields, Andre—420
Design for Living—186, 189, 217, 410, 411, 441
Designing for the Theatre—432
De Silva, Nina—45, 75, 121, 112, 208
Desire Under the Elms—126, 138, 177, 241, 278, 295, 340
Des Journees Entieres dans les Arbres—429
Desk Set, The—293
Deslys, Gaby—56, 57, 59, 66, 68, 74, 75, 83
Desmond, Dorothea—49
Desmonde, Jerry—235, 241, 248
Desmond, Florence—143, 158, 192, 222, 227, 236
Desmond, Jonny—309
Desperate Hours, The—293, 294, 297, 418
Dester, John—456
Destiny—429, 438
Destry Rides Again—314
d'Esti, Roberta—358
Detective Story—262, 265, 267
Detour, The—105, 303, 347
Deutsch, Ernst—373
Deutsche Schauspielhaus (Hamburg)—328
Deutsches Theater—389
de Valera, Eammon—363
Deval, Jacques—148, 196, 201, 210, 256, 338
de Valois, Ninette—120
de Vega, Lope—296, 302, 306
Develin, William—263
Devereaux, Jack—25, 31
Devereaux, John Drew—143, 217
Devereaux, William—22, 32, 48, 49, 82
Deverell, John—107
deVigny, Alfred—208
Devil and Daniel Webster, The—219
Devil Came From Dublin, The—283
Devil in the Cheese—142, 167
Devil Is an Ass, The—430, 438
Devil Passes, The—181, 185
Devil's Advocate, The—326, 331, 381
Devil's Disciple, The—68, 117, 174, 219, 223, 268, 302, 389, 416, 429, 430, 436, 445, 453
Devil's General, The—283
Devil's Island—437
Devils, The—327, 335, 336, 408, 446, 452, 467
Devil, The—42, 48, 51, 181, 412, 414
Devil Within, The—138
Devine, George—214, 222, 223, 269, 273, 278, 284, 285, 290, 295, 296, 300, 301, 302, 303, 305, 306, 307, 311, 312, 317, 318, 321, 334, 340, 346, 362
Devi, Ragina—112
De Vito, Danny—380
Devitt, Nina—157
Devlin, William—206

Devonshire Cream—128
Devour the Snow—452
De Vries, Joseph—304
DeVries, Peter—276
Dewhurst, Colleen—301, 307, 321, 339, 340, 341, 365, 391, 393, 404, 411, 429
Dewhurst, Dorothy—244
Dewhurst, Keith—368, 445, 453
de Wilde, Brandon—276, 281, 404
DeWolfe and Kindler—418
DeWolfe, Billy—282, 304, 327
de Wolfe, Drina—2, 15
de Wolfe, Elsie—6, 15, 21
Dews, Peter—316, 367, 381, 387, 388, 403, 415, 427, 431, 438, 453
Dews, Williams—437
Dexter, John—311, 317, 318, 333, 334, 335, 340, 342, 346, 348, 351, 361, 381, 395, 396, 398, 406, 407, 408, 411, 416, 422, 434, 452
Dexter, Lynn—227
Deyo, Blanche—27
De Young, Michael H.—39
Dhery, Robert—295
Diaghilev, Serge—451, 455
Dial "M" for Murder—276, 277, 286
Dialogues—353
Diamand, Peter—368
Diamond, I. A. L.—372
Diamond Lil—156, 258
Diamond Orchid—351
Diamond Studs—420
"Diamonds Are a Girl's Best Friend"—263
Diana of Dobsons—43
Diane—215
Diarmuid and Grainne—3, 160, 167, 172
Diary of a Madman, The—340
Diary of a Rat—444
Diary of a Scoundrel, The—264
Diary of Anne Frank, The—65, 293, 300, 430
Diary of Adam and Eve, The—358
Diary of a Superfluous Man—357
Dibdin-Pitt, George—449
Dicey, Paul—66
Dickens, Charles—61, 121, 122, 245, 291, 312, 440, 445, 455, 457
Dickerson, Glenda—447
Dickey, Paul—69
Dick Hope—2
Dickie, Murray—274
Dickinson, Emily—252, 426
Dickson, Dorothy—92, 101, 114, 120, 127, 133, 142, 201, 208, 231, 283
Dickson, Muriel—193
Dick Turpin—390, 391, 398
Dick Whittington—38, 45, 59, 122, 128, 137, 179, 184, 193, 198, 214, 225, 250, 265, 280, 313, 383, 408, 444, 449
Dick Whittington and His Cat—232
Dictator, The—19, 81
Dido and Aeneas—8, 274
Die Bruecke—376
Die Buchse Pandoras—391
Die Dreigroschenoper—303
Die Fledermaus—167, 182, 230, 245
Die Geschiedene Frau—53
Die Kino-Koenigin—72
Die Kluge—455
Die Mitschuldigen—360
Diener, Joan—194
Die Raeuber—64
Die Ratten—360
Dierdre—449
Dies Committee—215
Dietrich, Marlene—348, 435
Dietz, Howard—142, 148, 163, 171, 181, 191, 195, 201, 206, 257, 338
Dietz, Kyra—410
Die Unberatenen—367
Die Weber—27
Die Wildente—27
Diffen, Ray—454
Difference of Opinion—340
Diff'rent—101, 109, 136, 189, 213
Digby, Richard—381

Digges, Dudley—47, 96, 99, 101, 103, 117, 120, 121, 145, 152, 160, 163, 208, 211, 222, 232, 247
Dighton, John—272
Dignam, Mark—276, 409, 415, 443
Dignon, Edward—143
Dillingham, Charles—15, 34, 55, 56, 61, 62, 78, 82, 93, 98, 99, 112, 129, 130, 190, 194
Dillman, Bradford—298
Dillon, Gladys—88
Dillon, Melinda—332
DiLuca, Dino—276
Dime a Dozen—332
"Dinah"—119
Dinehart, Allan—92, 148, 221
Ding and Co.—193
Dingo—368, 429, 444
Dinner at Eight—181, 187, 189, 229, 361, 376
Dinner With the Family—305
Dinny and the Witches—325
Dinros, Dorothy—391
Dionisotti, Paola—453
Diplomacy—73, 128, 188
Dippers—114
Directions to Servants—444
Director of the Opera, The—409
Director, The—273
Dirtiest Show in Town, The—385, 394
Dirty Linen/New-Found-Land—427, 434, 441
Dirty Work—182
Disabled—395
Discher, M. Willson—228
Disciplines of War, The—316
Disenchanted, The—309, 319
Disher, Maurice Wilson—384
Disher, M. Willson—96
Dish Ran Away, The—267
Dishy, Bob—400
Disintegration of James Cherry, The—387, 424
Dispatches—452
Displaced Person, The—358
Disraeli—56, 98, 250
Disraeli, Benjamin—120
Distaff Side, The—188, 191, 199
Distant Drums—181
District Attorney, The—233
Ditrichstein, Leo—47, 52, 66, 67, 74, 102
Diversion—159
Divinas Palabras—439
Divorce a la Carte—340
Divorced Woman, The—53
Divorce Me, Darling*—346
Divorcons-nous—359
Dixey, Henry E.—25, 115, 122, 144
Dix, Frank—54, 59, 81, 85
Dixie to Broadway—125
Dixon, Adele—206, 213, 232
Dixon, Lee—234
Dixon, Marjorie—127
Dixon, Thomas, Jr.—30, 92
Dizenzo, Charles—376, 388
Dobbie, Alan—333, 395, 438
Dobe, John—455
Dobie, Alan—290, 292, 314, 316, 318
Doble, Frances—182, 191
Dock Brief, The—310
Dockstader, Lew—9
Doctor and the Devils, The—335
Doctor Faustus—53, 135, 249, 254, 207, 260, 329, 349, 373, 388, 391, 417, 454, 455
Doctor in Spite of Himself—241
Doctor in the House—299
Doctor's Boy, The—232
Doctor's Office, The—93
Doctor's Dilemma, The—33, 33, 150, 173, 185, 218, 228, 231, 297, 295, 302, 341, 360, 381, 402, 422, 428
Doctors of Philosophy—336
Doctor Without Medicine—241
Dodd, Lee Wilson—118, 130
Dodge Boys, The—440
Dodge, D. Frank—10

478

Dodger Theatre—448
"Do-Do-Do"—142
Dodsworth—190, 194, 212, 411
Dog Accident—379
Dog Beneath the Skin, The—201, 256, 412
Dogg's Hamlet/Cahoot's Macbeth—451
Dog Ran Away, The—439
Doherty, Brian—205
Do I Hear a Waltz?—351, 418
"Do I Love You?"—217
Dolan, Peggy—99
Dolan, Phil—206
Dolan, Robert Emmett—262, 332
Dolin, Anton—143, 159, 240
"Doll and the Golliwog, The"—178
Dollar Princess, The—47, 49
Doll House Fedora, A—220
Doll's House, A—44, 45, 173, 184, 209, 245, 249, 285, 340, 395, 399, 403, 408, 421, 456
Dolly, Edward—114, 116
Dolly Sisters—56, 101, 107, 108, 114, 125
Dolly Varden—10, 16
Dolman, Dorothy—127
Dolman, Richard—187
Dolorme, Daniele—353
Dolphin Theatre Company—397, 402, 407, 417, 422, 424, 440
Doltrice, Michele—348, 354
Dominant Sex, The—193
Dominican College—331
Dominion Drama Festival—189
Dominion Theatre, The—169
Domino Revue, The—285
Dom Kobiet (The House of Women)—306
Don—49
Donahue, Jack—164, 174
Donald, James—252, 253, 340, 341
Donaldson Award—391, 404, 412, 418
Donaldson, Walter—157
Donath, Ludwig—370
Donat, Peter—161, 421
Donat, Richard—413
Donat, Robert—159, 179, 188, 219, 245, 246, 250, 254, 283, 313
Don Carlos—97, 349
Donehue, Vincent J.—282, 309, 332
Dones, Gwendolyn—220
Don Giovanni—260, 360
Don Juan—188, 192, 301, 312, 340, 388, 404, 445
Don Juan Comes Back from War—445, 451
Don Juan in Love—410
Don Juan in Hell—37, 214, 249, 250, 275, 279, 335, 407, 408
Donkey's Years—427
Donlan, Yolande—247, 258, 268
Donleavy, J. P.—315
Donlevy, Brian—125, 186
Donnay—90
Donnelly, Donal—316, 324, 339, 357, 442
Donnelly, Dorothy—17, 87, 106, 118, 126, 129, 149
Donnelly, Ruth—73
Donner, Clive—90
Donohue, Jack—240, 298
Donohue, Nancy—421
Donohue, Walter—381, 403, 446, 453
Do Not Pass Go—360
Donovan Affair, The—141
Don Perlimplin—318
Don Quixote—37, 44, 382, 415
Don't Bother Me, I Can't Cope—400
Don't Drink the Water—358
Don't Just Lie There, Say Something!—394
Don't Let Summer Come—348
Don't Listen, Ladies—258
Don't Play Us Cheap!—400
Dooley Boys—101
Dooley, Ray—124, 157, 191
Doone, Rupert—197, 218
Doormats—63

Dora—128
Dorane, Ward—191
Dore, Alexander—328, 359, 371, 379
Dorelli, Johnny—444
Dormen Theatre—396
Doro, Marie—32, 61
Dorothea Baird Repertory—33
Dorothy—394
Dorothy and the Bitch—435
Dorothy Chandler Pavilion, The—350
Dorothy o' the Hall—26
Dorothy Vernon of Haddon Hall—26
D'Orsay, Dorothy—115
D'Orsay, Laurence—14, 43
Dors, Diana—387
Dorst, Tankred—408, 420
Dos Passos, John—140, 321
Dossor, Alan—414, 427, 437
Dostoievsky, Feodor Mikhailovich—53, 122, 249, 289
Dotrice, Roy—327, 330, 353, 354, 365, 366, 401, 434
Doty, Charles—30
Double Dealer, The—317, 379, 445
Double Door—186, 191
Double Edge—421
Double Image—299
Double Life, The—313
Doughgirls, The—230, 238
Douglas—269
Douglas, Cecil—366
Douglas, Craig—335
Douglas, Felicity—289, 315, 352, 366
Douglas, Jerry—399
Douglas, Kenneth—21, 26, 63
Douglas, Kirk—339, 396
Douglas, Lord Alfred—421
Douglas, Melvyn—171, 185, 190, 191, 262, 273, 276, 314, 320
Douglas, Michael—395
Douglas, Paul—364
Douglas, Robert—186, 187, 247, 318
Douglass, Margaret—240
Douglas, Stephen—244
Douglas, Tom—113
Douglas, Wallace—277, 288,, 289, 315, 365, 394
Douglas, Warren—379
Dove, John—417, 438, 443, 455
Dover Road, The—107, 114, 116
Dover Street to Dixie—120
Dove, The—144
Dovey, Alice—52
Dowager Duchess of York—303
Dowd, Elwood P.—422
Dowerrless Bride, The—44
Dowling, Eddie—112, 141, 149, 191, 212, 244, 297
Dowling, Jennette—276
Down, Angela—430, 450
Down by the River Where the Water-lillies are Disfigured Every Day—422
Downes, E.—4
Downey, Ella—145
Downie, John—416
Downs, Jane—372
Downs, Johnny—244
Down the Arches—390
"Down Where the Watermelon Grows"—51
Doyle, Arthur Conan—17, 27, 32, 48, 49, 53, 84, 120, 414
Doyle, Len—217
Doyle, Monte—333
Doyle, Tony—439
D'Oyly Carte, Richard—9. Opera Company—44, 127, 173, 184, 193, 202, 218, 224, 228, 249, 255, ,260, 264, 269, 273, 285, 296, 302, 306, 313, 330, 334, 335, 346, 349, 355, 366, 369, 373, 424, 429, 446
Do You Love Me?—440
Do You Turn Somersaults?—427
Drabble, Margaret—380
Dracula—135, 150, 189, 219, 401, 432, 434, 440, 447

Drago, Kathleen—63, 76
Dragon, The—96, 340, 368
Drain, Kate—90
Drake—63
Drake, Alfred—205, 216, 217, 221, 234, 238, 243, 247, 258, 282, 306, 347, 354, 406, 423
Drake, Charlie—330
Drake, Ervin—344, 371
Drake, Fabia—127, 151, 189, 212, 250
Drake, Temple—314
Drama—98
Drama at Inish—193, 285
Drama City—31
Drama Critics' Circle Award—195, 199, 217, 225, 233-4, 238, 252, 256, 261, 262, 266, 272, 280-1, 283, 287-8, 292-4, 298, 300, 305, 309, 311, 313-15, 319, 320-2, 325, 327, 350, 356, 378
Drama of the Nativity and the Massacre of the Innocents, The—98
Drama of Job, The—68
Drama Society—80
Dramatic Soundings—362
Dramatic Workshop—224
Dramatis Personae—383
Dramatists' Guild—98, 147, 154, 204, 256, 331, 350, 448
Dr. Angelus—253
Draper, Ronald—347
Draper, Ruth—46, 153, 176, 293, 303
Drawing Room Players—116
Drayton, Alfred—95, 99, 107, 178, 218
Dr. Dolittle's Play—153
Dream—131, 214
Dream Girl, The—124, 224, 251, 273, 412
Dreaming Dust, The—223, 316
Dream of Peter Mann, The—323
Dream on Monkey Mountain, The—395
Dream Play, The—306, 396
Dreams of a Mischievous Heart Shipwrecked on Illusion—451
Dreamy Kid, The—135
Dreiser, Theodore—107, 147
Dresdel, Sonia—263, 279
Dres, John—69
Dressed Like an Egg—440
Dresser, Louise—30, 71
Dressler, Marie—20, 30, 52, 62, 101, 117, 142, 194
Drever, Constance—48
Drewe, Evelyn—117
Drew, John—1, 10, 30, 35, 43, 57, 72, 78, 107, 122, 130, 131, 137, 153, 238
Drew, Larry—284
Drew, Louisa Lane—153
Drew, Louise—15, 71
Drew, Maurice—15
Drew, Mrs. John—55, 123, 194
Drexler Plays, The—388
Drexler, Rosalyn—373, 374, 388, 451
Dreyfuss, Richard—454
Drifters, The—102
Driller, Eleanore—49
Drink from an Amethyst Cup—366
"Drinking Song"—126
Drinkwater, John—90, 94, 104, 109, 114, 120, 122, 147, 152, 158, 183, 188, 193, 209, 237, 241, 242
Drischell, Ralph—345
Drivas, Robert—332, 371, 393, 413, 437
Drive-In—387
Driver, Donald—371, 382
Driver, John—449, 450
Driver, Tom—350
Driving a Girl to Destruction—60
Dr. Angelus—253
Dr. Jekyll and Mr. Hyde—22
Dr. Johnson and Monsieur de Paris—44
Dr. King—383
Dr. Knock—159
Dromgoole, Patrick—345, 451

Dr. Selvay's Magic Theatre—400
Drubows, Herbert—92
Drugger, Abel—254
Druid Circle, The—252, 424
Druid's Rest, The—241
Drummond, Alice—390
Drums in the Night—367, 387, 410
Drunkard, The—188, 190, 193, 208, 228, 260, 283, 319, 323, 332, 349, 388
Drunk Man Looks at the Thistle, A—366
Drury, Allen—321
Drury Lane Theater—9, 33, 46, 67 76, 79, 81
Drury, Major W. P.—43
Dryden, John—135, 192, 249, 317, 354, 438, 439
Dry Rot—289
Dubarry—7, 13
Dubarry, The—183, 255
DuBarry Was A Lady—130, 217, 231, 233, 398
Duberman, Martin—339, 374
DuBois, Raoul Pene—258, 282
DuBois, William—181, 213
Dublin Drama League—91, 89, 90, 91, 121
Dublin Festival Company, The—324
Dublin Gate Theatre—153, 160, 166, 167, 173, 175, 228, 232, 237, 242, 245, 249, 250, 255, 260, 264, 279, 283, 295, 296, 300, 301, 306, 311, 316, 335, 348, 373, 375, 380, 396, 402, 408, 416, 422, 428, 436, 447, 453, 455
Dublin Revue—178
Dublin Theater Society—28
Dublin Theatre Festival—394, 431, 440
DuBois, Raoul Pene—258, 282
DuBois, William—181, 213
Duck Variations—426, 446
Ducovny, Amran—365
Duc Song—415
Dude—400
Dudley, Bernard—126
Dudley, Bessie—192
Dudley, Bide—83
Dudley, John H. M.—85
Dudley, Philip—372
Duel of Angels—310, 320, 325
Duel, The—30
Duenna, The—128, 290
Duerrenmatt, Friedrich—309, 313, 318, 323, 325, 332, 339, 354, 359, 366, 395, 409, 410, 441
Duet for Two Hands—245, 249
Duet for Solo Voice—388
Duff, J. C.—10
Duff, Lesley—421
Duff-MacCormick, Cara—406
Duffy, Jimmy—132, 193
Duffy, Margaret—380
Dugan, William Francis—154
du Gard, Martin—89
Duguild, Peter—312, 317
Duhamel, Georges—121
Duke in Darkness, The—239
Duke of Killicrankie, The—20
Duke of York—376
Duke, Patty—314, 319
Dukes, Ashley—134, 165, 178, 179, 192, 197, 214, 132, 269, 273, 358
Dukes, David—409, 450
Dukes, Lulu—235
Duke, Vernon—158, 170, 182, 190, 201, 222, 227, 276, 300, 383
Dula, Tom—454
Dulcimer, Julian—186
Dulcy—105, 116, 120
Dullea, Keir—318, 378, 417
Du Marrier Festival—416
Dumas, Alexander—37, 44, 45, 50, 54, 90, 92, 156, 173, 208, 296, 306
Dumas, Alexander, fils—22, 23, 45, 323, 329, 341, 394, 411

du Maurier, Daphne—38, 222, 224, 244, 250, 259, 268
Du Maurier, George—2, 31, 103
Du Maurier, Gerald—7, 8, 16, 22, 30, 33, 38, 43, 47, 52, 53, 57, 63, 75, 79, 82, 84, 95, 102, 107, 114, 119, 127, 135, 142, 143, 147, 150, 158, 182, 188, 194
Du Maurier, Major—48
du Maurier, Muriel (Beaumont)—38
du Maurier Council for the Performing Arts—416
Dumb Show, A—445
Dumbwaiter, The—322, 332
Dumke, Ralph—349
Duna, Steffi—188
Dunaway, Faye—352
Dunbar, Paul Laurence—14, 98
Dunbar Theatre, The—123, 162
Duncan, Archie—253
Duncan, Augustin—92, 105, 111, 140
Duncan, Isadora—3
Duncan, John—417
Duncan, Martin—421, 440
Duncan, Ronald—246, 250, 253, 301, 306
Duncan, Rosetta—100, 126
Duncan, Sandy—372, 388, 455
Duncan Sisters—100, 126
Duncan, Todd—196, 212, 262
Duncan, Vivian—1200, 126
Duncan, William C.—110, 119
Dundee Repertory Theatre—317
Dundy Elmer—29
Dunham, Joanna—334
Dunham, Katherine—258
Dunlop, Frank—329, 341, 344, 346, 354, 361, 367, 368, 373, 375, 387, 388, 390, 395, 397, 403, 404, 406, 414, 415, 424, 436, 437, 445, 448, 455, 456
Dunmow Players—68
Dunn, Emma—36, 106
Dunnigan, Bill—210
Dunning, Philip—141, 155, 190
Dunn, Mary—218
Dunn, Michael—339
Dunnock, Mildred—244, 247, 262, 273, 282, 339, 342, 359, 386, 431
Dunsany, Lord Edward—54, 58, 68, 80, 95, 107, 218
Duplex, The—401
Dupont, Jacques—66
Dupree, Minnie—56, 112
Duquesnel, Felix—76
Durang, Christopher—403, 420, 429, 436, 437, 442
Durango Flash, The—436
Durante, Jimmy—171, 196, 200, 216
Durante, Ted—313
Duras, Marguerite—360, 379, 386, 396, 429, 431
Durbridge, Francis—394
Durbridge, Francis—394
Durning, Charles—342, 347, 379
Durrell, Lawrence—329
Duryea, Dan—216, 376
Dusa, Fish, Stas and Vi—431
Duse, Eleanora—3, 13, 16, 18, 27, 29, 122, 123, 238, 363
Dussarrat, Michael—452
d'Usseau, Arnaud—234, 238, 244, 251, 281
Dusseldorf Schauspielhaus—264
Dust Under Our Feet—284
Dusty Ermine—201
Dutch Courtesan, The—289, 316, 348, 349
Dutchman—347, 366
Dutch Uncle—379
Dutfield, Kenneth—114
Duty—90
Duvall, Robert—332, 353, 357, 434
Dux, Pierre—453
Dvorak, Anton—299
Dwarfs, The—342, 359, 417
Dwyer, Ada—35
Dyall, Franklin—114, 143, 151, 191, 192

Dyall, Valentine—339
Dybbuk, The—133, 145, 147, 297, 314, 347, 353, 436
Dyer, Charles—334, 343, 361, 408
Dyer, Doug—395, 398
Dylan—344, 350
Dylan Thomas Growing Up—294
Dynamo—163
Dynamo: The Story of the Vassar Theatre—384
Dynasts, The—72
Dyne, Michael—345
Dyrenforth, James—245
Dysart, Richard—340

Each Had Six Wings—347
Each His Own Wilderness—311
Eadie, Dennis—27, 47, 53, 56, 72, 79, 83, 99, 102, 103, 115, 137
"Eadie Was a Lady"—182
Eagels, Jeanne—87, 113, 128, 130, 148, 168
Eagle Has Two Heads, The—250, 252, 253, 453
Eagle, Oscar—19, 117
Eames, Clare—133, 145, 151, 152, 174
E. and O.E.—108
Earl and the Girl, The—16
Earl Carroll's Sketch Book—164, 195
Earl Carroll Vanities—116, 123, 125, 130, 132, 141, 157, 170, 176, 181, 225
Earle, Josephine—88
Earle, Virginia—25
Earl of Pawtucket, The—14
Early Morning—373, 379, 415
Early To Bed—234, 237
Early Worm, The—46
Earnshaw, Catherine—207
Earth Between, The—166
Earthly Paradise—385
Earthquake, The—52
Earth, The—77
Earthworms—430
Easiest Way, The—47, 98
East Cultural Centre—412
Easter—146, 245
Easter 1916—173, 183
East Is West—88, 116, 161
East Lynne—268, 376, 416
East of Suez—114
Easton, Richard—332, 373, 381
Easton, Wallas—268, 294
Eastward Ho—95, 185, 336
Eastward in Eden—252, 261
East Wind, The—366
Easy Come, Easy Go—133, 139
Easy Play in Three Acts—57
Easy Virtue—133, 143
Eaton, Mary—149
Eaton, Walter Pritchard—119, 307
Ebb, Fred—351, 358, 371, 410, 420, 434
Ebb Tide—279
Ebert, Joyce—328, 342, 395
Ebsen, Buddy—181, 216
Ebsen, Vilma—181
Eccentricities of a Nightingale, The—427
Eccentricities of Davey Crockett, The—261
Eccentric Lord Comberdene—53
Echegaray, José—12, 153
Eckert, Allan W.—409
Eckert, Jules—82
Eclipse—447
Ecole des Femmes, L'—273
Ecoutez Bien, Messieurs—284
Ecstasy of Rita Joe, The—365, 424
Eddinger, Wallace—47, 66, 96, 141, 143
Eddington, Paul—443
Eddison, Robert—207, 218, 219, 295, 354, 415
Eddowes, Joan—222
Edelstein, Gertrude—363
Eden—428
Eden End—192, 196, 260, 415

Eden, Guy—49
Eder, Richard—441
Edeson, Robert—6, 10, 25, 87, 112
Edgar, David—401, 415, 428, 429, 430, 438, 444, 450, 451, 453
Edgar, Mariott—192
Edge, George—295
Edge o' Beyond, The—108
Edge of Reason—348
Edginton, May—102, 114
Ediss, Connie—26
Edmondson, James—430, 441
Edney, Florence—52
Edouin, Willie—21, 26, 27, 45
Education of Mr. Pipp, The—25
Education of Skinny Spew, The—388
Edwardes, Felix—94
Edwardes, George—2, 48, 51, 53, 63
Edward, Gus—25, 36
Edward IV—341, 346
Edward, My Son—253, 257, 265
Edwards, D. Emyr—409
Edwards, George—63, 67, 72
Edwards, Gus—440
Edwards, Hilton—153, 160, 162, 166, 167, 174, 179, 184, 188, 192, 202, 223, 245, 259, 260, 273, 274, 275, 279, 285, 291, 296, 312, 316, 334, 341, 348, 368, 396, 402, 408, 416, 422, 447, 455
Edwards, Jack—120
Edwards, Jimmy—268, 276, 336, 359, 402
Edwards, Julian—10, 16, 20
Edwards, Rex—376
Edwards, Sherman—378
Edward the Second—27, 127, 301, 348, 373, 382, 417, 424
Edward VIII—401
Edwin, Grace—27
Ed Wynn Carnival, The—104
Effect of Gamma Rays on Man-in-the-Moon Marigolds, The—385, 403, 446
Egan, Michael—367
Egan, Peter—374, 388, 390, 435, 455
Eggar, Samantha—334
Eggerth, Marta—237, 295
Egg, The—337
Egnos, Bertha—421
Egoists—109
Eh?—346
Eight Bells—187
1808 Walnut Street Theatre—399
Eighty in the Shade—315
Eileen—82
Einen Jux will er sich machen—373
Ein Palast Revolution—27
Ein Rabensvater—27
Eisdell, Hubert—127
Eisengery, Emanual—206
Eisenhower, Dwight D.—313
Eisler, Hanns—221
Elaine—68
Elcar, Dana—310, 332
Eldee, Lilian—21
Elder Brother, The—69
Elder, Eldon—128, 293, 304
Elder Brother, The—69
Elder, Lonne III—379, 424
Elder Miss Blossom, The—198
Elder Statesman, The—311, 312
Eldest Son, The—73
Eldridge, Florence—111, 112, 140, 153, 216, 227, 269, 271, 247, 298
Electra—32, 44, 249, 273, 280, 348,

349, 361, 366, 397, 430
Electronic Nigger, The—373
Elephant in the House, The—402
Elephant Man, The—439, 449
Elevating a Husband—61
Eleven Plus—322
Elgar, Avril—366
Elgar, Edward—121
El Grande de Coca Cola—406
Eliot, Samuel Jr.—136
Eliot, Thomas Stearns (T. S.)—197, 202, 207, 214, 217, 250, 264, 266, 270, 283, 285, 301, 311, 312, 313, 325, 355, 359, 360, 374, 375, 376, 382, 403, 451, 454
Elizabeth of England—178
Elizabeth I—400, 428, 451
Elizabeth Steps Out—237
Elizabethans, The—391
Elizabeth the Queen—171, 180, 318, 361
Elizabethan Stage Circle, The—167
Elizabethan Stage Society, The—8, 54, 59
Elizabethan Theatre—110, 423
Elizondo, Hector—367
Elkins, Hillard—344, 395
Ellen—395
Ellen, Vera—237
Ellerbe, Harry—252
Elliman, Yvonne—393
Ellinger, Desiree—107
Ellington, Duke—247
Elliot, Arthur—83
Elliot, Colin—334
Elliot, Michael—316, 329, 336, 375, 451
Elliott, Denholm—247, 258, 263, 267, 272, 281, 285, 295, 316, 327, 414, 421, 437, 451, 452
Elliott, Gertrude—3, 9, 11, 13, 15, 27, 37, 43, 45, 57, 67, 69, 98, 101
Elliott, Madge—151, 158, 165, 242, 245
Elliott, Maxine—15, 80, 97, 108
Elliott, Patricia—381, 451
Elliott, Sarah Barnwell—21
Elliott, Shawn—371
Elliott, William—82
Ellis, A. E.—417
Ellis, Beth—57
Ellis, Catherine—400
Ellis, Charles—126
Ellis, Colin—329
Ellis, Edith—135
Ellis, Edward—68
Ellis, Evelyn—149
Ellis, Fred—73
Ellis, George—167
Ellis, Harold—27
Ellis, Mary—125, 156, 218, 236, 258, 264, 278, 289, 295
Ellis, Maurice—208
Ellis, Melville—30
Ellis, Michael—295
Ellison, Mary—108
Ellis, Vivian—133, 143, 144, 165, 166, 172, 177, 182, 188, 192, 207, 213, 242, 248, 253, 273, 282, 294
Ellis, Walter—75, 172, 236
Elmer Gantry—385
Elocution of Benjamin Franklin, The—443
Eloquent Dempsy, The—54
Elsie Janis at Home—129
Elsie, Lily—49, 57, 151, 159
Elsom, Anita—94, 141
Elsom, Isobel—72, 134, 218, 274
El Teatro Campesino—356
Eltinge Follies, The—185
Eltinge, Julian—23, 45, 56, 65, 71, 229
Elton, Jane—15
Elusive Angel, The—440
Elvis—435
Elwes, Eva—96
Embers—146
Embezzled Heaven—243
Emblin-Walker, J.—116

Embury, Phyllis—53
Emden, Henry—5, 49
Emens, Homer—11, 19, 25, 26, 41, 52
Emerson, Faye—269, 302, 311
Emerson, John—52, 118, 141, 143, 177, 302
Emery, Gilbert—106, 130
Emery, John—194, 273, 356
Emery, Katherine—191, 212
Emery, Winifred—12, 33, 49, 57, 107
Emigres—430
Emil and the Detectives—324, 336
Emily—68, 394
Emma—244
Emmanuel, Belita—293
Emmanuel, Ivor—293
Emney, Joan—114, 116
Emny, Fred—218, 231, 245
Emperor Henry IV—408, 412
Emperor Jones, The—100, 110, 135, 144, 189, 232, 368, 432
Emperor's New Clothes, The—281, 286
Empire Builders, The—335
Empire Theatre Stock Company—146
Empty Sleeve—75
Emu in Pantoland—432,
Enchanted, The—266, 290
Enchanted Aisles—237
Enchanted Cottage, The—113, 117
Enchanted Night, The—347
Enchanted Trousers, The—96
Enchanteur Pourrissant—408
Enchantress, The—56
Encounter in the Wilderness—447
End as a Man—281
Endecott and the Red Cross—373
En Deshabille—69
Endgame—312, 348, 389, 394, 396, 422, 429, 437, 447
End of Day—336
End of Me Old Cigar—422
End of Summer—200, 204
End of the Beginning, The—219
End of the War—442
Enemies—197, 396
Enemy in Our Midst, The—75
Enemy of the People, An—152, 193, 218, 269, 368, 394, 422, 423
Enemy, The—132, 147, 224
Enfants d'Edouard, Les—278
Engaged—422
Engel, Alexander—192
Engel, Erich—301
Engel, Susan—443, 451
England, Alfred—8
England, Barry—379
England Expects—72
Englander, Ludwig—10, 19, 15, 20, 31, 43
England My Own—447
England, Paul—126
Engle, Alexander—42
Engle, Lehman—208
Engles, Heinz—378
English Dramatic Critics, The—256
Englishman Amused, The—418
Englishman's Home, An—48
English National Opera—377
English Nell—2
English Opera Group, The—306
English Stage Company—300, 303, 306, 307, 312, 317, 318, 325, 329, 362, 363, 430
English Stage Society—307, 312, 314
Enlisted Men's Contest—234
Enquist, Per Olov—434, 445, 446
Enrico IV—408
Enter a Free Man—372, 455
Enter Kiki—107, 120
Enter Laughing—338
Enter Madame—99, 110
Enters, Agna—112
Enter Solly Gold—387
Entertainer, The—305, 309, 313, 417
Entertaining Mr. Sloane—345, 351, 421, 423
Enter the Hero—84

Ephron, Henry—64, 241, 327
Ephron, Phoebe—241, 327, 399
Epiphany—338
Episode, An—57
"Episode in Cavalry Barracks"—53
Epitaph for George Dillon—309, 310, 319, 402
Epsom Downs—439
Epstein, Alvin—368
Epstein, Julius—239
Epstein, Philip—239
Equity, Actor's—118, 392
Equity Library Theatre—297, 355, 362, 368, 376, 383, 390, 404, 410, 418, 424, 431, 440, 447, 455
Equity Players—119, 121
Equus—406, 413, 425, 429, 433, 436
Era Almanack and Annual, The—50
Erckmann—95
Erdegeist—391
Erdman, Jean—333, 452
Erdmann, Nikolai—453
Ergo—373
Eric, Elspeth—217
Ericson, John—271
Ericson, Leif—217, 281, 320
Erlanger, Abe (A. L.)—6, 7, 10, 13, 39, 70, 80, 86, 98, 130, 149, 154, 155, 168, 185, 203
Ernotte, Andre—452
Erpingham Camp, The—365
Errol, Leon—56, 62, 71, 78, 82, 107
Erskin, Chester—170
Erskine, James—7
Erskine, John—282
Erskine, Wallace—66, 88
Erstwhile Susan—78
Ervine, John—58, 59, 68, 76, 92, 104, 114, 115, 130, 136, 165, 166, 174, 197, 207, 212, 242, 398
Escapade—282
Escape—143, 184, 411
Escape Me Never—188
Escorial—347
Esmond, Annie—78, 107, 151, 159
Esmond, H. V.—7, 12, 16, 21, 57, 79, 89, 140
Esmond, Jill—172, 186
Espert, Nuria—439
Espionage—197
Essays in Mime—278
Esterman, Laura—414
Eternal City, The—12
Eternal Jew, The—145
Eternal Mystery, The—69
Eternal Road, The—205, 209
Ethan Frome—200, 204, 209
Ethel, Agnes—17
Ethel Barrymore Theatre, The—163
Etherege, George—396, 452
Ethiopia—204
Ethiopian Art Theatre—121
Etting, Ruth—148, 157, 170, 176, 447
Ettlinger, Don—394
Eubie!—442
Eugenia—304
Euripides—15, 27, 32, 63, 108, 166, 197, 208, 249, 255, 260, 347, 349, 353, 355, 360, 361, 366, 368, 388, 397, 407, 409, 417, 423, 436, 438, 439, 444, 453
Europeans, The—304
Eurydice—268
Eustace, Jennie—36
Evangeline—129, 248
Evangelist, The—35, 341
Evans, Alice—76
Evans, Dillon—381
Evans, Dorothea—76
Evans, Edith—68, 96, 100, 107, 111, 113, 123, 128, 130, 144, 145, 152, 159, 165, 179, 181, 183, 184, 194, 202, 207, 218, 222, 249, 250, 260, 263, 272, 289, 294, 311, 312, 316, 329, 344, 347, 349, 373, 433
Evans, Frank—341
Evans, George—45
Evans, Graham—302, 307
Evans, Hugh—283, 335, 341, 381
Evans, Jessie—274

480

EVans, Lyle—212
Evans, Madge—82, 150, 212, 234
Evans, Martin—262
Evans, Maurice—159, 188, 193, 197, 200, 207, 214, 215, 218, 228, 246, 255, 264, 265, 268, 269, 273, 277, 302, 318, 321, 335
Evans, Michael—272
Evans, Monica—351
Evans, Nancy—260
Evans, Norman—232
Evans, Peter—434, 451
Evans, Ray—309
Evans, Rex—159
Evans, Tenniel—452
Evans, Wilbur—262, 287
Evans, Will—113
Evans, Winifred—152, 156, 167, 244
Evaristi, Marcella—435, 444
Evasion of Women, An—380
Eveling, Stanley—340, 366, 379, 394, 396, 401, 410, 415
Evelyn, Clara—62
Evelyn, Judith—217, 276, 285, 369
Evelyn, Walter—122
Evening for Merlin Finch, An—376
Evening Light—
Evening of Cole Porter, An—416
Evening of Rubbish, An—339
Evening with Beatrice Lillie, An—276, 289
Evening with G.B.S., An—361
Evening With Hinge and Bracket, An—417
Evening With Joyce Grenfell, An—456
Evening with Mike Nichols and Elaine May, An—321
Evening With Quentin Crisp, An—430
Evening with Richard Nixon and . . ., —400
Evensong—183
Eve of Liege, The—75
Eve of St. Mark, The—230, 238
Eve on Parade—218
Eve, Oscar—8
Everage, Edna—427
Everbody's Welcome—176, 180
Everest, Barbara—159, 165, 207
Everest Hotel, The—428
Ever Green—173, 210
Ever Open Door, The—67
Evershed-Martin, Leslie—319
Ever Since Paradise—253
Every Good Boy Deserves Favour—446, 450
Everyman—37, 53, 90, 153, 197, 265
Everyman and Roach—397
Everyman Company—103
Everyman Street Theatre—397, 403
Everyman Theatre—127, 167, 173
Everything—87
Everything in the Garden—334, 365, 377
Everywhere I Roam—212
Evett and Klein—120
Evett, Robert—26, 32, 62, 115
Evillene—420
Evita—443
Ewell, Tom—50, 196, 212, 252, 276, 304, 320
Ewing, Max—148
Examination, The—444
Excelsior—137
Excersion—205
Excess Baggage—404
Excitement—277
Exciting Adventures of Queen Dan-iella, The—424
Excursio—210
Exiles—131, 165, 229, 245, 390, 396, 409, 436
Exit the King—340, 373, 447
Expeditions One—348
Expedition to Pick Mushrooms, An—366
Expeditions Two: Home and Co-

lonial—353
Experience—71
Experimental Theatre, Inc.—256, 255, 257, 259
Expert, Nuria—402
Explorer, The—43
Expressin' Willie—445
Expresso Bongo—310
Eyen, Tom—385, 408, 413, 435
Eyes of the Heart, The—27
Eyes of Youth—82
Eye Winker, Tom Tinker—401
Eyre, Marjorie—193
Eyre, Peter—415, 417
Eyre, Richard—397, 421, 427, 438, 439
Eyre, Ronald—389, 391, 396, 406, 415, 417, 453
Eyre, Wilfred—166
Eysler, Edmund—74
Eytinge, Rose—60
Eyton, Frank—171, 177, 197, 218, 222, 236, 258

Faber, Beryl—43, 53
Faber, Leslie—74, 102, 108, 115, 126, 144, 150, 159
Fables Then and Now—399
Fabray, Nanette—226, 252, 257, 271
Fabri, G.—75
Fabulous Invalid, The—211
Face the Music—2, 181
Face Value—110
Factory Birds—439
Factory Theatre Lab—389, 392, 397
Fade Out—Fade In—344
Fagan, Barney—149
Fagan, Bernard J.—33
Fagan, James B.—50, 58, 77, 83, 96, 103, 106, 108, 109, 113, 137, 143, 214, 273
Faggot, The—406
Failures, The—119
Fain, Sammy—176, 180, 211, 216, 221, 227, 271, 293
Fairbanks, Douglas—13, 19, 25, 30, 31, 42
Fairbanks, Douglas Jr.—427
Fairbank, Spring—424
Fairbrother, Sydney—26, 102, 145, 165, 197
Fairchild, William—315
Fair Co-ed, The—47
Fairfax, Lettice—2, 7, 21, 26
Fairfax, Marion—46, 61
Fairfield, Robert—308
Fair Maid of the West, The—97, 103
Fair Quarrel, A—452
Fair Slaughter—437
Fair Weather Friends—430
Fairy, Marise—58
Fairy Tales of New York—340
Faith, Adam—428
Faithful, The—77, 95, 369
Faithful Heart, The—108
Faithfull, Marianne—366, 373
Faith Healer, The—52
Faith of Our Fathers—269
Fake, The—125, 126
Falcon and the Lady, The—116
Falconbridge and Lewsley—91
Falconer, John—256
Falkenhain, Patricia—310
Falk, Peter—344, 394
Fallada, Hans—408
Fallen Angels—134, 265, 300, 367
Fallen Fairies—49
Fall Guy, The—131, 137
"Falling in Love With Love"—212
Falling Upstairs—72
Fall, Leo—47, 49, 53, 56, 62, 111, 121
Fall of the House of Usher, The—415
Fallon, Thomas—112
Falls, Gregory—356
False Confessions, The—390
False Gods—50
Falsely True—59
Falstaff—53, 354, 360
Family, A—443

Family Affairs—192
Family Album—201, 391
Family and a Fortune, A—421
Family Business—442, 453
Family Cupboard, The—66
Family Dance, The—427
Family Failing—64
Family Fun—302
Family Man, A—107, 197
Family Mishmash, A—154
Family Portrait—216, 220
Family Reunion, The—217, 250, 301, 312, 451, 454
Family Ties: Wrong First Time and Never Right, Yet Again—439
Famine—379
Famous Blackbird Choir—192
Famous Five, The—296, 302
Famous Mrs. Fair, The—94, 104, 146
Fan and Two Candlesticks, A—77
Fanatics, The—150, 383, 411
Fancourt, Darrell—167, 232
Fancy Ball, The—276
Fancy Free—240, 272
Fand—37
Fando and Lis—340
Fane, Dorothy—41, 103
Fane, Maud—126
Fanghorn—366
Fanin, Kay—257
Fanlights, The—422
Fanny—141, 288, 292, 299, 411
Fanny's First Play—57, 114, 242, 301, 313, 354, 409
Fantana—25
Fantasies Take Flight—455
Fantastic Fricasee, A—115
Fantasticks, The—2, 136, 188, 295, 320, 356, 392, 425, 457
Fantastical Feats of Finn MacCool, The—417
Faraday, Philip Michael—32, 63
Farango, Peter—435, 450
Far Country, A—326, 331
Fardeau de la Liberte—90
Farebrother, Violet—97, 145, 299, 384
Farewell, Farewell, Eugene—315
Farewell Performance, A—69
Farewell Supper, A—57
Farewell To Arms, A—170
Farfetched Fables—269
Farjeon, Eleanor—201, 284
Farjeon, Herbert—61, 84, 201, 212, 218, 231, 284, 422
Farjeon, J. J.—135
Farjeon Reviewed—422
Farjeon's Little Revue—219
Farkas, Karl—244
Farkoa, Maurice—12
Farleigh, Lynn—415
Farley, Frederick—290
Farley, Morgan—124, 141, 178
Farmer, Peter—418
Farmer's Wife, The—125, 126, 367
Farmer Takes a Wife, The—191, 199
Farm Show, The—377
Farm, The—145, 410, 431
Farnum, Dustin—19
Farnum, Frank—105
Farnum, Marshall—30
Farnum, William—30, 48, 286
Farquhar, George—152, 174, 210, 237, 249, 264, 301, 316, 455
Farquhar, Malcolm—342, 367, 368, 372, 388, 389
Farquharson, Robert—137
Farrand, Jan—283
Farrar, Gwen—119, 151
Farr, Derek—333
Farrell, Charles—212, 227
Farrell, Glenda—172, 221, 398
Farrell, James—445
Farrell, June—256
Farrell, M. J.—212, 241, 263
Farrell, Paul—329
Farren, Nelly—23
Farren, William—45
Farrow, Mia—403, 429, 450

Farson, Daniel—368
Farther Off from Heaven—254
Fascinating Flora—35
Fascinating Foundling, The—273
"Fascinating Rhythm"—126
Fascinating Widow, The—56
Fase, Berkeley—263
Fashion—166, 415
Fassbinder, Rainer Werner—415, 430
Fassett, Jay—176
Fassnacht, Adolph—166
Fassnacht Family, The—166
Fatal Weakness, The—250, 256
Fata Morgana—124, 127
Father and the Boys—55
Father Malachy's Miracle—205
Father's Day—454
Father, The—59, 166, 199, 260, 264, 283, 346, 397, 408, 436, 452
Father Uxbridge Wants to Marry—368
Fauchois, Rene—50, 181
Faucit, Helen—85
Faulkner, William—307, 314, 319, 340
Fauquez, Arthur—354
Faun, The—68
Fausses Confidence, Les—274
Faust!—452
Faust—45, 79, 130, 153, 160, 173, 238, 264, 316, 328
Faust, Lotta—6, 55
Faust on Toast—109
Faversham, Julie Opp—45
Faversham, William—16, 26, 43, 71, 72, 180, 224
Favieres, Guy—87
Fawcett, Owen—23
Faye, Herbie—230, 272
Faye, Janina—314
Fayer, Eleanor—236
Fay, Frank—87, 112, 118, 235, 240, 330
Fay, W. G.—3, 13, 16, 17, 22, 159, 160, 205, 212
Fazan, Eleanor—391
Fear—69, 108
Fear, Arthur—182
Fearful Joy, A—43
Fearnley, John—374
Fear of Heaven, The—428
Featherstone, Vane—2, 40, 43
Feathertop—56
Febrier, Henri—93
Federal Theatre Project—46, 110, 194, 199, 204, 207, 208, 213, 215, 220, 384, 404
Fedora—13, 16, 220
Fedorovitch, Sophie—274
Feedlot—436
Feely, T. J.—348
Feibleman, Peter—333
Feiffer, Jules—358, 364, 372, 374, 378, 385, 426, 428, 436
Feingold, Michael—436
Feist, Gene—409, 430, 437, 453
Feldshuch, Tovah—418, 420
Felice—69
Felix, Hugo—16, 32, 67, 78
Fellini, Federico—357
Fellowship—144, 423
Fellowship of Players—136, 144
Female Detectives, The—137
Female Hun, The—89
Fenholt, Jeff—393
Fenn, Charles—289
Fennelly, Parker—124
Fenn, Frederick—21, 32, 53, 61, 63
Fenoglio, Edmo—422
Fenston, Joseph—223
Fenton, Leonard—447, 454
Fenton, Norman—442
Fenwick, Irene—66, 119
Ferber, Edna—74, 125, 150, 181, 189, 200, 210, 246, 273, 361, 376, 403, 424
Ferguson, Elsie—6, 99, 128, 330
Ferguson, Robert V.—27
Fergusson, Dina—212
Fergusson, Francis—160

Ferman, James—305
Fernald, C. B.—68, 127, 269
Fernald, John—188, 193, 259, 264, 268, 269, 274, 275, 276, 277, 279, 282, 284, 289, 290, 291, 295, 299, 301, 312, 347, 388
Fernandez, Alfonso—300
Fernandez, Bijou—330
Fern, Peter—340
Ferrar, Beatrice—12, 20
Ferrau, Mimi Aguglia—44
Ferrell, Conchata—413
Ferren, Helen—120
Ferrer, Jose—200, 216, 217, 224, 244, 257, 259, 260, 269, 271, 276, 285, 286, 295, 309, 315, 339
Ferrer, Mel—287, 291
Ferris, Walter—159, 164, 168
Festa d'Aderno—53
Festival Lennoxville—405
Festival of Underground Theatre—389
Festoons—430
Fetter, Ted—205
Feudalismo—44, 53
Feuer, Cy—59, 293, 352, 358
Feuillere, Edwige—296, 306, 373
Feu la Mere de Madame—306, 369
Few Memories, A—224
Few More Memories, A—224
Feydeau, Georges—79, 89, 102, 301, 302, 306, 314, 316, 353, 359, 369, 375, 380, 382, 396, 403, 410, 416, 428, 439, 445, 447, 453
Ffolliot-Ffoulkes—248
Ffrangcon-Davis, Gwen—110, 111, 115, 130, 144, 152, 155, 159, 172, 173, 192, 213, 217, 263, 289, 290, 301, 304, 335, 355
Fialka, Ladislav—373, 382
Fiastri, Iaia—444
Fichhandler, Thomas—270, 365
Fichhandler, Zelda—270, 303, 365, 392
Fictional Account of the Lives of Richard and Sarah Allen, A—428
Fiddle-dee-dee—1
Fiddler on the Roof—344, 356, 365, 405, 432, 441, 457
Fidos—98
Field, Ben—101
Field, Betty—205, 211, 221, 235, 244, 281, 315, 412
Field, Crystal—323
Fielden-Kaye, Beatrix—219
Field God, The—148
Fielding's Music Hall—347
Fielding, Fenella—284, 311, 315, 359, 368, 402
Fielding, Henry—36, 317, 319, 373, 418
Fielding, Marjorie—253
Field, Nathaniel—72
Field, Ron—361, 385
Field, Salisbury—71, 93, 104
Field, Sally Ann—379
Fields and Chodorov—229
Fields, Benny—240
Fields, Dorothy—156, 158, 215, 216, 226, 234, 239, 244, 247, 271, 287, 314, 357, 406, 418
Fields, Gracie—158, 178, 199
Fields, Herbert—92, 132, 140, 148, 149, 156, 158, 164, 171, 186, 217, 222, 226, 234, 239, 244, 247, 263, 287, 314
Field, Sid—235, 240, 241, 248
Fields, Joseph—222, 227, 230, 233, 238, 281, 286, 287, 293, 298, 304, 334, 393
Fields, Lew—1, 6, 15, 20, 30, 35, 52, 56, 61, 62, 66, 70, 82, 83, 92, 99, 115, 116, 140, 142, 158, 199, 229
Fields, Sally—117
Fields, W. C.—28, 74, 82, 87, 93, 99, 105, 112, 118, 124, 157, 251
Field, Sylvia—141
Field, Virginia—257
Fierstein, Harvey—445, 451
Fifinella—64, 97

Fifteen Years of a Dancer's Life—161
Fifteen Years of My Life—161
Fifth Column, The—221
5th of July, The—445
Fifth Season, The—281, 288
Fifty-Fifty—183, 248
Fifty Miles from Boston—41
Fifty Million Frenchmen—164
59 Theatre Company—316
Fifty Years of Spoof—189
Figaro—373, 436
Fight for Barbara, The—368
Fighting Cock, The—315, 360
Fighting Hope, The—42
Fighting Mac—444
Figman, Max—132
Figure of Fun—273
Fiji Company—445
Filippi, Rosina—21, 27, 127
Filling Station—219
Fillmore, Clyde—200
Filtch, Arden S.—4
Filumena—298, 435
Finch, Peter—261, 266, 275, 279, 309
Finch, Robert—418
Finck, Herman—72, 74, 79, 83, 89, 102, 113, 134, 177
Fin de Partie (Endgame)—306
Findlater, Richard—251
Findlay, Thomas—93
Findon, B. W.—64, 130, 147
Find the Woman—63
Find Your Way Home—388, 413
Fine and Dandy—170, 231
Fineberg, Larry—392, 430, 446
Fine Feathers—245
Fine Fettle—315
Fine, Sylvia—217
Fingernails Blue as Flowers—399
Fings Ain't Wot They Used T' Be—316, 318, 321
Finian's Rainbow—130, 252, 253, 295, 323, 367, 383
Finishing Touches—406
Finklehoff, Fred—200, 235
Finlay, Frank—318, 333, 346, 353, 361, 388, 411, 427, 430
Finnegan's Wake—452
Finnerty, Warren—314
Finne, William—452
Finney, Albert—310, 316, 322, 328, 342, 354, 355, 359, 365, 409, 414, 422, 423, 428, 431, 436, 445
Finn, Marvin—452
Fiorello—98, 315, 325, 335, 431
Firbank, Ann—315
Firbank, Ronald—311
Firebird, The—106, 376
Firebrand, The—125, 142, 355
Fire-Bringers, The—102
Fire Eaters, The—289, 330
Firefly, The—62, 404
Fire in the Mind House—417
Fireman's Flame, The—205
Fire of London, The—361
Fires of Fate, The—48
Fires of St. John, The—23, 44
Fire That Consumes, The—437
Firkins, Yvonne—350
First American Dictator, The—216
First and the Last, The—107
Firstborn, The—276, 310
First Breeze of Summer, The—422
First-Class Passengers Only—153
First Cousins—235
First Edition—270
First Episode—189, 190, 191
First Flight—132
First Gentlemen, The—245
First Impressions—314
First Interval—376
First Lady—196, 204, 279
First Legion, The—191, 206, 210
First Man, The—111
First Monday in October—442, 457
First Mrs. Fraser, The—165, 411
First Night of Pygmalion, The—423
"First Rose of Summer"—114
First Stone, The—159

First Year, The—100, 110, 116, 144, 297
Firth, Peter—406, 415, 417
Firth, Tazeena—373, 415
Fischer, Paul M.—286
Fischer, Sebastian—373
Fisher, Bob—351
Fisher, Daisey—135
Fisher, J.—83
Fisher, John C.—11
Fisher, Jules—333, 434
Fisher, Lola—78
Fisher, Robert—385
Fisher, Rudolph—202
Fisher, Sallie—36
Fisher's Theater (San Francisco)—34
Fishing—422, 431
Fiske, Harrison Grey—11, 20, 24, 28, 31, 42, 51, 56, 57, 78, 152, 160, 184, 233
Fiske, Minnie Maddern—11, 16, 18, 20, 24, 27, 29, 31, 42, 51, 56, 78, 110, 130, 152, 160, 163, 180, 184, 233
Fitch, Clyde—1, 5, 6, 7, 8, 11, 12, 14, 15, 20, 25, 27, 32, 35, 41, 42, 44, 47, 50, 51, 52, 72, 77, 80, 97, 104, 132, 149, 209, 213
Fitzgerald, Aubrey—95
Fitzgerald, Barry—84, 96, 135, 145, 152, 193, 216, 223, 330
Fitzgerald, Desmond—96
Fitzgerald, F. Scott—140, 163, 225, 310
Fitzgerald, Geraldine—215, 234, 353, 396, 397, 441
Fitzgerald, Gerry—222
Fitzgerald, Percy Hetherington—138
Fitzgerald, S. A. J.—88
Fitzgibbon, Maggie—321
Fitzmaurice, George—58, 68, 389
Fitzsimmons, Bijou—62
Five Finger Exercise—310, 315, 325, 376
Five Hoffman Girls—151
5 O'Clock Girl, The—149, 256
Five on the Black Hand Side—382
Five Philadelphia Physicians—283
Five Star Final—180
Five Variations for Corno di Bassetto—381
Flacks, Niki—422
Flagan, Bud—315
Flag is Born, A—247
Flag Lieutenant, The—43
Flagstad, Kirsten—274
Flahooley—271
Flanagan and Allen—236
Flanagan, Bud—212, 218, 246, 248, 267, 322, 376
Flanagan, Hallie—199, 215, 445
Flanagan, Neil—413
Flanagan, Pauline—318
Flanders, Ed—335, 393
Flanders, Michael—272, 282, 291, 299, 305, 317, 390
Flannery, Peter—446, 447
Flare Path—231
Flashing into the Dark—359
Flatt, Ernest—450
Flavin, Martin—118, 144, 164, 370
Flea in Her Ear, A—381, 382
Flecker, James Elroy—120, 188, 274
Fledermaus, Die—290
Fleet's Lit Up, The—213
Fleetwood, Susan—366, 367, 403, 417, 436, 437, 443
Fleming, Atholl—197
Fleming, Carroll—56, 61
Fleming, George—15, 67
Fleming, Gordon—339
Fleming, Ian—114, 115, 134, 201, 383
Fleming, Rhonda—409
Fleming, Tom—395
Flemming, Claude—101
Flemyng, Gordon—352
Flemyng, Robert—212, 263, 264, 268, 304, 315, 362, 381, 439
Fler, P. L.—72

Flesh To a Tiger—311
Fletcher, Allen—260, 264, 279, 285, 290, 296, 301, 307, 323, 329, 347, 374
Fletcher, Bramwell—165, 214, 217, 244, 273
Fletcher, John—69, 335, 416
Fletcher, Lucille—400
Fletcher, Percy—108
Fletcher, Robert—296
Fleur d'Oranger—45
Flexner, Anne Crawford—297
Flicker, Theodore J.—324, 341
Flight Into Egypt—276
Flight To the West—222, 229
Flint—386
Flippen, J. C.—140, 148
Flip Side, The—366
Flo-Flo—83
Flood, Gerald—443
Flood-Tide, The—16
Flora Bella—78
Flora, The Red Menace—351
Florence, Evelyn—10
Florence, Mildred—133
Florence, W. J.—161
Florida Aflame—285
Flodorora—1, 4, 76, 103, 178
Flow—410
Flower Drum Song—309, 322, 424
Flower, Gilly—165, 172
Flowering Cherry, The—314
Flowering Peach, The—288, 297, 386
Flower, Mary—108
Flower of the Palace of Han, The—61
Flower of Yamato, The—44
Flowers—414, 419
Flowers for Algernon—450
Flower, Sir Fordham—362
Flowers of the Forest—192, 195
Flutter of Wings, A—174
Fly Away Home—362
Flying Colors—181, 185
Flying Doctor, The—290, 430, 445
Flying High—170
Flying Squad, The—159
Flynn, Billy—420
Fly With Me—103
Foch, Nina—128, 252, 266, 325
Fo, Dario—397, 446
Fodor—197
Fogerty, Elsie—58
Fogarty, Elsie—58
Fokine, Michael—93, 106, 111, 120
Folger, Henry Clay—174
Folies Bergere Revue—135, 263, 272, 276, 283, 347
Follies—393
Follies Parisiennes—204
Follies, Pelissier—58
Follow My Leader—222
Follow that Girl—322
Follow the Girls—239, 245
Follow the Sun—201
Follow Thru—163
Follow, William—415
Folly Theatre—419
Folly To Be Wise—177
Fonatine, Robert—371
Fonda, Henry—168, 181, 190, 191, 257, 272, 287, 309, 315, 321, 351, 382, 421, 442, 449
Fonda, Jane—449
Fonson, Jean—63, 75
Fontaine, Robert—266
Fontanne, Lynn—90, 105, 119, 121, 125, 137, 142, 144, 148, 150, 152, 156, 168, 171, 177, 186, 198, 200, 208, 214, 221, 241, 265, 277, 298, 309, 323, 441
Fontenelle—233
Fonteyn, Margot—255
Fool and the Wise Man, The—63
Foolish Gentlewoman, The—263
Foolish Notion—244, 246
Fool of Fortune, The—137
Fool's Paradise—315
Fools Rush In—248
Fools, The—373, 382, 421, 423
Fool, The—112, 123, 127

Fool There Was, A—47
Foot, Alistair—365, 394
Foot, Dingle—336
Foote, Horton—282, 301
Foote, John T.—92
Foot, Michael—363
Footsteps of Doves, The—357
For Adults Only—310
For All Eternity—75
For All Those Who Get Despondent—435
For Amusement Only—299
For Better, For Worse . . .—278
Forced Marriage, The—228, 445
Force of Habit—431
For Colored Girls Who Have Considered Suicide/When the Rainbow is Not Enuf—426, 428, 442
For Crying Out Loud—245
Forde, Hal—66
Forde, H. Athol—84
Ford Foundation, The—337, 456
Ford, Harriet—7, 11, 71, 106
Ford, Helen—99, 118, 132, 133, 142, 150
Ford, Henry—7, 106
Ford, Hugh—35, 48, 57, 71
Ford, John—121, 128, 329, 335, 403, 416, 422, 438, 444
Ford, Mick—447
Ford, Miriam—409
Ford, Nancy—364, 385, 445
Ford of the Hurdles, The—167, 188
Ford, Paul—244, 320, 333, 432
Ford, Paul L.—1
Ford, Ruth—247, 248, 293, 307, 314, 319, 361
Ford, Wallace—124, 205
Forefather's Eve—422
Foreign Affairs—184
Foreman, Richard—400, 424, 441
Forester, C. S.—180, 191
Forest Meadows Theater—331
Forest, The—139
Forever After—87, 91
For France—73
Forget-Me-Not Lane—395
For King and Country—75, 430
Fork, The—428
For Love or Money—252, 279
Forman, Milos—331
Formation Dancers—395
Formby, George—273, 283
For Mother Country—75
Fornes, Maria Irene—378
For None Can Tell—369
Forrest, David—444
Forrest, Edwin—86, 137, 139
Forrest, Frederick—92
Forrest, George—253, 264, 282, 367, 389
Forrest, Sam—105
Forrest Theatre, The—40, 162
Forristal, Desmond—402, 416, 422, 428, 455
For Russia—75
Forsberg, Rolf—317
Forsell, Lars—422
For Serbia—75
For Services Rendered—183, 453
Forsslund, Louise—78

Forster, E. M.—322, 340, 365, 432
For Sword or Song—15
Forsyth, Bruce—332, 443
Forsythe, Henderson—332, 345, 357, 364, 395, 404
Forsyth, James—373
Fortescue, Jack—59
For the Defense—94
For the Land She Loved—76
For the Love of Mike—178, 180
For the Use of the Hall—430
For the West—435, 437
Fortnightly Review—229
For Tonight—293
Fortune and Men's Eyes—355, 364
Fortune Hunter, The—47, 51
Fortune Teller, The—167
Fortune Theatre—387
Fortuny, Mariano—9, 46
Forty Carats—372, 384
Forty Five Minutes from Broadway—30, 34, 229
"Forty Minutes for Lunch"—235
'49ers, The—215
Forty Thieves, The—38, 64, 128, 198
Forty Years On—372, 389
Forum Theatre—380
Forward, Up Your End—390
Forwood, Antony—216
Fosse, Bob—287, 293, 298, 304, 314, 327, 329, 332, 340, 357, 400, 420, 442
Foss, George R.—90, 96, 122
Foster, Barry—334
Foster, Basil—62, 107, 127, 135, 143, 172, 177, 183
Foster, Claiborne—133, 163
Foster, Fredrick W.—40
Foster, Gloria—352, 355, 368, 386, 391, 401
Foster, Nanette—52
Foster, Pamela—235
Foster, Paul—353, 360, 365, 366, 400, 451
Foster, Peggie—84
Foster, Stephen—219
Foulds, J. H.—68
Fountain, The—69, 133, 137
Fourberies de Scapin, Les—274
Four Cohans, The—233
Four Degrees Over—360
Four, Five, Six!—258
Four Horsemen of the Apocalypse, The—153
Four Mortons—153
Four Musketeers, The—366
Fournier, Maurice—359
Fourposter, The—268, 271, 280, 295, 358
Four Saints in Three Acts—278
Four Seasons, The—352, 387
Foursome, The—395, 401
Fourth Day Like Four Long Months of Absence—417
Fourth Wall, The—158
Four To One—430
Four Walls—149
Fowle, John—405
Fowler, A. N. C.—35
Fowler, Keith—437
Fox and Geese—84, 90
Fox, Della—69
Fox, Edward—414
Fox, George—223
Fox, Harry—66, 131, 150
Fox, John Jr.—61
Fox, Moireen—102
Fox, Paul Hervey—184
Fox, Terry Curtis—445
Foxy—332, 344, 424
Foy, Eddie—10, 14, 16, 18, 19, 61, 161
Foy, Gloria—107, 113
Foy Jr., Eddie—171, 195
Foy, Peter—384
Fragments of a Trilogy-Medea, Electra and the Trojan Women—416, 424
France, Anatole—50, 56, 76, 84, 90
France, Charles—75, 102, 107, 112,

143, 172, 177, 181, 183, 191
Francesca de Rimini—13, 161
Frances, Kathleen—193
Francheville, Robert—75
Francine, Anne—410, 455
Franciosa, Anthony—294
Francis, Anne—212
Francis, Arlene—201, 230, 264, 273, 309, 361
Francis, Arthur—109
Francis, Derek—302
Francis, J. O.—73
Francis, Kay—376
Francis, William—352
Francis, W. T.—15, 25
Francke, Caroline—223
Frankau, Ronald—206, 222, 263
Frank, Bruno—207
Frank, Charles—273
Frankel, Gene—364, 378, 400, 402, 428
Franken, Rose—181, 185, 226, 229, 240, 243, 246, 424
Frankenstein—375, 409
Frank, Harrison J. L.—180
Frank, Leonard—167
"Franklin D. Roosevelt Jones"—211
Franklin, Irene—52
Franklin, J. E.—393
Franklin, Malvin—92
Franklin, Ronnie—328, 443
Franklyn, Leo—310
Franklyn, William—304
Frank, Melvin—298
Frank & Ruby—451
Franz, Eduard—233
Franzen, Ulrich—356, 377
Franz, Esther—453
Franzheim, H. Kenneth—116
Franz, Victor—453
Franz, Walter—453
Frapie, Leon—75
Fraser, Agnes—26, 32
Fraser, Bill—222
Fraser, C. Lovat—103
Fraser, George—355, 398
Fraser, Graham—267
Fraser, John—306, 310, 344
Fraser, Liz—339
Fraser, Moyra—282, 299
Fraser, Mrs. Kennedy—130
Fraser, Ronald—315, 322
Fraser-Simson, Harold—83, 101, 120, 127, 135
Fraser, Winifred—2, 3, 8, 48, 82
Fratricide Punished—317
Frawley, James—341
Frawley, Paul—92, 132
Frayne, Frankie—206
Frayn, Michael—397, 427, 443, 445
Frazee, H. H.—70
Frazier, Ronald—327
Frears, Stephen—409
Frechtman, Bernard—301
Frederick Douglass . . . Through His Own Words—402
Frederick, Pauline—13, 32, 42, 215
Fredericks, Charles—249
Fred Karno's Company—46
Fred Millar Theatre (Milwaukee)—337
Fredro, Aleksander—306
Free as Air—305
Freedley, George—369
Freedley, Vinton—155, 383
Freedman, David—202
Freedman, Gerald—367, 373, 374, 376, 379, 381, 383, 400, 404, 431, 446, 454
Freedom of Suzanne, The—22
Freedom of the City, The—407
Freedom of the Seas, The—89
Freehold, The—390
Freel, Aleta—186
Free Lance, The—30
Freeman—402
Freeman, Al Jr.—339, 344
Freeman, Dave—315
Freeman, David—392, 397, 412, 420, 427

Freeman, Gillian—380
Freeman, Morgan—364
Freeman, Stan—345
Free Soul, A—199
Free Theatre—384
Freeway, The—417
Freibrug Passion Play, The—166
Freid, Martin—400
Freitag, Dorothea—366
French as he Is Spoke—45
French, Bert—105
French, Daniel Chester—433
French, David—444
French, Dorothy—381
French, Elsie—103, 128
French for Love, The—218
French, Harold—101, 142, 216, 218, 316
French, Lawrence—142
French Leave—102
French, Leslie—296, 311
French Mistress, The—315
French Players—80, 84, 85, 102
French Revolution—316
French Without Tears—202, 205, 264, 415
Frenzy—258
Fresh Airs—299
Fresh Fields—187
Freska, Friedrich—59, 135
Fresnay, Pierre—192, 202
Freudenberger, Daniel—428, 431, 436, 444, 451
Freud, E. W.—114
Freund, Julius—72
Frey, Leonard—371, 398, 410, 418, 426
Friderici, Blanche—106
Fridolin—261
Friebus, Florida—184
Friedlander, William—135
Friedman, Bruce Jay—364, 386
Friedman, Charles—206, 262, 280
Friedman, Gary William—385
Friedman, Leon—365
Fried, Martin—375
Friel, Brian—348, 357, 363, 368, 373, 375, 407
Friendly Enemies—87
Friends—84
Friends, The—387, 389
"Friendship"—217
Friganza, Trixie—10, 30, 61
Friml, Rudolf—15, 62, 67, 74, 87, 92, 93, 105, 125, 132, 156, 404, 418, 424
Frings, Ketti—305, 313, 358
Frisby, Terence—359, 437, 456
Frisch, Max—330, 338, 343, 347, 348, 453
Frisco, Joe—157
Frisky Mrs. Johnson, The—14
Frochard—104
Froetz, Franz Xaver—415
Frogs, The—367
Frog, The—201
Frohman, Charles—1, 5, 6, 7, 11, 15, 22, 23, 33, 34, 37, 41, 42, 47, 53, 54, 56, 69, 72, 77, 80, 117, 118, 137, 203, 233, 237, 261, 286, 302
Frohman, Daniel—4, 6, 18, 77, 146, 194, 225
Frohman, Gustave—77
From Broadway to Bowery—104
From Dixie to Broadway—154
Frome, Hector—197
From Here and There—295
From Morn Till Midnight—103, 111
From Moses to Mao—415
From President to Postman—225
From the Second City—326
From the Stocks to the Stars—233
From This Day Forward—375
From Vienna—216
Front Page, The—157, 250, 302, 381, 382, 392, 402, 456
Frost, Rex—294
Frou-Frou—13, 16
Frow, Gerald—323, 324
Froyez, Maurice—97

Frozen Assets—439
Fruit—387, 390
Fruits of Enlightenment, The—452
Fruse, Roger—404
Fry, Christopher—38, 249, 250, 263, 266, 267, 268, 272, 274, 276, 279, 280, 283, 289, 294, 297, 310, 315, 320, 334, 335, 373, 376, 389, 403, 417, 444
Fry, Dwight—144
Frye, Revis—423
Fryers, Austin—13, 90
Fry, Jeremy—456
Fry, Reginald—79
Fuente Ovejuna—403
Fugard, Athol—340, 344, 360, 385, 396, 398, 410, 413, 414, 423, 424, 431, 435, 444
Fugitives, The—201
Fugitive, The—67
Fugue in a Nursery—451
Fuller, Charles—415, 432
Fuller, Dean—316
Fuller, Frances Golden—42, 157, 161, 181
Fuller, La Loie—8, 161
Fuller, Penny—385
Fuller, Rosalinde—140, 223
Fuller, Thomas—454
Full House—197
Full Moon, The—54, 58
Full Swing—231
Fulton Theatre—46
Fumed Oak—201, 265
Fun and Games—227
Fun and the Fair—283
Fun I've Had, The—237
Funke, Lewis—447
Funny Face—150, 155, 209, 383
Funny Girl—155, 344, 358
Funnyhouse of a Negro—374
Funny Peculiar—427
Funny Side Up—222
Funny Thing Happened to Me on the Way to the Forum, A—326, 340, 402, 441
Fun of the Fayre—108
Funt, Julian—2, 287
Fun To Be Free—228
Furber, Douglas—83, 95, 99, 114, 119, 127, 159, 166, 172, 177, 191, 207, 212, 213, 218, 222, 227, 235, 236, 245
Furniss, Grace Livingson—25
Furse, Jill—205
Furse, Judith—245, 246, 249, 268, 284
Furse, Roger—267, 274, 279, 295
Furst, William—36, 62
Furter, Frank N.—409
Furth, George—385, 394, 434
Futari-Daimyo—408
Future Indefinite—411
Futz!—366, 371, 384
Fuzz—382
Fyffe, Patrick—421
Fyffe, R. E.—27
Fywell, Tim—435

Gabel, Martin—221, 273
Gable, Christopher—367, 452
Gable, Clark—161, 325
Gabor, Eva—266
Gabriel, Master—42
Gaby—56
Gadd, Renee—187, 235
Gaelic League Amateur Dramatic Society—3
Gaffney, Liam—219
Gage, Margaret—121
Gagliono, Frank—353, 368
Gagnon, Louis Philippe—138
Gahagan, Helen—131, 133, 171
Gaieties, The—244
Gaiety of Nations, The—360
Gail, Zoe—222, 226, 235, 241, 263
Gaines, J. E.—415
Gaines, Pearl—250

Gaity Theater—13, 18, 46, 91, 95, 123
Gale, Jane—65
Galentine, Sydney—49
Gale, Peter—435
Gale, Richard—306
Gale, Zona—84, 101, 124, 215, 445
Galileo—255, 303, 366
Galitzine, Prince Nicholas—153
Gallacher, Tom—428, 444
Gallagher, Bernard—359, 361
Gallagher, Ed—64, 111
Gallagher, Helen—256, 262, 281
Gallatin, Alberta—136
Gallegly, David—420
Gallon, Tom—23
Galloper, The—30
Gallows Humor—347
Galsworthy, John—24, 33, 44, 48, 53, 60, 62, 67, 68, 73, 98, 101, 103, 107, 110, 113, 114, 122, 165, 127, 131, 139, 143, 184, 189, 193, 197, 273
Galway Handicap—254
Gamble, Rollo—214
Gamble, Ronald—354
Gamblers All—75
Gamblers, The—52
Gamble, Warburton—135
Gambon, Michael—444, 450, 453
Game Called Arthur, A—387, 395
Game of Love and Death, The—167
Game, The—69
Gam, Rita—260
Gang, Crazy—376
Gang's All Here, The—314
Gang Show of 1954, The—291
Gangway—227
Gannon, Kim—271
Gans, Sharon—358
Gant, David—450
Gantillon, Simon—155, 161
Gantry—385
Gantt, Cora Dick—100
Gaol Gate, The—38, 59, 185
Garcia, Victor—395, 439
Garde, Betty—234
Garden District—309
Gardenia, Vincent—122, 321, 390, 414
Garden of Allah, The—56, 102
Garden of Eden, The—151
Garden, The—403
Gardiens du Phare—76
Gardiner, Reginald—165, 196, 201, 276
Gardner, Dorothy—252
Gardner, Herb—337
Gardner, J. E.—48
Gardner, Kerry—345
Gardner, Rita—320
Gardner, Shayle—134
Garen, Leo—364
Garfein, Jack—281, 312
Garfield, John—259, 262, 273, 278
Garfield, Jules—205
Gargan, William—171
Garick's Head Pub—425
Garland, Geoff—330
Garland, Hamlin—138
Garland, Patrick—365, 366, 372, 391, 394, 395, 408, 409, 414, 427, 435, 438, 440
Garner, Herb—332
Garner, Jay—378
Garnett, Constance—237
Garnett, Edward—39
Garrard, Jim—377
Garrett, Betty—230, 247, 338
Garrett, Lloyd—120
Garrick, David—16, 37, 44, 274
Garrick Gaieties of 1926, The—140
Garrick Producing Company—76
Garrick Theater (New York)—34
Garrick Theater (Philadelphia)—9
Garrison, Gene—371
Garrison, Sean—333
Garroters, The—104
Garson, Barbara—364
Garson, Greer—193, 197, 201

Garvey, Marcus—224
Garwood-Jones, Trevor—412
Gary, Mary—41
Gas—122, 173
Gascoigne, Bamber—305
Gascon, Jean—317, 318, 325, 367, 374, 381, 389, 419
Gaskill, William—307, 311, 316, 318, 329, 342, 346, 359, 361, 363, 366, 373, 379, 388, 390, 395, 414, 436, 452
Gaslight—217, 223, 429
Gasman, Ira—409
Gaspers—108
Gass, Ken—392
Gassman, Vittorio—341
Gassner, John—218, 343, 362
Gates, Frank—11
Gates, Larry—272
Gateson, Marjorie—117
Gates, Tudor—443
Gate Theatre, The—155, 167, 232, 447
Gateway Company—301
Gateway To Gaiety—301
Gathering, The—431
Gatterburg, Gail—452
Gatti, J. M.—147
Gatti, R.—147
Gauguin, Paul—135
Gaul, George—152, 160
Gauntlet, The—166
Gaxton, William—112, 149, 164, 177, 191, 202, 342
Gay Deceivers—197
Gay Divorcé—182, 188, 440
Gay Dog, The—277
Gay Gordons, The—37
Gay Invalid, The—273
Gay, John—103, 115, 137, 188, 223, 232, 260, 269, 306, 312, 341, 361, 375, 377, 402, 411, 422
Gay Landscape—312
Gay Liberationists—393
Gay Lord Quex, The—423
Gay, Maisie—84, 95, 109, 120, 127, 134
Gay Men's Theatre Collective—442
Gay Morning Glories, The—229
Gay, Noel—196, 207, 212, 222, 236, 258
Gaynore, Charles—406
Gay Paree—132, 142
Gay Rosalinda—245, 250
Gay White Way, The—35
Gazebo, The—327
Gazzara, Ben—281, 286, 293, 294, 429
Gear, Luella—190
Geary Theatre, The—161
Geddes, Barbara Bel—116, 239, 244, 266, 271
Geddes, Norman Bel—185, 205, 240
Geddes, Vergil—166
Gee, George—151, 157, 197, 222, 244
Gee, Hazel—272
Gee, Lottie—105
Geer, Ellen—335
Geer, Will—160, 196, 211, 360, 447
Geese—378
Geeson, Judy—409
Geisha and the Knight, The—4
Geisha, The—178
Geisterbahn—428
Gelb, Arthur—331
Gelbart, Larry—326, 427
Gelber, Jack—314, 325, 327, 357, 401, 402, 410, 417, 452
Geld, Gary—420
Gelinas, Gratien—259, 261
Geliot, Michael—347, 360
Gellner, Julian—274
Gellner, Julius—323, 329, 342, 353, 359, 368, 415
Gem—436
Gemier, Firmin—129
Gemini—429, 434, 436
Gemmel, Don—269, 280, 286, 349
Gems, Barton—444
Gems, Pam—415, 431, 438, 444, 451

Genee, Adeline—41, 45
Gene Feist's Roundabout Theatre—453
General John Regan—67
General Post—83
Generation—351, 363
Genet, Jean—279, 301, 319, 320, 326, 329, 340, 387, 396, 397, 398, 414, 415, 417, 431, 444
Geneva—213, 221, 397
Genius and the Goddess, The—334
Genius, The—31
Gennaro, Peter—315
Genn, Leo—184, 223, 247, 272, 304, 326, 345, 366, 447
Gensler, Lewis—125, 132, 141
Gentleman from Mississippi, A—42
Gentleman Jack—199
Gentleman of France, A—7
Gentleman Caller, The—378
Gentlemen Prefer Blondes—141, 142, 262, 334, 337, 413
Gentle People, The—216
Gentle Shepherd, The—264
Gentry, Kishasha—393
Gentry, Minnie—393
Geoffrey, Wallace—258
Geography of a Horse Dreamer—424
Geordie's March—409
George, A. E.—27, 28, 48, 96
George and Margaret—205, 206
George, Colin—285, 389
George Dandin—285, 353, 374, 380
George, Edwin—68
George, Gladys—191, 292
George, Grace—14, 22, 30, 38, 47, 50, 54, 60, 66, 72, 76, 110, 153, 195, 226, 263, 330
George IV—60
George M!—371, 446
George, Marie—1, 2, 32
George, Muriel—213
Georgett Lemenunier—90
George Washington—103
George Washington, Jr.—30
George Washington Slept Here—222, 229, 263
George White Girls—157
George White's Scandals—105, 112, 118, 124, 131, 140, 157, 164, 176, 196, 209, 216, 376, 399
Georgie, Leyla—125, 216
Gerald, a Portrait—194
Gerard, Rosemonde—66, 69
Gerard, Teddy—89
Gerber, Alex—99
Gere, Richard—450
German, Edward—12, 15, 36, 49, 273
German Emigrants, The—104
German Skerries—436
German Spy, The—73
Gerrard!—74
Gerrard, Ernie—218
Gershe, Leonard—314, 334, 378
Gershwin, George—78, 87, 92, 99, 105, 112, 118, 119, 120, 124, 126, 127, 131, 133, 150, 151, 155, 156, 170, 177, 186, 196, 209, 284, 329, 374, 431
Gershwin, Ira—109, 126, 127, 131, 133, 141, 142, 150, 155, 156, 159, 170, 177, 185, 186, 187, 190, 195, 226
Gerson, Hal—258
Gerstad, John—276
Gerstenberg, Alice—77
Gertie—280
Gertrude—246, 401
Gertrude Hoffman Girls—131, 140
Gessner, Adrienne—373
Gessner, Clark—364
Gest, Morris—82, 91, 98, 111, 117, 202, 223, 233
Get A Load of This—227
Getaway—436
Geto, Alfred—235
Get-Rich Quick Wallingford—52, 60, 229
Getting Gertie's Garter—105, 161
Getting Married—43, 114, 115, 122,

152, 178, 184, 245, 273, 367, 383, 403
Getting On—394
Getting Out—443
Get Together—106
Geva, Tamara—171, 181, 200, 283
Gheon, Henry—144, 198, 202
Ghostley, Alice—276, 291, 320, 333
Ghost of Yankee Doodle, The—208
Ghost on Tiptoe—414
Ghosts—16, 72, 80, 122, 123, 152, 173, 184, 198, 223, 237, 259, 312, 330, 353, 367, 369, 415, 439
Ghost Sonata—402
Ghost Train, The—135, 168, 193, 269, 432
Gianni Schicchi—380
Giraudoux, Jean—208, 265, 310
Gibbons, Carol—245
Gibbons, Walter—5, 34
Gibbs, Armstrong—127
Gibbs, C. Armstrong—107
Gibbs, Emily—241
Gibbs, George—241
Gibbs, Leslie—236
Gibbs, Nancy—101
Gibbs, Wolcott—313
Gibney, Charles—136
Gibson, Charles Dana—25
Gibson, James—301
Gibson, John—306, 348
Gibson, William—73, 309, 313, 314, 319, 325, 344, 376, 406, 434
Giddens, George—53
Gide, Andre—260, 274, 287, 291, 319
Gideon—85, 327, 337
Gideon, Melville—167
Gielgud, John—113, 129, 136, 144, 167, 173, 177, 178, 179, 183, 192, 193, 198, 202, 203, 206, 208, 212, 213, 214, 218, 219, 223, 232, 241, 242, 249, 254, 255, 260, 263, 264, 268, 274, 278, 280, 283, 284, 289, 290, 295, 296, 299, 304, 306, 310, 311, 313, 317, 318, 319, 329, 330, 334, 340, 345, 347, 352, 354, 367, 372, 373, 386, 391, 393, 403, 410, 415, 417, 422, 423, 436, 437, 443, 448
Gielgud Repertory Company—369
Gielgud, Val—153, 169, 273, 375
Gierasch, Stefan—374
Giffith, Hugh—220
Gifford, Alan—272
Gigi—272, 280, 299, 406
GI Hamlet—246
Gilbert and Sullivan—37, 39, 44, 49, 63, 68, 97, 109, 136, 144, 145, 167, 173, 193, 199, 202, 203, 218, 228, 229, 232, 241, 245, 249, 255, 260, 264, 269, 274, 290, 296, 316, 323, 330, 331, 334, 335, 341, 346, 347, 349, 369, 374, 376, 421, 422, 424, 429, 446
Gilbert, Edward—220, 361, 367
Gilbert, G. H., Mrs.—20, 23
Gilbert, James—299
Gilbert, Jean—63, 71, 72, 113, 133
Gilbert, Michael—316
Gilbert, Ronnie—358
Gilbert, W. S.—21, 45, 46, 49, 53, 97, 422
Gilchrist, R. Murray—68
Gilder, Jeannette—1
Gile, Bill—424, 431, 436
Giles, David—381, 415, 417, 423, 447, 455, 456
Gilford, Jack—314, 382
Gilhooley, Jack—440
Gilky, Stanley—332
Gillam, Melville—294
Gill, Basil—32, 33, 67, 79, 192
Gill, Brendan—73
Gill, Dorothy—193
Gillen, Allyn—166
Gillespie, Robert—348, 431, 439, 452
Gillette, Anita—203, 354, 358, 434
Gillette, Helen—205
Gillette, Viola—15

Gillette, William—9, 12, 28, 42, 54, 73, 82, 86, 88, 90, 180, 209
Gillett, William—347, 414
Gill, Frank Jr.—239
Gillie, Jean—236
Gilliland, Helen—119, 158, 177
Gillingwater, Claude—87
Gill, Merton—246
Gillmore, Margalo—94, 102, 106, 111, 121, 145, 148, 156, 201
Gill, Paul—151
Gill, Peter—353, 361, 373, 379, 381, 387, 389, 395, 398, 410, 429, 448
Gilman, Mabelle—1, 16
Gilmore, Peter—322
Gilmore, Ruth—108
Gilmore, Virginia—234, 240, 247
Gilmour, Ian—143
Gilpin, Charles—100, 144
Gilroy, Frank D.—339, 344
Gilsa, A. V.—39
Gimme Shelter—436, 437, 448
Gin Game, The—434, 448, 451
Gingerbread Lady, The—386, 414
Gingerbread Man, The—456
Ginger Man, The—315
Gingham Dog, The—378
Gingham Girl, The—112, 303
Gingold, Hermione—68, 114, 201, 227, 231, 236, 241, 248, 265, 282, 314
Ginsberg, Allen—402
Ginsbury, Norman—245, 275
Ginty, E. B.—424
Ginzburg, Natalia—375
Gioconda Smile, The—266
Giordano, Tony—436
Giovanni, Paul—228, 316, 442
Gipsy Love—62
Gipsy Princess, The—107, 242
Girardot, Etienne—20, 33, 122, 148, 220
Giraudoux, Jean—174, 255, 258, 266, 267, 269, 270, 287, 289, 290, 294, 295, 302, 306, 325, 334, 349, 373, 378, 396, 438, 444
Girl and the Cat, The—152
Girl and the Judge, The—7
Girl Behind the Counter, The—35
Girl Called Jo, A—295
Girl Crazy—170
Girl Friend, The—140, 151
Girl from Ciro's, The—79
Girl from Maxim's, The—12
Girl from Up There, The—6, 7
Girl from Utah, The—67
"Girlie, Girlie"—97
Girl I Left Behind Me, The—179
Girl in Pink Tights, The—287
Girl in the Limousine, The—93
Girl in the Taxi, The—63
Girl in the Train, The—53
Girl of the Golden West, The—26, 29, 154, 179
Girl of the Pillow, The—178
Girl on the Film, The—67
Girl on the Via Flaminia, The—287, 291, 292
Girls—41
Girls of Gottenberg, The—37
Girls Upstairs, The—393
"Girl That I Marry, The'"—247
Girl Who Came to Supper, The—339
Girl with the Green Eyes, The—50
Giroux, B. M.—81
Gish, Dorothy—178, 217, 247, 252, 376
Gish, Lillian—66, 69, 205, 213, 266, 281, 321, 340, 371, 407, 420
Give a Dog a Bone—349, 355, 363, 369, 376, 383, 391, 398
Give and Take—117, 238
G.K.C.—389, 423
Glad Eye, The—58
Glad of It—15
Gladwin, John—199
Glad Tidings—440
Glandenning, Jessie—92, 93

Glaser, Lulu—10, 19, 41, 42, 313
Glasgow Citizens' Theatre—246, 269, 312, 317, 390, 392, 401, 403, 408, 428, 436, 444, 451, 452, 455
Glaspell, Susan—77, 80, 84, 90, 95, 137, 139, 152, 174, 180, 188, 223, 261, 445
Glass Blowers, The—66
Glass Cage, The—304, 307
Glassco, Bill—397, 413
Glass, Joanna—403, 431, 451
Glass Menagerie, The—244, 246, 302, 258, 297, 354, 355, 395, 396, 422, 432, 439, 451
Glass, Montague—66, 74, 82, 93
Glass, Philip—440
Glass Slipper, The—132, 243, 246
Glazer, Benjamin—221
Gleason, Jackie—239, 262, 314
Gleason, James—131, 156, 318
Gleason, Joanna—434
Glendinning, Ethel—183
Glendinning, Ernest—121, 203
Glendinning, John—30
Glen, John—301
Glenney, Charles—87
Glennon, Gordon—244
Glenny, Peter—147
Glenville, Peter—398
Glenville, Peter—69, 193, 224, 258, 260, 263, 266, 274, 276, 288, 293, 301, 314, 315, 344, 365, 387, 406
Glenville, Shaun—150
Glickman, Will—293, 298
Glimpse of Reality, The—274
Glittering Gate, The—54
Globe Revue, The—277
Globe Theater—34
Gloo Joo—443
Gloria and Esperanza—388
Glorious Days, The—282
Glorious Morning—212, 445
Glory Be!—328
Gloucester Road—386
Glover, John—32, 54, 85, 95, 440
Glover, Julian—359, 398, 409, 443
Glover, William—446
Gluckman, Leon—327
Glydebourne Festival Opera—260, 264
Glyn, Elinor—46, 84
Glynn, Mary—59, 83, 94, 111
Gnadiges Fraulein, The—357
Goat Alley—105
Goat Song—144, 246
Goblet Game, The—376
God Bless—372
God Bless the Major—422
Goddard, Charles—66, 69
Goddard, Malcolm—284
Goddard, Michael—284
Goddard, Paulette—146
Godfernaux, Andre—32
Godfrey, Derek—329, 348, 359, 364, 379, 382, 396, 417, 438
Godfrey, Isadore—218, 273
Godfrey, John—83
Godfrey, Peter—139, 155, 166
God Gentry—323
God is a (Guess What?)—376, 380
God, Man and Devil—198
Godney, Barry—328
God of Gods, The—97
God of Vengeance, The—113, 116, 198
God Save the Empire—73
God Save the King—73
God Sends Sunday—247
God's Favorite—414
God's Gentry—275
Gods of the Lightning—157
Gods of the Mountain, The—80
Godsong—430
Godspell—393, 398, 423, 430, 441
Goetz, Augustus—252, 287, 291, 308, 429, 453
Goetz, E. Ray—56, 82, 145, 157

Goetz, Ruth—252, 287, 291, 308, 429, 453
Goff, Ivan—248
Gog and MacGog—260
Gogol, Nikolai—103, 121, 144, 179, 197, 214, 259, 260, 340, 353, 359, 367, 409, 425, 439, 447, 455
Gohman, Don—394
Going Up—83, 129, 207, 431
Gold—105, 120
Golda—434
Goldberg, Dick—257, 442, 453
Goldbergs, The—257
Goldby, Derek—371
Gold Diggers, The—93, 161
Gold Eagle Guy—193
Golden Apple, The—102, 287, 292
Golden Arrow—197
Golden Bat, The—386
Golden Boy—205, 212, 215, 278, 344, 424,
Golden Crucible, The—317
Golden Dawn—150, 155
Golden Door, The—278
Golden Doom, The—80
Golden, I. J.—178
Golden, John—61, 82, 87, 130, 147, 163, 189, 235, 279, 297
Golden Land of Fairy Tales, The—59
Golden Legend of Shults, The—220, 348
Golden, Michael—242
Golden Moth, The—108
Golden Rainbow—371
Golden Six, The—319
Golden Toy, The—191
Goldfish, The—59
Goldie, Hugh—284, 352, 366, 374, 440
Goldie, Wyndham—264
Goldilocks—309
Golding, William—310, 409
Gold, Jack—429
Gold, Jimmy—218, 315
Goldman, Emma—451
Goldman, James—328, 357, 393
Gold, Michael—202
Goldner, Charles—226
Goldoni, Carlo—37, 122, 136, 145, 153, 241, 301, 312, 323, 354, 367, 374, 396, 408, 431, 455
Goldoni, Stephen—81
Goldsby, Robert—359
Goldsmith, Bea—230
Goldsmith, Clifford—211
Goldsmith, Eleanor—257
Goldsmith, Oliver—3, 8, 27, 33, 63, 64, 74, 80, 121, 160, 270, 323, 381, 398, 402, 403, 409, 416, 452
Gombeen Man, The—68
Gombrowicz, Witold—396
Gomez, Thomas—398
Gondoliers, The—37, 49, 97, 167, 184, 193, 228, 232, 245, 249, 255, 260, 264, 269, 275, 285, 290, 302, 313, 334, 335, 346, 366, 373, 424
Gone With the Wind—401
Gooch, Steve—409, 443, 457
Goodall, Edyth—46, 61, 79, 144
Goodall, Grace—47
Goodbody, Buzz—410, 417, 422, 424
Good Boy—157
"Goodbye Broadway, Hello France!"—82
Goodbye, Charlie—315
Goodbye, Mr. Chips—213
Goodbye, My Fancy—257, 265
Good Companions, The—177, 246, 414
Good Doctor, The—406
Good Earth, The—184
Good Evening—401, 406, 419
Good Fairy, The—177, 271, 369
Good Friday—84
Good Gracious, Annabelle—125
Goodhart, Al—207
Good Hope, The—37, 153
Good-Humored Ladies, The—452, 455
Goodie Two Shoes—59

Good, Jack—435
Good Lads at Heart—397, 403, 453
Goodliffe, Martin—288
Good Little Devil, A—66, 69
Good Little Fairy-Birds, The—280
Good Losers—303, 177
Good Luck—120
Goodman, Arthur—202
Goodman, Benny—171, 240
Goodman, Jules Eckert—74, 93, 205, 208
Goodman, Randolph—259
Good, Maurice—334, 347
Good Morning, Dearie—106
Good-Natured Man, The—80, 219, 398, 416
Goodner, Carol—181, 192, 213
Goodness, How Sad!—213
Good News—149, 425
Good Night Ladies—245
Good Old Bad Old Days, The—401
Good Person of Szechwan, The—436
Goodrich, Arthur F.—119, 229
Goodrich, Frances—293
Good Sailor, The—299
Good Sex!—430
Good Soldier Schweik, The—291, 300
Good Soup, The—320, 328
Goodspeed Opera House—431, 453
Goodtime Charley—425
Good Times—99
Goodwin, J. Cheever—1
Goodwin, Nat C.—17, 31, 61, 83, 97, 180
Goodwin, William—320
Good Wives—295
Good Woman of Setzuan, The—302, 391, 416, 424, 430, 436
Goody Two Shoes—243, 269, 302, 307
Goorney, Howard—291, 347
Goose Hangs High, The—124, 130
Goosens, Eugene—114
Gorcey, Leo—196
Gordin, Jacob—60, 368
Gordon, Barbara—236, 259, 272
Gordon, Charlie—450
Gordon, Colin—268, 272
Gordon, Douglas—91
Gordone, Charles—379, 382
Gordon, Eleanor—105
Gordon, Gavin—207, 248
Gordon, Josephine—328
Gordon, Kitty—21, 56
Gordon, Larry—334
Gordon-Lenox, Cosmo—35
Gordon, Leon—118
Gordon, Marvin—344
Gordon, Max—185, 447
Gordon, Michael—279, 287
Gordon, Noele—236
Gordon, Pamela—252
Gordon, Richard—299
Gordon, Robert—247
Gordon, Ruth—87, 131, 148, 163, 170, 186, 198, 200, 202, 209, 239, 247, 278, 289, 290, 320
Gordon, Stephanie—353
Gorelik, Mordecai—221
Gore, Patrick—96
Gorey, Edward—440, 443
Gorey Stories—443
Gorilla Queen—364
Gorilla, The—134
Goring, Marius—220, 223, 260, 284, 335
Gorky, Maxim—44, 94, 121, 122, 198, 259, 334, 347, 396, 403, 417, 418, 420, 422, 429, 437, 453
Gorman, Cliff—373, 393, 434
Gorman, Mari—382
Gorme, Eydie—371
Gorney, Jay—132, 148, 164, 181, 262
Gospel of St. Matthew—393
Goss, Bernard—408
Gossett, Lou—394
Gossip Column—284
Gotcha!—436

Gothenberg City Theatre—417
"Gotta Dance"—257
Gottschalk, Ferdinand—243
Gough, Michael—259, 273, 291, 379, 432, 435
Gould, Diana—264
Gould, Elliot—309, 332, 364
Goulding, Edmund—73, 124
Gould, John—360
Gould, Morton—244
Goulet, Robert—325, 371
Gourlay, Eileen—332
Government Inspector, The—103, 144, 179, 259, 359, 367, 408, 422, 455
Governor's Lady, The—61
Governor's Son, The—6
Gowers, Patrick—305
Gow, James—234, 238, 244, 251
Gow, Ronald—196, 263, 283, 372, 379
Gow's Watch—128
Gozzi—390
Grab Bag, The—125
Grabber, The—90
Grable, Betty—379
Grab Me a Gondola—299
Grace—53
Grael, Barry Alan—342
Graham-Browne, W.—188
Graham, Colin—318, 335, 336
Graham Crackers—338
Graham, Denys—339
Grahame, G. M.—21
Grahame, Ronald—96
Graham, Gloria—325, 446, 451
Graham, Harry—72, 75, 83, 88, 101, 102, 113, 114, 120, 121, 127, 134, 135, 144, 150, 158, 159, 177, 182
Graham-Jones, Sebastian—437, 453
Graham-Jones, Susanna—431
Graham, Martha—118, 194, 341
Graham, Philip—159
Graham, Richard—264, 274, 279, 285
Graham, Ronny—212, 276, 287, 338, 373
Graham, Shellah—158
Graham, Sonia—296
Graham, William—315
Grainer, Ron—346, 358
Grainger, Gawn—366, 430, 437
Grain of Mustard Seed, The—101
Gramm, Donald—290
Grand Army Man, A—36, 40
Grand Duke, The—106, 446
Grand Guignol Players—44, 58, 102, 108, 114, 122
Grand Harlequinade—228
Grand Hotel—171, 177, 180, 246, 411
Grand Kabuki—382
Grand Magic—444
Grand Magic Circus—415, 452
Grand Manouvres—417
Grandma, Uncle Iliko, Hilarion, and I—360
Grand National Night—248
Grand Opera House (San Francisco) —34
Grand Opera House (Chicago)—331
Grand Street Follies, The—128, 131, 140, 148, 156, 161, 164
Grand Theatre, The (Liverpool)—5
Granger, Farley—137, 219, 314, 223, 347
Granger, Stewart—219
Grania of the Ships—188
Granier, Jeanne—68
Granite—143, 224
Granny—20
Grant, Cary (Leach, Archie)—150, 167
Grant, Christina—248
Grant, Cy—336, 435
Grant, Joyce—339, 347
Grant, Lee—189, 262, 364, 394
Grant, Micki—400, 427
Grant, Pauline—289
Grant, W. F.—102

Granville Barker, Harley—33, 54, 107, 250, 279
Granville Barkers, The—173
Granville, Charlotte—163
Granville, Sydney—193
Grass, Gunter—353, 389
Grass Harp, The—276
Grasshopper—114
Grass is Greener, The—311
Grass, Laurence—110
Grasso, Giovanni—44, 53
Grattan, Harry—53, 75, 79, 80, 83
Grauer, Ben—131
Graves, Clotilde—2
Graves, George—21, 43, 54
Graves, Peter—268, 278, 289
Graves, Robert—401
Gray, Alexander—131
Gray, Charles D.—345, 453
Gray, Clifford—79, 89, 196
Gray, David—143
Gray, Dolores—240, 247, 256, 314
Gray, Dulcie—232, 235, 240, 263, 268, 315, 323, 330, 355, 362, 387, 391, 407, 435
Gray, Eddie—236, 322
Gray, Gilda—92, 111
Gray, Harold—434
Gray, Jack—277
Gray, Joel—300
Gray, John—443
Gray, Linda—231, 258
Gray, Madeleine—282
Gray, Mary—136
Gray, Nicholas Stuart—265, 361
Gray, Peter—208
Gray, Sally—222
Gray, Simon—366, 379, 388, 394, 421, 443, 444, 450, 451
Gray, Spalding—406
Gray, Timothy—344
Gray, T. J.—94
Grease—400, 406
Great Adventure, The—70, 67, 274
Great Broxopp, The—119
Great Career, A—376
Great Catherine—68, 80, 209, 273
Great Caper, The—417
Great Day—244
Great Day, The—95
Great Divide, The—30, 51, 146
Great English Eccentrics—444
Great Expectations—220, 323
Great Galeoto, The—153
Great Gatsby, The—140, 412
Great God Brown, The—140, 144, 147, 190, 318, 404
Great Goodness of Life—378
Great Lafayette, The—39
Great Lover, The—74
Great Macdaddy, The—415
Great Northern Theater, (Chicago)—331
Great Passion Play, The—374
Great Queen Street Theater—5, 40
Great Romancer, The—208
Great Sebastians, The—298
Great Society, The—415
Great Temptations—140
Great Wall, The—431, 432
Great Waltz, The—190, 194, 389
Great White Hope, The—365, 384
Greaza, Walter—190
Greek Art Theatre Company—353, 367, 380
Greek National Theatre—402, 411
Greeks Had a Word for It, The—170, 192, 411
Greek Theatre—193
Green, Adolph—244, 271, 281, 286, 298, 309, 321, 327, 339, 344, 364, 385, 413, 442
Green and Wright—229
Green Back, The—182
Greenbank, Percy—2, 10, 11, 16, 21, 26, 27, 43, 48, 53, 57, 62, 63, 67, 72, 79, 80, 84, 95, 127
Green Bay Tree, The—186, 194
Green, Benny—414, 437
Green Bundle, The—202

Green, Carolyn—294
Green Cockatoo, The—68, 380
Green, Dorothy—178, 237, 249, 277
Greene, Clay—10
Greene, Clayton—37
Greene, Daisy—1
Greene, Evie—11, 16, 32, 43
Greene, Graham—235, 282, 286, 297, 301, 304, 310, 315, 337, 346, 421
Greene, Isabelle—23
Greene, James—451
Greene, Lorne—295
Greene, Rosie—47
Green Goddess, The—105, 110, 120, 129, 250
Green Grow the Lilacs—176, 180, 234
Green Hat, The—132, 135, 147, 237, 303
Green Helmet, The—54, 455
Green, Henry—100
Greenish Man, A—447
Green, John—191
Green Julia—367
Green, Julien—295
Green, Mabel—26, 120
Green, Marion—94
Green, Martyn—167, 193, 273, 280, 424
Green, Mawby—379
Green, Michael—455
Green, Millicent—190
Green, Mitzi—205
Green Pastures, The—170, 198, 274
Green, Paul—138, 142, 148, 155, 179, 200, 202, 226, 254, 269, 273, 295, 311, 312, 317, 354, 360, 389
Green Pond—440
Green Revue—431
Green, Richard—15
Green Stockings—59
Greenstreet, Sydney—37, 56, 72, 100, 291
Greenwich Theatre Trust—384
Greenwich Village Follies, The—92, 100, 106, 112, 118, 123, 125, 130, 133, 137, 138, 282
Greenwich Village Players, The—90
Greenwich Village Theatre—96
Greenwillow—377, 384, 390
Greenwood, Charlotte—61, 66, 78, 112, 125, 183, 197, 267, 447
Greenwood, Joan—258, 263, 275, 282, 283, 299, 311, 328, 346, 347, 367, 379, 407
Greenwood, John—307
Greenwood, Walter—196, 245, 305
Greet, Ben—4, 22, 37, 76, 80, 84, 90, 193, 229
Greet, Clare—119, 134, 144, 161
Greet, Philip Ben—193, 203
Greewell, Peter—315
Gregg, Everley—217
Gregg, Hubert—193, 218, 272, 334
Gregorio, Rose—332
Gregory, Andre—390, 397, 421
Gregory, Gillian—435
Gregory, Lady Augusta—3, 13, 23, 28, 37, 38, 39, 44, 46, 50, 51, 54, 58, 59, 60, 64, 76, 89, 96, 110, 145, 160, 184, 192, 197, 220
Gregory, Paul—284
Gregory, Sara—284
Gregson, John—334, 340
Greig, Edvard—121, 239, 264, 367
Grein, J. T.—85
Grenfell, Joyce—218, 245, 253, 272, 456
Gresham, Herbert—14, 19, 20, 30, 41, 57
Grew, Mary—157
Grew, William—163
Grey, Beryl—255
Grey, Clifford—79, 88, 95, 101, 102, 114, 119, 132, 151, 156, 165, 178, 182, 191, 231
Grey, Eddie—173
Grey, G.—139
Grey, Harrison—29
Grey, Joel—351, 358, 371

Grey, Mary—96, 100
Grey, William Daniel—440
Grifasi, Joe—450
Griffen, Minnie—49
Griffies, Ethel—126, 252, 273, 322, 327, 424
Griffi, Giuseppie Patroni—373
Griffin, Hayden—417
Griffin, Jonathan—307
Griffin, Norman—114
Griffin, Russell—163
Griffith, Andy—293, 314
Griffith, Drew—435
Griffith, Eleanor—163
Griffith, Hugh—64, 272, 300, 316, 338
Griffith, Robert—200, 323
Griffiths, Herbert—206
Griffiths, Jane—289
Griffiths, Joe—409
Griffiths, Michael—357
Griffiths, Trevor—397, 398, 401, 411, 421, 427
Grigson, John—267
Grillo, John—401
Grimaldi, "Joey"—456
Grimes, Jerry—366
Grimes, Tammy—297, 300, 314, 321, 334, 344, 383, 420, 426, 444, 454
Grimston, Dorothy—21
Grimwood, Herbert—54, 58
Grip, The—75
Grist, Reri—301
Grizzard, George—161, 332, 334, 337, 354, 378, 401
Grodin, Charles—420
Grofe, Ferde—216
Groody, Louise—106, 134, 148
Groome, Stanley—227
Groom-Johnson, Austin—188
Gropper, Milton—126
Grosbard, Ulu—353
Gros, Ernest—2, 10, 20, 21, 25, 41
Gross, Bernard—418
Gross, Laurence—181
Grossman, Jan—373
Grossmann, Suzanne—373, 375
Grossmith, Ena—127
Grossmith, George, Jr.—8, 16, 21, 26, 37, 41, 43, 57, 62, 79, 94, 102, 114, 120, 127, 134, 143, 158
Grossmith, Lawrence—21, 30, 43, 48, 49, 58, 82
Grossmith, Weedon—7, 16, 21, 48, 57
Grot, Anton—229
Grotowski, Jerzy—375, 382
Grounds for Divorce—125, 215
Grounds for Marriage—366
Group Soup—369
Group Theatre—179, 181, 184, 193, 197, 200, 205, 214, 216, 217, 219, 221
Grout, Hugh—430
Grout, James—427
Grout, John—394
Grout, Philip—395
Groves, Fred—101, 178
G. R. Point—436
Grudeff, Marian—351
Gruen, Bernard—202
Gruendgens, Gustaf—264, 328
Grumpy—66
Grun, Bernard—299
Grundy, Lily—43
Grundy, Sydney—2, 43, 264
Grunwald—178
Gruppo Sperimentazione Teatrale—403
Gruppo Teatro Libero—430
Guardian Angel—241
Guardino, Harry—371
Guardsman, The—125, 134, 155, 381, 439, 444
Guare, John—374, 393, 396, 398, 428, 436, 449
Guarnieri, Gianfrancesco—382
Guerin—57
Guernon, Charles—82

Guernsey, Otis L., Jr.—246, 356, 363, 392, 399, 412, 419, 425, 433, 448, 457
Guerrero, Maria—144
Guest, Morris—166
Guest, Val—227, 236, 245, 248
Guetary, Georges—253, 263
Guevara—380, 381
Guild of Canadian Playwrights—441
Guild of Variety Artists (GVA)—98
Guillaume, Robert—430
Guillemand—62
Guilliat, Lee—400
Guilty Party—328
Guinea-Pig, The—247
Guinnan, John—152
Guinness, Alec—202, 207, 214, 218, 220, 222, 238, 248, 249, 254, 255, 259, 260, 264, 266, 274, 276, 285, 288, 301, 318, 322, 340, 344, 345, 361, 366, 374, 394, 406, 421, 427, 435
Guise, The—455
Guitry, Lucien—50, 110, 115, 122
Guitry, Sacha—84, 85, 87, 101, 103, 106, 115, 117, 122, 144, 145, 165, 198, 284
Guittard, Laurence—456
Gullan, Campbell—128
Gulliver's Travels—8, 376, 424, 445
Gunayadin, Erol—396
Gunn, Bill—421
Gunning, Louise—15, 36, 53
Gunn, Judy—187, 188
Gunn, Moses—367
Gunther, John—257
Gurdner, Paul—208
Gurney, A. R.—395, 415, 428
Gurney, A. R. Jr.—431
Gurney, Calud—248
Gurney, Rachel—247, 274, 279
Gustav III—417, 422
Guthrie, Judith—249
Guthrie Theatre (Minneapolis)—336, 399
Guthrie, Tyrone—154, 178, 182, 183, 184, 188, 189, 192, 197, 202, 207, 208, 213, 214, 218, 219, 228, 241, 242, 243, 249, 250, 260, 264, 268, 269, 274, 278, 279, 283, 285, 286, 290, 295, 296, 298, 300, 301, 302, 306, 307, 312, 314, 316, 317, 319, 323, 327, 329, 334, 336, 341, 343, 356, 361, 366, 367, 376, 398
Guthrie, Woody—404
Gutierrez, Gerald—434, 446
Guys and Dolls—130, 267, 270, 275, 282, 295, 353, 360, 384, 430
Gwatkin, Norman—319
Gwenn, Edmund—27, 28, 48, 49, 107, 119, 120, 143, 144, 172, 207, 226, 244, 318
Gwillim, Jack—366
Gwynne, Fred—400
Gwynn, Michael—272, 301, 417, 438
Gwynn, Nell—223
Gwyther, Geoffrey—127
Gyarmathy, Marcel—272
Gyarmathy, Michael—263
Gypsy—163, 314, 409, 417, 425
Gypsy Baron, The—220
Gypsy Love—56
Gypsy Rose Lee—230

Haas, Dolly—247
Haas, Tom—436
Habeas Corpus—406, 420
Habimah Troupe (Israel)—133, 145, 353
Hackaday, Hal—394
Hackett, Albert—47, 226, 293
Hackett, Buddy—288, 345
Hackett, James K.—11, 19, 22, 34, 45, 51, 80, 93, 103, 114, 146
Hackett, Joan—400
Hackett, Raymond—120
Hackett, Walter—48, 71, 79, 84, 89, 107, 153, 166, 172, 177, 187, 192, 197, 201, 206, 303

Hackin, Dennis—425
Hack, Keith—403, 431, 436, 439, 452
Hackman, Gene—344
Hackney, Mabel—49, 67
Hacks, Peter—387
Haddon, Peter—114, 127
Haddow, Jeffrey—450
Hadfield, Henry—33
Hadjidakis, Manos—364
Hadley, Henry—14
Hadrian the Seventh—372, 378, 381, 384
Hael, Joan—274
Hag—435
Hagan, James—186, 262
Hagar's Children—436
Hagedorn, Jessica—445
Hagedorn, W.—33
Hagen, Claude L.—4, 60
Hagen, Uta—217, 259, 262, 267, 268, 275, 279, 287, 293, 300, 302, 332, 373
Haggard, Stephan—218
Hague, Albert—293, 314
Hahn, Reynaldo—144
Haig, Emma—151
Haigh, Kenneth—299, 301, 302, 329, 335, 346, 354, 373, 417, 454
Hailey, Marian—374
Hailey, Oliver—424, 430, 454
Hailstone, John—361
Haimsohn, George—372
Haines, Herbert E.—26, 32, 36
Haines, William Wister—252
Hair—139, 364, 370, 372, 377, 392, 398, 405, 417, 437, 440
Haire, Wilson John—445
Hairy Ape, The—111, 112, 160
Haiti—213
Hajos, Mitzi—71, 78, 100, 200
Hale, Alan—270
Hale, Binnie—95, 102, 114, 126, 132, 134, 165, 182, 192, 206, 222, 258, 285
Hale, Georgina—451
Hale, John—317, 383, 389, 428
Hale, Robert—75, 93, 109, 182
Hales, Jonathan—416, 427
Hale, Sonnie—151, 158, 173, 178, 258, 273, 315
Hale, Willis—9, 204
Hale, Winifred—4
Haley, Jack—182, 230, 257
Half a Loaf—315
Half an Hour—66
Half-a-Sixpence—339, 351
Half-Life—437, 443
Half-past Eight—80
Halfway Up the Tree—365
Hall, Adelaide—156, 170
Hall, Adrian—333, 375, 388
Hallant, Henry—167
Hallard, C. M.—67, 79, 106
Hall, Bettina—176
Hall, Bob—434
Hall, Carol—442
Hall, Clay—287
Hall, Davis—390
Hall, Dorothy—170, 205
Halleck, Dan—378
Hallelujah—403
Hallelujah, Baby—364
Hall, Glenn—66
Halliday, Hildegarde—170
Halliday, John—100, 148, 196
Halliday, Lena—30, 102
Halliday, Richard—287, 411
Halliday, Robert—142, 157, 177, 203
Halliwell, David—361, 387, 407
Hall, John T.—43
Hall, Juanita—243, 288, 376
Hall, Katie—201
Hall, Laura Nelson—41
Hallman, William—99
Hall, Mary—109
Halloran, John—191
Hallor, Edith—82
Halloween—382
Hall, Owen—1, 7, 10, 15, 21, 31

Hallows, Lillian—68
Hall, Peter—290, 291, 295, 296, 300, 301, 304, 311, 316, 321, 323, 324, 334, 335, 336, 337, 341, 347, 352, 355, 359, 360, 361, 367, 373, 379, 386, 393, 394, 400, 415, 431, 435, 436, 439, 444, 451
Hall, Philip Baker—420
Hall, Thurston—93
Hall, Vyvian—272
Hall, Willis—316, 322, 335, 353, 382, 406, 414, 424, 430, 435, 440
Halstan, Margaret—49, 58, 94, 95, 183
Hamarskjold, Dag—394
Hambleton, T. Edward—286, 291, 395, 431
Hambling, Arthur—213
Hambourg, Mark—223
Hamilton, Aubrey—159
Hamilton, Bruce—277
Hamilton, Cicely—43, 136
Hamilton, Clayton—138, 251
Hamilton, Cosmo Gordon—21, 32, 53, 89, 159
Hamilton, Dorothy—236
Hamilton, Edith—329, 342
Hamilton, Guy—315
Hamilton, Henry—16, 21, 26, 28, 32, 37, 48, 49, 57, 62, 67, 79
Hamilton, John F.—124
Hamilton, Kim—314
Hamilton, Murray—244
Hamilton, Nancy—190, 216, 221, 291
Hamilton, Ord—187, 192
Hamilton, Patrick—165, 217, 239, 336, 429
Hamilton, Rick—354
Hamlet—3, 4, 13, 16, 22, 23, 27, 37, 49, 50, 53, 54, 58, 59, 63, 67, 68, 69, 70, 72, 73, 76, 80, 84, 90, 97, 98, 100, 103, 115, 122, 128, 135, 136, 137, 152, 160, 166, 167, 173, 179, 183, 188, 192, 193, 197, 202, 203, 207, 208, 209, 214, 215, 218, 219, 223, 228, 231, 232, 233, 241, 242, 246, 249, 254, 255, 256, 259, 260, 265, 268, 274, 278, 284, 285, 290, 296, 301, 306, 307, 309, 311, 312, 313, 317, 323, 328, 329, 341, 342, 343, 347, 348, 353, 355, 360, 363, 366, 369, 374, 375, 381, 384, 388, 390, 391, 394, 396, 397, 403, 415, 417, 421, 422, 423, 425, 428, 430, 433, 438, 439, 444, 445, 447, 452, 455
Hamlet and Ham-Omlet—401
Hamlet of Stepney Green, The—310, 319
Hamlett, Dilys—352
Hamlisch, Marvin—449
Hammerstein, Arthur—67, 88, 98, 110, 150, 155, 164
Hammerstein, James—344, 371, 395, 418, 421
Hammerstein, Oscar—5, 14, 52, 99, 155
Hammerstein, Oscar II—103, 104, 117, 119, 125, 132, 133, 150, 157, 164, 181, 196, 217, 234, 235, 236, 238, 244, 247, 249, 262, 266, 271, 309, 314, 324, 329, 348, 374, 376, 438, 447, 454, 456
Hammerstein, Reginald—150, 164
Hammerstein, William—290
Hammond, Aubrey—134, 224
Hammond, Kay—171, 178, 186, 227, 250, 264, 274, 277, 285, 300, 302, 305, 309
Hammond, Myra—59
Hammond, Percy—203
Hammond, Peter—288
Hammond, Ruth—148
Hammond, Virginia—92
Hamp—348, 364
Hampden, Walter—32, 36, 41, 52, 78, 84, 98, 103, 108, 122, 135, 137, 142, 152, 184, 238, 251, 262, 297
Hampshire, Keith—322

Hampshire, Susan—322, 345, 374, 403, 417, 418, 431, 439
Hampstead's Everyman Theatre—136
Hampstead Theatre—424, 426. Club —368, 372, 391, 395, 397, 403, 408, 409, 410, 439, 443, 445
Hampton, Christopher—359, 375, 389, 393, 395, 407, 415, 427, 430, 436, 440, 452
Hampton, Louise—127, 134, 177
Ham, Roderick and Partners—457
Hamsun, Knut—114, 122
Ham Tree, The—25
Hanaford, Phebe—5
Hanbury, Lily—6, 1
Hancock, John—335, 368, 373
Hancock, Sheila—318, 328, 334, 406, 418
Hancock, Tony—276
Handel, George F.—250
Handke, Peter—401, 402, 407, 410, 430, 436
Handl, Irene—219, 328, 417, 432
Handman, Michael—395
Hand Man, The—69
Handman, Wynn—350
Hand of Death, The—115
Hand of the Potter, The—107
Hands Across the Sea—201
Hands, C. E.—16
Hands, Terry—366, 372, 373, 374, 380, 382, 388, 389, 396, 397, 403, 415, 422, 427, 429, 437, 444, 453
Haney, Carol—287, 291, 315
Hanging Judge—277
Hanging Outlook, The—64
Hang of the Gaol, The—446
Hankin, John—260
Hankin, St. John—28, 33, 36, 44, 83
Hanky Panky—61
Hanky Park—395
Hanley, James—131, 141, 149, 380
Hanley, William—332, 345, 396
Hannan, Charles—7
Hanna, Philip—252
Hannay, Rev. J. O.—67
Hannele—44
Hannen, Hermione—223
Hannen, Lion—135
Hannen, Nicholas—119, 135, 143, 151, 158, 191, 212, 246
Hann, Walter—3, 61
Hanrahan's Oath—89
Hanratty in Hell—430
Hanray, Lawrence—121, 127, 188
Han, Reynaldo—145
Hans Anderson—418, 440
Hansberry, Lorraine—314, 344, 355, 378, 406
Hansel and Gretel—189, 214, 457
Hans Kohlhass—408
Hanson, Barry—375, 379
Hanson, Gladys—38
Hanson, Leslie—273, 274, 279, 285, 301
Hapgood, Norman—209
Happening—335
"Happening" Come—366
Happiest Days of Your Life, The—258
Happiest Millionaire, The—298, 305
Happiness—83, 368
Happiness Cage, The—390
Happy and Glorious—241
Happy Apple, The—386
Happy as a Sandbag—421
Happy as Larry—255
Happy Birthday—247, 450
Happy Birthday, Wanda June—386, 439
Happy Days—93, 326, 335, 354, 375, 384, 404, 422, 439, 454
Happy Day, The—75
Happy Days Are Here Again—353
Happy End—353, 408, 436
Happy Ending—352
Happy Family—192, 273
Happy Haven, The—323
Happy Holiday—291
Happy Hooligan—49

Happy Hunting—298
Happy Hypocrite, The—3, 12, 303
Happy Journey to Trenton and Camden, The—361
Happyland—25
Happy Marriage, The—47, 246, 277
Happy New Year, A—115, 454
Happy Prince, The—125
Happy Returns—212
Happy Time, The—266, 270, 276, 371
Happy Yellow—436
Harangues, The—383
Harbach, Otto—83, 85, 92, 93, 100, 106, 117, 119, 125, 132, 133, 134, 177, 187, 202, 342
Harbage, Alfred—432
Harben, Hubert—206
Harbord, Gordon—299
Harburg, E. Y.—164, 170, 181, 182, 190, 206, 221, 240, 252, 271, 304
Harcourt, Cyril—37, 90, 95
Harcourt, R. V.—32
Hardie, Russell—315
Harding, Ann—149, 185
Hardinge, H. C. M.—103
Harding, Huntly—395
Harding, Lyn—27, 32, 48, 49, 63, 82, 103, 160, 171, 181, 183
Harding, Sarah—452
Harding's Luck—417, 418
Hard Slog—415
Hardwicke, Cedric—111, 143, 144, 150, 159, 165, 178, 181, 183, 184, 196, 211, 249, 260, 265, 275, 288, 314, 340, 349
Hardwicke, Edward—359
Hardwick, Paul—438, 452
Hardy, Hugh—377
Hardy, Joseph—364, 378, 385, 386, 406, 450
Hardy, Robert—328
Hardy, Thomas—72, 137, 401, 430
Hare, Betty—188, 192
Hare, David—379, 390, 395, 414, 421, 427, 430, 437, 443
Hare, Doris—183, 212, 348, 368
Hare, Gilbert—16
Hare, Lumsden—57, 62, 67, 350
Harem, The—126
Hare, Robertson—201, 244, 253, 259, 268, 278, 289, 372
Hare, Sir John—16, 38, 85, 97, 110, 198
Harford, Betty—325
Hargrave, Roy—148
Hargreaves, John—239
Haricot Beans—108
Hari-Kari—69
Harker and Terraine—127
Harker, Gordon—140, 165, 192, 227, 294, 369
Harker, Joseph—3, 8, 53, 61, 62, 121, 127, 135
Harker, L. Allen—151
Harker, Phil—121, 127, 135
Harkers, The—126, 134, 143, 158, 159
Harkness, Edward S.—147
Harkness, Jean—53
Harland, Celia—102
Harlan, Otis—6, 31, 56
Harlem—163
Harlem Cavalcade—230
Harlequin and the Fairy's Dilemma—21
Harlequinade—228, 246, 258
Harlettes—420
Harley, Margot—405
Harling, Frank—141
Harlow, Jean—410
Harmonica Orchestra—142
Harned, Virginia—4, 7, 22, 35
Harnick, Sheldon—98, 128, 282, 315, 321, 338, 343, 344, 358, 386
Harold—159
Harper, Gerald—394, 435
Harper, Valerie—390
Harriet—234, 238, 242
Harrigan, Edward—15, 59

486

Harrigan, Nedda—92, 150, 224
Harrigan, Nes—104
Harrigan, William—156, 257
Harriman, Borden—124
Harrington, Alice—76
Harrington, Eva—385
Harrington, Hamtree—125
Harris, Anita—358
Harris, Barbara—326, 341, 351, 358, 388
Harris, Chris—437
Harris, Clare—249
Harris, Clifford—79, 80, 113, 126, 134
Harris, Cynthia—358
Harris, Eliza—313
Harris, Elmer—78, 221, 279
Harris, George II—364
Harris, Henry B.—56, 60, 70
Harris, Jed—186, 209, 241, 262, 281, 298, 456
Harris, Jim—145
Harris, Joan—379
Harris, Joel Chandler—72
Harris, Julie—138, 250, 260, 262, 266, 272, 273, 294, 307, 323, 327, 339, 352, 372, 393, 400, 407, 426, 439
Harris, Leonore—82
Harris, Lionel—290, 315
Harris, Neil—428
Harrison, Carey—379, 415
Harrison, Frederick—3, 29
Harrison, John—422
Harrison, Kathleen—188, 212, 289, 299, 315, 402
Harrison, Mona—105, 107, 235
Harrison, Paul Carter—415
Harrison, Ray—315
Harrison, Rex—105, 174, 186, 202, 216, 258, 266, 267, 296, 298, 315, 323, 407, 408, 435, 437
Harrison, Richard Berry—170, 198
Harrison, Tony—422
Harris, Richard—315, 316, 340, 407
Harris, Robert—126, 152, 156, 158, 183, 188, 218, 255, 306, 329, 361
Harris, Rosemary—276, 296, 300, 309, 319, 320, 334, 346, 357, 362, 366, 371, 394, 437
Harris, Sam H.—30, 36, 41, 45, 52, 56, 61, 106, 110, 116, 229
Harris Theatre—141
Harris, Winifred—49
Harrold, Orville—52
Harron, Donald—352
Harrow, Lisa—403
Harry, Noon and Night—351
Harry Outside—422, 439
Hart, Dolores—309
Harte, Bret—50, 272
Harter, Sarah—341
Hartford, Huntington—309, 350
Hartford Stage Company—350
Hart, John—329
Hart, Lorenzo—92, 99, 103, 131, 132, 140, 149, 151, 156, 163, 164, 170, 173, 196, 205, 206, 211, 217, 230
Hartman Foundation—425
Hartman, Grace—253, 266
Hartmann, Louis—29, 34, 60
Hartman, Paul—153, 253, 266, 279
Hart, Margie—230
Hart, Moss—170, 180, 181, 186, 190, 191, 196, 199, 200, 205, 210, 211, 216, 217, 220, 222, 225, 226, 227, 229, 238, 240, 243, 249, 256, 257, 262, 263, 265, 276, 286, 287, 311, 319, 331, 350, 355, 356, 445, 453
Hartnell, William—267
Hartne, Norman—159
Hart, Peggy—196
Hart, Richard—244
Hart, Roxy—420, 424, 449
Hart, Stan—357
Hart, Teddy—205, 212
Hart, Tony—59
Hartwig, Walter—121, 128, 138, 144, 152, 167, 210
Hart, William S.—26, 61

Hartzel, Rachel—191
Harvard Prize—66, 117
Harvard Theater Collection—9
Harvard University—325
Harvard Workshop—147
Harve, Paul—52
Harvest—54, 59
Harvest Moon, The—48
Harvey—65, 240, 246, 263, 276, 308, 412, 422, 433
Harvey, Frank—235, 401
Harvey, Georgette—216
Harvey, Gladys—53
Harvey, John Martin—2, 7, 45, 54, 58, 68, 75, 80, 97, 121, 130, 174, 188, 202
Harvey, Laurence—278, 290, 293, 300, 302, 307, 313, 321, 385, 412
Harvey, Martin—43, 45, 58, 122, 130
Harvey McLead—403
Harvey, Morris—79, 108, 114, 120, 126, 127
Harvey, Peter—326
Harvey, Rupert—109
Harwood, H. M.—75, 79, 83, 101, 127, 158, 172, 185, 188
Harwood, J. M.—201
Harwood, John—158
Harwood, Robb—15
Harwood, Ronald—414, 443, 451
Hasait, Max—123, 129, 138
Hasek, Jaroslav—291, 300
Haseltine, Fred—297
Hasenclever, Walter—307
Haskell, Loney—130
Hasnain, Arif—439
Hassall, Christopher—197, 201, 207, 218, 236, 263, 268, 279, 283, 285
Hassan—120, 125, 274, 447
Hassard Short's Ritz Revue—125
Hassett, Ray—422
Hastings, Basil M.—79, 94
Hastings, Charlotte—263
Hastings, Hugh—267, 407
Hastings, Michael—361, 435, 437, 443, 455
Hastings, Milo—202
Hastings, Patrick—253
Hasty Heart, The—244, 246
Has "Washington" Legs?—445
Hatch, Frank—87
Hatch, Tony—406
Hatfield, Hurd—220, 296
Hatfields and the McCoys, The—389
Hatful of Rain, A—294, 305, 383
Hats Off To Ice—239
Hatton, Fanny—74, 78
Hatton, Frederick—74, 78
Hatvany, Lili—171
Hauerbach, Otto (later Harbach)—41, 56, 62, 71, 74, 85
Haughton, Charlie—315
Hauptmann, Gerhart—24, 27, 44, 64, 74, 115, 359, 360
Hauptman, William—436
Hauser, Frank—294, 305, 310, 315, 322, 323, 330, 334, 352, 365, 366, 394, 410, 418, 424, 429, 438, 439
Havana—43, 51
Havel, Vaclav—373, 383
Havergal, Giles—356, 390, 403, 436, 452
Haverly Minstrels—137
Have You Met Our Rabbit—394
Haviland, William—7
Havoc—126
Havoc, June—239, 316, 339, 361, 391, 406
Hawdon, Robin—401
Hawkes, Sylvia—143
Hawkes, Tom—435
Hawkins, Ira—442
Hawkins, Iris—32
Hawkins, Jack—145, 159, 165, 172, 177, 182, 183, 193, 201, 207, 208, 213, 219, 249, 274, 411
Hawkins, John—372
Hawkins, Trish—406, 452
Hawk, Jeremy—222

Hawk, The—71
Haworth, Joseph—17
Hawthorne, Nathaniel—56, 85, 373
Hawthorne, Nigel—437
Hawthorne, Ruth—131
Hawthorn, Pamela—454
Hawtrey, Anthony—248, 253, 267, 273, 289
Hawtrey, Sir Charles—7, 12, 36, 43, 49, 53, 67, 83, 84, 95, 107, 123, 206, 212, 222, 289
Hawtrey, William—48
Hayd, Douglas—3
Hayden, Terese—269
Haydn, Richard—221
Haydon, Florence—27
Haydon, Julie—196, 211, 217, 244
Haye, Phyllis—108
Hayes, Albert—148
Hayes, Alfred—287, 292
Hayes, Anthony—288
Hayes, Bill—281
Hayes, David—325
Hayes, George—245
Hayes, Grace—119, 148
Hayes, Helen—48, 50, 52, 56, 83, 88, 93, 111, 124, 128, 136, 146, 149, 150, 159, 161, 172, 177, 189, 196, 217, 226, 234, 242, 244, 247, 248, 266, 276, 289, 290, 295, 296, 302, 308, 309, 335, 362, 399
Hayes, Joseph—293, 297, 332, 418
Hayes, Milton—151
Hayes, Patricia—213
Hayes, Peter Lind—309
Hayes, Robert—279
Hay Fever—132, 134, 189, 349, 373, 411, 439
Hay, Ian—94, 107, 120, 127, 165, 172, 177, 192, 201, 202, 211, 273, 280
Hay, Julya—295
Hay, Malcolm—457
Hayman, Carole—450
Hayman, Ronald—367
Hay, Mary—119
Haynes, Daniel—148
Haynes, Jim—340, 347
Haynes, Minna Gale—82
Hay, Richard L.—319, 441, 448
Hays, Bill—389, 432
Hays, David—380, 392
Hays, H. R.—221
Hays, Will—131
Hayward and Maynard—55
Hayward, Leland—258, 398
Hayward, Louis—171, 181, 195
Hazel Flagg—281
Hazell, Hy—253, 280, 294, 317
Hazelton, George—62
Hazzard, John E.—78, 99
He—179
Heade, Robert—447
Headmaster, The—67
Head Over Heels—120
Heads Up—164
Heal, Joan—294, 289, 295, 299, 351
Healy, Betty—148
Healy, Edgar—23
Healy, Eunice—191
Healy, Ted—132, 148, 164
He and She—104
Hearne, Chrystal—82
Hearne, Richard—227
Hearn, James—45, 49, 58
Heartbreak House—100, 108, 122, 184, 188, 213, 215, 237, 269, 318, 330, 348, 367, 368, 375, 396, 422, 431, 446
Hear Their Voices: Women Founders of the American Theatre, 1910-1945—445
Heart is a Highland, The—348
Heather Field, The—3
Heatherley, Clifford—197
Heatherton, Ray—174
Heath, Gordon—244
Heath, Thomas—25, 111
"Heat Waves"—186
Heaven and Earth—202, 265

Heaven and Hell—428
Heaven and Hell's Agreement—415
Heaven Grand in Amber Orbit—430
Heavy Traffic—243
Hecht, Ben—157, 182, 196, 208, 228, 247, 250, 269, 281, 302, 349, 381, 402, 442
Hecht, Paul—357
Heckart, Eileen—97, 288, 305, 340, 351, 378
Hector, A. B.—81, 146
Hecuba—360, 366
Hecube—80
Hedda Gabler—16, 50, 114, 159, 193, 203, 231, 232, 237, 256, 259, 273, 290, 324, 347, 374, 389, 395, 401, 417, 418, 422, 439
Hedgerow Repertory Theatre—123
Hedley, H. B.—151, 171
Hedley, Philip—421
Heeley, Desmond—340, 367
Heffernan, John—318, 368, 379
Heflin, Frances—116, 244
Heflin, Van—216, 293, 338, 398
Heggen, Thomas—257, 261, 302
Heggie, O. P. (Blayds)—49, 50, 67, 108, 125, 131, 203
"He Had Refinement"—271
Heidelberg—11, 16
Heifner, Jack—426
Heijermans, Herman—95, 153, 250
Heilman, John—379
Heimann, Philip—189, 191
Heimath—121
Heinemann, Ede—164
Heinreid, Paul—407
Hein, Silvio—71, 83
Heinz, A.—154
Heiress, The—252, 261, 263, 268, 308, 429, 453
He Is To Blame for Everything—153
Helburn, Theresa—84, 238, 252, 318
Held, Anna—6, 15, 20, 31, 43, 52, 90, 185
Held by the Enemy—54, 209
Helen!—182
Helena's Husband—77
Helen Come Home—455
Helen Goes to Troy—239
Helen Keller—319
Helen of Troy—99, 118
Hell—56, 75
Hellbent for Heaven—124, 130, 246, 430
Heller, Joseph—371
Heller, O.—261
Hellinger, Mark—181
Hellman, Lillian—138, 191, 199, 216, 220, 226, 229, 239, 246, 247, 256, 262, 271, 275, 280, 298, 302, 320, 325, 368, 410, 455, 456
Hellman, Wilbur, Latouche, Parker and Bernstein—308
Hello and Goodby—410, 444
Hello! Brixton!—76
Hello Broadway—71
Hello Daddy—158
Hello! Dolly!—155, 212, 344, 350, 353, 370, 373, 399, 424, 445, 455, 457
Hello, Out There!—323
Hello, Paris—56
Hello! Plymouth!—76
Hello! Ragtime!—63
Hello, Repertory!—76
Hell, Temptation and Gaby—60
Hellzapoppin'—211, 240, 258, 441
Helm, John Cecil—226
Helmond, Katherine—393
Helmore, Tom—248
Heloise—390
Heloise and Abelard: Love Letters from the Middle Ages—446
Helpmann, Max—374
Helpmann, Robert—50, 208, 241, 259, 274, 279, 283, 289, 290, 295, 301, 302, 306, 307, 318, 329
Help Yourself—202
Heming, Percy—127

Heming, Violet—111, 115, 119, 121, 136
Hemingway, Ernest—221
Hemmell, Don—296
Hemmerde, Edward—57
Hemmings, David—359, 421
Hempstead Theatre Club—353
Hemsley, Thomas—274
Henderson, Dickie—305, 316
Henderson, Florence—280, 285, 288, 339, 367
Henderson, Margo—334
Henderson, Ray—131, 140, 149, 157, 163, 170, 176, 181, 196
Henderson, Robert—254, 264
Hendra, Tony—406
Hendricks-Simon, Roger—379
Hendrie, Ernest—28
Hendry, Tom—381, 400, 405
Heneker, David—318, 339, 353, 359
Henie, Sonja—221, 239, 252
Henley, George—73
Henley, Joan—165
Hennequin, Maurice—68, 76, 94
Henning, Doug—413
Henrichs, Helmut—360
Henried, Paul—222, 223
Henrietta, The—45
Henri, Florette—279
Henry, Charles—113, 227, 272, 276, 280, 289, 322
Henry Irving—138
Henry IV Part 1—49, 109, 160, 183, 197, 218, 232, 246, 274, 285, 295, 296, 312, 322, 328, 329, 367, 387, 396, 423. Part 2—8, 68, 73, 76, 84, 109, 144, 145, 184, 232, 246, 274, 279, 295, 322, 329, 387, 403, 416. Parts 1 & 2—68, 73, 76, 84, 108, 135, 136, 184, 218, 224, 246, 249, 295, 335, 347, 348, 354, 360, 374, 389, 417, 422, 428, 454
Henry, Lee—317
Henry, Martha—374, 394
Henry, O.—52
Henry of Navarre—48
Henry, Peggie—400
Henry Pilk's Awesome World—436
Henry Savage's Grand Opera Company—38
Henry the Tenth Part Seven—455
Henry, Victor—359
Henry V—3, 4, 8, 45, 54, 58, 59, 63, 64, 68, 69, 73, 76, 80, 103, 109, 152, 192, 193, 194, 207, 208, 228, 237, 249, 265, 273, 274, 279, 285, 296, 301, 312, 313, 323, 335, 341, 347, 348, 354, 360, 381, 382, 396, 409, 422, 428, 429, 430, 437, 438, 444, 446
Henry VI, Part 1—121, 122, 285, 389, 444. Part 2—8, 121, 285, 290, 389, 430. Part 3—121, 285, 296, 361, 439. Parts 1 and 2—307. Parts 2 and 3—444. Parts 1, 2 and 3—33, 341, 346, 360, 423, 437
Henry VII—245
Henry VIII—12, 54, 58, 63, 80, 137, 182, 189, 214, 250, 251, 258, 264, 268, 283, 286, 307, 311, 329, 354, 375, 380, 390
Henson, Elizabeth—279
Henson, Gladys—284, 294
Henson, Leslie—79, 102, 113, 119, 120, 151, 158, 164, 199, 206, 207, 222, 231, 244, 258, 289
Henson, Nicky—358, 390, 416, 417, 452, 456
Hentschel, Irene—219, 227, 244, 254, 259, 264
Hepburn, Audrey—272, 287, 291
Hepburn, Katharine—216, 232, 268, 279, 306, 323, 378, 426, 433, 449
Hepple, Jeanne—357
Hepton, Bernard—317
Hepworth, Barbara—273
Herald Square Theatre, The—46
Herbach, Otto—176
Herbert, A. P.—143, 182, 187, 192, 206, 248, 253, 294

Herbert, Evelyn—133, 149, 157
Herbert, F. Hugh—234, 252, 271, 279, 298
Herbert, Henry—117
Herbert, H. H.—67
Herbert, John—355, 364, 379
Herbert, Joseph—30, 35, 41, 47, 100
Herbert, Victor—15, 17, 20, 26, 30, 31, 35, 42, 43, 46, 52, 56, 62, 66, 71, 74, 78, 82, 92, 97, 99, 105, 112, 114, 115, 124, 128, 129, 167, 253, 254, 424, 446
Herbie, Eileen—217
Her Cardboard Lover—148
Here Are Ladies—395, 407
Here Comes the Bride—172
Here Comes the Sun—430
Here Come the Boys—248
Here Come the Clowns—212, 220, 265, 355
Hereford, Oliver—65
"Here in My Arms"—132
Here's Love—338
Here, There and Everywhere—253
Heretic, The—386
Her Excellency—263
Her First Roman—371
Her Forbidden Marriage—76
Herford, Ann—104
Herfords, The—104
Her Honour at Stake—96
Her Husband's Wife—79
Herington, Julian—317
Heritage—and Its History, A—352
Her Ladyship—89
Herlie, Eileen—250, 253, 260, 269, 284, 307, 347, 401
Her Life of Pleasure—96
Herlihy, James Joe—309
Her Lord and Master—137
Herman, Jerry—326, 344, 357, 378, 413, 445, 455
Hermann, Henry—268
Her Master's Voice—187, 194
Herne, Chrystal—1, 15, 28, 47, 56, 87, 119, 129, 132, 270
Herne, James A.—1, 9, 32, 104
Herny, Charles—283
Herod—2, 58, 445
Heroes, The—341
Heroic Stubbs, The—32
Hero Is Born, A—208
Heron, Joyce—213, 231, 438
Heron-Maxwell, Beatrice—28
Hero Rises Up, The—382
Hero, The—106, 116
Her Own Way—15, 153
Herr, Michael—452
Hersee, George—22
Hersey, David—435
Hersey, John—240, 321
Her Soldier Boy—79
Herts, Henry B.—60, 70
Hertz, H. A.—68
Herve, Paul—66
Hervey, Frank—187
Hervieu, Paul—8, 38, 45, 90
Herz, Ralph—41, 91
Hess—445, 451
Hessian Corporal, The—366
Hess, Rudolf—445
Hester Crewe—184, 233
Hester, Hal—371
Heston, Charlton—255, 302, 320
Hestor, George—108
He That Plays the King—422
Heuer, John—417
Heureuse—33
He Wanted Adventure—187
He Was Born Gay—206
He Was Gone When They Got There—359
Hewer, John—340
Hewes, Henry—85, 311, 319, 325, 334, 337, 343, 350, 419
Hewett, Christopher—328, 341, 366
He Who Gets Slapped—111, 116, 144, 249, 348, 368
Hewitt, Muriel—144
Hewlett, Maurice—32
Hewlett, Monroe—60
Hey, Dennin—324
Heyward, Dorothy—149, 216, 224, 257, 330
Heyward, Du Bose—149, 176, 195, 216, 224, 284
Heywood, Donald—97, 103, 148
Heywood, Thomas—395
Hiatus—69
Hibbard, Edna—141
Hichens, Robert—8, 57, 58, 102
Hickerson, Harold—157
Hicklin, Margery—127
Hickman, Charles—236, 245, 248, 253, 258, 263, 268, 273, 276, 277, 278, 283, 288, 289, 294, 311, 345, 354, 368, 372, 410, 414, 453
Hicks, Barbara—304
Hicks, Edward Seymour—265
Hicks, Israel—383, 432
Hicks, Julian—5
Hickson, Joan—244, 435
Hicks, Patricia—244
Hicks, Seymour—1, 8, 12, 16, 21, 26, 28, 32, 36, 37, 72, 79, 84, 113, 120, 125, 177, 192, 223
Hicks Theater, The (London)—34
Hicky, William—351
Hidden Hand, The—89
Hidden Horizon—244, 248
Hidden King, The—307
Hide and Seek—207
Hi-De-Hi—236
Hi-Diddle-Diddle—192
Hier—261
Hieronymas, Clara—419
Higashi, Yutaka—386
Higgins, Michael—274, 341
Higgledy-Piggledy—20
"High and Low"—176
High Bid, The—43, 278, 368
High Button Shoes—252, 259
High Jinks—67, 79
Highland Fair, The—279, 285
High Museum of Art—377
High Road, The—151, 215
High Spirits—344
High Temperature—223
High Time—248
High Tor—205, 210, 297
Highwaymen, The—417
High Wind in Jamaica, A—235
Hiken, Gerald—332, 456
Hilary, Jennifer—328, 346, 365
Hilda, Irene—281
Hiley, Jim—394
Hill, Abraham—246
Hill, Arthur—221, 261, 264, 290, 305, 321, 332, 365
Hill, Benny—294
Hill, Billie—107, 150, 212, 296, 315
Hiller, Wendy—64, 196, 241, 252, 263, 272, 294, 296, 304, 320, 366, 386, 401, 438, 444
Hill, George Roy—314
Hill, Graham—43
Hilliard, Kathlyn—143
Hilliard, Robert—26, 47
Hill, Kenneth—390, 408, 456
Hill, Lucienne—268, 300, 345
Hillman, Philip—241
Hill, Paul—348, 375, 403, 455
Hill, Richard—372
Hill, Ronnie—290, 291
Hill, Ruby—247
Hills, Ruth—105
Hill, Steven—326
Hillyard, Eric—451
Hilton, Conrad—356
Hilton, James—213
Hilton, Tony—328
Hind, Archie—407
Hindle Wakes—62, 209, 264, 445
Hines, Barry—389
Hines, Elizabeth—106
Hines, Gregory—442
Hines, Maurice—442
Hines, Patrick—375, 381
Hinge and Bracket at the Ambassadors'—421
Hingle, Pat—305, 310, 329, 371, 385
Hingley, Ronald—408
Hinnant, Bill—351
Hinritze, Betty—310
Hinton, Mary—223
Hinton, Maxine—107
Hinze, Gerard—231
Hip! Hip! Hooray!—36, 40
Hipple, Hugh Herbert—59
Hippo Dancing—288
Hippodrome Theatre—29, 39
Hippolytus—23, 24, 32, 197, 353, 453
Hird, Thora—283, 305, 358
Hirschfeld, Al—246, 292
Hirsch, Hugo—127
Hirsch, John—363, 367, 371, 373, 374, 381, 383
Hirsch, Judd—364, 406, 434, 452
Hirsch, Louis—83, 88, 100, 106, 112, 129, 431
Hirsch, Robert—316, 328
Hirson, Roger O.—358, 400
His Borrowed Plumes—48
His Excellency—267, 278
His Excellency the Governor—91
His Honor, Abe Potash—93
His Honor the Mayor—30
His House in Order—30, 32, 39, 274
His Indian Wife—54
His Majesty's Servant—21
His Monkey Wife—397
History of English Drama, A—432
History of the American Film, A—437, 442
History Show, The—402
Hitchcock, Alfred—165
Hitchcock, Raymond—19, 30, 35, 48, 79, 82, 100, 105, 112, 125, 168
Hitchy-Koo—82, 362
Hitchy-Koo 1920—100
Hitler Dances—401
Hit the Deck—148
Hit-the-Trail-Holiday—74
Hitting Town—422
H. M. S. Pinafore—45, 63, 68, 72, 76, 123, 184, 193, 260, 264, 269, 273, 280, 285, 290, 306, 323, 330, 334, 349, 362, 366, 369, 374, 376, 424, 429, 446
H. M. Tennent Ltd.—325
Hoare, Douglas—67, 89, 95
Hobart, George V.—10, 25, 26, 41, 42, 48, 52, 71, 74, 78, 82, 112
Hobart, Rose—145, 213
Hobble, John—87
Hobbs, Jack—158
Hobson, Arthur—324
Hobson, Earl—323
Hobson, Harold—23, 292, 381
Hobson's Choice—74, 79, 279, 346, 358, 408
Hobson, Valerie—271
Hochhuth, Rolf—371
Hochwalder, Fritz—300
Hockney, David—361
Hockridge, Edmund—281
Hodge, Merton—186, 188, 212
Hodges, C. Walter—319
Hodges, Horace—66, 87
Hodge, William T.—1, 42, 184
Hodgson-Burnett, Frances—8
Hodiak, John—287
Hodson, Henrietta—55
Hodson, J. L.—364
Hoey, Dennis—159, 165
Hoey, Iris—57, 61, 89, 97, 161, 236
Hoffa, Portland—163
Hoffe, Barbara—102, 113, 171
Hoffe, Monckton—49, 70, 83, 108, 150
Hoffman, Aaron—87, 100, 117, 238, 248
Hoffman, Al—207
Hoffman and Henon—155
Hoffman, Bill—417
Hoffman, Carey—409
Hoffman, Dustin—346, 351, 357, 414
Hoffman, Jane—326
Hoffman, Max—25, 31, 35
Hoffman, Ted—381
Hoffman, Theodore—296
Hoffman, William—360, 445
Hofheimer, Moses Lafayette—60
Hofmannstahl, Hugo von—121
Hofreiter, Friedrich—451
Hofsiss, Jack—426, 449
Hogan's Goat—352
Hoggs, James—397
Hohl, Arthur—99
Hohnson, Ashton, Mrs.—21
Hoity Toity—6
Hokey-pokey and Bunty, Bulls and Strings—61
Holabird and Roche—110, 155
Holborn Empire Theater (London)—34
Holbrook, Al—30
Holbrook, Hal—319, 323, 340, 345, 347, 360, 371
Holden, Jan—353
Holden, Peter—211
Holder, Geoffrey—306, 347, 420, 442
Hold Everything—157
Hold Me!—436
Hold My Hand—178
Hold On To Your Hats—221
Hold, Thea—187
Hole in the Head, A—364, 371
Hole, John—450
Hole, The—311
Holiday—91, 157, 265, 410, 454
Holiday, Bob—357
Holland, Anthony—216
Holland, Edmund Milton—6, 69
Hollander, Jack—367, 373
Hollander, Victor—59, 61, 135
Holland Festival—390
Holland, George—69, 146
Holland, Joseph Jefferson—146
Holland, Norman—375
Hollenbeck, Webb Parmelee—363
Holliday, Judy—244, 247, 273, 298, 355
Hollis, Stephen—394, 430, 444, 451
Holloway, Baliol—59, 97, 150, 156, 135, 219, 223, 228, 237, 285
Holloway, Stanley—148, 159, 167, 222, 231, 290, 291, 298
Holloway, Sterling—131, 140, 170
Hollow Crown, The—329, 429
Hollow, The—272
Holly and the Ivy, The—267
Hollywood Pinafore—447
Hollywood Pirate—214
Holman, Libby—148, 163, 168, 171, 191, 211, 280
Holman, Robert—436, 444
Holman, Vincent—135
Holm, Celeste—97, 217, 234, 240, 266, 278, 406
Holmes, Amanda—456
Holmes, Fanny—247
Holmes-Gore, Dorothy—102, 188
Holmes, Helen—52
Holmes, John Haynes—195
Holmes, Oliver Wendell—247
Holm, Hanya—257, 260, 261, 287
Holm, Ian—352, 354, 387
Holm, John Cecil—138, 195
Holm, Klaus—310
Holofcener, Larry—298
Holst, Gustav—135
Holt, Stella—330
Holt, Will—420
Holtz, Hugo—41
Holtz, Lou—99, 230, 240
Holy Isle—238
Holzer, Adela—437
Homage to Shakespeare—347
Homans, Robert—50
Home—386, 399, 456
Home Again—87
Home and Beauty—94, 206, 232, 269, 375
Home at Seven—267
Home Chat—151
Homecoming, The—352, 364, 431, 446
Home for Christmas—428
Home Free—353, 374
Homeier, Skippy—234
Home is the Hero—398
Home is the Hunter—246, 341
Home, John—269
Home of the Brave—244, 251, 261
Home of the Free, The—84
Home on Leave—79
Homer—438, 439
Home, Sally—353
Home Sweet Homer—433
Home, William Douglas—207, 253, 256, 263, 264, 279, 282, 288, 294, 345, 372, 387, 401, 407, 414, 435
Homolka, Oscar—235, 240, 295, 314
Honeydew—100
Honey Girl—303
Honey in The Rock—329
Honeymoon Express, The—66, 129
Honeymoon Lane—141, 146
Honeymoon, The—58
Honneger, Arthur—291
Honours Easy—172
Hood, Captain Basil—2, 12, 15, 17, 32, 37, 45, 49, 57, 62, 67, 273
Hooker, Brian—132, 251
Hooker, Brian C.—122
Hook, Line and Sinker—311
Hooks, Bobby Dean—209
Hooks, Robert—209, 347, 383
Hooper, Ewan—383, 388, 390, 417
Hooray for Daisy—324
Hooray For What—206
"Hoosier Poet"—87
Hooters—439
Hooydonck, Hubert—9
Hope, Anthony—2, 45
Hope, Bob—200
Hope, Edward—187
Hope, Evelyn—111, 126, 151, 167
Hope for a Harvest—227, 233
Hope, Vida—258, 278, 284, 311, 342
Hopkins, Anthony—342, 348, 367, 395, 402, 407
Hopkins, Arthur—82, 86, 90, 94, 98, 103, 106, 108, 112, 115, 117, 128, 130, 132, 133, 141, 148, 150, 157, 195, 247, 250, 270
Hopkins, Charles—73, 74, 140, 170, 213
Hopkins, Joan—261
Hopkins, John—375, 388, 413, 415, 451
Hopkins, Linda—420
Hopkins, Miriam—118, 141, 163, 166, 404
Hop O' My Thumb—59
Hopper, De Wolf—6, 25, 76, 82, 87, 123, 198
Hopper, Edna Wallace—1, 11, 41, 66, 105, 319
Hopper, Louis—1
Hopp, Julius—184
Hoppla, Wir Leben—166
Hopwood, Aubrey—16, 28
Hopwood, Avery—30, 48, 52, 89, 93, 99, 100, 105, 106, 118, 124, 126, 133, 143, 151, 161, 183, 207, 224, 232, 245, 313
Horan, Charles—138
Horan, E. A.—101
Horan, Edward—190
Hordern, Michael—253, 268, 274, 278, 285, 289, 296, 310, 312, 316, 335, 357, 365, 372, 386, 388, 401, 408, 451
Horder, P. Morley—154
Horlock, David—421
Hornblow, Arthur J.—117, 141
Horne, David—236
Horne, Kenneth—207, 248, 267, 283
Horne, Lena—194, 216, 304
Horne, Marie—43
Horner, Harry—217, 279
Hornick, Neil—451
Horniman, Annie Elizabeth Fredericka—16, 24, 39, 46, 55, 63, 68, 91, 209
Horniman Company—44
Horniman, Roy—43, 84, 108

Horn in the West—279
Hornsby, Nancy—198
Horn, Stephen—116
Hornung, E. W.—30
Horowitz, Israel—220, 371, 372, 374, 381, 395, 410
Horst, Julius—42
Horton, Edward Everett—61, 220, 391
Horton, Joe—406
Horton, John—381
Horton, Robert—71, 113, 142, 339
Horwin, Jerry—221
Horwitt, Arnold—257, 293
Hosanna—409, 413
Hoschna, Karl—41
Hosford, Maud—21
Hosho Noh Theatre—403
Hospital Ward, A—59
Hostage, The—95, 316, 317, 320, 330, 331, 389, 402, 404
Hostile Witness—346, 357
Hot Buttered Rolls—388
Hot-Cha!—181
Hot Chocolates—164
Hotel in Amsterdam, The—374
Hotel Paradiso—301, 306, 416
Hotel Pimlico—102
Hotel Universal—170
Hot Grog—440
Hothouse—418
Hot Ice—415
HotL Baltimore, The—402, 406
Hot Mikado, The—219
Houdini, Harry—87
Hough, Julian—421
Houghton, Katherine—346
Houghton, Norris—255, 286, 290, 291
Houghton, (William) Stanley—46, 62, 63, 69, 73, 448
Hough, Will—35
Houp La!—80, 81
Hour Glass, The—38, 64
Hour of Love, An—380
House, Billy—203
House by the Lake, The—299
House, Eric—396
House in the Wood, The—291
Housekeeper, The—28
Houseman/Granville Barker—246
Houseman, John—13, 202, 207, 213, 255, 289, 296, 300, 301, 306, 312, 325, 368, 369, 375, 402, 403, 405, 407, 411, 421, 431, 446
Houseman, Laurence—13, 23, 32, 59
Housemaster—202
House of Atreus, The—376
House of Bernarda Alba, The—273, 408
House of Blue Leaves, The—393
House of Connelly, The—179, 185
House of Flowers—288
House of Glass, The—74
House of Mirth, The—31, 50, 209
House of Peril, The—94
House of Pierre, The—45
House of Temperley, The—49
House of Usher, The—140
House, Ron—406
Houses by the Green, The—375
House That Jack Built, The—100, 166
House Un-American Activities Committee—443
Housewife-Superstar!!—427
Housman, Laurence—68, 196, 204, 208, 318
Houston Community Players—204
Houston, Donald—317
Houston Grand Opera—431
Houston, Renee—263, 289
Howard, Alan—317, 339, 373, 381, 388, 395, 396, 432, 437, 453
Howard, Ann—391
Howard, Bart—282
Howard, Bronson—45, 77, 444
Howard, Catherine—182
Howard, Disney—190, 194
Howard, Donald—328, 417

Howard, Edward—297
Howard, Edwin—296
Howard, Eugene—61, 101, 112, 140, 164, 196
Howard, Frankie—280, 283, 326, 359, 411
Howard, Harry—205
Howard, Joe—330
Howard, Joseph—35
Howard, Keble—158
Howard, Ken—406
Howard, Leslie—108, 143, 148, 149, 159, 161, 181, 195, 203, 237
Howard, Michael—377
Howard, N. J.—45
Howard, Peter—355, 398
Howard, P. M.—434
Howard, Roger—457
Howard's End—365
Howard, Sidney—123, 126, 132, 133, 138, 145, 148, 151, 155, 167, 181, 186, 190, 195, 212, 218, 227, 247, 250, 286, 298, 302, 411
Howard, Stanley—208
Howard, Tom—118
Howard, Trevor—202, 255, 283, 290, 333, 346, 415
Howard, Walter—83
Howard, Willie—61, 101, 112, 140, 164, 196, 230
How Are They At Home?—242
"How Are Things in Glocca Mora?"—252
How Are Things With the Walking Wounded—405
How Are Your Handles?—388
Howarth, Don—368
Howarth, Donald—316, 387, 431, 440
How Brophy Made Good—379
How D'You Do?—187
Howell, Jane—359, 373, 375, 379, 417, 443
Howell, John—89
Howell, Lottice—141
Howell, William Dean—93, 104
Howes, Basil—135, 143
Howes, Bobby—151, 164, 165, 187, 192, 197, 206, 207, 218, 226, 248, 258, 272, 404
Howes, Sally Anne—272, 276, 299, 410
Howe, Tina—445, 455
Howett, John—289
How, George—159
How He Lied To Her Husband—19, 28, 80, 108, 273, 341, 387
"How High The Moon"—221
"How I Hate To Get Up In The Morning"—230
Howland, Jobyna—61, 81
Howland, W. Legrand—70
How Long Brethern—210
How Mad Tulloch Was Taken Away—423
How Now, Dow Jones—365
How Pleasant to Know Mr. Lear—366
How Say You?—315
How's Your Code—308
How the Other Half Loves—386, 446
How the Vote Was Won—50
How to Succeed in Business Without Really Trying—130, 326, 337, 339, 360, 384, 404
Hoyle, Fred—334, 336
Hoyt, Charles—2, 61, 128, 153, 161
Hoyt, Charles Hale—4
Hoyt, Henry E.—10
Hubbard, Esme—135
Hubbard, Philip—67
Hubell, Raymond—14, 25, 30, 36, 47, 61, 71, 82, 87, 99, 112
Huby, Roberta—236, 241
Huddersfield Thespians—144
Huddle, Elizabeth—341, 355
Huddleston, Will—430
Hudd, Roy—386, 440
Hudd, Walter—126, 182, 184, 188, 220, 222, 242, 249, 254, 255, 304, 306

Hudson, Eric—135
Hudson Guild Theatre—424, 445, 447, 449
Hudson, Henry—205
Hudson, W. H.—46, 122
Huff, Louise—117
Huffman, J. C.—42, 112, 117, 118, 125, 140, 142, 150
Hugen, Pauline—94
Huggett, Richard—423
Hughes, Annie—11, 26, 48
Hughes, Bernard—209, 445
Hughes, Charles Evans—155
Hughes, Dusty—430, 436, 439
Hughes, Gareth—84
Hughes, Glenn—349
Hughes, Hatcher—124, 130, 246
Hughes, Hazel—368
Hughes, Howard—452
Hughes, Langston—196, 254, 327, 369
Hughes, Patricia—252
Hughes, Richard—188, 235
Hughes, Ted—440
Hughie—345, 347
Hughs, Bernard—321
Hugo, Victor—105, 452
Huis Clos—340
Hulbert, Jack—72, 79, 108, 133, 144, 151, 158, 159, 166, 177, 213, 231, 236, 242, 245, 248, 263, 273, 279, 282, 283, 328, 368
Hull, Henry—59, 66, 78, 111, 126, 140, 149, 164, 171, 205, 244, 441
Hull House Players—18
Hull, Josephine—136, 200, 226, 282, 308, 352
Hullo! America—89
Hullo! Tango—68
Hull, Rod—432
Hull, Shelly—88
Hull Truck Company—430
Human Factor, The—136
Humboldt's Current—445
Hume, Benita—182, 370
Hume, Sam—85
Humoresque—122
Humperdinck, Engelbert—369
Humphrey and the Dumptrucks—425
Humphrey, Cavada—237, 367
Humphrey, Doris—173
Humphrey, John—306
Humphreys, Cecil—183, 234
Humphries, Alexander—49
Humphries, Barry—347, 427
Humphries, H.—126
Humphries, John—89, 95
Humpty Dumpty—17, 20, 38, 91, 209, 229, 232, 237, 260, 275, 280, 302, 318
Hunchback of Notre Dame, The—452, 456
Hundley, John—163
Hundred Years Old, A—219, 245
Huneker, James Gibbons—109
Hunger Demon, The—174
Hunger, Ian—119
Hung Yen, Hu—360
Hunt, Barbara Leigh—455
Hunter, Alberta—150
Hunter, Bernard—235
Hunter, Glenn—93, 113, 133, 163, 170, 246
Hunter, Ian—107, 112, 122, 143, 151, 166, 178, 192, 266, 274
Hunter, Ian McLellan—332
Hunter, Kermit—269, 279, 300, 317, 323, 329, 341, 374, 381, 423, 430
Hunter, Kim—116, 252, 280, 287, 327, 329, 409
Hunter, Louise—150
Hunter, Mary—257
Hunter, N. C.—272, 283, 310, 334, 398, 438, 444
Hunter, Reginald—108
Hunt, Helpmann—254
Hunt, Hugh—198, 219, 235, 249, 259, 260, 264, 268, 273, 278, 279, 283, 290, 374, 389

Hunt, Ida Brooks—48
Huntley, G. P.—12, 22, 27, 36, 95
Huntley, Raymond—111, 150, 213, 235
Hunt, Martita—167, 177, 184, 188, 193, 219, 220, 223, 254, 258, 384
Hunt, Peter—378
Hunt, Ruth—451
Hunt, William—400
Hurd, James—84
Hurgon, Austen—36, 83, 84
Hurlburt, William—42, 70, 96
Hurlbut, Jack—95, 147
Hurok, Sol—126, 197, 276, 290, 296, 418
Hurrah for the Bridge—366
Hurran, Dick—248, 263, 272, 276, 283, 294, 345
Hurry, Leslie—289, 447
Hurst, Fannie—105, 122
Hurt, John—342, 414
Hurt, Marybeth—454
Hurt, William—436
Hussein, Waris—437
Hussey, Ruth—244
Husson, Albert—281
Huston, John—249
Huston, Walter—124, 126, 133, 148, 190, 207, 211, 270
Hutchinson, Ernest—103
Hutchinson, Harry—152
Hutchinson, Josephine—152, 159, 160, 167, 184
Hutchinson, Ron—451
Hutchison, Percy—89
Hutton, Betty—221
Hutton, Laurence—23
Hutton, Michael—273
Hutt, William—295, 317, 374, 430
Huxley, Aldous—327, 334
Hyacinth Halvey—38, 50, 59
Hyams, John—6
Hyde & Behman's Theater (Chicago)—24
Hyde Park Corner—192, 376
Hyde, Robert A.—374
Hyde, Walter—15
Hyde-White, Wilfried—227, 241
Hyland, Diana—314
Hyland, Frances—365, 381, 454
Hyland, James—308
Hyland, Lily—128, 140
Hylton, Jack—151
Hylton, Richard—211
Hyman, Earle—276, 298, 306, 312, 314
Hymer, John B.—88, 143, 148
Hymn To the Rising Sun—202
Hynes, Katherine—302
Hypocrites, The—30
Hyson, Dorothy—196, 236

I Am a Cabaret—407
I Am A Camera—272, 280, 288, 308, 358
I and Albert—401
Ib and Little Christina—2, 45
Ibañez, Vicente Blasco—188
Ibsen, Henrik—3, 8, 16, 22, 24, 27, 44, 45, 50, 54, 58, 64, 68, 69, 72, 80, 90, 114, 121, 122, 123, 128, 129, 135, 136, 137, 145, 146, 147, 152, 159, 160, 173, 179, 184, 192, 193, 198, 199, 202, 203, 209, 218, 223, 229, 231, 232, 237, 242, 245, 249, 250, 254, 255, 259, 260, 268, 269, 273, 275, 285, 290, 295, 297, 312, 316, 318, 322, 324, 329, 330, 334, 336, 340, 341, 346, 347, 353, 366, 367, 374, 375, 381, 382, 388, 389, 391, 393, 394, 395, 401, 402, 403, 405, 408, 415, 416, 417, 421, 422, 423, 428, 430, 438, 439, 440, 445, 446, 451, 452, 453, 454
"I Cain't Say No"—234
I Can Get It For You Wholesale—332, 425
I Can't Sleep—197
Ice Age—420

Icebound—117, 123, 303
Iceman Cometh, The—247, 256, 310, 313, 410, 429
Icetime of 1948—252
I Claudius—401
"I Could Have Danced All Night"—298
"I Could Write a Book"—222
Idare et Cie. Ltd.—133
"Ida, Sweet as Apple Cider"—93
Ideal Husband, An—90, 184, 237, 246, 355, 361, 445
Iden, Rosalind—223, 228, 259, 285
Ides of March, The—340
"I Didn't Know What Time It Was"—217
Idiot's Delight—200, 204, 215, 273, 363
Idiot, The—360, 388
I'd Like to Do It Again—303
I Do! I Do!—358, 372, 409
I Don't Generally Like Poetry But Have You Read Trees?—403
I'd Rather Be Right—205, 233
I Due Gemelli Veneziani—354, 374
If—107
If Four Walls Told—115
Ifield, Frank—355
If I Were King—6, 12, 51, 64, 69, 132, 193
If I Were You—179
If Men Played Cards as Women Do—118
I Forgot—197
If This Be Treason—195
If You're Glad, I'll Be Frank—431, 436
"I Get a Kick Out of You"—191
"I Got Plenty O' Nuttin'"—196
"I Gotta Right to Sing the Blues"—181
I Gotta Shoe—432
I Had a Ball—345
I Have Been Here Before—207, 211, 219
I Knock at the Door—304
I Know My Love—265, 270
Ikoli, Tunde—435
Ik, The—428
Il Burbero Benefico—37
Il Campiello—431
'Ile—90, 114
"I Left My Heart At the Stage Door Canteen"—320
Il Faut Passer par les Nuages—373
Iliad—438, 439, 455
I Lived With You—182
I'll Be Home for Christmas—357
"I'll Build a Stairway to Paradise"—112
Illington, Margaret—21, 22, 26, 30, 35, 71, 194
Illington, Marie—21, 32, 42, 62, 75
Illinois Theater (Chicago)—5
I'll Leave It To You—102
Ill Met by Moonlight—249, 254, 264, 380
I'll Say She Is—124
Illuminating Engineering Society, The—34
Illuminatus—437
Illya Darling—364
Il Maestro Capella—29
Il Matrimonio Segreto—307
"I Love a Piano"—74
I Loved Your Wednesday—181
"I Love Louisa"—176
I Love My Wife—434, 441
"I Love Paris"—281
"I Love You"—239
I Love You Baby Blue—420
Il Ratto Sabine—37
Ilse, James—188
Il Teatro Stabile—354
I Made It, Ma—Top of the World!—435
Image, The—54, 59
Imaginary Conversation, An—50
Imaginary Invalid, The—167, 237, 359, 367, 374, 389, 416, 419

"I'm an Indian"—99
I Married an Angel—211
"I'm Falling in Love with Someone"—52
I'm Getting My Act Together and Taking It on the Road—445
"I'm Getting Tired So I Can Sleep"—230
I'm Herbert—357
"I'm Just Wild About Harry"—105
Imlay, Agnes—182
Immoralist, The—287, 291, 292
Immortal Garden—231
Immortal Hour, The—115, 144
Impact of the Broadway Theatre on the Economy of New York City, The—441
Imperial Court Theater (Tokyo)—8
Imperial Nightingale, The—324
Imperial Theater (London)—9, 18, 34, 46
Imperial Theater (St. Louis, Missouri)—13
Importance of Being Earnest, The—12, 50, 73, 76, 115, 188, 192, 204, 207, 214, 218, 220, 232, 254, 317, 373, 396, 411, 422, 423, 430, 436, 437, 440, 453
Importance of Being Oscar, The—323, 329, 336, 341, 349, 373, 375, 396, 408, 422, 447, 454
Impossible Years, The—351, 363
Impresario—418
Impresario from Smyrna, The—198, 290
Impromptu at Versailles, The—347
Improper Duchess, The—177
Improvisations in June—159
I'm Talking About Jerusalem—323
I Must Be Talking To My Friends—341, 348, 447
I Must Love Someone—216
In Abraham's Bosom—142, 155
In a Cottage Hospital—379
In a Country Scandal—323
Inadmissible Evidence—346, 352, 363, 447
In a Garden—133
In a Gondola—179
In Barnes—137
Inca of Perusalem, The—80, 85, 273
In Celebration—379
In Chancery—95
Incident at Vichy—345, 356, 358
In Circles—365
Inclan, Ramon del Valle—439
Incognito—23
Inconsistant Couple, The—446
Inconstant George—53, 58
Incorporated Stage Society—95, 96, 103, 137
Increased Difficulty of Concentration, The—383
Incubus, The—49
In Dahomey—14, 115
Index to the Story of My Days—363
Indiana Repertory—456
"Indian Love Call"—125
Indians—372, 415
Indian Wants the Bronx, The—371, 381
Indulgences in the Louisville Harem—454
Inedits—389
Inescort, Elaine—48, 94, 349
Inescourt, Frieda—108, 117, 122, 126, 134, 181, 432
I Never Sang for My Father—371
Infancy—332
Infanticide in the House of Fred Ginger—335
Infernal Machine, The—208, 224, 311
Inferno, The—403
Informer, The—312
Inge, William—254, 266, 270, 281, 286, 297, 305, 313, 315, 411, 412, 418, 429, 431, 454
Ingham, Barrie—342, 347, 358, 366, 372, 380, 421

Ingomar—22
In Good King Charles' Golden Days—223, 308
In Harvard—179
In Hayti—47
Inheritors, The—137, 152
Inherit the Wind—293, 322, 391, 456
In His House—65
In His Own Write—373
Inkster, Leonard—69
Inman, John—454
In Mizzoura—97
In My Father's Time—428, 431
Innaurato, Albert—403, 429, 430, 434, 436, 437, 447
Inner City—394
Inner City Mother Goose, The—394
Inner Journey, The—380
Innes, George—353
Innocent Eyes—129
Innocent Gems' Piaf, The—453
Innocent, Harold—453
Innocents, The—266, 268
Innocent Thoughts, Harmless Intentions—417
Innocent Voyage, The—235, 243
Inns, George—334
Inook and the Sun—409
In Order of Appearance—438
In Praise of Love—407, 414, 425
Inquest—180
Insect Comedy, The—260
Insect Play, The—113, 237, 360
Insideout—379
Inside the Lines—83
Inside the U.S.A.—257
Inspector Calls, An—250, 261, 409
Inspector General, The—121, 425, 445
Instant Sunshine—455
Instant Theatre—359
Institute of Journalists—70
Institute of Outdoor Drama—343
Insurrection—85
Interference—150
Interior—77
Interlude of Youth, The—39, 64
Intermezzo—302, 306
International Alliance of Theatricas Stage Employees, The—13
International Cup, The Ballet of Niagara, and The Earthquake, The—52
International Federation of Actors—415
International Ladies Garment Workers Union—65, 206
International Stud—445
International Turkish Players—446
Interview, The—358, 444
In the Bar of a Tokyo Hotel—378, 447
In the Deepest Part of Sleep—415
In the Hospital—20
In Their Wisdom—421
In the Jungle of Cities—321, 401
In the Lap of the Gods—284
In the Matter of J. Robert Oppenheimer—361, 380, 381
In the Next Room—119, 127
In the Night—95
In the Night Watch—89
In the Palace of the King—1
In the Recovery Lounge—445
In the Red—435
In the Shadow of the Glen—22, 341
In the Summer House—282, 292, 431
In the Train—290
In the Wine Time—424
In the Zone—84, 109, 128, 208, 452
Intimacy at Eight—280
Intimacy at 8:30—288
Intiman Theatre Company—405
Intimate Relations—273
In Time of War—76
In Time To Come—233, 249
Intrigues and Amours—367
In Trousers—452

Investigation, The—353, 357, 388, 451
Invisible Foe, The—84
Invitation to a Beheading—379
In Wall Street—179
In White America—339, 404
Iolanthe—45, 68, 76, 97, 144, 145, 167, 184, 193, 228, 232, 245, 249, 255, 260, 264, 269, 273, 280, 285, 290, 296, 316, 330, 334, 349, 355, 369, 376, 424, 446
Ionesco, Eugene—64, 295, 302, 306, 312, 319, 322, 329, 331, 340, 347, 353, 368, 373, 389, 409, 427, 447
Ionescu, Arrabal—410
Ionescu, Petrika—410
I Pagliacci—29, 44
Iphigenia in Aulis—108, 349, 366, 368
Iphigenia in Concert—398
Iphigenia in Tauris—63
Ipi Tombi—421
Irby, Dean—456
Iredale, Martin—102
Ireland, Anthony—165, 187, 222, 229
I Remember Mama—240, 246, 250, 308
Irene—93, 112, 116, 245, 406, 412, 430
Iris—8
I Rise in Flames Cried the Phoenix—319
Irish Dramatic Movement—184
Irish Eyes and English Tears—445
Irish Hebrew Lesson, The—444
Irish Jew, The—109
Irish Literary Theater—3, 13, 14
Irish National Theatre of Dublin, The—46
Irish National Theater Society—13, 16, 18, 22, 23, 24, 29, 49, 68, 220
Irish Players—59, 90, 145, 153, 306
Irma La Duce—310, 320, 456
Iron Curtain—273
Irons, Jeremy—423, 443
Iroquois Theater (Chicago)—18
Irregular Verb to Love, The—328
Irving, Ethel—21, 27, 37, 53, 88, 103
Irving, George—25
Irving, George S.—400
Irving, Henry Brodribb—2, 4, 7, 8, 12, 16, 17, 18, 27, 28, 33, 50, 53, 54, 55, 74, 79, 84, 85, 90, 97, 123, 233, 261, 268, 296, 363
Irving, Isabel—27
Irving, Jules—256, 280, 356, 360, 361, 380, 383, 394, 404, 405, 410, 456
Irving, Laurence—57, 67, 274
Irving, Lawrence Sidney—8, 16, 17, 49, 53, 63, 68, 73
Irvington, Washington—254
Irwin, Mary—24
Irwin, May—128, 215
Irwin, Wallace—35
Irwin, Will—227, 247, 251
Isaac, Bernard—154
Isaacs, Edith J.R.—302, 350
Isabel's a Jezebel—391
Isadora Duncan Sleeps with the Russian Navy—436
Iscove, Rob—455
I Sent a Letter To My Love—452
Isham, Frederick—78, 100
Isherwood, Christopher—201, 206, 217, 218, 256, 358, 412
Island of Goats, The—293, 412
Island of Saints: How to Get Out It, The—102
Island of the Mighty, The—401
Island, The (Fugard)—414
Island, The (Hodge)—212
Isle of Spice, The—19
Is Life Worth Living—285
Is Marriage a Failure?—37
Is Matrimony a Failure?—47
Is Your Doctor Really Necessary?—408

Is Your Honeymoon Really Necessary?—241
Is Zat So?—131, 142
Italian Girl, The—372
Italian Straw Hat, An—279, 296, 367, 396
Italian Theater Company—347
It Can Be Done—69
It Can't Happen Here—200, 204
It Depends Upon What You Mean—241
It Happened in Nordland—20
It Happened on Ice—221
It Is the Law—113
Ito, Yuji—112
It Pays to Advertise—71, 153
"It's a Bird It's a Plane It's SUPER-MAN"—357
It's All Right If I Do It—437
It's All Wrong—102, 302
"It's a Long, Long Day"—120
It's A Two Foot Six Inches Above The Ground World—386
It's A Wise Child—164
It's Called the Sugar Plum—371
"It's De-Lovely"—200
It's Foolish But It's Fun—235
It's Later Than You Think (Ornifle)—396
It's My Criminal—361
It's Never Too Late—289
It's Nothing Serious—451
It's Time To Dance—236
It's Up to You—404
It's You I Want—187
Itzin, Cathy—457
Ivan—22
Ivanov—137, 268, 319, 355, 429, 444, 447
Ivan the Terrible—27
"I've Got Rings on My Fingers"—47, 52
I've Got Sixpence—308
Ives, Arthur—213
Ives, Burl—212, 243, 265, 290
Ives, Kenneth—395
"I've Told Every Little Thing"—181
Ivor, Frances—88
Ivory, Apes and Peacocks—109
Ivory Door, The—149
I Wanted to be an Actress—418
"I Want To Be Happy"—134
I Was Shakespeare's Double—416
I Was Sitting on My Patio This Guy Appeared I Thought I Was Hallucinating—438
"I Wonder"—53
Ixion—123
Izenour, George—64, 325, 356

Jacchia, Paul—219
Jack and Jill—55, 203, 229, 232, 237, 280, 330
Jack and the Bald Soprano—319
Jack and the Beanstalk—38, 54, 59, 109, 122, 174, 184, 193, 198, 208, 214, 229, 250, 255, 261, 376, 411, 415
Jackdaw, The—37, 38, 59
Jack, Donald—329
Jacker, Corrine—422, 436, 439, 451
Jackie the Jumper—340
Jack-in-the-Box—232
Jackley, Nat—248
Jack O'Diamonds—196
Jack O'Lantern—82
Jackson, Anne—282, 298, 322, 332, 338, 344
Jackson, Arthur—92
Jackson, Barry—64, 68, 97, 111, 126, 130, 137, 143, 144, 152, 165, 168, 209, 249, 259
Jackson, Barry Vincent—330
Jackson, B. H.—4
Jackson, Brian—374
Jackson, Ernestine—406
Jackson, Fred—92, 120, 135, 195, 278
Jackson, Freda—248, 401

Jackson, Glenda—339, 345, 348, 353, 366, 435, 453
Jackson, Joe—74
Jackson, Josephine—148
Jackson, J. W.—151
Jackson, Leigh—447
Jackson, Nagle—354, 454
Jackson, Petunia—222
Jackson, "Stonewall" Billie—186
Jackson, Zaidee—148
Jack Straw—43
Jack the Ripper—414
Jacobi, Derek—367, 373, 381, 416, 432, 438, 439, 455
Jacobi, Lou—314, 326, 344, 358, 385
Jacobi, Victor—67, 78, 93, 110
Jacobowsky and the Colonel—239, 243, 245, 303, 411
Jacobs, Jim—400
Jacobson and Oesterreicher—134
Jacobs, Paul—420
Jacobs, Sally—388, 395
Jacobs, W. W.—21
Jacqueline—115
Jacques—329
Jacques Brel Is Alive and Well and Living in Paris—371, 412
Jacques, Hattie—275, 286, 310
Jacques, Yvonne—241
Jaeyes, Allan—342
Jaffe, Carl—218
Jaffe, Sam—84, 113, 171, 205, 216, 273
Jagger, Dean—212
Jail Diary of Albie Sachs, The—444, 451, 453
Jalousie—75
Jamaica—304
Jame, Dan—232
James, Cecil—75
James, David—440
James, Emrys—373, 396, 401, 403
James G. Carroll Players—138
James, Gordon—159
James, Henry—43, 46, 81, 84, 96, 143, 250, 252, 266, 278, 298, 304, 308, 315, 340, 368, 372, 380, 394, 429, 446
James, Jesse—420
James Joyce Memorial Liquid Theatre—397
James, Louis—55
James, Margo—247
Jameson, House—333
James, Peter—390, 394
James, Polly—352
James, Sidney—352, 407
James the First of Scotland—136
Janauschek, Francesca—23
Janauschek, Mme.—146
Jane—253, 276, 280, 309
Jane Clegg—68, 95, 99, 104, 115, 166, 209, 242, 398
Jane Eyre—201, 241, 250, 309
Janes, Hugh—443
Janice Meredith—1
Janie—230
Jani, Robert F.—455
Janis, Conrad—327
Janis, Elsie—25, 30, 47, 56, 74, 89, 102, 128, 302
Janis, Percy—25
Janitress Thrilled by Prehensile Penis—407
Janssen, Werner—117
January, Lois—216
Janus—294
Japanese Court Theater—4
Japanese Doll, A—38
Japanese Lady, A—38
Japanese Ophelia, A—38
Jarman, Robert—62
Jarrell, Randall—348
Jarry, Alfred—340, 361, 366, 373, 389
Jar, The—380
Jason—233
Jason, Mitchell—380
Jay, Charlotte—135
Jaye, Eddie—113
Jay, Ernest—183

Jay, F.—73
Jayhawker—265
Jay, Isabel—21, 32, 43, 49, 53
Jayston, Michael—372
Jay, William—380
Jazz Marriage—134
Jazz Singer, The—132
J.B.—310, 319, 327
Jealousy—260
Jean Cocteau Repertory—447
Jean de la Lune—329, 334
Jean III—85
Jeanne D'Arc—36, 303
Jeans, Isabel—148, 197, 201, 272, 278, 283, 284, 373, 376
Jeans, Ronald—76, 88, 89, 101, 108, 114, 120, 127, 133, 143, 144, 151, 166, 172, 177, 178, 182, 192, 201, 263
Jeans, Ursula—142, 148, 151, 165, 171, 182, 188, 191, 212, 218, 241, 253, 264, 273, 300, 355, 411, 452
Jeaves, Allan—126, 244
Jedd, Gerry—336
Jedermann—121, 238
Jeeves—421
Jeffcoat, A. E.—405
Jefferson, Joseph—28, 69, 85, 104, 137
Jeffers, Robinson—255, 260, 264, 269, 336, 355
Jefford, Barbara—279, 290, 302, 306, 311, 313, 316, 317, 323, 329, 334, 352, 364, 438, 439, 455
Jeffrey, Peter—285, 453
Jeffreys, Ellis—2, 20, 27, 31, 57, 113, 120, 187
Jeffries, Douglas—102, 195
Jeffries, Maud—3
Jellicoe, Ann—285, 311, 318, 333, 340, 416
Jenback, Bela—150
Jenkins, Allen—157
Jenkins, George—237
Jenkins, Gordon—262
Jenkins, Len—439
Jenkins, Megs—222, 235, 236, 277, 347, 382
Jenkins, Richard Walter Jr.—138
Jenkins, Steve—118
Jenkins, Warren—396
Jennie—338, 411
Jennings, Gertrude—101, 192
Jennings, Hazel—222
Jennings, John—333
Jenn, Myfanwy—366
Jens, Salome—198, 320, 374
Jeremiah—218
Jerome, Helen—196, 201, 204, 250
Jerome, Jennie—48, 65
Jerome, Jerome K.—2, 43, 67, 153, 167
Jerome, Sadie—38
Jerome, William—19, 25, 35
Jerrold, Douglas—268
Jerrold, Mary—122, 127, 134, 151, 181, 212, 226, 248
Jersey Lily, The—223, 225
Jesse and the Bandit Queen—420
Jesse, F. Tennyson—75, 83, 127
Jessel, George—92, 118, 130, 132, 171, 233
Jessel, Patricia—259, 269, 315, 376
Jessel, Raymond—351
Jesse, Stella—102
Jessup, G. H.—15
Jesters, The—41
Jest, The—104
Jesuit, The—428
Jesus Christ Superstar—393, 399, 401, 405, 440
Jeu de l'Amour et du Hasard, Le—284
Jew!—374
Jewel, Jimmy—277, 400
Jewel of Asia, The—14
Jewett, Henry—139
Jewish Drama League—137
Jewish State Theatre of Poland, The—368

Jewish Theatrical Guild of America, The—130
Jewison, Norman—317
Jew of Malta—114, 348, 353
Jews of York, The—219
Jew Suss—165, 179
Jezebel—404
Jig-Saw—101, 225
Jill Darling!—192, 242
Jillson, Joyce—351
Jim Bludsoe—129
Jimmie—104
Jimmy Shine—384
Jingo—421
Jitta's Atonement—135
Joan—400
Joan Littlewood's Theatre Workshop—341
Joan of Arc at the Stake—291
Joan of Lorraine—247, 256
Joan of Memories—96
Job, Thomas—230, 233, 245, 246
Jockey Club Stakes, The—387
Johannesburg Repertory Theatre—412
Johannesburg Workshop '71—435
Johansen, John—392
Johan, Zita—157, 176
John—149
John Brown's Body—284
John Bull's Other Island—22, 27, 28, 33, 64, 109, 255, 256, 259, 348, 395
John, Errol—312, 332, 340
John Ferguson—76, 92, 98
John Gabriel Borkman—58, 145, 146, 250, 268, 329, 422, 430, 446
John Gassner Award of the Outer Critics Circle—443
John, Graham—133, 144, 158, 197
John Loves Mary—252, 256
John Murray Anderson's Almanac—282, 418
Johnny—415
Johnny Belinda—221, 279
Johnny Johnson—200, 210
Johnny Jones—101
Johnny Noble—290
Johnny No-Trump—364, 390
John, Paul, George, Ringo . . . And Bert—414
John, Rita—127
Johnson, Albert—190
Johnson, Arte—293
Johnson, Bayn—365
Johnson, Bill—258
Johnson, Carroll—22
Johnson, Celia—165, 171, 178, 187, 188, 196, 222, 225, 255, 274, 289, 294, 305, 311, 322, 334, 346, 360, 365, 373, 414, 435
Johnson, Chic—211, 227, 240
Johnson, Choo Choo—234
Johnson, Edward—4
Johnson, Fred—186
Johnson, Grace—368
Johnson, Greer—288
Johnson, Hall—186
Johnson, Harold (Chic)—336
Johnson, Herman—415
Johnson, James W.—35, 118
Johnson, Janet—208
Johnson, Jill—217, 366
Johnson, Jimmy—156, 163
Johnson, J. Rosamond—20, 35, 47, 48, 56, 216
Johnson, Julian—70
Johnson, Justine—83
Johnson, Katie—166
Johnson, Kay—133
Johnson, Laurie—315, 317, 335, 366
Johnson, Louis—376
Johnson, Louise—97
Johnson, Margaret—231, 271, 315
Johnson, Mary—400
Johnson, Molly—142
Johnson Over Jordan—217, 246
Johnson, Owen—36
Johnson, Raymond Edward—234

Johnson, Richard—287, 299, 311, 315, 321, 329, 409, 430
Johnson, Robert—217
Johnson, Ruth—156
Johnson, Van—200, 217, 305
Johnson, William—97
Johnston, Denis—9, 183, 192, 193, 197, 213, 223, 228, 255, 316
Johnstone, Alick—166
Johnstone, Denis—259
Johnstone, Keith—323, 333, 359
Johnstone, Tom—124, 134, 138
Johnstone, Will B.—124
Johnston, Howard—105
Johnston, James—291
Johnston, Julie—149
Johnston, Margaret—217, 257, 259
Johnston, Mary—11
Johnston, Moffat—112, 182
John Tiller Girls, The—158
Joie de Vivre—322
Joint Stock Company—439, 450
Jokers Wild—289
Joking Apart—450
Jolly Roger—187
Jolson, Al—39, 56, 57, 61, 66, 71, 78, 87, 106, 131, 132, 221, 270
Jones, Barry—156, 197, 271
Jones, Bassett—60
Jones, Clifton—316
Jones, David—353, 362, 367, 374, 382, 388, 396, 401, 415, 417, 421, 422, 429, 439, 453
Jones, Dean—321
Jones, Dedwydd—366
Jones, Disley—318
Jones, Dudley—306
Jones, Edward—75, 116
Jones, Elinor—385
Jones, Emrys—277
Jones, Freddie—452
Jones, Gemma—365, 374, 394, 417
Jones, Gil—99
Jones, Griffith—156, 201, 294, 353
Jones, Guy—37
Jones, Henry Arthur—2, 15, 18, 20, 30, 32, 35, 67, 71, 73, 77, 85, 168, 215, 250, 268
Jones, Howard—180
Jones, Jackson—61
Jones, James Earl—326, 327, 329, 332, 335, 339, 341, 344, 365, 368, 385, 418, 442
Jones, John—29
Jones, John Price—149
Jones, Julia—403
Jones, LeRoi—345, 347, 366, 378, 383, 388
Jones, Leslie Julian—248
Jones, Lightnin' Bill—87
Jones, Margaret—204
Jones, Margo—129, 204, 209, 210, 247, 297
Jones, Paul—283, 379, 436
Jones, Peter—277, 278, 289
Jones, Preston—426, 456
Jones, Robert Edmond—76, 77, 81, 103, 115, 129, 131, 132, 133, 136, 140, 186, 207, 216, 219, 223, 291
Jones, Sandra—416
Jones, Shirley—306
Jones, Sidney—15, 32, 43, 67, 79
Jones, Silas—422
Jones, Stephen—118, 132
Jones, Tom—320, 339, 358, 378, 385, 418
Jones, Walton—436, 450
Jones, Winifred Arthur—20
Jongeyans, George—267
Jonic, Bettina—361
Jonson, Bari—383
Jonson, Ben—16, 97, 108, 121, 159, 198, 208, 215, 242, 254, 259, 269, 278, 285, 295, 301, 306, 323, 329, 336, 361, 366, 373, 381, 382, 388, 396, 409, 427, 430, 436, 438, 445
Jonson Tercentenary—208
Joplin, Scott—420
Joppolo, Major—240

Jordan, Joe—170
Jordan, Kate—45
Jordan, Richard—360
Jordan, Walter C.—110
Jordan, William—358
Jorrocks—359
Jory, Jon—354
Jory, Victor—235, 250
Jose, Juliette—94
Joselovitz, Ernest—436
Joseph and His Brethern—67
Joseph and the Amazing Technicolor Dreamcoat—403
Joseph, Claire—104
Joseph Entangled—20
Josephine—32
Joseph, Stephen—385
Josipovici, Gabriel—410
Joslyn, Allyn—118, 196, 226
Joullot, Eugene—76
Jourdan, Louis—287, 428
Journey by Night, A—229
Journey of the Fifth Horse, The—357, 368
Journey's End—297, 401, 411, 424
Journey, The—390
Journey to Jerusalem—221
Jouvet, Louis—255, 273, 274
Joy—189
Joy-Bells—94
Joyce Grenfell Requests the Pleasure—289, 293
Joyce, James—131, 229, 245, 317, 333, 390, 396, 414, 415, 436, 452
Joyce, Margot—79
Joyce, Michael—435
Joyce, Paul—428, 436
Joyce, Peggy Hopkins—118
Joyce, Robert—389
Joyce, Stephen—421
Joyce, William—216
Joyce, Yootha—316
Joy, Nicholas—236
J. Rosamond Johnson Singers—216, 222
Juan Jose—44
Juarez and Maximilian—145, 146
Jubilee—137, 196
Judas—54, 168
Judas Iscariot—128
Judd, Gerry—309
Judgement—63, 437, 446
Judgement Day—190, 206, 208, 209, 310
Judgment of Hippolytus, The—444
Judith—334, 349, 417
Judson Memorial Church—406
Judson Poets' Theatre—418
Juggernaut—166, 173
Jukes, Bernard—219
Julian, Leslie—186, 227
Julia, Raul—358, 367, 398, 418, 454
Juliet in the Rain—214
Julius Caesar—4, 37, 49, 50, 53, 54, 58, 63, 68, 69, 73, 76, 80, 84, 96, 102, 114, 115, 136, 160, 179, 183, 184, 192, 193, 198, 202, 208, 214, 219, 228, 229, 268, 279, 283, 285, 295, 296, 297, 306, 312, 319, 323, 334, 335, 341, 342, 349, 354, 360, 373, 376, 381, 389, 402, 403, 409, 416, 436, 438, 445, 446, 452, 453, 454
Julius Caesar AD 1957—306
Jullet, A.—138
Jumble Sale—102
Jumbo—196, 362
Jumpers—401
"June"—102
"June is Bustin' Out All Over"—446
June Moon—164, 398
Junior Miss—227, 233, 235
Junkin, John—328
Juno and the Paycock—128, 140, 152, 153, 192, 193, 208, 223, 359, 409
Jupiter Laughs—227
Jupiter's Night Out—289

Jupp, Kenneth—316
Jurado, Katy—298
Just a Little Bit Less Than Normal—451
Just Between Ourselves—435
Just Fancy!—101, 215
Just for Kicks—447
Justice—53, 114, 184, 189, 197
Justice, Barry—340, 360
Justice, James Robertson—424
Justin, John—268, 305, 317, 409
Just Like John—65
Just Married—127
"Just One of Those Things"—196
Just Out of College—25
Just, The—444
Juvenalia—430
"Juvenile Delinquents, The"—268

K—440
Kacer, Jan—388
Kaddish—402
Kadelburg, Gustav—27, 44
Kafka, Franz—367, 376, 440
Kagami-Jishi—382
Kahane, Eric—381
Kahan, Gerald—312
Kahn, Florence—22
Kahn, Gus—151
Kahn, Madeline—358, 442
Kahn, Michael—361, 367, 374, 381, 382, 389, 403, 404, 417, 434
Kahn, Sammy—352, 358
Kailling, Reed—434
Kaiser, George—87, 103, 111, 122, 173, 273
Kalcheim, Lee—447
Kalfin, Robert—377, 418, 420, 431, 448, 453
Kalich, Bertha—28, 60, 87, 144, 220
Kalita Humphreys Theatre—319
Kallman, Chester—412
Kalmar, Bert—141, 144, 149, 156, 157, 164, 256
Kalman, Emmerich—62, 71, 78, 79, 82, 102, 107, 112, 141, 148, 150, 242, 244
Kaminska, Ida—306, 368
Kamoku, William—61
Kanadehon Chushingura—374
Kanawa—85
Kander, John—153, 351, 358, 367, 371, 388, 395, 410, 420, 434
Kane, Helen—148, 157, 303
Kane, Marvin—328
Kane, Michael—386, 393
Kane, Whitford—62, 131, 191, 248, 230, 303
Kani, John—410, 413, 414, 435
Kanin, Fay—265, 314
Kanin, Garson—195, 196, 247, 251, 304, 320, 321, 327, 364, 408, 410, 454
Kanin, Michael—314
Kann, Lilly—232
Kannon Reigenki—374
"Kansas City"—234
Kantor, Tadeusz—431, 451
Kapell, Marty—439
Kaplan, Juliette—442
Kaplan, Richard D.—399
Kareda, Urjo—454
Karen—89
Karl and Anna—167
Karlin, Elizabeth—289
Karlin, Miriam—217, 273, 283, 285, 295, 310
Karl Marx Play, The—402
Karloff, Boris—226, 268, 383
Karlweis, Oscar—239
Karnilova, Maria—215
Karson, Nat—291
Karst, Anton—39
Kasakoff, E.G.—455
Kasha, Lawrence—361, 386
Kaspar—402, 407
Kass, Jerome—443
Kataki—319
Katayev, Valentine—195, 197

Katerina—144, 166
Katherine and Petruchio—123
Katherine Dunham Dancers—222
Kathleen ni Houlihan—50
"Katie Went to Haiti"—217
Katinka—74
Katja, the Dancer—133
Kauffman, Stanley—363
Kaufman and Connelly—116
Kaufman and Hart—211, 229, 232, 237
Kaufman, George S.—105, 111, 113, 118, 123, 124, 125, 130, 132, 133, 147, 150, 157, 164, 170, 177, 180, 181, 185, 189, 191, 196, 199, 200, 204, 205, 210, 211, 216, 217, 220, 222, 225, 240, 246, 249, 263, 266, 274, 279, 282, 293, 311, 330, 352, 355, 361, 366, 376, 387, 392, 397, 403, 424, 445, 453, 455
Kaufman, Leueen MacGrath—293
Kavanagh, Dorrie—359
Kay, Ada—354
Kay, Charles—359, 446
Kaye, A.P.—200
Kaye, Danny—69, 217, 226, 386
Kaye, Fred—21
Kaye, Stubby—298
Kayf Up West, A—347
Kay, Ray—97
Kay, T.—129
Kazan, Elia—221, 239, 244, 257, 260, 268, 276, 281, 305, 314, 344
Kazantzakis, Nikos—371
Kazsnar, Kurt—235, 339
Keach, Stacy—335, 341, 355, 364, 374, 381, 396, 403
Kean—37
Kean, Edmund—394
Keane, Doris—15, 17, 30, 47, 66, 73, 75, 89, 96, 108, 111, 246
Keane, George—252
Kearney, Patrick—141
Kearney, Peadar—81
Kearns, Allen—118
Keathley, George—429
Keaton, Buster—439
Keaton, Diane—378
Keats, John—297
Kedrova, Lila—368, 381
Kedrov, M.M.—311
Keeffe, Barrie—407, 423, 430, 431, 435, 436, 437, 439, 448, 455
Keegan, Ellen—144
Keeler, Ruby—149, 372, 395
Keel, Howard—234, 307, 394
Keenan, Frank—26, 36
Keen, Malcome—107, 114, 122, 135, 158, 184, 191, 197, 217, 235, 391
Keep 'Em Laughing—441
Keep it all in the Family—354
Keep Kool—124
Keep Shufflin'—156
Keep, The—323, 330
Keightley, Cyril—49, 58, 104, 117
Keitel, Harvey—353
Keith-Albee—29
Keith, Ian—121, 324
Keith-Johnstone, Colin—111, 151, 159, 191, 217
Keith, Penelope—394, 427, 440
Keith, Robert—145, 187
Keith Vaudeville Circuit—122
Kekona, Diamond—61
Kelcey, Herbert—35
Kellard, John—3
Kellaway, Alec—119
Kellerd, John E.—59
Keller, Helen—314
Keller, Jeff—450
Kelley, Bunty—252
Kelley, George—22
Kelley, Sheila—436
Kellgren, Ian—435, 445
Kellogg, Clare Louise—81
Kelly—351, 356
Kelly, Anthony Paul—87
Kelly, Barbara—288, 291
Kelly, Diarmuid—279
Kelly, Eamon—428, 431, 439, 452

Kelly, Eva—36
Kelly, Gene—211, 216, 217, 222, 226
Kelly, George—112, 116, 124, 130, 132, 142, 147, 150, 154, 155, 164, 200, 250, 256, 368, 375, 419, 456
Kelly, Harry—42
Kelly, Irene—84
Kelly, Judy—227
Kelly, Katherine Wick—85
Kelly, Margot—136
Kelly, Nancy—288
Kelly, Patrick—252
Kelly, Patsy—164, 170
Kelly, Paul—87, 112, 252, 267
Kelly, Renee—71, 78, 102, 105, 356
Kelly, Robert—99
Kelly, Seamas—96
Kelm, Jeannin—23
Kelso, Louis—10
Kelso, Mayme—56
Kelso, Vernon—206
Kelton, Pert—377
Kemble, Henry—26
Kembles, The—138
Kempinski, Tom—368, 437
Kemp, Jeremy—394
Kemp, Lindsay—347, 353, 387, 401, 407, 414, 432
Kemp, Robert—348
Kemp, Roger—443
Kemp's Jig—437
Kempson, Rachel—188, 200, 202, 266, 267, 301, 417, 435
Kempt, Robert—329
Kemp-Welch, Joan—218, 295
Kempy—111
Kenan, William R. Jr.—430
Ken Campbell's Road Show—390, 415
Kendal, Dame Madge—198, 227
Kendal, Felicity—443, 451
Kendall, Henry—126, 227, 244, 245, 263, 299
Kendall, Marie—59
Kendal, William Hunter—85
Kendrick, Richard—186
Kennedy, Adrienne—374, 379, 389, 424
Kennedy, Arthur—219, 252, 262, 281, 298, 371
Kennedy Center for the Performing Arts—350, 356
Kennedy, Charles Rann—13, 41, 61, 90, 121, 129, 270
Kennedy, Cheryl—359, 401, 450
Kennedy/Dean—237
Kennedy, E.J.—153
Kennedy, Harold—381
Kennedy, John—254
Kennedy, John F.—350, 381
Kennedy, Joyce—127, 128, 134, 183, 195, 289
Kennedy, Madge—118, 150, 172
Kennedy, Margaret—188, 207
Kennedy, Mary—131
Kennedy's Children—414, 415, 420, 423
Kenny, James—310, 317
Kenny, Margaret—143
Kenny, Sean—312, 316, 317, 318, 333, 343, 351, 376, 380, 409, 411
Kent, Edgar—44
Kentish, Elizabeth—274
Kent, Keneth—102, 151, 214, 231, 244
Kent, Larry—304
Kent, Nicolas—452
Kenton, Godfrey—220
Kentuckian, The—104
Kent, Walter—271
Kent, William—150
Kenwright, Ken—418
Kenyon, Doris—93
Kenyon, Leslie—41
Kerin, Nora—12, 44
Kerker, Gustav—2, 6, 7, 20, 30, 35, 96
Kermoyan, Michael—374
Kernan, David—427

Kern, Jerome—23, 31, 56, 62, 74, 79, 82, 87, 94, 99, 100, 106, 114, 120, 123, 132, 150, 158, 162, 164, 176, 181, 187, 217, 231, 246, 290, 329, 376, 397, 424
Kerr, Berilla—402
Kerr, Deborah—281, 401, 420, 439
Kerr, Fred—7, 26, 31, 120, 127, 144, 151
Kerr, Geoffrey—117, 118, 222
Kerr, Ian—406
Kerridge, Mary—274, 283
Kerrigan, J.M.—33, 53, 54, 58, 63, 76, 108, 121, 136, 148
Kerrigan, T.W.—102
Kerr, Jean—262, 282, 287, 309, 326, 331, 345
Kerr, John—276, 281, 287, 309
Kerr, Molly—108, 166
Kerr, Walter—243, 262, 268, 281, 287, 304, 309, 343, 441
Kerry, Anne—454
Kershaw, Wilette—108, 113
Kert, Larry—282, 420
Kesey, Ken—339, 396
Kesselring, Joseph—226, 229, 242, 312, 359, 370, 431, 438
Kessler, David—38
Kester, Max—236, 263
Kester, Paul—2, 6, 26, 100, 121, 192
Kestleman, Sara—388, 395, 398, 417, 435, 439, 452
Ketron, Larry—424, 431
Keuls, Hans—396
Kevin, Michael—454
Keyhole, The—348
Key Largo—217, 225
Keys, Daniel—450, 451
Keys, Nelson—80, 102, 149, 177, 192, 206
Khartoum 1971—401
Kholstomer: The Story of a Horse—453
Kick In—391
Kid Boots—119, 142
Kid Champion—422
Kidd, John—274
Kidd, Michael—281, 298, 314, 386
Kidd, Robert—359, 368, 375, 389, 393, 430, 431, 445
Kid from Stratford, The—259
Kidnapped at Christmas—424
Kid, The—402
Kiefert, Carl—8
Kiely, Benedict—447
Kiepura, Jan—237, 295
Kievman, Carson—452
Kift, Roy—401
Kiki—107
Kildare, Pat—248
Kiley, Richard—282, 291, 314, 321, 332, 345, 352, 371, 429, 439
Killbride, Percy—222, 356
Killdeer, The—415
Killer's Head—418
Killing of Sister George, The—352, 357
Killo, Walter—67
Kill That Story—190
Kill, The—108
Kilroy, Thomas—440
Kiltartan Moliere, The—185
Kilty, Jerome—296, 320, 340, 367, 406, 437, 453, 454
Kimball, Clara—324
Kimberley, F. G.—64, 96
Kimber, W. E.—161
Kimbler, Kay—252
Kimmin, Anthony—316
Kim, Willa—349
Kinch, Martin—377, 405
Kind Lady—195
Kind of Magic, A—376
Kind Sir—282
Kinema Club—121
Kinemacolor—60
King, Ada—46, 152
King, A. Fitzmaurice—2
King Ahaz—63
King, Alan—351, 353

Kern, Jerome—23, 31, 56, 62, 74, 79, 82, 87, 94, 99, 100, 106, 114, 120, 123, 132, 150, 158, 162, 164, 176, 181, 187, 217, 231, 246, 290, 329, 376, 397, 424

King and I, The—155, 271, 283, 301, 323, 348, 374, 410, 432, 438, 441, 454
King Argimenes and the Unknown Warrior—58, 80
King, Charles—124, 148, 156
King Charles I—8
King Charming—313
King, Coretta—383
King, Dave—299, 427
King, Dennis—105, 111, 125, 132, 156, 183, 195, 211, 239, 249, 398
Kingdom—428
Kingdom of God, The—121, 158, 318
King, Edith—106
Kingfisher, The—435, 443, 457
King-Hall, Stephen—165, 177, 192
King Herod Explains—380
King John—8, 68, 76, 80, 84, 136, 223, 228, 259, 260, 285, 301, 306, 317, 323, 329, 367, 374, 381, 388, 391, 416, 422
King Kong—327
King, Larry—442
King Lear—37, 54, 58, 76, 84, 90, 97, 128, 178, 184, 202, 208, 223, 224, 236, 237, 242, 249, 250, 254, 268, 269, 274, 278, 283, 284, 285, 295, 296, 300, 303, 307, 311, 312, 316, 334, 335, 336, 341, 342, 343, 347, 348, 354, 373, 376, 388, 397, 401, 403, 409, 412, 415, 416, 417, 422, 423, 429, 430, 432, 438, 444, 446, 454
King Lives—435
King, Mabel—420
King of Candonia, The—43
King of Hearts—287
King of Nowhere, The—213
King of Rome, The—254
King of Schnorrers, The—137
King, Philip—244, 263, 264, 332, 359
King Rene's Daughter—33
Kingsbury, Lillian—67
King's Head Theatre Club—410
Kingsley, Ben—437, 453
Kingsley, Charles—13, 68
Kingsley, Sidney—98, 186, 194, 196, 199, 203, 204, 217, 225, 234, 238, 262, 265, 271, 275, 288
Kingsley, Susan—443
King's Mare, The—359
King Solomon and the Cobbler—367
King's Rhapsody—263
King Stag—250, 390, 391
King's Theater (Edinburgh)—34
King's Threshold, The—16, 22
Kingston, Gertrude—7, 19, 27, 32, 48, 63, 68, 80, 120, 136, 151, 209
Kingston, Leonard—352
Kingsway Theatre—40
King, The—366
King Ubu—373
King, Woody, Jr.—358
Kinlan, Aideen—328
Kinnear, Roy—382, 444
Kinnian, Alice—450
Kinoy, Ernest—345, 371
Kinsolving, William, 375
Kipling, Rudyard—15, 67, 128
Kipness, Joe—239
Kipphardt, Heinar—361, 380, 381
Kipps—62
Kirby, Max—222
Kirkland, Alexander—195, 205
Kirkland, Jack—187, 211, 216
Kirkland, Muriel—156, 164, 170, 399
Kirkland, Sally—371
Kirk, Phyllis—264
Kirkwood, James—126, 445, 446, 452
Kirkwood, Pat—226, 253, 268, 272, 281, 286
Kirstein, Lincoln—219
Kirwan, Patrick—45, 72
Kismet—57, 58, 246, 282, 294, 354, 442, 445
Kiss and Tell—234, 238, 245, 404
Kiss Burglar, The—87
Kiss Call, The—95

Kiss for Cinderella, A—79, 85, 128, 208, 261
Kissing Time—94
Kiss in the Dark, The—69, 115
Kiss Me, Kate—258, 272, 301, 354, 391
Kiss the Boys Good-Bye—211, 220
Kiss Them for Me—244
Kistemaekers, Henri—75, 87
Kitchen, Michael—446
Kitchen, The—318, 357
Kitch, Kenneth—385
Kit-Kat Artists and Models Award—319
Kitt, Eartha—276, 288, 304, 442
Kitty Darlin'—15, 85
Kitty Grey—2, 8
Kivett and Myers—457
Kiyotsune—408
Klauber, Adolph—51, 189
Klaw and Erlanger—6, 7, 16, 23, 34, 51, 80, 86, 115
Klaw, Marc—39, 110, 154, 103
Kleigl Brothers—199
Kleiglight—199
Kleiman, Harlan—354
Klein, A.B.—104
Klein, Alan—404
Klein, Charles—15, 19, 26, 47, 52, 63, 77, 80
Klein, Manuel—31, 36, 56, 61, 71, 79
Klein, Robert—224, 266, 358, 372, 449
Kleinsinger, George—304
Kline, Kevin—449
Kliss, H. Paul—290, 296
Klondyke—354
Klugman, Jack—351
Knack, The—333, 344, 359
Knee, Allan—422
Knickerbocker Holiday—211, 398
Knickerbocker Theater (New York)—34
Knife, The—410
Knight, Albert—411
Knight, David—287
Knight, Esmond—166, 383
Knight for a Day, A—36
Knight, G. Wilson—228
Knight, Joseph—38
Knightley, Timothy—421
Knight of the Burning Pestle, The—23, 96, 97, 183, 307
Knight, Perdical—87
Knight, Shirley—348, 414, 436, 451
Knights of Madness—267
Knights, Rob—374
Knights, The—431
Knipper-Tchekhova, Olga—121
Knoblauch, Edward—See Knoblock, Edward
Knoblock, Edward—57, 62, 67, 68, 72, 75, 79, 88, 90, 104, 123, 128, 154, 171, 177, 183, 246
Knock Knock—426, 428
Knockout—449
Knots—410, 415
Knott, Frederick—277, 286, 327, 357
Knott, J.—17
Knowles, Christopher—420
Knowles, Richard—97
Knowles, Sheridan—38
Knox, Alexander—214, 296
Knox, Teddy—173, 218, 235, 267, 315
Knuckle—414
Kober, Arthur—138, 205, 276, 280
Koch, Frederick H.—91
Koch, Howard—233, 249
Koehler, Ted—181
Koestler, Arthur—271, 279
Kohler, Estelle—388, 417
Kohout, Pavel—426, 451
Kollmar, Richard—217, 239, 398
Koltai, Ralph—367, 435, 453
Komedie—140
Kominski, David Daniel—69
Komisarjevsky, Theodore—121, 179,

183, 184, 188, 192, 197, 202, 203, 214, 219, 291
Komisarzhevsky, Vera—44
Kongi's Harvest—373
Konieczny, Zygmunt—422
Konstantin, Leopoldine—59
Kootz, Samuel—246
Kopit, Arthur—329, 332, 337, 356, 372, 445, 449, 452
Kops, Bernard—310, 319, 323, 387
Kornfeld, Lawrence—365, 378, 379
Korngold, Erich Wolfgang—182, 239
Kossoff, David—284, 295, 326
Kosta, Tessa—92, 111, 117, 133, 136, 167
Koster, Dorothy—221
Kotcheff, Ted—346, 379
Koun, Karolus—353, 367, 380
Koun's Greek Art Theater—347
Kraft, Hy—272, 299
Kramm, Joseph—200, 276, 280, 285
Krannert Center for the Performing Arts—384
Krapp, Herbert J.—91, 98, 110, 123, 130, 154, 155
Krapp's Last Tape—308, 312, 320, 354, 375, 396, 404, 407, 449
Krasna, Norman—191, 210, 240, 246, 252, 256, 282, 309, 327
Krause, E. P.—34
Kreeger Theatre—428
Kreisler, Fritz—93
Krejca, Otomar—380
Kremlin Chimes—353
Kretzmer, Herbert—366
Kreutzberg, Harald—153
Kreutzer Sonata, The—39, 60, 329, 435
Kreymborg, Alfred—363
Krichon, V.—167
Kroetz, Franz Xaver—428, 424
Kroll, Jack—454
Kroll, Louis—241, 244
Kronenberger, Louis—286, 292, 297, 308, 319, 325, 331
Kruger, Alma—324
Kruger, Otto—78, 79, 93, 106, 111, 133, 150, 167, 172, 230, 419
Krumback, Peter—104
Krupa, Gene—171
Krutch, Joseph Wood—391
Ktshona, Winston—410
Kuhn, Walt—148
Kumagai Jinya—382
Kumalo, Alton—451
Kumalo, Stephen—402
Kummer, Clare—78, 82, 86, 98, 100, 107, 108, 125, 187, 194, 206
Kunneke, Edward—119, 159
Kyle, Barry—417, 422, 429, 438, 439, 444, 446, 453, 455
Kyle, Howard—35
Kyne, Peter B.—92

Labanowski, John—452
Laban, Rudolf—343
L'Abbe Constantin—27
La Beffa—54
La Belle Helene—182, 220, 239
La Belle Paree—56
Labiche, Eugene—25, 43, 279, 296, 367, 396, 430
Labiche-Martin—429
Lablache, Luigi—7
La Bonheur—76
Labor Stage—65
La Bouquet—260
Labour Leader, The—96
La Bugiarda—353
Laburnam Grove—188, 195, 202, 220, 318, 411, 440
La Carosse du Saint-Sacrament—85
La Carte, A—154
La Cenerentola—374
Lace on Her Petticoat—268
Lacey, Catherine—206, 217, 218, 219, 224, 241, 273, 279, 284, 312, 322, 371, 373

Lacey, Franklin—305
Lacey, Ronald—333
La Chance de Francoise—89
La Chauve Souris—214
La Chevalier au Masque—102
La Citta Morta—13, 18, 123
Lackaye, Wilton—7, 8, 19, 22, 66, 70, 144, 185
Lackey's Carnival, The—2
La Comedie Canadienne—261
La Commissaire est Bon Enfant—75
La Corporation du Grand Theatre de Quebec—261
La Coupe Enchantee—95
La Course de Flambeau—8
La Dame aux Camelias—16, 23, 50, 54, 80, 296, 306, 310
Ladder, The—141
La Delaissee—75
La Demoiselle de Magasin—75
La Derniere Soirée de Brummel—45
La Derniere Torture—75
La-Di-Da-Di-Da—235
Ladies in Retirement—218, 221, 228
"Ladies' Man, A"—95
Ladies Night—99
Ladies of the Corridor, The—281, 362, 412
Ladies of the Evening—126
Ladies Paradise, The—6
La Dispute—432
La Donna del Mare—122
La Douleureuse—23
Lad, The—159
Lady Aoi Hanjo, The—340
Lady Audley's Secret—264, 349, 446
Lady, Be Good—126, 143, 209, 374
Lady Billy—100
Ladybird, Ladybird—428
Lady Butterfly—117
Lady Chatterley—329
Lady Day: A Musical Tragedy—402
Lady Explorer, A—179
Lady Frederick—37, 250, 389
Lady from Alfaqueque—166
Lady from Edinburgh—244
Lady from Maxim's, The—439
Lady from the Provinces, The—121
Lady from the Sea, The—122, 123, 135, 249, 269, 329, 395, 428, 451
Ladyhouse Blues—431
Lady Huntsworth's Experiment—91
Lady in Ermine, The—113
Lady in the Dark—226, 229
"Lady Is A Tramp, The"—205
Lady Jane's Christmas Party—23
Lady Luck—151, 154
Lady Luxury—77
Lady Madcap—22
Lady Mary—158
Lady Mislaid, A—267
Lady of Belmont, The—174
Lady of Lyons, The—97
Lady of the Camellias, The—173, 329, 341
Lady of the Rose, The—113
Lady of the Slipper, The—62
Lady on the Barometer—316
Lady or the Tiger?, The—358
Lady Patricia—57
Lady Precious Stream—193, 202, 237, 242, 254, 269
Lady's Not for Burning, The—263, 267, 389, 403, 417, 444
Lady Susan—278
Lady's Virtue, A—133
Lady Teazle—24
Lady, The—73
Lady Windermere's Fan—23, 59, 72, 84, 179, 250, 289, 361, 408
Lady With a Lamp, The—165
La Fauteuil 47—144
Lafayette Players—98
Lafayette, S.—50
La Femme de Claude—90
La Femme Nu—53
La Femme X—54
Laffan, Kevin—382, 386
Laffing Room Only—240

Laff That Off—133
La Figlia di Jorio—44
La Flambee—75
La Foi—50
L' Age d' Aimer—27
La Gioconda—4, 13, 16
L'Aglais tel qu'on le Parle—45
La Grande Eugene—429
La Gringoire—90
LaGuardia, Fiorello—210, 246, 315
La Guerre de Troie N'Aura Pas Lieu (Tiger at the Gates)—294, 438
La Guerre, Yes Sir!—403
Lahmann, Beatrix—249
Lahr, Bert—157, 170, 181, 190, 196, 200, 217, 229, 237, 240, 250, 271, 298, 306, 332, 333, 360, 370
Lahr, John—229
Lahr, Mildred—229
L'Aiglon—1, 4, 8, 54, 80, 90, 193
Laine, Cleo—311, 336, 368
Laing, R.D.—410, 415, 440
La Jalousie du Barbouille—85, 90
La Joie Fait Peur—45
Lake, The—176
Lake of the Woods—399
Lakier, Gail—421
La Kommandatur—75
La, La, Lucille—92
Lalique, Suzanne—290
La Locandiera—145
Laloy, Louis—61
La Lupa—44, 380
La Main Passe—375
La Mama Experimental Theater Club —331, 385, 386, 388, 393, 403, 416, 420, 424, 430, 443, 445, 451
La Mama-Plexus II—381
L'Amante Anglais—379, 386, 396
Lamar & Rosita—227
La Massière—50
Lamas, Fernando—298
Lambert, Constant—178
Lambert, Particia—305
Lamberts, Heath—438
Lamble, Lloyd—285
Lamb, Myrna—388, 428
Lambrett-Smith, Frank—255
Lamb, Thomas W.—194
Lament for Rastafari—430
L'Ami Fritz—95
L'Amiral—85
Lamont, Duncan—401
LaMont, Margie—140
L'Amorcage—57
La Morte de Cleopatre—80
L'Amour Medecin—89
Lamp at Midnight—255
Lampell, Millard—97, 321
Lampert, Zohra—209, 347
La Navette—260
Lanchester, Elsa—113, 128, 143, 154, 180, 188, 203, 303
Landau, Cecil—263, 289
Landau, Jack—296, 300, 301, 306, 312, 329, 355, 369
Landau, Martin—289
Lan, David—415, 435, 452
Landeck, Ben—50
Landen, Dinsdale—347, 444, 445, 450
Lander, Charles—22
Lander, Jean Margaret Davenport—17
Land for the People, The—102
Landi, Elissa—127, 135, 170
Landis, Frederick—87
Landis, Jessie Royce—200, 223, 249, 267, 273, 286, 291, 404
Land of Fame—391
Land of Promise, The—67, 72
Land of Smiles, The—183, 317
Land of the Christmas Stocking—174, 246, 250, 261
Landone, Alice—267, 401
Landon, Margaret—271
Landscape—379, 387, 390, 395
Landscape of the Body—436
Landscape/Silence—379, 390
Land, The—28
Landy, Michael—373

Lane, Burton—179, 221, 240, 252, 351, 436
L'Ane de Buridan—53
Lane, Dorothy—172
Lane, Grace—127, 135
Lane, Lauri Lupino—119, 124, 232, 235, 264, 288
Lane, Rosemary—226
Lane, Terry—340
Lan-Fang, Mei—174
Langbridge, Rosamund—45
Langella, Frank—349, 355, 368, 376, 420, 431, 434, 440
Langer, Lawrence—153, 179, 336
Langham, Chris—437
Langham, Michael—268, 273, 274, 291, 295, 301, 306, 311, 312, 317, 323, 329, 335, 338, 348, 360, 367, 381, 389, 452
Lang, Harold—222, 351, 354, 368, 424
Langmire, Adele—222
Langner, Lawrence—80, 186, 188, 224, 252, 296, 424
Langner, Ruth—167
Lang, Robert—190, 334, 346, 381, 409
Langton, Basil—249, 254
Langton, David—248
Langtry, Lily—9, 13, 43, 46, 55, 168, 223, 225
Languirand, Jacques—392
Lanham, Florence—93
Lanier, Sidney—350
Lannin, Paul—120
L'Annonce Faite a Marie—334, 353
La Nouvelle Idole—89
Lansburgh, G. Albert—130, 185, 457
Lansbury, Angela—138, 306, 321, 357, 378, 393, 409, 449
Lansbury, Edgar—174
Lansky, Israel—219
La Nuit des Rois—85, 95
La Otra Hora—285
La Paix Chez Soi—75, 89
La Parisienne—23, 306
La Passerelle—23, 27, 75
La Perichole—85, 137
La Petite Marquise—27, 89
Lapine, James—452
La Plante, Laura—192
La Plume de Ma Tante—294, 309, 319
La Porta Chiusa—123
La Porte Close—75
Lapotaire, Dale—390
Lapotaire, Jane—381, 382, 388, 390, 429, 432, 444, 451, 453
La Poupee—178, 198
La Prisonniere—141, 194
La Puce a l'Oreille—453
La Rafale—33, 45
LaRampe—63
Lardner, Ring—111, 164
Lardner, Ring, Jr.—332
La Recommandation—76
LaRedd, Cora—163
La Reine Joyeuse—102
La Reine Morte—359
La Revenante—76
Large as Life—310
Larger Than Life—267
Larimore, Earle—145, 176, 190, 256
Lark Rise—445, 453
Lark, The—294, 296
Larner, Elizabeth—276, 321
Larnyoh, George—422
La Robe Rouge—23, 45, 99
La Ronde—447
Larrimore, Francine—83, 89, 105, 142, 163, 177, 424
Larry, Sheldon—455

Larson, Jack—374
la Rubia, Marga—75, 84
LaRue, Danny—359, 371, 386, 411, 424
La Rue, Grace—302
La Russo, Louis II—449
La Samaritaine—54
Lascelles, Ernita—111
Lasdun, Denys—433
La Seconda Moglei—27
Lasenby, May—376
La Serre, Edward—8
La Shelle, Kirke—14, 19, 28
Lashin, Orie—202
Lasky-Famous Players Stock Company—179
Lasky, Jesse—56, 60
La Sommnambula—307
La Sorciere—23, 54
La Souris—29
L'Association Francaise d'Action Artistique—329
L'Assommoir—50
Last Analysis, The—344
Last Call for Breakfast—455
Last Chance Saloon, The—381
Last Days of British Honduras, The—417
Last Days of the Dandies, The—8
Last Feast of Fianna—3
Last Meeting of the Knights of the White Magnolia, The—426
Last Mile, The—170
Last Night of Don Juan, The—133
Last of Mrs. Cheyney, The—133, 135, 147, 237, 242, 368
Last of Mrs. Lincoln, The—400
Last of Summer, The—241
Last of the Czars, The—360
Last of the Red Hot Lovers, The—378, 392, 451
Last P. M., The—341
Last Romantic, The—423
Last Rose of Summer, The—369
Last Stop—240
Last Straw, The—388
Last Street Play, The—431
Last Sweet Days of Isaac, The—385, 397
Last Waltz, The—105, 115
Last Warning, The—112
La Surprise de l'Amour—89
Late Christopher Bean, The—181, 187, 189, 220, 273
Late George Apley, The—240, 246
Late Joys—251, 349
Latell, Alfred—59
La Tendresse—112
Late Night Final—177
Latent Heterosexual, The—372
Later—451
Laterna Magika—348
Latham, Frederick G.—26, 47, 56
Lathbury, Stanley—144
Latimer, Edith—42
Latin Quarter—263, 267, 272
Latitude 15 Deg. S—108
La Tosca—16, 103
La Touche, John—216, 222, 227, 247, 257, 287, 292, 410
La Tourneaux, Robert—371
La Traverse—89
La Troupe du Roi—388
Lattimer, Hugh—283
Lattimore, Richard—360
La Turista—367, 379
Lauder, Sir Harry—50, 199, 270
Laugh, Clown, Laugh—119
Laughing Lady, The—117
Laughter!—443
Laugh Parade, The—176
Laughter—451
Laugh Time—235
Laughton, Charles—144, 145, 154, 159, 166, 172, 180, 188, 189, 192, 203, 255, 275, 284, 287, 302, 303, 310, 316, 323, 336
Launay, Andre—427
Lau, Patrick—453
Laura—419
Laurel and Hardy—428

Laurel, Stan—46
Laurence, Charles—391, 401, 414
Laurence, Paula—219
Laurents, Arthur—244, 251, 261, 286, 304, 308, 314, 332, 344, 351, 364, 418, 445, 455
Laurie, John—212, 219
Laurie, Piper—354
L'Avare—89, 95, 114, 285, 359
La Varres—221
Lavedan, Henri—30
Lave, Dilys—353
Lave, Evelyn—134
La Veine—95
Lavenar, Ladies—134
Lavender Blue—437
Lavender, Ian—450
L'Avenir est dans Les Oeufs—340
L'Aventuriere—115
La Verde, Belle—23
Laver, James—166
La Verne, Lucille—78, 117
Laverty, Maura—251, 273, 275, 278, 279, 290, 295
Lavery, Emmet—191, 247
La Vie Parisienne—416
La Vile dont le Prince est un Enfant—396, 437
Lavin, Linda—357
La Voile du Bonheur—90
Law, Alice—129
Law, Arthur—10, 11
Law Divine, The—89
Lawford, Ernest—22, 136
Lawful Larceny—111
Law, Harry Robert—130
Lawler, Ray—305, 313, 341, 373
Lawless, Sue—453
Lawlor, Mary—149
Law of Silence, The—53
Lawrence, Boyle—57, 113
Lawrence, Carol—276, 304, 327
Lawrence, D. H.—145, 152, 244, 329, 366, 368, 373, 410
Lawrence, Georgia—61
Lawrence, Gerald—49, 58, 103, 173, 308
Lawrence, Gertrude—89, 108, 117, 119, 120, 124, 133, 135, 142, 159, 172, 178, 183, 188, 201, 205, 217, 226, 259, 271, 280
Lawrence, Helen—236
Lawrence, Jack—345
Lawrence, Jerome—77, 257, 293, 298, 314, 351, 357, 378, 405, 442
Lawrence, Jordan—284, 360
Lawrence, Joseph—361
Lawrence, Margaret—93, 111
Lawrence, Peter—268
Lawrence, Reginald—195
Lawrence, Steve—344, 371
Lawson, Cristyne—327
Lawson, Denis—439
Lawson, Elsie—156
Lawson, John Howard—81, 90, 131, 184, 207
Lawson, Winifred—167, 193
Lawton, Frank—159
Lawton, Leslie—445
Lawton, Mary—67
Lay By—397
Lay, Dilys—286, 289, 299, 318, 382
Laye, Evelyn—95, 108, 121, 135, 157, 158, 165, 168, 182, 206, 236, 285, 288, 316, 354, 394
Layton, Joe—367, 371, 378, 386, 401, 420
Layton, Turner—112
Lazarus—348, 416
Lazarus, Frank—450
Lazarus, Milton—239, 367
La Zolfara—44
Leachman, Cloris—260, 287
Leach, Rosemary—435
Leach, Wilfred—401, 424, 436, 446, 454
League of New York Theatres and Producers—174, 204, 337, 431, 433, 441
League of Notions—107

League of Off-Broadway Theatres and Producers—297
League of Resident Theaters—356, 363
Leah Kleschna—20, 51
Lean, Cecil—41
Lean Harvest—177
Leap Year—126
Learner, Sammy—207
Learning, Walter—377
Leatherhead Repertory Company—312
Leave It To Jane—82
Leave It To Me—211
Leave It To Psmith—172
Leaven of Malice—423
Leaver, Philip—245
Leavitt, Paul—329
Le Baiser dans la Nuit—76
Le Barbier de Seville—245, 296, 373
LeBaron, William—93, 94
Lebensold, Frank—384
Leblanc, Maurice—47
Leblang, Joe—60
Le Bonheur, Mesdames—102
Le Bons Villageois—45
Le Bourgeoise Gentilhomme—45, 68, 97, 129, 249, 296, 348
LeBrandt, Joseph—59
LeBreton, Flora—156
Le Captif.—75
Le Carrosse du Saint-Sacrement—306
Le Cercle Moliere—138
Le Chandelier—218
Le Chauffeur—76
Le Chevalier au Masque—89
Le Chien du Jardinier—302, 306
Le Cid—312, 359, 369
Leclercq, Adolphe—75
Le Cloitre—75
Le Coeur Dispose—108
L'Ecole des Femmes—255, 264, 354
L'Ecole des Maris—218
LeCoq, Jaques—343
Le Corsaire—214
Le Coup de Telephone—95
Lederer, Charles—282
Lederer, Francis—176, 177, 181, 269
Lederer, George—10, 14
Lederer, Suzanne—440
Le Detour—45
Le Dindon—316
Lee, Auriol—48, 50, 58, 107, 115, 129, 159, 177
Lee, Belinda—301
Lee, Bernard—212, 248, 253, 267, 293
Lee, Bert—134, 148, 151, 157, 165, 187, 197, 206, 213
Lee, Canada—208, 224, 226, 232, 245, 247, 257, 280
Lee, Carl—314
Leech, Richard—273, 322
Lee, C.P. P.—437
Lee, C. Y.—309
Leeds, Phil—230
Leeds Playhouse—389, 422
Lee, Edith—201
Lee, Eugene—383
Lee, Gypsy Rose—200, 314, 391, 450
Lee, Ken—421
Lee, Leslie—422
Lee, Michele—406
Lee, Ming Cho—454
Lee, Pinkie—230
Lee, Robert E.—90, 257, 293, 298, 312, 314, 351, 357, 378, 405, 442
Lees, Martin—348
Lee, Sondra—327
Leeson, Georgia—307
Leeson, Sylvia—307
Lee, Valerie—338
Lee, Vanessa—263, 280, 289, 368
Lee, Will—217, 221
Le Fanu—183, 188
LeFeaux, Charles—208, 249
Le Fevre, Adam—410
Lefevre, Pierre—411
Lefevre, Robin—450, 453

Lefkowitz, Louis—343
Le Fourberies de Nerine—85
Le Frenais, Ian—414
Left Bank, The—176, 183, 185
Left-Handed Liberty—354
Left Theatre—187
Leftwich, Alexander—156
LeGallienne, Eva—75, 105, 118, 121, 132, 137, 145, 146, 147, 152, 159, 160, 162, 166, 167, 173, 174, 178, 180, 184, 188, 193, 230, 241, 245, 250, 251, 254, 259, 268, 307, 347, 366, 373, 433
Le Gallienne, Richard—63
Legend of Leonora, The—71, 153
Legend of Lizzie, The—399
Legend of Lovers—272
Legend of Pepito, The—295
Legend of Tom Dooley, The—454
Legend of Wu Chang, The—438
Le Gendre de M. Poirier—90
Legends—407
Leggatt, Allison—92, 151, 192, 213, 266
Legge, R. J.—15
Legge, Phyllis—62
Legnaioli, Louis—60
Le Grand Duc—115
Le Grande Eugene—429
LeGrand, Phyllis—62
Legras, Jacques—295
Lehar, Franz—37, 56, 57, 62, 74, 121, 126, 128, 150, 278, 295, 311, 317, 348, 380, 446
Lehman, Herbert—210
Lehman, Leo—366
Lehman, Liza—21, 32
Lehmann, Beatrix—142, 166, 177, 192, 202, 208, 219, 250, 255, 300, 309, 310, 312, 315, 349, 361
Leiber, Fritz—108, 148, 173, 179
Leibert, Michael—430, 454
Leibman, Ron—209
Leicester, Ernest—53
Leicester Square Theatre, The—175
Leigh, Andrew—76, 152, 159, 160, 166, 214, 228, 301
Leigh, Carolyn—288, 321, 332, 365
Leigh, Charlotte—218
Leigh, Eleonora—33
Leigh, Grace—21, 32
Leigh-Hunt, Barbara—329, 366, 372, 398
Leigh, Jenny—368
Leigh, J. H.—22
Leigh, Leslie—56
Leigh, Mary—127, 135
Leigh, Mike—388, 416
Leigh, Mitch—352
Leigh, Roland—159, 172, 206
Leighton, Frank—267
Leighton, Isabel—226
Leighton, Margaret—216, 242, 245, 246, 249, 250, 254, 274, 278, 283, 284, 285, 289, 310, 317, 321, 322, 327, 329, 344, 347, 357, 368, 402, 432
Leighton, Queenie—32, 45
Leigh, Vivian—197, 206, 208, 223, 230, 250, 253, 256, 264, 274, 283, 295, 299, 308, 310, 314, 320, 329, 338, 369
Leigh, Walter—187, 212, 218
Leinster Players—96
Leipziger, Leo—72
Leister, Fredrick—177, 202, 211, 222
Leivick, H.—219
Le Jeu de l'Armour et du Hasard—296, 369
Le Juif Polonais—50
Lekolight—209
Leland, David—439
Le Legataire Universel—218
Le Lys—57
Le Magician—423
LeMaire, Rufus—154
Lemaitre, Jules—50
Le Malade Imaginaire—97, 260, 273, 311, 312, 388, 408
Le Mariage de Barillon—427
Le Mariage de Figaro—45, 90, 340

Le Mariage de Mlle. Beulemans—63
Le Mauvais Bergere—89
Lembeck, Harvey—271, 295
Le Medecin Malgre Lui—90
Le Medicin Volant—408
Le Menteur—95
LeMesurier, Jen—421
L'Emigre—50
Le Misanthrope—95, 260, 302, 306, 329, 334, 453
Lemle, William—104
Lemmon, Jack—442
LeMoyne, Sarah Kamble—77
Lenard, Mark—323
Lend an Ear—258, 383
Lengyel, Melchoir—67
L'Enigme—90, 93
Lenihan, Winifred—94, 119, 160, 349
Leningrad Gorki Theatre—362
Lenin, Nikolai—414, 451
Lennard, Isobel—344
Lennon, John—373, 378, 424
Lennon-McCartney—414
Lennox-Ashley—219
Lennox, Cosmo Gordon—8, 12, 22, 75, 101
Lennox, Vera—97
Lenny—393
Leno, Dan—4, 17, 131
LeNoire, Rosetta—426
Lenormand, H. R.—119, 214
Le Nouveau Testament—198
Le Nozze di Figaro—255
L'Enterrement—274
Lenya, Lotte—205, 209, 226, 271, 290, 332, 335
Lenz, Jakob—375
Leocadia—289
Leonard, Bennie—117
Leonard, Billy—93, 95, 107, 115, 120, 177, 192
Leonard, Eddie—19, 22, 25, 45, 93
Leonard, Hugh—341, 379, 394, 430, 439, 445, 452
Leonard, Joseph—410
Leonard, Nellie—115
Leonard, Queenie—158
Leonard, Robert—66, 82, 111
Leonce and Lena—306
Leonidoff, Leonid—121
Leoni, Franco—189
Leontovich, Eugenie—116, 171, 182, 196, 203, 214, 304, 400
Leon, Victor—53
Leopold and Loeb murder cases—304
Le Pain de Manage—85
L'Epervier—108
Le Pharmacien—75
3Le Piege—75
Le Pieton de l'air—353
Le Plus Heureux de Trois—43
Le Poison Hindou—76
Le Proces de Jeanne d'Arc—54
Le Repetition ou L'Amour Puni(The Rehearsal)—307
Le Reviel—38
Lerne, Marion—201
Lerner, Allen Jay—90, 246, 252, 256, 257, 268, 272, 298, 321, 351, 374, 378, 406, 426, 455
Lerner, Sammy—207
Leroux, Gaston—57,423
Le Roux, Madeleine—385, 410
LeRoy, Hal—217
Le Roy, Ken—304
Les Adieux—306
Lesan, David—197
Le Satyre—62
Les Ballets Africaines—348, 362
Les Belles Soeurs—375
Les Bonnes (The Maids)—279, 301
Les Bouffons—54
Les Boulingrins—245
Les Caprices de Marianne—90
Lescarbot, Marc—337
Le Secret—68, 90, 102
les Efants Dansaient—261
Le Seul Bandit du Village—75

Les Fausses Confidences—260
Les Felines—128
Les Femmes Noirs—415
Les Femmes Savantes—316, 388
Les Folies de Paris—210
Les Fourberies de Scapin—85, 316, 328
Les Freres Karamazov—89, 95
Les Fridolinons—261
Les Hannetons—39
Les Liason Dangereuses—334
Leslie, Beth—273
Leslie, Fred—62, 120, 127, 159, 165
Leslie, Lew—143, 156, 187, 192, 201
Leslie, Marguerite—32
Leslie-Smith, Kenneth—212, 245, 276
Leslie, Sylvia—108
Les Maris de Leontine—63
Les Miserables—185
Les Nuits de la Colere—306
Le Soulier de Satin—353
Les Parents Terribles—223, 446
Les Precieuses Ridicules—45, 241
Les Rois en Exil—57
Les Romanesques—45, 90
Les Rouges et Noirs—96
Lessac, Michael—442
Lesser, Eugene—390, 404, 411
Lessing, Doris—283, 306, 311, 361
Lessing, Gotthold Ephiaim—44, 368, 376
Lessing, Madge—84
Lesson in a Dead Language, A—374
Lesson in Blood and Roses, A—410
Lesson, The—295, 312, 340, 368
Lester, Alfred—79, 107, 119
Lester, Claude—218
Lester, Edward—88, 117
Lester, Harry—218
Lester, Mark—107, 120, 127
Lester, Phil—101, 113
L'Estrange, David—127
L'Estrange, Julian—90
Les Trois Mousquetaires—323
Les Veuves—415
Les Violins Parfois—334
Le Systeme Ribadier—340
L'Ete de St. Martin—45
Let 'Em Eat Cake—187
Le Testament du Pere Leleu—89
Let Freedom Ring—196
Le Theatre du Nouveau Monde—301, 311, 312, 353
Let Him Have Judgement—277
Let My People Come—413, 433
Le Treteau de Paris—396, 438
Le Triangle—76
Le Triomphe de l'Amour—301, 312
Let's All Go Down the Strand—366
"Let's Be Buddies"—222
Let's Face It—226, 231, 418
Let's Get a Divorce—359
Let's Get Laid—414
"Let's Have Another Cup of Coffee"—181
Let Sleeping Wives Lie—365
Let's Make an Opera—336, 349
Let's Pretend—214
Letter for Queen Victoria, A—420
Letter of the Law, The—99
Letters from an Eastern Front—361
Letters from K—435
Letters from Stalingrad—361
Letters to Lucerne—233
Letter to the President, A—202
Letter, The—150
Let the Good Stones Roll—443
Let Them Eat Cake—315
Letton, Francis—276
Letty—16
Let Us Be Gay—163, 424
Let Wives Tak Tent—264, 329
Levant, Oscar—149, 182
Le Veilleur de Nuit—122
Level, Maurice—76, 108
Levene, Sam—153, 181, 195, 205, 217, 309, 344, 382, 400
Leveridge, Lynn Ann—359
Lever, Lady Arthur—102

Levesey, Jack—177
Levey, Ethel—20, 41, 297
Levey, Harold—100
Levi, Maurice—1, 41, 47
Levine, Beth—141
Levine, James—456
Levine, Richard—257
Levin, Herman—38
Levin, Ira—293, 321, 442, 449
Levin, Meyer—179, 304, 325
Levinson, Jesse A.—154
Levitt, Amy—385
Levitt, Saul—315, 325, 393, 431
Le Voleur—50
Le Voyage de Monsieur Perrichon —45
Levy, Ben W.—143, 161, 166, 170, 173, 177, 181, 185, 232, 248, 270, 305, 320, 412
Levy, Burton—179
Levy, Ethel—56
Levy, Jacques—364, 367, 374, 378, 393
Levy, Jonathan—431
Levy, Jose—58, 68, 79, 84
Levy, Joseph—209
Levy, Melvin—193
Lew Dockstader's Minstrels—22
Lewes, Eva—69
Lewes, Miriam—102, 152, 178, 202
Lew Fields Company—319
Lewine, Richard—205
Lewin, John—376
Lewis, Ada—41, 56
Lewis, Arthur—53, 87, 113, 174, 352
Lewis, Bertha—167
Lewis, Catherine—58
Lewis, Curigwen—202
Lewis, Eric—16, 89, 102
Lewis, Florrie—59
Lewis, Fred—107
Lewis, George—34
Lewis, Gillian—305, 371
Lewis, Henry—92
Lewis, John—264
Lewis, Kay—187
Lewis, Leopold—268, 428
Lewis, Lloyd—265
Lewis, Mabel Terry—2, 129
Lewis, Martin—108
Lewis, Morgan—221
Lewis, Nick—379
Lewisohn, Alice—77, 111, 133, 404
Lewisohn, Irene—77, 131, 243
Lewisohn, Victor—128, 143, 183
Lewis, Robert—168, 221, 262, 276, 304, 314, 332, 352
Lewis, Ronald—282, 340, 366
Lewis, Sinclair—106, 190, 200, 204, 212, 265, 385
Lewis, Stephen—323
Lewis, Ted—93, 106, 112, 150, 399
Lewis, Windsor—298
Lew Leslie's Blackbirds—171, 216
Leycester, Laura—120
Leyland, Noel—126
Leyton, Helen—32
Le Zebre—58
L'Habit Vert—68
L'Heroique le Cardunois—63
L'Hirondelle—23, 27
L'Holocauste—80
L'Homme et ses Fantomes—129
L'Homme qui Assassina—129
L'Hotel du Libre Exchange—102
Liars, The—76, 77
Liar, The—380
Libeau, Gustave—75
Libel!—191, 196
Liberated Woman, A—397
Liberson, Will—439
Liberty Belles, The—6, 137
Liberty Cart, The—430
Liberty Theater (New York)—33
Liberty Tree, The—374
Libin, Paul—367, 404
Libman, Yisrol—198
License, The—386
Licentious Fly, The—395
Lichtenstein, Harvey—437, 448

Lido Lady—144
Liebelei—408
Liebler and Company—7, 22
Liebman, Max—216, 230
Liebman, Yisrol Paul Mann—198
Liepolt, Werner—375
Lies About Vietnam—379
Lie, The—71
Lieven, Albert—236
Lifar, Serge—172
Life and Death of an American, The—219
"Life and Love"—92
Life and Times of Joseph Stalin, The—410
Life Begins at 8:40—190
Life Class—415, 424
Life in Bedrooms, A—366
Life in the Sun, A—296
Life in the Theatre, A—398, 434, 452
"Life is Just a Bowl of Cherries"—176
Life Machine, The—157, 177
Life of a Star, The—138
Life of David Garrick—138
Life of Edward the Second of England, The—409
Life of Galileo, The—323, 341
Life of Johnson—389
Life of Man, The—144
Life on the Stage—138
Life Price—379
Life with Father—217, 225, 233, 253, 256, 368, 376
Life with Mother—257, 265
Liffey Lane—273, 295
Liff, Samuel—374
Lifting the Lid—25
Liggat, James—360
Light Blues' The—79
Light Comedian, The—73
Light Failing—306
Light Fantastic—295
Light from St. Agnes, A—27
Lighting a Torch—280
Light, James—101, 224
Lightner, Winnie—124
Lightnin'—87, 104, 110, 116, 129, 180
Light of Heart, The—222, 228, 232
Light Opera of Manhattan, (LOOM) —424, 446
Lights O' London—246
Light Shining in Buckinghamshire —428, 431
Light That Failed, The—15, 67, 69
Light Up the Sky—257, 265, 350
Ligon, Tom—371
Likely Tale, A—299
Likes of Her, The—122
Li'l Abner—298
Lilac Domino, The—88, 242
Lilac Time—106, 160, 184, 189, 232
Lilies of the Field, The—120, 135
Liliom—105, 110, 145, 184, 192, 223, 224, 244, 383
Lillie, Beatrice—17, 75, 83, 88, 94, 95, 108, 114, 124, 133, 135, 156, 158, 172, 176, 182, 183, 188, 195, 200, 212, 216, 218, 231, 240, 248, 257, 298, 304, 344
Lillie, Muriel—114
Lillo, George—291
Lily, The—57
Lily White Boys, The—322
Limelight, Fred—443
Limited Mail, The—243
Limon, José—173
L'Impromptu de Versailles—245, 328
L'Impromptu du Vieux-Colombier— 85
Lincke, Paul—35
Lincoln—431
Lincoln, Abraham—77, 185, 209, 252
Lincoln Center Repertory Company—347, 349, 350, 355, 356, 362, 363, 368, 373, 376, 380, 383, 387, 391, 395, 398, 401, 404, 405, 407, 456
Lincoln Mask, The—400

Lindenberg, Paul—216
Linden, Hal—179, 386
Linden, Jennie—401
Linden Tree, The—253
Linder, Leslie, 294
Lindfors, Viveca—283, 291, 332, 340, 364
Lind, Geoffrey—198
Lind, Gillian—172, 179, 222
Lind, Jakov—373
Lind, Letty—123
Lindo, Olga—113, 126, 143, 212, 244, 246, 376
Lindsay, David—409
Lindsay-Hogg, Michael—447
Lindsay, Howard—105, 111, 121, 187, 198, 200, 206, 217, 225, 244, 251, 257, 265, 266, 280, 282, 298, 314, 332, 362, 368, 376
Lindsay, Jack—366
Lindsay, Margaret—244
Lindsay, Normal—292
Lindsay, Vera—219
Lindsey, Gene—364
Lineham, Fergus—328
Line of Least Existence, The—373
Link, John—431
Linklater, Eric—269, 317
Link, Peter—378, 398
Link, Ron—435
Linn, Bambi—237, 244
Linnebach projector—147
Linney, Romulus—437
Linn, Margaret—345
Linthicum, Lotta—82
Linton, N.—64
L'Invitation au Chateau—334
L'Invitation au Voyage—160
Lion and the Jewel, The—361
Lion and the Mouse, The—26
Lionel!—435
Lionel and Clarissa—135
Lion in Love, The—323
Lion in Winter, The—357
Lion, Lion M.—57, 61, 89, 103, 135, 158, 184, 191, 197
Lion Theatre—440
Lipman, Clara—61
Lippman, Sidney—252
Lipscomb, W. P.—207
Lipton, Celia—227, 246
Lipshitz, Harold—179
Lipton, Michael—346
Lisbon Story, The—236, 242
Listen Lester—88
Listen To Me—418
Lister, Eve—181
Lister, Francis—119, 143, 166
Lister, Lance—134, 143, 151
Lister, Laurier—253, 263, 272, 282, 289, 295, 299
Lister, Margot—258
Lister, Moira—264, 283, 296, 344, 394
Litchfield, Emma—54
Literature—77
Lithgow, John—246, 394, 428
Little Accident—157
Little Bit of Everything, A—19
Little Bit of Fluff, A—75, 236
Little Bit of Youth—89
Little Black Sambo and Little White Barbara—23
Little Black Sheep—421
Little Blue Light, The—273
Little Boxes—372
Little Cafe, The—66
Little Cherub, The—31
Little Christmas Miracle, A—64
Little Clay Cart, The—348
Little, Cleavon—364, 385, 414
Little Damozel, The—49
Little Dog Laughed, The—218
Little Duchess, The—6, 90
Little Dutch Girl, A—102
Little Elephant Is Dead, The—451
Little Eyolf—54, 173, 245, 341, 453
Little Father of the Wilderness, The—308

Little Foxes, The—216, 220, 231, 247, 262, 368, 377, 430, 455
Little French Milliner The—12
"Little Girl Blue"—196
Little Guy, Napoleon—359
Little Hans Andersen—17, 229
Little Hut, The—268, 281, 418
Little Idiot—285
Little Jessie James—118
Little Johnny Jones—20, 229
Little Lambs Eat Ivy—258
Little Lord Fauntleroy—8, 69
Little Malcolm—361
Little Man, The—166, 193
Little Man-What Now?—408
Little Mary—16
Little Mary Sunshine—140, 315, 319, 383, 391
Little Me—332, 346, 446
Little Men, The—361
Little Michus, The—26
Little Millionaire, The—56
Little Minister, The—23, 209
Little Miss Bluebead—118
Little Miss Llewelyn—63
Little Miss Muffet—265
Little Murders—364, 378
Little Nellie Kelly—113, 119
Little Nemo—42
Little Night Music, A—406, 412, 421
Little Old King Cole—330
"Little Old Lady"—201
Little Orphan Annie—434
Little Ray of Sunshine, A—5
Little Red Riding Hood—38, 45, 123
Littler, Emile—243, 255, 260, 265, 402
Little Revue, The—120, 218, 456
Littler, Prince—223, 325
Little Show, The—163
Little Stone House, The—64, 68, 116
Littlest Revue, The—300
Little Theatre of Dallas—138
Little Theatre Tournament—121, 128, 138, 144, 152
Little Town of Bethlehem—53
Little Whopper, The—93
Little Women—97, 228, 243, 246, 295, 369
Littlewood, Joan—279, 285, 286, 289, 290, 291, 295, 296, 300, 301, 308, 311, 312, 313, 316, 317, 318, 321, 323, 325, 328, 339, 347, 348, 364, 366, 367, 368, 390, 402, 404
Livanov, B. N.—388
Live Like Pigs—313, 357, 401
Liveright, Horace—189
Liverpool Playhouse—445
Liverpool Repertory Theatre Company—60, 68, 69, 76, 80, 137, 145, 233, 259
Livesey, Jack—156, 236
Livesey, Roger—89, 124, 128, 134, 218, 241, 253, 260, 273, 300, 330, 355, 432
Livin' Fat—428
Living Corpse, A—64, 167
Living Dangerously—192
Living for Pleasure—310
Living Newspaper: The—203, 204, 213, 214, 221
Living Room, The—282, 286, 288, 297
Livings, Henry—328, 334, 346, 379
Livingstone, Douglas—333
Livingstone, Robert—385
Livingston, Jay—309
Living Theatre, The—275, 292, 327, 335, 343, 348, 375, 389, 451
Living Together—414
Liza—72, 113
Liza of Lambeth—427
Llewellyn, Richard—212, 253
Lloyd, Alice—4
Lloyd, Doris—76, 108
Lloyd, Flora—58
Lloyd, Florence—16
Lloyd, Frederick—166
Lloyd George Knew My Father—401

Lloyd, Marie—9' 46, 116
Lloyd, Norman—255, 301
Loaded Questions—451
Loaves and Fishes—57
Local 802—425
Local Stigmatic, The—359
Locke, Edward—47
Locke, Katherine—205, 221
Locke, Philip—333
Locke, Robinson—104
Locke, W. J.—43
Lockhart, Gene—82, ,137, 140, 186, 308
Lockhart, June—137, 252
Lockhart, Kathleen—137
Lockridge, Frances—226
Lockrido, Richard—226
Lock Up Your Daughters—317, 319, 334, 335, 375, 380
Lockwood, Julia—291, 324, 362, 435
Lockwood, Margaret—265, 274, 289, 333, 355, 389, 410, 421
Loden, Barbara—344
Loder, Basil—148, 172
Loder, John—252
Lodge, John Davis—275
Lodi—197
Loeb Drama Center—325
Loeb, Philip—109, 131, 145, 221
Loesser, Frank—257, 267, 270, 275, 298, 316, 327, 337, 353 360, 384, 418
Loew, Arthur—421
Loew, Frederick—246, 252, 256, 268, 272, 298, 321, 374, 406, 455
Lofthouse, Gilbert—143
Loftus, Cecilia—3, 6
Loftus, Cissie—237
Loftus, Marie—237
Logan, Ella—171, 227, 230, 383
Logan, George—417, 421
Logan, Janet—241
Logan, Joshua—45, 224, 247, 252, 257, 261, 262, 266, 270, 276, 280, 281, 282, 288, 295, 298, 302, 309, 333, 411, 428
Logan, Olive—50
Logan, Sally—339
Logan, Stanley—79, 113, 133
Logue, Christopher—438
Lohner-Beda—178
Lohr, Marie—43, 44, 49, 57, 62, 63, 75, 79, 83, 88, 115, 119, 144, 165, 207, 213, 227, 248, 263, 285, 288, 424
Lolita—399
Lollipop—124
Lolotte—23
Lomas, Herbert—46, 105, 145, 158, 223, 267, 280, 284
Lomax, Alan—296
Lombardi, Ltd.—82
Lombard, Michael—418
Lom, Herbert—271, 272
Lonbard, Maxine—452
London Academy of Music and Dramatic Arts (LAMDA)—343, 346
London After Dark—206
London Assurance—27, 389, 418
London Coliseum, The—24, 29
London Council for the Promotion of Morality—146
London County Council Improvement Committee, The—13, 33
Londoners, The—402
London Festival Ballet—392
London Follies Bergeres—4
London Hippodrome—4, 5
London Laughs—276, 358
London, Paris, and New York—102
London Pride—80
London, Rex—89
London, Roy—410
London Shakespeare Festival—54, 58
London's Old Vic—283, 295, 296, 301, 302, 340, 438
London's Royal Court Theatre—340
London Theatre Council—199, 233
Lonely Lives—64

Lonely Romeo—92
Lonergan, Lenore—216
Lonergan, Lester—88, 99, 141
Lone Valley—186
Long and the Short and the Tall, The—316
Long, Avon—400
Long Christmas Dinner, The—188, 361
Long Day's Journey Into Night—298, 308, 311, 312, 381, 396, 398, 423, 424, 428
Longford, Earl of—179, 197
Longhi, Vincent—368, 400
Long, Huey—216
Long, John Luther—1, 2, 11, 25, 154
Long, Kenn—386
Long, Mark—439
Long Mirror, The—279
Long Road to Garranbraher, The—121
Longstreet, Stephen—252
Long, Sumner Arthur—333
Long Sunset, The—329
Long, Tamara—372
Longue, Christopher—316
Long Voyage Home, The—128, 136, 208, 452
Long Wharf Theatre—397
Longworth, Alice Roosevelt—196
Lonsdale, Frederick—43, 53, 75, 79, 83, 94, 113, 118, 119, 121, 126, 127, 134, 135, 141, 147, 151, 158, 194, 211, 231, 237, 242, 244, 248, 267, 285, 291, 315, 362, 368, 439, 424
Look After Lulu—314, 315, 446, 447
Look at the Heffernans—193
Look Away—406
Look Back in Anger—299, 302, 305, 313, 375, 402, 404, 452
"Look for the Silver Lining"—100
Look Homeward Angel—305, 313, 416
"Looking All Over for You"—114
Looking Glass," "The—62
Look, Ma, I'm Dancin'—257
Look Me Up—393
Look Out . . . Here Comes Trouble—446
"Look To the Rainbow"—252
Look We've Come Through—327, 410
Loomis, Clarence—219
Looneys, The—417
Loos, Anita—118,, 141, 143, 177, 247, 262, 263, 272, 280, 302, 314, 334, 359
Loose Ends—449
Loot—359, 371, 423, 436
Loper, Robert—296, 307, 312, 439
Lopez, Priscilla—409
Lopez, Vincent—125, 157
Lopokova, Lydia—120, 188, 217
L'Oracolo—189
Loraine, Robert—41, 43, 49, 57, 59, 96, 101, 128, 144, 199
Loraine, Violet—95
Lorca, Federico Garcia—219, 273, 290, 318, 361, 363, 402, 408, 454
Lord Arthur Saville's Crime—279
Lord Babs—158
Lord, Basil—289
Lord Byron Show, The—389
Lord Chamberlain—60, 65, 73, 146, 147, 154, 168, 174, 180, 209, 225, 249, 251, 286, 292, 301, 302, 313, 319
Lord Chamberlains Regrets. . . :, The—328
Lord, Freddie—178
Lord Harewood—308
Lord of Misrule, The—42
Lord, Pauline—61, 94, 106, 126, 128, 181, 200, 270
Lord Pengo—332
Lord Richard in the Pantry—95, 101
Lord, Tracy—216
Lorelei—413
Lorenzaccio—312, 403
Lorenzaccio Story, The—438, 444

Lorenz, Fred—216
Loretto-Hilton Theatre—356
Lorimer, Enid—285
Lorimer, Wright—60
Loring, Eugene—219, 226
Lorna and Ted—389
Lorne, Constance—244, 259, 268
Lorne, Marion—107, 166, 172, 177, 183, 192, 197, 206, 376
Lorraine, Lillian—47, 56, 87, 99
Lorraine, Robert—25
Lorraine, Ted—14, 92
Lorraine, William—14
Lorre, Petr—349
Lortz, Richard—410
Losch, Tilly—153, 158, 165, 176, 192, 425
Losee, Frank—31
Losey, Joseph—255, 294
Losing Time—451
Los Pobres Bilingual Theatre—446
Loss on Roses, A—15, 411
Lost Horizons—191, 199
Lost in the Stars—262, 270, 368, 402, 404
Lost Leader, The—97
Lost Ones, The—440
Lost Silk Hat, The—68
Lost Worlds—445
Lotis, Dennis—315, 340
Lotta—410
Louden, Dorothy—443
Louder, Please—210
Louise, Tina—293, 298
Louisiana—188
"Louisiana Hayride"—181, 195
Louisiana Purchase—221
Louisiana Purchase Exposition—13
Louis XI—17, 27, 49, 58, 76, 90
Lounsbery, G. Constant—67
Love and Death—137
Love and Lectures—311
Love, Bessie—161, 264, 295, 302, 316
Lovebirds, The—305
Love Birds, The—21
Love Charm, The—59
Love Child, The—108, 113
Love Duel, The—163
Love, Edmund—327
Love for Love—136, 192, 237, 242, 254, 418
Love from a Stranger—200, 201
Love from Judy—277
Love in a Cottage—88
Love in Idleness—241
"Love is Sweeping the Country"—177
Love is the Best Doctor—193
Lovejoy, Frank—336
Love Letters on Blue Paper—445
Love Letter, The—110
Love Lies—165, 243
Loveliest Night of the Year, The—451
Love Life—257
Lovel, Leigh—90
Lovell, Raymond—231
Lovely Ladies, Kind Gentlemen—386
Lovely Sunday for Creve Coeur, A—452
Love Match, The—283
Love Me, Love My Children—393
"Love Me Tonight"—132
Love of Four Colonels, The—272, 281, 285, 286
Love o' Mike—82
Love on the Dole—200, 232
Love Parade," "The—176
Love, Patti—446, 450
Love Play, A—428
Love Race, The—172
Lovers—368, 375, 384
Lovers and Friends—235
Lovers of Virone, The—396
Lover, The—342, 346, 347, 379
LuPone, Patti—443
Luscombe, George—318
Lute Song—247, 251, 259, 316
Luther—328, 329, 331, 338, 350
Lutyens, Edward—65
Luv—340, 344, 356

353, 354, 374, 375, 403, 409, 416, 422, 430, 438, 446, 453, 454
Love's Lottery—20
Loves of Lulu, The—136
Love's Old Sweet Song—223, 428
Love's Young Dream—96
Love Us and Leave Us—428
Love Without Licence—96
Love, Yorick—104
Loving, F. Bryan—399
Low, A. M.—286
Low and Behold—190
Lowe, Allen—10
Lowe, Enid—197
Lowell, Helen—62
Lowell, Robert—349, 350, 366, 373, 396
Lowe, Porter, H. T. Mrs.—260
Lower Depths as a Long Way from Home, The—259
Lower Depths, The—94, 121, 334, 347, 403, 404
Lowery, W. McNeil—337
Lowe, Stephen—439
Low Moan Spectacular—406
Lowndes, Mrs. Belloc—75, 94
Lowry, Judith—144, 145
Loy, Myrna—350, 409
Loyalist, The—4
Loyalties—112, 113, 123, 184
Loyola College—419
Lucas, Jonathan—287
Luccia, Donna—454
Luce, Claire—126, 148,' 149, 161, 182, 197, 201, 250, 273, 409
Luce, Polly—192
Luce, William—426, 439
Lucia Di Lammermoor—457
Lucia, Donna—224
Luc, Jean Bernard—277
Luckinbill, Laurence—426
Luck of Roaring Camp, The—50
Luck of the Navy, The—89, 193
Lucky Sam McCarver—132
Lucky Strike—294
Lucrece—182
Luders, George—55
Luders, Gustav—14, 15, 20, 47, 52
Ludlam, Charles—415, 418, 429, 438, 446, 455
Ludlowe, Henry—44
Ludlow Fair—366
Ludlow, Patrick—89
Luebben, Anita Lee—203
Lugg, William—62
Lugosi, Bela—142, 150, 186, 303
Lukas, Paul—226, 293, 398
Luke, Peter—97, 372, 381, 414, 447
Lullaby, The—123
Lulu—361, 391, 445
Lulu Belle—140, 147, 302
Lumet, Signey—221, 295, 297, 320
Lumpkin, Albert Bein Grace—196
Lumumba, Patrice—394
Luna Park—403
Lunatics and Lovers—288
Lund, Art—298, 332
Lund, John—234
Lunney, Eric—324
Lunt, Alfred—93, 119, 120, 121, 125, 137, 144, 145, 148, 150, 152, 156, 160, 168, 171, 177, 186, 195, 198, 200, 208, 214, 221, 241, 265, 277, 298, 309, 323, 362, 363, 411, 441
Lunts Are the Lunts," "The—270
Lupino, Barry—113, 218, 336
Lupino, Richard—360
Lupino, Stanley—59, 83, 101, 107, 120, 126, 134, 158, 165, 172, 178, 191, 213, 222, 232, 233, 235, 236, 243
Lupino, Tony—218, 235
Lupino, Wallace—113, 207, 232, 235

Lyceum Club Stage Society—129
Lyceum Company—90
Lyceum Theater (London)—24
Lyel, Viola—218
Lyles, Aubrey—105, 118, 148, 156
Lynch, Alfred—316, 320, 334, 349, 415, 424
Lynde, Paul—280
Lyndon, Barre—201, 217
Lynley, Carol—304, 309
Lynn, Ann—310, 395
Lynn, Diana—271
Lynne, Carole—218, 239, 248, 262
Lynne, Gillian—275, 351, 391, 437, 438
Lynn, Jeffrey—198
Lynn, Jenny—184
Lynn, Jonathan—439, 453, 456
Lynn, Judy—272
Lynn, Leni—235
Lynn, Lorelei—450
Lynn, Ralph—95, 101, 113, 134, 143, 151, 159, 165, 172, 241, 253, 278, 289
Lynn, Vera—227, 276
Lyon, Ben—227
Lyons, A. Neil—80
Lyons, E. D.—7
Lyons, I. N.—23
Lyons, Joe—156
Lyons, Johnny—367
Lyons Mail, The—33, 45, 174
Lyric Revue, The—274
Lyric Theatre (New York)—18
Lyric Theater (Philadelphia)—29, 40
Lysistrata—55, 137, 173, 204, 214, 250, 292, 307, 318, 380, 404, 418
Lysistrata Numbah, The—438
Lytell, Bert—191
Lytton, Doris—53
Lytton, Edward—46
Lytton, Sir Henry—44, 167, 203

McAllister, Blue—192
McAnally, Ray—390
McAnuff, Des—436, 448
McArdle, Dorothy—90, 434
McArthur, Susan—374
McAvoy, Dan—10
McBain, Kenny—410
McCahill, Angela—105
McCallum, John—288, 305, 317, 431
McCallum, J. T.—5
McCandless, Stanley—139, 147
McCann, Donal—379
McCann, Frances—254
McCann, Hamish—26
McCarthy, Desmond—20
McCarthy, J. B.—121
McCarthy, Joseph—93, 99, 113, 119, 148, 406
McCarthy, Justin Huntly—6, 12, 15, 49, 51, 53, 66, 69, 89, 132
McCarthy, Kevin—247, 248, 290, 321
McCarthy, Lillah—43, 45, 48, 53, 57, 58, 64, 102, 324
McCarthy, Mary—64, 257, 262
McCarthy, Sean—417
McCarty, Lawrence—62
McClain, John—369
McClanahan, Rue—364
McCleery, R. C.—49, 61, 107
McClendon, Rose—142, 196
McClintic, Guthrie—119, 131, 149, 157, 181, 194, 203, 235, 249, 250, 255, 257, 262, 263, 276, 330
McClure, Michael—375, 407, 410
McComas, Carroll—78, 122, 336
McComb, Kate—217
McConnell, Lulu—99, 125, 132
McConnell, Ty—378
McCord, Nancy—196
McCormack, Patty—288
McCormick, F. J.—145, 152, 256
McCormick, Langdon—70, 93, 110
McCormick, Myron—191, 240, 293
McCowen, Alec—269, 279, 282, 290, 306, 311, 317, 323, 329, 336, 340, 353, 354, 361, 372, 389, 393, 406,

408, 416, 422, 427, 438, 439, 444, 447
McCowen, George—317, 329
McCoy, Bessie—27, 41
McCoy, Mildred—164
McCracken, Joan—244, 330
McCraken, Esther—213, 241, 242
McCullers, Carson—266, 270, 306, 339, 404
McCullough, Paul—112, 141, 170
McCutcheon, Bill—338
McCutcheon, George Barr—31
McDermott, Hugh—244
McDevitt, Ruth—433
McDonald, Grace—217
McDonald, T. B.—43
McDowall, Roddy—161, 283, 304
McDowell, Malcolm—373
McDowell, Robert Emmett—341
McEnery, Peter—339, 415, 429, 437
McEnroe, Robert—258, 265
McEvoy, Charles—89
McEvoy, J. P.—119, 141, 181
McEwan, Geraldine—266, 277, 278, 279, 287, 295, 306, 311, 329, 334, 359, 367, 373, 375, 381, 382, 396, 406, 410, 414, 424
McEwan, Gertrude—272
McFadden, Elizabeth—186
McGavin, Darren—288, 304, 348, 361
McGinn, Francis D.—61
McGiver, John—320
McGlyn, Frank—94
McGooch, Daisy—75
McGoohan, Patrick—316
McGough, Roger—347, 366, 424
McGowan, John—157, 164, 170, 176, 285
McGowan, Kenneth—129
McGrath, George—400
McGrath, Harold—25
McGrath, John—389, 440
McGrath, Paul—205
McGrath, Russell—379
McGrath, Tom—428, 444, 451, 453, 455
McGuire, Biff—271, 383
McGuire, Dorothy—90, 221, 226, 272, 431
McGuire, Michael—381, 403
McGuire, W. A.—119, 156, 157
McGuire, William—116, 133
McGuire, William Anthony—452
McHugh, Florence—145
McHugh, Frank—137
McHugh, Jimmy—156, 158, 216, 383
McIlrath, Patricia—348
McIntosh, Madge—72
McIntyre and Heath—47
McIntyre, Dennis—450
McIntyre, James—25, 111
McIver, Ray—376, 380
McKay, Gardener—424
McKayle, Donald—339, 366, 406
McKay, Scott—306, 314
McKee, Frank—42, 128
McKee, Lillian—105
McKellan, Ian—359, 364, 365, 382, 389, 397, 417, 422, 437, 438, 439
McKelvey, John—289
McKenna, Kenneth—185
McKenna, Rose—89
McKenna, Siobhan—254, 278, 291, 293, 295, 304, 306, 324, 347, 353, 395, 407, 409, 436
McKenna, Virginia—272, 278, 279, 281, 282, 290, 295, 454
McKenny, Ruth—222
McKenzie, Julia—414, 427, 443
McKern, Leo—264, 294, 315, 340, 355, 366, 410
McKinnel, Norman—7, 21, 22, 48, 49, 50, 53, 54, 79, 83, 101, 106, 107, 108, 127, 172
McKinney, Eugene—318
McKinsey, Beverly—332
McLaughlin, Robert—113
McLaurin, Kate—112
McLean, Ian—207

McLellan, C. M. S.—20, 36, 61, 62
McLellan, Robert—307, 335
McLennan, Oliver—156
McLennan, Rod—351
McLerie, Allyn Ann—257, 262
McMahon, Frank—385
McMartin, John—347
McMaster, Anew—336
McMillan, Kenneth—434
McMullan, Frank—249
McMurtry, Alden—64, 70
McNally, James B.—319
McNally, John J.—1, 20, 179
McNally, Terence—220, 341, 351,
  371, 372, 374, 378, 393, 413, 439
McNally, William—203
McNamara, Brinsley—96, 102
McNaughton, Anne—404
McNaughton, Fred—123
McNaughton, Gus—123
McNaughton, Harry—148
McNaughton, Tom—52, 88, 93, 123
McNeil, Claudia—314
McNutt, Paterson—124
McOwan, Michael—249
McPherson, Thomas—363
McQueen, Butterfly—211, 217, 382
McRae, Bruce—118, 153
McShane, Ian—355, 365
McVicker, Horace—179
McWade, Robert—142
McWhinnie, Donald—312, 322, 336,
  339, 341, 352, 353, 429
Ma—394
Mabley, Edward—440
Mabley, Jackie "Moms"—217
MacAnna, Thomas—375, 385, 431
Macardle, Dorothy—135, 184
MacArthur, Charles—140, 157, 182,
  196, 228, 250, 269, 302, 381, 402,
  444
MacArthur, Charles G.—161
MacArthur, James—35, 36
MacArthur, W. W.—256
Macaulay, Pauline—352
Macaulay, Tony—408
Macauley, Charles—347
Macbeth—3, 16, 37, 49, 50, 53, 54,
  58, 59, 64, 76, 80, 84, 90, 103, 108,
  109, 121, 122, 136, 145, 152, 159,
  160, 166, 167, 173, 178, 183, 184,
  188, 198, 202, 208, 214, 228, 229,
  232, 242, 245, 249, 255, 256, 264,
  269, 278, 279, 283, 285, 290, 296,
  302, 307, 312, 317, 329, 334, 335,
  337, 347, 354, 360, 367, 373, 381,
  382, 395, 396, 402, 409, 415, 416,
  422, 424, 429, 430, 437, 439, 445,
  446, 452, 454
Macbeth in Camera—368
Macbeth, Robert—373, 436
MacBird!—364
MacColl, Ewan—279, 285, 290, 291,
  295, 300
MacDermot, Galt—364, 396, 398,
  400
MacDermot, Robert—206, 244
MacDonagh, Donagh—255, 275, 306,
  323
MacDonagh, John—109
MacDonald, Brian—360
MacDonald, Christine—32, 36, 52,
  66
MacDonald, Jeanette—115, 149
MacDonald, Kenneth—423
Macdonald, Murray—206, 207, 219,
  250, 258, 263, 267, 282, 294, 297,
  299, 316, 334, 362, 366, 373
MacDonald, Ramsey—437
Macdonald, Robert David—354, 390,
  428, 451, 455
MacDonnell, Kyle—262
MacDonough, Glen—1, 15, 26, 42,
  47, 52, 56, 57, 87, 128
MacDougall, Roger—268, 282
MacEntree, George—208
MacEvoy, J.P.—216
MacEwan, Molly—296
Macfarlane, Bruce—186
MacFarlane, Elsa—131, 151, 167

Macfarlane, Hazel—151
Macgill, Moyna—138, 150
MacGinnis, Niall—206, 274
MacGowan, Kenneth—132, 136, 140,
  342
MacGowran, Jack—133, 247, 306,
  312, 336, 390
MacGrath, Leueen—196, 224, 253,
  266, 330
MacGunigle, Robert—188
Machen, Arthur—159
Machiavelli, Niccolo—220, 388, 436,
  454
Machinal—157, 445
Machiz, Herbert—378
Macho, Carole—320
MacHugh, Augustin—61, 100
MacIntyre, Doris—106
MacIntyre, Tom—401
Mackail, Dennis—127
Mack and Mabel—413
Mack, Andrew—16
Mackay, Clarence—155
Mackay, Elsie—101
MacKaye, Percy—36, 56, 77, 78, 95,
  103, 104, 303, 447
Mackaye, Steele—303
Mackay, Frank Finley—123
Mackay, Fulton—382
Mackay, Gayer—101
Mackay, J. L.—6
MacKay, Robert—5
Mackay, Sheena—380
Mack, Cecil—118
Mack, Charles—125
MacKechnie, Donald—375, 380,
  381, 382, 394
MacKellar, Helen—93, 105
MacKendrick, John—437
MacKenna, Kenneth—191
Macken, Walter—254
MacKenzie, Donald—444
Mackenzie, Margaret—101
Mackenzie, Mary—299
Mackenzie, Ray—241
MacKenzie, Ronald—179, 192
MacKenzie, Scobie—187
Mackie, Philip—294, 427
Mackinder, Lionel—26
Mack, Lavinia—148
"Mack the Knife"—300
Mack, Willard—82, 141
Mack, William—105
Mack, William B.—61
Maclaine, Shirley—287
Maclaren, Ian—13, 131, 115
MacLarnie, Thomas—180
MacLean, R. D.—72
Macleish, Archibald—194, 199, 310,
  319
Macleod, Alison—312
MacLiammoir, Micheal—53, 59, 84,
  160, 162, 166, 167, 173, 179, 183,
  184, 188, 192, 214, 223, 228, 232,
  245, 249, 250, 255, 259, 260, 264,
  279, 285, 291, 296, 301, 306, 323,
  329, 334, 336, 341, 348, 373, 375,
  380, 396, 408, 422, 428, 447
MacMahon, Aline—122, 128, 145,
  230, 283
MacMillan, Roddy—341
MacMurray, Fred—171
MacNamara, Brinsley—193, 342
MacNaughton, Alan—274, 276, 284,
  417
MacNaughton, Elspeth—361
MacNiece, Louis—342
Ma Cousine—23
Ma Cousine de Varsavie—144
Macowan, Michael—208, 214, 218,
  253, 260, 263, 272, 274, 278, 283,
  284, 285, 288, 301
MacOwan, Norman—101, 212
Macrae, Arthur—187, 213, 231, 236,
  245, 258, 273, 282, 289, 296, 310
Macrae, Duncan—322
MacRae, Gordon—247
MacRae, Sheila—354
Macready, Eleanor—268

Macy, Bill—358
Macy, Gertrude—161, 216
Macy, W.H.—418
"Mad About the Boy"—183, 216
Madame Bovary—208
Madame Butterfly—1, 2, 38, 154, 179
Madame de . . .—316
Madame et son Filleul—94
Madame la Presidente—68
Madame Louise—244
Madame Pompadour—121
Madame Sans-Gene—8, 27
Madame Sherry—16, 52, 161
Madame X—48, 215
Madam, Will You Walk?—57, 286
Madcap Duchess, The—66
Madcap Princess, A—19
Madden, Cecil—148
Madden, Donald—328, 374, 378
Madden, Harry—190
Madden, John—445, 449, 453
Maddermarket Theatre—110
Maddern, Mary—20, 27
Maddern, Merle—167, 176
Mad Dog—409
"Mad Dogs and Englishmen"—176,
  183
Maddox, Lester—378
Maddox, Mary—453
Made in Heaven—423
Mademoiselle—201
Mademoiselle Colombe—272, 287
Madhouse Company—415
Madigan's Lock—341
Mad Magazine—357
Madman and the Nun, The—390
Madness of Lady Bright, The—374
Madras House, The—54, 137, 436
Mad Show, The—357
Madwoman of Central Park West,
  The—445
Madwoman of Chaillot, The—258,
  265, 269, 272, 295, 378, 384, 444
Mad World, A—447
Mad World My Masters, A—435, 436
Maedchen in Uniform—183
Maeterlinck, Maurice—12, 23, 24,
  28, 44, 63, 73, 76, 77, 88, 95, 107,
  115, 146, 245
Maeve—3
Magarshack, David—301
Magda—3, 4, 12, 13, 44, 121, 144,
  233
Magdalany, Philip—387, 410, 415,
  429, 447
Magdalena—265
Magee, Patrick—294, 312, 317, 318,
  345, 354, 359, 361, 429
Maggie—435
Maggie Flynn—424
Maggie May—346
Maggie the Magnificent—164, 456
Maggot, Gilly—122
Magic—136, 197
Magic Afternoon—428
"Magical Moon"—119
Magic and the Loss, The—287, 292
Magic Bell, The—64
Magic Carpet—236
Magic Glasses, The—68
Magic Lantern—331
Magic Marble, The—198
Magic Melody, The—93
Magic Show, The—413
Magic Slippers—168
Magistrate, The—84, 242, 316, 381,
  382
Magito, Suria—260
Magnani, Anna—380
Magnanimous Lover, The—68
Magnier, Claude—305
Magnificence—409, 417
Magnificent Yankee, The—247, 251,
  303
Maguire, Fred—108
Maguire, Leonard—422
Mahagonny—388
Maharis, George—320
Mahon, Christy—218
Mahoney, Will—164, 176

Maibaum, Richard—187, 216
Maid in America—74
Maid in the Ozarks—251
Maid Marian—10
Maid of France, The—90
Maid of the Mill, The—368
Maid of the Mountains, The—83,
  174, 231, 402
Maids, The—301, 340, 396, 415, 417,
  444
Maid's Tragedy, The—23, 108, 136,
  347, 404, 452
Mail Call—235
Mailer, Norman—364, 410
Main, Marjorie—201
Main Street—106
Mainwaring, Ernest—134
Maitland, Bill—447
Maitland, Jack—401
Maitland, Joan—333, 401
Maitland, Lauderdale—108, 119
Maitland, Lena—151
Maitlands, The—192
Majestic Theater (Chicago)—34
Majestic Theater (San Francisco)—34
Majestic Theater (Toronto)—18
Majilton, A.J.—114
Major Andre—15
Major Barbara—32, 76, 78, 108, 160,
  197, 198, 220, 301, 302, 312, 367,
  390, 403, 436, 446
Major, Charles—26, 37
Majority of One, A—314, 322, 363
Major, Leon—337
Major Molineux—349
Major Pendennis—78
Major, Roscoe E.—91
Make a Million—309
Make a Wish—271
Makeham, Eliot—159
Make It a Date—248
Make Me an Offer—318
Make Mine Manhattan!—257
Making of a Girl, "The—78
Making of Moo, The—305, 319
Makropoulos Secret, The—140, 307
Malcochon—380
Malcolm—357
Malden, Karl—69, 217, 221, 234,
  247, 273, 278, 293
Male Animal, The—221, 225, 263,
  264, 279
Maleczech, Ruth—440
Maley, Denman—153
Malia—44
Malina, Judith—275, 292, 314, 321,
  327, 338, 375, 451
Malin, Ella—405, 419, 425, 433, 441,
  448, 457
Malleson, Miles—84, 95, 122, 127,
  143, 145, 150, 223, 268, 316, 383
Mallin, Tom—397, 407
Malloch, George Reston—54
Mallory, Jay—192
Malmberg, Ingar—316
Malo, Gina—206
Malone, J.A.E.—53, 62, 63, 67
Malone, John T.—3
Malpede, Karen—429
Maltby H. F.—94, 102, 144, 178, 183,
  196
Maltby, Richard—405, 437
Maltz, Albert—187, 189, 197, 202
Malvaloca—112
Malvern Festival. The—169
Mama's Bank Account—240
Mamba's Daughters—216, 224
Mame—357, 379
Mamet, David—418, 426, 434, 436,
  445, 446, 452
Mamma's Affair—104
Mammon, Epicure—185
Mamoulian, Rouben—153, 160, 167,
  170, 234, 247, 262
Mam'selle Napoleon—15
Mam'selle Tralala—72
Mamsun, Knut—420
Mamzelle Champagne—30
Man and Artifact—451
Man and Boy—340

Man and Superman—25, 27, 29, 33,
  44, 59, 108, 152, 173, 178, 194,
  198, 214, 249, 255, 264, 274, 275,
  349, 359, 361, 438, 439
Man and the Masses—128
Man, Beast and Virtue—311
Manchester Repertory Theatre—46,
  63
Manchester Royal Exchange Theatre
  —451
Manchiz, Herbert—304, 309
Mandel, Frank—71, 100, 106, 124,
  132, 134, 142, 157, 196, 202
Mandel, Loring—16, 321
Manderson Girls, The—154
Man Dies, A—363
Mandley, Percy—187
Mandragola—220, 338
Mandrake, The—436
Manet, Edvardo—407
Man for All Seasons, A—322, 327,
  337, 347, 376, 396, 403, 404
Man from Blankley's The—7
Man from Home, The—42, 51, 86,
  184
Man from Mexico, The—53, 110, 137
Man from the East, The—406
Man From the Ministry, The—248
Man from Thermopylae, The—54
Man from Toronto, The—88
Mango-Leaf Magic—342
Mango Tango—445
Mangum, Edward—270
Manhattan Little Theatre Club—135
Manhattan Mary—149
Manhattan Project—390, 397, 421,
  438
Manhattan Theater—24
Manhattan Theatre Club—403, 405,
  410, 416, 424, 431, 440, 442, 443,
  444, 451, 456
Manheim, Kate—424
Manheim, Ralph—436
Manhoff, Bill—345
Manilow, Barry—388
Man in Dress Clothes, The—113
Man in Half Moon Street, The—217
Man in the Glass Booth, The—365,
  371, 447
Man in the Moon, The—342
Man in the Raincoat, The—264
Man in the Stalls—116
Man in the Wheel Chair, The—127
Manken, Helen—83, 195
Mankowitz, Wolf—129, 284, 289,
  310, 318, 402, 444
Man Most Likely To, The—372
Mann, Charlton—101, 165
Mann, Daniel—287, 315
Mannering, Lewis—89
Mannering, Mary—1, 11, 22, 52, 56
Manners, J. Hartley—13, 28, 42, 62,
  65, 83, 93, 108, 111, 121, 134,
  161
Manners, Jill—235
Manners, Lady Diana—124
Mannheim, Lucie—260
Mannheim, Ralph—387, 409, 428
Mann, Louis—117
Mann, Paul—198, 228, 276, 345
Mann, Theodore—275, 329, 367,
  372, 374, 404, 405, 410, 416, 418,
  437
Man of Destiny, The—7, 17, 28, 37,
  137, 232, 269, 273, 274, 296, 311,
  341, 361, 407, 446
Man of Distinction—307
Man of Honour, A—21
Man of La Mancha—352, 372, 412,
  439, 448
Man of Mode, The—396
Man of the Hour, The—31
Man on the Box, The—25
Manor, Daniel—64
Manor of Northstead, The—288
Man's a Man, A—335, 424
Mansfield, Herbert—89
Mansfield, Jayne—293
Mansfield, John—241

Mansfield, Richard—7, 9, 16, 22, 27, 38, 56, 146, 204
Mansfield Theater (New York)—325
Man's House, A—237
Man Speaking—368
Man's World, A—52
Mantell, Robert Bruce—23, 58, 76, 84, 90, 161
Mantle, Burns—9, 51, 60, 65, 70, 73, 77, 81, 86, 91, 98, 104, 110, 116-7, 123, 125-6, 130-1, 138, 141-3, 147, 180, 185, 190-1, 194, 199, 204, 210, 215, 217, 220, 225-6, 229, 232-3, 238, 241, 243, 246, 252, 256, 297
Mantle, Doreen—453
Mantovani, Annunzio—199
Man Who Almost Knew Eammon Andrews, The—379
Man Who Came Back, The—78
Man Who Came To Dinner, The—217, 225, 227, 232, 237, 249, 311, 453
Man Who Had All the Luck, The—240
Man Who Laughed, The—105
Man Who Let It Rain, The—347
Man Who Married a Dumb Wife, The—76, 77, 183
Man Who Never Died, The—319
Man Who Owns Broadway, The—48
Man Who Stayed Home, The—72
Man Who Stole the Castle, The—8
Man With a Load of Mischief—134, 178, 269, 358, 410
Man With Red Hair, A—232
Man With the Flower in His Mouth—380
Man with Three Wives, The—70
Many Loves—319
Many Mansions—205
Mapes, Victor—74
Maple, Audrey—62
Marais, Jean—446
Marasco, Robert—385
Marathon '33—339
Marat/Sade—345, 352, 363, 401, 402
Marble Arch—386
Marble, Emma—174
Marble, William—180
Marbury, Elizabeth—98, 189
Marceau, Felicien—320, 337
Marceau, Marcel—122, 260, 278, 285, 295, 296, 311, 312, 340, 389
Marchall, Norman—285
Marchand, Nancy—320, 393
Marchant, William—293
March, Elspeth—253, 274, 436
March, Frank—240
March, Frederic—153, 216, 227, 230, 247, 269, 271, 298, 327, 424
March, Hal—326
Marching Song—207, 288, 417
Marcin, Max—74, 82, 92
Marco Millions—156, 213, 347, 369
Marco Polo—431
Marco Polo Sings a Solo—436
Marcus, Frank—352, 366, 372, 379, 395, 401, 428, 444
Marcus, Fred—269, 285
Marder, Louis—350
Margetson, Arthur—131, 151, 178
Margin for Error—217, 222, 225
Margo—195, 205, 217
Margo Jones Theatre—254
Margot—38
Margules, Annette—118
Margulies, David—378, 417
Maria Golovin—309
Marianna—12
Maria Stuart—373
Maricle, Leona—191, 333
Marie and Bruce—454
Marie Lloyd Story, The—368
Marie-Odile—75, 246
Mariette—165
Marie Tudor—301, 312
Marigold—151
Mariners, The—166
Marinka—244
Marinoff, Fania—106

Marionettes—137
Marion, George—6, 19, 20, 30, 42, 105, 106
Marion, George Jr.—234, 237, 244
Marion, Sam—20
Maritana—5
Marivaux, Pierre—45, 89, 274, 296, 301, 369, 432, 446
Marjanie—69
Mark—403
Markey, Enid—92, 117, 140, 276
Markham, Barbara—428
Markham, Daisy—58
Markham, David—219, 279
Markheim—33
Markova, Alicia—240
Marks, Alfred—273, 394, 400
Marks, Edward—35
Marks, Maurice—156
Marks, Walter—345, 371
Mark Taper Forum, The—350, 370, 380, 430, 437, 449
Mark Twain Tonight!—319, 323, 360, 363, 441
Marland, Patricia—276
Marlene Dietrich—377, 384
Marleyn, Hugh—187
Marlowe, Charles—72
Marlowe, Christopher—27, 114, 121, 135, 207, 274, 300, 301, 329, 348, 353, 373, 382, 403, 409, 417, 424, 431, 454, 455
Marlowe, Derek—330
Marlowe, Gloria—293
Marlowe, Hugh—59, 222
Marlowe, Julia—5, 6, 22, 23, 26, 50, 53, 54, 58, 69, 97, 109, 122, 130, 132, 137, 146, 180, 229, 270
Marowitz, Charles—347, 364, 366, 388, 401, 402, 403, 408, 409, 410, 424, 428, 430, 438, 447, 452
Marquand, John P.—240, 246, 272
Marques of Keith, The—417
Marques, René—358, 422
Marquis, Dixie—358
Marquis, Don—112, 123, 202, 209, 304
Marquise, The—150
Marre, Albert—138, 214, 273, 283, 445
Marriage—197, 260
Marriage a La Mode—97, 103, 249
Marriage Brokers, The—353, 409
Marriage Game, The—7
Marriage-Go-Round, The—309, 315
Marriage is for Single People—251
Marriage Market, The—67
Marriage of Blood—219
Marriage of Columbine, The—73
Marriage of Figaro, The—348, 354, 417
Marriage of Kitty, The—12
Marriage of Mr. Mississippi, The—318, 354
Marriage of St. Francis, The—198
Marriage Proposal, The—245
Marriage, The—447
Marriott, Anthony—365, 394, 435
Marrowbone Lane—219, 228
Marrying of Ann Leete, The—422
Marry the Girl—172
Marsden, Betty—431
Marshall and Fox—60, 91
Marshall, Armina—116, 121, 148, 186, 224, 424
Marshall, Benjamin—24, 40
Marshall, Boyd—100
Marshall, Captain Robert—2, 3, 12, 20
Marshall, E. G.—230, 247, 248, 298, 314, 368, 437
Marshall, Eric—202
Marshall, Herbert—102, 107, 119, 127, 129, 132, 135, 143, 150, 158, 164, 172, 176, 181, 186, 362
Marshall, Norman—202, 222, 223, 244, 245, 258, 279
Marshall, Peter—320
Marshall, Sarah—189
Marshall, Tully—15, 25, 41, 61

Marshall, William—296, 312
Marsh, Edward Owen—305
Marsh, Howard—126, 150
Marsh, Linda—347
Marsh, Ngaio—269
Marsh, Reginald—118
Mars, Kenneth—328
Mars, Marjorie—151, 178, 207, 244
Marston, John—150, 285, 289, 316, 348, 349
Marston, Richard—19
Martell, Gertrude—359
Martell, Gillian—417
Martin, Amy—32
Martin, Christopher—402, 417, 431, 444, 455
Martindale, May—75
Martinez, N. H.—154
Martin, Fay—127
Martin-Harvey, John—121, 208, 265
Martin, Helen—78
Martin, Hugh—226, 257, 271, 277, 344
Martini, Faurto—119
Martin, J. Sackville—63, 64
Martin, Judith—369
Martin Luther King—383, 384
Martin, Manuel—408
Martin, Mary—69, 211, 235, 247, 248, 262, 282, 287, 296, 314, 338, 344, 358, 411, 427
Martin, Mel—453
Martin, Millicent—315, 328, 369, 374, 406, 427
Martin, Nan—318
Martinot, Sadie—7, 123
Martin, Rosemary—341
Martin, Trevor—341
Martin, Virginia—327, 332
Martin, William—387
Martson, Joel—239
Martura, Mustapha—416
Marty, Emilia—140
Martyn, Edward—13
Martyr, The—38
Marvellous History of Saint Bernard, The—144, 202
Marvellous Story of Puss in Boots, The—291, 296, 302, 330
Marvenga, Ilse—126
Marvin, Jean—64
Marvin, Mal—440
Marwig, Carl—11
Marx, Arthur—124, 351, 385
Marx Brothers—64, 133, 157, 385, 450
Marx, Chico—124, 330
Marx, Groucho—124, 133, 157
Marx, Harpo—124, 350
Marx, Herbert—124
Marx, Julius—124
Marx, Leonard—124
Marx, Minnie—385
Marx, Zeppo—124
Mary—100, 103, 447
Marya—368
Maryan, Charles—382
Mary Barnes—450
Mary Broome—64
Mary Goes First—67
Mary Jane McKane—119
Mary Magdalene—53, 63
Mary, Mary—326, 331, 339, 401
Mary, Mary, Quite Contrary—136, 179
Mary of Magdalen—18
Mary of Scotland—189, 194, 318
Mary Rose—101, 110, 273, 403, 447
Mary's Ankle—128
Mary Stuart—3, 114, 122, 188, 307, 312, 398, 452
Mary Stuart in Scotland—323
Mary's Wedding—63
Mary the 3rd—117, 123
Mas—417
Masada—445
Masaniello—430
Mascagni, Pietro—12
Maschwitz, Erik—202, 222, 231, 258, 273, 275, 277, 384

Masefield, John—24, 37, 43, 54, 68, 72, 77, 84, 95, 122, 237, 369
Masey, Cecil—55, 297
Masiell, Joe—344
Mask and the Face, The—88, 269
Masked Ball, The—1
Maske of the New World, The—317
Maskerade—27, 428
Mask of Virtue, The—197
Masks and Faces—8, 37, 54
Masks, Mimes and Miracles—432
Mask, The—75, 127, 275, 363
Masoch—422
Mason, A. E. W.—33, 53, 57, 59, 102
Mason, Beryl—244, 248
Mason, Brewster—328, 373, 376, 390, 396, 403
Mason, Delia—14
Mason, Ena—151
Mason, Florence—117
Mason, Frank—225
Mason, Jack—35, 95
Mason, James—207, 227, 256, 290
Mason, John—20, 31, 36, 56, 343
Mason, Judi Ann—428, 447
Mason, Marsha—364, 371, 386, 406, 418
Mason, Marshal W.—374, 402, 406, 410, 413, 431, 436, 452
Mason, Patrick—440, 452
Mason, Pauline—141
Mason, Reginald—142
Mason, Richard—309
Masque of Kings, The—205, 209, 224
Masque of Love, The—8, 12
Masquerader, The—82
Masquerade, The—237, 354, 398
Massay, Daniel—189
Massen, Louis F.—137
Massey, Adrianne (Allen)—189
Massey, Anna—294, 305, 311, 314, 334, 341, 355, 366, 394, 395, 421, 429, 450
Massey, Daniel—304, 310, 334, 339, 373, 406, 414, 423, 440, 444
Massey Foundation—189
Massey Gold Medal for Architecture—308
Massey, Josephine—322
Massey, Raymond—22, 128, 136, 144, 148, 170, 177, 178, 179, 187, 189, 190, 200, 211, 232, 235, 277, 284, 310, 371
Massey, Vincent—308
Massie, Paul—293, 334
Massine, Leonid—120, 134, 143
Massinger, Philip—114, 285
Master and Margarita, The—445
Master Builder, The—3, 44, 90, 137, 145, 167, 192, 237, 254, 256, 259, 295, 346
Master of Arts—263
Masteroff, Joe—97, 338, 343, 358
Master of the Revels—202, 209
Masters, Edgar Lee—338
Masters, Eric—83
Masterson, Peter—365, 442
Masters, The—339
Mata Hari—377
Matcham, Frank—4, 5, 18, 24, 29, 60, 457
Matchmaker, The—289, 290, 294, 373, 425
Maternite—39
Mathe, Edouard—89
Mather, Aubrey—144, 152, 165, 177, 191
Mather, Sothern—77
Mather, Sydney—137
Mathew, Frances Aymar—14
Mathews, Carmen—265
Mathews, Ray—348
Mathews, Richard—374
Mathis, June—153
Mating Game, The—401
Matlon, Vivian—355, 358, 361, 395, 397, 417, 429
Matriarch, The—165
Matshikiza, Todd—327
Matson, Norman—223

Matter of Fact Husband, A—45
Matter of Gravity, A—426, 433, 457
Mattes, Barbara—338
Matteson, Ruth—221, 248
Matthau, Walter—288, 293, 295, 309, 351
Mattheus, H. V.—76, 90
Matthews, Adelaide—127
Matthews, A. E.—12, 16, 28, 32, 107, 124, 135, 142, 212, 235, 248, 253, 273, 288, 324
Matthews, Brander—168
Matthews, Ethel—21
Matthews, Gerry—332
Matthews, Hale—374
Matthews, Jessie—151, 158, 165, 173, 178
Matthias, Rita—131
Matthison, Edith Wynne—2, 13, 22, 27, 41, 53, 54, 61, 90, 121, 129
Matura, Mustapha—397, 430, 431, 440
Maturin, Eric—57, 107, 113, 127, 143, 151, 159, 197, 241
Matzan, Otto—78
Maude, Charles—53, 59
Maude, Cyril—3, 12, 14, 16, 20, 21, 29, 32, 33, 39, 43, 54, 57, 66, 67, 95, 119, 132, 275
Maude, Gillian—207
Maude, Joan—127, 178, 197
Maude, Margery—54, 57, 58
Maude-Roxby, Roddy—333
Maugham, Diana—284
Maugham, Robin—305, 417
Maugham, William Somerset—21, 37, 43, 48-9, 52-3, 57-8, 67-8, 72, 79, 82, 88, 102, 107, 113-4, 116, 123, 135, 142, 144, 150, 155, 158, 172, 178, 183, 188, 227, 232, 242, 246, 250, 253, 255, 264, 267, 269, 274, 283, 285, 354, 356, 366-7, 375, 389, 410, 422, 427, 429, 431, 446, 453
Maurette, Marcel—283, 306, 431
Maurey, Max—75, 76
Maurice, Anthony—222
Maurice Harte—64
Mauricette—33
Max Gordon Presents—447
Maxine Elliot Theatre, The—46
Max i Zona (Husband and Wife)—306
Maxwell, Gary—369
Maxwell, H. R.—17
Maxwell, James—316
Maxwell, Roberta—317, 381, 382, 434, 451
Maxwell, Roger—148
Maxwell, W. B.—53
Maya—55, 161
May, Ada—124, 177
"Maybe"—142
May, Edith—150
May, Edna—2, 6, 7, 12, 16, 21, 32, 36
May, Elaine—321, 378, 417
Mayer, Edwin Justus—125
Mayer, Jean—290
Mayerl, Billy—171, 197, 218
Mayer, Marcus—4
Mayer, Margery—260
Mayer, Renee—59, 109
Mayeur, Eugene—27
Mayfair and Montmartre—116
Mayfair, Mitzi—200
May Fair Theatre—343
Mayfield, Julian—262
Mayfield, Katherine—200
Mayflowers—139
May, Hans—258, 288
Mayhew, Stella—163
May, Ian—183
May, Jack—285, 312
May, Maggie—14
Maynard, Theodore Mrs.—96
Mayne, Clarice—114
Mayne, Freddy—315
Mayne, Mildred—305
Mayne, Peter—328

Maynes, H. F.—138
Mayo, Frank—342
May, Olive—11
Mayo, Margaret—38, 52, 57, 61, 71, 232
Mayor, Beatrice—166
Mayo, Vrginia—227
Mayo, Winifred—45, 50
Mayro, Jacqueline—344
Maytime—82
May, Val—317, 329, 335, 340, 348, 352, 359, 366, 372, 379, 386, 403, 406, 430
May Wine—196
Mazumdar, Maxim—423
Meacham, Anne—324, 378
Meacham, Michael—360, 367, 438
Meade, Julia—161
Meadow Brook Theatre—366
Meadow, Lynne—416, 431, 436, 440, 444, 451
Meadow Sweet—96
Meals on Wheels—353
Me and Bessie—431
Me and Bessie Smith—420
Me and Juliet—281, 383
Me and Molly—257, 261, 363
Me and My Girl—207, 219, 264
Meanest Man in the World, The—100
Mears, Deann—437
Mears, Stannard—87
Meason, Beryl—309
Measure for Measure—44, 90, 121, 122, 178, 179, 188, 208, 223, 249, 254, 268, 274, 290, 296, 300, 301, 306, 307, 317, 323, 334, 340, 341, 347, 360, 366, 381, 388, 403, 409, 411, 416, 423, 430, 438, 439, 446, 453,
Meaton, Will—59
Mechanic's Institute—24
Meckler, Nancy—417, 431, 437, 445
Medal and the Maid, The—15
Medal of Honor Rag—439
Medcraft, Russell—132
Medea—69, 103, 166, 228, 255, 260, 264, 355, 388, 407, 438, 439, 446
Medford, Kay—104, 282, 358, 364
Media—361
Medical Review of Reviews, The—70
Medina, Patricia—332
Medium, The—102, 252, 260
Medoff, Mark—410, 413
Medusa's Raft—273
Medwin, Michael—430
Meehan, John—117, 120
Meehan, John Jr.—230, 239
Meehan, Thomas—434
Meek, Donald—105, 119, 164
Meeker, Ralph—104, 244, 281, 344
Meeking, Brian—384
Meek, Kate—137
Meers, Thomas—164
"Meet Me Down on Main Street"—120
Meet Me on the Corner—295
Meet Mr. Callaghan—277
Meet the Prince—163
Meighan, Thomas—15, 19
Meilhac, Henri—27, 38, 89, 182
Mein Leopold—27
Meinrad, Josef—373
Meir Ezofowicz—306
Meir, Golda—434
Meisel, Kurt—373
Meisner, Sanford—28, 131, 145, 149, 221, 228, 262, 295
Meister, Maurice—143
Meister, Phillip—343
Melfi, Leonard—198, 360, 366, 372, 374, 382, 389, 410, 443
Melford, Austin—79, 95, 99, 114, 127, 173, 183, 236, 258
Melford, Jack—143
Melia, Joe—365
Melians, The—179
Meller, Raquel—146
Mellish, Fuller—61

Melloney Holtspur; Or, The Pangs of Love—122
Mellon Foundation—405
Melly, Andree—299
Melodrama Play—366
Melody That Got Lost, The—203
Melting Pot, The—46, 47, 63
Melville, Alan—248, 258, 264, 276, 278, 376
Melville, Frederick—49, 62
Melville, Herman—271, 294, 349, 359, 403, 416
Melville, John—401
Melville, Walter—13, 89
Melville, Winnie—143, 167
Melvin, Ernest—113
Melvin, Murry—312, 339
Melvyn, Glen—283
Member of the Wedding, The—266, 270, 306, 404, 441
Memorandum, The—73
"Memories"—53
Memories of a Manager—225
Memory of Two Mondays, A—293, 428
Memphis Little Theatre—152
Men in Shadow—231
Men in White—98, 186, 192, 194
Menken, Adah Isaacs—208
Menken, Helen—87, 112, 140, 141, 362
Me Nobody Knows, The—385, 407
Menon, Aubrey—191
Menotti, Gian-Carlo—252, 260, 266, 288, 309
Men's Beano—455
Mental Athletes, The—121
Menzies, Archie—213, 231, 236, 263
Mercenary Mary—135
Mercer Arts Center—412
Mercer, Beryl—119, 148
Mercer, David—352, 359, 361, 386, 388, 415, 443, 452
Mercer, Johnny—70, 201, 216, 247, 262, 272, 298, 332, 414
Mercer, Marian—199, 449
Mercer, Tony—334
Merchant Of Venice, The—3, 8, 17, 22, 27, 37, 44, 49-50, 53-4, 58-9, 63, 67-9, 72-3, 76-7, 80, 84, 90, 96-7, 103, 109, 115, 122, 128, 137, 144-5, 152, 160, 166-7, 174, 179, 183-4, 188, 192, 197-8, 202, 214, 223, 228, 231-2, 237, 241-2, 245, 249, 254-6, 259-60, 269, 283-5, 295-6, 301-2, 306, 312, 323, 329, 335-6, 336, 348, 353, 367-8, 381, 388-9, 391, 396, 403, 407, 409, 430, 434, 436, 438-9, 444, 452-3, 455
Merchant of Yonkers, The—212, 289, 373
Merchants of Glory—133
Merchant, The—137, 279, 283, 434
Merchant, Vivien—322, 342, 352, 373, 382, 390, 394, 397, 436
Mercier & Camier—455
Mercier, Mary—364
Mercouri, Melina—364
Mercury Street—382
Mercury Theatre—46
Meredith, Burgess—195, 205, 223, 232, 250, 273, 282, 302, 317, 320, 344, 369
Meredith, George—54
Merely Mary Ann—15
Merevilleuses, The—32
Merimee, Prosper—85, 306
Merivale, Bernard—151
Merivale, John—85
Merivale, Philip—85, 113, 115, 118, 148, 165, 172, 189, 198, 212
Merkenschrift, Dietrich—449
Merlin, Frank—195
Mermaid Theatre (London)—23, 334, 362
Merman, Ethel—50, 170, 176, 182, 191, 200, 216, 217, 222, 234, 247, 266, 295, 315
Merola, Gaetano—52
Merrall, Mary—159, 218

Merriam, Eve—394, 426
Merrick, David—292, 304, 321, 325, 327, 331, 332, 339, 363, 377, 420, 433
Merrick, John—449
Merrick, Leonard—7
Merrie England—12, 242, 273
Merrill, Beth—126
Merrill, Blanche—132
Merrill, Bob—104, 326, 344, 400
Merrill, Gary—216, 262
Merrill, Robert—304, 314
Merrily We Roll Along—191, 199
Merrison, Clive—424
Merry Death, A—166
Merry-Go-Round—148, 410
Merry Malones, The—149, 155
Merry, Merry—165
Merry Roosters Panto—342
Merry Widow Burlesque, The—41
Merry Widow, The—37, 121, 128, 167, 236, 237, 242, 278, 295, 306, 311, 348, 380, 446
Merry Wives of Windsor, The—16, 50, 54, 58, 64, 68, 73, 76, 80, 96-7, 109, 121-2, 128, 144-5, 159-60, 167, 173, 179, 184, 189, 197, 208, 219, 223-4, 225, 228, 231-2, 237, 249, 273, 290, 295-6, 301, 317, 341, 348, 354, 367, 373, 374, 380, 396, 403, 409, 417, 422, 428, 438, 446, 453
Merson, Billy—114, 119, 126, 143, 144, 151, 158, 159
Merton of the Movies—65, 113, 120, 123, 246, 455
Mert & Phil—418
Mervenga, Ilse—167
Mervyn, William—320
Meschke, Michael—361, 368
Message for Margaret—248
Message from Mars, A—137
Messager, Andre—26, 96
Messages in Bottles—428
Messel, Oliver—23, 274, 277, 314, 315, 447
Messenger Boy, The—2
Messin' Around—163
Messingkauf Dialogues, The—366
Messiter, Ian—353
Metamorphoses of a Wandering Minstrel, The—408
Metaphors—374
Metaxa, George—176, 191
Metcalfe, James S.—153
Meteor—168, 359
Mexican Hayride—239, 418
Meyer-Forster, Whilhelm—11
Meyer, Gaston—29
Meyer, George W.—143
Meyer, Jean—315, 316, 396
Meyer, Joseph—131, 159
Meyer, Louis—68
Meyer, Michael—316
Meyer, Ruth—334
Meyers, Nicholas—428
Meyers, Patrick—436, 445
Meyrald, Georgette—84
Mia Moglie non Ha Chic—37
Mice and Men—11, 67, 69
Michael—84
Michael and Mary—164
Michaelis, Robert—49, 62, 108, 120, 127
Michael, Ralph—273
Michaels, Sidney—344
Michell, Keith—273, 290, 301, 302, 306, 346, 359, 386, 403, 406, 438, 440, 442
Michener, James—262
Michigan, The—456
Michlin, Barry—409
Mickiewicz, Adam—422
Microbe Hunters—190
Mid-Channel—49, 52, 255
Middle of the Night—298, 398
Middleton, George—82, 93, 104, 132, 146
Middleton, Guy—202

Middleton, Ray—38, 216, 247, 257, 340
Middleton, Thomas—65, 74, 279, 329, 349, 359, 389, 444, 447, 452
Middle Watch, The—165
Midgie Purvis—326
Midgley, Robin—346, 359, 368, 386, 395, 401, 435, 440, 455
Midler, Bette—420
Midnight Bridal, The—49
Midnight Sons, The—47
Midshipmaid, The—177
Mid-Summer—281
Midsummer Madness—127
Midsummer Nights Dream, A—3, 16, 17, 18, 27, 44, 53, 54, 58, 59, 63, 64, 69, 72, 73, 76, 77, 80, 96, 103, 109, 121, 122, 128, 130, 144, 145, 153, 160, 173, 179, 184, 188, 192, 193, 198, 208, 214, 217, 219, 224, 229, 232, 237, 238, 242, 245, 249, 254, 260, 264, 265, 274, 290, 295, 296, 301, 307, 312, 316, 317, 323, 324, 329, 334, 335, 341, 348, 350, 360, 361, 367, 368, 374, 388, 389, 395, 396, 416, 422, 430, 437, 438, 446, 447, 451, 454, 455
Midwife, The—295
Mielziner, Jo—199, 203, 276, 297, 356, 432
Mighty Gents, The—454
Mighty Reservoy, The—367
Mikado, The—39, 44, 63, 68, 76, 97, 136, 167, 184, 193, 228, 232, 245, 249, 255, 260, 264, 269, 273, 274, 275, 280, 285, 290, 296, 302, 313, 334, 335, 346, 355, 362, 373, 374, 376, 422, 424, 429, 446
Mildmay, Audrey—223
Mile—446
Miles, Bernard—274, 279, 284, 285, 317, 318, 324, 329, 334, 335, 342, 347, 348, 366, 368, 369, 375, 376, 380, 390, 401, 409, 411, 415, 430, 437
Miles Dixon—63
Miles, Joanna—367
Miles, Sally—329
Miles, Sarah—274, 387
Milestones—62, 90, 246
Miles, Sylvia—320, 357, 431
Milhaud, Darius—103
Milholland, Bruce—442
Milholland, Charles—182
Milk and Honey—326
Milkman's Round, The—215
Milk Train Doesn't Stop Here Anymore, The—338, 343
Millaire, Albert—384
Milland, Ray—346
Millard, Alexander—11
Millard, Bill—350
Millard, Evelyn—2, 3, 11, 12, 21, 43
Millar, Gertie—8, 26, 34, 37, 48, 53, 63, 80
Millar, Ronald—248, 288, 300, 328, 346, 358, 386, 421
Millar, Webster—62
Millay, Edna St. Vincent—84, 96
Millbank, Edith—120
Mill, Calum—347
Miller, Alice Duer—78, 101, 102, 187
Miller and Lyles—398
Miller, Ann—216, 450
Miller, Arthur—102, 107, 172, 240, 252, 256, 262, 265, 269, 273, 281, 286, 293, 301, 302, 303, 344, 345, 347, 349, 350, 353, 354, 362, 371, 384, 394, 400, 401, 402, 403, 417, 422, 423, 428, 430, 432, 440, 453
Miller, Betty—287, 310, 320, 366
Miller, Brian—444
Miller, Edith—13
Miller, Flournoy—105, 118, 156, 171, 230, 398
Miller, Gilbert—102, 105, 118, 130, 141, 142, 146, 148, 150, 158, 170, 172, 181, 191, 211, 214, 218, 255, 266, 267, 285, 289, 299, 383

Miller, Henry—22, 31, 33, 41, 52, 78, 91, 96, 112, 117, 118, 230, 383
Miller, Irvin—113
Miller, Jason—402
Miller, Joan—273, 383
Miller, Johnathan—323, 328, 334, 349, 388, 389, 396, 417, 430, 452
Miller, Marilyn—71, 74, 78, 87, 100, 129, 132, 156, 171, 186
Miller, Mary—379
Miller, Max—227
Miller, Quintard—113
Miller, Robert—111
Miller, Robin—372, 334
Miller, Ruby—108
Miller, Sonny—288
Milles, Sally—323
Millett, Jack—231
Mill Hill—386
Milligan, Alice—3
Milligan, Spike—339, 346, 347
Millionaire of Rough and Ready, The—272
Millionairess, The—242, 279, 354, 438, 447
Millionaire, The—90
Mills, Billy—113
Mills, Clifford Mrs.—89
Mills, Clifford—59
Mills, Florence—112, 120, 125, 154
Mills, Frank—3, 6, 12, 56, 109
Mills, Hayley—383, 391, 421, 453
Mills, Hugh—288, 299
Mills, John—206, 212, 218, 231, 245, 273, 282, 289, 322, 407, 414, 436
Mills, Juliet—381
Mills, Kerry—56
Mills, Paul—445
Mills, Stephanie—420
Mill, Watson—76
Milne, A. A.—83, 101, 102, 107, 108, 116, 119, 127, 145, 149, 152, 157, 158, 163, 164, 174, 188
Milne, Lennox—348
Milner Antony—452
Milner, Ronald—357, 378, 415
Miltern, John—190
Milton, David Scott—388
Milton, Edmund—146
Milton, Ernest—69, 113, 165, 171, 183, 188, 228, 242, 419
Milton, Harry—178
Milton, John—198, 208, 250, 279
Milton, Robert—102, 117, 121
Milward, Dawson—48, 83, 128
Mima—157
"Mind the Gate" Girl, The—62
"Mind the Paint" Girl, The—62
Mine Hostess—24
Mineo, Sal—271, 432
Mineral Workers, The—58, 59, 369
Miner, Jan—97, 374
Miner, Worthington—161, 218
Mines, Mabou—431, 440
Mines Volonakis—307
Miniatures—353
Minick—125
"Mini-Plays"—366
Minna von Barnhelm—44, 376
Minnelli, Liza—341, 351, 434, 441
Minnelli, Vincente—181, 195, 200
Minnesota Theatre Company—363, 376
Minnevitch, Borrah—142
Minnie's Boys—385
Minor, Philip—368
Minotis, Alexis—280, 360, 411, 431
Minsky Brothers—91, 104, 112
Minster, Jack—245, 247, 277, 294, 299, 305
Minto, Marie—181
Minton, Gus—100
"Mirabelle"—178
Miracle at Verdun—178
Miracle Play—410
Miracle, The—68, 124, 233, 313
Miracle Worker, The—314, 319, 327, 447
Mirage, The—100
Miramova, Elena—171, 234

Miranda, Carmen—216, 227
Miranda, Edward da Roche—307
Mirandolina—136, 145, 428
Mirbeau, Octave—89
Mirele-Efros—306, 368
Mirette a ses Raisons—75
Miron, Joseph—19
Mirren, Helen—373, 381, 382, 388, 397, 424, 427
Mirror Mann—359
Misalliance—53, 98, 114, 128, 173, 197, 283, 300, 340, 361, 409
Misanthrope, The—27, 375, 381, 408, 422, 436. See also *Le Misanthrope*
Miser, The—68, 268, 359, 380
Mishima, Yukio—340
Misleading Lady, The—66, 69
Misrock, Henry—203
Miss 1917—82
Miss Civilization—81
Miss Hobbs—2, 91
Miss Hook of Holland—36, 183
Miss in Her Teens—455
Miss Innocence—43, 90
Miss Julie—63, 300, 343, 354, 359, 398, 422, 428, 430, 439, 446, 451
Miss Liberty—262
Miss Lulu Bett—101, 215, 445
Miss Margarida's Way—434, 436
Miss Moonshine—125
Missouri Legend—424
Missouri Repertory Theatre—348
Miss Pell Is Missing—334
Miss Springtime—78
Miss Wingrove—29
Mister Biko—451
Mister Johnson—298
Mister Lincoln—430
Mister Roberts—257, 261, 268, 302, 424
Mistinguette—129
Mistress of the Inn, The—145, 241
Misunderstanding, The—303
Mitchell, Abbie—47
Mitchell, Adrian—359, 366, 396, 431, 438, 439
Mitchell, Basil—258
Mitchell, Cameron—262
Mitchell, Dodson—17, 28
Mitchell, Esther—122
Mitchell, Georges—20
Mitchell, Grant—71, 82, 118, 133
Mitchell, James—252, 326
Mitchell, Joseph—279, 345
Mitchell, Julian—10, 14, 31, 43, 56, 113, 124, 146, 248, 352, 421, 437, 443
Mitchell, Langdon—31, 77, 78, 437
Mitchell, Loften—426
Mitchell, Maggie—90
Mitchell, Marie—108
Mitchell, Margaret—278, 401
Mitchell, Millard—216
Mitchell, Norma—132, 191
Mitchell, Robert—434
Mitchell, Stuart—431
Mitchell, Thomas—157, 181, 248, 336
Mitchell, Warren—379, 453
Mitchell, Yvonne—241, 249, 265, 273, 284, 291, 296, 414
Mite, Tony—143
Mitford, Nancy—268
Mitropoulis, Dmitri—280
Mittleholzer, Edgar—276
Mixaels, Michael—344
Mixed Doubles—134, 358
Mixed Marriages—58, 59, 114, 398
Mlle. Mischief—42
Mlle. Modiste—26, 129, 167
Mnouchkine, Ariane—397
Moa, Lily—61
Mob, The—209
Moby Dick—294, 333, 401, 403, 455
Mockridge, R. W.—76
Mod Donna—388
Moddy, Michael Dorn—428
Modern Theatre in Revolt, The—383
Modigliana—450

Modiste—446
Modjeska, Helena—3, 146, 203, 237
Moeller, Phillip—76, 77, 96, 111, 136, 137, 160, 170, 176
Moels, James—454
Moffat, Dickson—54
Moffat, Donald—320, 328
Moffat, Graham—57
Moffat, Margaret—176, 188
Moffatt, John—339, 353, 359, 401, 424
Moffitt, John C.—204
Mogu of the Desert—179
Mohr, Max—159
Mohyeddin, Zia—366
Moiseiwitsch, Benno—73
Moiseiwitsch, Tanya—73, 267, 283, 285, 286, 290, 295, 296, 308, 389
Moissi, Alexander—153, 173
Mokae, Zakes—396
Molesworth Hall (Dublin)—18
Molette, Barbara—395
Molette, Carlton—395
Moliere in Spite of Himself—442
Moliere, Jean-Baptiste Poguelin—27, 33, 50, 58, 68, 85, 89-90, 95-7, 114, 145, 160, 167, 185, 188, 193, 218, 237, 241, 249, 255, 264, 268-9, 273-5, 285, 290, 301-2, 306, 311, 316, 328-9, 334, 347-8, 353-4, 359, 366-8, 374-5, 380, 383, 387-90, 392, 395, 404, 408, 415-7, 419, 422-3, 431, 436-7, 441, 445-6, 453
Mollison, Clifford—177, 183, 202, 248
Mollison, William—4, 7, 135, 143, 151, 165, 166, 218, 259
Moll, James—430
Molloy, M. J.—341
Mollusc, The—178, 264
Molly—419, 444
Molnar, Ferenc—42, 48, 105, 110, 118, 125, 130, 132, 142, 145, 155, 172, 177, 184, 192, 223, 224, 244, 254, 271, 285, 381, 409, 410, 439, 444, 445, 452, 454
Moloney, Helen—81
Molyneux, Eileen—120
Momiji-Gari—382
Mona Inglesby's International Ballet—250
Monck, Nugent—110, 249, 254
Monckton, Lionel—2, 8, 10, 11, 16, 21, 26, 37, 48, 53, 57, 63, 84
Mon Double et Ma Moitie—198
Monette, Richard—381, 413
Monk and the Woman, The—62
Monkhouse, Allan—46, 64, 69
Monkhouse, Bob—326
Monkhouse, Jo—108
Monk, Julius—332, 344, 351
Monkman, Dorothy—101
Monkman, Phyllis—83, 101, 127, 151, 167, 212, 222
Monk, Meredith—424
Monks, John Jr.—200
Monna Vanna—28, 73, 146
Monnier, Henry—274
Monnot, Margaret—310
Monologue—415
Monroe, George W.—184
Monroe, Marilyn—276
Monro, Robert—315
Monserrat—262, 276
Monsieur Artaud—379
Monsieur Beaucaire—9, 94, 160, 178, 184
Monsieur Perrichon's Travels—429
Monsters—437
Montague, Lee—276, 372, 451
Montalban, Ricardo—304, 407
Monte Cristo, Jr.—92, 123
Monte Cristo—4
Montel, Michael—440
Monterey, Carlotta—391
Montero, Maria—112
Montez, Lola—159
Montgomery and Stone—52, 246
Montgomery, David—14, 30, 85
Montgomery, Douglass—148, 262

Montgomery, Elizabeth—23
Montgomery, James—63, 78, 83, 93, 431
Montgomery, Robert—332, 395, 398, 410, 440
Month in the Country, A—170, 237, 265, 300, 354, 409, 416, 432, 447
Monty Python Live!—414
Monty Python's First Farewell Tour—414
Moody, John—197
Moody, Ron—285, 286, 289, 299, 310, 322
Moody, William Vaughn—30, 51, 52
Moon—422
Moon and Sixpence, The—135
Moonbeam—428
Moonchildren—400
Moonchildren in New York—390
Moon, Ena—206
Mooney, Ria—209
Mooney, Tom—178
Moon for the Misbegotten, A—308, 304, 356, 374, 411
Moon in the Yellow River, The—183, 193
Moon Is a Gong, The—140
Moon Is Blue, The—271, 282
Moon is Down, The—230, 233, 236
"Moon Love"—120
Moon of the Caribees, The—128, 208, 452
Moon on a Rainbow Shawl—312, 332
Moon Over Mulberry Street—195
Moonshine—26
Moor, Bill—364
Moore, Carlyle—62, 75
Moore, Carol—309
Moore, Carrie—27, 32
Moore, Carroll—69
Moore, Constance—230
Moore, Decima—15
Moore, Dennie—129
Moore, Dora Mavor—456
Moore, Douglas—219
Moore, Dudley—198, 318, 323, 328, 378, 401
Moore, Edward—410, 413
Moore, Eva—7, 11, 12, 21, 43, 89, 104, 130, 151
Moore, Evelyn—197
Moore, Florence—150
Moore, Geoff—452
Moore, George—3
Moore, Grace—100, 118, 126
Moore, Harry—368
Moore, Hilda—107, 150
Moore, Jill Esmond—158
Moore, Juanita—314
Moore, Leon—146
Moore, Mabel—135
Moore, Mary—2, 16, 18, 27, 43, 58
Moore, Mary Tyler—443
Moore, Melba—385, 442
Moore, Menlo—60
Moore, Robert—386, 413, 449
Moore, Sam—262
Moore, Sonia—146
Moore, Tim—201
Moore, Tom—413
Moore, Victor—30, 36, 133, 142, 150, 164, 177, 191, 211, 221, 336
Moor Gates, The—68
Moorhead, Agnes—275, 332, 406, 407
Moorhouse, A. H.—50
Morahan, Christopher—386, 435, 437, 439, 444, 445, 452
Moral Evening, A—359, 360
Moral Law, The—114
Morals of Marcus, The—34
Moran and Mack—99, 141
Morand, Patricia—357
Morange, E. A.—11
Moran, George—125
Moran, Lois—177
More—75
Moreau, Emile—16, 17, 45, 54
Morecambe—424

Morehouse, Ward—363
More Intimacy at Eight—286
More, Julian—291, 299, 310
More Just William—255
More, Kenneth—253, 267, 372, 391, 394, 439
Moreland, Mantan—156, 176, 306, 412
Morell, Andre—278
Moreno, Rita—338, 344, 413, 418
More Respectable—68
More Stately Mansions—364, 377, 417
More Than You Deserve—410
Morgan, Agnes—111, 128, 131, 140, 148, 156
Morgan, Carey—106
Morgan, Charles—278, 279, 288
Morgan, Claudia—214, 236
Morgan, Diana—206, 244
Morgan, Frank—141, 170
Morgan, Helen—131, 141, 150, 164, 176
Morgan, Joan—241
Morgan, Ralph—71, 111, 230
Moriarty, Michael—413, 418
Morill, Patricia—347
Morley, Christopher—367
Morley, Malcolm—167
Morley, Robert—45, 202, 208, 213, 217, 245, 253, 268, 283, 288, 299, 311, 314, 317, 365, 386, 414, 430
Mormon Miracle Pageant—368, 370, 377
Mormon Peril—59
Morning After Optimism—410
Morning Becomes Electra—208
Morning, Noon, and Night—166, 366, 371
Morning's at Seven—217, 225, 295, 297
Morning Star, The—227
Morosco, Oliver—28, 62, 78, 82, 85, 92, 98
Moross, Jerome—197, 257, 287, 292
Moross, John Latouche-Jerome—261
Morrell, Andre—295
Morrel, Olive—21, 26
Morrey, P.—256
Morris, Beth—451
Morris, Chester—146, 156
Morris, Clara—138, 146
Morris, Colin—268, 428
Morrisey, John J.—137
Morris, John—423, 428
Morris, Libby—326
Morris, Lloyd—230, 238
Morris, Margaret—295
Morris, Margery—213
Morris, Mary—126, 186, 276, 295
Morris, McKay—121, 140, 195
Morris, Melville—120
Morris, Nat—400
Morrison and Stewart—37
Morrison, Anne—124
Morrison, G. E.—44
Morrison, Jack—95, 107, 231
Morrison, Lewis—146
Morrison, Mary—64, 74
Morrison, Patricia—77, 258
Morris, Richard—321
Morris, Robert—352
Morris, T. B.—251
Morris, Wayne—304
Morris, William—22, 66, 77, 117, 130
Morrow, Doretta—282
Morrow, John—451
Morrow, Karen—345, 368
Morrow, Macklin—133
Morse, Barry—244, 361, 363, 429
Morse, Robert—179, 316, 326
Morte Civile—44
Mortimer, John—310, 321, 333, 386, 390, 394, 401, 428, 435, 439
Morton, Brooks—333
Morton, Cavendish—55
Morton, Clara—153
Morton, Clive—213, 294, 328
Morton, Edward—37

Morton, Frederic—386
Morton, Hugh—2, 6, 7, 96
Morton, John Maddison—373
Morton, Kitty—153
Morton, Leon—89
Morton, Lew—163
Morton, Martha—137
Morton, Michael—1, 16, 32, 35, 71, 83, 84, 89, 108, 159
Morton, Myra—206
Morton, Paul—153
Mosca, Gittel—313
Moscovitch, Maurice—96
Moscow Art Theatre—116, 117, 121, 122, 347, 353, 388
Moscow Art Theatre Company—311
Moscow Art Theatre Players—197
Moscow Bells—231
Moscow Drama Theatre—447
Moscowitz, Jennie—103
Mosel, George Ault Jr.—115
Mosel, Tad—115, 321, 455
Moser, Hans—153
Moser, Margot—244
Moses, Gilbert—383, 393, 422
Moses, Montrose—383
Moses, Robert—319
Moshinsky, Elijah—431
Moss, Ariel—245
Moss, Arnold—180, 221, 245, 250, 311
Moss Empires Ltd.—4
Moss, Paul—246
Moss, Peter—454
Moss, Robert—372, 399, 429, 439
Moss, Stradford—45
Moss, Theodore—5
Mostel, Josh—393
Mostel, Zero—247, 276, 317, 319, 322, 326, 344, 415, 432, 441
Moster, Margot—368
Most Happy Fella, The—289, 316, 322, 360, 384
Most Unwarrantable Intrusion, A—373
Motel—358
Mother Adam—408
Mother Courage—301, 316
Mother Courage and Her Children—341, 343, 353, 368, 390, 446
Mother Goose—15, 38, 64, 128, 184, 203, 224, 232, 237, 246, 250, 255, 261, 269, 291, 330, 436
Mother Goose at the Crystal Palace—59
Mother of Pearl—187
Mother's Day—431
Mother, The—69, 198, 289, 409
Motocar—435, 437
Motor Show, The—347
Motzan, Otto—78
Mouillet, Frederick—57
Moulan, Frank—20, 48
Moulton, Arthur J.—185
Moumou—379
Mound Builders, The—422
Mountaineers, The—49
"Mountain Greenery"—140
"Mountain High-Valley Low"—247
Mountain Man, The—107
Mountain Play Association—68
Mountains Look Different, The—260
Mount, Peggy—275, 294, 315, 359, 372, 409, 414, 427, 431, 444
Mourning Becomes Electra—176, 185, 214, 232, 295, 329, 366, 368, 375, 396, 404, 405
Mourning Bride, The—135
Mouse Trap, The—104, 278, 289, 337, 370, 405, 419, 432, 441, 457
Mousme, The—57
Mouth Organ, The—422
Move Over Mrs. Markham—394
Mowat, David—373, 455
Mowatt, Anna Cora—166
Moya, Natalie—148, 176
Moya, Stella—241
Moyes, Patricia—289
Moylan, Thomas King—96
Mozart—144, 145

Mozart, Constanze—451
Mozart, Wolfgang Amadeus—255, 256, 260, 264, 348, 360, 367
Mr. and Mrs. North—226, 229
Mr. Bluebeard—14, 18
Mr. Bolfrey—241, 302
Mr. Burke, M. P.—324
Mr. Chops—276
Mr. Cinders—165
Mr. Dickens Goes to the Play—237
Mr. George—36
Mr. Gillie—267
Mr. Hopkinson—26
Mr. Jarvis—57
Mr. Jiggins of Jigginstown—188
Mr. Joyce Is Leaving Paris—396, 444
Mr. Kettle and Mrs. Moom—294
Mr. Lode of Koal—48
Mr. Manhattan—79
Mrozek, Slawomir—347, 353, 359, 378, 389, 430
Mr. Pickwick—159
Mr. Pim—101
Mr. Pim Passes By—101, 105, 152
Mr. Pitt—124
Mr. Popple (of Ippleton)—27
Mr. Preedy and the Countess—48
Mr. President—332
Mr. Prohack—154
Mr. Punch's Pantomime—432
Mrs. Argent—407
Mrs. Bumpstead-Leigh—56, 98, 163
Mrs. Dally Has a Lover—332
Mrs. Dane's Defence—2, 250
Mrs. Dot—52, 274
Mrs. Gorringe's Necklace—16
Mrs. January and Mr. X—239
Mrs. McThing—276, 280
Mrs. Moonlight—170, 412
Mrs. Mouse, Are You Within?—372
Mrs. Partridge Presents—131
Mrs. Patterson—288
Mrs. Skeffington—53
Mr. Strauss Goes to Boston—425
Mrs. Warren's Profession—13, 28, 37, 38, 84, 144, 147, 178, 198, 268, '353, 391, 428, 429
Mrs. Wiggs of Cabbage Patch—19, 297
Mrs. Willoughby's Kiss—18
Mrs. Wilson's Diary—366
Mr. Whittington—191
Mr. Wix of Wickham—23
Mr. Wonderful—298
Mr. Wu—68, 261
Mr. Wu Looks Back—261
Msomi, Welcome—402, 408, 438
Mthoba, James—435
Much Ado About Nothing—3, 8, 16, 23, 33, 37, 44, 58, 64, 68, 72, 73, 80, 97, 103, 114, 115, 122, 136, 152, 166, 167, 173, 184, 188, 193, 202, 207, 219, 223, 225, 228, 245, 250, 264, 268, 278, 279, 296, 302, 306, 311, 312, 317, 318, 329, 341, 347, 353, 354, 373, 381, 389, 396, 397, 403, 423, 429, 430, 438, 439, 446
Mud and Treacle—161
Mueller, Hans—208
Mueller, Harold—401
Muir, Frank—268
Muir, Gavin—134
Mulatto—196, 369
Mulberry Bush, The—300
Mulcaster, G. H.—151
Muldoon, J. Malachi—59
Mulhare, Edward—407
Mullally, Don—133
Mullen, Barbara—264, 438
Mullen, George—28
Muller, Hans—177, 202
Muller, Kurt—399
Muller, Robert—1967/3
Mullholland, J. B.—55
Mulligan Guards—59
Multry, Lance—417
Mummenschanz—416
Mummers Theatre (Oklahoma City)—337, 392

Mummmers Troupe of Newfoundland—405
Mummy and the Hummingbird, The—10
Mumsee—104
Mundin, Herbert—135, 158
Mundy, Meg—203, 257
Municipal Theatre Company (Malmo Sweden)—316
Muni, Paul—141, 149, 177, 217, 232, 247, 262, 293, 370
Munro, C. K.—119, 127, 193
Munro, George—312
Munro, Nan—295
Munsel, Patrice—348, 420
Munshin, Jules—247
Munson, Ona—149
Murcell, George—429, 438, 453
Murder at the Vanities—186
Murder at the Vicarage—264, 423, 430
Murderer—421
Murder in Mayfair—192
Murder in the Cathedral—197, 202, 207, 214, 283, 313, 325, 360, 403
Murder is Announced, A—435, 453
Murder, Like Charity . . .—208
Murder on the Nile—248
Murder on the Second Floor—363
Murderous Angels—394
Murder Without Crime—231
Murdoch, Richard—196
Murdock, Iris—339, 372, 390
Murphy and Dana—73
Murphy, Barney—81
Murphy, Brian—408
Murphy, Dallas, Jr.—452
Murphy, George—149
Murphy, Melissa—364
Murphy, Michael—284
Murphy, Owen—156
Murphy, Ric—335
Murphy, Rosemary—321, 344
Murphy, Thomas—328, 379, 382, 410, 415
Murphy, Tim—161
Murray, Alfred—2
Murray and Mack—128
Murray, Barbara—335
Murray, Braham—381, 403, 414
Murray, Brian—329, 339, 365, 386, 410, 451
Murray, C.—128, 160
Murray, Douglas—88
Murray, Gilbert—23, 24, 27, 32, 45, 46, 58, 63, 69, 103, 122, 167, 197, 202, 249
Murray Hill—149, 237
Murray, J. Harold—117, 132, 141, 148
Murray, John—33, 205, 276, 402
Murray, John J.—128
Murray, Ken—195, 231
Murray, Michael—184
Murray, Paddy—328
Murray, Ruby—294
Murray, Stephen—274, 278, 279
Murray, T. C.—59, 64, 114, 144
Murrell, John—451
Murry, Barbara—304
Murry, Bill—420
Murry, Ellen—206
Museaum—445
Museum of Costume Arts—243
Musgrove, Gertrude—201, 232
Musical Chairs—179
Musical Jubilee, A—420
Music Box Revue, The—106, 112, 118, 120, 126, 404
Music Center of Los Angeles—350
Music Cure, The—274
Music in the Air—181
Music Man, The—154, 305, 313, 327, 354, 377
Music Mountain, The—283
Music Theatre of Lincoln Center—381
Musser, Tharon—137, 304, 364
Mussolini, Benito—239
Mutchmore, Dr. J.—292
Mutilated, The—357

Muzeeka—374
My Astonishing Self—442, 453
My Aunt Bridget—184
Mycho, Andre—76
"My Coal Black Mammy"—112
My Crystal Ball—189
My Cup Runneth Over—444
My Darlin' Aida—280
My Dear Children—221
Myer, Joan—109
Myers, Carmel—93
Myers, Henry—157, 253
Myers, Paul—369
Myers, Peter—295, 299, 310, 328
Myers, Richard—138, 165
My Fair Lady—155, 194, 298, 310, 347, 369, 374, 411, 429, 433, 455
My Fat Friend—401, 413
My Friend From India—110, 137
"My Funny Valentine"—205
My Gal Friday—163
My Girl—126
"My Heart Belongs to Daddy"—212
"My Hero"—48
My Heart's In the Highlands—221
"My Kind of Man"—268
My Kinsman—349
My Lady Frayle—79
My Lady Friends—93
My Lady Molly—15
My Lady's Dress—72
My Lady Virtue—12
My Life—361, 436
"My Mammy"—87
"My Man"—105
My Maryland—149
My Mother Was a Fortune Teller—445
My Name is Aquilon—264
My Old Dutch—102
"My Romance"—196
Myrtrl, Odette—120
"My Ship"—226
My Sister Eileen—222, 229, 233, 236, 281, 447
My Son John—144
Mysteries and Smaller Pieces—375
Mystic Writings of Paul Revere, The—416
My Three Angels—281, 286, 294
"My Way of Love"—101
My Wife—35, 391
My Wife's Lodger—272
My Years on the Stage—153

Nabokov, Vladimir—379
NAB Show, The—390
Nagel, Claire—92, 110
Nagel, Conrad—87
Nagrin, Daniel—230, 262
Naikowska, Zofia—306
Naismith, Laurence—45, 299, 338
Naives Hirondelles—340
Naked—136, 260, 340
Naked Truth, The—53
Naldi, Nita—99, 330
Nalone, Nancy—276
Naming of Murderer's Rock, The—318, 322
Nan—43
Nance Oldfield—8, 37
Nancy Brown—14
Nannie's Night Out—128
Nanteuil, Georges—76
Naomi Court—416
Napier, Alan—127, 136, 206
Napier, Frank—246, 249
Napier, John—437, 453
Naples By Night, Naples by Day—373
Napoleon—66, 96, 102, 254
Napoli Milionaria—402
Napolin, Leah—420
Nares, Owen—75, 78, 102, 107, 113, 128, 157, 158, 165, 182, 195, 197, 207, 222
Narizzano, Dino—320
Narrow Road to the Deep North—379, 401

Nash, Charlotte—179
Nash, Florence—38, 133, 144
Nash, George—36
Nash, N. Richard—69, 284, 321, 371
Nash, Ogden—235, 276, 300
Nash, W. J.—129
Natal Theatre Workshop—402
Nat Goodwin's Book—97
Nathan and Tabileth—368
Nathan, George Jean—69, 131, 313
Nathan Hale—97
Nathan the Wise—228, 368
National Academy of Dramatic Art—123
National Anthem, The—111
National Arts Foundation—343
National Association of Schools of Theatre—399
National Association of Theatrical Producing Managers—46
National Children's Theatre Association—399
National Endowment for the Arts, The—356, 363
National Foundation for the Arts and Humanities—356
National Health, or, Nurse Norton's Affair, The—382
National Health, The—418
National Historical Landmark—392
National Lampoon's Lemmings—406
National Lampoon Show, The—420
National Phonographic Company, The—39
National Register of Historic Places—86, 419, 433
National Repertory Theatre, The—367
National Theater Company (American)—22
National Theater, Habimah (Israel)—347
National Theater School of Canada, The/L'Ecole National de Théatre du Canada—325
National Theatre (British)—329, 338, 346, 349, 353, 365, 366, 380, 381, 382, 388, 391, 392, 395, 396, 398, 402, 407, 408, 409, 411, 415, 417, 421, 422, 428, 430, 431, 445, 452, 456
National Theatre Conference—230
National Theatre (Greece)—280, 362, 431
National Theatre of the Deaf—380, 387
National Theatre Owners' Association—55
National Theatre: Scheme and Estimates, A—251
National Theatre School—261, 319
National Velvet—248
National Youth Theatre, The1—317, 335, 342, 348, 354, 362, 367, 382, 397, 403, 409, 417, 423, 430, 436, 439, 447, 451, 453, 455
National Youth Theatre-Dolphin Theatre Company—399
Nation, The—318
Native Son—226, 229
Nattavo and Myrrio—126
Natural Law, The—419
Nature and Purpose of the Universe, The—420
Natwick, Mildred—45, 188, 227, 232, 276, 289, 300, 382
Naughton and Gold—253, 289, 300
Naughton, Bill—322, 339, 354, 359
Naughton, Charlie—218, 267
Naughton, Harry—311
"Naughty Baby"—127
Naughty Cinderella—133
Naughty Marietta—52, 129, 167, 424
Naughty Princess, The—102
Navette—85
Naylor, Ruth—245
Nazarene, The—104
Nazimova, Alla—35, 36, 54, 58,

90, 122, 137, 160, 166, 170, 176, 198, 203
Neagle, Anna—193, 208, 244, 282, 353, 435, 455
Neal, Patricia—146, 247, 280, 314
Neal, Sally—366
"Neapolitan Love Song"—74
Nearly a Hero—41
Ned and Jack—446, 454
Nederlander, David T.—370
Nederlander, James—457
Nederlander, Joseph—457
Nederlander Organization—405
Ned Kean of Old Drury—120
Ned Kelly—323
Ned MacCobb's Daughter—145
Ned Wayburn Dancing, Singing and Dramatic Schools—233
Needle—317
Neff, Hildegarde—293
Neglected Lady, The—69
Negro Ensemble Company—373, 376, 380, 383, 391, 394, 398, 400, 402, 406, 415, 422, 428, 432, 440, 447, 456, 479
Negro in the America Theatre, The—302
Negro Playwrights Company—224
Negro Theatre Guild—188
Negro Theatre Unit—202, 204, 213, 214
Neighborhood Players—122, 128, 243
Neighborhood Playhouse—147, 404
Neighbors, The—84, 86, 366
Neil, Hildegard—381
Neill, James—179
Neil, Roger—449
Neilsen, Herman—391
Neilson, Adelaide—104
Neilson, Francis—57
Neilson, Julia—15, 26
Neilson, Perlita—381
Neilson-Terry, Dennis—103,151
Neilson-Terry, Phyllis—192, 193, 208, 441
Neiman, Irvin—235
Nekrassov—307
Nelis, Sylvia—103
Nell Gwynne, the Player—43
Nellhaus, Gerhard—335
Nelligan, Kate—414, 437, 443
Nelly Neil—36
Nelson, Barry—271, 293, 326, 352, 365, 420
Nelson, Gail—442
Nelson, Gene—258
Nelson, Gwen—359, 451
Nelson, John—92
Nelson, Kenneth—271, 320, 371, 437
Nelson, Novella—385, 415
Nelson, Perlita—268
Nelson, Ralph—235
Nelson, Richard—452
Nelson, Ruth—186, 221, 395
Nemerov, Howard—314
Nemiroff, Robert—378, 406
Nemirovitch-Dantchenko and Galperin—137
Nemtchinova, Vera—143
Neptune Theatre Foundation (Halifax, Nova Scotia)—337
Nero—32
Nero and the Golden House—428
Nervo and Knox—126, 243, 245, 253, 289, 300, 322
Nervo, Jimmy—173, 218, 235, 267, 315
Nervous Wreck, The—127, 452
Nesbitt, Cathleen—59, 67, 101, 119, 129, 143, 159, 165, 172, 177, 183, 197, 206, 214, 219, 244, 250, 260, 264, 266, 272, 279, 282, 298
Nesbitt, Evelyn—33
Nesbitt, Harry—151
Nesbitt, Max—151
Nesbitt, Robert—192, 218, 222, 227, 231, 235, 236, 241, 245, 248, 253, 263, 267, 272, 273, 277, 282, 299, 305, 310, 315

Nest Egg, The—313
Nestroy, Johann—373, 380
Nest, The—116
Ne Te Promene doc pas Toute Nue—353
Nethersole, Olga—1, 4, 12, 28, 44, 53, 55, 110, 161, 189
Net, The—97
Nettlefold, F. C.—97
Neveaux, Georges—302, 306, 329
Never Had it so Good—323
Never Homes, The—56
Never on Sunday—364
Never Say Die—67
Nevertheless—80
Never Too Late—333, 343
Neville, Henry—2, 32
Neville, John—285, 289, 290, 295, 296, 300, 301, 302, 307, 311, 313, 317, 334, 339, 355, 433
Neville, Michael—431
Neville, Oliver—329
Neville, Sheila—392
Nevin, Arthur—1
Nevis Mountain Dew—447
Nevolin, Boris—231
New Adventures of Noah's Ark, The—383
New Alcazar Theatre—39
New Amsterdam Theater—18
New Arts Theatre—340
Neway, Patricia—266
Newberry, Barbara—157
Newberry, Len—390
"New Bill of Mini-Plays"—366
New Clothes for the Emperor—307, 342
Newcombe, Mary—193
New Drama Forum—425
Newell, Joan—272
Newell, Raymond—218
New Faces—190, 200, 222, 228, 276, 280, 298
New Federal Theatre—393
Newfoundland Night—405
New Girl in Town—304, 418
New Girl, The—192
New Gossoon, The—178, 184, 193
New Haven Repertory Theatre—428
Newhouse, Mitzi E.—410
Newlands, Anthony—296
Newley, Anthony—179, 286, 296, 300, 328, 343, 351, 401, 443, 446, 447
New Life, A.—235
New Lyceum, The (New York)—18
Newly-Married Couple, The—68
Newman, Charles—25
Newman, David—357
Newman, Greatrex—143, 151, 165, 167, 191
Newman, Paul—281, 293, 314
Newman, Phyllis—327, 445
Newman, Sidney—256
Newman, Stephen—451
Newmar, Julie—309
Newmark, Isadore—39
Newmeyer, Sarah—219
New Moon, The—157, 241
New Morality, The—115, 136
New Negro Theater Company, The—323
New Phoenix Repertory Company—404, 410 418
New Play Centre—392, 416
New Players—58
New Play Society—456
New Reekie—435
New Shakespeare Company—96, 97, 103
New Show of Improvisations—341
New Shylock, The—72
Newspaper Guild Page One Award—319
New Stages Company—255
Newsweek—413
New Tenant, The—302
New Theater, The (London)—18
New Theater, The (New York)—34
New Theatre League—202

New Theatre Repertory—48
New Theatre, The (Toronto)—167, 457
Newton, Christopher—377
Newton, Isaac—223
Newton, Robert—166, 192
Newton, Theodore—214
New Victoria Line—388
New Watergate Theatre Club—302, 312
New Way to Pay Old Debts, A—114, 285
New World, Old Friends, The—82
New York Actors Equity—377
New York City Center Theatre Company—269, 283, 374
New York City Opera—254
New York City Theatre Company—259
New York Commercial Advertiser—209
New York Daily Mirror—271, 305
New York Daily News, The—270, 363, 450
New York Drama Critics' Circle—204, 409
New York Drama Critics' Circle Award—297
New York Drama Critics' Circle Best Musical citation—393
New York Drama Desk—265
New York Dramatic Mirror—9, 60, 65
New York Dramatic News—90
New York Equity Library Theatre—398
New Yorkers, The—171
New Yorker Theatre, The—175
New York Exchange—147
New York Honours List—89
New York Hudson Guild—439
New York Idea, The—31, 77, 437
New York Philharmonic Orchestra—203, 274
New York Pro Musica—312
New York Public Library Theatre—29, 454
New York's Bread and Puppet Theatre—389
New York State Theater—350
New York Theatre Guild—101
Next—62, 378
Next of Kin—415
Next Religion, The—65
Next Time I'll Sing To You—339, 340, 350, 404, 411
Ney, Marie—144, 178, 182, 192, 198, 208
Niblo, Fred—14, 19
Niccodemi, Dario—27, 83
Nice, France—179
Nice People—105, 110
Nicholas, Mike—180, 394
Nicholas Nickleby—104, 121
Nicholas, Peter—382, 414, 417, 418
Nicholls, Anthony—290
Nichols, Anne—28, 11, 127, 200
Nichols, Anthony—218
Nichols, Beverly—172, 183
Nichols, Dandy—259, 386
Nichols, Guy—161
Nichols, Jay—268
Nichols, Josephine—320
Nichols, Joy—287
Nichols, Lewis—234, 241, 244
Nichols, Mike—321, 333, 339, 345, 358, 365, 371, 395, 397, 407, 434
Nicholson, Anthony—289
Nicholson, H. O.—49, 99
Nicholson, Kenyon—148, 186
Nichols, Peter—435, 440, 445
Nichols, Robert—160, 297
Nichtern, Claire—104
Nicht wi' Burns, A—54
Nicolaeff, Ariadne—444
Nicol, Alex—97
Nicoll, Allardyce—432
Nield, David—455
Nielson, Ada—28
Nielson, Adelaide—146

Nielson, Christine—53, 61
Nielson, Julia—2, 3, 26, 48, 57
Nielson, Perlita—355
Nielson-Terry, Phyllis—53, 58, 59, 63, 68, 113, 119, 132, 178
Niesen, Gertrude—239
Niggerlovers, The—364
Nigger, The—48
Night—430
"Night and Day"—182
Night and Day—443
Night and the Laughter, The—248
Night and the Music, The—245
Night Before Paris, The—387
Night Boat, The—99
Nightclub Cantata—434
Night Hawk—147
Nightingale and the Rose, The—282
Nightingale, Florence—379
Night in Paris, A—140
Night in Spain, A—148
Night in Venice, A—164, 242
Night Like This, A—172
Night Lodging—94
Night Music—221
Night Must Fall—197, 200, 208, 214, 237, 376, 416
Night of January 16, The—195, 408
Night of the Ball, The—294
Night of the Fourth—299
Night of the Garter—183, 232
Night of the Iguana, The—327, 337, 352, 361, 431, 432
Night of the Party, The—7
Night of the Tribades, The—434, 446
Night Out, A—102
Night Over Taos—181, 318
Nights of Cabiria—357
Night Thoreau Spent in Jail, The—405
Night Was Made for Love", "The—176
Night Watch—400
Night with the Pierrots—61
Nigro, Robert—447
Nijinsky, Kyra—192
Nikolaeva-Legat, Nadejda—231
Nil Carborundun—334
Nillson, Carlotta—26, 31
Nimmo, Derek—407
Nina—296
Nina Rose—177
Nine Girls—237
Nine O'Clock Revue, The—114
Nine Sharp—212
1940's Radio Hour, The—450
1931—179
Nine Till Six—171
90 in the Shade—74
Ningyo Shimai—445
Ninotchka—278, 293
Nirdlingers, The—86
Nivoix, Paul—133
Nixon, Fred G.—179
Nixon-Nirdlinger theatres—179
No. 17—135, 174
Noah—429
Noakes, John—333
Noble Land, The—2
Noble, Larry—268
Nobles, Dolly—129, 174
Nobles, Milton—129
Noble Spaniard, The—49
Noble, William—309
Nobody Home—74
Nobody Loves an Albatross—339
Nobody's Daughter—53
Nobody's Widow—52
No 'Count Boy, The—138
Noddy in Toyland—296, 302, 307, 313, 318, 336
Noel Coward in Two Keys—413
Noel, Craig—296, 301, 307, 374, 381, 389, 438, 454
No Exit—247
No Foolin'—146
No for an Answer—229
Noguchi, Isamu—295

Noh Theatre of Japan, The—367
Nolan, Doris—195
Nolan, Lloyd—186, 287
Nolan, Margaret—379
Nolan, Peter—84
No Laughing Matter—306
Nolen, Doris—230
Nolte, Charles—271, 360
No Man's Land—421, 427
No Medals—241
No More Ladies—190
No More Peace—213
Nono—122
No, No, Nanette!—132, 134, 202, 395
Noonan, John Ford—380, 417
Noone—408
No One Was Saved—391
No Orchids for Miss Blandish—231, 444
Noose, The—141, 253
No Place to be Somebody—379, 382
Norcross, Frank—146
Norcross, Joseph M.—137
Norden, Denis—268
Nordstrom, Marie—26
Norman Conquests, The—414, 415, 421, 454
Normand, Jacques—85
Norman, Frank—316, 321, 347, 379, 404
Norman, Karyl—118
Norman, Marsha—443
Norman, Monty—318
Norman, Mrs. George—101
Norman. Is That You?—385
Norman, Norman V.—137
Norman, Thirza—22, 23
No Room at the Inn—248
Norris, Frank—19
Norris, William—161
North, Alex—55, 230
Northampton Repertory Company—411
Northern, Michael—300
Norton, Deborah—451
Norton, Elliott—419
Norton, Frederic—45, 79
Norwich Players—68
Norwith, Jack—91
Norwood, Ellie—53, 72, 83, 120
Norworth, Jack—41, 47, 91, 185
No Sex Please-We're British—394
No Strings—332, 340, 398
Not Drowning but Waving—410
Not Enough Rope—417
Notes from the Underground—410
Notes on a Love Affair—401
Not for Children—198, 291
Nothing But the Truth—78
Nothing-Doing Bar—103
Nothing Like Leather—69
Nothing Sacred—281
Not I—404
No Time for Comedy—216, 220, 228, 411
No Time For Sergeants—293, 299
Not in the Book—310
Not Now, Darling—372, 456
Notorious Mrs. Ebbsmith, The—8, 12
No Traveller Returns—224
Notre Dame des Fleurs—414
Notre Jeunesse—27
Nottingham Playhouse—394, 423, 434
Nottingham Playhouse Company—264, 382, 388, 439
Novelist—397
Novelli, Ermete—37
Novello, Ivor—79, 84, 88, 95, 101, 108, 125, 126, 127, 145, 152, 159, 166, 172, 182, 187, 192, 197, 201, 207, 212, 217, 218, 236, 245, 254, 263, 374
Novelty Theater—5
November Night—422
Novotna, Jarmila—239
Now Barabas . . .—253
Nowhere to Run, Nowhere to Hide—415
No Why—348

Now Is the Time for All Good Men—364, 390
Ntshona, Winston—414, 435
Nude With a Violin—299, 305
Nue, Carrie—355
Nugent, Eddie—216
Nugent, Elliott—105, 111, 221, 225, 232, 235, 264, 279
Nugent, J. C.—111, 213
Nugent, Moya—102, 165, 183, 201, 206
Nugent, Nancy—234
Nugent, Ruth—111
Nuits de la Colere, Les—274
Nunn, June Trevor—377
Nunn, Trevor—354, 355, 359, 360, 367, 373, 374, 380, 381, 382, 388, 390, 409, 410, 429, 437, 438, 439, 444, 447, 453
Nuns, The—407
Nuova Compagnia de Canto Popolare—423
Nuria Espert Company—396
Nurse!—2
Nurse Benson—89
Nurse Cavell—191, 232
Nurse Macateer—380
Nusbaum, Nathaniel Richard—69
Nutcracker in the Land of Nuts, The—451
Nutcracker Suite, The—114, 392, 457
Nutmeg Tree, The—227
Nuyen, France—309
Nye, Carrie—329, 330, 342
Nyiri, Janos—374
NY Journal-American—369
Nymph Errant—188, 248
Nype, Russel—128
NY Post—363

Oaks, Larry—441
Oates, Cicely—182
Oates, Joyce Carol—390, 410
Oberammergau Passion Play, The—284
Ober, Philip—191, 244
Obey, Andre—109, 182, 192, 295, 429
Obie Award—301, 426
Objections to Sex and Violence—421
Oblomov—346
Obraztsov, Sergei—361
O'Brian, Pat—171
O'Brien, Conor Cruise—380, 394
O'Brien, David—234
O'Brien, Diedre—228
O'Brien, Edna—336, 401, 431
O'Brien, Flann—451
O'Brien Girl, The—106
O'Brien, Jack—381, 424, 429, 438
O'Brien, Justin—342
O'Brien, Kate—241, 262
O'Brien-Moore, Erin—163
O'Brien, Liam—282
O'Brien, Richard—409
O'Brien, Tim—373, 374
O'Brien, Timothy—367, 415
O'Bryan, Edward—159
Obsession in India—183
O'Casey, Sean—121, 128, 137, 140, 144, 152, 153, 166, 191, 192, 193, 208, 219, 223, 248, 250, 255, 304, 306, 312, 313, 316, 317, 318, 323, 329, 330, 335, 350, 354, 359, 360, 366, 375, 382, 394, 395, 402, 407, 409, 431, 436
Occupations—398, 401
Occupe-Toi d'Amelie—302, 314, 447
Ockrent, Mike—410, 421, 436, 437
O'Connell, Arthur—288
O'Connor, Bill—258
O'Connor, Flannery—358
O'Connor, Frank—290
O'Connor, Garry—348
O'Connor, Jeff—239
O'Connor, Joseph—386
O'Connor, Kevin—353, 366, 420

O'Connor, Una—59, 119, 144, 166, 178
O'Conor, Joseph—438
Octagon Theatre of Bolton—397
Octave—45
Octopus, The—368
Octoroon, The—328
O'Day, Alice—158
O'Day, Nell—277
Odd Couple, The—351, 356, 359, 377
Oddie, Bill—351
Oddly Enough—286
Odd Man In—305
Odds and Ends of 1917—83
O'Dea, James—36, 62
O'Dea, John—235
Ode to Liberty—191
Odets, Clifford—176, 179, 181, 195, 197, 199, 205, 215, 220, 221, 227, 232, 233, 262, 267, 275, 278, 285, 288, 297, 342, 344, 361, 386, 397, 400, 402, 424
Odette, Mary—108
Ododo—391
O'Donnell, Frank J. H.—102, 135, 108
O'Donovan, Desmond—340, 353, 355, 361
O'Donovan, Fred—54, 58, 63, 76, 166
O'Dowda, Brendan—453
Oebbecke, Ferdinand—104
Oedipe—274
Oedipus—249, 280, 283, 373, 390, 431, 440
Oedipus at Colonus—152, 283, 353, 360, 398, 431
Oedipus Now—403
Oedipus Rex—37, 58, 59, 60, 122, 202, 246, 265, 290, 296, 301, 360, 380
Oedipus The King—145, 295, 417
Oedipus the Tyrant—250
Oedipus Tyrannus—416
Oenslager, Donald—138, 147, 424
Oesterman, Philip—413
Oestreicher, Gerard—405
Offenback, Jacques—19, 137, 182, 239, 317, 416
Offence, The—166
Offering, The—440
Office Boy, The—15
Officer 666—61
Officers' Mess, The—89
Official State Theatre of Pennsylvania—319
Off-Off-Broadway Alliance—405
Off the Wall—403
O'Flaherty, Liam—312
O'Flaherty V. C.—103, 274, 361, 454
O'Flaherty, V. C. and his Press Cuttings—396
Of Love Remembered—369
O'Flynn, The—53
Of Mice and Men—205, 215, 412, 418
Of Thee I Sing—177, 185, 187, 209, 279, 376
Of Time and the River—318
Of V We Sing—23
Ogain, Sean—145
Ogilvy, Ian—453
Oglesby, Marshall—452
Ogodivelefthegason—368
O'Hanrahan, Kieron—248
O'Hara, John—222
Oh, Boy—82
Oh! Calcutta!—378, 399, 431, 433
Oh Captain!—309
Oh, Clarence—372
Oh Coward!—400, 421
Oh, Daddy!—172
Oh, Dad, Poor Dad, Mama's Hung You in the Closet, and I'm Feeling so Sad—329, 332, 337, 356
Ohee a Crook—228
O'Herlihy, Michael—285
"Oh, How I Hate to Get Up in the Morning"—87

O'Higgins, Harvey—71, 106
Oh, I Say!—67
Oh, Joy—94
Oh, Kay—142
Oh, Lady! Lady!—87, 410
Oh Les Beaux Jours—353, 379
Oh Men, Oh, Women—282, 424
Oh! Mr. Porter—437
Oh, My Dear!—88
Oh! Oh! Delphine—61
O'Horgan, Tom—338, 364, 366, 368, 371, 393, 394, 400, 414, 424, 438, 440, 445
Oh Starlings—394
"Oh, What a Beautiful Morning"—234
Oh! What a Lovely War—339, 344
O'Keefe Brewing Company—292
O'Keefe Center (Toronto)—325
O'Keefe, Richard—436
O'Keeffe, John—429, 432
O'Kelly, Seumas—84
Oklahoma—155, 176, 234, 238, 261, 285, 311, 340, 381, 447, 456
Okonhowski, George—63, 72
Olaf, Pierre—295
Old Acquaintance—222, 227
Old Adam, The—136
Old Bachelor, The—179
Old Bill—83, 87
Old Boston Museum Days—116
Old Boys, The—396
Old Colony Players—375
Old Country, The—435
Old Curiosity Shop, The—129
Old Dutch—48, 50
Oldenberg—368
Old English—126, 127
Old English Comedy Company—64
Oldest Living Graduate, The—426
Old Folks at Home, The—188
Old Friends—54
Old Garrick Theatre—337
Old Globe Theatre—396, 448
Old Glory, The—349, 350
Oldham, Derek—125, 132, 167, 177, 193, 376
Oldham, R. C.—64
Old Heidelberg—18, 22, 54, 126, 419
Old Homestead, The—23, 238
Old King Cole—432
Old Ladies, The—269, 273, 383
Old Lady 31—78
Old Lady Says No!, The—166, 178, 192, 197, 213, 228, 255, 259, 306
Old Lady Shows Her Medals, The—82
Old Maid, The—195, 199, 209, 445
"Old Man River"—184
Old Man, The—177
Old Movies—437
Old Ones, The—401
Old Soak, The—112, 123, 209
Old Story, The—108
Old Times—394, 408
Old Town, The—52, 55
Old Tune, The—347
Old Vic Company—152, 161, 167, 173, 233, 237, 241, 242, 243, 245, 246, 248, 249, 250, 251, 254, 255, 259, 260, 264, 268, 269, 270, 286, 285, 289, 296, 300, 306, 307, 311, 312, 313, 316, 317, 336, 455, 457
Old Vic Shakespeare Canon Cycle—121
Old Vic Theatre—323, 328, 329, 334, 381, 382, 388, 389, 390, 391, 395, 397, 398, 402, 408, 409, 411, 412, 415, 417, 422, 428, 432, 433, 444, 456
Old Women, The—108, 135
Old World—427
O'Leary, Con—96
Olimpia Theatre, The—40
Olimpic, The—46
Olive, Edyth—23, 27, 43, 58, 63
Oliver!—322, 435, 440
Oliver Cromwell—120
Oliver, Edna May—132
Oliver, Jean—119

Oliver, Rochelle—320
Oliver Twist—27, 61, 154, 440
Oliver, Vic—201, 218, 227, 253, 267
Olivia—4, 101, 311
Olivier, Laurence—114, 129, 137, 144, 150, 152, 159, 165, 166, 168, 172, 182, 186, 187, 192, 197, 198, 207, 208, 213, 214, 216, 223, 230, 242, 243, 245, 246, 249, 250, 253, 256, 260, 264, 267, 268, 274, 275, 283, 295, 305, 306, 308, 316, 320, 321, 322, 334, 335, 341, 342, 343, 346, 353, 355, 359, 366, 369, 375, 388, 391, 396, 398, 407, 411, 415, 436, 445, 452
Olivier Theatre—431
Olmos, Edward James—449
O'Loughlin, Gerald—300
Olsen and Johnson—211
Olsen, Ole—211, 216, 227, 240, 342
Olson, Nancy—240, 304
Olster, Fredi—396, 454
Olympia—285
O'Malley, Ellen—22, 26, 28, 49, 53, 102
O'Malley, J. Pat—236
O'Malley, Mary—435, 437, 446
O'Malley, Rex—119, 166, 211
Oman, Julia Trevelyan—366, 388, 396
Omero, Costas—393
O Mistress Mine—202, 241, 247, 251, 441
O'Morrison, Kevin—431
On a Clear Day You Can See Forever—351
On Approval—141, 231, 362, 424, 439
On Baile's Strand—23, 28, 38, 455
On Borrowed Times—211, 213, 215, 283
Once a Catholic—435, 437, 450
Once a Clown, Always a Clown—199
Once in a Lifetime—170, 180, 445, 453
"Once in a While"—114
"Once in Love with Amy"—257
Once is Enough—211
Once More, With Feeling—309, 317
Once Upon a Mattress—316
Once Upon a Time—429
Ondaatje, Michael—409
Ondine—255, 287, 327, 363
"One Alone"—142
O'Neal, Patrick—327
One at Night—395
One Crack Out—444
One Dam Thing After Another—151
One Day More—146
One Day of the Year, The—328
One Flew Over the Cuckoo's Nest—339, 396
One for the Money—216
One for the Pot—328
110 in the Shade—339
100 Years Old—180
O'Neil, Barbara—239
O'Neil, George—188
O'Neill, Barry—212
O'Neill, Eugene—77, 81, 84, 90, 99, 100, 101, 104, 105, 106, 109, 110, 111, 112, 114, 116, 123, 124, 126, 128, 129, 131, 132, 133, 135, 136, 138, 140, 142, 144, 145, 147, 156, 160, 162, 166, 176, 178, 185, 186, 189, 190, 192, 194, 203, 208, 210, 213, 214, 232, 233, 237, 241, 242, 247, 254, 256, 257, 259, 260, 275, 278, 283, 285, 295, 298, 304, 308, 309, 312, 313, 314, 318, 319, 329, 340, 345, 347, 356, 365, 366, 367, 368, 372, 374, 375, 391, 396, 398, 404, 405, 410, 411, 417, 422, 423, 424, 428, 429, 432, 438, 441, 452, 453
O'Neill, Henry—133
O'Neill, James—4, 38, 48, 67, 82, 123, 180
O'Neill, James, Jr.—11, 123
O'Neill, Maire—54, 58, 152, 153, 219

O'Neill, Michael—379
O'Neill, Rose—85
O'Neil, Nace—23, 99, 355
O'Neil, Peggy—53, 101, 135
O'Neil, Rose M.—53
O'Neil, Sheila—340
One Leg Over the Wall—322
One More River—315
One Mo' Time—450
One Night in Rome—93
One of the Family—133, 138
One Over the Eight—328
One Person—417
One Sunday Afternoon—186, 189, 416
One Third of a Nation—215
1001 Nights—452
One To One, The—394
One Touch of Venus—235
One Way Pendulum—318, 326
One Wild Oat—259
Ongley, Byron—31
On Golden Pond—447, 449
O, Nightingale—131
Onkel, Onkel—353
Only a Game—407
"Only a Rose"—132
Only Game in Town, The—377
Only Girl, The—71
Only Jealousy of Emer, The—401, 455
Only Way, The—45, 174
On Monday Next . . .—263, 264
On ne Saurauit Penser a Tout—284
O'Nolan, Fergus—102
On Strivers' Row—246
On the Frontier—217, 412
On the Harmfulness of Tobacco—316, 380
On the Level—358
On the Lock-In—436
On the Outside—415
On the Quiet—6
On the Rocks—188, 213, 422
On the Spot—172
On the Stage and Off—153
On the Town—240, 310, 339
On the Twentieth Century—442
Ontological-Hysteric Theatre—441
On Trial—71, 98
On Whitman Avenue—247
On With the Dance—134
On With the New—286
On Your Toes—200, 206, 291
Opatoshu, David—221
Open Air Theatre—269, 284, 335, 347, 354, 389
Open Circle—457
Open On Sunday—373
Open Theatre, The (New York)—368, 389
Open Window, The—378
Opera House, The (New London, Missouri)—46
Operation Iskra—415
Operation Sidewinder—387
Operette—212
Ophelia—188, 198, 223, 246, 311, 313, 318, 448
Oppenheimer, George—380, 441
Opp, Julia—7, 12, 109
Opportunity—99
Or—69
O'Ramey, Georgia—102
Orange Blossom—115
Oranges and Lemons—263
Orange Souffle—360
Orbach, Jerry—320, 326, 353, 364, 372, 400, 420
Orchestra Hall (Chicago)—24
Orchid, The—16, 18, 35
Ordeal of Gilbert Pinfold, The—451
Orders Are Orders—183
Ord, Robert—101
Ordway, Sally—430
O'Regan, Kathleen—149, 187, 212, 253
O'Regan, Terence—283
O'Reilly, Terry—440

Oresteia—176, 269, 329, 360, 376, 454
Oresteia and I—402
Oresteian Trilogy—22
Orestes—63, 366
Orff, Carl—455
Orison—340
Orison and Fando and Lis—330
Orkeny, Istvan—410, 422, 428, 444
Orlando Furioso—389, 391
Orlando, John—397
Orlob, Harold—88
Orlock, John—454
Orlov, Vassily—311
Orme, Denise—32
Orme, Michael—128
Ornadel, Cyril—340, 379
O'Rourke, J. A.—166
Orphan, The—407
Orpheum Theater (San Francisco)—34
Orpheus—403, 452
Orpheus Descending—304, 308, 316
Orpheus in the Underworld—317
Orr, Mary—239
Orsini, Victor—187
Orton, Joe—345, 359, 361, 365, 369, 379, 421, 423, 452, 455
Orwell, Sonia—360
Or When Queens Collide—455
Osato, Sono—240, 273
Osborn, Andrew—277
Osborne, John—313, 319, 328, 329, 331, 334, 346, 349, 350, 352, 359, 374, 375, 394, 396, 401, 402, 404, 417, 422, 427, 447, 452
Osborne, Vivienne—143
Osborn, Lincoln—117
Osborn, Paul—171, 211, 215, 217, 225, 235, 240, 243, 246, 272, 280, 283, 295, 308
Oscar, Henry—129, 223
Oscar Remembered—423
Oscar Wilde—202, 260
Osgood, Betty—369
Osgood, Charles—115
Osgood, Lawrence—353
O'Shaughnessy, John—248
O'Shea, Ethel—248
O'Shea, Milo—290, 328, 361, 378, 427, 441
O'Shea, Tessie—231, 248, 339
Osterman, Philip—378
Osterwald, Bibi—243
Ost, Geoffrey—259
Ostrovsky, Alexander—3, 44, 50, 122, 167, 197, 264, 361
Ostrow, Stuart—338
O'Sullivan, Denis—16
O'Sullivan, Maureen—333, 354, 394
O'Sullivan, Michael—353, 357, 404
Othello—3, 13, 23, 37, 53, 58, 63, 64, 67, 69, 72, 76, 80, 97, 103, 108, 114, 115, 128, 135, 173, 179, 183, 184, 197, 207, 213, 219, 228, 232, 237, 242, 245, 249, 254, 259, 260, 264, 274, 275, 290, 296, 300, 301, 306, 307, 312, 316, 317, 329, 335, 336, 340, 346, 348, 350, 361, 367, 389, 396, 397, 403, 409, 423, 424, 425, 429, 430, 432, 453, 454
Other Animals, The—295
Other Company—390
Other Girl, The—15
Other House, The—380
Other Men's Wives—376
Other People's Babies—68
Other People's Houses—227, 231
Other People's Lives—188
Other Place, The—416, 439, 444
Others—373
Otherwise Engaged—421, 434, 441
Otis, Elita Proctor—154
O'Toole, Peter—301, 316, 323, 342, 343, 352
Ottiano, Raphaella—128
Otway—97, 103, 284, 316, 366
Ould, Herman—166, 173
Our American Cousin—77
Our Betters—82, 123, 250

Our Father's Failing—410
Our Late Night—421
Our Little Cinderella—54
Our Miss Gibbs—48
Our Mr. Hepplewhite—94
Our Mrs. McChesney—74
Our Nell—126
Oursler, Fulton—148
Our Sunday Times—396
Our Town—73, 211, 215, 241, 248, 313, 319, 325, 382, 423, 425, 456
Our Wives—71
Ouspenskaya, Maria—121, 129, 167
Out Cry—84, 406
Outer Critics' Circle—449
Out from Under—360
Out of Bounds—334
Out of Hell—88
"Out of My Dreams"—234
Out of the Battle—182
Out of the Past—139
Out of the Question—344, 372
Out of the Sea—209
Out of the Whirlwind—285
Out of this World—267, 391, 447
Out on a Limb—427
Outrageous Fortune—243, 253
Outside Looking In—132
Outsider, The—124
Out to Win—107
Outward Bound—120, 130, 214, 224, 237
Outward Room, The—217
Over 21—239, 243
Overend, Dorothy—107
Over Gardens Out—379
Over Here!—413
Over Night—74
Overruled—63, 80, 274, 454
Over Sunday—96
Over the Moon—282
Over the River—61
Over the Top—83, 85
Overtones—77
Overture—136, 171, 180
Owen, Alun—316, 346
Owen, Bill—300
Owen, Catherine Dale—107, 142, 143
Owen, Cecil—105
Owen, Dan—456
Owen, Harold—68
Owen, Paul—377
Owen, Reginald—35, 57, 95, 142
Owen, R. Lichfield—114
Owen, Ruth Wynn—197
Owens, Elizabeth—366, 409
Owens, Reginald—43
Owens, Rochelle—371, 384, 402
Owens, William—146
Owl and the Pussycat, The—345, 358
Owl and the Pussy Cat Went To See . . .—383, 391, 398
Ox Cart, The—358
Oxford and Cambridge Theatre Company—396
Oxford Players—136. Playhouse—334, 340, 452
Oxford Union Drama Society (OUDS)—136
Oxford University Drama Society—135
Oxman, Philip—452
Oyston, Peter—366, 368

Pacey, Steven—391
Pacific 1860—248, 251
Pacific Overtures—426
Pacifists, The—85
Pacino, Al—371, 438, 454
Packard, William—359
Pack, Charles Lloyd—276, 401, 421
"Pack Up Your Troubles"—79, 235
Paddick, Hugh—310, 359
Paddy the Next Best Thing—101
Padilla, Sandy—400
Padlocks of 1927—148
Padlock, The—455

Padovani, Lea—271
Pagan Place, A—401
Page, Anthony—312, 346, 349, 374, 387, 394, 409
Page, Auston—88
Page from a Daughter's Diary, A—26
Page, Geraldine—101, 108, 278, 281, 287, 288, 295, 314, 348, 406
Page, Ken—430
Page, Norman—102
Paget, Dorothy—82
Page, Tilsa—234, 248
Paget, Nicola—427, 429
Paget, Rosamund—227
Paget, Violet—95
Pagnol, Marcel—133, 183, 288
Paid in Full—41
Paige, Elaine—443
Paige, Janis—287, 338
Pailleron, Edouard—29
Pain, Nesta—219
Pains and Penalties—59, 60
Painted Veil, The—178
Painter, Eleanor—74, 105
Painter's Palace of Pleasure—444
Painting the Town—294
Paint Your Wagon—272, 282
Pair of Sixes, A—141
Pair of Spectales, A—179, 264
Pair of Trousers, A—174
Pair of White Gloves, A—69
Pajama Game, The—287, 294, 306
Pakington, Mary—207
Palace of Truth, The—53
Palais Royal—63
Pal Joey—222, 286, 329, 340, 428
Palladium Pleasures—142
Palleas and Melisande—63
Palmer, A. M.—28, 203
Palmer, Betsy—427
Palmer, John—405
Palmer, Leland—371
Palmer, Lilli—216, 264, 265, 267, 358
Palmer, Peter—298
Palmer, Valentine—358
Palmetto Outdoor Historical Drama Association—374
Panama Hattie—222, 245, 424
Panama, Norman—298
Pan and the Young Shepherd—32
Panell, Beverly—409
Panell, Raymond—409
Pangborn, Franklyn—67
Panic—199
Panne—44
Pansy—164
Pantagleize—368, 375, 397, 451
Pantaloon—26
Panthea—70
Panther and the Unicorn, The—342
Pantomime Rehearsal, A—2
Pantomimes of Bip, The—278
Paolo and Francesca—11, 16, 76
Papas, Irene—368, 407
Paper Bag Players—369, 379
Paper Wheat—437
Paphnutius—72
Papp, Joseph—292, 301, 307, 312, 319, 323, 329, 335, 367, 369, 373, 374, 380, 381, 382, 383, 388, 389, 390, 395, 396, 398, 403, 410, 412, 415, 417, 418, 419, 422, 423, 426, 428, 430, 436, 445, 446, 448, 452, 454
Parade—197
Paradise—429
Paradise Lost—196
Paradise Now—375
Paralytic Hotel, The—39
Paramount Studios—189, 229
Pardoner's Tale, The—390
Pardon My English—186
Pardon My French—283
Parent, Gail—413
Parents and Children—378
Parents Terribles, Les—273
Parfitt, Judy—395
Pariah—219
Paris '90—276

Paris—96, 157
Paris Bound—150
Paris by Night—294
Parish, Mitchell—216
Parisian Love—154
Parisian Model, The—31, 90
Parisian Romance, A—22, 38
Parisienne, La—237, 269
"Paris Is a Paradise for Coons"—56
Paris to Piccadilly—276
Park—398
Parker, Alfred—197
Parker, Anthony—248
Parker, Cecil—187, 201, 218, 227, 230, 282
Parker, Dorothy—281
Parker, Flor—43
Parker, Frank—8
Parker, George D.—165
Parker, Harry—53
Parker, Lew—252, 252
Parker, Louis N.—3, 16, 20, 21, 30, 36, 50, 56, 58, 63, 67, 83, 95, 121, 127
Parker, Ross—280, 295
Parker, Steward—428, 431
Parker, Val—146
Parker, Will—234
Park Lane—376
Park, Phil—248
Parks, Trina—366
Park Theatre, The—46
Parlor, Bedroom, and Bath—83
Parlour Match, A—2, 90
Parnell—232
Parnell, Peter—455
Parnell, Val—295
Parnellite, The—84
Parolini, C.—116
Parone, Edward—347, 358, 374
Parr, Chris—379, 410, 436
Parr-Davies, Harry—218, 236, 263, 268, 282
Parrish, Elizabeth—333
Parrish, James—248
Parry, Dilys—245
Parry, Natasha—273
Parsifal—418
Parson, George—41
Parson, Hubert—119
Parson's Bride, The—166
Parsons, Donovan—126, 159, 166
Parsons, Estelle—332, 339, 357, 371, 381, 388, 393, 398, 418, 434, 436
Parsons, Geoffrey—263
Parsons, Nancie—120
Partage de Midi—274, 373
Partington, Jack A.—161, 162
Partners Again—111, 119
Party—182
"Party's Over, The"—216
Party Spirit, The—289
Party, The—310, 347, 411
Party With Betty Comden and Adolph Green, A—310, 434
Pasadena Community Playhouse—86
Pascal, Fran—371
Pascal, John—371
Pascal, Milton—239
Pascal, Stephen—451
Pasco, Richard—269, 273, 285, 302, 306, 366, 372, 379, 380, 389, 390, 396, 415, 417, 418, 439
Pasquin, John—430, 436
Passage to India, A—322
Passers-By—57
Passing Day, The—274
Passing of the Third Floor Back, The—43, 49, 67, 69, 153, 167, 209, 264
Passing-Out Parade, The—452
Passing Show of 1912, The—61
Passing Show of 1913, The—66
Passing Show of 1914, The—71
Passing Show of 1915, The—74
Passing Show of 1916, The—76
Passing Show of 1917, The—82
Passing Show of 1918, The—87
Passing Show of 1919, The—93

Passing Show of 1921, The—101
Passing Show of 1922, The—112
Passing Show, The—72, 118, 125, 432
Passionella—358
Passion Flower, The—99
Passion of Dracula, The—434, 443
Passion of Josef D.—344, 350
Passion, Poison, and Petrification—273, 366
Passion, The—395, 437, 445
Passmore, Walter—12, 15, 16, 26, 27, 32, 43, 121
Pasteur—115, 117, 146
Pastime of Monsieur Robert, The—359
Past Imperfect—345
Paston, George—53
Pastor, Tony—97, 215
Patachon—76
Patch, Blanche—154
Patch, Wally—268
Paternoster, G. Sidney—68
Paths of Glory—195
Patience—4, 63, 97, 167, 184, 193, 228, 245, 249, 255, 260, 264, 269, 285, 306, 330, 346, 362, 366, 373, 374, 376, 424
Patient, The—334
Patinkin, Mandy—426
Patmore, Derek—218
Paton, Alan—262
Patria II: Requiems for the Party Girl—403
Patriarch, The—147
Patricia—127
Patrick, Dora May—150
Patrick Henry Lake Liquors—424
Patrick, Jerome—123
Patrick, John—244, 246, 252, 256, 266, 281, 292, 302, 386
Patrick, Nigel—201, 206, 217, 253, 272, 282, 283, 309, 310, 322, 345, 347, 353, 365, 389, 402, 406, 427, 447
Patrick Pearse Motel, The—394
Patrick, Robert—374, 414, 417, 423, 444
Patriot for Me, A—292, 352, 398
Patriots—63, 64
Patriots, The—234, 238, 313
Patriot, The—42
Patsy, The—133
Patten, Francis Gray—139
Patterson, Dick—344
Patterson, Don—430
Patterson, James—333, 364
Patterson, Tom—286
Patton, Angela—359
Patton, Lucille—344
Patton, Pat—430, 439, 454
Patton, Shirley—396
Paturel, Dominique—373
Paul, Betty—267
Pauline—68
Paul, Kent—449
Paulo and Francesca—33
Paul Robeson—442, 448
Paulson, Arvid—235
Paulton, Edward A.—66
Paul Twyning—114
Paumier, Alfred—83
Pavek, Janet—288
Pavillion Theater—9
Pavlov, Harvey—290
Pavlow, Muriel—222, 290, 366
Pawle, Lennox—148
Pawley, William—149
Pawlings, Margaret—218
Paxinou, Katrina—223, 231, 273, 280, 360, 411
Payment Deferred—180, 202
Payne, B. Iden—82, 88, 127, 208, 214, 223, 228, 232, 296, 301, 307
Payne, Edmund—8
Payne, Laurence—264, 284
Payn, Graham—222
Pay the Piper—291
Payton, Lew—124

Payton-Wright, Pamela—385, 404, 420, 437
Peabody, Josephine Preston—54, 58, 116
Peace—379, 389
Peace in Our Time—253
Peacemaker, The—37
Peace on Earth—187, 189
Peach, C. Stanley—29
Peach, L. du Garde—69, 273
Peacock, Bertraum—106
Peacock, Kim—156, 191
Peacock, Thomas Love—276
Peacock, Trevor—331, 389, 439
Pearce, Vera—144, 206, 212, 218, 227
Peardon, Patricia—227
Pearle, Gary—439
Pearl Girl, The—67
Pearl, Jack—117, 140, 150, 163
Pearse, Ashton—57, 183
Pearson, Hesketh—126
Pearson, Richard—310
Pears, Peter—217, 260
Peasant Girl, The—74
Peaslee, Richard—359
Peck, Gregory—227, 234
Pecknold, Adrian—396
Peck, Raymond—30, 141
Peck, Sam—118
Peculiar Treasure, A—376
Pedagogue, The—348
Pedrick, Gale—218
Peebles, Melvin—400
Peepshow—266
Peep-Show, The—107
Peer Gynt—58, 114, 121, 135, 160, 184, 223, 242, 243, 273, 322, 336, 381, 388
Peggy—57
Peggy-Ann—142
Peggy From Paris—14
"Peg O'My Heart"—28, 62, 65, 66, 108, 116, 161, 179, 237
Peg Woffington—8
Pelham, Laura Dainty—18
Pelican Shakespeare, The—432
Pelican, The—127, 362
Pelissier, Anthony—267, 272
Pelissier, Constance—97
Pelissier Follies—69
Pelissier, Harry Gabriel—69, 447
Pelissier's Follies of 1938—212
Pelleas—58
Pelleas and Melisande—12, 95
Pelletier, Denis—432
Pell-Mell—79
Pember, Ron—373, 376, 387, 390, 414, 430
Pemberton, Brock—99, 112, 142
Pemberton, Madge—254
Pemberton, Max—79
Pemberton, Reece—278
Pendeleton, Austin—332, 368, 385, 421
Penders, The—54
Pendleton District Historical and Recreational Commission—423
Pendleton, Jack—236
Penelope—48, 285
Penfield, Roderic—23
Peniculescu, Radu—410
Penlay, W. S.—5
Penley, Graham—236
Penn, Arthur—321, 344, 427, 434
Pennington, Ann—66, 76, 87, 92, 99, 105, 124, 140, 157, 399
Penn, Leo—287
Penny for a Song, A—272, 335
Penny Plain—272
Penthouse Legend—408
Pentrass, Sari—78
People Are Living There—398
People of Our Class—212, 398
People Show, The—373, 379, 387, 390, 407
People's Theatre Society—103
"People Will Say We're In Love"—234
Peppard, George—309
Pepys, Samuel—143, 207

504

Perchance to Dream—245
Percival, T. Wigney—66
Percy, Edward—115, 218, 244, 296
Percy, Esme—45, 46, 72, 152, 153, 173, 177, 218, 250, 260, 263, 264, 269
Pere Goriot—291
Perelman, S. J.—182, 235, 333, 418
Perfect Alibi, The—157
Perfect Fool, The—106, 362
Perfect Gentleman, The—68
Perfect Woman, The—258
Performance Group—417
Performing Giant, The—359
Pericles—3, 109, 144, 219, 254, 307, 311, 368, 380, 409, 410, 416, 417, 453
Period of Adjustment—321, 331, 335
Peripherie—153
Perkins, Anthony—305, 358, 385, 413, 450
Perkins, Bobbie—140
Perkins, Julia—37
Perkins, Kenneth—194
Perkinson, Coleride-Taylor—376
Perkins, Osgood—124, 157, 189, 200
Perkins, Walter E.—5, 137
Perkin Warbeck—422
Perl, Arnold—295
Perlmutter, Mawruss—74, 82, 93
Peron, Eva—443
Perplexed Husband, The—57
Perr, Harvey—374, 422
Perrin, Sam—244
Perrins, Leslie—178
Perrottet, A.—270
Perry, Albert—100
Perry, Antoinette—36, 124, 125, 142
Perry, Clive—348, 382
Perry, Jimmy—421
Perry, John—212, 241, 263
Perry, Shauneille—393
Perry's Mission—395
Persians, The—353, 366, 367, 410
Personal Appearance—191
Persons, Julian—129
Persons, Nina—129
Persons, Truman Streckfus—129
Person Unknown, The—108
Perth Theatre Company—317
Pertwee, Bill—414, 421
Pertwee, Michael—366, 394, 435
Pertwee, Roland—72, 107, 148, 150, 172, 236, 242, 342
Peschkowsky, Michael Igor—180
Petch, Steve—454
Pete—76
Peter Grimes—246
Peter Ibbetson—75, 82, 103
Peterman, Joe—76
Peter Pan—22, 33, 50, 59, 69, 73, 77, 85, 90, 97, 109, 115, 122, 128, 129, 137, 145, 153, 160, 167, 174, 179, 184, 189, 193, 198, 203, 208, 209, 214, 228, 229, 232, 237, 243, 246, 250, 255, 261, 265, 268, 269, 280, 286, 287, 291, 296, 302, 307, 313, 318, 324, 330, 342, 349, 355, 362, 369, 376, 384, 404, 411, 418, 440, 447, 455, 456
Peter Pan and Emily—435
Peters, Bernadette—372, 413
Peters, Brock—402
Peters, Jean—211
Peters, Lauri—360
Peter's Mother—32
Peterson, Dorothy—150
Peterson, Eric—443
Peterson, Karen—201
Peters, Rollo—66, 112, 121, 127, 157, 190, 207, 369
Peter the Great—73
Petherbridge, Edward—365, 415, 423, 440
Petley, H. E.—152
Petrass, Sari—62, 107
Petrified Forest, The—195, 199, 231, 237
Petronella, Peggy—167
Petticoat Fever—195, 201
Petticoat Influence—172
Petticoat Rebellion, The—409
Pettitt, Wilfred—237
Pevney, Joseph—244
Peymann, Claus—439
Peyre, Andre—76
Pezet, Washington—202
Pfeiffer, Jules—251
Phaedra Britannica—422
Phantom of the Opera, The—423
Phedre—8, 13, 16, 54, 245, 306, 323, 342, 359
Phelps, Leonard P.—128, 180
Phelps, Pauline—36, 40
Phethean, David—360
Philadelphia, Here I Come—335, 348, 357, 363, 373
Philadelphia Story, The—216, 220, 265, 416
Philandere, The—37, 67, 128, 241, 359, 396, 430, 444
Philanthropist, The—389, 393
Philharmonic Society of New York—146
Philipe, Gerald—312
Philipp, Adolf—66
Philipp Hotz's Fury—347
Philips, Mary—200
Philip The King—72
Phillips, Andy—455
Phillips, Arthur—128, 198
Phillips, John—317
Phillips, Kate—12, 16, 33, 76
Phillips, Leslie—278, 294, 372, 435, 439, 456
Phillips Margaret—257, 268, 271, 300
Phillips, Mary—239
Phillips, Robin—386, 388, 390, 398, 401, 408, 410, 438, 454
Phillips, Sian—352
Phillips, Stephen—2, 11, 32, 33, 43, 45, 75
Phillpotts, Adelaide—143
Phillpotts, Ambrosine—294
Phillpotts, Eden—65, 69, 115, 126, 128, 143, 367
Philoctetes—319, 346
Philosophy in the Boudoir—381
Phi-Phi—114
Phipps, Charles John—33, 303
Phoenix '55—295
Phoenix Society—97, 103, 114, 121
Phoenix, The—108, 129
Phoenix Theatre—175, 286, 296, 297, 312, 318, 340, 349, 386, 395, 410, 426, 428, 429, 431, 436, 439, 440, 444, 451
Phoenix Too Frequent, A—249, 250, 266, 274
Photo Finish—333
Photograph, A—436
Physicists, The—339, 344, 356
Physioc, Joseph—11, 14, 20, 22
Piaf, Edith—256, 444, 451
Piazza, Ben—326, 354
Picard and Mirande—113
Picard, Andre—33, 107
Picardo, Robert—434
Picasso, Lamberto—136
Piccadilly Hayride—248
Piccadilly Theatre—162
Piccolo Della Citta di Milano—312
Piccolomini, The—59
Piccolo Teatro (Milan)—301, 323, 367
Picenardi, Sommi—95
Pichler, Maria—216
Pick a Number XV—351
Pickard, Helena—160
Pickens, Jane—221, 262
Picket Line—202
Pickett, George—151
Pickett, Mary—309
Pickles, Christina—440
Pickles, John—339
Pickles, Wilfred—277
Pick Up Girl—239, 243, 249, 251
Pickup, Ronald—359, 361, 367, 388, 390, 402, 436
Pickwick—340, 351, 363
Picnic—154, 281, 286, 411
Picnic on the Battlefield—340, 348
Picon, Molly—314, 326
Pictorial Smash—439
Picture of Dorian Gray, The—67, 245, 255, 300, 422
Pictures in the Hallway—318, 335, 360, 395
Pidgeon, Walter—129, 195, 298, 314, 361
Pieces of Eight—315
Pie Dish, The—58
Pied Piper, The—336
Pierre or the Ambiguities—416
Pierre Patelin—86
Pierrot the Prodigal—78, 135
Pietra Fra Pietre—53
Piff! Piff! Pouf!—19
Pigeons—353
Pigeons and People—186, 189
Pigeon, The—62, 68, 114
Piggot-Smith, Tim—414
Piggott, A. Stewart—88
Pignight—394
Pigott, J. Smith—8
Pig Pen, The—388
Pigs—124
Pike, Ivy—103, 184
Pilbrow, Richard—375, 381
Pilcer, Harry—56, 57, 74, 83, 330
Pilcher, Velona—155
Pilgrim—423
Pilgrim, Andrew—344
Pilgrim Players, The—39, 209
Pilgrim's Progress—423
Pilgrim, William Lepper—90
Pillars of Society, The—8, 22, 179
Pillars of the Community—438
Pinafore—167
Pinch-Me-Not—436
Pinchot, Rosamund—124, 153
Pinero, Arthur Wing—3, 4, 8, 12, 16, 21, 27, 30, 32, 43, 44, 46, 49, 54, 57, 62, 63, 68, 75, 84, 90, 95, 109, 110, 113, 114, 115, 128, 136, 153, 214, 242, 245, 255, 269, 274, 279, 316, 347, 354, 355, 360, 381, 382, 403, 409, 410, 423
Pinero, Miguel—415
Pinget, Robert—347
Pinkard, Maceo—113, 164
Pink Dominoes—75
Pinkie and the Fairies—45, 50
Pink Lady, The—40, 56, 59, 62
Pink String and Sealing Wax—236, 242
Pinkville—395
Pink, Wal—79, 83, 88, 94, 95, 97, 101, 107
Pinocchio—342, 349, 398, 403
Pins and Needles—107, 206, 219, 404, 424
Pinski, David—103
Pinter, Harold—283, 310, 315, 322, 332, 335, 337, 342, 343, 345, 346, 347, 348, 352, 359, 364, 365, 371, 379, 387, 390, 394, 395, 397, 401, 408, 415, 417, 421, 422, 424, 430, 436, 443, 444, 446, 450
Pinter Plays—371
Pinza, Carla—358
Pinza, Ezio—262, 288
Pioneer Days—31
Pioneer Players—59, 72, 84, 85, 95
Pious, Minerva—295
Pipe Dream—294
Piper, Aubrey—124
Piper, Frederick—182
Piper, John—300
Piper, The—54, 58
Pippa Passes—33
Pippin—400, 412
Pippin, Donald—415
Pip Simmons Theatre Group—390, 394, 432, 444
Piraikon Theatre—362
Pirandello, Luigi—114, 112, 135,
136, 148, 183, 260, 269, 285, 295, 301, 311, 316, 340, 341, 347, 348, 353, 360, 362, 380, 389, 396, 408, 416, 418, 452
Pirates—398
Pirates of Penzance—4, 45, 63, 145, 173, 184, 193, 228, 232, 245, 249, 255, 260, 264, 269, 274, 285, 290, 306, 316, 329, 330, 334, 349, 355, 362, 374, 376, 424, 429, 446
Piscator, Erwin—224, 228, 232, 240, 349, 362, 366
Pitlochry Festival—274
Pitt, Arthur—178
Pitt, George Dibdin—128
Pit, The—19
Pitts, Zasu—239
Pixly, Frank—1, 14, 20
Place des Arts—343
Place Without Doors, A—386
Plaice, Neville—431
Plaice, Stephen—431
Plain and Fancy—293, 299, 398, 455
Plaintiff in a Pretty Hat—299
Planche, J. R.—265, 275, 291, 296
Planchon, Roger—374, 380, 431
Planer, C.—17
"Plantation Company"—120
Plantation Revue—112
Plat du Jour—407
Platform—457
Platinum People, The—353
Platonov—323
Play—346, 347, 387
Play Actor's Society—39
Play and Other Plays—429, 440
Playbill—258
Playboy of the Western World, The—37, 50, 58, 59, 60, 65, 90, 137, 144, 193, 218, 250, 324, 375, 394, 402, 422
Player King, The—279
Player Piano—444
Player Queen, The—122
Players Classic Revival—313
Players, The—115, 122, 128, 136
Players Theater Club (London)—296, 297, 327
Player Under Three Reigns, A—209
Playfair, Arthur—63, 74, 83, 89
Playfair, Nigel—22, 32, 45, 50, 53, 67, 80, 83, 96, 103, 113, 115, 122, 127, 128, 135, 143, 145, 152, 173, 178, 179, 182, 188, 191
"Play Gypsies-Dance Gypsies"—141
Playhouse, The (Fredericton, New Brunswick, Canada)—350
Playing With Fire—335, 347
Play It Again, Sam—378, 384, 396
Playmakers—91, 319
Playpen—435
Play Pictorial—64, 130, 147
Plays and Players—307
Plays for Bleecker Street—332
Plays for England—334
Plays for Poem-Mimes—363
Play's the Thing, The—142, 155, 254, 409, 445, 452, 454
Play Strindberg—395, 409
Playwrights Company—217, 221, 222, 226, 230, 258
Playwright's Co-op—405
Playwrights Horizons—399, 425, 426, 429, 434, 439, 452
Playwrights Unit—387
Plaza Suite—371, 377, 379
Pleasance, Angela—389, 390
Pleasance, Donald—232, 249, 274, 294, 295, 300, 322, 345, 365, 366
Please—188
Please Get Married—92
Please Help Emily—79
Please Renew Your Membership—373
Please, Teacher!—197
Pleasure and Repentance—389, 403
Pleasure Bound—163
Pleasure Cruise—182
Pleasure Garden, The—166
Pleasure Man—162
Pleasure of His Company, The—315, 319, 427
Pleasure of Your Company, The—285, 309
Pleasure Principle, The—410
Pleasures Of A Gay City—60
Plebeians Rehearse the Uprising, The—119
Plenty—443
Plesch, Honoria—296
Pleshette, Suzanne—304
Pleydell, George—53, 75
Plotters of the Cabbage Patch Corner, The—398, 404
Plough and the Stars, The—144, 153, 193, 219, 323, 335, 407, 431, 436
Plowright, Joan—294, 298, 299, 301, 302, 305, 306, 311, 312, 317, 321, 322, 341, 342, 346, 367, 375, 380, 381, 382, 388, 395, 396, 407, 415, 424, 435
Plumber's Progress, The—421
Plumbers, The—53
Plummer, Christopher—296, 307, 310, 321, 323, 329, 339, 346, 396, 406
Plummer, Inez—100
Plumstead Players—382
Plunder—159, 428, 444
Plunkett, M. W.—86
Plus Fours—119
Plus Que Reiner—16
Pluta, Leonard—359
Pockriss, Lee—338
Podbrey, Maurice—384
Podgorny, Nikolai—121
Poe, Edgar Allen—415
Poel, William—8, 44, 68, 72, 96, 159, 167
Poetasters of Ispahan, The—63
Poet of the Anemones—379
Poets Theatre—406
Poil de Carotte—45, 89
Poindexter, H. R.—441
Pointing, Audrey—183
Point of Departure—268
Point of No Return—272, 280
Point, The—432, 440
Point Valaine—195
Poison Pen—212
Poitier, Sidney—250, 314
Pola, Eddie—206
Poliakoff, Stephen—394, 417, 421, 422, 428, 437, 444, 446, 452
Poliakoff, Vera—184
Polish Circot 2 Theatre—431
Polish Contemporary Theater—347
Polish Mime Theatre—353
Polish Popular Theatre—362
Polish State Jewish Theatre—306
Polish State Theatre—306
Pollard, Daphne—101
Pollock, Channing—19, 30, 94, 123, 132, 147, 148, 161, 224
Pollock, Ellen—242, 263, 273, 275, 279, 290
Pollock, John—83
Pollock, Sharon—416
Polly—115, 137, 422
Pollyanna—78, 128
Polly Preferred—117
Polly with a Past—82
Polsky, Abe—452
Polygamy—71
Pomander Walk—58
Pomerance, Bernard—394, 439, 449
Pompeii—403
Pompey the Great—54
Pom-pom—78
Ponder, Daniel—298
Ponder Heart, The—298, 384
Ponsonby, Claude—18, 307
Poole, G. W. S.—39
Poole, Roy—320
Poor Bitos—345, 356
Poor Little Ritz Girl—99
Poor Murderer—426
Poor Richard—126, 345

Pope, Muriel—102, 127
Popinjay, The—57
Poppelwell, Jack—294
Poppy—118, 127
Pop Theatre—362, 368
Popularity—31, 48
Porch—455
Porgy—149, 195, 224
Porgy and Bess—195, 209, 241, 279, 284, 329, 347, 431, 441
Porno Stars at Home—443
Portable Theatre—397
Porta, Elvio—430
Portage, Wisconsin—215
Porter, Cole—114, 125, 157, 164, 165, 171, 182, 188, 191, 196, 200, 211, 212, 217, 218, 222, 226, 233, 234, 239, 247, 258, 267, 281, 293, 301, 350, 391, 414, 437, 454
Porter, Don—344
Porter, Eleanor—78
Porter, Eric—274, 280, 284, 295, 318, 321, 373
Porter, Henry—72
Porter, Jimmy—302, 452
Porter, Neil—208
Porter, Nyree Dawn—431
Porter, Stephen—366, 368, 374, 375, 381, 383, 395, 404, 418, 428, 431, 437
Portfolio Revue—418
Portman, Eric—126, 144, 152, 159, 168, 188, 205, 208, 220, 258, 267, 289, 305, 309, 352, 384
Portmanteau Theatre—95
Portrait in Black—248
Portrait in Marble—202
Portrait of a Gentleman in Slippers—145
Portrait of a Madonna—316
Portrait of a Queen—352, 398
Portrait of Miriam—255
Portrait of Mrs. W.—116
Portrait of Van Gogh—395
Portraits of Women: From Chaucer to Dylan Thomas—312
Portrait, The—135
Posford, George—231, 202, 273
Posnick, Michael—436
Possessed, The—220, 342, 402
Posterity for Sale—367
Post, Guy Bates—7, 50, 61, 82
Postman Always Rings Twice, The—200
Post Office, The—68
Poston, Tom—260
Post Road—191
Post, W. H.—67, 132, 251
Po, Su Ting—188
Posy on a Ring, A—65
Potash, Abe—82
Potash and Perlmutter—66
Potash and Perlmutter in Society—74
Pot Luck—108
Pot of Broth, The—20, 44, 185, 445
Potter, Dennis—452
Potter, George—79
Potter, H. C.—258, 272
Potter, Paul—6, 16, 43, 50, 109, 268
Potter's Shop, The—103
Potters, The—119
Potting Shed, The—304, 308, 310
Poulton, A. G.—19
Pound on Demand, A—219, 250, 255, 316, 366
Pounds' Courtice—16, 58, 62
Pounds, Lorna—113, 134, 143
Pounds, Louie—15
Pounds, Toots—113, 134, 143
Pour Lucrece—310
Pour Vivre Hereux—66
Povah, Phyllis—100, 101, 117, 122, 125
Poverty Is No Crime—197
Powel, Clyde—209
Powell, Anthony—334, 340
Powell, Dick—372

Powell, Eleanor—163, 170, 195
Powell, Lovelady—333
Powell, Michael—277
Powell, Peter—241, 260, 273
Powell, Robert—395
Powell, William—99
Power, Ambrose—53
Power and the Glory, The—301, 310
Power, Hartley—272
Power of Darkness, The—24, 99, 166
Powers, Leona—30
Powers, James T.—43, 115, 121
Powers, Margaret—399
Powers, Marie—252, 260, 266
Powers, Tom—94, 170, 179, 192, 213
Power, Tyrone (1869-1931)—11, 22, 25, 30, 36, 41, 56, 79, 115, 180
Power, Tyrone—257, 284, 289, 302, 311
Pownall, David—428, 435, 437
Powys, Stephen—258
Prager, J.—219
Prager, Stanley—358
Prairie Outlaw, The—64
Prayer for My Daughter, A—436, 445, 447
Prayer Meeting or The First Militant Minister—378
Precedent—178
Prefaces to Shakespeare—251
Pre-Honeymoon—200
Prelude in Kazbek Street—408
Prelude to Exile—203
Preminger, Otto Ludwig—191, 214, 217, 321
Premise, The—324, 337
Prentice, Herbert M.—98, 196, 249
Prentiss, Paula—341
Presbrey, Eugene Wyley—1, 30, 179
Prescott Proposals, The—282
Present Arms—156, 222
Present from the Past, A—361
Present Indicative—411
Present Laughter—235, 247, 254, 299, 313, 353, 390
Preserving Mr. Panmure—57, 269
Presnell, Harve—321, 401
Press Cuttings—50, 65, 273, 366, 387
Pressly, Charles E.—180
Pressman, David—371
Preston, Robert—279, 287, 294, 305, 339, 340, 344, 357, 358, 413
Pretenders, The—68
Pretty Peggy—14
Pretty Sabine Women, The—96
Pretty Sister of Jose, The—15
Prevert, Jacques—260, 274
Previn, Andre—378, 414, 450
Price, Dennis—235, 344
Price, Evadne—122
Price, Gethin—421
Price, Gilbert—351, 378, 442
Price, Julius—55
Price, Leontyne—278, 279, 284
Price, Nancy—11, 12, 49, 53, 142, 156, 197
Price of Justice, The—401
Price of Peace, The—2, 5
Price of Thomas Scott, The—69
Price, Paul—395
Price, The—371, 377, 379, 384, 453
Price, Vincent—214, 217, 286, 423
Pride and Prejudice—196, 201, 204, 314, 360
Prideaux, James—400
Pride, Malcolm—295, 375
Pridmore, J. E. O.—60
Priestley, J. B.—177, 182, 188, 192, 196, 199, 202, 206, 207, 213, 214, 217, 219, 224, 228, 235, 242, 246, 248, 250, 253, 260, 261, 278, 279, 294, 304, 391, 409, 411, 414, 415, 440, 453
Prima Donna, The—43
Prime Minister, The—88
Prime of Miss Jean Brodie, The—358, 371, 377, 384, 416
Primrose—127

Primrose, Dorothy—246
Primrose, Peggy—212
Prince, Alonzo—88
Prince Charles Theatre—337
Prince Edward Theatre—175
Prince, Elsie—119
Prince, Harold—287, 323, 326, 327, 351, 357, 371, 375, 385, 393, 404, 406, 418, 426, 443, 449
Princely Fortune—188
Prince of Darkness—428
Prince of Homburg, The—431
Prince of India, The—30
Prince of Pilsen, The—14, 167
Princess and the Butterfly, The—109
Princess and the Swineherd, The—302, 318
Princess Caprice—62
Princess Charming—143
Princess Clementina, The—53
Princess Flavia—133
Princess Ida—136, 167, 184, 193, 290, 296, 316, 330, 346, 355, 373
Princess of Kensington, A—15
Princess Pat, The—74, 129
Princess Players—68, 69, 73
Princess Theater (Toronto)—9
Prince's Theatre, The—337
Prince, The—376
Prince There Was, A—88
Prince, William—230, 252, 272, 382
Pringle, Brian—348
Pringle, Casha—158
Printemps, Yvonne—115, 122, 144, 145, 165, 202
Prior, Allan—126
Priorities of 1942—230
Priscilla Runs Away—53
Prisoner of Second Avenue, The—394, 405
Prisoner of the Bastille, The—49
Prisoner of Zenda, The—45, 90, 133, 146, 194
Prisoners of War—195
Prisoner, The—288
Pritchett, John—295
Private Ear/The Public Eye, The—333
Privateer, The—233
Private Eye—366
Private Hicks—202
Private Life of Helen, The—282
Private Life of the Master Race, The—245
Private Life of the Third Reich—452
Private Lives—172, 176, 242, 260, 265, 340, 341, 383, 390, 403, 409, 411, 422, 425, 446
Private Parts—401
Private Prosecutor, The—312
Private Secretary, The—54, 123, 168, 174, 289
Privates on Parade—435, 445
Prividi, Joe—224
Problems of the Playwright—251
Proby, P. J.—435
Processional—131
Prochnik, Bruce—322
Proclemer-Albertazzi Company—348
Proctor, Catherine—109
Prodigal Son, The—27, 76, 78, 82
Prodigal, The—320, 325, 410
Producing Managers' Association—98, 121, 130
Productions d'Aujourdui—389
Professor Bernhardi—373
Professor Schelling—219
Professor's Love Story, The—122, 209, 232
Progress—114
Progress of Bora, the Tailor, The—374
Progress to the Park—316
Projector, The—390
Prologue to Glory—213
Promenade—378
Prometheus—451
Prometheus Bound—396
Promise—201

Promises, Promises—372, 379, 384
Promise, The—365, 380, 429
Pro Patria—59
Proposal, The—264
Proposition, The—393
Proscenium—187
Proscenium Productions—297
Prospect Theatre Company—382, 389, 397, 409, 410, 416, 417, 423, 432, 438, 439, 444, 447, 457
Proud, Frederick—409
Proud Prince, The—15, 18, 49
Proud Women, A—243
Prouse, Derek—322
Provincetown Players—77, 100, 129, 261
Provincial Life, A—361
Provincial Theatre Council—233
Provok'd Wife, The—95, 193, 208, 268, 341, 367, 409
Provost, Lord—256
Prowse, Juliet—357
Prowse, Philip—334, 390, 451
Proxopera—447
Prude's Fall, The—102
Prunella: Or, Love in a Dutch Garden—23, 32, 54, 68, 246
Pryce, Jonathan—421, 427, 453
Pryce-Jones, Alan—334
Pryde, Belinda—239
Pryer, Richard—21
Pryor, F. R.—151
Pryor, Maureen—396
Pryse, Hugh—272
P. S. 193—343
Psacharopoulos, Nikos—374
P.S. Your Cat is Dead—445, 452
Public Theatre, The—370, 379, 382, 383, 388, 390, 395, 398, 403, 407, 410, 415, 417, 420, 421, 446, 448, 454, 455
Puce a l'Oreille—89
Puerner, Charles—11
Pugliese, Armondo—430
Pulitzer Prize—98, 99, 101, 117, 124, 132, 138, 142, 147, 177, 186, 189, 191, 194, 195, 200, 204, 209, 211, 215, 217, 220, 224, 225, 230, 233, 238, 240, 244, 246, 251, 252, 256, 261, 262, 265, 266, 280, 286, 292, 293, 297, 298, 303, 305, 308, 313, 319, 321, 325, 327, 331, 337, 356, 378, 385, 402, 411, 420, 434, 443, 452
Pulman, Jack—386
Punchbowl—242
Punch, Judy and Co.—14
Puppet Plays—363
Puppet Prince, The—349
Puppets—126
Puppets of Passion—154
Purcell, Charles—92, 93, 99
Purcell, Harold—236, 245, 248, 273, 282, 317
Purcell, Henry—8, 274
Purchase, Bruce—397
Purdell, Reginald—183
Purdom, Edmund—274
Purdy, James—357
Purgatory—445
Purlie Victorious—326, 376, 385
Purnell, Louise—335, 367, 381
Purple Dust—335
Purple Mask, The—88, 89, 102
Purple Road, The—66, 186
Pursuit—380
Pursuit of Happiness—424
Pursuit of Pamela, The—68
Purvis, G.—9
Pushkin, Aleksander Sergeevich—137, 178
Puss in Boots—38, 77, 145, 168, 189, 203, 229, 261, 265, 307, 336, 401, 452
Puzzles of 1925—302
Pygmalion—72, 97, 142, 152, 179, 198, 208, 213, 219, 242, 249, 254, 273, 274, 285, 298, 309, 354, 398, 416, 423, 452

Pyjama Tops—379
Pyne, Natasha—436

Quadrille—277, 288
Quail Southwest—431
Quaker Girl, The—53, 242, 245, 369
Quality Street—7, 12, 110, 153, 223, 245, 268, 447
Quansan, Eddie—422
Quare Fellow, The—301, 319
Quartermaine, Charles—43, 49, 57, 113, 183, 206, 244
Quartermaine, Leon—3, 42, 67, 95, 107, 130, 134, 142, 206, 213, 253, 369
Quayle, Anna—451
Quayle, Anthony—183, 184, 188, 208, 249, 250, 255, 259, 264, 268, 269, 274, 276, 290, 295, 298, 301, 302, 322, 345, 365, 366, 373, 386, 388, 422, 427, 428, 444
Quayle, John—453
Queen and the Rebels, The—294
Queen Christina—438
Queen Elizabeth—269
Queen Elizabeth Playhouse—343
Queen Elizabeth Slept Here—263
Queen Gate Hall (London)—18
Queen High—141, 143
Queen of Hearts—189, 214
Queen of Scots—192
Queen of Spades, The—178
Queen of the Moulin Rouge, The—43
Queen of the Movies, The—71
Queen of the Stardust Ballroom—443
Queen Passionella and the Sleeping Beauty—376
Queens and Emperors—183
Queen's Comedy, The—269
Queen's Double, The—7
Queen's Enemies, The—80
Queen's Hall—40
Queen's Husband, The—156, 178
Queen's Minister, The—116
Queens of France—361
Queen's Theatre—40
Queen Victoria—116, 119
Queen Was in the Parlour, The—143
Queer Ones, The—96
Questa Sera Si Recita a Soggetto—301
Question of Age, A—32
Question of Fact, A—283
Question of Property, A—63
Quick, Diana—408, 443
Quick, Richard—430
Quiet Wedding—213
Quiet Week End—242
Quilley, Denis—282, 295, 299, 344, 395, 408, 411, 415, 435
Quilligan, Veronica—417
Quilter, Roger—59
Quinlan, Gertrude—342
Quinn, Anthony—135, 152, 235, 268, 269, 321, 322, 420
Quinn, Arthur Hobson—48
Quinney's—75
Quintero, Joaquin—112, 173
Quintero, Jose—278, 282, 298, 320, 327, 329, 332, 340, 345, 347, 351, 365, 371, 411, 423, 426, 438, 441
Quintero, Serafin—112, 144, 173, 245
Quitten, Sheila—417
Quoi Revent les Jeuenes Filles, A—218
Quotations from Chairman Mao—375
Quo Vadis—1, 5
Quo Vass Iss—229

Rabb, Ellis—319, 334, 347, 349, 355, 362, 368, 373, 374, 375, 381, 401, 424, 434, 437
Rabbit Race, The—341
Rabe, David—395, 398, 407, 410, 417, 419, 428, 436, 438, 444, 445

Rabelais—382, 396
Rabin, Leo—334
Raceward, Thomas—20
Rachel Lily Rosenbloom—419
Rachmaninoff, Sergei—137
Racine, Jean Baptiste—45, 54, 306, 323, 342, 353, 359, 380, 384
RADA Ex-Students' Club—129
Radd, Ronald—409
Rademacher, Gail—417
Radford, Basil—253, 280
Radio Rescue—313
Radnor, Gilda—420
Rado, James—364, 417
Rafferty's Chant—368
Raffles—39, 69, 179, 194
Raffles, the Amateur Cracksman—30
Raft, George—148
Ragland, Oscar—100, 203
Ragland, Rags—171
Ragni, Gerome—364, 400, 417
Ragotzy, Betty—251
Ragotzy, Jack—251
Ragotzy, Michigan—251
Rags—51
Rahn, Muriel—235
Rain—113, 117, 123, 124, 134, 232, 283, 391, 446
Rainbow Square—273
Rainbow, The—119
Raine, Jack—114
Raine, Lola—119
Rainer, Luise—269
Rain From Heaven—194
Rainger, Ralph—164
Rainmaker, The—288, 299
Rain or Shine—156
Rains, Claude—67, 103, 108, 113, 120, 144, 167, 170, 183, 184, 188, 271, 283, 369
Raisin in the Sun, A—314, 315, 319, 406
Raitt, John—244, 287, 354, 420
Rake's Progress, The—368
Rakhmanov, Leonid H.—311
Raleigh, Cecil—2, 5, 15, 16, 49, 57, 62, 67, 73, 79
Ralph, Jessie—88
Rambeau, Marjorie—82, 87, 105, 121, 391
Ramblers Quartet—151
Ramblers, The—141
Ramhackle Inn—239
Ramos, Richard—335
Ramsay, Allan—264
Ramsay, Remak—422
Ramsden, Molly—114
Ramsey, Ethel—206
Ramsey, John—59
Ramuz, D. F.—295
Ranalow, Frederick—103, 127, 177
Randall, Andre—182
Randall, Carl—87
Randall, Juliet—328
Randall, Rob—400, 413
Randall, Tony—309
Rand, Ayn—195, 408
Randell, Pamela—212
Randell, Ron—282
Randolph, Amanda—230
Randolph, Clemence—113, 123
Randolph, Elsie—159, 196, 213, 244
Randolph, John—221
Randolph, Louise—140
Random Happenings in the Hebrides—389
Rand, Sally—450
Rands, Leslie—193
Rand, Violet—7
Ranee of Sarawak, The—168
Ranevsky, Boris—172, 205
Rang Tang—148
Ranken, Fredrick—10, 14
Rankin, Arthur McKee—73, 194
Rankin, Phyllis—194
Rann Kennedy, Charles—173
Ransley, Peter—395, 415
Ranson's Folly—81
Raot, Nino—353

Rape of Lucretia, The—301
Rape of the Belt, The—305
Rape Upon Rape—317, 319, 375
Raphael, John—75, 103
Raphaelson, Samson—132, 191, 199, 217, 225, 233
Rapp, C. W.—77
Rapp, G. L.—77
Rapp, W. J.—163
Rapson, Ralph—343
Rasch, Albertina—221, 370
Rashomon—314, 334, 356, 410
Raskin, A. H.—331
Rathbone, Basil—102, 103, 108, 111, 112, 114, 118, 155, 168, 181, 194, 252, 268, 369
Rathbone, Guy—67, 72
Rathbone, Irene—103
Rathgeber, Ralph—104
Ratoff, Gregory—207, 325
Rats!—119
Rats Mass—389, 424
Rats of Norway, The—187
Rats, The—334, 374, 381
Rat, The—127
Rattigan, Terence—189, 191, 202, 218, 222, 231, 236, 241, 248, 251, 258, 261, 263, 264, 268, 277, 283, 289, 308, 310, 322, 340, 374, 387, 391, 403, 407, 415, 435, 436
Rattle of a Simple Man—334, 343
Rauh, Ida—99
Rau, Santha Rama—322
Rawdon, Willoughby—101
Rawlings, Margaret—178, 219, 254, 274, 296
Rawlins, Lester—378
Rawlinson, Brian—440
Rawls, Eugenia—244
Rawson, Graham—250
Rawson, Tristan—181, 217
Ray, Andrew—266, 329, 365
Rayburn, Joyce—372, 427
Ray, Carol—268
Raye, Carol—222, 227
Raye, Martha—221
Rayfiel, David—343
Ray, James—323, 333, 349, 374
Rayman, Sylvia—273
Raymond, Gary—309, 338
Raymond Hitchcock's Pinwheel Revel—112
Raymond, Maud—8, 30
Raymond, Paul—414, 427, 430
Rayne, Leonard—137
Rayner, Minnie—127, 207, 218, 229
Ray, Nicholas—247
Ray, Rene—227, 273
Ray, R. G.—68
Ray, R. J.—84, 114
Razaf, Andy—164, 171
Razzle-Dazzle—79
Read, Al—288, 295
Reade, Charles—33, 37, 45, 54, 174
Reader, Ralph—206, 213, 273, 291
Reader's Theater—321
Reading, Beatrice—311, 314
Ready Money—63
Ready Steady Go—416
Rea, Lawrence—21, 43
Real Charlotte, The—422
Real Inspector Hound, The—372, 431, 436
Realities—90
Real Thing, The—56
Reaney, James—367
Rear Column, The—443, 444
Reardon, Dennis—390, 407
Reardon, Marian—346
Re-Arrangements—451
Reason the Sun King—401
Rea, Stephen—429, 436
Rea, William—92, 120, 136, 185
Rebecca—222, 224, 225, 232, 237, 244, 429
Rebecca of Sunnybrook Farm—52
Rebellion in Ballycullen, The—96
Rebel, The—64
Rebel Women—426, 428

Rebori, Andrew M.—86
Reckford, Barry—311, 340, 396, 397, 417
Reckford, Lloyd—323
Reckoning, The—378
Reclining Figure—287, 292
Recluse Balls, The—366
Recluse, The—360
Recovery, The—347
Recruiting Officer, The—210, 237, 301, 342, 455
Reday, Horst—295
Red Bright and Blue—200
Red Buddha Theatre—406
Red Convertible, The—396, 399
Red Cross—374
Red Dawn, The—92
Red Devil Battery Sign, The—420, 433, 439
Redemption—90, 249
Red Eye of Love, The—326
Red Falcon, The—447
Redfarn, Robert—450
Redfarn, Roger—421, 427
Red Feather—15
Redfield, Billy—240
Redfield, William—262, 283, 400, 433
Redford, George—13, 60
Redford, Robert—327, 338
Redford, William—252
Red Fox/Second Hangin'—444
Redgrave, Corin—330, 333, 334, 394
Redgrave, Lynn—334, 353, 355, 364, 395, 401, 426, 437
Redgrave, Michael—202, 207, 208, 214, 217, 223, 230, 239, 255, 260, 264, 267, 268, 274, 284, 285, 294, 300, 310, 311, 315, 322, 346, 354, 396, 446, 450
Redgrave, Vanessa—310, 312, 316, 322, 329, 358, 398, 402, 409, 410, 451
Redgrave, Will—228
Redhead—314, 368, 418
Red, Hot, and Blue—200, 383
Red Magic—347
Redman, Joyce—235, 245, 254, 258, 260, 266, 273, 295, 310, 346, 353, 355, 359, 452
Red Mill, The—30, 34, 97, 246
Redmond, Johanna—59
Redmond, Liam—293
Redmond, Moira—373, 379, 386, 394
Red Moon, The—47
Redpath, Oliver—1
Red Pepper—111
Red Peppers—201, 391
Red Petticoat, The—62
Red Riding Hood—214, 250, 269
Red Roses for Me—248, 294, 330, 335
Red Runner, The—455
Red Rust—167
Redskin, The—30
Redstone, Willy—75, 102
Red, White and Maddox—378
Redwood, Manning—439
Reece, Brian—276, 287, 336
Reed, Alaina—442
Reed, Carol—151, 159
Reed, Florence—50, 82, 100, 123, 140, 160, 214, 244, 370
Reed, Gavin—402
Reed, Henry—375
Reed, John—76
Reed, Joseph Verner—412
Reed, Mark—195, 205, 206
Reed, Napoleon—235
Reed, Walter—190
Reel, Renee—113
Ree, Pamela—443
Rees, Roger—438, 447, 453
Rees, Roland—381, 382, 394, 397, 410, 431, 439, 455
Reeve, Ada—4, 15, 201, 241, 363
Reeve, Christopher—426, 436
Reeves, Bettina—437
Reeves, Geoffrey—372
Reeves-Smith, Henry—215
Reflected Glory—200

Reflections of Mark Twain, The—454
Reformer, The—37
Refugee Artists Group—216
Regan, Kathleen Patricia—104
Regan, Michael—56
Regan, Sylvia—278, 281
Regeneration—422
Regent's Park Open Air Theatre—279
Regiment, The—114
Regina—247, 262, 377, 455
Regnard, Jean-Francois—218
Regnis, Louise—108
Regy, Claud—379, 396
Rehan, Ada—22, 55, 85, 104, 146
Rehan, Arthur—104
Rehan, Mary Kate—104
Rehearsal, The—135, 328, 332, 350, 430
Reicher, Frank—111, 355
Reid, Alexander—388
Reid, Beryl—290, 291, 299, 352, 389, 415, 417, 431, 432
Reid, Carl Benton—257
Reid, Fiona—451
Reid, Hal—104
Reid, Kate—344, 357, 449
Reid, Sheila—361
Reid, Trevor—277
Reilly, Charles Nelson—327, 414, 449
Reilly, Frank—159
Reiner, Carl—257, 338
Reinhardt, Gottfried—239
Reinhardt, Heinrich—52, 58, 66
Reinhardt, Max—56, 58, 59, 61, 68, 113, 124, 135, 153, 182, 193, 230, 233, 234, 238, 205, 212, 265, 313, 425
Reis, Kurt—389
Reiss, Amanda—334, 354, 389
Reizenstein, Elmer—71, 84, 98
Rejane, Gabrielle—8, 23, 27, 29, 33, 76
Rejuvenation of Aunt Mary, The—55, 233
Relapse, or Virtue in Danger, The—269
Relapse, The—241, 255, 367, 374, 401
Relations Are Best Apart—289
Relatively Speaking—365
Relative Values—273, 410
Relph, George—67, 94, 105, 151, 282, 324
Relph, Phyllis—107
Reluctant Debutante, The—293, 294
Reluctant Heroes—268, 428
Reluctant Peer, The—345
Relyea, Marjorie—1
Remains to Be Seen—271, 278, 280
Reman, Richard—439
Remarkable Mr. Penny Packer, The—282, 294
Remember Louvain—76
Remember the Truth Dentist—417
Remick, Lee—357, 429
Remnant—83
Removalist, The—409
Renard, Jules—10, 85, 89
Renaud, Madeleine—260, 280, 306, 307, 347, 354, 373, 379, 396, 429
Rendel, Robert—93
Rendez-Vous de Senlis, Le—274
Rendle, Adrian—348
Rendle, Thomas McDonald—146
Rene, Louie—37
Renfield, Elinor—219, 439
Renga Moi—422
Rennie, James—140, 186, 356
Rents—451
Repertory Players, The—126, 128, 144, 208, 249
Repole, Charles—424, 452
Representative, The—340
Reprobate, The—96
Republic Frolics, The—185
Republic Theater (New York)—5
Request Program—415
Requiem for a Nun—307, 314, 319, 340

Requital—166
Resistible Rise of Arturo Ui, The—354, 375, 376, 381
Resnick, Muriel—344
Resounding Tinkle, A—307, 311
Respectable Wedding, A—447
Restoration of Arnold Middleton, The—368
Resurrection—16, 193, 249
Retford, Ella—336
Retrieved Reformation, A—52
Return Half, The—129
Return of A. J. Raffles, The—421
Return of Buck Gavin, The—97
Return of Imray, The—72
Return of Peter Grimm, The—56, 60, 109, 264
Return of Sherlock Holmes, The—120
Return of the Native—430
Return of the Prodigal, The—28, 44, 73, 260
Return, The—283
Return To My Native Land—435
Reud, Robert—235
Reunion—452
Reunion in Vienna—177, 185, 191, 396, 402, 441
Revel, Billy—195
Revel, Harry—244
Revelle, Hamilton—4
Revenge—379
Revenge of the Law—403
Revenger's Tragedy, The—360, 367, 382, 416
Revenge With Music—191
Revere, Anne—191, 320
Revill, Clive—322
Revisor—197
Revis, Victor—394
Revner, Katherine—111
Revue of Revues, The—59
Revue Russe—116
Reynard the Fox—354
Reynolds, Alfred—128, 143, 182, 384
Reynolds, Burt—327
Reynolds, Debbie—406, 412
Reynolds, Dorothy—289, 305, 322, 364
Reynolds, E. Vivian—21, 280
Reynolds, James—99, 105, 118, 126
Reynolds, John—68
Reynolds, Jonathan—418, 452
Reynolds, Thomas—36, 126, 183, 233
Reynolds, Tim—379
Reynolds, Virginia—61
Reynold, Walter—192
"Rhapsody in Blue"—142
Rhinoceros—322, 326, 331
Rhoades Opera House—46
Rhoda in Potatoland—424
Rhodes, Harrison—42
Rhodes, Marjorie—339
Rhodes, Miles—339
Rhodes, Nancy—455
Riano, Rene—106
Rianza, Yetta—95
Ribman, Ronald—351, 357, 368, 372, 399, 434
Ricardel, Molly—181
Riccardo, Rona—226, 227
Ricci, Mario—403
Rice, Alice Heggan—19
Rice, Andy—99
Rice, Edward Everett—23, 129
Rice, Elmer—40, 71, 94, 98, 113, 117, 156, 159, 163, 164, 166, 176, 185, 186, 189, 190, 191, 198, 204, 206, 208, 209, 210, 221, 222, 229, 232, 235, 244, 251, 254, 273, 291, 309, 369, 439
Rice, John C.—184
Rice, Peter—335
Rice, Tim—393, 403, 404, 440, 443
Rich and Famous—428
Richard, Amy—11
Richard Carvel—1
Richard II—3, 8, 54, 59, 80, 68, 73, 103, 128, 144, 145, 166, 167, 173,

188, 193, 207, 208, 228, 242, 254, 255, 264, 273, 274, 280, 285, 295, 301, 302, 317, 323, 335, 347, 348, 374, 375, 382, 389, 415, 416, 417, 453, 454

Richard III—8, 23, 44, 50, 54, 58, 63, 68, 76, 80, 84, 90, 96, 103, 109, 121, 122, 137, 160, 188, 193, 202, 208, 219, 228, 231, 242, 264, 284, 285, 286, 301, 303, 306, 307, 329, 334, 341, 346, 347, 360, 367, 368, 388, 389, 396, 402, 403, 408, 418, 422, 429, 437, 439, 445, 446, 452, 454, 455

Richard of Bordeaux—183, 190, 208, 292

Richards, Angela—427

Richards, Beatrix—218

Richard Schechner Performance Group—440

Richards, Cicely—189

Richards, Cliff—349, 362

Richard's Cork Leg—401

Richards, Lloyd—314, 345, 357, 358

Richardson, Douglas—354

Richardson, H. M.—69

Richardson, Howard—244, 455

Richardson, Ian—336, 345, 348, 367, 373, 380, 388, 390, 403, 415, 417, 422, 429, 455

Richardson, Jack—320, 325

Richardson, Jazzlips—164, 171

Richardson, Leander—90

Richardson, Lee—332, 413

Richardson, Ralph—143, 144, 159, 172, 178, 183, 184, 187, 188, 192, 196, 201, 208, 213, 217, 242, 243, 245, 246, 248, 249, 250, 252, 254, 255, 267, 278, 283, 300, 302, 305, 315, 334, 346, 359, 361, 368, 379, 386, 394, 401, 435, 445

Richardson, Robert—452

Richardson, Tony—266, 294, 299, 305, 306, 307, 311, 312, 314, 316, 321, 328, 329, 334, 347, 381, 401, 402, 409

Richards, Regina—92

Richards, Shelah—153

Richelieu—13, 23, 33, 49, 58, 68, 76, 84, 90, 229

Richie, George—49

Rich, Irene—261

"Rich Kid's Rag"—446

Richman, A.—112, 116, 139

Richman, Arthur—243

Richman, Charles—22, 31, 225

Richman, Harry—140, 176

Richmond, Brian—425

Richmond, David—434

Richmond, Fiona—427

Richmond, Susan—97

Richmond, Wyn—171

Rich Mr. Hoggenheimer, The—31

Rich, Roy—264, 268, 269, 273, 274, 278, 279, 283, 301

Ricketts, Charles—107

Riddle, Richard—173

Riddle: Women, The—87

Ride a Black Horse—395

Ride a Cock Horse—352, 359, 452

Ride Across Lake Constance, The—401, 410

Riders to the Sea—22, 38, 50, 59, 445

Ridge, Stanley—190

Ridge, Vimy—86

Ridiculous Theatre Company—415, 418, 429, 438, 446

Ridi, Pogliaccio—119

Ridley, Arnold—135, 151, 432

Rietti, Victor—285, 316

"Riff Song"—142

Rigby, Arthur—158, 165, 171, 243

Rigby, Edward—275

Rigby, Harry—256, 425, 450

Rigby, Terence—435

Rigg, Diana—327, 336, 386, 401, 402, 408, 416, 422, 443

Riggs, Lynn—176, 180, 200, 234, 269, 291

Right Christmas Caper, A—440

Right Honourable Gentleman, The—345, 352

Right To Strike, The—103

Right You Are If You Think You Are—136, 148, 347, 353, 362

Rignold, George—64

Rignold, Lionel—97

Rile, Lawrence—191

Riley, James Whitcomb—87

Riley, Joan—315

Rimbaud, Arthur—375

Rimers of Eldrich, The—424

Rinehart, Mary Roberts—48, 99, 100, 161, 207, 313

Ring—438

Ring and the Book, The—142

Ring Around the Moon—267, 422

Ring, Blanche—10, 14, 20, 21, 30, 36, 47, 52, 61, 330

Ringer, The—143

Ring for Catty—299

Ring in the New—275

Ringkmap, Jonathan—439

Ringland, Byron—425

Ringling Brothers—77

Ring of Truth—315

Ring Out the Bells—280

Ring Round the Moon—279, 296, 315, 376

Rintels, David W.—421

Rio Grande—429

Rio Rita—148

Rip Off—430

Rip Van Winkle—4, 44, 69, 104, 137, 229, 254, 428

Riquet with the Tuft—275, 324

Riscoe, Arthur—217, 291

Risdon, Elizabeth—313

Rise Above It—227

Rise and Fall of the City of Mahagonny, The—354, 456

"Rise 'n Shine"—182

Rise of Silas Lapham, The—93

Rising Generation, The—120

Rising of the Moon, The—36, 38, 44, 54, 59, 185, 445

Rising Sun, The—95, 250

Riske, Douglas—402

Risqué, W. H.—4, 7, 8

Risso, Richard—317, 375, 381

Ritchard, Cyril—142, 151, 158, 165, 172, 212, 218, 222, 231, 242, 245, 255, 263, 269, 279, 282, 283, 304, 309, 332, 340, 351, 367, 389, 420, 441

Ritchie, Adele—25, 35, 174

Ritchie, Anna Cora Mowatt—415

Ritchie, Carl—375, 381

Ritchie, June—401

Rites—380, 381

Ritman, William—364

Rittenhouse, Florence—161

Ritter, Thelma—304

Ritt, Martin—250, 257, 288, 293

Ritz, Al—356

Ritz, The—413

Rivals, The—3, 13, 33, 53, 54, 64, 68, 80, 115, 121, 135, 152, 188, 214, 228, 245, 259, 300, 361, 362, 396, 439, 444

Rivera, Chita—293, 298, 304, 320, 345

River Line, The—278, 279

River Niger, The—400, 406, 415

Riverside Nights—143

Riverside Studios—429, 431, 444, 448

Rivers, Max—127, 134, 151, 158, 165, 202, 206

Riverwind—333

Riviera Girl, The—82

Rix, Brian—268, 289, 310, 328, 345, 365, 394

Rizer, Elsie—99

Roache, Viola—74, 330

Road House—183

Roadside Theatre—444

Road, The—354

Road to Happiness, The—152

Road to Rome, The—148, 155, 207

Roar China—171

Roar Like a Dove—305

Roar of the Greasepaint—The Smell of the Crowd, The—351

Robards, Jason, Jr.—298, 309, 320, 326, 332, 344, 345, 371, 381, 402, 411, 428, 441

Robards, Jason, Sr.—342

Robber Bridegroom, The—424, 431

Robbers, The—417

Robbery, The—108

Robbins, A. E.—45

Robbins, Barbara—171

Robbins, Jerome—217, 240, 244, 252, 257, 262, 266, 271, 276, 287, 298, 304, 314, 332, 344, 374, 418, 454

Robbins, Rex—332, 351, 451

Robb, Lotus—83

Roberta—187

"Roberta"—246

Robert and Elizabeth—346

Robert E. Lee—119, 120

Robert, J. H.—259, 330

Roberts, Arthur—189

Roberts, Ben—248

Roberts, C. E. B.—191

Roberts, Cledge—176

Roberts, Evelyn—206, 336

Roberts, Florence—153

Robertshaw, Jerrold—21, 84, 229

Roberts, Howard A.—366

Roberts, J. H.—258

Roberts, Joan—234, 238, 244

Robertson, Bill—454

Robertson, Cliff—304

Robertson, Guy—148, 164, 190

Robertson-Hare, J.—143

Robertson, H. Brough—88

Robertson, Ian—3, 203

Robertson, J. R.—123

Robertson, Liz—455

Robertson, Margaret—198

Robertson, Pax—63

Robertson, Toby—285, 316, 334, 341, 375, 382, 389, 397, 403, 410, 416, 432, 438, 439, 455

Robertson, Tom—16, 166, 254

Robertson, T. W.—403

Robertson, W. Graham—45

Roberts, Pernell—27

Roberts, Rachel—285, 286, 290, 295, 296, 316, 346, 406, 435

Roberts, Ralph—79

Roberts, Rene—206, 222

Roberts, Theodore—11, 161

Roberts, Tony—344, 372

Roberts, Vera—270

Roberts, William—403

Robert's Wife—207

Robeson, Paul—100, 135, 141, 145, 150, 173, 184, 190, 237, 245, 316, 432, 442

Robespierre—8

Robey, George—79, 94, 101, 113, 120, 126, 134, 152, 292

Robin Hood—32, 59, 104, 167, 179, 232

Robin Hood and the Babes in the Wood—193

Robins, Edward—120

Robins, Elizabeth—280

Robins, Leo—165, 263

Robinson, Andy—381

Robinson, Bill "Bojangles"—156, 170, 219, 265

Robinson, Charles—186

Robinson Crusoe—4, 38, 59, 77, 78, 115, 153, 174, 184, 198, 243, 307, 362, 369, 391, 451

Robinson, Earl—291

Robinson, Edward G.—94, 117, 121, 144, 145, 148, 152, 298, 411

Robinson, Henry J.—63

Robinson, Joe—276

Robinson, John—253

Robinson, Lennox—58, 59, 63, 64, 76, 91, 97, 106, 110, 135, 145, 166, 179, 184, 188, 193, 202, 208, 224, 285, 313

Robinson, Margaret—85

Robinson, Norah—126, 150

Robinson, Percy—253, 369

Robinson, S. L.—54

Robins, Phyllis—218

Robins, Toby—366, 424

Robles, Emmanuel—262

Robman, Steven—440, 451

Robson, Eleanor—1, 7, 11, 15, 27, 35, 119

Robson, Flora—124, 126, 145, 178, 182, 183, 188, 192, 207, 208, 218, 230, 233, 248, 260, 263, 266, 274, 283, 296, 299, 312, 315, 373, 376, 383

Robson, James—439

Robson, May—25, 144, 233

Robson, Stuart—17

Roche, Arthur Somers—73

Roche, Dominic—272

Rochester, Eric Portman—309

Rochez, Harry—55

Rock, Charles—48, 49

Rockefeller Foundation—154, 405

Rockets—113

Rockets in Ursa Major—334, 336

Rocket to the Moon—220, 258

Rocking the Town—299

Rock, Jerry—315

Rockwell, Frederick—97

Rockwell, George "Doc"—99, 240

Rock, William—47

Rocky Horror Show, The—409, 425

Rodal, J. L.—398

Rodda, Peter—451

Roden, Illa—216

Roderick, William—347

Rodgers and Hammerstein—240, 252, 261, 264, 281, 285, 290, 291, 294, 301, 307, 313

Rodgers and Hart—131, 140, 142, 144, 200, 201, 210, 212, 429

Rodgers, Anton—345, 395, 408, 429, 439

Rodgers, David—450

Rodgers, Mary—357

Rodgers, Richard—92, 99, 103, 131, 132, 140, 149, 151, 156, 163, 164, 170, 173, 196, 205, 206, 211, 217, 230, 234, 237, 238, 244, 247, 262, 266, 271, 309, 314, 316, 329, 332, 348, 351, 366, 374, 381, 386, 418, 438, 447, 454, 456

Rodway, Norman—339, 388

Rodzinski, Arthur—238

Roe, Basset—83, 194

Roebling, Paul—338

Roe, Patricia—333

Roffey, Jack—299, 346

Rogers, Alex—30, 41, 48

Rogers, Ann—284, 288, 338, 358

Rogers Bros. in a Reign of Terror—179

Rogers Brothers in Central Park, The—1

Rogers Brothers in Harvard, The—10, 45

Rogers Brothers in Ireland, The—25

Rogers Brothers in London, The—14

Rogers Brothers in Panama, The—35

Rogers Brothers in Paris, The—19, 45

Rogers Brothers in Washington, The—6, 45

Rogers Brothers, The—45, 179, 215

Rogers, Doris—197, 207, 236

Rogers, Ginger—164, 170, 357

Rogers, Gus—1, 6, 10, 14, 19, 45

Rogers, Katherine—240

Rogers, Mary—316

Rogers, Max—1, 6, 10, 14, 19

Rogers, Paul—264, 269, 274, 283, 285, 290, 295, 296, 300, 302, 310, 311, 315, 352, 359, 371, 386, 417, 429, 436, 437, 447, 455

Rogers, Will—61, 82, 87, 107, 111, 124, 413

Rogueries of Scapin, The—58

Rohmer, Sax—113

Rolf, Frederick—352

Rolfe, Mary—239

Rolland, Romain—167

Rolle, Esther—380, 400

Rollicking Girl, The—25

Rollit, George—15

Rollo—100, 315

Rollo's Wild Oat—100

Rolls Hyphen Royce—435

Roloff, Michael—410

Rolyat, Dan—48

Roly-Poly—224

Roly-Poly and Without the Law—62

Roly-Poly Eyes—93

Romaine, Claire—8, 16

Romain, Jules—159, 283

Romance—66, 73, 75, 98, 108, 246

Romance of David Garrick, The—232

Romance of the English Stage, The—138

Roman, Lawrence—321

Romanoff and Juliet—299, 304, 409

Romantic Age, The—102, 113

Romantic Comedy—450

Romanticks, The—295, 301

Romantic Young Lady, The—103, 130, 152

Romany Love—253

Romberg and Goodman—141

Romberg, Sigmund—71, 74, 78, 79, 82, 83, 87, 92, 93, 99, 106, 111, 118, 125, 126, 133, 142, 149, 156, 157, 177, 196, 236, 244, 287, 367, 410, 424, 446

Rome, Harold—206, 211, 216, 230, 247, 288, 314, 332, 401, 424

Romeo and Jeannette—383

Romeo and Juliet—22, 23, 44, 49, 53, 54, 58, 59, 63, 68, 73, 76, 90, 96, 115, 122, 144, 145, 159, 167, 173, 174, 183, 184, 188, 193, 198, 199, 202, 208, 214, 219, 220, 223, 228, 249, 254, 255, 256, 264, 279, 290, 301, 302, 304, 311, 317, 323, 329, 334, 341, 360, 366, 367, 369, 374, 381, 389, 396, 402, 409, 416, 417, 422, 429, 433, 436, 437, 438, 439, 455

Romero, Cesar—164, 181

Romulus—332

Romulus the Great—323

Ronane, John—335

Ronan, Robert—390

Ronconi, Luca—389

Roof and Four Walls, A—119

Rooke, Irene—91, 108, 127, 120

Rookery Nook—143, 232, 456

Rook, Robin—291

Room for Two—213, 243

Room Service—65, 205, 209, 402

Room, The—322, 345

Room With a View, A—368, 432

Rooney, Mickey—193, 450

Rooney, Pat—6, 15, 35, 336

Roose-Evans, James—341, 348, 355, 359, 368, 369, 386, 403, 417

Roosevelt, Franklin—205, 309

Roos, Joanna—122, 128

Rooted—408

Rooting—444

Root, Lynn—222

Root of the Mandrake—454

Roots—317, 323, 366

Rope—165

Rope Dancers, The—304, 308, 313, 317

Rope's End—165

Rorem, Ned—341

Rorke, Kate—16, 22

Rorke, Mary—21, 43, 100, 103

Rosa, Dennis—440

Rosalee Prichett—395

Rosalie—76, 156

Rosalind—58, 63, 189, 301, 306, 317

Rosalinda—230

Rosamund Gilder Award—442

Rosa, Nera—104

Rosay, Francoise—253

Rose and the King, The—349

Rose and the Ring, The—122, 168
Roseanne—119
Rose Bernd—27, 115
Rose, Billy—29, 148, 164, 171, 196, 228, 240, 256, 362
Rosebud of Stingingnettle Farm, The—268
Rose, David—238
Rose, Edward E.—1, 2, 6, 7, 52, 92
Rose, Frank—68
Rose, George—274, 281, 345, 358, 455
Rose Girl, The—105, 110
Rose, Jerry—293
Rose, L. Arthur—120, 197, 207, 236, 245
Rose La Tulippe—360
Rose Maid, The—64
Rose Marie—125, 134, 232, 404
Rosemary—448
Rosenberg, James—153
Rosencrantz and Guildenstern Are Dead—45, 365, 377, 380, 381, 389, 390, 452
Rosenfeld, Sydney—25, 30, 42
Rosen, Michael—373, 374
Rosen, Sheldon—446
Rosenthal, Harry—134
Rosenthal, Jean—296, 383
Rose of Arizona—140
Rose of Stemboul, The—111
Rose of the Rancho, The—31
Rose, Philip—385, 420
Rose, Raymond—15
Rose, Reginald—345
Rose Tatoo, The—271, 275, 315, 361
Rose, The—27
Rosewicz, Tadeusz—436
Rose Without a Thorn, The—182, 199
Rosmer, John—145
Rosmer, Milton—46, 120, 217, 237, 242, 399
Rosmersholm—22, 90, 136, 145, 245, 260, 318, 334, 363, 405, 408, 416, 440
Rosqui, Tom—357
Ross—322, 327
Ross, Adrian—2, 10, 11, 16, 21, 26, 31, 32, 37, 43, 48, 49, 51, 53, 57, 62, 63, 67, 75, 79, 80, 84, 94, 95, 101, 102, 109, 119, 120, 134
Ross and Greenbank—8
Ross, Annie—300
Ross, Anthony—244
Ross, Carmel—340
Ross, David—297, 324, 330, 334, 336
Ross, Douglas—160
Ross, Duncan—230
Rosse, Herman—98
Rossellini, Roberto—291
Rossetti, Dante Gabriel—251
Ross, Frederick—61, 83, 95
Ross, George—310, 328, 340
Ross, Herbert—2, 87, 108, 288, 434
Rossini, Gioachino—374
Rossi, Richard—454
Rossiter, Leonard—381, 386, 417, 452
Ross, Jamie—400
Ross, Jerry—282, 287
Ross, Leslie—59
Rostand, Edmond—1, 8, 13, 54, 56, 90, 96, 122, 133, 136, 184, 188, 193, 250, 285, 295, 301, 320, 335, 341, 367, 373, 391, 423
Rostand, Maurice—66, 69
Rosten, Norman—298
Rostova, Mira—290
Roth, Lillian—148, 157, 176
Rothschilds, The—386
Rothwell, Talbot—263
Rougerie, Jean—389
Rouget de l'isle—2
Rough and Ready Lot, The—316
Roughwood, Owen—105, 151
Round About Piccadilly—345
Roundabout Theatre—430, 437
Round and Round the Garden—414
Round House, The—384

Round in Fifty—113
Rounding the Triangle—108
Rounds, David—332
Round Up, The—35
Rounseville, Robert—205
Roussin, Andre—268, 273, 282, 288, 296, 311, 418
Routledge, Patricia—339, 401
Rouverol, Aurania—398
Rowe, Frances—255, 294
Rowe, Iris—143
Rowell, George—403
Rowell, Kenneth—285
Rowland, Adele—27
Rowlands, Gena—298
Rowley, William—108, 192, 329, 349, 389, 444, 447
Rowntree, Douglas W.—270
Roxana—89
Roxanne—4, 313, 250
Royal Adelphi Theater, The (London)—9
Royal Alexandra Theatre—39, 343
Royal Alliance, A—102
Royal Avenue Theatre, The—39
Royal Charter—251
Royal Commission Revue, The—347
Royal Court Theatre—29, 280, 305, 306, 353, 356, 410, 423. Upstairs—390, 396, 410
Royal Divorce, A—76
Royal Dramatic Theatre of Stockholm—374, 396
Royale Avenue Theater—29
Royal Exchange Company—454
Royal Family, The—150, 192, 196, 273, 403, 424, 456
Royal General Theatrical Fund—97, 194
Royal Hunt of the Sun, The—346, 348, 352, 409
Royal Lyceum Troupe—389, 397, 423
Royal Mounted, The—41
Royal Necklace, A—9
Royal Peacock, The—152
Royal Rival, A—7
Royal Shakespeare, Aldwych—330
Royal Shakespeare Company, The—313, 321, 325, 327, 329, 331, 334, 335, 336, 337, 339, 340, 341, 342, 345, 346, 347, 348, 352, 353, 355, 362, 364, 366, 367, 372, 377, 379, 380, 381, 382, 388, 389, 390, 391, 393, 394, 395, 396, 398, 401, 402, 403, 409, 410, 414, 415, 416, 417, 418, 421, 422, 427, 428, 429, 437, 438, 439, 444, 445, 446, 447, 451, 452, 453, 455
Royal Shakespeare's Other Place—429, 422, 438, 444, 453
Royal Society of Literature—80
Royal Strand Theater—29
Royalty Theater—29, 325, 392
Royal Vagabond, The—92
Royal Winnipeg Ballet—362, 374
Royce, Edward—53, 62, 149
Royle, Edwin Milton—26, 51, 54
Royle, Selena—26, 121, 128, 146, 181
Royston, Roy—114, 151, 236
Roze, Raymond—21
R.S.V.P.—142, 147
Rubbers—418
Ruben, Jose—99, 144
Rubens, Bernice—452
Rubens, Maurice—140
Rubens, Paul—11, 12, 14, 15, 16, 21, 22, 27, 32, 36, 49, 53, 62, 67, 72, 74, 75, 79, 80
Rubicon, The—111
Rubinstein, H. F.—95, 279
Rubinstein, John—400
Ruby, Harry—141, 144, 149, 156, 157, 164
Ruby, Thelma—310, 359
Rudas, Tibor—384
Ruddigore—167, 184, 193, 264, 269, 285, 290, 302, 334, 346, 355, 362, 373, 390
Rudd, Paul—430, 437, 449

Rudel, Julius—290
Rudkin, David—348, 405, 409, 410, 415, 416, 427, 431, 436, 438, 444, 453
Rudman, Michael—387, 395, 410, 417, 427, 439, 443, 445, 453
Ruffian on the Stair, the—361, 365
Rugged Path, The—251, 285
Ruggles, Charles—87, 92, 93, 114, 141
Rule a Wife and Have a Wife—136
Rule, Janice—288
Rule of Three—334
Rules of the Game, The—295, 360, 396, 418
Ruling Class, The—379
Ruling the Roost—403, 416
Rum an' Coca-Cola—431, 440
Rumann, Siegfried—186
Rumbold, Hugo—103
Runaway Love—218
Runaways—415, 442, 445
Runaways, The—14
Runner Stumbles, The—405, 416, 421, 452
Running Dogs—202
Running for Office—14
Running of the Deer, The—444
Running Riot—213, 220
Runnin' Wild—118, 123
Runyan, Damon—198, 267
Runz, Ernest—9, 13
Rupert Christmas Show, The—404
Rupert of Hentzau—1, 4
R. U. R.—112, 123, 166, 179, 391
Rush, David—451
Rush Hour Revue, The—284
Rush, Peggy—106
Rushton, William—427
Rusidda—44
Ruskin, John—277
Russel, Henry—29
Russell, Anna—307, 326
Russell, Annie—7, 50, 53, 64
Russell, Billy—347, 368
Russell, Charlie—382
Russell, Hattie—41
Russell, Irene—151, 166
Russell, James—137
Russell, John—137
Russell, Lillian—6, 10, 23, 42, 115, 194, 231
Russell, Mabel—61
Russell, Marie Booth—23
Russell Market Dancers—157
Russell, Maud—125
Russell, Robert—143, 314, 351
Russell, Rosaline—281, 298
Russell, Sol Smith—238
Russell, William—381
Russell, Willy—414, 437
Russet Mantle—200
Russia—69
Russian People, The—233
Russians, The—237
Rustaveli Company—455
Ruta, Ken—454
Rutherford and Son—404
Rutherford, Margaret—212, 218, 222, 225, 227, 245, 258, 284, 299, 302, 315, 334, 352, 360, 361, 404
Rutter, Barrie—409
Ruy Blas—122, 245
Ryan, E. H.—62
Ryan, Irene—411
Ryan, Kate—116
Ryan, Madge—345, 353, 355, 366
Ryan, Mitchell—374, 453
Ryan, Robert—289, 323, 325, 332, 381, 396, 411
Ryder, Alfred—221
Ryecart, Patrick—452
Ryer, George—21
Ryerson, Florence—234, 238, 257
Ryga, George—365, 424
Rylands, George—313, 319
Ryley, Madeleine Lucette—11, 67

Ryskind, Morrie—133, 148, 157, 170, 177, 185, 187, 221
Ryton, Royce—401, 443

Sabatini, Rafael—57, 118, 134
Sabel, Josephine—149
Sabine, Lillian—93
Sabrina Fair—282, 289
Sacco-Venzetti!—376
Sach, Andrew—423
Sackler, Howard—342, 359, 365
Sacrament of Judas, The—67
Sacred and Profane Love—99
Sacred Flame, The—158, 366
Sacred Heart, The—246
Sacrifice to the Winds—295
Saddler, Donald—282, 400, 454
Sadler Wells Ballet, The—255, 260
Sadler Wells Opera Company—316, 317, 377, 391
Sadler Wells Theatre—260
Sadoff, Fred—315
Safety Match, A—107
Sagan, Francoise—334
Sagan, Leontine—202, 207
Saga of Jenny, The—226
Sager, Carole Bayer—449
Sag Harbor—1, 184
Sagi—408
Saidy, Fred—252, 271, 304
Saigon Rose—428
Sail Away—326, 334
Sailor, Beware!—186, 294, 398, 422
Sailors of Cattaro—191
Saint Denis, Michel—213, 214, 260, 265, 273, 325, 337, 354
Saint, Eva Marie—282, 400
Sainthill, Loudon—284, 306, 318, 334, 383
Saint Joan—119, 126, 135, 178, 193, 202, 219, 245, 247, 249, 255, 275, 285, 291, 295, 302, 316, 323, 334, 341, 342, 373, 390, 423, 437, 438, 444
Saint of Bleeker Street, The—288
Saints and Sinners—286
Saintsbury, H. A.—53, 79, 113, 120, 132
Saint's Day—274, 353
Saint, The—96, 129
Saks, Gene—314, 351, 426, 434
Salacrou, Armand—274, 291, 306
Salad Days—289, 300, 305, 429
Salakta Balloon Band, The—422
Salaman, Chattie—389
Salaman, Nicholas—409
Sale, Chic—82, 92, 93, 132
Salerno, Mary Jo—455
Salisbury Arts Theatre Company—312
Salle, Antoine—50
Salle Wilfred Pelletier—343
Sally—100, 101, 108, 112, 116
Sally in Our Alley—10
Sally, Irene and Mary—112
Salmi, Albert—293, 371
Salome—121, 160, 178, 180, 279, 290
Salomy Jane—35
Salt, Waldo—291
Salute to Negro Troops—232
Salute to the Chile of Pablo Neruda, A—415
Salvation—302, 378
Salvation Army Hall (Alberta Canada)—356
Salvation Nell—42
Salvini, Alexander—56
Salvini, Tomasso—77
Salvio, Robert—364
Salzburg Festival—238
Samaritan, The—397
Sambo—383
Same Time, Next Year—420, 425, 427
Sammy Cahn's Songbooks—413
Samples—80
Samson—42, 50
Samson and Delilah—104

Samson, Ivan—201
Samson Riddle, The—402
Sam, the Greatest Jumper of Them All—323
Samuel, Herbert—51
Samuels, Arthur—118
Sanchez, Jamie—353
Sanchocho—452
Sancho Panza—130
Sancho's Master—152
Sanctity—366
Sanctity of Marriage, The—452
Sanctuary—314
Sanders, Carlo—105
Sanderson, Joan—244
Sanderson, Julia—25, 32, 56, 67, 78, 87, 100
Sandhog—291
Sandoe, James—264, 274, 285, 290, 296, 307, 312
Sandow, Eugene—138
Sand, Paul—326, 357
Sandrich, Mark Jr.—344
Sands, Chris—223
Sands, Diana—345, 373, 378, 412
Sands, Dorothy—148, 156, 164, 312
Sands, Leslie—453
San Francisco—34
San Francisco Actor's Workshop—368, 456
Sangster, Alfred—259
Sanguineti, Eduardo—391
San Juan, David—272
Sankowich, Lee D.—396
Sanskrit, Kalidasa—96
Santa Anita '42—422
Santley, Fred—92
Santley, Joseph—118
San Toy—183
Sapho—1, 4, 5, 8, 12, 16, 54
Sappho—329
Sappington, Margo—378
Sara—194
Saratoga—45, 444
Saratoga Performing Arts Festival—405
Sardou, Victorien—8, 9, 16, 17, 20, 23, 27, 32, 38, 50, 54, 72, 73, 103, 128, 188, 189
Sargeant Brue—21
Sargeant of Hussars, The—45
Sargent, Franklyn H.—123
Sargent, Mary—187
Sargent School of Dramatic Art—123
Sari—71
Sarnoff, Dorothy—230
Sarony, Leslie—107
Saroyan, William—217, 221, 223, 225, 226, 232, 295, 304, 313, 322, 323, 336, 383, 417, 424
Sarruf, Valeria—368
Sartene, J.—75
Sartre, Jean Paul—247, 249, 257, 260, 290, 307, 311, 329, 340, 357, 394
Sass, Enid—89
Satire, Irony, and Deeper Meaning—340
Saturday Evening Post—66
Saturday Night—145, 146
Saturday Night at the Crown—305
Saturday Review—319
Saturday's Children—148, 155, 191
Saturday, Sunday, and Monday—407
Saturday to Monday—21
Satyricon—381
Sauce for the Goose—60
Sauce Tartare—263
Saul, Oscar—221
Saunders, Florence—99
Saunders, James—339, 346, 366, 372, 379, 382, 394, 445, 450
Saunders, Madge—113, 134
Sauter, Joe—344
Sauvajon, Marc-Gilbert—278
Savage Amusement—446
Savage, Henry—42, 98, 130
Savage, John—434
Savage/Love—455
Savages—407, 430
Savary, Jerome—415, 452

Saved—356, 359, 363, 379, 386
Savile, Jane—201
Saville, Edith—135
Saving Grace, The—84
Savoir, Alfred—106
Savo, Jimmy—124, 212, 230, 324
Savory, Gerald—206, 299
Savoy, Bert—100, 123
Savoy Havana Band—120
Savoy Theatre—39, 169
Sawyer, Mike—344
Saxon, Luther—235
Say, Darling—309, 316, 355
Saye, Maurice—75
Sayers, Dorothy L.—202, 278
Sayers, JoAnn—222
"Say It With Music"—106
Sayo, Bidu—238
Says I, Says He—451
Say Who You Are—353
Scaife, Isobel—197
Scala Theater (London)—29
Scale, Douglas—312
Scales, Prunella—290, 359, 382, 386, 394, 437, 455
Scandal—89
Scandalous Marriages and Afternoon Tea—422
Scandals—216, 383
Scandals of 1919—92, 376
Scandals of 1920—99
Scandal, The—115
Scanlan, Walter—82, 99
Scapin—58, 316, 347, 411, 436
Scapino—388, 390, 392, 415, 425
Scaramouche—118
Scarborough, George—93
Scardino, Don—364
Scarecrow, The—56, 303, 330, 447
Scarlet Pimpernel, The—26, 39, 160, 203, 214
Scarlet Sister Mary—441
Scase, David—437
Scenes from American Life—395
Scenes from Soweto—444
Scent of Flowers, A—346, 378
Schachter, Steven—418, 436
Schaefer, George—246, 275, 302, 400
Schafer, R. Murray—403
Schaffer, Jerry—379
Schaffner, Franklin—321
Schanzer and Welisch—67, 113
Schary, Dore—205, 309, 313, 316, 326, 331
Schauerein, Lewis—189
Schaufelberg, Ernest—130, 210
Schauspielhaus, Bochum—408
Schechner, Richard—375, 391, 406, 440, 445
Scheck, Max—151
Scheffauer, Herman—72, 122
Scheff, Fritzi—20, 26, 43, 130, 154, 167
Scheider, Roy—357
Schell, Maximillian—306, 352, 436
Scheming Lieutenant, The—250
Schenck, Joe—174
Schenck, Max—22
Schier, Ernest—419
Schifter, Peter Mark—434, 436
Schildkraut, Joseph—105, 121, 125, 191, 227, 230
Schildkraut, Rudolph—113, 174
Schiller, Friedrich—3, 59, 64, 307, 312, 349, 393, 396, 398, 417, 452
Schiller Theater (Berlin)—343, 347, 349, 396, 429
Schiml, Johann—449
Schippel—415
Schirmer, Gus—368, 388
Schisgal, Murray—338, 340, 344, 353, 414, 416
Schlamme, Martha—338
Schlegel, August—173
Schlesinger, John—348, 360, 401, 436
Schletter, Annie—94
Schmidt, Harvey—320, 339, 358, 378, 385, 418

Schnabel, Stefan—197, 272, 378
Schneider, Alan—259, 287, 301, 326, 332, 339, 345, 346, 347, 354, 357, 364, 371, 395, 400, 404, 426, 440, 446, 449
Schneider, George—45
Schneider, Vern—386
Schniff, Henry—35
Schnitzler, Arthur—20, 24, 57, 61, 68, 77, 90, 132, 373, 380, 408, 428, 447, 451
Schofield, David—408, 439
School for Brides—239
School for Scandal—8, 16, 22, 27, 49, 54, 76, 96, 109, 122, 128, 137, 166, 167, 179, 188, 202, 203, 208, 232, 237, 245, 264, 285, 334, 389, 402, 404
School for Slavery—231
School for Wives—275, 395
School Girl, The—16, 391
Schoolmistress, The—347
School of Husbands, The—188
Schrappnel, John—421
Schreiber, Terry—436, 452
Schubert, Franz—106, 264
Schulberg, Budd—309, 319, 344
Schulberg, Stuart—344
Schulman, Arnold—338, 371
Schulmann, Peter—381
Schultz, Charles—364
Schultz, Michael A.—373, 376, 378, 380
Schuman, Howard—440
Schumann, Robert—191
Schuman, Peter—403
Schummann-Heink, Ernestine—20
Schuster, Betty—148
Schwabe & Company—110
Schwab, Laurence—124, 132, 141, 149, 157, 163
Schwartz, Arthur—140, 163, 166, 171, 172, 176, 181, 191, 195, 198, 201, 206, 215, 216, 219, 257, 271, 287, 338
Schwartz, Eugene—340
Schwartz, Jean—14, 19, 25, 31, 35, 87, 92, 101, 118, 148
Schwartz, Maurice—121, 179, 198, 219, 324
Schwartz, Stephen—393, 398, 400, 413, 442
Schwartz, Yevgeny—368
Schwarzwald, Milton—125
Schweizer, David—439, 410
Schweyk in the Second World War—342, 429, 439
Scioto Society—409
Scism, Mack—392
Sclerosis—353
Scofield, Paul—230, 249, 250, 255, 259, 263, 264, 278, 279, 280, 283, 284, 289, 296, 301, 305, 310, 315, 322, 329, 334, 336, 347, 359, 361, 373, 374, 395, 396, 422, 436, 433, 451
Scognamiglio, Vincenzio—122
Scioto Society—409
Score—399
Scorsese, Martin—434
Scotch Mist—142
Scotia's Darlings—444
Scotsman, The—256
Scott, Clement—12, 146
Scott, Cyril—41, 117
Scott, Elizabeth—161, 185
Scott, George C.—321, 335, 337, 340, 371, 422, 427
Scott, Harold—365
Scott, Hazel—230
Scott, Helena—298
Scott, Hutchinson—285
Scottish Actors Company—382
Scottish Opera—303, 368
Scottish Repertory Theatre—51
Scottish Theatre Festival—220, 264
Scott, Joan Clement—127
Scott, John—395
Scott, Kevin—288
Scott, Margaretta—186, 207, 217, 223

Scott, Martha—211, 240, 241, 279, 320, 424
Scott, Michael—153
Scott, Noel—119, 151
Scott, Raymond—247
Scott, Rosemary—207, 268
Scott, Shepherd and Breakwell—185
Scott-Siddons, Mrs.—104
Scott, Zachary—234, 301, 307, 314
Scoular, Christopher—421
Scourby, Alexander—357
Scrabble—380
Scrambled Feet—449
Scrap of Paper, A—72, 73
Screen Actors Guild—98
Screens, The—398
Scribes—431, 436, 441
Scuba Duba—364
Scully, Anthony—405, 421
Scully, Terry—333
Sea Anchor, The—416
Sea at Dauphin—322
Seabrook, Jeremy—379
Sea Change, The—428
Seagulls Over Sorrento—207
Sea Gull, The—77, 167, 173, 184, 202, 214, 220, 264, 284, 290, 301, 323, 347, 362, 363, 374, 388, 409, 415, 416, 421, 424, 430, 444
Sea Horse, The—410, 413
Sealed Orders—67
Seale, Douglas—279, 285, 295, 296, 301, 306, 307, 311, 312, 316, 317, 326, 334
Seal, Elizabeth—289, 310, 380
Seall, Harry—191
Sea Marks—424
Searching Wind, The—239, 243
Searchlights—74
Searle, Humphrey—329
Sears, Zelda—41, 79, 92, 93, 100, 114, 124, 166, 173, 179, 188, 228
Seascape—420
Season Changes, The—243
Season in Hell—366
Season in the Sun—275, 313
Season of Choice—318
Sea, The—407
Seaton, Derek—439
Seattle Repertory Theatre, The—343
Sebastian, Hugh—187
Sebree, Charles—288
Secombe, Harry—299, 310, 318, 340, 358, 366, 421
Second Best Bed—284
Second City Review—338
2nd Greatest Entertainer in the Whole Wide World, The—438
Second Hand Rose—105
Second in Command, The—3
Second Man, The—148, 198, 411
Second Mrs. Tanqueray, The—4, 12, 44, 68, 115, 128, 269
Second Threshold—271, 275, 277
Second World Theatre, The—353
Secretary Bird, The—372
Secret of Polichinelle, The—19
Secrets—114
Secret Service—54, 209, 428
Secrets of a Savoyard—203
Secret, The—67
Secret Woman, The—65, 115
Section Nine—410, 415
Seduced—452
Seegar, Miriam—148
See How They Run—244
Seeing Stars—197
Seeing Things at Night—220
Seeley, Blossom—74, 418
Seely, Tim—301
See My Lawyer—216
See Naples and Die—164, 182
Seen but Not Heard—203
Seeniaya Ptitza—126
Seesaw—406
See-See—32
See You Again—278
Segal, Alex—304
Segal, George—333

Segal, Vivienne—74, 93, 112, 124, 141, 142, 156, 222, 237
Seidelman, Arthur—372, 434
Sejanus: His Fall—159
Sekulovich, Mladew—69
Selbie, Christopher—455
Selby, Nicholas—322, 359
Seldes, Gilbert—217, 240, 250
Seldes, Marian—321, 381, 382, 404, 411, 442
Sell, Janie—358
Sell-Out—437
Seltzer, Daniel—405
Selwart, Tonio—186
Selwyn, Beatrice—37, 100, 130
Selwyn, Edgar—1, 7, 11, 52, 56, 91, 96, 98, 100, 116, 124, 130
Semi-Detached—334, 452
Semi-Monde—436
Senator, The—179
Sennett, Mack—38
Sense of Detachment, A—401
Sense of the Past, The—143
Sentimentalists, The—54
Separate Rooms—221
Separate Tables—289, 299, 308, 436
"September Song"—211
September Tide—259
Seraphica—66
Serban, Andrei—416, 424, 430, 436, 439, 452, 454
Serena Blandish—163, 456
Serenade—167
Serenading Louie—428
Serf, The—102
Sergent, John W.—104
Serjeant Musgrave's Dance—318, 357
Serpent: A Ceremony, The—389
Serpent's Tooth, A—243
Serrano, Vincent—1, 6, 148
Serumaga, Robert—422
Servaes, Dagny—153
Servais, Yvan—83
Servant in the House, The—41
Servant-Master-Lover—81
Servant of Two Masters—153, 312, 323, 367, 376, 398, 408
Servants and the Snow, The—390
Servant, The—417
Service—183
Servoss, Mary—115, 163
Sesostra—61
Set My People Free—257
Settled Out of Court—322
Set To Music—216, 284
7½ Cents—309
Seven Blind Men—108
Seven Chances—78
Seven Days—48, 313
Seven Days' Leave—83
Seven Deadly Elements, The—438
Seven Deadly Sins of the Lower Middle Class, The—428
Seven Descents of Myrtle, The—371, 377
Seven Keys to Baldpate—66, 98, 153
Seven Lively Arts—240, 256
Seventeen—87, 271
1798-The French Revolution Year One—397
1776—130, 378, 386
Seventh Commandment, The—397
Seventh Heaven—112, 297
Seventh Man, A—431
Seventh Sin, The—428
Seventh Veil, The—272
70 Girls, 70—398
Seven Year Itch, The—276, 282
Severed Hand, A—339
Severin-Mars—45
Sex—140, 147, 154
Sextet—435
Sexton, Anne—382
Sexual Perversity in Chicago—426

Seyler, Athene—50, 107, 119, 130, 135, 178, 188, 212, 218, 279, 300, 310, 359
Seymore, William—1, 20, 22, 25, 35, 41
Seymour, Alan—328, 360
Seymour, Ann—309
Seymour, Felix—142
Seymour, May Davenport—15, 35, 370
Sganarelle—316, 387, 445
Sgt. Pepper's Lonely Hearts Club Band on the Road—413
Shadow and Substance—211, 215, 235
Shadow Box—457
Shadow of a Doubt, The—294
Shadow of a Gunman, The—121, 152, 306, 312, 354, 366, 402
Shadow of Heroes—311, 327
Shadow of the Glen, The—16, 59, 160, 193
Shadow of the Rockies—166
Shadow Play—201
Shadows Move Among Them—276
Shadows of the Evening—358
Shadow, The—69
Shadowy Waters, The—38
Shadwell, Charles—274
Shaffer, Anthony—386, 421, 445, 451
Shaffer, Peter—311, 333, 342, 346, 348, 354, 359, 364, 386, 406, 409, 429, 433, 451
Shaftsbury Theatre—337
Shaggy Dog Animation, The—440
Shairp, Mordaunt—166, 186, 188, 194
Shakespeare Anthology—313, 319
Shakespeare and Music—317
Shakespeare Birthplace—432
Shakespeare Club House—86
Shakespeare Festivals: American (Stratford, Conn.)—275, 296, 300, 301, 306, 312, 317, 323, 329, 335, 337, 341, 347, 354, 362, 367, 369, 374, 381, 382, 389, 396, 403, 409, 412, 417, 419, 423, 430, 432, 441, 446, 454. Canada (Stratford, Ontario)—285, 286, 290, 295, 301, 303, 308, 317, 323, 329, 335, 343, 348, 350, 362, 367, 370, 374, 381, 392, 396, 398, 399, 403, 409, 412, 416, 423, 430, 432, 438, 446, 454. Colorado (Boulder)—312. Marin (San Rafael, Calif.)—331. National (San Diego)—199, 264, 296, 301, 307, 312, 323, 329, 335, 341, 362, 367, 371, 374, 381, 389, 396, 403, 409, 416, 423, 429, 438, 446, 448, 454. New York (Central Park)—307, 312, 319, 323, 335, 341, 342, 348, 354, 362, 367, 374, 381, 383, 389, 396, 403, 409, 417, 419, 430, 439, 445, 446, 452, 454. Oregon (Ashland)—198, 202, 208, 224, 225, 255, 256, 260, 264, 269, 274, 279, 285, 290, 301, 307, 312, 313, 317, 323, 335, 341, 348, 354, 362, 368, 375, 381, 388, 392, 396, 402, 403, 409, 417, 423, 430, 439, 441, 446, 448, 454. San Francisco—317. Stratford-Upon-Avon (Stratford, England)—3, 8, 12, 16, 22, 27, 33, 37, 44, 58, 59, 60, 63, 64, 68, 72, 76, 80, 81, 96, 103, 114, 115, 121, 122, 128, 136, 138, 144, 145, 147, 152, 155, 160, 161, 166, 167, 169, 173, 178, 183, 184, 185, 188, 189, 197, 208, 219, 220, 223, 228, 232, 237, 242, 246, 249, 254, 259, 264, 284, 295, 301, 306, 307, 311, 313, 316, 319, 323, 329, 330, 331, 341, 367, 373, 374, 377, 380, 381, 388, 396, 402, 403, 409, 410, 416, 422, 429, 432, 437, 438, 444, 446, 453. Utah (Cedar City)—335.
Shakespeare Memorial Theatre—147, 167, 169, 237, 242, 254, 295, 296, 306, 308, 311, 316, 331, 412
Shakespeare Newsletter—350

510

Shakespeare Play, The—444
Shakespeare Quatercentenary—346
Shakespeare Revel—446
Shakespeare Revisited—335
Shakespeare's Happy Comedies—383
Shakespeare Survey—432
Shakespeare Theatre Company—184
Shakespeare Theater (London)—8, 9, 115
Shakespeare Theatre Workshop—301
Shakespeare, William (see play titles)
Shakespearewrights—297
Shakespeare Without Tears—405
Shake Your Feet—151
Shakuntala—96, 97
Shall We Join the Ladies?—268
Shameless Professor, The—316
Shame Woman, The—161
Sham Prince, The—274
Shand, Maggie—146
Shand, Phyllis—111, 159, 178, 188
Shangai Gesture—140
Shange, Ntozake—426, 428, 436, 454, 455
Shanks, Alec—253, 276, 280, 288, 289, 295, 300, 322
Shannon, Effie—35, 88, 105, 128, 157, 217, 223
Shannon, Frank—106
Shannons of Broadway, The—161
Shanwalla—76
Shapes and Shadows—396
Shapes of our Theatre—432
Shapiro, Dan—239, 293
Shapiro, Mel—393, 396, 398, 418, 436, 449
Sharaff, Irene—202, 221, 226
Sharaff, Veronica—221
Shar, Antony—450
Shared Experience Theatre—445
Share My Lettuce—305
Sharkey, Anna—435
Sharman, Jim—393, 409, 416
Sharma, Pratap—366
Sharp, Andrew—451
Sharp, Anthony—276, 322, 328, 421
Sharpe, Albert—252
Sharp, Lewen—9
Sharp, Margery—227, 263
Shatner, William—309
Shatzov, Sophie Sonia—146
Shaughnessy, Father—216
Shaughran, The—268, 374
Shavings—273
Shawan, April—369
Shaw, Anthony—212
Shaw Centenary Year—302
Shaw, Charlotte—24, 39
Shaw, David—314, 338
Shaw Festival (London)—301
Shaw Festival (Niagara-on-the-Lake, Canada)—335, 337, 341, 348, 362, 363, 367, 370, 375, 389, 396, 403, 409, 412, 416, 422, 429, 438, 446, 453
Shaw, George Bernard—2, 7, 13, 17, 19, 22, 23, 24, 25, 27, 28, 29, 31, 32, 33, 35, 37, 38, 39, 43, 44, 47, 50, 51, 53, 57, 58, 59, 63, 64, 65, 67, 68, 69, 72, 76, 77, 80, 83, 84, 85, 92, 95, 96, 98, 100, 103, 108, 109, 111, 114, 115, 117, 119, 121, 122, 123, 128, 129, 135, 136, 137, 138, 142, 144, 147, 150, 152, 154, 159, 160, 165, 167, 169, 170, 173, 174, 178, 183, 184, 189, 192, 193, 194, 197, 198, 199, 202, 208, 209, 210, 213, 214, 215, 218, 219, 220, 223, 228, 232, 237, 241, 242, 245, 249, 250, 251, 254, 255, 256, 259, 260, 263, 264, 265, 268, 269, 273, 274, 275, 278, 279, 283, 284, 285, 291, 295, 296, 297, 298, 300, 301, 302, 308, 311, 312, 316, 317, 318, 320, 323, 329, 330, 334, 340, 341, 342, 349, 353, 354, 359, 360, 361, 366, 367, 368, 371, 373, 374, 381, 382, 387, 388, 389, 390, 391, 396, 397, 398, 402, 403, 407, 411, 422,

423, 428, 436, 437, 438, 439, 440, 442, 444, 445, 446, 447, 454
Shaw, Glen, Byam—173, 188, 214, 250, 264, 273, 278, 284, 285, 290, 295, 301, 306, 311, 316, 322, 329, 345, 359, 361, 366, 368, 391
Shaw, Howard Van Doren—139
Shaw, Irwin—200, 202, 206, 216, 234, 244
Shaw, Kathryn—454
Shaw, Martin—8, 12, 72
Shaw, Mary—13, 16, 28, 37, 47, 115, 168
Shaw, Maxwell—291
Shawn, Dick—420, 438
Shaw, Norman—13
Shawn, Wallace—421, 436, 454
Shaw, Oscar—105, 106, 126, 142, 149, 176
Shaw, Robert—240, 274, 315, 322, 329, 339, 377, 385, 394, 398
Shaw, Sebastian—144, 165, 182, 183, 274, 329, 359, 417
Shaw Theatre—397, 399
Shay—439
Shdanoff, George—220
She—185
Sheaf, Robert—360
Shea, John—455
Shean, Al—64, 111, 167, 181
Shearer, Moira—290, 301
Shea, Robert—437
Shea, Steven—429
Shea's Theater (Toronto)—18
Sheen, Al—205
Sheen, Martin—344, 369, 374
Sheep Is Out, The—452
Sheep Well, The—296
Sheerluck Jones—8
Sheffield Repertory Company—98, 110, 130, 162, 220, 259
Sheiness, Marsha—429
Sheldon, Edward—42, 48, 56, 66, 71, 73, 75, 98, 111, 140, 145, 302, 428
Sheldon, Richard—108
Sheldon, Sidney—314
Shelley, Carole—351, 449
Shelley, Elsa—239, 243, 249, 251, 316
Shelley, Percy B.—115, 116
She Loves Me—338, 343, 345, 376
She Loves Me Not—187
Shelton, George—22
Shelton, James—217
Shelton, Reid—358, 434
Shelton, Timothy—406
Shelving, Paul—143
Shenandoah—45, 77, 420
Shepard, Sam—353, 360, 367, 374, 379, 387, 395, 403, 406, 407, 416, 417, 418, 422, 437, 439, 440, 443, 445, 452, 455
Shephard, Firth—109, 151, 212, 213, 227, 231, 248
Shephard Show, The—248
Shepherdess Without a Heart, The—168
Shepherd, John—361, 368
Shepherd's Pie—108, 218, 228
Shepherd's Play, The—444
Shepley, Ruth—45, 93
Sheppy—188
Sherek, Henry—266, 274, 301, 307
Sheridan, Dinah—435
Sheridan, Ivor—231
Sheridan, Mary—144
Sheridan, Philip Henry—121, 122
Sheridan, Richard Brinsley—3, 8, 13, 22, 33, 49, 54, 58, 64, 68, 76, 80, 96, 109, 115, 128, 135, 136, 137, 152, 166, 167, 179, 188, 202, 208, 214, 228, 232, 237, 241, 245, 246, 249, 250, 259, 264, 285, 290, 300, 361, 362, 389, 396, 402, 439, 444
Sherin, Edwin—365, 400, 403, 413, 416, 418, 427, 451
Sherlock Holmes—54, 90, 137, 180, 414, 425, 442
Sherman, Charles—276
Sherman, Geoffrey—452

Sherman, George—376
Sherman, Hiram—252, 293
Sherman, John—13
Sherman, Martin—387, 429, 439, 450
Sherman, Nathan—216
Sherriff, R. C.—200, 202, 210, 267, 269, 329, 401, 424
Sherrin, Ned—336, 359, 388, 427, 432
Sherry, Gordon—206
Sherwin, Jeannette—135
Sherwin, Manning—222, 227, 231, 236, 245, 259, 263
Sherwood, Garrison P.—51, 65, 70, 73, 77, 81, 86, 91, 297, 303, 308, 313, 342
Sherwood, Lydia—178, 274
Sherwood, Madeleine—281
Sherwood, Morgan—4
Sherwood, Robert E.—148, 155, 156, 170, 177, 185, 195, 196, 199, 200, 204, 207, 210, 211, 215, 220, 221, 225, 251, 262, 265, 271, 273, 279, 304, 338, 340, 362, 396, 402
She's My Baby—156, 256
She Stoops to Conquer—3, 8, 27, 33, 54, 63, 64, 73, 122, 128, 160, 203, 218, 223, 264, 265, 270, 313, 323, 381, 402, 403, 409, 452
Shevelove, Burt—257, 326, 347, 364, 395, 443, 454
Shewing-Up of Blanco Posnet, The—39, 50, 51, 59, 108, 122, 218, 273, 329
She Would If She Could—452
Shields, Arthur—81, 84, 96, 102, 106, 120, 135, 193, 212, 223
Shiels, George—114, 152, 178, 184, 193, 274, 285
Shillingford and Ellis—145
"Shimmy With Me"—114
Shinbone Alley—304
Shine, Bill—268
Shiner, Ronald—183, 267, 281, 305
Shine, Ted—380
Shining Hour, The—190, 193, 194, 398
Shipman, F.—251
Shipman, Samuel—61, 87, 88, 92, 111, 148, 205
Shipp, J. A.—14, 30, 41, 48
Ship, The—166
Shire, David—338, 437
Shirley, Florence—87
Shivvers—415
Shockheaded Peter—8, 168
Shock of Recognition, The—357
Shoemaker, Anne—156
Shoemaker's Holiday, The—213, 242, 347, 397, 403
Shoestring Revue—297
Shogun, A Tale of Old Japan, The—8
Sho-gun, The—20
Shoker, H. G.—120
Sholom Aleichem—424
Shoo-Fly Regiment, The—35
Shop at Sly Corner, The—244
Shop Girl, The—103
Shore Acres—32
Shore Leave—244
Shortchanged Review, The—428
Shortest Story of All, The—108
Short Eyes—415
Short, Hassard—11, 15, 106, 112, 118, 133, 175, 177, 183, 190, 194, 240, 257, 266
Short, Marion—36
Short Sleeves in the Summer—435
Shostakovitch, Dimitri—335
Shot in the Dark, A—327, 339
Shotter, Winifred—143, 151, 159, 165, 172, 177, 183
Shout Across the River—446, 452
Show Boat—150, 184, 236, 246, 249, 290, 329, 361, 376, 383, 397
Show Is On, The—200
Show (magazine)—350
Show Off, The—124, 130, 368, 375, 419

Show of Wonders, The—78
Show Time—230, 383
Shrew, The—424
Shrike, The—65, 276, 280, 285
Shriner, Herb—257
Shubert Brothers, The—18, 23, 29, 34, 35, 39, 52, 54, 55, 56, 57, 60, 61, 63, 68, 70, 73, 85, 86, 91, 93, 97, 98, 106, 110, 112, 118, 123, 129, 130, 131, 136, 138, 139, 140, 144, 147, 155, 162, 163, 167, 185, 193, 200, 216, 240, 243, 302, 342
Shubert Gaieties of 1919—92
Shubert, J. J.—125, 141, 142
Shubert, Lee—29, 39, 51, 55, 70, 93, 129, 155
Shubert Organization, The—449
Shubert, Sam S.—22, 23, 25, 28, 29, 51, 70, 91
Shubert Theatrical Company of New York—51
Shuffle Along—116, 154, 182
Shulin, Herman—456
Shulman, Arnold—364
Shulman, Max—252, 287, 365
Shumlin, Herman—181, 226, 278, 314
Shutta, Ethel—112, 432
Shut Your Eyes and Think of England—435
Shylock—80
Shyre, Paul—304, 318, 321, 335, 357, 360, 395, 413
Siamese Connections—407
Sibbald, George—440
Sicilian Players, The—44, 53
Siddons, Mary Francis—81
Siddons, Sarah—456
Sideshow—401, 437
Side by Side by Sondheim—427, 434
Sidewalks of New York—149
Sidney, Basil—163
Sidney Howard Memorial Award—232
Sidney, Sylvia—148, 157, 208, 434
Siebert, Charles—374
Siedle, C. F.—10
Siege—206
Siegel, Larry—357
Siegfried—174
Siegmeister, Elie—243
Sierra, G. Martinez—103, 121, 130, 152, 155, 158, 173, 241
Sieveking, Lance—365, 368, 432
Siff, Ira—400
Sifton, Clair—179
Sifton, Paul—179
Sigh No More—245
Sight of Glory, A—423
Sigler, Goodhart, and Hoffman—201
Signalman's Apprentice, The—396
Signal Man, The—276
Signals—430
Signed and Sealed—1976/2
Sign in Sidney Brustein's Window, The—344
Sign of the Cross, The—4, 295
Sign of the Seven Dials, The—177
Sign on the Door, The—94
Signoret, Simone—361
Signpost to Murder—333
Silence—387, 395
Silence of Lee Harvey Oswald, The—361
Silent House, The—151
Silent Night, Lonely Night—315
Silent Partner, The—400
Silk Stockings—293, 431
Sillitoe, Alan—387, 444
Sillman, Leonard—148, 190, 200, 276, 280, 298
Sills, Milton—174
Sills, Paul—338, 390, 436
Sillward, Edward—67
Sill, William Raymond—116
Silva, Carmen—33
Silvera, Frank—335, 391
Silver Box, The—33, 44, 68, 98, 114, 189, 273
Silver, Christine—62

Silver Cord, The—145, 151, 155, 220
Silver Curlew, The—265, 269
Silver King, The—268, 313
Silverman, Stanley—381, 400
Silver Slipper, The—7, 10
Silvers, Phil—252, 272, 321, 387, 402
Silvers, Sid—176, 182
Silver Tassie, The—162, 166, 382
Silver Whistle, The—257, 265
Silver Wings—172
Sim, Alastair—188, 222, 228, 241, 253, 260, 267, 302, 310, 316, 334, 342, 354, 360, 382, 387, 410, 433
Simenon, Georges—285
Sim, Millie—197
Simmonds, Herbert—115
Simmonds, Nikolas—452
Simmons, Jean—406
Simmons, Philip—127
Simms, Hilda—240
Simms, Margaret—113
Simone, Michael—380
Simon, John—449
Simon, Mayo—368
Simon, Neil—93, 139, 326, 332, 338, 350, 351, 357, 358, 371, 372, 377, 378, 386, 394, 400, 406, 414, 426, 434, 449, 451
Simonov, Konstantin—233, 237, 262
Simon, Robert—451
Simon, Roger Hendricks—390
Simon's Hour—144
Simonson, Lee—369
Simoom—173
Simple Simon—170
Simple Spyman—310
Simpleton of the Unexpected Isles, The—197
Simpson, Bland—420, 440
Simpson, Harold—114, 119, 120, 133, 134
Simpson, Harvey—114
Simpson, Joan—228
Simpson, N. F.—307, 311, 318, 326, 388, 401
Simpson, Reginald—192
Simpson, Ronald—244
Simpson, T.—9
Sim-Sala-Bim—204
Sims, George R.—7, 34, 59, 67, 95
Sim, Sheila—268, 278, 299
Sims, Hilda—154
Sims, Joan—289, 328
Sinbad—32, 87, 452
Sinbad the Sailor—193
Sinclair, Arthur—36, , 54, 58, 59, 63, 76, 90, 103, 152, 208
Sinclair, Edward—178
Sinclair, Hugh—122, 163, 188, 216, 299
Sinclair, Maud B.—41
Sinclair, Robert—216, 264
Sinclair, Upton—157
Sinclair, Ward—25
Sinden, Bert—32
Sinden, Donald—255, 305, 310, 328, 359, 372, 380, 389, 390, 406, 407, 418, 435, 438, 453
Sing a Rude Song—388
Singer, Campbell—310, 328, 340
Singer, Isaac Bashevis—418, 420
Singer, The—183
Sing for Your Supper—219, 220
Singher, Martial—317
Singing Dolphin, The—342
Singing Girl from Killarney, The—104
Singing Jailbirds—157
Singin' the Blues—176
Single-Ended Rope, The—380
Singles—436
"Sing Me A Song of Social Significance"—206
Sing Me No Lullaby—291
Sing Out Sweet Land—243
Sing Out the News—211
Sinners—130
Sins of Society, The—73
Sirena, Don—233
Sirens, The—410

511

Siren, The—56
Sir Gawain and the Green Knight—439
Sir Is Winning—437
Sirmay, Albert—67, 158
Sirocco—103, 152
Sir Walter Raleigh—49
Sissle, Noble—105, 120, 124, 143, 182, 230
Sisson, Rosemay Ann—414
Sissy—403
Sister Beatrice and the Miracle of Saint Anthony—44
Sisters of Mercy—409
Sisters' Tragedy, The—115
Sitwell, Edith—153
Sitwell, Osbert—153
Sitwell, Sacheverell—153
Siviter, F.—55
Six Characters in Search of an Author—112, 114, 136, 183, 269, 340, 341, 353, 360, 452
Six-Cylinder Love—105, 116
Six from La Mama—360
Six in the Rain—323
Six of Calais, The—193, 274
Six of One—340
6 Rms Riv Vu—400
Six Stokers Who Own the Bloomin' Earth—166
Sixteen—191
Sixteen Empire Girls—119
1600 Pensylvania Avenue—426
Sixth Commandment, The—32
Sixty Minute Queer Show, The—438
69 Theatre Company—375, 403
Six Who Pass While the Lentils Boil—77, 80
Sizwe Banzi Is Dead—410, 413, 414, 435
Skelly, Hal—149
Skelton, John—417
Skidding—398
Skillan, George—102, 183
Skin Game, The—101, 110, 197, 199, 391
Skinner, Alistair—394
Skinner, Cornelia Otis—456
Skinner, Otis—22, 30, 57, 130, 137, 160, 179, 180, 227, 239, 250, 276, 282, 302, 309
Skinner, S. T.—64
Skin of Our Teeth, The—230, 238, 245, 246, 250, 296, 374, 377, 423, 425
Skipper Next to God—259, 261
Skipworth, Alison—6, 33, 112, 118, 147, 213
Sklar, George—187, 189, 190, 197, 202, 219
Skowronnek, Richard—44
Skulnik, Menasha—281, 288, 298, 391
Sky High—134, 231
Skylark—217, 225, 231
Skyscraper—352
Skyvers—340, 396
Skywriting—374
Slab Boys, The—444, 445
Slade, Bernard—174, 420, 442, 450
Slade, Julian—289, 290, 300, 305, 322, 334, 403, 429
Slade, Mary—109
Slag—395
Slapstick Tragedy—357
Slater, Daphne—273
Slater, John—289
"Slaughter on Tenth Avenue"—200
Slaughter, Tod—184
Slaughter, Walter—8, 17
Slave Ship—383
Slave, The—345
Slavin, John—36
Sleak—437
Sleep—401, 402
Sleeper, Martha—200, 216
Sleeper's Den, The—353, 379
Sleeping Beauty—64, 145, 168, 184,

209, 214, 220, 237, 243, 246, 255, 275, 313, 369, 398
Sleeping Beauty and the Beast—4, 6
Sleeping Beauty in the Woods, The—291, 342
Sleeping Beauty: Or, What a Witch!—198, 203
Sleeping Clergyman, A—188, 193, 254
Sleeping Partners—84, 87
Sleeping Price, The—283, 374
Sleep of Prisoners, A—271, 272, 283
Sleep, Wayne—403
Sleuth—386, 399, 421, 445, 451
Slezak, Walter—181, 191, 196, 281, 288
Slight Ache, A—345, 408, 415, 424
Slight Case of Murder, A—198
Slipper for the Moon, A—291
Slip Road Wedding—397
Sloane, Alfred Baldwin—14, 23, 52, 56, 61, 100, 102, 137
Sloans, Winnie—197
Slow Dance on the Killing Ground—345, 356, 396
Sly, Christopher—390
SlyFox—427, 441
Small Craft Warnings—400, 408
Small Hotel—294
Small Miracle—191
Small, Paul—235, 240
Small, Robert Graham—436
Smalls, Charlie—420
Small War on Murray Hill—304
Small Wonder—257
Smile—83
Smiles—171
Smiles of a Summer Night—406
Smilin' Through—94
Smith—49, 255
Smith, Alexis—393, 409
Smith, Alfred E.—130, 147
Smith and Dale—141, 149
Smith, Andy—428
Smith, Arnold Dunbar—180
Smith, Art—197, 221
Smith, Augustus—188
Smith, Ben—157, 176
Smith, Bessie—164, 420
Smith, Betty—271
Smith, Boyd—147
Smith, Bruce—5, 49
Smith, C. Aubrey—7, 15, 26, 53, 71, 83, 89, 94, 107, 119, 127, 134, 142, 144, 166, 172
Smith, Charles—17
Smith, Clay—89
Smith, Cyril—16, 159, 197, 218
Smith, Dody—181, 207, 213, 224, 235, 368
Smith, Earl Hobson—348
Smith, Edgar—15, 31, 35, 36, 48, 52, 164
Smith, Euan—410, 415
Smith, F. Hopkinson—1
Smith, Frederick M.—85
Smith, George Totten—25
Smith, Harry B.—1, 6, 10, 15, 19, 30, 31, 35, 41, 42, 43, 47, 56, 74, 87, 88, 92, 114, 141, 148, 204, 208, 228, 439
Smith, Harry James—56, 163
Smith, H. Reeves—6, 82
Smith, Jack—151
Smith, Jane—444
Smith, Kate—146, 170
Smith, Kent—222, 266
Smith, Lillian—244
Smith, Maggie—298, 305, 317, 323, 326, 333, 342, 346, 353, 381, 388, 389, 403, 414, 422, 439, 443
Smith, Mel—452
Smith, Michael—395
Smith, Mrs. Sol—1, 15, 23, 25, 36, 56, 92, 114
Smith, Muriel—235, 301
Smith, Oliver—298, 374
Smith, Paul G.—134, 155, 164
Smith, Peter—448

Smith, Queenie—93, 125, 133, 164
Smith, R. D.—329
Smith, Robert Paul—287
Smith, Roger—437
Smith, Sally—351
Smith, Sebastian—149, 151, 183
Smithson, Florence—27, 32, 48, 57
Smithson, Frank—10
Smithson, Laura—119
Smith, Stevie—451
Smith, Sue—395
Smith, Sydney—323
Smith, W. Gordon—395
Smith, Winchell—7, 28, 31, 42, 47, 74, 78, 87, 106, 141, 170, 171, 193, 303
Smoke Persian—166
Smoky Mountain Passion Play—409
Smollett, Tobias—291
Smyrl, David Langston—436
Smythe, William G.—110
Snader, Edward—13
Snafu—240
Snap—114, 414
Snapdragon—224
Sneider, Vern—281
Snodin, David—387, 395
Snow—284
Snowangel—338
Snowdrop and the Seven Little Men—17
Snow Queen, The—260, 369
Snow Was Black, The—285
Snow White and the Chicken—422
Snow White and the Seven Dwarfs—265, 275, 455
Snyder, Ella—2
Snyder, William—332, 340
Sobol, Edward—212
Social Register, The—177
Social Success, A—396
Social Whirl, The—30
Society, A—26, 103
Society of American Dramatists and Composers—243
Society of American Magicians—104
Society of Stage Directors and Choreographers—337
Society of West End Theatre Managers—199
Soft Morning City—396
Sohlke, Gus—19, 88
Soho So What!—295
Sojourner Truth—259
Soldier Boy—447
Soldier For Christmas, A—241, 242
Soldiers—370, 371
Soldier's Fortune, The—366
Soldiers of Fortune—10
Soldier's Tale, The—295, 368, 390
Soldier's Wife—240, 246, 248
Sol Hurok Presents—418
Solid Gold Cadillac, The—282, 308, 352, 447
Solitaire/Double Solitaire—395, 397
Solitary Lover, The—259
Solkover, George—225
Solly, Billy—420
Solms, Kenny—413
Solomis, Alexis—264
Solomon, Louis—240
Solomon R. Guggenheim Museum—397
Solomos, Alexis—360, 431
So Long, Letty—78
"Somebody Loves Me"—124
Somebody's Sweetheart—88
Some Like It Hot—400
Some (More) Samples—79
Some of My Best Friends are Husbands—430
Someone from Assisi—332
"Someone to Watch Over Me"—142
Someone Waiting—283
Somer, Josef—450
Somerset, C. W.—11, 15, 120
Somers, Harry—423
Somerville, Reginald—49

Something for the Boys—234, 241, 418
Something in the Air—236, 242
Something's Burning—415
Something Unspoken—309
Sometime—87
Son, A—373
Son-Daughter, The—93
Sondergaard, Gale—160, 188
Sondheim, Stephen—304, 314, 326, 344, 351, 385, 393, 406, 410, 418, 424, 426, 449
Song and Dance Man, The—119
Song at Twilight, A—358, 413
Song of Lady Lotus Eyes, The—86
Song of Norway—239, 248, 253, 264, 367
Song of Norway Festival—367
Song of Songs, The—71
Song of the Centipede, The—278
Song of the Drum, The—177
Song of the Flame—133
Song of the Goat—354
Song of the Lusitanian Bogey—373, 380
"Song of the Mounties, The"—125
Song of the Sea—159
Songs from Milk Wood—387
Songspiel—429
So Nice They Named It Twice—428
Son of Heaven, The—136
Son of Oblomov—346
Sons and Soldiers—234
Sons of Adam—219
Sons of Light, The—427, 438, 444
Sons of Oedipus, The—436
Sons O' Fun—227
Sons O'Guns—164
Son, Son, Get the Gun—407
Sooner or Later—138
Sophocles—58, 60, 122, 145, 202, 246, 249, 250, 273, 280, 283, 295, 319, 346, 348, 353, 360, 361, 380, 390, 394, 397, 403, 416, 417, 431
Sorcerer, The—76, 173, 184
Sorceress, The—9, 20
Sore Throats—455
Sorrow Beyond Dreams, A—436
Sorrows of Stephen—455
Sorrows of Werther—455
Sorry You've Been Troubled—166
S.O.S.—158
Sothern, Ann—176
Sothern, E. H.—4, 6, 15, 23, 36, 50, 53, 54, 58, 59, 69, 97, 109, 122, 132, 270
Sothern-Marlowe Shakespeare Repertory Company—53, 447
Sothern, Sam—7, 16, 20, 43, 58, 84
So This Is London!—119
So This Is Love—158
Souchette, H. A.—53
Soule, Robert—333
Soul Kiss, The—41, 45
Soul of Nicholas Snyders, The—203
Soul of the White Ant—428
Sound of Hunting, A—256
Sound of Murder, The—315
Sound of Music, The—314, 328, 367, 376, 411, 455
Souris—33
Souris, Chauve—126
Sousa, John Philip—1, 30, 60, 87
Sous la Lumiere Rouge—76
"South American Way, The"—216
Southard, Henry D.—156
Southern Cross Players—215
Southerners, The—19
Southern Girl in the Sistine Chapel, A—179
Southern Maid, A—101
South Pacific—154, 262, 270, 273, 295, 306, 329, 354, 367, 376
South Sea Bubble—299
Soutter, Dan—206
Souvaine, Henry—141, 148
Sovey, Raymond—211, 362
Sowande, Fela—201
So Who's Afraid of Edward Albee?—340

Soyinka, Wole—360, 361, 365, 373, 409
So You're Writing a Play!—251
Space Is So Startling—336
Space/The Company, The—423
Spain, Elsie—53
Spaniard in the Works, A—373
Spanish Art Theatre—152
Spanish Love—99, 313
Spanish Theatre Repertory Company—285
Spanish Tragedy, The—444
Spanish Treasure—107
Spano, Lynn—440
Sparer, Paul—434
Spark, Muriel—336, 358, 384
Sparks, Ned A.—78
Sparrers Can't Sing—323, 402
Speaight, Robert—105, 159, 167, 197, 207, 214, 246, 249
Speckled Band, The—53
Speed Limit—166
Spegl, Fritz—342
Spell #7—455
Spelvin, George—31, 42
Spence, Ralph—134
Spencer, Helen—134
Spencer, Marian—248
Spender, Stephen—312, 398
Spenser, Jeremy—323
Spettri—122
Spewack, Bella—181, 196, 204, 211, 258, 281, 325, 428
Spewack Sam—181, 196, 204, 211, 258, 262, 265, 276, 281, 325, 399, 428
Spider's Web—289
Spider, The—148
Spiderwoman Theatre—438
Spigelgass, Leonard—314
Spike Milligan and Musical Friends—422
Spikes, John C.—65
Spinetti, Victor—339, 351, 380, 409, 414, 418
Spingarn Medal—198
Spirit of Parsifal Robinson, The—95
Spirochete—214
Spiser, Frank—413
Spithead—383
Splinters—96
Splits, The—329
Spohn, Walter—251
Spoiled—394
Spoilers, The—35, 38
Spokesong—428, 431
Spoleto Festival of Two Worlds—427
Sponge Room, The—335
Spong, Hilda—118, 129
Spook Sonata, The—130
Spoon River Anthology—338
Sporting Days—42
Sporting Duchess, The—154
Sporting Life—73
Sporting Love—191, 243
Sporting Times—73
Sport of Kings, The—127
Sport of My Mad Mother, The—311
Spot on the Sun, The—151
Spotted Dick—218
Sprague, W. G. R.—29, 34, 38, 70, 81
Spreading the News—23, 28, 59
Spread It Abroad—201
Spriggs, Elizabeth—373, 389, 390, 396, 415, 430
Spring—246
Spring Again—226
Spring and Port Wine—354
Spring Awakening—340, 353, 356, 367, 415, 446
Spring Chicken, The—26
Spring Cleaning—118, 133
Spring Is Here—163
Spring Maid, The—52, 58, 123
Spring Meeting—212
Spring Rites—416
Spring Song, A—348
Springtime for Henry—177, 183, 197, 220, 391, 412
Squall, The—142, 153

Squaring the Circle—195, 197
Squarzina, Luigi—374
Squat Betty—335
Squaw Man, The—26, 51, 251
Squire, J. C.—143, 173, 202
Squire Puntila and His Servant Matti—354
Squire, Ronald—95, 107, 119, 135, 177, 236, 248, 267, 272, 285
Sriosto, Ludovico—391
Srts Theater Club (Vancouver)—350
S.S. Glencairn—128, 254, 259
Stabb, Dinah—443
Stack, William—80, 89
Stacpoole, H. De Vere—101
Stadlen, Lewis—385
Stafford-Clark, Max—379, 409, 415, 417, 431, 436, 439, 449
Stage Blood—418, 446
Stage Confidences—138
Stage Door—200, 210, 376
Stage Door Canteen—233
Stage in America, The—209
Stage Is Set, The—369
Stageland: Curious Habits and Customs of Its Inhabitants—153
Stage Relief Fund—185
Stage Society, The—2, 24, 39, 54, 58, 63, 68, 72, 84, 104, 114, 117, 128, 134, 140, 144, 145, 152, 177, 178, 190, 195, 219
Stage Struck—451
Stage Year Book, The—98
Stag Movie—393, 430
Stainer, Annie—387, 415, 422, 435
Staircase—361, 371
Stalag 17—271
Stalin, Joseph—371
Stalin Peace Prize—432
Stallings, Lawrence—125, 132, 138, 141, 170, 318
Stallone, Sylvester—399
Stamper, Dave—82, 88, 93, 99, 105, 106, 112, 127, 342
Stamp-Taylor, Enid—241
Stamp, Terence—451
Standard Theater (Kansas City, Missouri)—5
Stander, Lionel—227
Standing, Aubrey—123
Standing, Guy—10, 30, 123
Standing, Herbert—123
Standing, John—360, 373, 376, 421, 422, 450
Standing, Percy—123
Standing, Victor—241
Standing, Wyndham—123
Stand Up and Sing—177
Stanford, Arthur—47
Stanford, Jack—227
Stange, Hugh—224
Stangel, Jo—229
Stange, Stanislaus—10, 16, 20, 48, 87
Stanislavsky, Constantin—121, 137
Stanislavsky's Moscow Art Theatre—111
Stanitsyn, Victor Y.—311
Stanley, Arthur—107, 127
Stanley, Audrey—454
Stanley, Blanche—89
Stanley Company—130
Stanley, Charles—38
Stanley, Kim—281, 293, 297, 309, 314, 348
Stanley, Pamela—196, 220
Stanley, Pat—309, 327, 338
Stanley, Phyllis—235
Stanley, Richard—39
Stanwood, Sheldon—118
Stanwyck, Barbara—141, 149
Stapleton, Jean—322
Stapleton, Maureen—250, 255, 262, 271, 281, 286, 293, 304, 310, 320, 354, 371, 385, 386, 402
Star and Garter—46, 230
Star for the Night, A—302
Stargazing—446

Stark, Graham—273
Starkie, Martin—372, 453
Starkweather, David—340
Starlight Roof—253, 256
Starr, Frances—31, 67, 123, 281
Stars and Stripes—374
Stars in My Crown—341
Stars in Your Eyes—215, 216
Star-Spangled Girl, The—358
Star Theater (Toronto)—18
Star Time—240
Starting Now—437
Star Turns Red, The—223
Star-Wagon, The—205, 215
Stary Theatre—422
"Stately Homes of England, The"—216
Statements After an Arrest Under the Immorality Act—414, 444
State of Emergency—401
State of Revolution—435
State of the Union—244, 251, 376
State Theatre of Northern Greece—439
Statham, Keith—305
Stavis, Barrie—255, 319
Stavrogin, Nicholas—342
Stayton, Frank—18, 45, 134
St. Claire, Perri—417
St. Clair, Lydia—241
St. Clair, Sylvie—267
St. Cyr, Dirce—35
Stead, Estelle—76
Steadman, Alison—450
Steambath—385
"Steam Heat"—287
Stearns, James Hart—380
Steele, Henry—59
Steele, Marjorie—282
Steele, Tommy—313, 339, 383, 418, 440
Steele, Vernon—59
Steel, Pippa—362
Steel, Wilbur Daniel—191
Steeplejack—109
Steer, Jeanette—7
Stehli, Edgar—103
Steiger, Rod—314, 333
Steinbeck, John—205, 211, 215, 230, 233, 266, 294, 418
Steinbock, Rudolf—373
Steiner, Andreas—177
Steiner, Eric—439
Stein, Gertrude—278, 365, 418
Stein, Joseph—293, 298, 314, 338, 344, 371, 406
Stein, Leo—150
Steinman, Jim—410
Stein, Peter—437
Stein unter Steinen—53
Stell, John—450
Stepanek, Karel—239
Stephen D.—339
Stephen Foster Drama Association—317
Stephen Foster Story, The—317
Stephens, Frances—325
Stephens, Nan Bagby—119
Stephenson, Henry—94
Stephens, Robert—310, 318, 346, 348, 353, 367, 375, 388, 389, 403, 410
Stephens, Yorke—2
Stephins, James—91
Step-in-the-Hollow—306
Stepping Sisters—170
Sterling, Jan—262, 304
Sterndale-Bennet, Joan—275
Stern, G. B.—165
Sternhagen, Frances—345, 346, 358, 404, 449
Sternheim, Carl—197, 421
Stern, Teddy—205
Stevedore—190
Stevens, Connie—358
Stevens, Craig—338
Stevens, David—66
Stevens, Edwin—42
Stevens, Elsie—89
Stevens, Emily—4, 123, 124

Stevens, Gavin—314
Stevens, George—71
Stevens, Gowen—314
Stevens, Leslie—309
Stevens, Michael—394
Stevenson, Charles A.—2, 25, 161
Stevenson, Richard—118
Stevenson, Robert Louis—53, 74, 318
Stevens, Onslow—252
Stevens, Rise—348
Stevens, Roger L.—268, 363
Stevens, Shakin'—435
Stevens, Thomas Wood—139, 264
Stevens, Virginia—221
Steward, Athole—101, 108, 182, 222
Steward, Ron—383
Stewart, Donald Ogden—170
Stewart, Ellen—331, 388, 403, 416, 424, 430, 438, 445, 451
Stewart, Grant—31, 161
Stewart, Jimmy—422
Stewart, Johnny—266, 274, 276
Stewart, Marion—244
Stewart, Melville—10
Stewart, Michael—320, 326, 344, 350, 371, 413, 434, 445, 455
Stewart, Shakespeare—59
Stewart, Sophie—217, 244
St. George and the Dragon—4
St. Helena—200, 202, 210
St. Helier, Ivy—101, 127, 151, 207, 399
Stickiness of Gelatine, The—11
Stickney, Dorothy—142, 157, 181, 217, 257
Sticks and Bones—398, 444
Stiers, David Ogden—413
Sti, John—273
Stiller, Jerry—310
Still Life—201
Still Life Story, The—366
Still Waters—278
Stimac, Anthony—415
Stinger, Michael—329
Stitt, Milan—405, 421, 452
Stix, John—295, 296, 453, 454
St. James Theatre—4, 39, 308
St. Joan of the Stockyards—329, 347, 415
St. John, Lily—102, 114
St. John, Marco—372
St. Leger, Margot—159
St. Louis Woman—247
St. Mark's Gospel—447
St. Moritz—206
St. Nicholas Theatre—418
Stocker, Willard—259, 265, 284
Stockfield, Betty—166
Stockholm Marionette Theatre, The—362, 368
Stockholm's Royal Dramatic Theatre—389
Stock, Nigel—187, 267, 281, 287, 311, 451
Stockton, Frank—358
Stockwell, Dean—235, 304
Stockwell, Guy—235
Stoddard, Haila—224
Stoddard, Lorimer—1
Stoddart, George—88
Stoker, Bram—135, 150, 219, 432, 434, 440
Stokes, Leslie—202, 260
Stokes, Sewell—202, 260
Stokes, Simon—447
Stoler, Shirley—353
Stoll, Oswald—13, 24
Stolz, Robert—113, 150, 151, 177, 183, 223, 273, 322
Stomp—383, 389
Stone—430
Stone, Allene—14, 30, 82, 100, 123
Stone and Star—337
Stone, Carol—244, 246
Stone, Charles—144
Stone, Dorothy—123, 155
Stone, Edward Durell—399
Stone, Elly—371
Stone, Ezra—211, 262, 265
Stone, Fred—155, 327

Stone, Gene—407
Stone, Irving—421
Stone, Louis—87
Stone, Paddy—315, 328
Stone, Peter—352, 378, 386, 400
Stop! Look! Listen!—74
Stoppard, Tom—359, 365, 372, 380, 388, 389, 390, 394, 401, 414, 427, 431, 436, 443, 446, 450, 451, 452, 455
Stop the Parade—429
Stop the World—I Want to Get Off—328, 332, 343, 447
Stop Thief—62, 75
Stop You're Killing Me—390
Storch, Arthur—336, 371
Storey, David—368, 379, 386, 394, 409, 410, 415, 424, 430, 431
Storey, Fred—44
Storm, Lesley—217, 244, 263, 305
Storm Operation—243
Storm Over Patsy—207
Storm Over Wicklow—188
Storm Song—192
Storm, The—3, 76, 93, 127, 167, 361
Storri, Terri—134
Story, Edith—19
Story of Mary Surratt, The—252, 256
Story of Waterloo, The—84
Story Theatre—390
Stothart, Herbert—99, 117, 119, 133, 150, 157
Stott, Judith—294, 309, 327
Stott, Mike—359, 415
Stowe, Harriet Beecher—8, 234, 242
St. Patrick's Day—188, 250
St. Petersburg Dramatic Company—27
Strachey, J.S.—136, 151, 172, 222
Strachey, Lytton—116, 136, 414
Straight, Beatrice—228, 252, 266, 291, 359, 365
Straight Up—387
Straight, Willard—368
Strange Bedfellows—257
Strange Fruit—244
Strange Interlude—156, 162, 169, 177, 190, 340
Strange, Michael—105, 146
Strange Orchestra—183
"Strangers in Paradise"—282
Strasberg, Lee—131, 149, 163, 167, 179, 259, 260, 262, 273, 339, 348, 362
Strasberg, Paula—362
Strasberg, Susan—289, 293, 312, 341
Stratford-upon-Avon Memorial Theater—324
Stratten, Gil Jr.—226
Straus, Oscar—41, 48, 105, 115, 134, 144, 165, 187, 244, 254
Strauss, Botho—437, 451
Strauss, Johann—167, 177, 182, 190, 250, 290, 316, 389
Strauss, Richard—423
Strauss, Robert—271
Stravinsky, Igor—240, 295, 368, 390
Strawberry Fields Forever—437, 444
Straw Hat Players—307
Straw Hat Revue, The—216
Straw, The—106, 419
Streamers—428, 445
Streamline—192
Streep, Meryl—430, 436
Streetcar Named Desire, A—252, 261, 263, 268, 300, 369, 381, 407, 416, 439
Street Fighting Man—444
Street, G. S.—73, 139
Street, James—281
Street Scene—163, 199, 254, 369
Street Singer, The—127, 164
Streets of London, The—184, 232
Streets of New York or Poverty is No Crime, The—179
Streets of New York, The—342
Streets of Paris, The—216
Strehler, Giorgio—307, 312
Streisand, Barbara—332, 344
Strickland, William—204

Strictly Dishonorable—164
Stride, John—334, 341, 355, 361, 365, 373, 437
Strider—456
Strider: The Story of a Horse—453
Strife—48, 60, 189, 445
Strike a New Note—235
Strike it Again—241
Strike Up the Band—170
Strindberg, August—50, 59, 63, 109, 130, 146, 166, 173, 199, 219, 250, 260, 264, 278, 283, 300, 306, 316, 334, 335, 343, 346, 347, 354, 359, 360, 366, 396, 397, 398, 402, 408, 409, 415, 417, 422, 428, 434, 436, 439, 444, 446, 451, 452
String—380
Stringer, Michael—319
Stringle, Berny—427
Strip-Stease—379
Stritch, Elaine—253, 291, 293, 309, 326, 385, 386
Strode, Warren—247
Stroecklin, E.—270
Stroll Theatre (London)—308
Stromber, John—1
Strong are Lonely, The—300
Strong, Austin—61, 66, 87, 117
Strong Breed, The—365
Strong, Edward—448
Stronger, The—300, 347, 408, 430, 436
Stronger Woman, The—50
Strong Hand, The—84
Strongheart—25
Stroud, Gregory—133
Strouse, Charles—320, 344, 357, 401, 434, 442, 450
Strudwick, Kate—159
Strudwick, Lucille—191
Strudwick, Sheppard—186, 371, 427
Struggle Everlasting, The—153
Strut Miss Lizzie—112
Stshona, Winston—413
Stuart, Aimee—171, 191, 245, 268
Stuart, David—199
Stuart, Jeanne—197
Stuart, Leslie—1, 7, 11, 16, 32, 43, 56
Stuart, May—75
Stuart-Morris, Joan—454
Stuart, Otho—27
Stuart, Philip—171, 191
Stubborness of Geraldine, The—11
Stubbs, Una—401, 414, 437
Student King, The—31
Student Prince, The—126, 142, 242, 374, 426, 446
Studholme, Marie—33, 36
Studies of the Nude—366
Studio Arena Theatre, The (Buffalo, N.Y.)—356
Studio Theatre—224
Sturges, Preston—164, 271
Sturua, R.—455
Stuttgart Opera—362
Styne, Jule—252, 263, 271, 281, 288, 298, 309, 314, 321, 327, 334, 344, 364, 400, 413
Sty of the Blind Pig, The—398
Subject to Fits—395, 398
Subject Was Roses, The—344, 356, 416
Suburbia Comes to Paradise—166
Subways Are for Sleeping—327
Subway, The—163
Successful Calamity, A—82, 86
Success Story—184
Such Is Life—295
Suddenly at Home—394
Suddenly Last Summer—309, 410
Sudermann, Hermman—3, 4, 12, 23, 44, 53, 71, 121, 144, 233
Sudlow's Dawn—435
Sugar—400
Sugar Babies—450
Sugar Bowl, The—40
Sugar in the Morning—316
Suggs—401
Suicide in B Flat—440

Suicide, The—453
Suitcase, The—366
Suite in Three Keys—358, 413
Sulky Fire, The—241
Sullivan, Arthur—4, 63, 68, 97
Sullivan, Dan—419, 429
Sullivan, Ed—230
Sullivan, Francis—222, 224
Sullivan, Frank—177
Sullivan, Henry—182, 206
Sullivan, Jo—298
Sullivan, John—56
Sullivan, Margaret—200, 235, 277, 282, 294, 324
Sullivan, Vincent—88
Sultan of Sulu, The—10, 11
Sumac, Yma—271
Summer and Smoke—257, 276, 278, 313, 142
Summer Brave—1972/3
Summer Days—396
Summerfolk—417, 422, 437
Summer Harlequinade—232
Summer, Keene—110
Summer of the Seventeenth Doll—305, 309, 313
Summers, Basil—219
Summers, Elaine—365
Summer Song—299
"Summertime"—196, 295
Summertree—371
Summer Widowers, The—52
Summit Conference—444
Sumurun—59, 61, 135
Sunday—20
Sunday Dinner—390
Sunday in New York—327
Sunday Play Society—117
Sunday Promenade—422
Sunde, Karen—444
Sunderland, Nan—190
Sunderland, Scott—172, 197
Sundgaard, Arnold—212, 214, 369
Sundown Beach—260
Sun Never Sets, The—212, 389
Sunny—132, 143, 363
Sunny River—236
Sun of York, The—296
Sunrise at Campobello—65, 309, 313
Sunset in Late Autumn—366
Sunshine—428
Sunshine Boys, The—93, 400, 412, 421
Sunshine Girl, The—62, 73
Sunshine Train, The—400
Sun Up—117, 130, 134
Superman—363, 394
Super Santa—377
Suppressed Desires—84, 109, 188
Suratt, Valeska—36
Surguchev, Ilya—207
"Surrey With The Fringe On Top, The"—234
Surtees, R. S.—359
Sus—455
Susan and God—205, 215
"Susanna, Don't Your Cry"—219
Suspect—296
Sutcliffe, Berkeley—277
Suter, Graham—278
Sutherland, Dan—290
Sutherland, Donald—381
Sutherland, Evelyn G.—7
Sutro, Alfred—21, 23, 46, 57, 76, 95, 116, 117, 146
Sutton, Dudley—345
Sutton, Julia—427
Sutton, Shaun—263
Suzanna and the Elders—224
Suzette—83
Suzman, Janet—355, 367, 373, 381, 389, 409, 430, 439
Suzuki, Pat—309
Svervo, Italo—422
Svoboda, Josef—331, 388
Swados, Elizabeth—424, 434, 436, 442, 445, 452
Swan, Durrant—70
"Swanee"—87
Swank—72

Swan, Mark—36, 39, 83
Swann, Donald—272, 282, 299, 305, 317
Swann, Russell—111
Swan, Scott—453
Swanson, Beatrice—105
Swanson, Gloria—269
Swanson, Marcella—105
Swan, The—118, 130, 172
Swashbuckler, The—3
Swayne, Martha—95
Sweatnam, Willis—174
Sweeney Agonistes—197
Sweeney Todd—128, 178, 184, 318, 408
Sweeney Todd, the Demon Barber of Fleet Street—449
Sweet Adeline—164
Sweet Alice—394
Sweet Aloes—192
Sweet and Low—171, 241, 248
"Sweet and Low Down"—133
Sweet Ann Page—313
Sweet Bird of Youth—314, 319, 424
Sweet Charity—357, 363, 366
Sweete, E. Lyall—2, 11
Sweeter and Lower—241
Sweet Eros/Witness—371
Sweetest and Lowest—248
Sweethearts—66, 167, 254
Sweet, Jeff—455
Sweet Kitty Bellairs—15
Sweet Little Devil—124
Sweet Madness—277, 278
Sweet Marie—137
Sweet Mr. Shakespeare—423
Sweet Nell of Old Drury—2, 11, 121, 192, 209
Sweet Talk—409
Sweet Thursday—294
Sweet Yesterday—245
Swenson, Inga—351, 374
Swenson, Karl—240
Swenson, Swen—332
Swerdlow, Robert—393
Swerling, Jo—267
Swete, E. Lyall—127, 134, 159
Swetland, William—395
Swift, Allan—423
Swift, Clive—348
Swift, Dean Jonathan—259
Swift, Johnathan—8, 68, 427
Swift, Kay—170
Swinarski, Konrad—422
Swinburne, Algernon Charles—58
Swinburne, Ann—66
Swinburne, Nora—119, 143, 158, 231, 244, 284, 315
Swineherd and the Princess, The—8
Swinging Down the Lane—315
Swingin' the Dream—217
Swing Mikado, The—218
Swinley, Ion—144, 198, 208
Swinstead, Joan—182, 264, 274, 279, 285, 289, 295
Swiss Family Robinson, The—384
Sword of Gideon, The—279
Sybil—78, 107, 422
Sydney, Basil—96, 112, 117, 137, 329, 376
Sykes, Eric—310
Sylvaine, June—259
Sylvaine, Vernon—201, 227, 232, 244, 259, 268, 283
Sylva, Marguerite—56
Sylvester, Harry—222
Sylvester, William—257
Sylvia Plath—410, 415
Symonds, Evelyn—53
Symonds, Norman—392
Symonds, Robert—355, 373, 376, 380, 391, 454
Symphony in Two Flats—166
Syms, Sylvia—355
Synchronous Winch System—325
Syncopated Sandy—233
Syndham, Charles—2
Syndicate, The—39, 86, 91
Synge, John Millington—16, 22, 28, 37, 50, 51, 58, 59, 60, 65, 84, 86,
90, 137, 144, 160, 193, 208, 218, 250, 341, 389, 422, 445
Szajna, Josef—451
Szirmai, Albert—143
Szorgyi, Alex—323

Tabbert, Bill—240
Taber, Richard—131
Taber, Robert—12
Table by the Window—289
Table Manners—414
Table Number Seven—289
Table of Cymbeline, The—396
Table Settings—452
Tabor, Desiree—148
Tabori, George—276, 281, 286, 311, 325, 332, 364, 375, 395
Tabori, Kristoff—413
Tabs—88
Tactics—90
Tafler, Sidney—310
Tagg, Alan—301, 386
Tagore, Radbindranath—68
Tahlequah, Oklahoma—381
Tailor Made Man, A—82
Tails Up—89
Tait, Michael—423
Taiz, Lillian—113
Takazauckas, Albert—426
Take a Chance—182
Take a Giant Step—292
Take a Life—329
Take Her She's Mine—327
"Take Him"—222
Take It From Us—268
Take Me Along—314
Taken in Marriage—452
"Taking a Chance on Love"—222
Taking of Miss Janie, The—422
Takis, Steve—221
Talbot, Howard—8, 27, 29, 35, 48, 57, 67, 79, 80, 84, 95
Talbot, Lyle—221
Talbot, Percy—43
Talbot's Box—440
Tale of Istanbul, A—396
Tale of Kasane, The—380
Tale of Two Cities, A—245, 418
Tales From the Vienna Woods—436
Tales of the Hasidim—436
Tales of the South Pacific—262
Taliaferro, Edith—35, 52, 79
Taliaferro, Mabel—19, 28, 33, 222, 456
Talker, The—61
Talking About Yeats—335, 380, 396
Talking To You—232, 336
Talk of New York, The—36
Talk of the Night—284
Talk of the Town, The—4, 26, 289
Talley's Folly—452
Tall Story—314
Tallulah—377
Tally-Ho!—7
Tally, Ted—439
Talmud, Blanche—131
Tamburlaine—401
Tamburlaine the Great—274, 300, 403, 431
Taming of the Shrew, The—8, 22, 23, 37, 45, 53, 54, 58, 59, 63, 68, 72, 73, 76, 80, 89, 96, 97, 103, 109, 114, 115, 122, 128, 129, 144, 152, 159, 160, 166, 167, 178, 183, 185, 188, 197, 198, 202, 207, 208, 209, 214, 218, 219, 223, 228, 232, 242, 255, 258, 259, 264, 269, 273, 283, 284, 285, 290, 296, 300, 301, 306, 311, 312
Tamiris, Helen—126, 257, 288
Tamiroff, Akim—121
Tancock, Blanche—143
Tandy, Jessica—154, 177, 179, 197, 202, 206, 207, 212, 213, 219, 223, 252, 268, 283, 286, 295, 316, 326, 329, 337, 357, 393, 404, 413, 434
Tangerine—105
Tango—359, 378
Tanguay, Eva—10, 15

Tannenbaum, Murray—351
Tannen, Julius—74, 132, 141
Tanner and Nicholls—8
Tanner, James—2, 10, 11, 16, 21, 53, 63, 67
Tanner, John—249
Tanner, Tony—426
Tanquerray, Paula—424
Tansy, John—41
Tapping, Mrs A.B.—91
Tarasova, Olga—121
Tarbell, Ida—142
Tarbuck, Jimmy—358
Tarkington, Booth—7, 42, 51, 87, 93, 94, 104, 177, 271
Tarnish—130
Tarot—396
Tarragon Theatre—397
Tarride, M.—58
Tartuffe—45, 245, 260, 269, 316, 328, 353, 356, 366, 367, 374, 381, 401, 417, 423, 431, 437, 446
Tarver, Ben—358
Tashman, Lilyan—117
Taste of Honey, A—311, 316, 320, 331, 390, 430, 441
Tate, James—113
Tate, J.W.—79, 80, 84
Tate, Neil—383
Tate, Reginald—202, 253, 258, 264
Tate, Richard—207
Tate, Sharon—391
Tattooed Man, The—35
Taubman, Lawrence—439, 444
Tavel, Ron—364
Tavel, Ronald—417
Tavern, The—100, 347
Tawson, Graham—264
Tawson, Tristan—264
Taylor, Bobby—434
Taylor, Cecil—360, 410
Taylor, C.H.—15, 16
Taylor, Charles—26, 28, 32, 287
Taylor, Christopher—340
Taylor, Clarice—382
Taylor, C.P.—353, 379, 410, 415, 421, 435, 439, 444
Taylor, Deems—182
Taylor, Don—359, 438, 445, 453
Taylor, Dwight—182
Taylor, Elizabeth—409
Taylor, Enid—114
Taylor, Horacena J.—447
Taylor, Ian—421
Taylor, Jabez—197
Taylor, Jack—218
Taylor, Jeremy—366
Taylor, Jeremy James—455
Taylor, John—353
Taylor, Laurence—393
Taylor, Laurette—52, 61, 62, 83, 90, 93, 108, 111, 121, 133, 134, 135, 136, 214, 244
Taylor, Malcolm—446
Taylor, Nellie—102
Taylor, Pat—218, 245
Taylor, Rosemary—239
Taylor, Ross—353
Taylor, Ruth—120, 206
Taylor, Samuel—266, 282, 309,421, 427
Taylor, Tom—8, 37
Taylor, Valerie—141, 191, 267, 315
"Tazzaganza"—120
Tchaikovsky—120
Tchin, Tchin—71, 322, 332, 343
Tea and Sympathy—281, 292, 301
Tea for Three—87, 153
"Tea for Two"—134
Teahouse of the August Moon, The—281, 288, 292, 302, 386
Teal, Ben—6, 10, 21, 35
Tea Party/The Basement—371
Tearle, Conway—7, 35, 61, 72, 181
Tearle, Godfrey—75, 102, 108, 122, 126, 136, 142, 183, 191, 192, 197, 201, 212, 222, 250, 255, 259, 264, 274, 277
Tearle, Noel—113
Tearle, Osmond—9

Teasdale, Verree—170
Teather, Ida—212
Teatro Libero—389, 391
Teatro Stabile di Genova—374
Teazle, Lady—23, 49
Tebelak, John-Michael—393, 398, 400
Tecosky, Morton—73
Tecumseh!—409
Teer, Barbara Ann—357, 382
Teeth 'n Smiles—412, 427
Tegel, Peter—379
Teichman, Howard—282, 352
Teitel, Carol—323
Telephone, The—252, 260
Telestar—337
Tell, Alma—106, 113, 132
Tell Charlie Thanks for the Truss—401
Tellegen, Lou—54, 67
Tell Me More—131, 134
Tell Me the Truth—161, 237
Tell, Olive—112
Temperamental Journey—66
Tempest, A. Vane—21, 27
Tempest, Marie—2, 8, 12, 16, 22, 35, 48, 58, 62, 67, 127, 134, 150, 151, 165, 171, 181, 188, 198, 213
Tempest, or The Enchanted Island, The—317
Tempest, The—45, 53, 59, 73, 80, 96, 108, 145, 173, 184, 192, 193, 208, 214, 223, 228, 232, 237, 245, 246, 249, 254, 264, 274, 278, 279, 289, 290, 295, 296, 306, 307, 317, 323, 335, 341, 360, 367, 374, 381, 388, 389, 396, 403, 415, 416, 417, 422, 423, 430, 444, 445, 446, 447, 454
Temple, Dot—94
Temple, Edward P.—19, 36, 110
Temple, Joan—248
Temple, Robert—409
Templeton, Fay—6, 19, 25, 30
Temporary Gentleman, A—94
Temptation—56
Tenderloin—321, 424
Tender Trap, The—287, 294
Ten Little Indians—236
Ten Little Niggers—236, 239
Ten Million Ghosts—203
Ten Minute Alibi—187
Tennant, Dorothy—35, 47
Ten Nights in a Bar-Room—173
Tennyson, Alfred—27, 159
Tenor, The—77
1066 and All That—196, 254, 384
Tenschert, Joachim—395
Tenth Man, The—53, 314, 325, 328, 368
Ten Times Table—443, 452
Terayama, Shuji—444
Terkel, Studs—442
Terminal—389
Terraces—415
Terraine, Alfred—13, 53, 121, 134
Terraine, Harkers—121
Terrible Meek, The—173
Terriford, Christopher—288
Terris, Ellaline—1, 8, 12, 16, 28, 32, 37, 398
Terris, Norma—140, 150
Terrorists, The—452
Terror, The—151
Terry, Beatrice—145
Terry, Charles—20, 27
Terry, Ellen—4, 8, 12, 16, 26, 33, 37, 46, 54, 72, 80, 96, 123, 256, 311
Terry, Ethelind—148, 177
Terry, Fred—2, 15, 26, 48, 57, 59, 97
Terry, J.E. Harold—74, 83, 120
Terry-Lewis, Mabel—119, 133, 181, 235
Terry, Marion—3, 12, 27, 32, 45, 59
Terry, Megan—358, 373, 418
Terry-Thomas—275, 283
Terson, Peter—367, 375, 382, 397, 403, 409, 423, 428, 430, 439, 447, 453
Tesich, Steven—390, 399, 402, 420
Tess of the D'Urbervilles—137

Testament of Critic—313
Test, The—154
Tetley, Dorothy—82, 92, 120, 124, 201
Tetzel, Joan—240, 257, 268, 339, 386
Tevie der Milchiger—306
Texas—360
Texas Dallas Players—144
Texas, Li'l Darlin'—262
Texas Panhandle Heritage Foundation—362
Texas, Steer, A—161
Texas Trilogy, A—426, 456
Texsmith, Vaughn—1
Teyte, Maggie—102, 274
Thackeray, William Makepeace—32, 78, 122, 250, 334, 349
Thais—56
Thank the Ladies—401
Thank You—106
Thank You, Miss Victoria—360
Thank You, Mr. Pepys!—207
Thark—151, 354, 438
Tharp, R.C.—119
That Brute Simmons—29
"That Certain Feeling"—133
That Championship Season—402, 412
Thatcher, Billy—227
Thatcher, Heather—114, 197
Thatcher, Torin—152, 159, 327
That Good Between Us—439
That Lady—262
That's A Good Girl—159
That's Gratitude—170
That's Us—330
Thaw, Evelyn Nesbit—369
Thaw, Harry K.—33, 369
Thaxter, Phyllis—260, 327
Theater and its Double, The—346
Theater Communications Group—331
Theater de France—347, 350, 373
Theater Royal (Bury St. Edmunds)—356
Theater Syndicate—10
Theater Workshop—323, 325, 328
Theater World Annual—325
Theatre—227, 267
Theatre 1969—375
Theatre Arts—302, 350
Theatre Arts Monthly—147
Theatre Arts of West Virginia—389
Theatre Behind the Gate—380
Theatre Collective—202
Theatre Company of Boston—438
Theatre Crafts—398
Theatre de la Cite—380
Theatre de la Grande Panique—389
Theatre de la Renaissance—50
Theatre de L'Atelier—274
Theatre DeLys—297
Theatre de Quat'Sous—409
Theatre Development Fund (TDF)—412
Theatre du P'tit Benheur—457
Theatre du Soleil—397
Theatre du Trident—398
Theatre du Vieux-Colombier—85, 89, 90, 95
Theatre for Shakespeare—432
Theatre Francaise—29, 114
Theatre-Go-Round—373, 388, 396
Theatre Group (UCLA)—325, 337
Theatre Guild—76, 92, 96, 99, 100, 103, 105, 117, 119, 121, 122, 124, 130, 131, 132, 133, 136, 137, 138, 142, 144, 145, 147, 152, 160, 162, 164, 167, 168, 169, 170, 171, 176, 177, 178, 179, 182, 183, 184, 186, 188, 189, 190, 192, 193, 194, 195, 197, 200, 203, 205, 207, 208, 209, 214, 216, 217, 218, 221, 223, 224, 225, 226, 227, 232, 233, 234, 235, 237, 238, 239, 243, 244, 248, 249, 250, 254, 256, 258, 259, 264, 265, 296, 311, 316, 318, 321, 369, 376
Theatre Guild School—146
Theatre Guild Shakespearean Repertory Company—249

Theatre Guild: The First Ten Years, The—307
Theatre-in-the-Round—297
Theatre Machine—390
Theatre Managers' Association—91
Theatre Michel, The—396
Theatre Nationale Populaire—301, 312, 431
Theatre New Brunswick—377
Theatre of Action—197, 202
Theatre of Cruelty—346
Theatre of the Open Eye—452
Theatre of the Riverside Church—415, 443
Theatre of the Soul—160
Theatre on the Balustrade—367
Theatre Passe Muraille—377, 384, 389
Theatre Populaire du Quebec—384
Theatre Projects—433
Theatre Row—399
Theatre Royal—5, 29, 34, 150, 196, 286, 289, 348, 353, 397
Theatre Union—187, 189, 192, 197, 198, 202, 207
Theatre Upstairs—387, 389, 399
Theatre Workshop—300, 301, 308, 311, 312, 316, 317, 318, 368, 390
Theatre World Award—319
Theatrical Censorship in Britain—251
Theatrical Ladies Guild—40
Theatrical Management Association—233
Theatrical Syndicate—13, 23, 29, 34, 51, 86, 154, 203
Theatrical Trust—24
Theatricum Botanicum—447
Thebom, Blanche—377
The Days and Nights of Beebee Fenstermacher—332
Their Very Own and Golden City—358
Theodore & Co.—79
Theodore, Lee—446
Theory of the Theatre—251
There and Back—12
There Are Crimes And Crimes—250
"There Are Fairies At the Bottom Of My Garden"—176
There Goes the Bride—414
There' Many a Slip—12
There's a Girl in My Soup—359, 364, 377
"There's a Great Day Coming Manana"—221
There's Always Juliet—176, 362
Therese—246
Therese Raquin—80, 184, 214, 246
There Shall Be No Night—221, 225, 236, 362
"There's No Business Like Show Business"—247
There's One in Every Marriage—396
There Was a Man—353
These Charming People—132, 419
These Foolish Kings—300
These Were Actors—256
Thesiger, Ernest—75, 80, 97, 143, 152, 179, 188, 191, 223
They Are Dying Out—430
They Came To a City—235
"They Didn't Believe Me"—75
They Knew What They Wanted—126, 138, 220, 298, 428
"They Knew What They Wanted Under the Elms"—131
They Might Be Giants—328
They're Playing Our Song—449, 457
They Shall Not Die—192, 194
They Walk Alone—264
Thief in the Night, A—313
Thief, The—35
Thie, Sharon—374
Thimig, Hans—153
Thimig, Hermann—153
Thimm, Daisy—41
"Thine Alone"—82

Things That are Caesar's—184, 188
Things That Count, The—66
Third Degree, The—47
Third Frontier, The—323
Third Little Show, The—176, 302
Third Man, The—260
Third Party Risk—219
Third Visitor, The—263
Thirkield, Rob—436, 445
Thirteen Clocks, The—362
13 Rue de l'Amour—428, 445
Thirteenth Chair, The—79, 84, 237
This and That—80
"This Can't Be Love"—212
This Fine-Pretty World—122
This Is the Army—230, 236
This is the Rill Speaking—360
This'll Make You Whistle—201
This Marriage—129
This Property Is Condemned—285, 320, 416
This Sceptered Isle—228
This Story of Yours—375
This Was a Man—142
This Was A Woman—241
This Was Burlesque—332, 351, 388
This Way to the Tomb!—246, 250
This Woman Business—143
This Year of Grace—158
Thoma, Herbert—88
Thomas, A.E.—78, 79, 101, 190
Thomas, Agnes—28, 107
Thomas, Augustus—1, 6, 7, 10, 11, 14, 15, 25, 36, 48, 51, 56, 87, 97, 121
Thomas, Basil—236, 259, 272, 289, 305
Thomas, Brandon—15, 33, 90, 224, 257, 289, 389, 416, 423, 431, 432, 438, 454
Thomas, Charles—367
Thomas, Dorothy—63
Thomas, Dylan—299, 301, 307, 313, 329, 335, 347, 359, 373, 387, 446
Thomas, Evan—89
Thomas, F.D.—73, 81
Thomas, Frank—55; 100
Thomas, Frank Jr.—190
Thomas, Gareth—409
Thomas, Gwyn—323, 330, 340
Thomas, Hugh—421, 428
Thomas, John Charles—66, 74, 93, 325
Thomas, J. Partivity—410
Thomas, Karri—34
Thomas, Majorie—291
Thomas, Marlo—339
Thomas, Mater Vivian—8
Thomas, Millard—170
Thomas Muskerry—54
Thomas, Nina—456
Thomas, Powys—325, 389
Thomas, Queenie—127
Thomas, Stephen—242, 246
Thomas, Terry—248, 310
Thom Company, The—166
Thompson, Alan—451
Thompson, Alex—57, 62
Thompson, A.M.—26, 27, 32, 48
Thompson, Annie—241
Thompson, Billy Jr.—144
Thompson, Brandon—398
Thompson, David—329, 348, 349, 431, 436
Thompson, Denman—23
Thompson, Derek—437
Thompson, Eric—401, 415, 421, 451
Thompson, Erik—406
Thompson, Ernest—447, 449
Thompson, Flora—445
Thompson, Franklin—23
Thompson, Fred—75, 79, 80, 84, 95, 108, 114, 126, 131, 133, 148, 149, 155, 164, 177, 182, 197, 201, 207, 213, 222, 239
Thompson, Frederick—29, 42
Thompson, Harlan—118, 126
Thompson, Jay—316
Thompson, Jimmy—418
Thompson, J. Lee—231

Thompson, Leonard—127
Thompson, Lydia—45
Thompson, Nina—418
Thompson, Paul—377, 412, 417, 438, 444
Thompson, Randall—140
Thompson, Sada—321, 364, 376, 381, 385, 394, 407
Thompson, Sadie—446
Thompson, S.P.—110
Thompson, Sylvia—197
Thompson, U.S.—125
Thompson, Venie—23
Thom, R.J.—412
Thomson, Beatrix—112, 119, 143, 144, 219
Thomson-Houston Company—225
Thomson, Virgil—219, 278
Thorndike, Eileen—76, 183, 193, 269
Thorndike, Russell—80, 103, 108, 183, 232, 404
Thorndike, Sybil—37, 46, 62, 68, 69, 71, 80, 95, 97, 108, 114, 115, 119, 122, 135, 137, 143, 145, 152, 166, 173, 178, 186, 188, 206, 208, 213, 228, 242, 245, 246, 249, 253, 263, 269, 272, 283, 301, 304, 315, 322, 334, 345, 359, 383, 433
Thorn, Geoffrey—4
Thornton, Jim—149
Thornton, Robert—415
Thorpe, George—272
Thor, With Angels—274, 411
Those Endearing Young Charms—234
Thoughts—403
Thoughts on the Instant of Greeting a Friend on the Street—374
Thousand Clowns, A—332, 337
Thou Shalt Not—214
Thread of Scarlet, A—455
Three Cheers—80
Three-Cornered Moon—186
Three Daughters of Monsieur Dupont, The—83
Three Faces East—87
Three Graces, The—126
Three Hearts, The—137
Three Homes—313
Three Hundred Club—136, 145, 152, 159
Three Leopards—197
Three Little Maids—13, 14, 363
Three Live Ghosts—100
Three Men on a Horse—195, 201, 227, 382, 412
Three Months Gone—387
Three Musketeers Ride Again, The—383
Three Musketeers, The—59, 60, 76, 87, 156, 189, 194, 199, 374, 418
"Three O'Clock in the Morning"—106
Three of Us, The—31
Three Penny Opera, The—188, 290, 300, 354, 361, 401, 402, 403, 439, 444
Three's a Crowd—171
Three's a Family—241
Three Sisters, The—103, 121, 144, 145, 198, 213, 232, 274, 297, 311, 325, 348, 353, 366, 367, 380, 381, 382, 408, 411, 424, 427, 430, 437, 453
Three Stooges—216
Three To Make Ready—247
Three Twins—41, 46
Three Waltzes—206, 244
Three Weeks—46, 84
Three Wise Fools—87
Three Wishes, The—349
Three Wonder Tales—53
Threlfall, David—453
Thrie Estaites, The—260, 264, 274, 317, 409
Throckmorton, Cleon—155, 181, 195, 232, 356
Through the Looking-Glass—184, 286, 300

Thulin, Ingrid—369
Thumbs—191
Thumb, Tom—146
Thunderbird, The—106
Thunderbolt, The—43, 245, 360
Thunder Rock—219, 228, 273, 404
Thunderstorm—438
Thurber Carnival, A—320, 325, 355, 432
Thurber, James—221, 225, 279, 320, 330, 362
Thurman, Wallace—163
Thurston, E. Temple—102, 119, 153, 283
Thurston, Howard—91
Thurston, Katherine C.—82
Thurston, Ted—378
Thwarting of Baron Bolligrew, The—355, 362
Thyestes—422
Thy Hostage—312
Tibbett, Lawrence—238
Tich, Little—161
Ticket-of-Leave Man, The—302
Tickets, Please—266
Tide Rises, The—197
Tidings Brought to Mary—84, 116
Tidmarsh, E. Vivian—241
Tierney, Dorothy—118
Tierney, Gene—221
Tierney, Harry—87, 93, 99, 113, 119, 148, 406
Tietjens, Paul—14
Tiffany, Maud—73
Tiger and the Horse, The—322
Tiger at the Gates—293, 294, 373
Tiger Cats—125, 128, 174
Tiger Rose—82
Tiger's Cub—79
Tiger, The—353
Tiger! Tiger!—88
Tiger, Tiger, Burning Bright—333
Ti-Jean and His Brothers—403
Tilbury, Walter—17
Tilden, Fritz—180
Tilford, Amelia—191
Tiller Girls—124, 138
Tiller, John—138
Tiller, Ted—440
Tilley, Vesta—4, 15
Tillie's Nightmare—52, 142
"Till the Clouds Roll By"—82
Till the Day I Die—195
Tilly of Bloomsbury—94
Tilton, George—184
Tilzer, Albert Von—112
Timberg, Herman—78
Timbuktu!—442
Time and the Conways—206
Time and Time Again—401
Time Gentlemen, Please—327
Time Limit!—298
Time of the Cuckoo, The—276, 286, 455
Time of Your Life, The—217, 225, 247, 295, 383, 417, 424
Time Out for Ginger—276
Time Present—374
Time Remembered—289, 304, 313
Times (London), The—24
Times Square—366
Times Square Theatre Centre—412
Time, The Place, And the Girl, The—35
Timon of Athens—22, 114, 160, 198, 278, 296, 302, 341, 350, 353, 396, 401, 438, 446
Tina—75
Tingalary Bird—349
Tinker's Wedding, The—68, 84, 86, 341
Tinney, Frank—118
Tin Pan Ali—455
Tin Pan Alley—224
Tinted Venus, The—235
Tiny Alice—345, 356, 381, 382, 386
Tiny Little—146
Tip-Toes—133, 143, 453
Tip Top—100

Tisa Chang's Pan Asian Repertory —438
'Tis Pity She's a Whore—121, 228, 329, 390, 403, 416, 438, 444
Titanic—429
Tit-Coq—259, 261
Titheradge, Dion—108, 114, 126, 127, 150, 151, 166, 172, 177, 182, 188, 191
Tear Paul—178, 237
Titheradge, Madge—79, 83, 88, 89, 102, 106, 108, 125, 127, 143, 151, 201, 330
Titheradge, Peter—218
Title, The—89
Titmuss, Phyllis—102, 107
Titus Andronicus—121, 122, 275, 295, 301, 306, 308, 367, 402, 409, 417, 446
Tivoli Opera House #3 (San Francisco)—34
Toad of Toad Hall—174, 179, 184, 189, 193, 291, 324, 330, 336, 342, 349, 355, 362, 369, 376, 391, 398, 432, 440, 447, 456
Tobacco Road—187, 224, 229, 238
Toba Circuit—450
To Be Continued—115
To Be Young, Gifted and Black—378
Tobias and the Angel—182, 208, 214, 219, 237, 284, 323, 436
Tobias, Charles—211
Tobias, George—125, 167, 192
Tobie, Ellen—454
Tobin, Genevieve—117, 149, 164
Tobin, Vivian—117, 121, 157
Toby's Bow—92
Tocher, E.W.—166, 178, 192
Todd, Ann—165, 172, 181, 201, 217, 272, 290, 302
Todd, Beverly—332
Todd, Clarence—156
Todd, Hal J.—301, 312
Toddles—32, 39
Todd, Mary—399, 400
Todd, Michael—219, 230, 238, 239, 261, 266
Tod, Kenneth—172
To Dorothy, A Son—268
To Fit the Crime—231
Together Again—253
To Have and To Hold—6
To Have the Honor—127
Toibin, Niall—385
Toilet, The—345, 356
Toke, John—43
Tokonogy, Gertrude—186
Tokyo Kid Brothers—386
Tokyo Kid Brothers Company—417
Tolan, Michael—350
TOLA (Theatre of Latin America) —382
Toledo Blade—104
To Live in Peace—264
Tolka Row—275, 278, 290, 295
Toller, Ernst—128, 166, 213
Toller, Rosalie—53
Tolstoy, Leo—16, 24, 27, 35, 63, 64, 69, 84, 90, 99, 121, 122, 153, 166, 167, 228, 249, 329, 335, 349, 435, 452, 453, 456
Toltons Theatre Company—295
To Make My Bread—196
Tom Brown's Schooldays—401
Tombs, J.S.M.—68
Tombstone Jake—243
Tomer, Ben-Zio—347
Tom Jones—36
Tomlinson, David—268, 289, 305, 315
Tomlinson, Paul—450
Tommy—450
Tomoika—445
Tomorrow and Tomorrow—176, 180, 362
Tomorrow the World—234, 238, 241
Tom Paine—366, 368, 371
Tompkins, Yewell—50
Toms, Carl—368, 390
Tomson, Bob—423

Tom Thumb the Great—418
Tone, Franchot—170, 176, 179, 181, 216, 221, 282, 295, 304, 376
Tonge, Philip—37
Tongues—455
Tong, Winston—451
Toni—127
Tonight at Eight—391
Tonight at 8:30—200, 201, 367, 396
Tonight in Samarkand—297
Tonight or Never—171
Tonight's the Night—75
Tonight We Improvise—416
Tons of Money—113
Tony Award—247, 312, 385, 394, 402, 406, 412, 414, 420, 449
Tony Draws a Horse—217, 219
Too Many Cooks—71, 113
Too Many Girls—217
Too Many Heroes—205
Too Much Johnson—54, 347
Tooth of Crime, The—403, 406, 416, 417
Too True To Be Good—103, 184, 242, 260, 340, 354, 416, 422
"Toot, Toot, Tootsie!"—106
Topaze—170, 183
Top Banana—271
Top of the World, The—36, 39
Topol—344
Topol, Josef—380
Top Speed—164
Topsy and Eva—126
To Quito and Back—208
Torchbearers, The—112, 134, 419
Toreador, The—8, 10
Toretzka, Ludmilla—234
Torjada, La—6
Torn, Rip—314, 344, 357, 364, 406, 452
Toronto Free Theatre—405
Toronto Opera House—18
Toronto's Theatre Passe Muraille—443
Toronto Workshop Productions—318
Torquet, Charles—76
Torrens, Grace—95
Tortilla Flat—211
Torture on a Train (Brain-Mechanisms of the Redistributed French Virgin)—441
Tosca—4, 13, 54
Total Eclipse—375, 415
Tot Family, The—428
To the Ladies—111
Totheroh, Dan—131, 181
To The Water Tower—338
To Those Born Later—437
Touch—386
Touch and Go—262, 267
Touched—439
Touch of Brightness, A—366
Touch of Spring, A—421
Touch of the Poet, A—309, 319, 365, 367, 416, 441, 448
Touch of the Sun, A—310
Touch Wood—192
"Toujours Gai"—304
Toumanova, Tamara—216
Tour—374
Tourner, Cyril—382
Tours, Frank—32, 56
Tovarich—196, 200, 210, 279, 338
Tovey, George—322
Towards Zero—421
Tower Beyond Tragedy, The—269
Towers, Constance—361, 367, 374, 438
Towers, David L.—9
Townsend, Marcia—190
Townshend, Pete—450
Toy, Barbara—264, 423
Toye, Wendy—191, 197, 241, 248, 253, 273, 317, 339, 346, 358, 389, 390, 397, 401, 402, 418, 437
Toymaker of Nuremburg, The—174
Toys in the Attic—320, 322, 325
Tozzi, Giorgi—367
Tracy, Lee—141, 157, 196, 376
Tracy, Spencer—149, 170

Tragedy of Nan, The—68, 237, 369
Tragedy of Pompey the Great, The —68
Tragedy of the Korosko, The—48
Tragedy of Thomas Andros, The—402
Tragedy of Truth—45
Trail of Tears, The—381
Trail of the Lonesome Pine, The—61
Trainer, David—375
Traitor, The—262
Tramp—403
"Tramp! Tramp! Tramp!"—52
Transfiguration of Benno Blimpie, The—437, 447
Transformations—424
Trantara! Tarntara!—421
Trap Play, The—428
Traps—435
Trask, Katrina—53
Traube, Shepard—276, 287
Trauble, Helen—294
Travails of Sancho Panza, The—382
Traveling Light—352
Traveller's Joy—258
Traveller, The—285
Traveller Without Luggage—316, 419
Travelling Music Show, The—443
Travelling Salesman, The—41
Traven—295
Travers, Ben—114, 126, 134, 138, 143, 151, 159, 165, 172, 177, 182, 187, 202, 212, 218, 253, 278, 349, 354, 424, 428, 430, 438, 444, 456
Travers, Bill—230
Traverse Company—407
Traverse Theater (Edinburgh)—347, 354, 366, 397, 445
Traverse Theatre of Edinburgh—395
Traverse Theatre Club—368, 375, 455
Travers, Henry—99, 103, 122, 137, 142, 200
Travers, Josephine—218
Travers, Linden—231
Travesties—414, 420, 433
Travolta, John—413
Treacher, Arthur—120, 171, 273
Treadwell, Sophie—131, 157, 186, 227, 233, 445
Treasure Hunt—263
Treasure Island—74, 115, 122, 128, 137, 145, 168, 174, 179, 189, 193, 203, 209, 214, 246, 250, 255, 261, 265, 269, 318, 330, 342, 348, 349, 355, 362, 369, 383, 404, 411, 424
Treasure on Pelican—278
"Treasurer's Report"—118
Treasure, The—103
Treats—427, 440
Trebitsch, Siegfried—135
Treble, Sepha—187, 197
Tree, Arthur Beerbohm—32
Tree, Beerbohm, Mrs.—16, 32, 44, 50, 143, 151
Tree Grows in Brooklyn, A—271, 355
Tree, Herbert Beerbohm—3, 4, 8, 11, 12, 16, 27, 32, 33, 39, 44, 45, 49, 50, 53, 54, 58, 59, 61, 63, 68, 72, 76, 80, 199, 303
Tree in the Crescent, A—279
Treemonisha—420
Tree, Viola—95, 102, 108, 135, 178, 187
Treewhela, Ralph—327
Trelawny—354, 403
Trelawny of the "Wells"—54, 91, 136, 153, 214, 279, 355, 390, 403, 421
Tremblay, Michel—375, 409, 413
Trembling Giant, The—440
Trench, Herbert—96
Trenkler, Freddie—239, 252
Trentini, Emma—52, 62, 74, 95
Trent, Jackie—406
Trespass—253
Treteau de Paris—353
Tretyakov, S.—171

Trevelyan, Hilda—22, 26, 33, 43, 63, 79, 122, 200, 202
Trevor—372
Trevor, Austin—176
Trevor, Claire—181
Trevor, Leo—43
Trevor, Michael—396
Trevor, Norman—82
Trevor, Spencer—158
Trial and Error—283
Trial by Jury—76, 173, 184, 193, 228, 232, 255, 260, 264, 269, 273, 290, 306, 316, 330, 349, 366, 369
Trial of Cobb and Leach—316
Trial of Lee Harvey Oswald, The—365
Trial of Mary Dugan, The—149, 237
Trial of Queen Caroline, The—455
Trial of the Catonsville Nine, The —393
Trials by Logue and Cob and Leach —323
Trials of Brother Jero, The—360, 365
Trial, The—367, 440
Triana, Jose—366
Tribades, The—445
Tribune—66, 442
Tribute to a Lady—428
Tribute to Lili Lamont, A—431
Tricks of Scapin, The—368
Trick To Catch the Old One, A—279
Trifles—80, 95
Trifles and Tomfooleries—366
Trilby—50, 109, 250, 268
Trilogy—316
Trimmingham, Ernest—114
Trimplet, The—80
Trinder, Tommy—227, 241, 253, 272
Trinity Square Repertory Company —350, 375, 388
Trinity Square Repertory Company (Providence, Rhode Island)—350, 353, 375, 388
Trinity Unity Methodist Church (Providence, Rhode Island)—350
Trio—241, 243, 246
Triple Image—368
Triple Play—316
Triplet, The—77
Trip to Bountiful, The—281, 301
Trip to Brighton, A—57
Trip to Chinatown, A—61, 116
Trip to Japan, A—47
Trip to Scarborough, A—179, 241
Trip to the Moon, A—97
Tristram and Iseult—166
Tritschler, Conrad—50, 61, 97
Triumph of the Egg—229
Trix, Helen—108
Trix, Josephine—151
Trix Sisters—108
Troilus and Cressida—68, 121, 202, 209, 249, 259, 290, 300, 302, 312, 313, 323, 325, 329, 335, 336, 341, 354, 373, 381, 403, 408, 410, 429, 430, 438, 455
Trojan Wars, The—366
Trojan Women, The—27, 208, 342, 349, 361, 430
Trolls—387
Troobnick, Gene—374
Trotter, Alan—241
Trotter, Frank—399
Trotter, Stewart—436
Troubled Island—369
Troubled Past, The—311
Trouble in Tahiti—293
Trouble with Ants, The—422
Trouncer, Cecil—198, 223
Troutman, Ron—420
Trovailoi, Armando—444
Trowbridge, Erwin—227
Troy, Daniel—64
Troy, Louise—344, 358
Truckline Cafe—247, 251
True Story of the Horrid Popish Plot, The—402, 422
Truex, Ernest—92, 100, 105, 125, 131, 137, 149, 181, 222, 250
Trumbo, Dalton—272

Trumpet In The Land—389
Trumpets and Drums—302, 423
Trumpet Shall Sound, The—142
Trumpets of the Lord—339
Truth About Blayds, The—108, 111
Truth Game, The—159
Truth, The—35, 50, 72
Trzinski, Edmund—271
Tsar Paul—178, 179, 237
Tschetter, Jane—434
Tschirkoff, Eugene—27
Tsubosaka—374
Tsuri Onna—374
Tsvel, Ronald—380
Tuberin 5—208
Tucci, Niccolo—367
Tucker, Don—378
Tucker, Sophie—47, 125, 211, 362
Tucker, Thomas—100
Tulip Time—197
Tulip Tree, The—334
Tull, Pat—96
Tully, George—83, 107, 134
Tully, Jim—141
Tully, May—128
Tully, Richard Walton—31, 61, 70, 91, 98
Tully, Tom—217, 221
Tumarin, Boris—332, 404, 411, 424, 456
Tumble In—92
Tumbler, The—320
Tunbridge, Joseph A.—113, 165, 166, 172, 178, 187, 191, 197, 206
Tune, Tommy—426
Tunnel Fever—452
Tunnel of Love, The—304, 305
Tuotti, Joseph Dolan—372
Tuppence Coloured—253
Turandot, Princess of China—67
Turgenev, Ivan Sergeyevich—121, 170, 237, 265, 300, 354, 357, 409, 416, 432, 447
Turkey Time—177
Turkish Bath—99
Turkish Clogs, The—446
Turleigh, Veronica—166
Turman, Glynn—357
Turn Again Whittington—324
Turnbull, Colin—428
Turnbull, Stanley—84
Turner, Bridget—451
Turner, David—452
Turner, Douglas—380
Turner, Holly—351
Turner, Jerry—317, 403, 430, 446, 454
Turner, J.H.—83, 89, 102, 108, 116, 120, 134, 135, 151, 158, 165, 201
Turner, John—69, 438
Turner, John Hastings—127
Turner, J.W.—5
Turner, Robert—203
Turner, Sam—333
Turner, Tubby—218
Turney, Catherine—210, 221
Turn of the Screw, The—250, 266, 306
Turn to the Right!—78
Turpin, Allan—250
Turquoise Pantomime, The—387
Tuscaloosa's Calling Me . . . But I'm Not Going!—420
Tushingham, Rita—333, 334, 390
Tussaud, Francois—96
Tutin, Dorothy—269, 272, 273, 274, 278, 282, 294, 297, 311, 317, 327, 329, 330, 352, 367, 394, 404, 418, 438, 439
Tutor, The—375
TV—358
Twain, Mark—149, 291, 358, 454
Twelfth Night—3, 8, 12, 22, 37, 49, 50, 53, 54, 58, 63, 64, 68, 72, 73, 76, 80, 85, 96, 97, 103, 109, 114, 115, 122, 136, 145, 152, 160, 166, 167, 173, 178, 180, 183, 184, 188, 189, 193, 198, 202, 207, 208, 214, 219, 223, 228, 232, 236, 237, 242, 245, 249, 254, 255, 260, 261, 274,

283, 284, 285, 289, 290, 295, 301, 306, 311, 312, 313, 317, 319, 323, 324, 329, 334, 335, 342, 348, 350, 360, 367, 371, 373, 380, 389, 396, 401, 402, 403, 409, 416, 417, 422, 429, 431, 436, 444, 445, 446, 447, 453, 454
Twelve Miles Out—133
Twelve-Pound Look, The—54, 56, 318
Twentieth Century—182, 269, 302
"Twentieth Century Blues"—178
20th Century Fox—229
Twenty Days in the Shade—46
27 Wagons Full of Cotton—293, 428
26 Efforts at Pornography—415
Twenty-to-One—197, 231
Twenty Years on Broadway and the Years it Took to Get There—233
Twiddle-Twaddle—30
Twigs—394
Twin Beds—71
Twirly Whirly—10
Two and Two—76
Two and Two Make Sex—407
Two Angry Women of Abington, The—72
Two Arts Ltd.—325
Two Black Crows, The—99, 125
Two Blind Mice—262, 265
Two Bouquets, The—201, 284
Two by Two—386
Two-Character Play, The—369
Two Children, The—241
Two Executioners, The—347
Two for the Seesaw—309, 311, 313, 340, 406
Two for the Show—221
Two Gentlemen of Verona, The—22, 54, 80, 136, 214, 264, 278, 279, 306, 307, 311, 360, 361, 374, 381, 388, 390, 396, 398, 409, 417, 423
Two Girls Wanted—141, 147
250th Anniversary Committee—323
Two Loves I Have. . .—279
Two Mrs. Carrolls, The—197, 235
Two Noble Kinsmen, The—159, 416
Two on an Island—221
Two on the Aisle—271, 383
Two Orphans, The—22, 104, 144, 154
Two Out of Time—65
Two Pierrots, The—136
Two Pins, The—45
Two Roses, The—20
Two Savants, The—64
Two's Company—276
"Two's Company, Three's None"—119
Two Shepherds, The—197
Two Stars for Comfort—333
Two Times One—388
2 x 2 = 5—153
Two White Arms—158
Tydeman, John—415, 421, 435, 436
Tyers, John—257
Tyger—396
Tyger! Tyger!—380
Tyler, George C.—98, 133 ,137, 160
Tynan, Brandon—124
Tynan, Kenneth—268, 274, 275, 309, 378, 427, 431
Tyneside, Theatre Company—427
Typhoon—67
Typists, The—338
Tyrant, The—134
Tyree, Elizabeth—153
Tyrell, Norman—246, 421
Tyrell, Susan—454
Tyrer, A.W.—102
Tyrone Guthrie Theatre (Minneapolis)—337
Tyson, Cicely—326, 332, 339, 378
Tyzack, Margaret—316, 388, 410, 417
Tzara, Tristan—414

Ubu in Chains—366
Ubu Roi—340, 361, 368, 374, 389
Udell, Peter—420
Uggams, Eloise—156
Uggams, Leslie—364, 371
Uhlanga (The Reed)—435
Ullmann, Liv—421, 438
Ulloa, Alejandro—285
Ulrich, Lenore—82, 93, 107, 126, 140, 158, 177, 391
Ulster Group Theatre—312
Ulysses—11, 317, 386, 415
Ulysses in Nighttown—317, 319, 415, 441
Ulysses in Traction—436
Umabatha—402, 408, 438
Umberger, Randolph—430
Umbrellas of Cherbourg, The—452
Umewaka, Manzaburo—408
Umewake Noh Troupe—408
Un Ballo in Maschera—264
Un Caprice—260, 296, 316, 340
Unchastened Woman, The—98
Uncle Harry—230, 233, 241, 245
Uncle Tom's Cabin—8, 123, 126, 189, 199, 308, 313
Uncle Vanya—72, 144, 247, 245, 249, 278, 311, 335, 341, 342, 387, 402, 403, 407, 416, 446
Uncle Willie—298
Uncommon Women and Others—440
Under Cover—15, 71, 153
Underdown, Edward—201, 311
Under Fire—153
Underground Hour—214
Underhill, John Garrett—96
Under Many Flags—61
Under Milk Wood—299, 301, 304, 313, 329, 373, 396, 446
Under Plain Cover—334
Undertaking, The—452
Under the City Lamps—90
Under the Clock—265
Under the Counter—245
Under the Gaslight—368
Under the Sycamore Tree—276, 325
Under the Yum-Yum Tree—321
Under Two Flags—6
Under Your Hat—213
Undiscovered County—451
Une Femme Charmante—76
Unexpected Guest, The—311
Unexpected Husband—176
Unexpected Years, The—318
Unexpurgated Memoirs of Bernard Mergendeiler, The—374
Unfair Sex, The—135
Un Fil a la Patte—359
Unforseen, The—12
Unger, Gladys—53, 67, 75, 80, 94, 141
Unguarded Hour, The—197
Un Honnéte Homme—45
Unicorn from the Stars, The—38
Uniform Theatre—223
Uninvited Guest, The—282
Union Jack and Bonzo—410
Union Square—194
Unitt, Edward—6, 7, 10, 11, 19, 25
Universal Film Corporation—104
University and College Theatre Association—399
University of Colorado at Boulder—312
University Resident Theatre Association—399
Unknown Soldier and His Wife, The—364, 374, 406, 412
Unknown, The—102, 122
Unknown Warrior, The—166, 297
Unknown Woman of Arras, The—291
Unquiet Spirit, The—264
Unseen Fear, The—108
Unseen Hand, The—407
Unseen Menace, The—369

Unshaven Cheek, The—341
Unsinkable Molly Brown, The—321
Un Sujet de Roman—122
Untermeyer, Louis—128
Untitled Play—366
Unto Such Glory—202, 311
Unto These Hills—269
Unvarnished Truth, The—443
Unveiling, The—220
Unwritten Law, The—53, 73
Up and Doing—222, 228
Up and Down Broadway—55
Up in Central Park—244, 418
Up in Mabel's Room—92
Up Pops the Devil—176
Up She Goes—113
Upstairs and Down—78
Up the Truncheon—439
Up the Years from Bloomsbury—250
Upton, Leonard—206
Up To Thursday—353
Uptown West—117
Uranium 235—279
Urban Arts—427
Urban, Charles—60
Urban, Joseph—65, 74, 78, 81, 105, 148, 154, 157, 170, 176, 181, 189
Urban Scenic Studio—65
Ure, Gudrun—275
Ure, Mary—289, 296, 299, 301, 302, 316, 320, 323, 329, 369, 394, 404
Urfaust—316
Urgent Hangman, The—277
US—89, 359
U.S.A.—321, 404
U.S. Amusement Company—39, 51
Ustinov, Peter—237, 241, 258, 264, 272, 285, 286, 299, 333, 364, 365, 374, 409
Ustinov, Tamara—364
Utopia—423

Vaccaro, Brenda—328
Vaccaro, John—438
Vachell, Horace—74, 75, 94 119
Vagabond King, The—132, 236, 398, 404, 424
Vail, Lester—163
Vajda, Ernest—124, 125, 126
Vakhtangov, Eugene—145
Valdez, Luis—356, 449
Vale, Martin—197
Valency, Maurice—266, 287, 290, 309
Valentina—240
Valentine, Anthony—394
Valentine, Sydney—6, 15, 21, 80, 91, 113
Valentino, Rudolph—154
Valentin, Thomas—367
Valery, Anne—452
Valiant, Stephen—391
Valjean, Jean—185
Valk, Frederick—232, 237
Vallee, Rudy—176, 196, 327
Vallen, May—83
Vallerand, Jean—423
Valley Forge—193, 318
Valli, Valli—47, 66, 77
Valmouth—311
Valor, Henrietta—415
Vampire, The—75, 436
Vamp, The—294
Van and Schenck—99
Van, Billy B.—42, 132, 140
Van, Bobby—291
van Bridge, Tony—273, 381, 389, 423, 438, 453
Vanbrugh, Irene—12, 16, 26, 32, 35, 49, 52, 53, 76, 79, 80, 91, 101, 108, 114, 144, 166, 172, 181, 207, 208, 212, 223
Vanbrugh, Sir John—23, 95, 179, 193, 241, 255, 268, 269, 341, 367, 409, 416
Vanbrugh, Violet—2, 3, 12, 21, 42, 49, 54, 57, 59, 63, 101, 135, 183, 207

Van Buren, A.H.—143
Vanburgh's Restoration—374
Van Call—289
Vance, Nina—256
Vance, Vivian—226
Vandam, Florence—362
Vanderbilt Cup, The—30
Vanderbilt, Gertrude—36, 88, 324
Vanderbilt, Gloria—295
van der Burgh, Margot—302
van Druten, John—129, 133, 159, 161, 176, 177, 183, 192, 199, 222, 230, 235, 240, 243, 246, 252, 267, 272, 275, 280, 308, 424
Vane, Sutton—120, 130, 136, 214, 224, 342
Van Fleet, Jo—249, 262, 276, 282, 305
van Griethuysen, Ted—329
van Gyseghem, Andre—145, 279, 283, 456
Van Heusen, James—352, 358
van Italie, Jean-Claude—358, 360, 374, 389
Vanities—146, 179, 186, 426
Vanities of 1923—118
Vanity Fair—73, 79, 250, 334
Vanne, Marda—107, 145, 151, 192, 214, 295
Van Patten, Dick—230
Van Patten, Joyce—338
VanPeebles, Melvin—393
Van Scott, Glory—301
Vantage Out—72
Van Tuyl—75, 206
Van Volkenburg, Ellen—103, 208, 252
Van Vooren, Monique—282
Varden, Evelyn—274, 305, 313
Vardi, David—133
Varesa, Nina—82
Variation on a Theme—310
Variety—265, 363, 384, 399, 405, 411, 412, 419, 425, 433, 441, 448, 456, 457
Vari, John—315
Vassilissa Melentieva—50
Vatzlav—389
Vaudeville Company—189
Vaughan, Frankie—336
Vaughan, Hilda—83
Vaughan-Williams, Alan—383
Vaughn, Gladys—329
Vaughn, Peter, 345
Vaughn, Stuart—307, 310, 312, 316, 318, 328, 389
Vaun, Russell—37
Vautrin—436
Vedrenne-Barker—20, 22, 23, 24, 27, 28, 32, 44
Vedrenne, John E.—24, 29, 39, 91, 104
Vegetable, The—163, 225, 237
Veiller, Bayard—61, 79, 84, 149, 237
Velez, Lupe—211
Velie, Janet—164
Velie, Jay—118
Velvet Glove, The—263
Velvet Lady, The—92
Venables, Clare—432
Veness, Amy—158
Veness, Molly—139, 145, 155
Venetian Twins, The—396
Venice Preserved—103, 284, 363, 401
Venne, Lottie—21, 43, 107
Venning, Una—127
Venora, Lee—354
Venture, Richard—395
Venturiloquist's Wife, The—446
Venus in Furs—452
"Venus in Ozone Heights"—235
Venus Observed—267, 268, 276, 280
Venuta, Benay—230
Vera-Ellen—230
Vera Violetta—57
Verdi, Giuseppe—255, 264, 280
Verdon, Gwenn—281, 293, 304, 314, 357, 420

Verga, Giovanni—380
Verge, The—137
Verhaeren, Emile—75
Verity, Frank T.—9, 154
Verlaine, Paul—375
Verlene, Marie-Claire—315
Verne, Jules—247
Verner, Gerald—277, 299
Verneuil, Louis—108, 144, 183, 206, 266, 275
Verney, Guy—244
Verno, Jerry—183
Vernon, Anne—268
Vernon, Barbara—202
Vernon, Dorothy—444
Vernon, Frank—72, 104, 165
Vernon, Gilbert—317
Vernon, Harry—68, 88, 101
Vernon, Margaret—146
Vernon, Marie—88
Vernon Rice Award—391
Veronica, Ann—379
Veronique—21
Very Good, Eddie—74, 363, 424, 428, 433
Very Idea, The—94
Very Naked Boy, The—80, 95
Very Special Baby, A—308
Very Warm For May—217, 246
Vestoff, Virginia—358
Veterans—401
Vetsera, Maria—205
Via Crucis—121, 122
Via Galactica—400, 405
Vian, Boris—335
Via Wireless—42
Vicar of Wakefield, The—32
Vicious Circle—249
Victims Anonymous—399
Victor—348, 374, 422
Victoria—208, 454
Victorian Music Hall—349, 353
Victorian Nights—154
Victoria, Queen—9
Victoria Regina—196, 202, 204, 206, 318
Victor, Josephine—66, 127, 190
Victor, Lucia—424, 455
Victory—94
Vida Es Sueño, La—285
Vidal, Gore—304, 308, 320, 325, 332, 400
Vienna Notes—452
Vietnamization of New Jersey; an American Tragedy, The—436
Viet Rock—358
Vieux Carre—434, 443
View from the Bridge, A—293, 302, 303, 353
View to the Common, A—366
Vigil, The—108
Vigny, Alfred de—95
Vikings at Helgoland, The—160
Vikings, The—16
Viktoria and Her Hussar—177
Vilar, Jean—274, 285, 301, 312
Vile Bodies—178
Village Players—456
Village Wooing—193, 242, 273, 274, 279, 301, 348, 387, 453
Villa Primrose—61
Villela, Edward—368
Villiers, George—135
Villiers, Mavis—301
Vinaver, Steven—346, 357
Vincent—395
Vincent, Ruth—15, 21, 32, 233
Vincent, Sean Patrick—372
Vine, Eileen—246, 249
Vinegar Tree, The—171, 182
Vines, Margaret—295, 301
Vintage '60—325
Vintage Wine—192, 237
Virginia Beach, Virginia—312
Virginia Courtship, A—179
Virginia Museum Theatre—297
Virginian, The—19
Virginius—38, 137, 180
Virgin Man, The—147, 154
Viroux, Arthur—85

Virtue in Danger—339, 381
Visitant, The—102
Visit of the Old Lady, The—309
Visitor from Forest Hills—371
Visitor from Hollywood—371
Visitor from Mamaroneck—371
Visit, The—313, 319, 322, 323, 325, 368, 410
Visit to a Small Planet—304, 308
Vitrac, Roger—348
Vittes, Louis—233
Viva! El Paso!—446
Vivat! Vivat Regina!—387, 388, 393
Vivian, Anthony—251
Vivian Beaumont Theater, The—343, 350, 356, 381
Viviani, Raffaele—373
Vivian, Mona—107
Vivian, Percial—184
Vivian-Rees, Joan—113
Vivian, Rene—134
Vivian, Robert—61, 128
Vodery, Will—112
Voegtlin, Arthur—26, 36, 71
Vogue—447
Vogues of 1924—124
Voice from the Minaret, The—115
Voice in the Dark, A—92
Voice In the Wind—300
Voice of Shem, The—416
Voice of the Turtle, The—235, 243, 253, 308, 424
Voice, The—347
Voight, Jon—353, 360
Vokes, May—36, 125
Vokes, Rosina—243
Volanakis, Minos—329, 347, 387, 398, 407, 438, 439
Volk, Frederick—295
Vollmer, Lulu—117 130
Vollmoeller, Karl—124
Volpe, Fred—37, 75, 149
Volpone—97, 108, 121, 160, 215, 231, 242, 254, 259, 278, 285, 295, 301, 306, 366, 373, 396, 427, 436
Volstead Act—146
Voltaire, Francois-Marie Arouet de —298
von Ambesser, Axel—373
von Furstenberg, Betsy—282, 293, 326
von Hoffmannstahl, Hugo—44, 153
von Horvath, Odon—436, 445, 451
von Kleist, Heinrich—49, 306, 311, 431, 439
Vonnegut, Kurt, Jr.—386, 439
Vonnegut, Marjorie—99
von Ottinger, Leonora—47
Von Rhau, Lee—380
Von Sacher-Masoch, Leopold—452
von Scherler, Sasha—381
von Seyfferitz, Gustav—61
Von Sydow, Max—316, 434
Von Tilzer, Albert—303
von Tilzer, Harry—250
von Trapp, Baroness Maria—314
Von Winterstein, Eduard—153
Voorhees, Donald—206
Vortex, The—127, 132, 278, 411, 422
Vosburgh, Dick—386, 450
Voskovec, George—332, 339, 451, 454
Vosper, Frank—134, 143, 177, 182, 201
Voss, Stephanie—317
Vostra, Alena—388
Votes for Women—39, 44, 47
Voyage Round My Father, A—390, 394
Voyage Theatre, The—368
Voysey Inheritance, The—27, 32, 193, 273, 279, 359
Voysey, Michael—442, 453
Vulgar Lives—451
Vulpius, Paul—202

Wade, Allan—96
Wadsworth, Charles Dr.—252
Wager, Michael—332

Wager, The—410, 413
Wagner, Frank—332, 344, 455
Wagner, Richard—187, 203, 438
Wagner, Robin—414, 454
"Wait a Bit, Susie"—127
Waite, Arnold—188
Waite, Ralph—352, 367, 381
Waiting for Gilain—288
Waiting for Godot—296, 298, 306, 349, 366, 374, 395, 417, 422, 429, 445, 451
Waiting for Lefty—195
Waiting in the Wings—322
Wait Until Dark—357, 364
Wajda, Andrzj—402, 422, 436
Wakefield, Gilbert—213
Wakefield, Hugh—102, 127, 213
Wakefield Mystery Plays—329, 353, 390
Wakefield Nativity, The—390, 391
Wakefield Tricycle Company—440
Wakeman, Frederic—244
Wake Up and Dream—49
Wake Up, It's Time To Go To Bed—452
Walbrook, Anton—226, 288, 370
Walcott, Derek—323, 380, 395, 403
Waldorf Theater—29
Waldron, Charles—71, 99
Wale, Terry—274
Walk a Little Faster—182
Walken, Christopher—360, 364, 374, 404, 410
Walker, Ada—41
Walker, Clara—400
Walker, C.P.—38
Walker, George—14, 30, 41, 115
Walker, Jack—180
Walker, James—147
Walker, J.G.—146
Walker, Joseph—383, 391, 400, 406
Walker, June—131, 132, 141, 170, 176, 189, 212, 287, 362
Walker, Kathryn—426
Walker, Laura—69
Walker, Margaret—1
Walker, Mildred—93
Walker, Nancy—241, 252, 257, 262, 295, 300, 321, 373
Walker, Polly—183
Walker, Robert—430, 431, 438
Walker, Stuart—77, 80, 95
Walker Theatre, The—38
Walker, William—192, 201
Walker, Zena—290, 296, 365, 450
Walking Happy—358, 358
Walking to Taldheim—368
Walk This Way—178
Walk Together Children—202
Walk Toward the Sunset—381
Wallace, Edgar—68 73, 95, 101, 119, 126, 143, 151, 158, 159, 165, 172, 177, 181, 182, 201, 212
Wallace, General Lew—12, 30, 80
Wallace, Ira—344
Wallace, Nellie—126, 134
Wallace, Pat—212
Wallace, The—323
Wallace, William Vincent—5
Wallach, Eli—250, 255, 271, 273, 281, 295, 302, 310, 322, 338, 344, 361, 407
Wallack's Theater—5
Wallbrook, Anton—186
Wall, Carolyn—211
Wallenstein—59
Waller, David—361, 367, 379, 382, 395, 415
Waller, Eugene—41
Waller, Jack—143, 165, 166, 172, 178, 187, 191, 197, 206
Waller, Lewis—4, 7, 21, 32, 43, 45, 46, 48, 49, 54, 57, 75
Waller, Thomas "Fats"—156, 164, 234, 237, 442
Wallflower—239
Wall, Harry—126
Wallis, Bertram—21, 43, 49, 53, 57, 101, 115, 120, 121, 150, 159, 236
Wallis, Bill—366, 445

Wallis, Shani—281
Wall, Max—151, 181, 182, 222, 248, 287, 361, 407, 417, 421, 431, 432, 436, 437, 438, 439
Wallop, Douglas—293
Walls of Jericho, The—21, 146
Walls, Tom—84, 113, 143, 151, 159, 165, 172, 177
Wall Street—153
Wall Street Girl, The—61
Wall, The—321
Walpole, Hugh—232, 269, 273, 383
Walser, Martin—341, 347
Walsh—416
Walsh, Blanche—25, 77
Walsh, Dermot—268, 289, 372
Walsh, Mary Jane—226
Walter, Bruno—274
Walter, Eugene—47, 61, 92, 98
Walter Mitty—404
Walters, Olive—207
Walters, Polly—187
Walter, Wilfrid—121
Walter, William—172
Walthall, Henry B.—33
Walton, Adan—401
Walton, Edna—99
Walton, Tony—315, 336, 382
Waltz Dream, A—41, 193
Waltzes from Vienna—177
Waltz of the Toreadors, The—300, 304, 308, 410, 415
Waltz Without End—231
Wanamaker, Sam—247, 257, 262, 269, 285, 294, 295, 300, 316, 338, 403, 409, 423
Wanamaker, Zoe—423, 429
Wanderer, The—82
Wandering—374
Wandering Jew, The—102, 153, 283
Wandering Minstrel, A—203
Wand, Jim—420, 440
Wanshel, Jeff—387, 403, 424, 436
Wappy Water Bus, The—355
War—360
Waram, Percy—37, 196, 212, 287, 330
War and Peace—228, 335, 349, 366
Warburton, Charles—103
Ward, Achurch—81
Ward, Aida—156
Ward, Donald—420
Ward, Dorothy—150
Ward, Douglas Turner—352, 373, 378, 380, 388, 391, 395, 422, 432, 440
Wardel, Geoffrey—294
Warden, Jack—291, 338
Warde, Shirley—146, 164
Warde, Willie—21, 53, 113, 127
Ward, Genevieve—54, 81
Ward of France, A—179
Ward, Penelope—250
Ward, Simon—359, 394, 443
Ward, Theodore—224
Wardwell, Geoffrey—246
Ward, Winifred—425
Ware Case, The—75
Ware, Helen—38, 47
Wareing, Alfred—51
Warfield, David—6, 19, 36, 40, 80, 109, 115, 275
Warfield, William—279
War God, The—59
Waring, Frances—245
Waring, Herbert—3, 40, 46, 158
Waring, Richard—213, 247
Wark, Colin—197
Warlock, Jim—172
War Music—439
Warner Brothers—139, 229
Warner, Charles—20
Warner, David—345, 346, 353, 355, 360, 401
Warner, H.B.—35, 87, 117
Warner, John—87
Warner, Sherman—448
Warning-A Theme for Linda, The —378
Warn That Man—227

Warrall, Lechmere—74
Warren, Brett—232
Warrender, Harold—197
Warren, Edith—141
Warren, Harry—176
Warren, Jennifer—364
Warren, Rod—358
Warren, Sheridan—190
Warrilow, David—440
Warrior's Husband, The—230
Warriss, Ben—277
Warsaw Theatre Studio—451
Warshawsky, Samuel—202
Wars of the Roses, The—341, 346, 347, 389
Warwick, Ethel—212
Warwick, Robert—47, 67, 115, 133, 144
War, Women and Other Trivia—396
Washbourne, Mona—288, 295, 322, 334, 386, 435
Was He Anyone?—401
Washington—95
Washington, Fredi—186
Washington, Isabell—163
Washington, Keith—436
Washington Square—252, 308, 429
Washington Square Players—46, 76, 77, 80, 84, 91, 233, 246
Wasserman, Dale—339, 352, 396
Wasserstein, Wendy—440
Waste—39, 203
Wasteland, The—359
Waste of Time III, A—422
Watch and Ward—372
Watched Pot, the—391
Watch It Come Down—427
Watch It, Sailor!—321
Watch on the Rhine, The—226, 229, 231, 246, 399
Watch Your Step—71
Water Babies, The—13, 307
Water Carrier, The—219
Watercolor—387
Water Engine, The—436
Waterford, Rose—135
Watergate, Presentations Ltd.—301
Water Gipsies, The—294
Water Hen, The—402
Waterhouse, Keith—322, 335, 353, 382, 406, 414, 427, 435
Waterloo—17, 27
Waterloo Bridge—170
Waterman, Dennis—346
Waters, Ethel—148, 171, 186, 195, 216, 222, 235, 441
Waters, Jan—438
Waters, Naomi—197
Waters of Babylon, The—307
Waters of the Moon—272, 398, 438, 444
Waters, Ronald—218
Waterston, Sam—373, 374, 403, 421, 423, 430, 440
Watford Civic Theatre Trust—356
Watford, Gwen—267, 365, 445, 450
Watford Palace of Varieties—46
Watford Palace Theatre—356
Wathall, Alfred G.—11
Watkin, Lawrence—211
Watkins, Linda—149
Watkins, Mary—233
Watkins, Maurine—142, 155
Watkins, Maurine Dallas—420
Watkyn, Arthur—278, 310
Watling, Jack—231
Watling, Peter—264
Watson, Betty Jane—234
Watson, Bobbie—93, 125
Watson, Donald—306, 312
Watson, Douglas—274, 278, 283
Watson, Elizabeth—37
Watson, Fred—335
Watson, Henrietta—57, 83, 102, 143, 151, 172, 236, 244
Watson, James Murray—256
Watson, June—451

Watson, Lucille—15, 100, 117, 191, 196, 205, 336
Watson, Malcolm—8, 12
Watson, Mamie—157
Watson, Minor—355
Watson, Ruth—190
Watson, Susan—378
Watt, Douglas—450, 454
Watters, George Manker—149, 161, 250
Watters, Marlys—304
Wattis, Richard—340, 359
Watts, Carrie—301
Watts, James—106
Watts, Jeanne—367
Watts, Lyonel—132
Watts, Michael—182
Waugh, Evelyn—178, 451
Wax—428
Waxler, John—192
Way, Brian—359
Wayburn, Agnes—1
Wayburn, Ned—14, 19, 20, 25, 42, 47, 52, 88, 93, 94, 100, 117, 168, 233
Way Down East—238
Wayne, David—252, 281, 298, 309, 340, 345, 347, 361, 371
Wayne, Jerry—267
Wayne, Naunton—196, 231, 248, 263, 283, 345, 366, 372, 391
Way of the World, The—6, 127, 184, 232, 260, 284, 302, 381, 410, 415, 430, 444
Way Out in Piccadilly—359
Wayrick Alexander—77
Ways and Means—201
Way Things Go, The—267
Way Things Happen, The—126
Way Through the Wood, A—288
Way To Treat a Woman, The—172
Wayward Saint, The—293, 301
Wayward Way, The—188, 349
We Americans—141
Weapons of Happiness—430
Wearing, Michael—389
Weaver, Fritz—310, 312, 318, 322, 351, 374, 431, 453
Weavers, The—74
Weaver, Wyn—120, 172, 197, 218
Webb, Alan—145, 201, 206, 212, 248, 253, 263, 272, 274, 283, 285, 300, 311, 340, 371, 435
Webb, Clifton—82, 88, 99, 108, 114, 156, 163, 171, 181, 816, 211, 218, 227, 235, 363
Webber, Andrew Lloyd—393, 403, 404, 421, 440, 443
Webber, Florence—77, 99
Webber, Robert—321
Webb, Geoffrey—136
Webb, June—108
Webb, Kenneth—138
Webb, Leonard—410
Webb, Lizbeth—267
Weber and Fields—1, 6, 15, 20, 30, 61, 62, 70, 83, 115, 116, 199, 229
Weber, Carl—373, 380, 401, 431
Weber, Joseph—1, 6, 15, 20, 30, 31, 35, 36, 40, 41, 61, 62, 70, 83, 115, 116, 199, 229
Webling, Peggy—68
We Bombed in New Haven—371
Webster, Annie—8
Webster, Ben—2, 13, 16, 23, 27, 44, 49, 75, 101, 145, 256, 261, 405
Webster, Jean—71, 277
Webster, John—97, 136, 250, 302, 306, 323, 324, 350, 355, 382, 395, 396
Webster, Margaret—145, 167, 179, 192, 241, 245, 246, 247, 250, 254, 256, 259, 275, 286, 301, 307, 345, 405
We Can't Pay? We Won't Pay!—446
We Comrades Three—362
Wedding Band—403
Wedding Bells—93, 104
Wedding Guest, The—2
Wedding in Paris—288

Wedding Morning, The—57
Wedding of Iphigenia, The—398
"Wedding of the Dancing Doll, The"—99
Wedding, The—273, 360
Wedekind, Frank—77, 340, 353, 356, 367, 391, 415, 417, 435, 445, 446
We Dig for the Stars—251
Wednesday's Child—190, 194
Wedwick, Daryl—405
Weeden, Evelyn—36
Weede, Robert—298
Weekley, The—226
Weeks, Ada Mae—88
Weese, Harry—331, 365, 392
Wehlen, Emmy—49
Weid, Gustav—153
Weidhaas, F.E.—168
Weidman, Charles—173
Weidman, Jerome—98, 315, 332
Weidman, John—426
Weidner, Paul—437
Weih, Dagmar—43
Weill, Gus—378
Weill, Kurt—188, 200, 205, 211, 226, 228, 235, 247, 254, 257, 262, 270, 290, 300, 353, 354, 388, 400, 402, 403, 456
Weil, Simone—382
Weingarden, Israel—50
Weingarten, Romain—396
Weinstein, Arnold—326
Weir, George R.—44
Weir of Hermiston—312
Weisenfreund, Muni—141
Weiser, Jacob—216
Weiss, George—298
Weiss, Jeff—451
Weiss, Peter—345, 353, 359, 373, 380
Weitzenkron, Louis—177, 180
Wekwerth, Manfred—395
Welch, Elisabeth—156, 241, 253, 263, 315, 336
Welch, Ethel—85
Welch, James—26, 32, 67
Welchman, Harry—62, 67, 127, 142, 157
Welcome Stranger—100, 108
Welded—124
Weldon, Ben—191
Welford, Nancy—156
Weller, Mike—381, 390, 400, 410, 422, 431, 449
Welles, Orson—46, 194, 202, 207, 208, 213, 215, 247, 274, 275, 294, 300, 330
Well, John—366
Well of the Saints, The—28, 560, 59, 193
Wells, Charlotte-87
Wells, Deering—151
Wells, Eileen—358
Wells, Frank—379
Wells, H.G.—62, 263, 379
Wells, John—417, 435
Wells, Karen—393
Wells, Sadler—189, 251
Wells, William K.—120, 126, 131, 140, 157
Wells, Yona—219
Wellwyn, Christopher—62
Welsh Drama Company—424
Welsh National Theatre—188
Welty, Eudora—298, 424
Welwyn Garden City Theatre Society—152
We Moderns—134
Wen, A—360
Wendel, Beth—334
Wenman, Henry—78
Wenning, Thomas H.—336
Wenrich, Percy—71, 141
We're Having a Ball—305
We're Not Just Practical—328
Werfel, Franz—144, 145, 146, 205, 209, 239, 246
Werther—16
Wescott, Marcy—217

Wesker, Arnold—312, 317, 318, 323, 333, 350, 352, 357, 358, 366, 387, 389, 401, 434, 445
Wesley, Richard—410, 431, 454
West, Christopher—307
Westcott, Edward N.—1
West End—90
Westerman, Nydia—141
West, Jennifer—347
Westley, Helen—76, 99, 100, 112, 117, 121, 122, 132, 144, 160, 170, 188, 233
West, Mae—59, 61, 87, 140, 150, 154, 156, 162, 239
Westman Family—391
Westman, Nydia—391
Westmoreland, Lillian—148
West, Morris—326, 386
West, Nathaniel—438
West of Suez—394, 396
Weston and Lee—172, 192
Weston, David—382, 451, 454, 455
Weston, Harris—165
Weston, Jack—413, 449
Weston, R.P.—134, 148, 151, 157, 165, 187, 197
West, Rebecca—145, 334
West Side Story—304, 311, 323, 344, 374, 418
West, Timothy—403, 432, 438, 446, 455
Westward Ho!—68
Westwell, Raymond—263, 317
West, William—6
We, the People—186, 189
Wetzel, Donald—287
We Were Dancing—201, 391
Wexley, John—170, 194, 202
Whale, James—97, 145
Whanslaw, H.W.—138
Whartan, Anthony P.—62
Wharton, Carley—221, 241
Wharton, Edith—31, 50, 195, 200, 209
What a Life—211, 215
What a Mouth—388
What Did Her Husband Say?'—102
What Every Woman Knows—43, 121, 146, 237, 238, 250, 290, 323, 418, 435
What Every Woman Wants—424
What Happened to Blake—390
What Happened to George—189, 193
What Happens in Hamlet—383
"What'll I Do?"—118
What Makes Sammy Run?—344
What Men Live By—84
What Might Happen—144
What Price Glory?—125, 138, 154, 318
What's A Nice Country Like You Doing in a State Like This?—409
What's Become of the Fairies?—203
"What Shall I Do"—211
What Shall We Tell Caroline?—310
What's In a Name?—99
What the Butler Saw—97, 379, 385, 390, 423, 428, 452, 455
What the Public Wants—49
What the Wine-Sellers Buy—415
Wheat King, The—21
Wheatley, Alan—249
Wheatley, William—86
Wheaton, Anna—105
Whedon, John—262
Wheelan, Alfred—2
Wheeler, Bert—148, 235, 376
Wheeler, Billy Ed—389
Wheeler, David—357, 438, 454
Wheeler, Hugh—326, 327, 331, 406, 410, 449
Wheeler, Lois—241
Wheeler, Penelope—68
Wheeler, Van Rensselaer—10, 36
Wheel of Life, The—113
Wheel, The—113
Whelan, Christopher—315
Whelan, Peter—421, 455

Whelen, Emmy—67
When Crummies Played—152
When Did You Last See My Mother?—359, 389
When Everything Becomes the City's Music—417
When Hair Was Long and Time Was Short—435
When in Rome—316
"When It's Apple Blossom Time in Normandy"—62
When I was a Little Girl—215
When Knighthood Was in Flower—6, 36
When Knights Were Bold—72, 145, 168, 179, 184, 189, 193, 198, 203, 208
When Ladies Meet—181, 187, 189
When Lovely Women—202
When Thou Art King—391
When We Are Married—213, 217, 228, 391, 453
When We Dead Awaken—245, 375, 402
When We Were Forty-One—25
When We Were Twenty-One—180
When You Comin' Back, Red Ryder?—410
"When You're Away"—71
When You Smile—138
Where Angels Fear to Tread—340
Where Do We Go From Here?—417
Where E'er We Go—235
Where Free Man Shall Stand—423
Where Has Tommy Flowers Gone?—393
"Where Or When"—205
Where Poppies Bloom—87
Where's Charley—257, 310, 360, 384, 418
Where Stars Walk—223, 232, 259, 279, 447
Where the Cross is Made—144, 178
Where the Rainbow Ends—59, 77, 81, 97, 109, 115, 122, 128, 137, 145, 160, 168, 174, 179, 184, 189, 193, 198, 203, 208, 214, 220, 224, 237, 255, 260, 265, 269, 275, 280, 291, 297, 302, 313
Which is Which?—243
Whiffen, Mrs. Thomas—144
While Parents Sleep—182
While the Sun Shines—236, 240, 403
Whims—77
Whip, The—49, 62, 76
Whirled into Happiness—113
Whirligig, The—95
Whirligig Theatre Company—457
Whirl of Society—61
Whirl of the Town, The—9, 71, 126
Whispering Friends—156
Whispering Well, The—68
Whispering Wires—112
Whisper into My Good Ear—332
"Whistle Away Your Blues"—138
Whistler, Rex—254
Whistling in the Dark—181, 328, 382
Whitaker's Almanack—5, 13
Whitbread, Peter—372
Whitby, Arthur—96
Whitby, Gwynn—120
White, Bert—22
White Blackbird, The—135
White Cargo—118, 127
White, Cat, The—23, 447
White Devil, The—136, 254, 355, 382
White Eagle—251
White, Edgar—415, 445
White Feather, The—74
Whitefield, Alice—371
White, Fisher—76
White, Frances—82
White, George—92, 99, 104, 105, 112, 118, 149, 157, 164, 170, 376, 383
White Guard, The—197, 214, 453
Whitehall Theatre—175

White-Headed Boy, The—106, 313
Whitehead, Paxton—340, 367, 370, 375, 381, 389, 395, 396, 401, 403, 416, 429, 442
Whitehead, Robert—296, 332, 350
White Heather, The—73
White Horse Inn—199, 202, 223
Whitehouse, Frances—70
White House Murder Case, The—385
Whitehouse, Pauline—334
White, Iris—159
White, Irving—362
White, Jane—310, 342
White, Joan—227
White, John—376
White, Josh—259
Whitelaw, Billie—429, 444, 454
White, Lee—89
White, Leonard—272
White Liars/Black Comedy—372
White Liars, The—364
White Lies—364
White, Madge—107
White Man, A—54
White Marriage—436
White, Miles—234
Whitemore, Hugh—435, 451
Whiteoaks of Jalna—201, 211, 231
White, Onna—385
White, Philip—111
White, Ruth—326, 332, 354, 357, 358, 364, 375, 384
White Sheep of the Family, The—273
White, Sisters, The—48
White Slaver, The—73
White Slave Traffic—13
White, Stanford—30, 33, 162, 369, 433
White Steed, The—216, 220, 254
White Suit Blues—438, 439
Whitewashing Julia—15, 18
White Whore and the Bit Player, The—403, 408
White, Wilfred Hyde—266, 274, 288, 294, 310, 334
Whitfield, June—427, 456
Whitford, Annabelle—47
Whiting, Jack—157, 191, 206, 221
Whiting, John—272, 274, 288, 295, 316, 327, 335, 336, 342, 348, 353, 367, 417
Whiting, Margaret—306
Whiting, Michell—306
Whiting, Richard—92, 182
Whitman Portrait, A—357
Whitman, Walt—362
Whitmore, James—252, 413
Whitnall, Timothy—435
Whitney, Arthur—431
Whitting, John—446
Whittington, Dick—302
Whittington Junior and His Sensational Cat—228, 362
Whitty, May—63, 197, 246, 256, 261, 405
Whitworth, Geoffrey—98
"Who?"—132
Who Goes There!—272
Who Is He?—75
Who Is Sylvia?—268
Who Killed "Agatha" Christie?—443
Who Killed Richard Cory?—428
Whole Town's Talking, The—118, 143
Whole Truth, The—294
Whole World Over, The—262
Who'll Save the Plowboy?—339
Whoop-Dee-Doo—15
Whoopee!—157, 452
Whorf, Richard—363
Who's Afraid of Virginia Woolf?—332, 343, 345, 374, 429, 443
"Whose Baby?"—108
Whose Life Is It Anyway?—457
Whose Turn Next—388
Who's Got His Own—357
Who's Happy Now—424, 454

Who's Hooper?—95
Who's the Lady?—68
Who's Who of Flapland, A—379, 387
Who, The—450
Who Was That Lady I Saw You With—309
Why Hanna's Skirt Won't Stay Down—413
Why Marry?—83, 98, 113
Why Not?—113, 123
Why Not Stay for Breakfast?—407
Why Not Tonight?—192
Whytal, Russ—36
Wiata, Ina—298
Wicheler, Fernand—63, 75
Wicked Age, The—150
Wicked Uncle, The—12
Wicked World, The—49
Wickwire, Nancy—334, 419
Widdoes, Kathleen—323, 329, 403
Widmark, Richard—241, 244
Widney, Stone—394
Widower's Houses—35, 178, 264, 353, 382, 387
Widowing of Mrs. Holroyd, The—145, 373
Widow of Wasdale Head, The—63
Widows and Children First—451
Widows of Clyth, The—451
Wieth, Mogens—311
Wife to a Famous Man, The—173
Wife Without a Smile, A—21
Wife with the Smile, The—109
Wiggin, Kate Douglas—52
Wigram, O. and I.—296
Wilbur, Crane—172
Wilbur, Richard—353, 367, 410, 423
Wilcox, Collin—327
Wilcox, Michael—451
Wilcox, Ron—402
Wild Animals from Memory—422
Wild Birds—131
Wildblood, Peter—315
Wildcat—321
Wild Decembers—187
Wild Duck, The—28, 90, 135, 136, 173, 255, 260, 275, 297, 366, 382, 391, 418, 452, 454
Wilde, Cornel—195, 218
Wilde, Marty—320
Wilde, Oscar—4, 12, 23, 50, 58, 59, 67, 72, 73, 84, 90, 115, 121, 125, 160, 178, 179, 180, 184, 188, 189, 192, 204, 207, 214, 218, 232, 237, 245, 246, 250, 254, 279, 284, 289, 290, 300, 317, 355, 361, 368, 373, 396, 402, 408, 422, 423, 430, 437, 440, 445, 446, 447, 453, 454
Wilde, Percival—286
Wilder, Billy—372
Wilder, Clinton—338, 361
Wilder, Gene—341, 315
Wilderness of Monkeys—264
Wilderness Road—295
Wilderness, The—7
Wilder, Thornton—142, 182, 188, 211, 212, 215, 230, 238, 241, 246, 250, 289, 290, 296, 319, 325, 337, 361, 373, 374, 382
Wildfire—42
Wildflower—117, 142
Wild Geese—101
Wild Horses—278
Wilding, Michael—201, 236
Wild, Michael—435
Wild Oats—212, 429, 432
"Wild Rose"—100
Wild Rose, The—10, 231
Wild Stunt Show, The—415
Wild Violets—183
Wiles, John—323, 410
Wilfred, Thomas—138
Wilhelm, Julius—58
Wilkes-Alcazar Company—60
Wilkes, Allan Tupper—127
Wilkie, Wendell—244
Wilkins, May—83
Wilkinson, Marc—359
Wilkinson, Norman—64

Wilkins, William—34
Will Any Gentleman?—268
Willard, Emund S.—16, 137, 144, 179
Willard, John—111, 209
Willet, John—436
William, David—295, 341, 360, 367, 402, 415, 427, 439, 453
Williams, Alan Vaughan—389, 390, 395, 451
Williams, Arthur—12, 21
Williams, Bert—14, 30, 41, 48, 52, 56, 62, 78, 115
Williams, Billy—92, 98, 105
Williams, Clifford—316, 318, 341, 348, 359, 360, 367, 373, 379, 381, 386, 390, 397, 396, 408, 415, 417, 418, 421, 427, 432, 434, 435, 439, 440, 446
Williams, David—335, 437
Williams, Dick—372, 388, 393
Williams, E. Harcourt—68, 167, 183, 190, 193, 235, 236
Williams, Eliot C.—129
Williams, Emlyn—166, 167, 181, 187, 197, 206, 208, 213, 222, 227, 237, 241, 245, 246, 253, 262, 268, 276, 279, 283, 294, 297, 300, 301, 307, 311, 340, 346, 348, 353, 354
Williams, Frances—140
Williams, George—70
Williams, Heathcote—359, 387, 395, 417, 435
Williams, Herschel—230
Williams, Hope—157, 171
Williams, Hugh—134, 143, 144, 151, 166, 182, 211, 248, 266, 289, 299, 311, 338, 345, 353, 360, 366
Williams, Ivy—115
Williams, Jack—289
Williams, Jesse Lynch—83, 113, 123, 138
Williams, John—102
Williams, Kenneth—285, 291, 294, 299, 305, 313, 315, 328, 333, 395, 427, 452
Williams, Lawrence—277
Williams, Margaret—299, 311, 328, 345, 353, 366
Williams, Michael—340, 373, 396, 451
Williams, Misha—394
Williams, Nigel—443, 445, 452
Williams, Noel—263
Williamson, David—409
Williamson, Hugh—269
Williamson, Laird—354, 402, 403, 438
Williamson, Nicol—334, 346, 347, 349, 380, 384, 407, 410
Williams, Pat—327
Williams, Rhys—239, 383
Williams, Robert B.—111
Williams, Samm-Art—456
Williams, Sonia—284
Williams, Sylvia—450
Williams, Tennessee—244, 252, 257, 261, 268, 271, 275, 278, 281, 285, 293, 300, 302, 304, 309, 314, 316, 320, 321, 327, 331, 335, 337, 338, 343, 354, 355, 357, 361, 362, 369, 371, 377, 378, 387, 395, 400, 406, 407, 408, 410, 417, 419, 420, 422, 424, 427, 428, 431, 432, 434, 439, 447, 451, 452
Williams, Treat—413
Williams, Walter—101, 102, 108, 119, 126
Williams, William—425
Willie—454
Willie Rough—407
Willie, West, and McGinty—119
Willingham, Calder—281
Willis, Hal—151
Willis, Mervyn—416
Willis, Ted—245, 299
Willman, Noel—254, 283, 288, 295, 302, 333, 376, 426, 429
Willman, Willman—357
Willmore, Alfred—59

Willner, A.M.—56, 58, 126
Willner and Gruenbaum—49
Willoughby, Kitty—166
Will Roger's U.S.A.—413, 419
Will Shakespeare—219
Willson, Meridith—305, 321, 338
Will Spoor Mime Company—422
Will Success Spoil Rock Hunter?—293
Wills, W.G.—4, 8, 49
Will, The—122
Will the King Leave the Teapot?—401
Wilmer, Steve—444
Wilner, Max—93, 194
Wilshin, Sunday—127, 176
Wilson and Marlow—5
Wilson, Angus—300
Wilson, Beatrice—143
Wilson, Billy—426, 430
Wilson, Clarence—295
Wilson, Dooley—222
Wilson, Earl, Jr.—413
Wilson, Edmund—129, 273
Wilson, Edwin—88
Wilson, Elizabeth—351
Wilson, Florence—164
Wilson, Frances—10, 25, 115, 121, 122, 142, 149, 176, 199, 202
Wilson, Hansford—88
Wilson, Harry Leon—42, 113
Wilson in the Promised Land—388
Wilson, John—364
Wilson, John C.—244, 260, 263
Wilson, John Dover—348, 383, 430
Wilson, John F.—78
Wilson, Josephine—153, 279, 347, 395
Wilson, Judy—352, 381
Wilson, Kate Denin—25
Wilson, Katherine—141
Wilson, Lanford—353, 360, 374, 378, 402, 406, 422, 424, 428, 445, 452
Wilson, Marie—1, 37, 231
Wilson, Mary Louise—332
Wilson, Maude—22
Wilson, Rathmel—63
Wilson, Robert—410, 420, 437, 438
Wilson, Sandy—278, 284, 285, 288, 299, 311, 315, 346, 368, 388, 397, 401, 456
Wilson, Snoo—394, 397, 401, 410, 418, 428, 436, 447
Wilson, W. Cronin—143
Wilson, William—79
Wilsrud, Astrid—340
Wilstach, Paul—56
Wilton, Marie—146
Wilton, Penelope—444
Wiltse, David—401
Wiman, Dwight Deere—163, 275
Wimperis, Arthur—32, 37, 48, 53, 57, 61, 62, 63, 72, 74, 79, 89, 99, 101, 102, 106, 143, 159
Wincelberg, Shimon—319
Winchelman, Fritz—224
Wincott, Geoffrey—201
Wind and the Rain, The—188
Windham, Donald—244
Windmill Man, The—115, 122, 128, 137, 145, 168, 174, 179
Windmill Theater, The (London)—350
Wind of Heaven, The—245
Wind o' the Moors—69
Windows—114, 122
Window, The—379
Windsor, Barbara—339, 407
Windust, Bretaigne—241, 244, 298, 324
Wine of Choice—214
Winesberg, Ohio—229
Wine, Women and Song—230, 233
Winged Victory—238, 243
Wingfield, Amanda—244

Wings—445, 449, 452
Wings of the Dove—298, 340
Wings Over Europe—160, 297
Winners and Losers—375
Winnie the Pooh—391, 398
Winninger, Charles—83, 99, 150, 191, 383
Winning Isn't Everything—447
Winsloe, Christa—183, 192
Winslow Boy, The—248, 252, 261, 391
Winsome Widow, A—61
Winter Dancers, The—435, 452
Winter, Jessie—95
Winter Journey—267
Winter, Keith—187, 190, 194
Winter, Marian—336
Winter Signs—452
Winter Soldiers—232, 238
Winters, Shelley—294, 338, 385
Winter's Tale, The—16, 53, 54, 64, 76, 80, 96, 109, 136, 178, 202, 208, 224, 232, 237, 242, 249, 259, 269, 274, 290, 296, 312, 323, 341, 354, 361, 380, 389, 404, 423, 429, 446
Winter, Virginia—235
Winter Visitors—428
Winter, William—16, 85, 203
Winthrop, Ethel—36
Winwood, Estelle—32, 53, 67, 82, 83, 119, 134, 192, 213, 218, 236, 258
Wirtz, Arthur—239, 252
Wisdom, Norman—257, 276, 294, 358
Wisdom of the Wise, The—3
Wisdom Tooth, The—147
Wise Child—366
Wise Have Not Spoken, The—249, 254
Wise, Herbert—347
Wise, Jim—372
Wiseman, Joseph—226, 380, 404
Wiseman, Philip—315, 367
Wiseman, Thomas—312
Wise, Sybil—127, 159
Wise, Thomas—42
Wise Woman, The—455
Wishengrad. Morton—304, 308, 313, 317, 342
Wish You Were Here—276, 280, 283
Wislack, Maria—424
Wisteria Trees, The—266, 270, 295
Wister, Owen—19
Witching Hour, The—36, 51
Witch of Edmonton, The—108, 202, 336
Witch, The—173, 241, 369
With a Load of Mischief—232
Withdrawal Symptoms—444
Withee, Mabel—117
Withers, George—315
Withers, Googie—235, 267, 288, 311, 431
Withers, Iva—244
Witherspoon, Cora—66
Within the Gates—191, 192
Within the Law—61, 62, 65, 98, 237
Without Love—232
Without Veils—398
Witkiewicz, S.I.—436
Witmark, Isidore—10
Witness for the Defence, The—57, 58
Witness for the Prosecution—283, 288, 289, 297, 355, 376
Wittow, Frank—303, 351
Wives of Henry VIII, The—179
Wizard of Oz, The—14, 250, 255, 368, 404, 420
Wiz, The—154, 420
Wobblies, The—430
Wodehouse, P.G.—36, 37, 78, 82, 87, 88, 94, 108, 114, 120, 142, 156, 172, 280, 372, 421, 424, 456
Wogan, Charles—53
Woldin, Judd—406
Wolfe, Friedrich-191
Wolfe, Howard—377

Wolfe, Karin—406
Wolfe, Linda—440
Wolfe, Monty—89
Wolff, Pierre—19, 27
Wolfit, Donald—134, 167, 192, 202, 203, 215, 223, 228, 229, 231, 236, 237, 241, 245, 249, 254, 259, 274, 278, 283, 285, 300, 339, 347, 376
Wolfson, Victor—202, 205, 210
Wolf of Gubbio, The—116
Wolheim, Louis—100, 106, 111, 125
Wolston, Henry—134
Wolf, The—376, 410
Wolveridge, Carol—288
Woman in Love, A—264
Woman in Room 13, The—92
Woman in the Case, The—7, 25, 77
Woman in White, The—290
Woman Is a Weathercock, A—72
Woman Killed With Kindness, A—395
Woman of Bronze, The—100
Woman of Destiny, A—202
Woman of No Importance, A—80, 284, 368, 446
Woman's Way, A—47
Woman, The—56, 409, 443, 454
Woman to Woman—108
Women Aren't Angels—228
Women Behind Bars—435
Women Beware Women—335, 380, 404
Women Have Their Way, The—173
Women of Twilight—273
Women-Pirates Anny Bonney and Mary Read, The—443
Women's Honor, A—90
Women, The—201, 210, 218
Wonder Boy—180
Wonderful Grandmother—64
Wonderful Lamp, The—302
Wonderful Night, A—167
Wonderful Time—278
Wonderful Town—281, 286, 294, 311, 340, 367, 431
Wonderland—26
Wonderland in Concert—445
Wonder Tales, The—85
Wong, Anna May—166, 172
Wontner, Arthur—83, 84, 94, 102, 108, 127, 219
Wood, Arthur—134
Woodbridge, George—208
Wood, Charles—353, 368, 401, 421, 429, 441, 445, 456, 457
Wood, Cyrus—164
Wood, David—360
Wood Demon, The—361, 410, 415
Wood, Douglas—73
Wood Edna—236, 241
Wood, Hayden—75, 166
Wood, H. Harvey—256
Wood, J. Hickory—4, 6, 14, 15, 20, 23, 32, 54, 59, 237
Wood, Joan-273
Wood, John—281, 365, 390, 396, 409, 414, 429, 437, 442, 451, 452
Woodland—20
Woodman, William—446
Wood, Metcalfe—28
Wood, Mrs. Henry—268
Wood, Nicholas—410
Wood of the Whispering, The—341
Wood, Peggy—55, 71, 82, 165, 176, 212, 222, 227, 273, 286, 447
Wood, Peter—302, 310, 312, 317, 323, 327, 329, 341, 346, 406, 414, 444, 451
Wood, Raymond—420
Woodruff, Robert—452
Woods, Al H.—65, 91, 98
Woods, Aubrey—366, 403
Woods, Donald—334
Woods, James—359, 406
Woods, Maxine—247
Woods, Ronald Edmundson—454
Woods, The—452
Woodthorpe, Peter—296, 322

Woodvine, John—329, 347, 453
Woodward, Edward—299, 334, 368, 387, 391, 410
Woody King Associates—378
Wooland, Norman—274
Woolf, Edgar Alan—30
Woolfe, Pierre—57
Woolf, Virginia—414
Woolf, Walter—105, 118, 124, 132, 141
Woolgar, Mark—430
Woollcott, Alexander—177 214, 217, 237
Woollens, Evans—456
Woolley, Monty—217, 342
Woolley, Reginal—414
Woolman, Edna—447
Woolsey, Robert—148
Wootten, Christopher—412
Woottwell, Tom—84
Wordplay—424
Words and Music—183, 216, 413
Wordsworth, Richard—317
Work and Other Dear Green Fables—444
Workhouse Donkey, The—341
Workhouse Ward, The—50, 59, 160
Working—442
Workman C.H.—48
Work Out, The—347
Works Progress Administrations—199
World-Journal-Tribune—363
World of Carl Sandburg, The—320
World of Charles Aznavour, The—363
World of Kurt Weill in Song, The—338
World of Lenny Bruce, The—413
World of Paul Slickey, The—315, 319
World of Percy French, The—453
World of Sholom Aleichem, The—295
World of Susie Wong, The—309, 316
Worlds, The—455
World Theatre—380, 396, 408, 422
World Theatre Festival—347, 389
World Theatre Season—362, 367
World Turned Upside Down, The—445
World We Live In, The—112, 116
World Well Lost, The—438
World We Make, The—217, 225
Worley, Jo Anne—357
Worlock Frederick—411
Worrall, Lechmere—68
Worster, Howett—150
Worth, Billie—266
Worthing, Frank—55
Worthing, Jack—218
Worthing, John—254
Worth, Irene—217, 235, 264, 266, 274, 283, 285, 294, 296, 304, 307, 312, 317, 320, 336, 339, 345, 358, 368, 373, 401, 416, 436, 454
Worth, Mary—100
Wouk, Herman—262, 287, 292
Would-Be Gentleman, The—145, 160, 167
Would You Look at Them Smashing All the Lovely Windows—373, 382
Woyzeck—360, 361, 381, 408, 410, 417, 428
Wozzeck—306
WPA—194, 204
WPA's Federal Theatre Project—202
Wray, George—212
Wray, John—224
Wray, Maxwell—188, 193, 236
Wrecker, The—151
Wrede, Caspar—316, 346, 375, 443
Wreford, Edgar—312, 360
Wren, Jane—22
Wren, Jenny—203
Wright, Cowley—80, 113
Wright, David—366, 373, 382
Wright, Frank Lloyd—264, 319
Wright, Garland—426, 440, 445
Wright, Geraldine—421

Wright, Haidee—102, 126, 150
Wright, Hugh—79, 80, 89
Wright, Huntley—11, 21, 32, 38, 43, 49
Wright, Nicholas—435
Wright, Norman—254
Wright, Peter—317
Wright, Richard—226
Wright, Robert—253, 282, 367, 389
Wright, Teresa—217, 305
Wright, Tom—353
Write Me a Murder—327
Writers Guild of America, The—292
Wrong Side of the Moon, The—361
Wrong Side of the Park, The—321
Wurzle-Flummery—83
Wuthering Heights—192, 197, 207, 218, 223, 242
Wyatt, Jane—191, 195, 221
Wycherley's Restoration—436
Wycherley, William—302, 307, 348, 355, 387, 409
Wycherly, Margaret—38, 66, 79, 99, 111, 112, 136, 181, 303
Wyckoff, Alexander—210
Wylie, Betty Jane—403
Wylie, Julian—113, 158, 159, 183
Wylie, Laurie—113, 120, 126, 134, 143, 166
Wylie, Maggie—418
Wymark, Olwen—368
Wymark, Patrick—316, 335, 368
Wyndham, Charles—3, 16, 17, 18, 27, 43, 97
Wyndham, Dennis—89
Wyndham, Gwen—151
Wyndham, Olive—92
Wyndham's Theatre—46
Wyngarde, Peter—369, 410
Wynn, Ed—71, 74, 78, 87, 104, 106, 125, 149, 170, 176, 206, 221, 362
Wynne, Nora—83, 134
Wynn, Keenan—216, 221
Wynyard, Diana—172, 179, 186, 187, 192, 208, 248, 268, 274, 281, 282, 288, 296, 301, 309, 310 318, 320, 349
Wyse, John—202
Wyspianski, Stanislaw—360, 382, 422

X—417
XXX's—417

Y'a d'Jolies Femmes—75
Yaffe, James—325
Yahoo—188, 197, 427
Yale Repertory Theatre—393, 413, 436, 445, 449
Yale School of Drama—139, 429
Yale University Theatre—147
Yamash'ta, Stomu—406
Yankee at the Court of King Arthur, A—149
Yankee Circus on Mars, A—25
Yankee, Consul, The—19
Yankee Girl, The—52
Yankee Princess, The—112
Yankee Prince, The—41
Yankee Tourist, A—35
Yankowitz, Susan—389
Yanks 3 Detroit 0 Top of the Seventh—418
Yarde, Margaret—197
Yates, Dornford—95
Yates, Margery—452
Yates, Peter—330
Yates, W. B.—16
Yavorskaya, Lydia—50, 63, 69
Yeamans, Annie—7, 8, 15, 38
Year Boston Won the Pennant, The—380
Years Ago—247, 256
Years Between, The—244
Years of the Locust—375
Year the Yankees Lost the Pennant, The—293
Yeastman, R.J.—182

Yeates, William Butler—3, 13, 19, 22, 23, 24, 28, 38, 44, 45, 50, 53, 54, 59, 60, 64, 89, 91, 95, 110, 122, 129, 145, 152, 185, 193, 220, 246, 249, 283, 390, 455
Yellen, Jack—156, 176, 196, 216, 227
Yellen, Sherman—386
Yellow—146
Yellow Jack—190, 250
Yellow Jacket, The—62
Yellow Mask, The—158
Yellow Sands—143
Yellow Star, The—245
Yellow Ticket, The—71, 84
Yentl—418, 420
Yentl the Yeshiva Boy—418
Yeo, Leslie—429, 453
Yeoman of the Guard, The—49, 76, 97, 167, 184, 193, 232, 245, 249, 255, 260, 264, 269, 274, 275, 285, 290, 302, 313, 334, 346, 366, 373
Yerma—361, 363, 402, 454
Yes and No—207
Yes, Madam ?—192
Yes My Darling Daughter—205, 206, 210
Yes, Yes, Yvette—149
Yiddish Theatre—121
Yip Yip Yaphank—87, 230
Yoicks—127
Yokel Boy—216
Yolk Life—444
Yordan, Philip—224, 240, 246
York Cycle of Mystery Plays—445
Yorke, Augustus—66, 82
York, Michael—355, 406
York Mystery Play—404
York, Susannah—336, 340, 440
Yorska—84
Yoshe Kalb—198
Yost, Herbert—82
You and I—91, 117, 123
"You And The Night and The Music"—191
You Can't Take It With You—200, 207, 210, 229, 245, 355, 363, 366, 397
You'd Be Surprised—120
You'd Better Think It Over, Giacomo—285
You Know I Can't Hear You When the Water's Running—357
You'll Be Lucky—288
You'll Come to Love Your Sperm Test—347, 353
Youmans, Vincent—117, 119, 124, 127, 134, 148, 171, 182, 202
You Never Know—211
You Never Know, Y'Know—89
Young Auchinleck—335
Young, Clarence III—395
Young, Douglas—361
Young Elizabeth, The—276
Young England—192
Younger Generation, The—63, 209
Youngest of the Angels, The—32
Youngest, The—126
Young, Gig—282, 321, 359
Young, Harold, 145, 160
Young, Herbert—84
Young Idea, The—115
Young in Heart—322
Young, Joan—230
Young, John—6, 10
Young Lyceum Company—410, 417
Young Man from Rathmines, The—114
Young Master Dante, The—375
Young People's Theatre—441
Young Person in Pink, The—101
Young, Phil—452
Young, Rida Johnson—30, 38, 52, 62, 79, 82, 87, 124
Young, Robert—429
Young, Roland—78, 82, 100, 135, 156, 187, 286
Young, Roy—55

Young, Stark—125, 129, 342
Young Vic Company—260
Young Vic Theatre (London)—388, 390, 391, 392, 394, 397, 398, 402, 403, 404, 408, 409, 410, 415, 417, 418, 423, 424, 430, 432, 436, 437, 440, 445, 455, 456
Young Visiters, The—101
Young, William—12
Young Wives' Tale—263
Young Woodley—133, 147, 159, 161, 246, 447
Your Arms Too Short To Box With God—427, 441
"You're a Goddam Liar"—51
You're a Good Man, Charlie Brown—364, 372, 383
"You're My Everything"—176
"You're the Top"—191
Your Own Thing—371, 416
You Said It—176
Youth—84
Youth's the Season—179, 184
Youth Theatre—417
You Touched Me—244
You've Had Your War—368
You Won't Always Be On Top—307, 308
Ypsilanti Greek Theatre—362
Yucca Flats—410
Yulin, Harris—367, 389, 454
Yuriko—374, 454
Yurka, Blanche—37, 47, 77, 109, 135, 142, 144, 418
Yu, Tsao—438
Yvonne Arnaud Theatre—354, 430
Yvonne, Princess of Burgundy—396
Zabelle, Flora—35
Zadek, Peter—279, 301, 408
Zaks, Jerry—437
Zala, Nancy—365
Zaltzberg, Charlotte—406
Zamacois, Miguel—41, 54
Zang, Edward—373
Zangwill, Israel—15, 46, 47, 59, 63, 65, 134, 137
Zaslove, Arne—420, 453
Zaza—2, 23
Zeami—408
Zeffirelli, Franco—323, 329, 334, 341, 348, 353, 380, 407, 435
Zeigler, Anne—227
Zeisler, Peter—363
Zerbe, Anthony—360
Zetterling, Mai—264, 268, 316
Ziegeunerliebe—56
Ziegfeld, Billie Burke—190
Ziegfeld, Florenz—6, 15, 20, 31, 41, 43, 46, 55, 56, 61, 71, 78, 90, 93, 98, 105, 119, 125, 138, 148, 154, 156, 157, 170, 171, 176, 181, 185, 189, 190, 275, 391
Ziegfeld Follies—35, 41, 47, 52, 55, 56, 62, 66, 71, 74, 78, 82, 84, 87, 98, 99, 100, 105, 111, 115, 123, 124, 129, 146, 148, 176, 185, 189, 190, 200, 234, 251, 304, 376, 432, 447
Ziegfeld Midnight Frolic—93, 106
Ziegfield 9 O'Clock Frolic, The—105
Zien, Chip—452
Zigger Zagger—367, 403, 423
Zilboorg, Gregory—111
Zimbalist, Efrem—100
Zimmerman, Ethel—50
Zindel, Paul—385, 393, 403, 446
Zingoro—4, 8
"Zing Went the Strings of My Heart"—191
Zion Passion Play—197
Zip Goes A Million—273
Zola, Emil—50, 80, 184, 214, 246
Zonneslag et Cia—75
Zoo Story, The—319, 320, 325, 347, 353, 354, 375
Zoo, The—303
Zoot Suit—449
Zoo Zoo Widdershins Zoo—382
Zorba the Greek—371, 410

Zorina, Vera—206, 211, 221, 245, 291
Zucca, Manna—67
Zucco, George—102, 177
Zuckmayer, Carl—191, 283, 349, 395
Zukovs, The—429
Zuleika Dobson—305
Zulu Macbeth—408
Zum of weissen Rossl—177
Zwar, Charles—248, 258, 276
Zwei Gluckliche Tage—27
Zweig, Stefan—160, 218
Zwei Wappen—27
Zwick, Joel—381, 420
Zykovs, The—418